Argumentation and Critical Decision Making

Eighth Edition

RICHARD D. **Rieke**

University of Utah

MALCOLM O. **Sillars**

University of Utah

TARLA RAI **Peterson**

Texas A&M University

PEARSON

Boston   Columbus   Indianapolis   New York   San Francisco   Upper Saddle River
Amsterdam   Cape Town   Dubai   London   Madrid   Milan   Munich   Paris   Montreal   Toronto
Delhi   Mexico City   Sao Paulo   Sydney   Hong Kong   Seoul   Singapore   Taipei   Tokyo

American River College Library
4700 College Oak Drive
Sacramento, CA 95841

Editor-in-Chief, Communication: Karon Bowers
Assistant Editor: Stephanie Chaisson
Editorial Assistant: Megan Sweeney
Project Manager: Debbie Ryan
Marketing Manager: Blair Zoe Tuckman
Art Director, Cover: Jayne Conte
Cover Designer: Karen Noferi
Cover Photo: Alamy
Full-Service Project Management: Nitin Agarwal
Composition: Aptara®, Inc.

Text Font: Sabon LT Std

Credits and acknowledgments borrowed from other sources and reproduced, with permission, in this textbook appear on appropriate page within text.

Copyright © 2013, 2009, 2005, 2001, 1997 by Pearson Education, Inc. All rights reserved. No part of this publication may be reproduced, stored in a retrieval system, or transmitted, in any form or by any means, electronic, mechanical, photocopying, recording, or otherwise, without the prior written permission of the publisher. Printed in the United States. To obtain permission(s) to use material from this work, please submit a written request to Pearson Education, Inc., Permissions Department, One Lake Street, Upper Saddle River, New Jersey 07458 or you may fax your request to 201-236-3290.

Library of Congress Cataloging-in-Publication Data

Rieke, Richard D.
  Argumentation and critical decision making/Richard D. Rieke, Malcolm
O. Sillars, Tarla Rai Peterson.—8th ed.
    p. cm.
  ISBN-13: 978-0-205-21059-6
  ISBN-10: 0-205-21059-7
  1. Debates and debating. I. Sillars, Malcolm O. (Malcolm Osgood),
1928– II. Peterson, Tarla Rai. III. Title.
  PN4181.R47 2012
  808.53--dc23

                                            2011047403

ISBN-10:   0-205-21059-7
ISBN-13: 978-0-205-21059-6

CONTENTS

Preface   xiii

PART 1   Principles

The domain of argumentation encompasses virtually every occasion in which people seek to make the best possible decision in spite of the inevitability of uncertainty. What are the principles that underlie the process of argumentation? Why do people advance unreasonable arguments? How do people make critical decisions? How do people evaluate arguments, telling good ones from bad? How can we make sense of the process of argumentation? What are the forms of argument available to us when we want to be reasonable? When people perceive a problem exists, how can they move from this feeling of concern to the statement of a proposition worthy of critical decision making? How can people prepare a presentation, paper, report, memorandum, editorial, blog, or other forms of an argumentative case that will facilitate decision making? These are the principles we discuss in this section.

CHAPTER 1
Defining Argumentation   1

Elements of Argumentation   2
    Adherence   2
    Appropriate Decision Makers   2
    Claims   3
    Issue   5
    Proposition   6
    Support   7
    Argument   8
    Criticism   9

Elements of Critical Decision Making   10
    Toleration of Uncertainty   11
    Critical Thinking—The Internal Dialogue   13
    Dialectic—The External Dialogue   15
    Spheres   17
    Rhetoric   20

Conclusion   23

Exercises/Projects   24

CHAPTER 2
Appraising Argumentation   25

Argumentation and Being Reasonable   27
    Why People Advance Unreasonable Arguments   27
    Beliefs Are Not Necessarily Reasonable   27

Thinking Is Not Necessarily Reasonable   28
The Mind Is Not Necessarily Reasonable   29
Social Influence Is Not Necessarily Reasonable   30
Characteristics of Reasonable Arguments   30
Why People Seek Reasonable Arguments   31

The Bases of Reason in Argumentation   32
Starting Points for Argumentation   32

Conclusion   36

Exercises/Projects   36

CHAPTER 3
Making Sense of Argumentation   37

Good Reasons   37
A Good Story   39
Science   40
Feminist Argumentation   41

Alternative Dispute Resolution   46
Classifying Alternative Dispute Resolution Processes   47
Alternative Dispute Resolution as Argument   49

Conclusion   50

Exercises/Projects   51

CHAPTER 4
The Nature of Arguments   52

The Model of an Argument   53
Claim   53
Grounds   53
Warrant   54
Backing   54
Qualifier   55
Rebuttal/Reservation   55

Reasoning Processes   56
Argument by Logic/Deduction/Syllogism/Enthymeme   57
Argument by Generalization   59
Argument by Cause   60
Argument by Sign   62
Argument by Analogy   63
Argument from Authority   64

Definitions as Argument   65
Formal Definition   66
Definition by Example   66
Functional Definition   66

Definition by Analogy *66*
Definition by Authority *67*

The Analysis of Arguments 67
Characteristics of Arguments *68*

Conclusion 69

Exercises/Projects 70

CHAPTER 5
Analysis in Argumentation 71

Critical Analysis to Find a Proposition 72
Identify the Question *73*
Search For New Information *73*
Survey Implicated Objectives, Values, and Biases *73*
Canvass Alternative Decisions *74*
Weigh the Costs and Risks to the Alternatives *74*
Select a Proposition *74*

Critical Analysis of a Proposition 75
Determining the Issues *75*
Rank-Order Issues *77*
What Critical Values Will Be Applied? *79*

Analysis of Claims 80
Clarify What Each Claim Asserts *80*
Locate the Points of Disagreement *81*

Conclusion 82

Exercises/Projects 82

CHAPTER 6
Case Building—Presentation Planning 83

Preliminary Steps in Case Building 83
Identify the Ultimate Purpose *84*
State the Proposition *84*
Assess Presumptions and Burden of Proof *85*

Preparing the Presentation/Case 89
Identify the Decision Contexts *89*
Locate Starting Points *90*
State Possible Issues *90*
Outline Your Arguments *91*

Developing a Convincing Vision 93
Learn the Decision Makers' Vision *93*
Tell the Story of Your Vision *94*
Consider an Example *94*

Communication to Specific Decision Makers   95
    What Are the Communication Constraints?   *95*
    What Counterargument Will Occur?   *95*
    What Argumentative Format Will Be Used?   *96*
    What Are the Rules of the Sphere?   *96*
    How Will the Decision Be Made?   *97*
    What Sequence of Claims Is Most Appropriate?   *97*

Conclusion   100

Exercises/Projects   101

PART 2 Tools

Aristotle said, "State your case, and prove it." In this section, we discuss how people do that. What counts as proof? Proof, called support here, consists of evidence, values, and credibility. The tools of argumentation include more than just locating support. They also include the critical process of what some people call "scrubbing arguments" or cleaning away the poor arguments through refutation and refutation by fallacy claims. Without these tools, argumentation lacks its full power.

CHAPTER 7
Support: Evidence   102

Forms of Evidence   103
    Example   *103*
    Statistics   *105*
    Combining Forms of Evidence   *107*
    Testimony   *108*

General Principles for the Use of Evidence   109
    Use Representative Instances   *109*
    Use a Sufficient Number of Instances   *109*
    Use only Relevant Instances   *110*
    Account for Negative Instances   *110*
    State the Value Characteristics of Instances   *110*
    Make Instances Seem Real with Details   *111*
    Use Decision Makers' Experience   *111*
    Use Current Examples and Statistics   *111*
    Use Credible Sources   *111*
    Carefully Consider Statistical Measures   *112*
    Use Comparison to Clarify Statistics   *114*
    Base Testimony on Credibility Measures   *114*

Sphere Dependence of Evidence   115
    Hearsay Evidence   *115*
    Ordinary and Expert Evidence   *115*
    Reluctant Evidence   *116*
    Negative Evidence   *117*

Documented Evidence   *117*
Assertion and Evidence   *118*

Conclusion   119

Exercises/Projects   119

CHAPTER 8
Support: Values   120

Characteristics of Values   121
   Stated and Implied Values   *121*
   Positive and Negative Values   *122*
   Terminal and Instrumental Values   *122*
   Abstract and Concrete Values   *124*

Values Appear in Systems   124
   Traditional Value Systems   *125*
   Values Are Graded in Systems   *126*

Values Define Ethics   127

General Principles for the Use of Values   128
   Values May Be Found Anywhere in an Argument   *128*
   Recognize Values in Warrants   *129*
   Find the Values in the Arguments of Others   *130*
   Recognize the Limits of Value Change   *130*
   Find the Best Point of Attack on Values   *131*
   Relate Your Values to Decision Makers   *132*
   Use Evidence and Argument to Develop Values   *133*

Sphere Dependence of Values   133
   Values in Scientific Argument   *134*
   Values in Religion   *135*
   The Relation of Science and Religion   *138*

Conclusion   139

Exercises/Projects   140

CHAPTER 9
Support: Credibility   141

Characteristics of Credibility   142
   Competence and Trustworthiness   *142*
   Good Will and Dynamism   *143*
   Homophily (Similarity)   *143*

Forms of Credibility   144
   Direct Credibility   *144*
   Secondary Credibility   *145*
   Indirect Credibility   *146*

General Principles for the Use of Credibility   146
   Develop Credibility from Reputation   146
   Be Sincere   147
   Identify with Decision Makers' Values   148
   Use Evidence to Build Credibility   149
   Use Organization to Build Credibility   149
   Argue Issues, Not People   150
   Understand Credibility as Dynamic   151

Sphere Dependence of Credibility   151
   The Reputation of the Arguer   152
   Secondary Credibility in Spheres   153
   Indirect Credibility in Spheres   154

Conclusion   154

Exercises/Projects   155

CHAPTER 10
Refutation   156

The Process of Refutation   156

Approaching Refutation   158

Setting a Framework for Refutation   159
   Assess the Argumentative Situation   159
   Analyze the Decision Makers   162
   Analyze Opponents   165

Selecting a Posture for Refutation   165
   Refute from a Constructive Basis   166
   Defend Your Position   166
   Keep the Focus on the Goals of Decision Making   167
   Engage in Framebreaking   167
   Test the Credibility of Other Factions   168
   Understand Momentum   169
   Deny Support   169

Communicating Refutation   170
   Probe Opponents   171
   Follow Good Communication Practices   172

Conclusion   173

Exercises/Projects   173

CHAPTER 11
Refutation by Fallacy Claims   174

Fallacy Began in the Study of Logic   175
   Fallacy Claims of Sophistry   177
   Fallacies as Violations of Discussion Rules   181

Social Guides to Fallacy Claims   182
   Intent to Deceive   182
   Refusal to Reason   183
   Breach of Conversational Cooperation   183

Using Fallacy Claims in Refutation   186

Conclusion   186

Exercises/Projects   187

PART 3   Applications

You know that argumentation and critical decision making occur within social entities called spheres. It is within the sphere that ultimate purposes are formed, forms of argument are specified, criteria for their evaluation are enforced, and the character of argumentative cases is defined. Although spheres are numerous and varied, there are some general areas of decision making that can be used to exemplify the way spheres shape argumentation. In this section, we discuss law, science, religion, business, and government and politics as highly generalized spheres.

CHAPTER 12
Argumentation in Law   188

Narratives in Legal Argumentation   189
   Narratives Construct the Facts   189
   Narratives Must Satisfy the Demands of a Prima Facie *Case   190*
   Ledbetter's Narrative   191
   Goodyear's Narrative   192
   The Jury's Decision   193
   Justice Alito's Narrative   194
   Justice Ginsberg's Narrative   194

Arguments on the Law   195
   Commonplaces in Legal Argumentation   196

Conclusion   202

Exercises/Projects   203

CHAPTER 13
Argumentation in Science   204

What Is Science?   204

Scientific Values   206

The Tradition of Argumentation in Science   207
   Claims of Fact   207
   Search for Truth over Personal Gain   208
   Testable Results   209
   Established Theory Changes Slowly   209

Scientific Use of Argument Types   211
   Argument by Generalization   211
   Argument by Cause   212
   Argument by Sign   213
   Argument by Analogy   214
   Argument from Authority   216

Scientific Use of Evidence   217
   Empirically Grounded Claims   217
   Specific Instances   217
   Statistics in Science   218
   Testimony   219

Scientific Method as Argument   220

Conclusion   220

Exercises/Projects   221

CHAPTER 14
Argumentation in Religion   222

Major Questions in Religious Argumentation   223
   What Is the Nature of God?   224
   What Is the Nature of Human Beings?   225
   What Is Moral Behavior, the Religious Life?   226
   What Are Sin, Evil, and the Meaning of Suffering?   226
   What Is the Human's Relationship to God?   227
   What Is the Nature of Salvation?   227
   What Is the Role of the Church?   228
   Values and Themes   228

Evidence in Religious Argumentation   229
   Text as Evidence   229
   Tradition as Evidence   232
   Experience as Evidence   232
   Revelation as Evidence   233
   Culture as Evidence   233

Preferred Argument Forms   234
   Argument from Authority   234
   Argument by Analogy   236
   Argument by Narrative   237
   Argument by Sign   238
   Argument by Paradox   238
   Argument by Generalization   239

Conclusion   241

Exercises/Projects   241

CHAPTER 15

Argumentation in Business   242

Starting Points for Business Argumentation   243
    Facts in Business Argumentation   244
    Presumptions in Business Argumentation   244
    Probabilities in Business Argumentation   246
    Commonplaces/Forms of Argument in Business Argumentation   248

Forms of Support in Business Argumentation   252
    Evidence as Support in Business Argumentation   252
    Values as Support in Business Argumentation   253
    Credibility as Support for Business Argumentation   255

Conclusion   256

Exercises/Projects   256

CHAPTER 16

Argumentation in Government and Politics   257

The Nature of Political Argumentation   258
    The Claims of Political Argumentation   258
    The Content of Political Claims   258
    The Development of Political Claims   259

Argumentation in Government and Politics   262
    Argumentation in Committee Hearings   262
    Characteristics of Hearings   263
    Using the Record in Hearings   263
    Focus for the Record in Hearings   263
    The Forms of Argumentation in Committee Hearings   264
    Telling Good Stories   265

Argumentation in Legislative Action   265
    Legislative Argument Is Usually Not Confrontational   266
    Legislative Argument Is Usually Not Personal   266
    The Amendment Process as Argumentation   267
    Argumentation Has an Important Credibility Function   267
    Relations between Legislature and the Executive   268

Argumentation in Political Campaigns   269
    Campaigns Involve Issues and Images   269
    Campaign Arguments Are Linked to "The People"   270
    Telling the Right Story   271
    Maintaining the Story   271
    Media and Political Argumentation   273

The Special Role of Debates   274

Refutation in the Political Campaign   275
   Refutation Is Usually about Testing Proposals with Values   275
   Evidence Is Important in Refutation   276
   Credibility Is Significant in Refutation   276
   The Story Is Significant in Refutation   277
   Leave No Shot Unanswered   277
   Refutation by Inoculation   278

Conclusion   278

Exercises/Projects   279

References   280
Name Index   295
Subject Index   298

PREFACE

The ultimate purpose of *Argumentation and Critical Decision Making* is to help people improve their understanding of how arguments and argumentation actually operate in practice, and to help them improve their ability to participate in argumentation. From the first edition to today, we have worked within a set of criteria: (1) the discussion of argumentation will reflect the world of practical affairs rather than intercollegiate forensics; (2) the examples used are from the contemporary "real-world" rather than silly old epigrams like, "if wishes were horses, beggars would ride;" (3) the discussion of argument theory and practice is rooted in classical thought, strengthened by modern philosophers, and buttressed by reference to contemporary scholarship; (4) argumentation is illustrated in practice both in general and in selected technical spheres.

When the first edition appeared, Roe v. Wade had recently been decided, the Vietnam War had just ended, unemployment in the United States was 9.2%, a gallon of gasoline cost 44 cents, Motorola got the patent for the first portable mobile phone, and Bill Gates and Paul Allen had just gotten together to form a new company they called Microsoft. The circumstances of communicating argumentation have extended its importance beyond where it was when we started the first edition and far beyond where it was when we were students. Obviously, since 1975, when the first edition was published, we have been constantly at work making the book responsive to our criteria and the changes in society.

NEW TO THIS EDITION

This new edition of Argumentation has undergone changes and acquired new material to bring it up-to-date and adhere to the needs of our students. Even after all this time, some reviewers for this edition told us we still sounded too much like we were writing for college debaters. As a result, we've updated the following:

- Chapter 6 on Case Building is substantially revised to remove those parts that were judged to be too oriented to college debate.
- Instead, we have focused on more common experiences people face in setting out a comprehensive set of arguments for a proposition in a presentation, essay, memorandum, paper, editorial, thesis, article, or blog.

Reviewers also recommended that the Nature of Arguments be discussed earlier in the text. Vital to the understanding of all argumentation it should come before analysis and case building, they said. In response, we've made the following changes:

- The Nature of Arguments is now Chapter 4. What's more, we have revised our discussion of arguments to make the material more clear and comprehensive.
- Chapter 3 is now entitled "Making Sense of Argumentation." Exchanging "in" with "of" is meant to communicate the purpose of the chapter: locating the process of argumentation in a wide variety of contexts that reflect and support the various perspectives about argument coming from different constituencies such as the feminist, non- confrontational approach to decision making.

An overall need for current information and examples cited by reviewers led us to the following updates:

- Chapter 3 is significantly revised from the last edition to reflect some of the practical applications of feminist and other scholarship that emphasize more collaborative approaches to disputes.
- We have added a section that introduces the most common types of alternative dispute resolution that have become widely accepted as a way to manage conflict in recent years.
- We also rewrote much of Chapter 13, Argumentation in Science, for this edition to offer updated information on scientific argumentation and evidence.
- Argumentation in Religion, Chapter 14, while still emphasizing religions of the Judeo-Christian-Islamic tradition, has been enhanced by acknowledging the role of other religions of the world that are increasingly important in western nations.

Some of our reviewers pointed out that we had presented the spheres of argumentation in an artificially disjointed manner. As a result,

- We have tried to address this concern by pointing out where argumentation from one sphere slips into another.
- We also have included specific links between strategies and tactics commonly used in scientific argumentation and basic concepts such as values and credibility introduced earlier.

Reviewers also said the text was too dense—too wordy—and we should introduce some visual variety. In response,

- In most chapters we have included figures set off from the text to break up the words, give the reader some relief, and highlight particularly important material.

GIVE YOUR STUDENTS CHOICES

In addition to the traditional printed text, *Argumentation and Critical Decision Making, 8/e* is available in the following format to give you and your students more choices—and more ways to save.

The **CourseSmart eTextbook** offers the same content as the printed text in a convenient online format—with highlighting, online search, and printing capabilities. **www.coursesmart.com**

CourseSmart eTextbook: ISBN: 0205864058

MySearchLab® with Pearson eText

MySearchLab is an interactive website that features an eText, access to the EBSCO ContentSelect database and multimedia, and step-by-step tutorials which offer complete overviews of the entire writing and research process. MySearchLab is designed to amplify a traditional course in numerous ways or to administer a course online. Additionally, MySearchLab offers course specific tools to enrich learning and help students succeed.

- eText: Identical in content and design to the printed text, the Pearson eText provides access to the book wherever and whenever it is needed. Students can take notes and highlight, just like a traditional book. The Pearson eText also is available on the iPad for all registered users of MySearchLab.

- **Flashcards:** These review important terms and concepts from each chapter online. Students can search by chapters or within a glossary and also access drills to help them prepare for quizzes and exams. Flashcards can be printed or exported to your mobile devices.
- **Chapter-specific Content:** Each chapter contains Learning Objectives, Quizzes, and Flashcards. These can be used to enhance comprehension, help students review key terms, prepare for tests, and retain what they have learned.

Learn more at **www.mysearchlab.com**

ACKNOWLEDGMENT

For each edition, we have been grateful to the colleagues throughout the nation who have told us and written us of ways to improve this book. Once again, with this eighth edition, we have been aided by reviewers who we must particularly thank: Benjamin Bates, *Ohio University*; Norm Fricker, *Orange Coast College*; Joshua J. Frye, *State University of New York*; Angela Hoppe-Nagao, *Cerrito College*; Pamela Kaylor, *Ohio University Lancaster*; Greg Leichty, *University of Louisville*; Kristopher Willis, *Appalachian State University*. They helped us improve our work while staying faithful to our criteria.

Defining Argumentation

KEY TERMS

adherence, p. 2

decision makers, p. 2

ultimate purpose, p. 2

claim, p. 3

subclaim, p. 3

factual claim, p. 3

value claim, p. 4

policy claim, p. 4

issue, p. 5

proposition, p. 6

support, p. 7

evidence, p. 7

values, p. 7

credibility, p. 8

argument, p. 8

argumentativeness, p. 8

verbal aggression, p. 8

criteria, p. 10

uncertainty, p. 11

fallacies, p. 12

language, p. 12

critical thinking, p. 13

dialectic, p. 15

spheres, p. 17

group structuration, p. 17

internal dialogue, p. 18

personal spheres, p. 18

technical spheres, p. 19

public spheres, p. 19

rhetoric, p. 20

audience, p. 20

probability, p. 21

proof, p. 22

When people need to make a decision, and they want to get it right, they use argumentation. By making arguments and then evaluating them, people are able to improve the quality of their thinking, communicating, and decision making, and that is what this book is about. You engage in argumentation whether you are aware of it or not, and you have been making arguments since you were about four years old. In fact, you still use a lot of reasons that came to mind when you were only a child

(Willbrand and Rieke 1991). As a kid, you probably reasoned on the basis of power authority, "Mom said I could play the game now, so move over!" As an adult, you still use power authority, although in a more grown-up way, "My advisor says this course will satisfy a major requirement, and she has the power to make that determination."

Argumentation may seem unfamiliar because people so rarely take time to reflect on what they mean and do under the heading of argument or argumentation. If we were to ask a group of people what argumentation means, we would get many different answers, and most of them would be fairly superficial.

The difficult part about studying argumentation is keeping your mind open to new ways of thinking about a familiar process. The objective of this book is to sensitize you to your own argumentation behaviors and provide new information and insight to help you be as effective as possible.

In the first four chapters, we will offer our perspective on argumentation for your consideration. Subsequent chapters will present information about engaging in argumentation that we expect will provide you with some valuable insights.

We begin by introducing you to the key elements of argumentation. Then, we will explain how argumentation is inherent in critical decision making.

ELEMENTS OF ARGUMENTATION

Argumentation is the communicative process of advancing, supporting, criticizing, and modifying claims so that appropriate decision makers, defined by relevant spheres, may grant or deny adherence. Let us briefly discuss the important terms in this working definition.

Adherence

The objective of argumentation, as Chaim Perelman and L. Olbrechts-Tyteca have noted, is to gain **adherence**, which is the informed support of others (1). By informed, we mean that people who have committed themselves to your claim are consciously aware of the reasons for doing so. By support, we mean that people stand ready to act on your claims, not simply grant lip service.

We have said that argumentation is a communication process, which means it involves engaging people's minds through interaction. As we will see in the next chapter, different people make different demands on arguments before committing themselves. The responsibility for decision making is shared, including the responsibility for bad decisions.

Appropriate Decision Makers

The appropriate **decision makers** are those necessary to the implementation of the decision and the achievement of the **ultimate purpose**. The judge or jury in court, the city council, state legislators, U.S. Congress, the President in making public policy decisions, the board of trustees or the C.E.O. in business, the admissions board at college, the driver's license examiner, the insurance adjuster, and many more are all appropriate decision makers in their context. Winning the adherence of people who are not in a position to move the decision toward the ultimate purpose of the decision is of little value.

At colleges and universities throughout the United States, when their football teams are having a good season, people begin arguing that the Bowl Championship Series (BCS) is unfair. Claims are advanced that the BCS gives unfair advantage to the six BCS conferences and independent Notre Dame at the expense of others who have truly outstanding teams only once in a while. For example, Tulane, Marshall, Utah, Boise State, Texas Christian, and Hawaii had undefeated seasons but were not able to compete for a national championship, while teams who had losses were allowed.

These arguments receive sympathetic responses from people from similar schools. However, most of those sympathizers have no influence over decisions related to selecting the national champion football team. And, the people who have the power to make decisions about football championships tend to be members of the BCS conferences and Notre Dame who are least interested in making changes.

The arguments must gain the adherence of those who really make the decisions. The senior Senator from Utah announced he was going to work to change the BCS system when the University of Utah had a perfect season but was denied entry into the championship game. The President of the United States said that he did not like the BCS system and called for a playoff process. But neither of these influential and powerful men changed the BCS even a little bit. When you make an argument, you must address it to the appropriate decision makers if you expect to achieve what you are trying to accomplish (your ultimate purpose).

Because argumentation functions as a social interactive process and because people's critical decisions are the products of argumentation, we speak of argumentation as audience-centered. The word audience is used in its broadest sense to include all argumentative situations ranging from interpersonal interaction between two people face-to-face or on social media to blogs that fly around the world being read by millions.

Claims

A **claim** is a statement that you want others to accept and act on (to grant their adherence). It may be linked to a series of other claims that constitute a case.

When a claim is used to justify another claim, it is called a **subclaim**. "Playing violent games for more than three hours a day makes children aggressive" is a claim. It becomes a subclaim when it is used to justify the claim, "Violent games should not be sold to anyone under 17 years of age."

We will talk about three kinds of claims: fact, value, and policy. Later in this chapter, we will see how they interrelate and are used to support one another. For now, let us see what they are.

Factual Claim.   A **factual claim** affirms that certain conditions exist in the material world and can be observed. Decision makers are asked to adhere to a factual claim because it is confirmed by objective data from reliable sources. The following are examples of factual claims:

- Cypress College is in Orange County, California.
- Twenty-four species of animals run faster than humans.
- New Mexico became a state in 1912.
- Playing violent games causes children to be more aggressive.
- The percentage of the U.S. population over 65 will significantly increase by 2020.

These are all factual claims. Each makes a claim that decision makers might verify by reference to some kind of data. The first two are claims of *present fact* and the third is a claim of *past fact*. The fourth claim about the cause of aggression in children is more complex since it must be verified by research, and research results are usually contested. The fifth claim about the U.S. population is worth special note as it is a claim of *future fact* (Cronkhite). A visit or a web site tells you that Cypress College is in Orange County, California, a count found in an almanac confirms that 24 species of animals run faster than humans, and a historical record shows that New Mexico became a state in 1912. But claims of cause and effect may be supported by objective data coming from scientific studies, but such research is always kept open to correction by new studies. And, a future fact cannot be confirmed by looking at objective data from reliable sources. Decision makers will require more extensive reasoning to give it adherence. However, it is still a factual claim because at some point you, or someone, will be able to check it by objective data or observation. For instance, current government statistics tell us how many people are over 65 years of age today. By examining the percentage of people who are 50 and over with the general population, today you can estimate the percentage who will be over 65 in 2020. Eventually, in 2020, you can check it, if you wish.

Nonetheless, whether of past, present, cause, or future, factual claims all have similar characteristics. All make assertions about what a situation was, is, or will be. All can be identified by some variety of the verb "to be." Note the examples above: "Cypress College *is* . . . ," "Twenty-four species of animals *run* . . . ," "New Mexico *became* . . . ," "Playing games *causes* . . . ," and "The percentage of the population over sixty-five *will* . . ." And, all are analyzed in the same way.

Value Claim. A claim that asserts the quality of a person, place, thing, or idea is called a **value claim**:

- Natural gas is our best energy source.
- Drugs and alcohol are a threat to public morality.

Both of these statements make claims about the value of something; they make a value judgment that cannot be checked against data. "Drugs and alcohol are a threat to public morality" is clearly a value claim. "Public morality" is a condition that can be defined only by the participants in argumentation. It has no generally accepted means of verification. Natural gas, however, might be shown to have fewer pollutants, may cost less per BTU than other energy sources, and may have other characteristics that seem to make this claim verifiable as a factual claim. But *best* means more than verifiable characteristics. Some people find gas *better* than electricity for cooking. How is that to be verified? So, value claims may vary from personal choice to definition in the strictest verifiable terms.

The value claim is frequently confused with the factual claim because it has the same form. It is built around some version of the verb "to be." Note the preceding examples: "Drugs and alcohol are . . . ," "Natural gas is. . . . " Furthermore, as we will show later in this book, the value claim is analyzed the same way as is the factual claim. But the value claim can always be distinguished from the factual claim because it has in it a value term ("public morality/immorality," "best/worst," "right/wrong," "just/unjust," "beautiful/ugly") that contains a judgment that cannot be objectively verified and depends on the decision makers' concepts of what is and what is not of value.

Policy Claim. A claim that tells someone or some agency how to behave is called a **policy claim**. Any statement of a rule, law, or regulation is a policy claim and is a proposed change in the way people or agencies currently behave:

- No left turn.
- Don't walk on the grass.
- The balanced budget amendment to the constitution should be passed.
- Medical marijuana use ought to be legalized.
- The United States must control undocumented immigration.

Because policy claims have to do with behavior, it will help you to identify them by checking to see if they state or imply the word *should*. The first two claims do not specifically state "You should not turn left" or "You should not walk on the grass," but they are commands based on policy decisions. The last two policy claims use terms *ought* and *must* that mean the same as *should*.

Note the differences in these three related claims:

- Left turns are against the law at Fifth and Elm Streets. (Factual claim)
- Left turns at Fifth and Elm are dangerous. (Value claim)
- You should not turn left at Fifth and Elm Streets. (Policy claim)

All three claims deal with the same subject matter, but they are quite different. They require different kinds of analysis and argumentation, primarily because asking for a change of behavior is more than asserting a fact or value.

Notice that a claim is a single statement, but it is possible that you could have a sentence with more than one claim in it. Consider this sentence: "The national average composite score for the ACT test in 2010 was 21, and that reveals a disappointing decline over the past few years," is a factual claim about the scores and a value claim about their significance. You may need to separate these two for your analysis.

Issue

The term **issue**, as frequently used in our society, can be confused with the term *claim*. A politician will argue, "My opponent has missed the issue; we need a balanced budget amendment." But an issue is more than an important claim. *An issue is the paralleling of two opposing claims stated as a question.*

To make analysis more pointed, you should always state issues in a hypothetical form allowing only two responses: yes or no. In this way, the statement of the issue points the response either toward one claim or a continued search.

For example, people might ask, "Did a mercury-based preservative used in many vaccines until 2001 actually cause a rise in cases of autism?" There is an issue: one faction claims the answer is yes, while opposing factions reject the idea. Issues are best stated with words such as *should, will, does, can, whether,* or *is* because such words clearly imply a yes or no answer. If the decision makers decide the answer is no, it does not mean the discussion of autism is over; it merely means that those trying to understand the causes of autism must revise their analysis and open another issue. For example, they might move to the question, "Did some Mumps and Measles vaccines given to children cause inflammation which led to a rise in cases of autism" (**About.com** 1)?[1]

By the same token, issues never begin with words such as *who, what, where, when, why,* or *how*. These and similar words lead to an open-ended question such as, "What is

---

[1]In some logic systems, this point is made by substituting for yes or no, yes or not yes. All you have decided to do was not to say yes to the question this particular issue poses, not to reject anything else on this subject.

the impact of livestock grazing on federal lands?" The response to such a question is wide open and does not focus the analysis. As you will see in Chapter 5, such general questions may be the point where analysis begins, but such analysis will look to find issues.

Many political leaders in western states oppose the wilderness designation for federal lands because that will restrict the economic development of those lands for livestock grazing, mining, and logging. Environmental groups favor a greater designation of wilderness to preserve more land in the natural state. They claim, "More federal land should be designated as wilderness." Others argue against such designation. Here, then, is a policy issue: "Should more public land be designated as wilderness?" No, opponents say, because designated wilderness land hurts the local economy. Supporters claim that it does not. Here is a value issue: "Does a wilderness designation of federal land hurt the local economy?" "Wilderness attracts tourists who strengthen the local economy," say the supporters. Opponents say, "Tourism adds less to the economy than do mining, grazing, and lumbering." This paralleling of claims results in an issue of fact: "Does tourism add more to the economy than mining, grazing, and lumbering?"

Not all claims result in issues, but any claim (policy, fact, or value) may become an issue. If you say to a friend, "We should go to the basketball game tonight," you have a claim. But if she says, "Sure, let's go," you have no issue. Issues are important because they identify the significant points where controversy exists and, therefore, where possible claim modification can be made to reach agreement. If such modification is impossible, these points become the places where you must concentrate your argument.

Proposition

A **proposition** is a claim that expresses the judgment that decision makers are asked to accept or reject. Generally speaking, like other claims, a proposition may be of fact, value, or policy.[2] Although other claims may serve as subclaims to one another and to propositions, a proposition cannot be a subclaim because it represents the point where you want the decision makers to be when your argumentation is finished.

Claims accumulate to form other claims. These claims support a proposition. You may change your proposition when new information is added or when your proposition is rejected. Argumentation is a continuing process of changing issues, claims, and propositions. But at the point you choose to build a case (see Chapter 6), you select a judgment for decision makers to accept or reject. The claim that states that judgment is the proposition.

---

[2]Among students of argumentation, there have been attempts to define a wider variety of propositions than the three most traditional ones we have identified here. However, these show that fact, value, and policy come in a variety of forms. As long as you recognize that all fact, value, or policy claims will not look exactly alike, you can be a successful arguer using these three.

There are definitional propositions (Ehninger and Brockriede 218–229) in which people argue how to define a term (e.g., "What is a democracy?"). We treat these as factual claims. Definition is discussed in Chapter 6. Some people treat some value claims that imply a policy claim ("War is immoral") as "quasi-policy claims." Some differentiate "comparative value claims" from value claims ("Rape victims are more important than a free press") and treat some value claims ("Television is an important literary genre") as what they call "value-object claims" (Zarefsky 1980, 13). "Historical/scientific claims" (Zarefsky) and "historical inference claims" (Church and Wilbanks 37) are sometimes used to identify a particular kind of claim of fact ("The Battle of the Little Big Horn was a military victory, not a massacre").

The following is a brief outline of a controversy to illustrate the relationship between a proposition and its supporting claims.

PROPOSITION OF POLICY: "The University should increase regulations to assure that animals in laboratories are protected from pain or distress."

I. The activist group Stop Animal Exploitation NOW has put our university on its top 20 most painful labs in the country (factual claim).

II. The Department of Agriculture's Animal and Plant Health Inspection service reported that the university used 1,504 guinea pigs in tests without the use of anesthesia (factual claim).

III. If no anesthesia is used, animals suffer unwarranted pain (value claim).

IV. The university should assure the community of the proper functioning of its labs (policy claim).

V. Tighter regulations would prevent unwarranted pain to animals (value claim).

FIGURE 1.1
Propositions and Claims

Support

Whatever communication (including both words and objects) is necessary and available to secure adherence, what it takes to get others to accept and act on your claim, falls within the concept of **support**. Support presents the decision makers with claims with which they already agree that will help them agree with your claim. Sometimes, nothing more than your own authority in stating the claim is required:

> JERI: This university should not torture animals in the name of research.
> MARY LOU: You're right!

We often put support alongside a claim without waiting to find out if others will demand it.

> JERI: This university should not torture animals in the name of research, because [support] wanton cruelty to living creatures is never acceptable.

It is also common to give reasons where the claim is understood but not spoken. In their conversation, Jeri might simply say, "Animals have rights against unnecessary suffering," and Mary Lou will understand from the context that it is a claim about university research. In more complex situations, where disagreement is expressed or anticipated, support of more explicit kinds is used. We will discuss the following:

Evidence.   You can strengthen a claim and increase its potential for adherence if you add to it examples, statistics, or testimony, the three broad categories of **evidence**. This is discussed in Chapter 7.

Values.   Claims are supported when they are identified with social **values**—generalized conceptions of what are desirable ends or ways of behaving—of the decision makers. Values are discussed in Chapter 8.

Credibility. Claims are more acceptable when the person making the claim, or the source reporting the claim, is regarded as credible, as believable, and worthy of adherence. **Credibility** is discussed in Chapter 9.

Essentially, support provides the answer to the question, whether asked or not, "Why should I take your claim seriously?" Anyone is free to make any claim they wish whether it makes sense or not. Someone says, "You know, the U.S. never really put people on the moon. It was just another government conspiracy." You might ask in reply, "What makes you think that is so?" Here, you are asking for support to help you decide whether or not to take the claim seriously.

Argument

An **argument,** in our usage, is a single unit of argumentation comprising a claim and its support. Both claim and support may be explicitly stated or one or both may be implied but understood by the persons participating in the argumentation process. To qualify as an argument, the support must potentially provide justification to relevant decision makers to grant adherence to the claim.

A caution is necessary here. In English usage, *argument* can also refer to the open expression of conflict, as in, "My roommate and I had a terrible argument last night." In fact, in western thought, arguments and argumentation are often associated with competition, a form of fighting. The idea of argumentation functioning in a competitive forum where the desire to win might overcome the search for the best answer has always been troubling. It was this concern that led Socrates to defend the dialectical approach to decisions and the need to wait for the discovery of truth. Although the inherent uncertainty pervading the domain of argumentation makes Socrates' position unworkable, as we explain shortly, the competitive (some say masculine) character of many decision making situations continues to be a source of concern. We discuss other rationales in argumentation that are intended to diminish the competitive impulse in Chapter 3.

However, argumentation does inherently involve a willingness to express your ideas, provide support for them, and allow others to respond in ways that are often in disagreement with you. And, engaging in argumentation requires you to consider others' disagreement and say why you do or do not find them worthy of your adherence. This is called **argumentativeness,** and some students in argumentation classes have reported that learning to do that is "exhilarating," and leads to a feeling of being "confident and knowledgeable and eloquent" (Goodwin 48). They have learned socially acceptable skills of openly expressing disagreement and standing up for what they believe in what has been measured as a construct of "self-perceived communication competence" (Teven et al. 264).

By contrast, **verbal aggression** is a construct found to be associated with people perceiving themselves as being less competent in communication skills (Teven et al. 268). As we explain in Chapter 11, trying to attack others' self-concept through the infliction of psychological pain rather than dealing with their arguments characterizes verbal aggression. "Aggressive people often use hostile, aggressive body language or other threatening behavior to bully and dominate people because they perceive themselves to be less successful in their communication with others . . . when one feels less competent, he or she is more likely to attack the competence of others through verbally aggressive messages" (Teven et al. 268). When we describe arguments and argumentation, we are talking about argumentativeness not verbal aggression.

In this book, argument includes the argument a lawyer prepares for a trial, the argument supporting a scientific principle, or the argument of a friend that you should join her in studying for the test. Daniel O'Keefe explains two meanings of argument other than the confusion with angry exchanges. What he calls argument 1 "is a kind of utterance or a sort of communicative act" (121). This speaks of an argument as a product as we have just defined it. What O'Keefe calls argument 2 is a communicative process, what we have defined as argumentation. Argumentation (argument 2) refers to the ongoing process of advancing, rejecting, modifying, and accepting claims, whereas argument (argument 1) refers to a single claim with its support. Our interest is in arguments functioning within argumentation in whatever context, ranging from informal interpersonal communication to complex situations such as law, politics, religion, business, or science.

Criticism

Argumentation involves criticism of claims with the open potential for modifying them. Dogmatic defense of positions is not argumentation; it is fanaticism. Criticism involves refutation, which is discussed in Chapters 10 and 11. Stephen Toulmin (1964) says that the test of an argument is its ability to "stand up to criticism" (9).

The Society for Personality and Social Psychology includes research on racial prejudice, homophobia, sexism, stereotype threat, and unconscious bias against minorities; so, the members pride themselves on being experts on bias in society. However, at the 2011 convention in San Antonio, Dr. Jonathan Haidt, a social psychologist at the University of Virginia, charged the society with being a "tribal-moral community" united by "sacred values" that damage their research and their credibility. He charged the scientists with being blind to the hostile climate they have created for nonliberals (Tierney 1). By a show of hands, the members revealed that of the 1,000 psychologists present, 80% identified themselves as liberals while only three members said they were conservatives. "Anywhere in the world that social psychologists see women or minorities underrepresented by a factor of two or three," claimed Dr. Haidt, "our minds jump to discrimination as the explanation. But when we find out that conservatives are underrepresented among us by a factor of more than 100, suddenly everyone finds it quite easy to generate alternate explanations" (Tierney 1). Locating deep-seated contradictions in an argument is a common and effective form of criticism, and Dr. Haidt identified a big one.

Starting with this evidence gathered on the spot in front of his audience, Dr. Haidt proceeded to develop a criticism of the social science sphere. Using fundamental values that provide a foundation for research arguments—that the studies are conducted from a position of scholarly independence and objectivity—Haidt claimed that another value— the commitment to redress the wrongs of racism—had turned social science blind to its own prejudices. He charged his colleagues with embracing "science whenever it supports their sacred values, but [ditching or distorting] it as soon as it threatens a sacred value" (Tierney 2). The professor went on to provide some high profile examples of instances in which social scientists had been shunned when they violated sacred values—good criticism usually requires examples as support for arguments.

Showing that the criticism was taken to heart, the members of the society agreed to some language changes in their category of "underrepresented groups" who are provided special funds to travel to the annual meeting. Instead of limiting the category to ethnic or racial minorities, first-generation college students, individuals with a physical disability and/or lesbian, gay, bisexual, or transgender students, the category is left open and may one day include conservatives in the list (Tierney 3).

This example comes from the sphere of academic research where fairness, objectivity, and thoroughness are fundamental values, and a criticism can be powerful when it shows a violation of one or more of them. In other formal spheres, such as law, business, or government, complex rules often determine the character of criticism. Argumentation in interpersonal spheres is based heavily on cooperation and the compromising of personal preferences.

ELEMENTS OF CRITICAL DECISION MAKING

A critical decision is one that survives the test of a relevant set of criteria. Choice is made on the basis of clearly articulated arguments that have been held open to refutation or disagreement. It stands up to criticism and it remains open to further criticism as long as possible. When the arguments change, when new arguments occur, when the criteria for decision change, the decision changes accordingly.

Criteria are standards, rules, algorithms, or tests on which a decision can be based. So, a critical decision is one for which you can state the standard, rule, algorithm, or test on which it is based, so that others can understand and accept or reject your criteria as a sufficient basis for the decision.

You may say, "I decided to buy the new iPad because I felt like doing it." You have shared the criterion on which your decision is based; now let's see if it stands up to criticism: Is your old iPad no longer good enough? Do you have plenty of money to afford such a purchase? Will you be unable to pay for something more important because of this expenditure? Did you do some comparison-shopping to see that the iPad is the best device to meet your needs? Did you check with *Consumer Reports* or other independent testing groups to see if they gave a high rating to your iPad? Did you talk with people who own the iPad to see how they like it? Did you take time to think about this decision in relation to others you must make to increase the likelihood you will be happy you did it? Some of your friends might conclude that this was more of an impulse purchase than a critical decision. In fact, if you were really pushed by such questions, you might admit the decision does not stand up to such criticism and is therefore not critical. But, you may still be glad you did it, because we don't always want to make a critical decision.

By contrast, consider a decision that almost anyone would want to make critically. Parents are urged to have their children vaccinated to protect them from disease, but now there are reports that vaccinating your child might be dangerous. The Centers for Disease Control and Prevention (CDC) reported in 2011 that about one in 150 children have autism spectrum disorder (ASD), and that is a higher number than estimates from the early 1990s. The CDC said, "Some people believe increased exposure to thimerosal [a mercury-based preservative] (from the addition of important new vaccines recommended for children) explains the higher prevalence in recent years" (Vaccine Safety). As a parent, you would want to weigh the risks to your child from either lacking protection from disease or potentially developing a disorder of ASD. The CDC concluded, based on a scientific review by the Institute of Medicine, "the evidence favors rejection of a causal relationship between thimerosal-containing vaccines and autism." But that may not be good enough for you. You may want to take the CDC conclusion into account along with other criteria. If you go online to research this question, you will encounter, among many other sites, **About.com** writing on the subject. They identify a number of issues that to date are unresolved, but they stress this caution: when doing your research, you must remember that what comes up in an Internet search may be produced by people trying to persuade you to their way of thinking, and they may use questionable fact claims and omit important considerations. It will be necessary for you to look beyond headlines and opening paragraphs to make a quality assessment of the material. In other words, they urge you to make a critical decision.

However, critical decision making does not demand certain knowledge or unanimous agreement. Within the domain of argumentation, questions have no sure answers to which all reasonable people must agree. When we say decisions must stand up to criticism, we mean that before action is taken, people must engage in a critical process and act, when the time comes, on the results of that process. You will be forced to decide whether or not to vaccinate your child without knowing with certainty that it is safe. If you wait, you are deciding to let your child go through highly susceptible ages without protection. Although there is no single way to make critical decisions, we will explain the process by focusing on some of the more important elements: *toleration of uncertainty*, *internal dialogue*, *dialectic*, *spheres*, *rhetoric*, and the *willingness to act* even though no certain answers or unanimous agreement.

Toleration of Uncertainty

To call decision making critical is to say that the claims of argumentation are inherently open to ongoing criticism. Decisions must be made and actions taken on them without knowing for certain that they are correct. In religion, politics, science, ethics, business, law, government, education, and many more pivotal areas of your life, you must decide and act without being able to wait until you are certain.

In ancient Greece, Socrates was sure that an absolute truth was out there waiting to be discovered, but he also recognized how very difficult it was to find. His solution was simply to continue searching, indefinitely if necessary, until absolute truth was found. Philosophers may have the luxury of an endless search for truth, but you rarely do.

Those human tasks that must be accomplished through reason within a context of **uncertainty** lie within the domain of argumentation. To engage in argumentation is to tolerate uncertainty.

Uncertainty Is Pervasive. As you proceed in the study of argumentation, you will probably be surprised to find uncertainty so pervasive. Throughout modern times, many scholars (followers of Socrates) have refused to teach argumentation because it operated in arenas of uncertainty, and they were interested only in the absolute. As those issues once thought to be susceptible to certain answers have proven to be, at best, uncertain, the study of argumentation has become increasingly important. Physicist F. David Peat characterizes the history of science in the twentieth century as moving from certainty to uncertainty. "We have left the dream of absolute certainty behind. In its place each of us must now take responsibility for the uncertain future" (213).

Uncertainty is partly the result of the constantly changing world we inhabit. The universe is expanding, the world continues to experience forces that push continents apart and mountains up and down, and living organisms are born, live, and die in continuous change. Michael Shnayerson and Mark J. Plotkin report that in 1969, the U.S.

surgeon general declared, "We can close the books on infectious diseases" because of the emergence of antibiotics (11). But the Centers for Disease Control announced in 2007 the presence of antibiotic-resistant strains of *Staphylococcus aureus* that were creating a health crisis, as reported in the *New York Times* on October 23, 2007. And, in 2010, the respected British medical journal *Lancet Infectious Diseases* claimed that the rapid spread of multidrug-resistant bacteria might mean the end of antibiotics altogether (Boseley 1). Within a half-century, antibiotics conquered infection and then infection conquered antibiotics. Of course, the issue remains open: keep an eye out for future developments.

Language Is Inherently Ambiguous.   Another source of uncertainty is the inherently ambiguous character of language. By language, we usually mean words, but the same principles apply to all signs, pictures, objects, mathematical symbols, musical sounds, and anything else that facilitates communication.

One of the things that allowed people in the past to think they could find certainty was the belief that language could convey precise meaning. They thought meaning was derived from a tight link between language and "reality" (the presumed but erroneous belief in the regularity of the universe). Aristotle's idea of **fallacies** (argument practices that are persuasive but illogical), which is still influential today, rests largely on such assumptions about language (Hamblin, *Fallacies* 50–63). Aristotle believed in language precision. He noted how many times argumentation is frustrated by ambiguity, frequently by people who intentionally hope to mislead, and so he labeled those instances as fallacies or sophistical refutations. Aristotle's system loses much of its force today, when we find that language cannot be made as precise as the system requires. Language is inherently ambiguous.

Language is a collection of noises, movements, and marks people utter or set down on a surface. Language is not connected to things "in the world"; it is simply a tool people use to interact with each other. These noises and marks become language only when we use them as such, and that use defines their nature (Kent 11). Words do not have meaning; people have meaning that they try to share through language. When you seek to communicate, there are at least three meaning processes at work: (1) the meaning you intend to communicate, (2) the conventional meanings stored in dictionaries or other databases, and (3) the interpretations made by the people with whom you are communicating (Anderson and Meyer 48). The junior Senator from Utah claims to be an expert on the U.S. Constitution. He says he knows just what the framers of the Constitution meant when they wrote it, and we should stick with that meaning today. What he "knows" is his own interpretation of what the framers meant. The subject of language is one's perception, not reality.

The Attraction of Certainty Is Powerful.   History documents a search for truth and certainty. Philosopher John Dewey in *The Quest for Certainty* observed that our society is obsessed with a quest for certainty (Dewey). Whether it is a genetic characteristic of humans or something learned, people deplore doubt. It is an uncomfortable state of mind from which people seek to free themselves (Peirce 7–18). Writing about the role of various parts of the brain on how we make decisions, author Jonah Lehrer says,

> It feels good to be certain. Confidence is comforting. This desire to always be right is a dangerous side effect of having so many competing brain regions inside one's head . . . This is why being sure about something can be such a relief. The default state of the brain is indecisive

disagreement; various mental parts are constantly insisting that the other parts are wrong. Certainty imposes consensus on the inner cacophony. It lets you pretend that your entire brain agrees with your behavior (210).

We like to think of science and mathematics as bedrock, certain reality. "We demand truths that are absolute, leaders who are blameless and doctors who are omniscient" (Salzer B5). We expect arguments that are true and valid for everyone.

Perelman and Olbrechts-Tyteca note that René Descartes, the influential seventeenth-century philosopher and mathematician, declared that anything that was not certain was false. "It was this philosopher who made the self-evident the mark of reason, and considered rational only those demonstrations which, starting from clear and distinct ideas, extended, by means of apodictic [incontestable] proofs, the self-evidence of the axioms to the derived theorems" (1). Descartes believed his certainty was divine because God would not mislead us. His ideas struck a chord with Europeans who had suffered long and terrible wars and were desperate for something secure to hold to (Kagan et al. 467–478).

The Future Is Inherently Uncertain. The primary reason for uncertainty in argumentation stems from the fact that decision making invariably commits you now to actions to be carried out in the future. Argumentation comes into play when you must choose, and choice inherently involves uncertainty. It may be uncertainty about future consequences of what you do today, future preferences, or how you will feel about today's actions tomorrow (Simonson 158).

Argumentation and Critical Decision Making describes a process by which you seek the best possible choices within a context of uncertainty and ambiguity. Most of the decision making people do occurs in this context. From trying to understand how your own mind works to characterizing the universe, from deciding what to do on Saturday night to pondering to what to do with your life, you engage in argumentation and critical decision making. The better you use the process, the better you are at making decisions. But unless you are genuinely willing to open your mind to alternative ideas (to become uncertain about the best decision) and accept the inevitable uncertainty of the outcome, you cannot make critical decisions.

Critical Thinking — The Internal Dialogue

A second element of critical decision making is critical thinking. Although argumentation is a social process (audience-centered), it involves engaging individuals in making up their minds about how to act through communication with other people. Many people speak of critical thinking alone, as if it were an end in itself. But critical thinking that is uncoupled from behavior has little value. Argumentation theory asserts that critical thinking is one important part of the larger process of making critical decisions. There may be times when you are satisfied simply to think critically, but we are talking about the incessant obligation to make a decision and act on it.

The term **critical thinking** calls attention to the fact that who you are, how your mind works, and what roles you play in society are inextricably linked. Self-awareness, or reflection on your own thinking and open-mindedness toward others, becomes an essential feature of critical thinking (Millman 48–49). Phrases such as "sensitive to context," "reflective," "thinking appropriate to a particular mode or domain of thinking," and "to assess the force of reasons in the context in which reasons play a role" are other ways to characterize critical thinking.

Many scholars argue that critical thinking means to follow the rules of formal logic, or at least to avoid fallacies that often turn on logical errors. Courses in logic are taught with the purpose of improving critical thinking. However, even those who have studied formal logic find it difficult to follow it in their thought processes. "Over the last 40 years there has been a great deal of work in cognitive psychology on people's logical reasoning abilities. . . . The conclusion of this work was that in many areas people seem unable to reason logically" (Oaksford and Chater 173–174). This should not be surprising because logic is the "calculus of certainty" and it was not designed to manage our thinking in the uncertain domain of argumentation. What is needed, say Mike Oaksford and Nick Chater, is a calculus of uncertainty that they identify as probability theory (13). Michael Scriven has suggested a theory of informal logic in which he rejects most aspects of formal logic in order to provide a rationale for critical thinking (21–45). At this stage of our discussion, it is enough to say that critical thinking employs the same process of argumentation that we describe throughout this book.

Critical thinking is the *personal* phase of critical decision making. It is the first step in the conscious reconciliation between your inner thoughts and your social experience. Critical decision making requires us to focus on our individual thinking as well as interact with others in developing and testing arguments. To rely totally on either your own thoughts or social influence is dangerous. If individuals engaging in argumentation are not willing and able to think critically, they will be unable to participate effectively in critical decision making.

When we say that critical thinking is the personal phase of critical decision making, we are not suggesting that it is all that different from the social act of argumentation. Indeed, research suggests that critical thinking is really a minidebate you carry on with yourself. What is often mistaken for private thought is more likely an "internalized conversation" (Mead 173), an "internal dialogue" (Mukarovsky), or an "imagined interaction" (Gotcher and Honeycutt 1–3). All of these concepts refer essentially to the same thing, which we will call an internal dialogue.

The idea is this: You are able to carry on a conversation in your mind that involves both a "self" that represents you and "others" who stand for those people, real or imagined, with whom you wish to try out an argument. In a sense, all of our communication behaviors are pretested in social simulations (internal dialogue) prior to being shared in actual social situations (Wenburg and Wilmot 21). It may be misleading, in fact, to distinguish between imagined and actual interactions. During any conversation, you may find yourself doing some of the dialogue mentally while some of it may be spoken aloud, and, at any moment, you may not be able to say with confidence which is which. Some societies make no such distinction (Regal 61–66).

In critical thinking, you become keenly aware of your internal dialogues. You identify and put aside the tendency to think only of how to justify your thoughts while denigrating the thinking of others. Instead, you must apply critical tests, reflect on what you are doing, and try to open your mind to the potential weaknesses in your position while truly looking for other and better ways of thinking. Ian Mitroff calls it "smart thinking" and says if you are adept at it you "know how to cut through complex issues, ask the right questions, and solve the right problems." He concludes, "The ability to spot the right problems, frame them correctly, and implement appropriate solutions to them is the true competitive edge that will separate the successful individuals, organizations, and societies from the also-rans" (Mitroff 6).

It is critical thinking that makes you able to become a working partner in the next element of critical decision making: *dialectic.*

Dialectic — The External Dialogue

Dialectic is an ancient process that is very much on the minds of contemporary scholars. As an element of critical decision making, **dialectic** is the social dialogue in which people seek to come to understanding by opening themselves to the thinking of others with an interest in learning and changing. Critical thinking is the internal dialogue and dialectic is an external, interpersonal, or intertextual dialogue (Montgomery and Baxter 2). In some contexts, dialectic is closely associated with using logic, but we are using the term in a different sense. Now, instead of an imagined conversation, you actually interact with one or more other people. The objective is to continue the development of your own thoughts by learning those of others, combining personal and social influences in a creative error correction process.

Aristotle defined dialectic as the counterpart of rhetoric—a companion in the critical decision making process, a philosophical disputation. He believed that people are inherently rational: "The function of man is an activity of the soul which follows or implies a rational principle" (*Nicomachean Ethics* 1098a).

In dialectic, individuals engage in conversation, one person advances a claim tentatively, seeks to point out the reasoning behind it, and then responds to the probing questions of the others. "Dialectic proceeds by question and answer, not, as rhetoric does, by continuous exposition" (Kennedy in Aristotle On Rhetoric 26). Michael Leff identifies four points of contrast between dialectic and rhetoric: (1) issues in dialectic are more general and abstract than those in rhetoric; (2) dialectic deals with the relationship of propositions to one another in a search for rationality, whereas rhetoric relates propositions to situations following social norms; (3) dialectic proceeds through question and answer with participants seeking to persuade one another, whereas in rhetoric there is relatively uninterrupted discourse in an effort to persuade an audience; and (4) "dialectic employs unadorned, technical language, whereas rhetoric accommodates and embellishes language for persuasive purposes" (57).

William Isaacs describes dialectic as a dialogue enabling a "free flow of meaning, which has the potential of transforming the power relationships among the people concerned" (395). His program, he says, can help business organizations change their patterns of behavior in productive ways. In many meetings, says Isaacs, people feel themselves or their actions being challenged and this generates a tendency toward defensiveness. However, in dialogue, Isaacs argues, one has the choice to "defend or suspend": to suspend one's defensiveness in order to listen and learn from others (365).

In the dialectical stage of critical decision making, truly important work is done. It is here that parties discuss the ultimate purpose of the decision making: What are we trying to accomplish? They discuss how the decision making will be carried out and what starting points will be available. They bring up (1) definitions of important terms; (2) the facts they can agree on; (3) what their presumptions will be and who will undertake the burden of proof; (4) what the key points of disagreement (issues) are; and (5) generally decide how arguments will be criticized: what criteria will be applied.

Although Aristotle characterized dialectic and rhetoric as counterparts, the distinguished rhetorician Wayne Booth claims that rhetoric plays a vital role during dialectic as well. He says a key function of rhetoric at its best is facilitating dialogue, moving people to listen to each other closely, and promoting reconciliation.

> At its best, serious rhetoric pursues understanding of the kind that results only when there is genuine listening to the opponent's position. Our goal as rhetoricians is to pursue a dialogue that, in contrast to our current militaristic rhetoric, leads the opponent to burst out with something like "Oh, now I understand your position." Or at least, "Oh, now I can see that we can get somewhere as we talk together." (9)

It is not only possible but it is also desirable that during dialectic, the issues are resolved and critical decisions made without the need for more adversarial rhetorical exchanges.

During dialectic, the parties involved in the decision making establish relationships with each other and set up ways of communicating that may or may not facilitate agreement. Dialectic can fail if parties become angry, belligerent, threatened, or frightened, allowing their differences to harden into non-negotiable positions. Dialectic succeeds if those involved consciously engage in what Kathy Domenici and Stephen W. Littlejohn call facework. They recognize that identity is socially constructed and requires people to pay attention to the "how" of communication and the manner of communication. This involves more than merely being concerned that people do not lose face during the dialogue. It broadly addresses the ways in which, during dialectic, people create the personas that will influence the entire process of decision making. Domenici and Littlejohn identify the following principles:

- Create positive communities through constructive communication. Communities and systems of all types are made in interaction.
- Understand that every act is part of a larger set of interactions that, over time, connects people in relationships and communities.
- Communicate with others in a way that honors the complex identities of each person (176).

Often, if dialectic occurs when strong differences already have been expressed, people find it difficult to engage in effective facework. Also, because this type of rhetorical behavior is difficult to perform, many people lack the understanding and ability to do it successfully. Failure at this stage can sour the relationships so that cooperative decisions are difficult, if not impossible, to reach. In this case, it is often wise to employ mediators, who are professionals in helping people through a successful negotiation leading to integrative decisions, as we discuss later in Chapter 3 under alternative dispute resolution methods.

Some contemporary scholars suggest that failure to understand and engage in dialectic is at the heart of some of our most painful difficulties. They suggest that the dogmatic rights-based diatribes that too often replace argumentation demonstrate the absence of dialectic in our society. We need to be aware, say Floyd W. Matson and Ashley Montagu,

> . . . that the end of human communication is not to command but to commune; and that knowledge of the highest order (whether of oneself, or of the other) is to be sought and found not through detachment but through connection, not by objectivity but by intersubjectivity, not in a state of estranged aloofness but in something resembling an act of love (6).

Richard H. Gaskins says that argumentation runs into trouble when debates boil down to an inability to prove any position to be superior to others, resulting in decisions being made not on solid, critical grounds, but by default (1–11). He proposes more effective use of dialectic through which values, presumptions, and criteria can be worked out in advance (240–272).

Derek Edwards and Jonathan Potter argue that psychological research into human cognitive behavior such as perception, memory, language and mental representation, knowledge, and reasoning must proceed from the fact that these processes are socially and culturally embedded (14). They are to be understood through an examination not of the individual mind but in naturally occurring conversation, an informal dialectic. "The phenomena of thought and reasoning, of mind and memory, are best understood as culturally formed, socially shaped and defined, constituted in talk and text. . . ." Cognitive processes, they say, ". . . are ideas generated within cultures, conceptions of sense, action and motive that people invent to mediate their dealings with each other and to engage in social forms of life" (18).

Spheres

We have spoken of appropriate decision makers as the object of your argumentation. Now, we will locate decision makers within decision making groups, forums, organizations, societies, professions, disciplines, generations, or other such arrangements, which we will refer to as **spheres**. We will provide a general definition of spheres first, and then discuss some of the ways spheres work in argumentation and critical decision making.

Definition of Spheres. Spheres are collections of people in the process of interacting on and making critical decisions. They are real sociological entities (Willard 28). You cannot make a critical decision completely alone. No matter how private you believe your thoughts to be, your internal dialogue involves a myriad of "voices" from your life's experiences.

Spheres function in the present tense: They are in the process of making critical decisions. Although they quite often have a history of the same or similar people doing similar activities, that history functions for the purposes of critical decision making only as construed in the present. Edwards and Potter argue that perception, memory, language, knowledge, and reasoning are neither fixed in our brains nor guaranteed in documents and protocols. They are to be found in our interactions in the present. What we recall as facts, they say, are really what we put into our present rhetorical accounts and accept as facts (44–57).

Spheres operate as decision making groups. Although millions of people may ultimately play a part in a single decision, in practical terms, the process occurs in multiple, overlapping small groups (see Frey 4–8).

John F. Cragan and David W. Wright define a small group "as a few people engaged in communication interaction over time . . . who have common goals and norms and have developed a communication pattern for meeting their goals in an interdependent manner" (7). Although the size of the group can vary widely, generally speaking at any time, a group probably involves enough people to provide a diversity of opinion, yet still allow the development of reasonably close interpersonal relations in which people know and react to every other member.

Donald G. Ellis and B. Aubrey Fisher describe **group structuration** as a process in which groups develop by making use of certain rules and resources while processing information.

Rules control how things ought to be done in the group and resources are materials and attributes the group can use, "such as special knowledge, money, status, equipment, and relationships" (56). Although groups develop highly individualized patterns of interaction and sets of rules and resources, they are still in constant tension with external constraints.

When we speak of spheres, then, we are talking about decision making groups with recognizable goals and norms and sets of rules and resources and patterns of interaction, most often under ongoing tension (direction, control, ultimate decision power) with external entities. For example, in a business setting, a task force in research and development may be working on how an invention might be transformed into a marketable product, but they do so within the constraints of the larger company organization. In law, two lawyers and a judge may generate a ruling, but it must be done according to the dictates of the appropriate laws and subject to the review of courts of appeal.

Although spheres operate in the present, their interactions observed over time demonstrate patterns that are related to one another and used time after time. In critical decision making, these patterns of interaction include the starting points of argument, the way argumentation is conducted, and the criteria used to evaluate arguments and form critical decisions. Because they are thus predictable, the patterns guide your guesses about how your arguments will be understood and criticized. Because they are predictable, patterns of argumentation come to be associated with some groups and serve to increase the likelihood that critical decisions will result. *Groups are called spheres when their predictable patterns of communicative behavior are used in the production and evaluation of argumentation.*

Spheres, then, consist of people functioning as a group who share a cluster of criteria for the production and appraisal of argumentation. People in spheres share language interpretation strategies, facts, presumptions, probabilities, and commonplaces. But remember that sharing is in the present, subject to ongoing change, and is never certain to yield a critical decision.

Location of Spheres.   Spheres may consist of only a few people or may constitute groups within complex organizations involving many people. Spheres may be transitory or enduring. At any time, you may be a member of many spheres. Your **internal dialogue**, because it includes many voices, can work as a sphere. Basic *social groups* such as families, friends, or people with common interests can function as spheres. Standing or temporary *task-oriented small groups* such as committees or task forces function as spheres.

Groups working within the rubric of a religion, profession, academic discipline, vocation, civic or charitable organization, business, or governmental unit may function as spheres. Sometimes, the defining characteristic of a sphere is an ethnic association, a social movement, or a political entity such as a state or nation. All spheres function within a culture and during a certain time or generation, both of which supply some of the argumentation patterns of a sphere.

Spheres and Level of Activity.   G. Thomas Goodnight identifies three levels of activity of spheres: personal, technical, and public. By level of activity, Goodnight means the "grounds on which arguments are built and the authorities to which arguers appeal" (216).

In **personal spheres,** the level of activity is more spontaneous, negotiated interpersonally or in your internal dialogues. The interstructured and repetitive patterns of argumentation tend to be less easily discerned and predicted, so the chances of a critical decision are lower than at other levels of activity.

Technical spheres are those in which formal argumentative patterns are enforced. The highly specialized criteria are appropriate to the nature of the decisions made by professional groups such as lawyers, managers, scholars, engineers, physicians, and technicians. Those with advanced education, possessing a special kind of knowledge, are most likely to be found in technical spheres. Toulmin (*The Uses of Argument*) uses the term *field* to describe special criteria for the appraisal of arguments within a particular technical sphere. Charles A. Willard notes that a technical sphere may restrict access to its patterns of argumentation by requiring decision participants to "master specialized codes, procedures, knowledge, and language to limit what can count as reasonable argument" (50). This may insulate it from interacting with other spheres without substantial translation.

Public spheres usually involve those people who seek participation in public debate and are recognized by the relevant decision makers. They may be elected politicians or publicly recognized spokespersons. Although politicians may use highly formalized arguments, their decision making must be comprehensible to the public. The chief problem with the public sphere is complexity. Public decision makers face complex organizations representing different values, interests, and influence.

Goodnight's idea of the personal, technical, and public spheres is useful in understanding that some issues require only the most informal and commonsense demands for support of arguments, whereas other issues demand highly specialized argumentation. The public sphere is neither as casual as the personal nor as specialized as the technical. Yet, as Goodnight says, "it provides forums with customs, traditions, and requirements for arguers" because the consequences of public disputes go beyond either the personal or technical spheres (257).

Ultimate Purpose.   Each sphere involves an ultimate purpose that provides a relatively enduring set of tests (criteria) of arguments. Toulmin speaks of this concept as "well-defined collective goals, which express the shared ideals of the discipline" (*Human Understanding*, 488). What critical tests arguments and decisions must satisfy are themselves rooted in " what we [people in the sphere] want now, constructed from our sense of purpose and what we are here for" (Willihnganz et al. 202). This generalized sense of purpose resists change to the extent that it is unlikely that one person or one argumentative interchange will have much effect on it. We refer to the ultimate purpose throughout this book as what the decision makers are *trying to accomplish*.

Chapter 16 discusses argumentation in government and politics, and that provides a good example of the need to identify what decision makers are trying to accomplish. In political campaigns, the ultimate purpose is to win elections. In government, the ultimate purpose is to establish laws and regulations that make the best policies for governing the country. When politicians make promises during campaigns that they later fail to act upon, people may complain, but realistically understand, that the arguments were aimed at winning the election. Once in office, the politician is now an office holder with a new ultimate purpose of governing well, and that may mean holding off on meeting campaign promises or even canceling them altogether. The Governor of Wisconsin promised during his 2010 campaign to restrict the ability of public employees' unions to bargain for anything other than wages and salary. Once in office, during the 2011 legislative session, the governor stuck to that promise even as protesting citizens occupied his state capitol, and the entire Democratic State Senate delegation had left the state to deny a quorum and object to the governor's efforts.

The arguments often centered on this question: what is the governor trying to accomplish? Initially, the governor said it was necessary to balance the state budget by asking the public employees to make concessions on health insurance and retirement plans. When the employee unions agreed to the concessions and the governor continued to call for reduced union negotiation rights, people asked, again, what are you trying to accomplish? Is it to balance the state budget, and if so, have not the unions granted the request? If the ultimate purpose is truly to balance the budget, then what will be accomplished by limiting union negotiation rights? Could weakening unions serve a political purpose rather than a government purpose? There seemed to be confusion over what was the ultimate purpose, and arguments could not be criticized apart from a clearly stated ultimate purpose. The governor kept saying, "I promised to do this during my campaign," as if getting elected was still the ultimate purpose (Krugman A23).

Complexity of Spheres. Our description of spheres may make them seem straightforward and clear, but that is not the case. In fact, there is considerable discussion among argumentation specialists about how to define spheres of argument and how they function. Scholars realize that the concept of spheres is just that—a concept. There have not been sufficient studies of people in the act of making decisions to make us as confident as we would prefer. For example, some commentators have argued that part of the concept of spheres involves the moral or ethical effect of how they function to empower some people and disempower or marginalize others. Shawn Batt reviews these comments in his article, "Keeping Company in Controversy: Education Reform, Spheres of Argument, and Ethical Criticism."

So, although the concept of spheres will help you come to understand argumentation and the decision making process, you need to keep your critical faculties in place. Remember the tentative nature of the concept and the hidden problems it entails.

Rhetoric

The fifth element in critical decision making is **rhetoric**. Aristotle defined rhetoric as the "ability [of a person, group, society, or culture] in each [particular] case to see [perceive] the available means of persuasion" (On Rhetoric 36). To perceive the available means of persuasion is to understand an issue from all points of view and ways of thinking. It is not necessary to use all of the available means, just take them into account (13).

Although the meaning of rhetoric has varied dramatically in the almost 2,500 years since Aristotle, we will discuss its contemporary relevance to argumentation and critical decision making. There are three key rhetorical elements we need to explain here: audience, probability, and proof.

Audience. Rhetoric is concerned with people, how they think, act, and communicate. When we say our perspective of argumentation is **audience**-centered, we are saying it is a rhetorical perspective. In dialectic, the focus is on the soundness of reasoning and availability of support for claims. In rhetoric, the focus is on the bases with which people will grant or deny adherence to claims. As we will see in the discussion of proof, people resort to a wide variety of bases in making up their minds.

In his discussion of rhetoric, Aristotle observed rhetoric occurring throughout society: deciding on public policy, resolving legal disputes, and developing and strengthening the values that underlie most arguments. He noticed that different people respond differently to arguments, so he talked about how rhetoric can be adapted to the young, middle-aged, and elderly; to the wealthy and the powerful; and to those in all stations of society.

Aristotle divided knowledge into two groups: scientific demonstration, which he believed was not audience-centered, and rhetoric, which dealt with those issues not susceptible to certain demonstration and thus turning on human judgment. Today, scholars are much less likely to accept this division. Scientists of all kinds are more inclined to see their work as audience-centered, and we now read of rhetorical analyses of almost all aspects of scientific endeavor. Thomas Kuhn speaks of scientific revolutions in discussing his contention that science rests on paradigms or groups of people with common models, perspectives, problems, and procedures. When paradigms come into conflict, they work it out, says Kuhn, by using what is essentially political rhetoric.

Probability. As we have said, argumentation deals with those tasks that require decision under uncertainty. In a condition of uncertainty, the best we can seek is probability. We need to talk about two different meanings for the word **probability**.

In statistics and other forms of mathematical analyses of frequencies or chance, objective calculations can be made of the probability with which a certain phenomenon will occur or the probability that the phenomenon that did occur was the result of pure chance. For example, serious gamblers can say with high confidence the frequency with which certain combinations of numbers will appear on dice or roulette. Weather forecasters can calculate the frequency with which certain weather patterns will occur. Experimenters can say that their results could have been explained by chance alone, say, once in a thousand times. But even these calculations are by no means certain. "Statistical analysis must find ways to expose and counterbalance all the many factors that can lead to falsely positive results—among them human nature" (Carey 2).

Rhetorical probability is a more general concept that embraces mathematical probability as well as what might be called human or subjective probability. Early research into decision making revealed that people do not necessarily stick to mathematical probability even when it is explained to them and guaranteed to produce greater profits (Edwards and Tversky 71–89). Psychologists coined the term *subjective probability* to describe the experience in which, for example, people were told to bet on a single outcome because it was certain to produce a victory where all other options would not. In spite of this information, people varied their bets because they *felt* like doing so. Feelings, intuitions, values, and emotions are part of rhetorical probability.

Economists Andrew W. Lo and Richard H. Thaler note that people are presumed to behave rationally when making such decisions as investing money. For example, before buying securities, you should "maximize utility" by seeking to receive the most satisfaction for your money, and rationally that means paying the "right price" based on the intrinsic value of the stock you are buying. Price-earnings ratios, charts of past performance, and the behavior of factors that influence stock performance can be studied to produce mathematical probabilities of future values. But, as Lo and Thaler say, people regularly reject such rational probabilities to act instead on, "behavioral assumptions such as overreaction, overconfidence, loss aversion, and other human foibles that each of us exhibits with alarming regularity" (Lo and Thaler 13–15). They conclude that markets are not rational in the traditional economic sense. Investors ultimately act on the basis of rhetorical (subjective) probability.

Rhetorical probability works in two ways: the extent to which one person is willing to advance a claim and be held responsible for it, and the extent to which people are willing to accept and act on a claim. In critical decision making, both of these probability judgments apply.

We have said that argumentation deals with the uncertain, but there is no law that says you cannot say you are certain about a claim. People do it all the time. We use words such as absolutely, certainly, unquestionably, or without a doubt to describe our claims. If your claim really cannot be advanced with objective certainty, how can you say it is so? Because you are not describing the mathematical probability of your claim or some other measure of reality, you are describing the extent to which you are willing to be associated with the claim and be held responsible for the outcome.

A stranger stops you and asks, "Can you tell me what time it is?" You reply, "Certainly, it's 10:00 o'clock." "Thanks," replies the stranger, "I'm setting a watch." "Oh," you interject, "If you're setting your watch, it's actually 10:03." "It's good you corrected that," the stranger says, "because the watch I'm setting is used to control locks on our vaults." Shocked to learn the importance of the original question, you blurt out, "Maybe you should ask someone else. I'm not sure my watch is accurate." What changed during the interaction? Not the time of day—it was your willingness to be held accountable for your claim, or the level of rhetorical probability you wanted to communicate toward the stranger's decision.

Consider the decision to drop atomic bombs on two Japanese cities during World War II. There were scientific probabilities about whether the bombs would work and whether they would cause extensive destruction. There were tactical probabilities about whether the Japanese would surrender once the bombs were dropped, or if they were about to surrender anyhow. The alternative, dropping the bombs on a deserted area while Japanese leaders looked on, was rejected as unlikely (improbable) to cause surrender. There was the military probability of how many lives would be lost on both sides if an invasion of the Japanese home islands occurred. There was the moral probability whether history would judge the dropping of the bombs to be justified.

The debate over this decision continues. There is sharp disagreement on most of these questions. President Harry S. Truman, however, could not wait more than a half-century to make the decision. He had little time and knew he would live forever with the consequences of the decision. He committed himself to those consequences, and that is rhetorical probability.

On the fifty-eighth anniversary of the dropping of the bombs, Nicholas D. Kristof reported in the New York Times that "there's an emerging consensus: we Americans have blood on our hands" (August 5, 2003). But he argued in reply that the consensus is "profoundly mistaken" and that the bombs helped end the war. On the other hand, Daniel Jonah Goldhagen, writing in 2009 on mass murder, included Truman alongside Adolph Hitler and Joseph Stalin as among history's leading killers.

Proof. Mathematical calculations and experimental demonstrations constitute proof for some scientific probability claims. Rhetorical **proof**, which includes such scientific proof, is more complex.

Aristotle included three forms of proof in his discussion of rhetoric. *Logos* represented the use of reasoning taking the form of logic as support for claims. In Aristotle's system, examples served as the rhetorical equivalent to induction, and the *enthymeme* (a rhetorical syllogism) served as rhetorical deduction. In a symbolic format, induction and deduction are forms of logic that work on problems outside the domain of argumentation. A pure induction requires itemization of 100% of the elements under consideration. A rhetorical induction or example requires sufficient instances to satisfy the audience. Simply demonstrating that it satisfies the rules of internal validity proves a symbolic deduction or syllogism. A rhetorical deduction or enthymeme depends on its link to established beliefs, values, and ways of thinking already held by the audience.

Pathos, for Aristotle, included the feelings, emotions, intuitions, sympathies, and prejudices that people bring to decisions. It suggested the fact that people accept or reject claims and make or refuse to make decisions on the basis of the values that are connected to the arguments. It is common for people to speak of separating reason from emotion, as if using emotion is bad. But the most current studies of our brains lead to the conclusion that "decision making is itself an emotional process" (Sternberg 69).

Ethos identified the extent to which people are inclined to go along with an argument because of who expresses it. In contemporary research, ethos is seen as part of credibility.

In the chapters that follow, we will discuss the various forms of support that are available to prove your claims. The important point to remember here is that rhetorical proof is addressed to people (audience-centered) and the quality of proof is measured by the extent to which the appropriate decision makers find it sufficient for their needs.

CONCLUSION

We have introduced you to the domain of argumentation by identifying the elements of argumentation and critical decision making. In argumentation, a key term is adherence, which characterizes the audience-centered focus of argumentation on the appropriate decision makers, who have also been defined. Claims, the points or propositions you offer for others' consideration and adherence, the support or materials provided to help others understand and subscribe to your claims, and the definition of argument as the intersection of a claim and its support have been discussed. Arguments serve to resolve issues of fact, value, and policy. Criticism, the give and take of making your claims and noting the weaknesses in alternative claims, has been explained as a key feature of argumentation.

To participate in critical decision making, you must understand that you will necessarily be working with uncertain knowledge, and you must keep your mind open to alternatives and resist the temptation to rush to belief. Critical thinking is a concept that describes reflective, open-minded attention to your own thinking and the search for alternatives and complete information. Dialectic and rhetoric are counterparts in the development of critical decisions. Dialectic is the question–answer process through which you and others inquire, seek to understand the values and criteria appropriate to your decision, and entertain various points of view. It is in spheres that people set the purpose and method of producing and critizing arguments leading to critical decisions. Rhetoric is the process of persuasion through which claims are presented to decision makers (audience) with the appropriate proof to help them understand and grant adherence.

In summary, we have said that argumentation provides the mechanism that mediates the tension between individual judgment (your mind) and social judgment (your culture) to bring the most powerful and relevant criteria to bear on any decision. The product is social (audience-centered) critical decision making.

EXERCISES/PROJECTS

Read the editorials in one issue of a newspaper and answer these questions for each:

1. What adherence is sought from the reader?
2. Who are the appropriate decision makers? Why?
3. What claims does the editorial make?
4. What support is provided for the claims?
5. What criticism can you make of the arguments?

Select a topic with which you are familiar that involves making a decision. Prepare an argument in which you label each of these parts:

1. In what kind of sphere is the decision to be made?
2. What is the ultimate purpose of the decision?
3. What proposition expresses your desired decision?
4. What issue do you want to address?
5. What claim do you wish to make?
6. What kind of support will you supply?

Appraising Argumentation

KEY TERMS

criteria, p. 25

critical decision, p. 26

reasonable, p. 26

belief system, p. 27

worldviews, p. 28

starting points, p. 32

interpretation strategies, p. 32

facts, p. 33

presumption, p. 33

probabilities, p. 34

commonplaces, p. 35

When you interview for a job, you and the interviewer are engaged in reasoned argumentation. The position announcement should set the broad **criteria** that will be used to judge your application, and the interview will flesh them out. Here is a position announcement:

We are looking for an administrator in our downtown office. This person will support our Information Technology consulting services operations for our national clients.

- Excellent MS Office solid Excel and PowerPoint skills
- Organized and detail-oriented
- General understanding of IT terminologies and technologies
- Good writing skills
- Good phone and interpersonal relationship skills
- Good typing skills
- Good conceptual skills with an ability to crunch numbers and generate reports

In return, you can expect the following:

- Join a stable, fast growing technology company
- To be treated with respect and make a contribution to our growth and success

When you go to the interview, they could well ask, "Why should we hire you?" This is an invitation for you to present arguments on your behalf, complementing those in your application. What will be the strongest arguments you can make? At this stage, your best bet is to follow the criteria set out in the job announcement and argue this way:

ULTIMATE PURPOSE: TO BE HIRED BY THIS COMPANY

PROPOSITION: I have the ability to be an excellent employee.

CLAIM #1: I have excellent MS Office and solid Excel and PowerPoint skills, and I have a general understanding of IT terminologies and technologies.

SUPPORT: My transcript shows courses in these areas;

CLAIM #2: I am organized and a detail-oriented person, with good conceptual skills and an ability to crunch numbers and generate reports,

SUPPORT: The letter from my last employer mentions these skills;

CLAIM #3: I am effective in writing, typing, phone, and interpersonal relationships,

SUPPORT: My letters of recommendation report on these skills, and I have samples of my written work.

FIGURE 2.1

Arguments Based on Criteria

If you can convince the interviewers of each of these points, and if they truly are the criteria being used to make this decision, it would be reasonable for them to hire you. It would be a **critical decision**. Of course, they could interview five people, all of whom meet these criteria. It would be reasonable to hire any one of them. So, a critical decision does not mean resolution of uncertainty. It does not necessarily mean finding the one correct decision. It means selecting and applying a set of criteria designed to generate the best possible decision.

What will probably happen is this: During the interview, the employer will refine the criteria as you develop your arguments. They will try to make value judgments about the quality of your credentials compared to other applicants, and, before making a hiring decision, they will probably discuss the applicant pool with other colleagues to add their particular criteria.

Before a job offer is made, still other criteria may be applied, partly in response to arguments you make. For example, you might comment on their promise of treating you with respect and allowing you to participate in their growth and success. You might say, "I value your promise of treating me with respect, and in return I commit myself to working for the growth and success of this company."

In Chapter 1, we defined a critical decision as one that can survive the test of a relevant set of criteria, one that can stand up to *criticism*. We also said that argumentation and critical decision making involve choice in a context of uncertainty.

In this chapter, we will talk about how people apply criteria to arguments, and how they can use such criticism to increase the quality of their decisions even in the face of uncertainty. We introduce the term **reasonable** to describe the process through which arguments are tested and finally granted adherence because they rest on reasons and reasoning that reflect the standards of the sphere within which they are being critically examined. First, we will identify some of the forces that tend to reduce the reasonableness of decisions. Then, we will give greater detail about how people make reasonable decisions.

ARGUMENTATION AND BEING REASONABLE

Critical appraisal of argumentation applies to you in two interacting ways: (1) When you *present* an argument, the better you understand the way it will be evaluated, the stronger you can make it; (2) When you *evaluate* an argument, the better you understand the relevant criteria (tests for argument evaluation), the better (more critical) will be your decisions. These two points interact in the sense that presenters and evaluators of argumentation do their jobs best when they consciously operate within a common set of criteria (described in Chapter 1 as a sphere).

Why People Advance Unreasonable Arguments

Unreasonable arguments cannot stand up to critical appraisal. Often, the sphere defines what counts as an unreasonable argument. For example, in hiring decisions, laws specify that the company may not use criteria based on age, gender, religion, race, national origin, marital status, and so forth, and to bring up arguments about these categories would not stand up to criticism. The laws were passed to counter the *beliefs* some people have about age, gender, religion, race, and many other discriminatory concepts that have been used to make unreasonable decisions.

Beliefs Are Not Necessarily Reasonable

The Wizard's First Rule tells us, "Given proper motivations, almost anyone will believe almost anything. . . . They will believe a lie because they want to believe it's true, or because they are afraid it might be true" (Goodkind 560). Even when no one actually believes something, if no one can disprove it, then "a lie unchallenged is very soon stronger than a truth unsupported" (Hill 238). Novelist and law professor Stephen L. Carter puts it this way: "We're reasoning creatures. . . . We're designed to breathe the truth. We need it to live. When the truth we crave is hidden away, we'll breathe the lies to keep from smothering" (436). Although your beliefs are important and meaningful to you, they may not have come from a reasonable foundation or they may be applied in a way that cannot survive critical scrutiny.

Patrick Colm Hogan reports a variety of studies showing that beliefs operating in systems are behind a good deal of our tendency to conform to political and ideological positions even when the beliefs are quite untrue or at least without clear support (58–86). People develop fundamental beliefs during childhood that continue to influence their decisions throughout life. "They distort people's perceptions and even their memories, reforming individuals' experience in their image. For many years, cognitive scientists have been aware of a broad human tendency to reinterpret experience in conformity with basic beliefs " (74).

Glenn D. Walters argues that criminal behavior can be best understood by examining the development of individuals' belief systems. He defines a **belief system** as a "group of interrelated convictions of truth or statements of perceived reality" (21). They involve, he says, not only cognitive elements but also behavioral, sensory, motivational, and affective features. Walters says that beliefs interact both with the internal elements just mentioned and with one's experience. Beliefs are, says Walters, "more than what fills a person's head. . . . [P]eople construct their own realities and then proceed to defend these realities against alternative perspectives" (21, 44).

Your beliefs function, as these authors suggest, in belief systems that we will call **worldviews**. It is from your worldviews that you experience stereotypes, prejudices, norms, folkways, language, and culture. Worldviews are neither inherently reasonable nor unreasonable. They enable you to make it through life more comfortably. Having a common language is obviously important. So is sharing common narratives, scripts, or stories of how to go about your daily life: how to dress, eat, play, worship, form relationships, educate children, and care for the elderly. What you perceive as commonsense in any occasion is determined by your worldviews. You may have noticed, however, that your commonsense is different from that of, say, your acquaintances from other parts of the world. You may feel that other people's commonsense is unreasonable; they may think the same of you.

Thinking Is Not Necessarily Reasonable

More than a half-century of psychological research supports the claim that people use a variety of biases and heuristics (shortcuts in thinking) to guide their decision making in ways that depart from what rational theory would predict (Gilovich and Griffin 4–16). For example, thinking may be guided by facts that happen to be readily available or easy to access rather than those most significant to supporting your point. For example, when you do an Internet search to prepare a research paper, you may be confronted with thousands of items. Do you evaluate all the hits and make sure you are using only the most reliable, or do you look just long enough to meet your immediate needs and then write the paper (a heuristic called *satisficing*)? No one expects you to look at all the many hits that come up, but you are expected to evaluate the quality of those you do use. Even numerical data presented in graphs can lead to less than optimal decisions when managers use their ideas of what is generally true in their experience to interpret the data. "A large body of evidence suggests that prior beliefs significantly distort perceptions of correlation, such that people overestimate relationships that are expected and underestimate relationships that are unexpected. . . . [This is] the failure of analytic thinking to overcome informal prior impressions" (Hutchinson et al. 628).

A study of juror decision making found that jurors' race, the interpretation of the presumption of innocence, and the amount of evidence they were expected to consider had the "potential to decisively alter the outcome of critical judgments" (Tamborini et al. 354). Researcher Ron Tamborini and his associates observed that people can approach decision making from two forms of cognitive processing: systematic processing (what we describe as critical decision making) or heuristic processing which they conceptualized as "a more limited mode of information processing that requires less cognitive effort and fewer cognitive resources than systematic processing" (342). For example, a juror might look at the defendant and decide on guilt or innocence simply because he or she was more or less attractive, of the same or different race as the juror, or consider the defendant's gender, dress, behavior, and so on. This would exemplify heuristic processing.

> [We were once told by a clerk of courts that he and his judge could tell just by looking whether the defendant was guilty or not. He thought it a special gift they had.]

FIGURE 2.2

The point is that while people are capable of systematic processing, the use of heuristic processing is easier and thus quite likely to be employed when motivation is low (Gilovich & Griffin 16).

The Mind Is Not Necessarily Reasonable

Ever since Plato assumed a separation of mind and body, and Aristotle proclaimed human beings to be rational animals, scholars have operated on the assumption that our mind functions in an inherently logical way. Aristotle's rhetorical system is premised on the assumption that people are able to find truth, even when it is mixed in with a great deal of nonsense, because they have a rational capacity. To this day, some logicians, linguists, psycholinguists, and cognitive psychologists continue to claim that the human mind operates according to formal logical rules or probabilities (Braine and O'Brien; Oaksford and Chater).

In his 1637 *Discourse on Method,* René Descartes announced, "I think, therefore, I am," giving his support to the notion that the mind can be separated from the body so as to operate logically. In his 1994 book, *Descartes' Error,* Antonio R. Damasio says this about Descartes' claim: "The statement, perhaps the most famous in the history of philosophy . . . illustrates precisely the opposite of what I believe to be true about the origins of mind and about the relation between mind and body." We should say, "I am, therefore I think" (248). He claims the mind cannot be understood apart from knowledge of neuroanatomy, neurophysiology, and neurochemistry. There is considerable evidence, says Damasio, that efforts to find an inherently logical function in the mind are doomed to failure.

Gerald M. Edelman, director of the Neurosciences Institute and chair of the Department of Neurobiology at the Scripps Research Institute, agrees. He reports that people are physiological and social beings capable of thinking and feeling, but there is no evidence of a rationality of mind that can be separated from our totality as human beings.

Our minds sort sensory stimuli into meaningful units. In this way, our mind creates its own reality to serve our needs. But no matter how helpful that reality may be, Philip Regal points out that it is an "illusion organ" (69). That means sometimes your reality could get you into trouble. In the summer of 1999, John F. Kennedy, Jr., his wife, and her sister died in a plane crash off Martha's Vineyard, Massachusetts. Investigation revealed that the plane dove straight into the water at a high speed and no mechanical problems were discovered. Our friend, a retired colonel in the U.S. Marine Corps who started his flying career in World War II fighters, said what probably happened is that Kennedy's mind told him he was flying level even though the plane was on its downward course. "A pilot," our friend said, "must learn to ignore personal reality and stick totally with what the instruments say. Kennedy just didn't have enough instrument flight experience to be able to do that."

Research is now able to "observe" the mind at work through various imaging technologies, and the results are discouraging. It appears as if when you need to make a decision, you receive inputs from different parts of your brain and nervous system ranging from the most evolutionarily advanced parts such as the prefrontal cortex to the most primitive parts such as the amygdala or the limbic system, and they rarely give a consistent message. When making a decision, you are bombarded with contradictory choices, and silencing the debate through the force of the executive power of the prefrontal cortex could well cause you to make the wrong decision: a possible explanation of the Kennedy crash (Lehrer 217).

Social Influence Is Not Necessarily Reasonable

Solomon Asch reports experiments in which he asked people to judge the length of one line compared to a series of other lines. He adjusted the task until people judging alone made almost no errors. He then selected four experimenters who were instructed to announce an incorrect answer and put them with a series of naive subjects who did not know the experimenters were being intentionally incorrect. One by one, the experimenters would announce an incorrect choice, and then the naive subject was asked to respond. Imagine the social pressure this placed on the naive subjects. They had just heard four apparently honest people give answers that seemed obviously wrong. In the research, about a third of the naive subjects chose to give the same incorrect answer rather than disagree with the others.

Some subjects later said they actually saw the incorrect response as correct, whereas others said they simply went along with the group rather than oppose the majority. In this instance, social influence moved people to doubt their personal judgment, which almost certainly would have produced a correct response.

The emergence of social media has demonstrated the power and danger in social influence. The rise of movements overthrowing autocratic leaders in the Arab world in 2011, according to some observers, could be traced to the availability of more widespread interaction than had been possible earlier. People could share experiences, learn of inequities, and discover social support that gave them the courage to revolt. By the same token, it was social media and the power of some opinion leaders that led many people, including Donald Trump, to believe that U.S. President Obama was foreign born and a Muslim long after clear evidence to the contrary was available. How many times have you abandoned what you thought was right when your friends said you were wrong? How many times have you stubbornly insisted you were right in the face of unanimous opposition? Maybe you were. Maybe you weren't.

Characteristics of Reasonable Arguments

So, what makes one argument more reasonable than another? From the examples we have given, you can see that arguments derive their force either from the criteria already in people's minds, or from criteria that emerge in their minds during an argument.

When your arguments—claims and support—square directly with the criteria in the minds of the decision makers, the arguments will draw power from those criteria and thus be more influential. In contrast to past philosophical thought, arguments are not necessarily more powerful by virtue of their internal logical validity or by passing some scientific test. As we will explain in Chapter 4, concepts of logical validity and scientific significance, *when they are part of the criteria decision makers apply*, will support the reasonableness of your arguments. But you cannot count on this process always happening.

If arguments are tested by criteria in the minds of decision makers, how does argumentation differ from persuasion in general? What makes argumentation different from what we see on TV, read on billboards, or hear from some fast-talking salesperson? The answer is, first, that argumentation is a relatively distinct dimension of persuasion that includes many of the strategies found in ordinary advertising or political campaigning (Willbrand and Rieke, "Reason Giving" 57).

Second, argumentation is a *distinct* dimension of persuasion, in that people tend to use it when they want to make wise decisions, and the strategies used in argumentation tend to be different from other forms of persuasion. Arguments employ more of the forms of criteria that we discuss in Chapter 4 than do common persuasive messages, and argumentation occurs within spheres that demand such criteria, as we discussed in Chapter 1 and illustrate in Chapters 12–16. Argumentation appeals to the reasonableness of the decision makers by consciously focusing on criteria that are carefully selected, subjected to criticism, publicly accessible, and open to continual reexamination. Many commentators on critical thinking and informal logic argue that *all* persuasion should be subjected to argumentative analysis. If this were done, they say, people would be less likely to be taken in by unreasonable persuasive efforts.

Argumentation serves as the process through which people seek to enhance the positive contributions of their personal reality while holding in abeyance its unreasonable tendencies. Argumentation is the process through which people take advantage of the positive influences in their society and culture while holding in abeyance the perilous social pressures that produce unreasonable behavior. By employing messages predicated on carefully chosen and socially scrutinized criteria, argumentation becomes that form of persuasion dedicated to making the best possible decisions. This almost always means taking advantage of types of criteria and social processes that have proved helpful over the years in yielding reasonable decisions.

Why People Seek Reasonable Arguments

The ultimate purpose of argumentation is to make the best possible decisions, where *best* is defined in various ways. At a basic level, best means to be able to state a basis for decision that satisfies the expectations and demands of the appropriate decision makers. When the decision is important enough to do more than trust chance (flip of a coin) or the of undefined influences of beliefs, thinking, mind, or society, best means to do the systematic processing or analytic thinking demanded by the sphere: to be able to assure the decision makers that they can rely on your arguments at the highest level and thereby produce a decision at the highest level. Another meaning of best is a pragmatic one: decisions that work or do what the sphere seeks to have done: to fulfill the ultimate purpose of the sphere, whatever that may be. To assure, for example, a sphere of medical specialists that your arguments and the resulting decisions will be consistent and effective in terms of their ultimate purpose of health/healing. In law, people are held responsible for their acts on the assumption that they had conscious choice or free will and were not simply at the mercy of their beliefs, thinking, mind, society, or chance. Our discussion of those forces could lead one to conclude that conscious choice is almost impossible, but we do not suggest that. In this context, best means to take responsibility for your arguments and authorize others to hold you accountable for them. Eliezer J. Sternberg, writing in his book *My Brain Made Me Do It*, rejects the implication of his title and argues instead:

> Our ability to go beyond the algorithms—to achieve understanding, to appreciate meaning, to imagine, to consciously deliberate, to reason through boundless problems, and to act as free agents—is what separates us from lower animals, from computers, and from all other machines. It is what makes us human (179).

THE BASES OF REASON IN ARGUMENTATION

Argumentation is the product of centuries of evolution in social practices aimed at resolving or creating uncertainty. We try to resolve uncertainty by making wise decisions that cannot be held absolutely, and we create uncertainty by raising doubts about ideas that may no longer deserve support (Goodnight 215). During this evolution, people have developed a number of systematic practices designed to improve the quality of argumentation and the decisions it produces. In this section, we identify some powerful concepts that provide the necessary common bonding for reasoned interaction to take place and that form a fundamental test of the strength of an argument.

Starting Points for Argumentation

Argumentation works by connecting understandings people possess with claims to which they are being asked to grant adherence. If they grant adherence to those claims, then the newly accepted claims can be used as the connectors to still other claims, leading finally to a decision. The energy or power that drives argumentation is found in people: that which they believe provides the foundation for that which they are asked to believe. In any argumentative interaction, then, some **starting points** (understandings people already possess) must be identified—those powerful concepts that will start the connecting process: language interpretation strategies, facts, presumptions, probabilities, and commonplaces.

A general focus for reasonable arguments is to examine the nature and quality of the powerful concepts invoked. If they are mistaken—either not shared by all the relevant decision makers, or controversial—then the arguments that flow from them become suspect.

Language Interpretation Strategies.   The most fundamental starting point is language and shared **interpretation strategies**. English is widely spoken in India because of the many years of British rule, and English is spoken in the United States for the same reason, but such sharing of a common language does not guarantee sufficient commonality for argumentation. With the development of calling centers in India, training sessions in speaking U.S. English are being conducted in India. The interactants will need to negotiate some common strategies for interpreting their common language before critical argumentation can occur.

Language is commonly referred to as human symbolic activity. The symbols that make up language are arbitrarily assigned meaning when people interpret them as part of interaction. You have meanings in mind when you speak or write, but they are based on your prior experience and education. In the immediate context in which you are speaking, writing, or reading, the meanings of the words will depend on the context in which you find yourself at the time, and the people with whom you are interacting.

The first step in evaluating arguments is to open up interpretation strategies for examination. Disagreements may dissolve as strategies are made to coincide, but so might agreements. Before advancing or evaluating an argument, you must satisfy yourself that you understand what is being communicated.

Facts.   In the discussion of analysis in Chapter 5, we observe that facts can become issues, questions around which controversy occurs. However, as starting points of argumentation,

facts are empirical knowledge (see, taste, touch, hear, smell) derived from observation or experience over which there is no controversy.[1] The morning sun appears in the east. Caviar costs more than chopped liver. Mothers who abuse drugs during pregnancy endanger the health of their babies. These are facts that could very well be the starting points of arguments because the decision makers regard them as facts beyond question.

There are profound differences in what is accepted as fact as you move from one sphere to another. Millions of people acknowledge the "fact" that Jesus is the Messiah, and millions reject the idea totally. Even among scientists, there is significant disagreement about what to count as fact, and advances in science are often based on revisions of what is fact. In assessing the reasonableness of arguments, one place to look is at the facts used as starting points because people may accept facts that, on reflection, they should not.

Think back to that Internet search when writing a paper. The sequence in which items appear in the search has nothing to do with the quality of the facts they allege. On the contrary, they may reflect what someone is willing to pay the search engine to put first. The Internet is a sea of garbage with occasional gems of value floating here and there. Special interests will do their best to have you accept what they say as fact. Even friends can forward messages with strange claims of fact that have been passed along without fact checking. People use techniques such as stating facts without justification, using spurious examples, or graphics such as this:

FACT: Eating asparagus can cure cancer.

Or they can beg the question (a fallacy, see Chapter 11, that assumes as fact that which has not yet been accepted as fact):

DID YOU KNOW that eating asparagus can cure cancer? It's true!

The Internet is filled with efforts to have you accept what they say as fact. When you accept their word without doing your own testing, your arguments may be rejected when others, who have done their homework, show you to be wrong.

Presumptions.   Another powerful concept that serves as a starting point for arguments is presumption. A **presumption** occurs when one statement occupies the argumentative ground or position "until some sufficient reason is adduced against it" (Whately 112). Like facts, presumptions may reflect considerable experience and observation, but they usually involve a broader generalization or a point taken hypothetically for the sake of argument.

Many presumptions have been formally stated in legal decisions. Children are presumed to have less ability to look out for themselves than adults; so, society demands more care for them. U.S. criminal law presumes people to be innocent until proven guilty. As this presumption suggests, all presumptions are subject to challenge and may be

---

[1]We do not mean to say that these so-called facts are beyond controversy. At one time, people held as fact that the world was flat. We use *fact* here to mean a powerful concept that is widely accepted without controversy, *at the time of the argument,* to the extent it can be invoked as the starting connection for further argumentation. Today, we might be able to invoke the "fact" that the universe is constantly expanding as a starting point for the argument, only to have people a hundred years from now laugh at the idea the same way we laugh at the idea that the world is flat.

overturned. In fact, people may start with a presumption they really do not believe, just to get the argumentation going. Without a presumption to work from (say, the presumption of innocence), they would not know who has to start the argument and who wins in the absence of clear superiority of one argument over another. The U.S. criminal law presumes innocence, so the state has to open with a claim of guilt: the burden of proof. The individual citizen does not have to prove innocence. If the state fails to win the argument, we choose to let the citizen go free rather than risk convicting the innocent. We expand the concepts of presumption, burden of proof, and *prima facie* cases in Chapter 6 during the discussion of case building.

Part of understanding the reasonableness of argumentation is examination of presumptions. Because presumption is more or less arbitrary, it is possible for one position in the discussion to claim presumption and use it as a tool to force others to defend their position. In a university class on argumentation, a student said, "There has never been an astronaut on the moon. If was faked by the government." The professor replied, "Can you prove that?" The student immediately came back, "Can you prove I'm wrong?" Who should have the presumption in this case? Putting an unreasonable burden of proof on one point of view can lead to an unreasonable decision (Gaskins).

Probabilities. As starting points of argument, **probabilities** consist of commonly held beliefs about what is likely to happen, what is ordinary, and what is to be expected. Such beliefs can be used as premises for arguments. After extensive observations, we hold powerful concepts of such probabilities as the times of the tides, the movements of the planets, the changing of the seasons, or the behavior of matter under various conditions. We reason from biological probabilities such as what plants will survive in certain climates, how animals will respond to loss of habitat, and how diseases disseminate. We hold concepts of how people will probably act under certain circumstances: They will look to basic needs such as food, clothing, and shelter before considering such abstract needs as self-fulfillment; they will seek pleasure and avoid pain; they will organize themselves into societies.

Like presumptions, probabilities vary from one sphere to another. Many hold the probability that human beings will seek to avoid death, but some spheres hold that death in a holy cause is desirable.

Where presumptions may be points that are taken for the sake of argument without solid proof of their validity, probabilities get arguments started because they are likely to be accepted as well established by proof while falling short of the confidence given to facts. Their susceptibility to challenge makes it necessary to present claims resting on probabilities with some statements of *qualification*.

Stephen Toulmin says that when people qualify claims, they "authorize . . . hearers to put more or less faith in the assertions . . . treat them as correspondingly more or less trustworthy" (*The Uses of Argument* 91). Because argument functions within uncertainty, there is always some degree of qualification on claims. Sometimes you use words: *likely, almost certainly, probably, maybe*. Sometimes you use numbers: 90% chance, $p < .05$, three to one odds. No matter how you express these probabilities, they communicate the force with which an argument is advanced, the degree of faith you authorize others to place on your claims.

The reasonableness of arguments, then, necessarily involves an examination of the probabilities on which they rest and the qualifications with which they are presented. A point of criticism is to ask the basis of the probability statement.

In deciding what and how much higher education you need, you may turn to statistics that indicate probabilities about what kinds of majors will be most in demand when you graduate and what value advanced degrees may produce. The U.S. Bureau of Labor Statistics projects that between 2008 and 2018, the careers most likely to increase, produce a high salary (ranging from $70,000 to $85,000), and require a bachelor's degree include biomedical engineers, network systems and data communication analysts, financial examiners, and computer software engineers. In the same time, a similar increase will occur in home health aids, personal and home care aids, skin care specialists, and dental hygienists, producing salaries between $20,000 and $66,000 but requiring only short on the job training or an associate's degree. Will the cost of an extra two or more years of college be worth it? Would you be just as happy to take one of the lower paying jobs that do not require college? What is the probability that after you complete college, no such high paying job will be available because economic conditions have changed?

Commonplaces.   In argumentative practice, various ways of putting arguments together become standardized, common, widely recognized, and accepted. These **commonplaces** are lines of argument or places from which arguments can be built. Aristotle spoke of logic in the form of induction or generalization: reasoning from specific instances to a generalization; or deduction (syllogisms or enthymemes): reasoning from a generalization to a specific application. Aristotle mentioned rationales such as opposites: What goes up must come down; You are either with us or against us. He called these processes, depending on which translation you use, *topoi,* topics, lines of argument, or commonplaces (Roberts, W. Rhys 1396). Perelman and Olbrechts-Tyteca call them *loci* (83). We will call them commonplaces.

The reasonableness of arguments is measured, in part, by the commonplaces on which they are developed. For centuries, logic was considered the prime example of how to put an argument together, but today we see that logic has a limited application in actual argumentation. We have mentioned the commonplace of opposites as an example. If one argues from this commonplace, the critic must test the assumption of opposition. Up and down do not work the same in the weightlessness of space, of which Aristotle never heard, and in the war on terror, for example, countries such as Pakistan seemed to be both with us and against us.

An argument based on genealogy was also common in Aristotle's time, but it is less likely to survive critical scrutiny today. To argue, for example, that people are suitable for high office because of the high status of their parents is not well received in a democracy. However, genealogy still functions as a commonplace in certain argumentative contexts. The selection of a British monarch or a Japanese emperor rests on it. Many people point with pride to their distinguished ancestors, and we pay attention to the children of celebrities and distinguished families.

A fortiori (more or less) argues, for example, that if you can perform the more difficult task, you can surely perform the easier one. Or, conversely, if you can't do an easy task, you won't be able to do a more difficult one. The argument "If we can put a man on the moon, we should be able to solve the hunger problem" rests on the commonplace of *a fortiori.* So does this one: If you cannot pass the introductory course, you surely will flunk the advanced one.

Considerations of *time* work as commonplaces. Professionals charge fees based on the time spent for a client or patient. Most wages are calculated on time. Forty hours is deemed enough work for a week, and any more deserves better pay. Students argue for a better grade on the basis of how much time was spent on an assignment. We presume that a person can't be in two places at the same time; so, the accused may argue an alibi based on the time to go from point A to point B. Commonplaces vary from sphere to sphere. For example, the commonplace of cause and effect is interpreted in quite different ways within different spheres.

Language interpretation strategies, facts, presumptions, probabilities, and commonplaces are powerful concepts that work as socially generated starting points for argument. When you make an argument, you will want to think carefully about where you can start it with reasonable assurance that there is common ground between you and your decision makers. In your critical appraisal of the argumentation of others, you must scrutinize the starting points to see whether they were well selected.

CONCLUSION

When you evaluate the reasonableness of argumentation, when you try to decide what arguments are acceptable, what ones are not, and what decision makes the most sense, you will necessarily make your judgments under the influence and within the limits of your genetic make-up, the environments in which you have lived, your worldviews, and the social interactions you have experienced. Sometimes these factors will help you act wisely, and sometimes they will get you into trouble.

Over many centuries, people have developed systematic argumentation practices that can increase the likelihood that you will make sensible decisions. When properly used, these will help you make critical decisions. Powerful concepts such as language interpretation strategies, facts, presumptions, probabilities, and commonplaces can serve as starting points for argumentation. They establish a foundation on which everyone can argue and provide some ready rationales on which to build claims.

EXERCISES/PROJECTS

1. Write a description of a job interview you have had. Did you understand the criteria to be used in making a hiring decision? Did you make arguments in response to the criteria? Did the job decision rest on the criteria? In all, do you think the decision was critical or uncritical, and why?

2. Identify the career choice you currently prefer, then do an Internet search of it. Keep a record of all the responses that come up, separating the unusual language usages: fact claims, presumptions, probabilities, and commonplaces (look particularly for generalizations, cause and effect claims, a fortiori, and opposites). Then write an argument supporting your career choice with material drawn from your search. Does your argument seem reasonable? Did your work change your career thinking? Where did you find unreasonable arguments?

Making Sense of Argumentation

KEY TERMS

good reasons, p. 37

good story, p. 38

science, p. 38

feminist theory, p. 38

alternative dispute resolution (ADR), p. 38

narrative, p. 40

feminist argumentation, p. 42

patriarchal reasoning, p. 42

personal testimony, p. 43

essentialism, p. 44

moral conflicts, p. 46

arbitration, p. 47

mediation, p. 47

negotiation, p. 47

collaborative law, p. 47

consensus, p. 49

In Chapter 2, we examined ways people appraise arguments, focusing on how they decide what is reasonable. We pointed out that criteria that are appropriate for evaluating an argument in some situations are not necessarily appropriate for all situations. Whenever people participate in argumentation, they strive to present themselves as reasonable, or as making sense. Notions of what makes sense, however, change as society changes. In this chapter, we will describe how people try to make sense of argumentation. You probably already use these approaches to analyze arguments every day. Careful attention to how you and others use these approaches may help you become a more effective advocate.

We will explain how these five ways of making sense of the world appear in some form or another in the communication patterns of many social interactions.

Good Reasons

In the rhetorical tradition, Aristotle (Roberts W. Rhys) focuses on reasoned discourse. What reasons are offered in support or justification of a claim? Are they **good reasons**, or good enough to warrant adherence to the claim?

(1) A sensible argument is based on **good reasons.** We will examine the ways claims are justified through reasoned discourse. You demonstrate that you have good reasons to support your claims by employing standard patterns of inference, drawn from logic. You also appear to be reasonable if your arguments are consistent and are not contradictory.

(2) A sensible argument has a **good story.** People have been using stories to make sense of social interaction since human communication began. When someone describes an event, you listen to "what happened" and decide if it makes sense on the basis of how coherent and believable the story is.

(3) Scientific argumentation is a more recent way to make sense of the world than logical reasoning or stories. Arguments derived from **science,** or systematic observation of the world through the senses of sight, sound, taste, touch, and smell, are assumed to make sense. By the twentieth century, science became predominant and appeared destined to outshine all other approaches. It still has persuasive power but has failed to produce the certain truth many people hoped for.

(4) Many people have recognized that men and women have been socialized differently and that this socialization process affects how people construct, deliver, and receive arguments. **Feminist theory** systematically examines these and other social differences, and uses them to suggest new possibilities for what counts as a sensible argument. Feminist approaches encourage us to carefully differentiate between argumentation and verbal aggression.

(5) **Alternative dispute resolution or ADR** has emerged as a way to make sense of argumentation in the world of fragmented identities and relationships that characterize the twenty-first century. Using some of the principles identified in Chapter 2, ADR helps people negotiate tensions within society without erasing important differences.

FIGURE 3.1

Some Ways of Making Sense

When children or adults are asked to generate reasons in support of a claim, they typically call on *personal authority* ("I believe it"); *power authority* ("The textbook says it's so"); *moral obligation* ("It's the right thing to believe"); *social pressure* ("Everyone believes it"); or *listener benefit* ("If you want to pass this test, you will be well advised to believe it"), among other kinds of reasons (Willbrand and Rieke, "Reason Giving" 420). Reasons generated in this way are learned from early childhood and reflect the enculturation each person has experienced (Toulmin, "Commentary").

Recent studies of the human mind hint at the possibility that some reasons are hardwired into the brain. Katarina Gospic of the Karolinska Institute in Stockholm analyzed brain scans of 35 subjects as they played a game. She concluded, "A sense of fairness is both cerebral and visceral, cortical and limbic" (Angier D2). Reasons, properly based on fairness, will probably be considered good reasons. David Brooks sums it up this way:

> Nobody has to teach a child to demand fair treatment; children protest unfairness vigorously and as soon as they can communicate. Nobody has to teach us to admire a person who sacrifices for a group; the admiration for duty is universal. Nobody has to teach us to disdain someone who betrays a friend or is disloyal to a family or tribe. Nobody has to teach a child the difference between rules that are moral—"'Don't hit'—and rules that are not—'Don't chew gum in school'." These preferences also emerge from somewhere deep inside us (Brooks 284–285).

We learn to come up with good reasons in response to challenges:

"Why did you do that?"
"Because."
"Because why?"
"Just because."
"That's not good enough!"
"The teacher said I could." (power authority)
"Okay."

Tests of Good Reasons. Some of the ways we test reasons to see if they are good enough are listed as follows:

---

(1) The reasons should speak with one voice (noncontradiction). This test advises you to look for contradictions. When the religious leader who preaches faithfulness in marriage is found in a motel room with someone other than a spouse, the sermon loses its punch. In reasons, the old cliché, "Don't do as I do; do as I say," does not overcome the contradiction.

(2) The reasons should be consistent. Here, the critic looks to see if all parts of the argument play by the same rules. If a politician argues for big reductions in defense spending but opposes the closure of a military base in the home district, the argument is weakened by lack of consistency. The pro-life advocate who supports capital punishment communicates inconsistency.

(3) The argument should locate starting points within the appropriate audience. Arguments should neither patronize the audience by telling them what they already know nor presume starting points that do not exist.

(4) The reasons should be expressed in language that communicates to the appropriate decision makers. Critics should check to see if everyone involved in the argumentation is using the same interpretation strategies.

(5) The reasons should be complete. A critic searches for points necessary to the claim that are not addressed, exceptions or variations to the materials included.

(6) The reasons must demonstrate consistent patterns of inference, drawn from logic. As we explain in Chapter 4, logic provides patterns that are commonly used to test the validity of argumentation.

(7) The reasons must be reasonably related to the point they support. As we explain in our discussions of evidence in Chapter 7, there are specific tests to which reasons must be put.

| **FIGURE 3.2**

A Good Story

Malcolm O. Sillars and Bruce E. Gronbeck observe that people judge the rationality or truthfulness of human behavior in terms of what actions make sense, and what makes sense to people rests on the stories that are told within a culture. People make sense of their world in terms of the stories they tell about themselves. Stories are symbolic actions that create social reality, and so, even when stories are fiction, they are not false because they reflect the experience of those who tell the stories and those who hear or read them.

A **narrative** has a sense of chronology with regard to a central subject, developed coherently, leading to a narrative closure or outcome. Narratives generally involve a *theme* (good triumphs over evil), *structure* (beginning, middle, end), *characters* (heroes and villains), *peripeteia* (a change of fortune or reversal of circumstances), *narrative voice* (the storyteller), and *style* (language including figures of speech; Sillars and Gronbeck, Chapter 10).

According to W. Lance Bennett and Martha S. Feldman, we organize our understanding around stories from early childhood. What counts as real and what makes sense is learned as central actions and the way those actions are characterized in relation to the people and motivations that make them up. People evaluate stories in part by asking whether they are coherent—whether the content and structure of the story hang together properly—and whether they are faithful to what people have come to believe to be true about the real world (Fisher). How would you evaluate the following narrative? Is the mother a murderer? Do a Google search to learn the outcome and more details:

Caylee Anthony, a 3-year old girl, was last seen at her grandparents' house on June 15, 2008. Six months later, the child's body was found in swampy wooded area not far from her grandparents' home. Her remains, wrapped in a bag with a piece of duct tape over her mouth and nose, were too decomposed for a determination of cause of death. At first, Caylee's mother, Casey, said the child had been kidnapped by a baby sitter. She said she had not notified the police of her missing daughter for a month because she was investigating on her own and was frightened. During that month, some people said they saw the mother at various parties, and that she had gotten a tattoo. At the trial where the mother was accused of murder, her lawyer said the child had fallen into an unguarded swimming pool and negligent grandparents had covered up the accident. What makes the mother's story believable? Unbelievable?

At the end of the twentieth century, many scholars in the social sciences concluded that narratives provided excellent data for their research. "Emphasizing the stories people tell about their lives, [they] construed narrative as both a means of knowing and a way of telling about the social world" (Montgomery and Baxter 43). Narrative, they believed, is how people experience and understand their own lives. Other researchers (Cobb) have found that narrative plays a central role in successful mediations. For these reasons, argumentation cast in the form of narrative is a powerful way to make connections with the appropriate decision makers.

Science

There are many versions of the "scientific method," depending on the particular sphere involved. However, we can identify the use of **science** as a means of evaluating arguments in a more general way. Simply put, scientific logic rests on carefully performed observations, successful predictions, and the ability of others to obtain the same results. Ronald Pine provides these essential elements of scientific arguments (42):

(1) Conduct empirical observations (use sight, sound, taste, touch, smell).
(2) Think creatively about the observations.
(3) Generate a hypothesis in the form of a prediction.
(4) Conduct tests or experiments based on the hypothesis.
(5) Advance a claim in support of the hypothesis; present in sufficient detail that others can repeat your work and get the same result.

Richard Parker advanced these steps as tests of scientific logic:

(1) The argument must be internally consistent.
(2) Its premises must be acceptable to the decision makers for whom it is intended.
(3) It must survive refutation.
(4) It must survive the critical examination of all arguments for and against.

FIGURE 3.3
Elements of Scientific Arguments

During the past 300 years or so, science has been recognized as a particularly powerful form of argumentation. Spectacular scientific and technological advances have led some to believe, as did Aristotle, that science stands outside the domain of argumentation because it deals in certainty. In 1970, however, philosopher of science Thomas Kuhn argued that scientific arguments operate within uncertainty and should be criticized as argumentation. Part of this shift in perspective comes from within science itself. F. David Peat describes the transformation of science wrought by quantum theory as, "chairs and tables dissolved into an empty space filled with colliding atoms. Then atoms broke apart into nuclei, nuclei into elementary particles, and finally, elementary particles into symmetries, transformations, and processes in the quantum vacuum" (52–53). Postmodernist, rhetorical, and cultural studies commentators have taken the point further to show social, political, and cultural influences on scientific claims (Condit; Fuller).

Physicist Alan Sokal notes the congruence between science and argumentation:

1. Science is a human endeavor, and like any other human endeavor, it merits being subjected to rigorous social analysis. . . . 2. Even the content of scientific debate—what types of theories can be conceived and entertained, what criteria are to be used for deciding among competing theories—is constrained in part by the prevailing attitudes of mind, which in turn arise in part from deep-seated historical factors. . . . 3. There is nothing wrong with research informed by a political commitment as long as that commitment does not blind the researcher to inconvenient facts (10).

Feminist Argumentation

The traditional rationale for studying argumentation is that if disputants are sufficiently willing and able to present their cases and respond to others thoughtfully and logically, they can achieve mutually satisfactory resolution. It assumes that, in most cases, argumentation and debate will lead to a mutually agreeable solution. Failure to settle a dispute by these methods is viewed as a symptom of unskilled communication, failure to engage in critical decision making, or just plain selfishness. The approaches to making sense of argumentation we have described thus far are grounded in this rationale.

The persistent and increasingly public nature of terrorist activities, such as the September 11, 2001, destruction of the World Trade Center in New York City, has persuaded many people that traditional orientations toward political diplomacy are not only insufficient but also misguided. One response to terrorism aimed at the United States has been a proliferation of legislation that curtails individual freedom in the interests of national security. Another has been a series of military invasions in the interests of rooting out terrorism from other nations. Criticism is kept to a minimum by accusations of anti-Americanism. A traditional orientation might consider both the actions we label as "terrorist" and those we label as "war" to be outside the realm of argumentation. A feminist account, however, urges people to understand terrorism as the argument of the powerless.

Ideas drawn from feminism offer a way of interpreting the sensibility of radical actions, which can contribute to better understanding and more effective responses to these deeply felt conflicts. Some argumentation scholars claim that feminist insights are antithetical, and even destructive, to the process of argumentation (Rowland). We find them fundamentally consistent with the perspective toward argumentation described in Chapters 1 and 2. Despite differences between approaches to argument, all are loosely grounded in a *social constructionist* orientation that views human realities as products of social interaction. At the same time, we recognize that feminism offers a useful orientation to our understanding of argumentation. For example, feminism offers approaches to sensibility that can encourage people who are engaged in argumentation to develop forms of communication that are especially appropriate to contemporary situations that may otherwise end in violence.

Feminisms.   We hope you noticed our choice to use the plural form, "feminisms," to head this section. The following discussion should indicate that there is no universally accepted **feminist theory**. This is consistent with the feminist project to dismantle nonreflective patterns of social expectation. Jean Bethke Elshtain reminds us that, to accomplish such a goal, "the nature and meaning of feminist discourse itself must be a subject for critical inquiry" (605).

Feminist approaches to argumentation enable us to follow up on a distinction introduced in Chapter 1. Using Daniel O'Keefe's distinctions between argument 1 and argument 2, we described utterances or claims as fundamental products associated with the argumentation process. Feminist critiques offer at least three possibilities for using this construct as a beginning point for reinterpreting argumentation and critical decision making.

First, they critique traditional methods for evaluating communicative acts (argument 1). Second, they suggest alternative descriptions for the entire process of argumentation (argument 2). Third, they insist that a fruitful argumentation theory must include analysis of how gender and sex influence the reception of arguments and how they constrain the presentation of arguments.

Despite the multiplicity of feminisms, some general tendencies can be identified. Here, we will define **feminist argumentation** as a process committed to critically analyzing patriarchal reasoning and revising argumentation (both theory and practice) to include considerations of gender. For additional clarity, we will define **patriarchal reasoning** as reasoning used to justify attitudes, beliefs, values, and policies that subordinate women to men.

The Role of Personal Testimony. One of feminism's earliest critiques of traditional approaches to appraising or evaluating arguments related to the use of evidence, or support. Traditionally, the use of **personal testimony** has been relegated to subsidiary status in argumentation, with forms of support such as deductive reasoning, statistics, and expert opinion considered more persuasive. Karlyn Kohrs Campbell studied women speakers and found that they tended to use "personal experience, anecdotes, and other examples" to support their arguments much more often than did male speakers (12–13).

Catherine A. MacKinnon claims that personal testimony is not only pervasive in women's arguments but also is the most valid form of evidence women can use because their experiences have occurred "within that sphere that has been socially lived as the personal" (535).

Linda Kauffman resists labeling personal testimony as the best form of evidence, however. She claims that it essentializes traditional women's roles, relying on the assumption that "all women share similar conditions and experiences" (163). For example, because the biological experience of bearing children is not available to males, some feminists have offered it as a fundamentally feminine experience that differentiates between forms of communication possible for women and men. This claim, however, isolates women who either cannot or choose not to bear children. Their experience has currency in neither the feminine nor the masculine category. Katrina Bell and her co-authors point out the danger of marginalizing African-American women's experiences, which have been significantly different from those of most white, middle-class women. Feminist critiques, such as those offered by Kauffman and Bell et al., illustrate why feminisms must remain plural, in order to avoid essentializing a grand narrative of what it means to argue as a woman.

Catherine Helen Palczewski found that when women used personal testimony to support public claims, their experience was recast in the masculine terms (claims, grounds, warrants) that dominate public spaces. For example, if a woman is raped and chooses to press charges, she must inscribe her personal experience of the rape into the structure of the legal system. If she tells her story in court, it becomes the property of legal and medical experts who will reshape it into the story they think will be most likely to achieve a conviction. Whether the experts are male or female, they will frame the story to fit the masculine legal system.

For example, in 2011, Dominique Strauss-Kahn, head of the International Monetary Fund, was charged with attempted rape of Nafissatou Diallo, a maid who came to clean his hotel room in New York City. Strauss-Kahn pleaded not guilty to the charge. Partially because Straus-Kahn was a leading contender in the upcoming French Presidential election, his arrest became an international media incident. In response to DNA identification of Strauss-Kahn's sperm on her uniform, the defense asserted that the sex had been consensual. Coverage quickly shifted from focusing on whether or not Strauss-Kahn assaulted Diallo to the personal credibility of Diallo. Apparently Diallo, an immigrant from Guinea, had associated with a convicted marijuana dealer, had fraudulently claimed two children on previous tax returns, and had understated her income to obtain cheap housing. This information, along with other details of her life story, was used to support Struass-Kahn's claim that the sex had been consensual. Over time, Diallo was required to tell her story multiple times, and inconsistencies began to emerge, leading prosecutors to give up on the case.

Feminist theorists have used examples such as the Strauss-Kahn incident to demonstrate the importance of giving credence to a broader variety of utterances used as claims, evidence, and other support. They do not agree among themselves, however, on a hierarchy of value among such utterances.

Argumentation as a Cooperative Process. Feminisms have also made important contributions to our understanding of the argumentation process. The metaphor of argument-as-war pervades the conceptual system of western culture. As George Lakoff and Mark Johnson point out, even in arguments that are considered nonadversarial, "there is still a position to be established and defended, you can win or lose, you have an opponent whose position you attack and try to destroy and whose argument you try to shoot down" (63). Michael A. Gilbert argues that we cannot change the way we argue unless we develop "a mode of thinking that recognizes all communication as situated and emphasizes agreement" (108–109). He labels such an approach as "coalescent argumentation."

Sonja Foss and Cindy Griffin offer feminist argumentation as a solution, characterizing it as nurturing and affirmative; promoting self-determination, mutual respect, and camaraderie; and viewing the audience as a friend (3–4). From this perspective, attempts to change someone's mind are considered patriarchal and coercive, whereas feminist argumentation refers to a friendly exchange of perspectives.

Palczewski and M. Lane Bruner, however, are concerned that this critique inappropriately emphasizes distinctions between argument processes traditionally engaged in by women advocates and those used by men, and threatens to "slip into [the same] biological **essentialism**" that has characterized traditional argumentation theories (Palczewski 162). For example, Karyn Charles Rybacki and Donald Jay Rybacki interpret feminism as saying "men use argumentation to make mono-causal position statements and tests of knowledge, whereas women engage in conversation, a more inclusive technique, that invites all participants to share their experiences" (2). This interpretation of feminism illustrates a danger Bruner associates with the practice of dichotomizing argumentation into masculine and feminine characteristics. Bruner writes that this practice "disempowers and unnecessarily constrains feminisms. . . . If feminist argumentation theory assumes that one cannot constrain and enable at the same time, or nurture and at the same time seek to change the perspective of another, then feminist argumentation is limited to a very narrow range of argumentative situations" (186–187). To avoid this trap, feminist theorists have attempted to develop new processes of argument that avoid the binary opposition between male and female. This means that feminism must always struggle against the tendency to essentialize, or naturalize traditional female experience as the defining essence of woman as opposed to man (Bell et al.).

The concern over essentializing differences between men and women does not mean that feminisms cannot offer a significant critique to traditional argumentation processes. For example, Stephen Toulmin, Richard Rieke, and Allan Janik have written that some types of argument rely on consensus whereas others involve adversarial processes (254–255). They offer science and art criticism as illustrations of consensual argument, judicial argument as an illustration of adversarial argument, and business and public policy as illustrations of argument that integrates adversarial and consensus forms. A feminist critique of their perspective would say it does not move far enough beyond adversarial models. It would direct our attention to the fact that consensus in science refers not to a process but to a temporary goal. For example, the competitive model used in the United States and Western Europe to distribute funds to conduct scientific research, as well as opportunities to publish the results of that research, is extolled as the basis for human progress. The notion that this competition will weed out the weaker proposals, leaving only the most reasonable arguments, is widely held in western society. This adversarial model positions scientists in competition against each other in a search for truth. Feminist critique can encourage public awareness of the implications of the adversarial model, as well as the possibilities for alternative models.

Gender Influences Reception and Presentation.   Although feminist argumentation discourages its participants from using sex as a controlling variable, it encourages recognition that gender matters in both the theory and practice of argumentation. Feminist analyses of the judicial system illustrate how the premise of the male norm has circumscribed argumentative outcomes by limiting the scope of available arguments in legal discourse. Carrie Crenshaw demonstrates that legal constructions of neutrality "are reflective of primarily male concerns." When legal advocates argue "that women should be treated the same as men, [they make] the supposedly neutral standpoint the male standpoint" (172).

The conversational style adopted by many female advocates also influences audience reception of their arguments. Despite significant improvements in professional opportunities available to women, society continues to train females to fulfill roles traditionally defined as feminine. A trip through the infants' clothing section of any department store illustrates just how early this socialization process begins. A visitor from another planet would quickly learn that baby girls are to be dressed in pastels, generously sprinkled with lace and ruffles. Baby boys, however, should be dressed in bright, primary colors, often figured with tools, animals, and trucks. Both in terms of fabric and style, girls' clothing is more suited to sitting and observing, whereas boys' clothing is more suited to active participation. When parents dress their infants in the "wrong" attire, some observers assume that the clothing is left over from an older sibling, and others worry that the children will become sexually confused. As girls and boys grow up, distinctions in the treatment of boys versus that of girls become increasingly marked.

We are not suggesting that the traditional model for raising boys is better than that used for raising girls. We simply want to point out that the differences have real consequences. These consequences mean that women face additional challenges when making a public argument. Audiences sometimes fail to take their conversational style seriously. In other situations, standards of objectivity and credibility pose challenges. Lorraine Code points out that the credibility of a female advocate suffers from society's tendency to believe that women are more intuitive than men, thus dismissing them as incapable of *producing* knowledge (65). However, the credibility of women who do not project intuitive, nurturing personas suffers because they have violated their audiences' expectations.

We hope the previous discussion has demonstrated to you why we use the plural "feminisms," rather than the singular "feminism." These feminisms offer new ways "to think through the forms and functions of, as well as attitudes toward, argument." Despite their differences, most feminisms encourage the search for "emancipatory forms of argument" (Allen and Faigley 162). They can help advocates and audiences recognize the constraining and enabling aspects in all forms of argumentation.

Feminist argumentation encourages recognition "both that existing argumentation is overly grounded on adversarial assumptions and binary oppositions, and that absolute abandonment of argumentation on feminist grounds may be unnecessary." Instead, it can provide guidance for both women and men who want to "engage in consensus formation, coalescent reasoning, and non-dualistic thinking as they critique and theorize argument" (Bruner 188). Ultimately, feminist argumentation can be conceptualized as a perpetual critique of the limits imposed by gender stereotypes. This critique puts advocates in a strong position for undertaking the integrative task of asking how apparently opposing arguments "mesh with other different experience sets, different belief systems, different value codes, and even different reasoning styles" (Ayim 189).

Feminist critiques do not signal the end of argument. Rather, they suggest ways that argumentation can be used to constitute a more just society rather than simply buttressing existing hierarchies. Feminist argumentation would reject the following defense of purely rational argument:

1. "In a pure argumentative encounter, it does not matter whether you are President of the United States or a college junior; all that is relevant is what you have to say. Of course, this ideal is rarely realized, but the principle . . . is one that recognizes the fundamental humanity in all people" (Rowland 359).
2. "As a rational problem-solving tool, argument has no gender; it belongs equally to men and women. Thus, far from being a tool of patriarchal oppressors, argument is one tool with which to free women and other oppressed groups from all forms of domination" (Rowland 362).

Feminist approaches to argumentation encourage you to resist the urge to retreat behind a principle of equality that "is rarely realized" and instead to engage in discourse for the purposes of changing existing patterns of privilege. They offer the surprisingly optimistic possibility that argumentation can do more than change people's ideas on a particular topic. It can alter the very context within which those ideas take shape.

ALTERNATIVE DISPUTE RESOLUTION

Ideas developed from feminist approaches to argument have motivated some people to explicitly apply argumentation theory to a wide variety of conflicts. Ordinary argument seems unable to resolve some particularly thorny disputes. Researchers have labeled these vexing conflicts as intractable, meaning that they are long running, and have been resistant to multiple attempts at resolution. W. Barnett Pearce and Stephen W. Littlejohn describe them as **moral conflicts**. They suggest that attempts to mediate such conflicts should focus on altering the political context rather than changing people's minds. Their goal is to discover ways of "managing moral disputes in a way that allows expression and without the violent, disrespectful, and demeaning outcomes of open clash" (6). Their work is part of the growing field of research and practice called **alternative dispute resolution (ADR)**.

Deborah Kolb described ADR as a set of procedures rooted in the belief that it is essential to "bring a different kind of process to the problems of overcrowded and unsympathetic courts; to changing, conflict-ridden communities; and to the stalemates that accompany long and contentious struggles over public policy and international affairs" (2). In ADR, participants negotiate a consensual agreement for the management of an issue. The trend toward ADR emphasizes facilitation of diverse sets of individuals in long-term relationships, where they establish mutually agreed upon goals and seek solutions to complex problems. ADR is especially useful for situations where parties needed to maintain a continuing relationship to solve future problems with one another.

ADR provides principles and strategies for creating a social climate that enables participants to learn from each other and cooperate across divergent perspectives. Characteristics that determine the legitimacy of an ADR process include the apparent ability of the process to (1) facilitate an ideological discussion across interest groups, (2) highlight the reality of power struggle, and (3) and provide strong leadership contributing to cooperation. Successful ADR practioners need a broad expertise in ADR principles (Lipsky and Seeber).

Despite resistance by many people, ADR has gained widespread acceptance among both the general public and legal professionals (Lipsky and Seeber). The term is used to describe both a set of informal methods for resolving disputes that is attached to, yet outside of, official judicial mechanisms, and a set of informal methods for resolving disputes that is completely independent from the formal judicial system. Whether attached to official judicial mechanisms or not, the basic methods and skills are similar.

Classifying Alternative Dispute Resolution Processes

Although there are many ways to categorize ADR, it usually is divided into at least three types: **arbitration, mediation,** and **negotiation.** Some practitioners differentiate a fourth type, **collaborative law,** which is a legal process used most often to enable people who want to end their marriage without the hostility that has come to be associated with traditional divorce litigation.

Arbitration.   The ADR approach that is most thoroughly integrated into the formal judicial system is arbitration, which is a legal technique for resolving disputes outside the formal court system. In arbitration, parties to a dispute refer it to a third party or panel of parties, who will make the final decision. All parties agree to be bound by the decision of the third party or arbiter. In formal arbitration, the decision of the arbiter is legally binding. Although arbitration is not the same as judicial proceedings, it may be legally mandated. The use of arbitration is frequently employed in consumer issues, where it may be mandated by commercial contracts. For example, the fine print describing the conditions under which you may use your credit card probably mandates the use of arbitration for disputes.

Mediation.   One of the most flexible ADR processes is **mediation.** Although mediations vary, all share the feature of having a third-party mediator (or facilitator) who assists disputants in reaching agreement. Mediation empowers the disputants by allowing them to deal directly with neutral facilitators of their own choosing, rather than with adversarial judges and lawyers who have been assigned to their case. Like arbitration, mediation has become a standard complement to legal systems of jurisprudence. The two processes differ in how they distribute responsibility for decision making. While the arbitrator makes the decision in an arbitration, the parties to the dispute retain full responsibility for decisions in mediation.

The flexibility of mediation may be the reason why some people have referred to it as the feminine face of dispute resolution. For example, Barbara Ashley Phillips explains that mediation offers an opportunity to reframe power relationships more consistently with the feminist understanding described earlier in this chapter. In mediation, the parties to a dispute work together to reason through the possibilities presented by a situation. Rather than relying on *power over* their adversary, they are encouraged to envision how sharing *power with* that person may be used to craft a common enterprise that will meet everyone's needs.

Negotiation.   Negotiation is a problem-solving process where two or more people voluntarily discuss their differences and attempt to reach a joint decision. For negotiation to be successful, all parties need to identify their disagreements, educate each other about their needs and interests, generate possible options, and debate the terms of an agreement. A negotiation may be relatively simple, as when a couple decides whether to spend the evening at home or go to a movie. On the other hand, it might be extremely complicated, as when the nations making up the Security Council of the United Nations decide whether to impose sanctions on Iran unless it suspends uranium enrichment. In this case, the members of the Security Council have multiple subdecisions to make: What level of sanctions should they levy, how much time should they allow before deciding, how are the sanctions likely to stabilize or destabilize the region around Iran, how will this impact their own internal security, etc.

There are many reasons why parties choose to negotiate. Although we are unlikely to be able to produce a complete list, a few of the most common reasons are:

(1) Gain recognition that their concern is legitimate;
(2) Obtain information about issues and other parties;
(3) Educate other parties;
(4) Change perceptions of themselves and/or others;
(5) Mobilize support for their perspective;
(6) Change an existing relationship;
(7) Make substantive gains.

FIGURE 3.4
Reasons to Negotiate

Parties may also refuse to negotiate. Common reasons why people refuse to participate in negotiation, or why they may drop out of negotiations, are as follows:

(1) Other important parties are not participating
(2) No sense of interdependence with other parties
(3) Belief that they have no means of influencing others
(4) No commonality with other parties to use as starting points
(5) No sense of urgency
(6) Issues in dispute are not negotiable
(7) Strong negative emotions about other parties
(8) Lack the authority to make decisions

FIGURE 3.5
Reasons to Reject Negotiation

High-profile groups such as the Harvard Negotiation Project (Fisher and Ury; Ury, *Getting Past No; The Third Side*) have developed procedures that have been used in successful international negotiations. For example, U.S. President Jimmy Carter used processes from the Harvard Negotiation Project as a guide to facilitating the Camp David agreements between Israel and Egypt (Fisher and Brown). It is important to note that, in the Camp David Accords (1978), as in most other international ADR "successes," the conflict was not resolved but reformed in a way that made it more amenable to humane management. Although the Israeli-Palestinian conflict continues to flare into violence with disappointing frequency, subsequent agreements, such as the Oslo Accords in 1993, the Israel-Jordan Treaty of Peace in 1994, and the Camp David 2000 Summit, used the Camp David Accords as a starting point for further negotiations.

Collaborative Law.   Stuart Webb, a family lawyer in Minnesota, pioneered collaborative law. Since 1990, it has gained widespread acceptance in the U.S. and other nations (Gregory R. Solun, Collaborative Law). Today, the New York State Unified Court System offers collaborative family law as an option designed to "reduce the pain, trauma, and expense of divorce on families" (Welcome to the Collaborative).

Alternative Dispute Resolution as Argumentation

Alternative dispute resolution (ADR) engages people in interactive, sustained communication and provides them with influence over the final decision. In ADR, participants negotiate an agreement for the management of an issue. ADR provides principles and strategies for creating a social climate that enables participants to learn from each other and cooperate across divergent perspectives. It may even use consensus building strategies and techniques such as those suggested in Lawrence Susskind, McKearnan, and Thomas-Larmer's popular *Consensus Building Handbook*.

Although it is certainly complementary with **consensus**, ADR should not be reduced to consensus. There are significant differences. At their best, ADR approaches encourage constructive debate and direct communication among parties in a dispute. Participants are expected to address issues, concerns, and values openly. Like consensus processes, ADR also includes exercises in joint learning and fact finding, and exploration of underlying value differences. The primary measure of whether a consensus process has succeeded, on the other hand, is whether agreement has been achieved. This focus may actually make change more difficult to achieve. As M. Nils Peterson et al. note, "management by consensus is dangerous because the attempt to placate everyone risks the attenuation of any impetus for change and reifies the status quo" (764). Given that one of the most powerful reasons to employ ADR is to change the status quo, it is important to remember that, while agreement is a frequent outcome of ADR processes, it is not the primary goal.

Robert L. Ivie reminds us that argumentation is a valuable tool for those who value democracy. He argues that, "the illusion of consensus and unanimity is fatal to democracy because a healthy democratic process requires the vibrant clash of political positions and an open conflict of interests" (277). Maintaining the idea that reasonable people engage in argumentation is especially important for anyone who is seeking changes that might threaten the authority of powerful economic interests or destabilize existing social arrangements. Because absence of argument allows elites to control deliberative processes, the existence of vociferous debate is not a "sign of hostility, alienation, misbehavior, inefficiency, or even impending chaos and ruin" (278) but rather a sign of a healthy, pluralistic democracy.

The rapid growth of ADR's popularity has resulted in a wide variety of processes. They range from approaches that are explicitly grounded in postmodern theory (Pearce and Littlejohn 168–216) to locally grown community groups that learn as they go (Peterson 148–157). Some explicitly include argumentation and debate in their practices (Daniels and Walker), whereas others seek consensus (Arthur, Carlson, and Moore; Susskind, McKearnan, and Thomas-Larmer). As you might expect, facilitators also run the gamut from those who have studied the theory behind the Public Dialogue Consortium (Pearce and Littlejohn 197–210) to those who simply have the knack of communicating well in difficult situations.

CONCLUSION

When you try to make sense of argumentation, your choices and evaluations will be influenced by your history as well as your current circumstances. The interaction between you, other participants in the dispute, and the larger political structure within which all of you engage will influence both your ability to present an argument and its reception. This does not mean that the outcomes are controlled by external forces. In fact, it suggests that the discursive patterns you choose have the power to fundamentally alter the available possibilities.

Every situation has established patterns of criteria that help participants evaluate the possibilities for argumentation. Common patterns such as good reasons, storytelling, and science have evolved to help people make and justify critical decisions and argumentation. Understanding and using these patterns will help you argue effectively in most settings.

During the last half of the twentieth century, feminist theory has contributed to new patterns of criteria that respond to social and political changes. These patterns bring an explicitly critical edge to the theory and practice of argumentation. They are especially useful to you if your goal is to change existing configurations of power. They also provide a theoretical basis for an explicitly nonadversarial approach to argumentation known as ADR.

Alternative dispute resolution (ADR) processes have emerged as an alternative to the acrimonious exchanges constructed with zero-sum outcomes that have led increasingly to gridlock and citizen outrage. They have the potential to enrich the overall quality of democracy by endowing governments and their regulatory agencies with additional legitimacy and providing communication channels for generating lively discussion among citizens.

EXERCISES/PROJECTS

1. Select an editorial from your local newspaper. Revise the editorial twice. First, write a version of the editorial that is persuasive from a scientific perspective. Be sure to use Pine's essential elements in your revision. Second, write a version of the editorial that uses a feminist sensibility to make the same argument.
2. Learn what rights you have in the event of a dispute with your credit card company. Find out if your credit card agreement mandates the use of binding arbitration in the case of a dispute. If you do not have a paper copy of your agreement, you can find the agreement on the URL for your credit card company. Discuss your response to what you have learned.

The Nature
of Arguments

KEY TERMS

claim, p. 53

grounds, p. 53

warrant, p. 54

backing, p. 54

qualifier, p. 55

force, p. 55

rebuttal, p. 55

reservation, p. 55

reasoning processes, p. 56

logic, p. 57

deduction, p. 57

syllogism, p. 57

enthymeme, p. 57

informal logic, p. 58

pragma dialectical discussion rules, p. 59

argument by generalization, p. 59

sample, p. 59

agreement, p. 60

difference, p. 60

correlation, p. 60

residues, p. 60

argument by cause to effect, p. 60

argument by effect to cause, p. 60

argument by sign, p. 62

argument by analogy, p. 63

argument from authority, p. 64

wisdom of crowds, p. 64

narrative, p. 64

argument by definition, p. 65

O n the playground, a little girl and boy are in an argument:

GIRL: "You're a liar."
BOY: "No I'm not, 'cause my pants aren't on fire."
GIRL: "Good point."

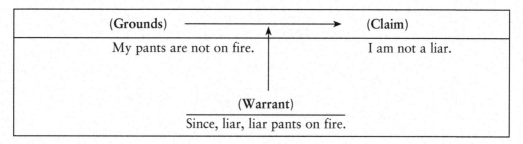

| **FIGURE 4.1**

What do people mean when they say, "Good point" or "That makes sense" or "That's reasonable" or "That's logical?" In the case of the little girl, the boy invoked a familiar refrain, "liar, liar, pants on fire," which many children learn. He connected his claim with knowledge already possessed by the girl so that she perceived it as a good point. Adults smile at the exchange because they have learned more complex and effective ways of telling if someone has supported a claim. It was an argument, but not a good argument. In this chapter, we will explain some of the ways people have developed, over thousands of years, of making arguments—connecting claims with knowledge possessed by decision makers so they can grant adherence.

THE MODEL OF AN ARGUMENT

We start by introducing you to a modification of a model developed by Stephen Toulmin (1963, iii) to help you understand the parts of an argument and their interrelationships. In the past half-century, Toulmin's layout of argument has become the standard pattern for examining arguments and his terminology of claim, grounds, warrant, backing, qualifier, and rebuttal/reservation has become widely adopted (Hitchcock and Verheis). The model we are using is useful to *analyze* an argument, but be aware that you will put an argument together for communication in a completely different format. We illustrate the model with this argument:

On May 23, 2011, *The Chronicle of Higher Education* reported new data from the U.S. Census Bureau revealing that the median income of people who graduated with a major in petroleum engineering was US $120,000, more than any other major. Students interested in maximizing their lifetime income should seriously consider majoring in petroleum engineering.

Claim

A **claim** states the idea or action for which you are seeking adherence—it is the end goal of the argument, and it is the place you begin:

(Claim) Students should major in petroleum engineering.

Grounds

Grounds provide the primary source of support in answer to the question: "Why should I agree with your claim?" "What have you got to back it up?" "What facts do you use to get there?" Grounds consist mostly of evidence as discussed in Chapter 7, as well as values discussed in Chapter 8 and credibility discussed in Chapter 9.

(Grounds) ──────────────▶	(Claim)
People who graduate with a major in petroleum engineering earn more than those with any other major.	Major in petroleum engineering.

❙ FIGURE 4.2

Warrant

Rarely, do the grounds alone allow the decision maker to grant adherence to the claim. Usually, an argument includes, either stated or implied, a general statement mostly in the form of a value as discussed in Chapter 8 or a variation of a value statement in the form of a reason, law, principle, rule, maxim, rationale, custom, procedure, rule of thumb.

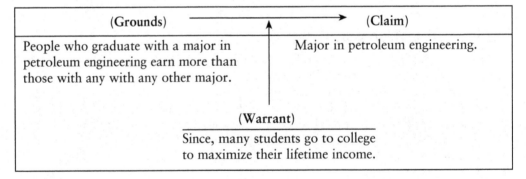

❙ FIGURE 4.3

Backing

For some people, "claims, grounds, and **warrant**" are all an argument would need. They would accept the reasoning and find the claim acceptable. Others, however, particularly on controversial questions, would want more. They would require backing for either the grounds or the warrant. **Backing** *is any support (specific instances, statistics, testimony, values, or credibility) that provides more specific data for the grounds or warrant.* In today's communication scene, characterized by blogs, social networking, commentators, as well as the usual interactions, it is quite common for people to assert facts without saying where they came from or how others can confirm their accuracy. In other words, they need to provide backing. Notice we have had to add backing to the warrant because none was originally supplied.

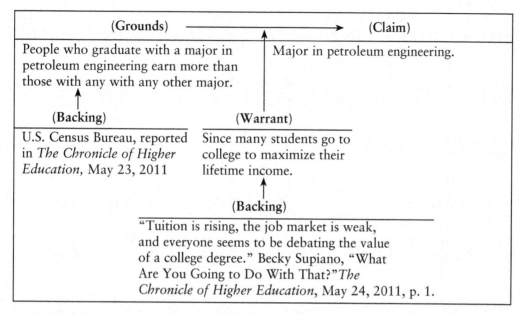

Within the figure:

(Grounds) ⟶ (Claim)

People who graduate with a major in petroleum engineering earn more than those with any with any other major.

Major in petroleum engineering.

(Backing)

U.S. Census Bureau, reported in *The Chronicle of Higher Education*, May 23, 2011

(Warrant)

Since many students go to college to maximize their lifetime income.

(Backing)

"Tuition is rising, the job market is weak, and everyone seems to be debating the value of a college degree." Becky Supiano, "What Are You Going to Do With That?" *The Chronicle of Higher Education*, May 24, 2011, p. 1.

| FIGURE 4.4

Qualifier

To be reasonable, an argument must have a claim and grounds for that claim, and the link between the two must be justified by a warrant. The grounds or warrant may need backing, depending on the level of questioning by decision makers. Sometimes, you have to look very carefully at the claim to see how much is being claimed. Some claims will have a **qualifier**, *a statement that indicates the force of the argument.* As we noted in greater detail in Chapter 1, words such as *certainly, possibly, probably, for the most part, usually,* or *always* show how forceful a claim is. The qualifier in this argument is "seriously consider" which shows less force than "certainly major in petroleum engineering" would have shown. Remember, the force of an argument is an expression of the confidence in the claim the arguer is willing to express, and the extent to which the arguer is willing to be held responsible for the claim.

Rebuttal/Reservation

The actual strength of this argument has to be judged as well by possible **rebuttal/reservation**, *the basis on which the claim could be questioned by decision makers and the limits the arguer puts on the claim.* The rebuttal reflects the arguments that detract from the claim, and the reservation explains the qualifier. It says "seriously consider," but with the reservation that only select students will do so. The rebuttal/reservation itself is another claim, for which you could develop an entire argument. It is possible that at a certain point, the rebuttal may become strong enough to replace the claim, at which point, the original argument would become the rebuttal. In this case, you have probably already started rehearsing rebuttals to the argument: not everyone goes to college just to make more money, you can make just about as much money in other majors, not everyone is qualified to major in engineering, petroleum engineering might not be a career you would enjoy, petroleum engineers usually have to work in places where oil is being pumped such as Saudi Arabia or Nigeria, which may not be where you want to live. You might have reservations about working in the petroleum industry because it has been charged with damaging the environment or because the importance of petroleum will decline in the future as alternative sources of energy are developed.

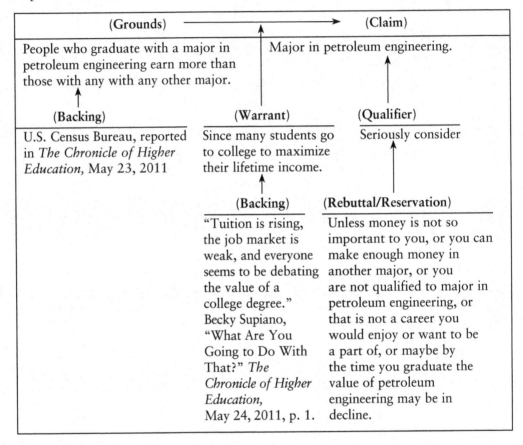

| **FIGURE 4.5**

Not all arguments are the same. Some will be found reasonable without backing. Some parts will not be stated. Some will be carefully developed. Some claims will be subject to significant rebuttal, others to little. Some warrants will be specific, others will be vague. You will find some arguments much easier and others more difficult to diagram than this one on choosing your college major. However, the Toulmin model should help you evaluate the argument when someone asks, "Is this a good argument?" It will be the basis for examining the problems with arguments in Chapter 11. It will also be useful to you in understanding the reasoning processes.

REASONING PROCESSES

In Chapter 2, we identified the commonplaces of arguments: those principles that are used to generate starting points of argumentation. Among the commonplaces were certain reasoning processes: **logic** or **deduction, generalization, cause, sign, analogy,** and **authority.**

These constitute the basis for most arguments. The purpose of this section is to look at those principles more carefully to see how they are applied in all but the most specialized situations and how they differ in the nature of their grounds, claims, and warrants.

There is no natural superiority of one type of argument over another. However, their relative usefulness will vary from sphere to sphere. Logic is still influential in technology, science, and law, but it rarely appears in other spheres. Authority is a crucial form of argument in religion but is less significant in science. Analogy, a strong force in legal and political argumentation, is frequently considered suspect by social scientists. Economists, epidemiologists, and weather forecasters consider sign arguments quite useful. Nonetheless, each type of argument has its use and the chances are that not a week goes by that you do not use them all.

Argument by Logic/Deduction/Syllogism/Enthymeme

Aristotle set out a pattern of formal relations by which arguments could be tested for validity. That is to say, if you begin with true premises, this **logic** can dictate the ways in which they can be combined to yield true conclusions. The pattern is called **syllogism** (**deduction**) and is taught, with the modifications that have been made over the years, as formal logic. We explain below, however, that logic works only with abstract terms such as A's and B's or P's and Q's. When practical arguments in ordinary language are put into the pattern, the logic loses its certainty and becomes a rhetorical syllogism or **enthymeme**. The pattern of arguments in logical form has been set for centuries and well before the advent of the Toulmin model. We will present logic as it has traditionally been displayed.

Typical examples of the validity patterns in syllogisms are the *categorical*, *hypothetical*, and *disjunctive*. We will give simple examples of each.

Categorical: If all A is B, If good students are good drivers,
And if all C is A, and if good drivers have fewer accidents,
Then all C is B then, good students have fewer accidents.

(There are many other valid forms of categorical syllogisms.)

Hypothetical: If A, then B If you have a degree, you will earn more money.
So if A exists You do have a degree,
Then B exists so, you will earn more money.

(Modus ponens—one of two valid forms of hypothetical syllogisms)

Or,
If B does not exist, You are not earning more money,
Then A does not exist) so, you must have no degree.

(Modus tollens—the other valid form of the hypothetical syllogism)

Disjunctive: Either A or B Either the team wins or the coach is fired.
So if A exists The team is winning,
Then B does not exist The coach is not fired.
or, if B exists The coach has been fired.
then A does not The team was not winning.

FIGURE 4.6

Valid Forms of Syllogisms/Enthymemes

You should see at once that when we put ordinary language in the place of abstract symbols, the arguments require grounds, backing, and qualifiers. Validity means only that there is no internal contradiction in the logic. It does not assure the conclusions can be held with confidence.

Modern formal logic texts (Smith, *An Introduction to Formal Logic*) illustrate the various valid forms of these syllogisms and show how validity can be tested symbolically in a method closely resembling mathematics. Because of different basic assumptions and requirements, this logic deals with tasks such as computer programming, which fall outside the domain of argumentation. That is to say, this logic is the calculus of certainty. The search for mathematical certainty grounded in logic goes back at least to Euclid in ancient Greece. Throughout the first half of the twentieth century, mathematical philosophers attempted to organize every possible assumption and principle used in mathematics into logical patterns, complete with strict rules for moving from one step to the next. Mathematics was fundamentally changed when, in 1931, Kurt Gödel published a paper arguing that mathematics "is both incomplete and inconsistent" (Peat, 41). The search for a "new" logic continues to this day.

Martin D. S. Braine and David P. O'Brien explain in detail their theory of mental logic consisting of "a set of inference schemas. For example, when one knows that two propositions of the form *p* or *q* and *not p* are true, one can assert *q*" (3). They provide an extensive list of such schemas, although it does not claim to be exhaustive. Although we disagree with their contention that the human mind naturally employs such logic, we agree that people are quite capable of learning and using it.

During the last half of the twentieth century, there was much philosophical discussion of the viability of formal logic in argumentation (Toulmin, *The Uses of Argument*; Perelman and Olbrechts-Tyteca). At the same time, work in artificial intelligence presented computer programmers with the need for a goal-directed, knowledge-based logic (a logic of uncertainty) suited to describing how people actually go about the business of practical reasoning (Walton 1990).

The result has been what is called **informal logic** (Johnson and Blair). In many ways, its contribution is directed toward the discussion of fallacies, as we explain in Chapter 11. In its more conservative form, informal logic employs the patterns of deductive logic to criticize arguments within the realm of argumentation. Thus, the concept of validity is retained, but the force of conclusions does not reach the certainty of formal logic. Perelman and Olbrechts-Tyteca speak of *quasi-logic*, meaning the use of syllogistic forms in presenting arguments to benefit from the widespread respect given to logic by many decision makers.

Douglas Walton (1990) offers a goal-directed pattern of informal logic appropriate for both artificial intelligence and practical reasoning. Walton sees informal logic, unlike formal logic, as working with reasoning in a problem-solving context, involving some value-laden mandate (must, should), premised on known requirements and consequences, projecting into the future, assessing costs and benefits, and calling for a shift or adjustment in the collective commitments of the relevant decision makers (*The New Dialectic* 83).

The argumentation scheme Walton offers is this:

A is the goal.
B is necessary to bring about A.
Therefore, B is necessary.

This is used, says Walton, to convince someone to take whatever action is entailed in B. Critical appraisal of such argumentation, according to Walton, follows these questions:

1. Are there alternatives to B?
2. Is B an acceptable (or the best) alternative?

3. Is it possible to bring about B?

4. Does B have bad side effects? (85)

Walton has described a new dialectic that returns to the dialectical writings of the ancient Greeks "as a general perspective and way of evaluating arguments in a context of dialogue." He seeks to provide "a new theoretical basis for logic which can be used to evaluate arguments that arise in everyday conversational exchanges" (*The New Dialectic* 4–36).

Frans H. van Eemeren and Rob Grootendorst have proposed a set of rules by which critical decision making can be guided. They speak of dialectical constituents of argument as the logical or reasonable foundation. They list 10 rules for critical discussion:

---

1. Participants must not try to silence each other to prevent the exchange of arguments and criticism.
2. If you make a claim, you must be willing to provide support if it is requested.
3. When you criticize someone's argument, you should be sure you are talking about what they really said.
4. You should defend your claims with arguments relevant to them.
5. You should not claim that others have presumed something they have not, and you should be willing to admit your own presumptions.
6. You should not try to start argumentation with a starting point others do not accept, and you should not deny a genuine starting point.
7. You should not say your claim has been established unless you have provided proper argumentative support.
8. You should stick to arguments that are logically valid or can be made valid.
9. If you fail to establish your claim, admit it; if others establish their claims, admit it.
10. Avoid unnecessary ambiguity, and try to interpret other's arguments as clearly as possible.

FIGURE 4.7
Pragma-Dialectical Discussion Rules

Argument by Generalization

Generalization, or rhetorical induction, is an argument in which individual instances are assembled to allow the assertion of a general principle. At its most basic, a generalization is formed by looking at individual elements so that a general statement can be made that fairly reflects the individual data. For example, the U.S. Federal Reserve divides the country into 12 districts. Economic activity in each district is examined regularly and a general statement on the nation's economic health is announced. Information collected on May 27, 2011 was published on June 9, 2011. According to *The New York Times* of that date, the nation's economy continued to grow but was held down by high food and energy prices and an earthquake and tsunami in Japan. Some districts performed better than others, but the generalization was faithful to the central tendency. On the basis of that information, arguments from generalization were then made about how well the economy would do in the future.

Argument by generalization is regularly made through a sampling process. If you want to make a general statement that fairly describes a large number of instances such as the entire population, you do not need to look at each person or instance. You can, instead, examine a **sample** of that population and generalize that what is so about your sample is also so about the entire population. The critical element in this is the selection of the sample, usually by a form of randomization, so that you can properly claim that all members of the total population had an equal chance of being included in the sample. When the Pew Research group said that only 32% of Americans believe that life has evolved over time, they only questioned 2,001 people (Fox, popsci.com).

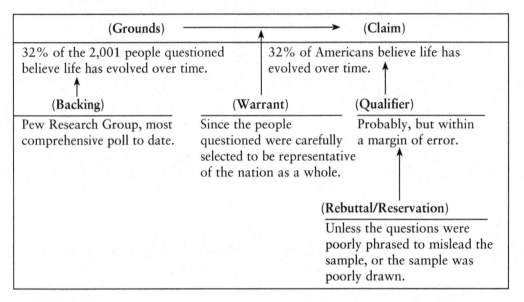

I FIGURE 4.8

Examples, discussed in Chapter 7, are also part of reasoning by generalization. Aristotle called examples rhetorical induction (40). You might advance a general claim, "The number of emergency-management programs in higher education has increased dramatically from 2001 to today." Then, you can provide grounds for the claim by citing examples: State University of New York, New Paltz, Fordham University, and Eastern Kentucky University (Foderaro A19). These three examples or individual instances (and there is rhetorical power in three as opposed to one or two) communicate support for the generalization and help the decision makers grant adherence.

Argument by Cause

Since well before Thomas Aquinas argued the existence of God by saying, "Things do not change unless some agent changes them," as we discuss in Chapter 14, people have acted on the presumption that effects have causes. Only God, claimed Aquinas, could be the unmoved mover. Captain Von Trapp, in the film *The Sound of Music*, sings "Nothing comes from nothing, nothing ever could." An **argument by cause** can reason from **cause to effect** or from **effect to cause**.

John Stuart Mill suggested that causal arguments can be developed by using the methods of **agreement, difference, correlation, and residues** (278–291). As we discuss in Chapter 13, scientific arguments are frequently based on cause and effect. We will illustrate Mill's methods with an example from epidemiology.

During the summer of 2011, a deadly outbreak of *Escherichia coli* bacteria occurred in northern Germany. Reasoning from effect to cause, the effect was obvious: 39 people died, around 3,500 people in 12 countries were stricken with serious illness, and farmers were hurt when people stopped eating vegetables they thought might be carrying the bacteria. The question was: What actually is the cause? Using the method of agreement, authorities asked, "What is the one and only thing common to all the people who have suffered?" If they could find, for example, that all had eaten the same food, it would probably be the cause. In fact, it was quickly found that people had probably come in contact with the bacteria after eating salads, but salads contain a variety of ingredients—which one was the culprit? At first, the suspect was Spanish cucumbers, but it was found that some people had eaten salads without cucumbers and still became sick. The method of difference was used to zoom in on salads as the cause because people in the same circumstances who had not eaten salads did not get sick. So, the question was what single ingredient was in all the salads (method of agreement)? It was, apparently, bean sprouts from a single farm (Rohan). More than a month later, the method of agreement led to a search for a shipment of 16 tons of tainted fenugreek (a version of bean sprouts) seeds sent from an Egyptian organic farm and used to grow the sprouts in the German salads, as well as those in France, Britain, Austria, and Spain.[1]

Reasoning from cause to effect, suspicion had fallen early on organic farms because they use manure as fertilizer. This helped investigators locate the farm that produced the tainted bean sprouts through correlation: *E. coli* is often found in and around manure. Using the method of residues, the various ingredients of salads including cucumbers, tomatoes, lettuce, and bean sprouts were tested. When cucumbers, tomatoes, and lettuce were found to be untainted, suspicion fell on the (residue) remaining ingredient: bean sprouts.

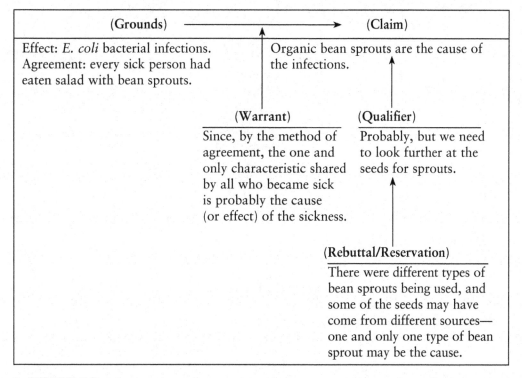

FIGURE 4.9

[1]William Neuman, "A Search Is Under Way For Tainted Sprout Seeds," *The New York Times*, July 6, 2011, B3.

Argument by Sign

Argument by sign is closely related to causal argument but is different. A sign argument is based on a warrant that most things, conditions, or ideas have characteristics that will signal their presence. The sign is closely associated, but is not necessarily the cause or effect, of the thing signaled. We have just mentioned correlation as involved in cause–effect reasoning, but it is also part of argument by sign. A correlation says that two phenomena vary together such that one may be the cause of the other or they both may be the result of an external cause. For example, auto insurance companies will typically reduce premiums for drivers under 25 years of age if they have maintained a B or better grade average. What research has told them is that good grades are significantly correlated with safe driving. That is, the good grades are a sign of safe drivers. Getting good grades does not necessarily cause safe driving, nor does safe driving cause good grades; they just seem to go together, and it is far easier and cheaper for insurance companies to get grade transcripts than it would be to come up with a measure of safe driving tendencies.

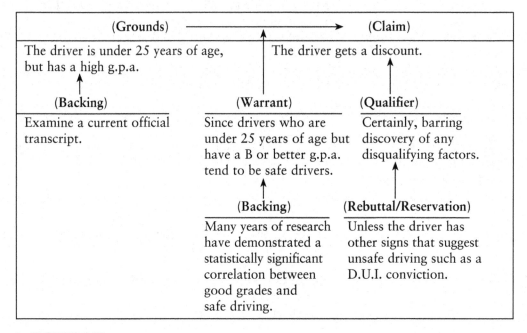

(Grounds)		(Claim)
The driver is under 25 years of age, but has a high g.p.a.	The driver gets a discount.	
(Backing)	**(Warrant)**	**(Qualifier)**
Examine a current official transcript.	Since drivers who are under 25 years of age but have a B or better g.p.a. tend to be safe drivers.	Certainly, barring discovery of any disqualifying factors.
	(Backing)	**(Rebuttal/Reservation)**
	Many years of research have demonstrated a statistically significant correlation between good grades and safe driving.	Unless the driver has other signs that suggest unsafe driving such as a D.U.I. conviction.

FIGURE 4.10

Specialists in business and finance make regular use of argument by sign. The *Composite Index of Leading Indicators* is an example. "The index is made up of 10 economic components, whose changes tend to precede changes in the overall economy" (Investopedia). The components, such as average weekly hours worked by manufacturing workers, the amount of new building permits, consumer sentiment, and the S&P 500 stock index, taken together have been shown to be reliable signs of the direction of the economy. There is no singular cause–effect relationship, but the 10 components function as a good sign of the economy. Notice also that by examining 10 individual signs and then generalizing about the economy as a whole, the index argues by generalization as well.

Argument by Analogy

In **argument by analogy,** you compare two situations that you believe have the same essential characteristics and reason that a specific characteristic found in one situation also exists in the analogous situation.

It has been traditional to differentiate between literal and figurative analogies. The literal analogy is presumed to be based on factual comparisons of situations, and the figurative analogy is based on more fanciful relations. No two situations can literally be identical. However, some comparisons are more material than others. For example, when a prize winning journalist announced that he was an undocumented resident in the United States, someone asked whether it would hurt anything to give him his citizenship. One answer was: no one is hurt by a single snowflake, but get enough of them and you can have an avalanche. This would be called a figurative analogy in traditional terms because undocumented residents and snowflakes are materially different. Still, it makes a point more rhetorically compelling.

From the perspective of reasoning, materially similar comparisons are more significant because decision makers tend to take them more seriously. A claim reasons that what is so about one point of comparison is arguably so about another, or can be used to argue a point based on comparison. DC Comics has renumbered its entire DC Universe line of comics. In September of 2011, 52 series started anew, each with an issue No. 1 (Gustines C1). Collectors buy these No. 1 issues of comics by making an analogy: The legendary Action Comics No. 1, which introduced Superman, has become quite valuable today, and readers in the past have shown increased interest in buying comics when they can start with No. 1. So, the claim is this: by restarting the numbering of all their comics, DC can significantly increase sales.

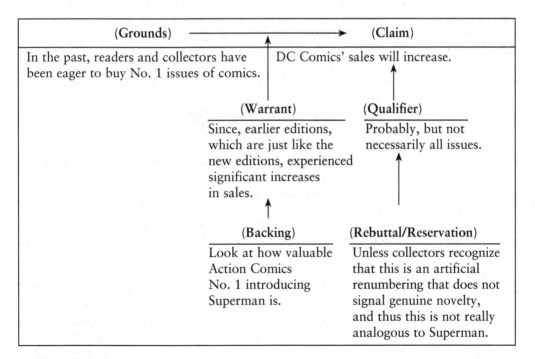

(Grounds) ⟶	(Claim)
In the past, readers and collectors have been eager to buy No. 1 issues of comics.	DC Comics' sales will increase.
(Warrant) Since, earlier editions, which are just like the new editions, experienced significant increases in sales.	**(Qualifier)** Probably, but not necessarily all issues.
(Backing) Look at how valuable Action Comics No. 1 introducing Superman is.	**(Rebuttal/Reservation)** Unless collectors recognize that this is an artificial renumbering that does not signal genuine novelty, and thus this is not really analogous to Superman.

| **FIGURE 4.11**

In Chapter 12, our discussion of argumentation in law reports how important reasoning by analogy is to lawyers and judges. Under the principle in which courts want regularity in law (*stare decisis*), arguments are based on comparing the present case with earlier cases that have already been decided. The argument is this: the court decided a previous case, which is analogous to our present case, in a certain way, and under *stare decisis*, the court should decide the present case in the same way.

Argument from Authority

In Chapter 9, we will discuss how your credibility can support the adherence decision makers give to your argument. Even persons of high credibility, however, frequently use the credibility of others to argue a claim. In **argument from authority**, you argue that a claim is justified because it is held by a credible person, ordinarily someone other than yourself. The most common way of presenting such an argument is to cite an authority.

When U.S. Army Private Bradley E. Manning was alleged to have helped pass thousands of classified prisoner dossiers and embassy diplomatic cables to WikiLeaks' founder Julian Assange, he was jailed and subjected to much public discussion. The questions turned on whether Manning should be considered a traitor for helping make government secrets public, or a patriot who exposed information that should not have been withheld from the public. Stephen M. Kohn, executive director of the National Whistleblowers Center, writing in *The New York Times*, claimed that Manning was a whistleblower and a patriot and supported his argument with the authority of the Congress of the United States acting in 1778. Kohn told the story of 10 revolutionary sailors and marines who reported the misdeeds of their captain. When the captain retaliated against his men, Congress enacted the first whistle-blower-protection law, stating, "That it is the duty of all persons in the service of the United States to give the earliest information to Congress of any misconduct, frauds, or misdemeanors." (Kohn A21). In the United States, the U.S. Congress is recognized as the ultimate authority concerning the military, and the first Congress, sitting in 1778, consisted of the founding fathers and other patriots who are regularly cited as the ultimate authorities on what it means to be a patriot. Congress even directed Sam Adams to ensure that the lawyers who represented the sailors and marines in the case were paid for their legal services (US$1,418).

There is another kind of argument from authority that is considered more questionable. It is called *bandwagon* or *ad populum*. It says that a claim is good because people believe it. Although it is considered a fallacy by many, its acceptability depends on the sphere in which it is used. Professor S.I. Hayakawa said, "Commonsense is that which tells you the world is flat (29–30). So, commonsense cannot be invoked as authority except in the most unsophisticated contexts. However, in a democratic society, it is a powerful kind of political argument. It rests on the authority of majority opinion, a strong political value. Or it could rest on the authority of those most involved. In Chapter 16, we include *The **Wisdom of Crowds*** as a valuable source of support for business arguments.

These five reasoning processes (logic, generalization, cause–effect, sign, analogy, and authority) constitute the arguments you are most likely to find in your own argumentation and that of most others, although there are special variations on these in some spheres. For example, *narratives* or stories carry a heavy burden of communicating reasoning in many instances. In Chapter 12, we discuss at length how legal argumentation appears in narrative form at many points in the decision making process. In the personal sphere, people reason with each other through narrative most of all. If you concentrate

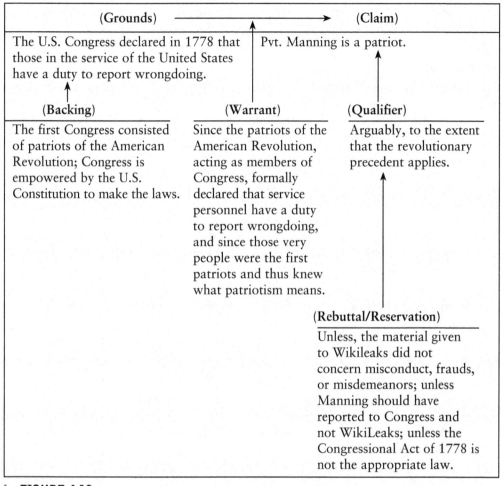

(Grounds) ——————→		(Claim)
The U.S. Congress declared in 1778 that those in the service of the United States have a duty to report wrongdoing.		Pvt. Manning is a patriot.

(Backing)	(Warrant)	(Qualifier)
The first Congress consisted of patriots of the American Revolution; Congress is empowered by the U.S. Constitution to make the laws.	Since the patriots of the American Revolution, acting as members of Congress, formally declared that service personnel have a duty to report wrongdoing, and since those very people were the first patriots and thus knew what patriotism means.	Arguably, to the extent that the revolutionary precedent applies.

(Rebuttal/Reservation)

Unless, the material given to Wikileaks did not concern misconduct, frauds, or misdemeanors; unless Manning should have reported to Congress and not WikiLeaks; unless the Congressional Act of 1778 is not the appropriate law.

| FIGURE 4.12

on reasoning processes, diagram them to see their parts and the reasoning that holds them together, you can better evaluate the quality of the arguments. Later in this chapter, we will look more carefully at how to analyze the arguments you encounter. First, however, you should consider an important special kind of argument: argument by definition.

DEFINITIONS AS ARGUMENT

In **argument by definition**, definitions serve to identify exactly what is being argued. Even in situations of strong disagreement, disputants should try to agree on the subject of the disagreement. Definitions are claims that must be supported by effective argumentation because meanings are based on consensus. Value-laden terms such as *love, knowledge, justice,* or *God* clearly have no single precise definition. Neither do such apparently straightforward terms as *climate change, gun control, abortion,* or *economic prosperity.* When you use words, you cannot appeal to a single correct definition. You must present a convincing argument to support your interpretation. Definitions can be used as support for your arguments only if you have a common interpretation with the decision makers and hopefully with opponents as well. There are several common ways to build an argument in support of your definition, and we will discuss some of them.

Formal Definition

A formal definition involves the development of an enthymeme or a deductive logic-based argument where a term is located within a general class for which there is a high probability of a common audience interpretation, and then differentiating it from other aspects of the class. The formal definition is usually the first one given in a dictionary.

> A *democracy*, as Americans use the term, is a form of government [general class] in which the people either directly or through elected representatives exercise power [differentiation].
> *Climate change* is long-term significant change in the weather patterns of an area [general class] influenced by the greenhouse effect [differentiation].
> *Fundamentalism* is a movement in American Protestantism [general class] based on a belief that the Bible is a literal historical record and incontrovertible prophecy [differentiation].

Definition by Example

Just as examples (see Chapter 7) can serve to support an argument and are essential to argument by generalization, they can define an unknown idea. In definition by example, you identify examples that decision makers are likely to know, and relate your concept to them.

> *Holocaust* is mass murder of Jews (and others) by the Nazis in World War II, any wholesale destruction, especially by fire, a great slaughter, or massacre.
> The *New Deal* is characterized by, for example, such programs as Social Security, the Federal Deposit Insurance Corporation, and the Securities and Exchange Commission.
> *Marsupials*, mammals that gestate their young in a pouch or marsupium, rather than in a uterus, comprise koalas, wallabies, kangaroos, and the only one found in North America, the opossum.

Functional Definition

Sometimes a good way to make a convincing definition is to illustrate how a concept functions.

> *Spark plugs* ignite the fuel mixture in an internal combustion engine.
> *Dental floss* cleans the areas between your teeth.
> A *heuristic device* gives students a guide to use for learning on their own.

Definition by Analogy

You can establish a clear meaning for a concept by using argument by analogy to show how a term is like or unlike other familiar concepts. Remember, arguments by analogy work by placing a concept under study alongside one on which there is agreement. If they can be shown to have significant similarities, the unknown concept can take on meaning from that which is already agreed on.

Definitions by analogy resemble formal definitions, but they are subtly different. In formal definitions, concepts are identified logically as part of a class. In definition by analogy, concepts are explained by their similarity to a more familiar concept.

School vouchers are like business vouchers that can be exchanged for goods and services. They differ in that they can be exchanged for private school attendance.

A *historical novel* is like a history book in that it is based on the study and interpretation of the past, but it differs in the fact that the author is free to include imagined characters, conversations, and events.

An *oboe* is like a clarinet in that it is a slender woodwind musical instrument, but it differs in that it has a double-reed mouthpiece.

Definition by Authority

Arguments based on authority are common in definition. The most obvious authority is a dictionary, which for many situations is all the authority you need. Resist being entrapped, however, by a veneration of authority leading you to believe that the dictionary is the final or only authority on word meanings. Often, it is the worst because dictionaries cannot possibly be updated fast enough to keep up with the dynamics of language. However, they will give you a general guide to three factors that will strengthen your argument in many situations.

Usage identifies how a word commonly appears in our communication, what people usually mean. Widespread use of a word for a certain meaning provides some authority for that meaning or definition.

Etymology reports the history of a word from the earliest languages. In the past, an argument for a definition that was based on what the root of a word meant, for instance in Greek or Latin, was more powerful than it is today. Today, such an argument is mostly effective with people who still believe that words possess inherent meaning.

Wordsmiths, or the people who create or modify words, can be used authoritatively to support a definition. When physicists theorized the existence of subatomic particles as the fundamental units of matter, they needed a new word for them. They turned to literature in James Joyce's *Finnegan's Wake:* "three quarks for Mr. Marks," and named their particles *quarks*. Academics, adolescents, gangs, ethnic groups, musical groups, artists, and others commonly create new words and can serve as the authorities on definitions.

Earlier, we used "democracy" to illustrate a formal definition. Now, we can point to a current political debate over whether the United States is a democracy or a republic. Richard W. Rahn, writing in *The Washington Times* for May 17, 2011, argues that Founding Fathers understood that unchecked democracy assigned what he called dangerous power to the majority of people. So, Rahn says, we actually created a republic that involved checks and balances to resist rapid changes that come from majority wishes. He bases his definition on the authority of the Founding Fathers and the U.S. Constitution.

THE ANALYSIS OF ARGUMENTS

You can see from the examples we have discussed in explaining the types of arguments that people do not organize their arguments exactly according to our model or any other model. That is because arguments are aimed at decision makers who know things about the subject, share values and credibility assumptions that the arguer need not mention, and respond to language structures that change the order of the model in actual use.

Consequently, the Toulmin model is a useful analytical tool to check your own arguments and the arguments of others for the kinds of problems discussed in Chapter 11. In this section, we will explain some of the characteristics of arguments that make the application of the model difficult, some guidelines for using the model to help you in analyzing arguments.

Characteristics of Arguments

Arguments are difficult to analyze, but if you recognize why that is the case, it will help you to use the model more effectively. They are difficult because they usually have parts missing, the order of the parts may vary, and they may overlap with one another.

Parts Missing.   Most arguments have parts left out. If the arguer believes the decision makers accept the grounds, then he or she will sometimes provide no backing. Warrants are frequently omitted because they are clearly implied by the other statements the arguer makes.

It is not the lack of a stated warrant that poses a problem for decision makers. The warrant is clearly implied. The real concern is on the level of adherence the decision makers give to the implied warrant.

Sometimes even claims are not stated. This is particularly true of argumentation that follows a strategy of telling stories. You could tell stories about people who defended themselves from assault by having a weapon in their possession without ever stating the claim that people should carry a weapon for self-protection. The claim is not stated but the decision maker knows that is the claim because the overall orientation of the argument clearly implies it.

Order in Arguments.   Arguments do not necessarily follow the order: grounds, warrant, claim. Indeed, they most frequently begin with the claim. However, in scholarly arguments, it is common to start with a discussion of the issues and the prior research on them, with claims coming toward the end. In argumentation in the sciences and social sciences, grounds are always developed first and the claim then developed from those grounds. Such an approach is seen by many as objective. The arguer wants to imply that the evidence is studied before a claim is made, although it is, of course, an argumentative strategy. The arguer knew the claim all along but chose to delay revealing it to decision makers. So, you must remember that analyzing arguments is different from communicating them, and technical spheres typically prescribe the organizational structure of arguments.

Overlapping Arguments.   Frequently, two or more arguments are developed in the same paragraph because the arguer sees them as linked. An argument, reported in *The New York Times*, claims that high school students use tranquilizers or prescription drugs for recreational use more than heroin and cocaine combined. It then adds another claim that in the past anti-drug laws have been able to oppose all use of drugs such as heroin and cocaine to reduce their recreational use, but that is not possible in relation to prescription drugs that also serve medicinal uses. The two arguments overlap in the same paragraph (Zuger, D1). In analyzing the argument, you need to separate the claims, grounds, and warrants, and so forth of each line of argument.

Frequently, arguments are linked to one another, their parts do not appear in any particular order, and parts are left out. Consequently, you may have trouble seeing in an article, television commercial, or speech what an argument is and what its parts are. Here is a useful sequence of guidelines for analyzing an argument:

---

1. Discover and state the claim or claims. What is it the arguer wants you to believe, value, or do? Claims may appear anywhere in the argument but they most likely appear at the beginning or the end.
2. Look for the subclaim of the grounds. It can best be determined if you know the claim first and then ask yourself "On what basis am I supposed to give adherence to the claim?"
3. Look for the warrant. Because it most frequently will be the part omitted, it will be the most difficult to find. But if you know the claim and the grounds you can find even an unstated warrant because it is the statement that would justify the movement from grounds to claim. If stated, it will frequently be identified by words such as *for*, *because*, or *since*.
4. Examine the warrant to determine the kind of argument you are analyzing. Look back over the examples we have used and you will see it is the warrant that identifies the kind of argument by identifying the commonplace (or principle) behind it. Here are a few of the warrants we have used:

    "The 12 Federal Reserve Districts are representative of the U.S. economy." [generalization (representative, comprehensive, overall)]
    "*E. coli* in bean sprouts caused illness." [cause (effect, generate, because, lead to, result in)]
    "The Index of Leading Indicators signals economic change." [sign (indication)]
    "The facts of an already decided case are just like the facts of this case." [analogy (parallel, like, alike)]
    "The patriots of the American Revolution in Congress know who is a patriot." [authority [expert (knowledgeable, trustworthy, skillful)]

5. Look for backing (evidence, values, credibility).

FIGURE 4.13
Guidelines for Analyzing Arguments

CONCLUSION

Arguments appear in a wide variety of situations, and they differ in their nature from one context to another. Yet, all arguments can be diagrammed by a variation of the Toulmin model, which illustrates how a claim can be justified only by showing that there are warranted grounds for it. In addition, grounds and warrants may need backing; claims may need to be qualified and stated with a reservation to avoid rebuttal.

Although the model provides a basis for the analysis of all arguments, not all arguments are alike. Certain types of arguments (commonplaces) can be observed. Arguments using logical forms present relationships such that conclusions are drawn validly. Argument by generalization attempts to draw a general claim from a series of instances. It is a rhetorical induction, the argument form closest to pure induction. Arguments may claim cause and effect relationships either of cause to effect or effect to cause. They may claim the existence of one condition as a sign of another. Arguments may claim that one condition is analogous to another, and they may be warranted by the credibility of an authority.

It is frequently necessary to develop an effective argument in support of a definitional claim before using it as part of the larger argumentation. Definitions can be formal or functional, by example, analogy, or authority. Definitions should be agreed to by decision makers and, if possible, by opponents.

The Toulmin model is an analytical tool. People do not organize their arguments according to the model because decision makers already know something about the subject. So, with most arguments, parts are missing, the order is different from the model, and arguments overlap. To analyze such arguments, start by stating the claim(s) and then find the grounds. Once this is complete, you should be able to find the warrant (frequently unstated) that justifies the supporting relationship between grounds and claim. This should also tell you what kind of argument is at hand.

Finally, take notice of the materials that serve as backing, qualifiers, refutation, and reservation. These pieces of information will permit you to evaluate the quality of the argument for the decision makers.

EXERCISES/PROJECTS

1. Bring to class one example of each of the types of arguments. Look for these in contemporary publications such as newspapers, magazines, advertising flyers, or on Internet sites. Be prepared to explain each argument by relating its parts to the Toulmin diagram. Your instructor may assign different types of arguments to different class members.

2. Select an argument supporting a claim that you **already agree with**. Do an analysis of the argument and then build a case for how reasonable and well-meaning people could disagree with this claim. Join with a group consisting of people who started either agreeing or disagreeing with the claim, and discuss the strengths and weaknesses of each others' reasoning.

Analysis in Argumentation

KEY TERMS

discover the proposition, p. 72
question, p. 73
identify the question, p. 73
objectives and values p. 73
costs and risks, p. 74
determining issues, p. 75
uncontroversial matter, p. 75
clarity, p. 79

significance, p. 79
relevant, p. 79
inherency, p. 79
consistency, p. 80
locate the points of disagreement, p. 81
criteria, p. 81
support, p. 81

M uch of your communication is an argument when you and others with whom you communicate seek to justify claims. The argument can be a simple inter- personal exchange about what to have for lunch, when to get a new cell phone, what features to have on it, or whether to go to Saturday's football game. Many other situations involving your health and well being, and the lives of others including matters of public policy produce claims that require more extensive justification.

Argumentation can even be a lengthy and involved process with hundreds of argu- ments and issues developing around a single proposition of fact, value, or policy. Consider, for instance the following:

There is a God. (fact)
Capitalism is the best economic system. (value)
Individual freedom should be guaranteed to all persons. (policy)

On such claims, there are potentially an infinite number of related arguments because by one chain of reasoning or another all potential arguments can be related. Certainly, that is the assumption of the theologian who looks at the factual proposition, "There is a God." But even the theologian will select from all the potential claims those that will build the best case for the proposition, "There is a God." Because your time is limited, some arguments are stronger than others for specific decision makers, and a smaller number of more powerful arguments gain adherence better than a large number of weaker arguments. To find the proposition you wish to argue, and the strongest claims that support it, requires *analysis: the examination of an argumentative situation for its claims and opposing claims to discover the issues and what arguments and support (evidence, values, and credibility) are most important.*

Analysis of argument is necessary, no matter at what point you enter the argumentation process. It may be your intention to seek the adherence of someone else to a claim, to refute another's claim, or to evaluate your own or someone else's argumentation.

Analysis should be undertaken systematically and in advance of presenting arguments to decision makers. Analysis is not simply a matter of acquiring knowledge. It is a process whereby all the constituents of the argumentative situation are examined in such a way that what needs to be argued and what it will take to gain adherence is revealed. With careful analysis, you can develop effective arguments supported by evidence, values, and credibility. And even more, analysis involves learning about the others with whom you will argue. What arguments might they make that could damage your position with the appropriate decision makers? Analysis, therefore, requires that you look at your own and opposing arguments with equal care.

Analysis has two somewhat distinctive parts. One part deals with developing a proposition from a problem that requires resolution but you are not sure what that resolution is—what Charles S. Peirce called a "feeling of doubt." The second part is used after the proposition has been identified. Then, the objective of analysis is to find the crucial issues, understand their relative importance, and examine the claims to see what you must prove to decision makers. These two can overlap and interact when changes are made in a proposition. A single analysis may move back and forth from one to the other, but we will treat them separately because they are rather different approaches. We will first look at how to develop the proposition you wish to argue from a general question about a problem.

CRITICAL ANALYSIS TO FIND A PROPOSITION

When you realize that there is some kind of a problem, when you have a "feeling of doubt," you frequently aren't sure what to do about it. Critical decision making can be used to help you **discover the proposition** you will argue. If you only express your feeling of doubt you may gain the adherence of some others who are equally frustrated, but to solve the problem you need a clearer statement of a proposition that provides a resolution. Statements such as the following have to be refined into propositions to which decision makers can respond:

> How serious is sexual harassment on this campus?
> Is global warming a serious threat to the planet?
> How should we deal with illegal immigration?
> Can we make good medical care available to all Americans?

Argumentation takes place in a broader societal context of decision making. There are stages that individuals, groups, and even whole societies go through to analyze a problem. Beginning with the problem, you move through the stages in critical analysis is intended to determine a proposition.

There are six stages to the selection of a proposition. However, an arguable proposition may appear at any time and you need not go through each stage. Your analysis should help you to decide at what point to enter the process. If no one recognizes that a problem exists, you must develop claims about the problem. But if everyone agrees that there is a problem, you may skip that stage. Suppose virtually all the decision makers agree that global warming is a significant threat to the health of the planet. In that case, you can slight the analysis of the problem and search for a proposition most likely to provide a solution. So, you will usually not need all six stages, depending on how advanced your knowledge is about the controversy in the question but all are potentially important to your analysis.

Those stages are: identify the question; survey implicated objectives, values, and biases; search for new information; canvas alternate decisions; weigh the costs and risks to alternatives; and then, select a proposition.

Identify the Question

The feeling of doubt that you have needs to be refined into a clearly stated **question** that represents the problem. In order to do this, you must entertain genuine doubt (Dewey, *How We Think*; Peirce). Ask yourself, "What are the potential meanings to my concern?" Entertain the possibility of alternatives. From these, identify and face squarely the question that represents that feeling of doubt (Browne and Keeley; Millman 45; Ruggiero 92). In recent years, there has been a concern over global warming. You obviously don't begin with nothing. You want to examine the question of global warming because you have heard some things about it. Here are some examples of the thoughts you might have about the question:,

> What is global warming and what problem does it pose to the world?
> Are the earth's surface temperatures rising?
> Will the problem cause threats to future ecology?
> Is global warming caused by humans?
> Will restricting fossil fuel use alleviate the problem?
> Does a solution require a radical change of society?

This is not a complete list of all the thoughts you might have, but it is a fair sample. Can you phrase a question from one or more of these that will define the problem and provide a basis for further critical analysis? For instance: Does global warming exist and does it pose a problem for the world?

Search For New Information

Using words such as facts or data often masks the complexity of information seeking. Information means overcoming ambiguity in language, developing a measure of the quality of evidence, searching for errors in discovery or measurement of data, and thinking about significant information that is missing (Browne and Keeley). The global warming question is a particularly difficult one to answer because the basic information is in complicated scientific studies. Not all questions will pose this problem but many questions of public policy do. The search for new information will frequently require a lot of effort on your part.

Survey Implicated Objectives, Values, and Biases

From your experience, research, and thought, identify those **objectives and values** that seem to be related to the question that concerns you. Locate the ultimate purpose of your argumentation—what in the long run are you trying to accomplish? You need to ask: What problems seem to need addressing? What might an ideal system look like? What values do you wish to see embodied in such a program? Knowing what is sought in the decision making and the values to be served sets up the criteria on which arguments will be tested (Janis and Mann 11). This includes your values and those of others involved as decision makers or critics. Pay particular attention to biases you may have and look carefully at objectives that you might be inclined to reject.

Canvass Alternative Decisions

Sometimes people look for alternative decisions only long enough to find the first one that fits; sometimes they look only for the alternatives that seem most attractive. Sometimes they use a small list of handy criteria and eliminate alternatives until one is left, and sometimes people just muddle through, choosing by hit or miss (Janis and Mann 21–41; Ruggiero 92). To be critical means to examine the widest range of alternative propositions, including some that you are tempted to dismiss at once. There seem to be four alternatives that are most prominently supported on the global warming question. They are:

1. Maintain the status quo: do nothing because there is no global warming.
2. People should develop voluntary programs to reduce carbon emissions by revising infrastructure, hybrid cars, more efficient electrical equipment, and so forth.
3. The U. S. government should encourage the development of alternate fuels such as nuclear, solar, wind, and biofuels to replace coal and oil.
4. The United States should enact a Cap and Trade program to reduce carbon emissions to the internationally agreed to levels.

Weigh the Costs and Risks to the Alternatives

Being critical means looking at the negative as well as the positive arguments on all alternative decisions (Janis and Mann 11). **Cost** means more than money; it means values and objectives sacrificed or modified by rejecting one alternative for another. **Risk** includes the degree of uncertainty involved in an alternative, and the strength of the worst-case scenario. Here is a sample of the weaknesses that might be argued about the costs and the risks of each of the possible solutions mentioned above:

1. If global warming exists then the *status quo* will bring the predicted negative effects to the world.
2. Voluntary programs will not do enough to restrict global warming.
3. Alternate sources of energy will be more dangerous, insufficient, or costly than coal and oil.
4. Cap and Trade will damage the American economy, cause a loss of jobs, and make government intrusive on the economy.

Select a Proposition

Selecting a proposition is the last of the six stages of critical decision making. In it a proposition is found that best answers the problem posed by a "feeling of doubt." The proposition you elect will be the product of considering the information, objectives, and values you have along with the costs and risks. Note that it is not a matter of selecting the "true" solution you will be looking for the proposition that has the greatest probability of solving the problem. There will still be claims that can be advanced against the proposition but you are looking for the most probable one. And you must also realize that you may modify your proposition as new information comes to light just as Congress, or other legislative bodies do. They amend proposals to eliminate troublesome objections.

Traditionally, after you have selected a proposition, you will be expected to consider three other steps: (1) make plans to implement the proposition, (2) prepare contingency plans, and (3) build a case for your decision. These will be covered in Chapter 6, "Case Building."

You will not always go through all six stages to find a proposition. Frequently, the proposition has already been identified. That is true of most public propositions. For instance, each of the four possible propositions identified earlier has been advanced as one or more groups in the political spectrum advocated alternate decisions at the time of President Obama's election in 2008. Cap and Trade was selected as the preferred proposition because of its broader base of support, its alleged less intrusive methods, and its claimed ability to deal with the problem with less risk to the economy than some others. So, we will use it as the example of the critical analysis of a proposition.

CRITICAL ANALYSIS OF A PROPOSITION

Any proposition is analyzed by identifying the various claims (fact, value, and policy) that are available to support or oppose it. Take note of what others are saying and what you can think of about the proposition, and then state the claims that are both expressed and implied. By matching up opposing claims you can find the crucial issues. These issues are generated by looking to the engagement of arguments, as in a debate. Not all argumentative situations are debates, but each is potentially a debate. If you wish to advance arguments, you must be prepared to answer objections to them. You need to meet even unstated objections that are likely to be known by decision makers.

Determining the Issues

A simple method for **determining issues** is to make a list of arguments for, and a list of arguments against the proposition and then match them up (see Table 5.1).

> Should the United States adopt a Cap and Trade program to reduce carbon emissions to the internationally agreed to levels?

These arguments, matched up for and against, are organized to determine issues—the places where opposing claims come together. First, look at the opposing claims that do not suggest an issue because they agree with one another. Such claims are called **uncontroversial matter**. Both sides agree to the claim. It is not an issue. One subclaim appears to be an **uncontroversial matter:**

> E.   There are international agreements to limit emissions in developed countries.

Although this claim is not contested, it may be used, as seen here, to support the proposition that the United States should adopt a Cap and Trade system. It might also be part an issue over the seriousness of the problem. Uncontroversial matter may be used

TABLE 5.1

Arguments For and Against

For	Against
A. Global surface temperatures have been increasing during the twentieth century. Climate models predict that temperatures will rise from 2.0 to 11.5 F during twenty-first century.	Some data suggest that earth is getting colder since 1998. Records of surface temperatures are unreliable.
B. This will cause sea levels to rise 7–21 inches causing flooding in Florida and New York City. Retreat of glaciers and sea ice. Expansion of subtropical deserts. More frequent and intense weather events. Species extinction will happen.	No evidence that rising sea levels are part of a long-term increase.
C. Caused by human activity. Attested to by 95% of scientists who study this phenomenon. All major science academies in the industrialized world support this claim.	In sharp dispute among scientists, natural factors such as solar output and El Nino account for warming since 1900.
D. Industrialized countries produce 10 times the CO_2 of undeveloped	China and India are increasing
E. International agreements to limit emissions in developed countries in US and Europe. Kyoto 2005 Copenhagen 2009. Cancun 2010. Designed to stabilize below 2005 levels.	
F. Possible solutions for the United States. Cut back on burning coal and oil. Changes to infrastructure, highways, transmission lines, and mining. Alternate fuels (nuclear, solar, wind, and biofuels). Cap and Trade.	Coal supplies half the electricity in the United States Nuclear dangerous, solar and wind unreliable.
G. Cap and Trade: Cap is ageed to for US to be 14% below 2005 levels by 2020, 83% below 2005 levels by 2050. Companies below their allocation can trade with others. Those over their quota pay a carbon tax.	Cap and Trade rewards heaviest polluters
In effect in Europe Same system used to control sulfur dioxide in 1990.	Minor problem compared with CO_2.
It is a free enterprise solution perhaps now but not by 2020.	H. It is socialistic. Government has final say in reorganizing the economy
New jobs new cleaner industries Economists agree Cap and Trade will not damage economy.	I. Will wreck the economy and cost 800,000 jobs. Fuel prices will soar. Will cause a depression and send American industry overseas.

to respond to issues but it does not constitute the basis of an issue on its own. Thus, although some claims may be uncontroversial, they still have to be accounted for in assessing claims that do become issues. On this score, examining Figure 5.1 we find that there are seven issues in the contrasting claims (notice that they start with these words: "Have," "Will," "Is," "Do," and "Would" that call for a yes or no answer):

---

1. Have global surface temperatures been increasing during the twentieth century and will they continue to rise?
2. Will rising temperatures threaten the ecology of the world?
3. Is the temperature increase caused by human activity of burning carbon fuels producing green house gases?
4. Do industrialized countries such as the United States produce 90% of worldwide CO_2 emissions?
5. Would a Cap and Trade system in the United States stabilize the level of greenhouse gas?
6. Is Cap and Trade a free enterprise solution?
7. Will the Cap and Trade system shrink the U. S. Gross Domestic Product, cut 800,000 jobs, and shift manufacturing overseas?

FIGURE 5.1

Issues in Global Warming

There are more arguments raised for and against an American Cap and Trade system, but these seven issues are a reasonable summary. They reflect the fundamental questions to be addressed in order to make a critical decision.

Rank-Order Issues

The first stage in the process of locating the issues more specifically is to rank-order them based on their significance—degree of involvement and disagreement—among decision makers. Permit us to illustrate how you might examine these issues based on what we know from following the topic.

The argument about global warming is an extremely complex question based on scientific analysis rooted in cause and effect that is always more difficult to prove. If an arguer could prove to the satisfaction of decision makers that (Issue 10) global temperatures are not increasing then none the subsequent issues would be important. There is no need to consider the effect of rising temperatures (Issue 20) or cause (issues 3 and 4) or a Cap and Trade system to control surface temperatures (Issues 5–7) if there is no rise in surface temperatures. There are people who claim that global warming is a hoax. However, the overwhelming scientific agreement and even countries that signed the Kyoto Protocol and participated in subsequent summits on the matter would make issue 1 difficult to argue against.

A similar situation exists with issues 2 and 4. It seems difficult to argue against the science that says the rising temperatures will threaten the ecology of the world or that industrial countries produce the most CO_2. However, issue 3 (Is the temperature increase caused by human activity of burning carbon fuels producing greenhouse gases?) is a more controversial point. To a significant extent, this is caused by the fact that it is so difficult to prove cause. Still a significantly large majority of the scientific community accepts CO_2 as the major cause.

Issue 5 is interesting because it stands at the crossroad between arguments about the nature and cause of global warming, and the possible solution. Arguments that claim Cap and Trade will seriously damage the American economy make it a vital issue of comparative advantage. If a Cap and Trade system in the United States would stabilize the greenhouse gas situation, then we would avoid the damage to the world ecology that proponents claim in Issue 3. At the same time, it might bring on the negative effects on the United States claimed in Issue7. This makes Issue 5 central to a comparative advantage case, which will be discussed in Chapter 6 (Case Building). It is central to an argument not about what is right or wrong but what is more (or less) advantageous.

It would seem that the first four issues, though still debatable, have stronger evidence to support them than some others. As for Issue 5, a Cap and Trade system might or might not stabilize the levels of greenhouse gasses. Issue 6 about free enterprise and socialism is an issue held important by a relatively small group of people, although some hold feverishly to the issue. It is probably the least important. The combination of questions about the extent and cause of global warming together with the fact that there are other proposed solutions pushes issue 7 to the head of the list. Even though Issue 5 points at the ultimate purpose of the debate—to protect the world from the effects of greenhouse gasses—it is the claimed disadvantage that Cap and Trade would damage the American economy that arouses the most controversy and demands the most serious search for evidence. So, Issue 7 is ranked first because of those factors.

The process of rank-ordering the issues requires you to consider not only what you think, or what an opponent might think, but also the preconceptions of the decision makers. Such speculation can lead to a number of different conclusions, but our analysis so far produces the following rank-order:

> Issue 7, first in significance: Would a Cap and Trade system significantly damage (or help) the American economy?
> Issue 5, second in significance: Would a Cap and Trade system in the United States stabilize the level of greenhouse gases?
> Issue 3, third in importance: Is the temperature increase caused by human activity?
> Issue 1, fourth in significance: Have global temperatures been increasing during the twentieth century (will they continue to rise)?
> Issue 2, fifth in significance: Will rising temperatures threaten the ecology of the world?
> Issue 4, sixth in significance: Do industrialized countries such as the United States produce 90% of worldwide CO_2 emissions?
> Issue 6, seventh in significance: Is Cap and Trade a free enterprise (or socialistic) solution?

This is not the sequence in which you will address these issues. That is discussed in Chapter 6 "Case Building." This arrangement of the issues indicates where you will need the most developed argument and evidence to overcome the opposition position with decision makers. Here, we have used a hypothetical situation with a general audience as we see it. With other groups, the order of significance may change. For instance, if your decision makers were more conservative, issues about free enterprise and socialism might be more powerful and an argument for Cap and Trade might require you to spend more time showing the free enterprise aspects of it.

Assuming this is the order of significance does not mean that you will want your case to develop the issues in the same order. It rather indicates where the greatest emphasis of argument and support must be placed.

What Critical Values Will Be Applied?

Because different demands will be placed on your case as you move from one context or sphere to another, it makes sense to pay attention to the way each set of decision makers approaches the decision task. We will identify five generic values usually relevant to decision making that can guide your analysis of each situation.

Clarity.   It may be belaboring the obvious to say your arguments should be clear to the decision makers, but **clarity** is tricky. Language meaning is socially based. If you ask people, "Is what I have said clear?" they may say it is when their understanding is not at all what you hoped it would be. You need to understand what interpretative strategies are typical of these decision makers, and then try to express your arguments so that they will be clear in a joint sense—satisfying you and them. It is also to your advantage to look at opposition arguments in the same way so that you can counter them.

Significance.   What is highly significant to you may be less so to your decision makers. We all have hierarchies of concerns. Special interest groups such as environmentalists or abortion opponents often seem to think that everyone shares their fervor, which is often not the case. For example, if someone asks you whether global warming is significant to you, you may say it is, but not significant enough to donate money to the cause or attend a conference. It helps to have an idea of where your **significance** coincides or does not coincide with that of the decision makers.

Relevance (or Salience).   One way you can decide what issues should be presented to a particular set of decision makers is by learning what is **relevant** (what some call salient) to them. There are related ecological issues about clean air, clean water, mercury pollution of lakes and streams, and so forth, but will these be considered relevant to the issue of the cost of global warming?

You need to be aware of decision makers' understanding of what is relevant and either adapt to it or strengthen your argument to accommodate it.

Inherency.   Decision makers might agree with an argument you make but be less inclined to follow your position because they do not believe you have identified a problem that is inherent in the system. **Inherency** means that a weakness is a permanent attribute or characteristic of something. For instance, in arguing for action on global warming, you would need to claim that the weaknesses in the status quo are inherent. They are so deeply imbedded that no minor modifications such as changing light bulbs and buying a hybrid car can solve them. Inherency puts a powerful obligation on an arguer, much more than significance or relevancy. Try to estimate how your decision makers perceive your arguments and the arguments that oppose you on inherency.

Consistency.   Gidon Gottlieb says, "One of the demands of rationality most often emphasized is the requirement of consistency" (171–172). "In our culture, there is a clear notion that the charge of inconsistency is a winning argument" (Sillars 3). Unfortunately, one person's consistency is another's confusion as different argument elements are identified as needing to be consistent with one another.

Although you want your decision makers to believe concepts you argue are consistent with one another, it will be important for you to learn the decision makers' standards of **consistency**. Remember that inconsistencies can be used against a position only if they exist in the decision makers' minds or are pointed out by the arguer. For instance, in the campaign leading up to the 2012 presidential election, Mitt Romney was charged with inconsistency in attacking President Obama's health care plan because as Governor of Massachusetts he had developed a state plan based on the same principles.

ANALYSIS OF CLAIMS

When the proposition is reduced to a workable series of issues of fact and value, the most significant identified, and the values by which they will be tested observed, you must further refine your analysis by focusing on each fact or value claim used to support or oppose the proposition. Your objective is to look closely at your ultimate purpose: What are you trying to accomplish with your proposition? We discussed the ordering of issues earlier in the chapter and will not repeat that here. But as we have observed, the most significant claim may be about the ability of a Cap and Trade system to stabilize the level of greenhouse gasses because that is the ultimate purpose of the debate, but the opposition claims that Cap and Trade would significantly damage the American economy will probably generate the most intense scrutiny.

Clarify What Each Claim Asserts

At this point, you have a rank-ordered series of issues, and you have recognized the relative importance of each. Next, you need to analyze each of them to locate the specific nature of the issue.[1] Some guidelines for such analysis involve establishing criteria for evaluating each claim and then finding the point at which the claim is most vulnerable to rebuttal. Disagreements may arise over the criteria themselves, the relationship of the claim to the criteria, or the relationship of the support to the criteria.

Each claim has a subject term and a judgment term. For instance, on the claim "Rising temperatures threaten the ecology of the world." there is little difficulty in understanding the subject term. The subject of the sentence is rising temperatures. However, the judgment term, threaten the ecology of the world, presents a problem in definition. That is where the criteria come in. Does "threaten the ecology of the world" mean retreat of glaciers and sea ice, expansion of subtropical deserts, more frequent weather events, flooding, or all of these and more?

---

[1]Some writers have called something similar to what we are suggesting here the four stock issues of propositions of value. For instance:

1. Identify the value object and value hierarchy?
2. Establish the criteria for the values?
3. Do the facts correspond to the definitions?
4. What are the applications of the values? (Freeley 55; Warnick, Inch, and Endres 233–236).

Locate the Points of Disagreement

To evaluate a claim you must **locate the points of disagreement** over it. As you do this work, you will be setting up the basis on which to evaluate the strength of the claim. We will suggest four locations for disagreement:

LOCATION I: By what criteria should the claim be judged?
LOCATION II: Which criteria are the most important?
LOCATION III: To what extent does the claim satisfy the criteria?
LOCATION IV: What is the strength of support for the claim?

By What Criteria Should the Claim Be Judged?   Let us assume that in arguing for a U. S. Cap and Trade emissions program you chose the following **criteria:**

It must reduce CO_2 levels 14% below 2005 levels by 2020.
It must not unduly damage the American economy.
It must allow for flexibility in a company's response.

The criteria in this case seem all inclusive. They ask for a plan to recognize the objections both the scientists, the governments of the world and the skeptical agencies who speak for American industries. But what if the opposition argued that no industry would be hurt by this plan? In that case, you would have an argument over criteria. The second criterion about damage to the economy is different from protecting each industry (coal, oil, and mining).

Which Criteria Are the Most Important?   Even when criteria are agreed on, there can still be a disagreement over which criterion is most important. For instance, suppose that proponents and opponents agree on three criteria as identified previously. They still could disagree over which criterion is most important. Those who support the proposition probably believe that reducing the CO_2 levels is the most important criterion. Opponents probably believe that the second criterion is the most important because of the damage to the economy. So, there is an issue over which criterion is most important.

To What Extent Does the Claim Satisfy the Criteria?   Even if both sides agree to the **criteria** for an acceptable government system, they still can disagree that Cap and Trade can satisfy the criteria. The program by these criteria will be so extensive as to strengthen other arguments against it such as bureaucracy and costs in taxes. Opponents might claim that Cap and Trade based on these criteria will break the U.S. economy and cost as much as 800,000 jobs in the manufacturing sector alone. This is probably where the main issue would exist in this question. Opponents would accept the criteria of the proponents not because they want the claim to succeed but because these criteria can be used to support their arguments about costs, bureaucracy, and socialism.

What Is the Strength of Support for the Claim?   Every argument must ultimately rest on some kind of support (evidence, values, or credibility). The arguments as we have stated them are not supported. To fully argue either for or against, there must be more than assertion. Therefore, it is necessary to find the available **support** and evaluate it as a part of the case.

Particularly on factual claims, the support necessary will usually emphasize evidence (examples, statistics, and testimony). An arguer needs to find the strongest possible evidence for a position. Although values and credibility can be strong bases to support arguments, they are most effective when linked to evidence.

What evidence is most trustworthy to decision makers on the global warming question: Personal examples? Scientific studies? Testimony of experts?

CONCLUSION

People determine where argumentation begins. They discover problems and determine how these problems will be resolved. They frequently do this in a hit-or-miss fashion from limited knowledge and analysis. The adherence of others can be more easily developed if the analysis of problems takes place systematically rather than haphazardly.

To understand how to engage in such analysis, some terms need to be understood. Because any statement may be linked to any other statement and thus generate an infinite number of claims, the number of arguments must be reduced to some workable basis. This is achieved in two parts: first, the critical process of finding a proposition when only a general problem (a "feeling of doubt") is recognized; and, second, the process of finding the crucial issues in the argumentation after the proposition has been identified.

Propositions are discovered through a process of analysis involving six potential steps: identify the question; survey implicated objectives, values, and biases; search for new information; canvass alternative decisions; weigh the costs and risks; and, then, select a proposition.

Once a proposition has been determined, it can be more specifically analyzed. A policy proposition is analyzed by looking for the clash of arguments as in a debate, rank-ordering the issues, and finding which of four critical values apply: clarity, significance, relevance, and consistency. Thus, by looking at both sides of the proposition, the arguer can discover the issues of fact or value that are likely to be most crucial. Each value and factual claim is analyzed by finding criteria for the judgment term in the claim with which to measure the subject term. Issues about fact and value claims will be found in one of four locations:

1. The formation of appropriate criteria.
2. The relative importance of various criteria.
3. Whether the claims meet the criteria.
4. The strength of support for the criteria.

When the proposition is identified, the issues discovered, and their specific natures identified, the arguer can then determine what must be argued and how best to build a case for it.

EXERCISES/PROJECTS

Many newspapers, including *USA Today*, have a regular feature of printing two opposing editorials on current topics. *Congressional Quarterly* also features such exchanges. Find one of these exchanges and determine the issues in the controversy.

With a small group of your classmates discuss a general problem area such as youth gangs, higher education costs, Mideast peace, racial tension, energy costs, and American health. How many possible policy claims can you generate? Which seems like the best? Why?

Case Building—
Presentation Planning

KEY TERMS

case, p. 83
ultimate purpose, p. 84
proposition, p. 84
presumption, p. 86
status quo, p. 86
burden of proof, p. 87
burden of rejoinder, p. 87
prima facie case, p. 88

stock issues, p. 88
counterargument, p. 88
incrementalism, p. 88
commonplace, p. 90
facts, p. 90
probabilities, p. 90
brief, p. 98
problem–solution, p. 98

In Chapter 4, we presented arguments in the form of relatively simple claims with limited supporting materials, but that is not how argumentation works. When people make arguments that they want others to take seriously, they develop more elaborated combinations of claims and support put together in a way that is meant to be persuasive. We call this a **case** in terminology borrowed from legal spheres, but it is more commonly called a presentation, an essay, memorandum, paper, editorial, thesis, article, blog, as well as other terms associated with certain spheres. It makes no difference whether the case is to be presented orally or written, or whether it is communicated in person, on paper, in a book, broadcast, or by new media. The important consideration is that the case uses well-developed arguments put together in a structure appropriate to the audience of decision makers and the context in which it will be presented.

PRELIMINARY STEPS IN CASE BUILDING

When you take on an assignment of preparing an argumentative case, the temptation is to start thinking of arguments—doing some research to find supporting materials and thinking up claims. That is a mistake. Before you start coming up with arguments, there is a good deal of preliminary work to be done, and failure to do this preliminary work usually leads to poor arguments.

Identify the Ultimate Purpose

First, be sure you understand what you are trying to accomplish with your case: the ultimate purpose. This is more than simply the desire that appropriate decision makers will grant adherence to your arguments. The question is this: what is the ultimate objective of your argumentation, or what would a successful outcome "look like?" If you are not sure what you are trying to accomplish, the chances are you will not accomplish it.

More than 40 years ago, many world leaders argued for a "war on drugs." The arguments quickly focused on how governments could catch and incarcerate people associated with certain drugs, whether they were major producers, transporters, sellers, or users. Great amounts of money and resources were assigned to law enforcement and the military to "go after" the drug dealers. But what was their ultimate purpose? To this day, the purpose is usually expressed as hunting down and punishing people involved in the drug trade, when in fact, the whole enterprise was started over a concern with how drugs were damaging the lives of so many people. They lost track of the ultimate purpose.

Former U.S. President and 2002 Nobel Prize winner Jimmy Carter argued on June 17, 2011 that failure to concentrate on the ultimate purpose of reducing the harm done by drugs had led to failure. Using data from the *Global Commission on Drug Policy*, Carter notes that, "global consumption of opiates increased 34.5 percent, cocaine 27 percent, and cannabis 8.5 percent from 1998 to 2008" (Jimmy Carter A31). Although tons of drugs have been seized, many drug lords killed or captured, and vast numbers of individuals have been imprisoned, the ultimate objective of reducing the harmful effects of drug use has not been fulfilled. Carter argues that the world should start over with a clear understanding of the ultimate purpose: help people who are suffering from the abuse of drugs. This will lead to claims that are more responsive to the ultimate purpose than the concept of "war on drugs." What would a solution "look like?" It would be a world where there are fewer abusers of drugs combined with the reduction of all the evils associated with the production, distribution, and sale of drugs.

The United States has participated in a number of armed conflicts since the end of World War Two where the ultimate purpose was either never clearly identified or it was allowed to shift in what has become known as "mission creep." If the ultimate purpose is unclear then there is no definition for victory or when the conflict is over. The Vietnam War developed year-by-year without a clear statement of ultimate purpose, leading Senator Richard Russell, Jr. of Georgia to recommend that the United States just declare victory and depart. In relation to the conflicts in Iraq, Afghanistan, and Libya, the question has regularly been asked, "What would victory look like?"

State the Proposition

In Chapter 1, we characterized a **proposition** as a claim that expresses the judgment that decision makers are asked to accept or reject. More specifically, the proposition represents the recommendation you want to advance in response to the ultimate purpose. The proposition makes no sense if, when agreed to, it does not make a direct contribution toward the ultimate purpose. It may take many steps resulting from granting adherence to a number of propositions, to reach the ultimate purpose, but each proposition must move the process along.

Suppose you are thinking about buying a new car. Like almost everyone, you would like to get the best car for the least amount of money, but you are not entirely confident of your ability to do so. In fact, many people dread buying a car because they are afraid of paying more than they have to. *Consumer Reports* is a magazine dedicated to helping people make critical decisions, and they have prepared a case designed to convince you to subscribe to their "New Car Price Service." Let's see how their arguments are presented. Their proposition is that car buying can be less of an ordeal for you if you subscribe to their service.

I. To negotiate effectively for a new car, you must know what the dealer paid for the car.
   A. The "sticker" price represents what the dealer wants you to pay.
   B. The "invoice" price is a guide to what the dealer paid.
   C. The New Car Price Service will provide you with the following:
      1. Invoice and sticker price for the car.
      2. Invoice and sticker price for all factory installed options and packages.
      3. Current rebates, unadvertised dealer incentives, and holdbacks.
II. To negotiate effectively for a new car, you need to understand how cars are sold.
   A. Salespersons want to bargain down from the sticker price, but you should bargain up from the invoice price.
      1. If the car you want is in tight supply, you may have to pay full price.
      2. Otherwise, 4 to 8 percent over the invoice price for popular models is reasonable.
   B. Salespersons want to sell extras that increase the price.
      1. For example, rustproofing, undercoating, fabric protection, extended warranty, windshield etching, and so on are generally overpriced or worthless.
   C. New Car Price Service will provide solid advice on how to negotiate your best deal.
      1. With invoice and sticker price comparisons, you have your negotiating room.
      2. You will have step-by-step professional car-buying advice.
      3. New car buyers who use New Car Price Service save an average of US$2,000 on their purchases.
      4. The cost of the service is US$14.[1]

The proposition claimed that you can achieve your ultimate purpose of buying the best car for the best price without the process being an ordeal, by subscribing to their service. Do you agree that there is a direct relationship between the proposition and the ultimate purpose? Of course, other factors will come into play in your purchase, but is this proposition well chosen?

Assess Presumptions and Burden of Proof

In Chapter 2, we introduced you to presumptions which, alongside shared interpretative strategies, facts, probabilities, and commonplaces, are starting points of argument. Now, we extend the concept of presumption to include decision makers' state of mind regarding

---

[1]This ad (case) appears regularly in *Consumer Reports*. We have modified the ad to suit our purposes, but it is drawn essentially from the July 2011 issue.

your proposition and introduce the concept of burden of proof to describe the challenge to overcoming presumption.

Presumption.   In any decision making situation, there is always the question of what will happen if no new decision is made, and there is the question of what to do if someone proposes an alternative decision, and after full discussion, the arguments for one point of view are about as good as those for other points of view. Then, what decision should be made? The answer to both questions is found in the concept of **presumption**. In 1828, Richard Whately defined a presumption in favor of any proposition as the "preoccupation of the ground, which implies that it must stand good till some sufficient reason is adduced against it; in short, that the burden of proof lies on the side [that] would dispute it" (Whately 112). Thus, if no new decision is made, the presumption favors a continuation of what is now being done: the **status quo**. Also, if arguments for all points of view are about equal, the presumption declares that the decision goes to those who have presumption.

Whately's metaphor of occupation of ground has led many to give a presumption to prevailing regimes. And this, in turn, has been criticized as giving strength to a conservative theory of hegemony or state power in contrast with those who argue against the legitimacy of some aspects of government or prevailing powers (Whedbee 172–173). Think of the "Arab Spring" of 2011, when people in Tunisia, Egypt, Bahrain, Syria, Jordan, Libya, Yemen, Morocco, and elsewhere charged their leaders with exercising illegitimate dictatorial powers. In some cases, the leaders held on to their positions through force or by spending billions to buy loyalty, but was there a true presumption in favor of the status quo? Obviously, there was not. A closer reading of Whately shows that his concept of presumption was not static, but dynamic, and it can be said that, "In any debate, there are multiple presumptions and counter-presumptions affecting audience perceptions; these presumptions and counter-presumptions shift from side to side and argument to argument as the debate progresses" (Whedbee 177).

Consider the question of marriage. For most of recorded history, marriage has involved a man and a woman (in some religious/cultural locations, it has involved more than one person of one sex with a single person of the other sex). Thus, the presumption in any discussion favored this concept of marriage: joining men and women. The idea of marriage between two people of the same sex has not been widely considered until recently, and it has always had the burden of proof.

Now, however, marriage between same sex partners has been made legal in a number of the states in the United States and in some other nations, while constitutional amendments have passed in other states declaring marriage is between one man and one woman. In still other states, law tends to favor the traditional concept of marriage. Who has the benefit of presumption and who has the burden of proof? Clearly, presumption must be decided on the basis of individual nations, states, locations, or discussions. If the question comes before the Congress or the Supreme Court of the United States, the first presumption to be considered is that marriage has traditionally been within the domain of the individual states.

Before advancing any claim, you should engage in a dialectical process as we describe in Chapter 1. Interact with those involved in the decision making, no matter what their preliminary point of view is. Ask questions about their preferences, group identities, primary sources of information, and what they hold as preferred facts, values, and policies. See, whether through the dialectical interaction, you can negotiate some agreement on presumptions and burdens of proof that will hold at least during the initial stages of decision making. J. Michael Sproule says this form of audience analysis, found in Figure 6.1, is actually what Whately was recommending (128).

---

1. To what groups do decision makers belong?
2. To what sources of information do decision makers accord deference?
3. What is the popular and unpopular opinion on the subject?
4. What information might hold the advantage of novelty?

FIGURE 6.1
Assessing Presumptions

In some situations, presumptions are agreed to for the sake of argument. In law or legal-like decision making, presumptions may be selected not because they represent the state of mind of the decision makers but because it will further a sphere value. For example, in criminal law, the accused is presumed to be innocent so that the state has the burden of making a charge and providing arguments. This is done for various reasons: (1) proving a negative (you did not commit a crime) is often difficult or impossible, (2) the state has resources such as investigators to develop arguments, (3) society generally prefers to set guilty people free rather than to convict the innocent. In many instances, presumptions and burdens of proof are prescribed by law. Although courts try to select jurors who have not already formed other presumptions, this is an uncertain process and nothing prevents decision makers from jumping to conclusion before the arguments have been heard.

Burden of Proof. **Burden of proof** identifies the responsibility to initiate an argument and set out a case sufficient in argumentative strength and breadth to bring the decision makers to doubt their presumptions and then see themselves, at least potentially, able to adhere to your proposition. Those who are challenging a presumed position typically have the burden of proof, or more generally, those who advance an assertion have the burden to prove it (Those who assert must prove).

Professor: "NASA put men on the Moon."
Student: "It never happened. It was faked by the government."
Professor: "Can you prove that?"
Student: "Can you prove I'm wrong?"

FIGURE 6.2
Burden of Proof

From a communicative perspective, fulfilling a burden of proof means moving decision makers to the point that if no further argument were to occur, they will grant adherence to your proposition. In that way, you will have shifted the initiative to your opponents, who now have the **burden of rejoinder**. If they do not reply to your case, their position will erode.

Prima Facie Case. What we have just described, a case that provides sufficient argument to justify adherence to its proposition if no **counterargument** occurs, is called a *prima facie* case. This is a Latin term still used in law that says, in essence, the case is sufficient on its face or at first examination to justify adherence. As in presumption, the meaning of *prima facie* is different in formal, legal decision making and other technical spheres than in policy making. In law, for example, what counts as a *prima facie* case is typically defined in statutes and legal decisions as we explain in Chapter 12.

In policy decision making, the traditional definition of a *prima facie* case has been the **stock issues,** so called because these generic questions can lead you to developing specific claims on any question so that you fulfill the burden of proof.

---

1. Is there something in our present policy that should be changed, that is causing harm or failing to achieve the ultimate purpose? Is there, then, a need for a change in policy?
2. Is this need or harm inherent in the present policy such that only a significant change will remedy it?
3. Is there a practical alternative policy that would satisfy this need?
4. Would the alternative policy be desirable, would it work with more advantages than disadvantages?

FIGURE 6.3
Stock Issues on Questions of Policy

The stock issues reflect the acceptance of the fullest possible burden of proof in policy analysis: to condemn the present policy in its entirety and argue for a complete replacement policy. This has been called complete or scientific policy analysis (Lindblom 517). The problem with stock issues, says Charles E. Lindblom, Sterling Professor of Economics and Political Science at Yale University, is that decisions rarely follow that pattern. There are, he says, too many values at stake, too many alternatives possible with too many consequences to be traced into the future and, with such complexity, it is rarely possible to win the adherence of a sufficiently large range of decision makers to put the new policy into effect (518).

In March of 2010, The Affordable Care Act became federal law. Now, it is usually called the Health Care Reform Law by its advocates or "Obamacare" by its critics. Here was an instance in which an attempt was made to accept the full burden of proving the harm in the current health policy and proposing a new policy replacement. While it did become law, it is criticized by one side as not doing enough to replace the old system, and by the other side as doing too much. It continues to be grist for political debate with threats to repeal it at the earliest opportunity. This is a good example of the difficulties in complete or scientific policy analysis as characterized in the stock issues.

For more than the past half century, an alternative to stock issues has been discussed: **incrementalism.** Sometimes known as "muddling through," incrementalism is a political change by small steps, "Analysis limited to consideration of alternative policies all of which are only incrementally different from the status quo" (Lindblom 517). Under the theory of incrementalism, the advocate does not accept the burden of condemning the present policy as whole—does not claim that the harms are inherent. Instead, the advocate argues that the status quo is not achieving the ultimate purpose of the policy as well as it could, and there is an available revision of the status quo that would do the job better without undue disadvantages. From a rhetorical perspective, incremental steps are more persuasive because, "They do not rock the boat, do not stir up the great antagonisms and paralyzing schisms as do proposals for more drastic change" (Lindblom 520). Look back to Figure 6.3. Under incrementalism, the *prima facie* case is achieved with a more restrained criticism of the status quo in the first point, and the second point on inherency is omitted.

Think back to the example of the Arab Spring, when people demanded the ouster of their leaders and government to be replaced by an entirely new constitution (complete policy analysis). In Morocco, by contrast, King Mohammed VI began moving slowly to achieve a sustainable change in his country (incrementalism), and the people never called for the fall of the regime (Audi). A similar incremental approach was pursued in Jordan by its king.

A *prima facie* case does nothing more than shift the burden of carrying the argument forward from you to those who previously were protected by presumption. They now have the burden of rejoinder: They must supply a counterargument to stay in contention. You should not expect that just because you have made a *prima facie* case you will win the adherence of the decision makers. It just means you are now a vital part of the decision process. Remember, also, that all these technical terms become meaningful only in what goes on in the decision makers' minds. In some abstract sense, you may have every reason to believe you have set out a *prima facie* case, when the decision makers remain unmoved.

The preliminary steps in case building, then, include the following: identify the ultimate purpose, state the proposition, assess the presumptions and burden of proof, and decide what will be needed for a *prima facie* case. Now you can proceed to prepare the case.

PREPARING THE PRESENTATION/CASE

There are two significant responsibilities in preparing a persuasive case: (1) clear, well-supported, and defensible arguments; and (2) a convincing vision of the rightness of your cause. Neither is sufficient alone. Since decisions are almost never made after one presentation, in one location, by a single set of decision makers, your presentation should be centered on the immediate context and adjusted for each new one.

Identify the Decision Contexts

Within a single decision-making sphere, there are frequently many contexts in which argumentation functions. Dennis Jaehne has found many different and complex contexts for argumentation just within the bureaucratic system of the U.S. Forest Service. An environmental group that wants, for example, to stop helicopter shooting of coyotes must carry its case from local Forest Service personnel all the way through several administrative levels ending in Washington, DC. The debate over turning millions of acres of public land into wilderness areas is even more complicated, involving many government bureaucracies, commercial interests, and citizen groups.

Before any idea such as expanding the wilderness becomes law, it will probably need to be argued among interested citizens, special interest groups, legislative research personnel, legislative committees, lobbyists, in formal floor debate, and among executive bureaucrats who must translate law into administrative policies. Each context is likely to bring up different arguments and issues, and all should be accounted for in your preparation.

Locate Starting Points

Consider the starting points for argumentation that we explained in Chapter 2: language interpretation strategies, facts, presumptions, probabilities, and commonplaces. You need to apply those concepts to your presentation. Remember, these concepts identify points of commonality that are shared and not controversial. The more you can rest your case on what is already shared by the decision makers, the stronger your case will be.

You should be familiar with **language usage** within the context being addressed to make yourself as clear as possible and to avoid embarrassing mistakes. A U.S. politician claimed the future of Afghanistan must be shaped by the "Afghanis." A reporter observed that an "Afghani" is the unit of currency in Afghanistan, and the people are known as "Afghans." The politician was made to appear ignorant. U.S. President John F. Kennedy famously proclaimed to the people of an endangered city, "Ich bin ein Berliner." Some commentators noted that in that sentence, Kennedy had actually said, "I am a jelly-filled pastry." Others said he really got it right, but it did show he was not a fluent speaker of German. The more your language choices match those common to your decision makers, the better you will communicate. We bought a set of luggage partly because of the argument they were, "guaranteed for life." We failed to learn what "life" meant: the expected lifespan typical to luggage. Familiarize yourself with how your decision makers use language by going online and reading their communications. Then, try to adopt their terminology.

At this stage of preparation, **facts** acknowledged by most or all of the decision makers are a potent source of support for your arguments. If you can say, "These are the facts . . . ." and the decision makers nod in agreement, you can move on with confidence using those facts as support for your claims, as we discuss in Chapter 7.

Presumptions and **probabilities** embrace the full range of worldviews held by the decision makers: values, customs, sense of how events occur and are to be evaluated, optimism or pessimism about the future, and more. The shared presumptions and probabilities help to locate the values and sources of credibility that you can use in support of your claims, as we discuss in Chapters 8 and 9.

Commonplaces or forms of argument that are typical to the decision makers will be more effective than ones that are foreign. In Chapter 4, we identify a variety of forms of argument available to you. Now, you need to match your choice of arguments with your immediate decision makers.

State Possible Issues

An issue is a question that identifies a significant point of difference among those engaged in the argumentation. We describe characteristics of issues in Chapter 1, and discuss how they are developed in Chapter 5. Look to the stock issues as guides to the possible issues in your case. The generic question, "Is there a need to change the present policy?" will lead you, perhaps, to the issue: "Is the present cost of higher education weakening the future of the United States?" You got there by listening to the participants in the arguments: some claim that college costs so much that the production of graduates is too low. Others say the present system is working well. So, you can frame the issue so that those who are criticizing the present system and thus have the burden of proof answer "yes" to the question: "Is the cost of higher education too high?" We call them possible issues because in different contexts points of difference may change. You need to be prepared to argue whatever point of difference emerges in the debate.

Outline Your Arguments

A case, presentation, or whatever it is called is first set up in outline form. If it is ultimately to be written in full, the outline will constitute the guide for the writing. If it is to be presented orally, the outline will constitute the speaking notes. The hard work is done in building the outline where the skeleton of the arguments can be easily seen and evaluated. If you see problems with the arguments, they can be corrected in the outline before they make it into the final product. Here we show an abbreviated sample of an outline.

SAMPLE ARGUMENT OUTLINE

ULTIMATE PURPOSE: The United States must produce a college-trained workforce sufficient to satisfy the national goals of meeting the economy's need for growth and reversing the rise of income inequality.

PROPOSITION: Resolved that a 3-year undergraduate degree program should be the standard in U.S. colleges and universities.

POSSIBLE ISSUES:

Is the United States under producing college-trained workers?

Is the high cost of college causing low graduation numbers?

Does the 4-year degree program reduce graduation numbers?

Will under production of college-trained workers increase an earnings gap?

Will under production of college-trained workers damage U.S. economic growth?

Would a 3-year undergraduate degree standard significantly increase college-trained workers?

Would a 3-year undergraduate degree standard be desirable?

STATEMENT OF ARGUMENTS (This is only a sample of how arguments might be arranged.)

I. The United States is failing to produce enough college-trained workers to meet the needs of the nation's economy or individual workers.

  A. The United States is losing ground in postsecondary education to its competitors,

    1. Only 42% of U.S. 25-34-year olds have college degrees, far below the 55% in Canada, Japan, and South Korea, according to Anthony P. Carnevale and Stephen J. Rose in *The Undereducated American,* from the Georgetown University Center on Education and the Workforce, 2011.

    2. To compete, the United States must increase the production of college-trained workers, according to Adam Cota, Kartik Jayaram, and Martha C.A. Laboissière, "Boosting productivity in US Higher Education, *McKinsey Quarterly,* April 2011.

  B. Low numbers of college-trained workers increase the income gap between the college-trained and those with high school only,

    1. The law of supply and demand means that if the demand exceeds supply, then the value of the supply (college-trained workers) will rise.

    2. Employers are now willing to pay Bachelor's degree holders 74% more than those with only a high school diploma, according to Carnevale and Rose.

(Continued)

II. Production of college-trained workers is diminished by the high cost of college,

A. "College prices are rising more rapidly than the prices of other goods and services. . . [a process] that has persisted over the entire 30-year period," according to *Trends in College Pricing 2010* published by The College Board. They conclude, "If college education is to become more affordable for more students, institutions will have to find ways to offer high-quality higher education in a more cost-effective manner."

B. Students have trouble paying the costs of college. The amount of money owed in student loans exceeds the nation's credit card debt and in 2010–2011 average student debt was US$27,204, according to a National Public Radio broadcast, "College Student Debt Grows. Is It Worth It?" June 29, 2011.

III. Three-year college degree programs will facilitate the production of college-trained workers,

A. Compressing a college degree into 36 months will lower the cost.

1. Hartwick College in Oneonta, NY says its 3-year bachelor's degree will reduce costs for students by 25% or more than US$40,000, according to Sara Lipka, "Facing Recession, Colleges Push 3-Year Degrees," *The Chronicle of Higher Education*, March 6, 2009. "Students will take 40 rather than 30 credits a year, keeping their summers free for study abroad, internships, or employment."

B. Three-year degrees are the next logical step in higher education,

1. According to Daniel de Vise, writing in *The Washington Post*, students are increasingly entering college having earned college credits from Advanced Placement or International Baccalaureate tests. This allows them to graduate sooner, and is part of the reason that three-year college degree programs are not proving to be as successful as hoped (June 23, 2011).

2. Three-year programs may not be for everybody, but they will help those who might otherwise not go to college. The University of Massachusetts, Amherst ultimately expects to graduate 100 students a year, according to Daniel de Vise.

C. Three-year degrees will increase the number of college-trained workers,

1. Students will start entering the workforce faster.

2. Students will start earning full salaries earlier.

3. The increased supply of college-trained workers will reduce the imbalance of supply and demand, narrowing the wage gap.

POSSIBLE REBUTTALS

I. Three-year degree programs have proved unpopular with students.

A. Most such programs have flopped,

1. The University of North Carolina at Greensboro only enrolled five students in its 3-year program, Manchester College in Indiana enrolled 20, and Ball State University enrolled only 29, according to de Vise.

B. Students value their college years and are reluctant to lose them.

II. Compressed study is appropriate only to a limited number of students.

A. Many programs require a high grade average from high school for entry.

B. Completing a high number of credit hours in a short time is difficult for most students.

C. Three-year programs do not allow for change of majors that many students want to experiment with.

D. Athletics, clubs, social life, employment, and other activities are sacrificed.

DEVELOPING A CONVINCING VISION

An outline provides you with a set of fully developed arguments. But as Karl Llewellyn observed about lawyers arguing before appellate courts, something more than fully developed arguments is required. He said that although courts accept a duty to the law, they also hold a vision of justice, decency, and fairness. So the obligation of a legal case is to combine what Llewellyn calls a technically sound case on the law (which the other side will probably also have) with a convincing vision that will satisfy the court that "sense and decency and justice require the rule which you contend for . . ." He says,

> Your whole case must make *sense*, must appeal as being *obvious* sense, inescapable sense, sense in simple terms of life and justice. If that is done, a technically sound case on the law then gets rid of all further difficulty: it shows the court that its duty to the Law not only does not conflict with its duty to Justice but urges along the exact same line (182).

Reread his statement. Notice that it is the vision that moves the decision maker in your direction, whereas the arguments merely dispel doubts that the vision is correct and provide a rationale for its promulgation.

What is sensible, just, decent, or right is a function of the worldview and values of the decision makers. To make a case is to engage and shape them on behalf of your cause. As Richard Rorty says, truth, goodness, and beauty are not eternal objects that we try to locate and reveal as much as artifacts whose fundamental design we often have to alter ("Philosophy" 143). Rorty believes that we satisfy our burden of proof by offering "sparkling new ideas, or utopian visions of glorious new institutions. The result of genuinely new thought is not so much to refute or subvert our previous beliefs as to help us forget them by giving us a substitute for them" ("Is Derrida" 208–209).

Robert Branham says that policy propositions necessitate imagination "of the alternative worlds in which the proposed actions would operate." They entail a comparison of alternative visions of the future emerging from policy alternatives. "At minimum," he says, "debaters must articulate a vision of the future world in which the plan exists and a future in which it does not" (247). They must tell a story that allows the decision makers to "see" what the ultimate purpose "looks like." Review the discussion on storytelling and narrative in Chapter 3 to see what it means to articulate a vision.

Learn the Decision Makers' Vision

The role of narratives, scripts, and scenarios is critical in evaluating argument. Many would argue that the most potent form of argument is narrative: telling a story that allows the decision makers to come to their own understanding that happens to coincide with yours. To do that, you need to listen to those who will be making the decision to learn their narrative world.

In the case of college education, it is common to speak nostalgically of the best 4 years of one's life—away from home and on your own, making new friends, learning new ideas, finding love, and becoming an educated person. For others, the narrative is one of struggle, frustration, being forced to do things against your will, running up a huge debt, and not wanting anything more than to get it over with. To argue a case for a 3-year bachelor's degree, you must know decision makers' narrative of college, and then craft your story accordingly.

Sometimes, telling your story means helping decision makers abandon their world-view. People often hold tenaciously to a policy because of tradition, "We've always done it that way," without re-thinking why we have always done so. Daniel de Vise, writing in *The Washington Post*, says that the 4-year college calendar was originally set up by Harvard College in 1652 because it was the pattern used in Britain and because it allowed students to take the summer off to work on the farms. In fact, de Vise says, Britain long ago switched to a 3-year degree calendar (2). If decision makers recognize that their vision has lost its relevance, they may be more willing to accept a new vision.

Tell the Story of Your Vision

The *Oldest Living Confederate Widow* tells us that, "Stories only happen to the people who can tell them" (Gurganus 256). Reality rests on the stories we take as accurate characterizations of the way things truly are. Visualization serves to intensify the feelings of the decision makers toward your proposition; it vividly projects them into a state in which your proposed decision is effectively in operation (Gronbeck et al. 128). When you tell the story of your vision, you make your proposed decision real.

Consider an Example

A member of the U.S. House of Representatives submitted a bill (proposition) asking that the Custer Battlefield National Monument in Montana should be renamed as the Little Bighorn National Battlefield Park and that a Native American memorial be erected. He had prepared his case carefully, but he also had to address a well-established vision of what happened between people coming to live in North America from the sixteenth century on and those who were already living there. Unless he could inspire members of Congress with his new vision, his proposition stood little chance of passing.

Randall Lake observes that contemporary civilizations make themselves legitimate by grounding their origins in historical processes, and that is the case in the United States today. Lake says there is a powerful and well-developed Euramerican narrative in place that renders Native Americans relics to the past and thus absent from the present and irrelevant to the future. In brief, the Euramerican narrative follows a "time's arrow" metaphor, suggesting events moving in a line from past to present to future. The Europeans arrived in North America, encountered a savage that had to be "civilized" and "saved," and ultimately produced a "vanishing red man." In this vision, the Battle of the Little Bighorn is merely an anomaly, a glitch in the steady movement toward the inevitable triumph of the Europeans. So, it makes sense to honor Custer, a martyr in a great cause. Because the Native American has vanished, there is no point in a memorial.

Those who would sustain a case for a Native American memorial must take the decision makers on a time-traveling expedition to establish an alternate vision to the time's arrow notion. They offer a "time's cycle" vision instead. Tribal life, says Lake, moved not along a linear chronology but in a cyclical pattern associated with the seasons and cardinal directions: the circle, not the line, is important. Thus, there is no beginning or end, but a constant cycling. We approached a young boy at the Taos Pueblo one time and asked, "How old are you?" He replied, "I do not measure my life with numbers."

In the Native American vision, the cycle now comes around to memorializing *all* those who fought at the Little Bighorn. The proposition to change the name of the memorial was proposed by then–U.S. Representative Ben Nighthorse Campbell of Colorado (he shortly became a U.S. senator), whose great-grandfather fought against General George Armstrong Custer and the Seventh Cavalry at the Little Bighorn River. In his vision, Native Americans did not vanish and become irrelevant; they have been here all along and were just made invisible by the Euramerican story.

Ben Nighthorse Campbell, by his very presence in the U.S. House of Representatives, represented the circle—what goes around, comes around—a Native American, whose ancestor fought and defeated Custer, stood before the nation as a symbol that there is no vanishing red man. The case would have been infinitely weaker had a Euramerican argued it.

The Congress chose Campbell's vision: a Little Bighorn National Battlefield Monument (Public Law 102–201), with monuments to both sides, such as we have at sites of Civil War battles. The once-invisible army that attacked Custer appears now as the victor in the battle.

COMMUNICATION TO SPECIFIC DECISION MAKERS

Preparing an outline of argument and a vision of the case are part of the overall planning and strategy in case preparation. They represent the vital research phase. However, each time a specific decision-making context is encountered, a specific adaptation of the case must be made. Is the case to be presented in writing, orally, or both? Will others present counterargument? What format of argument will be followed: discussion, presentation, debate, negotiation, mediation? What sphere-based rules apply? Will a decision be made immediately or after deliberation?

What Are the Communication Constraints?

Having done all the research on your case, there is a powerful temptation to present everything you have at every opportunity. Lawyers once wrote such long briefs that the appellate courts set page limits. In almost every situation, time limits apply, even if only by implication. The important point to remember is this: Say what you need to say to make your point, and no more. Do not expect the decision makers to hear or read volumes of material and select what is most relevant to them. It is your job to do the selecting and to make the difficult decision to leave out much material that is good but not the best for this group.

Use different media effectively. Because some people feel more comfortable writing their case than presenting it orally, they choose to bypass oral presentations. The reverse is also true. It is a mistake to presume that writing or speaking alone is as effective as a combination of the two plus any other appropriate nonverbal means such as charts, graphs, films, models, slides, or PowerPoint. Each medium of communication can serve a role in making a case and should be considered.

What Counterargument Will Occur?

In formal debates such as at trials or during legislative deliberations, speakers are followed by someone taking another point of view and likely to refute what has been said before. In other situations, such direct advocacy may be avoided. There are times when a speaker has been invited to present a case, only to learn later that others have also been invited to present alternative cases. On some television magazine programs, such as *60 Minutes*, people are interviewed individually, and later their remarks are edited together to make the interview appear to have been a debate.

The presentation of a case must be adjusted to meet the needs presented by **counter-argument**. The more powerful, direct, and sustained the counterargument, the more care-fully the case must be adjusted to withstand such criticism, to bolster weakened points, and to engage in counter-refutation. If there is to be such direct counterargument, it is important that you know that in advance, secure specific permission to respond to the rebuttal, and come prepared with backup support.

What Argumentative Format Will Be Used?

Veteran advocates do not walk into a decision-making situation without plenty of ad-vance notice of the order of the speakers, how long they will speak, how frequently they will speak, what the agenda will be, how the physical surroundings will be set up, what materials will be appropriate, who will attend, and so forth. Read the history of debates among candidates for major political office to see how much attention they pay to such details.

Political candidates carefully work to keep "debates" more on the order of press conferences or public forums in which a panel of reporters or members of the audience alternate in asking questions. They toss coins to see who speaks first and last because they know these are important speaking positions. They like to turn a reporter's question into an opportunity to make a short speech rather than answer the question, and they earnestly avoid any direct interaction with each other that might force them to address specific issues while on the defensive.

In business presentations, it is often the case that day-long sessions will be scheduled with one presenter after another coming to the front. It is also common in business pres-entations to present many charts, PowerPoint images, or DVDs in a darkened room. This means that unless you are one of the first presenters, your audience is likely to be lulled into a soporific stupor by the time your turn comes. If you follow the pattern of all the others, you will be unlikely to make much of an impression.

To bring the decision makers back to life, it will be necessary for you to violate the established pattern. It may be smart to turn up the lights, turn off the projector, and talk directly to the audience. Using other forms of visual aids such as handouts may also help. The important point is this: Do not let obedience to an established pattern work to your disadvantage.

What Are the Rules of the Sphere?

Among the mass of argument and support for your proposition, some will be quite in-admissible in certain spheres. Admissibility is most clearly defined in law, where some arguments, witnesses, documents, or comments simply will not be heard. However, many scholars become disturbed when their scientific research is presented in court in abbrevi-ated form, without the careful documentation required in science. Many legal arguments would never survive scholarly scrutiny. Of course, a scholarly argument that wins praise in one discipline might be considered nonsense in another discipline.

What counts as the starting point for argument and what counts as proper support will vary from sphere to sphere. In selecting your specific case for presentation, you must know what rules apply. A corporation may make a decision based on solid arguments within its context that would never win the adherence of government regulators. One case would have to be defended before company executives, with quite another ready for presentation before a regulatory agency. This is not to say that the company is being two-faced or devious; it merely recognizes that arguments and support that lead to a business decision may need to be combined with different arguments and support adjusted to another sphere.

How Will the Decision Be Made?

Rarely does a single case presentation lead to an immediate decision. Typically, some time passes between argumentation and decision making. The questions for case selection are how much time will pass, how many other deliberations will take place, how much of the ultimate decision will be made outside your presence?

The more time that will pass between your case presentation and the decision, the more your case must be designed to make a lasting impression. A complex case with many claims may be effective for relatively short-term recall, but the more time that will pass, the more the case must be encapsulated in a few memorable points that will stay in decision makers' minds.

It is here that vision, language, and focused argument come together to make powerfully memorable arguments. Few remember the legal intricacies of Justice Holmes's argument in *Schenck v. United States*, but many firmly "know" the prohibition against "falsely shouting fire in a theatre and causing a panic." He boiled his case down to a memorable statement that was combined with another: This speech act would present a "clear and present danger," which government has a right to punish, and thereby made a case for an interpretation of the First Amendment to the U.S. Constitution that retains currency well into another century. The more deliberations that will occur prior to the decision, the more your case must be designed to endure close scrutiny. If you have weaknesses that are sure to be exposed, it makes sense for you to bring them up first, acknowledge them, and then show why they do not fatally damage your case. Use a two-sided approach, giving full credit to other proposed decisions while showing clearly why they are not the best, and use more neutral language, which is unlikely to offend anyone.

What Sequence of Claims Is Most Appropriate?

Remember, the purpose of a case is to generate adherence to your proposition by the immediately appropriate decision makers. That means the series of claims included in the case must combine to move the decision makers from where they are to where you want them to be. The same proposition can be argued with different organizational structures that engage the minds of the decision makers through generalized forms of reasoning. The choice of organization for a presentation is largely a rhetorical one—what format is most likely to connect with the decision makers?

Technical spheres tend to have preferred organizational structures. Getting a graduate or professional degree is heavily oriented toward learning how to organize your arguments according to the typical pattern. Law students are told from the first semester that their primary assignment is to "learn to think like a lawyer." That means knowing how to write a **brief** or legal memorandum that presents convincing arguments. Graduate students are told that their task is to become scholars—to present the products of their research in a form suitable for publication. That means to make a scholarly case for their research. In the application chapters 12–16, we illustrate how argumentation is developed and structured in various technical spheres.

Here, we will show some generalized organizational patterns from which you can choose in preparing your presentation. These are only suggestions that have been commonly used over the years. Do not limit yourself to these options.

Stock Issues.   In the sample outline, we have illustrated how your presentation can be organized by the stock issues. Following the format for an incremental analysis, we have omitted the inherency issue. Each stock issue becomes a specific claim:

I. There is a need for a change.	I. The United States is failing to create enough college-trained workers.
II. There is a plan to meet the need.	II. A 3-year bachelor's degree will train enough workers.
III. The plan is desirable?	III. A 3-year bachelor's degree is desirable.
	1. It will save students money.
	2. It will put students into the labor force quickly.
	3. It will provide the skilled workers needed in new industries.

From a rhetorical point of view, a structure with three major claims or contentions is most desirable since decision makers are more likely to remember your points if you have managed to place your arguments into that configuration rather than setting out a long string of individual points. The downside of PowerPoint and similar presentation software is that it seems to encourage argumentation by bullet points. Avoid that tendency. Rhetoricians, social scientists, and neuroscientists have long argued that there are limits on people's ability to process and recall information, and three or four main points seem ideal (Miller).

Problem–Solution.   A way of expanding the stock issues case structure is to use a **problem–solution** format. It is widely used in journalistic writing and policy decision making. One of the most enduring formats for public speaking, called the *motivated sequence*, rests on this pattern. Kathleen German and her colleagues claim that it approximates the normal processes of human thinking and will move an audience toward agreement with a speaker's purposes. They describe the following sequence of claims:

ATTENTION: An opening claim aimed at generating the active involvement of decision makers—often this is a story about individuals' experiences.

NEED: A claim that identifies a condition in need of correction.

SATISFACTION: A claim that identifies a way the condition can be corrected.

VISUALIZATION: A claim that sets forth the vision of the case: the world in which the condition is corrected through the proposed method—what does success "look like?"

ACTION: A claim that calls for specific measures to put the proposed action into being (266–270)

Bill Gleason, writing in *The Chronicle of Higher Education*, makes an argument for more transparency in the costs of college. We will adapt his case to illustrate the problem–solution format.

ATTENTION: Contrast the cost of attending the University of Minnesota: US$11,268 with the student or the parents expected to borrow US$8,000 per year for a 4-year total debt of US$34,400—with the cost of attending the University of North Carolina where a student with comparable financial resources would face a net cost of US$2,700 and no outstanding debt at the end of the four years (1).

NEED: The actual cost of attending a particular college is difficult if not impossible to learn. The published figures cannot be trusted, and students need this information if they are to make critical decisions about college.

SATISFACTION: There is already movement toward transparency in college costs. The U.S. Department of Education, under a mandate of The Higher Education Opportunity Act of 2008, is working to put the information Online, and once the process settles down to more reliable figures, students and their parents will be able to make choices based on reliable information.

VISUALIZATION: Colleges and universities will no longer be able to engage in questionable practices in publishing tuition and total price figures. If students and their parents can rely on published college costs, they will be able to make their selections more specifically, reduce the number of applications submitted and paid for, and they will know going in what the financial aid package will be (Geason).

ACTION: Those interested in college cost transparency should speak out in blogs and in communicating with members of Congress and the U.S. Department of Education. They should also communicate to local colleges and universities that transparency is a necessity for critical decisions.

Comparative Advantages.   Sometimes policy analysis turns on a joint acknowledgement that the present system needs improvement, but there is difference over the best way to do that. So, the argumentation centers on comparing the advantages of two or more potential policy changes. The structure looks like this:

I. The United States must increase the production of college-trained workers, as we all agree.
II. A 3-year bachelor's degree would not significantly increase the production of college-trained workers,
   A. Many students already manage to finish college in 3 years through advanced placement, International Baccalaureate, and year-round study.
   B. Experiments with 3-year degree programs have failed to attract more than a handful of students.
III. Increased availability of Online degree programs will significantly increase the production of college-trained workers.
   A. Online degrees can be offered at lower cost than on campus, as proven by The Western Governors University.
   B. Students will be relieved of travel and living costs by being able to study at home.
   C. Online study is more consistent with twenty-first century information technologies that are appealing to college-age students.

We have not included in this example the discussion of comparative disadvantages of the two policy proposals. In the second point, in addition to showing that 3-year programs are unlikely to produce a significant increase in college-trained workers, you will need to discuss the disadvantages of the proposal as well. And, in point three, you will need to argue how Online degree programs are more desirable than other proposals, and would not produce significant disadvantages.

Criteria/Definition. A case organization that begins by arguing for a credible set of criteria or a definition of the ultimate purpose can lay the groundwork for presenting and defending policy arguments. Similar to stock issues, the case looks at what is not working in the *status quo*, and then argues that any policy proposal must meet a certain set of criteria or fulfill the expectations of a definition if it is to be successful. Look back at Chapter 4 where we discuss definitional argument.

I. The United States is not preparing enough college-trained workers, as we all agree.
II. What is needed is to fill the so-called, "skills gap,"
    A. The definition of the "skills gap" is, "A national problem that has left businesses without a crucial pipeline of the skilled workers they need in a rapidly changing economy" according to Erika Niedowski in *The Salt Lake Tribune*, July 3, 2011.[1]
    B. Being "college-trained" is not enough: the workers must be trained to meet the current demand for skilled workers, and that may require only an associate's degree, says Niedowski.
III. So, any proposed solution must satisfy the following criteria:
    A. Whatever the degree, the product must be workers ready to enter the new technology-demanding workforce.
    B. Career and technical education programs are not enough—they must be increased in quality and relevance to present demands.
    C. Community college associate degrees are not enough—community colleges must communicate with employers to learn their needs.
    D. "No Worker Left Behind" programs that allow " unemployed or low-wage workers to get up to US$10,000 in free tuition," or "lifelong learning accounts, which, like a 401(k) help workers save for education, training, or apprenticeships," must be made widely available (Niedowski).

CONCLUSION

Presentation or case building rests on thorough research and preparation. Before you are ready to support any proposition, you should identify the ultimate purpose or what it is you are trying to accomplish with your arguments. You should phrase your proposition to express your position clearly in relation to the particular decision context or sphere at hand and in relation to the ultimate purpose. You should fully understand the status of presumptions and burden of proof for each set of decision makers and what will constitute a *prima facie* case.

---

[1] Erika A. Niedowski, "Skills gap leaves firms without worker pipeline," *The Salt Lake Tribune, Sunday, July 3, 2011, E2.*

In preparing the presentation, you need to identify decision contexts and what starting points there are on which to support your claims. By engaging in dialectic, you can discover where the possible major points of disagreement will be—the issues. Then, you can outline your arguments.

Powerful arguments are only half of the job in preparing a case or presentation. The other half is developing a convincing vision through which you can tell the story of your ultimate purpose. This will need to be adapted to specific decision makers along with choosing the issues to be addressed. You need to know in advance all the constraints and procedures that will be associated with each presentation occasion.

Finally, you should review the various alternatives there are to organizing the outline or sequencing your claims. Stock issues on questions of policy lead to a common sequence of claims as do problem–solution, comparative advantages, and criteria/definition formats.

EXERCISES/PROJECTS

1. Interview a politician, scientist, lawyer, or businessperson. Ask your specialist how a case is made within the specialty. Ask to see a sample of one used in the past.
2. Along with a team of other students, select a proposition on which you will engage in a debate. Start with dialectic on the subject area so that you can discover where team members' beliefs, attitudes, values, fact acceptance, presumptions, and the like are located. Once a proposition is selected, go Online to learn the language usage common in the subject area and what seem to be common points of disagreement—issues. Then, prepare a case and conduct the debate.
3. Listen to the debates conducted by other students, and prepare a detailed critique. Be prepared to explain where the debate and various arguments worked well and where the debaters could have done a better job.

American River College Library

Support: Evidence

KEY TERMS

evidence, p. 103

example, p. 103

hypothetical example, p. 105

statistics, p. 105

raw numbers, p. 105

central tendency, p. 106

probability, p. 106

trend, p. 107

testimony of fact, p. 108

testimony of opinion, p. 108

sphere dependence, p. 115

hearsay evidence, p. 115

ordinary testimony, p. 115

expert testimony, p. 115

reluctant evidence, p. 116

negative evidence, p. 117

documented evidence, p. 117

assertion, p. 118

Studying the nature of arguments in Chapter 4 should have led you to understand that arguments do their work by putting information into widely recognized and respected ways of making sense. Throughout your life, you have learned that people make sense through formats such as logical deductions, generalization, cause, sign, analogy, authority, and definition. In Chapter 4, you also learned from the Toulmin model that the primary relationship in argumentation is between the claim and the grounds advanced in its support. Grounds include material that the decision makers are expected to acknowledge as acceptable, right, even correct. The argument, then, does its work primarily by connecting information that decision makers already accept with claims they are being asked to accept. In Chapters 7, 8, and 9, we focus on the three forms of support for arguments: evidence, values, and credibility. And by support, we mean the information that decision makers already accept that is used to help them grant adherence to the claims being advanced. In this chapter, we will introduce you to evidence, which is information that people use most often as grounds, or backing for grounds and warrants.

Evidence, as we will use the term in this chapter, is the support for a claim that the arguer discovers from experience or outside authority. It usually takes the form of examples, statistics, and testimony. As we stated in Chapter 1, different spheres have different definitions of what counts as evidence and which forms of evidence have the most significance. In some spheres, evidence plays an extremely important role, whereas in others values and credibility are more important. However, there are substantial empirical data and centuries of commonsense observation to support the idea that, when properly presented, most decision makers are influenced by evidence.

FORMS OF EVIDENCE

Evidence (examples, statistics, and testimony) supports a claim in such a way as to cause the decision maker to give adherence to that claim. Evidence need not be a part of the spoken or written argument in order to contribute to adherence, however. The simplest form of an argument is the statement of a claim: an assertion. Assertions are not usually considered good arguments, but they can gain adherence when decision makers already know the evidence.

> CAROL: "Pick me up at 5:00 so we can get to Sam's early and make sure we get to the game on time."
> DON: "Okay. Sam is always late, so that's a good idea."

Carol's assertion receives instant adherence from Don because of previous experiences with Sam's tardiness. If called on, Carol could provide examples such as the time they were late for the barbecue because of Sam. In this example, the decision maker already knows the specific examples, and thus, stated evidence is unnecessary.

In addition, decision makers sometimes are in possession of evidence that runs counter to the argument, yet they do not choose to state this negative evidence. The unstated negative evidence in the minds of the decision makers must be met as surely as the evidence of an outspoken opponent. Although the emphasis in this chapter is on the way in which you may strengthen arguments through the use of evidence, you should always consider possible responses to unstated evidence held by decision makers.

Example

Examples may refer to *undeveloped instances used in an argument by generalization.* Such examples may be short. Bruce Luecke argues that the U.S. space program has produced "30,000 spin-off products and technologies since its inception in 1958."

> to name a few that NASA lists there are: new fire-fighting suits with better breathing systems; a device that can warn of pending heart attacks; digital imaging that enables a more accurate medical diagnosis; a longer-lasting running shoe; and scratch resistant contact lenses (684).

He uses five short examples to illustrate the large number that he claims exist.

An extended example, or *illustration,* usually means *an extended instance that illustrates a general principle* (Perelman and Olbrechts-Tyteca 357). David Grann begins his article about the "Knowledge Is Power Program" (KIPP) at "a middle school in the heart of the South Bronx" across the street from the Andrew Jackson Housing Project with an extended example contrasting the regular students leaving in the afternoon with the KIPP students who continue working, chanting rhymes about reading, going "back to basics," and getting high success rates on academic tests (24). That extended example is used to support the claim that this is "a public school that works."

Examples aim at confronting others with what they will accept as bits of reality, things that happened. One of the most compelling and probably most commonly used examples occurs when you remind others of their own experiences.

Remember our earlier example of the argument of Carol and Don and the examples they might have used to support their claim about Sam? Those examples were of their own experiences. Such examples abound in an interpersonal argument.

> Let's go backpacking this summer. We had such a great time last year on the Kern Plateau and in the Wind Rivers.
> Don't buy beets. I've never had beets cooked a way I like them.
> Let's go see the new Colin Firth movie. He was awesome in *The King's Speech*.

Even in a public argument, it is common for a speaker to use examples taken from the experiences of decision makers.

On August 21, 2007, Wal-Mart announced that its online music store would start selling songs free of copy-protection technology for 94 cents per tune. The Associated Press (AP) explained that, "songs from the Rolling Stones, Coldplay and Maroon 5, among others, will play on most portable media devices, including Apple Inc.'s iPod." The article then proceeded to tell the story of the awkward relationship between the contemporary music industry and music consumers. This story was offered as justification for Walmart's new policy.

The article explains that, although independent musicians have long allowed those who purchase their music to share the tunes in whatever manner they choose, large music companies have maintained strict controls over music they sell, even after people have purchased it. Although the story mentions that the music industry has a potentially compelling economic motivation for these restrictions, that is only mentioned as a passing thought. Instead, the article lists name after name of music industry groups that either already have, or are considering a similar move. By the time they finish reading the article, readers are likely to recognize that Walmart's new music policy is not only attractive to consumers but also part of a trend among progressive members of the music industry.

Anyone familiar with the contemporary music business will recognize the examples given in this story and will understand how they support the claim that Digital Rights Management has caused consumer frustration and how the new practices in music retail activities, such as Walmart's new policy, will reduce the frustration.

In Chapter 3, we described how good stories function in argumentation. All examples, and particularly extended examples, need the characteristics of good stories. The story should ring true for the decision makers. The illustration must have characters, action, motives, and outcomes that make sense to them. In the case of a possible classroom argument about a change in the course registration system students must use, you might ask students to create their own stories. The scenarios of long lines, faulty telephone and computer instruction, failure to get classes, preferences for others, and payments that must be made just before payday, is a "story" that rings true to them.

In most public argumentation and many interpersonal argumentative situations, the specific instances you use will be outside the experience of the decision makers. Indeed, most frequently, they will be outside your experience. In those situations, it is important to make the specific instances as believable as possible, to make them seem real. Including specific details and the citing credible sources promote the idea that the instances are real because they can be verified by the decision makers.

Remember how Bruce Luecke argued that the space program had spun off 30,000 products and he gave examples of five of them? There is also a credibility argument, in that he says the list came from NASA. Part of the power of these examples comes from the credibility decision makers grant NASA. Specific details also help examples seem more real because detail makes it easier for a decision maker to visualize.

A special kind of specific instance, called the **hypothetical example,** is used where real examples are not available or when the available real examples are far removed from the decision makers' experience. It is important that a hypothetical example be perceived as equivalent to a real example. That is, it must have the detail and credibility to give it the characteristics of a real example.

Here is a hypothetical example that you might use to illustrate the problems of auto repair rip-offs:

Here's a not-very-far-fetched description of what you might be involved with. You take your Ford Escort in for repairs; there's something wrong in the engine or transmission. It's making a lot of noise that it didn't make before. You learn that the repair should take about ten hours and the charge is $50 an hour. The bill is $500 for labor. Sounds like simple arithmetic, right? Wrong! The actual work took only seven hours and that should save you $150. But, the service manager tells you they go by the *Flat Rate Manual* that says this repair should take ten hours, so you pay for ten hours of labor, even though it took only seven.

Statistics

Statistics are numerical summaries of examples. Statistics provide a means for talking about a large number of examples without citing every one. This means of summarizing examples is found in various forms in argumentation. The most common are raw numbers, central tendencies, probabilities, and trends.

Raw Numbers.   Some statistical references are clearly intended to emphasize significant numbers of examples. For example, the UN AIDS-fighting agency reported on November 20, 2007, that it had overestimated the size of the epidemic and that new infections with the deadly virus have been dropping each year since they peaked in the late 1990s. Donald G. McNeil, Jr., writing in the *New York Times* of that date, says that the estimated number infected would be reduced from 39.5 million to a more realistic figure of 32.2 million.

The 30,000 products NASA claimed as spin-offs of the space program offer another example of **raw numbers.** Raw numbers are also used to provide evidence of how significant a disaster is. During the summer of 2011, wildfires scorched much of the southwestern United States. CNN (Thousands evacuated) supported its claim that 2011 was one of the worst wildfire seasons to date by reporting that one fire in Arizona "grew by 40,000 acres Monday, forcing the evacuation of thousands as crews battled heavy winds in trying to prevent the 30-mile line from advancing further. . . . [The fire] has scorched 233,522 acres as of Monday evening—up more than 21% from the 192,746 acres reported that morning."

There are a number of points worth observing about these examples of raw numbers. First, where the numbers are large, they often are rounded off to make them easier to understand without damaging their accuracy: The UN AIDS-fighting agency said that there are 32.2 million people infected. These are not exact but rounded numbers. That is undoubtedly true of the 30,000 spin-offs. Second, the raw numbers are compared with other possibilities so the decision maker can tell, for example, that 32.2 million people infected is significantly lower than 39.5 million. The CNN audience can also tell not only that the number 233,522 describes the current size of the fire but also that the fire is continuing to grow, because this number is substantially different from the 192,746 acres reported as having burned less than 12 hours earlier.

Central Tendency. Some statistics go beyond raw numbers to provide an indication of what is normal in a larger population. **Central tendencies** are frequently called *averages*.

In 2007, research from the Washington, DC, nonprofit Excelencia in Education revealed that although Latinos constitute the fastest-growing segment of the U.S. population and will be one-fifth of the U.S. workforce by 2025, only 12% of Latinos aged 25 years and older have earned college degrees, compared with more than 30% of other adults. Moreover, in the next 15 years, two-thirds of all jobs in the United States will be filled by Latinos, but only 1% of them will be at the managerial level. These statistics are based on generalizations drawn from samples of the population, and they represent proportions, averages, or central tendencies. They help you understand the general trends in the United States, but they do not tell you anything about any one individual or group.

Statistical Probability. In Chapter 2, we talked about various meanings of the word **probability**, and statistics can represent one of them. Hilary Waldman used statistical probability to explain why doctors spent years misdiagnosing and prescribing wrong medications to Sofi Pagan, a young girl who was finally diagnosed with Batten, a genetic disease with 100% fatality, in November 2000. The gene for Batten disease is extremely rare, and a child must inherit one gene for the disease from each parent. The chance that two people who carry that gene "will marry and have children is about one in 25,000. Even if two carriers do find each other, their chance of having a sick child is one in four. It's so rare, in fact, that only 300 children in the United States have Batten disease" (83). The story went on to explain that Sofi's little brother, who was born before the Pagan family had any suspicion that Sofi was ill, also had Batten disease.

In another use of statistical probability, Alice Park reported that a drug known as letrozole offers additional hope to breast cancer survivors. Park explained that women who have been treated for breast cancer take the drug tamoxifen for five years to prevent recurrence. After five years, they must stop using tamoxifen, even though recurrences occur beyond the five-year mark. According to Park, a trial involving more than 5,100 women demonstrated that those who began taking letrozole after five years experienced 43% fewer cancer recurrences than those assigned to the placebo group" (81). The numbers in both of these examples are based on a concept of probability called *frequency*.

The statistics are an expression of the frequency with which events occur by pure chance, or the likelihood that something exceeds pure chance. That is, pure chance would predict that 30% of the population will get cancer by the time they are 70 years old, but if they smoke, their likelihood exceeds pure chance by a significant factor.

In the breast cancer study, pure chance would predict that the women treated with letrozole and those assigned to the placebo group would have the same rate of cancer recurrences, and changes from that seem to be related to use of letrozole. Forty-three percent is a significant movement beyond pure chance.

Statistical Trends.   Many times, statistics are used to compare a situation over time, to discover a **trend**. Genaro C. Armas noted that, in the United States, "the number of women 15 to 44 forgoing or putting off motherhood has grown nearly 10 percent since 1990, when roughly 24.3 million were in that class" (A11). Armas went on to explain that these numbers reveal the well-established "trends of women attending college, entering the workforce, choosing to adopt rather than conceive a child, or choosing not to have children at all." Armas cited David Popenoe, "co-director of the National Marriage Project, a research group at Rutgers University" to support her statement that this last trend was particularly pronounced among wealthy women, who "had the highest childless rates, in part a reflection of the increased professional options available to them." Armas reported a smaller trend in the overall birthrate among U.S. women in this age group, with "61 births per 1,000" in 2002, and "67 per 1,000 in 1990." During the same years, the "birth rate for women 15 to 19 rose from 40 per 1,000 to 56 per 1,000" (A11). Because women aged 15–19 are unlikely to have extensive college or other professional training, this apparent aberration supports Armas's interpretation that the larger trend among women from 15 to 44 is explained by the availability of increased professional options.

The direct comparisons in the article on childlessness among U.S. women are based on census data accumulated between 1990 and 2000. Direct comparison cannot extend before 1990, because the Census Bureau did not track childbearing among women under 18 until 1990. The claim of a trend, however, is based on similar data accumulated over several decades. The statistical strength of Armas's claim is further strengthened because the report was based on data from 50,000 homes spread across the United States.

Combining Forms of Evidence

Few arguments rely on only one form of evidence. Instead, successful arguments demonstrate careful use of several different forms. Las Vegas showman Roy Horn (of the duo Siegfried and Roy) was mauled by a tiger while performing at the Mirage hotel in October 2003. The attack led to a spate of news coverage about private ownership of tigers. Michael D. Lemonick argued that private ownership of tigers was widespread, cruel, and dangerous. He used several forms of evidence to make his point. He began by telling the story of a tiger kept in a Harlem apartment house until police rappelled down the outside of the building, tranquilized the tiger, and relocated it to an animal sanctuary. Lemonick followed with additional examples, then with statistics. He offered raw numbers, stating that between 1998 and 2001, the United States saw seven fatal tiger attacks "and at least 20 more that required emergency care" (63). He introduced statistical probability into his argument by claiming that these numbers should not be surprising because there are about 10,000 privately owned tigers in the United States, twice as many as live in the wild. Thus, the statistical probability of being near a "pet" tiger in the United States is greater than it is anywhere in the wild. Lemonick relied on the expert testimony of Richard Lattis, director of New York City's Bronx Zoo, to clinch his argument. According to Lattis, tigers always remain wild animals, and private owners subject themselves and everyone else to unwarranted danger (64).

So, statistics are summaries of examples that sometimes appear as raw numbers, are sometimes averaged, frequently rounded off, and usually compared if they are to have maximum force for decision makers. From the point of view of evidence, however, you must remember that no matter how much counting and predicting has gone into statistics, they still rely on the response of the decision makers to have value in argumentation. Many people acknowledge the statistical relationship of smoking to cancer and heart disease, for instance, but do not apply it to themselves.

Testimony

Testimony is the statement of another person or agency that is used to support a claim. It may be used with examples or statistics as backing for the grounds of an argument. It may also serve, as we noted in Chapter 4, by itself as the grounds for an argument from authority. Testimony adds the credibility of its source to the grounds or warrant of an argument.

Traditionally, testimony has been divided into two types: **testimony of fact** and **testimony of opinion**. Obviously, all testimony represents the opinion of the person or agency cited. However, testimony about facts that provide examples or statistics is seen by many as stronger than testimony that only expresses the opinion of the source. Indeed, there is a general view among the researchers in this area that example and statistical evidence are more powerful than opinion evidence (Reinard 38–40). This is in line with the common-sense notion that testimony of fact is preferable to testimony of opinion.

Testimony of fact adds to examples or statistics the credibility of the source of the testimony. Daniel S. Turner argues that "America's infrastructure is crumbling." He says that more than a trillion dollars will be needed to upgrade roads, bridges, mass transit, airports, schools, dams, water purity, and waste disposal facilities in the next century. In each of these areas, he argues that a series of facts exist that cannot be overlooked. On roads and bridges, for instance,

1. More than half of the roads in the United States are "substandard."
2. Substandard roads, bridges, and pavement are responsible for 30% of fatal accidents.
3. Passenger travel doubled between 1970 and 1995 and will increase nearly two-thirds by 2015.
4. Thirty-one percent of bridges are structurally deficient.
5. Eighty billion dollars will be required to eliminate the backlog of bridge deficiencies and maintain repair levels.
6. Full repair of the nation's roads and bridges would require $437,000,000,000.

These are not "his" facts, moreover; he presents them as the testimony of the Federal Highway Administration and the American Society of Civil Engineers (10–11). Turner makes a similar analysis of each of the areas of the infrastructure, and in each case, he identifies an authority for the facts (e.g., U.S. Department of Transportation, American Association of State Highway and Transportation Officials, Federal Aviation Administration, Environmental Protection Agency, Association of State Dam Safety Officials). These are not simply "facts" but testimony of fact. The power of the evidence rests in the detail of amounts and percentages but depends on the authority, not of the arguer, but of the sources of the testimony.

In truth, all these pieces of testimony represent opinion, although it is *expert* opinion. And there still is potential for bias, which is discussed later in this chapter. The crucial question for you as you use testimony is whether it will be perceived as fact and not "simply opinion." That judgment will depend on the credibility of the source and the specificity with which that source develops the information.

Some of the biases of these specialized spheres have been incorporated into our general practices. For this reason, we test factual testimony by asking about the testifier's experience, access to direct perception of the facts, and expertise on the matter at hand. As a general principle, good factual testimony comes from an expert source with direct knowledge. That source carefully delineates the fact testified to from its own and others' opinions. Even so, you must remember that the source is only testifying *about* facts and any time a human is involved, so is opinion.

GENERAL PRINCIPLES FOR THE USE OF EVIDENCE

It is difficult to prescribe how evidence should be used to support an argument because the believability of any argument is heavily influenced by who the decision makers are and the experience they bring to the situation. However, some principles have evolved that are generally accepted by most persons in our society. These principles serve as reasonable standards for tests of evidence. They help you to see the difference between forceful and questionable evidence.

Use Representative Instances

By using representative instances, you choose the best examples available to prove a generalization. Remember the use of examples by Bruce Luecke on page 103? He argues that the U.S. space program has produced 30,000 spin-off products that are useful to the general population. He supports this with five examples. All seem important, having to do with improved health and safety and running shoes. Are they representative of the 30,000? That is difficult to tell. His argument would be stronger, perhaps, if each of his examples had been representative of one of the five areas where products might be identified with the space program.

There is no mathematical formula for judging representativeness, although specialists in survey research have standard rules they follow. Recall from Chapter 4 that some form of sampling must be used to allow the claim that what is true of your examples is probably true of the general category. Ultimately, the key question is, to what extent will decision makers believe that these examples are representative and, therefore, provide reason enough to warrant adherence?

Use a Sufficient Number of Instances

To form a satisfactory generalization, enough examples must be provided to convince others that the argument is believable. There is no magic number for the amount of evidence needed, but there is a long-standing "rule of three." Where a claim is in contention, use at least three examples. It is clear that some evidence is useful even when the decision makers already agree to the claim. It is also clear that the argument is seen as more powerful when more high quality evidence from multiple sources is added.

Use Only Relevant Instances

Large amounts of evidence that is perceived as of low quality weakens an argument (Reinard 40). One of the most obvious examples of low quality evidence is information that is irrelevant to the argument. In fact, in some spheres, it can completely invalidate an argument. For example, in 2011, the Supreme Court of Georgia reversed the murder conviction of a teenage girl because the state had introduced irrelevant evidence about the defendant's Goth lifestyle (Boring v. State). The evidence included photographs of the appellant with dyed black hair and dark make-up; a document bearing the text of a "'curse' to be recited 'while burning the letter over a black candle'; and seven different inscriptions . . . of song lyrics . . . bearing themes of anguish, enslavement, atheism, and violence." The court found that the State had sought to use these items "simply because the jury would find these beliefs morally reprehensible," but did not establish any direct connection between the items and the crime. Although the use of irrelevant evidence will not always produce such a dramatic boomerang effect, it is a dangerous tactic that may threaten the credibility of any argument.

Account for Negative Instances

Particularly with knowledgeable decision makers, you make a mistake if you fail to account for instances that do not support the claim. The study we cited earlier that identified the trend among U.S. women to remain childless deals carefully with negative instances. In fact, it reported and explained negative instances. Recall it reported that the birthrate among women aged 15–19 actually rose between 1990 and 2002. This was explained by the presumption that such young women were unlikely to have extensive professional options. Armas also responded to the negative instance of an increase among never-married women in professional positions who chose to have a child. She pointed out that these women are economically capable of rearing a child without a partner and suffer much less social stigmatizing than in the past. Further, she was able to use this negative evidence to point out that even with the increased likelihood that never-married professional women will choose to have children, the trend for women to remain childless remains strong.

Arguers who fail to account for negative instances that decision makers know about will lose credibility. Even with people who do not know the negative instances, some acknowledgment of them may strengthen an argument because it makes the arguer seem more trustworthy.

State the Value Characteristics of Instances

It is important to let decision makers know what value judgments apply to the example. The following instances all provide a value clarifier (shown here in italics, though the words probably were not emphasized that way originally).

> The *best* example of the increase in violence against minorities is the shooting at a Jewish day care center in Granada Hills, California.
> That 54 percent of all high school seniors have smoked marijuana is a *good* example of the widespread use of drugs.
> A *recent* example of press censorship occurred in the *New York Times*.
> A *typical* example of the efforts to clear up water pollution is the activity on the Connecticut River.

Make Instances Seem Real with Details

As we noted earlier, people give greater adherence to more specific examples (Kline 412). Even hypothetical examples should be given the characteristics of real examples. Suppose you were to argue for new traffic regulations and develop a hypothetical example to explain how traffic congestion can be a serious imposition that needs new regulations. That hypothetical example might be stated like this: "Suppose you start home tomorrow night and find yourself in a massive traffic jam that delays you, and you miss an important appointment." Your example would be better if given the characteristics of a real example of streets and freeways your decision makers know: "Suppose as you leave work at 5:00 tomorrow night you turn onto the freeway at the Temple Street on-ramp. All that is needed to close down the Hollywood Freeway is one car out of gas just beyond Silver Lake Boulevard and there you are, stuck for hours in the sweltering heat, missing your important appointment."

Use Decision Makers' Experience

Although you should provide enough examples to support your claim with decision makers, the other side of that coin is also important. The tedious repetition of examples for people who already know them can injure the effectiveness of an argument. Therefore, you should remind decision makers of what they already know in support of your case. Phrases such as "as you already know," "your own experience has shown," and "as you learned last week" help strengthen your case.

Use Current Examples and Statistics

Clearly, the most up-to-date information is superior to less current information in assessing the present situation. Even for historical study, current information should be more useful because historical evidence is frequently cumulative. That is, every new piece of information makes the previous idea clearer. Also, more recent statistics may be more useful in historical argument because more sophisticated statistical measures have been employed.

Use Credible Sources

Avoid the bias of the source. This is important not only because of the danger of drawing a less accurate generalization but also because such bias, when recognized, will damage the argument. Even though it is sometimes possible to win adherence through the use of biased sources that some decision makers do not recognize as biased, it is not wise to do so. Evidence from such sources can only be successful in seeking short-term adherence. Even persons who initially gave adherence will learn from others of the biased sources and, in the long term, remove adherence. Such a discovery could weaken your credibility with them on many claims.

Even information that is not biased but *appears* to be from a biased source is poor evidence because of others' reactions. A company that produces pain relievers offers a free booklet that they claim explains about pain relievers. You have no way of knowing whether the information provided is accurate, but you may distrust it because it is offered by a source potentially biased by its own commercial self-interest.

For each example or statistical study that you take from someone else, ask yourself the extent to which that source is biased and the extent to which it may appear biased to others. Federal government agencies such as the Bureau of Labor Statistics are generally regarded as unbiased. But the claim cited earlier that there are 30,000 spin-offs from the space program is made by NASA and that agency may be trying to boost its image to get new funds. Regardless of whether sources are biased, the crucial issue is whether decision makers *think* they are or suspect that they may be.

Carefully Consider Statistical Measures

For our purpose, statistical measures basically answer the question: How typical are the examples? Darrell Huff, in the book *How to Lie with Statistics*, presents many of the problems of statistical argument in everyday language.

One could spend a lifetime of study and become an expert in statistical argument and its errors. For the moment, however, the following are a few of the mistakes to avoid.

"The Sample with the Built-in Bias."   If you asked your classmates what they thought about the federal ban on private possession of handguns and they approved it by a vote of 15 to 5, that would be impressive, but if 10 others had refused to answer your question, you might have a built-in bias for which you were not accounting. Thus, the potential actual split was 15 to 15 or 25 to 5. The real proportions could be as great as 5 to 1 or as little as dead even. Also, suppose some of the people who opposed the ban did so because they thought it was not strong enough. That would give you another built-in bias.

"The Gee-Whiz Graph."   Graphic representation of statistical data can provide a visual clarification. It can also mislead. All graphs should be carefully examined to be sure that they provide information in a form that reflects the best interpretation of the data. Figures 7.1 and 7.2 describe the impact of a recent earthquake in the Canterbury region of New Zealand. On September 4, 2010, the region was rocked by an earthquake. The earthquake was centered about 25 miles west of Christchurch, which is New Zealand's second largest city. The region suffered widespread damage and power outages. Perhaps

FIGURE 7.1

Number of people living in districts within the Canterbury region of New Zealand where the emergency operations were activated in response to the magnitude 7.0 (moment magnitude scale) earthquake of September 4, 2010.

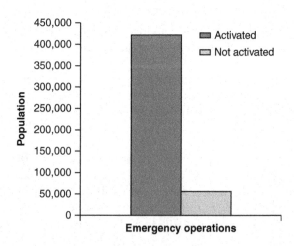

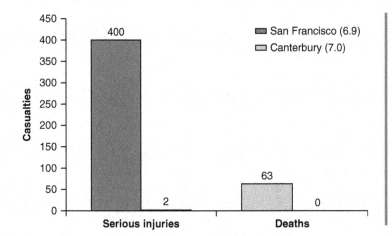

FIGURE 7.2

Casualties (i.e., serious injuries and deaths) associated with the 6.9 and 7.0 magnitude (moment magnitude scale) earthquakes that occurred on October 17, 1989, in the San Francisco Bay Area (USA) and September 4, 2010, in the Canterbury region of New Zealand, respectively; both locations employed modern, earthquake resistant building codes.

because it occurred at night, and in a rural area where most construction is intended to withstand such quakes, no deaths were verified as being caused by the September 2010 earthquake. In the aftermath of the earthquake, some coverage described the region as a disaster, while other coverage focused on how minimal the damage had been (both in terms of economic loss and human causalities). People who wanted to emphasize the severity of the situation, perhaps for the purpose of ensuring that their audience realized the region's need for assistance, might construct Figure 7.1. Other groups, perhaps wanting to encourage tourism and convention business, might construct Figure 7.2. Both figures use real information, but they make very different arguments. Figure 7.1 uses the fact that most residents of Canterbury lived in districts that were officially designated as emergency sites to focus attention on the widespread need for disaster assistance following the earthquake. Figure 7.2 uses the equally valid fact that no deaths and few serious injuries occurred to focus on the how minimal the damage was, as compared to another earthquake of similar magnitude that occurred in the U.S., a nation with similar safety standards to those in New Zealand. Remember that graphs such as these are arguments; they are constructed from carefully selected evidence, and they require thoughtful analysis. Think about the ethical dilemma presented by the two different arguments presented in these figures.

"The Well-Chosen Average." *Average* is a popular term standing for some measure of central tendency in data, but there are several ways of measuring it. One such measure is the *median*, the point above and below which 50% of the items fall. A second measure is the *mode*, the value that appears most frequently among the data. The third measure is the *mean*, an arithmetic average and the term most correctly applied to the term *average*. The mean is found by dividing the number of items in a series into the sum of all the items.

It's salary negotiating time at the place where you work, and the company president says that you shouldn't expect much of a raise because the average salary at this company is $20,000 a year and you already earn that. The average in this case is the mode. You check it out and find that the median salary is $30,000 and the mean salary is $57,000. Here are the salaries:

$450,000 × 1
$150,000 × 1

$100,000 \times 2$
$57,000 \times 1$ Mean
$50,000 \times 3$
$37,000 \times 4$
$30,000 \times 1$ Median
$20,000 \times 12$ Mode

Has your employer chosen the measure of central tendency well?

"Much Ado about Practically Nothing." There are groups in higher education who undertake the task of determining the quality of graduate programs in various disciplines. One hears the statement, "We are one of the top five communication [or psychology or political science] departments in the country." Statistical reports are published showing the relative ranking of all graduate programs by specialty. They make an impressive display, and people use them in arguments. The problem is that the data are gathered by sending questionnaires to people in the discipline who may have only limited knowledge of work in all the institutions to be considered. The results do not control the bias in favor of the department the largest number of surveyed faculty graduated from, bias toward schools with certain popular approaches to the field, bias in favor of larger schools, and the long time between periods of productivity in a department and when the results of those periods become part of its reputation. Those who understand these factors may well see the data as "much ado about practically nothing."

Use Comparison to Clarify Statistics

We noted earlier in the discussion of statistics that they can be more useful if compared. If you lived in Albuquerque, New Mexico, you could argue that your state and local tax burden is low for a family of four with a $50,000 a year income. It averages only $6,900, according to the *Statistical Abstract of the United States*. But $6,900 sounds like a lot of money, almost 14% of income, to some people. It would be best to compare it with other cities such as Des Moines, Iowa, $8,200; New York City, $13,200; Philadelphia, $15,200; or Bridgeport, Connecticut, $18,800 to show that the Albuquerque tax burden is the lowest surveyed in the Bureau of Census figures ("State and Local Taxes" 310).

If you wanted to argue that government projections for the fastest-growing occupations in the country show that those occupations are in the health care area, you might cite these examples by the Bureau of the Census: The number of home health aides is expected to increase 138.1% in the next few years, human service workers by 135.9%, physical therapists by 88%, and occupational therapists by 78.1%. Those percentages look impressive, but they become even more impressive when compared to some that are estimated to decline in the same period: machine operators—32.8%, telephone installers—50.3%, equipment operators—60.2%, and frame wirers—75.3% ("Civilian Employment" 411).

Base Testimony on Credibility Measures

The purpose of testimony is to provide credibility to a claim by adding a second person or agency to its support. The trustworthiness and competence of the source of the testimony is essential to its effectiveness. We discuss credibility in greater detail in Chapter 9. We will make only a few comments here.

Before you accept testimony, ask yourself if the person was in a position to know, either as an observer or with the expertise to make an intelligent observation. Ask if the source of the testimony has anything personal to gain by the acceptance of the facts testified to. Ask if this is firsthand knowledge or only a testimony about someone else's testimony.

A more specific source will add greater force than a vague one. Reports in the press are often attributed to unnamed or unknown sources, and readers have trouble assessing credibility. It is important for you to let decision makers know the source of any testimony. Of course, that will influence the argument you make because some sources will not be credible to decision makers and will need to be dropped. For instance, LaVarr Webb and Ted Wilson wrote that tax exemptions for credit unions violated "the first principle of fair tax policy." They went on to explain that this exemption hurts education. "Most Utah businesses, including banks, pay their fair share of taxes, contributing millions of dollars to educate Utah's children. Allowing a few large, profitable, expanding credit unions to avoid this responsibility increases the burden on all other businesses and citizens" (65). Readers might note that Webb and Wilson's article appeared in a publication that is edited by the senior vice president and public relations manager for a major bank, and is distributed at no charge to bank customers. This information might lead decision makers to judge Webb and Wilson's claims as biased in favor of the banking industry.

SPHERE DEPENDENCE OF EVIDENCE

Evidence may be evaluated differently depending on the sphere in which the argumentation occurs. The evidence necessary to provide grounds or backing for a claim may well change as the sphere of argument changes. **Sphere dependence** in evidence does not merely mean that some evidence will be accepted in one sphere and rejected in another but also that one kind of evidence may be used in two spheres but valued more in one than in the other. We will note some of the more common cases of sphere dependence of evidence.

Hearsay Evidence

Legal practice does not lend credibility to **hearsay evidence**, that is, testimony a person might give about a statement made by another person. It is usually not admissible. Only what a witness directly observes is admissible. The law makes this provision because only statements from witnesses who can be held responsible are accepted. But in politics, the reverse is frequently the case. When reporters say that the president of the United States (or even a "usually reliable source") told them something, it has a potential for developing a greater adherence to their arguments than if they claimed they observed it themselves.

Ordinary and Expert Evidence

A similar situation exists in the difference between **ordinary testimony** and **expert testimony**. In most professional spheres, the expert is preferred. In humanistic scholarship, a philosopher, such as Plato, John Locke, or Karl Marx, is preferred over the observations of ordinary people. In literary criticism, Jane Tompkins, Catherine Belsey, or Thomas Eagleton is expected to be more perceptive about literature than college students. In interpersonal argument, people probably trust folks they know better than they trust strangers. You may trust your friends to recommend a movie more than the expert critic in the local newspaper. You believe your friend "knows what you like."

Expert evidence for the behavioral social scientists is not a matter of differences in testimony. They frequently survey ordinary people, so the testimony is ordinary, but the means to draw conclusions from it is not. Behavioral social scientists draw their conclusions about human behavior through an elaborate system of statistical calculations. So, the evidence becomes not simply a collection of instances but a complex expert statistical demonstration.

There is an interesting situation involving expert and ordinary testimony in the court of law. Lawyers make a distinction between ordinary witnesses and expert witnesses and the legal system has careful distinctions as to when each is most acceptable. But as far as jurors are concerned, little distinction is made between ordinary witnesses, expert witnesses, and other members of the jury who can say, "Well, I have been there myself, and believe me, this is how things are done." In fact, other jurors may be the most powerful source of testimony (Hawkins).

Reluctant Evidence

Reluctant evidence, from those who are antagonistic to one's purpose, has long been considered the best evidence in public debates. In a court of law, witnesses are under oath and required to testify against their own interests. In a public argument, a person's own argument may be quoted by an opponent to attack the claim and make the person seem to have extreme views. In a political argument, an advocate may use the claims of persons who have been supporters of a particular policy to point out the errors of that policy.

During the months following the September 11, 2001, attack on the World Trade Center, Congress cooperated with the Bush administration to pass numerous pieces of legislation intended to protect the United States from further terrorist attacks. The USA Patriot Act, a centerpiece of that legislation, passed overwhelmingly, with only three Republicans and 62 Democrats in opposition. Two years later, Michael Tomasky used the testimony of conservative Republicans to argue that the Patriot Act had gone too far in its assault on American freedom.

Tomasky first cited Bob Barr, offering as his credentials the fact that this former Republican congressman from Georgia was an avid supporter of President Clinton's impeachment, voted for the Patriot Act, and currently holds an endowed position at the American Conservative Union. In July 2003, Barr participated in an interview with staff from the *Houston Chronicle* (a newspaper with strong pro-Bush leanings). The result of the meeting was a *Chronicle* editorial stating that "John Ashcroft and other Justice Department officials assure Americans that their liberties and privacy are not in jeopardy. They say the anti-terrorist Patriot Act passed after 9/11 does not apply to U.S. citizens. Ashcroft is wrong, and he knows he is wrong" (47). Tomasky went on to state that Barr no longer thinks that his decision to vote for the Patriot Act was the correct one.

Although the USA Patriot Act was heavily supported by Republican members of Congress and was a highlight of the Bush administration, by September 25, 2007, some parts of the law had become so widely criticized that amendments were introduced into Congress to restrict executive action under the act. Important from the concept of reluctant testimony is the fact that bills to reduce executive powers were cosponsored by Democrats and Republicans. For example, the National Security Letter Reform Act of 2007 was introduced by Senators Russ Feingold, a Democrat from Wisconsin, and John Sununu, a Republican from New Hampshire. A similar act was introduced in the House of Representatives by Jerrold Nadler, a Democrat from New York, and Jeff Flake, a

Republican from Arizona. The Republicans reluctantly joined with their Democratic colleagues when public criticism and court decisions could no longer be ignored.

Negative Evidence

Negative evidence, or the absence of evidence, is used in all spheres of argument, but it is used differently in different spheres. It is frequently used in historical scholarship. A historian who finds no evidence of women doctors, lawyers, or professors in early America will claim from this negative evidence that the professions were male dominated.

Scientists use negative evidence in the form of the null hypothesis. They try to prove that the data may be attributable to sampling error. When they cannot prove this null hypothesis, they believe the reverse—the hypothesis is true. So, a researcher who cannot prove that children do not grow more violent from seeing violence on TV (the null hypothesis) believes that they do (hypothesis).

Almost 800,000 prescriptions for Zetia and Vytorin, cholesterol-lowering drugs, are written each week according to Alex Berenson. Two years after the drugs' makers Merck and Schering-Plough completed a clinical trial, no findings have been released. Cardiologists complain that they need evidence on the effectiveness of the drugs and any possible side effects, such as heart disease, so that they can decide whether to continue prescribing the drugs or switch to others. The drug makers say they may release some, but not all, of the evidence within a few months. And, even if the entire clinical findings were made public, not all the questions will be answered one way or the other. Another bigger study, reported in 2010, failed to answer the most important questions, and now, lawsuits are underway. It is one thing to make decisions in the presence of uncertainty— we have said that is inevitable in critical decision making. It is another thing to know that evidence exists but is simply being withheld by the researchers or the drug companies. Cardiologists will necessarily wonder about what evidence is being kept from them and whether it is being held back because it contains bad news.

In another sphere, law, a federal judge warned that if the government did not allow lawyers to review classified material on possible wiretapping of an Islamic scholar who was convicted of inciting terrorism, she might order a new trial. Eric Lichtblau calls attention to problems emerging from the National Security Agency's wiretapping program. The government wants to keep classified information from becoming public, but lawyers for the convicted man need the information if they are to challenge his life sentence. The judge determined that absence of evidence could be grounds for forcing the government into a new trial, also something they do not want.

Documented Evidence

In law and in most scholarly fields of humanistic inquiry (e.g., literature, philosophy, history, theology), there is a clear bias for **documented evidence** over undocumented evidence, perhaps because written or recorded evidence seems more permanent.

Traditional historical scholarship provides a reasonable example of this emphasis. There is such a bias toward documents that elaborate methods have been defined by students of historiography to determine which documents are best and how they should be interpreted. For historians, for instance, there is a strong preference for "primary sources"—original documentary evidence. At the same time, there is a strong reservation about "secondary sources"—interpretations of evidence or events. This preference is related to the historian's interest in objective historical reconstruction (Gene Wise 59).

Documented evidence for historians has also meant documents that came from official sources or from the reports of well-educated and, presumably, more knowledgeable people. In recent years, there has been a growing interest in what has been called social history that tries to define how ordinary people were responding to events. Consequently, such persons have been interviewed (what is called oral history), and these interviews, along with diaries and letters, have been accorded greater weight. Still, there remains a strong bias for documented versus undocumented evidence.

Assertion and Evidence

Testimony as evidence means, as we indicated earlier, the testimony of someone *other than* the person making the argument. However, studies of arguments in conversational discourse reveal that people do use their own authority as grounds for claims (Willbrand and Rieke, "Strategies" 419–423).

Children argue by assertion more frequently than adults. However, the examination of the arguments of well-known adults shows that they use assertion frequently. Sometimes such assertions gain the adherence of decision makers who trust the person making the assertion. However, arguing by **assertion** is a questionable practice in any situation where the arguer does not have unquestioned credibility with decision makers.

You may be an unquestioned authority on some things when you talk with your friends or you might be an expert in an area that others don't know about, in which case you will need to let them know of your expertise. Most likely, you will want to provide evidence and not trust your argumentation to assertion.

Former Senator Mark Hatfield of Oregon presents us with an example of one who, because he is a Republican senator and conservative Christian, may not need evidence when he argues against legalizing public prayer in the schools.

> I must say very frankly that I oppose all prescriptive prayer of any kind in public schools. Does that mean that I am against prayer? No. It does not mean that at all. I am very strong in my belief in the efficacy of prayer. But I must say that there is no way [the Senate] or the Constitution or the President or the courts could ever abolish prayer in the public schools. That is an impossibility. Prayer is being given every day in public schools through this country—silent prayer, personal prayer that in no way could ever be abolished even if we wanted to.

Hatfield has no evidence to support his assertions, but his argument may be accepted because of his conservative credentials and his status. So, if the people hearing the claim accept the credibility of the person advancing the claim, assertion may function as if evidence were attached. It is a practice to be cautioned against because, for most people in public situations, assertion without evidence will not gain adherence.

Thus, each sphere will have its own interpretation of the degree of reliance that can be put into evidence: expert or ordinary, original or hearsay, willing or reluctant, positive or negative, documented or undocumented, substantial or asserted. There may be some general bias for one or the other in each of these pairs. You will do best to think clearly about the standards of the sphere in which you undertake to argue before you select the evidence you will use.

CONCLUSION

Arguments may be supported to gain decision makers' adherence using evidence, values, and credibility. Evidence—the traditional term for examples, statistics, and testimony—is the subject of this chapter.

Examples may be used to develop a generalization or illustrate a general principle. They can be real instances or hypothetical ones. Statistics provide a means for compacting examples, for talking about a large number of specific instances at one time. Statistical measures provide the basis for averaging and comparisons. Such measures can be simple or highly sophisticated. Testimony about fact or about opinion is a means of adding credibility to a message.

A number of general principles guide you in using examples, statistics, and testimony. All are based on the inclination of the decision makers, but the principles provide general guidelines:

1. Examples should be representative.
2. Examples should be in sufficient number.
3. Negative instances should be accounted for.
4. Value characteristics of examples should be given.
5. Detail should be given to make examples seem real.
6. The decision makers' experience should be used.
7. Examples and statistics should be current.
8. Examples and statistics should come from the most reliable sources.
9. Statistical measures should be carefully considered.
    a. Avoid the "sample with the built-in bias."
    b. Avoid the "gee-whiz graph."
    c. Avoid the "well-chosen average."
    d. Avoid "much ado about practically nothing."
10. Statistics should be made clearer through comparison.
11. Testimony should be based on credibility measures.

Some forms of evidence are sphere dependent, that is, they have different values depending on the sphere in which they are used. Hearsay evidence is suspect in a court of law but quite acceptable in political argumentation. Many fields regard the expert witness as superior to the ordinary witness, but this is not true for social scientists interested in human behavior or for interpersonal argument. Reluctant testimony depends for its value on the extent to which its author is clearly perceived to be reluctant. Negative evidence is useful in international relations but not in scientific argument. Documented evidence is preferred in most scholarly fields and in religion.

EXERCISES/PROJECTS

1. Deliver a short argumentative speech in which you state a single claim and support it with specific examples, statistics, and testimony.
2. Along with all class members, bring another claim with supporting evidence to class. One by one, present the arguments and then as a class talk about the evidence: how does it do the job of supporting the claim? How could the claim have been supported better?
3. Participate in a debate in class. Prepare your arguments with the best evidence you can find, and compare and contrast the evidence supporting your claims with that used to support opposing claims.

Support: Values

KEY TERMS

stated values, p. 121
implied values, p. 121
positive values, p. 122
negative values, p. 122
terminal values, p. 122
instrumental values, p. 122
abstract values, p. 124
concrete values, p. 124

value systems, p. 124
value hierarchy, p. 126
ethics, p. 127
changing values, p. 131
attacking value, p. 131
decision makers' value systems, p. 132
implied values, p. 133
sphere dependence of values, p. 134

Communication technology has made enormous strides in the past 50 years, especially in the past 20. Television satellites, cable, computers, fax machines, smart phones, iPads, iPods, iMacs, camera phones, Twitter, Facebook, and other electronics have increased by geometric ratios the availability of information to people while increasing their ability to communicate with one another. Many feel this has been a mixed blessing, particularly when the influence on children is measured.

Children can find sex and violence on media sites and communicate it to others. Most people believe this is a problem, but can it be solved? And how? Should media be censored? Should the government impose the restrictions on cable that are imposed on broadcast television? Would such restrictions infringe on freedom of speech? Can the media be censored for on-line communication? Does government censorship lead to restrictions on knowledge?

This problem is complex and made particularly difficult because it affects children. It is, as many have noted, a question of values. Think about the arguments that are generated on this question and note the values, stated and unstated, in this brief description: knowledge (information), communication, children (family, innocence), violence, sex, restriction, and freedom (freedom of speech).

Not all argumentation is so obviously based on values. But all argumentation has values in its development. Some would argue that values are the defining central factor of all argumentation (Sillars). One series of studies of unplanned reasoning by children and adults in various cultures indicates that values-based reasoning is pervasive (Willbrand and Rieke, "Reason giving in . . . ," 343). In this chapter, we will examine values as they serve as support for claims at the same time that we remember that claims themselves may be values.

"A *value*," says anthropologist Clyde Kluckhohn, "is a conception . . . of the desirable that influences the selection from available modes, means and ends of action." A value may be "explicit or implicit, distinctive of an individual or characteristic of a group" ("Values" 395).

In Chapter 1, we observed that there are three kinds of claims: fact, value, and policy. Value claims are those that directly involve values, and policy claims require value claims to support them. Only a factual claim, which asserts that certain conditions exist in the material world and can be observed, would seem to be value free, but it is not. Even the scientist's careful statement about laboratory observations implies the values of rationality and knowledge. Thus, values are important even to choose one factual claim over another.

Values obviously relate directly to claims of value, and they are vital to policy and factual claims as well. Values, together with source credibility and evidence, are the grounds and warrants by which decision makers judge claims to be worthy of adherence. However, understanding how values serve as support is not simply a matter of observing that they do. Values differ in their characteristics and in their applications. They appear in systems and they are adapted to spheres.

CHARACTERISTICS OF VALUES

Values, then, are concepts of what is desirable that arguers use and decision makers understand. Arguers use them with credibility and evidence to justify claims. But values have a variety of characteristics and fit together in various ways. We will examine those characteristics now so that you can better understand what goes into a value system in argumentation.

Stated and Implied Values

Some statements of value concepts are direct; these are called **stated values**. People sometimes say that *freedom, health*, or *wealth* is important. These words state directly the value concepts they hold. Some value concepts may be identified by several different words, as is the case with *liberty, freedom*, or *independence*. Furthermore, there can be variations of a single word as in *freedom, free*, or *freely* depending on the nature of the sentence in which they appear.

Value concepts are not always explicitly stated, however. Frequently, they are **implied**. Values are general concepts that define what arguers and decision makers believe are desirable, but many values are implied in what we call *belief statements*. Milton Rokeach defines a belief as "any simple proposition, conscious or unconscious, inferred from what a person says or does and capable of being preceded by the phrase, 'I believe that . . . '" (*Beliefs* 113). Many statements of what a person believes do not directly state value concepts but imply them.

Equality
STATED: *Equal* pay for *equal* work
IMPLIED: Women deserve the same pay as men for the same work.

Science

STATED: DNA research is a *scientific* triumph.
IMPLIED: DNA research is virtually unquestionable.

Self-Respect

STATED: Every child's well-being is based on *self-respect*.
IMPLIED: Children need to learn to like themselves.

When you directly and frequently state value concepts, you are more intensive in your use of values than if you imply values only through indirect statement. The closing argument of a trial frequently is more value intensive than is the examination of witnesses. In the legal sphere, there is an attempt to be value free during the collecting of evidence. Witnesses, even expert witnesses, are supposed to report only facts tied to demonstrable sources. These are values, of course, including values of accuracy, fact, and science, but they are implied rather than stated. A witness might say under questioning, "I saw the defendant take the money from the cash register and run from the store." The negative value of stealing is only implied. The closing arguments of a trial provide more freedom for an attorney to openly attach values to the evidence.

Positive and Negative Values

Our definition of a value as "a conception of the desirable" puts a clearly positive cast on value concepts. However, for every positive concept, there is at least one antithesis. So, a statement of a value can be either positive or negative. Earning opposes stealing, freedom opposes restraint, thrift opposes waste, knowledge opposes ignorance, and pleasure opposes pain. Depending on the strategy devised, if you argue against a specific proposal, you may do so by identifying **positive values** that oppose it or **negative values** that you associate with it. As a critic of argument, you will want to note the extent to which an arguer focuses on either negative or positive values.

On the Saturday before Easter 2011, Pope Benedict XVI used the vigil marking Jesus' transition from death to rebirth to speak out on evolution. He said:

> If man were merely a random product of evolution in some place at the margins of the universe, then his life would make no sense or might even be a chance of nature. But no, reason is there at the beginning, creative divine reason. (Winfield)

Note how he uses negative values to set up the argument for powerful positive values.

Negative values: "random," "at the margins of the universe," "no sense," "chance of nature."
Positive values: "Reason," Creative," "Divine" (God).

Terminal and Instrumental Values

Values will reflect the *ends* a person admires (wealth, health, happiness, security) or the *means* to attain the ends (hard work, faith, helpfulness, responsibility). Milton Rokeach called these "terminal and instrumental values" (*Beliefs* 160). He also found the terminal values to be the most central to an individual's value system (*Nature* 215).

A caution is necessary on that point, however. People frequently make a terminal out of an instrumental value. For instance, they recognize that they must work hard (means) to achieve economic security (end), but for many people, hard work becomes an end in itself. Retired people with secure financial situations frequently work hard at whatever they do because work has become a terminal value for them. For the scientist, a carefully worked out experiment brings pleasure. For the religious person, faith can become more than a means to salvation; it can be an end in itself. Instrumental values such as hard work or faith sometimes become terminal values. Even so, it is worthwhile to remember the distinction when you are building and analyzing arguments.

In his research, Rokeach identified 18 **terminal values** (Figure 8.1):

TERMINAL VALUES	
1. A comfortable life	10. Inner harmony
2. An exciting life	11. Mature love
3. A sense of accomplishment	12. National security
4. A world at peace	13. Pleasure
5. A world of beauty	14. Salvation
6. Equality	15. Self-respect
7. Family security	16. Social recognition
8. Freedom	17. True friendship
9. Happiness	18. Wisdom

FIGURE 8.1

Rokeach's "Terminal" Values

Note: He found these 18 values most central in an individual's value system.

Source: Rokeach, Milton. *The Nature of Human Values*. San Francisco: Free Press, 1972. Page 28.

Rokeach also identified 18 **instrumental values** (Figure 8.2):

INSTRUMENTAL VALUES	
1. Ambition	10. Imagination
2. Broad-mindedness	11. Independence
3. Capability	12. Intellect
4. Cheerfulness	13. Logic
5. Cleanliness	14. Love
6. Courage	15. Obedience
7. Forgiveness	16. Politeness
8. Helpfulness	17. Responsibility
9. Honesty	18. Self-control

FIGURE 8.2

Rokeach's "Instrumental" Values

Note: The instrumental values in this list have been adapted from Rokeach's original list to make them all nouns like his terminal values.

Source: Rokeach, Milton. *The Nature of Human Values*. San Francisco: Free Press, 1972. Page 28.

His lists are not exhaustive, but they illustrate terminal and instrumental value concepts that you are likely to find in your argumentation and that of others. More important here, they illustrate the difference between terminal and instrumental values.

Abstract and Concrete Values

A value is a conception, so it would seem that values are abstract. Words such as *freedom, justice,* and *truth* represent **abstract value** concepts in society. However, there are also times when particular people, groups, institutions, or objects serve as values. These are called **concrete values** (Perelman and Olbrechts-Tyteca 77). The flag, the family, the pope, the Star of David, and the Constitution are all concrete, yet they are value concepts. The Constitution is a good illustration. It is an actual document, but in an argument, it has all the power of an abstract value.

A statement that a law is unconstitutional is as value laden for most people, as it is to say that the law denies freedom. In a court of law, violation of the Constitution is a more forceful value argument than restriction of freedom. Civil justice frequently limits freedom. You have to leash your dog, drive at 20 miles per hour through a school zone, and restrict your speech when it maliciously damages another. However, no law can acceptably violate the Constitution. The Constitution is to U.S. legal argumentation what God (another concrete value for believers) is to religious argumentation.

In recent years, the First Amendment to the Constitution that says, "Congress shall make no law respecting the establishment of religion, or prohibiting the free exercise thereof," has been interpreted, through the Fourteenth Amendment applying the principles of the Constitution to the states to mean that the Establishment Clause applies to the states as well as the national government. This has led to a series of decisions by the Supreme Court that rule out state and local prayer in the schools, religious symbols in public parks and public buildings, and the like. In 2011, there were questions about crosses on the highway to commemorate fallen highway troopers and a challenge to the President proclaiming a National Day of Prayer. Although behind the arguments of both sides is an abstract value of freedom, the practices are all about the meaning of concrete values: The Constitution, the Cross, State Law, public buildings, presidential proclamations, and God. The realization that abstract and concrete values work together leads us to another: that values, abstract and concrete, terminal and instrumental, positive and negative, stated and implied, work in systems.

VALUES APPEAR IN SYSTEMS

Values do not appear alone in argumentation. They appear in **value systems,** that is, as a set of linked claims. Clyde Kluckhohn calls these "value orientations . . . generalized and organized conceptions . . . of the desirable and non-desirable" ("Values" 411). We hear people argue for better treatment of Native Americans, not on the basis of a single value of justice or equality but on the basis of a series of values like justice, freedom, family security, happiness, and self-respect that link together and reflect a unified system in which each value will be perceived as compatible with every other.

Indeed, one of our major disagreements in argumentation is over perceived inconsistency. When values are not compatible in a system, they are used to weaken a claim. People are charged with inconsistency if they argue for their own freedom and discriminate against minorities. We know of people who wonder how someone can object to marijuana (health) and still drink alcohol. Some people consider it inconsistent to argue for morality and deny a belief in God. Others find it inconsistent to support capital punishment but oppose abortion, and vice versa.

These are examples of arguments about the consistency of values in a given system. They come about because values do not stand alone. They work in integrated systems. The theoretical and experimental literature supports the idea that there is a limited and distinct group of value systems. There are many potential value patterns, Rokeach says, but the number will be limited because of the social factors involved (*Beliefs* 161).

In an extensive study of the value systems across cultures, Charles Morris found a dominant pattern of American value systems, although it was different from the value systems in other cultures (44). Shalom H. Schwartz of the Hebrew University of Jerusalem has found a core set of 10 values that his research shows are present in all cultures: Self-direction, Stimulation, Hedonism, Achievement, Power, Security, Conformity, Tradition, Benevolence, Universalism. However, he notes, the pursuit of achievement values may be in conflict with benevolence values. So, a person's own attempt to succeed might obstruct his or her interest in the welfare of others. Then again, the actions of successful and wealthy business leaders like Bill Gates, Mark Zuckerberg, and Steve Jobs would seem to make these values compatible. So, the question of inconsistency must be argued on a case-by-case basis.

A frequently cited cultural difference is between Japanese and American values in their emphasis on collectivism versus individualism. Three researchers examined the role of "commitment" in both cultures. In short, how do American and Japanese workers and family members perceive the commitment they have to the agencies of the society? What values characterize the Japanese and American value systems beyond the accepted collectivism/individualism? The values [they called them *themes*] found among Americans were dedication, obligation, integrity, and determination. Among Japanese, the values were connection, membership, responsibility, cooperation, and interest. The American values are all linked to individualism. They reveal what values an individual must have. The Japanese values are all ways of explaining a collective value system all except "interest," which reflects the individual's interest in a person or subject (Guzley et al.). Anyone who is going to engage in argumentation before decision makers whose value system comes from another culture must recognize and adapt to such differences.

Traditional Value Systems

There are several acknowledged U.S. value systems that scholars from a wide variety of fields identify (Kluckhohn, *Mirror* 228–261; Morris 185; Ruesch 94–134; Steele and Redding 83–91; Weaver 211–232). To illustrate, we will examine one value system that is probably the dominant value system in U.S. politics and government, the enlightenment value system.

The United States became a nation in the period of the Enlightenment, a new intellectual era based on the writings of scientists such as Sir Isaac Newton and philosophers such as John Locke. The Declaration of Independence is the epitome of an Enlightenment document. In many ways, the United States is an enlightenment nation, and if enlightenment is not the predominant value system, it surely is first among equals.

The Enlightenment position stems from the belief that there is an ordered world where all activity is governed by laws similar to the laws of physics. These "natural laws" may or may not come from God, depending on the particular orientation of the person examining them, but Enlightenment thinkers theorized that people could discover these laws by themselves. Thus, people may worship God for God's greatness, even acknowledge that God created the universe and natural laws, but they find out about the universe because they have the powers of observation and reason. The laws of nature are harmonious, and one can use reason to discover them all. They also can provide for a better life.

Restraints on humans must be limited because people are essentially moral and reasonable. Occasionally, people act foolishly and must be restrained by society. However, a person should never be restrained in matters of the mind. Reason must be free. Thus, government is an agreement among individuals to assist the society to protect rights. That government is a democracy. Certain rights are inalienable, and they may not be abridged: "among these are life, liberty, and the pursuit of happiness." Arguments for academic freedom, against wiretaps, and for scientific inquiry come from this value system. Some of the words representing concepts from the enlightenment value system are

POSITIVE: freedom, science, nature, rationality, democracy, fact, liberty, individualism, knowledge, intelligence, reason, natural rights, natural laws, progress, information

NEGATIVE: ignorance, superstition, inattention, thoughtlessness, error, indecision, irrationality, dictatorship, book burning, falsehood, regression

People use the enlightenment value system in a wide variety of spheres and situations. They make judgments about the desirable in science, in politics, and in everyday life. All value systems, like the enlightenment system, are a set of linked claims about desirable ends and means. But the values in a system are more than linked to one another. A **value hierarchy** defines their relationship to one another. In a particular argumentative situation, the values in a system are graded.

Values Are Graded in Systems

A particular set of decision makers is defined by the value system to which it adheres. Many residents of the United States follow what we will call a personal success value system. For many people, family, career, health, self-respect, satisfaction, freedom of choice, accomplishment, material possessions, friendship, and similar values are most important (Gallup and Newport). The personal success value system represents U.S. citizens as success oriented in an individual way that may not be found in other cultures (e.g., the Japanese culture).

However, as natural as such a value system is in the United States, it cannot be used in a particular argumentative situation until it has some kind of order to it. Any two values potentially contradict one another. A person may value both family and career as a part of personal success. Yet, an argument can be made that career can interfere with family. In such a case, the two values are not simply part of a value system; they have to be understood in relation to one another and the solution in this case involves using both.

"A particular audience," say Perelman and Olbrechts-Tyteca, "is characterized less by what values it accepts than by the way it grades them." If you think of decision makers' values in isolation, independent of interrelationships, you "may neglect the question of their hierarchy, which solves the conflicts between them" (81–82; Walker and Sillars 141–145). Therefore, a claim that two parents should cut back on their work schedules to spend more time with their children is a matter of emphasizing family over career without denying the legitimacy of either value. Such an argument may also mean a lower rank in the hierarchy of other personal success values, such as material possessions.

Values, therefore, are concepts of the desirable ends and actions that are stated directly or implied. They are stated positively or negatively. They are terminal or instrumental, abstract or concrete. They are found in clusters that are value systems and, when applied to a particular situation, are graded to reveal their relative significance, one to another. With this understanding, you are ready to see how you may use values in the argumentative situation.

VALUES DEFINE ETHICS

Societies, spheres, and professional groups have ethical rules by which they judge their own and other's behavior. For the arguer, in our society, **ethics** is the theory of the good and the right. Ethics define how one should behave toward others. Decision makers should be protected from unethical arguers. Therefore, responsible arguers will point out those arguers and arguments that are unethical. The standards by which arguers are judged to be ethical or unethical are rooted in values.

For instance, in western society, it is generally considered unethical to deny someone's freedom of expression, to tell people things that you know not to be true, to be unfair to an opponent, or to shirk your responsibility to provide a reasonable story. These are only examples. There are more, but the point to be noted here is that these are all derived from the enlightenment value system discussed earlier in the chapter. Individual spheres will also have their ethics, based again on their value systems. Chapters 12 through 16 present examples of how argumentation is carried on in various spheres and each has values that define the ethical system to which they adhere. Virtually, every professional group has a formal set of ethics.

The Society of Professional Journalists has a Code of Ethics for journalists. Notice some of the wording they use. "Seek truth and report it." "Test the accuracy from all sources and exercise care to avoid inadvertent error." "Diligently seek out subjects of news stories and give them the opportunity to respond to allegations of wrongdoing." "Ethical journalists treat sources, subjects, and colleagues as human beings deserving respect." It is clear that this code, like the Code of Legal Justice, is rooted in the enlightenment value system but is specific to journalism.

In 2006, the Duke University lacrosse team (all white men) had a party and hired two African-American women to perform a striptease at the party. Afterward, one of the women claimed that she had been raped. Subsequently, three of the players were arrested and charged by Durham, North Carolina, District Attorney (DA), Mike Nifong. A recent analysis of the case charges that the Duke faculty, the media, and the DA each violated their Code of ethics, but we will examine here the legal ethics of the DA (Feighery, Hasian, Jr. and Rieke), In December 2006, before the case came to trial, the North Carolina Bar Association filed ethics charges against the DA for making misleading and inflammatory statements to the media about the three lacrosse players. For instance, the DA told ESPN that the athletes were "a bunch of hooligans." He also said that their "wealthy daddies" could buy them expensive lawyers. "One would wonder," he said publicly, "why one needs an attorney if one is not charged and has not done anything wrong." These and other statements, the Bar Association charged, broke the ethics rule against any comments "that have a substantial likelihood of heightening public condemnation of the accused." Subsequently, DA Nifong was charged with breaking the ethics rule against "dishonesty, fraud, deceit, and misrepresentation." He had DNA evidence that cleared the men but did not make it available to the defense when he had said that all evidence had been given to the defense. The case was dismissed. Nifong resigned as DA and was disbarred. The important point to be noted here is that the legal ethics statements are specific applications of the values of fairness and honesty.

GENERAL PRINCIPLES FOR THE USE OF VALUES

Because they are so basic to argumentation, values are essential both for criticizing the arguments of others and developing your own arguments. In this section, we will examine seven principles for using values in argumentation. The first three apply most directly to criticizing the arguments of others. The last four are principles that will aid you in developing your own arguments.

Values May Be Found Anywhere in an Argument

We have already observed that there are no value-free arguments. Any part of an argument can state values. Arguments can be made where all parts openly state values. In this example, all the parts of the argument contain direct, positive values.

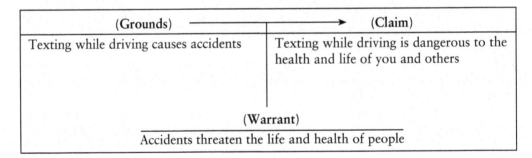

(Grounds) ————————➤	(Claim)
Texting while driving causes accidents	Texting while driving is dangerous to the health and life of you and others
(Warrant)	
Accidents threaten the life and health of people	

I FIGURE 8.3

Such a value-intensive argument is possible though not likely. In most arguments, many values will be implied, not stated, and in some arguments, one or two (warrants, grounds, or claims) will not be stated. Yet, to function as a critic of arguments (your own or others), you will need to be aware that values may be found anywhere. You need to understand where an argument fits in a value system. You can do that only by actively looking for an argument's values. As an arguer, you must be aware that you may be challenged at any time to state unstated values. That is a good reason for you to be aware of the values from which you and those who support them argue.

There has been an ongoing disagreement in this country, particularly in the western states over the federal government's management of the public lands. National Parks, National Forests, and Bureau of Land Management land make up a large portion of many western states. Local and state leaders in the western states who want the land to be available for development frequently clash with environmentalists who want development to be restricted. In 2009, the U.S. House of Representatives Sub-committee on National Parks, Forests, and Public Lands considered the Red Rock Wilderness Act that would protect millions of acres of Southern Utah as wilderness.

Robert Redford writing in the Huffington *Post* made this argument for protecting the public lands from development:

> I love the extraordinary lands encompassed in America's Red Rock Wilderness Act. I have spent decades exploring them, and I am still awed by the beauty of their serpentine canyons and alcoves filled with stone houses built by the ancestors of today's Pueblo people. I have profoundly inspiring memories of the time I've spent hiking with my family under scalped arches, through pink sand dunes and across mesas that open up to a sea of redrock vistas.

An article, by Scott Streater, posted on Utah Congressman Rob Bishop's web site states the opposing view:

> The 'American's Red Rock Wilderness Act' which preserves 9.4 million acres of pristine land across eastern Utah, isn't supported by a single member of the state's congressional delegation and might never be approved by Congress. But Uintah County leaders say the federal government is preventing them from tapping the vast oil and gas reserves beneath a 385,000-acre section of public land within the proposed wilderness boundaries, County Commissioner Michael McKee blames tough federal conservation measures . . . for scaring off drillers and contributing to the county's highest unemployment rate.

You can see from these two brief excerpts the values on each side of the debate: Beauty, Family, protection of nature, and ancient culture are opposed by: popularity, development, employment, and prosperity.

Recognize Values in Warrants

Warrants are the most likely place to find values. Their role in an argument is to justify the reasoned movement from the grounds to the claim. Justification is clearly a value-using procedure.

The debate over the protection of wildlife has centered on the Endangered Species Act (ESA). Those who oppose the act claim that the ESA violates private property, hurts the economy, and wastes tax money. A strong argument is also made that it doesn't work. This claim is supported by a study by Charles Mann and Mark Plummer in their book *Noah's Choice: The Future of Endangered Species*. Their studies show that "by the end of 1994, only 21 species had been struck from the list, and of those 21, only 6 were delisted because they had gained enough ground to warrant removal." Others were removed from the list because they became extinct or were not endangered in the first place. Even several of those whose status improved did not do so because of the ESA (Carpenter 43). Those who argue for the ESA claim that improvement has to be measured not only by delisting but also by other factors. Their argument is really about how success is defined, and the value of success remains central to the controversy even though not mentioned as such.

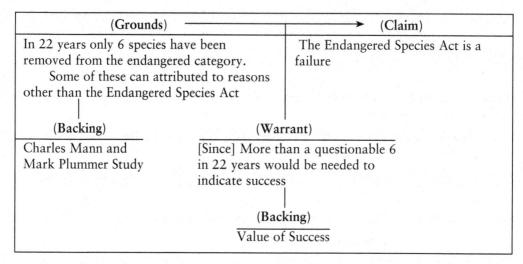

(Grounds) ─────────────────→	(Claim)
In 22 years only 6 species have been removed from the endangered category. Some of these can attributed to reasons other than the Endangered Species Act	The Endangered Species Act is a failure

(Backing)	(Warrant)
Charles Mann and Mark Plummer Study	[Since] More than a questionable 6 in 22 years would be needed to indicate success

(Backing)
Value of Success

I FIGURE 8.4

Find the Values in the Arguments of Others

Before you can decide whether to accept or refute arguments of others, you need to find the values they use. Here is a specific list of tools.

1. Look for specific language that directly states values.
   a. A statement ["I believe in *honesty*"]
   b. A word [*freedom, truth, nature*]
2. Look for negative terms [*waste, immoral, filth*].
3. Look for concrete values [*God, Constitution, Star of David*].
4. Look for indirect values ["Vaccination is essential for all children" or "A cure must be found for Alzheimer's disease" (health)].
5. Look for absent values that you might expect to find ["The purpose of government is to protect life and property"]. (Why have liberty and the pursuit of happiness been left out and property added to the traditional values found in the Declaration of Independence?)
6. Look for other factors that indicate values.
   a. Statistical evidence (science)
   b. Testimony of authorities who represent values [the Pope, Marx, Jefferson]
   c. Heroes and villains of stories
   d. Stylistic evidence [biblical, African-American, or scientific style]

When you examine someone's argument with these tools, you will have a good idea of the values in the arguer's value system.

Recognize the Limits of Value Change

Before you develop a case, you must think seriously about exactly what value changes you wish decision makers to make. Nicholas Rescher has pointed out that value changes usually take place by (1) making a value more or less widely distributed within the society, (2) changing its relative importance to another value, (3) altering the range of a value's application, and (4) raising or lowering what one expects a particular value to mean when applied to a specific belief (14–16). These four options all have to do with shifts in the hierarchy, in application, or in the meaning of a value. None involve the almost impossible act of **changing values** by adding a new one or dropping an existing one.

The current public controversy over abortion is irresolvable as long as it is seen as a conflict between two prominent values in our society—life ("pro-life") and freedom ("pro-choice").

It is virtually impossible for the pro-life forces to accept the pro-choice position, and vice versa. Yet, neither side denies the other's value. The pro-life position says a woman had a choice when she got pregnant, and the pro-choice group argues that quality of life must be considered, not only physical life. But it can be argued, a woman did not have a choice in the case of rape, and the life of the mother is important. Also, there are arguments about when life actually begins.

Although the abortion debate is a rare case of two values in a direct clash, there are at least two possible modifications that might be made: (1) limit abortions to the first trimester or (2) to cases such as rape, incest, health of the mother, or severe fetal deformity. If either of these were generally accepted, it would represent Rescher's third condition, altering the range of application. The first trimester proposal limits "life" to after the first trimester. The second proposal limits the freedom to choose abortion. Neither satisfies those who see either life or choice as an absolute value.

Find the Best Point of Attack on Values

The method for analyzing claims of fact or value discussed in Chapter 5 is used to determine the best point for **attacking value**. First, you must determine what values support the claim. Second, you must determine what criteria to use in judging those values. Third, you must determine how to grade the values (Tuman).

Traditional journalistic standards, such as those published in the Society of Professional Journalists' Code of Ethics, reveal a value system that has been labeled "accurate interpretation." That value system maintains that journalists should be truthful, communicate information, be objective, be fair, support freedom, and accept responsibility (Sillars and Gronbeck 68–76).

FAIR (Fairness and Accuracy in Reporting) is a liberal journalistic organization like the conservative one Accuracy in Media (AIM). (You might note that both groups use terms from this value system in their names.) FAIR published an analysis of the programs of popular conservative radio commentator Rush Limbaugh subtitled "Rush Limbaugh Debates Reality." That he is objective even Limbaugh would deny, but he does claim to be truthful and give people information ("I do not lie on this program"). He also believes that he supports freedom. He claims to accept responsibility ("if I find out that I have been mistaken, . . . I proclaim it . . . at the beginning of a program—or as loudly as I can"). FAIR argues that Limbaugh is neither truthful nor fair. Those two values are the basis of their criticism of Limbaugh.

FAIR claims that Limbaugh takes factual situations and draws untruthful and unfair conclusions. For instance, they claim that he says that human use of fluorocarbons does not destroy the ozone. It is a theory, says Limbaugh, developed by "environmental wackos," "dunderheaded alarmists," and "prophets of doom." FAIR's refutation, they believe, shows that these are unfair characterizations. To support his argument, Limbaugh claims that volcanoes, for example, Mount Pinatubo, cause more ozone depletion by a thousand times "than all the fluorocarbons manufactured by wicked, diabolical, and insensitive corporations in history." FAIR cites the journal *Science*, to claim that chlorine from natural causes, such as volcanoes, is soluble and, therefore, rain prevents it from getting to the upper atmosphere to release the carbons. FAIR also quotes an atmospheric chemist at the University of California, Irvine, who says, "Natural causes of ozone depletion are not significant." FAIR contrasts these experts with Limbaugh's expert Rogelio Maduro, who they claim only has a bachelor's degree in geology (10–11). The criterion for judging truthfulness in FAIR's analysis is clearly the quality of the scientific supporters.

This short summary of a piece of FAIR's argumentation illustrates the three steps necessary to determine the best way to attack a value claim. FAIR has found the values (truth, fairness, responsibility), found a criterion (science) for evaluating the argument, and determined how to grade the values (truthfulness is primary). Such a system, Joseph H. Tuman observes, leads to five alternative attack points on such an argument illustrated by examples of what a Limbaugh supporter might have argued:

1. Dispute the values.
   (Ex: "Fairness doesn't apply when attacking a dangerous falsehood.")
2. Concede the values and hierarchy but dispute the criterion.
   (Ex: Calling people "environmental wackos" and "dunderheaded alarmists" is just a joke. It is part of Limbaugh's style. People who are offended by this should get a life.)
3. Concede the value and criterion but dispute the hierarchy.
   (Ex: "The most important criterion is supporting freedom.")
4. Concede the value but dispute the criterion and hierarchy.
   (Ex: "There is a more important criterion for judging scientific truth. These so-called experts are part of the "agenda-oriented scientific community.")
5. Dispute all.
   (Ex: "Fairness is an inappropriate value in this case and even were it appropriate, attacking a joke doesn't make sense and freedom is more important than either of these values.") (93)

Obviously, the first and fifth alternatives are ones people would seldom use because, as we have already noted, values change very slowly. Still, this example illustrates how to challenge value claims. The three middle attacks (dispute the criterion, dispute the hierarchy, or both) are the most likely points at which Limbaugh supporters could attack the FAIR argument. They are also the most likely points for you to attack any value argument.

Relate Your Values to Decision Makers

The fact that limited options are available to you in a value dispute makes it clear that you will be most successful by arguing within **decision makers' value systems**. Adherence is most likely when the values in your arguments are ones that relate to decision makers. To achieve this, you must pay close attention to the particular social group or sphere to which decision makers belong. Values are social, shared among the members of particular groups. Indeed, to a large extent, interaction among the members of a group defines the value system and its potential hierarchy. This is true of all kinds of groups: social, political, religious. It is true of families, and it is true of gangs. The values of your family (e.g., love, respect, cooperation, security) are positive to you because you are a member of that group. You probably think that gangs who hang out, get in fights over turf, bully people, and threaten authority are negative. To most of society, they are. Some sociologists who have studied gangs say that their values are middle-class values stood on their heads. The gang members, however, have defined their values much as your family has, and their values are positive to them: "turf", respect, protection, harmony, toughness, smartness, excitement, fate, violence. (Carlie)

Use Evidence and Argument to Develop Values

We can talk about values by identifying specific words that reflect these values (e.g., *freedom, work, happiness, reason, salvation*). However, you need to keep in mind that you communicate values indirectly by the evidence and argument you use more than by a direct statement. This is what we mean by *implied values*. Rather than telling someone that your argument is "reasonable" or "factual," demonstrate that it is. Remember the old writing dictum: "Show, don't tell." Direct statements make more value-intensive arguments. There are times when you will want to make your arguments value intensive. However, for most of your argumentation, values will usually be communicated by evidence and argument.

Some extensive studies indicate that although people hold values, and hold them in systems such as those we have discussed in this chapter, they do not hold them in clearly defined systems. They live in a "fragmented intellectual culture" and a "fragmented popular culture" (Bellah et al. 282–283). In the words of Conal Furay, Americans "dance around their values" (19). Although individuals and groups can frequently identify values, they do not use them in a fully rational fashion. Consequently, care must be taken in stating values in too absolute a manner. You need to make clear to decision makers that your values are their values, but if you overuse values, you will make your case too obvious and open it to rejection.

A *Sports Illustrated* article in March of 2011 revealed the results of a six months' investigation by SI and CBS into the "alarming number" of football players at major programs who have criminal records. There aren't so many direct statements of the negative value of crime or positive values like law and morality. The values are carried by examples of individual cases of assault, robbery, or sex offenses by statistics of the number of players on each of the 25 top ranked teams in Division I who had criminal records. It is a powerful value argument because it is built on examples and statistics (Dohrmann and Benedict).

Making value-based arguments and examining the arguments of others involves finding values, understanding the limits of value change, learning to find a point of attack, relating values to decision makers, and using evidence and argument to develop values. However, these practices are tempered by a realization that value systems will differ from sphere to sphere.

SPHERE DEPENDENCE OF VALUES

Probably, no other function of argumentation defines spheres so well as values. We have defined a sphere as a collection of people in the process of interacting on, and making critical decisions. The criteria by which the people in a sphere appraise arguments form a value system. People are not admitted seriously to the sphere unless they have the credibility identified by appropriate credentials (e.g., J. D., M. D., a successful election, ordination, a Ph.D. in the right discipline). The permitted evidence, as we noted in Chapter 7, is regulated by the criteria of the sphere. The preferred kinds of argument, how one argues, and appropriate language all depend on the criteria of that sphere. These criteria make up a system of a **sphere dependence of values.** So, in one sense, a sphere is defined by its system of values.

Science and religion are two spheres that have frequently been at odds with one another. A comparison of the values in these two spheres helps to make their disagreements clearer. Not only are their claims sometimes at issue but also their defining values are much different.

Values in Scientific Argument

Scientific argument, as we use the term here (and in Chapter 13), refers to those disciplines that use the physical sciences as a model to explain how physical, biological, human, and social entities function and interact. From this definition, we could say that the scientific narrative provides an "objective account of the natural world based upon measurement and quantification. So, that structure, process, movement, and transformation can be described mathematically in terms of fundamental laws" (Peat 208). Scientific argument can be characterized by the values of order, usefulness, prediction, rationality, and knowledge.

Order in Science.   What we have called scientific argument assumes there is some *order* in phenomena. This means that a scientist builds "a world picture" (Toulmin et al. 328–330). Thus, scientific argumentation is judged by how well it can prove that the theory explains all related phenomena. Any sign that there is an inconsistency between one explanation and another must be accounted for or the explanation is deficient.

Scientists assume an order to data when they argue that one set of data will identify the natural state of related phenomena. For example, a social scientist will claim that an experimental examination of one group of children will provide a generalization about all similar children.

It is the rupture of order that interests scientists. A communication researcher discovers that TV takes up a good deal of a child's time until age 14. Then, viewing time drops off sharply. Why? Because other factors interfere? Because parents monitor TV viewing more? Because TV programming is less interesting to teenagers? One does not decide to develop a theory about something that is explained by current theories. Theories are developed to explain a phenomenon that is different, and developing or revising a theory to explain the change and accommodate the previous lack of change returns order returned to the sphere.

Usefulness in Science.   Closely related to order is the value of *usefulness*. If order is sustained by research, then it is useful because it can be applied at other places and other times, the assumption goes. When a theory, no matter how much order it has, ceases to be useful, it is abandoned for another theory of greater usefulness.

Anthropologists in the nineteenth century considered it useful to know if people of different races and social status had different shapes and sizes to their heads. They used calipers to measure head sizes to explain their perceived differences in achievements. They believed that head size represented brain size and, thus, factors such as intelligence, social action, and language.

Today, serious social scientists consider such measurement humorous because the theory that head size determines intelligence has been rejected. There is a similar debate today over whether the Graduate Record Examination (GRE) is a useful predictor of success in graduate school. Thirty years from now, the GRE may be as useless as determining graduate school admission on the basis of hat size.

Prediction in Science. Implied in both order and usefulness is the value of *prediction*. It means that the theory represented in a claim will tell one not merely about the instance under consideration but also it will predict how similar instances will occur. The theory of evolution is a good example of such a claim. It does not merely claim that a particular biological species changes. It predicts that all biological species evolve. It claims that they have evolved, are evolving, and will evolve according to certain principles. It asserts a high level of predictability.

Rationality in Science. Although it is an ambiguous term, *rationality* is the clearest way to explain this value. It relates directly to the assumption that order exists. Abraham Kaplan distinguishes between what he calls "logic-in-use," which describes the actual patterns of thinking used by scientists, and "reconstructed logic," which describes the discourse through which scholars justify their conclusions (8–18). In the process of discovery, says Kaplan, imagination, inspiration, and intuition play enormous roles, but the discoveries must be justified to other scientists by reconstructing the imagination, inspiration, and intuition into a rational explanation that other scientists can follow and test as an intellectually coherent commentary. The rational explanation must provide a set of refined practices based on empirical evidence for the justification of claims.

Knowledge in Science. Nonprofessionals frequently describe science as the search for "scientific truth." Medical science has had a strong influence on this kind of thinking by suggesting that there are certain diseases that it is learning to conquer one by one. Curiously, there is always plenty to work on, even after hundreds of years of conquest. A better term than *scientific truth* for this value is *verifiable knowledge*: an extended explanation based on repeated attempts to justify related claims. Scientists seek knowledge that, when lodged in theories, links to the other values. It gives order to the subject under study and predicts what other useful knowledge may be known. Knowledge, then, is not some once-and-for-all final truth. Rather science, as Toulmin puts it, makes "the course of Nature not just predictable but intelligible—and this has meant looking for rational patterns of connections in terms of which we can make sense of the flux of events" (*The Uses of Argument* 99).

The values of science identified here (order, usefulness, prediction, rationality, and knowledge) only begin to define the scientific value system. In addition, there are adaptations in the value system from one scientific discipline to another. Nonetheless, these five identify the value system of the sphere well enough to be used to contrast it with another major sphere: religion.

Values in Religion

The Judeo-Christian-Islamic tradition of religion is examined in greater detail in Chapter 14. In this chapter, we briefly discuss seven values of argumentation in the religious sphere. Not all religious argumentation will cover all seven values we will discuss here, and other values are sometimes added. These seven, however, reasonably define the theological system: God, authority, human beings, morality, faith, salvation, and the church.

God. The most forceful value in the Judeo-Christian-Islamic theological value system is the concrete value of God. God is understood as an entity of some kind with complete control over the world and all who inhabit it. For some, God controls every action. For others, such as deists, God is the source of natural law who sets the system into motion. In Christianity, God is frequently understood to consist of a trinity—Father, Son, and Holy Ghost—in which the son, Jesus Christ, is seen as a primary source for the understanding of the religion. So, people speak of a "Christ-centered religion" to define the value of God.

The three religions of the Judeo-Christian-Islamic tradition are monotheistic—they believe in one God—although some, such as Christian Trinitarians, have one God in three persons. This one God, therefore, is all-powerful and all knowing. God is usually perceived as an eternal father figure, judge, and provider. There is currently a movement to add a mother figure.

Authority. As we note in Chapter 14, in the religions of the Judeo-Christian-Islamic tradition, the starting point of much religious argumentation is an authoritative figure (God, prophet, pope) or text (the Torah, the Bible, and the Qur'an being the most obvious examples). This explains the desire among religious writers to find the earliest texts, those that are closest to the actual statements and actions of the originators of the religion.

Conflicts over the criteria for judging texts abound in theological argument. Conservative Protestants believe the Bible to be inherently and literally true. For them, almost as important as being "Christ-centered" (the value of God) is that religion be "Bible based" (the value of authority). More liberal Protestants accept the Bible as a metaphor in many cases. Roman Catholicism uses specialized analysis to explain the meaning of biblical texts. For most Christians, the New Testament is more significant than the Old Testament. For Jews, of course, the Torah is the authoritative text. Some groups, such as Roman Catholics and Latter Day Saints, find a pope or prophet to be authoritative in some specialized situations. These differences among interpretive versions clearly illustrate the importance of authority to religious argumentation.

Humans. There is general agreement in the Judeo-Christian-Islamic tradition that humans are more important than other animals. But do humans get this status from nature? From the ability to reason? From their possession of a soul? Thus, a persistent question in religious argumentation is about the basic nature of the human.

Despite all the disagreement about the nature of humans, the religions of this tradition clearly value humans over earth, sea, air, and all other creatures. God loves humans above all others, speaks to humans, designs laws by which humans are to live, and gives dominion to humans over everything else in the world:

> And God blessed them [Adam and Eve], and God said to them, "Be fruitful, and multiply, and fill the earth, and subdue it; and have dominion over the fish of the sea, and over the birds of the air, and over every living thing that moves upon the earth." (Genesis 2:28)

Morality.   Although humans in most of the Judeo-Christian-Islamic tradition are more important than all other creatures in the natural world, they still are subservient to God. They must acknowledge God and follow the commandments God gives them. Thus, a very important value for religious persons is morality and how it is defined. Even people who have no religious affiliations have obligations because the rules of religious morality have been built into the laws and customs of the society. This general value of morality begins with texts such as the Ten Commandments, which contain a series of values that govern the relation of humans to God and to one another.

Faith.   Faith is an instrumental value unique to religion. It extends human reason beyond rational observation. To it is linked the "power of prayer," the ability of the believer to communicate with God. Faith in God, faith in prayer, and faith in authority are vital links between God and humans. Faith provides the important function of answering questions that fill in the gaps of traditional knowledge and reinforces the authority of text and spiritual leader (e.g., is there a God? Does God answer prayer? Is there life after death?). However, one looks at it, faith that allows for this relationship of human to God is a very special and important value in any system of religious argumentation.

Salvation.   For some people, salvation is the most important benefit one receives from religious belief. For others, salvation is less important or even personally nonexistent. For believers in salvation, it answers the question of immortality by not only granting it but also by making it a happy existence in a postexistent state (such as heaven), sometimes with a spiritual oneness with God and sometimes with a physical resurrection in paradise. For some others, it means escape from the horrible eternity of suffering known as hell. Salvation is more than a spiritual condition for those people who believe; it is an earned reward for a lifetime of following the other values in this system.

The Church.   Like salvation, the concrete value of the church is a value to which some religious people give little power. In Islam, Judaism, and much of Protestant Christianity, religious leaders get their status from their ability to gain the adherence of worshippers. Religious leaders are chosen and dismissed by the congregation. The church authority is in the members of an individual congregation.

For Roman Catholics and some other Christian denominations, however, the church interprets the essential texts of the religion, provides an understanding of the traditions of the religion, and administers holy sacraments in an authoritative way. In some ways, the church is still a value, even for those who do not grant it such authority, because the church grants to individuals the right to become a part of something greater than they are. There is a sense in which all members of religions in the Judeo-Christian-Islamic tradition are members of a spiritual church. *Islam, Judaism,* and *Christianity* are terms representing more than a series of values. They see themselves as a fellowship of believers.

This discussion of religious values has been brief, but it points out that any theology is a case that must be built using a value system for interpreting and grading these values. The decisions one makes on one value will affect what is possible for another. Thus, if humans are incapable of making proper decisions, some agency, such as the church or direct fellowship with God, must be available to do so. The nature of God affects the nature of fellowship with God. How one interprets salvation relates to the nature of humans. These are only a few examples of how building a case for a particular theology involves the interrelationship of these values.

The Relation of Science and Religion

We have examined these two spheres of argumentation (science and religion) to illustrate how different two value systems can be. None of the value terms of one are found in the other. Religion, unlike science, has concrete values as four of its seven values (God, authority, humans, the church). In some ways, science has the most abstract value system of all. Its five primary values (order, usefulness, prediction, rationality, and knowledge) are abstract. The only terminal value for science is knowledge and the usual terminal values for religion are God and salvation. How, then, do they coexist? An examination of the relationship between these two very different value systems provides a useful example of how values interact across spheres.

These two value systems have been the subject of controversy for many years. Early disciples of science, such as Copernicus and Galileo, found themselves in disputes with the Roman Catholic Church. In 1633, Galileo was forced to recant the publication of his belief in the Copernican theory that the earth rotates on its axis and, with the other planets in the solar system, revolves around the sun. The basis for judging the Copernican theory a Christian heresy was the authority of the Church and the Bible that, taken literally, says that the sun revolves around the earth (Genesis 114–118; Joshua 10: 12–14). This controversy between religion and science can be extended far beyond the Copernican theory. However, the controversy illustrates at least a clash between the scientific values of rationality and knowledge and the religious values for authority in sacred text, faith, and Church.

For many people, the sharp contrast in value systems between science and religion makes the two fundamentally antagonistic. For a natural system of order, there is the counterpart of God and the centrality of humans. Prediction is opposed by faith and salvation. Rationality is opposed by authority in sacred texts and the interpretation of the church. Accepting one value system can make the other its secondary value system. For instance, deists acknowledge God as a first cause. For them, God created the universe with natural laws, wound it up like a clock, and set it to working. The working of the universe is rational because God's principles are rational. The scientific value system is, therefore, the dominant one for deists because humans are to be scientists continually unraveling those laws. There are no miracles, answered prayers, or moral laws that are not rational and predictable. Faith is in the process, and the church is an institution that helps us to understand this gloriously ordered system.

The second way of using both value systems is to acknowledge the existence of two spheres of argument that can complement one another. Scientific order, rationality, and predictability are maintained and explained as science. God's role with humans, morality, and salvation cannot be explained by science because it is in a different argument sphere. An occasional miracle, for instance when prayer saves someone from a predicted death from disease, is just that—an occasional event. It may be celebrated as an act of God, but it does not refute the essential validity of scientific order. Neither does scientific rationality refute God because God, operating in a sphere where science cannot argue, is seen by the religious person as the first cause of natural law.

Such a separation between spheres is not unusual. The separation of religion and science is one of the most dramatic, having received considerable attention, but the same is true with other spheres. Literary scholarship following a humanistic qualitative orientation can be seen as a different sphere and, therefore, not in conflict with behavioral psychology. Law and morality are frequently separated. Someone may not be seen to have broken the law but to have broken a moral code. Examples abound of people avoiding conflict by separating the values they live by into spheres of argumentation.

However, when spheres of argument are seen to overlap, serious value problems occur. A. J. S. Rayl and K. T. McKinney asked scientists if science proves that God exists. Many argued that the question remains outside the sphere of scientific argumentation, but a few did not. One mathematical physicist said, "If science can't reach God, then God doesn't exist" (44). Such a point of view represents a total commitment to the scientific value system. This can be seen in his further statement: "Nature will tell us what sort of definition we have to use. . . . Physical evidence could greatly alter our view of God, but we need to redefine God in terms of physics, which won't be easy" (44–48).

Statements such as these clearly indicate that this mathematician believes that an argument about anything, even something as total as God, has to be argued by the values of science.

A similar situation occurs in the area of creation science. The Creation Science Association is a research and teaching organization that claims to provide scientific proof through research that the literal six-day creation of the earth stated in Genesis is scientifically correct. However, a careful examination of their arguments shows that the proof is clearly based on textual authority, God, and faith. David Klope shows the relationship of science and religious values in one presentation of the Institute of Creation Research's (ICR) "Worldview":

> In the transcendent portion of the ICR worldview, "creation" and "revelation" have priority over "science," . . . The emphasis in this entire speech is that defense of "creation" comes first from the Bible, and the speech tries to show the ICR as acting in this manner through phrases such as "what we're saying at the Institute for Creation Research is this: look, we have a revelation from God who knows everything. . . ." Although the ICR maintains the value of "science," they are careful to prioritize theology. In this view a "creationist" must first be Biblical. (123–124)

Some people, therefore, can bring these two spheres together, but they do so mostly by acknowledging that each deals with different issues. When spheres come together and claim to deal with the same subject, however, it is clear that argument becomes the unusual case we noted earlier of a direct clash of values.

CONCLUSION

Values are an essential part of the analysis of every argumentative situation. They share with evidence and source credibility the grounds and warrant for a claim. No matter what kind of claim (fact, value, policy) is being argued, decision makers use values to judge whether it is worthy of adherence. A value is a general conception of a desirable mode, means (instrumental), or end (terminal) of action. It is differentiated from a belief, which is a simple statement about a specific situation. Many times, values are openly stated (freedom) or implied in statements about specific beliefs ("people should vote").

Although values are usually treated as positive (freedom), they may be stated in the negative (restraint). They are usually thought of as abstract (freedom), but they can be concrete (the Constitution).

The values and beliefs used in an argumentative situation can be seen as a value system. That is, they work together and define each other's relation to the particular claim being argued. Because values are social as well as personal, decision makers can share them with the arguer. They can, therefore, be used in arguments to gain adherence. To gain adherence, however, decision makers must believe that the values in a particular system are consistent with one another.

There are a number of traditional value systems in the United States. Each of these systems not only has to be seen as having values consistent with one another but they also must be graded. That is, the decision maker must be able to see the hierarchy of values. It has been said that more important than which values are in the system is how each is graded in relation to every other value in the system.

Societies, spheres, and professional groups define ethical systems. These ethical systems indicate what is good and right for that group. They serve as standards to identify correct and incorrect behavior and speech. They are based on values. They convert values into ethical principles by which people and actions are judged.

There are some general principles for the use of values. Values may be found anywhere in an argument, although their use as warrants is probably most important. You can find the values in the arguments of others by using six specific tools discussed in this chapter. At the same time, you need to recognize the limits of value change. Changes in value systems rarely result from adding a new value or eliminating an old one. Most often, changes will come through changing a value's distribution, rescaling it, redeploying it, or restandardizing it in the value system.

The best point of attack on a value system is found by using the procedure suggested in Chapter 5 for analyzing the claims of fact or value: Determine the values, the criteria for judging them, and the grading of them. This usually results in one of three attack points: dispute the criteria, dispute the hierarchy, or dispute both.

All arguments have values in them, but the most effective are those where the values are related to decision makers. However, even well-chosen values are not simply stated; they must be developed through evidence and argument.

All spheres depend on values. This is illustrated by a comparison of science and religion. Scientific argumentation is characterized by the values of order, usefulness, prediction, rationality, and knowledge. Religious argumentation is characterized by the values of God, authority, humans, morality, faith, salvation, and church. These two spheres have frequently been in conflict with one another. There is no overlap in their value systems. Conflicts between them are resolved by making one a secondary value system to the other or by treating the two spheres as having completely different roles.

EXERCISES/PROJECTS

1. Analyze a newspaper or magazine editorial. Look for its stated and unstated, positive and negative, terminal and instrumental, abstract and concrete values. On the basis of your analysis, how would you characterize the value system the writer follows?
2. Using a speech or essay provided by your instructor, diagram some of the key arguments to discover unstated values.
3. From contemporary magazines, collect six or so different picture and written text ads for the same type of product (e.g., pain relievers, perfume, clothing, drinks, automobiles) and observe to what extent a single value system emerges.
4. Note the value differences between two magazines, web sites, or television programs that aim at different audiences (e.g., *People* and *Ebony*, *Sunset* and *Better Homes ad Gardens*, *Playboy* and *Field and Stream*).

Support: Credibility

KEY TERMS

ethos, p. 142
credibility, p. 142
competence, p. 142
trustworthy, p. 143
good will, p. 143
dynamism, p. 143

homophily, p. 142
direct credibility, p. 144
secondary credibility, p. 145
indirect credibility, p. 146
reputation, p. 146

The Great Recession that hit the world in the early part of the twenty-first century created a crisis of confidence that made recovery extremely difficult. Financial institutions, banks, housing lenders, and others were accused of having misled investors by saying investments were sound when they knew that was not true. They sold securities to customers even as they were betting that the securities would soon prove to be almost worthless. Some big institutions made enormous profits as millions of people lost money and some venerable firms went out of business or were bought out by competitors. Rating agencies such as Moody's or Standard and Poor's came under suspicion for having given highly positive ratings to financial products that a reasonable investigation would have revealed to be highly risky. The slow recovery was due, in part, to the fact that people had lost confidence in the leading agencies of the economy, including government. The problem was a profound loss of credibility.

James M. Kouzes and Barry Z. Posner, researchers into business leadership, argue, "Managers, we believe, get other people to do, but leaders get other people to want to do. Leaders do this first of all by being credible. That is the foundation of all leadership. They establish this credibility by their actions" (276). So, in at least one major sphere of argumentation, business, credibility is a major factor. But *credibility*, as Kouzes and Pozner argue, is not "some gift from the gods (as *charisma* is defined) but a set of identifiable (and hence learnable) practices, strategies, and behaviors" (275).

Whereas **credibility** may serve as a claim in argumentation, its most important role is as a means to support a claim, just as evidence (Chapter 7) and values (Chapter 8) do. You will see as you read this chapter that credibility is closely related to evidence and values.

When Aristotle (1991) first defined credibility as one of the three forms of proof, he used the term *ethos*. For Aristotle, *ethos* is "proof" that is generated in the mind of the decision makers "whenever the speech is spoken in such a way as to make the speaker worthy of credence" (38). The likelihood that adherence will be granted is increased, according to Aristotle, as the arguer is perceived as having "practical wisdom, virtue, and good will" toward the listener (121).

It is also worth noting that *ethos* is used to refer to the spirit of a whole culture as well as to individual character. The characteristics that Aristotle defined for the speaker are characteristics that will make the speaker compatible with the group, and these characteristics, "wisdom, virtue, and good will," are values that are approved of by decision makers, at least in Aristotle's day and probably today as well.

CHARACTERISTICS OF CREDIBILITY

Modern social scientists have worked to find an empirical definition for credibility. Although there are differences among their studies, their judgments are not much different from Aristotle's. It is reasonable, therefore, to use Aristotle as a basis and, adapting to modern research on the subject, define *credibility* as *the support for a claim that is developed by the decision makers' perception that the arguer reveals competence, trustworthiness, good will, and dynamism.*

The first thing to observe about this definition is that it is the decision makers' perception that defines an arguer's credibility. When you say that someone has high **credibility**, you mean you find that person credible. Your perception of a person's credibility may also be influenced by the context of the argument. Your friend, your mother, your religious leader, and your professor may all be credible to you but on different subjects at different times. On the other hand, when you are dealing with a person or persons whom you perceive to be similar to you in one or more ways, you may find them more credible. This is called **homophily**. There are some characteristics, then, about decision makers' perceptions that serve as a broad basis for the credibility judgments they make. So, we will examine the most often-perceived characteristics of credibility: competence, trustworthiness, and to a lesser extent, good will and dynamism. And, we will report on recent social science research that finds homophily (similarity) to be a driver of credibility judgments.

Competence and Trustworthiness

A primary dimension that decision makers seek out is competence. A variety of value words have been used since ancient times as synonyms for **competence**: *wisdom, sagacity, reliability, authoritativeness, expertise,* and *qualification.* Commonsense experience would confirm that decision makers find an argument more worthy of adherence when it is advanced by a person they believe competent on the subject.

Persons who are perceived as trustworthy also have high credibility. In the literature on credibility since classical times, other value words have been used to define the meaning of **trustworthy**: *virtue, probity, character, evaluative, honest, sincere*, and *safe*. Common sense is that ideas are more readily accepted from persons you trust.

Good Will and Dynamism

The first two dimensions of credibility—competence and trustworthiness—are discussed by all writers. Two other factors—each of which is accepted by some and not by other writers—are *good will* and *dynamism*. Value terms such as *open-minded, objective, impartial, kind, friendly*, and *caring* have been used to characterize the **good will** dimension. **Dynamism**, the only one of the four terms to be strictly modern, is characterized by words such as *showmanship, enthusiasm, inspiration*, and *forcefulness*.

It is easy to see how the research might have shown either good will or dynamism to be weak or nonexistent as separate dimensions. Good will could easily be classified as a subcategory of trustworthiness. People find trustworthy those persons whom they perceive to have good will toward them. Likewise, dynamism, when it functions in a positive manner, may well be a judgment about competence. Research shows that dynamism in a speaker increases audience retention of an idea (Schweitzer). A dynamic speaker would also appear more self-assured, and self-assurance conveys the impression that the persons who posses it "know what they are talking about." Even written argument that is direct in stating a claim with a sense of authority carries with it a dynamic quality.

Movie and television stars are sometimes reported in the news for bad behavior which could lead people to reject them. But when they appear in films, their acting talent makes us forget about any off-screen hijinks, and we accept them as the characters they are portraying. They can play pirates, ship captains, lovers, and even geniuses and we grant credibility to each character.

However, dynamism has a feature not possessed by competence, trustworthiness, or even good will. Dynamism may be perceived negatively. The overly enthusiastic salesperson who calls at dinnertime promising a way for you to save money on your car insurance and persists even when you aren't interested is dynamic ("You mean you don't want to save money?") but not credible to many people.

Although individuals' definitions of credibility vary, there is enough agreement to identify decision makers' judgments of trustworthiness, competence, and good will as support for a claim. With some reservation about overdoing it, dynamism also serves as a credibility factor in support of a claim.

Homophily (Similarity)

Homophily, or the degree of similarity you perceive between yourself and the person making the argument, has been considered a factor in persuasion for many years (McCroskey et al.). It is claimed that the more you find the arguer to be similar to you, the more you are likely to accept the argument. Research in health communication has examined the way people use the Internet in seeking health information. This has raised a potential conflict among dimensions of credibility. Traditionally, people have looked to health professionals for medical advice because they were considered to be most competent. But, on second thought, people have always talked among themselves about health concerns and often followed that advice because they thought it came from people who were trustworthy and had their goodwill in mind. Moreover, doctors have been perceived as notoriously distant, hypertechnical, and uncommunicative—thereby damaging their credibility (Harris).

Online sources for health information range from, "Web sites run by organizations, home pages owned by individual doctors, online support groups where people actively exchange health information, and blogs authored by health advocates, caregivers, or those pursuing self-help" (Hu and Sundar). One study found results that led to this claim: "We argue that homophily is really the factor that grounds credibility and drives the whole persuasive process in the context of online health information" (Wang et al.). This may be unique to online health information seeking, but it suggests that homophily is involved in credibility judgments more generally.

FORMS OF CREDIBILITY

What decision makers know about an arguer's **reputation** will influence their perceptions of the claim. For instance, at the first meeting of your argumentation class, most of the members of the class probably know little about you. Your reputation is probably minimal. As time goes on in the class, they know more and more about you. You develop a reputation. An arguer's reputation is important to credibility but cannot be changed instantly. Therefore, what you do to develop credibility in your argument is most important. Aristotle, when he discussed credibility, did not include a person's reputation, position, or actions outside the argument. For him, *ethos* was a product of what happened in the argument. The three forms of credibility that can be built into actual arguments are direct, secondary, and **indirect credibility**.

Direct Credibility

The most obvious form of credibility is what we call **direct credibility**. This is the kind of credibility that you develop by making direct statements about yourself.

Every arguer brings a reputation to the decision making process. The president of the United States, the Speaker of the House, a company executive, an embezzler, a musical performer, and a prominent athlete each has a reputation: the opinion that decision makers have about a person's credibility before that person begins to argue. Advertisements for products frequently feature celebrities because of the images they have before they make the argument: their reputations.

Hawai'i is a state separated from the rest of the world both by miles of Pacific Ocean and a distinct culture. Andrew Gomes, writing in the *Honolulu Advertiser*, says, "Being perceived as 'local' is a sensitive and valuable quality for companies doing business in Hawai'i. It's the Good Housekeeping Seal of kama'aina" (a true resident, in contrast to outsiders). This is so, Gomes reports, because the Native Hawaiian host culture is joined by an ethnically diverse population, all of whom have grown up together. If the person or company advancing an argument can provide direct evidence of local roots, credibility is likely to follow.

When Clint Arnoldus, the chief executive of Central Pacific Bank, criticized rival First Hawaiian Bank as being less than local, First Hawaiian Bank's chief executive Walter Dods responded giving direct evidence of his local credentials. He said he was born and raised in Hawai'i, was a graduate of a prominent local high school (Saint Louis), and that, unlike Arnoldus, he had not just gotten off the boat from California. His final proof was a challenge to Mr. Arnoldus to a debate in pidgin, a language that combines bits and pieces of many languages and is not likely to be spoken by anyone who is not kama'aina. Arnoldus did not accept the challenge.

Accounting firms were among the most damaged entities in business and financial scandals early in this century. Some accountants, who were supposed to be the guardians of honesty, accuracy, and fairness, were exposed as co-conspirators in dishonest dealings. PriceWaterhouseCoopers, wanting to distance themselves from the discredited accounting firms, engaged in direct credibility through an advertising supplement in *Business Week*. Under a heading of "truth as a business opportunity," they list a series of shareholder rights such as meaningful information, explanations of numbers in plain language, and the facts managers use to make significant decisions. Considering that many companies are being sued by shareholders, the accounting firm says, some might argue that less rather than more openness is called for. "Not a bad argument," they reply to their own question, "but not a good argument if the overall objective is to regain public confidence." "What would companies get for all this honesty?" the ad continues. "A clear conscience and an opportunity to build credibility and trust with the investor." By directly associating themselves with these recommendations for building business credibility, PriceWaterhouseCoopers builds its own credibility as well.

Secondary Credibility

We call another form of credibility **secondary credibility**. The arguer uses another person's credibility as the grounds for the argument, thus the term *secondary*. By associating the credibility of someone else with yourself, you strengthen your own credibility.

Online health information seeking reflects a complex process of assigning credibility. A 2005 Pew survey revealed that more than a third of respondents believe that information on the Internet cannot be trusted (Wang et al.). So, how do people select health information they feel they can trust? They use primary credibility by judging the credentials of the person or persons originally presenting the information. Then, research has found, people heavily rely on Web sites, which are typically edited selectively as opposed to blogs, home pages, or the Internet in general, which reflect the choices of single individuals (Hu and Sundar 121). It is the secondary credibility of the editorial selection by reliable organizations that creates trust.

A problem inexperienced arguers frequently miss is that credibility is not enhanced for decision makers simply because the argument is supported by a number of well-known people and agencies. Prominent people are not necessarily credible. The National Fluid Milk Processor Promotion Board sponsors ads that argue that people should drink milk. Each ad features a celebrity with a milk mustache and the slogan, "Got milk?" Athlete David Beckham, actress Elizabeth Hurley, Superman, and other celebrities were featured in the ad campaign. The celebrities drew our attention to the ads, but the real question was whether they did anything to increase milk consumption. A study published by Milk ProCon.org entitled, "Milk Consumption Compared to Milk Advertising, 1978–2005," revealed that milk consumption fell steadily during the ad campaign and did not vary as more or less money was spent on advertising.

Think of the reputation the quoted person has with decision makers. You may want to review the discussion in Chapter 7 about testimony evidence. At this point, you should be able to see the close connection between evidence and credibility as forms of support for a claim. Secondary credibility is established from the testimony of sources the decision makers respect, not necessarily from the testimony of well-known sources.

Indirect Credibility

Unlike direct and secondary credibility, you develop indirect credibility without using the testimony of authorities or direct personal statements about your experiences that illustrate your trustworthiness, competence, or good will. **Indirect credibility** is developed by the way you develop, support, and argue your claims. The evidence and values you use influence decision makers' perceptions about you. The more effectively you argue, the more credible you become. This is sometimes called message credibility.

Indirect credibility is probably the most forceful kind of credibility. Although decision makers might rate you lower for speaking openly about your qualifications, they will not rate you down for making an argument that gains adherence. In a sense, then, this entire book is about how to gain indirect credibility.

GENERAL PRINCIPLES FOR THE USE OF CREDIBILITY

The credibility you generate to support your claims—direct, secondary, or indirect—can play an important part in the response you get. However, there are no easy rules for how you should use it because this changes as decision makers and spheres change. Like beauty, it is in the eye of the beholder. Still, there are some general principles of credibility that apply to most situations.

Develop Credibility from Reputation

Reputation is the credibility you have with decision makers before you argue. It may be influenced by the success you are perceived to have (Andersen and Clevenger 73) and by the perception that you are from the same group as the decision makers (Andersen 220; Myers and Goldberg 174–179).

O. J. Simpson, who was acquitted of the murder of his wife and her male friend many years ago, decided to publish a book under the title *If I Did It*. It was not to be a confession but a hypothetical account of how he might have committed the crimes. When the public learned of this plan, many were outraged at his seeking to profit from tragedy, and they criticized the publisher, who decided to cancel the book. His editor at the publishing house of HarperCollins, Judith Regan, said, "I made the decision to publish this book, and to sit face to face with the killer, because I wanted him, and the men who broke my heart and yours, to tell the truth . . . and to amend their lives. Amen" (Carr). Simpson's credibility, already low, merely dropped further, particularly after he was convicted of robbery in Las Vegas. If Casey Anthony, who was found not guilty in the murder of her 3-year-old daughter in 2011 to the outrage of the blogosphere, tries to make money out of the case, she will be as roundly condemned as O. J.

Difficulty occurs when arguers come to the argumentation situation with little credibility—not because they are unworthy of credibility, but because it is not recognized by decision makers. What we have said thus far about reputation would seem to at least reinforce half of the line from an old song, "The rich get richer and the poor get poorer."

A person who comes to an argumentative situation with a favorable reputation in the area of the argument has an advantage over one who does not. Yet, the person with a good reputation can make mistakes to damage his or her credibility. So, it is important to reinforce your good reputation with decision makers.

Even if your reputation is limited, it can be improved. You must make special efforts, at least indirectly and with the use of secondary credible sources, to enhance your credibility. It is not uncommon for arguers to introduce statements of direct credibility about themselves that tend to increase credibility, if they are not too self-congratulatory (Andersen 228; Ostermeier).

Men's Health is a magazine that caters to young men who perceive themselves (or want to be perceived) as masculine, adventurous, sexy, and daring. In a section called, "Men's Health Challenge—We Dare You to Try This," Bill Stump, under the title "Scull Session," wants to challenge readers to, "Leave the silly canoe at home this weekend. It's time to row a real boat." To develop his own reputation as willing to take a challenge, he begins his article by reporting his own experience: "The jockstrap full of cold river water actually relaxed me. I was learning to scull—a 50-cent word for rowing a $5,000 boat—and had been preoccupied with the thought of falling in" (103). He goes on to detail his own learning experience, which did not turn out so bad, and ends with a set of instructions for his readers to follow, his credibility strengthened by the implied, "If I can do it, so can you."

Arguers' reputations can be enhanced in a formal situation by the way they are introduced (Andersen and Clevenger 64; Haiman). For instance, the fact that Bill Stump was writing an article in this self-proclaimed "guy magazine," was writing under the subtitle "We Dare You to Try This," and in his first sentence used a "guy" term (*jockstrap*) introduced him to the reader as a man's man.

Take stock of your reputation. It is the starting point of your credibility. You can enhance it even if it is minimal. Your reputation is a benchmark that helps you to determine what you must do in your argument to enhance your credibility.

Be Sincere

Sincerity is probably the most commonly mentioned characteristic of credibility. It would seem a simple rule that to build credibility one should be sincere, but there is clear evidence that sincerity cannot be determined by decision makers (Andersen and Clevenger; Eisinger and Mills). But people believe they can judge sincerity or insincerity.

In preparation for the 2012 presidential election, a group of Republicans was competing for the opportunity to oppose President Barack Obama. At one point, the front runner was former Massachusetts Governor Mitt Romney who worked diligently to convince people of his sincerity. However, he was constantly confronted with an apparent shift in position regarding health care as he attacked the Obama administration health law and sought to distance himself from a similar plan in Massachusetts enacted when he was governor. Inconsistency, he found, is associated with insincerity in the minds of many people.

We are not saying that you should not be sincere. We have already noted that *sincerity* is frequently used as a synonym for *trustworthiness*. You need to be aware that sincerity alone does not mean that you will be perceived as sincere. However, your sincerity is a first step to convincing others that you are sincere.

Take care to avoid obvious signs that you mean to manipulate the decision makers. When you have a bias, and it is known, a clear and honest identification of it may actually advance your credibility. Decision makers usually put greater trust in the person who openly admits a bias. It is the decision makers' discovery of covert bias that is most damaging to sincerity (Mills and Aronson).

Identify with Decision Makers' Values

Perhaps the strongest means of indirect credibility is the arguer's identification with the values of the decision makers. A more complete discussion of social values and their role in argumentation is in Chapter 8.

Unless you choose to speak or write on noncontroversial points ("Motorists should slow down in school zones," "Cancer is a dangerous disease," "Everyone should have a friend"), you will find controversy. Indeed, as we have observed before, you cannot have argumentation without issues and decisions to be made. Those issues must be addressed as decision makers see them.

When you address issues, you will be taking some positions with which some decision makers disagree. That result is to be expected, and you will lose credibility if you try to agree with the audience on every point. Such a strategy will be transparent, and your sincerity will be questioned. A chameleon-like approach is in sharp contrast to what we mean by identification with decision makers' values.

Remember that audiences are collections of individuals. You can define a group of decision makers as an entity ("This is a Republican audience," "This is an audience of concerned parents," "This audience is pro-choice"), but this is *your* definition. The members are still individuals, and though they have some things in common, they are not identical. Furthermore, many audiences are segmented. Because it is "a Republican audience" does not mean they all agree on taxes, education, welfare, or foreign policy.

You must, of course, search for common ground with the majority of decision makers. Find as many points as you can on which to agree. Most important, show that your proposal is in keeping with their values (Reinard 44). Or construct a system of values showing clearly that, although your proposal is contrary to some of their values, it is still consistent with others, and those other values are more important. In addition, show that those who would oppose your position have opted for a misleading system of values.

Consider how different members of your audience might respond to values, and address the various segments. In this hypothetical argument for building a new community medical clinic, the values are linked to segments of the audience:

A new medical clinic should be established in Porterville because it would bring new medical specialties into the town that are not now there (health—medical people). It will provide services for people who find it difficult to drive to other cities (safety, health—elderly). People from small surrounding communities will come to town and will shop here instead of going to Fresno or Bakersfield (commerce—businesspeople). The new center will open up fifty new jobs (employment—youth).

None of these values is likely to be questioned by any segment of the audience, yet each has a particular appeal to a particular segment. Identifying with decision makers' values can be complex at times but usually can be done without damage to your credibility.

The use of strong value-intensive arguments, in which heavy and repeated use of directly stated values dominates the argument, may have a negative effect on credibility. The research on fear appeals (e.g., appeals to fear of murder, rape, or mutilation) illuminates what probably happens with all value-intensive appeals. Such appeals, it seems, are accepted only from an arguer with high credibility. Strong value-intensive appeals may boomerang when used by an arguer with modest credibility (Hewgill and Miller). Credibility is weakened when it is invested in values that decision makers question and when it is used in too many value-intensive arguments.

Use Evidence to Build Credibility

Evidence appears to strengthen credibility, especially of a low-credibility arguer, and particularly if the evidence is not known to the decision makers (McCroskey 175). This idea is easy to understand. A highly credible arguer is much more likely than an arguer with lower credibility to be effective using assertion without evidence.

An interesting example of this is a speech by Alan Greenspan, former chair of the U.S. Federal Reserve Board, to an economic conference in Washington, DC. He used no direct or secondary credibility. His only mention of himself was at the opening of the speech when he told what he would do in the speech ("I will offer my perspective. . . . [and] I will delve into some of the pitfalls. . . .") or when calling attention to his previous stated beliefs ("As I have indicated on previous occasions . . ."). But Alan Greenspan had a tremendous reputation on the economy and he was one of very few people who did not need to build credibility.

People are less likely to wonder, "Where did you get that idea?" or "How do you know that is true if you have high credibility?" Consequently, evidence becomes more important to a person with less credibility. One study shows that with apathetic decision makers, it takes twice as much evidence for an arguer with modest credibility to produce a movement toward adherence as it does for an arguer with high credibility (Lashbrook et al. 262). Furthermore, evidence in the form of examples that are close to decision makers' experiences are more believable and, therefore, are more likely to enhance perceived credibility.

An authoritative source connected to an argument will make that argument more believable. Studies show that an authoritative group has higher credibility than an authoritative individual (Andersen and Clevenger 71; Myers and Goldberg; Ostermeier; Warren). An interesting phenomenon known as a *sleeper effect* seems to operate in the use of authoritative sources as secondary credibility. A source with high credibility tends to produce a strong initial change in peoples' views. In time, that initial change weakens and a lower source gains in credibility (Andersen and Clevenger 67). This suggests that the credibility of the source has immediate impact, but for long-range adherence, the quality of the argument and the evidence take on greater significance. The lesson you could learn from all this is that you need to build your competence with evidence and argument that your decision makers respect.

Use Organization to Build Credibility

Well-organized cases may not increase credibility, but disorganized ones clearly weaken it, especially for low-credibility arguers. Furthermore, showing disorganization by using phrases such as "I should have mentioned this earlier" creates the impression that speakers are disorganized and, therefore, less credible (Baker; McCroskey and Mehrley; Sharp and McClung).

In Chapter 6 ("Case Building"), we discussed a number of different ways that a case can be organized. It is clear that the perception of disorganization can damage credibility. But what makes argumentation appear organized? One characteristic is that the decision makers know explicitly what claims are being made. When claims are vague, decision makers restructure information to correlate with their beliefs, even perhaps in the opposite direction of that intended by the speaker (Tubbs 18). First, therefore, explicit claims are preferred.

Second, a small group of well-developed arguments is preferable to a large number of unsupported arguments. Unsupported arguments invite decision makers to concentrate on their weaknesses. Well-developed arguments imply greater competence on your part. They also should be the arguments that are closest to decision makers' experience and knowledge. Thus, you are seen as having developed the most important issues.

Finally, show that you understand issues by acknowledging both sides of an argument. Even among decision makers who tend to disagree with your proposition, such two-sided argumentation creates the impression that you are fair and are not "dodging the issues." It is true that some decision makers who already support the arguers' proposition and who are less well informed respond better to being shown only one side. However, showing both sides has better long-term impact. The arguer is seen as being fair, and credibility is increased. This approach also provides the basis for what is called "inoculation." Two-sided argumentation strengthens the decision makers' resistance to later refutation. This has been demonstrated in a variety of situations, including public arguments and advertising (Pfau 27–28).

Recent research puts a more nuanced interpretation on the instruction to use a two-sided argument. Martin Eisend reports that when decision makers are under a cognitive load (are engaged in other cognitive tasks or otherwise distracted by such things as time pressure), "a two sided message clearly enhances brand attitudes compared to a one-sided message" (4). This is not so true for decision makers who are not under a cognitive load. Also, in two-sided presentations that do not seem voluntary, such as tobacco companies reporting that smoking is hazardous to health or that a prescription drug has some negative side effects, there is no credibility enhancement. People tend to see these as required admissions for which the arguer gets no credit.

Argue Issues, Not People

It is easy, when argumentation leads to sharp differences of opinion, to believe that your opponent is not fair, is biased, or has ulterior motives. Resist this tendency. Center your argument on your claims; let *your* credibility show. Attempts to attack the credibility of an opponent have been shown to weaken, not strengthen, credibility. In one study, persons who initiated such attacks were seen by decision makers as less credible with less acceptable arguments, whereas the credibility of the person attacked was rated higher (Infante et al. 1993, 188–189).

This phenomenon can be seen in political argumentation where people who raise claims about an opponent's credibility are found to be less credible, even with decision makers who agree with them on issues. Notice that most successful politicians carefully qualify attacks on opponents' credibility, emphasizing their records and positions on the issues. Direct attacks on a candidate's credibility are usually made by others, not the candidates themselves.

Understand Credibility as Dynamic

You must realize that the process of argumentation is dynamic. Decision makers reject or accept your arguments based on the interaction of credibility, values, evidence, and arguments that are both internal and external to the argumentation.

After studying two decades of credibility research, Jesse Delia concludes that the lack of consistent results can be explained in part by the failure to measure what takes place during the argumentative exchange itself. He says, "It is necessary to recognize that the communicator's image will, at least in part, consist of constructions made during the interaction itself" (375). He goes on to claim that the decision to grant credibility to someone involves mental processes in which slight changes in the situation, for example the addition of another person to the discussion, may result in a decision to raise or lower that person's credibility.

A friend had just about convinced you to see a movie that she thought was great when another friend whom you consider an expert joins the conversation to point out the many flaws in the picture. Credibility granted on the basis of the first friend's opinion dissolves in the presence of an expert (Delia 375).

Decision makers are not given neat choices between highly competent and trustworthy arguers who show good will and are dynamic, versus their opposites. Thus, credibility is a composite of responses to the dimensions, and it may change even as the message is being received. Readers may know nothing of an author, but as they read a book they develop an appreciation for the author's competence based on what they have read. Similarly, experience with an arguer can change the trustworthiness dimension. To complicate matters further, there is reason to believe that, for given decision makers, low credibility is not simply the opposite of high credibility but a new configuration of dimensions (Schweitzer and Ginsburg).

The whole process of decision making, from the highest level down through the single minor argument, constantly changes in the interaction among the elements that make it up. What we see when we talk about particular functions of credibility are arbitrarily frozen bits of information. Decision makers see a generalization or a movement in argumentation in which all the factors are seen together and simultaneously. They are always related to a particular argument, the arguers, the circumstance, and the decision makers. In politics, this is called *image*.

Your reputation is a benchmark of your credibility. No matter how limited it may be with the decision makers, it is the basis on which credibility is built. To make your argument more credible to decision makers, be sincere; identify with their values, use your evidence and organization to build credibility; and argue issues, not people. In all of your plans to enhance your credibility and use it to support your argumentation, keep in mind that credibility is a dynamic process, not a series of set rules.

SPHERE DEPENDENCE OF CREDIBILITY

Credibility is a dynamic process that must be seen in relation to particular circumstances, so different spheres of argumentation develop various standards for credibility. General principles such as those we have discussed will hold for most situations. They are modified, however, by the particular sphere in which the argumentation occurs.

Gary Cronkhite and Jo Liska have observed that credibility involves not only the inferred attributes that decision makers give to a particular source of an argument but also the specific subject matter and differing criteria of source acceptability. This point of view corresponds closely to our contention that credibility is influenced by the sphere of argumentation in which it operates.

You will recall that we defined a sphere of argumentation as a group of persons whose patterns of communicative behaviors are used in the production and evaluation of argumentation. Credibility is subject to those criteria on which people operating in a particular context or purpose agree.

Spheres are oriented around common needs, purposes, or what Stephen Toulmin calls the ultimate purpose, "doing what there is there to be done" (1972, 485). We have defined ultimate purpose as what you are ultimately trying to accomplish. In a television hospital drama, a young woman is told that she must have a mastectomy or die. It is unfair. "Why me?" is her reasonable response. But this is a question that medicine cannot answer. It has its own evidence, values, and ways of arguing that define its sphere of knowledge. The physician has tests that show the breast tumor is malignant, and medical knowledge indicates that the only solution is to remove it surgically. The only alternative she has to death or surgery, he says, is a faith healer. It is clear that he is not serious about that alternative. The young woman eventually relies on the credibility of the physicians and has the operation.

In another part of the same drama, the hospital attorney questions a surgeon's decision to do a controversial brain operation. The physician tells the attorney he is not a doctor and is not qualified to make such a judgment. The attorney argues that he must defend the hospital from malpractice suits. Here, in one hour, three spheres are introduced: medicine, religion, and law, all with different ways of arguing and different standards of credibility. Cronkhite and Liska claim that arguers who show promise of helping spheres do "what there is there to be done" or to achieve what they are trying to accomplish will be granted high credibility. As you may have guessed, if you didn't see the drama, in this television show, the highest credibility goes to those who know and act in the medical sphere.

Although competence, trustworthiness, good will, and dynamism may be general terms that cover all uses of credibility as support, they will look different from one sphere to another. What may be competence to a scientist will differ from competence in a law court, politics, or on popular television. The three areas of credibility, and how spheres influence them, that we will examine here, are the arguers' reputation, secondary credibility, and indirect credibility.

The Reputation of the Arguer

Some spheres, such as science, have firm definitions of who is competent. A beginning sign is the possession of advanced degrees (usually the doctorate) in the specific science being argued. Increased competence is assumed when a scientist's research is published in prestigious refereed journals, rewarded with research grants, and cited by other researchers. In the sphere of law, an individual or group's status alone increases credibility. For example, a decision by the U.S. Supreme Court is more credible, and has more persuasive value, than a decision by a lower court.

Consider the debate between scientists and religionists over the Genesis story of creation. Scientists with all the necessary credentials argue that the biblical story of the earth's creation in seven days is inaccurate because it conflicts with the theory of evolution and the evidence of science. Some groups, such as the Institute for Creation Research, have organized to argue for the scientific validity of the biblical account. Their members, who call themselves creation scientists, argue that scientific evidence supports the biblical account of creation.

They have degrees in science, and they make arguments based on the analysis of scientific data. For some people, they have the reputation of scientists because of their professions and the fields in which they have their degrees. But for the established scientific community, their reputations are suspect because of the nature of their research and their lack of credentials. Why? Some have only masters' degrees, and those with doctorates have degrees in applied fields of engineering or mineral science, rather than basic research-oriented fields such as physics or genetics, and they have no record of refereed research (Klope 124). They are, therefore, seen by those in the sphere of traditional science as not having competence.

Secondary Credibility in Spheres

Much of what we have noted about reputation holds as well for secondary credibility. When an arguer uses the credibility of others to support claims, those others need to be seen as credible by the standards of the sphere of the decision makers. Scientists acting as scientists need to be told about other scientists who support their views.

Lawyers frequently support their arguments with the testimony of people who are experts: psychiatrists, physicians, forensic experts, psychologists who study eye-witnesses, and professors of communication whose research area is freedom of speech. There are areas, however, where credibility takes a serious shift and one of them is in the court of law.

Reluctant witnesses, in most situations, are not considered trustworthy. If you pressure a reluctant friend to tell you something against his or her will, the potential for a distorted story is great. Such a person has a bias, so to speak; but reluctant testimony is believable in a law court. The person giving it is forced by the potential of legal penalty to testify against personal biases and interests.

Secondary credibility is not simply a product of persons. Institutions also have credibility as a part of the evidence they provide. *The New York Times, The Washington Post*, and the *Los Angeles Times* are respected newspapers that lend their reputations to those who write for them and those who quote them.

In business, the *Wall Street Journal* and *Forbes* magazine have great credibility, although the fact that the *Wall Street Journal* is owned by Rupert Murdoch's media conglomerate has weakened its credibility. In 2011, Murdoch's London-based paper, *News of the World*, was exposed for hacking into personal cell phones of crime victims, important people, and even the royal family. Murdoch had to shut the paper down because its credibility was fatally damaged, and this raised questions about all of his empire.

In the sphere of humanistic scholarship, other institutional publications such as the *American Historical Review* or the *Publication of the Modern Language Association* (PMLA) are more powerful sources of secondary credibility.

An interesting source of credibility in the human and social sciences is the number of times a particular piece of research is cited by others. For instance, the *Citation Index* provides a record of how many times a particular research article is cited and in what sources. The understanding is that research is more valuable if it is used by others who publish in the most prestigious journals.

Indirect Credibility in Spheres

Arguers gain credibility from all they do in making the argument. All that we have said about the influence of spheres of argument on evidence and values applies here. For instance, we noted that hearsay evidence is usually not admissible in a court of law and its use will decrease the credibility of a lawyer who tries to enter it. If the lawyer attempts this too often, the competency of the lawyer will be questioned by the judge. But in interpersonal argument, where such rules are not established, arguers frequently increase their credibility because they have heard the report from a prestigious secondary source.

The use of values and evidence appropriate to a sphere supports the claims of arguers and provides indirect credibility for the arguer. You will learn as you study and become expert in your chosen profession how decision makers assign credibility in that sphere.

CONCLUSION

People give adherence to arguments because they perceive them as reasonable, as employing values with which they agree, and as coming from a credible individual or group. Credibility has an important role in argumentation. It may serve as a claim in its own right, but most often it serves as support. It is generally considered to be developed by the decision makers' perception that the arguer is competent and trustworthy and reveals good will and dynamism.

There are three forms of credibility in arguments: direct credibility, used when arguers make direct statements about themselves designed to increase credibility; secondary credibility, from associating another's credibility with the argument; and indirect credibility, when the argument is developed in a way that makes the arguer more believable. Reputation adds to the likelihood of winning adherence, but only the first three forms of credibility can be directly controlled by the arguer at the time of any specific argumentation. Homophily or perceived similarity between arguer and decision maker can generate credibility.

Credibility is very changeable because it is so related to the perceptions of the decision makers. However, there are some general principles for the use of credibility. You should use whatever reputation you have and build on it to develop credibility. Be sincere in expressing your own ideas. Identify yourself with the decision makers' values. Use evidence and organization to build credibility; argue issues, not people; and recognize that credibility, like argumentation, is a dynamic process that is changed by what happens in the argumentative exchange itself.

Credibility will be defined differently by decision makers in different spheres. Reputations are established by criteria that are different, in medicine, religion, and law, for instance. Credibility is given to the person believed capable of "doing what there is there to be done" in a particular sphere. Reputation will be built by different credentials in different spheres. Secondary and indirect credibility will differ from sphere to sphere.

EXERCISES/PROJECTS

1. Spend an evening watching television, reading magazines, or surfing websites with a note pad in hand. Write down all the ways you can find that advertising agencies work to build credibility for their products. Engage in a discussion with others in class who have done the same. How well did what you see correspond to what is discussed in this chapter? Did you find additional principles about credibility not mentioned in this chapter?

2. Do a series of searches on the Internet. Record the first items that come up in each search. Then, do some research to find out whether it is likely that the position of the item was influenced by payments to the search engine. Now, make a determination of how your perception of credibility is or is not influenced by knowing it was a paid position.

3. Do another Internet search this time in preparation of an argument you will make in a class project. Evaluate the credibility of all the items you want to include in your argument. How did you decide on these credibility decisions? How will you help the audience grant high credibility to these sources when you use them in your argument?

Refutation

KEY TERMS

faction, p. 156
processes, p. 157
cooperative, p. 157
framework, p. 159
assessment, p. 159
critical decision making, p. 160
decision makers, p. 163
goals, p. 163
presumption, p. 164
burden of proof, p. 164
viable constructive position, p. 166

framebreaking, p. 168
momentum, p. 169
support, p. 169
probing, p. 171
questioning, p. 171
defense of the status quo, p. 166
defense of the status quo with minor
    repair, p. 166
counterplan, p. 166
flowsheet, p. 172

Criticism is inherent in critical decision making, and *refutation* is the term we use to describe the process through which one person or **faction** (group of people) involved in a decision criticizes arguments advanced by another person or faction. The criticism may be addressed to other members of the same faction, to members of other factions, or to decision makers who are not a part of any faction.

THE PROCESS OF REFUTATION

Although it is often useful to say that every issue has two sides, our concept of refutation embraces the idea of many factions subscribing to some point of view or advocating one decision over another. Refutation may need to move in several directions at once.

Some commentators have characterized refutation as a destructive process: one side tearing down the arguments of the other in a game of repartee. In our view, refutation is a constructive process. Just as the sculptor must chip away stone and smooth over rough places to produce a work of art, critical decision makers must put their arguments to the most severe tests possible to make the best decisions. Gordon R. Mitchell, in a study of attempts to improve intelligence reports through a form of competitive debate, describes the CIA process as seeking to "scrub the arguments" (160). This is a metaphor for refutation.

It is in this vein that Douglas Ehninger and Wayne Brockriede characterize debate as a cooperative enterprise. They say a debater is "not a propagator who seeks to win unqualified acceptance for a predetermined point of view while defeating an opposing view" (vii). Instead, they say refutation serves an investigative purpose in the search for the best possible decision.

The concept of refutation as cooperative and constructive becomes clearer when we call attention to fundamental **processes** that have been socially constructed over centuries of practice. In critical decision making, refutation implies the following minimum essential principles:

---

1. All interested parties are given fair notice of an impending decision so that they can prepare their responses.
2. Each faction has an equal opportunity to be heard.
3. Each faction grants the others the right to examine and criticize its arguments, including access to supporting persons and materials.
4. Decision makers hear arguments only in the presence of other interested parties.
5. People are not decision makers in their own causes.
6. Each faction accepts the delay of the final decision until the critical process has taken place.
7. All factions agree to accept the final decision no matter how far removed it is from their preference.

| FIGURE 10.1

In Chapter 11, we will discuss a view of fallacies that is based on rules such as these. The theory is that any action that impedes progress toward a critical decision is a fallacy, and violating such rules does impede progress.

The constructive and ultimately **cooperative** character of refutation is evident in some spheres such as legislation, law, and science. People often become impatient with legislative decision making as Democrats and Republicans debate each other, constantly finding weaknesses in the other's positions, but they accept that such delay is a price well worth paying in the interest of making critical decisions. Totalitarian government operates much faster, but most people prefer the "agreement to disagree" that characterizes partisan legislation.

In law, attorneys are instructed to disagree and criticize each others' claims in the overall cooperative search for justice. Failure to do their best to refute the opposition is a violation of legal ethics.

In scholarship, the presentation of research findings at conventions and in journals is only one phase in ongoing criticism. To be open to refutation, indeed to seek it out, is the very essence of scholarship in the cooperative search for knowledge.

Refutation as we use it in this book must be seen in contrast to many practices that reject opposing viewpoints uncritically. The history of political decision making is filled with examples of governments silencing the opposition by putting leaders in jail, exile, or graves. *McCarthyism* denotes uncritical rejection of opposing ideas through accusation and intimidation. A criticism of current politicians suggests they are more interested in securing their jobs, their political power, and their political philosophies than making decisions that best serve the nation and its citizens. When this happens, when even a minority of members in, for example, the U.S. Senate can prevent a critical decision being made for uncritical reasons, they behave much like totalitarian leaders.

Political commentators show themselves to be uninterested in critical interaction. They use their positions to talk over or cut off callers with whom they disagree, and then the audience hears the host's side of the issue when the caller has no further chance to speak. Professors who silence students' opinions are equally disinterested in critical behavior.

Refutation can be most unpleasant when it identifies weaknesses in ideas you believe in fervently, and many people lack the courage to listen to it. That is uncritical behavior.

In this chapter and the next, we set out basic processes of critical behavior. We cannot provide a "manual," and there are no litmus or pH tests of argument available, but we do provide a sequence of considerations and potential strategies from which to draw and adapt to each decision.

APPROACHING REFUTATION

Refutation requires *the open expression of disagreement with an argument made by someone else.* Social rules in force in many cultures discourage such expressions. It is commonly considered impolite to question or challenge others, and linguists say people have a preference for agreement. Scott Jacobs and Sally Jackson say that in interpersonal argument this preference for agreement operates like a presumption in favor of the validity of what others have said. Because of this, "disagreement requires some compelling rationale, something definite enough and significant enough to overcome this presumption" (235–236). Jacobs and Jackson say that refutation is not a general attitude of skepticism, but the application of a specific argument to a specific decision.

A general attitude of skepticism may be a useful approach to refutation at times, but incessant challenging of others' statements can be obnoxious. Benjamin Franklin reports in his autobiography that challenging and refuting almost everything others say can be an ego-building practice for bright youngsters, but it should be set aside with maturity:

> I found this method safest for myself and very embarrassing to those against whom I used it but gradually [I] left it. For, if you would inform, a positive and dogmatical manner in advancing your sentiments may provoke contradiction and prevent a candid attention. (25–26)

Franklin concludes his discussion of this phase of his childhood with this quote from Alexander Pope: "Men should be taught as if you taught them not, And things unknown propos'd as things forgot."

Some former championship college debaters, in response to a survey conducted by the American Forensic Association in 1981 concerning the National Debate Tournament, said debate had merely reinforced what they now consider to be antisocial behaviors. They describe a tendency "to turn every conversation, whether social or academic, into a contest [in which they] always had to have the last word." "Truth, logic, tact, and just good manners were more often than not sacrificed for the sake of argument." They describe "mindless, knee-jerk" argumentation as an "insidious habit of pushing informal discussions to the argument stage," ego gratification gained by winning, showing a superiority over others. One person says, "Debate made me over argumentative, always finding problems with others' ideas. It took a long time to get over it. It [debate] may have increased my inability to work well with people on an interpersonal level." They found themselves seeking to conquer opponents rather than work out decisions through negotiation. One former debater concludes this way:

> The road to agreement is not always won by argument; every encounter is not a debate. I undoubtedly applied techniques irrelevantly and inappropriately. Even in an argument, I subsequently learned, it is unnecessary, perhaps even counter-productive, to refute *all* of your opponent's case. The main points are enough, and humiliation is costly.[1]

Approaching refutation requires finding a working point somewhere between these extremes: a preference for agreement and silent acknowledgment of the validity of what others say; and the brash, hypercritical, competitive, and destructive practices described by Benjamin Franklin and some former college debaters. If you keep in mind that refutation is a cooperative part of the critical process, rather than a noncontact sport, you should fare well.

SETTING A FRAMEWORK FOR REFUTATION

Each decision and the arguments related to it require a new analysis from which to construct refutation. There must always be an inextricable link among the goals sought in decision making, the specific decisions proposed to meet the goals, and the arguments advanced in support of the proposed decisions. Before you can engage in refutation, then, you must lay a **framework** from which criticism will emerge. Just as the architect must adapt the structure of a building to meet the demands of the setting and its intended use, arguers must adjust their practices to the specifics of the situation at hand.

Assess the Argumentative Situation

Refutation is a response to the argumentative situation, an **assessment**; unless you understand the situation at hand, you are not ready to participate in refutation. Even though people tell stories about talking the police out of tickets, for the most part interactions with police do not represent an argumentative situation. It is better to present your refutation of the charges to a judge. Dinner parties in which your politics or religion differ dramatically from everyone else are probably not the place to launch into an attack on their views. Conversely, when you are part of an impregnable majority, there is little point in refuting the minority arguments when those arguments stand no chance of influencing the decision.

Silence is often the most effective refutation. Remember that humiliation can be costly. But remember, too, that the decision to remain silent is always a gamble: You are

---

[1]All quotations cited came from an anonymous data pool shared with the authors by Ronald J. Matlon, Lucy Keele, and others associated with the National Debate Tournament and the American Forensic Association. We stress that these critical comments reflect only a minority of those responding to the survey.

resting your case on an assessment of the state of mind of the decision makers. If your judgment proves to be wrong, you will probably kick yourself for not speaking out. It's a tough choice because speaking out can sometimes do more harm than good. Only the most insightful have the courage to use silence as a refutation.

Think of the last essay exam you took. Did you find yourself trying to put down everything you could think of, turning the booklet in only when the time was up? This technique can either help you stumble on the correct answer or muddle it up. Next time, take a look at the students who finish before the time is up. They have chosen to write their best answer and stop. They have the same kind of courage needed to use silence as a refutation (or they simply didn't have much to say).

The steps in **critical decision making** provide a guide in assessing the argumentative situation. As you check off each step, you should become more sensitive to the potential paths for refutation.

Identify the Question or Claim.   Keep your eyes on what the decision process is all about, the ultimate purpose—what are we trying to accomplish with the decision? When people lose sight of the key issues, bring them back. Constantly look at issues in relation to the proposition, and the proposition in relation to the ultimate purpose. If the issues are decided, will the proposition follow reasonably? If the proposition is adopted, will the ultimate purpose follow reasonably?

Ask about the status of the discussion. Where does the present argumentation stand in relation to deciding the proposition? During the preliminary interactions around any topic or decision, the focus of decision makers is likely aimed at gathering information and identifying and sorting relevant values. They are tuning in, paying attention, comprehending, generating relevant cognitions, and acquiring relevant skills (Trenholm, 56). This is probably not the time to start refutation. It is possible that the search for a decision will move inexorably toward the decision you propose, and no refutation will be required. At this point, the best argumentative approach is to make a good impression on the decision makers: Establish a rapport, obtain commitments, preview your point of view, and generally build high credibility (Rieke and Stutman, 68–71, 109–116).

As alternative decisions begin to emerge and compete for the decision makers' attention, as the attractiveness of the alternatives approaches parity, forcing decision makers to struggle with discriminating among them, the time for refutation has arrived (Festinger, 154–155). If you advance your refutational points too soon, the effect may be lost because the decision makers are too early in their search to appreciate your points. If you wait too long, the opportunity to reduce adherence to other positions may have passed.

Survey Objectives and Values.   Inherent in each sphere are overall objectives sought from argumentation and the values that will control the process. For example, find out about the rules of procedure. Different spheres prescribe different procedures of argumentation. In law, for example, refutation is restricted to specific stages in the trial and attempts to use refutation outside those limits may be denied. In business settings, criticism of a presentation is usually restricted to questioning rather than direct attack, and often this is limited to people in a high position. A lower-level person attacking a colleague may have what they call at IBM a "career-limiting experience." Before launching into your refutation, you are well advised to know the procedures.

A young negotiator going up against a seasoned veteran was determined to get the upper hand and decided to attack the other side's arguments immediately. The negotiators entered the room and had barely taken their seats when the younger man stood and delivered an impassioned, five-minute attack on the other side. There was a moment of silence, and then the seasoned veteran said, "Does anyone want a Coke before we get started?"

What are the operative cultural values? If you are familiar with film and television characterizations of lawyers at work, you may believe it is common to trash and brutalize the other side and then go out for drinks. If you have been a debater in high school or college, you may believe that tough, uncompromising attacks on others are appropriate behavior. Loud talking, rapid speech, ridicule, and other tactics make for good drama, but they are forbidden in many settings. Gordon R. Mitchell's study of intelligence debates revealed a flawed system in which, "What begins as a seemingly benign debate to 'scrub the arguments' can quickly evolve into a politicized campaign to manipulate public opinion" (160). The people who were brought into the process for the debate acted as if winning at any cost, even by intimidation and distortion, was acceptable. In doing so, they reduced the quality of the resulting decisions.

In most business settings, professional interactions, and even government sessions, restrained language, quiet voices, courtesy, and consideration for the "face" of opponents are demanded (Lim, 75–86). You may deliver a devastating refutation of another's position only to find you have alienated the decision makers. In countries other than the United States, this is often even more the case. Refutation, to be successful, must not exceed the cultural boundaries of the decision-making situation.

Canvass Alternative Decisions.   Refutation can be powerful when it exposes the fact that little effort has been made toward testing a range of alternative decisions. Further discussion can be delayed pending research that may well uncover better approaches. A common approach in criminal defense is to expose the fact that the police, thinking they had the culprit, really didn't seriously consider other suspects.

Weigh the Costs and Risks.   Proposals may seem attractive on their face but lose support when the costs or risks are made clear. There are plenty of government services people would support if they did not require increased taxes. Many people who believe that more help should be provided to the homeless lose their enthusiasm when they learn that a shelter will be built in their neighborhood. In trying to craft an acceptable national health policy, Congress and the president discover great support for good health care but powerful opposition to letting the federal government run it and pay for it with taxes.

Search for New Information.   Refutation does not mean merely expressing your opinion. If you have not done your homework, you're not ready for refutation. In 1999, the Kansas Board of Education decided to change the status of teaching on evolution in its public schools. Immediately, outraged refutation was leveled at the board on the charge that their behavior was an ignorant attack on modern science and a step toward mixing religion with public education. Robert E. Hemenway, chancellor of the University of Kansas, wrote an essay entitled "The Evolution of a Controversy in Kansas Shows Why Scientists Must Defend the Search for Truth." Hemenway devoted his argument to criticizing the board for eliminating the teaching of evolution. By failing to do his homework, however, he set himself up for refutation by Phillip E. Johnson, a professor of law at the University of California at Berkeley. Johnson merely noted that the board had only removed evolution from mandatory state standards and did not insist that students be taught biblical or creationist interpretations. By attacking the wrong issue, Chancellor Hemenway allowed his arguments to be dismissed with the wave of a hand.

Note Biases Underlying Positions.   Identifying biases is an important part of refutation in critical decision making. Roadblocks can often be pushed aside by exposing preconceived notions and biases.

The ongoing debate about reducing unemployment reveals many biases. On the surface, conservatives inevitably claim that private business must be allowed to create jobs because of their inherent bias in favor of free enterprise. By contrast, liberals inevitably claim that re-training grants, support for education, funding for infrastructure projects such as roads, bridges, rails, and ports will do the job because of their inherent bias in favor of government action. Support or opposition to unemployment compensation extensions often turns on biases about the nature of workers: will people be more or less likely to look seriously for jobs if they are still getting government checks that provide less money than they get from working? Opinions are often held without solid grounds for support.

Make Plans to Implement the Decision.   Often, the best refutation is to take other proposals seriously and set out precisely what will be needed to implement them. The act of implementation often proves so complex, costly, or plagued with onerous side effects that enthusiasm for the decision vanishes.

Enthusiasm for national health programs frequently starts out high only to dissipate as problems associated with implementation become clear. The American people generally favor a program of insurance, but there is wide variance in what kind of program is favored. When The Affordable Care Act of 2010 required people to have some form of health insurance, there was outrage over this as the federal government exceeding its authority. Others replied that if healthy people were able to avoid buying health insurance, only sick people would be left and that would make insurance too costly. Everyone wants cost-efficient programs but most people also want to choose their own physician and have their medical procedures paid for. Finding a way to satisfy all values in the same program is the key problem.

Analyze the Decision Makers

How will the decision be made? The tone of refutation varies with the proximity to the decision and the likelihood of opposing points being stated after yours. If you are making the last statement, after which the decision makers will immediately make their choice, a more flamboyant, exhortative, and arousing style of refutation may be appropriate. If the decision will not be made for months or years after your refutation, as in congressional hearings, appellate courts, or businesses, the style and content of your refutation should be geared toward lasting impressions and specific recall that decision makers can use during their long deliberations.

If decision makers will not be exposed to counterargument, if they are not very well informed, if they are unlikely to raise objections to your position in their own minds, or if they clearly favor your position, you may concentrate on a one-sided, highly partisan refutation. If these conditions do not apply, however, you will probably be more effective if your refutation takes a multisided approach resembling an objective analysis of the alternatives (Trenholm, 242).

Who Are the Decision Makers?   We are constantly amazed to discover people debating each other without knowing who ultimately are the **decision makers**. In academic debate, courts of law, and other highly formalized decision systems, this does not occur, but in the vast majority of decisions made each day, who finally decides may be obscure.

The police union was negotiating with the city government over their new contract. The city's negotiating team included a professional negotiator, the city attorney, a personnel officer, and a major of police. The union side included a professional negotiator, the president of the police union, and members of the executive committee of the union. After months of talks, the issues were narrowed to one: salary. It proved impossible to reach agreement on this issue, and at that point, the question of who would really make the city's decision on pay raises became salient. The union asked for a conference with the mayor, and that produced no progress. It was only when the city's negotiator asked to leave the room every time, a new proposal was presented that the police discovered it was the city director of personnel, a former aide to the governor, who was calling the shots. When she was asked to join the negotiations so she could hear the positions debated, she declined and talks broke off without agreement. It accomplished nothing to refute positions without her presence.

In many business settings, decisions are addressed and arguments exchanged with none of the participants knowing who will ultimately decide. People are asked to attend meetings without knowing their role or the purpose of the meeting. Curiously, our experience is that often the participants themselves are expected to decide, but *they do not know it*. Unless you know who will actually make the decision, you cannot generate useful refutation.

In legislation, the decision makers can be quite difficult to discover. On the surface, it is the elected representatives, senators, or members of Congress, for example, who vote and thus decide. But a glance beneath the surface says the real clout may be in the hands of a few people who are recognized experts in the particular area of legislation, senior members holding party power, leaders of state delegations, or powerful lobbies (Matthews and Stimson, 45). Unless your refutation gets to the real decision makers, it may have no impact at all.

What Are Decision Makers' Goals?   Refutation must not focus solely on the particular strengths and weaknesses of alternative decision proposals; it must relate ultimately to what is sought from the decision, the **goals**—ultimate purpose. It is possible that alternatives can be rejected *as a whole* rather than criticized point-by-point simply by showing that they fail to address the objective of the decision making. In law, the defense may reject the opponent's entire position by successfully arguing that no *prima facie* case has been advanced. What this means, simply, is that the judge could accept everything claimed by the prosecution and still not grant a decision in their behalf. In the midst of refutation, it is easy to lose sight of what the debate is about. Tit-for-tat argumentation may obscure what it is that constitutes the objective of all involved.

In legislation, for example, the overarching objective may be to manage the national economy, and opposing bills may call for deficit reduction, tax relief, controlling costs in

Medicare or Social Security, or reducing the size of the military. Although each of these proposals has specific strengths and weaknesses that need attention, the ultimate goal, an effective national economy, must be the primary criterion by which they are assessed.

In partisan bickering, refutation often is focused on trivial issues to the point that everyone seems to have lost sight of what the debate is really about. Although you should criticize the arguments within the web of subissues on which the primary purpose rests, refutation should be based on criticism relevant to the decision objectives.

What Are the Presumptions of the Decision Makers?

What Are the Presumptions of the Decision Makers?   In the chapters on making sense of argumentation and on case building, we discussed the concepts of presumption, probability, and burden of proof. These concepts are also crucial to refutation. There may be formal statements of **presumption**, such as that of innocence in U.S. criminal law, and there may be widely accepted presumptions, such as that in favor of the status quo, but each decision must be analyzed for the actual presumption in place.

In law, jurors who can truly accept the presumption of innocence of a particular accused may be so hard to find that the court will grant a change of venue. Time may be expended on behalf of proposed legislation that seems widely popular when the real decision makers have a strong negative presumption. After years of experience with television interviews of the leaders of a state legislature, we learned to ask off camera about specific bills under consideration, and almost invariably the leaders could accurately predict the outcome. Proponents would blithely continue their campaign, ignorant of a presumption against them that had to be refuted if they were to have any chance of success at all.

The character of your refutation must be responsive to the status of presumption. If your decision carries the weight of presumption, then your refutation should consist primarily of two components: (1) constantly demanding that all other positions accept the **burden of proof** and defining the nature of their burden and (2) constantly showing how they have failed to meet their burden of proof. The other side of that coin is this: If your position carries the burden of proof you may attempt a refutation that shifts the burden to the others.

After the uprising in Egypt in 2011 that caused the removal of the president, the military created what was expected to be an interim government pending a new constitution and elections. After time passed with no apparent progress, the people demanded that the temporary government prove it was moving in the right direction. The people successfully shifted the burden of proof to the government leaders who had to satisfy the demands.

Remember, both of these approaches rely on the fact that you *know the presumption of the real decision makers*. In Egypt, it was difficult to know at any time who the decision makers would be: the interim government leaders, the leaders of political parties, the mob in Tahrir Square? Also, at any point in decision making, presumption can change, and with it the burden of proof or rejoinder. Candidates for office have been known to shoot themselves in the foot by continuing a campaign based on early data showing a powerful lead even after research reveals that presumption has changed.

Are Involved Factions Trying to Act as Decision Makers?

Are Involved Factions Trying to Act as Decision Makers?   The problem about arguing with police is that they are actually involved in the issue: They aren't judges; they are givers of tickets. When you complain to a business or government agency about their products or services, chances are you will be talking to someone who has an interest in the outcome but who is also playing judge. You may be talking to the very person whose job it is that you are criticizing. If this is the situation, the solution is to find someone else with a smaller stake in defending the opposing point of view and more interest in resolving the dispute. Asking to talk with supervisors, managers, or a regulating agency often helps.

Similarly, such interactions may often involve question-begging tactics (see Chapter 11), such as "Our policy is that . . ." Instead of trying to refute the policy, ask to talk with a person who has the authority to make an exception to the policy.

Finally, you need to get around what Tom Wolfe calls "the flak catchers." These are people in organizations whose job it is to listen to complaints (take the flak) and send people away. They are often programmed to mislead: "I wish I could help you, but there is nothing I can do." Instead of trying refutation on such people, you must get around them to real decision makers.

A woman allowed a teenage neighbor to repair her car in the high school shop class, and with the teacher's help he managed to cause US$600 worth of damage. She went to the school district and spoke with the person in charge of all shop classes. He said, "I'm sorry, but the law does not allow us to carry insurance for this sort of problem. We are legally unable to help you." The woman asked a professional negotiator to go back to speak to him. He gave the same response, but this time the negotiator simply refused to accept the explanation. The administrator asked to be excused for a moment and returned with another person who introduced himself as the district insurance officer, who proceeded to give instructions about how to make a claim. The first administrator was merely acting as a flak catcher. If the woman had stopped with her first encounter, the district would have saved money. When the flak catcher failed to put off the negotiator, he brought in a real decision maker.

Analyze Opponents

Law provides "discovery" procedures that inform opponents in advance of a trial what witnesses or evidence will be presented. Opposing counsel have a chance to talk to each other's witnesses at length and to review documentary or physical evidence. The principle is that justice will be better served if opponents have time to prepare refutation carefully. The principle should be carried into all refutation: Know as much as possible about opponents and their probable arguments.

SELECTING A POSTURE FOR REFUTATION

One of the most common mistakes of inexperienced debaters is the use of a "the more you throw, the more will stick to the wall" theory of refutation. It's the same theory we spoke of earlier in relation to students writing essay exams: not enough courage to stop when you've said enough; not enough knowledge to know when enough is enough. This is a tactic used by the inexperienced or the desperate. We will suggest a variety of postures from which refutation can be conducted, in the hope of convincing you to think before you refute and to quit when you have done what you planned, even if you still have time, space, or arguments unused.

We posit a general theory of refutation: *Address refutation at the highest conceptual level possible.* Turn the water off at the main valve; don't run from faucet to faucet trying to stem the flow. A corollary of that theory is this: *When the decision is in your hands, shut up.* We have seen times when defeat has been snatched from the jaws of victory simply because the obvious victor could not remain silent. Continued refutation actually moved decision makers to change their minds.

Refute from a Constructive Basis

Whether you are defending an established position with the protection of presumption or attacking it, refutation is most powerful when it comes from the perspective of a **viable constructive position**. It is one thing to hammer away at the prevailing policy, but its defenders are unlikely to abandon it without an alternative. In fact, defenders of the status quo will probably not even perceive your refutations for what they are because of selective perception.

Thomas Kuhn reports on what he calls scientific paradigms (subsets of spheres) such as Ptolemaic astronomy, Newtonian physics, and quantum mechanics. Kuhn argues that "Once it has achieved the status of paradigm, a scientific theory is declared invalid only if an alternative candidate is available to take its place" (77).

In law, the defense can technically rely totally on refutation of the plaintiff's case, but that is less powerful than generating at least a plausible alternative theory of the case. In public policy, naysayers are often turned aside with: "We know of all the weaknesses of our system, but it's the best there is." In the health care debate, it is common for people to claim, without evidence, that the U.S. health system is the best in the world. It does little good to challenge that claim, even with solid support showing that many other countries have better health care. What is needed is the presentation of a constructive alternative that is demonstrably better. Challenges to public policy are strongest when they emanate from persuasive alternatives.

Defend Your Position

If you have constructed a viable alternative position or if you are defending the presumed position, stick with it. Generally speaking, defenders advance one of three positions: **defense of the status quo**, **defense of the status quo with minor repair**, or **counterplan**.

Defense of the Status Quo. When you defend the status quo, you put attention on the refutation of the arguments advanced against it. By showing that the arguments do not stand up to criticism, you leave yourself standing on unchallenged ground. This is sometimes called "straight refutation," since you are putting all your efforts on rejecting the others' arguments. This is the approach typically used in health care debates. Arguers claim that the U.S. health system is the best in the world and, "It ain't broke and it don't need fixen," to use a colloquial expression.

Defense of the Status Quo with Minor Repair. Often, there are legitimate problems with the policy you are defending, and you may as well acknowledge them. However, you reject any claim of inherency—that the problems are so great and so much a part of the present system that the only solution is to make significant changes. Instead, you argue that an incremental approach is called for: minor changes in the present policy can deal with the problems without making significant changes. In this way, you need not refute all the arguments leveled at you. In the health care debates, when it was argued that older people and poor people had genuine problems in obtaining medical attention, minor repairs in the form of Medicare and Medicaid could be adopted without essentially changing the private, fee-for-service system in place.

Counterplan.   When the challenges to the present policy seem overwhelming, defenders have to choose: accept the arguments and support the proposed new policy, or argue for another new policy. If you decide there is clearly a need for a change in policy but the proposal being presented is unacceptable, then you have the option of arguing for a counterplan. So, you do not try to refute the arguments claiming there is harm in the present policy that presents a need for a change. You stipulate (acknowledge) the need. Then, you argue that the proposed new policy is not appropriate because (1) it will not be a practical way of solving the need, (2) it will produce disadvantages that outweigh any advantages. Finally, you present your counterplan and argue that it does solve the need and produces more advantages than disadvantages. This is pretty much what is happening in the U.S. health care debate. The challenges to the present system have not been effectively refuted, a new policy has been put in its place—The Affordable Care Act of 2010—but opponents have announced a counterplan of "repeal and replace," saying they can come up with a better new policy.

Too often, the heat of debate draws attention away from your home position as you level criticisms at others. We suggest that every communication you produce in the debate begin with a restatement of your position and a discussion of how it remains intact despite the refutation of other factions. This may require some repairs. Your position may have been damaged by refutation, so your first priority is to put it back together. Remember, other factions will be trying to pull you away from your position and get you to debate on their ground. If they have the burden of proof, they will be trying to shift it to your shoulders.

Keep the Focus on the Goals of Decision Making

The highest conceptual level toward which refutation can be aimed is the goal of decision making. Constantly return the focus of the discussion to the goals sought from the decision to be made—the ultimate purpose—and demonstrate any point at which other factions fail to generate those goals.

In debating the U.S. deficit, arguments go back and forth about whether cutting spending and/or increasing revenue is the proper policy. One side claims that any tax increase is unacceptable because it will put a burden on the people who are "job creators," and they are the ones who will generate new revenue, thus reducing the deficit. The other side argues that it is unfair to cut benefits for ordinary people so that business people can hire more workers. Moreover, they say, we passed tax cuts last time and unemployment got worse. Often, the debate becomes so focused on the tax/spend conflict that no one demands that the question must always be what will do the best job of reducing the deficit?

Engage in Framebreaking

Chris Argyris reports research findings that suggest that people are able to detect and understand inconsistencies, errors, and other problems with decision proposals of others, *but not their own*, when under pressure to decide and act. Moreover, when they tried to refute other positions, "they created conditions that led to escalating error, self-fulfilling prophecies, and self-sealing processes" (39).

Argyris proposes **framebreaking** as the response to this problem. Helping others break their typical frame of reference in considering decision proposals allows them to see, for the first time, the problems with their positions.

Similarly, decision makers who are not otherwise involved in the argumentation need help breaking their frames of reference to see the problems you are pointing out in your refutation. Under pressure to decide, says Argyris, people disconnect from their reasoning process. These are the usual characteristics: people do not understand when their premises or inference processes are problematic, people perceive their analyses as concrete when they actually rely on abstractions and a complex series of inferences, people rarely see a need to test their own reasoning through interaction with others because they "know" their reasoning is clear and correct.

Michael Fernandes, in a letter to the editor of *The New York Times*, on June 2, 2011, talks about how to measure success in cancer treatment. He says the traditional frame of reference is the size of the tumor and success is measured by how much reduction in the size of the tumor is achieved. Fernandes claims this overlooks the fact that the real danger in cancer is "invasion and subsequent metastases, which are unrelated to tumor size" (A22). He argues that "progression" must be redefined to include invasion. Continuing in the usual frame of reference will overlook critical aspects of cancer treatment.

Thomas L. Friedman, writing in *The New York Times* on July 13, 2011, claims that politicians are framing their debate on how to reduce unemployment in their typical ways: liberals calling for stimulus and conservatives demanding tax cuts. Friedman says that if they do not break their old frames of reference and go after unemployment in a new way, they will fail. "I think something else, something new—something that will require our kids not so much to find their next job as to invent their next job—is also influencing today's job market more than people realize" (A25). Friedman notices that the most dynamic sector of our economy consists of such firms as Facebook, Twitter, Groupon, Zynga, and LinkedIn, which all combined employ only about 20,000 workers. Unlike old factories that needed thousands of employees, the new businesses need fewer, highly specialized people. Even GE, an old line firm with 133,000 employees, says this in their ads: "Through advanced manufacturing technology, GE employees lift thousands of people in the air, light up entire cities, bend steel and wield lasers. Because no matter what it is they're making, they're manufacturing the future" (ad appeared in *The New York Times*, July 14, 2011, A9). "Manufacturing the future" reinforces Friedman's frame—today's jobs are unlike the past and involve individual innovation to invent and keep jobs. Unless politicians can engage in framebreaking, says Friedman, they will not select policies that will help this generation of workers find, or to quote Friedman, *invent* their jobs.

Test the Credibility of Other Factions

Review the discussion of credibility in Chapter 9, and think about how challenges to others' credibility might form the basis of refutation. The credibility of key proponents may be used to damage a proposal. The credibility of evidence can be challenged by exposing bias, exclusion of important reservations, outdatedness, imprecision, or other criteria discussed in Chapter 7. Credibility of sources of support can be the object of refutation.

In the long battle between the tobacco companies and their critics, credibility of evidence has played an important role. Critics claim research shows that smoking damages health, but the tobacco interests continually reject this research by pointing out that the studies found only correlations, not causal connections. In return, when the tobacco companies produce research that suggests smoking is not the cause of health problems, critics note that researchers who are paid or otherwise supported by grants from tobacco interests are not reliable neutral scientists.

When a former lobbyist for the Tobacco Institute was diagnosed with cancer and decided to speak openly about his work, his testimony was granted high credibility. He was admitting he had participated in misleading the public by withholding information and providing inaccurate information. A former insider "coming clean" in a way that reflects badly on his own work has the highest credibility.

Similarly, *The Journal of the American Medical Association* has published claims that "Academic scientists have put their names on papers that are actually ghostwritten by for-profit companies and then published in medical journals" (Guterman). The argument focuses on evidence claimed in support of anti-inflammatory drug Vioxx marketed by Merck & Company. The credibility of the evidence is destroyed if it turns out that the academic scientists merely allowed their names to be put on research actually done by a private company.

Understand Momentum

In decision-making groups, **momentum** describes a state of mind regarding critical attention to arguments. When a long and arduous debate has taken place over one proposition, those to follow may well pass with little or no comment because the decision makers have more or less exhausted their critical energy. The last proposition to come up just before the usual time for adjournment may whip through easily because people want to leave. It is said that during World War II, General Douglas MacArthur held back certain issues until just before 5:00 P.M. when officers were anxious to get to "happy hour," thus often avoiding scrutiny.

In refutation, you must understand momentum. Trying to get people to listen to objections when momentum is running in favor of the proposition may be futile. You may need to find some way to stop action until another meeting. Proposing amendments, calling for testimony from absent witnesses, suggesting that objections need to be heard from those unaware of the proposal, or other delay tactics may keep the question open long enough for refutation to be truly heard. Try to reschedule consideration of the proposition for the first item of business at the next meeting when momentum will not have built up. Of course, if momentum is running in favor of a proposition you support, remain silent.

Deny Support

The refutation aimed at the lowest conceptual level of analysis is a point-by-point criticism of the **support** used by other factions. Review Chapters 7, 8, and 9 on the various means of support, and consider how they can be the basis of refutation. Essentially, you proceed by denying other factions' support through challenges of authenticity, relevance, or sufficiency and by producing countersupport that neutralizes or overcomes their material.

The problem with this sort of refutation should be clear by now. You are concentrating on the lowest level of an argument—the individual pieces of evidence advanced in support. If you find fault with one reference, quotation, statistic, or example, the arguers can usually replace the criticized item with other, maybe stronger, evidence. And the focus of the discussion will be shifted away from the important levels that ask about what you are trying to accomplish and how you intend to accomplish it and toward relatively insignificant points of difference.

Sometimes debaters sandbag the opposition by presenting their weaker support first to draw an attack that they then replace with secondary support so powerful that decision makers discount any further challenges. Pilots talk of "sucker holes"—patches of apparently clear sky that lure them in and who then find themselves in worse weather than that which they were trying to escape. Apparently weak support can be a sucker hole. Your refutational energy is drawn toward what appears to be a weakness, and later you find to your horror that you have exhausted your opportunity for refutation on trivia, having overlooked more significant refutational opportunities. Then you are confronted with powerful secondary support the others had held in reserve.

COMMUNICATING REFUTATION

It is exciting to read about daring feats written in ways that make them sound easy; it is quite another thing to try them yourself. Racing down a steep, powder snow-covered mountain that has been untouched by other skis or boards sounds exciting. When you are actually at the top looking down, it doesn't seem so attractive. Refutation sounds like more fun than it usually turns out to be.

What we often forget when reading about debates is that others will be trying to do to you what you are trying to do to them. In a Walter Mitty fantasy, you may picture yourself delivering a brilliant and powerful refutation to an opponent who cringes under your eloquence and bows to your superior analysis. When you really try it, the opponent will probably give you just as much in return.

The first time you are forced to hear or read what others think of your ideas, and their comments are not complimentary, you may find yourself gravitating toward escape from the process or giving an angry, flailing response. It will take considerable cool to stay on course. Because our society does not typically condone refutation, preferring agreement or silence instead, you may lack the emotional preparation for it. As a result, there are important steps to take in communicating your refutation. The more prepared you are, the more you will be steeled against the emotions that necessarily are involved. Simulations, practice sessions, are an absolute necessity. Even the president of the United States conducts practice sessions before major press conferences. Here is a basic format for communicating refutation that works in most situations:

1. State the point to be refuted.
2. State your claim relevant to the point.
3. Support your claim.
4. State explicitly how your criticism undermines the overall position of those you are refuting.

FIGURE 10.2
Steps in Refutation

These four steps make clear what is being refuted and why, and link your individual refutation to a higher conceptual level. This approach makes clear how this refutation weakens not only this one point but also the whole case. In the remainder of the chapter, we will discuss refutation processes that fall within this general pattern of communicating your refutation.

Probe Opponents

In debate, early refutation should send out tentative questions and challenges to discover where other factions are weak, where they are sandbagging, and where they are loaded for bear. Listen carefully for questionable support or repetition of original support rather than secondary support. At the same time, use a continued analysis of the decision makers to learn where they perceive weaknesses in other positions as well as your own.

Based on this **probing**, you can match your strengths against others' weaknesses. Choose your challenges to bring together your greatest strengths opposite others' greatest weaknesses *as defined by your reading of the decision makers*. If you have already won decision makers' support on a major point, don't keep going over it; simply review it from time to time to keep it on their minds. Concentrate refutation on those points in other positions that remain open in decision makers' minds and on which you have some reasonable expectation of success. Don't waste time pursuing an issue you cannot win.

Use Questioning to Probe. In most decision-making situations, there is some opportunity for interrogation, and if it is used properly, it can be powerful. The most frequent mistake is to confuse probing questions with refutation itself. Rarely do you seriously damage another's position during actual **questioning**. Instead, you discover weaknesses, expose contradictions, challenge credibility, and extract admissions that can then be used as part of your refutation. This will strengthen your refutation because you can remind decision makers that your point is based on what the opponents themselves have said. Follow basic rules of questioning:

1. Prepare and practice questions in advance.
2. Phrase questions to allow a reasonably brief, preferably yes or no, answer.
3. Ask questions to which you know the probable answers from prior research.
4. Be courteous in tone of voice and content of question, unless you want a dog fight.
5. Don't ask a question that demands that the other side capitulate—Perry Mason is pure fiction.
6. Ask the question and shut up; if you don't get the expected answer, move on rather than try to give your preferred answer yourself.
7. If the response is evasive, rephrase and try again, courteously.

FIGURE 10.3
Basic Rules of Questioning

The paradigm of ideal confrontation, according to Scott Jacobs, is for the questioner to elicit a declarative statement and then request a series of brief informative replies, followed by a rhetorical question that is, at once, a reply to the original declaration and a demonstration of its contradiction. Here is an example:

Mother:	I have a perfectly good will.
Daughter	(a law professor): Will it have to go to probate?
Mother:	I don't know.
Daughter:	Is it subject to estate taxes?
Mother:	I don't think so.
Daughter:	Will it adjust to your changing circumstances?
Mother:	I'm not sure.
Daughter:	Mother, don't you think it would be a good idea to have your will checked out for these things?

FIGURE 10.4

Prepare to Respond to Questioning. Answering questions well is a part of refutation, though few prepare for it. Lawyers spend plenty of time preparing witnesses and politicians prepare to answer the press, but few others do so. Follow these principles:

1. Never answer until you understand the question.
2. Take your time.
3. Recognize that some questions don't deserve answers.
4. If the questioner interrupts, allow it.
5. Don't elaborate if it won't help you.
6. Ask permission to elaborate if it will help you. (If permission is denied, remain silent.)
7. Answer only those parts of the question that you believe deserve an answer.
8. Answer a question that was not asked, if that makes more sense to you.
9. If given an opportunity to repeat your argument, accept it in full.
10. Remember that during your refutation you will have a chance to explain or discount the effect of your answers; don't try to do this during questioning as it will only make you appear to be whining.

FIGURE 10.5
Principles for Answering Questions

Follow Good Communication Practices

The most fundamental rules of good communication should be used in refutation, even though excitement often works against such clear practices. One way to keep yourself together even under pressure is to take notes that keep you informed at a glance on what arguments have emerged around each issue.

A **flowsheet** is a form of note taking or outlining that shows the progress of arguments and their various refutations. Divide the paper in half. Put arguments for one side on the left, and arguments on the other side on the right. Try to arrange the arguments so that they match: arguments for a claim on the left—arguments against the same claim on the right. This will allow you to see at a glance how the arguments are proceeding.

CONCLUSION

Refutation must come from a balanced posture that is neither too silent nor too brash. It should be approached as a cooperative, critical process important to good decision making. Before you can begin refutation, you need to assess the argumentative situation to learn the way the argumentation is functioning in the particular sphere, including who the appropriate decision makers are and what are their presumptions.

Before refutation begins, you should prepare yourself for it by assessing the situation in light of the steps in critical decision making. You should also analyze the decision makers and your opponents to gain the necessary information to select a posture for refutation.

Once refutation begins, it should be aimed at the highest conceptual level possible. Often it will include a constructive basis for your criticism that you can defend. Sometimes refutation rests on framebreaking, or helping decision makers adopt a different way of thinking about the issues. You may also test opponents' credibility, stop momentum, and deny support.

In communicating refutation, it is well to follow a format of stating the point to be refuted, then your refutation and support, and finally show how it undermines the opponent's position. To prepare for refutation, it is a good idea to build refutational blocks that summarize each argument to be refuted and your refutation of it. A flowsheet will help you keep track of an argument and visually identify what you must refute.

EXERCISES/PROJECTS

1. Select a newspaper editorial with which you disagree. Prepare a refutation of it with the aim of convincing the other members of the class to sign a letter to the editor rejecting the editorial.
2. Write an argument for a proposition that you truly support. Make it as strong as you can. Then, write a counterargument that engages in refutation of your own argument, again doing your best. Finish the paper by discussing how difficult it was to refute your own argument and what you might do differently in the future.
3. Within your team or in front of the class, engage in a debate over a topic you have agreed on. Prepare to engage in refutation of the other arguments, and then present your refutation as well as you can. After the debate, discuss what went well and what could have been done better in the refutations.

Refutation by Fallacy Claims

KEY TERMS

fallacy claim, p. 174
incorrect logic, p. 176
sophistry, p. 177
tu quoque, p. 177
begging the question, p 177
authority, p. 178
popularity, p. 178
post hoc, p. 179
ad hominem, p. 179
verbal aggression, p. 180

appeal to pity, p. 180
pragma-dialectical, p. 181
deception, p. 182
refusal to reason, p. 183
cooperation, p. 183
irrelevant, p. 183
obfuscation, p. 184
quantity maxim, p. 184
conflict of interest, p. 185
reckless disregard, p. 185

In Chapter 10, we discussed the process of refutation and how to build a refutation case and communicate it. In this chapter, we examine what traditionally have been seen as individual errors in reasoning that are subject to refutation. They are known as fallacies. The concept of fallacy originally came from the study of logic. Logic was closely related to mathematics and not particularly applicable to decision making. Thus, for most of argumentation we use the term **fallacy claim** because fallacy is not automatic but must be argued like any other claim. A *fallacy claim* asserts that *an argument must be rejected because it violates a significant rule of argumentation relevant to the appropriate decision makers.* Central to the concept of fallacy are three characteristics:

1. Charging that an argument commits a fallacy requires that you undertake the burden of proving it to the satisfaction of the decision makers. This is in contrast to pointing out, for example, that a computational error has been made in solving a mathematical problem or that a word has been misspelled. In mathematics or spelling, the error may well be self-evident once attention is focused on it. In argumentation, a fallacy claim is rarely self-evident (Lyne 3). Therefore, it must pinpoint the issue that needs resolution.

For example, we often hear in conversation the claim, "You're being inconsistent." And the other person merely replies, "No, I'm not." If you intend to make the fallacy claim of inconsistency, you need to say something like this: "When you argue we should reduce the power of the federal government and then call for strengthening the Environmental Protection Agency, you argue against yourself. That is inconsistent." When you state the fallacy claim that directly, the other person must do more than deny the charge.

2. A fallacy claim charges significant deviance from appropriate argumentation practices; it does not make nit-picking criticisms that score debate points rather than advance critical decision making. Sometimes people trounce on a slip of the tongue, a minor error, or an overstatement as though it were a triumph. In 2011, in a U.S. Senate debate, Senator Jon Kyl of Arizona was arguing to end federal subsidies to Planned Parenthood. He argued that 95% of the money was used to fund abortions. In reality, only 5% or less was used for abortion services (Peralta). That difference, when pointed out significantly, weakens his argument and is subject to a fallacy claim. But, what if he had said 10%? That would have been an insignificant difference and not worthy of a fallacy claim.

3. Although a fallacy claim rests on a significant rule of the sphere, the appropriate decision makers must reaffirm the rule for the claim to succeed. For example, The U.S. Office of Science and Technology defines fabrication as "manipulating research materials or changing or omitting data or results such that the research is not accurately represented in the research record" (55722–55725). But over the multiyear life of a research project, there will be many instances of omitting data that were not deemed relevant and material at that point in the research. A fallacy claim must be significant enough that decision makers (in this case scientists) will reaffirm and specify the rule that the research be accurate.

In the remainder of the chapter, we discuss four different views of fallacy: incorrect logic, sophistry, social guides, and breach of conversational cooperation as guides to the development of fallacy claims.

FALLACY BEGAN IN THE STUDY OF LOGIC

Aristotle is credited with formalizing logic, and his work in the *Sophistical Refutations*, *Prior Analytics*, and *Rhetoric* is cited as the origin of the concept of fallacy (Hamblin 50–88). As logicians sought to make sense of Aristotle's ideas, they did so from a worldview powerfully shaped by a sense of order and certainty. They were sure that the universe is orderly and that humans possess the rational capacity to understand and deal with it. Logic was perceived to be the tool of that rationality.

Logicians believed that just as numbers and abstract symbols, such as P and Q, could be manipulated within mathematical or logical analyses with certain and consistent meaning, so could ordinary language. For most of our intellectual history, people have believed that words have precise meaning and the primary task of the arguer is one of interpretation: discovering meaning and using the correct word to say what is meant.

The view of logic that has emerged during the past 500 years in Europe and ultimately in the United States is one that seeks order and certainty by removing the disorderly and unpredictable aspects of human behavior. In this view, dialogue, conversation, and human feeling are "mere nuisances" (Ong 251). Logic is a system existing outside of human discourse (Howell 350–361). It has little patience for the pragmatics of language as practiced by ordinary people where the meaning of words is negotiated through usage and may vary within a single argument.

From this worldview, it is no wonder that some philosophers understand Aristotle's idea of fallacy as identifying **incorrect logic**. In logic, the task is to locate logical errors, for example, the fallacy of the undistributed middle term in a categorical syllogism (described in Chapter 4):

> Japanese eat raw fish.
> Sharks eat raw fish.
> Therefore, Japanese are sharks.

The logical fallacy is that the middle term does not link Japanese with sharks, making the third claim invalid. If you care, consider the fallacy claim for the same argument in this form: Americans and dogs both eat meat, so, Americans are dogs.

In the discussion of informal logic in Chapter 4, we introduced you to the hypothetical syllogism that takes the "If A, then B" form. For example, "If it rains, then the streets will get wet." You can validly use this in two ways: (1) affirm the antecedent (a *modus ponens*) "it did rain, so the streets are wet" or (2) deny the consequent (a *modus tollens*) "the streets are not wet, so it did not rain".

However, drawing a claim from affirming the consequent or denying the antecedent can be subject to a fallacy claim because they may not yield valid conclusions. That is, if you see that the streets are wet and conclude it must have rained, you could be making an error. There is more than one way the streets can become wet. Similarly, if you know it has not rained and presume, therefore, that the streets are dry, you could be committing a fallacy.

A fundamental logical fallacy in the eyes of some is to mistake validity for truth (Fearnside and Holther 126). This may occur when ordinary language and real issues are presented in logical form (what we call quasi-logic in Chapter 4). For example, this argument follows a valid form: Any structure built on my property belongs to me, and your fence is on my property, so it belongs to me.

Although the claim seems clear-cut and logically valid as stated, the real problem is with the substance of the argument, not its form. Any lawyer will tell you that fences and property lines are not simply a matter of a surveyor's report. To make good on this claim, you must successfully argue not only that the property line is where you claim it is, but also that you have consistently and publicly continued to claim the property. If you have allowed the fence to stay there without asserting your claim, you may have no case. A critic who stopped with the observed validity of the argument would miss the key issues.

In one view, it is not worthwhile to study fallacies based on violations of the rules of formal logic because strengths and weaknesses in argumentation are addressed to decision maker's judgment not arbitrary standards (Ehninger and Brockriede 99–100). Gerald J. Massey claims that there is no theory behind logical fallacies and the subject should be sent to psychology if anywhere (170–171).

In another view, although argumentation is admittedly inexact and ambiguous, taking note of such fallacies serves as a point of reference by which arguments "might be critically analyzed" (Lyne 4). The more knowledgeable you are on the rules of logic and the ways they can be violated, the more likely you are to sniff out some of the problems in people's arguments and come up with effective refutation. But you must keep in mind that argumentation does not conform to strict rules of logic, and logical incorrectness may not be an effective fallacy claim.

Fallacy Claims of Sophistry

A fallacy, to some, is more than a logical error. It is an error that leads, or could lead, rational people toward mistaken or dangerous conclusions. Those holding to this view are dedicated to more than correctness. They seek to rid the world of **sophistry**, the use of plausible but fallacious reasoning.

A typical introduction to a textbook on fallacies predicates the study on the rising intensity in the "constant battle for our minds and allegiances that is such a distinctive feature of life through the mass media particularly" (Engel 4). W. Ward Fearnside and William B. Holther say "it would be a good idea if the community could somehow develop a serum against some forms of persuasion" (1). Howard Kahane believes the study of fallacies is the serum that attempts to "raise the level of political argument and reasoning by acquainting students with the devices and ploys which drag that level down" (xi). He says persuasion is often successful when it ought not to be, and so he defines a fallacy as an "argument which *should not* persuade a rational person to accept its conclusion" (1).

We will briefly introduce you to some commonly mentioned fallacy claims arising from the concern over sophistry. This is not a complete list, nor are these forms of argument always sophistic, each must be argued as a fallacy claim.

Responding to a Charge with a Countercharge.   When the attorney general of the state announced an investigation of the university president for possible misuse of funds because it had been discovered the president had lavishly remodeled his office, the president responded by revealing that the attorney general had recently spent $10,000 just for a new door into her office. This *tu quoque* argument (responding to a charge by making a countercharge) is a fallacy in the eyes of some because first, it is logically erroneous in not addressing the issue of the university president's actions and, second, it may seem plausible to the public.

Although pointing to another wrong rather than dealing with the immediate issue may be objectionable in some contexts, it may not always be so. Dennis Rohatyn notes that "He that is without sin among you, let him first cast a stone at her" (John 8:7), the New Testament quotation attributed, with widespread approbation, to Jesus, is a *tu quoque* argument. Jesus used it to spare a woman accused of adultery while avoiding damage to himself for seeming to violate the Mosaic law that stoning was appropriate for adultery. We know of no one who has charged Jesus with committing a fallacy. Rohatyn is not approving of *tu quoque* in general; he is merely saying it is not always a fallacy to use that argumentative form (1).

Begging the Question.   When an answer or definition seems plausible but, on closer examination, assumes as fact that which is not proved, it may be **begging the question** (*petitio principii*). To beg the question is to assume as true that which you are trying to prove. It is also called circular reasoning. Circular definitions fall within this classification. Douglas N. Walton says that an argument "...that commits the fallacy of begging the question uses coercive and deceptive tactics to try to get a respondent to accept something as a legitimate premise that is really not, and to slur over the omission, to disguise the failure of any genuine proof" (*Begging* 285). Walton says this is like pulling yourself out of the quicksand by your own hair (290). A *New Yorker* cartoon (March 24, 2003; 71) put it humorously: "It could go badly, or it could go well, depending on whether it goes badly or well."

In law, the defense may successfully object if the prosecutor says, "At what time did the murder occur?" The object of the trial is to determine whether a murder occurred, and the prosecutor assumed it into fact. We may know someone is dead, but whether it is *murder* is still at issue.

Similarly, to condemn abortion as murder because it is taking the life of a human being is to beg the question. The statement uses the point at issue (At what point does life begin?) to support the claim and thereby fails to carry the discussion any further along.

Appeal to Authority.   To assume a claim is a fact simply because someone with high credibility says it is may constitute a fallacious appeal to **authority**. Argumentation by its nature relies heavily on support from authority, and using that kind of support does not necessarily make it a fallacy. A fallacy claim on authority can occur when the so-called authority is not an authority on the question at issue or is biased. One may also claim a fallacy when an appeal to expert opinion is used "as a tactical device for preventing the respondent from raising the appropriate critical questions" (Walton, *Appeal to Expert* 228). That is to say, authority may be abused if it is used to silence the dialogue. Our discussion of testimonial evidence in Chapter 7 develops these ideas.

The common use of celebrities in advertising is subject to a fallacy claim. Actress Sally Field is not an authority on bone loss therapy, nor is former NBA star Michael Jordan an expert on underwear, or championship golfer Phil Mickelson an authority on arthritis, or Actress Jamie Lee Curtis on healthy Yogurt. Their celebrity status, when it is all that is used, is subject to a fallacy claim. When the celebrity makes an argument and provides evidence, it is more difficult to argue it as a fallacy claim because it is not clear whether it is a raw appeal to celebrity status or an argument about the subject. Such was probably the case when the actor with Parkinson's disease, Michael J. Fox, campaigned for several U.S. Senate candidates in 2006 because they supported stem cell research. His arguments may have been a fallacy, but a fallacy claim would be difficult to argue. Perhaps the most interesting case deserving a fallacy claim is the commercial wherein the celebrity says, "I'm not a doctor but I play one on TV."

Appeal to Popularity.   Similar to the objection to uses of authority is that over appeals to **popularity**. Claiming that something is good because it is popular runs the risk of a fallacy claim. Douglas Walton writes that the traditional interpretation that any appeal to popularity is a fallacy, under the Latin name *argumentum ad populum*, no longer can be accepted because in a democracy it is relevant and proper to take into account public opinion and preferences (*Appeal to Popular* 276). However, the appeal to popular opinion is only applicable to a fallacy claim when it claims more than that people favor or do not favor it. A poll showing that seniors favor keeping Medicare as it is can stand for just that. It would be subject to a fallacy claim to say that a change would, or wouldn't work.

Unpopular policies can still be better for the country than popular ones. Certainly, we learned that about raising children. So-called "tough love" is frequently better than giving in to every child's wish. In theology, as we will discuss in Chapter 14, that a religion is growing in popularity, or that it is one of the largest, is not a legitimate basis for claiming that it is correct.

Post Hoc Fallacies. Many arguments rest on a claim of causality, as we explained in Chapter 4. A fallacy may be claimed when it is believed that a faulty causal relationship is at hand. The Latin phrase *post hoc, ergo propter hoc* (after this, therefore because of this), from which the fallacy gets its name, calls attention to the tendency to assume a causal relation among events because they are related in time or space.

This kind of reasoning is common in politics. During the term of President George H. W. Bush, the economy went into a slump. Bill Clinton used it as an argument for his election. The economic slump was a major part of his campaign. The slogan at his campaign headquarters was "It's the Economy Stupid!" After the election, the economy improved and Democrats claimed the improvements were caused by President Clinton's policies. Then, George W. Bush became president and presided over a relatively successful economy. But, just as Barack Obama became President the Great Recession occurred. Although at first he claimed that it was caused by his predecessor, after a couple of years most observers said he owned the recession. The causes of the recession were complex and not directly and singularly the result of any president's actions, but charges of causality were made. Every one of the last four presidents has been subject to some claim based on post hoc fallacies.

People are quick to ascribe causes, often with little or no justification. You come down with a cold, and your mother says, "I told you not to go outside without your coat." You get in trouble, and your father says, "I told you not to run around with that bad crowd." Your grades go up at the same time that you are frequently absent from class, and you announce, "Attending class doesn't have anything to do with getting high grades." College officials often claim that going to college will cause you to earn more money because, on average, those with college educations do earn higher salaries. Whether graduates would have done as well without higher education remains unclear. Such pat causal arguments invite close scrutiny and may deserve the label of *post hoc* fallacy.

Fallacies in Language. Following Aristotle's lead, a great many fallacy claims are based on problems with the language in which an argument is expressed. Because argumentation uses ordinary language to deal with questions within the realm of uncertainty, ambiguity is always present. Still, a critic can sometimes find instances in which language problems are of such significance as to warrant a fallacy claim.

Article II of the Bill of Rights reads: "A well regulated Militia, being necessary to the security of a free state, the right of the people to keep and bear Arms, shall not be infringed." This has been used by some to claim that no restriction on the private ownership of weapons can be constitutional. Others claim that "a well regulated Militia" puts a limit on who may bear arms (law officers and National Guard perhaps?) and what does the term "Arms" mean in today's situation? Are automatic weapons, bombs, attack helicopters, that are a far cry from the flintlock rifles of those who wrote the Bill of Rights, part of the people's "right to keep and bear arms" There is plenty of room for fallacy claims based on language meaning on all sides of this ongoing dispute.

Ad Hominem Fallacies. When people turn their criticism against a person rather than the person's ideas, they may be subject to an *ad hominem* fallacy claim. There is plenty of evidence that we do this regularly in our own minds by giving more credence to the arguments of attractive people and less to the unattractive (Rieke and Stutman 128–129). It would be as if you said, "Your argument is weak because you're ugly." Although you may not be as blatant as that in using *ad hominem* arguments, they are still popular.

On February 12, 2007, in Salt Lake City, an 18-year-old boy armed himself with a shotgun, a handgun, a backpack of ammunition; went into Trolley Square Mall; and began shooting randomly at anyone who was in his path. By the time he was killed by police, he had killed five people and wounded four more. When it was learned he was an immigrant Bosnian Muslim, some people began threatening all Muslims in the city. The *ad hominem* fallacy here was to assume that any Muslim was capable of similar acts.

Verbal aggression constitutes a special form of *ad hominem* fallacy. In conversational argument, there is a presumption for agreement (Jackson and Jacobs 253). So attacking the self-concept of another person instead of, or in addition to, the person's position on a topic of communication is verbal aggression (Infante and Wigley 60). This aggression has the effect of inflicting, and may be intended to inflict, psychological pain (Infante 51). These attacks can take many forms: questioning others' intelligence, insults, making people feel bad, saying others are unreasonable, calling someone stupid, attacking character, telling people off, making fun of people, using offensive language, or yelling and screaming (Infante and Wigley 64). These are all *ad hominem* fallacies and should be the subject of a fallacy claim.

In politics, voters follow a generally held precept that a personal attack on someone may be seen as an ad hominem fallacy unless the personal weakness complained of is related to a candidate's policies or his or her approach to the office sought.

President Barack Obama was the subject of many negative claims about his health plan, his stimulus policy, his conservation policy, his war plans, and so forth. Although he was harshly criticized these were not ad homenem arguments because they centered on objections to his policies. But many of the charges against him were personal—some said racist—causing a prominent conservative commentator to call for an end to a whole group of other charges (Schneider).

All of us have at one time or another resorted to these forms of attack. However, even when decision makers think your charges are accurate, verbal aggressiveness reduces your credibility (see Chapter 9). In some cultures, even the direct expression of disagreement is perceived as in bad taste.

In western culture, what is important to emphasize is the difference between assertiveness and argumentativeness, which do not give rise to fallacy claims, and hostility and verbal aggressiveness, which do. Assertiveness involves being interpersonally forceful in expressing your ideas. Argumentativeness is characterized by presenting and defending positions on issues while attacking others' positions (Infante 52). Hostility is manifest by the use of the language of negativity, resentment, suspicion, and irritability. Verbal aggressiveness involves using language to inflict pain and weaken or destroy another's self-concept (Infante 52). When this occurs, a charge of committing an *ad hominem* fallacy is to be expected.

Appeal to Pity. Arguments that are based on the elicitation of pity (*argumentum ad misericordiam*) have traditionally been considered inherently fallacious. Such a broad condemnation cannot survive within an audience-centered rhetorical approach to argumentation. As our discussion of forms of support makes clear, values, including feelings such as pity, compassion, or sympathy, are important to argumentation.

Douglas Walton agrees that the traditional approach to this fallacy must be set aside in favor of a case-by-case approach. A fallacious **appeal to pity** might be sustained in relation to the way the argument is used in context: Did it further or damage the requirements of the argumentation? In general, Walton argues that the historical and pragmatic meaning of *pity* includes negative elements: A person is pitiful because of suffering from some undeserved evil (*Appeal to Pity* 73). So, concludes Walton, although sympathy and compassion are usually appropriate in argumentation, pity may be used in an irrelevant and distracting manner that inhibits the objective of argumentation.

Pity for a criminal guilty of a serious crime who had a difficult childhood will frequently be seen as inappropriate. But it is not considered a fallacy to ask for pity for poor children in Africa who have AIDS when it is not their fault. Pity is usually acceptable when it is directed at those who are innocent and have no control over their situations.

These are only a few illustrative forms of fallacies commonly mentioned in the efforts against sophistry. Other potential fallacies are appeals to fear, ignorance, force, prejudice, and the pressure of the mob.

We have discussed two theoretical foundations on which fallacies can be identified: incorrect logic and sophistry. Both of these premises have come under attack in recent times.

The relevance of logic to practical argumentation is in serious doubt. Although its patterns are still recognized and used, as we discuss in Chapter 4, as a way to structure argumentation, its rules of validity are generally seen as inapplicable to arguments based on probability and addressed to decision makers. Logic is useful as a guide to what is acceptable but in social situations it can never constitute an absolute ground for a fallacy claim.

Sophistry has always been a difficult posture from which to identify fallacies because of the extreme ambiguity of the concept. What is sophistic to one is often acceptable to another. Who is to say an argument "ought not to be persuasive?" Who has the authority to say an authority ought not to be believed in this instance? Who decides when responding to a charge with a countercharge is okay and when it is fallacious? By what rule do we say that a claim and the argument against a person is an inappropriate *ad hominem* argument and is, thus, fallacious?

If you accept these criticisms of fallacy theory, you might wonder why the study of fallacy continues to hold interest. The concept of fallacy is useful in two respects. First, by locating frequently employed mistakes in argument and giving them a name, we make it easier for you to keep them in mind and put them to use. Pedagogically, it is easier to teach people to be critical decision makers if we can use this memory device. Second, it is easier rhetorically to communicate to decision makers that a mistake in argumentation has occurred if there is a common vocabulary of fallacy to use.

Fallacies as Violations of Discussion Rules

Because of concerns with traditional approaches, contemporary scholars have sought a new and acceptable theoretical basis on which to rest the concept of fallacies. Frans H. van Eemeren and Rob Grootendorst of the University of Amsterdam have developed what they call a **pragma-dialectical** approach to argumentation. By this phrase, they mean a combination of normative rules (a philosophical ideal of reasonableness) with a pragmatic study of speech acts (what people actually say and mean in argumentation).

From the pragma-dialectical perspective, van Eemeren and Grootendorst develop a theory of fallacies that first sets out 10 rules for critical discussion (see Chapter 4). They include such prescriptions as allowing everyone to speak, requiring that claims be supported, demanding relevance of arguments, calling for honesty in representing arguments presented, expecting that arguments be logically valid or capable of being validated, and avoiding confusing arguments (209).

The concept of fallacy follows directly from these 10 rules: For them, any move in argumentation that blocks critical discussion by violating one of these rules is a fallacy. They conclude their discussion by arguing that all the traditional fallacies, including those we discussed under incorrect logic and those we discussed under sophistry, can be reasonably organized under one of the 10 rules of critical discussion.

Frans van Eemeren has elaborated on the concept of "strategic maneuvering," which attempts to recognize the tension you may feel between the desire to argue with perfect reasonableness and your desire to win the debate. If you allow your commitment to reasonable argumentation to be overruled by the desire to be persuasive, says van Eemeren, you may "victimize the other party. Then, the strategic maneuvering has got 'derailed,' and is condemnable for being fallacious" (142). If this move to persuasiveness is intentional, van Eemeren claims, it will be necessary for arguers to reaffirm their commitment to reasonableness before they can effectively continue.

Drawing on all of these views of fallacy as well as our own thoughts in the remainder of the chapter, we will discuss how fallacy claims are a part of refutation. You should remember that the contemporary image of fallacy is tied to the actual rules governing argumentation and the willingness of decision makers to see an argument as a violation of one of those rules.

SOCIAL GUIDES TO FALLACY CLAIMS

Although it is impossible to identify inherently fallacious ways of arguing, we can list some relatively enduring patterns on which fallacy claims can be based. You can use these guidelines in the development of fallacy claims.

Intent to Deceive

Earlier we said that simple errors or misunderstandings do not form the basis of fallacy claims because they can be brought up, discussed, negotiated, and corrected. But errors or misunderstandings that can be shown to intend **deception** are commonly seen as fallacious. People may forgive the former but not the latter.

Chris Raymond, in the *Chronicle of Higher Education*, reports that studies of patient histories suggest that Sigmund Freud suppressed or distorted facts that contradicted his theories. He rested his case heavily on the case histories of six people, of whom one left therapy dissatisfied after three months, two were never treated by Freud or any psychoanalyst, and another never really had therapy. Of the two remaining cases, Freud's claims of effecting a cure were refuted by a confession of Freud himself and a denial by one of the patients. Raymond quotes a research professor of psychiatry at the University of Pittsburgh as saying, "It is clear that Freud did what euphemistically might be called editing of his case material [but that] isn't tantamount to dishonesty" (4–5). Again, there was deception, leading to a debate over intent. To establish a fallacy claim, the critics must show that Freud doctored his cases with the intent to deceive.

Advertisers come in for considerable criticism because of their apparent willingness to deceive people to win them over. Communication scholars who specialize in the study of advertising, however, do not identify deception as central to advertising. They do say it relies on the force of *our own* self-deceptions, fantasies, values, personal realities, or worldviews. Loose analysis may lead you to charge deception when an advertiser is merely using intense language, hyperbole, and dynamism alongside appeals to our own realities. However, there are examples of those who have knowingly sought to deceive us in order to gain our adherence, and these become the object of fallacy claims.

Refusal to Reason

In a pure sense of the term, critical decision making means having a basis for a decision that can be examined critically. It does not demand any particular kind of rationale; it merely demands *a* rationale. To make a claim but refuse to give reasons in its support may give rise to a fallacy claim. Even to rely on altruism or one's own authority—"Believe it because I ask you to"—is a reason that can be critically examined. To say, "Believe it just because," or "Believe it for no particular reason," is to deny others (including yourself) the opportunity for critical appraisal.

Children about the age of three years use the word *because* as a reason, whereas older children and adults almost never do so. This is not so much a refusal to reason as it is a childish understanding of the process of reasoning (Willbrand and Rieke, "Strategies" 435).

By the same token, when someone older than the age of four years asserts a claim without any support, or with "because, just because" as a basis, we conclude it is a refusal to reason and may form the basis of a fallacy claim. Parents do their children no good by answering the multitude of "why" questions with "just because" answers. Government does citizens no good by answering challenges to public policy with a refusal to reason, hidden behind national security. Critical decision making rests on the ability to consider reasons, so **refusal to reason** denies the critical process and constitutes a potential fallacy.

In the debate leading up to the 2003 invasion of Iraq, arguments about the alleged weapons of mass destruction held by Saddam Hussein were often cloaked in national security claims. Administration spokespersons frequently said that although they were prevented from revealing details, they were absolutely confident the weapons would be found. When no weapons of mass destruction were found, many people felt angry. Because the administration had not presented its evidence and allowed the critical process to take its course, they may have been guilty of a refusal to reason.

Breach of Conversational Cooperation

H. P. Grice says that when people engage in argumentation, they do so within a presumption that anything said is intended to be "cooperative," that it contributes toward the goal of the interaction. He posits four conversational maxims of such **cooperation** that govern each utterance: the utterance is topically relevant; it is expressed clearly; it is sufficient for the meaning needed at that juncture, says neither too much nor too little; and it is believed to be true ("Logic"; "Further Notes"). Robert Sanders says that breaches of this process of conversational implicature may constitute the bases of fallacy claims (65). We will discuss each briefly, again focusing on intent. Innocent breaches of conversational implicature can, presumably, be repaired through further dialogue.

Irrelevant Utterance.   Because the cooperative principle guides people to presume comments are relevant, it is possible to damage the critical process by making **irrelevant** statements with the intent that they be taken as relevant. We stopped at a small-town gas station recently, only then noticing that the price was 10 cents a gallon more than the place across the street. The attendant, in response to our request for a justification for his high prices, said, "Well, you can go across the street if you are willing to put cut-rate gas in your car." We were supposed to presume that the quality of the cheaper gas was lower and even dangerous to use. An acquaintance who runs a station in the city says the difference in price was probably a function of one station being a "name" outlet and the other a cut-rate place. He says the gas at both places was probably about the same because cut-rate stations often buy their gas from major name producers. That the other place was cut-rate was relevant but not to gas quality.

Obfuscation. The cooperative principle leads us to presume that our interlocutors are doing their best to be clear and as easy to understand as possible. **Obfuscation**, as we use it here, is an intent to make communication unclear in order to secure adherence from those who trust in the commitment to clarity. The common paradigm case of unclarity—the IRS tax instructions and other publications of the federal government—probably would not count as obfuscation as defined. Bureaucrat-ese may be a disease, but it is usually not *intended* to confuse.

Today, many food products include some variation of the word *light or lite* in their name or description. *Diet* is used similarly, as are *low-fat* and *no-cholesterol*. In these instances, there is the possibility of obfuscation by oversimplification. A diet or light product may contain a few calories, a hundred, or more. A no-fat product may still be fattening, and a diet product may contain dangerous cholesterol, whereas a no-cholesterol product may contain dangerous fat. The government required statement of "Nutrition Facts" on food packages are designed to provide facts that may be the basis of a fallacy claim for consumers.

Violations of the Quantity Maxim. The cooperative principle says we presume that our communications say enough to make sense and no more. Violations of this **quantity maxim** seek adherence by taking advantage of that presumption while saying more or less than would otherwise be appropriate. Closely related to this potential fallacy claim is the concept of conflict of interest, in which some information that would be significant to a critical decision is withheld to mask multiple motives.

Tax advisors say that people get themselves in more trouble than necessary during audits with the Internal Revenue Service by saying too much. They advise people to answer questions with the minimum necessary to respond, and no more. The problem comes, say the advisors, when the audit seems over, people are standing up to leave, and the urge toward normal conversation returns: "Well," says the taxpayer, "I'm glad that's over because I'm leaving tomorrow for my place in the Bahamas." "What place in the Bahamas?" asks the tax auditor. "Maybe we'd better sit back down."

There is a fine line between an honest withholding of information that is not legally required, as is recommended by tax advisors, and saying more or less than is reasonably needed for understanding simply to secure adherence. In court, this took place:

> PROSECUTOR: Did you sleep with this woman?
> DEFENDANT: No.

The answer is true in one sense (they did not sleep) but untrue in the meaning communicated. If exposed, the defendant may be the subject of a fallacy claim of violating the quantity maxim. The waste disposal company that publishes data showing that a shipment contains "no hazardous waste" without saying that the shipment was originally hazardous by government standards but has barely fallen out of that definition through chemical changes is the potential object of a fallacy claim.

This maxim can be violated by overstatement as well. The incessant commercials for prescription drugs usually include a person, speaking far too rapidly to follow, listing a bewildering array of possible side effects. While such statements may be accurate, they lump rare occurrences with ones that might be worth considering. In the end, most viewers ignore these dangers because of the too fast overstatement. This, too, may be the basis of a fallacy claim.

Conflict of Interest. Withholding of relevant information is usually the basis for charging a **conflict of interest**. When the ophthalmologist recommends an optical shop nearby, it is relevant to know it is owned by the ophthalmologist.

An acquaintance went to a lawyer to discuss a suit against a local company she believed had cheated her. The attorney advised her to forget about the incident and sent her away. Only later did she discover that the attorney had for many years been on retainer to represent the company in question. That discovery could count as the basis of a fallacy claim through conflict of interest.

A prominent law firm was retained by the state of Utah to defend an anti-abortion law that was under challenge by such entities as the Utah Women's Clinic. After billing the state for $170,000 in fees, the firm was discovered to represent the Utah Women Clinic in tax and employee benefit matters. Was it a conflict of interest to serve as attorneys for the clinic in some legal matters while opposing them in the suit over the anti-abortion law? The firm claimed there was no conflict of interest and refused to withdraw, but the state attorney general fired them.

More to the point is the question of why the firm had not notified the state at the outset about its representation of the clinic. Their failure to be "up-front" about the matter was probably more damaging than the fact of the representation itself. Knowing that the same firm had been ordered to withdraw from another case by the state Supreme Court because of conflict of interest simply added to their low credibility (House).

Reckless Disregard for the Truth. We have already discussed the intent to deceive; however, here we interpret the cooperative principle from a concept developed in law (see *New York Times* v. *Sullivan*). When someone participates in communication by providing information, we presume through the cooperative principle that they not only believe what they say but also have some basis for that belief. In law, it may be considered malicious to communicate facts with **reckless disregard** for the truth, and that is the basis of this fallacy claim.

Newspapers usually make a practice of verifying stories before printing them, particularly when reporting sensitive facts such as that a banker is a heavy gambler. Independent sources are sought along with parallel confirmation. To make little or no effort to confirm a story may constitute reckless disregard for the truth, a fallacy claim. The CBS program *60 Minutes* interviewed people who claimed to have been paid as sources for news stories for which they had no information. What CBS was doing was making a fallacy claim of reckless disregard for the truth against some supermarket tabloids.

USING FALLACY CLAIMS IN REFUTATION

Claims of logical incorrectness, sophistry, and violations of discussion rules must be considered in your plan of refutation. Recall from Chapter 10 that you should always aim at the highest conceptual level and that pointing out specific mistakes or embarrassing slips may not do much to criticize other positions.

The highest conceptual level can usually be found by looking for the ultimate purpose sought from the argumentation. In debating the pros and cons of the death penalty, Jonathan D. Salant claims racism plays a significant role in deciding guilt. Although the same number of African-Americans and whites are murdered, murderers of white people are more likely to receive the death penalty. Since 1977, he says, 80% of the people executed were convicted of killing a white person. Kent Scheidegger, legal director of the pro-death–penalty Criminal Justice Legal Foundation, "blamed racial differences on fewer prosecutors in heavily minority areas willing to seek the death penalty" (Salant A20). He claims that prosecutors in more conservative counties use the death penalty more often. The highest conceptual level on which to base refutation must be whether the judicial process is operating fairly and properly or whether racism either in the form of convictions or the decisions of prosecutors is distorting justice.

Before using refutation by fallacy claim, be sure it is consistent with your overall critical pattern. If you decide to argue a fallacy claim, we remind you here of the format for communicating refutation discussed in Chapter 10.

1. State the claim you find fallacious in this circumstance.
2. Identify the fallacy claim you make about it.
3. Provide the support for your fallacy claim.
4. State explicitly how your fallacy claim undermines the overall position you are refuting.

David Cay Johnson, Pulitzer Prize winning economist from Syracuse University responded to a statement by Gretchen Carlson, Fox News Host, that 47% of Americans do not pay taxes. Johnson asserted the fallacy claim of obfuscation: the word "taxes" in this context means federal income taxes and that is intentionally misleading. While many people do not pay income taxes, they do pay, "plenty of other taxes, including federal payroll taxes [as well as] gas taxes, sales taxes, utility taxes, and other taxes." "In every state except Vermont," he said, "they bear a heavier burden than the rich." "In Alabama, for example, the burden on the poor is more than twice that of the top one percent (11 percent of income compared to 4 percent)". This is part of the reality that provides a basis for "questioning tax cuts for wealthier Americans," he said (16).

CONCLUSION

Fallacies are violations of significant rules of argumentation relevant to the appropriate decision makers. They are expressed in fallacy claims. The notion of fallacy as incorrect logic is identified with the tradition of formal logic. Although this perspective is generally not appropriate for the realm of argumentation, knowledge of specific fallacies within the system may serve as a critical guideline. Three formal fallacies are as follows: affirmation of the consequent or denial of the antecedent, undistributed middle term, and mistaking validity for truth.

Identifying fallacies with sophistry has been a key element of informal logic. Here fallacies are seen as arguments that are persuasive when they should not be. Some specific fallacies are as follows: responding to a charge with a counter charge; begging the question; appeal to authority; appeal to popularity; *post hoc, ergo propter hoc*; fallacies in language; *ad hominem*; appeal to pity. Although you cannot be sure a fallacy is present simply by noticing these argumentative forms, they can direct your attention toward such questions as whether intent to deceive can be argued successfully.

Contemporary theories tend to see fallacies as violations of discussion rules. In critical interactions, there are some basic rules of rationality that can be suggested through a dialectical perspective. Fallacies occur when one of these discussion rules is violated. Mere blunders or misstatements of fact are not classified as fallacies. A fallacy must occur within argumentation and serve as a deliberate violation of accepted rules in order to gain an improper advantage.

There are also enduring, socially negotiated guidelines for the development of fallacy claims that, although they do not point to certain fallacies, can be used to discern what may prove to be convincing fallacy claims: intent to deceive, refusal to reason, breach of conversational cooperation, irrelevant utterance, obfuscation, violations of the quantity maxim, conflict of interest, and reckless disregard for truth.

We suggest that in making a refutation by fallacy claim, you integrate it with your overall refutation strategy. First, arguing a fallacy should make a substantial contribution to critical analysis at the highest conceptual level. Second, the fallacy claim must be effectively argued. You must accept and satisfy your burden of proving not only that a fallacy is present, but also that its presence constitutes a significant and relevant consideration to the appropriate decision makers at the time.

EXERCISES/PROJECTS

1. Select a letter to the editor published in a newspaper that commits what you believe to be a fallacy. Identify the fallacy and develop your argument proving why.
2. Exchange your paper with another student. Each of you writes a response to the other's paper that argues one or both of these claims: (1) the alleged fallacy really is not fallacious or (2) the alleged fallacy would not be a fallacy used in another sphere.
3. Search on the Internet for arguments that you believe represent three different kinds of fallacies (incorrect logic, answering a question with a question, begging the question, false appeal to popularity, etc.) Be prepared to defend your fallacy claim.
4. Join in a small group discussion where you share the fallacies you have found with others in the group.

Argumentation in Law

KEY TERMS

narratives, p. 189
burden of proof, p. 190
preponderance of evidence, p. 190
equipoise, p. 191
prima facie case, p. 191
commonplaces, p. 196
decide only enough to dispose, p. 196
consider only questions posed, p. 197
file in a timely manner, p. 197
definition, p. 197
stare decisis, p. 198

analogy, p. 198
logic, p. 199
consistency, p. 199
noncontradiction, p. 199
validity, p. 199
syllogism, p. 199
legislative intent, p. 200
policy arguments, p. 200
reductio ad absurdum, p. 200
laches, p. 201
authority, p. 201

Nine days after being sworn in as President of the United States, Barack Obama signed his first Act of Congress into law: the Lilly Ledbetter Fair Pay Act of 2009. The new law, an amendment to the Civil Rights Act of 1964, specifies that the 180-day statute of limitations on filing legal claims of discrimination, included in the Civil Rights Act, resets after every discriminatory paycheck. The law was a direct rebuttal to the argument made by Justice Samuel Alito, Jr. in rejecting Lily Ledbetter's claims against the company where she worked for almost 20 years. This interaction between the legislative, executive, and judicial branches of the federal government exemplifies the judicial dialogue (Rieke, "Judicial Dialogue") in which significant factions on the Supreme Court reveal sharp differences through their argumentation, and policy argumentation interacts with legal argumentation within complex cultural concerns. Paul Stob says, "Legal decision making and the form and content of judicial opinions are influenced by the political and legal cultures in which they are embedded" (139). *Ledbetter* emerged alongside several decisions that for the first time reflected the influence of two new justices, Chief Justice John Roberts and Associate Justice Samuel A. Alito, Jr., appointed by President George W. Bush.

In this chapter, our focus is on argumentation in legal spheres, and *Ledbetter* will serve as a case study. Obviously, our discussion will be selective in seeking to demonstrate how legal argumentation can proceed rather than to examine the case in its entirety. And we will expose argumentation in only one of the many spheres that can be found within the concept of law: federal civil law. Federal law differs from that of the various states and localities in the argument spheres that can be found, and what comes up in civil cases, such as patents, taxes, estates, divorce, Internet, labor, environment, torts, and so on, differs from the varieties of criminal argument spheres.

NARRATIVES IN LEGAL ARGUMENTATION

Aristotle distinguished between deliberative (policy) and forensic (legal) rhetoric by noting that deliberative rhetoric addresses questions of the future: What policies should we adopt to serve people best in the coming years (1991, 47–49)? It often happens, though, that the policies arising from deliberative decision making are interpreted as questions of law. Forensic rhetoric, said Aristotle, addresses questions of the past: What happened back then and how can we decide about it in a way that best serves the needs of justice today? Part of that decision making, as revealed in *Ledbetter*, can rest on interpreting the intent of the legislators. When courts try to advance claims about congressional intent, however, they may find themselves forced to make deliberative arguments. So, Aristotle's distinction is not quite as precise as he suggested.

Because legal argumentation deals with claims about what has happened in the past, it must, as the law puts it, find the facts about what happened. The expression, "find the facts," makes the process sound like crime scene investigators zealously searching for any piece of paper, witness, or other items that might help explain what happened. And in some ways, that is what happens. During pretrial research and discovery (looking at what the other side will claim as fact), questions are asked of potential witnesses. Documents and physical objects are obtained. Experts are consulted and their judgments are solicited (review the steps in critical analysis and case building in Chapters 5 and 6). Lawyers representing all involved clients work to put together **narratives** that incorporate the information that is produced in a way that provides support for their argumentative case.[1]

Narratives Construct the Facts

Even after the most diligent research and discovery process, however, there are rarely enough facts to dictate a decision, and that is why argumentation is required. It is always possible to construct different narratives that seem faithful to what appear to be the facts, and there are almost always contradictory versions of the facts. Anthony G. Amsterdam and Jerome Bruner conclude, "We now understand that stories are not just recipes for stringing together a set of 'hard facts'; that in some profound, often puzzling way, stories

---

[1]To sample the results of the discovery process in *Ledbetter v. Goodyear*, examine the "Joint Appendix" in the Petition for Certiorari filed with the U.S. Supreme Court on February 17, 2006. http://supreme.lp.findlaw.com/supreme_court/briefs/05-1074/05-1074.mer.joint.app.pdf.

construct the facts that comprise them. For this reason, much of human reality and its 'facts' are not merely recounted by narrative but *constituted* by it" (111).

The materials turned up during research and discovery put constraints on the kinds of narratives that can be woven around them, but the structure of the narrative, what answers it gives to such questions as these posed by Amsterdam and Bruner, in return construct what will be recorded as facts:

1. What is ordinary and legitimate?
2. What constitutes time?
3. What human beings strive for?
4. What comprises *Trouble*?
5. What makes character?
6. What shape human plights can take? (112–113)

Each narrative presented in law—during opening statements by plaintiff and defendant, during the trial questioning of witnesses and examination of other evidence, during the review by courts of appeal, during review by the media, during reconsideration by legislators—the so-called facts will be shaped and reshaped over and over. Janice Schuetz, writing in *Communicating the Law*, says,

> Persuasive opening statements are not just descriptions, they are carefully organized, framed, and condensed stories that meet specific legal constraints. Describing the scene, characters/actors, and their motives, disputed action, and outcomes of the action are not persuasive unless attorneys frame the descriptions as assertions that relate to themes, sequence the narrative into distinct story categories, draw causal connections between parts of the story, and establish direct connections between the elements of the story and the [legal issues]. (110–111)

Narratives Must Satisfy the Demands of a *Prima Facie* Case

In November of 1998, Lilly Ledbetter filed suit against the Goodyear Tire and Rubber Company, Inc., in U.S. District Court for the Northern District of Alabama, Eastern Division. She claimed that during the almost 20 years she had worked as a supervisor and area manager in the Goodyear tire production plant in Gadsden, Alabama, she had been discriminated against through low salary because of her sex. She claimed, among other charges, that Goodyear had violated Title VII of the Civil Rights Act of 1964 as amended:

UNLAWFUL EMPLOYMENT PRACTICES
SEC. 2000E-2 [Section 703]
(a) It shall be an unlawful employment practice for an employer—
(1) to fail or refuse to hire or to discharge any individual, or otherwise to discriminate against any individual with respect to his compensation, terms, conditions, or privileges of employment, because of such individual's race, color, religion, sex, or national origin[2];

Title VII places the burden of proof on the plaintiff, Lilly Ledbetter (review the discussion of burden of proof and *prima facie* case in Chapter 6). Here, **burden of proof** means that after hearing all the evidence, to decide for the plaintiff, the jury must conclude by a *clear preponderance of the evidence*[3] that Goodyear discriminated against Lilly Ledbetter.

---

[2]To review Title VII of the Civil Rights Act go to http://eeoc.gov/policy/vii.html.

[3]The burden of proof in civil cases tends to be less stringent than that applied in criminal cases, where the jury must conclude *beyond a reasonable doubt* that the accused committed the crime.

If the jury remains uncertain, or as Justice Ruth Bader Ginsberg put it, in "**equipoise**," they must find in favor of the defendant, Goodyear.

Based on the language of the law and the subsequent interpretations of it by courts, Ledbetter had to persuade a jury of a yes answer to each of the following issues, which are the elements of a *prima facie* case (in law, the word *elements* designates the issues that must be affirmed by the party with the burden of proof in order to make out a *prima facie* case):

1. Whether the salary decisions applied to Ledbetter constituted an employment practice;
2. Whether the salary decisions were made with discriminatory intent.

More specifically, meeting the burden of proof requires successfully persuading a jury to grant adherence to these claims:

1. Ledbetter is a member of a protected class (female).
2. She performed work substantially equal to work of the dominant class (males).
3. She was compensated less for that work.
4. The disparity was attributable to gender-based discrimination.

Ledbetter's Narrative[4]

My story began in 1979, when Goodyear hired me to work as supervisor in their tire production plant in Gadsden, Alabama. I worked there for nineteen years. During that time, there must have been eighty or so other people who held the same position as me, but only a handful of them were women. But I tried to fit in and to do my job. It wasn't easy. The plant manager flat out said that women shouldn't be working in a tire factory because women just made trouble. One of my supervisors asked me to go down to a local hotel with him and promised if I did, I would get good evaluations. He said if I didn't, I would get put at the bottom of the list. I didn't say anything at first because I wanted to try to work it out and fit in without making waves. But it got so bad that I finally complained to the company. The manager I complained to refused to do anything to protect me and instead told me I was just being a troublemaker. So I complained to the EEOC [Equal Employment Opportunity Commission]. The company worked out a deal with the EEOC so that supervisor would no longer manage me. But after that, the company treated me badly. They tried to isolate me. People refused to talk to me. They left me out of important management meetings so I sometimes didn't know what was going on, which made it harder to do my job. So I got a taste of what happens when you try to complain about discrimination. When I started at Goodyear, all the managers got the same pay, so I knew I was getting as much as the men. But then Goodyear switched to a new pay system based on performance. After that, people doing the same jobs could get paid differently. Goodyear kept what everyone got paid confidential. Over the following years, sometimes I got raises, sometimes I didn't. Some of the raises seemed pretty good, percentage-wise, but I didn't know if they were as good as the raises other people were getting. I got a "Top Performance Award" in 1996.

Over time, I got the feeling that maybe I wasn't getting paid as much as I should, or as much as the men. I heard rumors that some of the men were getting up to $20,000 a year extra for overtime work. However, I volunteered to work as much overtime as any of them, but I did not get anywhere near that much pay in overtime. I figured their salaries must be higher than mine, but I didn't have any proof—just rumors. Eventually one of my managers even told me that I was, in fact, getting paid less than the mandatory minimum salary level put out in the Goodyear rules. So

---

[4]For convenience, we have excerpted elements from Lilly Ledbetter's testimony before the U.S. House of Representatives Committee on Education and Labor, June 12, 2007. For the entire text go to http://web.lexis-nexis.com/congcomp/document?_m=91c42c61ea7dbdf2d62a55e6dlaa395.

I started asking my supervisors to raise my pay to get me up to Goodyear's mandatory minimum salary levels. And after that, I got some good raises percentage-wise, but it turned out that even then, those raises were smaller in dollar amounts than what Goodyear was giving to the men, even to the men who were not performing as well as I was. I only started to get some hard evidence of what men were making when someone anonymously left a piece of paper in my mailbox at work, showing what I got paid and what three other male managers were getting paid. Shortly after that, I filed another complaint of discrimination with the EEOC in 1998, when I got transferred from my management job to a job doing manual labor, requiring me to lift 80-pound tires all shift long.

It turned out that I ended up getting paid what I did because of the accumulated effect of pay raise decisions over the years. In any given year, the difference wasn't that big, nothing to make a huge fuss about all by itself. Some years I got no raise, when others got a raise. Some years I got a raise that seemed OK at the time, but it turned out that the men got bigger percentage raises. And sometimes, I got a pretty big percentage raise, but because my pay was already low, that amounted to a smaller dollar raise than the men were getting.

For example, in 1993, I got a 5.28 percent raise, which sounds pretty decent. But it was the lowest raise in dollars that year because it was 5.28 percent of a salary that was already a lot less than the men's because of discrimination. The result was that at the end of my career, I was earning $3,727 per month. The lowest paid male was getting $4,286 per month for the same work. So, I was actually earning 20 percent less than the lowest paid male supervisor in the same position. There were lots of men with less seniority than me who were paid much more than I was.

Goodyear's Narrative[5]

Petitioner [Ledbetter] worked at Goodyear's Gadsden, Alabama, tire plant for nineteen years as a Supervisor and later as an area manager. She was hired on February 5, 1979, and was initially paid the same salary as a similarly situated male employee. In 1980 and 1981, Petitioner received the same pay increase as all other area managers at the plant. Beginning in 1982, Goodyear determined the salaries of its managerial employees using a system of annual merit-based raises. Raises were based on individual performance appraisals that incorporated an employee's performance ranking, present salary, and salary range. . . . Petitioner and her co-workers thus had their salaries reviewed at least once annually by plant management.

Petitioner worked in several different departments under several different supervisors before 1992. Earlier in her career, she was included in two general layoffs. Her longest layoff started in 1986 and lasted into 1987. She did not receive salary increases in 1986 or 1987 because of that layoff. She was also included in another general layoff in 1989.

Petitioner conceded that the manager who established her raises in 1990, 1991, and 1992 did not discriminate against her because of her sex. She also offered no evidence of "who, prior to 1992, the other area managers in [her] immediate areas of the plant were, how [she] fared against them in end-of-year performance rankings, or how her salary or the merit-based raises she received compared to theirs."

From mid-1992 until 1996, Petitioner was supervised by Mike Tucker, who also supervised three male area managers. Based upon Tucker's recommendations, Petitioner received a 5.28 percent salary increase in 1993, a 5 percent increase in 1994, and a 7.85 percent increase in 1995. Petitioner's cumulative salary increase for this period was higher than the increases for all three of the male area managers working under Tucker's supervision.

Petitioner was ineligible for a salary increase in 1996 because her 1995 raise had not yet been in effect for the minimum time interval required between raises at that time. . . . She was

---

[5]For convenience, we have excerpted this statement contained in the "Brief in Opposition," to the Petition for a Writ of Certiorari, submitted in the U.S. Supreme Court, No. 05-1074. References and citations have been omitted.

also ineligible for a raise in 1997 because she was slated to be included in an upcoming general layoff. She did not receive a salary increase in 1998 because her manager at the time concluded that her performance did not warrant an increase.

In August 1998, Goodyear announced that it planned to downsize the Gadsden plant and offered an early retirement option. Petitioner applied and was accepted for early retirement, and she retired effective November 1, 1998.

An important aspect of Goodyear's story was that Ledbetter's salary was set through performance reviews, and the supervisor whom she claimed had openly discriminated against her was dead and thus unable to testify. Goodyear implied that he would have denied the discrimination charge and would have claimed, instead, that his review was proper and Ledbetter's performance simply did not deserve a higher salary. After all, Goodyear suggested, the alleged discrimination by this supervisor occurred years ago and Ledbetter is only now complaining about it.

The Jury's Decision

The trial court in Alabama reported the jury's decision this way[6]:

> The Jury rendered a $3,843,041.93 verdict in this case, concluding that Plaintiff Lilly M. Ledbetter had proved that Defendant Goodyear probably paid her a disparate salary because of her sex. The jury's finding that Plaintiff was subjected to a gender disparate salary is abundantly supported by the evidence. It found that Plaintiff lost $223,776.00 because of this disparity. The jury could reasonably have found that Terry Amberson is an appropriate comparator. Apparently both he and the Plaintiff were paid the same salary on April 1, 1979. The jury could reasonably have concluded that but for the gender discrimination, their salaries would have been the same up to November 1, 1998. It could have found that in the 1996–1998 period, Plaintiff's base annual salary was $44,724; and that Amberson's base annual salary was $59,028.
>
> Assuming that the jury found the facts concerning damages in the most favorable light to Plaintiff that it reasonably could have, the maximum award for the salary differential would have been $60,000—including overtime pay and prejudgment interest.
>
> The Court concludes therefore that to the extent that the jury's award for the disparate salaries exceeds $60,000, it is not supported by the evidence.
>
> The jury's award of compensatory damages for mental anguish in the amount of $4,662 is solidly supported by the evidence.
>
> The jury's punitive damage award of $3,285,979 must be reduced. The punitive damages, coupled with the compensatory damages may not [according to the law] exceed $300,000.00.
>
> A reasonable jury could have found $500,000 to be a reasonable amount sufficient to punish and deter Goodyear. Given the statutory limitation and the compensatory damage award, it follows that the punitive damage award must be reduced to $295,338.00.

After taking relevant laws and defense arguments into account, the judge concluded that an award of no more than US$360,000 was appropriate in this case. The Ledbetter narrative thereby forms the basis for what the law will call the facts in the case because the winning side's narrative is what the jury "found" to be fact. The judge edited the jury decision/narrative so that it would coincide with the Court's judgments of what is reasonable in the eyes of the law.

---

[6]*Ledbetter v. Goodyear*, Civil Action Number 99-C-3137-E U.S. District Court for the Northern District of Alabama, Eastern Division 2003 U.S. Dist. LEXIS 27406, September 23, 2003 Decided; September 24, 2003, Entered.

Goodyear, however, was by no means ready to give up. It is one thing to win the right to craft the narrative that constructs the facts; it is another to survive the clash of arguments on the law. The appropriate decision makers now shifted from a jury of Ledbetter's peers to a panel of nine justices, two of whom were recently appointed and not well known. The appellate process is more complicated than we describe here. In reality there are always various levels of courts of appeal, and cases must follow the prescribed route step-by-step, and only rarely do they end up in the U.S. Supreme Court.

Generally speaking, courts of appeal do not reconsider the so-called facts determined by the jury and the trial judge as they appear in the official transcript or record. Instead, appellate judges use the facts to form the grounds of the claims about the law. But, in doing so, the judges select, from the record, their own narrative of the facts to suit the legal argument being supported. So, it is useful to look at the narrative as it emerged in the decision of the U.S. Supreme Court. Justice Alito's majority narrative is followed by Justice Ginsberg's dissenting narrative.

Justice Alito's Narrative[7]

Petitioner Lilly Ledbetter worked for respondent Goodyear Tire and Rubber Company at its Gadsden, Alabama, plant from 1979 until 1998. During much of this time, salaried employees at the plant were given or denied raises based on their supervisors' evaluation of their performance. In March 1998, Ledbetter submitted a questionnaire to the EEOC alleging certain acts of sex discrimination, and in July of that year she filed a formal EEOC charge. After taking early retirement in November 1998, Ledbetter commenced this action, in which she asserted, among other claims, a Title VII pay discrimination claim.

The District Court granted summary judgment in favor of Goodyear on several of Ledbetter's claims but allowed others, including her Title VII pay discrimination claim, to proceed to trial. In support of this latter claim, Ledbetter introduced evidence that during the course of her employment several supervisors had given her poor evaluations because of her sex, that as a result of these evaluations her pay was not increased as much as it would have been if she had been evaluated fairly, and that these past pay decisions continued to affect the amount of her pay throughout her employment. Toward the end of her time with Goodyear, she was being paid significantly less than any of her male colleagues. Goodyear maintained that the evaluations had been nondiscriminatory, but the jury found for Ledbetter and awarded her backpay and damages.

Justice Ginsberg's Narrative[8]

Lilly Ledbetter was a supervisor at Goodyear Tire and Rubber's plant in Gadsden, Alabama, from 1979 until her retirement in 1998. For most of those years, she worked as an area manager, a position largely occupied by men. Initially, Ledbetter's salary was in line with the salaries of men performing substantially similar work. Over time, however, her pay slipped in comparison to the pay of male area managers with equal or less seniority. By the end of 1997, Ledbetter was the only woman working as an area manager and the pay discrepancy between Ledbetter and her 15 male counterparts was stark: Ledbetter was paid $3,727 per month; the lowest paid male area manager received $4,286 per month, the highest paid, $5,236.

---

[7]This narrative and subsequent quotations are taken from the majority opinion in *Ledbetter v. Goodyear* written by Justice Samuel Alito. References and nonessential material have been omitted.

[8]This narrative and subsequent quotations are taken from the dissent in *Ledbetter v. Goodyear* written by Justice Ruth Bader Ginsberg. References and nonessential material have been omitted.

Title VII provides that a charge of discrimination "shall be filed within [180] days after the alleged unlawful employment practice occurred." Ledbetter charged, and proved at trial, that within the 180-day period, her pay was substantially less than the pay of men doing the same work. Further, she introduced evidence sufficient to establish that discrimination against female managers at the Gadsden plant, not performance inadequacies on her part, accounted for the pay differential.

Because the facts, as determined at trial, constitute the grounds for arguments on the law, it is instructive to read each version of the narrative to notice how each is constructed. Although the essential features of Lilly Ledbetter's experience with Goodyear remain reasonably steady, Rieke and Stutman observe the focus of each narrative—what material is included and what is excluded, the language employed, the identification of the central action, the implications of individuals' motives and behavior, and the values implicated—tends to shift subtly to reflect the narrator's argument (93–103). With these narrative factors in mind, we will reexamine the two justices' versions of the narrative to discover how they subtly directed them toward their opposing claims.

Justice Alito used the impersonal reference to "Petitioner Lilly Ledbetter," and focused on a central action of performance evaluations and quality of work. Justice Ginsberg mentioned Ledbetter's name in what could be seen as a personal reference and emphasized the gradual degradation of her salary over time. Justice Alito reported that the lower court threw out some of Ledbetter's claims, and he spoke of "certain acts," "past pay decisions" that "continued to affect." Justice Ginsberg, by contrast, said, "over time her pay slipped." She observed that Ledbetter was "the only woman" in the plant whose pay discrepancy with the men "was stark," whose low salary was the result of discrimination, not poor performance, and the 180-day statute of limitations had been met by the continued issuing of low paychecks.

ARGUMENTS ON THE LAW

Those differences in narrative become quite important as justices build the arguments on the law. The legal argument we will primarily discuss centers on the 180-day statute of limitations in Title VII:

> ENFORCEMENT PROVISIONS
> SEC. 2000E-5 [Section 706]
> (e) (1) A charge under this section shall be filed within one hundred and eighty days after the alleged unlawful employment practice occurred .

Justice Alito, along with four other justices, concluded that Ledbetter had failed to meet the 180-day demand: The unlawful employment practice occurred more than 180 days before she filed her claim. Therefore, her claim must be dismissed. Even her own story, Alito observed, includes the fact that toward the end of her work with Goodyear she was receiving high percentage raises. Justice Ginsberg, along with three other justices, argued that every time a paycheck was issued that was lower than that of the men because of sex discrimination another "unlawful employment practice occurred." So, her claim was filed within the 180-day requirement. Therein lies the debate we shall examine.

When arguments are presented to courts of appeal, the claims focus on errors alleged to have occurred in the trial. With the fact situation more or less set in the record, lawyers now claim that the application of the law to the facts was improper. Goodyear argued that the Court should have thrown out the Title VII charge, along with others that were rejected, because of the failure to satisfy the time limits. Thus, the Court erred, made a mistake, which the appellate court should correct. We will survey the commonplaces that typically help locate legal arguments, all of which can be found in the *Ledbetter* decision. In the course of this discussion, we will identify the lines of argument supporting the majority decision and the dissent.

Commonplaces in Legal Argumentation

In Chapter 2, we introduce the concept of **commonplaces** as standard, common, widely recognized, and accepted ways of putting arguments together. We identify them as part of the starting points for argument because people need to establish forms of common ground in language, facts, presumptions, probabilities, and commonplaces if they are to interact reasonably and effectively. Within spheres, then, it is possible to locate the commonplaces that are used with sufficient regularity as to become part of the characteristics of the sphere. In Chapter 4, we discuss the nature of arguments. There we discuss a number of types of arguments that have appeared in argumentation across many spheres and over thousands of years. They include such standard commonplaces as logical deduction, generalization, cause, sign, analogy, and authority. In legal argumentation, we will find some of these more typical commonplaces along with some that are generally found only in legal arguments.

Decide Only Enough to Dispose of the Case.   Appellate courts are presented with many questions in complicated cases, and the decisions they make will affect future cases as well as the one immediately presented, as we explain under *stare decisis*. For this reason, courts typically respect an argument that narrowly tailored decisions are to be preferred, they **decide only enough to dispose.** If a case can be disposed of on a simple issue, that is preferable to addressing more difficult questions. In popular parlance this is often called a "technicality," but to the courts it is consistent with following the law. If the *Ledbetter* case can be disposed of by finding that it was not filed in a timely manner, then the other, thornier, issues need not be addressed.

An example of this outside our present case can be found in the instance of a challenge to the phrase "under God" in the Pledge of Allegiance recited in a school. A father filed an objection to his daughter having this religious phrase forced on her. The court, probably wary of opening up a divisive discussion of the separation of church and state, dismissed the claim because the father was not the legal guardian of the daughter at the time he filed the claim and, therefore, lacked standing before the court. In a manner of speaking, the court dodged a bullet by making this simple decision rather than tackling the more explosive one.

The Court Will Consider Only Questions Posed.   Justice Alito opened his opinion by observing that Ledbetter could have asked the court to consider a number of questions, but she limited herself to only one, and that is the only one that will be addressed:

> Whether and under what circumstances a plaintiff may bring an action under Title VII of the Civil Rights Act of 1964 alleging illegal pay discrimination when the disparate pay is received during the statutory limitations period, but is the result of intentionally discriminatory pay decisions that occurred outside the limitations period.

Courts will be receptive to arguments that claim that the petitioner might have been successful by appealing other questions, but if the petitioners do not ask the questions, the court should not do it for them. The courts **consider only questions posed**. On the one hand, it might seem frustrating to learn that Ledbetter might have won the case if only she had made other arguments. On the other hand, it is not uncommon, and may have been so in this case, that the purpose of the appeal is less motivated by a desire to win an award for Ledbetter than it is to set a precedent for all similar cases that will come in the future, as we explain under the commonplace of *stare decisis*. It might be instructive to note that by the time the case was decided by the Supreme Court, the combined expenses of the plaintiff and defendant far exceeded US$360,000. Thus, the money involved was less important than the opportunity to set a precedent that would affect subsequent claims.

Claims Must be Made in a Timely Manner. The narrative that Justice Alito reviewed from the facts of the case put emphasis on "past pay decisions" that occurred outside the 180-day limitation period that continued to affect her pay within the limitation period. Courts of appeal tend to be strict in enforcing time limits set in the laws. Cases must be **filed in a timely manner**. Lawyers are expected to take timely steps demanded by the law, and if they fail to do so, the court will almost certainly make the simple and restricted decision to reject the claim, even if a lawyer's failure punishes a client. The Supreme Court rejected a claim that was not timely filed even when it was accepted as fact that the judge had given lawyers the wrong deadline.[9] Ledbetter's case was rejected, including the US$360,000 award, because the majority of the court concluded she had not filed her claim within the required 180 days.

Definitions Form Important Warrants. What constitutes *time* is frequently a contested concept in law. In this case, the crucial determination is at what point the clock on the statute of limitations began to run. And this question turned on the **definition** of an unlawful employment practice. The law is clear, as quoted previously: A claim must be filed within 180 days after the alleged unlawful employment practice. The definition of unlawful employment practice—whether what happened to Ledbetter is better defined as a discrete act of discrimination that occurred at a specific point in time or as the gradual emergence of something resembling a hostile work environment—will govern the starting point of the clock.

Justice Alito argued that, to satisfy the demands of the statute of limitations, Ledbetter had to satisfy both of the elements of the law—an employment practice and discriminatory intent—both occurring within the 180-day period. The central element of a disparate treatment claim such as Ledbetter made, said Justice Alito, is discriminatory intent. And, he continued, Ledbetter could not prove that the low paychecks Goodyear issued during the limitation period came with discriminatory intent. That, said Alito, happened earlier, and "current effects [low paychecks] cannot breathe life into prior, uncharged discrimination."

Justice Ginsberg, in her dissent, argued that the paychecks were discriminatory because they would have been larger if Ledbetter had been evaluated in a nondiscriminatory manner prior to the 180-day limitation period. Ginsberg argued that "each payment of a wage or salary infected by sex-based discrimination constitutes an unlawful employment practice; prior decisions, outside the 180-day charge-filing period, are not

---

[9]*Bowles v. Russell*, No. 06-5306; 127 S. Ct. 2360; 2007 U.S. LEXIS 7721.

themselves actionable, but they are relevant in determining the lawfulness of conduct within the period." This definition, Justice Ginsberg claimed, is more faithful to precedent, more in tune with the realities of the workplace, and more respectful of Title VII's remedial purpose. This argument, replied Justice Alito, "is squarely foreclosed by our precedents."

Stare Decisis: *Precedents Should be Respected.* Within the argument sphere of the U.S. Supreme Court, there is a powerful commonplace identified as *stare decisis*, a Latin term proclaiming that prior decisions of the court should be respected and, in most circumstances, should be allowed to stand. Even when justices might not like the outcome of a particular case, they will be reluctant to overturn a precedent that clearly applies. Of course, there will be argumentation around the questions of whether the current case is enough like the precedent case that what was decided then should rule now. Also, there will be argumentation around claims attempting to interpret the intended rule contained in the precedent.

Analogy: Present Case Is Analogous to a Precedent. When we say a precedent "applies," we refer to an argument based on the commonplace of **analogy**. Justice Alito argued that Lilly Ledbetter's case is analogous to the facts of a case previously decided by the U.S. Supreme Court, *Nat'l R.R. Passenger Corp. v. Morgan* (2002 U.S. LEXIS 4214). In that case, Abner J. Morgan, Jr., an African-American male, claimed "that during the time period that he worked for Amtrak he was 'consistently harassed and disciplined more harshly than other employees on account of his race.' While some of the alleged discriminatory acts about which Morgan complained occurred within [180] days of the time that he filed his charge with the EEOC, many took place prior to that time period" (12). In *Morgan*, the U.S. Supreme Court decided

> that the statute precludes recovery for discrete acts of discrimination or retaliation that occur outside the statutory time period. We also hold that consideration of the entire scope of a hostile work environment claim, including behavior alleged outside the statutory time period, is permissible for the purposes of assessing liability, so long as any act contributing to that hostile environment takes place within the statutory time period. (11)

Also in *Morgan*, the Court explained that the statutory term *employment practice* generally refers to "a discrete act or single 'occurrence'" that takes place at a particular point in time. Discrete acts are defined as decisions to terminate, failure to promote, denial of transfer, and refusal to hire, among others.

Justice Alito argued that the time limit period is triggered when a discrete unlawful practice occurs. Because the discrete decision to grant a lower pay raise because of her sex occurred much more than 180 days prior to her filing of charges, Ledbetter's claim cannot be considered because it was not timely filed and is thus time barred.

Justice Ginsberg replied that the Alito definition of Ledbetter's experience as coming from discrete acts of discrimination that occurred years prior to the claim is incorrect. She said that the *Morgan* decision defined two kinds of unlawful employment actions: discrete acts that are easy to identify as discriminatory and acts that recur and are cumulative in impact. She argued,

> Different in kind from discrete acts are claims based on the cumulative effect of individual acts. The *Morgan* decision placed hostile work environment claims in that category. Their very

nature involves repeated conduct that cannot be said to occur on any particular day. It occurs over a series of days or perhaps years and, in direct contrast to discrete acts, a single act of harassment may not be actionable on its own. The persistence of the discriminatory conduct both indicates that management should have known of its existence and produces a cognizable harm. Pay disparities, of the kind Ledbetter experienced, have a closer kinship to hostile work environment claims than to charges of a single episode of discrimination. Ledbetter's claim, resembling Morgan's, rested not on one particular paycheck, but on "the cumulative effect of individual acts."

Logic Provides a Respected Set of Criteria. Arguments on law are traditionally written so they can be criticized by the rules of **logic** (Aldisert). Justice Alito's argument could be set out logically this way:

Major Premise: The law, as expressed in our decision in *Morgan*, says that discrete acts of discrimination that occur outside the 180-day statute of limitations are time barred from consideration.

Minor Premise: Ledbetter's alleged acts of discrimination occurred outside the 180-day statute of limitations.

Conclusion: Ledbetter's alleged acts of discrimination are time barred from consideration.

Logical criteria center on **consistency** and **noncontradiction**. By using precedent to decide present cases, the Court seeks to apply the law consistently and to speak with a single voice. The law for *Morgan* should not be different from the law for *Ledbetter* and any future case that comes forward with an analogous set of facts. Logical form (thus called formal logic) provides for tests of **validity**, or whether the argument satisfies internal tests of consistency and noncontradiction. In this instance, Justice Alito can be said to be employing a form of categorical **syllogism** called a universal affirmative deemed inherently valid since the time of Aristotle (Aldisert, 43–47).

The shortcomings of logical analysis alone are revealed in the fact that Justice Ginsberg's argument can be set in an equally valid syllogism:

Major Premise: The law, as expressed in our decision in *Morgan*, says that consideration of the entire scope of a hostile work environment claim, including behavior alleged outside the statutory time period, is permissible for purposes of assessing liability as long as any act contributing to that hostile environment takes place within the statutory time period.

Minor Premise: Ledbetter's experience was recurrent and cumulative, and paychecks infected with discriminatory intent were issued within the statutory time period and thus is within the concept of a hostile work environment claim.

Conclusion: Ledbetter's claim can consider behavior alleged outside the statutory time period for purposes of assessing liability and thus is not time barred.

The question is clearly one of definition. If *Morgan* is the controlling law, and both sides accept it (we have omitted lengthy discussions of other cases both sides cited to keep our discussion focused on the argumentation process), then the decision turns on whether Ledbetter's experience is better defined as constituting a discrete act of discrimination or a recurrent and cumulative creation of a hostile work environment. And this discussion, of course, rests on competing narratives of Ledbetter's experience.

Courts Should Respect Legislative Intent. In the constitutional history of the United States, the three coequal branches of government—legislative, executive, and judicial—have continually engaged in contests over power and prerogative. Traditionally, the judicial branch has been defined as only interpreting the Constitution, not making law, which is the prerogative of the legislative branch. But just as the Court can be selective and editorialize in framing the narrative produced in the facts of a certain case, it can also be interpretative in defining the legislative intent behind any law. In the *Ledbetter* case, both the majority and the dissent claimed to be more faithful to the intent of Congress in passing the Civil Rights Act. Because courts do not engage in a conversation with legislators to iron out intent, the dialogue takes place at long distance: courts deciding and Congress legislating. Thus, in this case, the Lily Ledbetter Fair Pay Act of 2009 was enacted by Congress to correct an erroneous interpretation of their intent. Of course, this Congress included different people than those who passed the Civil Rights Act of 1964, and a future Congress might have a different "intent." The dialogue is ongoing.

With that said, arguments predicated on being faithful to **legislative intent** carry weight. Justice Alito argued that to accept Ledbetter's claims, "would distort Title VII's 'integrated, multistep enforcement procedure." He recounted how different factions argued during the debate over passage of the Civil Rights Act and how many compromises were necessary to win passage. He quoted language from other Court decisions to the effect that the Court should be "respectful of the legislative process that crafted this scheme (multistep enforcement procedure) [and must] give effect to the statute as enacted." He noted that the Court has "repeatedly rejected suggestions that we extend or truncate Congress' deadlines."

"A clue to congressional intent," replied Justice Ginsberg, "can be found in Title VII's backpay provision. The statute expressly provides that backpay may be awarded for a period of up to two years before the discrimination charge is filed. This prescription indicates that Congress contemplated challenges to pay discrimination commencing before, but continuing into, the 180-day filing period."

Policy Arguments Can Support Legal Arguments. Although courts are expected to rest decisions on legal arguments alone, it is not uncommon to find **policy arguments** brought in to explain and give support to legal decisions. Having argued that the court must respect legislative intent, Justice Alito proceeded to advance the policy arguments that give reason to the intent.

Employers, claimed Alito, must be protected from "the burden of defending claims arising from employment decisions that are long past." He continued, "Certainly, the 180-day EEOC charging deadline is short by any measure, but 'by choosing what are obviously quite short deadlines Congress clearly intended to encourage the prompt processing of all charges of employment discrimination.' This short deadline reflects Congress' strong preference for the prompt resolution of employment discrimination allegations through voluntary conciliation and cooperation."

Taking direct aim at Justice Ginsberg's defense of the *Ledbetter* claim, Justice Alito, using the commonplace of *reductio ad absurdum*,[10] claimed that if Ledbetter's

---

[10]Taken from studies of logic, the strategy of *reductio ad absurdum* proceeds by carrying an argument's premises to their logical extreme so as to expose their inherent weakness or fallacy.

position were adopted, it would mean that an employee could file a timely charge over a single discriminatory pay decision made 20 years ago, if it continued to affect the employee's pay today. In law, a doctrine labeled *laches* (pronounced la/chey) embraces a commonplace that "equity aids the vigilant and not those who procrastinate regarding their rights."[11] The idea is that waiting to make a charge until much time has passed causes a disadvantage to the other party. So, Justice Alito argued, statutes of limitation are good policy. Ledbetter's delay, he suggests, disadvantaged Goodyear because the supervisor who committed the alleged discrimination had died and could not testify in his own defense.

Justice Ginsberg argued that Ledbetter did not procrastinate unduly. Although discrete acts of discrimination can be readily identified and should bring a quick complaint, what Ledbetter experienced was different. "Compensation disparities" argued Justice Ginsberg, "are often hidden from sight. It is not unusual for management to decline to publish employee pay levels, or for employees to keep private their own salaries. Tellingly, Goodyear kept salaries confidential." This is a policy, Justice Ginsberg argued, that benefits an employer because when a woman is paid less than a similarly situated man, "the employer reduces its costs each time the pay differential is implemented." This makes pay discrimination different from most other forms of discrimination, concluded Justice Ginsberg. The **authority** of the EEOC was invoked by Justice Ginsberg to give weight to her argument. She observed that EEOC policy says that "each paycheck that complainant receives which is less than that of similarly situated employees outside of her protected classes could support a claim under Title VII." And, in fact, the EEOC had urged the courts to adopt that policy in the *Ledbetter* case. Justice Ginsberg argued, "the EEOC's interpretations mirror workplace realities and merit at least respectful attention."

In the last paragraph of Justice Ginsberg's dissent, which she uncharacteristically delivered orally from the bench, she said, "This is not the first time the Court has ordered a cramped interpretation of Title VII, incompatible with the statute's broad remedial purpose. As in 1991, the Legislature may act to correct this Court's parsimonious reading of Title VII."

Michael Starr and Christine M. Wilson, lawyers chosen to write an explanation of the *Ledbetter* decision to help the legal profession put it to use, report that in 1991 Congress had amended Title VII to overrule a Supreme Court decision.[12] This is apparently what Justice Ginsberg is calling for with regard to *Ledbetter*. They go on to observe that the "every paycheck" concept argued by Justice Ginsberg was first articulated before compensatory and punitive damages were available in Title VII cases. They continue,

> The prospect of stale claims is less daunting for employers when all that is at stake is back pay for the period of disparity. But when compensatory damages are also allowed and the underlying events occurred so long ago that critical defense witnesses are unavailable or dead [as was the case in *Ledbetter*], the balance shifts decidedly against asserting today claims of discrimination based on intentional acts committed long ago. (12)

---

[11]This definition can be found at www.lectlaw.com/def/1056.htm.
[12]See 42 U.S.C. 2000e-5(e)(2).

Starr and Wilson also acknowledge the charge by Justice Ginsberg that "victims of pay discrimination are not likely to know how much less they are paid than their counterparts or that discriminatory animus was at play." They suggest that the policy must be amended to clarify the time limits or to place some limit on compensatory damages.

CONCLUSION

Argumentation in law involves questions of fact and of law. When Lilly Ledbetter made her claim of discrimination, the steps in critical decision making were invoked to decide what had happened to her. Lawyers for Ledbetter struggled to find documents, such as records of pay for other employees doing similar work, records of performance evaluations, recollections of assignments, comments, attitudes, and the like, that might give evidence that she had been treated differently because of her sex. At the same time, lawyers for Goodyear looked at the same records and talked to employees and managers, all with the aim of showing that the evidence that Ledbetter's pay was lower than all others doing her kind of work could be explained by proper behavior such as performance appraisals.

From this work, narratives were created that accounted for the artifacts of the research process in a way that favored the side writing the narrative. Ledbetter's lawyers told a story of a woman who had been mistreated from the start because she was a woman in a man's world. Goodyear's lawyers told a story of an employee who had been treated properly but who had simply not done the job well enough to merit a higher salary.

In reviewing this phase of legal argumentation, we discovered that the so-called facts that emerge from the research may constrain the narratives that are created, but in a remarkable way, the narratives that are told may well work in return to constitute the facts. We saw how reality shifted from narrative to narrative as the storytellers sought to influence the decision making.

Although the research leading to the competing narratives went on, legal research also occurred. Lawyers on both sides read the appropriate statutes such as the Civil Rights Act of 1964, they read appellate court decisions on cases that seemed to be analogous to the *Ledbetter* narrative, and they read commentaries by legal authorities.

Goodyear's lawyers discovered that the Civil Rights Act has a 180-day statute of limitations, and they moved to have the case thrown out because Ledbetter's claim did not include acts of discrimination that happened within 180 days of her complaint. The trial judge rejected that motion and allowed the case to go to trial. The jury found in favor of Ledbetter, and ultimately she was awarded US$360,000.

On appeal, Goodyear argued that the trial judge had made a mistake by rejecting their motion to dismiss because of failure to timely file. When the case reached the U.S. Supreme Court, a majority agreed with Goodyear, and the claim was rejected.

In making its decision, the majority and the dissenters on the court used a variety of commonplaces in their arguments that tend to characterize legal argumentation. Courts try to decide only enough to dispose of the case and no more, and they will not consider questions the petitioner does not ask. Meeting time limits, or failing to do so, can be a quick way to dispose of a case. Arguments over interpretations and definitions consume a great deal of legal argumentation as courts try to satisfy the demands of *stare decisis*, and this involves many arguments from analogy. Traditionally, logic has been important to law, and it remains so today.

Although questions of law are the focus of courts, they bring in arguments that could be seen as policy claims to give strength to their decision. A major policy/legal argument is that courts should respect legislative intent.

EXERCISES/PROJECTS

1. Find a 2-hour period either from 9:30 to 11:30 A.M. or from 1:30 to 3:30 P.M. to spend in your local court—municipal, state, or federal. It would be a good idea to call the clerk of courts a few days in advance and ask about what trials will be going on. Tell the clerk you are a student interested in observing legal arguments, and you want to see a good example. Take notes on what you observe, and write a critical analysis of what you learn.

2. On the Internet, go to www.supremecourt.gov and click on the decision in the following case: Albert Snyder, Petitioner v. Fred W. Phelps, SR., ET AL. 562 U.S. _____ (2011); 2011 U.S. LEXIS 1903. Read the syllabus that summarizes this case involving members of the Westboro Baptist Church picketing the funeral of Marine Lance Corporal Matthew Snyder. The picketers had signs saying, "God Hates the USA/Thank God for 9/11," "America is Doomed," "Thank God for Dead Soldiers," Pope in Hell;" "Priests Rape Boys," "God Hates Fags," and other similar expressions. Albert Snyder, the father of the dead Marine, sued the church and its members for intentional infliction of emotional distress, intrusion upon seclusion, and civil conspiracy. Write an argument supporting your position on this case, using legal arguments as much as possible, and prepare for an in-class debate on it.

Argumentation in Science

KEY TERMS

science, p. 204
hypotheses, p. 206
theory, p. 206
scientific law, p. 206
natural order, p. 207
claims of fact, p. 207
peer review, p. 209
empirical, p. 209
replicate, p. 209
hypothetico-deductive method, p. 210

positionality, p. 210
generalization, p. 211
retroduction, p. 211
conditional cause, p. 213
homology, p. 215
specific instances, p. 217
decision rule, p. 218
testimony, p. 219
operationalizing, p. 220

For many people, scientific methods stand as the most competent way to understand what is going on in the world. Scientific standards for evidence and argument are held up as the way to understand what the natural world is like. Arguments that fail such tests are easily disregarded, not only by the scientists who work in the sphere but by lay persons as well. The sphere of science has great credibility in our society, and an examination of its understanding of evidence and argument will provide insight into the standards people frequently seek in public arguments.

WHAT IS SCIENCE?

First, let us define **science**. There are, after all, terms such as *physical science, human science, political science, life science, natural science*, and so on. There is the distinction made by many between quantitative and qualitative science. In this chapter, we take our definition of science from physicist F. David Peat. Peat described science as "that story our society tells itself about the cosmos." It you think back to Chapter 3, you may recall our statement that stories, or narratives, are important forms of argument. The science narrative provides a supposedly "objective account of the material world based upon measurement and quantification so that structure, process, movement, and transformation can be described mathematically in terms of fundamental laws" (208). Most of the scientific endeavors that fall within this account are quantitative, using physical science as a model and mathematics as a foundation to develop explanatory theories of how entities function. Science is more than method, however, as outlined in C. P. Snow's classic book *Two Cultures*, which describes the different modes of understanding that separate science from the arts and humanities. Thus, science refers to a way of understanding ourselves and the universe that differs from humanistic (literary, historical, philosophical) inquiry. Science also differs from *research*, which includes science, but also includes examination of individual phenomena rather than natural laws, and which is more likely to rely on qualitative and critical methods.

Some postmodern and feminist scholars have challenged the scientific narrative described in the previous paragraph. Their critique argues that, because scientists are members of society, scientific knowledge cannot be the outcome of completely neutral and objective rational thought. Therefore, the understanding gained through science is no more accurate than understanding gained through other approaches such as astrology or palm reading. From this perspective, science is a game with a set of rules created by scientists, and apparent successes of science in understanding the universe would not be defensible if society did not accept the rules of the scientific game. Postmodern critiques of science sometimes question whether a natural world exists outside of the mental constructs that humans erect. According to these critiques, science is no more than an elaborate social construct dedicated to maintaining existing patterns of hegemony.

Less extreme forms of postmodernism and feminism shift from challenging whether objective reality exists to challenging "magical notions of scientific objectivity" (Peterson et al. 2007, 75). This line of argument claims that everyone's—including scientists'—interpretation of reality is partial, and is influenced by their perspective. They have argued for more rigorous self-examination by scientists, an activity that is in harmony with science's basic tenets. For example, feminist critiques of science have argued that scientific theory and practice marginalize women. In response to this claim, the National Science Foundation has developed educational programs that affirmatively encourage young girls to study science and mathematics, has developed grant programs exclusively for women scientists, and has hosted seminars designed to encourage feminist scholars and traditional scientists to engage in critical discussions about the philosophy of science. The story of science, as modified by postmodern and feminist critique, has expanded to include alternative ways of asking questions about the universe. F. David Peat claimed that as long as these approaches "engage in disciplined argument and deduction, and that there is an element of careful attention to an observation, then the knowledge systems of other cultures have the right to stand as scientific viewpoints" (209).

This does not mean science has given up its search for understanding, nor does it translate into science as social construct. If you fall down the stairs, you are likely to get at least a few bruises. If you spend all of Saturday and Sunday partying, you will be less able to comprehend the 8:00 A.M. lecture on Monday morning than if you had taken time to sleep over the weekend. Notice that the expected results in these two examples include uncertainty—as does all scientific prediction. Although this chapter focuses on the use of argumentation in science as defined by the traditional markers of objectivity and quantification as a means of discovering fundamental laws, it is important to realize that the values of objectivity and quantification are merely markers, and that discovery is the goal.

The sphere of quantitative science can sometimes be identified by academic departments (e.g., physics, chemistry, geology, biology) in the natural sciences. Many social sciences departments (e.g., anthropology, communication, psychology) include both quantitative and qualitative science. The science that we discuss in this chapter ranges over a wide variety of fields with the physical sciences as its model.

We also need to distinguish between what we call *scientific argumentation*, political argumentation, and legal argumentation that is frequently associated with science. Scientists may be motivated to see that federal funding goes to their particular research. In addition, they may argue before public agencies for certain policy options. They may even argue that particular scientists are not competent or have falsified data. These are all part of the political and legal roles that scientists frequently play. These roles are illustrated in their public arguments over climate change, health care availability, child safety restraints in automobiles, and a host of other policy matters.

In this chapter, we examine not the political and legal roles of scientists, but what kind of argument and evidence they use in scientific journals, research papers, and grant applications. Although scientists frequently argue in the public sphere as experts, we look here at how they argue where other scientists are the decision makers. We will examine how science is integrated into political argument in Chapter 16.

SCIENTIFIC VALUES

One reason science presents such a persuasive narrative (as noted in Chapter 3) is that it appears consistent with many of society's core values, which we discussed in Chapter 8. The values of scientific study include knowledge, order, prediction, rationality, and usefulness. The individual values in this suite work together within scientific argumentation, although many of the values remain unstated. Sir Francis Bacon (1561–1626), who was one of the leading figures in the development of scientific philosophy and method, saw science as a means of constructing a better world for humans, through understanding natural truths. Although much has changed in the ensuing centuries, science in the twenty-first century remains consistent with this goal. Science begins from the premise that, where *knowledge* is concerned, more is better. This knowledge enables people to discover natural *order*. Once we understand the proper order of things, it becomes easier to *predict* future events, which should enable us to make more *rational* choices. All of this is important because it is *useful* for improving the human condition.

Natural order is first engaged through observation (empiricism), and is systematized and modeled by rational (mathematical and logical) means. In scientific argument, empirical observations are represented through agreed-on procedures in numerical forms of evidence that support **hypotheses**, or tentative assumptions made in order to draw out and test their empirical and/or logical consequences. Ideally, science proceeds from hypothesis testing, to theory development, to discovery of natural law. In this context, a **theory** refers to a hypothesis that has been subjected to testing, and thus offers greater likelihood of truth. A *law* refers to a statement about how some aspects of the natural world are organized or ordered. To refer to something as a **scientific law** is to claim that it is invariable under the same conditions.

Even if the **natural order** cannot be directly observed (i.e., you cannot observe a quark, a neutron, or an attitude), scientists still require that there be *empirical adequacy*. That is, the signs of the phenomenon must be observable. The procedures for finding these claims of fact must be clearly defined so that they may be replicated or questioned. These **claims of fact** are linked together to provide theoretical propositions of explanation. Such propositions are in turn used to predict another specific situation that has not been observed. That is, the signs of the phenomenon must be either directly or indirectly observable.

It is stated in claims of fact combined with other claims of fact already acknowledged to provide a *proposition of cause*. In the same way, a scientist could argue that the same causes will function in the future on another phenomenon that can never be directly observed. The same assumption, of the ability of theory to predict, holds for theories about gene structure, compliance gaining among humans, or social structure.

From this perspective, a theory about climate change is built from careful observation of the geological record. The case of global climate change is a useful place to begin our discussion of how the scientific method functions argumentatively because there is widespread interest in this issue. In this chapter, we will limit the discussion to argument within the scientific community. In Chapter 16, we will show how the argument changes when it moves into the sphere of government and politics.

Global climate change is a complex phenomenon that is planetary in scope and operates on a timescale that exceeds seasons, political terms, and the human life span. Global climate change differs from *weather* in both its spatial and temporal expanse. During the twentieth century, the earth's annual mean temperature increased by about 2°F. Given this small number, you may be wondering what all the fuss is about. After all, the temperature fluctuates more than that between noon and midnight, and between winter and summer. Physiological mechanisms have evolved that enable living things to adjust to short-term (easily up to a year) and localized changes in temperature. The problem is, however, that a small change is a serious matter to the global climate system. Temperatures that continue to increase over a long time and across the entire planet influence a complex system of intertwined processes that absorb or reflect sunshine, transport heat around the globe through the atmosphere and oceans, and exchange chemicals to and from different parts of the system. And humans depend on that system to support their lifestyles, not to mention their biological survival. Thus, it is no wonder that global climate change has been the subject of extensive scientific investigation (Intergovernmental Panel on Climate Change).

THE TRADITION OF ARGUMENTATION IN SCIENCE

There are several ways that the climate change debate helps to define the tradition of argumentation in the science sphere, four of which serve as a preliminary definition of scientific argumentation. They are that science (1) deals in claims and propositions of fact, (2) searches for truth over personal gain, (3) reveals results that are complete enough to test, and (4) establishes theory that changes slowly.

Claims of Fact

First, traditional scientific argument, in its central concern, argues claims and propositions of fact. The focus on facts is especially consistent with the scientific values of knowledge and rationality. Stephen Toulmin et al. identify four "broad and familiar issues" of science that focus on claims of fact.

1. What kinds of things are there [or were there] in the world of nature?
2. How are [or were] these things composed, and how does this makeup affect their behavior or operation?
3. How did all these things come to be composed as they are [or were]?
4. What are the characteristic functions of each such natural thing and/or its parts? (315)

In the case of global climate change, scientists deal with issues such as the following: (1) Is it occurring? (2) What has been causing it? (3) Does it pose dangers or problems to human society as a whole, as well as to specific segments of human society? (4) How serious are those dangers? And (5) What can be done to either slow or stop the warming trend?

All these questions must be answered by claims of fact. The policy questions that might come up move the argument into the realm of government and politics, which we discuss in Chapter 16.

Henry N. Pollack, a professor of geophysics who has studied global climate change for more than 40 years, described questions of fact that summarize the scientific debate about global climate change (216):

1. Has earth been warming over the past few centuries?
2. How has the rate of warming changed over time?
3. What is causing the warming?
4. What have been and will be the consequences of global warming?
5. What can be done to remediate the change?

By the early 1980s, most scientists had answered the first question affirmatively and had begun to explore the details of the others. At the beginning of the twenty-first century, there is a strong consensus among scientists that the earth has been warming during the past few centuries; that human activities associated with industrialization have caused a significant increase in the rate of warming since about 1850 (with another sharp increase about 1950); that consequences of this change already are being felt by some segments of society, while other consequences are expected; and that these consequences will have negative impacts on most segments of society. Scientists also tend to agree that human society can remediate this problem by reducing greenhouse emissions, particularly carbon dioxide (CO_2). Note that, although climate scientists have not focused on whether society *should* take measures to reduce greenhouse emissions, their work does include explicit value statements. Scientists tend to characterize climate warming in negative ways, using phrases such as "will get *worse*," "is increasingly *severe*," and "is a growing *problem*." It would be somewhat difficult, however, to maintain completely neutral language when one is describing widespread crop failure, inundation of coastal communities, and loss of glacial water supplies.

Search for Truth over Personal Gain

Scientists are not supposed to act for personal gain, but for the betterment of society. This is especially consistent with the scientific values of knowledge and usefulness; given that knowledge refers to true understanding of nature, and usefulness refers to improving the human condition. Yet public identification of discoveries has been, since the early eighteenth century, the basis on which scientific achievement is credited (Gross 90). Robert K. Merton identified the "paradox at the heart of the scientific enterprise" years ago:

> While the general progress of scientific knowledge depends heavily on the relative subordination of individual efforts to communal goals, the career progress of scientists depends solely on the recognition of their individual efforts. (Gross 89)

The paradox has always been there, yet scientists are expected to have their work subjected to **peer review** in which evidence and argument are tested by the scientific value of developing new knowledge, not the professional advancement of the scientist. This is one reason the scientific community is leery of climate research funded by the petroleum industry, which has lobbied successfully to prevent U.S. energy and environmental policies from responding to mainstream science on climate change. For example, Dr. Willie Soon and Dr. Sallie Baliunas presented a study that found twentieth-century warming "unremarkable compared with other climate shifts over the last 1,000 years." Other scientists were skeptical of their results, pointing out that the two researchers were funded by the George C. Marshall Institute, which "has long fought limits on gas emissions, [and that] the study in Climate Research was in part underwritten by US$53,000 from the American Petroleum Institute, the voice of the oil industry" (Revkin).

Testable Results

Science exists, according to its own rules, in an atmosphere of the free exchange of ideas, and to withhold information inhibits scientific progress. This claim is especially congruent with the scientific values of prediction and order. Probably most important, this argument calls attention to the fact that science is far more than a collection of observations or theories. Science is a comprehensive system of **empirical** knowledge building. So, the theory revealed, the methods followed, and the evidence used are all part of a comprehensive system. The results of climate science studies address climate questions in various ways, and those studies that pass the test of peer review are published in scientific journals such as *Science* and *Nature*, or more specifically focused journals such as *Climatic Change*, *Climate Research*, and *Transactions of the American Geophysical Union*. Details of the hypotheses tested and methodologies used for data analysis are provided so that other researchers can **replicate** (conduct an exact repetition of) the study to determine whether the claims were sufficiently and appropriately supported.

Established Theory Changes Slowly

Scientific theory evolves slowly over time, and requires significant argumentation to achieve change. The resistance to sudden change relates directly to the scientific value of order, in that it requires overwhelming evidence to change established patterns. Even Thomas Kuhn, who used the term *scientific revolution* to characterize major changes in theory, agrees that there is no sudden overturning of theory (Suppe 135). The replacement of Newtonian physics by the theory of relativity did not come suddenly when Albert Einstein said "$E = mc^2$." There was a continual building of the theory, as one anomaly after another was found in Newtonian physics. Newtonian mechanics were being dismantled for many years before Einstein. Likewise, the theory of evolution had been around for some time before Charles Darwin. He provided evidence and the unifying explanation and got credit for it. These were not scientific revolutions; rather, they were theoretical statements that built on, and made sense of, previous theory and findings.

One reason established theory changes so slowly is that the *scientific* or **hypothetico-deductive method** requires scientists to ground any new research in past research. Unlike the descriptive method, the scientific or hypothetico-deductive method focuses on hypothesis testing and the use of a methodology (usually statistical) designed to maximize accuracy in the interpretation of research results. This approach requires scientists to move through a predetermined series of steps, all of which should be quite clearly described for fellow scientists. This method encourages scientific endeavor to focus on questions of fact and to ensure the production of testable results. It is grounded in an assumption that is remarkably similar to that found in both postmodern and feminist thought: *Despite endeavors to maintain objectivity, all investigators are finite beings, positioned in time and space.* They cannot observe everything all the time. Instead, what they discover will be influenced by their focus. By beginning with a specific hypothesis to be tested, investigators provide their audience with a rationale for the research focus. Or, in stating the hypothesis to be tested, investigators reveal their **positionality**. Scientists using the hypothetico-deductive method generally follow a specific set of steps when developing and delivering an argument to their peers.

1. Identify the research problem.
2. Conduct literature review.
3. Identify broad research objectives.
4. Collect preliminary data if needed.
5. Conduct exploratory data analysis.
6. Formulate research hypotheses.
7. Formulate testable (usually statistical) hypotheses.
8. Design methodology.
9. Prepare research proposal.
10. Obtain peer review and revise.
11. Perform experiment, collect data.
12. Analyze data.
13. Evaluate, interpret, and draw conclusions.
14. Submit manuscript to peer-reviewed journal.
15. Respond to additional reviewers' suggestions.
16. Systemically repeat the process, beginning from step 5 above.

FIGURE 13.1

Hypothetico-deductive Argumentation

Scientists observe physical, biological, human, or social phenomena for factual claims. These claims are combined with existing knowledge to form theories that serve as general laws or rules about the natural condition. The theories develop in a system of peer review where others can see the claim, the evidence, and the method of argumentation and test them to confirm or deny. Because theories are built up of many subtheories and empirical confirmations, they are not, according to scientific tradition, easily overturned. New major theories are slowly infused into the system until, at some point, there is a realization among scientists that a crisis exists and they need a new theory to account for all the contradictions in the original theory. With this clearer understanding of scientific argument, we will look more carefully at the roles that the different types of argument, forms of evidence, value systems, credibility, and refutation (covered in Chapters 6 through 11) play in it.

SCIENTIFIC USE OF ARGUMENT TYPES

All six of the types of arguments discussed in Chapter 4 appear in scientific argument: logic, generalization, cause, sign, analogy, and authority. Generalization, cause and sign—particularly cause and sign—are the most important. In addition, scientists apply each of these types by their own value system based on empiricism, logic, and mathematics.

Argument by Generalization

In one sense, all scientific argument is by **generalization**. The goal of such argument is to make observations that will explain a class of phenomena. Those explanations generalize about how individual cases behave or about what properties individual cases have in common. Until well into the nineteenth century, using induction or experiments to form generalizations that would serve as theories to explain the natural world was the dominant tradition of science known as Baconianism after Francis Bacon, its chief architect (Campbell, *Man Cannot Speak* 500). Generalization in modern science functions by what C. S. Peirce first called *abduction*, and later referred to as *retroduction*. Because scientists more commonly use the second term, we will use it in this chapter. **Retroduction** refers to developing a hypothesis that would, if true, best explain a particular set of observations. Retroductive reasoning begins with a set of observations or facts, and then infers the most likely or best explanation to account for these facts. Consider the following: All the eggs in a bird nest disappeared overnight. There were no shell fragments, animal tracks, or disturbance of leaf litter at the nest site; therefore, a snake is the most likely predator; or, the earth's glaciers have melted at an extremely rapid rate ever since the Industrial Revolution was well established. Since that time, people have been burning large amounts of coal, oil, and natural gas, the waste from which emits large amounts of CO_2 into the atmosphere. When the atmosphere of a planet is made up of more, rather than less CO_2, that planet will be hotter than it otherwise would be. Therefore, the emissions from burning fossil fuels are likely to be a significant contributor to global climate change.

Although both deduction (see Chapters 3 and 4) and induction (see the discussion of examples in Chapter 7) are important to scientific argumentation, retroductive reasoning is, in many ways, the most interesting because it is more likely to result in novel explanations for puzzling phenomena than are induction or deduction. It also is much more likely to be wrong! Inductive reasoning is an effective way to derive important principles of association and is less likely to prove incorrect than retroduction. It has been the workhorse of science for centuries. Deductively derived conclusions are uninteresting in themselves; after all, they follow deterministically from the major premise. Instead, the value of deductive reasoning is that it allows scientists to devise ways to critically challenge and evaluate retroductively developed hypotheses.

So, the scientist begins with a hypothesis formed from limited cases. This hypothesis *may be* a valid generalization. But the generalization must be tested for what it might be expected to show. To some extent, this is a matter of replication (repetition of an experiment to see whether the results are the same).

Other confirmation is based on what can be generalized, based on past research. Initially, scientific debate about climate change focused on whether the earth was warming. Climate scientists answered this question by generalizing from historical, archeological, and geological records. They examined materials such as the polar ice shield, samples taken from the ocean floor, and samples from the earth's core. When the hypothesis of global warming became an established theory, the debate turned to how quickly the earth was warming. When research indicated that warming during the twentieth century was unusually fast, the debate shifted to *causes* of the rapid warming.

Although tests are part of the generalization process, they are not argument by generalization themselves, but argument from sign, as we will explain shortly. Scientific argument should build theories that will provide the scientific community with the most rational explanation of the natural order. This requires extensive experimentation and evidence, but generalization is only part of the process. Perhaps more important is the examination of anomalies in the theory. Toulmin, Rieke, and Janik provide an example from weather forecasting:

> Weather forecasting, for instance, presents some serious challenges to science, to find ways of squaring the observed course of meteorological events with the accepted principles of physical science. But that does not mean that scientists feel any responsibility for explaining every last day-to-day or minute-to-minute change in the weather. Presumably, such changes are brought about in a perfectly intelligible way by some minor local fluctuation in the atmospheric conditions, but normally no real scientific interest will be served by tracking down exactly what that fluctuation was. Only if a *significant* anomaly can be demonstrated—for instance, a storm that "blew up out of nowhere" under atmospheric conditions that apparently ruled out such a possibility—will there be a genuine *scientific issue* to face. (319)

Argument by generalization is, on the face of it, crucial to science. The generalizations (theories) require testing to make them more powerful. That testing is not always by replication. It will more often rely on the next two kinds of argument: cause and sign.

Argument by Cause

The assumption of science is that there is order in nature and that order is held together by cause-and-effect relationships. High- and low-pressure changes cause changes in the weather. Changes in the social order cause changes in the way individuals live their lives.

Once climate scientists began to focus on causes of climate change, they discovered that natural factors dominated climatic fluctuations up to somewhere between the years 1750 and 1850. From about 1850 to 1950, human factors associated with industrialization grew to sufficient potency to rival natural factors, leading to climate variability derived from a complex blend of natural and technological causes. In the latter half of the twentieth century, the technologically derived causes outpaced natural factors by a large margin.

Usually, a cause comes before the effect and is both necessary and sufficient for the effect to occur. Thus, the cause must always be there. A cause is sufficient if no other factor is necessary. It takes combustion, fuel, and oxygen for there to be fire. These three together are necessary and sufficient cause for fire. Fuel alone, however, is a necessary but not a sufficient cause. The force of a scientific argument is determined by the extent to which necessity and sufficiency approach certainty.

This requirement of approaching certainty poses an increasing problem in all sciences, but particularly in the human sciences. No cases of human behavior meet certainty standards. Consequently, the human sciences use a more open statistical probability as the basis for judging cause, called a **conditional cause**. The claim is the best explanation, but it is conditional because it is supported at a statistical level that admits of some evidence to the contrary. For example, Beatrice Schultz studied several variables to see how persons who were trained in argumentation would evaluate themselves as leaders in decision-making groups compared with the self-evaluation of those who had not been so trained.

> Self-ratings for argumentative trainees and other participants were compared by t-test, with results showing that trainees perceived themselves as significantly more self-assured ($t = 2.78$; df 36; $p < .01$), more goal-oriented ($t = 2.65$; df 36; $p < .01$), more quarrelsome ($t = 2.85$; df 36; $p < .01$), and in the direction of significance for summarizing ($t = 1.81$; df 36; $p = <.08$). Untrained participants did not significantly alter their ratings after the second session. (560)

Before the training, there was no difference between the experimental group and the control group, but after the experimental group was trained, they showed a significant difference in the perception of their leadership qualities versus the control group. The only difference between the two was the training that became the necessary and sufficient cause for the change. How well do we know that? Consider one leadership characteristic: "self-assured ($t = 2.78$; df 36; $p < .01$)." A t-test is a statistical procedure to compare the means of two groups. The t value of 2.78 with the recorded degrees of freedom (df 36) tells the researcher that chance alone was unlikely to be the source of the difference they found; probably, less than one time in a hundred.

If the design of the experiment was perfect, the elimination of chance as an explanation should leave only the "treatment" (training) as the cause. But this experiment does not prove that the training caused everyone to change as would be expected in a traditional understanding of cause. As a matter of fact, some participants changed, some did not, and a few probably regressed. Statistically, however, the total group changed. The change was dependent on an unknown characteristic, so we can say there is cause but the cause (training) is conditional.

The *Challenger* spaceship disaster was caused by an O ring that failed when the temperature fell below 53°F, the minimum for which the engineers had tests (Gouran 439). A decision was made to go ahead with the launch even when the temperature fell below that level. Dennis Gouran explains that the odds were against failure in that technological system. However, as the tragedy illustrates, this conditional cause could not predict an individual case—only a probability.

Scientists look for the necessary and sufficient causes of phenomena. There is always some question, but certain causal relationships, particularly in the physical and biological sciences, come closest to producing the ideal relationship between cause and effect. For much of science, a conditional relationship is the best that can be expected.

Argument by Sign

A major way to test a theory is to look for observable phenomena that the theory predicts should be there. The theory of global warming relies heavily on sign argument. Because the theory is based on propositions of past fact, the types of evidence all are signs of what has happened throughout earth's history. The Intergovernmental Panel on Climate

Change noted several signs to support its argument. For example, the global average sea level rose between 0.1 and 0.2 meters during the twentieth century, global ocean heat content has increased since the late 1950s, the thickness of the Arctic sea ice has declined by about 40% during late summer in recent decades, and the increase in temperature in the twentieth century is probably the largest of any century during the past 1000 years. These claims are not advanced as causes, but as signs, of global warming.

The argument from sign becomes particularly crucial in the human sciences. All survey research is a sign argument. The sample of the population is taken as a sign of the whole population. It is also an important part of experimental research in the social sciences. For instance, Cynthia Hoffner and Joanne Cantor wanted to find out what factors affect "children's enjoyment of a frightening film sequence." They studied 5- to 7-year olds and 9- to 11-year olds. The children viewed a sequence from *Swiss Family Robinson* in which two brothers encounter a snake. The researchers varied the introduction and the ending to provide either a threat or happy circumstances.

First, note that a video of the Robinson boys encountering a snake is taken to be a sign of a frightening film sequence. After viewing the sequence, the children were asked if they felt happy, scared, or just OK. They were also asked a number of questions such as how worried, scared, and so on they were. Note that what the children said is taken as a sign of what they actually felt.

In addition, Hoffner and Cantor monitored skin temperature and heart rate to measure the children's "residual arousal to enjoyment." Here is one example of their sign argument on this subject: "Skin temperature changes accompany peripheral vasoconstriction, which is a measure of [sign of] sympathetic arousal" (46–48). We have simplified the procedure they used, but it should be clear that sign argument is used at every stage of the study's design.

Social scientists cannot show you "enjoyment" or "frightening," and they cannot show you an "attitude," "violence," "communication conflict," or "deception." They must test their theories against things, events, or behaviors that are signs of those abstract concepts. In Chapter 2, we talked about worldviews that some people believe guide human mental processes. However, no one has ever seen a worldview, held one up to the light, or poked it with a finger. So, what makes the concept believable? Worldviews are accepted because numerous studies using outward signs point to the existence of such organizing principles.

Argument by Analogy

Scientists usually argue from generalization, cause, and sign. They also use analogy. In one sense, all argument is by analogy because claims are not the same as the incidents, things, or beings on which they are based. For example, a sign can be seen as an analogy for what it represents. Scientists use analogy extensively to explain a phenomenon; but only very carefully to help build an empirical argument to be tested.

Physicist Roger S. Jones uses a simple example of the scientific activity of measurement. To measure the length of a table top, he says,

> All I need to do is decide between which two marks on the meter stick the right end of the table lies. Deciding whether two points are coincident boils down to making judgments about the distance between two points. Point A on the table and point B on the meter stick cannot literally be coincident, for two objects cannot occupy the same place at the same time. (21)

In that sense, even measurement is an analogy. Analogy serves in this system as an explanation. There are quarks in physics, DNA in genetics, and attitudes in communication. They help explain phenomena that cannot literally be seen.

Science also uses the analogy of mathematics as a model of the natural world. Gene Shoemaker estimates that "an asteroid more than six-tenths of a mile in diameter will hit earth once every 40 million years" (Lessem 293). From this generalization, you could reason by analogy that the earth is overdue for an impact that might kill three-fourths of all living things.

In the scientific tradition we are examining here, analogy, although useful as explanation, is not as useful in making an empirical argument. Because scientists try to understand the natural world, there is a problem with the comparison of two things that are not the same. This problem applies particularly to figurative analogy, as in the example (in Chapter 4) in which undocumented immigrants are compared with snowflakes. Even a literal analogy, such as the one drawn between the oil industry's treatment of poor African-Americans in Norco, Louisiana, and its treatment of aboriginal inhabitants of Ogoniland, Nigeria, has its problems. There are at least as many differences as similarities between the treatments accorded the two populations. It is very unlikely that residents of Norco would be hanged for organizing a peaceful protest, even if it caused a work stoppage at the local factory. Protesters might be ignored, or even taken to jail, but few observers would equate those punishments with the hanging that occurred in Nigeria. In a scientific argument, the usefulness of this analogy would be based on a determination of what conditions are most appropriate for determining the industry's ability to influence the relevant economic, political, and legal structures so as to maximize its advantage.

Although analogy is not as forceful a scientific argument as the three we discussed before, analogy *is* argued, particularly in the biological sciences. The term used for an analogous relationship in biological sciences is *homologous*, which means there are extensive similarities of structure and evolutionary origin between two biological entities. In genetics, for instance, **homology** means having the same linear sequence of genes as another chromosome. So for a paleontologist to claim an analogy (homology) between a dinosaur and a bird requires detailed evidence and generalization.

John Lyne and Henry F. Howe use the example of E. O. Wilson, who moved far from his own area of expertise as an entomologist ("his publications prior to 1971 concern such topics as chemical communication among ants, and castes within insect societies"). In 1975, Wilson wrote *Sociobiology: The New Synthesis*. In it, and subsequently, he and his followers argue for the existence of genes for moral principles such as "altruism" (Lyne and Howe 136–140). Lyne and Howe criticize Wilson because sociobiology reveals a "superficial relationship." To say, for instance, that "certain human behavior is 'like' a certain baboon behavior" provides a basis for an analogy in public argument but not the homology necessary to a geneticist (142). It is probably most significant that sociobiology has had considerable popularity outside biology in the public sphere. Decision makers in the public sphere hold analogy to less rigid standards than scientists do.

However, scientists interested in the effect of carcinogens on rats believe there is a homology between rats and humans. To develop statistical analyses of the effects of smoking and cancer on humans when large amounts of tars and nicotines are ingested in a short period of time, rats are used rather than humans. Decisions are made about amounts necessary and periods of time based on assumptions about comparative body weights. More important is the basic assumption that humans and rats are homologous. That is, the analogy is based on extensive similarities of structure and evolutionary origin between rats and humans.

Unless a very strong analogy (homology) can be established, argument by analogy in science looks more like generalization. It serves as an explanation of a phenomenon.

Argument from Authority

An argument warranted by the authority of scientific principle is considerably different from argument from authority in public argument. In public argument, you might use authority to prove a claim ("Lower interest rates stimulate the economy, according to the chair of the Federal Reserve Board"). A scientist, however, is likely to use something more like a refutational argument. For instance,

1. The established theory has a lot of strength because of its long-standing success in predicting situations.
2. The countertheory has little evidence for its position.
3. Therefore, the established theory is still valid.

Whether as a constructive claim or a refutational one, such an argument does not look like the typical argument from authority found in public argument (Albert Einstein is a credible scientist, so we can trust his theory $E = mc^2$). For scientists making arguments in the scientific sphere, the only authority is the authority of established theory. It is probable that in private they are more likely to pay attention, if not give adherence, to arguments advanced by highly reputable scholars over unknowns, or to place greater weight on theories advanced by persons with better credentials.

By the usual rules of scientific argumentation, then, argument from authority is based on the authority of the theory, rather than of an individual. Recall our earlier claim that traditionally, scientific advancement subordinates individual effort to the search for knowledge. Individuals do have their names attached to theories (Haley's Comet, Heisenberg's uncertainty principle, Newton's laws, Darwin's theory) and scientists recognize the outstanding achievements of others, with the Nobel and other prizes. However, in the presentation of scientific arguments in scholarly papers and journal articles, you will not find the argument "X is true because Y said it."

Of course, each scientific paper includes a review of the literature in which the scientist identifies the significant findings to date and shows how the current research fits with it. The review of the literature gives the appearance of argument from authority because the most significant contributions must be by the most authoritative researchers. However, the argument advanced in the review of the literature is about the findings and theories of the research. The authority of the author is secondary. The authority of the theory is primary, yet it is not sufficient to maintain a claim in the face of conflicting empirical evidence.

There is also the authority of established theories. Earlier we noted that E. O. Wilson takes on an extensive burden of proof because his findings challenge established theory. The assumption in science that the established theory should remain until significant evidence is generated against it gives one who wishes to overturn it a tremendous burden of proof. The presumption for the status quo is particularly strong in the sciences.

Argumentation in the sphere of science concentrates on argument by generalization, cause, and sign. Its use of generalization is somewhat different from the usual understanding of that term because it is oriented to testing theory rather than simply replicating it. Scientific arguments depend particularly on cause and, to a lesser extent, sign. Argument by analogy is used mostly as a method of explanation. In empirical argument it is rare, found in a form more like generalization. Argument by authority is considered insufficient, although established principles have a kind of authority, and personal authority may play a role in private thought or discussion. Argumentation in science, as we have mentioned several times, is based on empirical evidence and we now turn to the subject of evidence.

SCIENTIFIC USE OF EVIDENCE

There are three forms of evidence, as we noted in Chapter 7: examples, statistics, and testimony. All can be found in scientific argumentation. We noted earlier that science is not simply a collection of observations or theories. It is a comprehensive system of empirical theory building. As we begin to examine the nature of scientific evidence we must look at that term *empirical* more carefully.

Empirically Grounded Claims

Traditionally, to be empirically grounded means that a claim must be based on sensory experience. Scientific explanations are empirical arguments when the evidence can be seen, heard, touched, smelled, or tasted. That understanding seemed reasonable in earlier centuries when our scientific theories were limited by our immediate senses, augmented by instruments such as microscopes and telescopes. Such limits are no longer applied to the term *empirical* because there is too much of what is known as reality that cannot be observed through even the augmented senses.

Quarks in physics, universes in astronomy, traits in biology, and the Jurassic period in paleontology are not available to the senses. "Nevertheless, science remains empirical in that its justification is in the interpretation of the material reality in which we function. In short, science makes sense of what we see, hear, and touch even though its explanation may incorporate much beyond that" (Anderson 12).

Specific Instances

Specific instances provide the empirical grounding for a scientific claim. That should be obvious. Colonies of bees, strata of rocks, actions of individuals all provide the empirical bases for forming generalizations about those phenomena that lead to hypotheses. Further examination of other instances serves to replicate, modify, or reject a theory.

A *New York Times* article about climate change research illustrates how several specific instances can strengthen, or specify, an existing claim. The instances included claims that Alaska has warmed by eight degrees over the past 30 years, today's Arctic temperatures are the highest in at least the past 400 years, and Arctic ice volume decreased 42% during the past 35 years. Based on these instances (in addition to other supporting evidence), the Office of Naval Research warns that it is plausible "that the summer Arctic ice cap will disappear completely by 2050" (Kristof A13).

Most of the scientific controversy about global warming surrounds different scenarios that are projected by computer models (Intergovernmental Panel on Climate Change). One set of scenarios assumes rapid economic development and globalization; rapid diffusion of new technologies; a global human population demographic that stabilizes, then slightly declines after 2050; and a shift in energy choices away from fossil fuels. Another set of scenarios assumes slower diffusion of new technologies, continuation of existing fertility patterns, and energy usage remaining dependent on fossil fuels. As you can imagine, each of these combinations of economic development, population trajectory, and energy choice predicts different greenhouse gas concentrations in the atmosphere and the accompanying increase of the global mean temperature. Scientists have attempted to incorporate in the climate models information from diverse disciplines including at least biology, chemistry, geology, communication, economics, and political science. Given the differences in scale, technique, and philosophy among these diverse disciplines, there is considerable controversy over both the data that are used in the models and the feedback loops that are hypothesized.

Such questioning is not unusual in science. No matter how many replications are achieved, the conditional nature of theories means that arguments are frequently based on statistical probability and are always open to further questioning.

Statistics in Science

We noted in Chapter 7 that statistics are essentially a numerical compacting of specific instances. They provide a means of talking about many specific instances without citing every one. That approach to explanation is common for most public, even legal, argumentation. But science uses statistics in many more ways.

In scientific argumentation, statistics are not simply a form of support. Ranging from relatively simple content analysis using some measure of an average to complex computerized programs of statistical analysis, statistics become a way of reasoning. Statistical reasoning provides the basis for generalizations about data, and arguments about the cause for the evidence assembled.

The numbers that comprise statistics serve as a sign for conditions in the natural world. Their usefulness to science is determined by the extent to which they actually are representative (signs) of what they propose to measure. No one can ever "know" many natural phenomena, as we observed in the previous section on specific instances. To use statistics, the scientist has to make assumptions about what makes a certain configuration of numbers a legitimate sign of the natural world. The three tasks of statistics are as follows:

1. *To quantify a set of observations into a set of numbers.* This is the descriptive use of statistics. Statistics reveal the central tendency of the numbers or the averages (mode, median, or mean), the distribution of certain characteristics, the dispersion of them, and the association among different characteristics in the set of numbers. Perhaps there are 15,000 students in your university and 54% of them are women. The average age is 23.7 years. These are all numbers that describe.

2. *To determine whether the sample is representative (a sign) of the population from which it was drawn.* A poll on your campus says that 58% of the students favor national health insurance. Were the students questioned representative of your student body?

3. *To determine by a decision rule whether the characteristics found can be attributed to an error in sampling* (the null hypothesis) or, if not, whether an alternative explanation, usually the hypothesis, is confirmed (Anderson 175–176).

Recall the study of children and the film sequence from *Swiss Family Robinson*. The researchers used a statistical test to determine how significant the results were.

The first task is to quantify observations into a set of numbers and relationships that will tell the researcher how to describe a population. The first task concerns measurement much like the general use of statistics discussed in Chapter 7. The second and third tasks are concerned with meaning. These statistics are used to develop knowledge about a population.

For these tasks, a **decision rule** is necessary to decide what is and what is not worth knowing. For the scientist, tasks two and three are at least as important as task one.

A look at these three tasks illustrates that there are assumptions that cannot be proven but must be taken as givens. For example, in measurement a primary assumption is that the numbers represent the phenomena. If not, then one's statistical descriptions have no real meaning. Another is that there is such a thing as a representative sample. If not, studies of public opinion, the behavior of chimpanzees, the effect of carcinogens on rats, or the physical properties of granite, would not be possible. If there is no such thing as a random sample that can be taken to be representative (a sign) of the population, the understanding of a natural phenomenon is impossible. But scientists do assume that a representative sample is possible. Another assumption is that the rate of error (the chance of being wrong) will identify the occasion of error (that the finding is false). Statistics are important sources of evidence that link with argument by generalization, cause, sign, and analogy to form a composite system of argument.

Testimony

Testimony is a form of evidence that can stand alone as grounds for an argument from authority. For instance, you could argue that because E. O. Wilson is a respected scientist, his theory that there are genes for moral principles should be accepted. But Lyne and Howe criticize that view because his theory is outside his expertise and, more important, he does not present sufficient evidence for the theory. Is there a place for testimony in scientific argument? The answer in the human sciences is yes. In such human sciences as psychology, communication, sociology, anthropology, and political science, testimony is at least a significant basis of evidence. It is used, however, in a special way.

Testimony functions as evidence when, in surveys or experiments, people express an opinion or indicate the facts that they know about a situation. For instance, Pamela and William Benoit were interested in discovering how people account for failure or success in an interpersonal argument and how they perceived the consequences for self and other relationships. They asked 27 students to write essays describing occasions of success and failure in interpersonal argument and answer questions about the consequences. Those written responses constituted the testimony that, when analyzed, provided the categories of explanations for success or failure.

Sometimes the evidence is taken from a set of categories that people judge. For instance, in Chapter 8, we introduce a series of value terms by Milton Rokeach to represent the 18 major terminal and the 18 major instrumental values. People are given one or both lists and asked to rank-order them, and the group's composite response is taken as a hierarchy of that group's values. Like Benoit and Benoit, Rokeach used open-ended testimony to discover the values. But both studies rely on testimony in defining categories and in forming generalizations about their use by a group. The evidence is testimony (and hangs on the scientist's assumptions that the testimony is both true and real). It reflects the opinion and knowledge of the persons engaged in the experiment.

What you can see from this brief summary is that all three of the evidence forms are found in scientific argument. Statistics are clearly the most critical. Specific instances and testimony (in the human sciences) are the raw material from which statistical inferences are made. Statistical inferences are essentially linked to argument by generalization, cause, sign, and sometimes analogy.

SCIENTIFIC METHOD AS ARGUMENT

The steps of the hypothetico-deductive method are intended to guide researchers in producing the most credible argument possible. *Identifying the research problem* requires scientists to use generalization, cause, sign, and sometimes analogical forms of argument. For example, when scientists argue that increased levels of CO_2 lead to global warming, they are claiming that CO_2 is a *cause*, and global warming is its effect. When they provide evidence that glaciers in South America are retreating, that the ice sheet in arctic regions is thinning, and that sea levels are rising, they are claiming that these events are *signs* of global warming. When they explain that global climate change is a complicated system response to multiple individual events and behaviors, they are *generalizing* from the few data points they have collected. The requirement to conduct a *literature review* indicates how differently authority is used in scientific argument. Researchers do not need to review the previous research of any individual scientist so much as they need to review the primary theoretical perspectives (of course, certain names do become connected with certain theoretical claims). If they attempt to argue for something that counteracts established theory, their burden of proof is significant. Most often, they will use the literature review to identify one small weakness within existing theory, and then argue that the current (or proposed) research takes care of that small weakness.

Identifying research objectives and formulating hypotheses are fundamental to the values espoused by science. In Chapters 8 and 9, we discussed values and credibility. Science values both order and the discovery of new knowledge. You may recall we emphasized that values function systematically, rather than individually. Without the necessity of identifying specific objectives and formulating testable hypotheses, the discovery function of science could easily destroy its orderliness. Further, without these steps, scientific replication would be impossible. Formulating hypotheses in a way that allows someone to test them also is referred to as **operationalizing** them. When you operationalize something, you provide a way to measure, or evaluate it. Most commonly, scientists operationalize hypotheses by identifying the statistical tests they will use, as well as the rejection range. The rejection range operates as a decision rule.

Suppose you wanted to know whether class attendance was correlated with the grades students earn in a class. You might hypothesize that students who attended more classes would earn higher grades. You could design a methodology that enabled you to compare daily attendance with final grades for all students. To make your hypothesis testable, you would need to decide what statistical test you would use to make this comparison. Further, you would need to designate a level beyond which you would assume that the correlation between attendance and grades should or should not be attributed to chance. That level is your decision rule. As you continue to move through the steps of the scientific method, you will rely on the value system common to most scientific endeavors to guide you in determining which forms of argument and evidence will provide the greatest credibility.

CONCLUSION

As examined in this chapter, science refers to the "objective account of the material world based upon measurement and quantification so that structure, process, movement, and transformation can be described mathematically in terms of fundamental laws" (Peat 208). Scientists often use the physical sciences as a model and mathematics as a foundation for explanatory theories. Scientists play a significant political role, but here we are interested in how they argue to one another as scientists. Scientific study begins with the value that there is order in nature that can be discovered. Order is explained through observation, and observations are characterized in claims of fact. They are combined with other already acknowledged claims of fact to develop a proposition that is a theory about fact. That theory can then be used to predict what will happen at another time or in another place.

The tradition of argumentation in the scientific sphere can be preliminarily defined by four observations: scientific argument deals in claims of fact, it searches for truth over personal gain, it reveals results that are complete enough to test, and its theories change slowly.

Generalization, cause, and sign are the most important argument types in the scientific sphere. Generalization, in contemporary times, functions as abduction. That is, a generalization is established on the basis of its greatest probability rather than certainty.

Argument by cause is basic to scientific argumentation. When study reveals some previously unrecognized condition, the scientist wants to know its cause. To be established in theory, it must be both necessary and sufficient to produce the effect. Argument by sign is important in establishing a scientific theory. Signs in biology indicate that an organism belongs to a particular species. All survey research is sign argument, as is most social science argumentation.

Argument by analogy is used primarily to explain a phenomenon. To be the basis for an empirical argument, the analogy must have extensive similarities. In biology, it must be homologous. Argument from authority is the least used type of argument in science. The review of literature sections of research papers and articles and the authority of established theories function as a kind of argument from authority. Outward statements of authority as a basis for argument are not made, although they may be used in private.

Evidence in scientific argumentation is used to provide empirical grounding for claims. This relationship is indicated in the specific instances that form the base of scientific reasoning. Statistics constitute the most elaborate kind of evidence and they have three tasks: (1) to quantify a set of observations into a set of numbers, (2) to determine whether the sample is representative, and (3) to determine whether the characteristics found can be attributed to an error in sampling. Testimony has a function in the human sciences, in which people are called on in surveys or experiments to express opinions.

EXERCISES/PROJECTS

1. Interview a faculty member at your college or university who would be considered a scientist as we have defined a scientist in this chapter. Ask questions about the kinds of arguments and evidence he or she uses with peers (not those that might be used to convince non-scientists). Write a short paper (no more than five double-spaced pages) about what kinds of argument and evidence apply. Does the person you interviewed agree with what has been said in the chapter? How different is the interviewee's position from that in this chapter? Why do you suppose the difference exists?

2. Read a research article from the journal *Science*. You can find the journal at www.sciencemag. org. Identify phrases, sentences, and/or sections of the article that demonstrate how the scientific research it reports exemplifies the values of knowledge, order, prediction, rationality, and usefulness. Which values are emphasized in this article? Which do you have difficulty identifying? What might be the reasons for these differences?

Argumentation in Religion

KEY TERMS

God, p. 223
revealed theology, p. 224
natural theology, p. 224
human beings, p. 225
moral behavior, p. 226
evil, p. 226
sin, p. 226
suffering, p. 227
salvation, p. 227
church, p. 228

sacred documents, p. 229
tradition, p. 232
experience, p. 232
revelation, p. 233
culture, p. 233
argument from authority, p. 234
argument by analogy, p. 236
narratives, p. 237
argument by sign, p. 238
paradox, p. 238

Religious argumentation is probably as old as human history, surely at least since 4000 BCE in the form of Chinese religions. Hinduism dates back to 2500 BCE and Judaism to 2000 BCE (Patheos). Today, religious groups constitute a bewildering variety of faiths that can be grouped into major religious categories.

It is reliably estimated that something like 85% of the adult population identify themselves with one religion or another. Christianity in all of its manifestations (Roman Catholic, Eastern Orthodoxy, protestant, Latter Day Saints, evangelicals, etc.) is the largest of the world's religions with approximately 2.1 billion adherents. Second is Islam in all its varieties at 1.5 billion. Hinduism has approximately 900 million followers. Chinese traditional religions (including Confucianism) have something under 400 million. Buddhism is slightly under that number. The third largest group of the world's peoples is the nonreligious (secular/nonreligious/agnostic/atheist) something over 1.1 billion persons (Patheos).

Each religion has a "unified system of beliefs and practices relative to sacred things . . . which unify into one single moral community," in the words of Emil Durkheim, and as such leads to many subcategories of each major religious tradition. These in turn lead to claims and counterclaims that one or another is not a religion but a vague philosophy of life, is or is not Christian, or Muslim, or what have you. It also leads to a wide variety of argumentative practices that make religion a unique sphere of argumentation.

Because we write primarily for people in western society, this chapter will be concerned primarily with the religions in the Judeo-Christian-Islamic tradition. They constitute something over 50% of the world's population. These religions, George Kennedy has observed, are all highly verbal religions (120). As such, they all have the primary ingredients for argumentation. But religious argumentation is quite different from argumentation in other spheres. The questions investigated and the values, evidence, and argument used to gain adherence in religious argumentation differ considerably from those of legal, legislative, or scientific argumentation, for instance. Our purpose, therefore, is to examine the factors that make religious argumentation unique.

John Macquarrie has observed that religious language can include praying, blessing, testimony, and nonverbal symbols such as crucifixes, paintings, music, and the like. With the modern technological innovations, this can include all kinds of printed and electronic messages: cartoons, movies, blogs, email, etc. To examine all of this for religious information, one must be concerned about what Macquarrie calls "theological language." It is narrower; it "arises out of religious language as a whole, and it does so when a religious faith becomes reflective and tries to give an account of itself in verbal statements" (19).

Many discussions conducted in religious situations do not seem much different from other public argumentation. Politicians speak at churches; Church leaders lead campaigns for social justice or aid to the poor, but they are not speaking to theological issues. In this chapter, we will investigate how religious argumentation is used to resolve theological issues.

In order to understand such religious argumentation, we will need to look at the major questions that identify where issues and values will be found. We will then examine sacred texts, the most important source of evidence, and tradition, experience, revelation, and culture as evidence. Finally, we will see how certain forms of argument are preferred over others.

MAJOR QUESTIONS IN RELIGIOUS ARGUMENTATION

The existence of a wide variety of religious groups holding different interpretations is evidence enough that religious questions abound. We will briefly identify seven questions adapted from two lists (one developed by Harry Emerson Fosdick, another by Peter C. Hodgson and Robert H. King) that constitute a fair summary of what has to be explained for a system of theology to be complete. Not all religious argumentation will cover all seven questions and other questions may arise, but these seven reasonably define religious argumentation: (1) what is the nature of **God**? (2) What is the nature of human beings? (3) What is moral behavior, the religious life? (4) What are sin, evil, and the meaning of suffering? (5) What is the human's relationship to God? (6) What is the nature of salvation? And (7) what is the role of the church?

What Is the Nature of God?

One important distinction in religious argumentation is between natural and revealed theology. **Revealed theology** comes from the examination of sacred texts, which reveal that there is a god and what God's relation is to humans and nature. **Natural theology** attempts to prove the existence of God from nature, that is, from observation and reasoning apart from revealed scripture. The arguments of natural theology began in Jewish theology (Epstein 86). Perhaps the best known example of natural theology is the five ways by which Thomas Aquinas proved the existence of God. We will summarize them here.

1. The world changes; things do not change unless some agent changes them; change cannot go on without end; there must be a first agent.
2. Patterns of cause and effect are observed in the world; it is not possible to conceive of a series of causes and effects without an initiating cause.
3. All things in the natural world are contingent on other things; nothing can be observed in the universe that is unnecessary. Therefore, it must exist because of something necessary: God.
4. All things have differences in value one from another. Nothing is perfect, but we cannot know the imperfect unless there is a perfect.
5. Since the natural world exhibits order and cause, there is design. A universe that exhibits design must have a designer: God (Anderson, *Natural Theology*, 25–66).

These arguments are based on what Aquinas believed are universal natural principles; they do not depend on sacred texts.

Such argumentation about the existence of God and the logic of belief still takes place today. However, although natural theology is important in religious argumentation, it is not as prevalent as is revealed theology. Natural arguments are most frequently used, when they *are* used, to reinforce arguments about revealed religion. Even Thomas Aquinas, for instance, made his five arguments when he was already a believer.

Much of religious argumentation, says George Kennedy, begins with the authority of texts and has to do with understanding God through the clear explication of these texts (158). Probably those who engage in religious argumentation easily accept the existence of God and the more difficult part of the question is the nature of God.

Many of the major religious traditions are based on polytheism, the existence of several Gods; even gods who war with one another. Others, like Confucianism, have no deities. The Hindu tradition sees a unity of all nature including humans with no special creator God (Patheos). The religions of the Judeo-Christian-Islamic tradition, on the other hand, are all monotheistic religions. They believe in one God. All accept the concept of monotheism, but it still constitutes an area of argumentation.

In Islam, the defining claim is "There is no God but Allah and Muhammad is his messenger." The inscription on the Dome of the Rock in Jerusalem, from the Qur'an, says, "Praise to God, who begets no son, and has no partner. He is God, one, eternal. He does not beget, he is not begotten, and he has no peer" (Lewis, *Crisis* 44). Mormons are frequently attacked for the statement, "As man is now, God once was. As God now is, Man may be" (Smith 46). Critics interpret this to mean that for Mormons, there is, or can be, more than one god.

As early as the second century CE, Celsus argued that Christianity affirms three Gods: Father, Son, and Holy Ghost. Trinitarians are obliged to argue that there is only one God, but God is found in three persons. Other issues also come under the theme of the nature of God. Does God intervene in human activity? Is God jealous, revengeful, or loving? Is God a person, a spirit, a world force? Is Jesus God? Does God still reveal himself to humans? Is God found in nature?

What Is the Nature of Human Beings?

Some religious traditions, like Hinduism, have animals as equal to humans in the unity of all nature. Among most arguers in the Judeo-Christian-Islamic tradition, there is a general agreement that human beings are more than other animals, as is argued in the *Holy Bible* Genesis 1:28:1

> And God blessed them [Adam and Eve], and God said to them, "Be fruitful, and multiply, and fill the earth, and subdue it; and have dominion over the fish of the sea, and over the birds of the air, and over every living thing that moves upon the earth."

Such a view has led some to argue that certain religions believe humans should exploit other living things, whereas others argue that it means that humans are called on to exercise stewardship. However, it is interpreted, there is no doubt that **human beings** are above all others, having been made in the image of God and given dominion (Genesis 1:26). But do humans get this status from God? From nature? From the ability to reason? From the possession of a soul? Thus, a persistent question in religious argumentation is about the basic nature of the human being.

There is, moreover, a long-standing and still active issue of free will versus determinism. Simply stated, it raises the issue of the extent to which God determines human conduct before a person is born, or is it subject to individual choice? Some will choose one or the other of these positions, but much religious argumentation is addressed to combinations of the two. For instance, a religion that attempts to convert others to its view usually is a religion which believes that individuals have the ability to make the choice (free will). Islam is such a religion. Yet Islam has a strong tradition of *kismet* (fate). When a loved one dies, consolation is provided by the belief that it was fate, that the person had no control over the situation.

After the tragic crash of Egypt Air Flight 990 in November of 1999 in the waters off Nantucket, relatives gathered at an interfaith memorial service for the 217 passengers who had died. Ahmed El Hattab of the Islamic Society of North America asked the mourners to submit to God's will. "Lo, we belong to God," he said, "and lo, we are returning. Let us remember it is God who grants life, and it is he who takes us back" (Chivers).

Many members of other religions hold similar views. Some resolve the seeming inconsistency between free will and determinism by arguing that one has free will to accept the religion but after that, one's destiny is in the hands of God. Others argue that even the decision to choose the religion was somehow predetermined. Still others believe God gives people control over some parts of their lives but not over others.

The question about the nature of human beings also involves an issue of the extent to which humans are basically good or evil. "In Adam's fall we sinned us all," says the Puritan *New England Primer*, thus expressing the concept of original sin, which sees human beings as basically evil and unable to "save" themselves. In such a view, humans can only be "saved" by God's grace. Other people will reject such a view and see human beings as basically good; capable of making moral choices; and sometimes led astray by evil forces (such as the Devil) but capable, with the support of God, of being good. Obviously, many different modifications of these positions may be argued.

What Is Moral Behavior, the Religious Life?

Knowing what is right and wrong is related to a perception of the nature of human beings. This question deals with such issues as how a person can know what is right. It may even be asked; can a person know right and wrong?

Some theologians would argue that there are specific tests that can be applied to discover what is morally right for a religion person. The *Catholic Catechism* says:

> The moral quality of our actions derives from three different sources, each so closely connected with the other that unless all three are simultaneously good, the action performed is morally bad. . . . The object of the act must be good. . . . Circumstances . . . can make an otherwise good object evil. . . . Finally, the end or purpose . . . also affects the moral situation. (Hardon 283–284)

Others would argue that determining morality from a religious perspective is more complicated and more tentative than this statement implies.

There are also specific issues of interpretation. An important example is in the interpretation of the basic law, "You shall not kill" (Exodus 20:13). Is such a law an absolute injunction against any form of killing? Animals? Fetuses? Criminals? Enemies in war? The problem of interpretation is further complicated by recent translations that substitute "murder" for "kill." Practitioners of religious argumentation will differ on this and a host of other issues about what constitutes **moral behavior** and how the most sacred documents, such as the Ten Commandments, are to be interpreted.

What Are Sin, Evil, and the Meaning of Suffering?

One of the most complicated and perplexing questions in religious argumentation is the nature of evil and the role of sin in the production of evil. Protestant theologian John Hicks has argued that "the enigma of evil presents so massive and direct a threat to our faith that we are bound to seek within the resources of Christian thought for ways, if not of resolving it, at least rendering it bearable by the Christian conscience" (ix). Hicks calls the issue created by the concept of a loving God in the presence of evil a "dilemma."

Evil is usually defined by human self-centeredness that leads to negative values such as cruelty, ruthless ambition, pride, murder, and rape. In modern times, mass versions of evil such as slavery, poverty, starvation, genocide, indiscriminate war, and terrorism make it a social institution. The holocaust is the most obvious example of mass evil in modern times, but evil has existed throughout world history and in virtually all cultures.

For many religions, evil is an expression of **sin**, which is a "disorientation at the very center" of the human self (Hicks 300). Ryszard Kapuscinski notes that most African aboriginal religions have no concept of sin or evil. There are only evil actions that become evil only when recognized and identified (294). Zen has no sense of suffering or evil (Patheos). But for those in the Judeo-Christian-Islamic tradition, the question must be answered, why has an infinitely good and loving God created sin in people and, therefore, evil in the world? The various answers provided to this question take one into many other questions. Does God grant the individual free will, and, if so, to what extent? What is a sin?

For instance, is homosexuality a sin or a natural representation of human diversity? This is a growing question in the religious community today.

Suffering means different things to different people. For Buddhists, suffering is a normal part of life, so there is no problem of evil. In the Judeo-Christian-Islamic tradition, some find the meaning of suffering in the claim that God punishes individuals or societies for their transgressions against divine laws. Certainly, that view can be seen in the sermons and writings of New England Puritan leaders. By their view, sin is inherent in human beings ("In Adam's fall we sinned us all"). Or suffering may be a test that God provides to strengthen one's faith. Certainly, that is one meaning of the story of Job's tribulations in which the most faithful person was one the most tested by suffering.

The Book of Job is a debate among Job, his friends, and finally God, who argue various positions about suffering and God's nature and power. In the end of the story, "the Lord blessed the latter days of Job more than his beginnings" (Job 42:12) because he was faithful to God even in his adversity. There are many answers to the question of suffering and all are related to the questions about the nature of God, humans, evil, and sin.

What Is the Human's Relationship to God?

"The meaning attributed to prayer," said Harry Emerson Fosdick, "is one of the most reliable tests of any religion" (201). For some people, God is unapproachable. A person's relation to God is simply that of giving praise and homage. One acknowledges God, attempts to find out as much as possible about, and stands in awe of, the deity. For others, God is very personal, and through prayer and other sacraments, a person can communicate with God. Some claim they actually talk directly with a divine being as if they were carrying on a conversation. For many people, such communication is an illusion. For others, such communication marks a human being as a special person: a prophet, for instance.

Dietrich Bonhoeffer was a German Protestant theologian. While he was in a Nazi prison in 1943, he wrote to his parents of a more socially oriented idea of the fellowship of God and humans:

> I have also been considering again the strange story of the gift of Tongues. That the confusion of tongues at the Tower of Babel, as a result of which people can no longer understand each other . . . should at last be brought to an end and overcome by the language of God, which everyone understands and through which alone people can understand each other again. . . . (Woelfel 197)

However, one looks at it, this relationship of human to God is a very special and important relationship in any system of religious argumentation.

What Is the Nature of Salvation?

There are great differences of view about the question of immortality in the Judeo-Christian-Islamic tradition. For some, it is the most important question in theology because **salvation** is the most important benefit one receives from belief, and its absence may be the most horrible punishment. Others view this issue as less important or even nonexistent. Like the followers of Confucius, they concentrate on the personal and social benefits of living a moral life on earth. In Hinduism, life is governed by the principle of Samsara, or rebirth. An individual is reborn to a new life. He or she grasps for an understanding of self. When one stops grasping, individuals are absorbed into the ultimate, what believers in Zen call Nirvana (Patheos).

Immortality can be seen as social, that is, the preservation of society. In such a view, individuals live on in what they contribute to others or through their children. Reformed Judaism has a concept of immortality, but it is a spiritual union with God. There is no resurrection of the body, no physical torment for sinners, no pleasures for those who are saved. Heaven is not a place but a state. Such a view is much less specific than the view held by most Christians, Muslims, or Orthodox Jews (Cohen 34–36).

What Is the Role of the Church?

In Islam, there is no church hierarchy. Religious leaders come from the people, and they get their status from their ability to gain the adherence of others. Jews and most Protestant Christians hold a similar view. Rabbis and ministers are chosen and dismissed by the congregation. The **church,** when it can be called such, is either an individual congregation or a loose confederation of individual congregations. The American Baptist Convention, for instance, is such a confederation that takes theological positions, but they are not necessarily binding on individual congregations. Individuals or congregations that disagree may drop out and be unaffiliated or join another confederation such as the Southern Baptist Convention or the General Association of Regular Baptists. A similar relationship exists between an individual and a congregation.

In Roman Catholicism, however, the church is an essential agency of the religion. Tradition is very important in Catholicism. So, in order to avoid error, church authorities must interpret what God's word means. Someone who rejects interpretations sanctioned by the church may, in extreme cases, be excommunicated. A similar condition exists in the Church of Jesus Christ of Latter-day Saints. In contrast, among Baptists, there is no concept of excommunication. Instead, there is the process of disfellowship from an independent congregation. One is not removed from the sacraments of God but only from that fellowship of believers.

Other churches have varying degrees of control over the religious claims their members may hold and still be regarded as members. The stricter the church control, the more likely it may be subjected to the rebuttal that it denies the fellowship of humans with God. The more individualistic the theology, the more it is subject to the rebuttal that it has no control over ignorance and error.

In Islam, there is no concept of the separation of church and state as there is in much of Christianity. The history of Judaism is one of separation from the state until the founding of Israel in 1948. The same was true of Christianity until Constantine I was converted in the third century CE. In modern western democracies, the tradition of the separation is preserved by enlightenment thought and statements such as Jesus' "Render unto Caesar the things that are Caesar's and unto God the things that are God's." But many issues abound about how far the separation of religion from the state can or should be carried. This is a particular problem in Islam, where its founder Muhammad was both a prophet and a ruler.

Values and Themes

The themes of religious argumentation are contained in the answers to the questions posed at the beginning of this section. Each person or group develops a series of linked themes that define their theology. Embedded in these themes are the values that warrant the theological claims. Every arguer does not use all of these values. We have already noted, for instance, that Islam has a restricted concept of a church hierarchy, that some Christians reject the idea of a sinful human, and that Judaism has a restricted concept of immortality. Furthermore, the values that warrant a religion are not limited to the values contained in this limited discussion of themes. Yet, our discussion has revealed a significant set of values that are prominent in religious argumentation: God (Jesus for some), human beings (sometimes a negative value), moral behavior, evil (a negative value), sin (a negative value), suffering (sometimes a negative value), prophet, salvation, and church.

This discussion of the seven major themes and values of religion has been necessarily brief. Its purpose is to provide a basis for the analysis of religious evidence and arguments. Any theology is an argumentative case that must answer these questions to be acceptable. The decisions one makes on one question will affect what is possible on another.

EVIDENCE IN RELIGIOUS ARGUMENTATION

At least in the religions of the Judeo-Christian-Islamic tradition, religious claims usually are grounded in a text, the Torah, the Bible, and the Qur'an being the most obvious examples. But the interpretation of these texts is based on interpreting them in the light of other kinds of evidence. Increasingly, in modern theology, these other kinds of evidence are used alone or with one another, sometimes without text as evidence, or even in opposition to text. Thus, we can identify five forms of evidence in religious argumentation: text, tradition, experience, revelation, and culture.

Text as Evidence

Robert Grant observes of Christian theology, "the interpretation of scripture is the principal bond between the ongoing life and thought of the Church and the documents which contain its earliest traditions" (9). This explains the desire among religious writers to find the most accurate, trustworthy, and best interpreted texts.

Accuracy.   The importance of **sacred documents** as evidence accounts for the significant arguments over the accuracy of translation. When the Revised Standard Version of the Bible was first published, it produced considerable controversy. Some argued that it destroyed the essential beauty of the King James Version. More important for our purposes here, its translation of certain passages involved changes in wording with far-reaching implications for Christianity. For instance, in Isaiah 7:14, which many Christians consider a prophecy of Jesus' birth, the King James version says "a virgin shall conceive," the Revised Standard version says "a young woman." The New English Bible, unlike either the Revised Standard Edition of the Bible or the King James version, even uses the term *girl* for *virgin* in Luke 1:27 in describing Mary, the mother of Jesus. These differences among three versions clearly lead to sharp differences in religious argumentation about the miracle of virgin birth.

In recent years, an organization of Catholic and Protestant biblical scholars known as the Jesus Seminar has undertaken to provide a new translation of the synoptic gospels (Matthew, Mark, and Luke) and to determine the relative legitimacy of words attributed to Jesus. In this translation, they employed "colloquialisms in English for colloquialisms in Greek. When the leper comes up to Jesus and says, 'If you want to you can make me clean,' Jesus replies, 'Okay—you're clean!'" instead of "I will; be clean" (Mark 1:40–41). Needless to say, this use of colloquialisms is only one practice that makes their work controversial (Funk et al. xiii).

Trustworthiness.   Even when wording is agreed on, there can still be argumentation about texts. It has to do with the issue, what is the "canon"? What part of the text is acceptable as "sacred" evidence? Certain books are left out by some scholars and councils and included by others. Even some books that are included in the canon are regarded as less reliable. Books of doubtful authorship or authenticity are excluded from both the Hebrew and Christian scriptures and are known as the Apocrypha. Even some books that are in the Bible, but whose authenticity was debated, are considered of less value than others. "Theologies," says John H. Leith, "that have depended overwhelmingly on books such as Revelation, whose admission to the canon was widely debated, have always been questioned" (235).

However, for most Christians, statements have more authority if they are actually identified as the word of God. In the fourth chapter of Joshua, there is a "narration of what God has done in Jewish history, put in the mouth of God himself and therefore given heightened authority." God's words are followed by Joshua's charge to the people, which is of less authority because it is an interpretation of the meaning of God's words (Kennedy 124).

In Islam, a similar distinction is made between the Qur'an, which is the revelation given to Muhammad by Allah, and the Hadith (Sayings). The Hadith reports the actions and utterances of the Prophet and, therefore, has less authority than the revealed text (Lewis, *Islam and . . .* 25). To add to the importance of the text of the Qur'an, it is untranslatable from the Arabic according to most of Islam.

Thus, in the Judeo-Christian-Islamic tradition, at least, texts are the best evidence in religious argumentation. There is, therefore, a desire to know the earliest texts, to translate them accurately, to make sure that only the inspired texts are included in the canon, and to determine the relative importance among parts of those texts, with God's own words given the highest authority.

Interpretation.   After one knows, even in a general way, what texts are most accurate and which parts are to be taken more seriously, there is a further problem of interpretation. How does one know what interpretation is justified?

The first deliberate attempt to systematize a method of interpretation was probably the seven rules of the Rabbi Hillel at about the time of the birth of Jesus (Farrar 18). From the earliest times of the Christian church, this problem of interpretation was important. Paul argued from texts in his letter to the Galatians (4:21–23):

> Tell me now, you who desire to be under law, do you not hear the law? For it is written that Abraham had two sons, one by a slave and the other by a free woman. But the son of the slave was born according to the flesh, the son of the free-woman's through promise. Now this is an allegory: These women are two covenants. (Galatians 4:21–23)

The Jewish scholar Philo of Alexandria observed in the first century CE that there were different ways to explain the meaning of a text. A century later, Clement of Alexandria was probably the first Christian to attempt to systematically explain the method of arguing by analogy from textual evidence. For him, the scripture had meaning, but the meaning was not the obvious one.

Clement of Alexandria found five kinds of meaning in a text. They are useful, we believe, to illustrate not a complete understanding of how to interpret religious argument but as a starting point to illustrate the potential validity of textual evidence:

1. *Historical meaning:* One uses a biblical story to inform oneself about history.
2. *Doctrinal meaning:* Biblical statements are taken as moral laws. The Ten Commandments are frequently treated this way.
3. *Prophetic meaning:* Specific prophesies are made, as when Daniel prophesied, "the God of Heaven will set up a kingdom which shall never be destroyed" (Daniel 2:44).
4. *Philosophical meaning:* Specific events or things are interpreted as symbolizing a more general principle, as when Hagar and Sarah stand for pagan philosophy and true wisdom.
5. *Mystical meaning:* Specific events or things are taken to mean something quite different from what they would literally mean to the novice. In this way, Lot's wife is seen to symbolize an attachment to earthly things that causes blindness to God's truth (Grant 80).

These textual meanings are arranged in an order from the most literal to the most metaphorical. For some scholars, as religious argumentation moves down the list from the most to the least literal, it becomes more questionable as evidence. A theology grounded in historical and doctrinal meanings is the easiest to defend. Yet, such a theology would face the refutation that it weakens the authority of the text by ignoring its most meaningful interpretation.

John Leith has argued that interpretation can only be made in terms of some organizing principle. "When a theologian seeks to work out his [or her] theology under the canon of scripture, he [or she] agrees to find warrant for theological assertion in the broad base of scripture, whether the datum for this theological reflection is text or symbol or theme" (237).

If, for instance, there are three repetitions in a pattern, they constitute more forceful evidence. Such is the case according to Robert C. Tannenhill (42), in Mark (14:66–71), when Peter denied he had known Jesus:

> "I neither know nor understand what you mean."
> But again he denied it. . . .
> But he began to invoke a curse on himself and to swear, "I do not know this man of whom you speak."

This repetition establishes a *pattern* to give more force to the evidence that Peter denied Jesus. In addition, a new piece of evidence is introduced that creates a tension and a fuller meaning:

> And immediately the cock crowed a second time. And Peter remembered how Jesus had said to him, "Before the cock crows twice you will deny me three times." And he broke down and wept.

It is in the identification of patterns and tensions and the interaction among them that a particular text can be seen as a unified piece of evidence. Thus, whatever the emphasis of the theologian on each of the five kinds of meaning, that emphasis will be governed by some organizing principle.

Text, then, is the most important source of evidence in religious argumentation. Its accuracy, trustworthiness, and method of interpretation can be issues. In addition, text is subject to adaptation, increasingly so in modern times by tradition, experience, revelation, and culture.

Tradition as Evidence

In long-standing religious organizations—the Roman Catholic Church, for instance—**tradition** is an important source of evidence. Over the centuries, certain interpretations have been accepted and others rejected. A body of interpretations constitutes a tradition by which new interpretations must be judged. Some Protestant theologians have argued against interpreting by tradition. Each argument, they say, must return to original texts.

One Protestant writer argues that a denial of the use of tradition is seriously flawed. It is subject to the rebuttal, he says, that "none of the New Testament writings, in its present form, was authored by an apostle or one of his [Jesus'] disciples." The essential substance of Christian witness came before the scriptures (Ogden 138–151). Thus, if one is to ask what a Christian should believe, it should be realized that even the text of the New Testament is an interpretation of the meaning of Christ. So, the argument goes, tradition, the accumulated body of interpretations, is fundamental to most contemporary Christian religious argumentation.

Even the Christian theologian who rejects this argument because the Bible was inspired by God and is, therefore, a literal statement of the Christian faith has to meet another argument: that theologians are a product of their environment. Even when they attempt to go back to the original text, they are unable to erase all traditional knowledge from their minds. The Hindu tradition admits that its many sacred writings, like the Veda, Upanishad, and Bhagavad-Gita epics, are an evolving tradition that has changed and adapted other views over the years.

All of these arguments about tradition point to a general issue. Most theologians agree that tradition plays some part in argumentative evidence. The issue among them is, how much?

Experience as Evidence

A principle of interpretation closely related to tradition is experience. It is also a source of considerable controversy. The argument for **experience** is that because the text does not speak to one generation but to every generation, it must be interpreted by succeeding generations on the basis of experience. In finding the meanings of texts for contemporary times, one asks not what they meant historically but what they mean today.

Thus, the religious experiences of the individual, such as answered or unanswered prayer, or the spiritual understanding in a congregation or community, or even secular knowledge, may become evidence in a religious argument. Experience is the basis on which religion might be reconciled with science. Indeed, a theology that relies heavily on experience is frequently called "empirical theology." By such a theology, one might accept religious claims that do not have a basis in scripture. Today, some theologians and scientists meet to discuss the gaps in scientific thought that do not explain the cause of such phenomena as the Big Bang theory, subatomic particles, DNA, and the human genome (Easterbrook).

If religion is applicable to people's lives, as believers contend, then its principles ought to be observable there. Many are quite suspicious of experience, however, because of the danger that one may respond to secular experience that leads away from religious interpretation.

Revelation as Evidence

Revelation involves a special kind of experience when the individual is presumed to have faith to aid in understanding a text. Augustine argued, and many Christians agree with him, that God deliberately made the meaning of scripture obscure so that it could be understood only by someone who had faith (Kennedy 132). Others do not go so far, but all religious argumentation contains in it the idea that one who has faith is a better interpreter of the text than one who does not. The idea is expressed for Christians in Hebrews 10:1 and 11:1:

> For since the law has but a shadow of the good things to come instead of the true form of these realities, it can never, . . . make perfect those who draw near. . . .
>
> Now faith is the assurance of things hoped for, the conviction of things not seen. For by it the men of old received divine approval. By faith we understand that the world was created by the word of God, so that what is seen was made out of things that do not appear.

Some religious groups, such as the Roman Catholic Church and the Church of Jesus Christ of Latter Day Saints, are led by individuals believed by their followers to have a special ability to produce revelations not necessarily connected to scripture. Many religious people believe that even ordinary individuals have revelations by faith. In most cases, faith clarifies text. A major thesis of the reform tradition in Protestant theology is that the Holy Spirit enables one to make a correct interpretation.

Culture as Evidence

Judaism and Christianity reflect a historical culture in the sense that they see the entire cosmic process as the temporal unfolding of a divine plan with a beginning, a series of crucial events, and an end. Judaism, however, is the more historical religion. And Islam is a more legalistic religion in which the law is defined by the Qur'an, which was written at one time by one person. It is less historical, though it is related to the Arab culture from which it comes.

Although Christianity has a history both before and after the life of Jesus, it is so dominated by that life that it has an ahistorical character to it. But even a person such as Martin Luther, who believed that "Christ is the point in the circle from which the whole circle is drawn," said that historical understanding is most important in giving meaning to Isaiah. For Luther, all the books of the Bible teach about Christ, but their historical context is still important (Grant 181). Interpretation that follows this line of argument will need to take into account the **culture** of the audience for which a text was written. For instance, was it written for Jews or Greeks or Romans, all of whom had different ways of looking at the world and, therefore, different possible rebuttals? What were the particular issues that concerned people at the time? How much did they know?

Chapter 11 of the Letter to the Hebrews, quoted previously, argues for faith but does so by linking it to a long series of events in Jewish history.

> By faith Abel offered to God a more acceptable sacrifice than Cain. . . . By faith Enoch was taken up so that he should not see death; . . . By faith Noah, . . . By faith Abraham, . . . And what more shall I say? For time would fail me to tell of Gideon, Varak, Samson, Jephthah, of David and Samuel and the prophets.

The Letter to the Hebrews is an argument probably aimed at anyone who might drop by the wayside, but it uses the Old Testament to amplify its argument from ancient text, and these ancient texts refer to events in Jewish history. That is why it came later to be called "The Letter to the Hebrews."

A major controversy in Christian theology is over the relative importance of Hebrew and Greek interpretations. "It is the characteristic of Greek thought to work with abstractions. It is not enough to know that it is a good horse or a good table, you must find out what is 'the Good.' . . . to get at reality you abstract the problem from the particular time and place, . . . Hebrew thought . . . argues . . . by presenting a series of related situation-images" (Barr 11–12). In this controversy of Hebrew and Greek interpretations is found the basic issue of the relative importance of history in understanding texts.

Islam provided rules for the proper treatment of slaves, women, Jews, Christians, and others of lesser social rank. As such, these rules were a liberalization of previous practices. However, those rules still accepted slavery, plural marriage, concubinage, and second-class citizenship for nonbelievers. Similar situations have existed in Judaism and Christianity. Christian acceptance of slavery, even in the original Constitution of the United States, is an obvious example. Today, in a different culture, religious arguments abound, sometimes textually linked and sometimes not, rejecting slavery, supporting women's equality, calling for equal treatment of all religions, and defending gay and lesbian rights. Those who argue against such practices are likely to make some of their arguments based on the culture with or without scriptural evidence.

Thus, evidence in religious argumentation is traditionally from texts. But it is necessary to discover which texts are most accurate, and of the accurate texts, which are most trustworthy. Those texts must be interpreted for meaning and they must be defined as evidence by some organizing principle. Such texts are influenced by evidence from tradition, experience, revelation, and culture. In some cases, particularly in modern times, these four in combination or alone may function as evidence without text.

PREFERRED ARGUMENT FORMS

The evidence developed from texts, traditions, experience, revelation, and culture form the grounds and warrants from which one makes arguments for a claim. At this point, we will examine the types of arguments that are preferred in religious argumentation. The preferred argument forms are by authority, analogy, narrative sign, paradox, and, less often, generalization.

Argument from Authority

Traditionally, the primary form in which religious arguments are found is **argument from authority**. God, texts, and special humans serve as a universal principle, authority, that warrants the argument and justifies the claim:

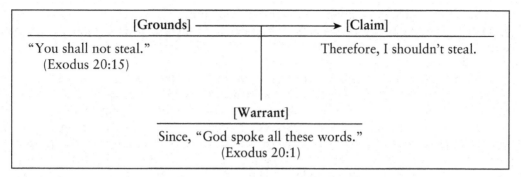

I **FIGURE 14.1**

This argument from the Ten Commandments is particularly powerful because it is warranted directly by God. Similar arguments, that are not direct statements of God's words, are warranted by the authority of the text itself, an apostle, or a prophet. Tradition, experience, revelation, and culture can also warrant an argument from authority. For instance, in the current debate over whether LGBT (Lesbian, Gay, Bisexual, and Transgender) persons can be equal members, or leaders, in Christianity, the tradition of Christian love is used as a warrant to say that they are. Even though specific statements in sacred texts identify the unrighteousness of homosexuals (see, for instance, Leviticus 18:22, and 20:13) I Corinthians 6:9 says, "Do not be deceived; neither the immoral, nor idolaters, nor adulterers, nor homosexuals, . . . will inherit the Kingdom of God." Such texts are overcome, for some, by the overwhelming tradition of Christian love.

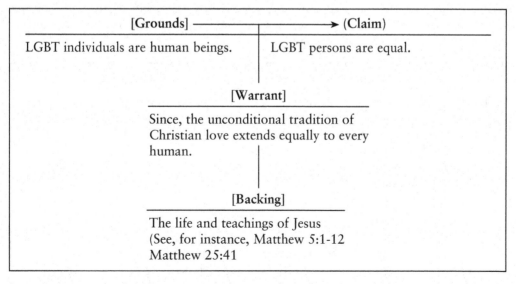

I **FIGURE 14.2**

These are simple illustrations of argument from authority, a form that is used over and over again in varying complexities of potential rebuttal and qualification. It is the argumentation form that reflects most closely the purely logical form of the formal syllogism discussed in Chapter 4.

Where the text is taken as authoritative, there is little need for verification. Consequently, generalization from sense evidence, in order to prove the value of the grounds or warrant, is less necessary than in some other kinds of argumentation. As we have seen, interpretation is not a simple process but is influenced by tradition, experience, revelation, and culture. It is quite different from argumentation in science, which frequently requires generalization to serve as warrants and observable phenomena as grounds. It is more like argument in law, where the text of a law or precedent is accepted and interpreted. Indeed, much of Hebrew and Islamic theology is rooted in law, and Christianity is heavily influenced by its association with Roman law.

Argument by Analogy

Throughout the Bible, there are indications of the importance of the parable, the analogy. The Psalmist says, "I will open my mouth in a parable" (Psalms 78:1). Mark says that Jesus spoke to the scribes and "said to them in a parable. . . ." Even the staunchest literalists do not argue that there is no metaphor in the Bible. Although they argue for a literal interpretation of the Bible, they do not argue, for instance, that when Jesus said, "You are the salt of the earth" (Matthew 5:13) he meant that his disciples were literally made of salt, nor that the parable of the prodigal son must be taken merely as a literal historical event. The very recognition that it is a parable means that it reveals a principle that can tell a person how to behave in a number of analogous situations. The main issue of most denominational argumentation is how far can one go in arguing by analogy to new interpretations of textual meaning?

Thus, although there are differences in how, and how extensively, **argument by analogy** is used, it is quite significant in religious argumentation. Many texts are not as straightforward in the assertion of principles from which to build claims as a law such as "You shall not murder." Indeed, many are quite clearly arguments by analogy. Parables are an obvious example. When an argument is identified as a parable, it means that one must argue by analogy to a useful claim.

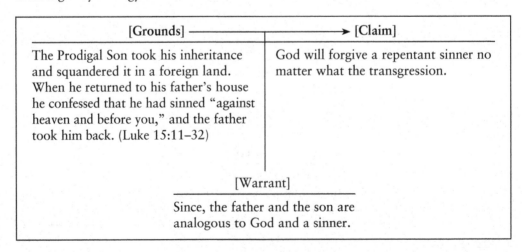

[Grounds] ⟶	[Claim]
The Prodigal Son took his inheritance and squandered it in a foreign land. When he returned to his father's house he confessed that he had sinned "against heaven and before you," and the father took him back. (Luke 15:11–32)	God will forgive a repentant sinner no matter what the transgression.

[Warrant]

Since, the father and the son are analogous to God and a sinner.

❙ FIGURE 14.3

The prodigal son analogy is supported by many specific references in the Bible to God as Father. But in religious argumentation, many uses of analogy will reach far beyond such an obvious example. It is here that disagreements about analogy will take place. John Macquarrie puts the problem very well:

> Just how wide a gulf can this symbolism bridge? One can see that an analogy, for instance, may very well be illuminative for another situation of the same order—for instance, one legal situation may help toward understanding another analogous one. But how could an everyday situation be illuminative for another one of quite different order—or, to make the point more concrete, how could things we can say about kings, portraits or the sun be illuminating for something so remote from these relatively intelligible matters as the incarnation? (184)

One solution is to return to the literal interpretation of texts. The early church father Tertullian as well as Augustine and Aquinas argued that analogy functions appropriately only when it has a final basis in the literal statements of text (Ayers 6). This relates to a point made earlier that the text must be taken as a unified statement. That is, an analogy is justified when it reflects a general understanding of meaning. The example given previously of the extensive use of "Father" for God in the text makes it easier for the prodigal son analogy to gain adherence.

However a theologian feels about a particular argument by analogy, no theologian would deny that analogy is a primary means of argumentation in religion. Paul's statement in 2 Corinthians 3:6, "The letter kills, but the spirit makes alive," has been used to justify all manners of analogy. Think of all the other possibilities where metaphor (analogy) functions. Is the serpent in the Adam and Eve story literally a snake? Was the fruit of the tree literally that of the knowledge of good and evil? Did God literally kill every living creature except Noah, his family, and the creatures he took in the Ark? Consider all of these stories and many more and consider how one could argue that they are bases for an argument by analogy.

Argument by Narrative

In Judaism and Christianity, much of the sacred literature is in the form of stories. The creation story, the story of Abraham, or the story of the Exodus from Egypt, when the grounding principles of both Judaism and Christianity were established, comes to mind. The story of Abraham is fundamental for Judaism, Christianity, and Islam. In the Qur'an, God says, "Salam (peace) be upon Abraham" (37:09) He is an ancestor to Muhammad, and to Jesus (John 8:33). The story of the life of Jesus, his followers, and his opponents is the central explanation of Christianity. **Narratives** of the Torah and the Bible can be interpreted as one of the traditional forms of argument. Earlier, we identified the story of Moses and the Ten Commandments as arguments from authority, and the parable of the prodigal son as argument by analogy.

However, there are times when interpreting a narrative as a single claim is seen to weaken and oversimplify the argument. In such a case, the theologian will see a story not as a piece of evidence to prove a claim but as a complex development of a theme. The Gospels of Matthew, Mark, Luke, and John tell the story of Jesus' life. But that life, for the believers, cannot be summed up in one claim or even a series of related claims. For them, the narrative brings to its receivers a combination of personal experience, culture, and revelation. It is more than a literal story told. It is a narrative that links to the individual and community through a theme with a deep personal meaning.

Theologian Sallie McFague TeSelle notes that the parable of the prodigal son develops the theme of divine love (although never mentioned in the story) "through stretching the surface of the story with an extreme imagery of hunger and feasting, rejection and acceptance, lost and found, death and life" (13). The oppositions created in this narrative develop the theme of divine love.

In some religious organizations, personal narrative is a central element in the religion. Such is the case with the Church of Jesus Christ of Latter Day Saints. At testimony meetings about once a month, members "bear testimony" (tell their stories) to elaborate the theme of the "truth of the gospel." Such a way of seeing a story permits a believer to use a narrative to reinforce the larger story of the religion. The believer looks to a personal story, or a story from sacred texts, and judges it by its consistency in developing a meaningful theme. For personal testimony, one frequently judges a story by its consistency with the narratives of others. The Christian who claims to have seen Jesus relates that experience to the story of Paul on the Damascus Road, for instance. In such a case, narrative provides a deep personal understanding of God, salvation, or brotherhood rather than a specific claim (Haverwas and Jones).

Argument by Sign

Closely related to argument by analogy is **argument by sign**. It is common to view one event as a sign of another. Miracles are taken as signs of the existence of God. It is argued that when Jesus fed the multitudes or raised a girl from the dead, it was a sign that he was God because only God could do these things. Sign argument has its problems in determining what sign is valid. We observed in discussing experience as a factor affecting interpretation that many argue that religion should be applicable in people's lives and, thus, the principles should be observable in experience. But many signs used in popular argument would be difficult for theologians to accept. Particularly subject to skepticism is the sign argument that gets away from text. A common argument that God supports his chosen people by giving them material wealth is a sign argument that is easily refuted by reference to the story of Job. Many practitioners of religious argumentation accept the claim that God answers prayers but not on the sign: "I prayed for a bicycle and on my next birthday my parents gave me one." Such arguments are made by laypersons but not by theologians.

Argument by Paradox

Paradox is a special kind of argument that is closely related to analogy. It is a special type of religious argument that is not mentioned in Chapter 4 ("The Nature of Arguments") because it is seldom found in other spheres of argumentation. But it is a characteristic of, particularly Jewish, religious argumentation. James Barr argues that there has always been a unity in Hebrew scriptures. But, he says, Christian scholars have difficulty seeing the unity because of the failure of western educated people to "perceive the unitary though paradoxical Hebraic mind" (9).

In Hebrew culture, reasoning is a process of considering alternate views of the same phenomenon. Even God is not knowable in a strictly literal sense. David Frank points out that "unlike the arguments in many western texts, those in the Hebrew Bible are often indeterminate, confused and can yield a host of reasonable but incompatible interpretations" (73). Abraham, Moses, and Job all argue with God, and God changes in response to their arguments that are warranted in God's values. Thus, divergent interpretations of God's words are acceptable, and paradox is a reasonable argument. Paradox comes into Christianity naturally from its Hebrew scriptural and cultural roots.

Paradox is also found in Islam. Most particularly, it has been observed by the acceptance of free will and determinism together. The Qur'an says that it is the best scripture without inconsistencies (39:23). It is written in Arabic a language that is free of faults (39:29), and it is free of contradictions (4:82). However, it accepts both free will and determinism as Allah misleads some and puts others on the right path (6:39). Those who follow will have nothing to fear, but those who deny will be punished (6:48) even though it is impossible for a person to correct the error Allah has set them to (4:98) (*The Noble Qur'an*).

A paradox is a riddle. The Hebrew psalmist (78:2) says, "I will open my mouth in a parable; I will utter dark sayings from of old." The Hebrew word that is translated "dark sayings" is also commonly translated as "riddle." "A riddle is a dark or obscure saying because it gives a deliberately obscure and puzzling description of something, a description which at first sight may well seem nonsensical but is not nonsensical when one hits upon the correct solution" (Macquarrie 29). In short, paradox is used to force a new way of thinking that makes the contradictory noncontradictory.

Religious argumentation employs such paradoxes, such riddles, frequently. Paul said, "We are afflicted in every way, but not crushed; perplexed, but not driven to despair; persecuted, but not forsaken; struck down, but not destroyed . . . for while we live, we are always being given up to death for Jesus' sake" (1 Corinthians 13:12). Ignatius argued, "Of flesh and spirit, generate and ingenerate, God in man, true life in death, son of Mary and Son of God, first possible and then impossible" (Macquarrie 29).

In a way, all analogy is paradoxical. Because argument by analogy compares unlike things, it is possible to have conflicting and, therefore, contradictory meanings. Furthermore, because religious argumentation starts from the interpretation of texts, several analogies when taken together can provide a paradox. The New Testament gives a number of images of Christ—"Son of man," "Son of God," "Messiah," "Lord," "Word." "It is impossible," says Macquarrie, "to 'harmonize' all these ideas, but from them something of the mystery of the incarnation finds expression" (228).

How does one solve the "riddle"? How is sense found in this nonsense, the paradox? By looking at the paradoxical argument in its context, as a part of the complete argumentative process, it can be done. We noted previously that the seemingly contradictory statements describing Christ come together to describe the mystery of something beyond language: incarnation—of God become man. Likewise, single paradoxical arguments make sense from context. So, "He that loveth his life shall lose it; and he that hateth his life in this world shall keep it unto life eternal" (John 12:25) is a paradox that makes sense in the context of the greater value of eternal life that can be secured by giving up the lesser value of mortal life. Such a meaning is understandable only in the context of the other major arguments in a system of religious argumentation.

Argument by Generalization

Because most of the grounds espoused in religious argumentation are given by the text and claims are reasoned from them by authority, analogy, narrative, sign, or paradox, generalization is rarely used. Unlike scientific argumentation, that searches through specific details to find rules or laws which will predict the nature of any other case of the same kind, religious argumentation has its warrants given and reasons mostly to find specific application. The most significant exception to this rule is the idea of unity mentioned earlier. It is essential that a religious argument not be in conflict with the text *taken as a whole*. Taking the text as a whole is, in a sense, a crude form of argumentation by generalization, for one argues that all the events in the text lead to a general principle.

Natural Theology (discussed on page 224, is an example of argument by generalization. The natural condition is observed and a principle drawn from it. Indeed, as we have noted, theologians frequently call this an "empirical argument."

But Thomas Olbricht has observed that most religious arguments, which look at first glance like generalizations, are not this at all. He found that, in his homilies, Basil the Great used the text as a source of beginning points for arguments and reasoned about specific claims by general principle. The many statements taken from the text are not for proof but for *amplification*. Olbricht cites an example from Pope Innocent III to show this amplification:

> Just as the sea is always stormy and turbulent, so the world remains always in storm and stress; nowhere is there peace and security, never is there rest and quietness, but everywhere toil and trouble. "For the whole world is seated in wickedness" (1 John 5:19). "Laughter shall be mingled with sorrow, and mourning taketh hold of the end of joy" (Prov. 14:13). With reason, therefore, the apostle laments: "Unhappy man that I am, who shall deliver me from the body of this death?" (Rom. 7:24). And the Psalmist said, "Bring my soul out of prison" (Ps. 142:7). "Man is born to labour and the bird to fly" (Job 5:7). "All his days are sorrows and miseries, *even in the night he doth not rest in mind.*" (Eccles. 2:23)

In a sense, this is argument by generalization, but some of the statements seem to have little to do with the main claim. So, says Olbricht, it is more like amplification of a claim already accepted than support for a generalization that is being argued. Early in the formation of a religion, argument by generalization may be necessary, but after its establishment it is not. It may even be considered foolish because why should one argue a principle that is already accepted?

Generalization by statistics is especially open to question. T. Dewitt Talmadge, an orthodox preacher of the late nineteenth century, used an argument from statistics to refute Robert G. Ingersoll's popular arguments for agnosticism. In his sermon, "Victory for God," he cited the increasing number of Christians in each century, the number of New Testaments distributed the number of converts, and so forth to prove the popularity of Christianity (290–292). Most theologians would quickly identify that as the fallacy of *argumentatum ad populum*. It is inappropriate to religious argumentation because religious argumentation does not attempt to know what is popular but what is true, and a true religion may be unpopular, as were early Judaism, Christianity, and Islam.

The issue created by the clash of some conservative Christians and evolution scientists illustrates this difference (see pp. 138–139 in Chapter 8 for a discussion of conflicting values). For such Christians, God created the universe and all in it (Genesis 1). For most scientists, "random mutation and natural selection" is the basis of creation. There is a clear disagreement between literal interpretation of text and generalization. Biochemist and Anglican priest Arthur Peacock claimed that evolutionary theory reveals something about God's nature. God limited his omnipotence and provided evidence of a "divine humility." By his reasoning, evolution grounds the claim that God created the universe. Such a view is a case of religion using generalization, but it is not the usual case (Begley 45).

There are, in summary, five and occasionally six forms of argument used in religious argumentation. Argument from authority, argument by analogy, and argument by narrative are the most frequently used. Argument by sign is probably less frequently used. Argument by paradox is not as frequently used as some other forms of argument, but it poses a "riddle" that can be central to the meaning of a religion. Except as natural theology, argumentation by generalization is rarely used and is open to question.

CONCLUSION

Something like 85% of the world's adult population identify with some religion. The largest are Christianity, Islam, Hinduism, Chinese religion (including Confucianism), and Buddhism. Religious argumentation is among the oldest spheres known to humans. The Judeo-Christian-Islamic tradition (the emphasis of this chapter) operates from an elaborate system of texts and other evidence to ground specialized theological arguments.

Theological argumentation is found in seven major questions. The explanation of most, if not all, of them will usually define a complete theology: (1) What is the nature of God? (2) What is the nature of human beings? (3) What is moral behavior, the religious life? (4) What are sin, evil, and the meaning of suffering? (5) What is the human's relationship to God? (6) What is the nature of salvation? And (7) what is the role of the church? The themes that arguers develop in answering these questions will identify the strongest values and serve as warrants for religious argumentation. These include God, human beings, moral behavior, evil, sin, suffering, prophet, salvation, and church.

In religious argumentation, texts are traditionally the most central kinds of evidence. The theologian must first decide which texts are most accurate, which texts are most trustworthy, and how these texts may be interpreted. In the interpretation of texts, and sometimes independent of texts, tradition, experience, revelation, and culture may also serve as evidence.

Argument from authority and argument by analogy are the preferred forms of argumentation among theologians. Argument by narrative has a special role in religious argumentation. Argument by sign is also used but less so. Argument by paradox is a special kind of argument prevalent in religious argumentation but uncommon elsewhere. It involves finding a new meaning in seemingly contradictory statements. Argument by generalization is usually not used except in the sense that the text must be taken as a whole. Some of what seems like generalization is actually a kind of amplification of a claim established by some other kind of argument.

EXERCISES/PROJECTS

1. Choose a short text that is important to your religion or to your nonreligious beliefs. Explain what it means to you. Evaluate your own answer. On what bases did you make your interpretation? Is it based on the principles discussed in this chapter? What different bases did you find?
2. Write a short essay on how you come to believe there is or is not a God, or what God is like. Consider the question of natural theology and any texts you deem appropriate.
3. With a small group of classmates, conduct a group discussion on one of the major themes of religious argumentation? Can you come to an agreement on what that theme means? How do you differ? How are your agreements or disagreements a product of your religious or nonreligious position?
4. In that discussion or a subsequent one, note what kinds of arguments you use. Are you arguing in the religious sphere or some other?

Argumentation in Business

KEY TERMS

basic beliefs, p. 243
respect the individual, p. 243
best customer service, p. 243
drive for superiority, p. 243
success, p. 243
burden of proof, p. 244
booms and busts, p. 246
change, p. 247
comparison and contrast, p. 248
differentiation, p. 249
cause and effect, p. 249

cost/benefit, p. 250
sign, p. 251
penetration, p. 251
wisdom of crowds, p. 252
evidence, p. 252
examples, p. 252
statistics, p. 252
testimony, p. 252
values, p. 253
credibility, p. 255

When Thomas J. Watson, Jr., CEO of IBM Corporation, delivered a series of lectures at the Graduate School of Business at Columbia University in the spring of 1962, his company was already 51 years old and stood at the pinnacle of successful industrial organizations. The thesis (proposition) of his lectures was this: "I firmly believe that any organization, in order to survive and achieve success, must have a sound set of beliefs on which it premises all its policies and actions." He continued,

> Next, I believe that the most important single factor in corporate success is faithful adherence to those beliefs.
>
> And finally, I believe that if an organization is to meet the challenges of a changing world, it must be prepared to change everything about itself except those beliefs as it moves through corporate life. (5)

Watson went on to detail the **basic beliefs** which, he asserted, made the difference between success and failure for any business:

1. **Respect the individual.**
2. Provide the **best customer service** of any company in the world.
3. **Drive for superiority** in all things (13–39).

Success, defined in various ways, constitutes the ultimate purpose of all business argumentation. In this chapter, we will discuss argumentation in business by looking closely at the experience of what began as a group of small companies that joined together to form International Business Machines Corporation, known today simply as IBM. Business is far too complex to be discussed as a single sphere. And business argumentation is far too complex to be covered in a single chapter. So, our look at IBM will examine only some of the characteristics and contexts for argument that occur within that company.

Why use IBM as a model for business argumentation? First, IBM, for about three-quarters of a century, was extraordinarily successful, held up as "the model of an all-conquering American multinational . . . it prevailed in every market it was allowed to enter; it was more widely visible, more scrutinized, more admired. It was the lodestar for other companies" (Mills and Friesen, citing *The Economist* 7). Second, IBM almost became extinct not because it fell behind the curve of remarkable technological change at the end of the twentieth century but because it broke its promises, stated in the basic beliefs, to respect individuals and provide the best customer service (Mills and Friesen 8–9). Third, IBM has, in the twenty-first century, recovered its world dominance as exemplified by its challenge to the two most successful human champions of the TV quiz show Jeopardy! In February of 2011, Ken Jennings and Brad Rutter took on an IBM computer named Watson, and lost. On May 8, 2011, bloomberg.com announced that the value of the IBM brand had risen to third place in the world behind Apple, Inc. (valued at US$153 billion) and Google (valued at US$111.5 billion). Celebrating its 100th year in business on June 16, 2011, IBM noted, of 25 thriving U.S. corporations in 1900, only two were still on the list in 1960. Similarly, 2011 saw only six companies retained from the Fortune 500 list of 25 thriving companies in 1961 (*The New York Times*; June 16, 2011; A16). Finally, IBM, more than any other business of which we are aware, has explicitly set out the guiding values on which all argumentation is to be based: the basic beliefs.

STARTING POINTS FOR BUSINESS ARGUMENTATION

Over the years, business spheres have developed elaborate systems designed to establish accepted language interpretation strategies, facts, presumptions, probabilities, and commonplaces on which argumentation could be based. Recall that without starting points, argumentation is not possible; the greater the shared starting points, the easier it is to develop an argument. Starting points are a springboard for argumentation. For example, the more facts we share at the start of our decision making, the more we will be able to use as support for our claims, and the fewer claims we will need to argue. We can reach the proposition faster with a head start. Review our discussion of starting points in Chapter 2.

It was language interpretation strategies that made the Watson computer competition in *Jeopardy!* so challenging. You may have thought that of course a computer can store and retrieve more information than humans, but think again. As IBM said, the nature of the game *Jeopardy!* is particularly challenging for a computer because it is filled with puns, irony, complexity, ambiguity and double meanings. If human beings find that difficult, think how much harder it is to program a computer to deal with such subtleties of ordinary language. Computers of the future will need to deal with the language of everyday life and business—e-mails, tweets, Ims, journals, blogs, and more, because every day the world creates over 2.5 extabytes of data and half of that come in a form that is not neat database language (A13). IBM boasted that the impressive performance by Watson's remarkable technological intelligence is already being applied in medicine, law, academia, and business, and they invite you to learn more at ibmwatson.com.

Facts in Business Argumentation

In his 1962 lectures, Thomas Watson, Jr., wanted to cite facts that would quickly describe his company since 1914 in ways that would be familiar to his business college audience. What categories of fact did he select? Number of employees: from 1,200 to 125,000; revenues: from US$4 million to US$1.6 billion; profits: from US$500,000 to US$200 million; dividends: not since 1916 has the company missed paying a cash dividend; number of stockholders: from 800 to 225,000; shareholder value (share price): 100 shares purchased in 1914 for US$2,750, if left untouched until 1962, would be worth US$5,455,000; product type and quality, from tabulating machines with Queen Anne legs to high-powered computers (9).

In 1995, after mostly restoring IBM to a successful path, Lou Gerstner, the CEO, cited these facts: revenues up 12% from US$64 billion to US$72 billion; net earnings per share grew by 40%, US$7.23 versus US$5.02; hardware, which produced half the company's sales, grew by 10 points, the System/390 was selling well and software, producing the most profitable revenue stream, was up by double digits (Garr 241). He could have noted that even after reducing the number of employees in the face of weak business activity, there were still some 350,000 IBM employees (known universally as IBMers), and he could have announced that there were about 600,000 shareholders. In 2011, IBM advertised its success by reporting that 100 shares purchased in 1915 would now be worth about US$200 million dollars (*The new York Times*; June 16, 2011; A17).

As a starting point for argumentation, then, the appropriate facts to be examined for a business argument would include those we have found listed by Watson, Gerstner, and the IBM Centennial announcement. Company size, earnings, profitability, shareholder value, and products are commonly recognized as appropriate to understanding a business. An important fact they did not mention, but which has become more important today is market share—a measure of how large a share of the total sales in any given market is held by one company. When a development team at an IBM site in Minnesota began creating a new product, they quickly realized that today businesses must consider two additional fact questions if they have any expectation of success: Who are our customers, and what do they want (Bauer et al. 7–9, 58–80)?

Presumptions in Business Argumentation

In the discussion of presumptions in Chapter 2, we say that, in any argumentative sphere, it is necessary to have agreement from the start on who has the **burden of proof** and what the decision will be if that burden is not met. In policy questions, people generally presume that the status quo will continue to be the policy of choice unless someone successfully proves that the policy should change. In law, people are presumed to be innocent of any crime unless the appropriate government agency assumes the burden to prove that they are not. And if the prosecutor fails to sustain a *prima facie* case of guilt, the accused will walk free even though some may suspect he or she really is guilty.

In business argumentation, presumptions are usually not so clearly established as these we have mentioned. Yet, without presumptions, business argumentation could not assign burdens of proof and clearly understand what will be done if no *prima facie* case is sustained. In the case of IBM, we can call attention to some presumptions that played a key role in their history. Specifically, IBM's basic beliefs defined the company's presumptions.

The basic beliefs outlined by Watson form the basis of many presumptions at IBM. The belief in *respect for the individual* was particularly powerful in placing the burden of proof in many decision-making situations. For example, it was presumed that once an individual was hired by IBM, "He or she was set for life. Benefits were good; salaries competitive; and the working environment excellent" (Mills and Friesen 9). In a decision concerning the performance of an IBMer, anyone arguing that the employee be fired carried a significant burden of proof. Most likely, poor performance in one IBM operation would result in a transfer to another corporate job along with training. The result of this presumption was that low turnover and protection of less-than-superior employees drastically reduced the company's flexibility and contributed to their ultimate downfall. "Had IBM managers dismissed ineffective employees at less than half the rate common at other firms," claim D. Quinn Mills and G. Bruce Friesen in their book, *Broken Promises: An Unconventional View of What Went Wrong at IBM*, "it could have significantly reduced its massive financial losses in the 1990's for early retirement and layoffs" (9).

By the same token, when a new process, product, or support needed to be developed, the presumption was that it would be done either in-house or using outside vendors. Anyone arguing to hire more IBMers to meet new needs carried a big burden of proof. Because employment was meant to be for life and because layoffs were anathema, increasing the number of IBMers was a difficult argument to sustain. It was virtually impossible to argue successfully for hiring new employees who would be needed only for a specified period of time and then let go.

In choosing new leaders from supervisors to the CEO, the presumption was that someone already a part of the IBM family would be selected. When Thomas Watson left the leadership of IBM, he was replaced by his son Thomas Watson, Jr. Years later, when IBM faced a crisis so dire that its very existence was at stake, a new CEO was desperately needed. Those who argued that an outsider should be chosen because a complete change in direction was demanded bore a significant burden of proof. In fact, except for poor health, Dick Gerstner, who was a full-fledged, lifetime IBMer who had risen through the ranks to a high level appointment, would have been a competitor for the assignment. Instead, it was his brother Lou Gerstner, who had never worked at IBM, who got the job. This was a clear sign of change. But when Gerstner retired, he was replaced by Samuel Palmisano, a lifetime IBMer.

From its beginning, International Business Machines or IBM was a manufacturer of machines, as its name implies. It made measuring/timing devices, tabulators, typewriters, mainframe computers, and the like. The presumption was that hardware would always be the defining characteristic of the firm's products. More particularly, again as the name implies and as its experience proves, IBM presumed that good-sized businesses and government agencies needing large systems would be its primary customers. And IBM had always been a superior marketing company. They did not lead in the development of technology as much as they had a strong customer base and a superior sales staff. The presumption was that IBM could always outperform their competitors, even those with better technology.

When the personal computer emerged as a major new product, IBM entered the competition and produced a PC that quickly took command of the market. Based on the presumptions that the machine itself combined with superior marketing would be key to IBM's success, and urged to avoid the appearance of monopolizing a market by the U.S. Department of Justice antitrust charge then being pursued, it was decided to use an open-systems approach that made the details of the PC's functions publicly available, and the company chose to use outside vendors for the computer chip (Intel) and the operating system (Microsoft). When other companies found they could produce a clone of the IBM PC that could run all its software more effectively and cost less, IBM lost its edge. Ultimately, in 1989, a decision was made with Microsoft to concede the small machine market to Microsoft while IBM concentrated on midrange and large computers (Garr 189). In retrospect, it seems as if the presumption by IBM in favor of its marketing superiority was misplaced: The PC was aimed at a retail market in which IBM had little experience. And its presumption that the hardware rather than the software was the key to success also proved wrong. At one point early on, Bill Gates had offered to sell the MS/DOS to IBM outright for a reasonable price, but IBM declined (Garr 188).

Probabilities in Business Argumentation

Among the many probabilities that provide starting points for business argumentation, the most prominent are (1) the inevitability of cycles of booms and busts, (2) the expectation of upward movement in economies, and (3) the inevitability of change.

Booms and Busts. A look at any graph of economic activity—stock markets, consumer prices, business earnings, housing, exports and imports, personal income, rates of inflation, and so on—over time will show that good economies are followed by bad (or less good) economies, which are followed by good (or better) economies, and so on. These are called the **booms and busts**. When and to what extent the economy will change direction is always a matter of speculation. There is money to be made by predicting accurately no matter what the new direction will be.

At any time, whether the economy is more bust than boom or vice versa, there can be strange arguments in the effort to predict the new direction. Eamonn Kelly, Peter Leyden, and members of Global Business Network note in their 2002 book *What's Next: Exploring the New Terrain for Business*, "Busts and Booms are equally irrational" (20). By this they mean that most people, when thinking rationally, would acknowledge the probability that no matter what is happening now, boom or bust, it will be followed sooner or later by its opposite. The irrational part comes in convincing ourselves the probability will not hold true *this time*. In the late 1990s, year after year of economic expansion led many to speculate that maybe, for the first time ever, people had learned how to maintain a continuously upward economy. Arguments were predicated on the rejection of the cyclical probability: Keep investing in almost anything because it will go up. Then, in 2000–2003, the dotcoms began to collapse and people realized, too late, they had been pouring money into companies that had never produced a profit and had virtually no intrinsic value.

Then there is the Great Recession of 2008–2012. This is far too complicated an event for us to review here, but we can use this downturn as another example of probabilities in business argumentation. The Financial Crisis Inquiry Commission, appointed to explain the causes of the financial crisis, released its report on January 27, 2011—while acknowledging that the recession was not yet over. Early on, the report recognizes the inevitability of booms and busts, "While the business cycle cannot be repealed, a crisis of this magnitude need not have occurred" (xvii). Having recognized the regularity of ups and downs, the commissioners wondered what made it so severe this time, and their answer was an excessive faith in the continued rise in housing prices alongside the emergence of a global economy. Quoting the Chair of the Federal Reserve, Ben Bernanke, the report says, "At some point, both lenders and borrowers became convinced that house prices would only go up." "For a time," the report continues, "rising house prices became a self-fulfilling prophecy, but ultimately, further appreciation could not be sustained and house prices collapsed" (423). So, once again, there is the inevitability of booms and busts and the apparently inevitable irrationality in thinking it will not hold true this time.

But even in the face of the probability of cycles in business activity, there is also a probability of a long-term upward trend. Frequently noted is the fact that various economic measures, such as those by Dow Jones, show a steady rise in value since, say, the end of World War II. Even factoring in the years of bust, a steady upward line in the price of securities can be shown. Thus, the probability is that, in the long term, values will rise. People invest in individual retirement policies with the idea that when they retire, their funds will have increased in value sufficient to support them. Unless, of course, they retire just as the economy goes down once more.

Upward Economic Movement.   Businesses predicate arguments about their success on comparisons with the past quarter or year or more. Because of the probability of a continuing rise in the economy, the expectation is that successful companies will report more earnings, more profits, more shareholder value, more command of the market, more sales, and so on than in the past. In 2011, IBM could report significant growth in its business: it is the largest technology and consulting employer in the world with over 400,000 employees; it does business in 170 different countries; it offers complex infrastructure, hosting, and consulting services; a portfolio of middleware for collaboration, predictive analytics, software development, and systems management; and the world's most advanced servers and supercomputers. IBM holds more patents than any other U.S. technology company with 17 straight years of patent leadership. And, LinkedIn, a business-oriented social networking site, concludes "IBM has pioneered the corporate operating model for the twenty-first century, changing from a classic 'multinational' to a global integrated company with a highly skilled global workforce managed by a common set of values." This is a powerful testimony in support of the claim that IBM has truly bounced back from its previous weakness to regain its dominance in the business world, again by relying on its basic beliefs as interpreted for a new century.

Probability of Change.   Along with the probability of booms and busts, and the long-term growth in business, is the probability of **change**. Jeffrey Garten says the world is now experiencing extraordinary changes in technology and globalization that have "created a level of competition that will lead to new categories of winners and losers and for a transformation in how companies are organized and led" (19). We are now, he says, in the third such revolution. He labels England between 1750 and 1840 and the United States between the 1860s and the 1920s as the Industrial Revolutions. Now, we are in the information, communication, or knowledge age, depending on who is speaking. Business argumentation uses the probability of change as a starting point for claims about what businesses and entire industries must do to anticipate and profit from the impending change, whatever it turns out to be. Remember that Thomas Watson, Jr., said in his lectures,

> And finally, I believe that if an organization is to meet the challenges of a changing world, it must be prepared to change everything about itself except those beliefs as it moves through corporate life. (5)

Fred Balboni of IBM says Watson's win over Jeopardy! champions was remarkable, but the real effect was to pull "back the curtain to reveal a glimpse into a world of new potential, for real people, cultures, and societies, as this capability finds its way into practical applications in health care, energy, transportation, education, and telecommunications." "Watson," says Balboni, "embodies the power of massively scaled analytics." He claims Watson can, "parse a problem across thousands of processors, race through its massive data reserves, evaluate a near-infinite number of options, make the relevant correlations, narrow the possibilities, and arrive at what it identifies as the highest-probability correct answer. And it does all that in less than three seconds" (Forbes.com). IBM will lead as the world changes.

Commonplaces/Forms of Argument in Business Argumentation

In Chapter 2, we define commonplaces as lines of argument, forms of argument, or places from which arguments can be built. In Chapter 4, we explain various forms of argument and we observe that spheres define the patterns of argument that are preferred and the criteria by which they will be evaluated. It is possible to identify some commonplaces that are generally characteristic of business argumentation. We will rely on reports about IBM and a research report written by IBMers about telecom providers in a digital content market to illustrate the commonplaces.

Comparison and contrast can be found in the argument of The Motley Fool that IBM is strong and worthy of investment. The question was, "How does IBM compare or contrast with its peers and competitors?" Using the measure of market capitalization for evidence, IBM with US$160.3 billion is contrasted with Oracle with US$113 billion, Accenture with US$23.7 billion, BEA Systems with US$7.2 billion, and TIBCO Software with US$1.6 billion (October 16, 2007). The Motley Fool went on to support the comparison and contrast argument in support of IBM by considering a bid by Oracle for another company that would amount to US$6.6 billion, and a bid by Google to buy YouTube for US$2 billion. Contrast that, said The Motley Fool, with the fact that at IBM when they have extra cash they invest it back in their own business. IBM, they said, is wise to keep its focus on its well-established business plan of internal growth and smaller acquisitions, in contrast with these newer firms that seem determined to spend money lavishly.

Considering what current telecom companies will need to accomplish technologically if they are to enter the digital content market, a report prepared by three IBMers, Ekow Nelson, Howard Kline, and Rob van den Dam, entitled, *A Future in Content(ion): Can Telecom Providers Win a Share of the Digital Content Market,* calls attention to the need to upgrade their systems considerably. For example, they say that there is talk of providing six simultaneous HDTV streams, which would need a huge 120 megabits (Mbit/s). "Delivering this kind of bandwidth over an access network that was fundamentally designed to carry narrowband voice traffic is not straightforward." They compare and contrast the current capabilities in various parts of the world:

> Only 50 percent of households in Western Europe could attain speeds of at least 10 Mbit/s over today's DSL networks. The Challenge is even bigger in North America, where some of the incumbent local exchange carriers can only manage to provide speeds of 2 Mbit/s—and then to only 60 percent of households. Conversely, in Singapore and Korea, about 95 percent and almost 100 percent of households, respectively, can obtain very high speed access. (9)

Another argument from comparison and contrast is found in the business concept of **differentiation.** Differentiation is seen as critical to telecom providers who wish to profit from new media markets. The report on *A Future in Content(ion)*, says "The most successful operators will thus be those that can simultaneously control their costs and drive penetration by differentiating themselves from their rivals with high-value offerings to content owners, advertisers, consumers, and third-party service providers" (2). The report emphasizes the challenge to companies that have traditionally profited from providing voice communication only, a business that will, at best, show little growth in the future, to moving into the full range of digital communications. They say

> If traditional telecom providers do not differentiate themselves from their competitors in the cable and satellites sectors, they will likely end up locked in a price war—and quite possibly risk alienating their institutional investors, too, since the capital markets will not support oversupply. (11)

AT&T, T-Mobile, Sprint, Verizon, Cingular, Qwest, and other voice communication companies have expended great amounts of money to secure subscribers and distinguish themselves from their competitors. Cingular bought the oldest communication company, AT&T, and then adopted its name and dropped the use of "Cingular." Apparently, the company leaders believed that the old brand was a more viable way to differentiate themselves from the other made-up names than their own made-up name. Most people in the twenty-first century have no idea that AT&T started out standing for American Telephone and Telegraph, any more than they remember that IBM stands for International Business Machines. In the comparison and contrast argumentation, a distinguished and venerable name seems to carry weight.

Cause and effect is a widely used commonplace in business argumentation. At the Computer Dealers Exposition (COMDEX), a conference in Las Vegas of 200,000 makers and purveyors of microchips and related wares, Lou Gerstner, IBM CEO, addressed the large gathering. In his talk, he reasoned from cause to effect, effect to cause, and cause to effect to cause.

> Every now and then, a technology or an idea comes along that is so profound, and so powerful, and so universal, that its impact changes everything. The printing press, the incandescent light, the automobile, manned flight. It doesn't happen often, but when it does, the world is changed forever. (Garr 4)

He said that information technology (IT) is such a cause of worldwide effect. If the cause is the IT revolution, Gerstner proceeded to identify processor power, memory, disk capacity, and bandwidth as effects that will in turn cause the profound effects throughout the world in information, communication, and technology. Members of his audience, representing all his competitors, were aware that one of the causes of IBM's decline at the end of the twentieth century was a protracted antitrust suit pursued by the U.S. Justice Department. From 1969 to 1982, the suit drained resources and weakened IBM's ability to conduct business. Those representing Microsoft, including Bill Gates, were already feeling the effects of such legal action because they had achieved the degree of market dominance that had brought IBM to the attention of the government (Garr 6).

Gerstner, who was not a technology-savvy person, charged that computer geeks are fascinated with complexity, and that causes them to produce products that consumers find difficult, if not impossible, to operate and include features few can ever use. And, said Gerstner, by the time the customers figured it out, new computers with new complexity are on the market requiring the customer to start all over. "There is," said Gerstner, "a disconnect between taking on technical challenges and meeting the customer's needs" (Garr 9).

IBM suffered serious effects from forgetting one of its prime beliefs: Provide the best customer service in the world. Instead, IBM technicians were focused on the technology rather than the customer. An IBM team in Rochester, Minnesota, charged with developing a new product, realized that they had become product-driven rather than customer-driven or market-driven. "We'd forgotten how to do something we'd always done so well before. We didn't listen to our customers" (Bauer et al. 6). They had been reasoning from cause to effect: We produce a fine product and the customers will buy it. But that reasoning had not worked. Instead, they had to reason from effect to cause: What utility does the customer need? How can we produce a product that meets that need? In the retail market today, the company that seems to be doing the best job of producing products the customers need and want is Apple with its iPod, iPhone, and iPad, and the effect is Apple's standing as the most valuable brand in the world.

Cost/benefit is found in virtually every business argument. Businesses must maintain close control over all aspects of their operations to ensure that profits (benefits) exceed costs. At the most simple level, if the total cost of doing business exceeds the total benefit derived in terms of earnings, then a business will fail. Lou Gerstner, in his COMDEX speech, spoke of what he called, "a near death experience" for IBM when, over the course of 3 years, IBM lost US$16 billion. Few businesses could experience that outcome and survive (Garr 4).

A key aspect of IBM's business over the years has been to provide ever more sophisticated machines to help businesses do the calculations needed to keep track of costs and earnings. On October 11, 2007, IBM announced in a press release that Merkur Group, a Slovenian-based retailer, had decided to use IBM Tivoli to manage its critical IT assets and systems:

> IT assets and systems are vital to a retail environment and ensure that sales and inventory data are readily available to help management make quick decisions. Due to Merkur's strong growth—IT assets within the organization had tripled in just three years—the company was challenged to deliver the same high levels of service while reducing costs. Existing manual, ad-hoc solutions for tracking and managing assets were expensive, error-prone and not scalable. . . . Merkur has started to roll out the software, with some 16,000 IT assets, including notebook computers, cell phones, monitors, point-of-sale devices and network equipment, now being managed by the Tivoli software. By the end of 2007, plans call for 30,000 assets to be managed.
>
> "By providing a single platform for asset and service management, Tivoli technology enables us to finally understand the true cost of our IT services and its impact on profitability," says Simon Znidar, CIO, Merkur Group. "With this information, we can proactively reduce operational costs while maintaining exceptional service quality." (IBM.com)

IBM reported that plans call for Merkur to use the Tivoli technology to measure service delivery, track incident response times, and evaluate the performance of individual assets. In this way, they can keep close track of costs and profitability.

At the same time, another IBM press release announced that AXA Group, a worldwide leader in financial protection and wealth management, had extended its Infrastructure On Demand contract with IBM. The AXA Group Managing Director said,

> By partnering with IBM, AXA will have access to the world's leading research and technology for an on demand operating environment, allowing AXA to significantly reduce its IT operational costs and increase productivity while focusing on their core business and clients. (IBM.com)

In this way, IBM has returned to its roots: providing customers with the means of doing their businesses more efficiently, thereby producing greater benefit at lower cost.

Sign reasoning occurs throughout economic and business argumentation. Remember, sign reasoning differs from cause and effect in that the sign may indicate something without having played a major role, or any role, in its cause. For example, surveys of consumer confidence are reported as signaling future business activity. The causes of the activity may be many and complex, including products, pricing, weather, fashion, and so forth, but the consumer confidence index has proved, over the years, to be a reliable predictor (sign) of what consumers will actually do. The various market indexes, such as Dow Jones, Standard and Poor's, and NASDAQ, take a sample of the stocks of selected businesses and report the average price, direction, and degree of change. Observers and investors tend to take these averages as signs of the economy's health, or lack thereof. Movement in the price of a single company's shares may signal the health of the company, or the likelihood that some other company is buying the shares with the plan of taking control. Or as our discussion of the irrationality of booms and busts suggests, a rapid rise in share price may simply signal the presence of a lot of wealth seeking an investment.

Sign reasoning can also be used to enhance the reputation of a company. For example, on November 2, 2007, an IBM press release announced Project Big Green, a US$1 billion investment toward dramatically increasing the efficiency of IBM products. The project included a five-step approach to "energy efficiency in the data center that, if followed, could sharply reduce data center energy consumption and transform clients' technology infrastructure into 'green' data centers" (IBM.com). Clearly, this effort was not aimed at increasing IBM's profits or reducing its costs. The energy consumed would be paid for by clients who were using IBM products. However, the green project was intended to be a sign of IBM's commitment to energy efficiency and that it was a good citizen in helping overcome the effects of global warming. As a part of the project, IBM announced a program that allows mainframe customers to monitor their systems' precise energy consumption in real time. In doing so, IBM signaled its further willingness to encourage its customers to take part in the green movement.

Penetration of markets is a commonplace used to argue a business' control of sales of certain products and to argue the future potential of a product in relation to the current level of adoption. For example, the IBM study of telecommunications companies' future potential in traditional voice telephony in Europe reports that the demand for wireless services is slowing down, as mobile penetration in Western Europe nears 100%. At the same time, the report says, "the prospective market for Internet Protocol Television (IPTV) is large because fewer than four million households currently have IPTV, but the number of subscriptions is expected to rise to over 30 million by 2010" (Nelson et al. 5–6). There is not much point in pursuing a line of business for which demand is dropping rapidly. There is good reason to pursue an expanding market.

The **wisdom of crowds** is a commonplace that has emerged recently. Traditionally, the idea of using what "everybody believes" as support for an argument has been denounced as mere bandwagon propaganda. The IBM report argues, however, that today consumers are demanding ubiquitous access; they want to control their own schedules, publish their own materials, and share content easily. Yahoo!, Google, MySpace, Amazon, and Wikipedia have "capitalized on the 'wisdom of crowds' to create ratings and recommendations." Consumers want to "reuse content legally and easily for mashups, fan sites, and create their own interactive Web applications" (Nelson et al. 20). The report claims that telecom operators will need to accommodate the wisdom of crowds.

FORMS OF SUPPORT IN BUSINESS ARGUMENTATION

Evidence, values, and credibility constitute the forms of support for arguments, as we explained in Chapters 7–9. In this section, we will discuss some of the ways business arguments are supported. Our primary focus will be on how IBM has used its basic beliefs as value support for its argumentation.

Evidence as Support in Business Argumentation

You learned in Chapter 7 that the common forms of **evidence** in arguments are examples, statistics, and testimony. All three forms are used widely in business decision making.

Examples abound in business argumentation. When IBM argues that in recent years it has presented the world with significant new technology and products, it can point to the example of the number of patents held by the company: more than US$1 billion earned each year from royalties. It can identify individual products introduced within the past few years, for example, the IBM System i5, an "all-in-one" IT platform for small and midsize businesses. They can give the example of the IBM System z9 Business Class mainframe. They can point to the U.S. Department of Energy's National Nuclear Security Administration's announcement of a joint production with IBM of the BlueGene/L— the world's fastest computer. They can brag about the IBM prototype compact storage "blade" that can hold more than 500,000 times more information than a magnetic hard-disk drive in a space not much larger than a briefcase.

Statistics are a vital part of business argumentation, as we have reported in the discussion of facts as starting points. Other than the science spheres, business is probably the largest user of quantitative data as support for arguments. For example, in the study of telecom providers and the digital content market, the IBM report presents a graph showing emerging content revenue in billions of U.S. dollars growing from US$56 billion in 2006 to US$135 billion in 2010 and breaking out the income according to source: Mobile TV, IPTV, in-game advertising, Mobile advertising, online advertising, digital streaming, interactive TV promotions, television, wireless games, online games, Mobile music, and licensed digital music content. These statistics vividly support the IBM argument that the future is not in voice communication but in the digital content market.

Testimony is given particular importance in business argumentation when the leaders speak. The CEO and other corporate chiefs are given a great deal of credibility, almost to the extent of personifying the business itself. An IBM press release dated July 25, 2007 reported on IBM CEO Samuel J. Palmisano's announcement of the Global Citizen's Portfolio. This is a suite of investments and programs to help IBM employees enhance their skills and expertise in order to become global leaders, professionals, and citizens. Palmisano said,

> to be competitive, any individual—like any company, community or country—has to adapt continuously, learning new fields and new skills. This package of capabilities enhances the ability of IBMers to acquire new skills and capabilities. (IBM.com)

This testimony formed the support for a variety of arguments. Since the CEO was addressing a conference of IBMers, they understood the argument that they were obliged to adapt and learn new skills. The old days of protecting less than excellent performance were over. The press release went out to the world, and the argument was understood that the IBM brand would be dominant around the world and the firm would be an attractive player in the emerging global market. The days of weakness at the end of the twentieth century were over. The fact that the announcement was made by the CEO communicated strongly that these commitments were real and not just window dressing.

Values as Support in Business Argumentation

We have spoken of the basic beliefs that have governed IBM decision making for almost a century, and we have said that IBM more than any other business of which we are aware explicitly states and relies on its **values** (basic beliefs) to develop and evaluate argumentation. In a personal conversation with an IBM vice president at an Austin, Texas, site in the 1990s, we asked what profound changes in their way of doing business IBM would consider. The answer came quickly, without apparent consideration, "I would give serious consideration to any proposed change." He paused, and then added as if an unnecessary addendum, "Except, of course, a change in the basic beliefs." We never doubted his sincerity because strict dedication to those beliefs has been the bedrock of support for argumentation for IBM's entire existence. In their 2011 advertisement on the occasion of their centennial, they said,

> "But Watson's most enduring contribution to business was his intentional creation of something that would outlast him—a shared corporate culture. He showed how the basic beliefs and values of an organization could be perpetuated—to become its guiding constant through time. By values we do not mean ethics or morals, which are requisites for every enterprise. We mean the characteristics that identify what is both unique and enduring about any particular enterprise . . . it's about institutionalizing *why* the organization does what it does. When we have lived our values, IBMers and our company have thrived. When we haven't, it hurt us" (*The New York Times*; June 16, 2011; A16).

In an internal study of the decision making at the Austin site, and by extension of the decision making throughout IBM because there is great conformity to process throughout the huge company, Richard Rieke found more than 50 specific value statements employed in IBM decision making.[1] We will identify a few of these that played significant roles in decision making, and we will illustrate how they can come into conflict to complicate decisions.

The specific value statements are derived from the three basic values outlined by Thomas Watson, Jr.: Respect the individual, provide the best customer service in the world, and drive for superiority in all things. For example, based on the mandate to respect the individual are these preferences: We prefer experienced individuals, the person or team most prepared and ready to go, the person or team with the most market experience,

---

[1]Richard D. Rieke, Analysis and Reasoning in Contention and Presentation, Being Effective in Management Communication. A training seminar created exclusively for the IBM Corporation, Austin, Texas.

the lowest headcount (never hire more people than will be needed to avoid layoffs at all costs), to treat all people with dignity and respect, people neatly dressed, forthrightness, optimism, loyalty, building from within, an open door (any IBMer can talk to any manager including the CEO), managers who help and train their people, wild ducks (people with an instinct for innovation and drama), multiple open channels of communication, team play, letting managers manage their units.

Emerging from the mandate to provide the best customer service in the world are these preferences: We prefer long-term to short-term effects, brevity to length, ease of use to difficulty, being competitive, ease of update, doing a job well, the best schedule, sooner to later, lowest cost, satisfied customers, adapting our equipment to our customers' businesses rather than asking them to adapt their business to our equipment, avoiding complacency, improved effectiveness.

From the demand for superiority in all things come these preferences: We prefer making more rather than less money, high quality, excellence, maximum utilization of our skills and resources, competence to incompetence, being competitive, superior products and performance, education and retraining, the future to the status quo, improving the image of the company, what has already succeeded, serving the stockholders, the free enterprise system, responding to markets, improving effectiveness.

In Chapter 8, we describe how values work in argumentation, particularly the fact that they most often appear as warrants and they operate in hierarchies. In IBM, the three major values stated by Watson in 1962 are not given more or less importance in relation to each other. Accordingly, the numerous specific values we have just listed do not carry any inherent superiority in relation to one another. In making a business decision, then, it is quite possible that two or more specific value warrants will be relevant and in conflict. We will present some scenarios to illustrate this situation without saying what decision should be made. That will depend on the other factors in the argumentative process: grounds, backing, qualifier, rebuttal, and reservation.

Price versus Schedule

Manufacturing is charged with the responsibility of getting the lowest per unit cost and thereby keeping down the product price. However, this leads them to refuse to bend: They won't pressure vendors to speed up because they have negotiated that low unit price. If they go back to the vendors and ask for more speedy delivery, they will jeopardize their low price agreements. Then again, if we speed up the schedule the products will reach the market faster and the money will start rolling in sooner.

How might the conflict between the two values be resolved? Under what conditions might low prices be more or less important than schedule?

Profit versus Compatibility

If we go in the direction Team A is recommending, clearly we can bring the product in precisely within set margins and profit will be just where management wanted it. However, Team B can show rather persuasively, that if we go in their direction, the new product will be more compatible with products that are currently being used by our customers, even though it will require eating into profits more than management wanted.

How might the conflict between the two values be resolved? Under what conditions might achieving compatibility be more or less important than profit?

Schedule versus Customer Acceptance
We can meet the schedule as per our original public announcement, but our surveys show that if we make the upgrade that has now become possible, customer acceptance will be significantly increased. However, if we make those changes, we will miss the announced schedule by a good deal.

How might the conflict between the two values be resolved? Under what conditions might improved products be more or less important the meeting announced schedules?

Credibility as Support for Business Argumentation
Credibility is defined in Chapter 9 as the perception that the arguer is competent and trustworthy, and has good will toward the decision makers. Dynamism is also frequently mentioned as a factor in credibility. In business argumentation, credibility plays a role in arguments addressed to customers, shareholders, employees, the government, other businesses, and special interest groups such as environmentalists.

Thomas L. Friedman, the international affairs op-ed columnist for the *New York Times*, describes at length what is happening throughout the world in business practices, communication, argumentation, and business decision making in *The World Is Flat: A Brief History of the Twenty-First Century*. He argues that there have been three great eras of globalization. The first started in 1492 when Columbus sailed, and lasted until about 1800. The second era lasted from 1800 until about 2000. The current era for globalization began in 2000 and continues to today. Friedman characterizes what he calls Globalization 3.0 as,

> the newfound power for *individuals* to collaborate and compete globally. And the phenomenon that is enabling, empowering, and enjoining individuals and small groups to go global so easily and so seamlessly is what I call the *flat-world platform* . . . [which] is the product of a convergence of the personal computer (which allowed every individual suddenly to become the author of his or her own content in digital form) with fiber-optic cable (which suddenly allowed all those individuals to access more and more digital content around the world for next to nothing) with the rise of work flow software (which enabled individuals all over the world to collaborate on that same digital content from anywhere, regardless of the distances between them). (10–11)

Credibility in business argument, from Friedman's perspective, will come from those organizations prepared to succeed in this new flat world. The old image of the successful business organization—large, nation centered, manufacturing oriented, and vertically structured from making parts to marketing a finished product—is rapidly losing credibility. You might think that such twentieth-century U.S. business leaders as GM and IBM would fall into that category. About GM, you might be correct. In the hundreds of pages of Friedman's book, there are only two pages on which he mentions GM. However, there are 35 pages on which IBM is discussed.

IBM has maintained credibility by restoring its commitment to providing the best customer service in the world (good will). As we learned earlier in this chapter, the software, technology, hardware, and technical service that is the foundation of the flat-earth platform is dominated by IBM. It is perceived as highly competent because it has regained the lead in its various markets. It is perceived as trustworthy because over its 100-year history it has consistently done what it promised to do. And despite its late twentieth-century slip, it now appears as dynamic a business as exists anywhere. And its presence is felt throughout the world.

CONCLUSION

IBM Corporation has proved to be an excellent case study in business argumentation primarily because it uses its basic beliefs of respect for the individual, best customer service in the world, and striving for superiority in all things to generate warrants and criteria for evaluating arguments and making decisions. The basic beliefs help us identify starting points for argumentation, particularly in locating presumptions that assign burdens of proof and help make decisions when no clear superiority of argument sets aside the presumption. IBM provided examples of facts, probabilities, and commonplaces as other starting points in business argumentation. We learned that such commonplaces as comparison and contrast, cause and effect, cost/benefit, and sign appear in arguments by and about IBM. As forms of support in business argument, IBM was most fruitful in demonstrating how the basic beliefs constitute the values that function powerfully in their decision making. Evidence and credibility also appear in the arguments. The fact that IBM, an old, established American corporation, has managed to enter the twenty-first century with high credibility is a testament to its being able to locate the foundation of the flat-earth platform and situate its business at the center and throughout the world.

EXERCISES/PROJECTS

1. Pick some businesses you know about or have heard of, and do a Google or other search for them. Notice arguments the businesses make about themselves and their products or services. Then, go to some websites that make critical commentaries about businesses such as Motley Fool (www.Fool.com), and find arguments about the businesses you have selected. Write a report about the argumentation you have found, notice how the arguments are constructed, and how they come together to allow a more reasoned decision about whether this is a business you would like to work for, or whether you would feel good about being their customer.
2. Identify a business in which you have some interest and go to their website. Note the arguments they make supporting their claims of being a good place to do business. Write an analysis of their arguments using the organization of this chapter as your guide.

Argumentation in Government and Politics

KEY TERMS

public sphere, p. 258
public screen, p. 258
political claims, p. 259
committee hearings, p. 262
good story, p. 265
majoritarianism, p. 266
amendment process, p. 267
credibility function, p. 267
issue and image, p. 269

the people, p. 271
the public, p. 271
media, p. 273
political debates, p. 274
values, p. 275
evidence, p. 276
leave no shot unanswered, p. 277
inoculation, p. 278

Political argumentation is the oldest recorded argumentation sphere. It can be found in the ancient myths of the Babylonian king Gilgamesh, the Homeric debates of the *Iliad* and the *Odyssey,* ancient Chinese records, and the Old Testament record of the ancient Jews. One modern form of political argumentation has taken its name from an Old Testament prophet: the Jeremiad. If you could penetrate fully to the earliest actions of our species, you would probably find that political discussion emerged virtually with language itself.

Wherever groups exist in the form of families, communities, organizations, states, or nations, political decisions are necessary. It is impossible to be apolitical, for inaction is also a decision. If the people who live across the street beat their children mercilessly and you do not report the fact to the authorities because you do not want to get involved, you have taken a political action based on a political reason. However, the political action we are interested in here is *political argumentation:* the process of using verbal and visual arguments among citizens, leaders, and government agencies to influence the policy decisions of a political community. This argumentation produces "consequences that are widespread and enduring; and affect persons other than oneself for good or evil" (Bitzer 230–231).

THE NATURE OF POLITICAL ARGUMENTATION

In its broadest sense, political argumentation is synonymous with argumentation. However, we will be talking about argumentation that directly involves what has been called the "public's business." It is the argumentation that G. Thomas Goodnight says is characteristic of the **public sphere**:

> A public forum is . . . a sphere of argument to handle disagreements transcending private and technical disputes. . . . [It] inevitably limits participation to representative spokespersons [and provides] a tradition of argument such that its speakers would employ common language, values, and reasoning so that the disagreement could be settled. (219–220)

Kevin DeLuca and Jennifer Peeples argue that the public sphere has morphed into a public screen, whether a computer or a television screen. They argue that the current emphasis on the **public screen** has shifted participation away from the top-down constraints seen in the traditional public sphere to areas of virtual interest, such as information dissemination, increased publicity, and virtual venues for dissent.

Whether political argumentation is characteristic of the public sphere, the public screen, or both, it can be further defined by examining its claims, its content, its development, and its refutation.

The Claims of Political Argumentation

In Chapter 5, we identified three kinds of claims—factual, value, and policy. One of the defining characteristics of political argument is that it always aims at policy. A lawyer may argue the factual claim that a chemical spill was harmful to a client and subsequently argue for a legally appropriate remedy. Both claims are treated in law as factual claims. When the same lawyer appears before a state legislative committee on the same subject, the aim is to bring about regulations that will constitute a new policy. Policy claims are argued by building a case on subclaims of fact and value, but the aim is to gain adherence to the policy claim.

The Content of Political Claims

When Aristotle referred to the relatively simple society of ancient Greece, he defined five general categories of political argumentation that are still important today: (1) finance, (2) war and peace, (3) national defense, (4) imports and exports, and (5) the framing of laws (53). Finance refers to issues emerging from consideration of fiscal and monetary policies. War and peace includes all of our foreign policy and national defense programs. Imports and exports suggest the full range of issues arising from interstate and foreign commerce—whether free trade agreements such as the North American Free Trade Agreement (NAFTA) or the General Agreement on Tariff and Trade (GATT) are beneficial to the U.S. economy. The framing of laws ranges from modification of the Constitution to statutory revisions. Legislatures must set policies as general as legal rights for women and as specific as the use of "low fat," "fat free," or "diet" labels on food.

Equal rights for women and informative food labels are good examples of the degree to which the content of **political claims** has expanded. Decisions such as these and many others that would have been personal then are political today. We have reached the place in our complex society where every policy question is potentially political.

Political argumentation is, as J. Robert Cox says, "a normative sphere." That is, it is not defined by a specific set of claims with which it deals. Rather, the participants in political argumentation generate reasons "for a course of action and in interpreting the consequences of their decision . . . invoke a notion of 'the public'" (131). There is always implied in argumentation the idea that its policy claims are designed for the common good of some social collective that we call the public. The usefulness of such public policy is determined by the immediate needs of the community. Should local communities censor cable television? Should the federal government regulate airline prices? Should the United States participate in an international agreement to regulate carbon dioxide emissions? These are all claims about what the public is and wants. However, community needs frequently have to be defined because members of the public are unaware or unclear about them. So, part of argumentation is the actual construction of the situation so that the public may identify with it and respond to the specific political claims being advanced. This process of creating the community has been with us throughout political history. Christine Oravec found that the arguments for environmental conservation that emerged from Theodore Roosevelt's presidency included a subtext that constructed "the kind of public required to justify and implement" conservation policies. The needs and desires of the public constructed by this discourse provided the necessary justification for government policies designed to slow the destruction of the United States' natural resources.

The Development of Political Claims

Initially, political claims are vague. They become more specific as argumentation develops. No court of law would tolerate a claim as unclearly stated as most political claims initially are, and no scientists could proceed without a firm statement of a hypothesis. Yet, most political claims begin the argumentative process in a very general form (Cobb and Elder 400):

> Air quality in U.S. cities should be improved.
> Taxes should be reduced.
> The potholes in Atlanta's streets should be repaired.
> The reading level of children in Denver should be improved.

These are examples of claims with which government agencies usually begin. They represent (as we noted in Chapter 5) the recognition of a problem, a "feeling of doubt." Frequently, they are almost issueless because they are claims with which everyone will agree. However, as public bodies examine these claims and interest groups argue them, they become more specific. To become a working policy, the claim must become more specific. Take the reading example. Virtually, no one in Denver would object to improving the reading level of children. But how? At what cost? What will the new policy replace? And how will improvement be measured? The answers proposed to these questions make the policy more specific and more controversial. Compare these two claims:

1. The reading level of children in Denver should be improved.
2. With funds now used for the education of children with disabilities, the Denver school board should hire 50 reading specialists to provide individualized reading programs for third grade students.

Issues Emerge as Claims Become More Clearly Phrased. Some people, even those who want the reading ability improved, will object to taking funds away from children with disabilities. They may argue that the money should come from other sources or new taxes, and a whole host of issues will emerge. Other people will argue that direct attention to reading is not the best way to improve reading. Rather, reading instruction should be integrated into other instruction. Issues that did not seem very important when the original general claim was advanced will arise. Some parents at a public hearing may be frustrated, saying, "I'm interested in better reading instruction for my children. Why are we talking about cutting programs for children with disabilities?" Their frustration comes from the need for claims of political argument to become specific.

Claims and Issues Will Change as Argumentation Emerges. Policies need the widest possible consensus of the members of the affected group. Therefore, claims are often amended to protect them from possible refutation. So, a school board may propose that social studies time be cut and more time allotted to reading instruction. Then, they may propose greater emphasis on reading in all instruction. As a matter of fact, they may come out with a curriculum revision that seems completely at odds with the original intent to improve reading instruction. The new revision may actually cut the amount of time specifically devoted to reading instruction!

Most Claims Do Not Become Policy, and Most That Do Are Noncontroversial. Many interest groups expend great amounts of money and time researching and arguing policy claims, yet most policy claims never become policy. Even those policy claims that become legislative bills have a high rejection rate. More than 20,000 bills are proposed each session to the U.S. Congress, yet less than 6% of them ever become law. Of those bills that pass, two-thirds are supported by both major parties (Matthews and Stimson 6–7).

Many bills, both simple and complex, are passed without argument. Although it is difficult to characterize those claims that pass easily, they most probably represent efforts to reduce conflict, reconcile varying interests, and compromise opposing goals. Political decisions that go through the modification process we have described are the product of a broad compromise-based consensus. The dramatic case of a hard-fought partisan argument on a well-defined policy claim is unusual.

On March 23, 2010, President Obama signed the *Patient Protection and Affordable Care Act*. This law, along with the *Health Care and Education Reconciliation Act of 2010*, was pushed through by the 111th U.S. Congress and the Obama administration. Health care has long been a controversial issue in the United States. Supporters of reform argue that the United States should join the ranks of other socioeconomically comparable nations in ensuring availability of health care to all citizens, while opponents have argued that health care is not an appropriate concern for the federal government. Previous attempts at reform had failed, despite evidence of broad public support. The controversial legislation passed in 2010 improved insurance coverage for those with pre-existing medical conditions, expanded access to care for over 30 million Americans, and reduced the long-term costs of the United States health care system. Although the Democrats controlled both the House and Senate at the time of the votes, both bills required multiple changes in their original wording to get the votes necessary to pass them.

Perhaps in part because of this controversial legislation, the House switched to a Republican majority and the Democratic majority in the Senate was dramatically reduced in the election of 2010. Members of the Tea Party Caucus, Republicans who swept into office in 2010, claimed that they would return government to "the American people." They pledged to do this by reigning in government spending and preventing tax increases. Although the Tea Party Caucus was not successful in passing desired legislation during its first year in office, it did succeed in stalling bipartisan compromise on the federal budget during this period, despite the fact that the national debt was a serious bipartisan concern.

The legislative process has more than a dozen points in committee and floor action where legislation may be delayed or defeated (Wise 22). The political party system, the presidential veto, and outside pressure all serve to make most political claims develop through continual cooperative modification until a consensus is reached.

Perhaps, this is one reason why moderation and middle-of-the-road options tend to be preferred by many Americans. For example, Gallup polls from 1992 to 2008 have found remarkable ideological consistency among the U.S. electorate, with more Americans identifying themselves as "moderate," than either "conservative" or "liberal." Of course, ideologies shift, and may have contributed to the outcome of the 2010 elections. Results of Gallup's 2009 and 2010 polls found that most Americans identified themselves as "Conservative," rather than "moderate," with "liberal" identification coming in a distant third (Gallup 2010).

Politicians emphasize their ability to contribute to consensus building whenever possible. The website of long-time Senator Pete Domenici (R–New Mexico), who retired in 2009 following six terms as a United States Senator from New Mexico, the longest tenure in his state's history, included a list of complimentary statements referring to his consensus building ability, many from members of the Democratic party. For example,

> I remember I was a young staff person in 1973, and he was a newly elected Senator from New Mexico, formerly the mayor of Albuquerque. Even back then many of us recognized—because of his intelligence, his good will, and the way he was able to demonstrate his ability to work across the aisle—that we would have the good fortune to work with him for a long, long time.
>
> *Democratic Minority Leader Tom Daschle, May 2003*

> He is a Republican and a strong Republican, but in the end, to govern, it seems to me, . . . to govern, you have to somehow work in toward the center. And that's been his strength. That's basically where he is on the political spectrum when it comes to fiscal policy. I think he sees a role for government, trying to bring, as I say, those disparate folks together, producing something that will keep government operating and functioning.
>
> *G. William Hoagland, former Senate Budget Committee staff director,*
> *National Public Radio, February 2003*

That "Politics is the art of the possible" is nowhere clearer than in the history of the U.S. House and Senate.

To say that cooperative modification to consensus is the nature of political argumentation is not to maintain that there are no issues, no debates. The modifications necessary to consensus are discovered when issues are revealed in debate. The issues are likely to be over modifications of policy, but issues are there nonetheless.

ARGUMENTATION IN GOVERNMENT AND POLITICS

Even in political campaigns, where conflict would seem most likely, disagreements are more likely to be over the degree or nature of a proposition than over a direct yes or no. On health care, taxes, foreign policy, or environmental protection, for instance, disagreements are over the degree of governmental action. In political campaigns, a diverse electorate usually makes it difficult for a politician with an absolutist position to win.

When a debate is present, refutation of opposing arguments is essential to the decision making process. Much of the legislative process is taken up with identifying potential rebuttals to a policy proposal. If the rebuttals come with political clout, the legislative policy is usually revised to accommodate them. The final draft of a bill will sometimes seem to lack clarity and coherence because it includes so many changes inserted in order to win votes.

The approval in 1999 of the final installment of the $1.8 trillion annual budget was supported in the House with a 196 to 135 vote and with a vote of 74 to 24 in the Senate. The 74 votes in the Senate were evidence of bipartisan effort, with 42 Republicans and 32 Democrats supporting the bill. It was praised by both Republican and Democratic congressional leaders and President Clinton. But to get the agreement, the budget had to include a number of compromises such as a 0.38 across-the-board budget cut, a one-day delay in the September military payday, some "accounting gimmicks," and some tax credits for research and development (Toedtman; Pianin).

Argumentation in government and politics includes a variety of situations, from a televised presidential campaign commercial to a newspaper advertisement for a local city council candidate, from a congressional hearing to a mayors' debate. Although there are similarities, there are also differences. We will try to deal with these differences by looking at how argumentation functions in three subspheres: committee hearings, legislative action, and political campaigns.

Argumentation in Committee Hearings

In recent years, people have been able to see firsthand how **committee hearings** function. Segments have been shown on television, particularly on C-SPAN. The most dramatic, such as the hearings on the federal raid on the Branch Davidian compound in Waco, Texas; the 1991 Senate Judiciary Committee hearings over the appointment of Judge Clarence Thomas to the Supreme Court and the charges of sexual harassment against him by Professor Anita Hill; the 1995 congressional investigations of the Ruby Ridge, Idaho, 11-day standoff between federal agents and white separatist Randy Weaver; and the 1998 House Judiciary Committee hearings on the impeachment of President Clinton, have had significant viewership. The Clarence Thomas–Anita Hill hearings were covered live on ABC, CBS, NBC, CNN, and C-SPAN and were seen in more than 14 million homes ("Viewers"). The impeachment hearings of President Clinton were seen in 4.4 million homes ("People's Choice").

Involving highly controversial charges about the actions of governmental personnel, they provided extensive examples of how refutation can function in committee hearings. The same principles apply to thousands of other hearings in Congress, state legislatures, and city and county government. Committee hearings are vital decision making scenes where the claims of argumentation are modified through debate.

During the ninety-sixth Congress, the House Appropriations Committee and its subcommittees "held 720 days of hearings, took testimony from 10,125 witnesses, published 225 volumes of hearings that comprised 202,767 printed pages" (Davidson and Oleszek 220). Committee hearings offer an opportunity to get the input of society on the scope of laws. Interested individuals, groups, businesses, and the like discuss what the law ought to be.

When you add to congressional policy and personnel hearings the many administrative hearings that administrative agencies hold to involve the public in the actual application of laws once written, you realize how important hearings are to defining and applying policy. We will look now at the characteristics of such hearings and the form that argumentation takes in them.

Characteristics of Hearings

Hearings are characterized by the need to convert solutions into law to develop and focus on a record that will justify the action taken. Argumentation in this setting involves the legal questioning format and telling good stories.

Hearings involve controversy over policy. Controversy leads to debate that is blunted because claims are made through a questioning process. This process resembles the type of fact-finding questions used in a court of law (Asbell 108). That is, those who hold the hearings ask questions rather than make claims. The format implies that they are gathering evidence. Frequently, it is evidence they already have. The testimony of witnesses is used to "build a record" from which specific provisions of laws or administrative decisions are justified.

Using the Record in Hearings

Although the questioning format limits how one may argue, there is still considerable potential. This potential comes mostly from the committee members who wish to establish their position. For instance, when the Senate Environmental Protection Subcommittee held hearings on the reauthorization of the 1977 Clean Air Act, Senator Max Baucus of Montana asked questions designed to prepare arguments for refutation. He asked four presidents of health organizations what the best arguments were against their conclusions and how they would respond to them (Boynton, "When Senators" 11).

Later, Chairman George Mitchell used this record when questioning an electric utility executive who claimed that there was no health problem requiring new legislation. George Mitchell asked the executive to read the testimony (that Senator Baucus had solicited) of the four presidents of the health organizations. Mitchell told him that he would change his mind about the seriousness of the problem if he read that testimony (Boynton, "When Senators" 143).

Focus for the Record in Hearings

In most hearings (the Ruby Ridge, Waco, Thomas, and Clinton impeachment hearings are exceptions), there is little disagreement among the members of the committee. Those who serve on committees generally agree on the basic direction of legislation. Everyone on the

Senate Agriculture Committee wants to help the farmer and generally they know how they want to do this and what the pitfalls are. They are there to find the best way to do it (Boynton, "When Senators" 10). This focus restricts the arguments that can be made.

Dennis Jaehne illustrates this restriction on arguments of wilderness groups in the administrative appeals of Forest Service implementation decisions. The conflict he observed between the Utah Wilderness Association and the Forest Service involved a basic value disagreement "between the idealistic concept of *preserving* land in its 'natural' state and the pragmatic concept of *protecting* land in . . . administrative rules and regulations" (496). However, in the cases he studied, the Utah Wilderness Association became pragmatic and technical in arguing modification of administrative practice in order to influence changes. He found that collaboration has problems for participants with "environmental ideals, particularly in the degree of cooptation of environmental ideals by administrative discourse. Speaking like the natives [bureaucrats] makes you rather more like the natives than not speaking like the natives" (501).

Even though witnesses might have idealistic views of the situation, they must adapt to the pragmatic questions of policy building or administration. Witnesses must follow the focus of the questioners or be without influence.

The Forms of Argumentation in Committee Hearings

The questioning format that produces a focused record of testimony works from specific forms of refutation. G. R. Boynton has identified four main questions that are used ("When Senators" 145–147). They are based on the record and, although questions, serve to refute the testimony of a witness.

1. The questioner reminds the witness of what he or she has said, then notes someone else's countertestimony and asks how the witness would answer the objections. The example given earlier when presidents of health organizations were asked what opponents might say and how they would respond to these opponents is an example of such an argument. Here is a case where friendly witnesses are asked to refute their own positions to bring out the positive answer the questioner wants.

2. The same line of questioning may be used with opponents. This form looks very much like the first, despite the fact that it is addressed to hostile, rather than friendly, witnesses. Boynton gives the example of a Department of Energy witness who said that installing scrubbers on old power plants would be too expensive. Senator Mitchell noted that another witness had testified that the Germans had installed scrubbers that cost only $100 per kilowatt hour. What would they cost in this country, he asked, and why would they be more costly than in Germany? ("When Senators" 146).

3. The questioner reminds the witness of what he or she has said but claims to have counterknowledge and asks the witness to justify his or her position. This is a simple variation on the second form except that the questioner uses his or her credibility rather than previous testimony. This method poses a difficult problem for the witness because, for the moment at least, the person asking the question is the decision maker. Thus, it is difficult for the witness to answer that the questioner is wrong. Furthermore, the traditions of the Senate ("the world's most exclusive club") are such that open attacks on a senator will usually bring even political opponents to the senator's defense. Thus, it's doubly difficult to come up with an acceptable response to this question.

4. The questioner compares what the witness said at this hearing with earlier statements or actions and asks the witness to justify the discrepancy. Inconsistency, as we have discussed in Chapter 5, is a serious charge. Some believe it is the most powerful because it uses one's own arguments (or actions) against one's position. In the Clean Air Act hearings, Senator George Mitchell argued to the auto industry representatives:

> Today you have said that the improvements we are proposing are impossible for you to meet and even if you could meet them the improved health would not be worth the cost. But, that is exactly what your industry has said every time the law has been changed from 1965 to [the] present, and despite these claims you have met the standards of each new law. Why should we take seriously what you are saying today? (Boynton, "When Senators" 146)

Telling Good Stories

G. R. Boynton's examination of the Senate Agricultural Committee hearings illustrates that all this building of a record, focus, and refutation can be put in a narrative argument:

> The "good story" told in the hearings of the Senate Agriculture Committee is "a" story. The individual narrative accounts are bits and pieces of this larger story. They do not stand alone. You cannot understand any one of these stories without understanding the larger story of which each is a part. An important role for the narratives is carrying the cognitive complexity which is the "good story." ("Telling" 437)

Many bills are omnibus measures that cover a number of subjects. A farm bill has to have narratives about potatoes, cotton, corn, and wheat; about regions; about size of farms; and about methods of harvesting. These narratives have to fit together into a **good story**. These stories have real characters in them: farmers, workers, and market specialists. They proceed through a series of events that lead to a satisfactory conclusion for all under the proposed policy. If they do not, the policy is modified to make the story right.

In a situation such as the Clarence Thomas hearings, the story is primarily about the credibility of a person. So, the day after Hill and Thomas testified, their supporters came forward to confirm their statements. The *New York Times* headlined: "PARADE OF WITNESSES SUPPORT HILL'S STORY, THOMAS'S INTEGRITY." Friends of Anita Hill affirmed that as long ago as 10 years earlier, she had mentioned the sexual harassment to them. These bits of testimony supported and became a part of her story. In the same way, those who testified that Clarence Thomas was completely businesslike and could never be guilty of sexual harassment supported his story.

Committee hearings, the first of the three subspheres of political argumentation discussed here, serve as a means to clarify policy legislation, confirm participants in the process, and define administrative action. They are characterized by applied legal practice and building and using a record. These same characteristics are carried forward into the second subsphere: legislative action.

ARGUMENTATION IN LEGISLATIVE ACTION

Committee hearings are a vital and time-consuming part of congressional action. They serve to define a proposition from a more general question and to make that proposition (a bill) more immune to opposition. After a bill is drafted, it must pass both houses of Congress and be approved by the president (or overridden by the president's veto). In addition, public opinion, spurred on by specific events, special interest groups, and sometimes legal action can influence what will happen.

As we noted earlier, most of the problems on about two-thirds of all legislation are worked out in the committee hearings. Therefore, controversy or rebuttal in their passage through the legislative process is limited. For the one-third of the bills that are the subject of controversy, refutation is an important part of their movement through the system.

Legislative Argument Is Usually Not Confrontational

You will recall from Chapter 10 that refutation should not be seen as an attack on an opponent to win a decisive victory. Nowhere is this principle more true than in the legislative process. It is a reflection of what has been called the first cardinal rule of politics: "Don't make enemies you don't need to make" (Dowd). More than that, however, an important value of the legislative process is **majoritarianism**. Sponsors of legislation try to get the greatest support that they can. They want a significant majority. The larger the better. Noncontroversial legislation is the ideal.

Argumentation in this system is frequently about resolving small problems in the legislation to make it acceptable to a larger majority. For instance, a clean air act that emphasizes acid rain may be criticized for not doing enough about ambient air quality, a point of interest to more states than acid rain. The following is a paraphrase of an actual argument. It refutes the proposed law by agreeing with it but supporting an amendment.

> We need to pass this bill to deal with the problem of acid rain. The chief sponsors of the bill have understandably, considering the problems in their New England states, emphasized acid rain. However, in the Middle West and West, ambient air quality is of greater concern. Because of the seriousness of that problem, I support the amendment to the Clean Air Act that would require modifications for ambient sulfur dioxides, sulfate, and particulate standards.

The argument is not against what is in the bill (acid rain control); it argues for an addition to the bill to regulate ambient air quality.

Legislative Argument Is Usually Not Personal

We have noted that much legislation depends on as large a majority as possible. Such majoritarianism is important because larger majorities provide political protection. If a legislator can say that the law was supported by most Republicans and Democrats, its supporters are less vulnerable to the charge that they are "too liberal" or "too conservative." In addition, the tradition of treating one another without personal rancor is a part of the American legislative tradition.

In the floor debate over the confirmation of Clarence Thomas and in response to Republican Arlen Spector of Pennsylvania who had led the questioning of Professor Hill, Senator Edward Kennedy said, "There's no proof that Anita Hill has perjured herself and shame on anyone who suggests that she has." Senator Spector replied, "We do not need characterizations like shame in this chamber from the senator from Massachusetts." To this, Senator Kennedy responded, "I reiterate to the senator from Pennsylvania and to others that the way that Professor Hill was treated was shameful" (Apple A13). That exchange is about as personal as you will find in a congressional debate.

The Amendment Process as Argumentation

The amending process has always been active in committees. When a bill came to the floor of the House or Senate, amendments were usually extensions of committee hearings. However, in recent years, the **amendment process** has been used more as a basis of refutation. Former Arizona Congressman Morris Udall noted a few years ago that the House of Representatives has become a "fast breeder reactor. . . . Every morning when I come to my office, I find that there are twenty more amendments. We dispose of twenty or twenty-five amendments and it breeds twenty more amendments" (Keefe and Ogul 208).

Many amendments are friendly. They are designed to strengthen, without changing in any significant way, the bill's essential purpose. Other amendments may look innocent enough but will actually weaken a bill and make it less likely to pass. Political scientists William Keefe and Morris Ogul explain how this can work:

> A favorite gambit in attacking a bill is to "perfect" or amend it to death. Under this plan, amendment after amendment is submitted to the bill, ostensibly to make it a "better" bill. With each amendment a new group can be antagonized and brought into opposition to the bill. Nor is it very difficult to make a bill unworkable, even ridiculous. Thus the president of the Illinois Retail Merchants Association succeeded in getting a committee in the Illinois House to adopt an amendment to a minimum-wage bill, a measure he vigorously opposed, setting up a $500,000 fund to be used in enforcement of the law. This move was calculated to stimulate new opposition to the bill. . . . Many a bill has been threatened or emasculated by a carefully drawn and skillfully maneuvered amendment. (209)

By such procedures, amendments become the basis on which a bill is refuted. If an arguer is not careful, a bill can be amended to refute its original intention.

Argumentation Has an Important Credibility Function

Although debate is important to a democratic society and refutation is central to it, floor debate has limited influence on legislation. A well-developed argument, or a new way of looking at an issue that strikes at the center of a policy, can influence undecided members. Mostly, however, floor debates, like committee hearings, are oriented to establishing a record. Speakers say what they say in supporting or refuting arguments to demonstrate their positions for their constituents.

The C-SPAN coverage of debates in the House of Representatives, though few people watch them, have aided some, such as Georgia Republican Congressman Newt Gingrich who used his appearances in C-SPAN-covered speeches attacking Democratic leaders to build a record that increased his credibility among some voters, eventually leading to his election as Speaker of the House. However, his subsequent actions and those of his partisan majority in the House of Representatives led to his downfall.

Perhaps more important than building a record or influencing a few fence sitters to move one way or another is a frequently overlooked **credibility function** of floor debate:

> It is a good way for members to persuade their colleagues of their competence in a public policy field; it enables them to affirm a personal position or to support or back off from a past position; it presents an opportunity to gain publicity, to consolidate old support, and perhaps to attract new followers. (Keefe and Ogul 218)

Relations between Legislature and the Executive

In recent years, the federal government has been characterized by what has been called "divided government," where the Congress is controlled by one party whereas the president is from another. In the 50 years between 1950 and 2003, a Democrat was president for only 22 years. The Democrats have controlled both houses of Congress for a majority of those years. In 1994, the situation was reversed and a Democrat was president while both houses of Congress were controlled by the Republicans. Although not as dramatic, similar divided government has occurred in some state governments. Even where the same party controls both legislative and executive branches, differences between the branches can occur.

In such situations, debate can be quite vigorous and even acrimonious. The president or governor has a veto that is difficult to override. So, even when the opposition has a majority in the legislative branch, its power is curbed. Some presidents (Harry S. Truman holds the record with 250) earned reputations for their frequent vetoes (Keefe and Ogul 329). The debate between a hostile majority in Congress and the president increases as an election nears.

During much of the administration of President George W. Bush, there was a debate concerning whether the United States was in a recession and what to do to prevent further economic problems. Political progressives and other opponents of the president used this discussion to highlight what they viewed as presidential incompetence. For example, *Think Progress* posted the following:

> In December of 2006 President George W. Bush held a news conference where he discussed the "way forward" for the economy in 2007. Renowned Morgan Stanley economist Stephen Roach says the "odds of the U.S. economy tipping into recession are about 40% to 45%." *New York Times* columnist Paul Krugman notes that "the odds are very good—maybe 2 to 1," that the U.S. will teeter toward a recession in 2007. Bush's solution? "Go shopping more." ("With Recession")

Following is a portion of the transcript from President Bush's speech in response to the recession charges.

> As we work with Congress in the coming year to chart a new course in Iraq and strengthen our military to meet the challenges of the twenty-first century, we must also work together to achieve important goals for the American people here at home. This work begins with keeping our economy growing. . . . And I encourage you all to go shopping more. (Bush 1)

Not surprisingly, Democrats found Bush's recommendation for stabilizing the economy by going shopping inadequate.

As 2007 drew to a close, huge waves of foreclosures on home loans hit the U.S. economy. The *Washington Post* reported that regardless of whether the country was experiencing a recession, something needed to be done about the rash of mortgage foreclosures (Cho and Irwin). When Bush proposed managing the crisis with a voluntary freeze by lenders on interest rate resets for a small fraction of subprime loans, Democrats claimed this was inadequate. They countered by proposing more vigorous measures, including a temporary moratorium on foreclosures on subprime owner-occupied homes, a freeze on interest rate resets for subprime adjustable rate mortgages, and federal funds to help at-risk borrowers stay in their homes. The Bush administration ended up with a plan that had support from many Democrats and Republicans, as well as key mortgage lenders such as Citigroup. The required five-year freeze represented a compromise between banking regulators, who argued for seven years, and mortgage firms, who argued for either one or two years. Of course, this did not end the debate. Some, such as Senator Hillary Rodham Clinton (D–New York), argued that the plan was too limited and failed to provide the support needed by homeowners. Others, such as John Berlau, from the politically conservative American Enterprise Institute, argued, "it's going to make investors think twice about investing in America again" (Cho and Irwin A1).

As we noted earlier, political arguments focus on policy. They begin with fact claims (such as those made in the *New York Times*), then incorporate values into the fact claims to justify a particular policy. In this case, the issues began with a definition: Is this a recession? They also involved process: Are economic conditions getting worse or better? They dealt with credibility: Is the president uninterested in the poor and middle class? Do the Democrats actually want to solve the problem or simply make political points? Does the issue threaten the country's international credibility? Value issues were actively involved: Is the suffering serious? Will high rates of mortgage foreclosures increase economic insecurity? And, of course, there were policy issues: Should the federal government get involved in an economic issue? Should the costs of a relief program be borne by mortgage lenders, tax payers, or some other party? The debate frequently emphasized the support and refutation of the fact and value claims behind the policy claims, such as whether the nation was in a recession, and how the mortgage crisis related to such a recession.

Eventually, some compromises were worked out between Congress and the administration. The lesson to be learned from observing this process is that argumentation is a complex problem because single issues have implications on a wide variety of claims along with a host of other apparently unrelated issues (e.g., limits on the military budget and damage to foreign investment) linked to these policy decisions. Political debate involves party politics, public opinion, the media, and the responsibilities of government.

For the most part, problems of legislative and administrative disagreement are worked out in some system of compromises. This generality holds true at all levels of government: national, state, and local. But compromise is required because there are different points of view. So, political parties and individuals with different worldviews vie for the support of the public. This is most clear in political campaigns where candidates compete for offices and propositions are put on the ballot.

ARGUMENTATION IN POLITICAL CAMPAIGNS

A political campaign is a complex mixture of activities. It includes speeches, debates, mailings, television and radio ads, sound bites for the media, person-to-person campaigning by candidates and supporters, telephone contacts, getting people to the polls, and many more activities. They all are argumentative in their nature and involve refutation. A closer examination of campaign argumentation is in order.

Campaigns Involve Issues and Images

All argumentation in the political sphere has, hidden in its attention to policy questions, an element of the personal: is this person (or party) a fit representative of his or her constituents? This dual emphasis on **issue and image**, present throughout the legislative process, becomes increasingly important as campaign and election time nears. The process described earlier of "building a record" becomes more focused on how that record will influence voters.

Candidates look to their opponents' records to find a basis for attack. In 2007, the Democratic Party had a bevy of presidential hopefuls, all attacking different aspects of President George W. Bush's management of the war in Iraq. Although the attacks all portrayed a negative image of Bush, they were also about the issues.

Some argue that image takes over and the issues are pushed aside by the image constructed through short commercials and media sound bites. Even debates, they argue, emphasize the candidate's image and play down the public policy issues. Says Lloyd Bitzer, "the stuff of ordinary campaigns consists of arguments, position statements, testimonials, commercials, and other materials relating to the prudence, good character, and right intentions of the candidates—to the image. . . . Thus, discussion of issues . . . tends to be subsumed under the discussion of images" (242–243).

It is natural that political campaigns should be seen as image centered. After all, the central issue of every campaign is personal: Should the candidate be elected? Some studies have shown that, in presidential and senate races, at least, "exposure to even small doses of campaign advertising is a significant educational experience." "We conclude," say Stephen Ansolabehere and Shanto Iyengar, "that negativity does not bolster the information value of political advertising. How much voters learn about the candidates' positions and the extent to which they think about political issues when evaluating the candidates does not depend on the tone of the advertising campaign" (51).

Candidates are usually reluctant to attack an opponent directly with charges about character. In 1999, when media sources began reporting that Governor George W. Bush of Texas, the Republican front-runner for president, had used cocaine, his opponents from both parties refused to comment or did little more than suggest that he clear up the issue. The 2000 election and subsequent polls seemed to show that the electorate was not unduly bothered by concerns about Bush's character. Backlash against negative advertising is less likely when negative advertisements are based on issues than on the personal characteristics of an opponent (Roberts, "Political Advertising" 181).

Another image problem that has to be contended within this era of heavily mediated campaigns is the tendency of journalists to change "the story of the election from 'who should govern' to 'who can win'" (Ansolabehere and Iyengar 38; Smith 295). The image that a candidate is a loser decreases the attention paid to the candidate and thus decreases the chance that the candidate can refute this or any other charge. Refutation obviously functions only if it is communicated, and it can only be communicated when the journalists pay attention or when the candidate has a lot of money to purchase rebuttal advertisements.

The decision of the electorate on the proposition: Should the candidate be elected? looks like a simple question of image. It is not. It is influenced significantly by a candidate's record and position on issues. Credibility may be more important in political campaigns than in some other situations, but credibility is influenced by the arguments and values an audience comes to associate with a candidate. Even negative ads have more influence if the credibility of a candidate is linked to issues.

Campaign Arguments Are Linked to "The People"

A political campaign is based on an argumentative strategy. The strategy has to cast the candidate as a leader who will achieve the public policy that the people want. Terms like

the people and **the public** are myths constructed by candidates to define the whole population as embodying the candidate's point of view (McGee). The biography on Senator
Frank Lautenberg's (D–New Jersey) website demonstrates this strategy:

> Senator Lautenberg has written landmark laws that are making a real difference in our lives.
> He stood up to Big Tobacco and wrote the law to ban smoking on airplanes. He stood up to
> the liquor industry and wrote the law to get more drunk drivers off our roads. Senator Lauten-
> berg worked to get cancer causing asbestos out of our schools. . . . Senator Lautenberg has built
> a record of uncommon accomplishment rooted in common sense. He stands up for his beliefs
> and he's standing strong against powerful interests to take on problems that concern everyday
> families. And the best is yet to come. (New Jersey)

Such strategies can be seen in every campaign. Candidates defend their claims as designed to support "the people," and refute opponents' claims as attacks on "the people."
Even though "the people" is a campaign myth, it is an important base for the story that a
candidate must tell and maintain at the center of the campaign.

Telling the Right Story

Each campaign should add up to a convincing story of a candidate whose record shows,
and statements reinforce, that he or she is in tune with the people to provide a wise public
policy. Developing such a story has been transformed in many cases into "the speech"
where the same arguments, values, credibility, and even examples are used by a candidate throughout a campaign. Emphasis can be shifted; introductions or conclusions are
changed to orient a speech to a particular audience. However, the campaign speeches turn
out to be essentially one speech. The term *the speech* was first used in Ronald Reagan's
precampaign for governor in 1966 (Ritter). It is a standard campaign procedure now. It
defines the story of the campaign.

In 1992, Ross Perot was the most successful presidential candidate from an independent or third party since Theodore Roosevelt in 1912. He was a successful billionaire businessperson who had never run for office but had gained some fame through Ken Follett's
book, commissioned by Perot. *On Wings of Eagles* was the story of Perot's rescue of his
company's hostages held in Iran at the same time that the government could not free the
American embassy hostages. Perot's campaign was built around the use of half-hour infomercials where Perot used charts and interviews to tell his story.

Ross Perot's story was of a man from a poor family who rose to be a leader in business. He did this by applying the things he learned in his close-knit family. There he
learned that self-sacrifice and working for others, for community, was the way to make
things better, not only for others but also for the individual. In this way, he got things
done, as he did in Teheran and in business. He is no politician because he does not complicate and confuse things as traditional candidates do. He analyzes the situation, sees what
has to be done, and does it. He can take these principles of analysis, family, self-sacrifice,
and community and use them to solve the deficit, increase employment, free MIAs, and
restore people's trust in the American government and confidence in themselves (Kern).

Maintaining the Story

The story does come under attack, and when that happens, a campaign must use
refutation to answer the charges and restore the story. George Bush and Bill Clinton,

realizing that they had more to lose than gain, did not attempt to refute Ross Perot's story. However, after the election Perot was hurt badly, and his story began to come apart when he debated Vice President Albert Gore on the NAFTA agreement in 1993. Gore attacked Perot's story that he would use the principles of self-sacrifice and community. He pointed out, for instance, that the Perot family had a tariff-free airport in Texas that they used to benefit themselves while denying the free trade advantages of NAFTA to others. Perot was unable to refute such charges. His inability to maintain his story undoubtedly contributed to his drop in popularity after the debate.

Frank Luntz is a political strategist for the Republican Party. In 2003, he was asked for advice on how to refute negative images regarding the party's environmental stance. After noting that "the environment is probably the single issue on which Republicans in general—and President Bush in particular—are most vulnerable," Luntz suggested that they should "think of environmental (and other) issues in terms of 'story.' A compelling story," Luntz wrote, "even if factually inaccurate, can be more emotionally compelling than a dry recitation of the truth" (132).

The strategy crafted by Frank Luntz responded to concerns that Republican candidates, especially George W. Bush, were having difficulty maintaining their environmental story. Luntz devoted an entire section to the issue of global warming. As we indicated in Chapter 13, the scientific community already had reached consensus that global warming was occurring, that certain human activities were a significant cause, and that the effects on society have been (and are expected to continue to be) largely negative. Scientific argument has moved on to questions of how best to address this problem. Despite strong scientific consensus, the George W. Bush administration consistently argued that global warming was not a serious issue and opposed any regulation of emissions thought to be primarily responsible for global warming. In fact, when the Environmental Protection Agency produced a report on the state of the environment, White House editors removed most of the section on global warming, and rewrote the rest. For example, they deleted information from "a 1999 study showing that global temperatures had risen sharply in the previous decade compared with the last 1,000 years," and replaced it with information from a study financed by the American Petroleum Institute that questioned the previous study's conclusions. Science writer Andrew Revkin and Katharine Seelye reported that "EPA staff members, after discussions with administration officials, said they decided to delete the entire discussion," rather than leave the selectively filtered material (Revkin and Seelye).

Frank Luntz offered a way to present a convincing story about global warming. He urged Republicans to maintain control over the argument by emphasizing scientific uncertainty: "voters believe that there is no consensus about global warming within the scientific community. Should the public come to believe that the scientific issues are settled their views about global warming will change accordingly. Therefore, you need to continue to make the lack of scientific certainty a primary issue in the debate" (137). He added that, although the Bush argument was out of line with the scientific consensus, this could be overcome with effective communication. "The scientific debate is closing [against us] but [it is] not yet closed," wrote Luntz. "There is still a window of opportunity to challenge the science" (138).

Politicians from presidents to city council members build a record through legislation and public argumentation. It is combined, in the political campaign, with the candidate's credibility, policy claims, and values to sustain a reasonable story. Defending that story is the central focus of political argumentation.

Media and Political Argumentation

Media attention is very important to defending the story. The higher the office, the more important it becomes. Many local races, such as city council or state legislature, get little media attention unless something unusual happens in the campaign. Those campaigns are usually tied to the coattails of a party or higher official, who does have media exposure, and to neighborhood campaigning. But at the higher level of office seekers, there is a continual adaptation to media sources. Speeches and announcements are timed to make the evening news and the morning newspaper. Beginning in 1992 when Bill Clinton went on *The Arsenio Hall Show* and played the saxophone, it has become common for candidates for president to appear on the talk shows of hosts such as Jay Leno, David Letterman, and Oprah Winfrey. Candidates use such appearances to reinforce the story and to refute the attack on it. Barak Obama has pushed this trend further, when he became the first sitting president to appear on a late-night talk show in 2009 (*The Tonight Show*), and then on October 10, 2010, the first sitting president to appear on Comedy Central's *Daily Show*, where he traded barbs with host Jon Stewart. One study of such nontraditional news sources indicates that they have more influence than traditional news sources in the early stages of a presidential campaign (Pfau and Eveland).

The press can also become an adversary, as when representatives of the press sometimes use what J. Michael Hogan calls "preemptive refutation" in debates. They attack a candidate with a question he or she would rather not discuss. In 2008, Mitt Romney was one of the Republican candidates for the presidency. Because he was a member of the Mormon Church (Church of Jesus Christ of Latter-day Saints), the "Mormon question" played a large role in the campaign. Although the 1960 election of John F. Kennedy was supposed to have taken care of the religion question in presidential politics, Romney faced a different kind of religious question. Kennedy had successfully argued that he supported the separation of church and state and that his religious views would not control his conduct while president. Romney's conservative Republican constituency had spent the past eight years (under George W. Bush) successfully arguing that church and state need not be separated and that a person's religious views were fundamental to his conduct as president. With religious beliefs no longer tucked away in a separate and private realm, Romney was repeatedly faced with probing questions about his religious beliefs. Despite his attempts to focus on other issues, the "Mormon question" dominated his interactions with the media. No candidate wants to debate the reporter, particularly when she or he can say, "I was just asking a question," but that is what the candidate has to do.

Successful political campaigns no longer rely primarily on traditional media to take their argument to the public. In late 2007, all of the U.S. presidential candidates had their own official web sites. Furthermore, there were numerous unofficial websites dedicated to building up or tearing down various candidates. On December 6, 2007, for example, a simple Google search for "presidential candidates website" came up with 314,000 hits.

In addition to traditional web sites, members of the public could "Face the candidates on YouTube." YouTube exemplifies the public screen discussed in Chapter 3 (under postmodernism). For any candidate, viewers could watch numerous short videos, ranging from personal testimonials to formal speeches and excerpts from television appearances. In December 2007, viewers could choose from hundreds of videos, including 335 videos tied to Barack Obama, 522 associated with Mitt Romney, 106 connected to Mike Huckabee, and 287 for John Edwards. Viewers also can leave comments. For example, on the John Edwards page, we read comments ranging from, "I hope he wins" to "Go John

Edwards! I trust you" to "Trust no one in government. They exist and live off the hard work and backs of every working American" to "The Associated Press has just reported that Dick Cheney will be dropped from the Ron Paul blimp this New Year's Eve over Times Square!" It is clear that the Internet plays an important role in political argumentation; just what that role is, however, remains in question.

The media at every level and of every kind pose a challenge for a campaigner who wants to make any argument. Especially with traditional media, managers can control the extent to which an argument gets covered. Although the Internet provides increased access, that does not necessarily lead to a favorable political climate. We have already noted the problem of local candidates in what are considered unimportant races. It is the media sources that decide that the mayor's race is important, but the second district city council's race isn't. They may do this because the race isn't close or because they believe nothing interesting is going on. To a lesser extent that same condition holds at every level of an election. Candidates, even for president, are restricted in how well they can reinforce and refute challenges to their stories by the media's willingness to carry their copy. This is true in less visible or less highly financed campaigns. It is also part of the reason campaigns are increasingly more expensive. Candidates believe that they need expensive media campaigns to get the message out.

Media not only controls what the story will be but may also construct a story for a candidate. Kathleen Hall Jamieson points out that media reporters tell voters the principles by which they should interpret the campaign. She found 15 principles, such as "Candidates believe that symbols win more votes than substance" and "At the end of a campaign those ahead in the polls adopt the motto: 'No news is good news'" (163–164). All of these principles, in one way or another, tend to portray the candidate as an actor with no concern for issues, only the strategy for winning.

This discussion may seem too negative about the role of media. In a society that prizes freedom of speech and the press, the media is certainly doing its job when it asks questions that the candidate doesn't want asked, reports events that a candidate doesn't want reported, and questions the accuracy of candidates' claims. In a campaign, the ability of a candidate to tell an appealing story is influenced by the willingness of the media to participate in the telling of the story. It is a reality to which candidates must adapt.

THE SPECIAL ROLE OF DEBATES

Increasingly, politics involves debates. There was a time not too many years ago when **political debates** were rare. Incumbents would not debate their lesser known opponents because they had nothing to gain. The first presidential debate was between two nonincumbents, Richard Nixon and John Kennedy, in 1960. The next presidential debate was in 1976, when Gerald Ford, although an incumbent, agreed to debate Jimmy Carter because Ford was vulnerable in the polls and because he was not an elected president. Since that time, it has been an expected routine. Also since that time, debates have become an expected part of campaigning in most state and local races.

Debate experts and others have examined these debates and found them less than ideal. The general agreement is that they are not debates in the sense that candidates directly confront, question, and refute one another. Rather, they are seen as "joint appearances" with minimum exchange between candidates. The Lincoln–Douglas Illinois senatorial debates of 1858 are held up as models against which contemporary political debates are judged negatively. However, as David Zarefsky has noted, those debates had some of the characteristics we decry in contemporary political debates.

The Lincoln–Douglas debates "were often repetitive; they are characterized by the trading of charges, often without evidence; the arguments were incompletely developed . . . the moral question received scant attention in the debates. . . . With rare exceptions, moreover, the candidates set out their own beliefs but did not grapple with the opponent's conception" (*Lincoln–Douglas* 224).

People believe that political debates will provide information about the candidates and their stands on issues (Rowland and Voss 239). Campaign debates have greater attendance or viewership than any other campaign messages (Jamieson and Birdsell 121).

The argumentation in these debates is determined by the diverse nature of the electorate. Voters hold a variety of positions on issues, and candidates who expect to be successful rarely take a strong stand on controversial issues.

REFUTATION IN THE POLITICAL CAMPAIGN

We have already discussed several implications for argumentation in the political campaign, but we now look at refutation specifically. Refutation in the political campaign is concerned with values, evidence, and credibility. It must preserve the story of the campaign and it must leave no shot unanswered.

Refutation Is Usually about Testing Proposals with Values

Favoring a controversial policy can damage a political candidate or officeholder. Although eventually specific policies must be implemented, these usually come through compromise so that the controversy is muted. Candidates, even when they argue for specific proposals, make sure that they are linked to **values** that a strong majority of the decision makers hold.

Candidates usually argue from values they share with the public (Werling et al. 231). But "the Devil is in the details" and so the specific proposals are difficult to argue. Bill Clinton was able to make a strong value argument that health coverage should be guaranteed for all. But as the Clinton health plan emerged and was subjected to refutation on the specifics of how it would work, it fell in popularity and was abandoned. Polls still indicated that health was an important value for most Americans, but finding a plan and paying for it is no easy task. Opponents of Clinton's health plan did not argue against the idea that everyone should have good health care. In fact, they argued that public funding would reduce the quality of health care available. Years later, opponents of President George W. Bush's plan to provide partial pharmaceutical coverage for Medicare recipients did not argue against providing coverage for prescription medications. In both cases, opponents based their refutation on grounds of the best way of attaining a generically acceptable goal.

Arguments against gun control are not in favor of violence, they are about how to control it and claim that better law enforcement will control violence and gun control will not. They will also argue on the basis of a constitutional right to "keep and bear arms." The questions abound in *which* values are the central concern of refutation. Most people oppose abortion but accept it because they believe a woman's right to the value of choice is more important. Protecting the environment is a widely held value, but people argue about how to do it without destroying financial security.

Therefore, refutation in politics is usually not a matter of refuting the values an opponent develops as part of his or her campaign story. Those values are usually shared by most people. Instead, refutation usually focuses on how specific proposals violate accepted cultural values. For instance, Republicans argue for across-the-board tax cuts that are "fair" to everyone. Democrats respond that such cuts provide great benefits to the most wealthy and are not fair to the middle class and the poor.

Evidence Is Important in Refutation

In refuting the specific proposals or the attack on such proposals, campaigns generate a surprising amount of **evidence**. A successful campaign will provide examples, statistics, and testimony to support the value orientation of the campaign. There is considerable use of evidence in speeches and debates.

Evidence used in political refutation can take many forms. A *USA Today* article about George W. Bush's tendency to deflect tough questions includes a series of examples. When asked about the failure to find any weapons of mass destruction (which had been used to justify invading Iraq), Bush responded by asking, "who could possibly think that the world would be better off with Saddam Husein still in power?" Bush answered inquiries into the administration's involvement in leaking the name of a CIA operative whose husband had made public statements critical of the Iraq war by stating that the threat of terrorism "has not passed," and "the terrorists who threaten America cannot be appeased. They must be found, they must be fought and they must be defeated" (Keen 4A).

Refutation in local political campaigns also includes the use of evidence. Mike Joseph wrote an article criticizing county commissioners of Centre County, Pennsylvania, for supporting a sports facility that would increase local tax rates. Joseph used statistical evidence to support his claim that the commissioners' decision was not responsive to their constituents. The "county commissioners split 2–1 in approving the allocation on Oct. 2," wrote Joseph. "In an unscientific poll of *Centre Daily Times* readers this week, more than 80% of respondents said they disagreed with the decisions" (A1, A6). Joseph used these statistics to support his claim that voters should not reelect the commissioners who had voted for the sports facility.

Credibility Is Significant in Refutation

In any political campaign, credibility is important because, as we have noted, the overarching proposition is about the candidate: Should this candidate be elected? Therefore, all that we have said about issue and image is appropriate here. Credibility becomes important as a candidate works to sustain an image. Sometimes credibility is attacked directly, as in an article "exposing pro-abortion Catholic politicians." Mark Stricherz names pro-choice Catholic politicians and describes them as full of "anger, hostility, insincerity, and silence." He charges that, "through their support of the horrors of abortion, the souls of countless Catholic politicians are in danger." The continued existence of these "culture-of-death politicians" reflects badly on all Catholic voters, for "we get the public officials we deserve. Their virtue—or lack thereof—is a judgment not only on them, but on us." Attacks on credibility are happily bipartisan. In a 2008 fund-raising letter for the Democratic Party, actor Paul Newman writes:

You can take your pick of issues where Republicans are seriously damaging this country: Iraq, global warming, civil liberties. But I resent them most for how they've destroyed the American spirit by using xenophobia and fear to hold onto power. It's scare-mongering pure and simple, and it is the only thing Republicans have left to offer.

Frank Luntz understood how essential it was for his clients to maintain credibility. In the memo on environmental argument that we discussed earlier, he explained that "the first (and most important) step to neutralizing the problem and eventually bringing people around to your point of view on environmental issues is to convince them of your *sincerity* and *concern*" (italics in original, 132). Luntz then went on to explain that no amount of logic or evidence would make up for a failure to appear sincere and caring.

It is indirect credibility, however, that most often causes problems for candidates. When candidates are seen as being on the wrong side of, confused about, or ignorant of issues, credibility problems are serious. A candidate in danger of such credibility problems must take immediate action to refute the charges to restore the story crafted for the campaign.

The Story Is Significant in Refutation

When we say the candidate must "restore the story crafted for the campaign," we acknowledge refutation as more than simply saying, "that's wrong." Each argument has a place in the campaign. You will recall from Chapter 10 that one needs a posture for refutation, a constructive base from which to refute the position of others. We also observed that the framework of refutation that works in most situations follows these steps: State the point to be refuted, state your claim relevant to the point, support your claim, and state explicitly how your criticism undermines the overall position (the story) of those whom you are refuting. We might add to this last point that the undermining of an opponent's position (story) should reaffirm yours.

David Kusnet argued that, although those who were campaigning for the Democratic presidential nomination in 2004 offered statements that undermined George W. Bush's position, they did not simultaneously strengthen their own positions. According to Kusnet, they failed to advance the debate, to provide new arguments, and to tell a convincing story about the positive leadership a Democratic president could provide.

Leave No Shot Unanswered

If the story of the campaign is to be sustained, then the dictum of Chris Matthews, television political commentator and a former political aide with considerable inside experience in the political campaign process, is worth remembering: **"Leave no shot unanswered"** (117). Perhaps, no election represents this maxim so well as the election of 1988. In that election, the George Bush campaign chose a strategy of devoting 50% of its efforts to "negative campaigning" or attacks on Michael Dukakis. It was late in the campaign when the Dukakis campaign adopted a similar strategy. Republican strategist Roger Ailes had said, "There are three things that get covered: visuals, attacks, and mistakes" (Bennett 129). The Bush campaign attacked Dukakis on conservation (the pollution in Boston Harbor), his membership in the American Civil Liberties Union (a "liberal" organization for a person who said he was not a "liberal"), crime (the Massachusetts prisoner furlough plan that came to be known as the Willie Horton case), softness on defense, and other issues. These attacks came in commercials (turnstiles of released and returning prisoners, Bush boating on Boston Harbor, pictures of medical waste in the water), speeches, and debates. And, as we noted earlier, Bush maintained the story of his opponent. In one debate, for instance, he said that one of Dukakis's answers was "as clear as Boston Harbor" (Frana 202).

Dukakis, virtually every political observer agrees, waited too long to respond. He somehow believed these were superficial charges that voters would see through and concentrated on his own "positive" campaign. He was wrong. Some negative campaigning backfires, but it always has to be refuted. Since that time, candidates may have passed up a few possible responses, but, in general, they have left no shots unanswered.

Refutation by Inoculation

Refutation is usually thought of as something that takes place after a candidate has had a story and the image it projects attacked. However, there is considerable evidence to show that answering the argument before it is made can have a significant effect and even prevent it from being used. Such a refutational strategy is called **inoculation**. It is a metaphor based on the inoculating of humans against disease in which a weakened form of a virus is introduced into the body to stimulate resistance to the disease. There are two factors in political inoculation: First there is a warning of an impending attack that causes a voter to be motivated to strengthen support, and then to establish resistance to any future attack arguments (Pfau and Kenski 85).

Studies of a South Dakota senatorial race and the 1988 Bush–Dukakis presidential election by Michael Pfau and Henry C. Kenski show that inoculation "deflects the specific content of the attacks, and it reduces the likelihood that the political attacks will influence receiver voting intention. In addition, because inoculation precedes attack, it even provides defenses against attacks that are launched late in the campaign" and therefore are particularly difficult to refute (100).

The major difficulty of such a strategy is that it brings out charges that might not have been made and is, therefore, subject to the credibility claim that the refuter is putting up a "straw man," manufacturing an argument that no one would use, in order to refute it. Still, where a candidate knows that a challenge is likely, inoculation against it is a useful refutational strategy.

CONCLUSION

Political argumentation is the oldest recorded argumentation sphere. It is the process of using verbal and visual arguments to influence the policy decisions of a political community. Political argumentation is characterized by the use of policy claims. The content of those claims emphasizes finances, war and peace, national defense, imports and exports, and the forming of laws, according to Aristotle, though those categories have expanded meanings in modern times. In addition, many things that would have been considered personal in other times are public now. Political claims begin in a vague form, but they become more specific as argumentation about them develops. Claims and issues also change as argumentation emerges. Most claims that are advanced do not become policy, and most that do are noncontroversial.

The first of three major subspheres of political argumentation is committee hearings. There, argumentation is characterized by applying legal practice. Arguments are developed as questions as if the questioner was only searching for facts. However, the questions are designed to build a record that can be used in subsequent hearings and legislative debates. The actual forms these questions take reveal the argumentative intent of their use. The overall objective of the questioning, record building, and refutation is to tell a good story that will stand up to criticism.

In the second subsphere, legislative action, argumentation is usually nonconfrontational. Under the influence of the value of majoritarianism, the objective is to get the largest possible majority. Argumentation is usually not personal. The amendment process serves as a kind of argumentation. Argumentation has an important credibility function in building a reputation for the legislator. This practice of resolving differences through the amendment process is extended to the relationship between the legislature and the executive.

In the third subsphere, political campaigns, there is a complex mixture of activities. Campaigns involve both policy issues and the images of the candidates. Campaign arguments are made in the light of an understanding of "the people" or "the public." These concepts are used as a basis for telling the right stories about the candidate and about the opponent. These stories together form the story of the campaign and its relationship to the people. That story must be maintained, not only against the claims of opponents but those of the media as well.

Debates have a special role in political campaigns. They are probably the single most important campaign activity, despite frequent complaints that they do not involve extensive attention to the issues. Debates reflect the mixed political condition in the country.

Refutation in a political campaign tends to be about testing proposals with values. Evidence and credibility are important to refutation because they help to sustain the story propagated by the campaign. To maintain that story, a candidate and campaign must answer attacks on the story. Sometimes that refutation comes in the form of inoculation before the attack is actually made.

EXERCISES/PROJECTS

1. Attend a committee hearing of a campus or local government group. Write a short analysis of the argumentation used there. To what extent does it reflect the principles of committee hearings discussed in this chapter? What is your opinion of the quality of the hearings?
2. Select a current political issue that interests you. Using an internet search engine (http://www.thesearchenginelist.com), first, identify Senators and Representatives who are involved in the issue. Then, identify any legislation regarding the issue that passed within the past four years. What compromises occurred between the legislation's introduction and its passage? If no legislation has been passed, at what stage has it been stopped? Have any of the Senators and Representatives you identified proposed legislation? What has happened to the proposals? How have the media been used in support or opposition to the proposal?

REFERENCES

About.com. *"Autism Spectrum Disorders."* Accessed February 7, 2011, from http://autism.about.com/od/whatisautism/a/vaccinequestion.htm? p = 1.

Adarand Constructors, Inc. v. Federico Pena. United States Court of Appeals for the Tenth Circuit, No. 93-1841 (June 12, 1995). Remanded by the Supreme Court of the United States, 515 US 200 (1995).

Aldisert, Ruggero J. *Logic for Lawyers.* New York: Clark Boardman, 1989.

Allen, Julia M., and Lester Faigley. "Discursive Strategies for Social Change: An Alternative Rhetoric of Argument." *Rhetoric Review* 14 (1995): 142–172.

Amsterdam, Anthony G., and Jerome Bruner. *Minding the Law.* Cambridge, MA: Harvard UP, 2000.

Andersen, Kenneth. *Persuasion: Theory and Practice.* Boston: Allyn and Bacon, 1971.

Andersen, Kenneth, and Theodore Clevenger Jr. "A Summary of Experimental Research in Ethos." *Speech Monographs* 30 (1963): 59–78.

Anderson, James A. *Communication Research: Issues and Methods.* New York: McGraw-Hill, 1987.

Anderson, James A. *Natural Theology: The Metaphysics of God.* Milwaukee: Bruce, 1962: 25–66.

Anderson, James A., and Timothy P. Meyer. *Mediated Communication: A Social Action Perspective.* Newbury Park, CA: Sage, 1988.

Angier, Natalie. *"Thirst for Fairness May Have Helped Us Survive."* The New York Times, July 5, 2011: D2.

Ansolabehere, Stephen, and Shanto Iyengar. *Going Negative.* New York: Free P, 1995.

Apple, R. W. Jr. "Senate Confirms Thomas 52–48, Ending Week of Bitter Battle; 'Time for Healing,' Judge Says." *New York Times,* October 16, 1991: A1, A3.

"Are We in a Recession: Six Experts Assess the Current State and Forecast the Future Direction of the American Economy." *New York Times,* December 16, 2007. Accessed from www.nytimes.com/2007/12/16/opinion/16recession.html.

Argyris, Chris. *Reasoning, Learning, and Action.* San Francisco: Jossey-Bass, 1982.

Aristotle. "Nicomachean Ethics." *Works of Aristotle.* Ed. by Richard McKeon. New York: Random House, 1949: 935–1112.

Aristotle. *On Rhetoric: A Theory of Civic Discourse.* Trans. George A. Kennedy. New York: Oxford UP, 1991.

Armas, Genaro. C. "Record Number of Women Childless, Census Shows." *Deseret Morning News,* October 25, 2003: A11.

Arthur, Jim, Christine Carlson, and Lee Moore. *A Practical Guide to Consensus.* Policy Consensus Initiative, 1999.

Asbell, Sally L. "Understanding the Rehabilitation Act of 1973: A Rhetorical Analysis of Legislative Hearings." Diss., University of Utah, 1989.

Asch, Solomon E. "Effects of Group Pressure upon the Modification and Distortion of Judgments." *Groups, Leadership and Men.* Ed. Harold Guetzkow. Pittsburgh: Carnegie, 1951: 171–190.

Associated Press. "Wal-Mart Offers Online Tunes Free of Copy Protection for 94 Cents Per Track." *The International Herald Tribune,* August 21, 2007: C1.

Audi, Nadim. *"Offering Slow, Small Changes, Morocco's King Stays in Power."* The *New York Times.* July 11, 2011: A4.

Ayers, Robert H. *Language, Logic, and Reason in the Church Fathers: A Study of Tertullian, Augustine, and Aquinas.* New York: Olms, 1979.

Ayim, Maryann. "Violence and Domination as Metaphors in Academic Discourse." *Selected Issues in Logic and Communication.* Ed. Trudy Govier. Belmont, CA: Wadsworth, 1988: 184–1950.

Baker, Eldon E. "The Immediate Effects of Perceived Speaker Disorganization on Speaker Credibility and Audience Attitude Change in Persuasive Speaking." *Western Speech Journal* 29 (1965): 148–161.

Balboni, Fred. *"What's Next For IBM's Watson?"* Accessed March 14, 2011, from Forbes.com/2011/03/14/Watson-ibm-business-leadership-managing-future_prin.

Barr, James. *Semantics of Biblical Language.* London: Oxford UP, 1961.

Batt, Shawn. "Keeping Company in Controversy: Education Reform, Spheres of Argument, and

Ethical Criticism." *Argumentation and Advocacy* 40 (2003): 85–104.

Baucus, Max. *Montana's Senator*. Accessed from www.maxbaucus2008.com.

Bauer, Roy A., Emilio Collar, and Victor Tang, with Jerry Wind and Patrick Houston. *The Silverlake Project Transformation at IBM*. New York: Oxford UP, 1992.

Beach, Wayne. "Temporal Density in Courtroom Interaction: Constraints on the Recovery of Past Events in Legal Discourse." *Communication Monographs* 52 (1985): 1–18.

Begley, Sharon. "Can God Love Darwin Too?" *Newsweek*, September 17, 2007: 45.

Bell, Katrina E., Mark P. Orbe, Darlene K. Drummond, and Sakile Kai Camara. "Accepting the Challenge of Centralizing without Essentializing: Black Feminist Thought and African American Women's Communication Experiences." *Women's Studies in Communication* 23 (2000): 41–62.

Bellah, Robert N., Richard Madsen, William M. Sullivan, Ann Swindler, and Steven M. Tipton. *Habits of the Heart: Individualism and Commitment in American Life*. Berkeley: University of California Press, 1985.

Bennett, W. Lance. "Where Have All the Issues Gone? Explaining the Rhetorical Limits in American Elections." *Spheres of Argument*. Ed. Bruce Gronbeck. Annandale, VA: Speech Communication Assoc., 1989: 128–135.

Bennett, W. Lance, and Martha S. Feldman. *Reconstructing Reality in the Courtroom*. New Brunswick, NJ: Rutgers UP, 1981.

Benoit, Pamela J., and William L. Benoit. "Accounts of Failures and Claims of Successes in Arguments." *Spheres of Argument*. Ed. Bruce Gronbeck. Annandale, VA: Speech Communication Assoc., 1989: 551–557.

Berenson, Alex. "After a Trial, Silence." *The New York Times*, November 21, 2007: A1.

Bitzer, Lloyd F. "Political Rhetoric." *Handbook of Political Communication*. Eds. Dan D. Nimmo and Keith R. Sanders. Beverly Hills: Sage, 1981: 225–248.

Blackman, Paul H. "Armed Citizens and Crime Control." Accessed October 7, 1999, from www.NRAILA.org: 1–9.

Booth, Wayne. "Introduction: The Rhetoric of War and Reconciliation." *Roads to Reconciliation Conflict and Dialogue in the Twenty-First Century*. Eds. Amy Benson Brown and Karen M. Poremski. Armonk, NY: M. E. Sharpe, 2005.

Boseley, Sarah. "Are you ready for a world without antibiotics?" guardian.co.uk 12 August 2010. Accessed February 7, 2011, from http://www.guardian.co.uk/society/2010/aug/12/the end-of-antibiotics-health-infections.

Bowden, Mark. "The Dark Art of Interrogation." *The Atlantic Monthly*, October 2003: 51–76.

Boynton, George R. "Telling a Good Story: Models of Argument; Models of Understanding in the Senate Agriculture Committee." *Argument and Critical Practices*. Ed. Joseph W. Wenzel. Annandale, VA: Speech Communication Assoc., 1987: 429–438.

Boynton, George R. "When Senators and Publics Meet at the Environmental Protection Subcommittee." *Discourse and Society* 2 (1991): 131–155.

Braine, Martin D. S., and David P. O'Brien. *Mental Logic*. Mahwah, NJ: Erlbaum, 1998.

Branham, Robert. "Roads Not Taken: Counterplans and Opportunity Costs." *Journal of the American Forensic Association* 25 (1989): 246–255.

Brown v. Board of Education of Topeka, Kansas 347 US 483.

Brooks, David. *The Social Animal*. New York: Random House, 2011.

Bruner, M. Lane. "Producing Identities: Gender Problematization and Feminist Argumentation." *Argumentation and Advocacy* 32 (1996): 185–198.

Bureau of the Census. "Civilian Employment in the Fastest Growing and Declining Occupations: 1992 to 2005." *Statistical Abstract of the United States*, 1994. 114 ed. Washington, DC: Bureau of the Census, 1994: 411.

Bureau of the Census. "State and Local Taxes Paid by a Family of Four in Selected Cities, 1994." *Statistical Abstract of the United States*, 1994. 114 ed. Washington, DC: Bureau of the Census, 1994: 310.

Business Week, Special Advertising Section, March 31, 2003.

Bylund, Anders. "Foolish Forecast: IBM Will Rock for Ages." *The Motley Fool*. Accessed October 16, 2007, from www.fool.com.

Campbell, John Angus. "Poetry, Science, and Argument: Erasmus Darwin as Baconian Subversive." *Argument and Critical Practices*. Ed. Joseph W. Wenzel. Annandale, VA: Speech Communication Assoc., 1987: 499–506.

Campbell, John Angus. "The Polemical Mr. Darwin." *The Quarterly Journal of Speech* 61 (1975): 375–390.

Campbell, Karlyn Kohrs. *Man Cannot Speak for Her: A Critical Study of Early Feminist Rhetoric.* Vol. 1. New York: Praeger, 1989.

Cardozo, Benjamin N. *The Nature of the Judicial Process.* New Haven: Yale UP, 1921.

Carey, Benedict. *"You Might Already Know This."* *The New York Times* on the Web, January 10, 2011. Accessed January 11, 2011, from http://www.nytimes.com/2011/01/11/science/11esp.html?_r=1&paagewanted.

Carlie, Mike. *"Into the Abyss: A Personal Journey into the World of Street Gangs."* Accessed from people.missouristate.edu. 2002.

Carpenter, Betsy. "Is He Worth Saving?" *U.S. News and World Report,* July 10, 1995: 43–45.

Carr, David. "This Time, Judith Regan Did It." *The New York Times,* December 18, 2006.

Carter, Jimmy. "Call Off the Global Drug War." *The New York Times,* June 17, 2011, A31.

Carter, Stephen L. *New England White.* New York: Alfred A. Knopf, 2007.

CDC Centers for Disease Control. *"Vaccine Safety."* Accessed February 7, 2011, from http://www.cdc.gov/vaccinesafety/concerns/Autism/Index.html.

Chivers, C. J. "Mourners Seek Solace in the Rituals of Faith." *New York Times* on the Web, November 8, 1999.

Cho, David, and Irwin, Neil. "Bush Wins Agreement to Freeze Mortgages: Hard-Up Owners Won't See Adjustable Rates Soar." *Washington Post,* December 6, 2007: A1.

Church, Russell T., and Charles Wilbanks. *Values and Policies in Controversy: An Introduction to Argumentation and Debate.* Scottsdale, AZ: Gorsuch Scarisbrick, 1986.

City of Richmond v. J.A. Croson 488 US 469 (1989).

Cloud, Dana L. "The Materiality of Discourse as Oxymoron: A Challenge to Critical Rhetoric." *Western Journal of Communication* 58 (1994): 141–163.

Clover, Charles. "Climate Change Is Like World War Three." *Telegraph.* Accessed from www.telegraph.co.uk/earth/11 May, 2007.

Cobb, Roger W., and Charles D. Elder. "Communication and Public Policy." *Handbook of Political Communication.* Eds. Dan D. Nimmo and Keith R. Sanders. Beverly Hills: Sage, 1981: 391–416.

Cobb, S. "A Narrative Perspective on Mediation: Toward the Materialization of the Storytelling Metaphor." *New Directions in Mediation: Communication Research and Perspectives.* Eds. Joseph P. Folger and Trish S. Jones. Thousand Oaks, CA: Sage, 1994: 44–66.

Code, Lorraine. *What Can She Know? Feminist Theory and the Construction of Knowledge.* Ithaca: Cornell UP, 1991.

Cohen, Simon. *Essence of Judaism.* New York: Behrman's Jewish Book House, 1932.

Condit, Celeste Michelle. *The Meanings of the Gene.* Madison: University of Wisconsin Press, 1999.

Cox, J. Robert. "Investigating Policy Argument as a Field." *Dimensions of Argument.* Eds. George Ziegelmueller and Jack Rhodes. Annandale, VA: Speech Communication Assoc., 1981: 126–142.

Cragan, John F., and David W. Wright. *Communication in Small Groups.* Belmont, CA: Wadsworth, 1999.

Crenshaw, Carrie. "The Normality of Man and Female Otherness: (Re)producing Patriarchal Lines of Argument in the Law and the News." *Argumentation and Advocacy* 32 (1996): 170–184.

Cronkhite, Gary. "Propositions of Past and Future Fact and Value: A Proposed Classification." *Journal of the American Forensic Association* 3 (1966): 11–17.

Cronkhite, Gary, and Jo R. Liska. "The Judgment of Communicants Acceptability." *Persuasion: New Directions in Theory and Research.* Eds. Michael E. Roloff and Gerald R. Miller. Beverly Hills: Sage, 1980: 101–139.

Culpan, Tim. *"Apple Brand Value at $153 Billion Overtakes Google for Top Spot."* Accessed June 6, 2011, from http://www.bloomberg.com/news/2011–05–09/apple-brand-value-at-153-billion-overtakes-g.

Czubaroff, Jeanine. "The Deliberative Character of Strategic Scientific Debates." *Rhetoric in the Human Sciences.* Ed. Herbert Simons. Newbury Park, CA: Sage, 1989.

Damasio, Antonio R. *Descartes' Error: Emotion, Reason, and the Human Brain.* New York: Avon Books, 1994.

Daniels, Steven E., and Gregg B. Walker. *Working through Environmental Conflict: The Collaborative Learning Approach.* Westport, CT: Praeger, 2001.

Davidson, Roger, and Walter J. Oleszek. *Congress and Its Members.* Washington, DC: Congressional Quarterly, 1981.

de Kluyver, Cornelis A., and John A. Pearce II. *Strategy: A View from the Top.* Upper Saddle River, NJ: Prentice Hall, 2003.

Delia, Jesse G. "A Constructivist Analysis of the Concept of Credibility." *Quarterly Journal of Speech* 62 (1976): 361–375.

DeLuca, Kevin Michael. *Image Politics the New Rhetoric of Environmental Activism.* New York: Guilford P, 1999.

DeLuca, Kevin M., and Peeples, Jennifer. "From Public Sphere to Public Screen: Democracy, Activism, and the 'Violence' of Seattle." *Critical Studies in Media* 19 (2002): 125–151.

Derrida, Jacques. *The Postcard: From Socrates to Freud and Beyond.* Chicago: U of Chicago P, 1987.

Dewey, John. *The Quest for Certainty.* New York: G. P. Putnam, 1928.

Docherty, Thomas (Ed). *Postmodernism: A Reader.* New York: Columbia UP, 1993.

Dohrmann, George and Jeff Benedict. *"Rap Sheets, Recruits, and repercussions."* Sports Illustrated. 110: 10 (March 7, 2011), 37–38.

Domenici, Kathy, and Stephen W. Littlejohn. *Facework: Bridging Theory and Practice.* Thousand Oaks, CA: Sage, 2006.

Domenici, Pete. *About the Senator: Senator Pete V. Domenici.* Accessed from http://domenici.senate.gov/about/index.cfm.

Dowd, Maureen. "Sununu Sayonara: He Broke 7 Cardinal Rules." *New York Times,* December 5, 1991: A14.

"Drug Use: America's Middle and High School Students." *World Almanac and Book of Facts.* Mahwah, NJ: World Almanac Books, 1999: 878.

Easterbrook, Gregg. "The New Convergence." *Wired Magazine* 10, December 12, 2002.

Edelman, Gerald M. *Bright Air, Brilliant Fire on the Matter of the Mind.* New York: Basic Books, 1992.

Edwards, Derek, and Jonathan Potter. *Discursive Psychology.* Newbury Park, CA: Sage, 1992.

Edwards, Ward, and Amos Tversky, Eds. *Decision Making.* Baltimore: Penguin, 1967.

Ehninger, Douglas, and Wayne Brockriede. *Decision by Debate.* New York: Harper, 1978.

Eisend, Martin. *"Explaining the joint effect of source credibility and negativity of information in two-sided messages."* Psychology and Marketing 27:11 (2010) 1032–1049. Accessed July 11, 2011, from http://onlinelibrary.wiley.com/doi/10.1002/mar.20372/full.

Eisinger, Richard, and Judson Mills. "Perceptions of the Sincerity and Competence of a Communicator as a Function of the Extremity of His Position." *Journal of Experimental Social Psychology* 4 (1968): 224–232.

Elisou, Jenny. "Music Biz Misery Continues." *Rolling Stone,* August 7, 2003: 15–16.

Ellis, Donald G., and B. Aubrey Fisher. *Small Group Decision Making.* New York: McGraw-Hill, 1994.

Elshtain, Jean Bethke. "Feminism Discourse and Its Discontents: Language, Power, and Meaning." *Signs* 7 (1982): 603–621.

Engel, S. Morris. *With Good Reason.* New York: St. Martin's, 1986.

Epstein, Isidore. *The Faith of Judaism.* London: Soncion P, 1954: 86.

FAIR. "The Way Things Aren't: Rush Limbaugh Debates Reality." *Extra!* July/Aug. 1994: 10–17.

Farrar, Frederic W. *History of Interpretation.* Grand Rapids, MI: Baker Book House, 1961.

Fearnside, W. Ward, and William B. Holther. *Fallacy: The Counterfeit of Argument.* Englewood Cliffs, NJ: Prentice Hall, 1959.

Feighery, Glen, Marouf Hasian, Jr., and Richard Rieke. "The Search for Social Justice and Presumption of Innocence in the Duke University (USA) Lacrosse Case of 2006–2007." *Handbook of Communication Ethics.* Eds. George Cheney, Steve May, and Debashish Munshi. New York: Routledge, 2011: 258–272.

Festinger, Leon. *Conflict, Decision, and Dissonance.* Stanford: Stanford UP, 1964.

Financial Crisis Inquiry Commission. *Report on the Causes of the Financial Crisis.* Washington, DC (January 27, 2011). Accessed March 9, 2011, from FCIC.gov.

Fischman, Josh. "Feathers Don't Make the Bird." *Discover* 20 (Jan. 1999): 48–49.

Fisher, Roger, and Stephen Brown. *Getting Together: Building a Relationship That Gets to Yes.* Boston: Houghton Mifflin, 1988.

Fisher, Roger, and William Ury. *Getting to Yes: Negotiating Agreement without Giving In.* Boston: Houghton Mifflin, 1981.

Fisher, Walter R. *Human Communication as Narration: Toward a Philosophy of Reason, Value, and Action.* Columbia: University of South Carolina Press, 1987.

Foderaro, Lisa W. *"On Campus, Students Get a Lesson in Disasters."* The New York Times, June 10, 2011: A19.

Follett, Ken. *On Wings of Eagles*. New York: W. Morrow, 1983.

Fosdick, Harry Emerson. *A Guide to Understanding the Bible*. New York: Harper Bros., 1938.

Foss, Sonja, and Cindy Griffin. "Beyond Persuasion: A Proposal for an Invitational Rhetoric." *Communication Monographs* 62 (1995): 2–18.

Foucault, Michel. *The Order of Things*. New York: Vintage Books, 1973.

Fox, Stuart. *Most Comprehensive Poll to Date Finds Americans Actually Love Scientists, Science. Unfortunately, they still don't believe in evolution or climate change*. Accessed June 9, 2011, from http://www.popsci.com/scitech/article/2009–07/new-poll.

Frana, Adrian W. "Characteristics of Effective Argumentation." *Argumentation and Advocacy* 25 (1989): 200–202.

Franklin, Benjamin. *The Autobiography of Benjamin Franklin*. Ed. Gordon S. Haight. New York: Black, 1941.

Freeley, Austin J. *Argumentation and Debate: Critical Thinking for Reasoned Decision Making*. Belmont, CA: Wadsworth, 1990.

Frey, Lawrence R. "Group Communication in Context: Studying Bona Fide Groups." *Group Communication in Context*. Ed. Lawrence R. Frey. Mahwah, NJ: Lawrence Erlbaum, 2003.

Friedman, Thomas L. *The World Is Flat: A Brief History of the Twenty-First Century*. New York: Farrar, Straus & Giroux, 2006.

Frank, David. "Arguing with God, Talmudic Discourse, The Jewish Countermodel: Implications for the Study of Argumentation." *Argumentation and Advocacy* 41 (2004): 71–86.

Fuller, Steve. *Philosophy, Rhetoric, and the End of Knowledge: The Coming of Science and Technology Studies*. Madison: University of Wisconsin Press, 1993.

Funk, Robert W., Ray W. Hoover, and the Jesus Seminar. *The Five Gospels: The Search for the Authentic Words of Jesus*. New York: Scribner, 1993.

Furay, Conal. *The Grass Roots Mind in America: The American Sense of Absolutes*. New York: New Viewpoints, 1977.

Gallup, George, Jr., and Frank Newport. "Americans Most Thankful for Peace This Thanksgiving." *Gallup Poll Monthly*, November 1990: 42.

Garr, Doug. *Lou Gerstner and the Business Turnaround of the Decade*. New York: HarperBusiness, 1999.

Garten, Jeffrey E. *The Mind of the C.E.O.* New York: Basic Books, 2001.

Gaskins, Richard H. *Burdens of Proof in Modern Discourse*. New Haven: Yale UP, 1992.

German, Kathleen, Bruce E. Gronbeck, Douglas Ehninger, and Alan H. Monroe. *Principles of Public Speaking*. New York: Longman, 2001.

Gilbert, Michael A. "Feminism, Argumentation and Coalescence." *Informal Logic* 16 (1994): 95–113.

Gilovich, Thomas, and Dale Griffin. "Introduction—Heuristics and Biases: Then and Now." *Heuristics and Biases*. Eds. Thomas Gilovich, Dale Griffin, and Daniel Kahneman. Cambridge: Cambridge UP, 2002: 1–16.

Gleason, Bill. *"Is College Worth It? Answer May Depend on Accurate Net-Price Estimate." The Chronicle of Higher Education*. Accessed June 30, 2011, from http://chronicle/blogs/brainstorm/is-college-worth-it-.

Glover, J., Vidal, J., and Clark, A. "Blair Told: Act Now on Climate." *Guardian Unlimited*. Accessed from http://politics.guardian.co.uk/polls/story/0,11030,1511097,00.html#article 21 June, 2005.

Goldhagen, Daniel Jonah. *Worse than War: Genocide, Eliminationism, and the Ongoing Assault on Humanity*. New York: Public Affairs, 2009.

Gomes, Andrew. *The Honolulu Advertiser*. May 4, 2003: A1–A3.

Goodkind, Terry. *The Wizard's First Rule*. New York: A Tom Doherty Associates Book, 1994.

Goodnight, G. Thomas. "The Firm, the Park, and the University: Fear and Trembling on the Postmodern Trail." *The Quarterly Journal of Speech* 81 (1995): 267–290.

Goodnight, G. Thomas. "The Personal, Technical, and Public Spheres of Argument: A Speculative Inquiry into the Art of Public Deliberating." *Readings on Argumentation*. Eds. Angela J. Aguayo and Timothy R. Steffensmeier. State College, PA: Strata Publishing, Inc., 2008: 253–265.

Goodwin, Jean. *"Theoretical Pieties, Johnstone's Impiety, and Ordinary Views of Argumentation."* Philosophy and Rhetoric 40.1 (2007): 36–50.

Gotcher, J. Michael, and James M. Honeycutt. "An Analysis of Imagined Interactions of Forensic Participants." *The National Forensic Journal* 7 (1989): 1–20.

Gottlieb, Gidon. *The Logic of Choice*. New York: Macmillan, 1968.

Gouran, Dennis S. "The Failure of Argument in Decisions Leading to the '*Challenger* Disaster': Two Level Analysis." *Argument and Critical Practices.* Ed. Joseph W. Wenzel. Annandale, VA: Speech Communication Assoc., 1987: 439–447.

Gozic, Charles, P. Ed. *Gangs: Opposing Viewpoints.* San Diego, CA: Greenhaven P, 1996.

Grann, David. "Back to Basics in the Bronx." *New Republic,* October 4, 1999: 24–26.

Grant, Robert M. *A Short History of the Interpretation of the Bible.* New York: Macmillan, 1963.

Gratz et al. v. Bollinger et al. 02–516 U.S. (2003).

"Great Moments in Presidential Speeches." Accessed from YouTube.com.

Greenspan, Alan. "Measuring Financial Risk in the Twenty-First Century." *Vital Speeches of the Day* 66, November 1, 1999: 34–35.

Grice, H. P. "Further Notes on Logic and Conversation." *Syntax and Semantics, 9: Pragmatics.* Ed. Peter Cole. New York: Academic, 1978: 113–128.

Grice, H. P. "Logic and Conversation." *Syntax and Semantics, 3: Speech Acts.* Eds. Peter Cole and Jerry L. Morgan. New York: Academic, 1975: 41–58.

Gronbeck, Bruce, Kathleen German, Douglas Ehninger, and Alan H. Monroe. *Principles of Speech Communication,* 13th Brief Edition. Boston: Allyn & Bacon, 1997.

Gross, Alan G. "The Rhetorical Invention of Scientific Invention: The Emergence and Transformation of a Social Norm." *Rhetoric in the Human Sciences.* Ed. Herbert Simons. Newbury Park: Sage, 1989: 89–107.

Grutter v. Bollinger et al. U.S. (2003).

Gustines, George Gene. "*Restarting Comics' Clock Is Issue No. 1.*" *The New York Times,* June 13, 2011: C1.

Gurganus, Allan. *The Oldest Living Confederate Widow Tells All.* New York: Ivy, 1989.

Guterman, Lila. "*Scientists May Have Put Their Names on Papers Written by Drug Companies.*" *The Chronicle of Higher Education April 25, 2008.* Accessed July 14, 2011, from http://chronicle.com/article/Scientists-May-Have-Put-Their/28363.

Guzley, Ruth M., Fumiyo Arkai, and Linda E. Chalmers. "Cross-Cultural Perspectives of Commitment: Individualism and Collectivisim as a Framework for Conceptualization." *Southern Communication Journal* 64 (1998): 1–19.

Haiman, Franklin. "An Experimental Study of the Effect of Ethos on Public Speaking." *Speech Monographs* 16 (1949): 190–202.

Hamblin, C. L. *Fallacies.* London: Methuen, 1970.

Honeycutt, James M., Kenneth S. Zagacki, and Renee Edwards. "Imagined Interaction and Interpersonal Communication." *Communication Reports* 3 (1990): 1–8.

Haney, Daniel Q. "Rabies: Rare but Deadly." *Salt Lake Tribune,* October 21, 1999: B1–B2.

Hardon, John A., S. J. *The Catholic Catechism.* Garden City, NY: Doubleday, 1975.

Harmon, Fred. *Business 2010.* Washington, DC: Kiplinger Books, 2001.

Harris, Gardiner. "*New for Aspiring Doctors, the People Skills Test.*" *The New York Times,* July 11, 2011: A1.

Harris, Thomas. *Hannibal.* New York: Delacorte P, 1999.

Harvey, David. *The Condition of Postmodernity.* Cambridge, MA: Basil Blackwell, 1989.

Hatfield, Mark O. "Remarks on a School Prayer Amendment to the Improving America's School Act, 1994." *Congressional Record,* July 27, 1994: S9894.

Haverwas, Stanley, and L. Gregory Jones. *Why Narrative? Readings in Narrative Theology.* Grand Rapids, MI: Eerdmans, 1989.

Hawkins, J. "Interaction and Coalition Realignments in Consensus Seeking Groups: A Study of Experimental Jury Deliberations." Diss., University of Chicago, 1960.

Hayakawa, S. I. *Language in Thought and Action.* New York: Harcourt, Brace, Jovanovich, 1978.

Hemenway, Robert E. "The Evolution of a Controversy in Kansas Shows Why Scientists Must Defend the Search for Truth." *The Chronicle of Higher Education,* October 29, 1999.

Hendershott, Anne. "Redefining Rape—Expanded Meaning Robs Women of Power." *The San Diego Union-Tribune,* August 15, 2003: B7.

Hewgill, Murray A., and Gerald R. Miller. "Source Credibility and Response to Fear-Arousing Communications." *Speech Monographs* 32 (1965): 95–101.

Hicks, John. *Evil and the God of Love.* New York: Harper and Row, 1966.

Hill, Reginald. *Death Comes for the Fat Man.* New York: HarperCollins Publishers, 2007.

Hitchcock, David, and Bart Verheis (Eds.). *Arguing on the Toulmin Model.* Dordrecht, The Netherlands: Springer, 2006.

Hodgson, Peter C., and Robert H. King. *Christian Theology: An Introduction to the Traditions and Tasks*. Philadelphia, PA: Fortress, 1985.

Hoffner, Cynthia, and Joanne Cantor. "Factors Affecting Children's Enjoyment of a Frightening Film Sequence." *Communication Monographs* 58 (1991): 41–62.

Hogan, J. Michael. "Media Nihilism and the Presidential Debates." *Argumentation and Advocacy* 25 (1989): 220–225.

Hogan, Patrick Colm. *The Culture of Conformism*. Durham: Duke UP, 2001.

Holbrook, Thomas M. *Do Campaigns Matter?* Thousand Oaks, CA: Sage, 1996.

House, Dawn. "Law Firm Fired, But Utahns Will Still Pay Abortion-Defense Bill." *Salt Lake Tribune*, October 10, 1991: A1–A2.

Howell, William S. *Logic and Rhetoric in England, 1500–1700*. Princeton: Princeton UP, 1956.

Hu, Yifeng, and S. Shyam Sundar. *"Effects of Online Health Sources on Credibility and Behavioral Intentions." Communication Research.*Accessed July 11, 2011, from http://crx.sagepub.com/content/37/1/105 November 25, 2009.

Huff, Darrell. *How to Lie with Statistics*. New York: Norton, 1954.

Hutchinson, J. Wesley, Joseph W. Alba, and Eric M. Eisenstein. "Heuristics and Biases in Data-Based Decision Making: Effects of Experience, Training, and Graphical Data Displays." *Journal of Marketing Research XLVII* (August 2010): 627–642.

IBM. *"Let's go, humans." The New York Times*, February 14, 2011: A13.

Infante, Dominic A. "Teaching Students to Understand and Control Verbal Aggression." *Communication Education* 44 (1995): 51–63.

Infante, Dominic A., and Charles J. Wigley, III. "Verbal Aggressiveness: An Interpersonal Model and Measure." *Communication Monographs* 53 (1986): 61–69.

Infante, Dominic A., Andrew S. Rancer, and Deanna F. Womack. *Building Communication Theory*, 2nd ed. Long Grove, IL: Waveland Press, Inc., 1993.

Intergovernmental Panel on Climate Change. *Climate Change 2001: The Scientific Basis*. A Report of Working Group I of the Intergovernmental Panel on Climate Change, 2001.

Investopedia. *Composite Index of Leading Indicators*. Accessed from http://www.investopedia.com.

Irwin, Neil, and Tomoeh Murakami. "Economy Shows New Signs of Stress: Merrill Lynch Loss, Homes Sales Expose Weaknesses." *The Washington Post*, October 25, 2007: D1.

Isaacs, William. *Dialogue and the Art of Thinking Together*. New York: A Currency Book, 1999.

Jackson, Sally, and Scott Jacobs. "Structure of Conversational Argument: Pragmatic Bases for the Enthymeme." *The Quarterly Journal of Speech* 66 (1980): 251–265.

Jacobs, Scott. "How to Make an Argument from Example in Discourse Analysis." *Contemporary Issues in Language and Discourse Processes*. Eds. Donald G. Ellis and William A. Donohue. Hillsdale, NJ: Erlbaum, 1986: 149–167.

Jacobs, Scott, and Sally Jackson. "Conversational Argument: A Discourse Analytic Approach." *Advances in Argumentation Theory and Research*. Eds. J. Robert Cox and Charles A. Willard. Carbondale: Southern Illinois UP, 1982: 205–237.

Jaehne, Dennis. "Administrative Appeals: The Bureaucratization of Environmental Discourse." Diss., University of Utah, 1989.

Jamieson, Kathleen Hall. *Dirty Politics: Deception, Distraction, and Democracy*. New York: Oxford UP, 1992.

Jamieson, Kathleen Hall, and David S. Birdsell. *Presidential Debates: The Challenge of Creating an Informed Electorate*. New York: Oxford UP, 1988.

Janis, Irving L., and Leon Mann. *Decision Making*. New York: Free, 1977.

Johnson, Phillip E. "The Religious Implications of Teaching Evolution." *The Chronicle of Higher Education*, November, 12, 1999: B9.

Johnson, David Cay. *"9 Reasons the Rich Get Richer." City Weekly*, April 14, 2011: 16–18.

Johnson, Ralph H., and J. Anthony Blair. "The Recent Development of Informal Logic." *Informal Logic*. Eds. J. Anthony Blair and Ralph Johnson. Inverness, CA: Edge, 1980: ix–xvi.

Jones, Roger S. *Physics as Metaphor*. Minneapolis: University of Minnesota Press, 1982.

Joseph, Mike. "Ballpark Plans Up for Review: Shaner Complex Expansion Swells into Campaign Issue." *Centre Daily Time*, October 11, 2003: A1, A6.

Kagan, Donald, Steven Ozment, and Frank M. Turner. *The Western Heritage*. New York: Macmillan, 1983.

Kahane, Howard. *Logic and Contemporary Rhetoric*. Belmont, CA: Wadsworth, 1971.

Kaplan, Abraham. *The Conduct of Inquiry.* San Francisco: Chandler, 1964.

Kapuscinski, Ryszard. *The Shadow of the Sun.* New York: Vintage Books, 2001.

Kauffman, Linda S. "The Long Goodbye: Against Personal Testimony, or an Infant Grifter Grows Up." *American Feminist Thought at Century's End.* Cambridge: Blackwell, 1993: 258–277.

Keefe, William J., and Morris S. Ogul. *The American Legislative Process: Congress and the States.* Englewood Cliffs, NJ: Prentice-Hall, 1985.

Keen, Judy. "Bush on Offensive over War Critics: White House Moves Fast to Manage the Debate." *USA Today,* October 10, 2003: A4.

Kelly, Eamonn, Peter Leyden, and Members of the Global Business Network. *What's Next: Exploring the New Terrain for Business.* Cambridge, MA: Perseus, 2002.

Kennedy, George A. *Classical Rhetoric and Its Christian and Secular Tradition.* Chapel Hill: University of North Carolina Press, 1980.

Kent, Thomas. *Paralogic Rhetoric: A Theory of Communicative Interaction.* London: Associated UP, 1993.

Kern, Montague. "The Question of a Return to Basic American Values: 'My Mother and Winston Churchill' in the Heroic Narrations of Ross Perot's Infomercials." *Presidential Campaign Discourse.* Ed. Kathleen E. Kendall. Albany: State U of New York P, 1995: 157–178.

Kline, John A. "Interaction of Evidence and Reader's Intelligence on the Effects of Silent Message." *Quarterly Journal of Speech* 55 (1969): 407–413.

Klope, David C. "The Rhetorical Constitution of the Creationist Movement." Diss., University of Utah, 1991.

Kluckhohn, Clyde. *Mirror for Man.* New York: McGraw-Hill, 1949.

Kluckhohn, Clyde. "Values and Value-Orientations in the Theory of Action." *Towards a General Theory of Action.* Eds. Talcott Parsons and Edward A. Shils. New York: Harper and Row, 1951: 388–433.

Kohn, Stephen M. *"The Whistle-Blowers of 1777."* *The New York Times,* June 13, 2011: A21.

Kolb, Deborah. *When Talk Works: Profiles of Mediators.* San Francisco: Jossey-Bass, 1994.

Kouzes, James M., and Barry Z. Posner. *Credibility: How Leaders Gain and Lose It. Why People Demand It.* San Francisco: Jossey-Bass, 1993.

Krauss, Laurence M. "Words, Science, and the State of Evolution." *The Chronicle of Higher Education,* November 29, 2002: B20.

Kristof, Nicholas. "Baked Alaska on the Menu?" *New York Times,* September 13, 2003: A13.

Kristof, Nicholas. "Blood on Our Hands?" *New York Times,* August 5, 2003: A19.

Krugman, Paul. *"Shock Doctrine, U.S.A."* *The New York Times,* February 25, 2011: A23.

Kuhn, Thomas S. *The Structure of Scientific Revolutions.* Chicago: University of Chicago Press, 1970.

Kusnet, David. "Talking American: The Crucial First Step in Taking Back the White House." *The American Prospect,* September 2003, 22–25.

Laclau, Ernesto. "Politics and the Limits of Modernity." *Postmodernism: A Reader.* Ed. Thomas Docherty. New York: Columbia UP, 1993a: 329–343.

Laclau, Ernesto. "Power and Representation." *Politics, Theory, and Contemporary Culture.* Ed. Mark Poster. New York: Columbia UP, 1993b: 277–296.

Lake, Randall A. "Between Myth and History: Enacting Time in Native American Protest." *The Quarterly Journal of Speech* 77 (1991): 123–151.

Lakoff, George, and Mark Johnson. *Metaphors We Live By.* Chicago: University of Chicago Press, 1980.

Lashbrook, William R., William B. Snavely, and Daniel L. Sullivan. "The Effects of Source Credibility and Message Information Quantity on the Attitude Change of Apathetics." *Communication Monographs* 44 (1977): 252–262.

Lavasseur, David, and Kevin W. Dean. "The Use of Evidence in Presidential Debates: A Study of Evidence Labels and Types from 1960–1988." *Argumentation and Advocacy* 32 (1996): 129–142.

Leatherdale, W. H. *The Role of Analogy, Model, and Metaphor in Science.* Amsterdam: North-Holland, 1974.

Lecocq, F., J. C. Hourcade, and M. Ha-Duong. "Decision Making under Uncertainty and Inertia Constraints: Sectoral Implications of the When Flexibility." *Energy Economics* 20(5/6) (1998): 539–555.

Ledbetter v. Goodyear Tire and Rubber Co. 550 US xxx (2007).

Leeds, Jeff. "Universal in Dispute with Apple Over iTunes." *The New York Times,* July 2, 2007: C7.

Leff, Michael. "The Relation between Dialectic and Rhetoric in a Classical and Modern Perspective." *Dialectic and Rhetoric.* Eds. Frans H. van Eemeren and Peter Houtlosser. Dordrecht: Kluwer Academic, 2002: 53–63.

Lehrer, Jonah. *How We Decide.* Boston: Houghton Mifflin Harcourt, 2009.

Leiserowitz, A. A. "American Risk Perceptions: Is Climate Change Dangerous?" *Risk Analysis* 25(6) (2005): 1433–1442.

Leith, John H. "The Bible and Theology." *Interpretations* 30 (October 1976).

Lemonick, Michael D. "Never Trust a Tiger." *Time,* October 20, 2003: 63–64.

Lessem, Don. *Kings of Creation.* New York: Simon and Schuster, 1992.

Levasseur, D., and K. W. Dean. "The Use of Evidence in Presidential Debates: A Study of Evidence Levels and Types from 1960–1988." *Argumentation and Advocacy* 32 (1996): 129–142.

Levy, Leonard W. *Origins of the Bill of Rights.* New Haven: Yale UP, 1999.

Lewis, Bernard. *Islam and the Arab World.* New York: Alfred A. Knopf, 1976.

Lewis, Bernard. *The Crisis of Islam.* New York. Modern Library, 2003.

Lichtblau, Eric. "Wiretap Issue Leads Judge to Warn of Retrial in Terror Case." *The New York Times,* November 21, 2007: A1.

Lim, Tae-Seop. "Politeness Behavior in Social Influence Situations." *Seeking Compliance.* Ed. James P. Dillard. Scottsdale: Gorsuch Scarisbrik, 1990: 75–86.

Lindblom, Charles E. *"Still Muddling, Not Yet Through."* Public Administration Review From the Professional Stream (November/December 1979): 517–526.

LinkedIn.com/company/ibm. Accessed March 14, 2011.

Llewellyn, Karl N. "The Modern Approach to Counseling and Advocacy—Especially Commercial Transactions." *Columbia Law Review* 46 (1946): 167–195.

Lo, Andrew W., and Richard H. Thaler. "Two Views on Stock Market Rationality." *Investment Forum* 3 (December 1999): 13–15.

Luecke, Bruce. "Hang on for a Wild Ride." *Vital Speeches of the Day,* September 1, 1999: 682–685.

Lubell, Jennifer. "CMS Wants Ownership Disclosure: Doc-owners Would Have to State Their Stake Upfront." (The Week in Healthcare). *Modern Healthcare,* April 23, 2007: 5.

Luntz, Frank. *The Environment: A Cleaner, Safer, Healthier America.* The Luntz Research Companies. Accessed from www.ewg.org/briefings/luntzmemo/pdf/LuntzResearch_environment.pdf (2003).

Lyne, John. "Argument in the Human Sciences." *Perspectives on Argumentation.* Eds. Robert Trapp and Janice Schuetz. Prospect Heights, IL: Waveland, 1990: 178–189.

Lyne, John R. "The Pedagogical Use of Fallacies." *Iowa Journal of Speech Communication* 13 (1981): 1–9.

Lyne, John, and Henry F. Howe. "The Rhetoric of Expertise: E. O. Wilson and Sociobiology." *The Quarterly Journal of Speech* 76 (1990): 134–151.

MacKinnon, Catherine A. "Feminism, Marxism, Method and the State: An Agenda for Theory." *Signs* 7 (Spring 1982): 515–544.

Macquarrie, John. *God-Talk.* New York: Harper and Row, 1967.

"Making Money the Nonprofit Way." *U.S. News and World Report,* June 26, 1995: 19.

Massey, Gerald J. "The Fallacy behind Fallacies." *Fallacies: Classical and Contemporary Readings.* Eds. Hans V. Hansen, and Robert C. Pinto. University Park: Pennsylvania State UP, 1995.

Matson, Floyd W., and Ashley Montagu, Eds. *The Human Dialogue.* New York: Macmillan, 1967.

Matthews, Christopher. *Hardball.* New York: Summit, 1988.

Matthews, Donald R., and James A. Stimson. *Yeas and Nays: Normal Decision-Making in the U.S. House of Representatives.* New York: Wiley, 1975.

Max: Montana's Senator. Accessed October 30, 2007, from www.maxbaucus2008.com/index.html.

Mayors Climate Protection Center. The United States Conference of Mayors. Accessed October 30, 2007, from http://usmayors.org/climateprotection/.

McCroskey, James C. "A Summary of Experimental Research on the Effects of Evidence in Persuasive Communication." *The Quarterly Journal of Speech* 55 (1969): 169–175.

McCroskey, James C., and Jason Teven. "Goodwill: A Reexamination of the Construct and its Measurement." *Communication Monographs* 66 (1999): 90–103.

McCroskey, James C., and R. Samuel Mehrley. "The Effects of Disorganization and Nonfluency on Attitude Change and Source Credibility." *Speech Monographs* 36 (1969): 13–21.

McCroskey, J.C., V.P. Richmond, and J. A. Daly. "The Development of a Measure of Perceived Homophily in Interpersonal Communication." *Human Communication Research* 1 (1975): 323–332.

McGee, Michael C. "In Search of 'The People': A Rhetorical Alternative." *The Quarterly Journal of Speech* 61 (October 1975): 235–249.

McGrath, Ben. "The Talk of the Town." *The New Yorker,* July 28, 2003: 27–31.

McNeil, Donald G. Jr. "U.N. Agency to Say It Overstated Extent of H.I.V. Cases by Millions." *The New York Times,* November 20, 2007: A1.

Mead, George Herbert. *Mind, Self, and Society.* Chicago: University of Chicago Press, 1934.

Meador-Woodruff, James H. Meador-Woodruff Lab. About Schizophrenia. Accessed from www.personal.umich.edu/jimmw, 1999.

Milk ProCon.org. "Milk Consumption Compared to Mild Advertising, 1978–2005."

Miller, G. A. "The Magical Number Seven Plus or Minus Two: Some Limits on our Capacity for Processing Information." *The Psychological Review* 63: 81–97.

Miller, Greg R. "Incongruities in the Public/Private Spheres: Implications of the Clinton Presidential Campaign." *Argument and the Postmodern Challenge.* Ed. Raymie E. McKerrow. Annandale, VA: Speech Communication Assoc., 1993: 345–351.

Mill, John Stuart. *A System of Logic, Book III.* New York: Harper & Brothers, 1881: 278–291.

Millman, Arthur B. "Critical Thinking Attitudes: A Framework for the Issues." *Informal Logic* 10 (1988): 45–50.

Mills, D. Quinn, and G. Bruce Friesen. *Broken Promises: An Unconventional View of What Went Wrong at IBM.* Boston: Harvard Business School P, 1996.

Mills, Judson, and Elliott Aronson. "Opinion Change as a Function of the Communicators' Attractiveness and Desire to Influence." *Journal of Personality and Social Behavior* 1 (1965): 173–177.

Mitchell, Gordon R. "Team B Intelligence Coups." *Quarterly Journal of Speech* 92 (May 2006): 133–173.

Mitroff, Ian. *Smart Thinking for Crazy Times: The Art of Solving the Right Problems.* San Francisco: Berrett-Koehler P, 1998.

Montgomery, Barbara M., and Leslie A. Baxter, Eds. *Dialectical Approaches to Studying Personal Relationships.* Mahwah, NJ: Erlbaum, 1998.

Morris, Charles. *Varieties of Human Values.* Chicago: University of Chicago Press, 1956.

Morton, Kathryn. "The Story-Telling Animal." *New York Times Book Review,* December 28, 1984: 1–2.

Mukarovsky, Jan. *Structure, Sign and Function.* Trans. Peter Steiner and John Burbank. New Haven: Yale UP, 1976.

Myers, Michele Tolela, and Alvin A. Goldberg. "Group Credibility and Opinion Change." *Journal of Communication* 20 (1970): 174–179.

National R. R. Passenger Corp. v. Morgan 2002 U.S. LEXIS 4214.

Nelson, Ekow, Howard Kline, and Rob van den Dam. *A Future in Content(ion): Can Telecom Providers Win a Share of the Digital Content Market?* IBM Institute for Business Value, IBM Global Business Services, 2007.

Newell, Sara E., and Richard D. Rieke. "A Practical Reasoning Approach to Legal Doctrine." *Journal of the American Forensic Association* 22 (1986): 212–222.

New Jersey's Senator Frank Lautenberg. Accessed October 30, 2007, from www.lautenbergfornj.com/home

New York Times v. Sullivan. 376 US 254 (1954).

O'Keefe, Daniel J. "Two Concepts of Argument." *Journal of the American Forensic Association* 13 (1977): 121–128.

Oaksford, Mike, and Nick Chater. *Rationality in an Uncertain World: Essays on the Cognitive Science of Human Reasoning.* Hove, East Sussex: Psychology Press, Taylor & Francis, 1998.

Office of Science and Technology, "Proposed Policy on Research Misconduct to Protect the Integrity of the Research Record." *Federal Register,* October 14, 1999 (Volume 64, Number 198): 55722–55725.

Ogden, Schubert M. "The Authority of Scripture for Theology." *Interpretations* 30 (October 1976).

Olbricht, Thomas H. *Medieval Instruction in Rhetoric* (unpublished). n.d.

Ong, Walter J. "Ramist Rhetoric." *The Province of Rhetoric.* Eds. Joseph Schwartz and John Rycenga. New York: Ronald, 1965: 226–254.

Oravec, Christine. "Presidential Public Policy and Conservation: W. J. McGee and the People." *Green Talk in the White House: The Rhetorical Presidency Encounters Ecology.* Ed. Tarla Rai Peterson. College Station, TX: TAMU Press, 2004.

Ostermeier, Terry H. "Effects of Type and Frequency of Self Reference upon Perceived

Source Credibility and Attitude Change." *Speech Monographs* 34 (1967): 137–144.

Palczewski, Catherine Helen. "Argumentation and Feminisms: An Introduction." *Argumentation and Advocacy* 32 (1996): 161–169.

Park, Alice. "Cancer Fighter," *Time,* October 20, 2003: 81.

Parker, Richard. "Toward Field-Invariant Criteria for Assessing Arguments." Western Speech Communication Association Convention. Denver, 1982.

Patheos Library of World Religions and Spirituality – patheos.adherento.com.

Pearce, W. Barnett, and Stephen W. Littlejohn. *Moral Conflict: When Social Worlds Collide.* Thousand Oaks, CA: Sage, 1997.

Peat, F. David. *From Certainty to Uncertainty: The Story of Science and Ideas in the Twentieth Century.* Washington, DC: Joseph Henry P, 2002.

Peirce, Charles S. "The Fixation of Belief." *Philosophical Writings of Peirce.* Ed. Justus Buckler. New York: Dover, 1955: 7–18.

"People's Choice: Cable's Top 25." *Broadcasting and Cable* (129) January 4, 1999: 67.

Peralta, Eyder. *"Sen. Jon Kyl Corrects Erroneous Statement on Planned Parenthood."* Accessed from NPR.org.

Perelman, Chaim, and L. Olbrechts-Tyteca. *The New Rhetoric: A Treatise on Argumentation.* Notre Dame: University of Notre Dame P, 1969.

Perrin, Norman. *Parable and Gospel.* Minneapolis, MN: Augsburg Fortress Publishers, 2003.

Peterson, Tarla Rai. *Sharing the Earth: The Rhetoric of Sustainable Development.* Columbia: University of South Carolina Press, 1997.

Pfau, Michael. "The Potential of Inoculation in Promoting Resistance to the Effectiveness of Corporate Advertising Messages." *Communication Quarterly* 40 (1992): 26–44.

Pfau, Michael, and Henry C. Kenski. *Attack Politics: Strategy and Defense.* New York: Praeger, 1990.

Pfau, Michael, and William P. Eveland, Jr. "Influence of Traditional and Non-Traditional News Media in the 1992 Election Campaign." *Western Journal of Communication* 60 (1996): 214–232.

Pianin, Eric. "Congress Ends with a Flurry." *Salt Lake Tribune,* November 20, 1999: A1, A5.

Pine, Ronald. *Science and the Human Prospect.* Belmont, CA: Wadsworth, 1989.

Pollack, Henry N. *Uncertain Science. . . Uncertain World.* Cambridge: Cambridge UP, 2003.

Popkin, James, and Gloria Borger. "They Think They Can." *US News and World Report,* April 10, 1995: 26–32.

Rayl, A. J. S., and K. T. McKinney. "The Mind of God." *Omni,* August 1991: 43–48.

Raymond, Chris. "Study of Patient Histories Suggests Freud Suppressed or Distorted Facts That Contradicted His Theories." *Chronicle of Higher Education,* May 29, 1991: A4–A6.

Redford, Robert. *"The Red Rock Wilderness Act: Our Chance to be Present at The Creation."* Huffingtonpost.com. 2009.

Regal, Philip J. *The Anatomy of Judgment.* Minneapolis: University of Minnesota P, 1990.

Regents of the University of California v. Bakke 438 U.S. 265 (1978).

Reinard, John C. "The Empirical Study of the Persuasive Effects of Evidence: The Status after Fifty Years of Research." *Human Communication Research* 15 (1988): 3–59.

Rescher, Nicholas. "The Study of Value Change." *Journal of Value Inquiry* 1 (1967): 12–23.

Revkin, Andrew C. "Politics Reasserts Itself in the Debate over Climate Change and Its Hazards." *New York Times,* August 5, 2003: F2.

Revkin, Andrew C., and Katharine Q. Seelye. "Report by the E.P.A. Leaves Out Data on Climate Change." *New York Times,* June 19, 2003: A1.

Rieke, Richard D. "The Judicial Dialogue." *Argumentation* 5 (1991): 39–55.

Rieke, Richard D., and Randall K. Stutman. *Communication in Legal Advocacy.* Columbia: University of South Carolina Press, 1990.

Ritter, Kurt W. "Ronald Reagan and The Speech: The Rhetoric of Public Relations Politics." *Western Speech* 32 (1968): 50–58.

Roberts, Marilyn S. "Political Advertising: Strategies for Influence." *Presidential Campaign Discourse: Strategic Communication Problems.* Ed. Kathleen E. Kendall. Albany: State U of New York P, 1995: 179–200.

Roberts, W. Rhys. "Rhetorica." *The Works of Aristotle.* Ed. W. D. Ross. Oxford: Clarendon, 1945: 1354–1462.

Rohan, Brian. *"Germany finds E.coli on farm's bean sprout packet."* Accessed June 10, 2011, from chicagotribune.com/news/natonalworld/sns-rt-us-ecolitre7591hw.

Rohatyn, Dennis. "When Is a Fallacy a Fallacy?" International Conference on Logic and Argumentation. Amsterdam, June 4, 1986.

Rokeach, Milton. *Beliefs, Attitudes and Values*. San Francisco: Jossey-Bass, 1968.

Rokeach, Milton. *The Nature of Human Values*. San Francisco: Free P, 1972.

Rokeach, Milton. *Understanding Human Values*. New York: Free P, 1979.

Rorty, Richard. "Is Derrida a Transcendental Philosopher?" *Yale Journal of Criticism* 2 (1989): 207–215.

Rorty, Richard. "Philosophy as a Kind of Writing: An Essay on Derrida." *New Literary History 9* (1978): 141–160.

Rowland, Robert C. "In Defense of Rational Argument: A Pragmatic Justification of Argumentation Theory and Response to the Postmodern Critique." *Philosophy and Rhetoric* 28 (1995): 350–364.

Rowland, Robert C., and Cary R. W. Voss. "A Structural Functional Analysis of the Assumptions behind Presidential Debates." *Argument and Critical Practices*. Ed. Joseph W. Wenzel. Annandale, VA: Speech Communication Assoc., 1987: 239–248.

Ruesch, Jurgen. "Communication and American Values: A Psychological Approach." *Communication: The Social Matrix of Psychiatry*. Eds. Jurgen Ruesch and Gregory Bateson. New York: Norton, 1951: 94–134.

Ruggiero, Vincent R. *The Art of Thinking*. New York: Harper, 1964.

Rybacki, Karyn Charles, and Donald Jay Rybacki. *Advocacy and Opposition: An Introduction to Argumentation*. 5th ed. Boston: Pearson, 2004.

Salant, Jonathan D. "Race Study Points to Death-Penalty Imbalances." *The Honolulu Advertiser* 27 April 2003:A20.

Salzer, Beeb. "Quotable." *The Chronicle of Higher Education,* July 21, 1995: B5.

Sanders, Robert E. *Cognitive Foundations of Calculated Speech*. Albany: State University of New York Press, 1987.

Schemo, Diana Jean. "Private Loans Deepen a Crisis in Student Debt." *The New York Times,* June 10, 2007: A1.

Schenck v. United States. 249 US 47, 1919.

Scheutz, Janice. *Communicating the Law*. Long Grove, IL: Waveland P, 2007.

Schlegel, John Henry. *American Legal Realism and Empirical Social Science*. Chapel Hill: University of North Carolina Press, 1995.

Schneider, Matt. *"Bill O'Reilly Debunks Obama Myths: Does Have a Legitimate Birth Certificate."* Mediaite.

Schultz, Beatrice C. "The Role of Argumentativeness in the Enhancement of the Status of Members of Decision-Making Groups." *Spheres of Argument*. Ed. Bruce E. Gronbeck. Annandale, VA: Speech Communication Assoc., 1989: 558–562.

Schwartz, Shalom H. *"Basic Human Values: An Overview."* Schwartzpaper pdf.

Schweitzer, Don A. "The Effect of Presentation on Source Evaluation." *The Quarterly Journal of Speech 56* (1970): 33–39.

Schweitzer, Don A., and Gerald P. Ginsburg. "Factors of Communication Credibility." *Problems in Social Science*. Eds. Carl W. Backman and Paul F. Secord. New York: McGraw-Hill, 1966: 94–102.

Scriven, Michael. "The Philosophy of Critical Thinking and Informal Logic." *Critical Thinking and Reasoning Current Research, Theory, and Practice*. Ed. Daniel Fasko, Jr. Cresskill, NJ: Hampton P, 2003: 21–45.

Seattle.gov. Office of the Mayor. *U.S. Mayors Climate Protection Agreement*. Accessed October 30, 2007, from www.seattle.gov/mayor/climate/quotes.htm#quotes

Sharp, Harry, Jr., and Thomas McClung. "Effects of Organization on the Speaker's Ethos." *Speech Monographs* 33 (1966): 182–183.

Shnayerson, Michael, and Mark J. Plotkin. *The Killers Within: The Deadly Rise of Drug-Resistant Bacteria*. New York: Little, Brown, 2002.

Sillars, Malcolm O. "Values: Providing Standards for Audience-Centered Argumentation." *Values in Argumentation*. Ed. Sally Jackson. Annandale, VA: Speech Communication Assoc., 1995: 1–6.

Sillars, Malcolm O., and Bruce E. Gronbeck. *Communication Criticism: Rhetoric, Social Codes, Cultural Studies*. Prospect Heights, IL: Waveland, 2001.

Sillars, Malcolm O., and Patricia Ganer. "Values and Beliefs: A Systematic Basis for Argumentation." *Advances in Argumentation Theory and Research*. Eds. J. Robert Cox and Charles Arthur Willard. Carbondale: Southern Illinois UP, 1982: 184–201.

Simonson, Itamar. "Choice Based on Reasons: The Case of Attraction and Compromise Effects." *Journal of Consumer Research* 16 (1989): 158–159.

Smith, Eliza R. Snow. "Biography and Family Record of Lorenzo Snow." *Deseret News* 1884: 46.

Smith, Peter. *An Introduction to Formal Logic,* Cambridge: University of Cambridge P, 2003.

Snow, C. P. *Two Cultures and the Scientific Revolution*. Cambridge UP, 1963.

"Soft Touches." *Time*, June 5, 1995: 20.

Snyder, Albert, Petitioner v. Fred W. Phelps, SR., ET AL. No. 09–751, 562 U.S. ____(2011).

Sokal, Alan D. "What the Social Text Affair Does and Does Not Prove." Noretta Koertge, Ed. *A House Built on Sand: Exposing Postmodernist Myths about Science*. Oxford: Oxford UP, 1998.

Sproule, J. Michael. *"The Psychological Burden of Proof: On the Evolutionary Development of Richard Whately's Theory of Presumption."* Communication Monographs 43.2 (June 1976) 115–129.

Starr, Michael, and Christine M. Wilson. "Employment Law: *Ledbetter v. Goodyear*." The *National Law Journal* 29, no. 43 (July 2, 2007): 12.

Steele, Edward D., and W. Charles Redding. "The American Value System: Premises for Persuasion." *Western Speech* 26 (1962): 83–91.

Sternberg, Eliezer. *My Brain Made Me Do It*. New York: Prometheus Books, 2010.

Stob, Paul. "*Chisholm v. Georgia* and the Question of the Judiciary in the Early Republic." *Argumentation and Advocacy* 42 (2006): 127–142.

Stone, Brad, and Matt Richtel. "Silicon Valley Start-Ups Awash in Dollars, Again." *The New York Times*, October 17, 2007: A1.

Stossel, Scott. "Uncontrolled Experiment." *New Republic*, March 29, 1999: 17–22.

Streater, Scott. *"Public Lands: Utah County Sues for Access to Energy Treasure Chest."* Accessed from Robbishop.house.gov. 2010.

Stricherz, Mark. "Blood on Their Hands: Exposing Pro-abortion Catholic Politicians." *Cri-sis Magazine*. Accessed May 22, 2003, from www.crisismagazine.com/may2003/feature1.htm.

Stump, Bill. "Scull Session." *Men's Health*, October 2003: 103–104.

Suppe, Frederick. *The Structure of Scientific Theories*. Urbana: University of Illinois P, 1974.

Susskind, Lawrence, Sarah McKearnan, and Jennifer Thomas-Larmer. *The Consensus Building Handbook: A Comprehensive Guide to Reaching Agreement*. Thousand Oaks, CA: Sage, 1999.

Talmadge, R. Dewitt. "Victory For God." *American Forum*. Eds. Ernest J. Wrage and Barnett Baskerville. New York: Harper and Bros., 1960.

Tamborini, Ron, Ren-He Huang, Dana Mastro, and Reiko Nabashi-Nakahara. "The Influence of Race, Heuristics, and Information Load on Judgments of Guilt and Innocence." *Communication Studies* 58.4 (December 2007): 341–358.

Tannenhill, Robert C. *The Sword of His Mouth*. Philadelphia: Fortress, 1975.

TeSelle, Sallie McFague. *Speaking in Parables: A Study in Metaphor and Theology*. Philadelphia: Fortress, 1975.

Teven, Jason J., Richmond, Virginia P., McCroskey, James C. and McCroskey, Lynda L. "Updating Relationships Between Communication Traits and Communication Competence." *Communication Research Reports* 27: 3 (2010): 263–270.

The New York Times. *"Nearly all the companies our grandparents admired have disappeared (IBM Centennial ad)."* June 16, 2011: A16–A17.

The Noble Qur'an. University of Southern California Compendium of Muslem Texts. Accessed from www.USC.edu/dept/msa/Quran.

Thompson, Kevin. "The Anti Clause." *California Farmer*, January 1995: 12.

Tierney, John. *"Social Scientists Sees Bias Within."* The New York Times on the Web, February 7, 2011.

Toedtman, James. "Clinton, Congressional Leaders Laud $4,000 Billion Spending Deal." *Salt Lake Tribune*, November 19, 1999: A12.

Tol, R. S. J. "Safe Policies in an Uncertain Climate: An Application of FUND." *Global Environmental Change*, 9 (1999): 221–232.

Tomasky, Michael. "Strange Bedfellows: Conservative Civil Libertarians Join the Fight." *The American Prospect*, September 2003: 47–49.

Toulmin, Stephen E. "Commentary on Willbrand and Rieke." *Communication Yearbook* 14. Ed. James A. Anderson. Newbury Park, CA: Sage, 1991: 445–450.

Toulmin, Stephen. *Foresight and Understanding*. New York: Harper and Row, 1963.

Toulmin, Stephen. *Human Understanding*. Princeton: Princeton UP, 1972.

Toulmin, Stephen E. *The Uses of Argument*. Cambridge: Cambridge UP, 1964.

Toulmin, Stephen E., Richard Rieke, and Allan Janik. *An Introduction to Reasoning*, 2nd ed. New York: Macmillan, 1984.

Trenholm, Sara. *Persuasion and Social Influence*. Englewood Cliffs, NJ: Prentice, 1989.

Tubbs, Stewart L. "Explicit versus Implicit Conclusions and Audience Commitment." *Speech Monographs* 35 (1968): 14–19.

Tuman, Joseph H. "Getting to First Base: *Prima Facie* Arguments for Propositions of Value." *Journal of the American Forensic Association* 24 (1987): 84–94.

Turner, Daniel S. "America's Crumbling Infrastructure." *USA Today,* May 1999: 10–16.

Tyndal Centre for Climate Change Research and Environment Agency, UK. "New Science Shows Urgent Action Needed Today on Climate Change." Accessed from www.tyndall.ac.uk/media/press_releases/pr45.pdf 16 Feb. 2006.

Ury, William. *Getting Past No: Negotiating with Difficult People.* New York: Bantam Books, 1991.

Ury, William. *The Third Side: Why We Fight and How We Can Stop.* New York: Penguin, 1999.

U.S. v. Miller 307: 174 1939.

van Eemeren, Frans H. "Fallacies." *Crucial Concepts in Argumentation Theory.* Ed. Frans H. van Eemeren. Amsterdam: Amsterdam UP, 2001: 135–164.

van Eemeren, Frans H., and Rob Grootendorst. *Argumentation, Communication, and Fallacies: A Pragma-Dialectical Perspective.* Hillsdale, NJ: Erlbaum, 1993.

"Viewers Tune In." *New York Times,* October 14, 1991: A17.

Visser, H., R. J. M. Folkert, J. Hoekstra, and J. J. de Wolff. "Identifying Key Sources of Uncertainty in Climate Change Projections." *Climatic Change* 45 (2000): 421–457.

Waldman, Hilary. "Watching Lily." *Readers Digest,* April 2003: 81–87.

Walker, Gregg B., and Malcolm O. Sillars. "Where Is Argument? Perelman's Theory of Values." *Perspectives on Argumentation: Essays in Honor of Wayne Brockriede.* Eds. Robert Trapp and Janice Schuetz. Prospect Heights, IL: Waveland, 1990: 134–150.

Walters, Glenn D. *Criminal Belief Systems An Integrated-Interactive Theory of Lifestyles.* Westport, CT: Praeger, 2002.

Walton, Douglas N. *Appeal to Expert Opinion: Arguments from Authority.* University Park: Pennsylvania State UP, 1997a.

Walton, Douglas N. *Appeal to Pity: Argumentum ad Misericordiam.* Albany: State University of New York P, 1997b.

Walton, Douglas N. *A Pragmatic Theory of Fallacy.* Tuscaloosa: University of Alabama Press, 1995.

Walton, Douglas N. *Begging the Question: Circular Reasoning as a Tactic of Argumentation.* New York: Greenwood, 1991.

Walton, Douglas N. *Practical Reasoning.* Savage, MD: Rowman & Littlefield, 1990.

Walton, Douglas N. *The New Dialectic.* Toronto: University of Toronto Press, 1998.

Wang, Zuoming, Joseph B. Walther, Suzanne Pingree, and Robert P. Hawkins. "Health Information, Credibility, Homophily, and Influence via the Internet: Web Sites Versus Discussion Groups." *Health Communication* 23 (2008): 358–368.

Warnick, Barbara, and Edward S. Inch. *Critical Thinking and Communication.* New York: Macmillan, 1994.

Warren, Irving D. "The Effect of Credibility in Sources of Testimony of Audience Attitudes Toward Speaker and Message." *Speech Monographs* 36 (1969): 456–458.

Watson, Thomas J., Jr. *A Business and Its Beliefs: The Ideas That Helped Build IBM.* New York: McGraw-Hill, 1963.

Weaver, Richard. "Ultimate Terms in Contemporary Rhetoric." *The Ethics of Rhetoric.* Chicago: Regnery, 1953: 211–232.

Webb, LaVarr and Ted Wilson. "Understanding the Bank and Credit Union Battle." *Community* Nov./Dec. 2003: 65.

Wenburg, John R., and William Wilmot. *The Personal Communication Process.* New York: Wiley, 1973.

Werling, David S., Michael Salvador, Malcolm O. Sillars, and Mina A. Vaughn. "Presidential Debates: Epideictic Merger of Issues and Images in Values." *Argument and Critical Practices.* Ed. Joseph W. Wenzel. Annandale, VA: Speech Communication Assoc., 1987: 229–238.

Whately, Richard. *Elements of Rhetoric.* Ed. Douglas Ehninger. Carbondale: Southern Illinois UP, 1963.

"With Recession Looming Bush Tells America to 'Go Shopping More.'" *Think Progress.* Accessed from http://thinkprogress.org/2006/12/20/bush-shopping/20 Dec. 2006.

Whedbee, Karen. "Authority, Freedom and Liberal Judgment: The 'Presumptions' and 'Presumptuousness' of Whately, Mill and Tocqueville." *Quarterly Journal of Speech* 84.2 (May 1998): 171–189.

Willard, Charles A. "Argument Fields." *Advances in Argumentation Theory and Research.* Eds. J. Robert Cox and Charles A. Willard. Carbondale: Southern Illinois UP, 1982: 22–77.

Willbrand, Mary Louise, and Richard D. Rieke. "Reason Giving in Children's Supplicatory Compliance Gaining." *Communication Monographs* 53 (1986): 47–60.

Willbrand, Mary Louise, and Richard D. Rieke. "Strategies of Reasoning in Spontaneous Discourse." *Communication Yearbook* 14. Ed. James A. Anderson. Newbury Park, CA: Sage, 1991: 414–440.

Willihnganz, Shirley, Joy Hart Seibert, and Charles Arthur Willard. "Paper Training the New Leviathan: Dissensus, Rationality and Paradox in Modern Organizations." *Argument and the Postmodern Challenge.* Ed. Raymie E. McKerrow. Annandale, VA: Speech Communication Assoc., 1993.

Winfield, Nicole. *"Pope Marks Christianity's Holiest Night."* *Salt Lake Tribune,* April 24, 2011: A14.

Wise, Charles R. *The Dynamics of Legislation.* San Francisco: Jossey-Bass, 1996.

Wise, Gene. *American Historical Explanations: A Strategy for Grounded Inquiry.* Minneapolis: University of Minnesota Press, 1980.

Woelfel, James W. *Bonhoeffer's Theology.* Nashville: Abingdon P, 1970.

Wong, Kathleen. "Bringing Back the Logjams." *U.S. News and World Report,* September 6, 1999: 60.

Wright, Beverly. "Race, Politics and Pollution: Environmental Justice in the Mississippi River Chemical Corridor." *Just Sustainabilities: Development in an Unequal World.* Ed. Julian Agyeman, Robert D. Bullard, and Bob Evans (2003). Cambridge, MA: MIT Press: 125–145.

Zarefsky, David. *Lincoln–Douglas and Slavery.* Chicago: University of Chicago Press, 1990.

Zuger, Abigail. *"Profiles in Science: Nora D. Volkow A General in the Drug War."* The New York Times, June 14, 2011: D1.

NAME INDEX

A

Alba, Joseph W., 28
Aldisert, Ruggero J., 199
Allen, Julia M., 46
Amsterdam, Anthony G., 189, 190
Andersen, Kenneth, 146, 147, 149
Anderson, James A., 12, 217, 218, 224
Angier, Natalie, 38
Ansolabehere, Stephen, 270
Apple, R. W. Jr., 266
Argyris, Chris, 167, 168
Aristotle, 12, 15, 16, 20, 21, 23, 29,
    35, 37, 41, 57, 60, 142, 144,
    175, 176, 179, 189, 199, 258
Arkai, Fumiyo, 125
Armas, Genaro C., 107, 110
Aronson, Elliott, 148
Arthur, Jim, 50
Asbell, Sally L., 263
Asch, Solomon E., 30
Audi, Nadim, 89
Ayers, Robert H., 237
Ayim, Maryann, 46

B

Baker, Eldon E., 150
Balboni, Fred, 248
Barr, James, 238
Batt, Shawn, 20
Baucus, Max, 263
Bauer, Roy A., 244, 250
Baxter, Leslie A., 15, 40
Begley, Sharon, 240
Bell, Katrina E., 43, 44
Bellah, Robert N., 133
Benedict, Jeff, 133
Bennett, W. Lance, 40, 277
Benoit, Pamela J., 219
Benoit, William L., 219
Berenson, Alex, 117
Birdsell, David S., 275
Bitzer, Lloyd F., 258, 270
Blair, J. Anthony, 58
Booth, Wayne, 16
Boseley, Sarah, 12
Boynton, George R., 263, 264, 265
Braine, Martin D. S., 29, 58
Branham, Robert, 93
Brockriede, Wayne, 6, 157, 176
Brooks, David, 38
Brown, Stephen, 49

Bruner, Jerome, 189, 190
Bruner, M. Lane, 44, 46

C

Camara, Sakile Kai, 43, 44
Campbell, Karlyn Kohrs, 211
Cantor, Joanne, 214
Carey, Benedict, 21
Carlie, Mike, 133
Carlson, Christine, 50
Carpenter, Betsy, 129
Carr, David, 146
Carter, Jimmy, 49, 84, 274
Carter, Stephen L., 27
Chalmers, Linda E., 125
Chater, Nick, 14, 29
Chivers, C. J., 282
Cho, David, 268, 269
Church, Russell T., 6
Clevenger, Theodore, Jr., 146,
    147, 149
Cobb, Roger W., 259
Cobb, S., 40
Code, Lorraine, 45
Cohen, Simon, 228
Collar, Emilio, 244, 250
Condit, Celeste Michelle, 41
Cox, J. Robert, 259
Cragan, John F., 17
Crenshaw, Carrie, 45
Cronkhite, Gary, 4, 152

D

Daly, J. A., 143
Damasio, Antonio R., 29
Daniels, Steven E., 50
Davidson, Roger, 263
Delia, Jesse G., 151
DeLuca, Kevin Michael, 258
Derrida, Jacques, 93
Dewey, John, 12, 73
Dohrmann, George, 133
Domenici, Kathy, 16
Dowd, Maureen, 266
Drummond, Darlene K., 43, 44

E

Easterbrook, Gregg, 232
Edelman, Gerald M., 29
Edwards, Derek, 17
Edwards, Ward, 21

Ehninger, Douglas, 6, 94, 98,
    157, 176
Eisend, Martin, 150
Eisenstein, Eric M., 28
Eisinger, Richard, 147
Elder, Charles D., 259
Ellis, Donald G., 17
Elshtain, Jean Bethke, 42
Engel, S. Morris, 177
Epstein, Isidore, 224
Eveland, William P., Jr., 273

F

Faigley, Lester, 46
Farrar, Frederic W., 230
Fearnside, W. Ward, 176, 177
Feighery, Glen, 127
Feldman, Martha S., 40
Festinger, Leon, 160
Fisher, B. Aubrey, 17
Fisher, Roger, 49
Fisher, Walter R., 40
Foderaro, Lisa W., 60
Follett, Ken, 271
Fosdick, Harry Emerson, 223, 227
Foss, Sonja, 44
Fox, Stuart, 60
Frana, Adrian W., 278
Frank, David, 238
Franklin, Benjamin, 158, 159
Freeley, Austin J., 80
Frey, Lawrence R., 17
Friedman, Thomas L., 158, 255
Friesen, G. Bruce, 243, 245
Fuller, Steve, 41
Funk, Robert W., 230
Furay, Conal, 133

G

Gallup, George, Jr., 126
Garr, Doug, 244, 246, 249, 250
Garten, Jeffrey E., 247
Gaskins, Richard H., 16, 34
German, Kathleen, 94, 98
Gilbert, Michael A., 44
Gilovich, Thomas, 28, 29
Ginsburg, Gerald P., 151
Gleason, Bill, 99
Goldberg, Alvin A., 146, 149
Goldhagen, Daniel Jonah, 22
Gomes, Andrew, 144

Goodkind, Terry, 27
Goodnight, G. Thomas, 18, 19, 32, 258
Goodwin, Jean, 8
Gotcher, J. Michael, 14
Gottlieb, Gidon, 79
Gouran, Dennis S., 213
Grann, David, 103
Grant, Robert M., 229, 231, 233
Greenspan, Alan, 149
Grice, H. P., 183
Griffin, Cindy, 44
Griffin, Dale, 28, 29
Gronbeck, Bruce E., 39, 40, 94, 98, 131
Grootendorst, Rob, 59, 181
Gross, Alan G., 209
Gurganus, Allan, 94
Gustines, George Gene, 63
Guterman, Lila, 169
Guzley, Ruth M., 125

H

Haiman, Franklin, 147
Hamblin, C. L., 12, 175
Hardon, John A., 226
Hasian, Marouf, Jr., 127
Hatfield, Mark O., 118
Haverwas, Stanley, 238
Hawkins, J., 116
Hawkins, Robert P., 144, 145
Hayakawa, S. I., 64
Hemenway, Robert E., 161, 162
Henry F. Howe, 215, 219
Hewgill, Murray A., 149
Hicks, John, 226
Hill, Reginald, 27
Hitchcock, David, 53
Hodgson, Peter C., 223
Hoffner, Cynthia, 214
Hogan, J. Michael, 273
Hogan, Patrick Colm, 27
Holther, William B., 176, 177
Honeycutt, James M., 14
Hoover, Ray W., 230
House, Dawn, 185
Howell, William S., 176
Hu, Yifeng, 144, 145
Huang, Ren-He, 28
Huff, Darrell, 112
Hutchinson, J. Wesley, 28

I

Inch, Edward S., 80
Infante, Dominic A., 150, 180
Isaacs, William, 15
Iyengar, Shanto, 270

J

Jackson, Sally, 158, 180
Jacobs, Scott, 158, 180
Jaehne, Dennis, 89, 264
Jamieson, Kathleen Hall, 274, 275
Janis, Irving L., 74
Johnson, David Cay, 186
Johnson, Mark, 44
Johnson, Phillip E., 161–162
Johnson, Ralph H., 58
Jones, L. Gregory, 238
Jones, Roger S., 214
Joseph, Mike, 276

K

Kagan, Donald, 13
Kahane, Howard, 177
Kaplan, Abraham, 135
Kapuscinski, Ryszard, 226
Kauffman, Linda S., 43
Keefe, William J., 267, 268
Keen, Judy, 276
Kelly, Eamonn, 246
Kennedy, George A., 223, 224
Kenski, Henry C., 278
Kent, Thomas, 12
Kern, Montague, 271
King, Robert H., 223
Kline, Howard, 248, 251, 252
Kline, John A., 111
Klope, David C., 139, 153
Kluckhohn, Clyde, 121, 124, 125
Kohn, Stephen M., 64
Kolb, Deborah, 47
Kouzes, James M., 141
Kristof, Nicholas D., 22, 217
Kuhn, Thomas S., 21, 41, 166, 209
Kusnet, David, 277

L

Lake, Randall A., 94
Lakoff, George, 44
Lashbrook, William R., 149
Leff, Michael, 15
Lehrer, Jonah, 12, 30
Leith, John H., 230, 231
Lemonick, Michael D., 107
Lessem, Don, 215
Lewis, Bernard, 224, 230
Leyden, Peter, 246
Lichtblau, Eric, 117
Lim, Tae-Seop, 161
Lindblom, Charles E., 88
Liska, Jo R., 152
Littlejohn, Stephen W., 16, 46

Llewellyn, Karl N., 93
Lo, Andrew W., 21
Luecke, Bruce, 103, 105, 109
Luntz, Frank, 272, 277
Lyne, John R., 175, 176, 215, 219

M

MacKinnon, Catherine A., 43
Macquarrie, John, 223, 237, 239
Madsen, Richard, 133
Mann, Leon, 74
Massey, Gerald J., 176
Mastro, Dana, 28
Matson, Floyd W., 16
Matthews, Christopher, 277
Matthews, Donald R., 163, 260
McClung, Thomas, 150
McCroskey, James C., 8, 143, 149, 150
McCroskey, Lynda L., 8
McGee, Michael C., 271
McKearnan, Sarah, 49
McKinney, K. T., 139
McNeil, Donald G. Jr., 105
Mead, George Herbert, 14
Mehrley, R. Samuel, 150
Meyer, Timothy P., 12
Michael, Sproule, J., 87
Mill, John Stuart, 60
Miller, G. A., 98
Miller, Gerald R., 149
Millman, Arthur B., 13, 73
Mills, D. Quinn, 243, 245
Mills, Judson, 147, 148
Mitchell, Gordon R., 157, 161, 263, 264, 265
Mitroff, Ian, 14, 15
Monroe, Alan H., 94, 98
Montagu, Ashley, 16
Montgomery, Barbara M., 15, 40
Moore, Lee, 50
Morris, Charles, 125
Mukarovsky, Jan, 14
Myers, Michele Tolela, 146, 149

N

Nabashi-Nakahara, Reiko, 28
Neil, Irwin, 268, 269
Nelson, Ekow, 248, 251, 252
Newport, Frank, 126

O

O'Keefe, Daniel J., 9, 42
Oaksford, Mike, 14, 29
Ogden, Schubert M., 232
Ogul, Morris S., 267, 268

Olbrechts-Tyteca, L., 2, 13, 35, 58, 103, 124, 126
Olbricht, Thomas H., 240
Oleszek, Walter J., 263
Ong, Walter J., 176
Oravec, Christine, 259
Orbe, Mark P., 43, 44
Ostermeier, Terry H., 147, 149
Ozment, Steven, 13

P
Palczewski, Catherine Helen, 43, 44
Park, Alice, 106
Parker, Richard, 41
Pearce, W. Barnett, 46
Peat, F. David, 11, 41, 58, 134, 204, 205, 220
Peeples, Jennifer, 258
Peirce, Charles S., 12, 72, 73, 211
Peralta, Eyder, 175
Perelman, Chaim, 2, 13, 35, 58, 103, 124, 126
Pfau, Michael, 150, 273, 278
Pianin, Eric, 262
Pine, Ronald, 40, 51
Pingree, Suzanne, 144, 145
Plotkin, Mark J., 11
Pollack, Henry N., 208
Posner, Barry Z., 141
Potter, Jonathan, 17

R
Rancer, Andrew S., 150
Rayl, A. J. S., 139
Raymond, Chris, 182
Redding, W. Charles, 125
Redford, Robert, 129
Regal, Philip J., 14, 29
Reinard, John C., 108, 110, 148
Rescher, Nicholas, 130, 131
Revkin, Andrew C., 209, 272
Richmond, Virginia P., 8, 143
Rieke, Richard D., 2, 31, 38, 118, 121, 127, 160, 179, 183, 188, 195, 253
Ritter, Kurt W., 271
Roberts, Marilyn S., 270
Roberts, W. Rhys, 35, 37
Rohan, Brian, 61
Rohatyn, Dennis, 177
Rokeach, Milton, 121, 122, 123, 125, 219
Rorty, Richard, 93
Rowland, Robert C., 42, 46, 275
Ruesch, Jurgen, 125
Ruggiero, Vincent R., 73, 74
Rybacki, Donald Jay, 44
Rybacki, Karyn Charles, 44

S
Salant, Jonathan D., 186
Salvador, Michael, 275
Salzer, Beeb, 13
Sanders, Robert E., 183
Schneider, Matt, 180
Schultz, Beatrice C., 213
Schwartz, Shalom H., 125
Schweitzer, Don A., 143, 151
Scriven, Michael, 14
Seelye, Katharine Q., 272
Seibert, Joy Hart, 19
Seminar, Jesus, 230
Sharp, Harry, Jr., 150
Shnayerson, Michael, 11
Sillars, Malcolm O., 39, 40, 80, 121, 127, 131, 275
Simonson, Itamar, 13
Smith, Eliza R., 224
Smith, Peter, 58, 270
Snavely, William B., 149
Snow, C. P., 205
Sokal, Alan D., 41
Starr, Michael, 201, 202
Steele, Edward D., 125
Sternberg, Eliezer J., 23, 31
Stimson, James A., 163, 260
Stob, Paul, 188
Streater, Scott, 129
Stricherz, Mark, 276
Stump, Bill, 147
Stutman, Randall K., 160, 179
Sullivan, Daniel L., 149
Sullivan, William M., 133
Sundar, S. Shyam, 144, 145
Suppe, Frederick, 292
Susskind, Lawrence, 49
Swindler, Ann, 133

T
Talmadge, R. Dewitt, 240
Tamborini, Ron, 28
Tang, Victor, 244, 250
Tannenhill, Robert C., 231
TeSelle, Sallie McFague, 238
Teven, Jason J., 8, 143
Thaler, Richard H., 21
Thomas-Larmer, Jennifer, 49
Thompson, Kevin, 292
Tierney, John, 9, 10
Tipton, Steven M., 133
Toedtman, James, 262
Tomasky, Michael, 116
Toulmin, Stephen E., 9, 19, 34, 44, 48, 53, 56, 57, 58, 134, 135, 152, 208, 212

Trenholm, Sara, 160, 163
Tubbs, Stewart L., 150
Tuman, Joseph H., 131, 132
Turner, Daniel S., 108
Turner, Frank M., 13
Tversky, Amos, 21

U
Ury, William, 49

V
van den Dam, Rob, 248, 251, 252
van Eemeren, Frans H., 59, 181, 182
Vaughn, Mina A., 275
Verheis, Bart, 53
Voss, Cary R. W., 275

W
Waldman, Hilary, 106
Walker, Gregg B., 50, 127
Walters, Glenn D., 27
Walther, Joseph B., 144, 145
Walton, Douglas N., 58, 59, 177, 178, 180, 181
Wang, Zuoming, 144, 145
Warnick, Barbara, 80
Warren, Irving D., 149
Watson, Thomas J., Jr., 242, 243, 244, 245, 248, 253, 254
Weaver, Richard, 125
Webb, LaVarr, 115
Wenburg, John R., 14
Werling, David S., 275
Whately, Richard, 33, 86, 87
Whedbee, Karen, 86
Wigley, Charles J., III, 180
Wilbanks, Charles, 6
Willard, Charles A., 17, 19
Willbrand, Mary Louise, 2, 31, 38, 118, 121, 183
Willihnganz, Shirley, 19
Wilmot, William, 14
Wilson, Christine M., 201, 202
Wilson, Ted, 115
Winfield, Nicole, 122
Wise, Charles R., 261
Wise, Gene, 118
Woelfel, James W., 227
Womack, Deanna F.
Wright, David W., 17

Z
Zarefsky, David, 6
Zuger, Abigail, 68

SUBJECT INDEX

A

Abduction, 211
Abstract values, 124
Adherence, 2
Ad hominem fallacy claim, 179–180
Ad populum, 64
ADR. *see* Alternative dispute
  resolution (ADR)
Affordable Care Act, 88, 162, 167
Agreement method, of development of
  argument, 60, 61
Alternative decisions, 160, 161
  in finding propositions, 74
Alternative dispute resolution (ADR),
  38, 46–50
  arbitration, 47
  as argumentation, 49–50
  classification of, 47–49
  collaborative law, 47, 49
  defined, 46–47
  mediation, 47–48
  negotiation, 47, 48–49
  popularity of, 50
Ambiguity, language, 12
Analogy
  argument by, 63–64, 214–216,
    236–237
  commonplace of, 198–199
  definition by, 66–67
Analysis, arguments, 67–69, 71–82
  of claims, 80–82
  critical (*see* Critical analysis)
  guidelines for, 69
  parts of, 72
Appeal to pity, 180–181
Appraising argumentation, 25–36
  critical decision, 26
  reasonableness in, 27–31 (*see also*
    Reasonableness)
Arbitration, 47
Arguer, reputation of, 152–153
Argumentation
  alternative dispute resolution as,
    49–50
  analysis in (*see* Analysis, arguments)
  appraising in, 25–36 (*see also*
    Appraising argumentation)
  bases of reason in, 32–36
  in business (*see* Business)
  contexts for, 89–90
  as cooperative process, 44–45

defined, 2, 9
disagreements in, 124
elements of, 2–10 (*see also*
  Elements, argumentation)
formats for, 96
in government and politics (*see*
  Government/politics)
in law, 188–202 (*see also* Law)
pragma-dialectical approach to,
  181–182
in religion (*see* Religion)
scientific, 38, 40–41, 204–220
  (*see also* Science)
sense of, 37–50 (*see also* Sense, of
  argumentation)
starting points for, 32–36, 90 (*see also*
  Starting points, argumentation)
Argumentation ad populum, 178
Argumentativeness, 8, 180
Argumentative situation
  alternative decisions, 160, 161
  biases and, 162
  decision implementation plans, 162
  identifying questions/claims in, 160
  information seeking, 161–162
  refutation and, 159–162
  survey objectives/values, 160–161
  weigh costs/risks, 161
Argument by analogy, 63–64
  in religion, 236–237
  scientific use of, 214–216
Argument by cause, 60–61
  scientific use of, 212–213
Argument by cause to effect, 60
Argument by definition, 65–67
Argument by effect to cause, 60
Argument by generalization, 59–60,
  109–115
  in religion, 239–241
  scientific use of, 211–212, 220
Argument by narrative, in religion,
  237–238
Argument by paradox, in religion,
  238–239
Argument by sign, 62
  in business argumentation, 251
  in religion, 238
  scientific use of, 213–214
Argument from authority, 64–65
  in religion, 234–236
  scientific use of, 216–217

Arguments, 8–9
  by analogy, 63–64
  analysis of (*see* Analysis,
    arguments)
  from authority, 64–65
  by cause, 60–61
  characteristics of, 30–31, 68–69
  defined, 8
  definitions as, 65–67
  to develop values, 133
  force of, 55
  by generalization, 59–60, 109–115
  on law, 195–202
  by logic/deduction/syllogism/
    enthymeme, 57–59
  model of, 53–56
  nature of, 52–69
  order in, 68
  outline, 91–92
  overlapping, 68
  petitio principii, 177–178
  policy, 200–202
  scientific, 38, 40–41
  scientific method as, 220
  by sign, 62
  tu quoque, 177
  unreasonable, 27
Argumentum ad misericordium,
  180
Assertions
  of claims, 80
  and evidence, 118
Assertiveness, 180
Assessment
  of burden of proof, 87
  of presumption, 85–87
Attacks, on values, 131–132
Audience, rhetoric and, 20–21
Authority, 201
  appeal to, fallacy claim and, 178
  argument from, 64–65, 216–217,
    234–236
  definition by, 67
  as religious value, 136
Averages, 106, 113–114

B

Backing
  in model of argument, 54–55
Baconianism, 211
Bandwagon, 64

Basic beliefs, in business argumentation, 243
Begging the question, 177–178
Belief systems
  defined, 27
  reasonableness of, 27–28
Biases
  in critical decision making, 162
  in statistics, 112
Bill of Rights
  Article II of, 179
Booms and busts, 246
Burden of proof, 164
  assessment of, 87
  in business argumentation, 244–245
  in fallacy claims, 174–175
  and *prima facie* case, 191
Business, 242–256
  basic beliefs, 243
  commonplaces, 248–252
  credibility and, 255–256
  evidence and, 252–253
  facts in, 244
  forms of argument in, 248–252
  presumptions in, 244–246
  probabilities in, 246–248
  support in, 252–256
  values and, 253–255
Business cycles, probability of, 247

C

Case, 83
  building (*see* Case building)
Case building, 83–100
  communication to specific decision makers in, 95–100
  developing vision in, 93–95
  preliminary steps in, 83–89
  preparing presentation, 89–92
  ultimate purpose and, 84
Cause and effect, in business argument, 249–250
Cause to effect arguments, 60, 61
Central tendencies, 106
Certainty, attraction of, 12–13
Changes
  probability of, 247–248
  in scientific theory, 209–211
Church
  as religious value, 137
  role of, 228
Circular reasoning, 177
Claims, 3–5
  analysis of, 80–82
  clarifying assertions of, 80
  defined, 3

differences in, 5
empirically grounded, 217
of facts, 207–208
factual, 3–4
fallacy (*see* Fallacy claims)
identifying, 75, 77, 160
issue *vs.*, 5
locations for disagreement, 81–82
in model of argument, 53
policy, 4–5, 121, 259–261
political (*see* Political claims)
of political argumentation, 258
propositions and, 7
public morality and, 4
sequence of, 97–100
strength of support for, 81–82
subclaim, 3
value, 4, 121
Clarity, as generic value, 79
Collaborative law, 47, 49
Committee hearings, 262–265
  characteristics of, 263
  forms of argumentation in, 264–265
  records in, 263–264
  storytelling, 265
Commonplaces
  of analogy, 198–199
  in business argumentation, 248–252
  consider only questions posed, 196–197
  decide only enough to dispose, 196
  in legal argumentation, 196–202
  legislative intent, 200
  stare decisis, 198
  as starting point for argumentation, 35–36, 90
Communication
  constraints on, 95
  counterargument in, 95–96
  to decision makers, 95–100
  good, rules of, 172–173
  of refutation, 170–173
Comparative advantage analysis, 99–100
Comparison and contrast, 248
Competence, and credibility, 142
Concrete values, 124
Conditional cause, 213
Conflict of interest, 185
Consensus, 49
Consider only questions posed, 196–197
Consistency, 79–80, 199
Constructive approach, to refutation, 166
Context
  in decision-making, 89–90
Convincing vision, 93–95

of decision makers, 93–94
example of, 94–95
story of, 94
Cooperation
  breach of conversational, 183–185
  conflict of interest, 185
  in feminisms, 44–45
  obfuscation, 184
  quantity maxim, violations of, 184–185
  reckless disregard for truth, 185
Cooperative, 157
Correlation method, of development of argument, 60
Cost/benefit, in business argument, 250–251
Costs, in finding propositions, 74, 161
Counterargument, 88
  and presentation of case, 95–96
Counterplan, 167
Credibility, 8, 141–154
  characteristics of, 142–144
  competence and, 142
  decision makers' values, identification of, 148–149
  defined, 142
  direct, 144–145
  dynamism and, 143, 151
  evidence and, 149
  of factions, 168–169
  forms of, 144–146
  goodwill and, 143
  homophily and, 142, 143–144
  indirect, 146
  legislative action, 267
  opponent's, attack on, 150–151
  organizations and, 149–150
  in political campaign, 270, 276
  principles for use of, 146–151
  in refutation, 276–277
  reputation and, 146–147
  secondary, 145–146
  sincerity and, 147–148
  source of, 153–154
  sphere dependence of, 151–154
  as support for business argumentation, 255–256
  of testimony, 114–115
  trustworthiness and, 143
  verbal aggressiveness and, 180
Criteria, 25, 31
  arguments based on, 26
  in case patterns, 100

Criteria (*continued*)
defined, 10
for judging claims, 81
logic and, 199
Critical analysis
alternative decisions and, 74
costs/risks in, 74
of decision makers, 162–165
to discover proposition, 72–75
identifying questions/claims in, 73
information seeking and, 73
of proposition, 75–80
surveying objectives/values in, 73–74
Critical decision making. *see also*
Decision makers
biases in, 162
context in, 89–90
defined, 10
elements of, 10–23 (*see also*
Elements, critical decision making)
to find proposition, 72–75
goals of, 167
in government/politics, 262–265
rules for, 59
stages of, 73–75, 160–162
Critical thinking, 13–15
Criticism, 9–10
Culture, as evidence, 233–234

D
Debates, 96, 157
political, 274–275
Deception, 182–183
Decide only enough to dispose, 196
Decision makers. *see also* Critical
decision making
analyzing, 162–165
appropriate, 2–3
communication to specific, 95–100
(*see also* Communication)
credibility and, 151
and decision-making process, 97
defined, 163
experience with instances, 111
factions acting as, 164–165
goals, 163–164
identification of values, credibility
and, 148–149
presumptions of, 164
values to, 132–133
and value system, 126
vision of, 93–94
Decision makers' value systems,
132–133
Decision making. *see* Critical decision
making

Decision-making groups, 17, 18
Deduction
arguments by, 57–59
Definitions, as argument, 65–67
by analogy, 66–67
by authority, 67
by example, 66
formal, 66
and formation of warrants,
197–198
functional, 66
Determinism, free will *vs.*, 225
Dialectic, 15–17
defined, 15
vs. rhetoric, 15, 16
Dialogue
external, 15–17
internal, 13–15, 18
Difference method, of development of
argument, 60, 61
Differentiation, 249
Direct credibility, 144–145
Disagreement
in argumentation, 124
locations for, 81–82
Discourse on Method (Descartes), 29
Discover the proposition, 72
Discussion rules
fallacies as violations of, 181–182
Divided government, 268
Doctrinal meaning, in text, 231
Documented evidence, 117–118
Dynamism, and credibility,
143, 151, 255

E
Effect to cause arguments, 60
Elements, argumentation, 2–10
adherence, 2
appropriate decision makers, 2–3
argument, 8–9
claims, 3–5 (*see also* Claims)
criticism, 9–10
issues, 5–6
proposition, 6–7
support, 7–8 (*see also* Support)
Elements, critical decision making,
10–23
critical thinking, 13–15
dialectic, 15–17
rhetoric, 20–23 (*see also* Rhetoric)
spheres, 17–20 (*see also* Spheres)
toleration of uncertainty, 11–13
Empirical adequacy, 207
Empirical knowledge building, 209
Empirically grounded claims, 217

Enthymeme, 23
arguments by, 57–59
Equipoise, 191
Ethics
defined, 127
values and, 127–128
Ethos, 23, 142, 144
Etymology, 67
Evidence, 7, 102–117
assertion and, 118
to build credibility, 149
to develop values, 133
documented, 117–118
expert, 115–116
forms of, 103–109 (*see also* Forms,
evidence)
hearsay, 115
negative, 117
ordinary, 115–116
principles for use of, 109–115
and refutation, 276
in religious argumentation, 229–232
reluctant, 116–117
role, in spheres, 103
scientific use of, 217–219
sphere dependence of, 115–118
as support in business
argumentation, 252–253
Evil, 226
Example
of convincing vision, 94–95
definitions by, 66
as form of evidence, 103–105, 252
Experience, as evidence, 232–233
Expert evidence, 115–116
External dialogue, 15–17

F
Factions
acting as decision makers,
164–165
credibility of, 168–169
defined, 156
Facts
in business, 244
claims of, 207–208
narratives and, 189–190
as starting point for argumentation,
32–33, 90
testimony of, 108–109
Factual claim, 3–4
Faith, as religious value, 137
Fallacy claims, 174–186
ad hominem, 179–180
appeal to pity, 180–181
burden of proof in, 174–175

characteristics of, 174–175
defined, 174
as incorrect logic, 176
and logic, 175–177
post hoc, 179
in refutation, 186
social guides to, 182–185 (*see also*
Social guides, fallacy claims)
of sophistry, 177–181
violations of discussion rules and,
181–182
Fanaticism, 9
"Feeling of doubt," 72
Feminist argumentation, 41–46
cooperation in, 44–45
and defense of purely rational
argument, 46
gender influences on reception/
presentation, 45–46
personal testimony role, 43–44
and recognition, 46
Feminist theory, 38
Filed in a timely manner, 197
Flowsheet, 172–173
Force, of argument, 55
Formal definition, 66
Formal logic, 58
Forms, evidence, 103–109
combining, 107–108
example, 103–105
statistics, 105–107
testimony, 108–109
Fortiori, A, 35
Framebreaking, 167–168
Free will *vs.* determinism, 225
Frequency, 106
Functional definition, 66
Future, uncertainty of, 13
Future facts, 4

G

Gender, and audience reception/
presentation, 45–46
Generalization, arguments by, 59–60,
109–115
scientific use of, 211–212, 220
God
human beings relationship to, 225, 227
nature of, 224–225
as religious value, 136
Good reasons, 37–39
tests of, 39
Good story, 38, 39–40
in committee hearings, 265
in political campaign, 271–272
Goodwill, and credibility, 143

Government/politics, 257–278.
see also Political argumentation
committee hearings, 262–265 (*see also*
Committee hearings)
legislative action, 265–269 (*see also*
Legislative action)
political campaigns, 269–274
(*see also* Political campaigns)
role of debates in, 274–275
Graphs, and statistical data,
112–113
Grounds
in model of argument, 53–54
Group structuration, 17–18

H

Hearsay evidence, 115
Historical meaning, in text, 231
Homology, 215
Homophily, 142, 143–144
Human beings
nature of, 225–226
relationship to God, 225, 227
as religious value, 136
Hypothetical example, as form of
evidence, 104
Hypothetico-deductive method,
210, 220

I

Illustrations, as form of evidence,
103–105
Image, 151
in political campaign, 269–270
Implied values, 121–122, 133
Incorrect logic, fallacy claims as, 176
Incrementalism, 88
Indirect credibility, 146
in spheres, 154
Information seeking, 73, 161–162
Inherency, as generic value, 79
Inoculation, refutation by, 278
Instances. *see also* Evidence
credible sources for, 111–112
decision makers' experience, 111
examples/statistics, 111
negative, 110
real, 111
relevant, 110
representative, 109
specific, 217–218
sufficient number of, 109
value characteristics of, 110
Instrumental values, 122–124
Rokeach's list, 123

Internal dialogue, 13–15, 18
Interpretation
of sacred documents, 230–232
strategies for language, 32, 90
Irrelevant statements, 183
Issues, 5–6
argument on, 150–151
defined, 5
determination, 75–77
in political campaign, 269–270
in political claims, 259–261
possible, 90–91
rank-order, 77–79
stock, 88
stock issue analysis, 98

L

Laches, 201
Language
ambiguity of, 12
defined, 12, 32
fallacies in, 179
interpretation strategies, 32, 90
Language usage
as starting point for
argumentation, 90
Law, 188–202
arguments on, 195–202
commonplaces in, 196–202
defined, 206
narratives in, 189–195 (*see also*
Narratives)
"Leave no shot unanswered,"
277–278
Ledbetter v. Goodyear, 188–202
Goodyear's narrative, 192–193
jury's decision of, 193–194
Justice Alito's narrative, 194
Justice Ginsberg's narrative,
194–195
Ledbetter's narrative, 191–192
Legislative action, 265–269
amendment process, 267
credibility, 267
as impersonal, 266
as nonconfrontational, 266
relations between legislators/
executives, 268–269
Legislative intent, 200
Level of activity, spheres and, 18–19
Lincoln–Douglas debates, 275
Listener benefit, 38
Literature review, 220
Locate the points of disagreement,
81–82
Loci, 35

Logic
  arguments by, 57–59
  and criteria, 199
  and fallacy claims, 175–177
  formal, 58
  informal, 58, 176
Logos, 23

M
Majoritarianism, 266
Markets, penetration of, 251
McCarthyism, 158
Mean, 113
Media, and political argumentation, 273–274
Median, 113
Mediation, 47–48
Mind, reasonableness of, 29–30
Missing parts, in arguments, 68
Mode, 113
Modus ponens, 176
Modus tollens, 176
Momentum, 169
Moral behavior
  nature of, 226
  as religious value, 137
Moral obligation, 38
Motivated sequence, 98
Mystical meaning, in text, 231

N
Narratives, 40, 64
  argument by, 237–238
  and construction of facts, 189–190
  in law, 189–195
    Ledbetter v. Goodyear (see *Ledbetter v. Goodyear*)
    and *prima facie* case, 190–191
    Nat'l R.R. Passenger Corp. v. Morgan, 198–199
Natural theology, 224
Negative evidence, 117
Negative instances, 110
Negative values, 122
Negotiation, 47, 48–49
  causes of, 48
  rejection, reasons for, 49
New York Times v. Sullivan, 185
Noncontradiction, 199

O
Obfuscation, 184
Objectives, in finding propositions, 73–74, 160–161
Operationalizing, 220

Opinion, testimony of, 108–109
Opponents
  analyzing, 165
  attack on, and credibility, 150–151
  probing, 171–172
Order
  in arguments, 68
  in science, 134, 206–207
Ordinary evidence, 115–116
Organization, to build credibility, 149–150
Overlapping arguments, 68

P
Paradox
  argument by, 238–239
  defined, 238
Parts missing, in arguments, 68
Past facts, 4
Pathos, 23
Peer review, 209
Penetration, of markets, 251
People, political campaign linkage to, 270–271
Personal authority, 38
Personal gain *vs.* Truth, 208–209
Personal spheres, 18–19
Personal testimony
  role in feminism, 43–44
Persuasion, 30–31
Petitio principii argument, 177–178
Philosophical meaning, in text, 231
Pity, appeal to, 180–181
Policy arguments, 200–202
Policy claims, 4–5, 121, 260–261
Political argumentation. *see also* Government/politics
  claims of, 258
  media and, 273–274
  nature of, 258–262
  overview, 257–258
Political campaigns, 269–274
  credibility in, 270, 276
  issues/images in, 269–270
  linked to people/public, 270–271
  media and, 273–274
  refutation in, 275–278
  storytelling in, 271–272
Political claims
  content of, 258–259
  development of, 259–261
Political debates, 274–275
Politics. *see* Government/politics
Popularity
  appeal to, fallacy claim and, 178
Positionality, 210

Positive values, 122
Post hoc fallacy, 179
Posture, for refutation, 165–170
  constructive approach, 166
  and criticism of support, 169–170
  framebreaking, 167–168
  goals of decision making, 167
  momentum and, 169
  position, defending, 166–167
  testing factions' credibility, 168–169
Power authority, 38
Pragma-dialectical approach, 181–182
Prediction, in science, 135
Preponderance of evidence, 190
Present facts, 3
Presumptions
  assessment of, 85–87
  in business argumentation, 244–246
  of decision makers, 164
  defined, 33
  as starting point for argumentation, 33–34, 90
Prima facie cases, 88–89, 190–191
Priority
  of claims, 97–100
  of issues, 77–79
  order in arguments, 68
  of values, 126–127
Probability
  in business argumentation, 246–248
  of change, 247–248
  rhetoric and, 21–22
  as starting point for argumentation, 34–35, 90
  statistical, 21–22, 35, 106–107
Probing, opponents, 171–172
Problem-solution format, 98–99
Process
  refutation, 157
Proof, rhetoric and, 22–23
Prophetic meaning, in text, 231
Proposition of cause, 207
Propositions, 6–7
  arguments for/against, 76
  and case building, 84–85
  and claims, 7
  defined, 6
  find, critical analysis to, 72–75
  selection of, 74–75
Public, political campaign linkage to, 270–271
Public morality, 4
Public screen, 258
Public spheres, 19, 258

Q

Qualifiers, in model of argument, 55
Quantitative science, sphere of, 206
Quantity maxim, violations of,
    184–185
Quasi-logic, 58
Quest for Certainty, The (Dewey), 12
Questions/questioning
    identification, 73, 160
    in probing opponents, 171–172
    in religious argumentation, 223–229

R

Rationality, in science, 135
Raw numbers, 105–106
Reasonableness, 27–31
    of belief systems, 27–28
    good reasons in, 37–39
    of mind, 29–30
    of social influence, 30
    of thinking, 28–29
    unreasonable arguments and, 27
Rebuttals, in model of argument,
    55–56
Reckless disregard, for truth, 185
Record, in committee hearings,
    263–264
Reductio ad absurdum, 200
Refusal to reason, 183
Refutation, 156–173
    approaching, 158–159
    communication of, 170–173
    cooperative character of, 157
    credibility in, 276–277
    defined, 156
    evidence and, 276
    fallacy claims in (*see* Fallacy claims)
    in government/politics, 262–265
    by inoculation, 278
    "leave no shot unanswered,"
        277–278
    in political campaigns, 275–278
    posture for, selection of, 165–170
        (*see also* Posture, for refutation)
    process of, 156–158
    setting framework for, 159–165
    silence in, 159–160
    steps in, 170–171
    storytelling in, 277
    testing proposals with values,
        275–276
Relevance, as generic value, 79
Religion, 222–241
    argument by analogy in, 236–237
    argument by generalization in,
        239–241

argument by narrative in, 237–238
argument by paradox in, 238–239
argument by sign in, 238
argument from authority in,
    234–236
evidence in, 229–234
science and, 138–139
values in, 135–137
Reluctant evidence, 116–117
Reluctant witnesses, 153
Replication, 209
Reputation
    of arguer, 152–153
    defined, 146
    developing credibility from,
        146–147
Reservations, in model of argument,
    55–56
Residues method, of development of
    argument, 60
Retroduction, 211
Revealed theology, 224
Revelation, as evidence, 233
Rhetoric, 20–23
    audience and, 20–21
    defined, 20
    dialectic *vs.*, 15, 16
    probability and, 21–22
    proof, 22–23
Risks, in finding propositions, 74, 161

S

Sacred documents
    as evidence, 229
Salience, as generic value, 79
Salvation
    nature of, 227–228
    as religious value, 137
Sample, 59
Schenck v. United States, 97
Science
    argumentation, 38, 40–41, 204–220
    argument by analogy in, 214–216
    argument by cause in, 212–213
    argument by generalization in,
        211–212
    argument by sign in, 213–214
    argument from authority in,
        216–217
    critiques of, 205
    defined, 204–206
    and evidence, 217–219
    order in, 134, 206–207
    prediction in, 135
    quantitative, 206
    rationality in, 135

and religion, 138–139
statistics in, 218–219
testimony in, 219
tradition of argumentation in,
    207–210
usefulness in, 134–135
values in, 206–207
Scientific revolution, 209
Scientific theory
    changes in, 209–211
Secondary credibility, 145–146
    in spheres, 153–154
Sense, of argumentation, 37–50
    alternative dispute resolution (*see*
        Alternative dispute resolution
        (ADR))
    feminist theory and, 38, 40–46
        (*see also* Feminist argumentation)
    good reasons and, 37–39
    good story and, 39–40
    ways of making, 38
Sign, argument by, 62, 213–214, 238,
    251
Significance, as generic value, 79
Silence, in refutation, 159–160
Sin, 226–227
Sincerity, and credibility, 147–148
Skepticism, and refutation, 158
Skills gap, defined, 100
Sleeper effect, 149
Social constructionist, 42
Social groups, 18
Social guides, fallacy claims, 182–185
    breach of conversational
        cooperation, 183–185
    intend deception, 182–183
    refusal to reason, 183
Social influence, reasonableness of, 30
Social pressure, 38
Sophistry, fallacy claims of, 177–181
Specific instances, 217–218
Sphere dependence
    of credibility, 151–154
    of evidence, 115–118
    of values, 133–139
Spheres, 17–20
    complexity of, 20
    defined, 17–18
    dependence (*see* Sphere dependence)
    indirect credibility in, 154
    and level of activity, 18–19
    location of, 18
    personal, 18–19
    public, 19
    of quantitative science, 206
    role of evidence in, 103

Spheres (*continued*)
  rules of, 96–97
  secondary credibility in, 153–154
  technical, 19
  ultimate purpose, 19–20
Stare decisis, 196, 197, 198
Starting points, argumentation,
    32–36
  business, 243–252
  commonplaces, 35–36, 90
  facts, 32–33, 90
  language interpretation strategies,
    32, 90
  presumptions, 33–34, 90
  probability, 34–35, 90
Stated values, 121–122
Statistics
  bias in, 112
  central tendencies, 106
  comparison, 114
  as form of evidence, 105–107, 252
  graphic representation of data,
    112–113
  measure, 112–114
  probability, 21–22, 35, 106–107,
    246–248
  raw numbers, 105–106
  in science, 218–219
  trends, 107
Status quo, defending, 166–167
Stock issue analysis, 98
Stock issues, 88
Storytelling
  in committee hearings, 265
  as form of evidence, 104
  in political campaign, 271–272
  in refutation, 277
Subclaim, defined, 3
Success, in business argumentation, 243
Suffering, 227
Support, 7–8
  in business argumentation, 252–256
  credibility (*see* Credibility)
  criticism of, refutation and,
    169–170
  defined, 7
  evidence (*see* Evidence)
  strength, for claims, 81–82
  values (*see* Values)
Syllogism
  arguments by, 57–59
  logical analysis, 199

T

Task-oriented small groups, 18
Technical spheres, 19
Terminal values, 122–124
  Rokeach's list, 123
Testimony
  in committee hearings, 265
  credibility of, 114–115
  of fact, 108–109
  in feminism, 43–44
  as form of evidence, 108–109,
    252–253
  of opinion, 108–109
  in science, 219
Text
  as evidence in religious
    argumentation, 229–232
  meanings in, 231
Themes, of religious argumentation,
    228–229
Thinking
  critical, 13–15
  reasonableness of, 28–29
Time, as commonplace, 35–36
Topoi, 35
Tradition, as evidence, 232
Trends, statistical, 107
Trustworthiness
  and credibility, 143
  of sacred documents, 230
Truth, personal gain *vs.,* 208–209
T-Test, 213
Tu quoque argument, 177

U

Ultimate purpose
  identification, 84
  spheres, 19–20
Uncertainty
  ambiguity of language, 12
  of future, 13
  as pervasive, 11–12
  toleration of, 11–13
Uncontroversial matter, 75, 77
Underrepresented groups, 9
Unreasonable arguments, 27
Usage, 67
Usefulness, in science, 134–135

V

Validity, 58, 199
Value hierarchy, 126

Values, 7, 120–139
  abstract, 124
  attacks on, 131–132
  changes, limits of, 130–131
  characteristics of, 121–124
  in claims, 121, 128–129
  concrete, 124
  critical, 79–80
  of decision makers, 148–149
  to decision makers, 132–133
  defined, 121
  development, evidence/arguments
    and, 133
  and ethics, 127–128
  in finding propositions, 73–74,
    160–161
  implied, 121–122, 133
  instrumental, 122–124
  negative, 122
  positive, 122
  principles for use of, 128–133
  recognization, in warrants,
    129–130
  in religion, 135–137, 228–229
  in scientific argument, 134–135
  sphere dependence of, 133–139
  stated, 121–122
  as support in business
    argumentation, 253–255
  terminal, 122–124
  testing proposals with, 275–276
  in value systems, 124–127
Value systems, 124–127
  grading of values in, 126–127
  of science, 138–139
  traditional, 125–126
Verbal aggression, 8, 180
Viable constructive position, 166
Vision, convincing, 93–95

W

Warrants
  formation of, definitions and,
    197–198
  in model of argument, 54
  values reorganization in, 129–130
Wisdom of crowds, 64
  as commonplace in business
    argumentation, 252
Wizard's First Rule, The, 27
Wordsmiths, 67
World views, reasonableness, 28

PCL COMM 311 #1
Rieke, Richard D.
Argumentation and critical
decision making

P9-CKY-789

LIBRARY

Linguistics *for* Everyone

An Introduction

Second Edition

Kristin Denham
Western Washington University

Anne Lobeck
Western Washington University

CENGAGE

Australia • Brazil • Mexico • Singapore • United Kingdom • United States

American River College Library
4700 College Oak Drive
Sacramento, CA 95841

Linguistics for Everyone: An Introduction, Second Edition
Kristin Denham, Anne Lobeck

Senior Publisher: Lyn Uhl

Publisher: Michael Rosenberg

Development Editor: Joan M. Flaherty

Assistant Editor: Erin Bosco

Editorial Assistant: Rebecca Donahue

Media Editor: Janine Tangney

Marketing Program Manager: Gurpreet Saran

Marketing Communications Manager: Linda Yip

Senior Content Project Manager: Michael Lepera

Art Director: Marissa Falco

Senior Print Buyer: Betsy Donaghey

Rights Acquisition Specialist: Jessica Elias

Production Service/Compositor: PreMediaGlobal

Text and Cover Designer: Maxine Ressler

Cover Art: iStockphoto

© 2013, 2010 Cengage Learning, Inc.

ALL RIGHTS RESERVED. No part of this work covered by the copyright herein may be reproduced, transmitted, stored or used in any form or by any means graphic, electronic, or mechanical, including but not limited to photocopying, recording, scanning, digitizing, taping, Web distribution, information networks, or information storage and retrieval systems, except as permitted under Section 107 or 108 of the 1976 United States Copyright Act, without the prior written permission of the publisher.

For product information and technology assistance, contact us at
Cengage Customer & Sales Support, 1-800-354-9706
For permission to use material from this text or product, submit all requests online at **www.cengage.com/permissions**
Further permissions questions can be emailed to
permissionrequest@cengage.com

Library of Congress Control Number: 2011940389

ISBN-13: 978-1-111-34438-2

ISBN-10: 1-111-34438-8

Cengage
20 Channel Center Street
Boston, MA 02210
USA

Cengage is a leading provider of customized learning solutions with office locations around the globe, including Singapore, the United Kingdom, Australia, Mexico, Brazil and Japan. Locate your local office at: **international.cengage.com/region.**

Cengage products are represented in Canada by Nelson Education, Ltd.

To learn more about Cengage platforms and services, register or access your online learning solution, or purchase materials for your course, visit **www.cengage.com.**

Printed in Mexico
Print Number: 09   Print Year: 2020

Contents

PREFACE   XVII
ACKNOWLEDGMENTS   XXIII

1   What Is Language and How Do We Study It?   1

WHAT IS LANGUAGE?   3
   Our Language Expertise   3
   Acquiring versus Learning a Language   4

HUMAN LANGUAGE AND ANIMAL COMMUNICATION   4
   Can Other Animals Learn Language?   6
   Two Case Studies: Washoe and Nim   6
   Did You Know . . . ? Rico and Chaser, Smarter Than the Average Dogs   7

WHAT IS GRAMMAR?   7
   The Components of Grammar   8
   What Is Grammatical?   9
      Prescriptive and Descriptive Grammar   10
      When Prescription and Description Overlap   10
      Modification: Another Overlap   11
   Grammar across Space and Time   12
   Universal Grammar   13
   Linguistics in the News The Language Blog and Eggcorns   14
      Parameters   15
      Sign Language Grammar   16
      Sign Language versus Body Language   17
   Language Alive! Sign Language Diversity   17

THE SCIENTIFIC STUDY OF LANGUAGE   18
   Noam Chomsky and Generative Grammar   18
   Did You Know . . . ? Noam Chomsky   19
   Influences on Modern Linguistics   20
      Rationalism and Empiricism   20
      Structural Linguistics   21

LINGUISTICS TODAY   22
   Accent on The Linguistic Society of America   23
Summary   24
Sources and Resources   25
Review, Practice, and Explore   25

2 The Human Capacity for Language   31

OUR CAPACITY TO ACQUIRE LANGUAGE   32

What Children's "Mistakes" Tell Us   33

Mouses and *Foots*: Overgeneralizing Rules   33

Language Alive! One *Wug* and Two . . . *Wugs*?   34

Evidence for Universal Grammar   34

Children Don't Learn by Analogy   36

Stages of First Language Acquisition   37

The Prelinguistic Stage: The Early Months   37

The Babbling Stage: 4 to 8 Months   38

Did You Know . . . ? How Do You Study an Infant?   38

The One-Word Stage: 9 to 18 Months   38

The Two-Word Stage: 18 to 24 Months   39

Language Alive! Hardwiring and Order of Acquisition   40

The Early Multiword Stage: 24 to 30 Months   40

The Later Multiword Stage: 30 Months and Older   41

A Critical Period for Language Acquisition?   43

Did You Know . . . ? Baby Talk and Parentese   43

Did You Know . . . ? What about *Baby Einstein*?   44

Acquisition and Isolation: Victor and Genie   45

Sign Language Acquisition   45

SECOND LANGUAGE ACQUISITION   46

Is It Learning or Acquisition?   46

Interlanguage Grammar   46

Social Aspects of Second Language Acquisition   47

Second Language Acquisition and Universal Grammar   48

TWO NATIVE LANGUAGES: BILINGUALISM   48

Misperceptions about Bilingualism   48

OUR CAPACITY TO CREATE LANGUAGE   49

Pidgins and Creoles   50

Nicaraguan Sign Language   52

Linguistics in the News A Gene for Language?   53

LANGUAGE AND THE BRAIN   54

Language Intelligence?   54

Specific Language Impairment   54

Linguistic Savants   54

Williams Syndrome   55

A Language Center in the Brain?   55

Did You Know . . . ? Poor Phineas Gage   58

Broca's Aphasia   58

Wernicke's Aphasia   58

More Evidence for Lateralization   59

           Dichotic Listening 60

           Split-Brain Patients 60

           Brain Imaging 61

      Accent on Clinical Linguistics 61

Summary 62

Sources and Resources 63

Review, Practice, and Explore 65

3 Phonetics: Describing Sounds 69

SOUNDS AND SYMBOLS 71

PHONEMES 72

CONSONANTS 72

      Voiced and Voiceless Consonants 73

      Did You Know . . . ? Visible Speech 75

      Place of Articulation 76

           Bilabial 76

      Language Alive! A Disappearing Sound 76

           Labiodental 77

           Interdental 77

           Alveolar 77

           Palatal 77

           Velar 78

           Glottal 78

      Manner of Articulation 78

           Stops 78

           Fricatives 79

      Language Alive! Why Do We Spell Words with *-ough*? 79

           Affricates 79

      Linguistics in the News Peter Ladefoged: Pioneer in Phonetics 80

           Nasals 81

      Did You Know . . . ? Mom Is Bob 81

           Glides 81

           Liquids 81

      Language Alive! Forgotten Clusters 82

      Why All These Distinctions? 82

      Slips of the Tongue 84

VOWELS 85

      Language Alive! Do *Dawn* and *Don* Rhyme? 86

      Diphthongs 86

      Syllabic Consonants 88

      Other Vowel Distinctions 88

      Language Alive! Double Is Not Long 89

Vowel Shifts 90

The Great Vowel Shift 91

The Northern Cities Chain Shift 92

The Southern Vowel Shift 92

PHONEMES AND ALLOPHONES 94

Accent on Product Naming 95

Summary 96

Sources and Resources 97

Review, Practice, and Explore 97

4 Phonology: The Sound Patterns of Language 103

PHONEMES AND ALLOPHONES 104

Did You Know . . . ? Babies Are Better at Language 107

Language Alive! Long-Lost English Allophones 108

ASSIMILATION RULES 109

Vowel Nasalization 109

Alveolar Nasal Assimilation 109

Nasal Assimilation 109

Palatalization 110

Did You Know . . . ? Invented Spelling 110

Voicing Assimilation 111

DISSIMILATION RULES 113

Dissimilation of Liquids and Nasal Sounds 113

Dissimilation of Fricative Sounds 114

INSERTION RULES 114

Insertion of Vowels 114

Insertion of Consonants 115

Insertion of Voiceless Stop 115

Insertion of /y/ 115

DELETION RULES 116

Deletion of /r/ after Vowels 116

Language Alive! Where the Heck Is <h>? 116

Deletion of Fricative Next to Fricative 117

Did You Know . . . ? Where Do You Get Tenashoes? 117

Deletion of Like Sounds or Syllables 117

Simplification of Consonant Clusters 117

Simplification of Syllable-Final Consonant Clusters 118

FRONTING RULES 118

Fronting of Velar Nasal to Alveolar Nasal 118

Fronting in Child Language 118

Fronting of /x/ 119

EXCHANGE RULES 119

Exchanging /s/ and a Consonant   119
Language Alive! What's Wrong with *Aks*?   119
Exchanging /r/ and a Vowel   120
Exchanging Syllable Onsets   120

MULTIPLE-RULE PROCESSES 120

Language Alive! Going Nucular   121

SUPRASEGMENTALS 122

Syllables   122
The Structure of the Syllable   123
    Phonotactics   123
    Children's Syllables   124
    Syllable Structure Variety   125
    Slips of the Tongue and Syllables   126
Stress   127
Intonation   128
Linguistics in the News Tone Languages and Perfect Pitch   129
Did You Know . . . ? Abbish versus Ubby Dubby   132
Accent on Linguistics and Reading   132

Summary   134
Sources and Resources   134
Review, Practice, and Explore   134

5   Morphology: Words and Their Parts   141

MORPHEMES AND MEANING 143

Morphemes and Syllables   144
Recognizing Morphemes   144

WORD CLASSES 146

Content Words   146
Function Words   146
Did You Know . . . ? Pooh on Pronouns   147
Word Classes and Our Mental Lexicon   148
Free and Bound Morphemes   149
Affixes   149
Language Alive! Embiggen His Soul!   150
Roots   151

DERIVATIONAL AFFIXATION 152

Language Alive! What about *Cranapple*?   153
Language Alive! Word-*orama*!   154

AFFIXATION AND OUR MENTAL LEXICON 155

Drawing Word Trees   156

Word Trees and Ambiguity   159
Inflectional Affixation   159
Inflectional Affixation of English Nouns   162
Number   162
Linguistics in the News Arkansas's Apostrophe   163
Case   164
Did You Know . . . ? Linguists in Hollywood   165
Language Alive! The Battle over *Whom*   167
 Gender   167
Inflectional Affixation of English Verbs   168
 Infinitives, Present Tense, and Past Tense   168
 Present and Past Participles   170
Suppletive Verbs and Adjectives   172
Language Alive! *Ain't* Ain't Had It Easy!   173
Accent on Field Linguistics   174
Summary   175
Sources and Resources   175
Review, Practice, and Explore   176

6 Morphological Typology and Word Formation   183

MORPHOLOGICAL TYPOLOGY   184
Synthetic Languages   185
Did You Know . . . ? Solid Roundish Objects and Mushy Matter   188
Analytic Languages   189
Mixed Typological Systems   189

THE MORPHOLOGY OF OTHER LANGUAGES   191

WORD FORMATION PROCESSES   191
Slang versus New Words   192
Linguistics in the News F***ing Brilliant! FCC Rulings on Profanity   193
Recent New Words   194
Did You Know . . . ? The Truth about *Truthiness*   195
Coining   196
Compounding   197
Eponyms   199
Retronyms   199
Blends   200
Conversions   200
Language Alive! Blimey!   201
Acronyms   201
Language Alive! Ms.   203
Clipping   203

Backformation   204
Reduplication   205
Accent on Lexicographers   206
Summary   207
Sources and Resources   208
Review, Practice, and Explore   208

7 Syntax: Heads and Phrases   215

NOUNS AND NOUN PHRASES   217
A Phrase Structure Rule for Noun Phrases   218

VERBS AND VERB PHRASES   219
Language Alive! How Many Modals?   220
A Phrase Structure Rule for Verb Phrases   221
Evidence for the Aux Position   221
Language Alive! Don't Use Double Negatives. NOT!   222
Subject-Auxiliary Inversion   222
English Do Insertion   224
Language Alive! English Didn't Always Do   225
Emphatic and Main Verb Do   225
A Phrase Structure Rule for Clauses   226

ADJECTIVES AND ADJECTIVE PHRASES   227
Adjective Phrase Positions   228
Did You Know . . . ? The Root of Trees   229
A Variable Phrase   230
Linguistics in the News What's the Right Answer?   231

ADVERBS AND ADVERB PHRASES   232
Adverb Phrase Positions   232

PREPOSITIONS AND PREPOSITIONAL PHRASES   233
Prepositional Phrase Positions   234
Did You Know . . . ? Syntax in the "Real" World   236

SUMMARY OF PHRASE STRUCTURE RULES   236

MORE CLAUSES   237
Subjects and Predicates   237
Independent and Subordinate Clauses   238
What Is a Sentence?   239
Accent on Teaching with Trees   241
Summary   242
Sources and Resources   242
Review, Practice, and Explore   243

8 Syntax: Phrase Structure and Syntactic Rules   251

HIERARCHICAL STRUCTURE AND AMBIGUITY   254

Ambiguity   255

Recursion   256

Linguistics in the News Starling Syntax?   259

SILENT SYNTAX   260

EVIDENCE FOR PHRASES AND CLAUSES   262

Substitution   262

Language Alive! Silent Pronoun?   264

Pronouns and Ambiguity   265

Pronoun Reference   266

Did You Know . . . ? Who Are *They*, Anyway?   267

Language Alive! Pronouns, Prestige, and Illogical Rules   268

Conjunctions and Coordination   269

Coordination and Ambiguity   270

Language Alive! Sex and Syntax   271

MOVEMENT AND DELETION   272

Deep and Surface Structure   272

Deletion Rules   273

Verb Phrase Deletion   273

Did You Know . . . ? "Does She . . . or Doesn't She?"   274

Gapping   275

Constraints on Deletion   275

Reordering Phrases: Movement   277

Did You Know . . . ? Passive Should Be Avoided?   278

Constraints on Movement   278

Wh-Movement   279

Accent on Psycholinguists   282

Summary   283

Sources and Resources   283

Review, Practice, and Explore   284

9 Semantics: Making Meaning with Words   291

MAKING MEANING   292

Semantic Deviance   292

LEXICAL SEMANTICS   294

Meaning Classifications: Semantic Features   296

Noun Classes   296

Language Alive! *Is* the Team Playing? *Are* the Team Playing?   298

Entailment and Markedness   298

Meaning Subclassifications: Semantic Fields   300

MEANING RELATIONSHIPS: THE NYMS 301
　　Opposite Meanings: Antonymy 301
　　Did You Know . . . ? Can Something Be *Very Dead*? 302
　　Similar Meanings: Synonymy 303
　　　　Euphemisms 303
　　Meaning Categories: Hyponymy 304
　　Related Meanings: Polysemy 305
　　Different Meanings: Homonymy 306
　　Many Meanings: Lexical Ambiguity 306
　　Vagueness 306
　　Linguistics in the News Talking Right . . . and Left 307

MEANING CHANGE: SEMANTIC SHIFT 308

MAKING NEW MEANINGS: FIGURATIVE LANGUAGE 310
　　Language Alive! Shifts in Meaning: Progress or Decay? 310
　　Connecting Meanings: Metaphor 312
　　　　Types of Metaphors 312
　　Did You Know . . . ? Hearing Colors 315
　　Comparing Meanings: Simile 315
　　Idioms 316
　　Accent on Linguistics and Computers 317
Summary 318
Sources and Resources 319
Review, Practice, and Explore 320

10 Semantics and Pragmatics: Making Meaning with Sentences 329

SENTENCE SEMANTICS: THE LINGUISTIC MEANING OF SENTENCES 331
　　Propositions and Truth Conditions 332
　　　　When Sentences Don't Express Propositions 332
　　　　Analytic and Synthetic Sentences 333
　　When Meanings Overlap: Entailment and Paraphrase 333
　　　　Sentences That *Can't* Be True: Contradictions 335
　　　　Presupposition 335
　　When Semantics and Syntax Overlap: The Structure of Meaning 336
　　　　Thematic Roles and Argument Structure 337

PRAGMATICS: HOW CONTEXT SHAPES MEANING 339
　　Linguistics in the News Watson the Computer Plays "Jeopardy!" 340
　　Saying What You Mean and Meaning What You Say: Speech Acts 341
　　Cooperative Talk: Conversational Rules 343
　　Did You Know . . . ? The Cooperative Principle and Language Acquisition 344
　　　　Manipulating Maxims 344

The Power of Politeness   345
   Honorifics and Forms of Address   347
Language Alive! Culture Clash and Pragmatic Failure   348
   Register   350
Language Alive! Register as a Literary Device   351
When Semantics and Pragmatics Overlap   352
   Definiteness   352
   Deixis   353

LANGUAGE AND THOUGHT   354
Did You Know . . . ? Does Culture Count?   355
Linguistic Relativity and the Sapir-Whorf Hypothesis   355
Did You Know . . . ? Lost in Translation   356
   Examining the Evidence   357
   Mentalese   358
Accent on Forensic Linguistics   358
Summary   359
Sources and Resources   360
Review, Practice, and Explore   361

11 The Early Story of English   367
FINDING FAMILIES: THE COMPARATIVE METHOD   368
Did You Know . . . ? Pretty Grimm Tales   371
Indo-European Language Families   371
   Celtic   371
   Italic   371
Language Alive! False Cognates   372
   Hellenic   372
   Baltic   373
   Slavic   373
   Indo-Iranian   373
   Armenian   374
   Albanian   374
   Germanic   374
Beyond Indo-European: Other Language Families   374
The Germanic Branch of Indo-European   375

ENGLISH EMERGES IN THE BRITISH ISLES   377
Language Alive! Pagan Fossils   378
   Old English Vocabulary   378
Did You Know . . . ? Why Was Alfred So Great?   379
Did You Know . . . ? Runic Writing and the Futhorc   381
Old English Morphology   381

Strong and Weak Nouns   382
Strong and Weak Adjectives   382
Strong and Weak Verbs and a Two-Tense System   383
Old English Syntax   384
Old English Word Order   384
Interrogative and Negative Sentences   385
Old English Phonetics and Phonology   385

ENGLISH MEETS FRENCH: MIDDLE ENGLISH   387
Did You Know . . . ? The Black Death, Rats, and Fleas   388
Middle English Vocabulary   388
Middle English Morphology   389
Loss of Inflection   389
Middle English Syntax   390
Fixed SVO Order   390
Middle English Auxiliary and Modal Verbs   390
Interrogative and Negative Sentences   391
Middle English Phonology   391
From Synthetic to Analytic   392

ENGLISH ESTABLISHED   392
Linguistics in the News Languages and Land Bridges   393
The Birth of "Correct" English and Prescriptive Grammar   394
Did You Know . . . ? The Word According to Johnson   395
Early Modern English Grammar   397
The Early Modern English Vocabulary Explosion   398
Accent on Philologists 399
Summary   400
Sources and Resources   400
Review, Practice, and Explore   401

12 English Goes Global   407

WHAT IS A DIALECT?   409

THE ORIGINS OF AMERICAN ENGLISH   409
British English Goes to the New World   409
British English Influences on American English   410

AMERICAN REGIONAL DIALECTS   411
Dialects and Settlement Patterns   411
Drawing Dialect Boundaries   412
Appalachian English   414
New England English   415
American "English" Vocabulary   415

ETHNIC DIALECTS   417

    African American English   418

    Did You Know . . . ? The Ann Arbor Trial   420

    Native American English   420

        Lumbee English   422

    Chicano English   422

SOCIAL DIALECTS   424

    Social Networks   424

    Communities of Practice   425

    Social Class and Language Attitudes   425

    Linguistics in the News Linguistic Profiling   426

ENGLISH KEEPS TRAVELING   426

    Australian English   427

    Caribbean English   427

    English in Asia   428

    Did You Know . . . ? Aladdin Speaks Standard English?   429

    English in Africa   429

    English as a Global Language   430

LANGUAGE VARIATION AND LANGUAGE DISCRIMINATION   431

    Language Alive! German Goes from Good to Bad   432

    Standard English and "General American"   432

    Dialect Pride   433

    Language Alive! Urban Dictionary   434

THE FUTURE OF ENGLISH DIALECTS   435

    Accent on Dialect Coaches   435

Summary   436

Sources and Resources   437

Review, Practice, and Explore   439

13 **Representing Language: The Written Word   441**

A BRIEF HISTORY OF WRITING   442

    Logograms and Phonograms   443

    Did You Know . . . ? Hieroglyphics   443

    Did You Know . . . ? Cuneiform   444

    Alphabets   444

THE DEVELOPMENT OF ENGLISH SPELLING   445

    Old English Writing and Spelling   445

    Language Alive! Ye Olde Confusion   446

    Middle English Spelling   447

    Toward Modern English Spelling   447

    Attempts at Spelling Reform   449

Linguistics in the News The CSIs of Language   451

THE DEVELOPMENT OF ENGLISH PUNCTUATION   452

Early Punctuation   452

Modern Punctuation   453

Punctuation "Errors"   455

WRITING RULES, STANDARDIZATION, AND AUTHORITY   457

Language Alive! Autocorrect Isn't Always   458

The Power of the Dictionary   458

Did You Know . . . ? The Oxford English Dictionary   459

Writing Registers and Forms   460

Electronic English   460

Written Standards in Flux   462

Language Alive! Smileys   463

Language Alive! Are You Ever Alright?   465

The Effects of Print   465

Accent on Copy Editors   468

Summary   469

Sources and Resources   469

Review, Practice, and Explore   471

14 **The Life Cycle of Language**   477

LANGUAGE ORIGINS   479

A Mother Tongue?   479

Language Alive! The Origins of American Sign Language   479

A Linguistic Big Bang?   482

Why Don't Apes Do It?   482

LANGUAGE GENESIS   485

Creoles Revisited   485

Did You Know . . . ? Chinook Jargon   487

Jamaican Creole   488

Hawaiian Creole English   489

Tok Pisin   490

Gullah and African American English   491

LANGUAGE SHIFT   492

Linguistics in the News Sundance Features *The Linguists*   493

Latin   494

Native American Languages   495

Norman French in England   496

Language Alive! Esperanto: A Failed Lingua Franca   497

Language Planning   497

English-Only Laws   498

Did You Know . . . ? Ketchup-Only Law   498

LANGUAGE REVITALIZATION   499
    Hebrew   499
    Welsh   500
    Hawaiian   501
    Native American Languages   502
        Cherokee   502
        Lushootseed   503
    Did You Know . . . ? Language Preservation in Action   504
        Navajo   504
    Accent on What Linguists Can Do   505
Summary   506
Sources and Resources   507
Review, Practice, and Explore   508

CREDITS   511
BIBLIOGRAPHY   515
GLOSSARY   529
INDEX OF LANGUAGES   537
INDEX   539

Preface

Linguistics is the scientific study of language. You might think, when you see the word *scientific*, that linguistics is not for you and that a scientific approach to language will be dry, technical, and of no real relevance to your everyday life. In fact, just the opposite is true: the scientific study of language is not just interesting but far more fun than peering into a test tube, because the "laboratory" in which we construct experiments, gather data, and form theories is everyday life, where we use language all the time.

Linguistics for Everyone will lead you through the story of language, of how we acquire it as children and how it changes over time. We look at how language varies from country to country, region to region, and even city to city. Drawing on both scholarship and experience, we discuss what's true about language and what's not. Some exciting research is under way (e.g., Is there a gene for language? Is the left side of the brain better at language than the right? Does watching TV help babies learn language?), and misconceptions abound (e.g., French is more romantic than German, English descended from Latin, some languages are more advanced or more primitive than others, people who say "gonna" are using sloppy speech). We explore many of our ideas about language, not all of which are based on linguistic facts; many are rooted in social and cultural (mis)perceptions. We also take a new look at grammar, which you might think of as the list of rules you learned in school, but you will learn about the rules of language that allow you to produce and understand sentences you've never said or heard before. Language is part of almost everything we do, and knowing more about it tells us more about ourselves.

Innovative Approach

Linguistics is a relatively young field, and for a long time it has been confined to linguistics departments in universities. But this is all changing as linguistics becomes more and more interdisciplinary; everyone is interested in language, and linguistics isn't just for linguists anymore. Linguistics contributes to our understanding of anthropology, sociology, computer science, speech pathology, communications, journalism, history, political science—you name it. In short, language is everywhere, and linguistics is for everyone. *Linguistics for Everyone* is intended for anyone with an interest in language, and its goals are twofold: to pique your interest in language and to familiarize you with the core areas of linguistics, the science of language. To that end, we present theoretical concepts in ways that capture the interest of the nonspecialist while providing solid background for someone who wishes to study linguistics in more depth. This balance is reflected in the topics we choose to treat and how we treat them, in the wealth and variety of exercises at the end of every chapter, and in the groundbreaking special features that offer information on "living language" and connect linguistics with life in the real world.

Organization of Content

The book begins with an introductory chapter that addresses such basic issues as defining this thing we call language, prescriptive versus descriptive grammar, and differences between the human language system and other animal communication systems. The second chapter is devoted to language, mind, and brain and addresses both psycholinguistic and neurolinguistic evidence for humans' innate capacity for language. Chapters 3 through 10 address the core areas of linguistics in detail, with two chapters devoted to each area (phonetics and phonology, morphology, syntax, and semantics). Chapters 11 and 12 focus on the history and development of English and language change, variation, and dialects. But these topics are not confined to these chapters; language change and variation are recurrent themes throughout the book. Chapter 13 explores writing systems from pictographs to text messages and discusses the development of spelling, punctuation, and standardization. Chapter 14 is the capstone chapter on the life cycle of language: language genesis, language endangerment, and language death. This final chapter ties together important issues and themes addressed throughout the book. And, of course, the glossary and bibliography are very helpful tools.

Hallmark Features

To present both the science of linguistics and the language of communication, we have designed and arranged the material in a variety of formats with unique features to facilitate navigation through the chapter, to show relationships among elements, and to aid in study and review.

The first page of every chapter offers an overview of the chapter's content:

- Specially rendered line art shows one or more humanlike characters engaging in an activity related to the chapter's main topic.
- "Chapter at a Glance" is a chapter outline listing the main headings.

- "Key Concepts" prompts consideration of the major ideas explored in the chapter.
- A list of special features and their titles previews the chapter's "living language" topics.

RPE 1 ▷ A brief, relevant epigram offers a spark of humor or pith (or both) before the introduction to the core material. The core material is presented in a fresh, accessible manner and offers many examples in English and several other languages to clarify the linguistics at work. To facilitate study and review of the material, key terms appear in boldface in the text and are repeated in the adjacent margin with their definitions. To give students the opportunity to practice and explore concepts as they are introduced in the text, notes "tacked" in the margins indicate the numerals of the related exercises in the "Review, Practice, and Explore" section at the end of the chapter.

To show the language at work and in life, the core material is enhanced with five special features that present information related to the topics discussed in the text. They highlight language as an immediate, changing, varied, and fascinating entity.

Language **Alive!** "Language Alive!" considers the way we speak, the way we used to speak, and the way some but not all people speak. It highlights language change, variation, and diversity as it explores the mystery of such issues as why words spelled with -ough are pronounced so many ways, whether women and men really speak differently, whether there's really anything wrong with aks, and whether double negatives are really ungrammatical.

"Did You Know . . . ?" offers background and commentary on interesting and relevant topics, such as whether Rico the Talking Border Collie can really talk, whether someone can be *very dead*, whether baby talk promotes or hinders language development, and why the Grimm brothers really wrote all those tales.

LINGUISTICS IN THE NEWS "Linguistics in the News" calls attention to the moments in which linguistic science crops up in the public eye. The media limelight shines on such news items as the controversy over grammar in the Scholastic Aptitude Test, political language, linguistic profiling, and the premiere of *The Linguists* at the Sundance Film Festival.

Accent on "Accent on . . ." shows how linguistics is actually used in such varied professions as software development, speech pathology, forensics, and psychology. Linguistics informs how we teach reading and spelling, study and interpret law, evaluate and treat language disorders, and even name new products.

hwæt! *Hwæt!* (rhymes with *that*) is Old English for "Hey! Listen up!" You might recognize it as the first word of the epic poem *Beowulf*. Our *hwæts* are sprinkled in the margins to alert you to such entertaining tidbits as these: The Washington State House of Representatives adopted a resolution to honor Washoe as the first nonhuman to acquire a human language; Navajo has more than a hundred thousand native speakers; and Steven Spielberg's four grandparents came from the Ukraine and spoke Ukrainian.

Every chapter has a summary that offers quick review of the main points as well as a list of sources and resources for further investigation.

"Review, Practice, and Explore" closes every chapter with an abundance of exercises and activities that target issues of broad interest rather than restricting the focus to traditional scientific linguistic analysis. It includes not only linguistics puzzles on English and other languages but also topics for research, ideas for classroom activities, and suggestions for fieldwork (surveys, interviews, and so on).

Our goal in writing this book is to share with you our own fascination with language, to introduce you to fundamental insights and advances of linguistic science, to raise your awareness of this uniquely human phenomenon, and to provide you with some tools with which to explore language on your own. Have fun!

New in the Second Edition

Based on very valuable feedback from instructors, we have revised and updated *Linguistics for Everyone* to keep it current and accessible. We have inserted new examples in more languages, updated maps, clarified explanatory diagrams and symbols, and improved charts and tables. We have revised chapter exercises (RPEs) to provide more practice of key concepts and in more languages. We have replaced some content in the hallmark features with current topics (e.g., the language Na'vi, Watson the computer on *Jeopardy!*), inserted new hwaets, and updated sources and resources.

Each chapter of *Linguistics for Everyone* has been carefully reviewed, and expanded in some cases and condensed in others.

In Chapter 1, about defining and learning language, new examples of parameters clarify the principles of Universal Grammar, and condensed sections on Noam Chomsky, generative grammar, and influences on modern linguistics clarify those aspects of modern grammatical theory relevant to this book.

In response to positive feedback, we kept the introduction to the brain in Chapter 2 to pique students' interest in the biological foundations of language right away. We remain unique in introducing pidgins and creoles here, along with Nicaraguan Sign Language.

Chapter 3, on phonetics, includes alternative IPA symbols, clarified articulation of consonants, and new information on glottal stops, mid-central vowels, lip-rounding, and bunched liquids.

Chapter 4, on phonology, has clarifications of assimilation and deletion/simplification and new RPEs on phonemes and allophones in Korean and Hungarian.

Revisions of Chapters 5 and 6, on morphology, focused on clarification. In Chapter 5, that includes word classes, affixation (new example of Icelandic verb), inflection (for gender), and a new section on clitics, as well as new RPEs on morphemes in Quiché and Turkish. Chapter 6 has a new chart of two Greek verbs, new acronyms in French and German, a new section on retronyms, and new RPEs on morphemes in Yoruba and Arabic.

Chapters 7 and 8, on syntax, are substantially revised, with more accurate phrase structure rules including a new section on clauses and a discussion of Aux as a separate constituent, additional examples of coordination, revised tree diagrams, and clarified explanations. Improved RPEs, and a new one to practice diagramming, focus more accurately on concepts in the chapters.

Chapters 9 and 10, on semantics, are streamlined, notably the discussion of metaphors. Yet they contain some additional information about metaphors, markedness, common/proper nouns, degree modification, and the meaning of polysemy and retronyms. The section on argument structure has been revised for clarification.

Chapter 11, "The Story of English," needed little revision. We added a bit of information on Hellenic languages and some history about Alfred the Great, and we replaced the Old English version of the Lord's Prayer with an excerpt from *The Battle of Maldan*.

Likewise, Chapter 12, "English Goes Global," required only some fine-tuning, although we did add detail on the AAVE verb system to the discussion of systematic rules.

Chapter 13, on the written language, benefitted from additional details about alphabets, punctuation (new section on apostrophe), the Great Vowel Shift, the *OED*, electronic English, and changing standards.

Chapter 14, "The Life Cycle of Language," needed only updates of some data as well as sources and resources.

Instructor's Resource Manual and Answer Key

An Instructor's Resource Manual and Answer Key is available with the text. Here you will find the answers to the "Review, Practice, and Explore" activities along with suggested discussion questions and research topics.

You can also find sample course schedules here that suggest ways to organize the textbook material.

Introduction to Linguistics Resource Center

The Introduction to Linguistics Resource Center has been carefully designed to enhance the instruction in *Linguistics for Everyone*. Clearly organized around the major subject areas in linguistics, the Resource Center offers web links, quizzes, flash cards for key terms, extensive sound files showcasing pronunciations by native speakers, PowerPoint slides, and more.

Acknowledgments

Writing a textbook turned out to be far more demanding than either of us anticipated, and we are deeply indebted to our families, friends, colleagues, and students for both their contributions and their support.

Thanks to Robert Denham for reading and editing sections of the manuscript, finding quotations for us, and sharing his invaluable literary insights; to Scott Denham for help on German data; to Hugh Conroy for reading and editing sections of the manuscript and helping us with a title (*Linguistics Unplugged* was a memorable contribution); to Hideo Makihara for help with Japanese; to the students at Willowwood School for data in Abbish and Ubby Dubby; to our own children (Ella, Ivy, and Jack Denham Conroy and Shellane, Schuyler, and Julia Jensen) for providing us with examples and for listening to countless explanations of linguistic phenomena; to our students for finding typos, commenting on chapter drafts, and testing exercises; to Russell Hugo for his computer expertise, help with pictures, and much other support; to Jason Cuniff and Chelsea Brandon, students who caught typos and offered suggestions; to the Sarahs for offering their *skinneded* data way back in '96; to Christopher Bryant for working on permissions and art and probably some other stuff; and to Kim Thiessen for help with American Sign Language.

A special thanks to our tireless development editor, Joan Flaherty, who guided us through what in the best of circumstances is a very intense and demanding editorial process. Joan's creativity made this a much better book. Her sense of humor kept us afloat when we thought we'd never see the light at the end of the tunnel. And her expertise in areas too many to list left us in awe. In fact, she contributed so much to the writing of this book that we sometimes thought she should be a third coauthor. Her invaluable input, suggestions, and advice have really shaped this final product in a way we would never have envisioned on our own.

Thanks also to everyone at Cengage Learning, including publisher Michael Rosenberg, Michael Lepera, Erin Bosco, and Rebecca Donahue, and to Kathleen Allain and her team at PreMediaGlobal. And a special thank-you goes out to Steve Dalphin at Cengage Learning, who sought us out in our out-of-the way corner of the country, convinced us that writing this book was a good idea and that we should do it, and promoted the project to Cengage Learning. To him, we are very grateful. It's been fun, rejuvenating, and rewarding.

We have been fortunate to have the support of the excellent staff of Western Washington University's Research and Sponsored Programs and of our colleagues in the WWU English Department (a very linguistics-friendly place) and Linguistics Program. Thanks as well to many of our colleagues in linguistics beyond our home institution, from whom we have learned over the years and whose scholarship and teaching inform this book. If we've borrowed anything unknowingly, we're sorry. We thank you and acknowledge you here. Any errors of interpretation or understanding are, of course, our own.

During the process of writing the first edition of this book, the manuscript was extensively reviewed numerous times, and reviewers gave us excellent insights, criticisms, and commentary. We thank the following colleagues for the time and effort they have committed to this project and for the invaluable feedback. We usually took their excellent advice, which has doubtless improved this book:

Dennis Baron	*University of Illinois, Urbana*
Edward (Rusty) Barrett	*University of Chicago*
Ellen Barton	*Wayne State University*
Catherine Bates	*Arizona State University*
Edwin Battistella	*Southern Oregon University*
Mark Canada	*University of North Carolina, Pembroke*
Shobhana Chelliah	*University of North Texas*
Linda Di Desidero	*University of Maryland University College*
Karen Dykstra	*Eastern Michigan University*
Paul Fallon	*University of Mary Washington*
Anna Feldman	*Montclair State University*
Joseph Galasso	*California State University, Northridge*
Kirk Hazen	*West Virginia University*
Andrew R. Hippisley	*University of Kentucky*
Ronald Kephart	*University of North Florida*
Sharon Klein	*California State University, Northridge*
Thomas M. Lambert	*University of Texas at Dallas*
Geraldine Legendre	*Johns Hopkins University*
John Levis	*Iowa State University*
Bruce Long Peng	*State University of New York at Oswego*
Megan Melançon	*Georgia College and State University*
Rod Moore	*Los Angeles Valley College*
Karen Mullen	*University of Louisville*
Lynette Nyaggah	*Rio Hondo Community College*
Mary Paster	*Pomona College*
Nataliya Semchynska-Uhl	*Purdue University*
Mary Shapiro	*Truman State University*
Cynthia Vigliotti	*Youngstown State University*
Rachelle Waksler	*San Francisco State University*
Rebecca Wheeler	*Christopher Newport College*

In writing the second edition, we have benefitted from excellent feedback from instructors who have used the book in class, from our students, and from colleagues who have taken the time to contact us with their comments and ideas. We are particularly grateful to Eric Hyman (Fayetteville State University), for his very useful and detailed critique of the first edition, and to Frederick Newmeyer, for sharing his expertise on the history of generative grammar. And finally, we owe a great debt to the following reviewers for this second edition.

Katie Crowder, Coordinator, Introduction to Linguistics, Department of Linguistics and Technical Communication, University of North Texas

John Fitzer, Humanities Division, Fresno City College

Thomas J. Hudiak, School of Human Evolution and Social Change (formerly Anthropology), Arizona State University

Eric Hyman, Graduate Coordinator, English Department, Fayetteville State University

Owen Mordaunt, English Department, University of Nebraska at Omaha

Johanna Rubba, Linguistics Minor Advisor, California Polytechnic University

Latricia Trites, ESL/Linguistics, English Department, Murray State University

Douglas J. Wulf, Linguistics Program, English Department, George Mason University

Finally, we thank each other, once again, for being terrific co-authors. Without us, we couldn't have done it!

Chapter at a Glance

What Is Language?
 Our Language Expertise
 Acquiring versus Learning a
 Language

**Human Language and Animal
Communication**
 Can Other Animals Learn Language?
 Two Case Studies: Washoe and Nim

What Is Grammar?
 The Components of Grammar
 What Is Grammatical?
 Grammar Across Space and Time
 Universal Grammar

The Scientific Study of Language
 Noam Chomsky and Generative
 Grammar
 Influences on Modern Linguistics

Linguistics Today

Summary

Sources and Resources

Review, Practice, and Explore

What Is Language and How Do We Study It?

Key Concepts

- Human language has numerous features that distinguish it from other communication systems.
- People have unconscious knowledge of language and use this knowledge to speak and understand language.
- All languages have grammar, a system of phonological, morphological, syntactic, and semantic rules.
- A language is really a continuum of language varieties that change over space and time.
- Children are hardwired to acquire a linguistic rule system, and they do so while very young, without direct teaching.
- All languages have the same basic framework: Universal Grammar.

Did You Know . . . ?

 Rico and Chaser, Smarter Than the Average Dogs
 Noam Chomsky

Language Alive! Sign Language Diversity

Linguistics in the News The Language Blog and Eggcorns

Accent on The Linguistic Society of America

> *Language is a means of getting an idea from my brain into yours without surgery.*
>
> —MARK AMIDON

L anguage is what makes us human, and we all seem to be naturally curious about it. We do much more than just communicate with language: we play games with it (pig latin, jump-rope rhymes, jokes, *Scrabble*, and even spoken-word poetry are all types of language games); we use it to identify each other (we can sometimes guess where someone is from by their accent or by the words they use for things); we have many questions and often very strong feelings about it. We value some ways of speaking over others, and we all have our pet peeves about language. Numerous websites, newspaper columns, books, and entire radio and television programs are devoted to interesting facts and musings about language as well as to critiques of language "misuse" and "deterioration."

Have you ever wondered:

- Does my dog *really* understand what I'm saying?
- Is sign language different from body language?
- Why do some people say "ahnt" rather than "ant" for *aunt*?
- Where did English come from, and is it really related to Latin?
- Why do the words *Yeats* and *Keats* sound different when they're spelled almost the same?
- Do people who are bilingual ever mix up their languages?

After reading this book, you will be able to answer these questions about language and, we hope, many others you may have.

In addition to the many questions we might have about language and how it works, most people have strong opinions about it. We have definite ideas about how language sounds, how we learn it, the right way to use it, and what it says about people's intelligence or education.

Do you agree with any or all of the following opinions?

- French sounds more romantic than German.
- The sentence *I don't know nothing* is sloppy English.
- Some languages are more primitive than others.
- People who say *aks* instead of *ask* are being lazy.
- We are taught language by our parents and teachers.
- Writing is more perfect than speech.

Each of these statements is probably familiar to you, but none of them happens to be true. What such statements, or language myths, really tell us is that ideas about language are deeply woven into culture. The way we talk, just like the way we act and dress, shapes how we think of ourselves and how we think of others. A thorough understanding of language equips us to answer our many questions about this uniquely human phenomenon and to separate linguistic fact from fiction.

What Is Language?

hwæt!

Hwæt (rhymes with *that*) was an attention-getting interjection used in Old English. You may recognize it as the first word of the Old English poem *Beowulf*. Our *hwæts* will appear throughout the text to alert you to interesting tidbits.

One of the first questions we need to answer is, 'What is this thing called *language*, anyway?' Even though we use it every day, language is actually hard to define. And though we can't immediately answer the complex question 'What is language?' each of us is already an expert in the language we grew up speaking. We don't have to stop and think about how to pronounce words, or how to form questions, or how to talk about something that will happen in the future or something that happened in the past. Still, each of these tasks, among thousands of others, is actually pretty complex. And it's amazing that we know how to do it—effortlessly, without direct instruction from anyone.

Our Language Expertise

Perhaps a more interesting question about language is, 'What is it that we know about language?' What does a speaker of English, for example, have to know about English in order to speak the language and understand the English spoken by others?

For instance, every speaker of English usually knows that the following sentences are not "normal" sentences in English. (Sentences that are not "normal" or possible in a language are marked with an asterisk, *.)

*Destroyed the city the hurricane.
*Sick Lionel seems.
*Chicago a large city in the Midwest is.

Any English speaker also knows how to rearrange the words in the impossible sentences to make them fully acceptable English sentences.

The hurricane destroyed the city.
Lionel seems sick.
Chicago is a large city in the Midwest.

So we know, as English speakers, what is a possible utterance in our language and what is not. This suggests that we know rules of English word order, even if we can't define these rules any more specifically than to say that we just *know* them. Indeed, we don't learn these rules in school, but we all mastered them before kindergarten. We acquire the rules of our language at an early age just by being exposed to it.

Acquiring versus Learning a Language

language acquisition natural, unconscious process of language development in humans that occurs without instruction

The process of **language acquisition** is different from the process of **language learning**. Acquisition takes place unconsciously, without direct instruction. Any of us who has studied a second language in school knows that learning a language is a conscious (and often difficult!) process requiring practice and study. Our ability to acquire our native language, on the other hand, is similar to a bird's ability to fly. Birds don't teach their offspring to fly; the young birds just do it when they reach a certain developmental stage and are in the appropriate environment. Similarly, children who are exposed to language acquire it regardless of race, class, or culture.

language learning process of gaining conscious knowledge of language through instruction

This is not to say that in addition to *acquiring* our languages, we don't also *learn* many language rules. Think about some of the language rules you've learned in school or from family and friends. You may have learned when to use *who* and when to use *whom*, for example, or to avoid saying *ain't* or *I don't got none*. You may have learned to avoid saying *John and me went to the store* and to say instead *John and I went to the store*. These rules of language also form part of our linguistic system, but they are consciously learned rather than unconsciously acquired.

Human Language and Animal Communication

design features of language proposed by Hockett, the features that distinguish human language from other communication systems

One way to gain more insight into our linguistic system is to take a look at the communication systems of other species. Let's examine the ways in which some of the more sophisticated animal communication systems differ from human language. Linguist Charles Hockett proposed a list of **design features** that characterize human language and distinguish it from other communication systems (other animal systems, traffic signals, etc.). Hockett's list has been revised and reexamined by many linguists, but the features of human language that remain on almost every researcher's list include the following.[1]

- **Semanticity** Specific signals can be matched with specific meanings. In short, words have meanings.
- **Arbitrariness** There is no logical connection between the form of the signal and the thing it refers to. For example, *dog* in English is *Hund* in German and *perro* in Spanish.

---

1. More current treatments of the unique characteristics of human language include Hauser et al. (2002), who argue that *recursion*, the ability to embed one sentence within another, is what makes human language unique. We take this (rather technical) argument up in Chapter 8 ("Linguistics in the News: Starling Syntax?").

- **Discreteness** Messages in the system are made up of smaller, repeatable parts rather than indivisible units. A word, for example, can be broken down into units of sound.
- **Displacement** The language user can talk about things that are not present—the messages can refer to things in remote time (past and future) or space (here or elsewhere).
- **Productivity** Language users can understand and create never-before-heard utterances.
- **Duality of patterning** A large number of meaningful utterances can be recombined in a systematic way from a small number of discrete parts of language. For example, suffixes can be attached to many roots, and words can be combined to create novel sentences.[2]

Many animals have complex communicative interactions that do not share Hockett's design features of human language. Consider, for example, the communication system of the African vervet monkey, as studied by Struhsaker (1967). In this system, there are three types of predators (leopard, eagle, and snake), and there is a distinct call for each. A loud bark signals a leopard; a coughing sound signals an eagle; a chutter sound signals a snake. The vervet's packmates respond appropriately to the calls (running up a tree to safety from a leopard, diving into brush to hide from an eagle, or scanning the ground for a snake) even if they cannot see the predator.

How many of Hockett's design features does the vervet monkeys' communication system meet? There seems to be semanticity: the signals or calls do have a meaning. There is also arbitrariness; just as there is no logical connection between the English word *monkey* and the animal, there is no logical connection between the chutter call and a snake or between the coughing sound and an eagle. Calls are distinct for each predator but can't be broken down into smaller parts, so the vervet system seems to lack discreteness (and also note that the calls are all of the same type: to indicate alarm). No calls are used out of context, so there is no displacement. The species relies on a single set of calls, so there is no productivity; and calls are not combined to form new calls, so there is no duality of patterning.

Zoologist Karl von Frisch (1967), in a series of well-known studies, found that honeybees appear to have displacement; by performing a "dance", they are able to communicate to their hivemates how to get to the pollinating flowers. And some birdsongs seem to have some degree of duality of patterning. Discrete pieces of song may be combined in different ways to indicate distinct meanings. The communication systems of many primates, birds, bees, and cetaceans have all been studied extensively. Though they are amazingly sophisticated, intricate, and fascinating systems, and though there is still much to be learned about them, they all lack some of the design features of human language.

RPE 1.1

RPE 1.2

---

2. Based on Hockett (1960).

Can Other Animals Learn Language?

hwæt!

Though whether animals can acquire human language is subject to debate, in February 2008 the Washington State House of Representatives adopted a resolution to honor Washoe as "the first nonhuman to acquire a human language." She died in October 2007 at the age of 42.

Whether animals can learn language is a question separate from whether animals have humanlike communication systems. Numerous researchers have attempted to teach intelligent apes various systems of communication, with the goal of enabling the apes to use those systems to communicate with humans and with each other. These attempts have had varying degrees of success, but each offers insights into the learning capacity of these primates as well as into some of their limitations.

The question of whether chimpanzees or gorillas have the same mental capacity as humans to learn language is difficult to answer. For one thing, primates lack the same vocal apparatus as humans, so they must be taught language in another modality, or means by which language is produced. Some have been taught to manipulate symbols of some kind; others have been taught manual signs. Such research requires experiments designed to measure, for example, whether a primate's understanding of a word or symbol is comparable to a human's.

More basic questions are whether Hockett's design features of language accurately capture the features of human language and whether they are an accurate yardstick for assessing a different species' understanding of human language. Yet another issue is the role of the trainer in such experiments; humans acquire language when exposed to it and have no trainers, so how does one measure language learning versus language acquisition? Experiments that measure language learning in species other than humans are thus extremely difficult to design, and results are hard to observe and measure. Two well-known studies of chimpanzees illustrate some of the complexities involved in this kind of research.

RPE   1.3 ▷

Two Case Studies: Washoe and Nim

In the 1960s, Allen and Beatrix Gardner embarked on their study of the chimpanzee Washoe (Gardner et al. 1989). The Gardners raised Washoe much like a human child and communicated with her in signs from American Sign Language. The Gardners' idea was to see whether Washoe, given the same language acquisition environment as a child, would acquire sign language. Washoe mastered around 200 signs and was thought to understand many more. She was even thought to have produced some creative combinations of signs on her own. At the time, the Washoe experiment was considered a great success.

hwæt!

The 2011 documentary "Project Nim" describes Nim Chimpsky's life with humans.

In the late 1970s, Herb Terrace taught the chimp Nim Chimpsky (a play on the name of world-famous linguist Noam Chomsky) 125 signs and argued that Nim had mastered some rudiments of grammatical structure as well (Terrace 1979). But after viewing videotapes of Nim's signs, Terrace saw

Did You Know...?

Rico and Chaser, Smarter Than the Average Dogs

In 2004, psychologists Juliane Kaminski, Joseph Call, and Julia Fischer (2004) of the Max Planck Institute for Evolutionary Anthropology in Leipzig, Germany, found that a border collie from Germany called Rico exhibited an extraordinary ability to learn new names for things. When presented with a new toy and told its name, Rico was able to retrieve it from a pile of other toys with almost 100 percent accuracy. This ability is similar to one seen in children, a process called *fast mapping*. Rico was also able to remember the names of about 200 toys, even after a month of neither hearing the name nor seeing the toy. More recently, another border collie, Chaser, trained by researchers John Pilley and Alliston Ried (2010) of Wofford College, learned the names of 1,022 objects. Chaser also clearly understood the distinction between the names of objects (proper nouns) and the commands to fetch a particular object (verbs). Another experiment revealed that Chaser also understood names for categories of objects (common nouns). She learned, for example, that "toy" referred to the 1,022 objects she was allowed to play with, each with a different proper name. She also learned to understand which "toys" fell into the subcategory "Frisbee" and which into the subcategory "ball". According to researcher Reid, "This research is important because it demonstrates that dogs, like children, can develop extensive vocabularies and understand that certain words represent individual objects and other words represent categories of objects, independent in meaning of what one is asked to do with those objects." Rico's and, to an even more astonishing extent, Chaser's abilities share design features with human language, namely semanticity and arbitrariness.

that Nim almost never produced signs spontaneously; rather, his signs were repetitions of his trainers'. Nim also signed only in response to food, and his combinations of signs did not exhibit consistent word order patterns, suggesting that he had not, in fact, mastered grammatical rules. Terrace reversed his position that Nim had acquired language, concluding not only that the Nim study was flawed but that many others, including the Washoe study, were flawed as well for similar reasons.

RPE 1.4 ▷

RPE 1.5 ▷

What Is Grammar?

Hockett's design features describe the basic properties of the rule system shared by all human languages. In particular, the ability to combine discrete units into larger units forms the foundation of what linguists call **grammar**. A grammar is a complex system of rules that governs how speakers organize sounds into words and words into sentences. (Sign languages also have grammar and differ from spoken language only in terms of modality. We

grammar linguistic rule system that we use to produce and understand sentences

talk more about sign languages later in the chapter.) It is our knowledge of grammar that allows us to create sentences we've never heard or uttered before. No other communication system (birdsong, whale songs, bee dances, or monkey calls) appears to have the equivalent of human language grammar. Note that this use of the term *grammar* is different from nonlinguists' use of the term. The term *grammar* actually has quite a few distinct, though related, meanings. The dictionary *Merriam-Webster Online* (http://www.merriam-webster.com) defines *grammar* this way:

> **1 a:** the study of the classes of words, their inflections, and their functions and relations in the sentence **b:** a study of what is to be preferred and what avoided in inflection and syntax

> **2 a:** the characteristic system of inflections and syntax of a language **b:** a system of rules that defines the grammatical structure of a language

> **3 a:** a grammar textbook **b:** speech or writing evaluated according to its conformity to grammatical rules

> **4:** the principles or rules of an art, science, or technique <a *grammar* of the theater>; *also:* a set of such principles or rules

Under a separate entry, *Merriam-Webster Online* offers *generative grammar:* "a description in the form of a set of rules for producing the grammatical sentences of a language." This is the definition we use here. (We discuss why this definition of grammar includes the term *generative* later in the chapter.)

RPE 1.6

The Components of Grammar

The grammar of a language can be divided into components. Each component interacts with the others, but each can also be studied on its own.

- **Phonetics** The inventory of sounds in a language
- **Phonology** Rules of how sounds are combined in a language
- **Morphology** Rules of word formation in a language
- **Syntax** Rules of sentence formation in a language
- **Semantics** Rules that govern how meaning is expressed by words and sentences in a language

We'll illustrate each component briefly with examples from English and other languages.

First, let's look at phonetics and phonology. The phonetic system of English has (basically) twelve vowels, and the Hawaiian system has five. In Hawaiian, sounds are combined in such a way that all words end with vowel sounds; this is not the case in English, where many words end with consonants. English and Hawaiian thus differ both phonetically (in their inventory of sounds) and phonologically (in how the sounds are combined).

Turning next to morphology, in English we form the past participle of many verbs by attaching the suffix -*ed* to the root. For example, we attach -*ed* to the root word *learn* to derive *learned*. In German, on the other hand, the past participle of the verb *lernen* 'to learn' is *gelernt*, where the prefix *ge-* and suffix -*t* are attached to the root, *lern*. Although both English and German have past participles, the languages differ morphologically in the rules to form them.

Languages also differ syntactically in the ways words are arranged in the sentence. For example, in English color adjectives precede the nouns they modify, as in *red skirt* or *black cat*. In French, on the other hand, color adjectives follow the noun: *jupe rouge* 'skirt red' and *chat noir* 'cat black'.

And finally, we find that languages differ semantically as well. Although all languages have kinship terms, the meanings expressed by these terms can differ, sometimes rather dramatically. In English, for example, the term *grand*- (*grandmother, granduncle*, etc.) refers to relatives who are two generations distant, *great*- refers to relatives three generations distant, *great-great*- refers to relatives four generations distant, and so on. The Australian aboriginal language Njamal, on the other hand, has a term that refers to "any relative two generations distant," *maili*. This term can refer, for example, to a father's father (two generations before) or a daughter's son's wife's sister (two generations after).

What Is Grammatical?

When we talk about the grammar of a language, we mean the set of rules a speaker knows that allow him or her to produce and understand sentences in the language. A *grammatical* sentence is therefore a *possible* sentence in the language. An *ungrammatical* sentence is one that is impossible in a given language, one that a native speaker of that variety would never utter naturally. (Remember that ungrammatical sentences are marked with an asterisk, *.) For example, of the two following sentences, the second sentence is ungrammatical because it is not a natural sentence that a speaker of modern English would use.

Sheba watched Murdock playing the banjo.
*Sheba wonders Murdock playing the banjo.

This definition of grammaticality is probably quite different from other definitions you might be familiar with. Consider, for example, the following sentence.

Sheba don't know nothing.

Some of you might think this sentence is ungrammatical because you have been taught that double negatives (*don't . . . nothing*) are to be avoided. Some of you might be aware that this sentence is typically considered "incorrect" or "bad" English. Others of you might find this sentence perfectly natural in your own dialect, whether or not you are aware of the social stigma attached to double negatives. In fact, double negative constructions are grammatical (in the sense we are talking about here) in many varieties of English, and for speakers of those varieties, this sentence is certainly a possible sentence of English. So a sentence is grammatical if a speaker would naturally produce it, regardless of its social value.

Prescriptive and Descriptive Grammar

descriptive grammar set of grammatical rules based on what we say, not on what we should say according to some language authority

prescriptive grammar set of grammatical rules prescribed by a language authority

Given the complexity of the term *grammatical*, it's useful to make yet another distinction between the concept of grammar that forms the basis of the study of language and the more everyday meanings of the term. The kind of grammar we are talking about here is called **descriptive grammar** because it *describes* the rule system we use to produce sentences, regardless of the social value we may attach to those sentences. **Prescriptive grammar**, on the other hand, is a set of rules that *prescribes* or defines how we are supposed to speak, typically according to some authority (your older sibling, your teacher, your parents, a writing or grammar handbook). Prescriptive rules have positive social value, and sentences that do not conform to prescriptive rules often have negative social value.

To make the difference between descriptive and prescriptive grammar clearer, let's consider another example.

I don't know who to see.
I don't know whom to see.

According to the rules of prescriptive grammar, the second sentence, with *whom* rather than *who*, is considered grammatical and therefore correct. Yet most of us would probably be more likely to say the first sentence, with *who*, in our everyday speech. According to our descriptive grammar, then, the sentence with *who* is grammatical, a sentence we'd produce naturally and that sounds perfectly natural to us. Notions of correctness and incorrectness don't really come into play here—descriptive grammatical rules simply describe what we actually say; they do not assign a social value to one construction over another.

(And here's the prescriptive rule for the distinction between *who* and *whom*, in case you are curious: Use the objective or accusative form *whom* when the pronoun is functioning as a direct object, as in *I don't know whom to see*, or as the object of a preposition, as in *I wonder to whom I should address this letter*. Use *who* when the pronoun functions as the subject: *Who left?*)

RPE 1.7 ⟩

When Prescription and Description Overlap

Now, though we may be able to cite examples of rules that are clearly prescriptive (rules you've been taught in school, for example) and rules that are clearly descriptive (rules that you probably can't even describe because they are unconscious and therefore not obvious to you), the distinction between prescriptive and descriptive grammar can be rather fuzzy. Many prescriptive rules are simply unnatural; they don't conform to rules of natural language and can be learned only consciously. Others, however, are actually descriptive rules for some speakers—the descriptive rules of the language variety that has higher social value. In this case, description and prescription overlap.

First, let's take an example of a prescriptive rule of English that is not a natural rule of any variety of English. It is completely natural in English to "split infinitives," that is, to insert an adverb between *to* and the verb, as in *to boldly go* or *to quickly run*. There is a long-standing prescriptive rule, however, that says split infinitives are to be avoided and that only *to go boldly* or *boldly to go* are prescriptively grammatical or "correct." This prohibition against split infinitives (which is now enforced less often than it used to be, and some of you might not even be aware that it is a prescriptive rule) originally grew out of the desire for English grammar to conform to the grammar of Latin, the language of prestige in eighteenth-century England. At that time, prescriptive grammarians proposed that because it is impossible in Latin to "split" infinitives, they should also not be split in English. But this prohibition was based on faulty logic; it is impossible to split infinitives in Latin because infinitives are single words! The infinitive 'to precede, go out before, lead', for example, is *praecedere* (the *-re* suffix, rather than an independent word, *to*, tells us that this form of the verb is the infinitive) and is impossible to split. Thus, applying this rule to English is an example of a prescriptive rule that is completely arbitrary and not based on the rules of natural language.

Some prescriptive rules, however, can also be descriptive rules. For example, you are likely aware of the prescriptive rule "Don't use double negatives." In fact, speakers of all English dialects do use so-called double negatives, though some varieties of English form negatives with a negative verb (such as *don't know*) and an *any-* word, such as *anyway, anyone,* and *anywhere* (*I don't know anything*), while other varieties form negatives with a negative verb and a *no-* word, such as *no one, nothing* (*I don't know nothing*). The *no-* variety of negative is stigmatized, and it is the one that is considered prescriptively ungrammatical and incorrect. The *any-* variety, on the other hand, is considered prescriptively grammatical and correct and is an example of a prescriptive rule that is also a natural descriptive rule for some speakers, one to which positive social value happens to be attached.

Modification: Another Overlap

From the discussion of prescriptive and descriptive grammar, you can see that the grammatical system we acquire is influenced by a variety of factors. It is shaped by what we learn in school, what we read, our desire to conform or impress, what our parents and friends tell us, the desire to belong to one group but not another, and so on. We are constantly modifying our language, sometimes to the extent that we revise and reshape our system of grammatical rules. **Modification** is also at work when we expand our vocabularies and shift from childish language to adult speech. It also plays an important role in the emergence of different dialects and in language change over time. We might modify our language to conform

modification
adjustment, change, and modification of grammatical systems based on various social factors

to the variety that has higher social status, adopting descriptive rules that are more highly valued (we may begin to use *any-* negatives instead of *no-* negatives), and we may learn "unnatural" language rules (and avoid splitting infinitives) for the same reason. Modification therefore once again complicates the distinction between prescription and description, and we explore this complex issue from different perspectives throughout the book.

Grammar across Space and Time

For illustration, we've assumed that the grammar of English is the same for all speakers, but of course this is not the case. Not everyone speaks English in exactly the same way. How do we account for differences among, for instance, British English, Irish English, and North American English, or even for the differences between how English is spoken in Boston, Massachusetts, and Birmingham, Alabama? What about the English spoken in South Africa and the English spoken in India and Jamaica? Do different varieties of a language share one grammar?

RPE 1.8

Let's complicate the matter even further. So far, we've raised the question of whether different varieties of a language, which vary over *space* or geographical area, share one grammar. What about different varieties of a language that vary over *time*? We use the word *English* for several varieties of English: Old English (the language of the famous epic poem *Beowulf*) is a variety of English, as are the Middle English spoken by Chaucer and even the Early Modern English spoken by Shakespeare. Speakers of Present-Day English can't even understand Old English, so is Old English still English? And do forms of English that vary over time or space all have the same grammar?

continuum of language varieties grammars that share enough of a historical and grammatical relationship to be recognized as varieties of one language

Well, yes and no. "English" is actually a general label under which a number of language varieties fall. English is spoken all over the world—in India, Africa, Jamaica, Barbados, and Australia, as well as in the United States and the British Isles and in many other countries. English also has a long history and has changed (rather dramatically) over time. What we call English, then, is really a **continuum of language varieties** rather than one language with a single set of grammatical rules. When we talk about the grammar of English, we include a variety of grammars of English that all share enough of a historical and grammatical relationship to be recognized as varieties of the same language, English. Throughout the book, our examples of English might not always be familiar to you, but they are nevertheless English in terms of the continuum of language varieties we're discussing here. We will discuss how English has changed over time (evolving from Old to Middle to Early Modern to Present-Day English) in Chapter 11, and we will discuss global varieties of English (also called "world Englishes") as well as varieties of North American English in Chapter 12.

RPE 1.9

RPE 1.10

dialect a variety of a language that differs from other varieties in grammar, pronunciation, and vocabulary and that is spoken and understood by a particular group, which might be identified by region, ethnicity, social class, etc.

Linguists generally consider two language varieties to be **dialects** of the same language if the speakers of each can understand each other, that is, if the language varieties are *mutually intelligible.* This distinction between language and dialect can get fuzzy because sometimes the linguistic differences are so great that the speakers of two varieties cannot, in fact, understand each other very well, but the two are still considered varieties of the same language. In other cases, the linguistic differences between two varieties can be fairly small and the speakers *can* understand each other, but the two are nevertheless called distinct languages for political, social, or geographic reasons. This is the case for speakers of Swedish and Norwegian, Macedonian and Bulgarian, Malaysian and Indonesian—each is considered a different language because they are spoken in different countries and the speakers' sense of identity is partly defined by their language. Some groups of people may go to great lengths to distinguish themselves from their linguistic relatives across a border; for instance, Serbs and Croats can understand each other perfectly well but consider their languages distinct and even use different writing systems. (The Eastern Orthodox Serbs use the Cyrillic alphabet, while the Roman Catholic Croats use the Latin alphabet.) Other groups use the writing system to help unite them. In China, more than a billion people speak at least seven mutually unintelligible varieties of Chinese; thus, the varieties could be considered different languages. Speakers of Cantonese, for example, cannot understand speakers of Mandarin unless they learn it as a separate language, and vice versa. However, because the people are in a single nation and because they use a single writing system, speakers consider all the varieties to be Chinese.

Many varieties of language fall somewhere in the middle of a language–dialect continuum, and only time will determine whether they land more firmly in the language camp or the dialect-of-a-language camp. We must keep in mind that every language variety is always changing, so the difficulty we have in classifying some is usually a result of their youth and continually changing forms.

Universal Grammar

We've seen that grammar involves the complex interplay of prescriptive grammar and descriptive grammar and that there is some overlap between the two. In the end, however, we all acquire a complex grammatical system, regardless of how and where we are raised. This suggests that we all tackle language acquisition with the same basic cognitive hardwiring to accomplish that task. Think about it—if we weren't predisposed to acquire this complex grammatical system, then we would have to learn it consciously. If this were the case, we'd expect to find a great deal of variation across cultures and individual speakers in how they learn language, but this is not the case (as you'll see in more detail in Chapter 2).

LINGUISTICS IN THE NEWS

The Language Blog and Eggcorns

The Language Log, a blog created in 2003 by professional linguists Mark Liberman and Geoff Pullum, has a few thousand daily visitors and is one of the most popular language sites on the Internet. The blog even made national news as the subject of a *New York Times* article by Michael Erard. As Erard observes, much of the commentary on The Language Log is devoted to debunking myths about language by countering them with linguistic fact, often with a "healthy dose of subversive humor." The posts do much to undermine the image of linguists as "finger-wagging eggheads" and address a range of issues about language. Titles of some of the posts are "No word for sex," "If wine and stew can always,

why can't toast?" "Stupid, contentless political blather," "Ray Charles, America, and the subjunctive," "Latte lingo: Raising a pint at Starbucks," and "Tighty-whities: The semantics."

The blog is also the birthplace of the term *eggcorn*, a word or phrase erroneously used in place of another word or phrase. Crucially, eggcorns make sense, often more than the original words. So, some examples of authentic eggcorns are *all intensive purposes* instead of *all intents and purposes*, and *cut to the cheese* for *cut to the chase*. However, spelling errors such as *they're* for *there* don't qualify as eggcorns (and the eggcorn *eggcorn* only works for you if you pronounce the initial vowel in both *eggcorn* and *acorn* the same way).

Eggcorn itself comes from (logically) misspelling *acorn*; an acorn is shaped like an egg and is the seed of an oak tree and therefore cornlike, right? There is even (now, thanks to Language Log) an entire site devoted to the discussion and cataloguing of eggcorns, called The Eggcorn Database, and as of September 2010, *eggcorn* appears in *Oxford English Dictionary*.

For more information
http://eggcorns.lascribe.net/about/
http://languagelog.ldc.upenn.edu/nll/
http://www.nytimes.com/2006/06/20/science/20lang.html?_r=1&scp=1&sq=geoff+pullum&st=nyt&oref=slogin
http://oed.com/news/updates/newwords1009.html

So, if we are all hardwired in some way to acquire language, what is the nature of this hardwiring? The study of descriptive grammar provides insights into this question because it helps us understand the core grammatical rules that we use to produce and understand language. These core grammatical rules must have similar properties across languages, forming a kind of basic grammatical "blueprint." These core properties make up what linguists refer to as **Universal Grammar (UG)**. One of the goals of modern linguistics is to study languages in order to learn more about what they have in common and to learn more about UG.

For example, all languages seem to combine subjects and predicates to form larger units, clauses. Word order within the clause, however, can differ across languages. The two most common word orders in the world's languages are the following:

Universal Grammar (UG) the set of linguistic rules common to all languages; hypothesized to be part of human cognition

Subject	**Verb**	**Object** (SVO, as in English)
The cat	ate	the rat

Subject	Object	Verb (SOV, as in Japanese)
Nekoga	nezumio	tabeta
Cat	rat	ate

It seems to be a principle of Universal Grammar that clauses in all languages have subjects, though languages may differ in how the subject is expressed. In some languages, clauses can have a subject that is pronounced; in others, the subject can be unpronounced but clearly interpreted. Such languages are called *null subject languages*. Italian, for example, is a null subject language.

> Isabella non vuole mangiare. (subject pronounced)
> Isabella not want to eat
> 'Isabella does not want to eat'
>
> Non vuole mangiare. (subject not pronounced)
>
> not want to eat
> '[She/he] does not want to eat.'

French is not a null subject language, and neither is English, so such sentences are ungrammatical in those languages.

There are many more examples of possible principles of Universal Grammar, and much current work in linguistics is devoted to discovering, through the study of what seem like differences among languages, the universal principles that all languages share.

Parameters

As you can see from the examples of principles of Universal Grammar, each principle can be characterized in binary terms: languages are most likely SVO or SOV, and languages either allow null subjects or they don't. Linguists have found evidence that basic universal principles can be defined more accurately as **linguistic parameters**. We can think of a parameter as a metaphorical on–off switch. We can account for certain facts about the differences between languages by proposing that in one language a parameter might be set "on" and in the other, "off." This means that the differences among languages, which seem dramatic, are really fairly trivial. Whether a language has SVO or SOV order is a possible parameter: in English, this parameter is set to "on" (and the language is SVO); in Japanese, it is set to "off," and the language is SOV. The same goes for null subjects; a language can have the null subject parameter set either to "on" (e.g., Italian) or to "off" (e.g., English and French).

The notion of such a setting makes the language acquisition task of the child much simpler. The difference between acquiring English and acquiring Japanese or Italian boils down to figuring out how parameters are set.

linguistic parameters binary (on–off) settings of universal grammatical principles proposed to account for differences among languages

All languages also appear to share these universal principles:

- They all have subjects and predicates.
- They all have nouns and verbs.
- They all use a subset of sounds from a much wider possible group of sounds humans make that could be used for language.
- They all have similar ways of categorizing meaning distinctions.

The study of which aspects of languages are universal principles and which are parameterized variations is the topic of a great deal of current research.

Sign Language Grammar

We've noted that sign languages are full linguistic systems with grammar. They differ from spoken language only in modality, the medium by which the language is produced. The study of sign languages provides important insights into UG and parameters and provides important evidence for what is common among all languages of the world.

We mentioned that sign languages exhibit all of the design features of spoken languages. Although some signs in American Sign Language (ASL) are nonarbitrary (the pronoun *I* is indicted by pointing at oneself, for example), most signs are arbitrary, without an obvious logical connection to meaning. (See Figure 1.1.) Sign languages therefore have the same features of arbitrariness and semanticity as spoken languages.

Sign languages such as ASL have complex syntax, morphology, and semantics, and the equivalent of phonology (a system of *primes*, including hand shape, location of sign to the body, and motion of sign to or from the

Figure 1.1 American Sign Language for *eat* is iconic, but the sign for *mistake* has no obvious connection to the meaning of the word and is thus arbitrary.

Source: From *A Basic Course in American Sign Language* by Tom Humphries, Carol Padden, and Terrence J. O'Rourke (1994). Used by permission of the authors.

EAT, FOOD   MISTAKE, ERROR

body). Sign languages therefore have discreteness, productivity, and duality of patterning, just as spoken languages do.

Sign languages also have displacement; signers can easily communicate about things in the past, present, or future. Deaf children even acquire sign languages at basically the same rate as hearing children acquire spoken ones; sign languages, like spoken languages, have different varieties (there are many different sign languages, and each has various dialects); and sign languages change over time. Sign languages also provide us with additional evidence for parameters. For example, linguist Diane Lillo-Martin has shown that ASL is a null subject language much like Italian, Hindi, and Japanese (Lillo-Martin 1991).

hwæt!

Gallaudet University is the only college in the world where every program is designed for deaf and hard-of-hearing students.

Sign Language versus Body Language

Sign language differs quite dramatically from what we call body language—the physical gestures we make, such as smiling, waving, winking, crossing our arms, or clapping. Although these motions and gestures convey meaning and might be argued to be arbitrary and to express semanticity, we don't combine different gestures and motions to create novel "utterances." Body language has no grammar (so there is no duality of patterning or productivity). There is no displacement; a wave or a handshake is just that, an expression of greeting or leave-taking, in the moment. Moreover, much body language is instinctive (smiling, for example, and crying) and stimulus bound, as in other species. Recall that vervet monkeys, for example, produce certain calls only in the presence of a predator,

Language Alive!

Sign Language Diversity

Many of you are aware of and may be signers of American Sign Language, but you might not know that there are many different sign languages around the world and that sign languages have different dialects. Sign languages are full-fledged linguistic systems separate from spoken languages. *Ethnologue*, a well-known compendium of world languages (with both print and web versions: see http://www.ethnologue.com/) lists 121 sign languages around the world. Sign languages are different from signed versions of spoken languages, also called *manually coded systems*. One such coded system is Signed Exact English (SEE), which is a sign system designed to visually represent English syntax and vocabulary as closely as possible, unlike American Sign Language, which has a grammar entirely different from English (and thus from SEE). Teaching SEE is somewhat controversial but is usually intended as a bridge to help ASL signers learn standard written English.

and Rico the border collie is responding to stimuli when he retrieves the toy associated with a particular name. So, though body language (also called *nonverbal behavior*) is highly expressive, it does not have the same structure or features as spoken or signed languages.

RPE 1.11 >

The Scientific Study of Language

So far, much of our discussion has focused on the question, 'What is language?' or more specifically, 'What is it that we know about language?' Here are some of the basic facts we've learned about language.

- We all have unconscious knowledge of a linguistic rule system.
- Languages exist independent of writing systems.
- All languages have grammar (morphology, syntax, semantics, phonetics, and phonology).
- All languages have the same expressive power.
- All children acquire language if exposed to it, without instruction.
- All languages change over time, no matter how hard we try to stop that change.
- A language is really a continuum of language varieties.
- All languages have a common set of basic grammatical properties (Universal Grammar), and some may be parameterized.

The properties of language listed here are relatively recent discoveries and are the result of subjecting language, like other natural phenomena, to rigorous scientific analysis, or the **scientific method**. As in physics or chemistry, language scientists examine data, form hypotheses about the data, test those hypotheses against additional data, and formulate theories, or collections of hypotheses, that can be tested against competing theories. (We talk more about how to study language scientifically throughout the book, and you will have numerous opportunities to be a language scientist yourself.) **Linguistics**, the scientific study of language, is informed by a long history of the study of grammar, and many of the ideas central to current linguistic theory go back to ancient times. Though many of you have heard the term *linguist*, your definition of this term might not be 'language scientist'. You probably think of a linguist as someone who speaks many languages or someone who is a professional translator (a linguist in the U.S. military, for example). Most people are unaware of what linguistics is and of what linguists do, partly because the field of linguistics is so young and also because the scientific study of language represents a significant departure from better-known ways in which language has been studied in the past.

scientific method formation of hypotheses that explain data and the testing of those hypotheses against further data

linguistics the scientific study of language

generative grammar system of grammatical rules that allow speakers to create possible sentences in a language

Noam Chomsky and Generative Grammar

In 1957, graduate student Noam Chomsky wrote a short book called *Syntactic Structures*. In so doing, he introduced **generative grammar**, now the most visible linguistic theory in the world. In *Syntactic Structures*, Chomsky outlined a theory of grammar based on questions about language that were very different from those asked by the scholars before him. Chomsky sought to explain what underlies the human ability to speak and understand language. He wondered what makes up a human language and whether we can construct theories about linguistic systems that can be scientifically tested (Chomsky 1957).

Chomsky's theory of grammar is called *generative* because it is designed to describe a precise and finite set of rules that generates (or has as its output) the possible sentences in a language. Mathematical operations such as division and multiplication are also generative; though many of you had to memorize multiplication tables in school, what you also learned was how to multiply, and the knowledge of that operation allows you (now) to multiply any numbers you want to. We can think of generative grammar in the same way; we don't memorize all the sentences in a language in order to speak it; rather, we learn or acquire a system of rules that allow us to produce and understand the possible sentences in the language. Chomsky proposed that some of these generative rules might also be grounded in Universal Grammar and thus be common to all languages.

Chomsky's approach to language was an enormous departure from the thinking of the time, and this is why Chomsky's influence on the study of

Did You Know...?

Noam Chomsky

No book on modern linguistics would be complete without mention of Noam Chomsky, the best-known linguist in the world. Chomsky was born December 2, 1928, in Philadelphia. His father, William Chomsky, was an eminent teacher and scholar of Hebrew who introduced his son to historical linguistics. Chomsky continued his education at the University of Pennsylvania, where he studied linguistics, mathematics, and philosophy. He earned his Ph.D. from the University of Pennsylvania, though much of his research was done at Harvard between 1951 and 1955. Since then, Chomsky has taught linguistics at the Massachusetts Institute of Technology and is now Institute Professor Emeritus of Linguistics there. Chomsky is also famous for his left-wing political activism and his critique of American foreign policy. He is the author of numerous books and articles on linguistics and on politics. According to the *1992 Arts and Humanities Citation Index*, Chomsky was cited as a source more often than any other living scholar from 1980 to 1992. He is the eighth most-cited scholar in any time period. Chomsky's 1959 review of psychologist B. F. Skinner's book *Verbal Behavior* was an aggressive challenge—an attack, really—that changed the whole approach to the study of language and contributed to what has been called the "cognitive revolution" in psychology.

hwæt!

Noam Chomsky's parents spoke Yiddish and his father, William Chomsky, was a Hebrew scholar from Ukraine.

language is sometimes referred to as the "Chomskyan revolution." In his view, in order to answer the question, What is a language? it is necessary to study language from the inside out, as a system, rather than as a corpus, a list of words and sentences in the language. For Chomsky, the most interesting question to ask about language was, 'What is it that we know about language in order to speak it and understand it?'

Influences on Modern Linguistics

Scientific theories don't crop up overnight; they grow out of research and ideas that precede and even compete with them. The study of language has a rich intellectual history that helped set the stage for the Chomskyan revolution. Chomsky's key ideas about language can be traced back to the thinking of the eighteenth-century rationalist philosophers of the Enlightenment and to the work of the great Swiss linguist Ferdinand de Saussure and other scholars in the structuralist tradition, the movement that examined how the elements of language related to each other in the present (synchronically) rather than comparing present forms to past forms (diachronically).

Rationalism and Empiricism

rationalism
philosophy based on the idea that we use innate knowledge, or reason, to make sense of the world

Rationalism is a philosophy based on the ideas that humans make sense of the world through reason and that reason provides the means of acquiring knowledge. Rationalists argue that in principle all knowledge can be gained through the use of reason. Much of the work that led to this hypothesis was based on geometry; rationalists hypothesize that from knowledge of the axioms of geometry one can derive much other mathematical knowledge. Prominent rationalist philosophers include René Descartes, Gottfried Leibniz, and Benedict Spinoza. An opposing (and also overlapping) school of thought, **empiricism**, is based on the idea that humans learn through experience rather than reason. Prominent empiricist philosophers include John Locke, Thomas Hobbes, and David Hume.

empiricism
philosophy based on the idea that we gain knowledge not through reason but through experience and that the mind starts out as a blank slate

Chomsky proposed a rationalist approach to language, arguing that humans (and not other species) are endowed with the biological capability to acquire the rules and principles that allow us to produce and understand language. He argued, in particular, that evidence from child language acquisition suggests that what speakers know about language cannot be learned simply from experience. Chomsky's ideas were supported by other work at the time. Neuropsychologist Eric Lenneberg argued in his book *Biological Foundations of Language*, published in 1967, that humans are predisposed to acquire language in the same way that behaviors emerge in other species. Lenneberg compared the emergence of human language to the emergence of eyesight in cats or flight in birds, which, he argued, could only be explained by innate biological capabilities. We talk more about Lenneberg's work and the innateness of language in Chapter 2.

Structural Linguistics

Another important influence on modern linguistics was the work of Ferdinand de Saussure (1857–1913). Saussure's work is now known as **structural linguistics**. Saussure's famous *Course in General Linguistics*, based on his students' lecture notes, was published in 1916. The central idea is that language is a structural system—an idea that still holds today.

Saussure focused on the linguistic **signifier**, a spoken, written, or signed form, and the **signified**, the concept, idea, or meaning of the signifier. The linguistic **sign** is the link that connects sound and idea and is abstract rather than concrete. The connection between signifier and signified is also arbitrary (except, in his framework, for onomatopoeia). Saussure argued that languages were complete systems made up of interconnected relationships among signs.

Key to his theory was the distinction between **langue** and **parole** (French words for 'language' and 'speech', respectively). *Langue* is the set of organizing principles of signs, including rules of combination, and *parole* is the physical utterance itself, the use of a sign or a set of signs. *Parole* is only the manifestation of *langue*.

We see Saussure's influence in Chomsky's distinction between **linguistic competence** and **linguistic performance**. In Chomsky's theory, our linguistic competence is our unconscious knowledge of language and is similar in some ways to Saussure's concept of *langue*, the organizing principles of a language. What we actually produce as utterances is similar to Saussure's *parole* and is called linguistic performance. The difference between linguistic competence and linguistic performance can be illustrated by slips of the tongue, such as "noble tons of soil" for "noble sons of toil." Uttering such a slip doesn't mean that we don't know English but rather that we've simply made a mistake because we were tired, distracted, or whatever. Such "errors" also aren't evidence that you (assuming you are a native speaker) are a poor English speaker or that you don't know English as well as someone else does. It means that linguistic performance is different from linguistic competence. When we say that someone is a better speaker than someone else (Martin Luther King Jr., for example, was a terrific orator, much better than you might be), these judgments tell us about performance, not competence. Native speakers of a language, whether they are famous public speakers or not, don't know the language any better than any other speaker in terms of linguistic competence.

That we attach positive value to speakers we characterize as well spoken or articulate shows that social attitudes about language are not necessarily consistent with linguistic fact. Such labels illustrate how we value certain types of linguistic performance over others. The scientific study of language tells us otherwise; none of us "knows" the language

structural linguistics study of the relationship between signifier and signified and of how signs get their meanings from structure

signifier a spoken or signed word or a word on a page

signified the concept, idea, or meaning of the signifier

sign the abstract link that connects sound and idea

langue the set of organizing principles of signs, including rules of combination

parole the physical utterance itself; the use of a sign or a set of signs

linguistic competence unconscious knowledge of grammar that allows us to produce and understand a language

linguistic performance the language we actually produce, including slips of the tongue and other missteps

RPE 1.12

ƕɯæȝ!

Anthropologist Claude Lévi-Strauss (1908–2009) applied Saussure's structural linguistics to the study of culture, arguing for definitions of "family" beyond the traditional father, mother, children structure.

RPE 1.13 ⟩

better than another, and such value judgments are just that: opinions based on our social perceptions and attitudes. Although such labels may seem innocuous enough, attaching social values to language use often leads to linguistic discrimination and even to linguistic "profiling." Such social attitudes about language may make someone less likely to rent an apartment to a speaker of a variety of English that he or she thinks of as lazy, and such negative perceptions based on language may keep someone from getting hired, being considered a competent employee, or even being perceived as a credible witness in court. A better understanding of how language works can help us recognize and challenge such discriminatory practices.

Linguistics Today

Now, linguistics is firmly situated as its own field. Linguistics departments have emerged in universities around the world, increasing in size and number nearly every year. Linguistics is also found in other areas of study, including philosophy, anthropology, computer science, psychology, and speech pathology. Linguistics is becoming more and more central to the study of language and literature in English departments and to the study of language acquisition, learning, and teaching in modern languages departments (sometimes called foreign or world languages departments). And since Chomsky came on the scene, other theories of grammar have emerged, some generative and some not. Some generative theories other than the principles and parameter or transformational grammar introduced

Table 1.1	Subfields of Linguistics

- **Grammar** The study of phonetics, phonology, semantics, syntax, and morphology
- **Pragmatics** The study of language use in context, including rules of conversation and politeness conventions
- **Sociolinguistics** The study of how social factors—including class, race, and ethnicity—influence language
- **Neurolinguistics** The study of language and the brain, how brain damage (aphasia) affects language, and the location of language centers in the brain
- **Psycholinguistics** The study of how we acquire our first language, how we acquire second languages, and how we produce and understand sentences
- **Computational linguistics** The study of artificial languages, computer programming, and modeling of natural language by computers, including voice production and recognition
- **Historical linguistics** The study of language change over time, including the study of language families and relationships among the world's languages
- **Anthropological linguistics** The study of language and culture, including the study of kinship terms and how language shapes cultural identity

here include categorical grammar, lexical functional grammar, head-driven phrase structure grammar, and relational grammar. Some nongenerative theories include cognitive grammar and functional grammar.

As you'll see by the number of topics covered in this book, linguists study a wide range of aspects of language within a range of theoretical frameworks to learn more about how language works and how we use it. Table 1.1 shows some of the subfields of linguistics.

hwæt!

Founded in the mid-1930s, the Department of Linguistics at the University of Chicago is the oldest linguistics department in the United States.

Throughout this book, you will learn how language is studied across these different subfields. In the course of the discussion, we will pique your interest with related facts and commentaries about language in features called "Language Alive!" and "Did You Know . . . ?" Features called "Hwæt!," with interesting tidbits about language and linguistics, are also sprinkled throughout the book. In each chapter, we highlight some way in which linguistics is relevant in everyday occupations ("Accent on") and how it crops up in the public eye from time to time ("Linguistics in the News"). As you'll see, linguistics is everywhere and indeed for everyone.

Accent on *the Linguistic Society of America*

Linguistic Society of America

The largest professional organization of linguists in the United States, the Linguistic Society of America (LSA), was founded in 1924 and now has nearly 6,000 members. The LSA publishes the journal *Language* and holds annual meetings at which linguists from all over the world present papers; attend symposia, workshops, and invited lectures; and share ideas about the scientific study of language. A number of subcommittees of the LSA convene during the annual meeting, including the Committee on the Status of Women in Linguistics, the Undergraduate Program Advisory Committee, the Committee on Social and Political Concerns, the Committee on Language in the School Curriculum, and the Committee on Endangered Languages, among others.

Other important national linguistics organizations typically hold their annual meetings alongside the LSA annual meeting. These include the American Dialect Society, the American Name Society, the North American Association for the History of Language Sciences, the Society for Pidgin and Creole Linguistics, and the Society for the Study of the Indigenous Languages of the Americas.

The LSA also hosts summer linguistics institutes for graduate and undergraduate students and is committed to educating the general public about the science of language. Another important function of the society is as a "linguistic watchdog" on press reports and city, state, and federal policies that concern language and languages in the United States. The LSA has issued statements and resolutions on language rights, the English-only movement, bilingual education, and Ebonics and promotes the revitalization of endangered languages both inside and outside of the United States.

The LSA website is full of information about the field of linguistics, what linguists do, and how to become a linguist yourself. The site provides detailed information on the many areas of study in the field (subfields of linguistics to which we devote chapters in this book), as well as information on linguistics programs and departments across the United States and Canada and on careers in linguistics.

Though you may think that being a linguist limits you to being a linguistics professor in a university, this is not at all the case. Some of the many careers that a background in linguistics prepares you to pursue include teaching foreign languages; translating or interpreting; working in the computer industry or for a product naming company; working on a dictionary (becoming a lexicographer); doing fieldwork and documenting languages of the world; working in publishing, testing, and technical writing; being a dialect coach on a movie set; and many, many more.

For more information
Linguistic Society of America website, http://
    www.lsadc.org/index.cfm
The Linguist List, http://www.linguistlist.org/

Summary

In this chapter, we've taken a close look at language, how to define it, and how to study it. We've found that it is one thing to ask, 'What is a language?' and quite another to ask, 'What do we know about language?' This latter question forms the core of the field of linguistics, the scientific study of language. Research in linguistics attempts to discover and describe the grammatical system we use to produce and understand language beginning when we are very young. That language acquisition proceeds fairly uniformly in all children who are exposed to language suggests that we come to the language acquisition task cognitively set up to do it, hardwired with a set of core grammatical rules and principles called Universal Grammar. The language acquisition task may be made even easier if certain grammatical principles and rules are parameterized, restricting the number of options available to the child. In the following chapter, we explore language acquisition in much more detail, and we investigate other evidence for our linguistic hardwiring based on studies of language and the brain.

Sources and Resources

Bauer, L. & P. Trudgill. 1998. *Language myths*. New York: Penguin.

Chomsky, N. 1957. *Syntactic structures*. The Hague: Mouton.

Chomsky, N. 1981. *Lectures on government and binding: The Pisa lectures*. Dordrecht, The Netherlands: Foris Publications.

Gardner, R., B. Gardner & T. Van Cantfort (eds.). 1989. *Teaching sign language to chimpanzees*. Albany, NY: State University of New York Press.

Hauser, M., N. Chomsky & W. Fitch. 2002. The faculty of language: What is it, who has it, and how did it evolve? *Science* 298(5598). 1569–1579.

Hockett, C. 1960. The origin of speech. *Scientific American* 203. 88–96.

Kaminski, J., J. Call & J. Fischer. 2004. Word learning in a domestic dog: Evidence for "fast mapping." *Science* June 8. 1682–1683.

Klima, E. & U. Bellugi. 1979. *The signs of language*. Cambridge, MA: Harvard University Press.

Lenneberg, E. 1967. *Biological foundations of language*. New York: John Wiley.

Lillo-Martin, D. 1991. *Universal Grammar and American Sign Language: Setting the null argument parameters*. Dordrecht, The Netherlands: Kluwer Academic Publishers.

Merriam-Webster Online. 2008. http://www.merriam-webster.com.

Newmeyer, F. 1986. *Linguistic theory in America*. Orlando, FL: Academic Press.

Pilley, J. W. & A. Reid. 2010. Border collie comprehends object names as verbal referents. *Behavioural Processes*. DOI: 10.1016/j.beproc.2010.11.007.

Pinker, S. 1994. *The language instinct: How the mind creates language*. New York: William Morrow.

Rizzi, L. 1982. *Issues in Italian syntax*. Dordrecht, The Netherlands: Foris Publications.

Savage-Rumbaugh, E. 1986. *Ape language: From conditioned response to symbol*. New York: Columbia University Press.

Searchinger, G. 1995. *The human language series*. Video. New York: Ways of Knowing.

Slobodchikoff, C. 1998. The language of prairie dogs. *Kinship with the animals*, ed. by M. Tobias & K. Solisti-Mattelon, 65–76. Hillsboro, OR: Beyond Words Publishing.

Struhsaker, T. 1967. Behavior of vervet monkeys and other cercopithecines. *Science* 156(3779). 1197–1203.

Terrace, H. 1979. *Nim*. New York: Alfred A. Knopf.

von Frisch, Karl. 1967. *The dance language and orientation of bees*. Cambridge, MA: Harvard University Press.

Wade, N. 2011. Sit. Stay. Parse. Good Girl. *New York Times*, Jan. 17. http://www.nytimes.com/2011/01/18/science/18dog.html.

Review, Practice, and Explore

RPE 1.1 Onomatopoeia and Arbitrariness

One of Hockett's design features of language is *arbitrariness*. Arbitrary signs or symbols have no connection to what they represent. In language, the connection between words and meanings is arbitrary, which is illustrated by the fact that different languages have different words for the same concept ('horse' is *cheval* in French and *Pferd* in German). What about onomatopoeia? Think about words like *buzz* and *woof*. Is the connection between these words arbitrary or not? Look up some examples from other languages. What do such examples tell you about onomatopoeia and arbitrariness?

RPE 1.2 ❯ **Sign Systems**

Investigate some of the different sign systems that we use other than language. Examples are traffic signs, Morse code, and the hand signals referees and umpires make at sports events. These systems can sometimes be quite complex. What design features do they have, and how are they similar to or different from the human language system?

RPE 1.3 ❯ **Prairie Dog Language**

Researcher Con Slobodchikoff of Northern Arizona University has studied prairie dogs for more than twenty years and has concluded that their communication system has many of the same features as human language. According to Slobodchikoff (1998), prairie dogs have different barks ("nouns") for different predators, and they combine these "words" with other sounds, or "modifiers," that indicate size, color, and other features. He also claims that prairie dogs coin new "words" by assigning new barks to new objects or animals in their environment. Prairie dogs, he argues, have words for coyotes, skunks, and badgers, as well as for such non-predators as deer, elk, cows, and even for "the man with the yellow coat." Investigate Slobod-chikoff's work on prairie dogs and determine which of Hockett's design features prairie dogs seem to possess and which they don't. (See http://www.animallanguageinstitute.net/AboutUs/tabid/64/Default.aspx)

RPE 1.4 ❯ **Animal Communication Systems**

Investigate the communication system of a species other than one belonging to the primates. Much research exists on the systems used by dolphins and whales, different varieties of birds, bees, wolves and other canines, and so forth. Discuss which of the design features the system exhibits and how it is similar to and different from human language.

RPE 1.5 ❯ **Primate Experiments**

Conduct some research on the attempts to teach primates communication systems, and discuss the ways in which they challenge Hockett's design features. The most debate centers on whether primates can recombine symbols to create new expressions (duality of patterning) and whether they can acquire the system from other primates. Here are the primary primates with the names of the primary researchers: Washoe (Gardner, Fouts), Nim Chimpsky (Terrace), Kanzi (Savage-Rumbaugh), Koko (Patterson), Lana (Rumbaugh), and Sarah (Premack).

RPE 1.6 ❯ **What Do You Mean by *Grammar?***

As we've pointed out in the chapter, the term *grammar* has many meanings. Explain the distinct meanings of *grammar* in the following sentences. If you can think of others, discuss them as well. You may use a dictionary if you like, but do not rely on it alone.

    a. I better watch my grammar around you!
    b. Please proofread your paper for grammar and style.
    c. I'm taking a class on Spanish grammar.
    d. There have been three grammars written on the language Quechua.
    e. Our innate capacity for the grammar of a language is quite amazing.

RPE   1.7   >   Is That Ungrammatical?

Which of the following sentences are ungrammatical in terms of your own *descriptive* grammar and which are ungrammatical in terms of *prescriptive* grammar? Briefly explain why you analyzed each sentence the way you did.

   a.   Rosie a beautiful pony is.
   b.   Maurice and me are going to the movies tonight.
   c.   John put the book.
   d.   All the tulips are coming up in the garden.
   e.   The all tulips are coming up in the garden.
   f.   Purple big pillows were on her bed.
   g.   I don't have no idea.
   h.   Who did you talk to?
   i.   I saw a cat climb up tree.
   j.   I have drank six glasses of water in a row.

RPE   1.8   >   Correct according to *Who or Whom?*

All of us can probably remember when someone corrected our language, and many of us can also probably think of examples where we have corrected someone else's language. Sometimes this correction can lead to modification; we adopt the "new" form in order to be more socially acceptable. What is a rule of grammar that you have learned is the correct or proper way to say something but that you do not always (or ever) use in speaking? For example, you may have learned that *It's me* is incorrect, and the correct form is *It is I*; however, you may use *me* anyway, and *I* sounds odd to you. Have you modified your speech to say *It is I?* Who corrected you? How would you respond to someone who tells you that your way of speaking is wrong? Write a short paragraph on the language authorities in your life and what modifications you've made (or not made).

RPE   1.9   >   Language in Different Places

The following sentences are grammatical in some variety of English but perhaps not in yours. Do you recognize each as English? Why or why not?

   a.   He is joking only. (Indian English)
   b.   Those cats were just a-playing. (Appalachian [American] English)
   c.   They might could make a deal. (Southeastern American English)
   d.   Ought she to walk the dog soon? (some British English varieties)
   e.   They have made a good life for theirselves. (various varieties)
   f.   This car needs washed. (various varieties)
   g.   We've already boughten some bread. (various varieties)
   h.   The child has learnt the alphabet song. (some British English varieties)
   i.   She done told you. (various varieties)
   j.   They be late. (African American English)
   k.   We happy. (various varieties)

RPE 1.10 ▷ Language in Different Times

Below are some examples of varieties of English that are no longer spoken but are the ancestors of Present-Day English. Do you recognize each variety as English? Why or why not? Which sentences are "older" than the others? Try to put them in order, and explain why you ordered them the way you did. (An answer key is at the end of this "Review, Practice, and Explore" section.)

a. Untill you had gave me an account of what you had Cutt . . .

b. That I ne knew therwith thy nycetee

   'That I knew not thereby your foolishness'

c. Hiericho seo burh wæs mid weallum ymbtrymed & fæste belocen

   'Jericho the city was with walls surrounded and firmly locked'

d. Cecile answerede, "O nyce creature!"

   'Cecile answered, O foolish creature!'

e. Thou sydest no word syn thou spak to me

   'You said no word since you spoke to me'

f. I have thoughts of what you Said to me Concerning them fish.

g. I wonder you had not wrote to me.

h. For ðes folces tocyme, and hi ne dorston ut faran ne in faran

   'Against the people's arrival, and they no dared out go nor in go'

RPE 1.11 ▷ Sign Language versus Body Language

Find at least four examples of arbitrary signs in American Sign Language or another sign language. Also find a few examples of nonarbitrary signs. What are some grammatical features of the sign language you are researching? How do your examples illustrate the difference between sign language and body language?

RPE 1.12 ▷ Linguistic Competence and Linguistic Performance

Record 2 to 5 minutes of casual conversation among friends or family members. (You must by law have their permission to do so. However, try to make the recording as unobtrusive as possible—you don't want their speech to be stilted or formal as a result of the taping. So tell them you're taping them but then try to get them to forget about it.) Now transcribe the tape, writing down everything that was said, including "ums" and "ahs," false starts, and other features. (Please leave out names and other identifying characteristics.) You will likely find that the speaker very rarely uses complete sentences. What does this simple exercise tell you about the distinction between competence and performance?

RPE 1.13 ▷ Language Myths and Stereotypes

Learning more about language allows us to recognize misperceptions about language when we hear them. While some "language myths" are rather benign, some can be very discriminatory. Based on what you've learned in this chapter, choose four of the following language myths (none of the statements below is true) and explain why they are misperceptions. Why do you think such misperceptions persist? Try to explain.

a. Some languages have no grammar.
b. French is much more romantic than German.
c. English descended from Latin.
d. Aborigines speak a primitive language.
e. Teenagers are ruining the English language.
f. Children are taught language by their parents.
g. We'd speak better English if schools would teach more grammar.
i. Some kids learn language better than others.
j. People who use double negatives are just lazy.

Answers to Exercise 10

Old English (from the OE Heptateuch): c, h
Middle English (from Chaucer's *Second Nun's Tale*): b, d, e
Early Modern English: a, f, g

The Human Capacity for Language

Our Capacity to Acquire Language
What Children's "Mistakes" Tell Us
Stages of First Language Acquisition
A Critical Period for Language
Acquisition?

Second Language Acquisition
Is It Learning or Acquisition?
Interlanguage Grammar
Social Aspects of Second Language
Acquisition
Second Language Acquisition and
Universal Grammar

Two Native Languages: Bilingualism
Misperceptions about Bilingualism

Our Capacity to Create Language
Pidgins and Creoles

Language and the Brain
Language Intelligence?
A Language Center in the Brain?
More Evidence for Lateralization

Summary

Sources and Resources

Review, Practice, and Explore

Key Concepts

- Children figure out complex rules of grammar just from hearing (or seeing, in the case of sign language) language around them.
- Evidence suggests that language acquisition proceeds in the same stages, over the same period of time, across languages.
- Second language acquisition differs from first language acquisition and from bilingualism, but all provide evidence for Universal Grammar.
- Universal characteristics of pidgins suggest that all languages share one blueprint.
- Language seems to be in some ways separate from other cognitive abilities, as the language capacity of linguistic savants indicates.
- Language may be lateralized on the left side of the brain, and specific areas may be responsible for specific linguistic tasks.

Did You Know . . . ?

How Do You Study an Infant?
Baby Talk and Parentese
What about *Baby Einstein*?
Poor Phineas Gage

Language Alive!   One *Wug* and Two . . . *Wugs*?

Hardwiring and Order of Acquisition

Linguistics in the News   A Gene for Language?

Accent on   Clinical Linguistics

31

> *When we study human language, we are approaching what some might call the "human essence," the distinctive qualities of mind that are, so far as we know, unique to man . . .*
>
> —NOAM CHOMSKY, *LANGUAGE AND MIND*

The previous chapter outlined some of what we can learn by studying language scientifically. It presented some evidence that humans are uniquely adapted to acquire language when exposed to it and that our unconscious knowledge of our own linguistic system (syntax, phonetics and phonology, morphology, and semantics) allows us to produce and understand sentences we've never heard before. In this chapter, we will explore in more detail our unconscious knowledge of language—or more specifically, of grammar—and what the scientific study of language tells us about how we think and about how our brains work. We will explore evidence from **psycholinguistics**, the study of the comprehension and production of language and its development in children. We will discuss how we acquire our first language and how this process differs from how we acquire a second or third language. We'll discuss what it means to be bilingual, or to have more than one first language. We'll explore evidence from the spontaneous emergence of language, or language genesis, to see what this phenomenon tells us about language acquisition and our unique capacity for language.

We'll then investigate how our brains are actually organized for language. We'll examine evidence from people with cognitive impairments who still develop language normally. We'll also look at the other side of the coin—people whose language is impaired but who otherwise function relatively normally. We will look at evidence for "language areas" of the brain and how the brain might be *lateralized* for language on the left side. The study of the human brain mechanisms underlying language is called **neurolinguistics.**

psycholinguistics study of how we acquire, produce, and understand language

neurolinguistics study of the mechanisms of the brain that underlie how we acquire, produce, and understand language

Our Capacity to Acquire Language

Contrary to popular belief, children do not learn language because we teach it to them or because they imitate us. If they did, we would expect a great deal more variation in the rate at which children acquire language and in the degree of acquisition. Some children would simply opt out of the learning process altogether, like, say, opting out of learning to play the piano. But that doesn't happen. In fact, all children are able to acquire an extremely complicated grammatical system by the time they are 4 or 5 years old, and they all, under normal circumstances, accomplish this task without being directly taught. Noam Chomsky was first to argue that first language acquisition in human infants proceeds the way it does because we are cognitively predisposed to acquire language. He observed that the input available to children—the language they hear around them—does not provide enough information alone for the child to learn the complex set of grammatical rules needed to produce and understand a language. Much research in the field of first language acquisition supports this **poverty of the stimulus argument**, that children do not receive enough data to acquire language simply from what they hear spoken around them.

poverty of the stimulus argument position that children do not receive enough data to acquire language simply from what they hear

What Children's "Mistakes" Tell Us

Children hear speakers stop and start, cough, fail to complete sentences, and trail off—but children seem to tease out the rules of language regardless of this mass of confusing data. The mistakes they make (which, as we'll see, aren't really mistakes at all) tell us that they are experts at the acquisition of linguistic rules, even if those rules don't correspond (yet) to the rules adults use.

Mouses and Foots: Overgeneralizing Rules

Most of you have probably heard a child say a word that you would never say. For example, children acquiring English routinely produce verbs like *bringed* and *goed* or nouns like *mouses* and *foots*, and they certainly haven't learned these forms from the adults around them. So they aren't imitating adult speech, but they are figuring out grammatical rules, in this case the way to form past-tense verbs and plural nouns. This process of figuring out a grammatical rule and applying it generally is called **overgeneralization**. Children later modify their natural rules of past tense and plural formation to accommodate the exceptions, including *brought, went, mice,* and *feet*. Moreover, they modify their language only when they're good and ready. Children are fairly impervious to correction, as the following exchange between an adult and a child illustrates:

overgeneralization application of a grammatical rule more broadly than it is generally applied

Child: Want other one spoon, Daddy.
Father: You mean, you want the other spoon.
Child: Yes, I want other one spoon, please, Daddy.
Father: Can you say "the other spoon"?
Child: Other . . . one . . . spoon.
Father: Say "other."
Child: Other.
Father: "Spoon."
Child. Spoon.
Father: "Other spoon."
Child: Other . . . spoon. Now give me other one spoon?

One *Wug* and Two . . . *Wugs*?

A famous example of overgeneralization is the deceptively simple-looking *wugs* experiment, devised by Jean Berko Gleason (1958). Here's how the experiment went. Children aged 4 through 7 years were shown a drawing and told, "This is a wug."

Then they were shown another drawing and told, "Now there is another one. There are two of them."

They were then led to fill in the blank.

There are two _____.

Children invariably responded, as you might expect, with *wugs* as the plural form of *wug*. What this shows, though, is that we do not have to hear words in the plural first in order to learn the plurals; rather, we learn the plural *rule*, namely, add *-s* to a singular noun, and we can then apply that rule to any new noun we hear.

_____

Wugs are copyrighted by Jean Berko Gleason and reprinted with permission.

Evidence for Universal Grammar

The evidence for overgeneralization tells us that children formulate grammatical rules when exposed to language, teasing these rules out of the mass of data they hear even when they are very young. Children's acquisition of language also provides us with evidence for Universal Grammar, the set of grammatical rules and principles common to all languages.

In English, we can form questions by putting a question word (such as *who, what, when, which,* etc.) in sentence-initial position.

Who did John see Mary with ____?

Here, we've questioned the object of the preposition *with*. The answer to such a question would be a sentence like the following (where *her friend* is the object of the preposition):

John saw Mary with <u>her friend</u>.

Now, children who have mastered this question rule (which takes some time) can form questions out of any sentence, producing, for example, *Where is the dog?* or *Why can't I go?* And children make many "errors" along the way to acquiring the adult version of this rule; you may have heard a child say something like *Where the dog is?* or *Why I can't go?* because they have yet to develop the adult form of the rule. But here's an error a child *never* makes:

*Who did John see Mary and ___?

Compare this question with the preceding one. In the first example, we've questioned the object of the preposition *with*, and the result is a grammatical sentence of English. In the second example, we've questioned part of a *coordinated* phrase, a phrase that is made up of two phrases connected with the conjunction *and*. The result is a sentence that no speaker of English would ever utter.

We won't go into a detailed discussion of the syntactic difference between these two sentences, but the basic point is this: Speakers simply *know* that the question formation rule works in sentences like the first one, with the preposition *with*, but not in sentences like the second, which involve coordination with *and*. Obviously, no one teaches us this kind of complex grammatical concept in school, nor do we learn this kind of thing from our parents. That young children never make this kind of error suggests that they already have the relevant grammatical information in their heads, wired into their brains as part of Universal Grammar.

Now let's look at another "error" involving the rule of question formation we've just introduced. This example is from research done by Stephen Crain, Rosalind Thornton, and Gabriela Tesan (2008) and is captured in a video clip at http://www.uga.edu/lsava/Crain/Crain.html. Consider the following question, produced (consistently) by a child of about 2 years. (What's odd to adult English speakers is the presence of the second *what*.)

What do you think what's in there?
What do you think what she said?

Several things about these questions are noteworthy. First, the child has never heard questions of this form in the English she is exposed to, yet she routinely produces them (regardless of the researchers' numerous attempts to elicit questions with adult word order). This tells us that the child has certainly formulated a rule of question formation, but it's one that differs from the adult version. That the child doesn't simply modify her grammatical rule to conform to the adult version when she hears adults talk tells us that children formulate their own versions of grammatical rules and that they don't learn by imitation or through correction. But perhaps the most interesting thing about the child's question rule is that it isn't idiosyncratic at all; her rule conforms to the way questions are formed in German:

Was denkst du was darin ist?
what thinks you what therein is
'What do you think is in there?'

Was denkst du was sie gesagt hat?
what think you what she said has
'What do you think she said?'

So the child's rule is a "possible" question formation rule, but it's just not the English one (yet). This provides evidence for Universal Grammar; the child is acquiring a linguistic rule that conforms to the options available to her via UG.

Children Don't Learn by Analogy

We have just discussed the notion that humans do not learn language simply by imitation; children produce words and phrases that they have never heard before.

The cat goed out already.
The mouses ate the seeds.

analogy learning rules and applying them to other similar expressions; learning through comparison

So, clearly language is not learned simply through imitation. Some have suggested, though, that children learn by **analogy**, by comparing partially similar forms and by using more general knowledge (rather than innate linguistic knowledge) to acquire language.

This analogy theory of language acquisition looks like a good one at first glance. Children may not have ever heard *goed* or *mouses*, but they have heard plenty of other words that end with those regular endings: past tense *-ed* and plural *-s*. So they simply extend those patterns to apply to all verb and noun forms. If this is how children acquire grammatical rules, it makes sense to think that rather than being equipped with Universal Grammar, they are simply very good at making connections, recognizing patterns, and making extensions. However, this kind of pattern extension breaks down upon closer examination.

Noam Chomsky gives several kinds of examples of analogies that break down in language acquisition. For instance, if we learned the patterns of language by hearing language, recognizing the patterns, and then extending those patterns to new constructions, we would expect to find the following kinds of sentences. Say that a child hears a sentence like this one:

We painted the green chair.

They might also hear a sentence like this one:

We painted the chair green.

On the basis of hearing sentences like that, the child could infer that the last two words, a noun and an adjective (*chair . . . green*) can be switched (*green . . . chair*), and either order results in a grammatical sentence. So the language learner then takes a sentence with a different verb, such as

> We saw the green chair.

and then deduces that the order of the final two words, a noun and an adjective just like in the previous examples, can be switched:

> *We saw the chair green.

This sentence is, of course, not a sentence of English (at least not if we understand *green* as an adjective, as in the other sentences). And neither children nor adults ever make this error or one remotely like it. We'd expect them to, though, if all they are doing is learning by analogy. Rather, it seems that children have some kind of knowledge of linguistic rules, rules that block production of such sentences.

RPE   2.1 ▷

In the following section, we turn to even more evidence that the human mind is specifically designed to approach the task of language acquisition and that it accomplishes much of this task relatively quickly and also at relatively the same rate across languages and cultures. Evidence from the stages of language acquisition provides us with additional evidence for our linguistic hardwiring and for Universal Grammar.

Stages of First Language Acquisition

In nearly all cases, children's acquisition of language follows a predictable sequence. Linguists study how children of all ages (even before they're born!) acquire sounds, words, and their meanings and how they combine words into sentences. Although children don't all progress through each stage in exactly the same way, it is possible to identify a general progression, beginning with the prelinguistic stage in the earlier months and progressing through what we'll call the *later multiword stage* at about 3 to 4 years old.

The Prelinguistic Stage: The Early Months

There is evidence that by the time hearing babies exposed to oral language are 2 months old, they can recognize the intonation patterns of their native language. This is perhaps not surprising, given that babies can hear in the womb after around 7 months and are exposed in this way to the sounds of language (and other sounds as well, of course) early on. This may also be why babies seem to be able to produce the intonation patterns of language before they can actually form words. Other studies have shown that babies can distinguish human language sounds from other sounds (car engines, doors slamming, dogs barking). Interestingly, babies during the prelinguistic stage differentiate the sounds of any language from nonlinguistic sounds regardless of whether that sound occurs in the child's native language. For example, a baby born in the United States to English-speaking parents, exposed only to English, can tell the difference between a sound that does not occur in English (but does occur in, say, Chichewa, a Bantu language of Africa) and nonlinguistic sounds.

The Babbling Stage: 4 to 8 Months

By about the time they are 6 months old, babies seem to have mastered many of the sounds of their own language, and up until they are about a year old they produce these sounds consistently during what is called the *babbling stage*. All hearing babies capable of vocalization babble, which shows that it is a universal process. Deaf children exposed to signing babble with their hands (their signs are rhythmic and signed consistently in front of the body). Babies in the babbling stage tend to produce the same consonants, no matter what language they are exposed to: /p, b, t, m, d, n, k, g, s, h, w, j/. The consonants /f, v, l, r/ and others are only infrequently produced during this period. Such evidence suggests that even at the babbling stage, babies are predisposed to language.

Did You Know...?

How Do You Study an Infant?

All kinds of experiments are conducted on infants—those that test perception, cognition, language abilities—but preverbal infant psychology is actually a very difficult thing to study. How can the baby convey what he or she is thinking? Andrew Meltzoff and his colleagues began using a technique in the 1970s for eliciting infants' responses to various stimuli: measuring babies' sucking on a pacifier. When the infants become accustomed to a stimulus, their sucking rate slows down. When a new stimulus is shown, they begin to suck more vigorously again.

The One-Word Stage: 9 to 18 Months

After about a year, hearing babies recognize the word as the link between sound and meaning. They begin to produce their own words, particularly nouns and verbs, around this time. Between the ages of about 12 and 18 months, they are attempting to produce the fifty or so most common words in their everyday environment. These first words typically show tremendous variability in pronunciation. Some may be adult-like productions, while others may be so distorted that only family members can understand them.

overextension use of words to apply to things beyond their actual meaning

underextension use of words to apply to things more narrowly than their actual meaning

At this stage, children tend to employ both **overextension**, in which they extend the meanings of words, and **underextension**, in which the meanings are narrower than for adults. An example of overextension is the word *moon* used not only for the moon but also for grapefruit halves, cakes, and the letter *o*. Another example is *candy* used not only for candy but for anything sweet. An example of underextension is use of the word *kitty* for a particular cat but not for other cats. This stage of acquisition is also called the *holophrastic stage*, in which a single word can function as a sentence or proposition. Children during this stage can produce about fifty different words (but understand many more than that), and most of their words are consonant + vowel combinations no matter what language they speak. The meanings conveyed by the single word seem to be more than just labels for an object or action; *ball* might convey something like "I want that ball." *Juice* means "I want juice." *Moon* means "I see the moon."

The Two-Word Stage: 18 to 24 Months

During the next stage, usually between 18 and 24 months, children seem to go through a 'naming explosion', when they grasp the idea that things have names. This process is called *fast mapping* (the same process the border collies Rico and Chaser appear to exhibit, as we discussed in Chapter 1). Children at this stage also begin to combine words into two-word utterances (which are distinguished from two one-word utterances by the intonation patterns). The utterances have fairly consistent word order, and their structure seems to be determined by semantic relationships rather than by syntactic ones as in adult speech. There are very few endings on words to indicate syntactic or morphological relationships. Some examples of speech produced during this two-word stage include the following:

agent + action	mama sleep
action + thing	kick ball
action + location	sit couch
thing + location	kitty bed
possessor + possession	dada boat
thing + attribute	mama big
determiner + thing	my sock

As you can see in the examples, at this stage children speak "telegraphically"; they leave out function words (articles such as *the*, *a*; prepositions such as *in*, *on*; verbs such as *don't*, *is*) and inflectional endings (such as plural *-s* or past tense *-ed*). They tend to rely on content words, such as nouns, verbs, and adjectives (which convey more meaning, so perhaps this isn't surprising). Though they seem to be limited in the number of words they can string together in a single phrase, they nevertheless can communicate (with limited vocabulary and syntax) quite expressively, and what children can understand far outstrips their language production at this stage. Deaf babies also go through a comparable stage, producing two-sign combinations during this developmental period.

Language  Alive!

Hardwiring and Order of Acquisition

Roger Brown, in an in-depth study of children's acquisition of certain *function* words (words with grammatical meanings, such as prepositions and auxiliary verbs, as opposed to *content* words, such as *cat* and *house*) and certain inflectional endings (such as *-ed* and *-s*) found that children acquire these in a particular order. Brown proposed that this order of acquisition provides evidence for linguistic hardwiring because the order is remarkably consistent regardless of the child's circumstances.

1. present progressive (*-ing*)
2. the preposition *in*
3. the preposition *on*
4. plural inflections (*-s, -es*)
5. irregular past tense verbs (*went, fell*)
6. possessive inflections (*the dog's ball*)
7. uncontractible copula (*is, am,* and *are*)
8. articles (*the, a, an*)
9. past inflections on regular verbs (*-ed*)
10. regular third-person forms (*-s* as in '*Suzi sings*')
11. irregular third-person forms (*has, does*)
12. uncontractible auxiliary forms (*did*)
13. contractible copula (*she's happy, they're sad*)
14. contractible auxiliary forms (*he's going*)

For more information

Brown, R. 1973. *A first language: The early stages.* Cambridge, MA: Harvard University Press.

The Early Multiword Stage: 24 to 30 Months

We mentioned previously that as children begin to acquire different grammatical rules, they often overgeneralize those rules. We gave the examples of *mouses* and *foots* (and *wugs*) to illustrate the overgeneralization of the rule for forming plurals in English.

Children also begin to acquire more complex syntactic structure and rules at this stage, though their grammatical patterns do not yet approximate those of adult grammar. From around 2 to 4 years, children form questions by placing such question words as *where* and *what* at the front of the sentence (data adapted from Foss & Hakes [1978] and Clark & Clark [1977]):

Where kitty?
What me think?

Children at this stage rely on intonation to form questions, producing utterances such as these:

> That mine?
> See doggie?

Acquisition of negative sentences during this stage also follows a certain pattern. At the one-word stage, children typically simply use *no* or a word such as *allgone* to indicate negation. During this early multiword stage, *no* appears at the beginning of more complex statements:

RPE 2.2

> no eat
> no sit down
> no do that

The Later Multiword Stage: 30 Months and Older

Right around 30 months begins what Steven Pinker (1994) refers to in *The Language Instinct* as "all hell break[ing] loose." Development is so rapid that it's hard to distinguish stages, and children begin to produce sentences of varied length and complexity.

During this stage, children begin to use more question words, such as *why* and *how*, and they at first continue to use intonation rather than inversion to form questions:

> Why doggie run?
> How she can do that?

Children produce more complex negative structures with *no* or *not* and some auxiliary verbs or modals, such as *don't* and *can't*. Interestingly, children acquire auxiliary verbs in negative sentences before positive ones, producing *can't* and *don't* before *can* and *do*.

> I can't move it.
> He not tall.
> Mommy no play.
> I don't know him.

Later, children produce negative sentences with *not* in the position after a wider range of auxiliary verbs, consistent with the rule of adult grammar; auxiliary verbs begin to appear in positive sentences during this stage as well:

> I didn't do it.
> Mommy won't play.
> I should not go.

And finally, children invert the subject and auxiliary verb in questions, as in adult grammar:

> Why did doggie run?
> How can she do that?

Table 2.1	Children's Speech Production	
Stage	**Approximate Age (mo.)**	**Typical Patterns**
Babbling	5–9	consonant–vowel patterns: *ma ma ma, da da da, ba ba ba*, etc.
One-word	9–18	single words: 50 or so common words in environment
Two-word	18–24	combinations of words, mini-sentences *mommy go, want juice, allgone, no eat*
Early multiword	24–30	more complex structure in sentences *where doggie? No eat that.*
Later multiword	30+	adult-like phonology, morphology, and syntax; still many overgeneralizations (*goed, mouses*, etc.)

As they progress through this later multiword stage, children gain command of function words (such as prepositions), coordination (with words such as *and* and *or*), and dependent clauses:

> He was stuck and I got him out.
> Look at the train Ursula bought.
> I like to play with something else. (Adapted from Pinker [1994])

There are several ways one could summarize the developmental sequence most children go through in acquiring language, but Table 2.1 shows a common way of describing children's production of speech.

Similar stages and patterns occur in all languages. Children seem to progress through the process of first language acquisition at relatively the same rate and through similar stages regardless of their environment: how much or how little they are spoken to, how much they speak, how many books are read to them, or how much TV they watch.

RPE 2.3

Table 2.2	Characteristics of Biological Behavior

- The behavior emerges before it is necessary.
- Its appearance is not the result of conscious decision.
- Its emergence is not triggered by external events (but the surrounding environment must be appropriate for it to develop adequately).
- Direct teaching and intensive practice have relatively little effect on the behavior.
- There is a regular sequence of milestones as the behavior develops, and these can usually be correlated with age and other aspects of development.
- There is likely to be a critical period for the acquisition of the behavior.

Data from Lenneberg, E. 1967. *Biological foundations of language.* New York: Wiley.

So language, like other biological behaviors, appears to simply emerge in children when they are exposed to it. In his book *Biological Foundations of Language*, published in 1967, neuropsychologist Eric Lenneberg compares the acquisition of language and what he argues are innate abilities in other animals, such as eyesight in cats or flight in birds. You can see from the list of characteristics of such behaviors in Table 2.2 that language acquisition fits in quite well.

A Critical Period for Language Acquisition?

One common assumption about learning a second language, at home or in school, is that it is easier the younger you are and that after you grow up, learning a second language is much harder. What about first language acquisition?

Did You Know...?

Baby Talk and Parentese

Do you think it matters how your parents talked to you when you were a baby? Can parents help children acquire language or even hinder that process? Do parents talk to children differently across cultures? If they do, and if "parentese" matters, wouldn't we expect to see differences in rates of language acquisition?

Much research has been done on the role of parents or caregivers in babies' language acquisition. Here are some of the basic characteristics of this kind of speech.

- Slower, exaggerated articulation, intonation, and stress; higher pitch, pauses
- Restricted, concrete vocabulary with fewer verbs and lots of nouns
- Complete, short sentences
- More commands and questions than declaratives
- Repetitive and focused on here and now—what's happening in child's immediate environment

Some people discourage so-called baby talk, believing it may hinder a child's language development, but in fact using such techniques in speaking to babies and small children may help language acquisition along. Kuhl and colleagues (1997) studied the parentese of native speakers of English, Swedish, and Russian and found that across languages, parentese has a unique acoustic signature that "stretches" vowels, a process that may make vowels more distinct to babies than those they would hear in typical adult speech. Such stretching of vowels, the researchers suggest, may facilitate language acquisition. There may also be a correlation between how rapidly a child acquires auxiliary verbs and the number of questions the child hears (*Is that your kitty?*). But children who do not have the same input will still end up fully acquiring the grammar of the language and therefore are not at a disadvantage.

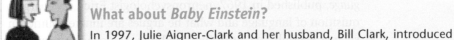

What about *Baby Einstein*?

In 1997, Julie Aigner-Clark and her husband, Bill Clark, introduced their line of *Baby Einstein* (marketed under the name *Language Nursery*) products to an enthusiastic public. *Baby Einstein* became a multimillion-dollar franchise, which is now owned by The Walt Disney Company. The *Baby Einstein* series is promoted as an educational tool to boost children's knowledge and language skills and includes such titles as *Baby MacDonald* (on agriculture), *Baby Wordsworth*, *Baby Mozart*, *Baby Galileo*, and *Baby da Vinci*. The series has been criticized by the Campaign for a Commercial-Free Childhood, however, for promoting television watching for young children. (The American Academy of Pediatrics recommends no television for children younger than 2 years.) An even more critical study by Frederick Zimmerman and colleagues (2007) concluded that infants aged 8 to 16 months exposed to educational DVDs aimed at them had *lower* scores on standard language development tests. Older babies studied showed no negative effects from watching DVDs but no positive ones either. But daily reading and storytelling did lead to higher language scores for toddlers. In an interview in *Newsweek*, Zimmerman suggested that the lower verbal scores might be due to the fact that watching DVDs takes the child away from interaction with parents and siblings, all of which facilitates language development.

For more information

Campaign for a Commercial-Free Childhood. http://www. commercialexploitation.org.

American Academy of Pediatrics. http://www.aap.org.

Interlandi, J. 2007. Learning: Turn it off, baby. *Newsweek*, August 20–27. http://www.newsweek.com/id/32243.

---

critical period for language acquisition early childhood to prepuberty; according to some, the best, maybe only, time in which humans can acquire a first language

Is there, as many (including Lenneberg) have argued, a **critical period for language acquisition**, just as there are critical periods for other types of behavior? For example, Banks et al. (1975) found that there appears to be a critical period for the development of a human child's binocular vision (from 1 to 3 years). And the well-known Austrian scientist Konrad Lorenz (1950) argued as early as the 1930s that baby birds form social bonds, *imprinting* on adult birds, during a critical period, after which imprinting becomes impossible (often with disastrous results for the baby bird). Studies have since shown that imprinting is not necessarily restricted, as Lorenz claimed, to a particular developmental phase or critical period (Hoffman 1996). The critical period for language acquisition is somewhat controversial as well. It is also quite difficult to study, given that under normal circumstances, children are not raised isolated from language. Cases of such isolation do exist, and we will discuss a few of them as well as other experiments that provide insights into the critical period for first language acquisition.

Acquisition and Isolation: Victor and Genie

hwæt!

A 1970 film by François Truffaut called *L'Enfant Sauvage* ("The Wild Child") is based on Itard's work with Victor.

There are some (rather horrifying) cases of children who were deprived of language during their early years and who were never able to fully acquire it. In 1797, a boy who was believed to be about 12 years old was discovered in the woods in Aveyron, France, where he had apparently survived on his own since childhood. The boy, called Victor, ultimately ended up in the care of a young doctor named Jean Marc Itard. Itard worked with Victor for years, carefully documenting his progress. Victor's language remained quite impaired, and Itard made very little progress with him.

Probably the best-known case of a child isolated from language is that of a girl called Genie. She was discovered in 1970 at the age of about 13. She had not been allowed to speak or to be spoken to for about 12 years. Despite subsequent years of direct instruction, she never fully acquired language. Susan Curtiss (1977), the linguist who worked most with Genie, wrote that Genie's utterances remained telegraphic and that what language she did acquire differed greatly from that of normal children.

Because social isolation can result in mental retardation and emotional problems, cases such as Victor's and Genie's are problematic for what they can really offer about the critical period and language acquisition. The fact that neither Victor nor Genie ever acquired language might be due to a number of factors other than lack of language development in the critical period—isolation, abuse, and deprivation among them. Other studies, however, provide us with some interesting insights into the critical period.

Sign Language Acquisition

Acquisition of sign language can shed additional light on the critical period hypothesis. Deaf children of hearing parents may not be exposed to sign language from birth for a variety of reasons. It may be that they are not diagnosed as deaf right away, or there may be limited opportunities to expose the child to sign language. Studies by Newport (1990) and others show that early exposure to sign language is crucial in order to fully acquire the grammar of the language. It has been found, for example, that the grammar of deaf children who were exposed to sign language after age 13 systematically differs from the grammar of signers exposed to sign language from birth. Although signers in both groups can communicate expressively, those acquiring the language later in life use different verbs of motion and also differ in their use of verb agreement. (For further discussion of a critical period for the acquisition of sign language, see Newman et al. 2002.)

Additional evidence for the critical period for language acquisition comes from Nicaraguan Sign Language, which we discuss later in the chapter. We will also return to the critical period hypothesis when we discuss the anatomy of the brain and what brain development tells us about how easy or how hard it is to acquire language. But first, we turn to second language acquisition and what this tells us about mind, brain, and language.

Second Language Acquisition

Now that you know something about how children acquire their native language, think about how this acquisition process differs from *second language acquisition*, the process by which, for example, you learn another ("foreign") language in school. You might sit in a classroom for an hour a day and be exposed to the language and have a teacher explain different grammatical rules, and after class you might study some of the grammatical rules you've learned, or you may practice speaking the language with some classmates, and so on. This situation is entirely different from the way in which you are exposed to your first language as a child, when you are immersed in your native language.

Let's suppose you're an adult, and you travel to another country and are immersed in the language there. You already speak a native language, so how does the process of becoming proficient in this second language proceed? Does your first language help you learn a second language, or does it hinder that process? How do you keep the grammar of each language, the native one and the second one, straight? If you are learning a second language as an adult, your brain is already mature, so do you go through the same developmental stages learning that language as you do acquiring your native language as a child? Let's look at what the research tells us and what questions it raises about this complex process.

Is It Learning or Acquisition?

First, should we call this phenomenon we're talking about second language *learning* or second language *acquisition*? The terminology here is rather controversial and boils down to whether one can gain the same proficiency in a second language as in a first one. This in turn depends on what we mean by *proficiency* and how we define such terms as *fluency* and what it means to be a "native" speaker. Native speaker judgments are not always clear; they do not consistently identify nonnative speakers, and sometimes they identify native speakers as nonnative!

We will use the term *second language acquisition* here, abbreviated SLA, and refer to those acquiring a second language as second language acquirers. Bear in mind that we are not talking here about simultaneous acquisition of two or more languages by children; that's *bilingualism*, discussed later in the chapter.

Interlanguage Grammar

As a second language acquirer, you already have a first language, and you are being exposed to a second one (you can still be a child, but you have had significant exposure to a first language). SLA can be characterized by

interlanguage
grammar
intermediate
grammar that is
influenced by both a
person's native and
second languages

what is called **interlanguage grammar**, the grammar that is influenced by both the first language (L1) and the second language (L2) and has features of each (for more discussion see White 2003).

L1 → interlanguage grammar → L2

The fact that you can tell what someone's first language is even though they are speaking a second one illustrates the influence of L1. The speaker *transfers* the phonology of the first language to the second one. So someone whose native language is Hindi will sound different speaking English as a second language than someone whose first language is Croatian. Interlanguage grammar is also influenced by L2; a speaker whose L1 is French may place adjectives after the noun in English, consistent with French placement. So they may say *coat long,* rather than *long coat.* Speakers of Japanese learning English often do not use determiners and articles such as *the* and *a,* producing such utterances as *dog barked* or *I like car.* This is because in Japanese the information expressed by these English words is indicated in other ways than by separate words preceding nouns.

RPE   2.4

Much more is involved; as you'll see throughout this book, knowing a language involves far more than knowing a list of grammatical rules. And just as in the case of first language acquisition, we can learn much about second language acquisition from studying the "mistakes" second language learners make, as well as the ones they don't make even though we might expect them to.

Social Aspects of Second Language Acquisition

The social aspect of learning a second language is crucial. Adults learning a second language bring to this task a much different set of tools (and inhibitions!) than those that children bring to the acquisition of their L1—and to the acquisition of L2 as well, for that matter. Adults are more conscious of cultural codes and rules, which can both help and hinder the language learning process.

Second language acquirers may also have been exposed to *metalanguage,* a way of talking about language that we often learn in school. So they may have some understanding of grammatical terms and concepts, which will affect acquisition of a second language.

Another important factor is motivation; we acquire our first language without conscious motivation, but we often learn a second language for a specific reason: a job, interest in a culture, cultural integration, and so on (Selinker 1972). (Interestingly, studies have shown that success in SLA requires motivation, but it doesn't matter much what *kind* of motivation.) In other words, how you feel about the SLA process plays a crucial role in your success at the task. How self-conscious you are, how much you do or do not identify with the cultural community that speaks the language you are attempting to acquire—such factors contribute to second language acquisition. There is a lot of anecdotal evidence that children can acquire second languages more easily than adults. Think about families from non–English-speaking countries who immigrate to North America; the children often quickly become fluent in the language and then serve as translators for their parents, whose second language acquisition typically lags behind that of their children.

Second Language Acquisition and Universal Grammar

One very interesting question that arises when we consider the differences (and similarities) between acquiring L1 and acquiring L2 is the role of Universal Grammar. We've seen that there is evidence that we rely on UG to acquire our first language as children. We've also seen that there may be a critical period for language acquisition, after which our window of opportunity for gaining native proficiency in a second language may narrow. Does this mean that we have less access to UG after that window closes? Is this what makes acquiring a second language as an adult more difficult than doing so as a child? There are many such questions, and the answers we ultimately find to them will contribute to our understanding of the complex human capacity for language and how we learn it and teach it.

RPE 2.5

Two Native Languages: Bilingualism

bilingualism (bilingual language acquisition) native ability to express oneself in two languages acquired simultaneously, usually at a very young age

Second language acquisition is different from **bilingualism** or **bilingual language acquisition**. Bilingual acquisition is the *simultaneous* (or nearly so) acquisition of more than one first language. Even though more than half of the world's population is bilingual, there are many misconceptions about what it means to be a native speaker of more than one language. One reason for this is that bilingualism itself is difficult to define: proficiency in the languages spoken can depend on, for example, opportunities for use, cultural attitudes toward bilingualism in school, the developmental stage of each language, and so on. As a result of the complexity of even defining what it means to be bilingual, many myths surround this linguistic phenomenon. Often, these misconceptions are linked with social attitudes about the bilingual speakers themselves and with ideas about cultural identity, attitudes about immigration and immigrant populations, and so on. (See Adger et al. 2002; MacGregor-Mendoza 2005.)

hwæt!

Bilinguals have higher IQs, by about ten points, than monolinguals!

Misperceptions about Bilingualism

One common myth about bilingualism is that bilingual speakers can't keep the two languages they speak straight. Perhaps (monolingual) people think this because they simply can't imagine knowing two languages, and they assume that doing so would inevitably cause confusion. But in fact, studies have shown that bilingual children possess a number of cognitive advantages over monolingual children. Bilinguals have a wider range of linguistic tools at their disposal and learn how to use them earlier than their monolingual peers. They often have superior communicative sensitivity and acquire other cognitive skills earlier and faster than monolinguals.

Negative perceptions about bilingualism can have detrimental effects. A child who is not allowed to speak his or her heritage language at school (or at home, in an effort to increase the child's success in school) can lose self-esteem and may come to think of the language of his or her parents and family as bad or stupid. A child who loses his or her heritage language also loses the means of communication with his or her parents and family.

codeswitching
switching between two languages during one conversation

Another myth is that switching between two languages, a process called **codeswitching**, means that the speaker doesn't know either language very well. But being able to codeswitch requires a great deal of grammatical and conversational expertise, and in two languages! Speakers codeswitch for a variety of reasons. A Spanish–English bilingual, for example, may use an English word or phrase because it has meanings a Spanish word doesn't, or he or she may switch from Spanish to English (or vice versa) because of the social context. For example, codeswitching may depend on who is being spoken to, what is being talked about, and when the conversation is taking place.

Codeswitching involves two or more distinct languages and is therefore distinct from *borrowing*, where a speaker uses a word from another language (that he or she may not even speak). An English speaker who says, "He has great *joie de vivre*" is borrowing a French phrase meaning 'enjoyment of life' but is not codeswitching.

Codeswitching can happen at the word level or can involve longer phrases of several words and even sentences. Here are some examples of speakers' codeswitching with Spanish and English. (Spanish words are italicized.)

Entonces, I will say *¿dónde está el diccionario?*
Then I will say, where is the dictionary?
Es muy beneficial.
It is very beneficial.
Yo empecé después del kindergarten.
I started after kindergarten.
Porque en español they play so many soap operas, *es ridículo.*
Because in Spanish they play so many soap operas, it's ridiculous.

RPE 2.6

Our Capacity to Create Language

creole native language with full grammatical complexity that develops (over time) from a pidgin

The spontaneous creation of new languages—called *language genesis*—is another piece of evidence for our innate linguistic ability.

The popular notion of **creole** varies greatly. Most North Americans likely think of the people, culture, and language of Louisiana. Within Louisiana, *creole* is used to describe people of African, Haitian, French,

Spanish, and Native American heritage or a mixture thereof and belonging to a cultural group known as the Creoles in southern Louisiana. For linguists, however, *creole* refers to a kind of language genesis, or language birth. Creoles typically evolve from **pidgin** languages, or *contact* languages.

pidgin a simplified, nonnative "contact" language that develops to enable speakers of distinct languages to communicate

Pidgins and Creoles

Pidgins and creoles are intimately connected. When speakers of different languages come into contact and need to communicate, a (usually) temporary, rudimentary form of language develops. The speakers maintain their native language(s) but use the pidgin language to communicate between the two (or more) groups. Pidgins generally have the following characteristics:

- Have no native speakers
- Are the result of contact between two or more languages
- Have a grammar of their own, but it is a simple grammatical system
- Have a small vocabulary (words are borrowed from the contributing languages)
- Are not mutually intelligible with the contributing languages

The development of a pidgin usually requires a situation that involves at least three languages, one of which is dominant. If only two languages are involved, there is likely to be a direct struggle for dominance. A direct struggle for dominance did take place between English and French after the Norman Conquest of England in 1066—a struggle won, in that case, by the socially inferior language (English) only after two or more centuries of coexistence (we talk more about this situation in Chapter 11). More typical is a situation in which the language of the people in power becomes the dominant language, as happened after English speakers came to the New World and the many Native American languages in North America became minority languages.

The dominant language usually contributes most of the vocabulary of the pidgin; this language is called the *superstrate* language. The other languages that contribute to the pidgin are called the *substrate* languages.

A creole language is the result of contact involving two or more languages, as with a pidgin, but it develops into a more fully formed, complete language and has native speakers. Creoles often result when the children of speakers of pidgins develop them into complete languages with larger vocabularies and more complex grammatical systems.

Tok Pisin (whose name comes from the English words *talk pidgin*) is a language of Papua New Guinea that began as a pidgin and developed into a creole, with influences from English, German, Portuguese, and various Austronesian languages. Here are some sentences in Tok Pisin:

Tok Pisin	English
Ken i *bin* wok asde.	Ken worked yesterday.
Ken *bai* i wok tumora.	Ken will work tomorrow.
Ken i wok *i stap* nau.	Ken is working now.
Ken i wok *pinis*.	Ken is finished working.
Ken i *save* wok long Sarere.	Ken works on Saturday.
Ken i *ken* wok.	Ken can work (he is allowed to).
Ken *inap* wok.	Ken can work (he has the ability).

hwæt!

Papua New Guinea, where Tok Pisin is spoken, is about the size of California, but it has some 800 languages, many of them completely unrelated to one another.

Though we can see—and especially hear, when these words are read aloud—the similarities in vocabulary to English, the words have very different functions in Tok Pisin. *Bin*, borrowed from English *been*, is a past tense marker; *bai*, from English *by*, indicates futurity; and so on. Because much of the vocabulary of pidgins and creoles is borrowed from one of the contributing languages, it can sound like a 'bad' version of that language. However, when a pidgin develops into a creole, it becomes a unique language with distinct phonology, morphology, syntax, and semantics. Linguist Derek Bickerton, who has studied pidgins and creoles since the 1960s, shows that there are similarities among new languages—creoles—that do not even share contributing substrate or superstrate languages. (See Bickerton 1984 for more discussion.)

Table 2.3 shows some comparisons of creole languages. Two of them, Hawaiian Creole and Sranan (spoken in Suriname), are so-called English based creoles; that is, English is the superstrate language, from which the creoles take much of their vocabulary. The other, Haitian Creole, is French based; French is the superstrate language, contributing much of the vocabulary.

This table demonstrates some of the similarities of these three creole languages. You don't need to worry about what *anterior, irreal*, and *nonpunctual* mean here; rather, notice the fact that these grammatical markers all occur and that they all occur in the same order in these three new, diverse languages. The anterior marker precedes the irreal marker, which precedes the nonpunctual marker. This same order occurs in other creoles around the world as well. Bickerton argues that similarities such as these among unrelated creole languages cannot be explained by contact with other languages; rather, he believes they provide strong evidence for the innate human capacity to create language. We return to a discussion of creoles in Chapter 14.

RPE 2.7

Table 2.3	Comparison of Creoles		
	Hawaiian Creole	**Haitian Creole**	**Sranan**
he walked (base form)	he walk	li maché	a waka
he had walked (anterior)	he bin walk	li té maché	a ben waka
irreal (he will/would walk)	he go walk	l'av(a) maché	a sa waka
nonpunctual (he is/was walking)	he stay walk	l'ap maché	a e waka
anterior + irreal (he would have walked)	he bin go walk	li t'av(a) maché	a ben sa waka
anterior + nonpunctual (he was/had been walking)	he bin stay walk	li t'ap maché	a ben e waka
irreal + nonpunctual (he will/would be walking)	he go stay walk	l'av ap maché	a sa e waka
anterior + irreal + nonpunctual (he would have been walking)	he bin go stay walk	li t'av ap maché	a ben sa e waka

From Bickerton, D. 1985. Creole languages. *Language: Introductory readings,* 4th edn., ed. by V. Clark, P. Escholz & A. Rosa, 134–151. New York: St. Martin's.

Nicaraguan Sign Language

A striking example of creolization is Nicaraguan Sign Language (*Idioma de Señas de Nicaragua, or ISN*). ISN differs from other creoles in having emerged essentially out of nothing rather than out of contact among existing languages. The discovery of this new language has been a boon not only for its signers but for linguists as well, as it provides a wonderful example of humans' ability to create language.

The short story of Nicaraguan Sign Language is as follows. Deaf people who had had no exposure to a language, by virtue of not having heard the spoken language around them and not having been exposed to a sign language, were brought together in the 1980s in a school for the deaf in Nicaragua. They quickly developed a pidgin sign language based on no input except a few individual *home signs*. (Linguists define *home signs* as a gestural communication system, though not a fully developed grammatical system. It is fairly common for some deaf children—those who have hearing parents and no access to a sign language community—to develop home signs.) In this case, the pidgin sign language emerged from human contact but not from *language* contact.

Most of the students in the school were teenagers, and although they were eventually able to communicate quite well, the "language" they developed had a great deal of grammatical variability and variation across signers, and it lacked grammatical complexity. However, the younger

LINGUISTICS IN THE NEWS

A Gene for Language?

During the 1990s, it came to the attention of the scientific community that over three generations about half the members of a particular family, called the KE family, have suffered from a unique language disorder. Members with the disorder have largely unintelligible speech together with other cognitive and physical problems, including problems controlling the face and mouth. Scientists have uncovered what appears to be the source of this disorder, a mutation in a gene called FOXP2. Prior to the discovery of FOXP2, there had been no evidence of a molecular source for speech and language disorders, and the discovery sparked a media frenzy over a "language gene." For example, *Wired*, an online magazine, announced "First Language Gene Found," and *National Geographic* magazine proclaimed "Scientists Identify a

Language Gene." Although the mutation in FOXP2 does seem responsible for the deficits in language suffered by the KE family, to call it a language gene is an oversimplification. More interesting, perhaps, is that a version of FOXP2 is also found in apes and that the human version of the gene seems to have appeared around the time associated with the development of language in humans, some 50,000 years ago. It has recently come to light that not only do humans and apes have a version of FOXP2, but so do mice and mushrooms!

For more information
Enard, W., et al. 2002. Molecular evolution of FOXP2, a gene involved in speech and language. *Nature* 418. 869–872.
    Fisher, S., et al. 1998. Localisation of a gene implicated in a severe speech and language

disorder. *Nature Genetics* 18. 168–170.
    Kenneally, C. 2001. First language gene found. http://www.wired.com/. (3 October, 2001.)
    Lai, C., et al. 2001. A forkhead domain gene is mutated in a severe speech and language disorder. *Nature* 413. 519–523.
    Pinker, S. 2001. Talk of genetics and vice versa. *Nature* 413. 465–466.
    Trivedi, B. 2001. Scientists identify a language gene. *National Geographic Today*. http://news.nationalgeographic.com/news/2001/10/1004_TVlanguagegene.html. (4 October, 2008.)
    Vargha-Khadem, F., et al. 1995. Praxic and nonverbal cognitive deficits in a large family with a genetically transmitted speech and language disorder. *Proceedings of the National Academy of Sciences USA* 92. 930–933.

students in the school saw the pidgin being signed and quite quickly began to develop that pidgin into a full-fledged language—a creole. This distinction between older and younger signers seems to be evidence for a critical period, as well as for another important aspect of language: It does not develop on its own in isolation but takes two, a speaker and a hearer, to develop spontaneously. (So, this answers the "desert island question": Would a human who was never exposed to language, stranded on a desert island alone, develop language? No.)

Linguist Judy Kegl was the first to observe the signing by these students, and she and other researchers have gone back to Nicaragua numerous times over the last two decades. It should be noted that because the data on many early creoles are rather incomplete, many facts about creoles remain a mystery. However, the data and resulting research on ISN are nearly uncontroversially an example of the human capacity for the creation of language out of essentially nothing.

Language and the Brain

So far, we've seen that there is ample evidence that humans have a unique cognitive ability to acquire language. A logical question to ask next is, What does this mean about our brains? Is language *located* somewhere in the brain, or is it simply part of our general intelligence, our all-purpose learning strategies? This question raises a range of others: If someone's language is impaired, are his or her other faculties also necessarily impaired? Can language alone be affected? Can someone's language be unaffected by a brain disorder, trauma, or impairment while his or her other cognitive abilities seem disrupted? And what does all this mean about the anatomy of the brain?

Language Intelligence?

In this section, we will take a look at three cases, each of which provides evidence that our capacity for language is in some ways separate from our other cognitive abilities. We'll look at specific language impairment; the case of Christopher, the linguistic savant; and Williams syndrome.

Specific Language Impairment

Do all children acquire language if they are exposed to it? With only a few exceptions, children are extremely competent language learners. People with impaired cognitive abilities (from various kinds of mental retardation, for example) generally develop language exceptionally well, which suggests that linguistic ability may be separate from other parts of cognition. One exception to natural language ability occurs in children who have **specific language impairment (SLI)**, a disorder in which children do not acquire language in the normal way and who continue to have low language performance as adults. For those with the disorder, language is disrupted while other cognitive abilities are not affected at all.

specific language impairment (SLI) disorder in which children do not acquire language in the normal way but are otherwise not generally cognitively impaired

Linguistic Savants

Does anyone have "extra" linguistic ability? Yes, a few do. A man named Christopher, though extremely challenged in other ways (for example, he needs help dressing himself, finding his way, and tying his shoes) has a nonverbal IQ of about 40 (depending on how IQ is measured, the average is about 100, and low is 55) but is quite gifted linguistically. Christopher is known as a **linguistic savant**. He can read, write, and communicate in a number of languages and has knowledge of many more, though he may not speak them fluently. Some of the languages Christopher is familiar with are French, German, Spanish, Italian, Modern Greek, Dutch, Hindi, Berber, Turkish, Finnish, and Welsh.

linguistic savant person who is linguistically gifted but whose other cognitive abilities are below average

Neil Smith (1995), a linguist who has worked with Christopher for years, says that what is striking about Christopher is his ability to master languages

ˈhwæt!

When Christopher was given a postcard with *thank you* written in 100 languages, he was able to immediately identify twenty-nine of them.

RPE   2.8 ▷

and his inability to solve ordinary problems. Smith invented a language that violated rules of Universal Grammar, making it an "impossible" human language, although it was still quite logical. The invented language started off following rules of Universal Grammar, but then after several months, Smith introduced ways of marking past tense and negation that are unlike the ways that any languages in the world mark these, though the rules were logical and simple. The people of average or higher verbal IQs whom Smith tested did perfectly on this task, using their logical reasoning to figure out the how to form past-tense verbs and negative sentences in Smith's made-up language. Christopher couldn't do it. Smith argues that this is because Christopher doesn't have a logical, rational power that enables him to work out things that fall outside his innate language capacity. Because of his innate (and in his case, exceptional) linguistic ability, acquiring languages is no problem for him. Smith claims that Christopher is a very good example of a person learning a language in exactly the way that Chomsky says we do, equipped with UG.

Williams Syndrome

Williams syndrome rare genetic disorder that involves severe retardation, distinct physical characteristics, and uniquely expressive language ability

Williams syndrome is a very rare genetic disorder that typically results in severe retardation; people with the disorder have an IQ of about 50. Though they cannot tie their shoes or tell left from right, people with Williams syndrome are unusually socially expressive and linguistically adept. Here is an excerpt from the conversation of Crystal, an 18-year-old woman with Williams syndrome (reported in Pinker 1994: 52).

> And what an elephant is, it is one of the animals. And what the elephant does, it lives in the jungle. It can also live in the zoo. And what it has, it has long, gray ears, fan ears, ears that can blow in the wind. It has a long trunk that can pick up grass or pick up hay. . . .

Crystal, like others with Williams syndrome, has what appears to be the linguistic competence of a normal person, a fact that can only be explained if we assume that language ability is, at least in some aspects, separate from other cognitive abilities.

So it appears that intelligence alone is not what leads to language acquisition. The ability to acquire language appears, instead, to be a biologically endowed human behavior, a behavior that can be disrupted, and also one that, in very rare cases, can be exceptional in some people. Such evidence suggests that whatever cognitive ability we use to acquire language is in some way separate from other cognitive abilities.

A Language Center in the Brain?

In this section of the chapter, we turn to how the brain is structured for language, the topic of study called *neurolinguistics*, to further investigate the innate human capacity for language. People have been interested in how the brain works for centuries, and the study of language provides a unique opportunity to deepen our understanding of this complex organ. We've come a long way since the practices of the early Egyptians, who considered the heart, not the brain, the center of intelligence (and even removed the "waste product" brain during the embalming process before mummification). We've also moved forward since the early nineteenth century, when Franz Joseph Gall proposed that certain areas of the brain control certain behaviors. Though this idea of **localization** is still of use today, Gall's work led to the (quite unscientific) theory of *phrenology*, the study of the connections between personality traits and the bumps on the skull. Now, with electroencephalography (EEG), positron emission tomography (PET) scans, and functional magnetic resonance imaging (fMRI), we've come a long way! (See Figure 2.1.) As we'll see in this section, language disorders that result from trauma to the brain provide a rich resource for information leading to our understanding of the brain and at the same time expand our knowledge of the innateness of human language.

People who experience damage to the brain, particularly to the frontal lobe of the left hemisphere, typically experience certain kinds of language disorders and deficits. Such language-related disorders and deficits, called **aphasia**, provide us with insights into the areas of the brain that seem to be primarily responsible for language. The two major types of disorder are **Broca's aphasia**, named after Paul Broca, a French physician, who first

localization theory that different parts of the brain are associated with or control particular behaviors and functions

aphasia language disorder resulting from trauma to the brain

Broca's aphasia form of aphasia characterized by labored speech and general agrammatism

Figure 2.1   A. Cover of the *American Phrenology Journal* of 1848. B. Science has come a long way in determining how the brain controls human behaviors!

A.

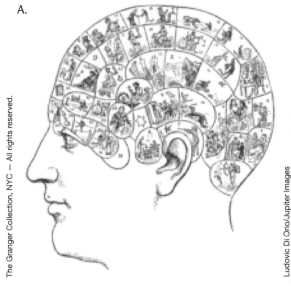

B.

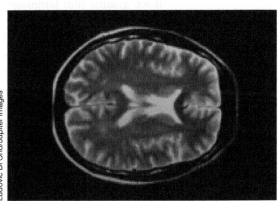

The Granger Collection, NYC — All rights reserved.

Ludovic Di Orio/Jupiter Images

Figure 2.2 Lateral view of the left hemisphere of the human brain, showing the positions of Broca's and Wernicke's areas.

Broca

Wernicke

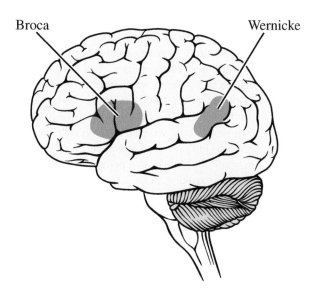

Wernicke's aphasia form of aphasia characterized by fluent speech that makes little sense

hwœc!

You can find Phineas Gage's brain and the tamping iron that went into it on display at Harvard Medical School.

lateralization idea that cognitive functions reside in or are controlled by either the left or the right side of the brain

described it in the 1860s; and **Wernicke's aphasia**, named after German physician Karl Wernicke, who first described this type of language deficit in the 1870s. (See Figure 2.2.) Their research led to a new field of neuroscience. There are many different aphasias, including *agraphia* (the inability to write), *alexia* (the inability to read), and *anomia* (the inability to name things in a particular category or categories).

Both Broca's and Wernicke's aphasias provide evidence for the separation of language from other cognitive abilities, for patients with these language disorders can be in command of other faculties that aren't closely tied to language. They test well on nonverbal IQ tests, and they can set clocks, read maps, make things, and carry out commands, suggesting that at least in some ways, language abilities are separate from other cognitive abilities. Aphasia results from damage to the frontal lobe of the left hemisphere, suggesting that language is **lateralized** on the left side of the brain. In addition, people with Broca's aphasia experience language deficits that are different from those suffered by people with Wernicke's aphasia, which suggests that not only is the brain lateralized for language but that particular regions are associated with specific linguistic behaviors. (Seventy percent of people with damage to the left hemisphere experience aphasia, but only 1 percent of those with damage to the right hemisphere do.)

Did You Know...?

Poor Phineas Gage

Phineas Gage was the foreman of a construction gang preparing the way for the railroad in Vermont. In 1848, an accident occurred in which a tamping iron (more than 3 feet long, weighing 13½ pounds) passed through Gage's skull. The tamping iron went in point first under his left cheekbone and came out through the top of his head, landing 25 to 30 yards behind him. The front left part of his brain was destroyed, but Phineas recovered. It is remarkable that he not only survived but was able to continue to work (although not at his previous job) and lead a relatively normal life. Unfortunately, his personality was dramatically altered, to a point where people said that he was "no longer Gage." This was striking evidence of how brain injury and trauma can affect some behaviors but not others, and for the possible localization of the brain: that the brain is divided into areas that have certain functions.

Broca's Aphasia

agrammatism
disorder caused by trauma to Broca's area so that word order does not conform to grammatical rules of the language

Broca's aphasics tend to have labored speech and general **agrammatism**; they have trouble with word order and difficulties with function words (prepositions, articles, auxiliary verbs) and inflectional affixes (*-ed*, *-s*). (Remember that children in the early stages of language acquisition also produce such "telegraphic" speech, and Genie's speech is often described as agrammatic.) They have frequent word-finding pauses, and though they appear to understand language quite well, they have great difficulty producing grammatical utterances. Broca's aphasia is often called *nonfluent aphasia*; speakers have difficulty producing language but not necessarily comprehending it.

Here is a patient with Broca's aphasia trying to explain how he came to the hospital for dental surgery:

> Yes . . . ah . . . Monday . . . er . . . Dad and Peter H . . . (his own name), and Dad . . . er . . . hospital . . . and ah . . . Wednesday . . . Wednesday, nine o'clock . . . and oh . . . Thursday . . . ten o'clock, ah doctors . . . two . . . an' doctors . . . and er . . . teeth . . . yah

RPE 2.9

Wernicke's Aphasia

Wernicke's aphasia is called *fluent aphasia*. People with Wernicke's aphasia produce fluent speech, but it makes little sense. They speak with good intonation and also pronounce and order words accurately, but they often use nonsense words and make other lexical errors. Their speech can also seem fragmented: one utterance seems unrelated to another. They also have difficulty comprehending speech. More extreme cases of Wernicke's aphasia are called *jargon aphasia*, in which a speaker uses correct intonation but few real words.

Here is an example from a patient with Wernicke's aphasia:

> Well this is. . . . mother is away here working her work out o'here to get her better, but when she's looking, the two boys looking in other part. One their small tile into her time here. She's working another time because she's getting, too.

Evidence from aphasia suggests that the brain is lateralized for language on the left hemisphere, and also that certain areas of the brain are localized specifically for language. Aphasia also tells us much about how our grammatical knowledge is organized. Broca's aphasics have trouble with word order (syntax) but not meaning (semantics), and Wernicke's aphasics exhibit almost the opposite behavior, speaking fluently with appropriate word order but in sentences that make little sense. Such evidence suggests that certain linguistic abilities or functions may be located in different areas of the brain.

Evidence from aphasia also tells us something about how our mental dictionary, or lexicon, is organized. People with Broca's aphasia often omit function words such as articles, pronouns, and auxiliary verbs, and they also often omit inflectional endings on words such as plural -s, progressive -ing, and past tense -ed, while people with Wernicke's aphasia have no trouble with these function words and affixes, and their sentences exhibit close to normal word order. This evidence suggests that function words are stored separately from content words in our mental lexicon and that brain trauma can affect the loss of one class of words but not the other. *Anomia* is a type of aphasia that affects semantic classes of words. People with anomia are unable to find words, which leads to substitutions—such as *wing* for *bird*—or circumlocutions, such as describing something but not being able to name it. They also may not be able to name objects in the same semantic category, such as fruits or different pieces of photography equipment. That aphasia can affect different semantic classes of words tells us that these classes form a component of our grammar.

RPE 2.10

RPE 2.11

More Evidence for Lateralization

We can gather further evidence for the organization of language in the brain from dichotic listening and brain imaging. But first, we need a bit more information on the structure of the brain.

The two central hemispheres of the brain are connected by a bundle of fibers known as the *corpus callosum*, which transmits information between the two hemispheres. The brain is controlled contralaterally, meaning that sensory information is received in the contralateral (opposite) side of the brain from the side of the body from which it is sent—the left side of the body is controlled by the right hemisphere, and vice versa. So if you scratch your ear with your right hand, the left side of your brain has sent the signal to do so. We have seen that the left hemisphere is the dominant side for language, and in what follows we'll discuss two types of evidence for this lateralization.

Dichotic Listening

dichotic listening
method of testing
processing of
linguistic stimuli
wherein people
hear different
sounds in two ears
simultaneously

Dichotic listening demonstrates how the left hemisphere is dominant for language. For this task, two different sounds (or words) are played simultaneously, one into each ear, through earphones. For example, the word *cat* may be played into the right ear and *cup* into the left. The listener then tells the examiner what he or she hears first (and best); this is typically the word played in the right ear, for that sound travels directly to the left hemisphere, where it is processed, whereas the word played in the left ear travels to the right hemisphere, then back over to the left hemisphere for processing, resulting in a slight delay.

The right ear even seems to have an advantage for decoding linguistic stimuli, regardless of whether those stimuli are in the form of words in the listener's language; nonsense words, single syllables, and even words played backwards seem to be processed more quickly through the right ear and hence through the left side of the brain. (This behavior is referred to as right ear advantage, or REA.)

This right ear advantage may be because of something larger than language; research has shown that the left hemisphere may be better at tasks involving temporal order, and language is simply one such task. Morse code, which requires temporal processing but is a nonlinguistic stimulus, is also processed more accurately through the right ear.

Split-Brain Patients

split brain severed
corpus callosum,
usually to relieve
epileptic seizures

Other interesting evidence for the lateralization of the brain for language (and contralateralization of the brain in general) comes from **split-brain** patients. Such patients have their corpus callosum severed in order to control seizures, usually from epilepsy. Though such an operation is a drastic measure, results are overall very positive. In the 1960s and 1970s, Michael Gazzaniga (1970) studied the language behavior of split-brain patients. They could talk normally (and he could cue patients verbally because they could hear his cues through both ears). But as soon as he devised experiments that required each side of the brain to communicate with the other, he got some surprising results. He found that a split-brain patient who held something in his left hand couldn't name that object. Gazzaniga knew already that each eye and hand sends its signal to the opposite side of the brain, so something held in the left hand sent a signal to the right side of the brain. When the patient put the object in his right hand, sending the signal to his left brain, he could name the object without a problem. When Gazzaniga showed the patient a printed word through the patient's left visual field, the patient couldn't read it. Shown the word through the right visual field, the patient read the word without a problem. Gazzaniga's work supports the hypothesis that the left brain is lateralized for language and that the corpus callosum transmits the signals between the two hemispheres.

Brain Imaging

Research on language and the brain also involves PET scans, MRIs, and EEGs, all of which are used for (among other things) studying brain activity while the person being tested performs specific tasks. Ongoing research involves studying how we process words we read and hear, how we learn words and

Accent on *Clinical Linguistics*

© Mary Kate Denny/Photo Edit

Linguist David Crystal defines *clinical linguistics* as "the application of linguistic sciences to the study of language disability in all its forms" (2003: 673). "Disability" here refers to anything that would fall under the description of abnormal language use and thus includes a wide range of phenomena. The range of professionals involved in this field is also very broad and includes speech and language pathologists, teachers, social workers, psychologists (including educational and clinical psychologists), and neurologists.

The goal of clinical linguistics is to accurately describe, diagnose, assess, and treat language deficits and communicative disorders, using the tools of linguistic science. Research and practice in clinical linguistics therefore not only tell us more about language disabilities and how to treat them but also shed light on the nature of language itself. Clinical linguistics therefore contributes much to our understanding of how language is processed, perceived, and produced and has much to tell us about our grammatical system.

Clinical linguistics is a relatively young but growing field with a major professional journal, *Clinical Linguistics and Phonetics* (published by Informa Healthcare), books specifically devoted to the subject, and departments and programs across the United States and Europe dedicated to its study. Some of the areas of study that fall under clinical linguistics include phonetic disorders in speech perception and production; communication disorders in multilingual populations; pragmatic aspects of speech and language disorders; disorders related to hearing impairment; sign language and lip-reading; and the study of language production, perception, and use by children and adults with autism, Williams syndrome, traumatic brain injury, and cleft palates.

The need for clinical linguistics is clear: not only to provide effective therapies for those diagnosed with language disorders and deficits but also to guard against misdiagnosis. To take an individual example, Crystal reports that a child who fails to respond to questions may be considered rude and uncooperative. However, such behavior may have its source in the child's inability to understand and process rules that govern conversation. Fillmore and Snow (2002) point out that in school, teacher evaluations of students' ability are largely based on language. Nonnative English speakers or speakers of stigmatized varieties of English can be declared to be slow learners. Once sorted this way, children receive substantially different instruction, reinforcing any initial differences among them in speed of learning and eagerness to learn. They also note the overrepresentation of African American, Native American, and Latino children in special education placements, which suggests that normal language features associated with a vernacular variety of English or with learning English as a second language are often misinterpreted as an indication of developmental delay. So, the broad field of clinical linguistics provides a wealth of very practical applications for linguistic knowledge.

For more information

Ball, M. 1993. *Phonetics for speech pathology*, 2nd edn. London: Whurr.

Ball, M., et al. (eds.). Forthcoming. *The handbook of clinical linguistics*. Malden, MA: Wiley-Blackwell.

Crystal, D. 2003. Clinical linguistics. *Handbook of linguistics*, ed. by M. Aronoff & J. Rees Miller, 673–682. Malden, MA: Blackwell.

Department of Human Communication Sciences, University of Sheffield, http://www.shef.ac.uk/hcs/research/clinling.

Fillmore, L. & C. Snow. 2002. What teachers need to know about language. *What teachers need to know about language*, ed. by C. Adger, C. Snow & D. Christian, 7–53. McHenry, IL: Delta Systems.

Grundy, K. (ed.). 1995. *Linguistics in clinical practice*, 2nd edn. London: Whurr.

associate them in categories, and how we parse sentences, among many other fascinating topics. Research on sign language and the brain also promises to tell us things about language beyond what is revealed by studying oral language alone. Are the same areas of the brain activated by (visual) signs as by (auditory) speech? What can we learn about lateralization from sign language aphasia?

Summary

In this chapter, we've explored a variety of different evidence for the human capacity for language. We've seen that as children, we seem to tease out complex rules of grammar from the (rather chaotic linguistic) stimuli we're exposed to, whether the stimuli are oral or gestural. That language acquisition proceeds at basically the same rate and through the same stages with both hearing and deaf children supports the idea that we are hardwired for language in some way, which allows us to accomplish this complex task at an early age. We have taken a look at some of the differences between first language acquisition and the acquisition of a second language, exploring evidence for a critical period of language acquisition and for Universal Grammar. We have also considered what it means to be bilingual—to have two native languages—and what we can learn about the human capacity for language from the study of creolization—the creation of language from a contact language, or pidgin. We've introduced the extraordinary story of Nicaraguan Sign Language, a language that emerged essentially out of nothing except the drive to communicate. We have then turned to what all of this means about our brains. We have looked at a variety of evidence that our capacity for language may be in some ways separate from other cognitive abilities and that in linguistic savants such as Christopher this capacity may be more highly developed than in those of us with normal intelligence. The study of aphasia tells us even more about the anatomy of the brain, how language may be lateralized on the left side of the brain, and how specific areas may be responsible for specific linguistic tasks. Evidence from dichotic listening also suggests that the left brain is lateralized for language, and the technology of brain imaging continues to deepen our understanding of this uniquely human capacity.

Sources and Resources

Adger, C., C. Snow & D. Christian (eds.). 2002. *What teachers need to know about language.* McHenry, IL: Delta Systems.

Banks, M., et al. 1975. Sensitive period for the development of human binocular vision. *Science* 190(4213). 675–677.

Berko, J. 1958. The child's learning of English morphology. *Word* 14. 150–177.

Bickerton, D. & commentators. 1984. The language bioprogram hypothesis. *Behavioral and Brain Sciences* 7. 173–221.

Bickerton, D. 1985. Creole languages. *Language: Introductory readings,* ed. by V. Clark, P. Escholz, and A. Rosa, 4th edn., 134–151. New York: St. Martin's.

Brown, R. 1973. *A first language: The early stages.* Cambridge, MA: Harvard University Press.

Caplan, D. 1987. *Neurolinguistics and linguistic aphasiology.* New York: Cambridge University Press.

Chomsky, N. 2006. *Language and mind,* 3rd edn. New York: Cambridge University Press.

Clark, H. & E. Clark. 1977. *Psychology and language: An introduction to psycholinguistics.* New York: Harcourt Brace Jovanovich.

Crain, S. & D. Lillo-Martin. 1999. *An introduction to linguistic theory and language acquisition.* Oxford, UK: Blackwell.

Crain, S., R. Thornton & G. Tesan. How children ask questions. Video. LSA: Videos on the Web. http://www.uga.edu/lsava/Crain/Crain.html. (1 March, 2008.)

Crystal, D. 2003. Clinical linguistics. *Handbook of linguistics,* ed. by M. Aronoff and J. Rees Miller, 673–682. Malden, MA: Blackwell.

Curtiss, S. 1977. *Genie: A psycholinguistic study of a modern-day "wild child" (Perspectives in neurolinguistics and psycholinguistics).* New York: Academic Press.

Fillmore, L. & C. Snow. 2002. What teachers need to know about language. *What teachers need to know about language,* ed. by C. Adger, C. Snow, and D. Christian, 7–53. McHenry, IL: Delta Systems.

Foss, D. & D. Hakes. 1978. *Psycholinguistics.* Englewood Cliffs, NJ: Prentice-Hall.

Gardner, H. 1978. What we know (and don't know) about the two halves of the brain. *Harvard Magazine* 80.24–27.

Gazzaniga, M. 1970. *The bisected brain.* New York: Appleton-Century-Crofts.

Geschwind, N. 1979. Specializations of the human brain. *Scientific American* 206. 180–199.

Haussamen, B., et al. 2003. Non-native speakers in the English classroom. *Grammar alive! A guide for teachers*, 53–55. Urbana, IL: NCTE.

Hoffman, H. 1996. *Amorous turkeys and addicted ducklings: The science of social bonding and imprinting.* Boston, MA: Authors Cooperative.

Honda, M. & W. O'Neil. 2008. *Thinking syntactically.* Malden, MA: Wiley-Blackwell.

Interlandi, J. 2007. Learning: Turn it off, baby. *Newsweek*, August 20–27. http://www.newsweek.com/id/32243.

Kegl, J. 1994. The Nicaraguan Sign Language Project: An overview. *Signpost* 7(1). 24–31.

Kegl, J., et al. 1999. Creation through contact: Sign language emergence and sign language change in Nicaragua. *Comparative grammatical change: The intersection of language acquisition, creole genesis, and diachronic syntax*, ed. by M. DeGraff, 179–237. Cambridge, MA: MIT Press.

Klima, E. & U. Bellugi. 1979. *The signs of language.* Cambridge, MA: Harvard University Press.

Kuhl, P., et al. 1997. Cross-language analysis of phonetic units in language addressed to infants. *Science* 277. 684–686.

Lane, H. 1975. *The wild boy of Aveyron.* Cambridge, MA: Harvard University Press.

Lenneberg, E. 1967. *Biological foundations of language.* New York: Wiley.

Lorenz, K. 1950. The comparative method of studying innate behavioural patterns. *Sym. Soc. Exp. Biol.* 4. 221–268.

MacGregor-Mendoza, P. 2005. Bilingualism: Myths and realities. *Language in the schools: Integrating linguistic knowledge into K-12 teaching*, ed. by K. Denham and A. Lobeck. Mahwah, NJ: Lawrence Erlbaum.

Meltzoff, A. & R. Borton. 1979. Intermodal matching by human neonates. *Nature* 282. 403–404.

Newman, A., et al. 2002. A critical period for right hemisphere recruitment in American Sign Language processing. *Nature Neuroscience* 5. 76–80. http://www.nature.com/neuro/.

Newport, E. 1990. Maturation constraints on language learning. *Cognitive Science* 14. 11–28.

Newport, E. & T. Supalla. 2000. Sign language research at the millennium. *The signs of language revisited*, ed. by K. Emmorey and H. Lane, 103–114. Mahwah, NJ: Lawrence Erlbaum.

Obler, L. & K. Gjerlow. 1999. *Language and the brain.* Cambridge, UK: Cambridge University Press.

Pinker, S. 1994. *The language instinct: How the mind creates language.* New York: HarperCollins.

Ritchie, W. & T. Bhatia (eds.). 1996. *The handbook of second language acquisition.* San Diego, CA: Academic Press.

Rymer, R. 1993. *Genie: An abused child's flight from silence.* New York: HarperCollins.

Searchinger, G. 1995. *The human language series*, part 2. Video. New York: Ways of Knowing.

Selinker, L. 1972. Interlanguage. *International Review of Applied Linguistics (IRAL)* 10(3). 209–231.

Smith, N., with I.-M. Tsimpli. 1995. *The mind of a savant.* Oxford, UK: Blackwell.

Sperry, R. 1968. Mental unity following surgical disconnection of the cerebral hemisphere. *The Harvey Lectures,* Series 62, 293–323. New York: Academic Press.

Sperry, R. 1974. Lateral specialization in the surgically separated hemispheres. *Neuroscience 3rd Study Program*, ed. by F. Schmitt et al., 5–19. Cambridge, MA: MIT Press.

Springer, S. & G. Deutsch. 1981. *Left brain, right brain.* San Francisco: W. H. Freeman.

Stemmer, B. & H. Whitaker (eds.). 1998. *The handbook of neurolinguistics.* San Diego, CA: Academic Press.

Wanner, E. & L. Gleitman (eds.). 1982. *Language acquisition: The state of the art.* New York: Alfred A. Knopf.

Wei, L. (ed.). 2000. *The bilingualism reader.* London: Routledge.

White, L. 2003. *Second language acquisition and universal grammar.* New York: Cambridge University Press.

Zimmerman, F., et al. 2007. Association between media viewing and language development in children under age 2 years. *Journal of Pediatrics* 151. 364–368.

Review, Practice, and Explore

RPE 2.1 > Children's Rules

Children often produce forms that they don't hear in adult speech—forms that nevertheless follow a systematic rule. In the following examples of children's language, what systematic rule is evident here? How do these data support the human capacity for language? Do children learn by imitation?

a. I bought a fire dog for a grillion dollars.
b. Hey, Horton heared a Who.
c. My teacher holded the baby rabbits and we patted them.
d. Daddy, I stealed some of the people out of the boat.
e. Once upon a time, a alligator was eating a dinosaur and the dinosaur was eating the alligator and the dinosaur was eaten by the alligator and the alligator goed kerplunk.

What do the following examples of conversations with children tell us about how children acquire language, and how do they provide evidence for our linguistic "hardwiring"?

Child: I taked a cookie.
Adult: Oh, you mean you took a cookie.
Child: Yes, that's right, I taked it.

Adult: Adam, say what I say: Where can I put them?
Child: Where I can put them?

RPE 2.2 > Two-Year-Olds Have *No* Words

Even though children seem limited in the number of words they can string together in the early stages of acquisition, their utterances can express a range of complex meanings. For example, negative utterances at this stage can express denial, rejection, or nonexistence. Study the following sets of negative utterances of children in the early multiword stage. What kind of negation is being expressed in each set? (Adapted from Foss & Hakes 1978.)

a. Allgone juice, no hot, no more light anymore play
b. No dirty soap, no meat, no go outside
c. No morning (it was afternoon), no daddy hungry, no truck

RPE **2.3** ⟩ Adult Speech to Children

Here are some examples of interactions between adults and children. What kinds of correction or reinforcement does the adult offer the child? What does the adult *not* correct? Do you think these interactions might help or hinder language acquisition? Why?

Child: [picking up toys].
Adult: Thanks for picking up your toys!

Child: Sally goed to the store.
Adult: No, Sally went to *work*.

Child: Doggy gone.
Adult: Yes, Rover went for a walk with your sister.

Child: I want a cookie.
Adult: You want a cookie? Well, here you go!

Child: Him ride bike.
Adult: Yes, he's riding a bike.

RPE **2.4** ⟩ How Would They Say It?

Here are some examples of issues that arise for speakers learning English as a second language. Based on the information given about each language, try to come up with what the learner might say. (Adapted from Haussamen 2003.)

a. In Vietnamese, there is no article before the word for a profession (*student, teacher, doctor*, etc.). What is a sentence a Vietnamese speaker learning English might say?

b. In Korean, pronouns aren't marked for gender, so you might hear a Korean speaker learning English use *it* in places where native English speakers might not. What is a possible sentence the Korean speaker might utter?

c. In Japanese, pronouns don't have to have to match the noun they refer to, so a singular pronoun can refer to a plural noun and vice versa. What kind of sentence might a Japanese speaker learning English utter?

d. In Cantonese, Japanese, and Korean, there are no plural forms of nouns (plurality is marked in other ways). What sentence might a speaker of one of these languages who is learning English produce?

RPE **2.5** ⟩ Acquiring or Teaching a Second Language

Explore one of the following questions about second language acquisition in more detail in a short research paper.

• What are some of the leading theories about how we acquire a second language, and how do these theories differ from one another?

• What are some of the theories about how to teach a second "foreign" language (now more frequently called *world language*) in school?

• Investigate English as a Second Language (ESL), Teaching English as a Second Language (TESL), and Teaching English to Speakers of Other Languages (TESOL). What are some of the theories about how to teach English language in a multilingual classroom?

- How does the U.S. system differ from the Canadian or British systems? How are heritage languages (the speakers' first language, or L1) treated in such systems?

RPE   2.6   > Bilingual Education

Bilingualism is a fascinating linguistic phenomenon of interest not only to linguists but also to educators. Bilingual education is both much studied and controversial. Many states and organizations want to limit bilingual education, and other organizations and states promote it. Do some research on the pros and cons of bilingual education. What are the arguments in favor of it, and what methods and approaches seem to be most effective? Where has bilingual education been argued to be ineffective, and why?

RPE   2.7   > Creole Grammar

Some tourist guidebooks describe pidgins and creoles as *baby talk, broken English, improper,* or *grammarless.* But as we've seen, creole languages have systematic rules and are fully developed linguistic systems. Below is a set of data that illustrate the rule of plural formation in Nicaraguan Creole English (from Honda and O'Neil 2008).

Nicaraguan Creole English	**Standard English**
a. The boat-dem de in the river.	The boats are in the river.
b. Ronald send to me two turtledove.	Ronald sent me two turtledoves.
c. Is many dog in Bluefields?	Are there many dogs in Bluefield?
d. These dog-dem in the street.	These dogs are in the street.
e. He want seven case of beer.	He wants seven cases of beer.
f. He did see the case of beer-dem.	He saw the cases of beer.

The word *dem* is borrowed from the English word *them*; however, it has a different meaning and use in Nicaraguan Creole English. When do you use *–dem* in Creole?
    Is the following sentence grammatical in this language?

g. The man-dem a plaant kann.	The men are planting corn.

RPE   2.8   > Linguistic Savants

The Linguistic Society of America maintains an archive of language-related short videos at the University of Georgia. At the website http://www.uga.edu/lsava/Smith/Smith.html are several clips about Christopher taken from the movie *Het Talenwonder.* Watch the clips and write a one- to two-paragraph response. Consider what Christopher's language ability tells us about the following:

- the human capacity for language
- our language "intelligence" and its relation to other cognitive abilities
- Universal Grammar

RPE   2.9   > Genie Says

Here are some examples of the speech of Genie, the child who was not exposed to language until age 13. Her speech has been described as *agrammatic.* What kinds of word order errors does Genie make, and does her speech resemble aphasia in any way? Does it resemble any of the stages of acquisition we've discussed in the chapter? Explain. (Data from Curtiss 1977: 31.)

Adult: Where are the graham crackers?
Genie: I where is graham cracker.

(or)

I where is graham cracker on top shelf.

Genie's way of forming questions:
   Where is tomorrow Mrs L?
   Where is stop spitting?
   Where is may I have ten pennies?
   When is stop spitting?

Other examples of Genie's language:
   Man motorcycle have.
   Genie full stomach.
   Genie bad cold live father house.
   Want Curtiss play piano.
   Open door key.

RPE   2.10 > Broca's and Wernicke's Aphasias

Look up some examples of aphasic speech. Find examples of both Broca's aphasia and Wernicke's aphasia and also of one other disorder we have discussed here (agraphia, alexia, anomia). Explain how each of your examples fits the description of a particular type of aphasia or language disorder.

RPE   2.11 > Sign Language Aphasia

Conduct some research on sign language aphasia. How does it differ from oral language aphasia, and how it is similar? What does sign language aphasia tell us about the brain and how it is lateralized for language?

Phonetics: Describing Sounds

Key Concepts

- You know a great deal about the complex sounds and the sound system of English; much of this knowledge is not something you usually need to think about, as you produce and manipulate the sounds of your language effortlessly.
- There is not a one-to-one correspondence between sound and spelling, so linguists use a system for describing the sounds of language in which each sound is represented by a single symbol.
- Sounds can be classified into groups based on similarities in the ways they are produced.
- Each language has a distinct set of phonemes, the sounds of a language that result in meaning differences in that language.
- Sounds change and vary over time in patterned ways.

Did You Know . . . ?

Visible Speech
Mom Is Bob

Language Alive!   A Disappearing Sound

Why Do We Spell Words with *-ough?*
Forgotten Clusters
Do *Dawn* and *Don* Rhyme?
Double Is Not Long

Linguistics in the News   Peter Ladefoged, Pioneer in Phonetics

Accent on   Product Naming

Sounds and Symbols
Phonemes
Consonants
   Voiced and Voiceless Consonants
   Place of Articulation
   Manner of Articulation
   Why All These Distinctions?
   Slips of the Tongue
Vowels
   Diphthongs
   Syllabic Consonants
   Other Vowel Distinctions
   Vowel Shifts
Phonemes and Allophones
Summary
Sources and Resources
Review, Practice, and Explore

The pleasure of Shawn's company
Is what I most enjoy.
He put a tack on Ms. Yancey's chair
When she called him a horrible boy.
At the end of the month he was flinging two kittens
Across the width of the room.
I count on his schemes to show me a way now
Of getting away from my gloom.

— A POEM CONTAINING ALL THE SOUNDS OF
ENGLISH, BY NEAL WHITMAN.
REPRINTED BY PERMISSION.

hwæt!

A version of Neal Whitman's poem appears in the film *Mission: Impossible 3*.

In this chapter, we describe the sounds of language. You will learn the sounds and their descriptions so that we can have a vocabulary to talk not only about the sounds but also about the sound systems of the language. As a literate person, you are used to thinking about the alphabet that we use to write our language as matching up with the sounds we produce. Although it does in some cases, we will talk about some of the many mismatches between sound and spelling, why those exist, and why we're stuck with them.

It will also be quite revealing to discover how much you, as a speaker of a language, know about the complex sounds and the sound system of English; much of this knowledge is not something you usually need to think about, as you produce and manipulate the sounds of your language effortlessly. You ignore nonspeech sounds, eliminate variations in speech sounds that are not relevant, and do a surprising amount of gymnastics with your lips, tongue, and teeth.

phonetics study of speech sounds

Thus, we will be studying the sounds of speech, **phonetics**. For the most part, we will be concerned with North American English. We will determine what the sounds are, how they vary, and how to describe them. The applications of phonetic knowledge are important for many other fields. An understanding of phonetics is crucial for teachers of reading and spelling because of the complexity of the English spelling system, a system that is not wholly phonetic. (Not surprisingly, phonetics and phonology instruction is a requirement for teachers in many states.) This understanding is part of the knowledge required for speech pathologists and speech therapists who work with those who have various language delays and disabilities, including loss of speech abilities due to injury or stroke. Phonetics is used by forensic linguists in legal cases for speech identification or to authenticate recordings. And anyone who is a speaker of a language should appreciate the complexity of the phonetic system; you will be surprised by how much you know about manipulating this system to convey meaning.

People have long been concerned with describing the sounds of their languages. Consider the following section of the text called *Marsanes* from *The Nag Hammadi Library*, a group of Gnostic texts likely written around the end of the third century CE.

> But know that the oxytones exist among the vowels, and the diphthongs which are next to them. . . . The sounds of the semivowels are superior to the voiceless (consonants). And those that are double are superior to the semivowels, which do not change. But the aspirates are better than the inaspirates (of) the voiceless (consonants). And those that are intermediate will accept their combination in which they are; they are ignorant of the things that are good. They (the vowels) are combined with the intermediates, which are less. Form by form, (they constitute) the nomenclature of the gods and the angels, not because they are mixed with each other according to every form, but only (because) they have a good function. It did not happen that (their) will was revealed. (Robinson 1990)

Many of the terms in the quotation that describe the author's Coptic language are terms we still use to describe English today.

Sounds and Symbols

Our first step in phonetics will be to learn to use a system of written symbols that linguists have developed for representing the speech sounds of any language. In this system, one sound is represented by one symbol, and each symbol represents only a single sound. Though the English spelling system is somewhat phonetic (that is, the symbols correspond to sounds in a fairly systematic way), it is full of inconsistencies. (We return to a discussion of spelling in Chapter 13, "Representing Language.") Young children learning to read illustrate the distinction between sound and symbol when they misspell words such as *bags* and *pushed* as *bagz* and *pusht*, but once we become literate, we tend to forget about the mismatch between sound and symbol.

Consider the following mismatches between the spelling system and the sound system.

- The same sound can be spelled using quite a variety of letter combinations. Consider the "ee" sound in each of the following and how it is spelled: *plea, tee, deceive, tangy, key, ski, brie, people,* and *algae.* And consider the letter <c>, which can represent the initial sound in *candy, cent, cello,* and *ocean.*
- Several single sounds are spelled using more than one letter: <u>th</u>in, <u>th</u>at (yes, those are two distinct sounds at the beginning of those words), and <u>ch</u>in, <u>sh</u>in.
- A single letter can represent more than one sound: <u>u</u>nite, <u>u</u>ntie and a<u>x</u>e, <u>x</u>ylophone.

- Sometimes letters aren't pronounced and so stand for no sound at all (though most of them did at some point in the history of English): *know*, *gnat*, *dumb*, *yolk*, *mouse*, *island*, and *psychology*.
- The same letter combination can result in a range of different sounds. Consider -*ough* in the following: *cough*, *enough*, *bough*, *through*, and *though*.

So the English spelling system is not a good system for representing sound. Instead, we will be learning and using a system to transcribe sounds to symbols that is based on the International Phonetic Alphabet, or IPA, which is used by linguists to transcribe any language.

Most dictionaries include some sort of phonemic transcription as a pronunciation guide, and although most dictionaries use a system of transcription similar to the IPA, they often develop their own system. It would be much easier if they all used the same one! And as you'll see, the IPA is really not very hard to learn.

Phonemes

phoneme unit of sound that makes a difference in the meaning of a word

Phonemes are the distinctive sounds in a language. Every spoken language has phonemes, but they differ from language to language. The number of phonemes in any given language can vary slightly depending on the speaker and the dialect; English has about forty distinctive phonemes, which is more than the average number of phonemes across languages, though not extraordinarily so. Almost every language has more consonant sounds than vowel sounds, though to varying degrees. Pirahã, spoken in Brazil, has about ten consonants, and !Xu, spoken in southern Africa, has 141! The most common consonant sounds across languages are /p,t,k/, but not all languages have them. (Sounds are represented enclosed in slashes to distinguish them from letters of the alphabet.) Hawaiian doesn't have /t/, and Mohawk doesn't have /p/. Hupa, a nearly extinct language of California, lacks both /p/ and /k/.

consonant sound characterized by closure or obstruction of the vocal tract

vowel sound characterized by an open vocal tract, with no closure or obstruction

We all know what the **consonants** and **vowels** of the English alphabet are, but what makes a sound a consonant sound or a vowel sound? What is the difference between them? The distinction has to do with how we produce them, with the restriction of airflow. A vowel sound is produced in such a way that the airstream can pass through the vocal tract without a noticeable obstruction. A consonant sound has some degree of air restriction.

Consonants

There are many consonant sounds in English, but there are only twenty-four consonant *phonemes* of English—the sounds that make a difference in the meanings of words to English speakers. For example, in English the sounds

/b/ and /p/ are *distinctive*, which means we hear the difference between them, and we know that the words *bit* and *pit* have different meanings. *Bit* and *pit* are a **minimal pair**, two words that differ by only a single phoneme in the same position. The version of the IPA we use in this chapter is a representation of the phonemes of English, the sounds that we recognize as distinct from one another. When we write words using the IPA, we are doing **phonemic transcription**. (It is a little confusing that we call the IPA a *phonetic* alphabet when the version we're using is really a *phonemic* alphabet. This distinction will be made clear in Chapter 4.) With phonemic transcription, there's always a one-to-one correspondence between sounds and symbols. It's important to remember that these symbols are not the same as letters and that they represent the sounds of language, not the letters of a writing system.

We will describe each consonant in terms of each of the following:

1. **Voicing** controlling the vibration of the vocal cords as air passes through to make speech sounds
2. **Place of articulation** the places in the oral cavity where airflow is modified to make speech sounds
3. **Manner of articulation** the way we move and position our lips, tongue, and teeth to make speech sounds

The ways in which we describe sounds within each of these categories—where and how the sound is made and whether there is vibration of the vocal cords—isolates a particular group of sounds, described as a **natural class** of sounds; sounds in a natural class share some set of phonetic characteristics, or phonetic features. Table 3.1 contains the consonants of English only. (We will discuss each descriptive label in Table 3.1 in the following sections.) Some of the symbols are adaptations of the IPA used by many North American linguists. The complete IPA consonant chart is shown in Table 3.2.

Voiced and Voiceless Consonants

All consonants are either *voiced* or *voiceless*. The airflow coming out of the lungs can meet resistance at the *larynx*, or voice box. The resistance can be controlled by the different positions of and tensions in the vocal cords or vocal folds, which are two muscular bands of tissue that stretch from front to back in the larynx, behind the Adam's apple. When you're just breathing, the vocal folds are relaxed and spread apart to allow air to flow freely from the lungs. When you have the right amount of air and tension of the muscles in the cords, they vibrate when you speak. This is called **voicing**.

You can feel this vocal fold vibration when you are producing a sound that you can make last several seconds. Put your hand on your throat and make the sound [s]. Keep your hand there and switch to [z]. (We are using

---

minimal pair pair of words that differ only in one sound in the same position (e.g., *pit* /pɪt/ and *bit* /bɪt/).

phonemic transcription written recording of sounds using the distinctive phonemes of a language, resulting in a one-to-one correspondence between a sound and a symbol

natural class set of sounds that have certain phonetic features in common

RPE   3.1

voicing vibration of the vocal folds

Table 3.1		Consonant Phonemes of English						

	Bilabial	Labiodental	Interdental	Alveolar	Palatal	Velar	Glottal
Stop	p b			t d		k g	
Fricative		f v	θ ð	s z	š ž		
Affricate					č ǰ		
Nasal	m			n		ŋ	
Glide	ʍ w			l	y		h
Liquid				r			

= voiceless	= voiced

Note: You may prefer to use the following alternative symbols for the palatal affricates and fricatives: š = ʃ, ž = ʒ, č = tʃ, and ǰ = dʒ.

Table 3.2		The International Phonetic Alphabet—Consonants									

	Bilabial	Labiodental	Dental	Alveolar	Postalveolar	Retroflex	Palatal	Velar	Uvular	Pharyngeal	Glottal
Plosive	p b			t d		ʈ ɖ	c ɟ	k g	q ɢ		ʔ
Nasal	m	ɱ		n		ɳ	ɲ	ŋ	N		
Trill	ʙ			r					ʀ		
Tap or Flap		ⱱ		ɾ		ɽ					
Fricative	ɸ β	f v	θ ð	s z	ʃ ʒ	ʂ ʐ	ç ʝ	x ɣ	χ ʁ	ħ ʕ	h ɦ
Lateral fricative				ɬ ɮ							
Approximant		ʋ		ɹ		ɻ	j	ɰ			
Lateral approximant				l		ɭ	ʎ	ʟ			

Note: Where symbols appear in pairs, the one to the right represents a voiced consonant. Shaded areas denote articulations judged impossible.

Source: Courtesy of International Phonetic Association (Department of Theoretical and Applied Linguistics, School of English, Aristotle University of Thessaloniki, Thessaloniki 54124, Greece).

brackets here to simply refer to a sound without reference to whether or not it is a phoneme.) You can feel the vibration of your vocal cords—that's voicing. It happens with other sound pairs too, but it can be harder to feel because the sounds are shorter. For example, [p] and [b] differ only in vocal cord vibration, but because the sounds are so short, it's harder to feel them. (Beware: When we produce these sounds, we tend to add a vowel to them, making it more like "puh" or "buh." All vowels are voiced, so you will feel the vibration during production of the vowel. Try to isolate just the [p] and [b], and you should feel the vibration during [b].)

The various parts of the mouth and throat used to make speech sounds (indicated in Figure 3.1) are called the **articulators**.

articulators parts of the human body involved in speech production: tongue, teeth, lips, glottis, velum, vocal folds

RPE   3.2

 Did You Know...?

Visible Speech

Visible Speech is a writing system invented in 1867 by Alexander Melville Bell, father of Alexander Graham Bell, the inventor of the telephone. Melville Bell was a teacher of the deaf and intended his writing system to help deaf students learn spoken language. Visible Speech was one of the first notation systems for the sounds of speech independent of a particular language or dialect and was widely used to teach students how to speak with a "standard" accent. In the 1860s, Melville Bell's three sons, Melville, Edward, and Alexander, went on a lecture tour in Scotland to demonstrate the Visible Speech system. In the show, one of the brothers would leave the room while the others brought volunteers from the audience to speak either in another language or in a nonstandard dialect. They would record the speech in Visible Speech on the board on stage. When the other brother returned, he would be able to replicate the sounds made by the volunteers by reading the Visible Speech notations. People would flock to see the Bell brothers' performances! The modern equivalent of Bell's Visible Speech is the International Phonetic Alphabet (IPA). In 1886, the International Phonetic Association was founded in Paris and has been the official keeper of the IPA ever since.

Figure 3.1   Places of Articulation

Source: Courtesy of Russell Hugo.

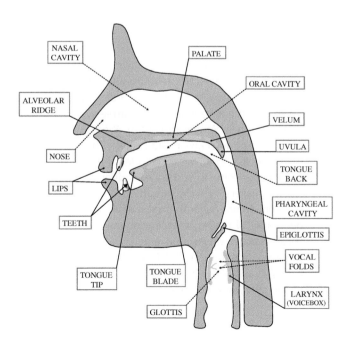

hƿæꞇ!

A bilabial fricative, /β/ in IPA, is not a phoneme in English but appears in most dialects of Spanish. It's similar to a /v/ but instead of top teeth on bottom lip, air comes through both lips. Try it!

Place of Articulation

In addition to the vocal cords, all the other organs of the mouth and throat (lips, tongue, teeth) have roles in making sounds. It's also possible to describe where in the vocal tract a constriction—a tightening of muscles—is made.

Bilabial

The bilabial (from the Latin *bi-* 'two' and *labial* 'lips') sounds are made with both lips. The sounds in this group are all made by bringing both lips together or almost together. The bilabial sounds are underlined in the following words.

Symbol	Sample Word
/p/	p̲ink
/b/	b̲all
/m/	m̲ake
/w/	w̲ash
/ʍ/	w̲hich (for some speakers)

/ʍ/ and /w/ are also sometimes classified as *velar* or *labiovelar* because the back of the tongue is raised toward the velum during production of the consonants.

Language Alive!

A Disappearing Sound

How do you pronounce *when, where, what,* and *whistle*? Have you noticed that words that begin with *wh* have two pronunciations? One way is just to sound the /w/, as you would in *weather, watt, was,* and *winter*. The other way is to make a little puff of air with the *w* sound. This *w*-with-a-puff sound, called a *voiceless bilabial glide*, is disappearing in American English. Words spelled with *wh-* came from a group of words spelled with *hw-* in Old English. The <h> has been preserved in the spelling for many words—*what, when, whistle, whale, where*—but the puff of air (called *aspiration*) that accompanies the /w/ is disappearing from most speakers' pronunciation. Many speakers over the age of 55 or so maintain the sound, while most younger speakers do not have this sound at all. Its disappearance does not seem restricted to geographical region or socioeconomic factors as many other variations are. Some speakers acquire the sound later as a result of a *spelling pronunciation* (changing one's pronunciation to more closely match the spelling) so words that start with *wh-* would have /ʍ/ as the result of direct instruction in speech or acting classes. Despite these factors, the /ʍ/ does appear to be on its way out of American English.

Labiodental

The two sounds in the labiodental (from the Latin *labio* 'lip' and *dent* 'tooth') group are made with the lower lip against the upper front teeth. The labiodental sounds are underscored in the following words.

Symbol	Sample Word
/f/	fast
/v/	valley

Interdental

The two sounds in the interdental (from the Latin *inter* 'between' and *dent* 'tooth') group are made with the tip of the tongue between the front teeth. The interdental sounds are underlined in the following words.

Symbol	Sample Word
/θ/	thick
/ð/	though

It can be difficult at first to distinguish between these two sounds because we aren't used to doing so (since they are both written with <th>). The name of the /θ/ symbol is *theta*, which itself begins with the voiceless /ð/ sound, and the name for the /ð/ symbol is *eth*, which itself contains the voiced /ð/ sound.

Alveolar

The sounds in this group are made with the tongue tip at or near the *alveolar ridge*. To find your alveolar ridge, put your tongue on the back of your top teeth and slide it upward. That bump, or ridge, is the alveolar ridge. The alveolar sounds are underlined in the following words. (It might not be obvious to you that /r/ is an alveolar sound because your tongue seems to be rather scrunched up. We'll explain this in more detail later.)

Symbol	Sample Word
/t/	teeth
/d/	dog
/s/	sea
/z/	zenith
/n/	nut
/l/	leer
/r/	red, bar

Palatal

The sounds in this group are made with the tongue near your *palate*, the hard part of the roof of the mouth. Slide your tongue back from your alveolar ridge to find your palate. The palatal sounds are underlined in the following words.

Symbol	Sample Word
/š/	shell
/ž/	genre, measure
/č/	cheers
/ǰ/	jam
/y/	yellow

The alternative symbols ʃ, ʒ, tʃ, and dʒ maybe be substituted for š, ž, č, and ǰ, respectively.

Velar

The sounds in this group are made with the tongue near the *velum,* the soft part of the roof of your mouth, behind the palate. The velar sounds are underlined in the following words.

Symbol	Sample Word
/k/	kiss
/g/	gear
/ŋ/	sing

Glottal

This is a sound made at the *glottis,* the space between the vocal folds. The glottal sound is underlined in the following word.

Symbol	Sample Word
/h/	happy

The sound /h/ is sometimes classified as a glottal fricative.

There is another sound of English, though it is not typically counted as a distinct phoneme, represented by the symbol /ʔ/. It is the sound in the middle of the word *uh-oh,* where there is a stoppage of airflow at the glottis; it is, therefore, classified as a glottal stop.

RPE   3.3 ▷

Manner of Articulation

Each consonant sound is also described by means of its *manner of articulation,* that is, *how* the sound is made, especially with respect to airflow.

Stops

The sounds in this group are made by obstructing the airstream completely in the oral cavity. All the symbols shown here have the same pronunciation as they do in the example words given with the places of articulation. The stop sounds are underlined in the following words.

Symbol	Sample Word
/p/	pink
/b/	ball
/t/	teeth
/d/	dog
/k/	kiss
/g/	gear

Fricatives

The sounds in this group are made by forming a nearly complete stoppage of the airstream. The fricative sounds are underlined in the following words.

Symbol	Sample Word
/f/	fast
/v/	valley
/θ/	thick
/ð/	though
/s/	sea
/z/	zenith
/š/	shell
/ž/	genre, measure

Language Alive!

Why Do We Spell Words with -ough?

How many ways can you say -ough? Think of the words you know that are spelled with these letters, usually at the end. Did you ever wonder why one set of letters can be pronounced so many ways? The -gh digraph was used in Old English to represent a voiceless velar fricative, represented in IPA as [x]. This sound is still found in other Germanic languages (like the final sound in German *Bach*). However, in English the sound was lost during the Old English period, though this took place after the spelling of these words had been standardized. In some words, the [x] became [f], as in *laugh, tough, rough, cough,* and *enough*; in others, the sound simply disappeared, as in *though* or *night,* even though the letters didn't.

Affricates

The sounds in this group are made by briefly stopping the airstream completely and then releasing the articulators slightly so that friction is produced; these sounds start as stops and finish as fricatives. The affricate sounds are underlined in the following words.

Symbol	Sample Word
/č/	cheers
/ǰ/	jam

Peter Ladefoged: Pioneer in Phonetics

When he died, word of his passing appeared in newspapers around the world—the *New York Times*, the *Los Angeles Times*, the *Daily Telegraph*, and the *Independent*, among others—and his death was reported worldwide by the Associated Press. Professor Peter Ladefoged, a remarkable man and a pioneer linguist, was mourned greatly within and outside of linguistics.

Among the many linguists who deserve mention for their impact on the field, Peter Ladefoged stands out as a true pioneer whose work has influenced the very way we look at language. Professor Ladefoged was widely regarded as the world's premier phonetician, whose life was devoted to the study of the acoustics and physiology of speech.

Born in 1925 in England and educated in Edinburgh, Scotland, Ladefoged was a member of the linguistics faculty at the University of California at Los Angeles from 1962. He established the UCLA Phonetics Laboratory, foremost of its kind in the world. Some of the areas Professor Ladefoged studied there include speech production, the electromyography of speech respiration, tongue positions of vowels, and articulatory–acoustic modeling.

Professor Ladefoged was committed to phonetics fieldwork.

In the days before laptops and more technologically advanced instruments, he carried into remote villages around the globe a camera, a tape recorder, an oscilloscope, and an instrument that measures airflow. He used these to document and describe how native speakers make the sounds of a variety of languages. One technique was to paint speakers' palates with olive oil and powdered charcoal; when the tongue came in contact with the palate during production of a particular sound, it would wipe away the charcoal, leaving a record of tongue position. Ladefoged would then photograph and catalog the tongue position. For another experiment, Ladefoged showed villagers how to put an air tube up their noses so that it would come out their mouths. One of his many works is *The Sounds of the World's Languages* (with Ian Maddieson 1996), widely considered the best catalogue to date of the consonants and vowels of some 6,000 languages.

Professor Ladefoged was a tireless advocate for the preservation of endangered languages, some of which he encountered during his years of fieldwork all over the world—in Nigeria, Botswana, Ghana, Uganda, Tanzania, Sierra Leone, Senegal, India, Yemen, Papua New Guinea, Nepal, Thailand, Brazil, Mexico, Australia, Korea, Scotland, the Aleutian Islands, and China.

The International Phonetic Alphabet also benefited from Ladefoged's expertise when he worked on expanding it to include more sounds and making sure that it would be available in computer fonts.

Ladefoged also found time to consult on many forensics cases. In an influential short paper in the journal *Language and Speech*, he showed that, in fact, we do not recognize each others' voices with the degree of accuracy we think we do, thus shedding doubt on such testimony in legal proceedings.

Perhaps his most "popular" work was as advisor on the movie *My Fair Lady*. He taught Rex Harrison, who portrayed the fictional phonetician Henry Higgins, to indicate the correct phonetic symbols on charts and to use the nineteenth-century phonetics equipment. Ladefoged's voice is heard pronouncing the recorded vowels in the film.

For more information
http://www.linguistics.ucla .edu/people/ladefoge (Peter Ladefoged's life and work)
http://www.humnet.ucla .edu/humnet/linguistics/faciliti/ uclaplab.html (UCLA Phonetics Lab and to see pictures of Ladefoged on the set of *My Fair Lady*)

hwæt!

The American English /r/ is the least common of the world's phonemes, popping up in less than 5 percent of languages; the American English /m/ is the most common, occurring in 97 percent of languages.

Nasals

The sounds in this group are made by lowering the velum and letting the airstream pass primarily through the nasal cavity. The nasal sounds are underlined in the following words.

Symbol	Sample Word
/m/	make
/n/	nut, bun
/ŋ/	sing

Did You Know...?

Mom Is Bob

When you have a cold, a word like *mom* sounds something like *bob*. Now you can explain why that is. The sounds /b/ and /m/ are made in the same way, except that when you are producing /m/, the air is pushed out through the nose rather than through the mouth. However, when your nose is plugged up, as it can be when you have a cold, very little air can go through, and the airflow defaults to your mouth. Thus, *mom* becomes *bob*, and *non* becomes *dod*.

Glides

The sounds in this group are made with only a slight closure of the articulators—if the vocal tract were any more open, the result would be a vowel. The glide sounds are underlined in the following words.

Symbol	Sample Word
/y/	yellow
/w/	wash
/ʍ/	which (for some speakers)
/h/	happy

Liquids

The sounds in this group result when an obstruction is formed by the articulators but is not narrow enough to stop the airflow or to cause friction. The /l/ is often described as a *lateral* liquid, because for most speakers the tongue touches the roof of the mouth near the alveolar ridge, and air flows around the sides of the tongue. As mentioned above, the /r/ is described

RPE   3.5 ▷

as a *bunched* liquid because for most American English speakers the tongue is just that—bunched up under the palate—during the production of the sound.[1]

Symbol	Sample Word
/l/	l̠eer
/r/	r̠ed

Forgotten Clusters

Besides the *wh-* and the *-ough*, Old English had several other consonant combinations that don't occur in Present-Day English pronunciation, but the letters for them are preserved in the spelling. We have lost the Old English consonant combinations of /k/ plus /n/ and /g/ plus /n/, though these clusters remain in our spelling—*knee*, *knight*, *knock*, *knife*, *knit*, *knot*, *gnash*, *gnarl*, *gnome*, *gnaw*, and *gnat*. In Old English, the *kn* and *gn* at the beginning of these words were all pronounced, as were all of those so-called silent *b*s in words like *dumb*, *climb*, and *comb*.

Why All These Distinctions?

Again, remember that the sounds in the chart in Table 3.1 are the consonant sounds used in English. Other languages have other combinations of voicing, place, and manner of articulation, resulting in distinct sounds as shown in Table 3.2. Some dialects of Spanish, for example, have a voiced bilabial fricative, /β/; German has a voiceless velar fricative, /x/; and Japanese has a uvular nasal, /N/. And Tsonga, a Southern Bantu language spoken in Mozambique, South Africa, and Swaziland, has what are called plain voiced nasals and breathy voiced nasals. Most Salish languages, spoken (or formerly spoken) in the Pacific Northwest (United States) and in lower British Columbia (Canada), have ejective stops and affricates. (*Ejectives* are voiceless consonants that are pronounced with simultaneous closure of the glottis.) Mazatec, a language of Mexico, has what are called creaky voiced consonants and breathy voiced consonants. (You can hear all of these contrasts at the UCLA phonetics site: http://phonetics.ucla.edu/.)

Because many of these symbols overlap with the symbols (letters) we use to spell English, learning the system is not difficult. Only the following symbols are new. The sounds are grouped according to where they occur in

---

1. A *bunched r* is sometimes called a *retroflex r*, though the two sounds are actually distinct. Bunched r is produced by having the tongue bunched in the region of the palate, while for retroflex the tongue tip is curled so that the underside faces the alveopalatal part of the roof of the mouth. The use of these appears to be quite variant for speakers of American English.

a word: at the beginning, or *word-initially*; in the middle, or *word-medially*; or at the end, or *word-finally*.

Symbol	Word-initial	Word-medial	Word-final
θ	thin, thank, thought	author, Arthur	bath, breath
ð	then, though	wither, feather	bathe, breathe
š	ship, charade	dishes, nation	fish, rash
ž	genre	measure, casual	rouge, garage[2]
č	chip, cello	riches, kitchen	ditch, which
ǰ	gem, jump	bludgeon, bridger	ridge, judge
ŋ	N/A	ringer, singing	wing, tongue
ʍ	what, which[3]	awhile	N/A

As previously noted, we call any of the various groupings of sounds in the consonant chart natural classes: groups of sounds in a language that share some articulatory or auditory feature(s). For a group of sounds to be a natural class, it must include all of the sounds that share a particular feature or group of features and must not include any sounds that don't. So all of the consonant chart groupings are natural classes, but some larger groupings are also natural classes. Some of these are shown in Table 3.3. For example, bilabials are a natural class, but so are *labials*, which include bilabials and labiodentals. Nasals are a natural class, but so are *sonorants*, which include not only nasals but also liquids and glides. We can distinguish sonorants, those consonants produced with a relatively open passage for the airflow (which include nasals, liquids, and glides) from *obstruents*, those sounds produced with a greater obstruction of airflow (which include stops, affricates, and fricatives). These labels are simply descriptions of groups of sounds that share some phonetic features. The groups of sounds pattern together in other languages too, not just English.

Table 3.3   Consonant Phonemes of English with Additional Natural Classes

	Bilabial	Labiodental	Interdental	Alveolar	Palatal	Velar	Glottal
Stop	p b			t d		k g	
Fricative		f v	θ ð	s z	š ž		
Affricate					č ǰ		
Nasal	m			n		ŋ	
Glide	ʍ w				y		h
Liquid				l r			

| = obstruent | = sonorant | = labial | = labial and sonorant |

---

2. In some dialects, these words would have /ǰ/ rather than /ž/.
3. These words begin with /w/ rather than /ʍ/ for most American English speakers.

ƕƿæᴛ!

Freudian slips are named after Sigmund Freud, the famous psychoanalyst who described such slips in his 1901 book *The Psychopathology of Everyday Life*. Freud argued that such slips came from repressed thoughts and desires.

Describing sounds in terms of natural classes is helpful for lots of reasons, as we'll see throughout the book. The natural groupings of sounds are relevant for understanding some of the things children do when acquiring language (which classes of sounds seem to be easier to acquire and which are more difficult and therefore often emerge later). Natural classes also help us understand language variation and language change. Vowels seem to shift and change over time, for example, and the shifts affect classes of vowels rather than individual sounds.

Slips of the Tongue

Slips of the tongue provide a fascinating illustration of our unconscious knowledge of sounds and show that we are able to manipulate features of sounds, pieces of sounds smaller than the sounds themselves. First, consider a common type of slip, the exchange of whole sounds, such as in the following actual examples, in which either initial consonants or consonant clusters have been exchanged. Carefully study what is going on in each example.

Intended Utterance	Actual Utterance
tall man	mall tan
sick fish	fick sish
take her snow pants off	snake her toe pants off

Now consider the following examples in which vowels have been exchanged.

Intended Utterance	Actual Utterance
pass the toast	poas the tast (/æ/ and /o/ exchange)
fill the pool	fool the pill (/ɪ/ and /u/ exchange)

In these next two examples, a whole segment—that is, an entire sound—doesn't move, but a piece of that sound, a *feature*, does. See how the voicing switches in the following example.

Intended Utterance	Actual Utterance
black cat	plack gat

In this voicing exchange, the voicing from /b/ moves to the /k/ of *cat*, resulting in /g/. Removing the voicing from /b/ results in /p/.

The next example shows a *nasality exchange*, where the intended utterance is *banana*; only the nasal feature moves from one segment to another.

Intended Utterance	Actual Utterance
banana	madana

The nasality from the first /n/ in *banana* moves to the /b/, making it a bilabial nasal. Removing the nasality from /n/ results in the alveolar stop /d/.

Though we call slips of the tongue "errors," they are actually quite systematic, affecting classes of sounds. Slips are not arbitrary; rather, they are patterned and reflect how we unconsciously organize sounds in our mental grammar.

RPE 3.6

Vowels

Most languages have between three and seven vowels. English, however, has between fourteen and twenty vowels, depending on the dialect. Table 3.4 includes the vowels of most dialects of American English (though not the diphthongs—we'll get to those soon). The position labels (high, back, etc.) are descriptions that refer to the position of the tongue in the mouth.

Though it may be slightly more difficult to determine where your tongue is with vowels than with consonants, your tongue does move. Say the words *beet, bet, bat,* and feel how your tongue lowers with each word.

Table 3.5 gives a sample word for each vowel of the chart. Keep in mind, however, that we do not all pronounce these words in the same way—there is a tremendous amount of variation in the pronunciation of vowels across dialects

Table 3.4	Monophthongal Vowel Phonemes of English		
	Front	Central	Back
High	i I		u ʊ
Mid	e ɛ	ə ʌ	o ɔ
Low	æ		a

unrounded	rounded

Table 3.5	Monophthongal Vowels with Example Words		
	Front	Central	Back
High	i (beat) ɪ (bit)		u (boot) ʊ (put)
Mid	e (bait) ɛ (bet)	ə (tun<u>a</u>) ʌ (but)	o (boat) ɔ (bawdy)
Low	æ (bat)		a (body)

of English—so the word used as an example may not be accurate for your own pronunciation. It can sometimes be difficult to distinguish the mid central vowels, /ə/ and /ʌ/. /ə/ is the vowel that occurs in unstressed syllables, and /ʌ/ in stressed syllables. See if you can detect the difference when comparing the sounds of *bun* /bʌn/ and the unstressed, final vowel of *Cuba* /kyubə/. Although this distinction may seem subtle at this point—and maybe not that important—such differences become more important when we learn more about stress later in the chapter.

Another natural class distinction we make for vowels is to distinguish the *tense* vowels from the *lax* vowels. The tense vowels are made with more muscular constriction: /i/ as in *beet*, /e/ as in *bait*, /u/ as in *boot*, and /o/ as in *boat*. The rest are said to be lax. And a final natural class distinction we make with vowels is lip rounding. English has rounded vowels only for the high and mid back vowels (/u, ʊ, o, ɔ/), but other languages, like French, have rounded front vowels.

RPE   3.7 ⊳

Language Alive!

Do *Dawn* and *Don* Rhyme?

Say *Don* and *Dawn* out loud. Do they sound the same? How about *caught* and *cot* or *stock* and *stalk*? For some people, there is no distinction in the pronunciation of the words in each pair—they all have only the [a] vowel sound. In many dialects of English, a distinction between the vowels /ɔ/ and /a/ has been lost. This loss is known as a *merger* of sounds because the two vowel sounds have come together, which is different from a vowel shift. The *low back merger* is well established in parts of the Midwest and eastern New England, where it has been going on for generations. It is more recently found in the speech of most western United States speakers and is characteristic today of most speakers under the age of 35 anywhere west of the Mississippi.

Diphthongs

diphthong
two-part vowel sound consisting of a vowel and a glide in one syllable

In addition to the vowels in the English vowel chart in Table 3.5, English has phonemic **diphthongs**, two-part vowel sounds consisting of a vowel and a glide in one syllable. In many dialects, if you say *eye* slowly, you can feel the two parts of the vowel sound. Diphthongs are distinguished from two single vowels. Compare Japanese, for example, which does not have diphthongs. *Aisu*, borrowed from the English word *ice cream*, is a three-syllable word in Japanese: /a/-/i/-/su/. Its counterpart /ays/ in English combines /a/ and /i/ to make the diphthong /ay/.

Most dialects of American English have the three phonemic diphthongs /ay/ (as in *wide* and *sky*), /aw/ (as in *loud* and *cow*), and /oy/ (as in *toy* and *foil*). These phonemes are distinct from the corresponding monophthongs

ƕƿæᴛ!

The standard pronunciation of the word *diphthong* is /dɪfθɔŋ/ with the <ph> as /f/, though the pronunciation /dɪpθɔŋ/ is becoming more common and therefore more accepted; *Merriam-Webster* now includes both pronunciations.

/a/ and /o/. (In some dialects, however, the /ay/ diphthong is a monophthong, so *wide* is closer to /wad/ and *sky* is something like /ska/, and the /oy/ in *foil* or *oil* is /o/, giving /fol/ and /ol/.) These sounds are distinct—no dialect has two words that differ only by those vowels; every dialect has either the diphthong /ay/ or the monophthong /a/ in a particular word, but not both. So the chart in some dialects would have all the tense vowels as diphthongs rather than monophthongs.

The most common diphthongs in American English are[4]

/ay/ as in *wide* and *sky*
/aw/ as in *loud* and *cow*
/oy/ as in *toy* and *foil*

Many people refer to a "Southern drawl" and have the impression that Southerners speak more slowly and "draw out" many of the vowels. Though some Southern dialect speakers have some diphthongs where speakers of other dialects have monophthongs, there are also monophthongs where other dialects have diphthongs. So a word like *fire* contains a diphthong in most non-Southern dialects, /fayr/; but in some Southern dialects, it contains a monophthong, /far/. So the dialect does not, in fact, "draw out" vowel sounds any more than other dialects.

We can write just /e/ and /o/ for the vowel sounds in *stay* and *go* when transcribing our own English speech. However, these tense vowels are often pronounced as diphthongs in English—they actually have a following glide. In many dialects of English, all of the tense vowels are usually diphthongized. Thus, the vowel sounds in words like *beet* and *peak* are better transcribed as /iy/ because of the diphthongization, as in the following examples.

iy—beat	uw—boot
ey—bait	ow—boat

It is this tendency to diphthongize vowels that can make English speakers sound like they have an "American accent" when they are speaking another language that does not have as many diphthongs. Spanish, for example, has shorter monophthongs in its vowel system. Consider a word like *perro* 'dog'. In Spanish, this is pronounced [pɛro], but an English speaker might pronounce it more like [pɛyrow], diphthongizing both of the vowels. One does this unconsciously, adopting the closest match of the sounds in one's own language. It can take a great deal of practice to acquire the sounds of another language without substituting the sounds of one language for the closest match in the other language. This substitution is what gives us a "foreign accent."

RPE 3.8

---

4. Sometimes these diphthongs are written with different symbols. Here are the alternative symbols: The /oy/ is written /ɔy/, /ɔɪ/, or /oɪ/; the /aw/ is written /æw/, /æʊ/, or /aʊ/; and the /ay/ is /aɪ/ or /ai/.

Syllabic Consonants

In English, the liquids /l/ and /r/ and the nasals /m/ and /n/ can be *syllabic consonants.* Syllabic consonants are sounds that are identified as consonants but that may fill a vowel slot in a syllable when no vowel is present. (More on syllables follows in the final section of the chapter.) Linguists indicate a syllabic consonant by a small mark under the consonant, like so:

/ṛ/ or /ṇ/

In some pronunciations of words like *runner* and *ribbon,* the final syllables contain no vowel sound, only the syllabic consonant sounds:

/rʌnṛ/	runner
/rɪbṇ/	ribbon

Because syllabic consonants can sometimes be confusing for beginning transcribers, and because it can be difficult to determine whether a vowel is present in a given syllable or not, you may find it easier when transcribing to use either /ər, əl, əm, ən/ or /ṛ, ḷ, m̩, ṇ/ to represent these syllabic sounds.

/šʊgər/ or /šʊgṛ/	sugar
/bərd/ or /bṛd/	bird
/bʌtən/ or /bʌtṇ/	button

RPE 3.9 ▷

Be sure to use syllabic consonants in transcription *only* when the consonant is syllabic. The liquids and nasals can be "regular" nonsyllabic consonants too. (So, though /n/ is syllabic in *ribbon,* it is not in *nonsense* or *nine.*)

Other Vowel Distinctions

Another way in which vowel sounds can be distinctive is with respect to *length,* that is, the actual duration of the sound. Some speech sounds are longer than others. In English, a vowel preceding a voiced consonant is longer than the same vowel before a voiceless consonant. Can you hear the length difference in word pairs such as *bit/bid* and *beat/bead*? The vowels that precede the voiced consonants are longer—actually last longer—than the ones preceding the voiceless consonants.

Though we have length variations in English, they are not distinctive; that is, the variation in length of a vowel sound does not change a word's meaning. (So Table 3.4 does not indicate long vowels as distinct from short vowels.) So, there's not one word [bɪt] and another one [bɪːt] (where ː indicates a longer duration of a vowel sound).

Length is distinctive in other languages, however. In Finnish, the difference in vowels and consonants can make a difference in the meaning of a word, as the following three sets of examples illustrate:

[muta]	mud
[muːta]	some other

[mut:a]	but
[tapan]	I kill
[tapa:n]	I meet
[tule]	come!
[tule:]	comes
[tu:le:]	is windy

Japanese also has consonant and vowel length distinctions, as these three sets of examples show:

[to:kai]	collapse
[tokai]	city
[kokaku]	a customer
[ko:kaku]	wide angle
[ko:to:]	oral, verbal
[koto:]	an isolated island
[kotto]	antique

Even though English doesn't have long consonants as phonemes, English speakers can get an idea of what the long (also called *geminate*) consonants are like by comparing the English words *bookend* and *bookcase*:

bookend	/bʊkɛnd/
bookcase	/bʊkkes/

The /k/s in the compound word *bookcase* are usually pronounced as one long, extended /k/ rather than either a single /k/ or two separated /k/s. Length, however, is not distinctive in English, so there is not one word /bʊkɛnd/ and another word /bʊkkɛnd/; consonant length can never make the difference in the meaning of a word. Another word that allows you to hear this "length" in a consonant is the word *except*, which sounds as if it has two occurrences of /s/, one from the /ks/ of <x> and one from the /s/ of <c>: /ɛkssɛpt/.

RPE   3.10

RPE   3.11

Language Alive!

Double Is Not Long

Old English also had phonemically long consonants. These were typically indicated in the spelling system by doubling the letter, so there were pairs such as *bed* 'prayer' and *bedd* 'bed', and *fȳlan* 'to befoul' and *fȳllan* 'to fill.' This phonemic distinction has dropped out of the language now, and double letters no longer reflect a different sound; for example, we would pronounce *bed* and *bedd* the same way, just as we would pronounce *Jen* and *Jenn*, both possible spellings for short versions of *Jennifer*, the same way.

tone variation in pitch that makes a difference in the meaning of words

Another way in which language sounds are distinctive is with respect to **tone**. In many languages, the pitch at which the syllables in a word are pronounced can make a difference in the word's meaning. These are called *tone languages*, and they include Thai, some Chinese dialects, Vietnamese, some African languages, and some South American Indian languages.

Mandarin Chinese has four tones, illustrated in these minimal pairs:

[ma]	mother	pronounced with a high level tone
[ma]	hemp	pronounced with a high rising tone
[ma]	horse	pronounced with a low falling rising tone
[ma]	scold	pronounced with a high falling tone

The following examples are from the Nupe language, spoken in Nigeria, which has three tones, indicated by the diacritic marks ` and ´. Vowels without a diacritic are mid tones.

ebà	place	èdù	Niger river
eba	penis	èdu	kind of yam
ebá	husband	edu	thigh
edú	kind of fish	edù	deer

stress relative emphasis given to syllables in a word

All aspects of languages are continually changing, and it is well documented that some tonal languages have changed into nontonal languages. Such languages generally develop a **stress** system as they lose the tonal distinctions. Swahili is one such language. Korean is in transition; currently, some dialects of Korean are tonal, and others, such as the variety of Korean spoken in Seoul, are not.

nasalization production of a speech sound with the velum lowered so that most of the airflow passes through the nose rather than the mouth

Another way in which vowels are distinctive across languages is with respect to **nasalization**. When a sound is nasalized, the air passes through the nasal cavity (the nose). This phonological feature is not distinctive in English; though we have nasalized and nonnasalized vowels, nasalization cannot make the difference in the meaning of an English word. Nasalization of vowels is, however, distinctive in some other languages, such as Navajo, Ijo (spoken in Nigeria), and French. For example, in French, *lot* 'prize' is pronounced /lo/, and *longue* 'long' is pronounced /lõ/, where the diacritic ~ marks the nasalization.

Navajo has only four vowels, /a, e, i, o/, which may contrast in length (so there are short and long versions of each vowel, indicated by doubling: a vs. aa), nasalization (so: a vs. ą, where the "hook" on the <a> indicates nasalization in Navajo), and tone (a vs. á).

RPE 3.12

Vowel Shifts

As noted already, vowels vary greatly among English dialects, much more than consonants do. Some of the better-studied vowel variations and vowel shifts are discussed briefly here.

The Great Vowel Shift

During the Middle English period, the seven tense vowels of the predominant dialect in the language underwent a shift known now as the Great Vowel Shift. It was a gradual process that began in Chaucer's time (the fourteenth century) and continued through the time of Shakespeare (the early seventeenth century). Table 3.6 illustrates the shift: One vowel's articulation point was raised, and this shifted the next vowel up; however, the highest vowels had no higher place to go, so those two vowels, /u:/ and /i:/, became diphthongs. So the early English speakers lived in a /hu:s/, milked a /ku:/ for /swe:t/ milk. Some English speakers, primarily in Scotland, still maintain the pre–Great Vowel Shift pronunciation. The table illustrates all of the shifts and sample words' preshift and postshift pronunciations.

One of the primary reasons that this vowel shift has become known as the 'Great' Vowel Shift is that it profoundly affected English phonology, and these changes coincided with the introduction of the printing press; William Caxton brought the first mechanized printing press to England in 1476. Prior to mechanized printing, words in the handwritten texts had been spelled pretty much however each particular scribe wanted to spell them, according to the scribe's own dialect. Even after the printing press, however, most printers used the spellings that had begun to be established, not realizing the significance of the vowel changes that were under way. By the time the vowel shifts were complete in the early 1600s, hundreds of books had been printed that used a spelling system that reflected the pre–Great Vowel Shift pronunciation. So the word *goose*, for example, had two <o>s to indicate a long /o/ sound, /o:/—a good, phonetic spelling of the word. However, the vowel had shifted to /u/; thus *goose, moose, food,* and other similar words that we now spell with <oo> have mismatched spelling and pronunciation.

Table 3.6	The Great Vowel Shift				
		Front	Central	Back	
High	[fi:f] → [fayf] 'five'	i:		u:	[hu:s] → [haws] 'house'
Mid	[swe:t]→ [swit] 'sweet' [dɛ:g] → [de] 'day'	e: ɛ:		o: ɔ:	[fo:d] → [fu:d] 'food' [stɔ:n] → [ston] 'stone'
Low			ay aw	a:	[na:mə] → [nem] 'name'

Why didn't printers just change the spelling to match the pronunciation? Because by this time, the increased volume of book production, combined with increasing literacy, resulted in a powerful force against spelling change. We discuss spelling more in Chapter 13.

Other vowel shifts are going on all the time, in all dialects of English, all over the world. A large-scale project to create a dialect atlas of the United States, based on pronunciation and including a detailed discussion of vowel shifts, is underway at the University of Pennsylvania under the direction of linguist William Labov. Figures 3.2 and 3.3 are taken from an online report of this work (http://www.ling.upenn.edu/phono_atlas/home.html), which gives a detailed account of many regional dialects.

RPE   3.13 >

The Northern Cities Chain Shift

The Northern Cities Chain Shift is a series of changes in the vowels of the variety of English spoken in such cities as Chicago, Detroit, Rochester, Cleveland, and Buffalo. Each vowel shifted to a new place of articulation, thus pushing the next vowel along to yet another new place of articulation, just as the Great Vowel Shift did. The arrows in the vowel chart in Figure 3.2 indicate the direction of the shift of these vowels in certain words for the majority of speakers in these major, inland, Northern urban regions.

The Southern Vowel Shift

Another vowel shift has been going on among some speakers, primarily in the southeastern United States, for quite some time. The vowel shifts shown in

Figure 3.2   The Northern Cities Chain Shift (Vowels with Examples)

Source: William Labov, The Organization of Dialect Diversity in North America, paper presented at the Fourth International Conference on Spoken Language Processing, Philadelphia, PA, October 6, 1996. Updated at http://www.ling.upenn .edu/phono_atlas/ICSLP4.html.

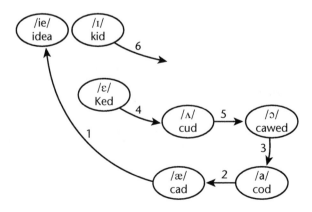

Figure 3.3 The Southern Vowel Shift

Source: William Labov, The Organization of Dialect Diversity in North America, paper presented at the Fourth International Conference on Spoken Language Processing, Philadelphia, PA, October 6, 1996. Updated at http://www.ling.upenn .edu/phono_atlas/ICSLP4.html.

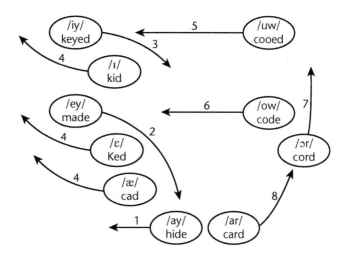

Figure 3.3 involve seven vowels, the same number of vowels involved in the Great Vowel Shift.

The fronting of the back vowels /u/ and /o/, as shown here, is taking place in the speech of many young people, regardless of region or other dialectal factors; it is quite widespread throughout the western United States. A word like *boot* /but/ is beginning to be pronounced more forward in the mouth—try it!

Another vowel shift, called the Northern California Vowel Shift, is being investigated by linguists. You can explore this shift in the 'Review, Practice, and Explore' section of this chapter.

RPE 3.14 >

The variations among the consonants across dialects are quite few compared to the vowel variations. Some Hispanic English dialects vary in the place of articulation of the alveolar consonants; they are dental rather than alveolar. Some dialects have no /ð/, replacing it with /d/, as in *this* /dɪs/ or *mother* /mədər/. There are certainly other variations involving consonants, such as the lack of [r] following vowels in many dialects ("Pahk the car in Hahvid Yahd"), but these are phonological rather than phonetic variations. In the next chapter, which deals

RPE 3.15 >

with phonology, you will come to better understand this distinction.

Phonemes and Allophones

As you transcribe words, you will likely notice that some details are difficult to represent with the symbols we have learned. As we will discuss throughout the next chapter, sounds vary depending on what other sounds occur around them. Consider the /p/ of English, for instance. Hold your hand or a piece of paper in front of your mouth and say the words *pat* and *spat*. When you pronounce *pat* you should feel a puff of air on your hand that you do not feel when you say *spat*. Making this puff of air is called **aspiration**. The difference in the way the two [p]s are pronounced results in two phonetically distinct [p]s, but native speakers are not even aware of that (unless they've had a linguistics class!) because the differences in those two sounds don't matter in English—they never occur in the same position. The [p] with the aspiration always occurs at the beginning of a stressed syllable; the other [p] occurs everywhere else.

aspiration puff of air that accompanies the initial voiceless consonants in such words as *pat* and *tick*

The consonant chart in Table 3.1 has only one /p/. That's because there is only one /p/ phoneme in English. However, we'll see that it's useful to indicate that there are two **allophones** of /p/—two predictable pronunciations of the phoneme /p/—and it is completely predictable when we get one and when we get the other. Let's see how this works.

allophone predictable phonetic variant of a phoneme

Consider the data in the following two columns, and determine whether you have the aspiration or not on each of the /p/s:

A	B
pat	spell
pickle	special
Peter	spare

The words in column A all have an aspirated [p]. Those in column B have an unaspirated [p].

Here's one way to illustrate this fact:

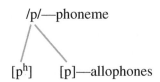

The superscript *h* in [pʰ] indicates the aspiration. This aspiration of the [p] occurs automatically in English when the /p/ is in a certain position with respect to other sounds and is what we will call a *phonological rule* of English. The following is one way to formally write the rule (the generalization) for the preceding data with the /p/s:

/p/ becomes aspirated when it occurs at the beginning of a stressed syllable. Otherwise, it is unaspirated.

The aspiration rule of English applies not only to /p/ but to the natural class of voiceless stops in English, /p/, /t/, and /k/. So, the /t/ of *tack* is aspirated, but the /t/ of *stack* is not. The /k/ of *cat* is aspirated, but the /k/ of *scat* is not. However, in certain other languages, aspiration does make a difference to speakers and can result in distinct phonemes. We'll see that phonemes are psychological constructs that vary depending on a person's native language. We continue our discussion of phonemes and allophones in the next chapter.

RPE   3.16 ⟩

Accent on **Product Naming**

The marketing, advertising, and sales of some very profitable companies and products owe some of their success to the work of linguists. The name of a company might have to convey the company's personality, expertise, track record, innovativeness, status, and so on. The name of a product usually has to carry a lot of information that gives an impression favorable enough to make people want to buy it. At the very least, its name should not deter people from buying it! Many linguists work at companies that specialize in naming things (companies, buildings, parks, campaigns, and such products as food, medication, electronics, fashion, cars—just about anything you can think of).

Researchers have showed conclusively that certain sounds convey specific attributes better than others. They can accurately predict the semantic associations likely to result from sound and spelling patterns and can then employ those sounds to create names. Answer these questions from Lexicon Branding's original pilot study. Do you agree with the survey findings?

- Which headache tablet sounds faster: Pavil or Bavil?
- Which computer sounds more compact: Gortan or Kortan?

© South West Images Scotland/Alamy

- Which car sounds faster: Sarrant or Tarrant?
- Which car sounds faster: Faldon or Valdon?
- Which computer sounds faster: Taza or Paza?
- Which car sounds more dependable: Bazia or Vazia?
- Which computer sounds more dependable: Gamza or Damza?

The results for most respondents: Pavil, Kortan, Sarrant, Valdon, Taza, Bazia, Damza. The researchers found that most English speakers made the following associations:

- Voiceless stops /p, t, k/ carry a greater connotation of speed than do voiced stops /b, d, g/.
- Fricatives /v, f, s, z/ connote speed better than stops /b, p, d, t/.

- Voiced fricatives /v, z/ connote speed better than voiceless fricatives /f, s/.
- Stops /b, p, t, d/ connote dependability better than fricatives /v, f, s, z/.
- Alveolars /t, d, s, z/ connote speed better than labials /p, b, f, v/.

Lexicon Branding (Sausalito, California) has a team of fifty-five linguists working in thirty-eight countries. They conduct research and ensure that the names are acceptable to speakers of languages in countries where the products might be sold. Catchword (Oakland, California, and New York City), another branding company, also recognizes the importance of knowledge of sounds. "When developing names . . . for the global market, we're keenly aware of pronunciation issues, such as consonant clusters, which are difficult for Japanese speakers, and vowel sounds that don't exist in Arabic. Our names generally do not require translation; they're pronounceable, if not meaningful, in every required language" (http://www.catchwordbranding.com/).

Factors other than *sound symbolism*— images, qualities, and emotions unconsciously associated with sounds—enter into product naming, too. Will Leben, director of linguistics at Lexicon and professor of linguistics at Stanford University, describes the process of naming the BlackBerry PDA. Someone at the company noted that all the buttons on the PDA were like seeds, so they began brainstorming fruit words. Someone suggested *strawberry*, but the sounds in *straw-* didn't convey the right message and seemed too 'slow'; *berry* was good, though, with the /b/ connoting both speed and dependability. Also, there is the 'friendliness' of the fruit word, good in a technical product so as not to make it intimidating, the 'lightheartedness' of the alliteration, the symmetry of the two /b/s, and the diminutive quality provided by the final <y>, suggesting compactness.

For more information
Lexicon. http://www.lexicon-branding.com/index.html.
Catchword. http://www.catchwordbranding.com/.

Summary

In this chapter, you have learned how linguists describe and categorize speech sounds—sounds that we produce effortlessly, without even thinking about it. You have learned a system of transcribing speech using a version of the International Phonetic Alphabet, and you have learned how speech sounds are made and how we can distinguish among sounds based on their phonetic features, distinguishing them by natural class. We have discussed how sounds change over time (the Great Vowel Shift), how they are changing right now (the Northern Cities Vowel Shift), and how these shifts and other sound changes happen in systematic and patterned ways. We have also glimpsed some of the ways in which these English sounds differ from those of other languages. In the next chapter, when we begin our study of phonology, we will see how the phonemes introduced in this chapter are combined into larger units by systematic rules.

Sources and Resources

Clark, J. & C. Yallop. 1990. *An introduction to phonetics and phonology.* Oxford, UK: Blackwell.

Fry, D. 1979. *The physics of speech.* Cambridge, UK: Cambridge University Press.

Ladefoged, P. 2001. *A course in phonetics*, 4th edn. Toronto: Harcourt.

Ladefoged, P. & I. Maddieson. 1996. *The sounds of the world's languages.* Cambridge, MA: Blackwell.

Robinson, J. (ed.). 1990. *The Nag Hammadi Library*, rev. edn. San Francisco: Harper Collins.

TELSUR Project 2011. http://www.ling.upenn.edu/phono_atlas/home.html

UCLA Phonetics Lab Archive. 2011. http://archive.phonetics.ucla.edu/

Review, Practice, and Explore

RPE 3.1 — Describing Consonant Sounds

Using Table 3.1, describe the following sounds in terms of voicing, place of articulation, and manner of articulation. Example: /p/ is a voiceless bilabial stop.

1. /f/	**7.** /ŋ/
2. /h/	**8.** /b/
3. /g/	**9.** /š/
4. /θ/	**10.** /č/
5. /n/	**11.** /t/
6. /r/	**12.** /m/

RPE 3.2 — Voiced or Voiceless?

Come up with four minimal pairs of words in which a sound differs only in voicing status; for example: *pin* /pɪn/ and *bin* /bɪn/. Refer to the vowel chart in Tables 3.4 and 3.5 for help with transcribing vowels.

RPE 3.3 — Different Places of Articulation

Looking at the consonant chart in Table 3.1, come up with three sets of three words, the words in each set differing only in the place of articulation of one of the sounds in the same position. For example, in the words *pit, tit, kit,* /pɪt/ /tɪt/ /kɪt/, the initial sounds are all voiceless stops, but /p/ is bilabial, /t/ is alveolar, and /k/ is velar.

RPE 3.4 — Different Manners of Articulation

Looking at the consonant chart in Table 3.1, come up with three sets of two words each that differ only in the manner of articulation of one of the sounds in the same position. For example, in the words *ship* and *chip*, /šɪp/ /čɪp/, the initial sounds are a voiceless palatal fricative /š/ and a voiceless palatal affricate /č/. The differing sounds do not have to occur at the beginning of the word.

RPE 3.5 > Place and Manner Natural Classes

For each group of words, write a three-part description (voicing, place of articulation, and manner of articulation) for the underlined sound in each word. Then determine which single natural class of sounds describes the underlined sounds in each group.

Group 1	Group 2	Group 3	Group 4
p̲izza	t̲hink	f̲avorite	sin̲g̲
m̲alice	t̲hough	s̲oap	bar̲k̲
b̲ashful	t̲hrash	v̲aporize	g̲et
w̲ash	t̲histle	z̲enith	
f̲ather	t̲here	s̲hape	
v̲alise		t̲hatch	

RPE 3.6 > Oops! That's Not What I Meant!

Slips of the tongue involve accidental manipulation of the building blocks of language. The slips can be phonetic, phonological, morphological, or syntactic. In the following phonetic slips, either a whole phoneme or only a piece—a feature—of each sound is involved. Describe what happens from the intended utterance to the actual utterance and why you think each slip occurs.

	Intended Utterance	Actual Utterance
Example:	black cat	plack gat

The voicing from /b/ moves to the /k/ of *cat,* resulting in /g/. Removing the voicing from /b/ results in /p/. This switch provides evidence for the features of these phonemes and for a speaker's ability to manipulate those features unconsciously.

	Intended Utterance	Actual Utterance
a.	pity the new teacher	mity the dew teacher
b.	mismatched	mitchmashed

(Before attempting an analysis, transcribe this one to see the correct phonemic representation.)

c.	bad, naughty kitten	mad, daughty kitten
d.	coin toss	toin coss

RPE 3.7 > Fiddle-Faddle!

Why do you think we say *fiddle-faddle* and not *faddle-fiddle*? Why is it *ping-pong* and *pitter-patter* and not *pong-ping* and *patter-pitter*? Here are some more:

dribs and drabs, spic and span, riffraff, zigzag, singsong, mishmash, ding-dong, crisscross, seesaw, hee-haw, flip-flop, hippity-hop, ticktock, eeny-meeny-miney-moe, bric-a-brac, clickety-clack, splish splash, dillydally, blither blather, tip-top, chitter chatter, shim sham, flimflam

Come up with more examples of similar kinds of singsong (there's one!) phrases. In the examples given and in your own, which vowel sounds seem to come first? Why do you think these vowels come before others? Is this pattern likely to hold for other languages? Why or why not?

RPE　3.8 ⟩　Mono or Di?

Recall that whether vowels are diphthongs or monophthongs varies quite a bit across English dialects. Write the following words in phonemic transcription of your pronunciation. (It might be easier to listen to someone else's pronunciation, since it can be difficult to reflect on your own.)

a.　foul
b.　bawdy
c.　coffee
d.　toil
e.　reign
f.　tine
g.　frame
h.　fire
i.　taught

RPE　3.9 ⟩　Syllabic Consonants

The transcription of words with syllabic consonants can cause some trouble when you are just learning to transcribe. Transcribe the following words phonemically, using syllabic consonants where relevant. Remember that not all instances of /r/, /l/, /m/, and /n/ are syllabic consonants.

a.　purple
b.　bludgeon
c.　furtive
d.　kittens
e.　bottom
f.　cycle
g.　cursive

RPE　3.10 ⟩　Phonemic Transcription

A.　Transcribe the following words using phonemic transcription:

1.　monkey
2.　though
3.　crabs
4.　fangs
5.　physics
6.　thanks
7.　badger
8.　think
9.　useful
10.　uncle
11.　measure
12.　pinch
13.　shaved
14.　wiggle
15.　huge
16.　prestige
17.　cured
18.　wart

B.

1.　Write your name in phonemic transcription.
2.　Write a sentence in phonemic transcription.

RPE　3.11 ⟩　Reverse Phonemic Transcription

Write the following sentences in regular English orthography. Keep in mind that this transcription may not match your pronunciation of some of the words. Also keep in mind that some of these sentences might not actually make a whole lot of sense—we don't want context to give away the words, so some of them are a bit, well, wacky.

a.　/ə maws slɛpt θru may lɛkšər əbawt bʌkəts ǰʌmpiŋ ɪntu ðə læps əv bebz/
b.　/ðə mʌnθ əv eprɪl wʌz pr̩tɪkyulərli lʌvli dont yu θiŋk/
c.　/ɪmæǰɪnɛri kričərz lɛpt tɔrd ʌs frəm al dɪrɛkšənz/
d.　/gulz ænd wɪčəz mayt rɔmp θru rɛd skwɛr ɔn sʌnde/
e.　/mɪsəz bizli wakt kwɪkli dawn ðə krʊkɪd bɔrdwak/
f.　/ðɪs ɛgzæmpəl ɪz ɛntɛndɪd tu bi mɔr kənfyuzɪŋ/

RPE 3.12 ⟩ Who Has "Creaky Voice"?

In a phonetic feature of voicing known as *creaky voice* (also called *laryngealization* and *vocal fry*), only the front part of the vocal folds are vibrating, giving a very low frequency of vibration. Sometimes you can even hear vibration of individual vocal folds. This feature seems to be on the rise in American English speakers; some researchers suggest that it happens more frequently in young people. It also appears to happen more at the end of an utterance. Look up 'creaky voice' online and listen to an audio recording of it. (There's one at http://seattlepi.nwsource.com/local/225139_nwspeak20.html.)

In some languages, creaky and noncreaky sounds are distinctive; Mazatec, a language of Mexico, has consonants and vowels that can be creaky or noncreaky (laryngealized or not) and that can make a difference in the meaning of a word. Hear this contrast at the following link: http://hctv.humnet.ucla.edu/departments/linguistics/VowelsandConsonants/vowels/chapter12/mazatec.html.

Do you think you or any of your friends use creaky voice? If so, do you do it all the time or more often in particular circumstances? Do you agree that it happens more with young people than with older people? Consider these questions and any others this leads you to. Summarize your discussion.

RPE 3.13 ⟩ The Great Vowel Shift

Consider the following words reflecting Middle English pronunciation before the Great Vowel Shift took place. Determine the Present-Day English pronunciation of these words after the Great Vowel Shift. (The symbol : indicates a long vowel and can be ignored for this exercise.)

- **a.** /luːs/
- **b.** /meːd/
- **c.** /kniːxt/
- **d.** /blaːmə/
- **e.** /gɔːt/
- **f.** /roːt/
- **g.** /duːn/

RPE 3.14 ⟩ Northern California Vowel Shift

Read about the Northern California Vowel Shift at http://www.stanford.edu/~eckert/vowels.html. This project also focuses on the adolescent peer social order in order to understand how it emerges from a child social order, how gender differences in phonology come about, how adolescent linguistic styles emerge from kid talk, and how to theorize style as social practice. Read about this research and write a one-paragraph response to it.

RPE 3.15 ⟩ Perceptions Based on Pronunciation

Consider the following common pronunciations among varieties of North American English.

agate	/ɛgət/—Northwest and Midwest
	/ægət/—elsewhere
both	/bɔθ/—Northwest and Midwest
	/boθ/—elsewhere
can't	/kent/—South
	/kænt/ or /kɛnt/—elsewhere
pen	/pɪn/—South
	/pɛn/—elsewhere

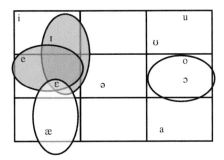

Discuss the variations, and determine which is most noticeable. What are your perceptions of people who pronounce these words either one way or the other?

The variation in the vowel sounds is only one step on the vowel chart, as indicated by the ovals, but we nevertheless find some distinctions more noticeable than others, and these are typically more stigmatized. Are your opinions about each variant linguistically or socially determined? Explain.

RPE 3.16 ⟩ Is There a "Right" Way to Say It?

Think of some words that have more than one common pronunciation (*coupon, pajamas, apricot, economic*). Practice transcribing by writing each pronunciation in phonemic transcription. After you have done the transcription, discuss the varying pronunciations and the characteristics you associate with each pronunciation. What factors (age, race, gender, class, ethnicity, education, etc.) correlate with each pronunciation, and why do you think you have those associations? Are there some words for which you do not have a preferred pronunciation? Are there some words for which you adopt the pronunciation of the person you're speaking with?

American River College Library

Phonology: The Sound Patterns of Language

Key Concepts

- Phonology is the study of the sound system and the processes we use to discover the unconscious systems underlying our speech.
- Linguistic sounds are not generally used in isolation; we string sounds together to make words and sentences.
- Rules also govern pieces bigger than single sounds, including the stress system of words and phrases and the structure of syllables.
- Pitch and loudness can affect meaning in systematic ways.

Did You Know . . . ?

Babies Are Better at Language!
Invented Spelling
Where Do You Get Tenashoes?
Abbish versus Ubby Dubby

Language Alive!   Long-Lost English Allophones

Where the Heck Is <h>?
What's Wrong with *Aks*?
Going Nucular

Linguistics in the News   Tone Languages and Perfect Pitch

Accent on   Linguistics and Reading

Phonemes and Allophones
Assimilation Rules
    Vowel Nasalization
    Alveolar Nasal Assimilation
    Nasal Assimilation
    Palatalization
    Voicing Assimilation
Dissimilation Rules
    Dissimilation of Liquids and Nasal
      Sounds
    Dissimilation of Fricative Sounds
Insertion Rules
    Insertion of Vowels
    Insertion of Consonants
    Insertion of Voiceless Stop
    Insertion of /y/
Deletion Rules
    Deletion of /r/ after Vowels
    Deletion of Fricative Next to
      Fricative
    Deletion of Like Sounds or Syllables
    Simplification of Consonant Clusters
Fronting Rules
    Fronting of Velar Nasal to Alveolar
      Nasal
    Fronting in Child Language
    Fronting of /x/
Exchange Rules
    Exchanging /s/ and a Consonant
    Exchanging /r/ and a Vowel
    Exchanging Syllable Onsets
Multiple-Rule Processes
Suprasegmentals
    Syllables
    Stress
    Intonation
Summary
Sources and Resources
Review, Practice, and Explore

> *A linguistic system is a series of differences of sound*
> *combined with a series of differences of ideas.*
>
> —FERDINAND DE SAUSSURE

phonology system
of rules underlying
the sound patterns
in a language

In Chapter 3, we learned about the sounds of English in isolation. In reality, however, linguistic sounds are not generally used in isolation; we string sounds together to make comprehensible words and sentences. When sounds are used together, they affect and influence each other in predictable and systematic ways. Recall that **phonology** is the study of the sound system and the ways we can discover the unconscious systems underlying speech. You will be surprised at the vast amount of unconscious knowledge you already possess about the sounds of your language and how they interact.

You've seen how to distinguish and represent the sounds of English. When we speak, however, we don't utter each sound separately with a neat break in between. The word *fact*, for example, is not /f/ + /æ/ + /k/ + /t/; rather, each sound blends into the next. Sometimes that blending leads to neighboring sounds affecting one another. When that happens, it does so in predictable and rule-governed ways. In this chapter, we also examine aspects of phonology bigger than single sounds; we explore syllables, variation in pitch, and variation in loudness to understand how these processes can affect meaning and how and why the rules change and vary.

Recall the discussion of phonemes versus allophones from Chapter 3. You learned that the environment in which a sound occurs can affect the way it is produced. For example, we saw that voiceless stops that occur at the beginning of a stressed syllable are aspirated (as in *top* /tap/), and they are unaspirated when they occur in other positions (as in *stop* /stap/).

phonological rule
description of
when a predictable
variation of a
particular sound
occurs

All of these elements in the sound system are governed by rules. Our main task in this chapter is to explore these **phonological rules** to understand how and why sounds affect each other and to understand our unconscious knowledge underlying these processes.

Phonemes and Allophones

Remember that each language has its own set of phonemes. In fact, in some languages the voiceless aspirated and unaspirated bilabial stops are the separate phonemes /pʰ/ and /p/, respectively. To speakers of Hindi and Korean, for example, these two sounds sound as different as /p/ and /b/ do to English speakers, and the two sounds can make a difference in the meaning of a word. For instance, in Korean, /pʰal/ means '*arm*', while /pal/ means '*foot*'. The same aspiration contrast exists for the other voiceless stops, /t/ and /k/.

tʰal	mask	kʰal	knife
tal	moon	kal	will go

The following chart compares Korean and English /t/s.

Phoneme	English	Sound/Allophone	Korean	Phoneme
	[**tʰ**æk]	[tʰ]	[**tʰ**al]	/tʰ/
	(*tack*)		(*mask*)	
/t/				
	[s**t**æk]	[t]	[**t**al]	
	(*stack*)		(*moon*)	
/d/	[**d**ak]	[d]	[man**d**u]	/t/
	(*dock*)		(*dumpling*)	

Hindi's aspiration distinctions are given here, illustrating that the aspiration on a voiceless stop makes a difference in the meaning of a word:

pʰal	knife blade
pal	take care of
kʰal	skin
kal	era
tʰal	plate
tal	beat
ʈʰal	wood shop
ʈal	postpone

Instead of an alveolar stop /t/ like English has, Hindi has a voiceless dental stop /t/, in which the tongue is on the back of the teeth rather than the alveolar ridge, and a voiceless postalveolar stop, /ʈ/. Both of these have aspiration contrasts that result in phonemically distinct sounds.

We can think of phonemes as our unconscious representations of the phonological units of a language. Though we aren't consciously aware of the phonemes of our language, we are perfectly aware unconsciously and are able to follow the "rules" of the phonology of the language effortlessly. Linguists sometimes say that phonemes are the "psychologically real" sounds of a language and allophones are the actual sounds. Put another way, phonemes are the sounds we think we are physically saying, and allophones are what we are actually saying.

Take, for example, the phoneme /t/ in English. If you are asked whether there is a /t/ in the word *Batman*, you most likely would say "of course!" But now pronounce the word—and you can see that although we are quite certain there is a /t/ in this word, we don't pronounce it as we would in the word *top*. So what's going on? Well, the /t/ of English has a set of allophonic variations. For American English speakers, the /t/ in such words as *little*, *battle*, *butter*, and *writer* is a sound called a **flap**, indicated by the symbol [ɾ]. This sound occurs between vowels when the second vowel is unstressed. (We'll return to a discussion of stress later in the chapter.) So if we indicate the phonetic detail, *little* would be transcribed [lɪɾəl]. In many British dialects, the /t/ in such words is not a flap but is instead a glottalized stop [tʔ], [lɪtʔl̩] or a glottal stop /ʔ/, [lɪʔl̩]. For many American English speakers, the /t/ in a word like *Batman* is glottalized as well, /bætʔmæn/. Also, as previously discussed, in all English dialects /t/ becomes aspirated when it is at the beginning of a stressed syllable, as in *tack* [tʰæk]. However, a speaker *thinks* of all of these sounds simply as /t/ and doesn't pay attention to the phonetic differences because they don't matter in English.

flap manner of consonant articulation similar to a stop, but with no air pressure build-up and therefore no air release

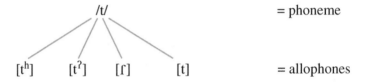

We will not go through a complete list of the allophonic variations for each phoneme. Simply be aware that such variations exist and also that some phonemes have just *one* principal allophone.

Let's consider the distinction between the sounds /l/ and /r/. In English, these are distinct phonemes, and to English speakers, then, the sounds seem quite different from each other, even though you can see by looking at the consonant chart (on the inside front cover of your book) that the /l/ and /r/ phonemes are similar in terms of their place and manner of articulation. However, other languages—such as Japanese, Korean, and Hawaiian—do not have a phonemic distinction between [l] and [r] because in those languages the sounds are allophones of one phoneme. In Japanese, there is only one /r/ phoneme, though it is a bit different from the American English [r], and one of the allophones of /r/ sounds more like an [l] to English speakers. And Hawaiian has no /r/, so when English words are borrowed into Hawaiian, a closest-match phoneme substitutes. In Hawaiian, therefore, the English borrowing *Merry Christmas* is pronounced Meli Kalikimaka (Hawaiian also lacks the /s/ phoneme).

Another example of sounds that are phonemes in English but not in another language is /z/ and /s/. These two sounds are distinct phonemes in English but allophones in some varieties of Spanish. And in most dialects of English, /n/ and /ŋ/ are separate phonemes (as in *run* and *rung*), but in Italian and Spanish they are allophones. Many sound pairs are phonemes in other

RPE 4.1

RPE 4.2

languages but not in English. Consider Lushootseed, for example, a Salish language spoken in the state of Washington. This language has a voiceless palatal affricate /č/ like English, but it also has an ejective version of that sound (a voiceless ejective palatal affricate) that is a distinct phoneme, so there are words that differ only in having /č/ instead of /č'/, and the two words mean different things: /čəɬ/ 'we' and /č'əɬ/ 'tear', for example.

Perhaps the following analogy will be useful for thinking about phonemes and allophones. Imagine that you are a naturalist working in Alaska. You go twice a year to catalog the animals there. In the summer, you find a large number of short-haired weasels, among other animals, and in the winter you find a large number of ermines. However, you never find ermines when you find short-tailed weasels, and you never find short-tailed weasels when you find ermines. It soon becomes clear: short-tailed weasels and ermines are the same animal; the ermine is a short-tailed weasel with a winter-white coat, or a short-tailed weasel is an ermine with a summer-brown coat. One animal, whose scientific name is *Mustela erminea*, shows up in different ways according to its environment. A phoneme is likewise one "animal" that shows up in different

Did You Know...?

Babies Are Better at Language

Until babies are about 6 months old, they perceive all allophonic contrasts of the world's languages (Werker and Desjardins 1995). Although an English-speaking adult, for example, has a difficult time hearing differences that are not English phonemes, any baby can do it. So Japanese babies perceive the contrast between [r] and [l], even though this phonetic contrast does not exist in Japanese. Babies who will grow up to be English speakers can perceive the distinction between [t] and the retroflex [T], a difference that exists in Hindi, among other languages, but not in English. Another example comes from the Salish language Nthlakampx, spoken in British Columbia, which makes a distinction between the glottalized velar and uvular stops [k'] and [q']. Experiments show that English-speaking babies perceive the contrast, but English-speaking adults cannot. After they are 10 to 12 months old, however, babies perceive only the phonemic contrasts of the language or languages spoken around them.

For more information

Jusczyk, P. 1993. From general to language-specific capacities: The WRAPSA model of how speech perception develops. *Journal of Phonetics* [Special issue on phonetic development], 21(1–2). 3–28.

Werker, J. & R. Desjardins. 1995. Listening to speech in the first year of life: Experiential influences on phoneme perception. *Current Directions in Psychological Sciences*, 4(3). 76–81.

ways according to its "environment"—the sounds with which it occurs and its position in relation to them.

Because phonemes are important units of linguistic structure, linguists must have a general method for identifying them in all languages, but the task of determining the phonemes of a language and the allophones assigned to them is not always straightforward. Imagine that you are listening to a language you have never heard before. You could record the sounds in narrow phonetic detail, but you would have no idea which sounds were the phonemes of that language and which were allophones of other phonemes. By a method of comparison and contrast, we can isolate the phonemes of language.

Note: We have been using slashes to indicate the phonemes in a particular language. Brackets are used to indicate words that are transcribed with more phonetic detail, the allophones. In transcription, you will use only phonemes (/t/ rather than its many allophonic variants, for example)—those are the distinct sounds that make a difference in the meaning of a word in English.

Neighboring sounds affect each other. Some phonemes change to make the sound combinations easier to pronounce, and some change to make them easier to perceive. These same processes—or unconscious "rules"—are at work in all languages and are at the heart of language variation, language change, and language acquisition. We illustrate some of the most common types of phonological rules here.

RPE 4.3

RPE 4.4

Language Alive!

Long-Lost English Allophones

Old English /h/ had several allophones that Present-Day English does not: in Old English, /h/ was [h] word-initially before vowels (except front vowels) and before the consonants /l, r, n, w/; but /h/ was the palatal fricative [ç] after front vowels and the velar fricative [x] elsewhere. Present-Day English has lost these allophonic variations of /h/. There were also more allophonic variations of /g/. Now we simply have /g/, but in Old English the voiced velar fricative, represented by the symbol [ɣ], occurred after a vowel or a liquid, while the voiced velar stop [g] occurred elsewhere. So the word *dagas* 'days' was pronounced [daɣas] because the /g/ followed a vowel. Also, as mentioned in Chapter 3, some sounds that were allophones only in older forms of English have now become distinct phonemes. For example, /ŋ/ was an allophone of /n/ that occurred before the velars /k/ or /g/. In Present-Day English, it is a distinct phoneme, as in *sing* /sɪŋ/.

Assimilation Rules

assimilation
process of making
one sound more
like a neighboring
one with respect to
some feature

One of the most common phonological rules across all languages is **assimilation,** the process of making one sound more like a neighboring one with respect to some feature. Here are some examples of assimilation.

Vowel Nasalization

When most English speakers say the word *man,* we begin to lower the velum so that air can pass through the nasal cavity for the /n/ while we are still saying the vowel /æ/. This opening of the velum has the effect of nasalizing the vowel, marked by ~.

> pan   /pæn/ as [pæ̃n]

This rule of nasalization in English holds for all vowels in that position: A vowel becomes nasalized when it precedes a nasal consonant (n, ŋ, or m).

Speakers of some dialects, especially those in the Northeastern United States and parts of the Midwest, have more nasalization (allow more air to pass through the nasal cavity and also to pass through earlier in the production of the vowel) than other speakers do.

Alveolar Nasal Assimilation

Many adults, especially in casual speech, and most children assimilate the place of articulation of the nasal to the following labial consonant in the word *sandwich*:

> sandwich   /sænwɪč/ → /sæmwɪč/

The alveolar nasal /n/ assimilates to the bilabial /w/ by changing the alveolar to a bilabial /m/. (The /d/ of the spelling is not present for most speakers, though it can occur in careful pronunciation.)

Nasal Assimilation

Another example of the assimilation of /n/ to what follows can be seen when the /n/ of a word like *can* (among others) can assimilate to the place of articulation of the following consonant. Compare the following:

I can be ready in five minutes.	can be /kæn bi/ → /kæm bi/
I can go with you.	can go /kæn go/ → /kæŋ go/
I can see the palace from here.	can see /kæn si/ → /kæn si/

Sometimes we are so influenced by the spelling that we don't realize that such assimilation is going on, though it is for most English speakers in casual speech.

Palatalization

palatalization
process that results
from an interaction
between either front
vowels or a /y/ glide
and a neighboring
alveolar consonant,
resulting in a
fricative or affricate
palatal consonant

Palatalization is a common process that results from an interaction between either front vowels or a /y/ glide and a neighboring alveolar consonant, resulting in a fricative or affricate palatal consonant. This phonological shift varies across dialects as well as across careful versus casual speech.

alveolar stop + high front vowel or glide → palatalized fricative or affricate

t + yu → č   *mature, nature*

/mətyur/ → /məčur/

d + y → ǰ   *could you, would you, did you*

/kʊd yu/ → /kuǰu/

hwæt!

Palatalization is reflected in informal spellings such as *wudja* (for 'would you') and *didja* (for 'did you'). Do you think these are likely to become standard spellings?

Similarly, alveolar stops that are followed by /r/ become palatalized:

d + r → ǰr   *drink*
t + r → čr   *truck*

These next examples involve an across-the-board pronunciation shift; that is, because most speakers make these assimilations all the time, we can say that the language has changed. Native English speakers don't say /netiən/ or /gresiəs/; rather they now say /nešən/ and /grešəs/, where the alveolars have become palatalized.

t + i   →   š   as in *nation*
s + i   →   š   as in *gracious*

Did You Know...?

Invented Spelling

Young children often misspell words because they spell them "as they sound." (See Figure 4.1.) That is, they use the symbol that most commonly represents a sound, and they try to write down in letters what they hear. So they might spell *called* as *kald*, *pushed* as *pusht*, *trip* or *truck* as *chrip* and *chruck*, and *drop* as *jrop*. They are actually making very good matches between spelling symbols and sound. Such "invented spelling" is often allowed in early grades now (kindergarten and first grade) to allow children to focus on getting their thoughts down on paper and on beginning to make the connections between sound and symbol (what's known as *phonics*). Then, later, the student and the teacher can focus on spelling correctly.

Figure 4.1 Children spell things as they hear them. This young student has written 'Room 12 is a good class. We do lots of art. In art we do pictures. Lots of reading too. We read from our book box and from our. . . .' (Used by permission of Brian Pahl.)

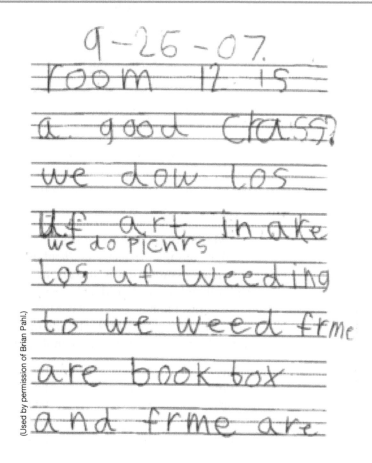

(Used by permission of Brian Pahl.)

Voicing Assimilation

Voicing assimilation occurs quite frequently in English. The following example shows how voiced /v/ of the word *have* assimilates to the voiceless /t/ following it in the expression *have to*:

$$/hæv \ tu/ \ \rightarrow \ /hæf \ tu/$$

The same assimilation happens for the /d/ of *used to*, which becomes /t/, and the /z/ of *has* in *has to*, which becomes /s/.

In children's acquisition of language, assimilation is a very common process. One example of this process is assimilation of voiced sounds, so a word like *paper* with two voiceless /p/s may

hwæt!

Some recent product names use <z>, including Bratz, Myntz, Squirtz, Catz, and Dogz. Of these examples, however, only Dogz mimics pronunciation, the others being nearly impossible to pronounce with a /z/ rather than an /s/ since assimilation is hard at work!

assimilate to the voicing of the neighboring vowels, resulting in a pronunciation like the following:

paper   /bebə/

The child changes the voiceless /p/s to voiced sounds to assimilate to the voiced vowels, resulting in voicing across the board. This also happens in adult variations. So for some speakers (including adults), an /s/ between two vowels becomes voiced, resulting in /z/:

| casserole | /kæsərol/ | → | /kæzərol/ |
| Leslie | /lɛsli/ | → | /lɛzli/ |

In fact, much dialectal variation is a result of assimilation. Another example of this assimilation is that some speakers pronounce the word *thanks* with a voiced /ð/ rather than the voiceless /θ/:

thanks   /θæŋks/   →   /ðæŋks/

And sometimes the /k/ and /s/ may assimilate with respect to voicing as well, resulting in /ðæŋgz/ or *Thanksgiving* /ðæŋgzɪvɪŋ/.

Voicing assimilation is at work in the production of the English regular plural ending -*s*. Consider the ways in which this most common plural ending varies phonologically according to the ending sound of the word it attaches to. Make each of the following words plural, and determine how you would transcribe each plural ending phonemically.

fig	fad	fly
top	fang	jig
tack	church	ball
fifth	judge	staff
dam	bib	kiss
buzz	car	bat
dish	can	garage

RPE 4.5

You should have three different endings: /s/, /z/, and /əz/. (The vowel of this final ending could be slightly different, sometimes closer to /ɪ/, giving /ɪz/. What's important is that a vowel must be inserted before the plural ending in some of the words.) It is the final sound in each word that determines which form of the plural morpheme, or **allomorph**, attaches. Determine which natural class of sound leads to each ending.

allomorph
predictable variant of a morpheme

You should have come up with the following generalizations:

RPE 4.6

/s/ follows /p, t, k, f, θ/ = voiceless sounds
/z/ follows /b, m, d, n, g, ŋ, l, r, ay/ = voiced sounds
/əz/ follows /s, z, š, č, ž, ǰ/ = sibilants

sibilants the natural class of "hissing" or "hushing" sounds in a language, which includes alveolar and palatal fricatives and affricates

Sibilants is the name for the natural class of sounds that are "hissing" or "hushing" sounds. Sibilants group together in many languages. Table 4.1

Table 4.1	Consonant Phonemes of English with Sibilants						
	Bilabial	Labiodental	Interdental	Alveolar	Palatal	Velar	Glottal
Stop	p b			t d		k g	
Fricative		f v	θ ð	s z	š ž		
Affricate					č ǰ		
Nasal	m			n		ŋ	
Glide	ʍ w				y		h
Liquid				l r			

voiceless	voiced
sibilants	

shows our consonant chart with the natural class of sibilants (alveolar and palatal fricatives and affricates) indicated.

Even when we encounter new words or made-up words, we know which plural ending to use, as you can see if you pluralize the following nonsense words.

tark   bab   blutch
blick   carg   clush

RPE 4.7 In the "Review, Practice, and Explore" section, you will investigate some variations on this rule of plural formation from child language acquisition.

Dissimilation Rules

dissimilation
process causing two neighboring sounds to become less alike with respect to some feature

Rules of **dissimilation** cause two neighboring sounds to become less alike with respect to some feature.

Dissimilation of Liquids and Nasal Sounds

Historically, Latin *turtur* was borrowed into English, but the second /r/ changed to /l/. Latin *purpura* and Middle English *purpre* became *purple* in Present-Day English.

turtur → turtle
purpre → purple

Consider a similar example of dissimilation of liquid consonants that took place when the suffix *-al* attached to some Latin nouns to make adjectives.

The regular suffixation process gives us pairs like the following: *orbit/orbital, person/personal, culture/cultural, electric/electrical*. However, when an /l/ precedes the ending anywhere in the root, the ending is changed from *-al* to *-ar* as a result of dissimilation: *single/singular, module/modular, luna/lunar.*

Latin *marmor* became Present-Day English *marble* via two dissimilations: the second *r* changed to *l*, then the second *m* changed to *b*, to dissimilate the two bilabial nasals, /m/.

$$\text{marmor} \quad \rightarrow \quad \text{marmle} \quad \rightarrow \quad \text{marble}$$

Another example of sonorant dissimilation comes from the Appalachian dialect, in which the word *chimney* is pronounced /čɪmli/ rather than /čɪmni/. The /n/ becomes an /l/, remaining an alveolar but losing its nasality to dissimilate the /m/ and /n/ with respect to nasality.

Dissimilation of Fricative Sounds

Many speakers avoid neighboring fricatives by changing one to a different place of articulation, so a word like *months* /mʌnθs/ becomes /mʌnts/, in which the fricative /θ/ becomes /t/. This happens frequently in casual speech and can disappear in more careful speech. (Also, the /t/ here may be assimilating to the same alveolar place of articulation as the preceding /n/, so perhaps both assimilation and dissimilation are at work.)

RPE 4.8

Insertion Rules

insertion process causing a segment not present at the phonemic level to be added to the phonetic form of a word

Rules of **insertion** (also called *epenthesis*) cause a segment not present at the phonemic level to be added to the phonetic form of a word.

Insertion of Vowels

From Old English to Middle English, vowels were inserted between consonants in certain positions. These insertions are indicated in these Middle English spellings.

Old English		Middle English	Present-Day English
þurh[1]	→	thorow	'thorough'
setl	→	setel	'seat'
æfre	→	ever	'dream'

---

1. The þ is a symbol used in Old English to represent the interdental fricatives /θ/ and /ð/.

In Present-Day English, many variations across dialects involve insertion (or not) of vowels. Do you have a vowel in *realtor* between the /l/ and the /t/? Often, too, a vowel is inserted between the consonants of a consonant cluster, as when a /ə/ occurs between /p/ and /l/ in words like *paraplegic* or *quadriplegic*. Other contemporary examples of vowel insertion are found in the "Review, Practice, and Explore" section.

RPE   4.9 >

Insertion of Consonants

Another example of an insertion that happened during the Middle English period is the insertion of /d/ in what now appears as *thunder*. (The <þ> is an Old English symbol representing /ð/ in this word.)

Old English *þunor*   →   Present-Day English *thunder*
(compare German *Donner* 'thunder')

The alveolar stop with the same place of articulation as the nasal /n/ (alveolar) was inserted in Old English speakers' speech to ease transition to the vowel. This /d/ was also inserted into the spelling and eventually became the standard spelling. The *d* in Present-Day English *thunder* is no longer considered an insertion for current speakers, as it is present phonemically.

Insertion of Voiceless Stop

A common insertion takes place between a nasal and a voiceless fricative when a voiceless stop with the same place of articulation as the nasal is inserted.

hamster	/hæmstr̩/	→	/hæmpstr̩/
something	/sʌmθɪŋ/ or /sʌmθɪn/	→	/sʌmpθɪŋ/ or /sʌmpθɪn/[2]
strength	/strɛŋθ/	→	/strɛŋkθ/

This insertion rule also led to the two common spellings of the surname *Thomson/Thompson*. Both derive from the English and Scottish first name *Thomas*. The *p* was inserted in the spelling by some because it sounds as if it is there. (And remember, it's *Chomsky*, not *Chompsky!*) The word *empty* underwent this insertion process; in Old English the word was *æmtig*, with no /p/ between the /m/ and the /t/.

Insertion of /y/

In some dialects of English—most British dialects and some southeastern American dialects—a /y/ is inserted after initial alveolar consonants and preceding high vowels, so words like *news*, *Tuesday*, and *duke* are pronounced /nyuz/, /tyuzde/, and /dyuk/. This insertion—which used to be the norm

---

2. Note the further deletion and assimilation that can occur in this word's pronunciation: /sʌmpm̩ /

in American English (so maybe it's not insertion but is better described as deletion)—appears to be gradually on its way out of the language, with the /y/ disappearing following certain kinds of consonants, as in *news*, but not yet lost in others, like *few*, /fyu/, and puny, /pyuni/.

Deletion Rules

deletion process causing a segment present at the phonemic level to be deleted at the phonetic level of a word

Rules of **deletion** cause a segment present at the phonemic level to be deleted at the phonetic level of a word.

Deletion of /r/ after Vowels

In many English dialects, /r/ is deleted when it follows a vowel. So words like *car* and *yard* are pronounced like /ka/ and /yad/. The "dropping of /r/s" in words like *car*, *park*, *hard*, and *court* is usually perceived as somewhat nonstandard in American English. It occurs most frequently in some dialects of New England and some dialects of the Deep South. However, in Britain, the dropping of /r/s in the very same words is considered characteristic of the standard dialect and is viewed favorably not only by British speakers but also by most American English speakers. This contrast in the attitude toward the same linguistic feature illustrates that standard and nonstandard features of dialects are socially, not linguistically, determined.

RPE 4.10

RPE 4.11

Language Alive!

Where the Heck Is <h>?

Why are words spelled with <h>s that we never say or hear? Many words spelled with <h> have no /h/ in the pronunciation for any English speaker: *hour, honor, honest*. These examples, then, are not examples of phonological deletion, though they would have been at some earlier point in the history of English. Although the letter <h> comes from the Roman alphabet, the /h/ sound was eventually lost in Latin and in the Romance languages that came from Latin. However, it is retained in the spelling of some words that English has borrowed from those languages, primarily French. So *honor, honest, hour*, and *heir*, borrowed from French, do not have the initial /h/, just as French does not. However, in Old English, <h> at the beginning of words and before vowels was pronounced /h/. In Middle English, the /h/ in those positions seems to have weakened and was often not pronounced, but in Present-Day English, perhaps due to the influence of spelling, the /h/ is usually pronounced not only in such Anglo-Saxon words as *happy* and *hot*, but in some French borrowings as well: *hostel, hotel, haste*. In some other English words borrowed from the French, there is dialectal variation such that in certain dialects the /h/ is pronounced in the words *herb, human, humor,* and *humble,* and in others it is not.

Deletion of Fricative Next to Fricative

The same process that leads to dissimilation can lead instead to deletion of one of the like sounds. For example, in words like *fifths* /fɪfθs/ and *sixths* /sɪksθs/, in which three fricatives occur in a row, one or two of them frequently are deleted.

/fɪfθs/ → /fɪfs/ or /fɪθs/ or even /fɪs/

Did You Know...?

Where Do You Get Tenashoes?

Tennis shoes are not just shoes for tennis. The word is likely stored as a single word in the mental lexicon of most speakers (especially those who do not use the word *sneakers*). When *tennis* precedes another word like *shorts*, the /s/ is not likely to delete because that is not a single lexical entry, and the word *tennis* needs to be made clear to the hearer in order to maintain communicative efficiency: *tennis shorts* remains /tɛnɪs šɔrts/ and does not become /tɛnə šɔrts/. The fricative deletion in *tennis shoes* doesn't typically happen across word boundaries; for example, *fresh start* would be /frɛš start/, not /frɛ start/ or /frɛš tart/. This fact provides evidence that *tennis shoes* is a single compound word. Also compare the compound word *tennis shoes*, /tɛnɪs šuz/ → /tɛnɪ šuz/, to a phrase such as *tennis balls*, in which a stop /b/ follows the /s/, /tɛnɪs balz/. There is no /s/ deletion on *tennis* in *tennis balls* because the /b/ does not use the same manner of articulation as /s/. (Compounds are discussed more in Chapter 5, 'Morphology'.) There is also semantic evidence for *tennis shoes*'s compound status; it is not just the sum of the meanings of its parts.

Deletion of Like Sounds or Syllables

Repeated consonants or entire syllables containing similar sounds are often deleted in casual speech:

probably /prabəbli/ → /prabli/
mirror /mɪrər/ → /mɪr/

Simplification of Consonant Clusters

There was historical deletion of /k/ and /g/ before /n/, as in *knight, knob, gnat*, as well as other consonant clusters. Realize that these are not currently considered deletions, however; though the letters appear in the spelling, they are not there phonologically for any modern-day speaker of English. Old and Middle English speakers would have pronounced these consonants before /n/, but this pronunciation had gradually dropped out by the late seventeenth century, during the Early Modern English period. As this simplification of a consonant cluster took place, there was a time when some speakers had the cluster /kn/ and others did not.

Compare the Old English and Early Modern English pronunciations of the following words.

Old English		Middle English		Early Modern English and Present-Day English
cnawan /kn/	→	knowe(n)	→	know /no/
gnagan /gn/	→	gnawe(n)	→	gnaw /na/

Simplification of Syllable-Final Consonant Clusters

Simplification of syllable-final consonant clusters is a common phonological process, though it does happen more in some dialects than others and much more frequently in fast speech.

fast pitch	/fæst pɪč/	→	/fæs pɪč/
friend	/frɛnd/	→	/frɛn/
M&M	/ɛmændɛm/	→	/ɛmənɛm/
softball	/saftbal/	→	/safbal/
grandma	/grændma/	→	/grænma/ or /græma/
			(with deletion of the first nasal)

Fronting Rules

fronting process causing a segment produced in the back of the mouth to change to a segment produced at the front of the mouth

Rules of **fronting** cause a segment produced in the back of the mouth to change to a segment produced at the front of the mouth. There are more front consonants than back consonants across the world's languages, and front consonants are acquired before back consonants in most children's language.

Fronting of Velar Nasal to Alveolar Nasal

In many speakers' casual speech, words ending in -*ing* are pronounced with /ɪn/ rather than /ɪŋ/. The velar nasal has fronted to become an alveolar nasal.

running	/rʌnɪŋ/	→	/rʌnɪn/

Fronting in Child Language

Many children front most velar sounds during the first few years of language acquisition.

goat	/got/	→	/dot/
OK	/oke/	→	/ote/

Fronting of /x/

A historical example of velar fronting is the velar fricative /x/ becoming a labiodental fricative /f/ in words such as *tough* and *enough*. The letters *h* and later *gh* were used to represent the velar fricative /x/ in Old English. In some modern English words that formerly had /x/, the consonant fronted to /f/, but in others it disappeared completely (*though*, *bough*, *night*, etc.).

OE /x/   →   /f/

Exchange Rules

Exchange rules reorder sounds or syllables. This exchange process is also known as *metathesis*.

Exchanging /s/ and a Consonant

The two consonants /s/ and /k/ spend a lot of time switching around in English. The same process that leads to the much-stigmatized metathesized pronunciation of *ask* also occurs in the less-stigmatized pronunciation of *asterisk*.

ask	/æsk/	→	/æks/
asterisk	/æstərɪsk/	→	/æstərɪks/

Historical switching of /s/ and /k/ also occurred, leading to both the modern English words *tax* and *task*:

Latin *taxa*   /taksa/   →   /tæsk/   'task'

Historical switching of /s/ and /p/ also took place:

wasp   OE wæps   →   PDE wasp

Language Alive!

What's Wrong with *Aks*?

As many of you are probably aware, the pronunciation *aks* for *ask* is quite stigmatized in U.S. English. This is for social reasons, however, not for linguistic ones. The form *aks* actually has a long and rich history. The Old English word from which we get *ask* had two forms that coexisted, *acsian* and *ascian*. The pronunciation and spelling of this word as "aks" was quite standard up to the nineteenth century and is still common in dialects both in the United States and in Britain.

Exchanging /r/ and a Vowel

Another common kind of metathesis occurs with /r/ and a neighboring vowel. This can be seen in current dialect variation, in historical examples, and in child language:

Old English		Present-Day English
brid	→	bird
drit	→	dirt
thridda	→	third

Modern English dialect variations include metathesized versions of *children* as /čɪldərn/ and *pretty* as /pərti/, and the more common /intərdus/ for /intrədus/ 'introduce'.

Exchanging Syllable Onsets

The onsets (beginning consonants or consonant clusters) of syllables commonly metathesize. This manipulation of the first sounds of syllables is especially common in child language, as in these common examples.

animal	/ænɪməl/	→	/æmmnəl/
cinnamon	/sɪnəmən/	→	/sɪmənən/

Such metatheses are also at work in adult language. The pronunciation of *nuclear* as /nukyələr/ involves metathesis, perhaps, but there's more than meets the eye (the ear?) with this word.

RPE 4.12 ▷

Multiple-Rule Processes

Sometimes more than one phonological process is employed in a phono-logical variation or change. Consider the following example, which involves both deletion and assimilation.

pumpkin	/pʌmpkɪn/	→	/pʌŋkɪn/

The second /p/ deletes (as a result of dissimilation) and then the /m/ assimilates to the same place of articulation (velar) as the following /k/.

Another example is the word *something*:

something /sʌmθɪŋ/ or /sʌmθɪn/	→	/sʌmpθɪŋ/ or /sʌmpθɪn/

When the word is pronounced in casual speech as /sʌmpm̩/, there is not only insertion of /p/ (discussed previously) but also assimilation (of the /n/ to /m/) and deletion (of /θ/).

Language Alive!

Going Nucular

Geoff Nunberg

Former President George W. Bush took a lot of ribbing (even from his wife!) for pronouncing the word *nuclear* as "nucular." But he was not the first president to do so. That one has been getting on people's nerves since Eisenhower made the mispronunciation famous in the 1950s. In Woody Allen's 1989 film *Crimes and Misdemeanors*, Mia Farrow's character says she could never fall for any man who says "nucular.". . . On the face of things, "nucular" is a typo *par excellence*. People sometimes talk about President Bush "stumbling" over the word, as if this were the same kind of articulatory problem that turns *February* into "febyooary." But *nuclear* isn't a hard word to pronounce the way *February* is—try saying each of them three times fast. Phonetically, in fact, *nuclear* is pretty much the same as *likelier*, and nobody ever gets that one wrong. ("The first outcome was likular than the second"?) That "nucular" pronunciation is really what linguists call a folk etymology, where the unfamiliar word *nuclear* is treated as if it had the same suffix as words like *molecular* and *particular*. It's the same sort of process that turns *lackadaisical* into "laxadaisical" and *chaise longue* into *chaise lounge*.

For more information

From Nunberg, G. 2004. Going nucular. *Fresh air*. National Public Radio. October 2. Published in *Going nucular*. 2004. New York: Public Affairs.

It's not always clear exactly why a phonological process has taken place. Sometimes the rules aren't easily motivated by a process. For example, in some dialects of English in the United States (in the South, parts of the Midwest, and more recently, parts of the West), the vowel /ɛ/ has become /ɪ/ when it occurs before a nasal consonant, /m/, /n/, or /ŋ/.

wren	/rɪn/
pen	/pɪn/
gem	/ĵɪm/
temper	/tɪmpər/
length	/lɪŋθ/
strength	/strɪŋθ/

Though this a rule-governed process—we can see that the vowel changes only when a nasal follows—it's not entirely clear what it is about the nasal that leads to the vowel change.

In this section, you have seen how phonological language variation and language change are motivated by the same kinds of natural phonological processes. Children's language acquisition (and the variation that is a part

ʰwɑɛʈ!

Perhaps someone should have thought a bit more about the phonology of some arguably bad product names: Blosxom (a weblog application), Fauxto (an editing tool, which has recently changed its name to Splashup), and Cuil (a search engine). They all involve combinations of letters that English readers just aren't sure how to pronounce.

of it) also is motivated by assimilation, dissimilation, deletion, insertion, metathesis, and fronting. You should be aware that the variety of rules introduced here is not exhaustive and that the set of rules can vary across dialects and even among individuals—each person has a slightly different set of phonological rules and processes in his or her speech.

You may have noticed in reading through and thinking about the examples of phonological processes discussed in this section that some are much more noticeable than others. Some you may have been aware of—and bothered by; others you didn't realize were occurring. Sometimes we never even hear the 'alternative' pronunciation as a contrast, and sometimes we simply don't notice the phonological changes because the variations are subtle and are assimilated by our ear and brain. Vowel variations are much more common and are fairly happily tolerated, while consonant variations are typically more stigmatized. The stigmatization is stronger for consonant variation primarily because the consonant sounds correlate more directly with spelling than do vowel sounds.

ease of articulation making something easier to say

Though the motivation behind many of these phonological processes is **ease of articulation**—that is, making something easier to say—that motivation is always competing with other factors. If ease of articulation were the sole motivation for language change, then presumably we would all be moving toward the same kinds of changes, not only in English but in other languages. However, we will see in the "Review, Practice, and Explore" section how certain variation, motivated by ease of articulation (such as assimilation), can vary, and we will discover other factors that can affect the change or lack of change. This is a topic we will continue to investigate throughout the book. Also, it is an ongoing area of research among phoneticians and phonologists to discover the motivation for phonological processes in general.

Suprasegmentals

suprasegmentals phonological phenomena that are larger than a single sound; includes syllables, stress, and intonation

In this section, we will explore some aspects of phonology bigger than the single sound, the "segment"; these are called **suprasegmentals**, and they include syllables, stress, and intonation.

syllable basic unit of speech generally containing only one vowel sound (*nucleus*) and also possibly an *onset* and a *coda* (called the *rime*)

Syllables

It is actually difficult to provide a neat definition of a **syllable**, though we all have awareness of syllables naturally and unconsciously. Very young children are able to tap out syllables; many phonological processes refer to the syllables of words; and children (and adults) manipulate syllables quite skillfully in all sorts of ways.

The Structure of the Syllable

onset consonant(s) at the beginning of a syllable

Languages have varying syllable structures. The group of consonants at the beginning of a syllable is called the **onset**, and the vowel and any consonants following it at the end of the syllable are called the **rime**. The symbol traditionally used by linguists for a syllable is the Greek letter sigma, σ.

rime vowel and any consonants following it at the end of the syllable

```
            σ
          /   \
     onset     rime
     /  \      /  \
    C    C    V    C
```

nucleus vowel that is the minimum unit of the rime

The rime can be further divided into a **nucleus**, a vowel that is the heart of the rime, and a **coda**, the consonant(s) at the end of the rime.

coda consonant(s) at the end of the rime

```
            σ
          /   \
     onset     rime
       C       /  \
          nucleus  coda
             V      C
```

Vowels are almost always the nucleus of a syllable. However, if the syllable lacks a vowel, certain consonants are able to take over as the nucleus of the syllable; recall the discussion in Chapter 3 of the syllabic consonants, /r̩, l̩, m̩, n̩ /.

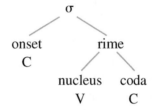

The word *strengths* may have the most complex syllable structure of any English word: /strɛŋkθs/, with three consonants in the onset and four in the coda!

In English, an onset can consist of a cluster of consonants. Certain groups of two phonemes can occur next to each other at the beginning of a syllable: /fl/, /sp/, and /tr/, among others. Consider which three sounds can occur as the onset of a syllable in English: /spl/, /spr/, /skr/, /str/, and the rare /skl/, as in *sclerosis*. You must remember to ignore spelling when considering cluster combinations and focus on only the sounds (so *thistle* and *psychology*, for example, do not contain word-initial consonant clusters, even though they are spelled with initial consonants).

Phonotactics

Note that all the consonant clusters just discussed must occur in a particular order and in a particular position within the syllable. So although /spl/ may occur at the beginning of a syllable, /pls/ cannot. And though /spl/ may occur as the onset of a syllable, it may not occur as the coda of a syllable.

phonotactics branch of phonology dealing with natural and unconscious restrictions on the permissible combinations of phonemes in a language

Such restrictions are known as **phonotactics**; this is the branch of phonology that deals with natural and unconscious restrictions on the permissible combinations of phonemes in a particular language. English, for example, may have /ŋ/ at the end of a syllable as the coda but not as the onset:

sing   /sɪŋ/   */ŋɪs/   (* indicates an impossible word)

On the other hand, /kt/ is a possible coda, as in *kicked* /kɪkt/, but not a possible onset. We are quite aware of these restrictions as speakers of a language, as evidenced by our knowledge of the related **graphotactic** constraints (as these use letters, not sounds) of anagrams or jumbles, like those typically found in many newspapers and other word game collections. So it doesn't take most people long to unscramble the letters here to make a word:

graphotactic
related to the
spelling and writing
system

irgn

We know that <ng> is not a possible combination at the beginning of the word or in the middle, so we quickly come up with *ring* or *grin*, rather than randomly trying the many possible combinations of the letters.

Even slips of the tongue reveal our knowledge of phonotactic constraints. Consider the following intended and actual utterance pair:

scratching Daddy's back   snatching graddy's back
/skræčɪŋ dædiz/   /snæčɪŋ grædiz/

In this example, the /kr/ of *scratching* and the /d/ of *Daddy* exchange. However, since /sd/ is not a possible combination in English, the alveolar stop /d/ becomes the alveolar nasal /n/, which is the only voiced alveolar allowed following /s/; thus /skr/ has become /sn/, and the velar /k/ that is now in initial position in the second word becomes the voiced velar /g/. So even when we "mess up," we do not violate our language's phonotactic constraints.

The rime in English can consist of a vowel followed by a consonant, as in *bat* /bæt/, or a cluster of two consonants, as in *toast*, *lift*, and *kicked* /kɪkt/; three consonants, as in *wasps* /wasps/; or even four, as in *prompts* /prampts/ or *sixths* /sɪksθs/. Despite English allowing syllables with complex onsets and codas, speakers often tend to reduce those clusters; consider the /rst/ of the word *first* in a compound word like *first grade*, which typically is pronounced /fʌrs gred/ rather than /fʌrst gred/, and the cluster in *sixths* /sɪksθs/, which most speakers would reduce to /sɪks/ except in careful speech. In many dialects of English, including African American English and Navajo English, word-final consonant clusters are reduced, so words such as *desk*, *toast*, and *walked* are pronounced /dɛs/, /tos/, and /wak/. This phenomenon is sensitive to morphological information, so if the cluster reduction would eliminate a grammatical marker, such as past-tense information, *-ed*, then it is less common. For example, the reduced form of the past tense *walked* would be /wak/, which would be the same form as the present tense *walk* /wak/, and thus such a reduction is less common.

Children's Syllables

Children acquiring English and other languages prefer consonant–vowel (CV) syllables and alter many syllables to make them conform to that structure. So CVC syllables often reduce to CV syllables for young children; for example, *cat* /kæt/ might be pronounced as /kæ/, *play* /ple/ as /pe/. Another common syllable-structure process in child language acquisition is deletion of unstressed syllables; for example, *banana* is pronounced as /nænə/, with the less-stressed /bə/ deleted. Similarly, *potato* might be /dedo/ or /dedə/ (with voicing assimilation occurring as well). Another very common syllable-structure process is the doubling of a syllable, known as **reduplication**. Typically, the initial CV syllable is reduplicated; for example, *water* is /wawa/.

reduplication
doubling of a syllable; a common syllable structure in children's language

Let's consider a certain child's rule of consonant-cluster reduction. Following are the pronunciations of some words containing consonant clusters by a child named Jack when he was between the ages of 2½ and 3½.

spoon	/pun/
stick	/tɪk/
stupid	/tupɪd/
skate	/ket/
Spencer	/pɛnsəʷ/
scared	/keəd/
scrape	/kwep/
slide	/slayd/
swipe	/swayp/
snail	/snel/
small	/smal/
play	/ple/
flag	/flæg/
three	/θri/
shrink	/šriŋk/
crowd	/krawd/
crab	/kræb/

First, consider which combinations of /s/ + consonant exist in most adult dialects. (Remember to think phonemically here, not orthographically.) So in adult English, the voiceless stops /p, t, k/ are allowed following /s/ syllable-initially, as in *stop*, *spot*, and *skate*. Also, sonorants may follow /s/, as in *slide*, *sway*, *snake*, and *smile*. This child, however, allows only a sonorant to be the second consonant in the initial consonant cluster. If an obstruent is the second consonant in the cluster, he deletes the /s/.

These examples illustrate that even when children alter their pronunciation of syllables, they are doing so in a rule-governed, patterned way, thereby illustrating their sophisticated command of the language even though it does not yet match an adult version of the language.

Syllable Structure Variety

In Maori and other languages, an onset can have only a single consonant and a rime must be just a vowel, so the basic structure of the Maori syllable is simply CV. CV syllables are the most common type of syllable in the world's languages. Japanese also has only CV syllables (with the exception of /n/ as a coda), so when a word is borrowed from another language into Japanese, speakers will make that word conform to the phonotactics, the syllable structure, of Japanese. Consider the following English borrowings, which have been adjusted to conform to the syllable structure of Japanese.

(1) strike /strayk/ → su-to-ra-i-ku
(2) merry Christmas /mɛ ri krɪs məs/ → me-ri ku-ri-si-ma-su
(3) strawberry ice cream /stra bɛ ri ays krim/ → su-to-ro-be-ri a-i-su-ku-ri-mo

** hwæt!**

Visit http://www.spoonerism-fun.com/belief.html to find a bunch of spoonerisms that result in words after the exchanges have taken place; for example, *answer to my prayers → prancer to my heirs*, or *part of the cure → cart of the pure.*

However, consonant clusters in loanwords do not necessarily follow the borrowing language's cluster limits. The Ubykh language (an extinct language of Turkey) had a word *psta*, a loan from Adyghe (a North Caucasian language of Russia) that violates Ubykh's rule of allowing no more than two initial consonants in an onset; also, the English words *sphere* /sfir/ and *sphinx* /sfinks/, which are borrowed from Greek, violate the constraint that two fricatives may not appear adjacently word-initially. Despite their existence in English now, they remain odd-sounding words for most English speakers.

The South Caucasian languages, also called the Kartvelian languages, are spoken primarily in Georgia, with smaller groups of speakers in Turkey, Iran, Azerbaijan, Russia, and other countries. These languages are among the most permissive in the world in terms of the size of consonant clusters they allow. Here is an example of four consecutive consonants from Georgian:

brt'q'eli 'flat'

and even six consonants:

mts'vrtneli 'trainer' (/ts'/ is a single phoneme in Georgian)

Slips of the Tongue and Syllables

Slips of the tongue reveal that speakers have a keen unconscious awareness of the structure of the syllable and are able to manipulate its parts quite judiciously. One of the most common types of slip of the tongue is an **exchange error**, a simple example of metathesis as previously discussed, or what is also called a **spoonerism**, named for William Spooner, who apparently made many of these exchange errors. Some of the better-known errors attributed to Spooner include the following:

exchange error (spoonerism) common type of slip of the tongue involving the exchange of one part of a syllable for another in two different words

lighting a fire	→	fighting a liar
missed all my history lectures	→	hissed all my mystery lectures
dear old queen	→	queera old dean
blow your nose	→	know your blows

As the final example indicates, it is typically not just the first sounds of two words that are exchanged but the onsets, here /bl/, not just /b/. Also, syllable nuclei may exchange, as in the following examples:

ad hoc   →   odd hack
/æd hak/   →   /ad hæk/

In this example, the onsets and codas remain in place, and only the nuclei are exchanged.

Another piece of evidence for our unconscious knowledge of syllables is the aspiration rule that we previously discussed for English: Voiceless oral stops are aspirated when they occur at the beginning of a word (the *pit/spit* contrast). Note that this aspiration applies to beginnings of stressed syllables, not just to the beginning of words, again providing evidence for our unconscious awareness of syllable structure and the ways in which phonological rules interact with them.

Aspiration		No Aspiration	
account	[a-kʰawnt]	backpack	[bæk-pæk]
append	[ə-pʰɛnd]	napkin	[næp-kɪn]

RPE   4.13

Stress

stress relative emphasis given to the syllables of a word

Stress refers to the relative prominence or emphasis of certain syllables in a word. This prominence can be achieved in several ways, depending on the language; stress is usually produced by an increase in articulatory force, by an increase in the airflow, and sometimes by increased muscular tension in the articulators. The results of this are higher pitch, longer duration, and greater intensity in stressed syllables than in unstressed syllables.

Stress has several linguistic functions in languages. Some languages have predictable and fixed word stress; for example, in Hungarian and Finnish, stress is always on the first syllable; in Quechua, Swahili, and Polish, stress is always on the next-to-last syllable. In these languages, such predictable stress patterns would serve as a signal of word boundaries, presumably aiding in language acquisition. In other languages, such as English, the position of stress is relatively free and may also be contrastive; that is, the changing position of stress may result in meaning and category differences.

Nouns		Verbs
récord	compared to	recórd
ímpact	compared to	impáct

(In these examples, changing the stress patterns also changes the quality of the vowels, so the words are not *homophones*; they are not pronounced identically.) Also, degrees of stress may be distinguished, so one can determine primary, secondary, and even tertiary stress.

rùdiméntary (ˋ indicates secondary stress, and ´ indicates primary stress)

English, Russian, and Arabic, among others, are called *stress-timed languages*, which means that the stressed syllables occur at a fairly constant rate, and the unstressed syllables are shorter. Other languages, such as Spanish, Telugu, and Yoruba, are *syllable-timed languages*, which means that syllables are produced at a fairly constant rate regardless of stress.

Syllable stress in English is less predictable, though it used to be quite regular; stress in Old English was fixed, with primary stress on the first syllable, but gradually shifted away from the first syllable due primarily to the influence of French.

Chomsky and Halle (1968) describe many of the rules of Present-Day English stress (ending up with forty-three rules of word-level stress for English!), discovering a complexity of patterns and rules beyond what we can tackle here. Compare the effects of Latinate and Germanic affixation.

Germanic affixes don't affect stress placement:

éarth   eárthly   unéarthly   unéarthliness

But Latinate suffixes do affect stress placement:

témpest   tempéstuous   tempestuósity
grámmar   grammátical   grammaticálity

Stress patterns vary across dialects of English as well; for example,

ínsurance with stress on the initial syllable in Southern American English compared to *insúrance* with stress on the second syllable in most other dialects

cárburetor with stress on the initial syllable in American English compared to *carburéttor* (spelled with two <t>s) with stress on the third syllable in British English

Poetry in English uses stress to establish the *meter* of the poem. Iambic pentameter, a common poetic pattern in English, is a *weak–strong*, or unstressed–stressed, pattern that is repeated five times in a line of verse. Other patterns, such as the following *dactyls* (a stressed syllable followed by two unstressed syllables), are also used in children's language play and nursery rhymes, as in the following example:

W S W W S W W S W W S
The cock's in the woodpile a-blowing his horn.
The bull's in the barn a-threshing of corn.
The maids in the meadows are making of hay.
The ducks in the river are swimming away.

RPE   4.14

RPE   4.15

Intonation

In the previous chapter on phonetics, tone—variation in pitch—was discussed. Some languages can vary the pitch of a syllable, and this variation can result in meaning differences; Mandarin and Nupe examples were given. Varying the pitch

LINGUISTICS
IN THE NEWS

Tone Languages and Perfect Pitch

Psychologist Diana Deutsch defines *perfect pitch*, also called absolute pitch, as the ability to name or produce a musical note of particular pitch without any kind of prompt, such as a reference note. People with perfect pitch are very rare in the United States and Europe, a fact that piqued Deutsch's interest— why would this be? Her research suggests that the ability to acquire absolute pitch is universal at birth and that it can be accomplished if children are encouraged to develop perfect pitch during the critical period of language acquisition. And how do you develop perfect pitch during the critical period of language acquisition? By acquiring a tone language.

Deutsch began to study the relationship between perfect pitch and language acquisition in a 1999 study that tested native speakers of two tone languages, Mandarin and Vietnamese. The researchers found that speakers of Mandarin and Vietnamese were extremely precise in recognizing absolute pitch, suggesting that speakers of tone languages naturally acquire this ability early on, during the critical period. So then the question arose, Do more speakers of tone languages have absolute pitch than speakers of non-tone languages such as English? And if so, what does this tell us about the language you speak and your ear for music?

Deutsch and her research team tested the prevalence of absolute

pitch in 88 students (ages 17 to 34) at the Central Conservatory of Music (CCOM) in Beijing, China. All of the students spoke Mandarin. The researchers also tested a group of 115 students (ages 17 to 23) at the Eastman School of Music (ESM) in Rochester, New York. These students spoke non-tone languages.

The test consisted of thirty-six notes spanning the three-octave range beginning on the C below middle C, a span designed to test absolute pitch (rather than relative pitch based on reference notes). The chart below shows the results.

In both groups, students who had started musical training early had a better chance of acquiring perfect pitch. But overall, the prevalence of absolute pitch was much higher among the CCOM students than the ESM students. (Gender had no effect on the results.)

The striking difference between the CCOM and ESM groups, Deutsch and her colleagues claim, supports the hypothesis that infants can acquire absolute pitch as a

feature of speech and that this feature can carry over to music. The earlier the child is exposed to music, the better, supporting the idea that there is a critical period for this carryover of perfect pitch from language to music. Children who speak non-tone languages are at a disadvantage for acquiring absolute pitch, even if they begin music studies very early, perhaps because there is no option for carryover from language to music.

For more information

Deutsch, D., et al. 1999. Tone language speakers possess absolute pitch. *Acoustical Society of America (ASA)* 138. Columbus, OH.

Deutsch, D., et al. 2006. Absolute pitch among American and Chinese conservatory students: Prevalence differences, and evidence for a speech-related critical period. *Journal of the Acoustical Society of America* 119. 719–722.

National Public Radio. 2006. Behaves so strangely. *Radio Lab.* Show 202, April 21. http://www.wnyc.org/shows/radiolab/episodes/2006/04/21. (17 October, 2008.)

Perfect Pitch

Age of first musical training (yr)	Chinese students (%)	American students (%)
4 to 5	60	14
6 to 7	55	6
8 to 9	42	0

intonation variation in pitch across an utterance

across a longer stretch of speech is known as **intonation**. Many languages, including English, use such pitch variations to convey surprise, irony, and questioning. American English typically has rising intonation across the utterance for what are called *yes–no* questions (*"She bought a new car?"*) and falling intonation for information-seeking questions (also called *wh-* questions) (*"What does she want to buy?"*), although there is much variation of these patterns in both American and British dialects.

Stress and intonation can interact at the sentence level; word-level stress patterns and pitch can be modified to indicate which part of the sentence is in focus or which word should receive special emphasis. In English, new and important information is typically placed at the end of a clause; therefore, utterance stress, when used neutrally—what we consider "normal" intonation contour—is usually associated with the end of a clause.

In the following sentence, "neutral" intonation means that the utterance stress does not make any major changes to the interpretation of the sentence:

Three children were sitting on the gray couch.

intonation nucleus most prominently stressed syllable in an utterance

In any given utterance, one stressed syllable stands out as most prominent. This stressed syllable is called the **intonation nucleus** (not to be confused with the nucleus of a syllable). This intonation nucleus can be moved and result in meaning changes; thus the phonological system interacts with meaning, the semantic system. Consider the change in meaning when various other words of the utterance receive more stress. (In these examples, the capitalized words indicate the intonation nucleus. They receive primary utterance stress and accompanying higher pitch.)

a. Three CHILDREN (not women, elves, men, etc.) were sitting on the blue couch.
b. Three children were sitting on the blue COUCH (not the chair, steps, etc.).
c. Three children were sitting on the BLUE (not the purple, gray, black, etc.) couch.

RPE   4.16

Contrastive stress like that indicated by these examples rejects something and suggests that what is being rejected has been already introduced into the discourse or is implied.

There is evidence that intonational contours and patterns are stored in a distinct part of the brain from the rest of language. When someone experiences brain damage to the left side of the brain that seriously affects their linguistic abilities, making them unable to produce fluent or grammatical speech, they often maintain the appropriate intonation patterns of their language. When right-hemisphere damage takes place, the result may be that the patient speaks with a monotone. And when babies who have not yet acquired any words begin to babble at around 6 months of age, they often utter nonsense syllables using the appropriate intonation pattern of the language they are acquiring.

Other evidence of our unconscious knowledge comes from *ludlings* (from Latin *ludus* 'game' and *lingua* 'language'). Children all over the world invent and pass on these ludlings (also called language games or secret languages), which distort the native language in some way, usually to prevent understanding by those who have not learned the language game. They are thus used primarily by groups attempting to conceal their conversations from others. Some common examples are Pig Latin, which is used all over the globe; the Gibberish family, prevalent in the United States and Sweden; Verlan, spoken in France; and numerous others.

Many of these ludlings show children's awareness of and sophisticated manipulation of syllables, stress, and meter (or prosody). Pig Latin is one such language game, and it illustrates speakers' awareness of the structure of syllables. The rules of the game are to remove the initial sounds of each word, move them to the end of the word, and add /e/ or /ey/. So *Pig Latin* is pronounced in the following way:

ig-pay atin-lay   /ig-pe ætən-le/

When the word begins with a consonant cluster, the majority of speakers of Pig Latin move the whole onset to the end of the word, so a word like *splash* would be:

splash = ash-splay   /æš-sple/

although some speakers separate the cluster, producing variations such as these:

plash   =   plash-say   /plæš-se/
lash   =   lash-spay   /læš-spe/

Such easy manipulations of syllable structure provide evidence for the speaker's unconscious knowledge of syllables and syllable structure.

Consider another ludling called Ly, written first in phonemic transcription:

a.   /hirli ɪzli ʌli mɔrli kamli plɪli ketli ʌdli gemli/

and here alphabetically:

b.   Here-ly is-ly a-ly more-ly com-ly pli-ly cate-ly ed-ly game-ly.
      'Here is a more complicated game.'

So the rules of speaking the Ly language are to insert /li/ after each syllable. Here's another ludling called Op.

a.   /ðapə fapʊt bapɔl stape dapi apəm blapu dapawn/
b.   th-op-e f-op-oot b-op-all st-op-a d-op-i op-um bl-op-ew d-op-own
      'The football stadium blew down.'

In the Op ludling one inserts /ap/ after the onset of each syllable. Note that when there is a consonant cluster, as with *blew* /blu/, the inserted /ap/ comes after that onset cluster and before the rime.

Did You Know...?

Abbish versus Ubby Dubby

In one elementary school, some children aged 7 to 11 were speakers of Abbish and others of Ubby Dubby, though they all called their language Abbish (Denham 2005). The Ubby Dubby speakers thought they were just "bad" speakers of Abbish, saying that they didn't know it very well, that their version was different, or that certain speakers knew it better. All the children were able to understand each other. When the children discovered the rules of the language and realized that they were two different varieties, they all got very excited. They discussed the difference in stress and the ways in which the two varieties were like two dialects of the same language. Some of the younger children began to blend the two dialects, developing a third version of the ludlings. It was a genuine language community doing the things that languages do!

Comparing two common language-game languages, Ubby Dubby and Abbish/Obbish, illustrates children's knowledge of both syllables and stress. Consider the rules of each.

Abbish: Insert /ab/ between onset and rime. Stress is on the initial syllable.

/mábay nábem ábíz mábɔrgəbə́n/   'My name is Morgan.'

Ubby Dubby is very similar to Abbish but has a different vowel inserted and a different stress pattern.

Ubby Dubby: Insert /əb/ between onset and rime. Stress is on syllable following insertion point.

RPE 4.17

/məbáy nəbém əbíz məbɔ́rgəbə́n/   'My name is Morgan.'

Accent on *Linguistics and Reading*

Think about all the things you read as you travel through your day—newspapers, text messages, textbooks, street signs, menus, e-mail, magazines, blogs, T-shirts, food labels, directions, and many other things. How well could you live your life if you couldn't read?

Monkey Business Images/Shutterstock.com

Have you ever thought about who taught you to read? As it turns out, teaching reading requires extensive knowledge of the sound system of language and of how sounds are represented on the page. Knowledge of phonetics and phonology is not only useful but in many ways essential in teaching children to read.

Many aspects of linguistic knowledge contribute to how we learn to read, but one key aspect is *phonemic awareness*—the understanding that words can be broken into units of sound. Learning to read requires understanding how phonemes can be mapped onto spellings of words. Though we think of reading as a visual activity, phonemic awareness is a crucial *acoustic* element of reading. Readers must decode the words, but this depends on being able to decode the sounds inside words, the sounds represented by letters. For example, learning to read requires understanding that in the word *bat* there are three sounds, that *bat* begins with the same sound as the word *boy*, that if you take away the first sound of *bat*, you have *at*, and so on. Children who have trouble with phonemic awareness also have trouble learning to read, and children who struggle learning to talk also have difficulty breaking words into their "sound parts."

Learning to read also requires understanding the writing system of the language. The alphabetic English spelling system is obviously not phonetic (think of the ways that the spelling <gh> is pronounced in *ghost*, *through*, and *rough*).

Nevertheless, there is a system, and we have to understand this system to read. An understanding of phonemes and allophones helps teachers explain how different phonemes are represented by different spellings. Teaching spelling from a phonological perspective can show that the spelling system has a kind of logic. For example, teachers can approach teaching the spelling of the sound /m/ by showing students that the sound /m/ is spelled <m> at the beginning of a word (*mat*) but <m, mb, mn> at the end (*ram, dumb, autumn*).

What about teachers who teach children to read in a second language? Teaching reading to monolingual children has been a topic of much investigation, but we have yet to fully understand the best ways to teach reading to bilingual children. Knowledge of phonetics and phonology is crucial in understanding the kind of "transfer" a bilingual child might encounter in learning to read in a second language. Does literacy in one language help or hinder acquisition of literacy in a second language? Can literacy skills acquired in one language be transferred to acquisition of literacy in another language? Which skills transfer, and which don't? Which methods and conditions favor transfer, and which don't? This is a topic of study for many linguists and educators, and the Center for Applied Linguistics is devoted to providing resources and promoting research on literacy in our increasingly multilingual, multicultural society.

So, the next time you pick up a novel or magazine or log on to check e-mail, think about who taught you to read. Have you ever thanked him or her?

For more information

Center for Applied Linguistics. http://www .cal.org/.

Treiman, R. 2003. *Linguistics and reading. The handbook of linguistics,* ed. by M. Aronoff & J. Rees-Miller, 664–672. Malden, MA: Blackwell.

Summary

In this chapter, we've examined some common phonological rules of English—assimilation, dissimilation, insertion, deletion, fronting, and metathesis. We've seen examples of these rules at work in our "standard" language, in child language, and in different North American dialects, as well as in earlier varieties of English. We have also examined some of the phonological processes that affect larger units of sounds, including syllables, stress, and intonation. We have seen that all of these processes are systematic and patterned and that they occur unconsciously.

Sources and Resources

Anderson, S. 1974. *The organization of phonology*. New York: Academic Press.
Berko, J. 1958. The child's learning of English morphology. *Word* 14.150–177.
Chomsky, N. & M. Halle. 1968. *The sound pattern of English*. New York: Harper & Row.
Clark, J. & C. Yallop. 1990. *An introduction to phonetics and phonology*. Oxford, UK: Blackwell.
Cowan, W. & J. Rakušan. 1985. *Source book for linguistics*. Philadelphia/Amsterdam: John Benjamins Publishing.
Denham, K. 2005. Ludlings teach language diversity and change. *National Council of Teachers of English (NCTE)* Annual Meeting, Pittsburgh, PA.
Deutsch, D., et al. 1999. Tone language speakers possess absolute pitch. *Acoustical Society of America (ASA)* 138. Columbus, OH.
Deutsch, D., et al. 2006. Absolute pitch among American and Chinese conservatory students: Prevalence differences, and evidence for a speech-related critical period. *Journal of the Acoustical Society of America* 119. 719–722.
Jusczyk, P. 1993. From general to language-specific capacities: The WRAPSA model of how speech perception develops. *Journal of Phonetics* [Special issue on phonetic development], 21(1–2). 3–28.
Kenstowicz, H. 1995. *Phonology in generative grammar*. Oxford, UK: Blackwell.
McMahon, A. 2002. *An introduction to English phonology*. Oxford, UK: Oxford University Press.
National Public Radio. 2006. Behaves so strangely. *Radio Lab*. Show #202. April 21. http://www.wnyc.org/shows/radiolab/episodes/2006/04/21. (17 October, 2008.)
Nunberg, G. 2004. Going nucular. *Fresh Air*. National Public Radio. October 2. Published in *Going nucular*. 2004. New York: Public Affairs.
Treiman, R. 2003. Linguistics and reading. *The handbook of linguistics*, ed. by M. Aronoff & J. Rees-Miller, 664–672. Malden, MA: Blackwell.
Werker, J. & R. Desjardins. 1995. Listening to speech in the first year of life: Experiential influences on phoneme perception. *Current Directions in Psychological Sciences* 4(3). 76–81.

Review, Practice, and Explore

RPE 4.1 > Allophones of [l] in English

There are three distinct allophonic forms of the phoneme /l/ in many English dialects, shown here as [l], [l̩], and [ɫ]. Figure out the rule that determines when each allophone of the phoneme /l/ occurs. To do so, look at the sounds that occur on either side of the [l]s, and write what determines when each sound occurs.

[lɪp]	lip	[pɪɫ]	pill
[lay]	lie	[ayɫ]	isle
[pl̥ei]	play	[blu]	blue
[kl̥u]	clue	[glu]	glue

Now look up each of the symbols and write the description of each of these allophones (in terms of place and manner of articulation and voicing).

RPE   4.2   Italian [n] and [ŋ]: Phonemes or Allophones?

Using the following words, determine whether [n] and [ŋ] are allophones of one phoneme or separate phonemes in Italian. Do the sounds occur in the same positions? Determine the environment in which each sound occurs; that is, look at the sounds that occur on either side of [n] and [ŋ] to see what determines when each sound occurs. If one sound always occurs before a certain natural class of sound, then the occurrence of that sound is determined by a phonological rule. What is that rule?

[nero]	black	[rana]	frog
[jʲente]	people	[aŋke]	also
[tenda]	tent	[faŋgo]	mud
[tinta]	dye	[tiŋgo]	I die

RPE   4.3   Korean [s] and [š]: Phonemes or Allophones?

Using the following words, determine whether [s] and [š] are allophones of one phoneme or separate phonemes in Korean. Do the sounds occur in the same positions? Determine the environment in which each sound occurs; does the sound always occur before a certain natural class of sound, and if so which one? (Adapted from Cowan and Rakušan 1985, 42)

[son]	hand	[šihap]	game
[sɔm]	sack	[šipsam]	thirteen
[sosal]	novel	[šinho]	signal
[sɛk]	color	[maši]	delicious
[us]	upper		

RPE   4.4   Hungarian [a] and [a:]: Phonemes or Allophones?

Consider the sounds [a] and [a:] (where : indicates a long vowel). Are these sounds allophones of one phoneme or separate phonemes? Determine the environment in which each sounds occurs; do they occur in the same positions or different ones? (Adapted from Cowan and Rakušan 1985, 66)

[bamba:n]	foolishly	[a:g]	branch
[cafatol]	tear	[a:da:z]	furious
[aga:r]	greyhound	[ba:mul]	wonder
[fɛlad]	to give up	[ca:pa]	shark
[cimborafa]	collar beam	[cikornʲa:š]	over-ornamented
[holta]	posthumously	[fɛla:za:š]	soaking up
[oldal]	side	[ra:k]	crayfish
[ado:š]	in debt	[a:bra]	illustration
[kortina]	curtain	[olda:š]	solution
[rak]	to put	[ča:]	to the right

RPE 4.5 > A Variation of the Pluralization Rule

In the text, you saw the three plural endings involved in plural formation for most adult speakers of English. Children acquiring English sometimes have variations on this rule. Consider the following pronunciations of some plural words by a child between the ages of 2½ and 3 years.

a.	bath	+	plural	=	/bæθəz/
b.	knife	+	plural	=	/nayfəz/
c.	cliff	+	plural	=	/klɪfəz/
d.	self	+	plural	=	/sɛlfəz/
e.	sleeve	+	plural	=	/slivəz/
f.	horse	+	plural	=	/hɔrsəz/
g.	fuzz	+	plural	=	/fʌzəz/
h.	fish	+	plural	=	/fɪšəz/
i.	church	+	plural	=	/čʌrčəz/
j.	cat	+	plural	=	/kæts/
k.	dog	+	plural	=	/dagz/
l.	pup	+	plural	=	/pʌps/
m.	pad	+	plural	=	/pædz/
n.	kick	+	plural	=	/kɪks/
o.	stamps	+	plural	=	/stæmps/
p.	bib	+	plural	=	/bɪbz/
q.	lamb	+	plural	=	/læmz/
r.	can	+	plural	=	/kænz/
s.	camel	+	plural	=	/kæməlz/
t.	caterpillar	+	plural	=	/kælərpɪtərz/

This child's rule of plural formation seems to match the adult rule for the data in items (j) through (t)—although notice his metathesis of syllables in his pronunciation of *caterpillars*. However, the adult rule that adds /əz/ after sibilants is slightly different for him. After which sounds does the child add /əz/? Briefly discuss how this rule is similar to and different from the adult rule of plural formation, and consider how this child might have come to acquire this rule.

RPE 4.6 > A Different Variation of Pluralization

A well-known psycholinguistic experiment that has come to be known as the *wug* test, first conducted by Jean Berko Gleason (Berko 1958), presents children with made-up words and asks them to make them plural. For example, a child might be shown a picture of a fantasy creature and be told, "This is a wug. Imagine there are two of them. There are two __."
The children then fill in the blank. Very young children are able to do this quite easily, supplying the adult forms: /s/ after voiceless Cs, /z/ after voiced Cs, and /əz/ after sibilants.

In one experiment, the 4-year-old subjects produced a slight variation of the adult plural rule; again, as with the other child variation, the variation was only with the /əz/ form. The attachment of /s/ and of /z/ matched the adult rule, as shown in items (a)–(g):

a.	cats	/kæts/	**c.**	pups	/pʌps/
b.	dogs	/dagz/	**d.**	pads	/pædz/

e. kicks   /kɪks/   **g.** bibs   /bɪbz/
f. stamps   /stæmps/

Made-up words demonstrated a similar pattern:

h. wug   /wʌgz/   **i.** biff   /bɪfs/

However, the plural forms in items (j) and (k) indicate that these children have a different rule when the word ends in a sibilant:

j. fish   /fɪš/   **k.** bunch   /bʌnč/

Again, made-up words demonstrated a similar pattern:

l. clush   /klʌš/   **m.** tazz   /tæz/

What is these children's rule of plural formation, and how does it differ from the adult rule? Briefly discuss how this rule is similar to and different from the adult rule of plural formation, and discuss how these children might have come to acquire this rule.

> **RPE   4.7** > **They Hissed, Banged, and Faded**

A. Determine the past-tense form of each of the following words. Remember to think phonemically here—ignore spelling. For example, the past tense of *dance* is /dænst/.

crush	turn	weed	wish	thrive	sift
kick	plow	hate	tuck	bag	bait
hiss	play	demand	botch	nab	import
heap	climb	pit	possess	breathe	relate
cinch	singe	tote	winch	bang	sand
pass	kill	pat	face	faze	fade

What are the three phonological forms of the regular English past tense? What natural classes of sounds determine the past-tense form used? What natural class of sounds does /t/ follow? What natural class of sounds does /d/ follow? What natural class of sounds does /ɪd/ (or /əd/) follow?

Notice that some of this assimilation has come into the spelling system. Consider *crept, slept, wept, leapt*. Can you think of others? Some words, such as *dreamed* and *dreamt*, have two distinct standard spellings and pronunciations in the past tense. Can you think of any others?

B. In some dialects, there is a slight variation of the rule you have discovered already for past tense. Consider the following data from some high school students in Seattle (Dialect B):

	Dialect A	Dialect B
skinned	/skɪnd/	/skɪndɪd/
boned	/bond/	/bondɪd/
burned	/bʌrnd/	/bʌrndɪd/

How is this past-tense rule different from the rule you already described?

RPE 4.8 > Dissimilation

The word *cardomom*, a kind of spice, is frequently pronounced as if spelled *cardomon*, with an /n/ at the end. Look up the following words in a good etymological dictionary to determine their origins. Explain the process of dissimilation that occurred to achieve the Present-Day English forms: *seldom, random, pilgrim*.

RPE 4.9 > Schwa Insertion

In many people's speech, a schwa sound is commonly inserted after a syllable ending in /l/ or preceding a syllable beginning with /l/.

| realtor /riltər/ | → | /rilətər/ |
| athlete /æθlit/ | → | /æθəlit/ |

Conduct a survey among your peers to determine whether the following words have a schwa inserted: *athletic, biathlon (decathlon, pentathlon), jewelry*. Can you think of others?

RPE 4.10 > Where Have All the /l/s Gone?

The deletion of /l/ before other consonants is in a state of flux in English. In most words in which /l/ is followed by another consonant, the /l/ is not pronounced by most speakers: *half, calf, walk, salmon, would, could, should*. This /l/ before a consonant had disappeared across the board by the time of Early Modern English (1500–1800), though it remained in the spelling. However, some people now pronounce the /l/ because of what we call a "spelling pronuncia-tion," an effect of seeing the /l/ in the word in print. (This has also happened with the /t/ of *often*, which used to not be pronounced but now is by some speakers, though not in *soften* or *fasten*.) Some words with an /l/ have two standard pronunciations, so you may hear *folk* or *psalm* with or without the /l/, though other /l/s before consonants are not pronounced by most speakers, such as in *yolk*. And though most speakers do not pronounce the /l/ in *half* or *calf*, those same speakers might pronounce the /l/ in *wolf* and criticize those who do not have an /l/ in *wolf*.

Consider the following and determine whether you have an /l/ in your pronunciation:

half, calf, walk, salmon, salve, palm, calm, talk, golf, wolf, Rudolph, elf, shelf, myself, always, folk, psalm

Are there some words that you can pronounce either with or without the /l/? If so, what do you think determines which pronunciation you use? What factors do you associate with particular instances of /l/-dropping in these words? Try to come up with other examples of words that have an <l> in the spelling but may or may not have an /l/ in the pronunciation.

RPE 4.11 > Deletion of /r/ in American English

Even the so-called standard American dialect that doesn't traditionally delete /r/ after vowels may delete /r/s elsewhere. Some Americans who regularly pronounce /r/ elsewhere do not have it in the middle of the word *governor*, for instance, although they may have it in *governing* or *government*. Can you suggest any reason for the loss of /r/ in the one word when it is retained in the other two?

Say the following words; in which ones do you pronounce the /r/s? Be careful not to be fooled by the spelling—you may think you have an /r/ where you really do not pronounce one. Then describe the circumstances under which the loss of /r/ occurs. Consider the position of the stress in the words and also whether there are other /r/s in the word.

surprise	mirror	February
thermometer	gubernatorial	temperature
vernacular	spectrograph	caterpillar
reservoir	southerner	particular
repertory	formerly	Arthur
wintergreen	paraphernalia	kindergarten

RPE 4.12 > Switching Sounds Around

Some words commonly involve sound exchanges, either as slips of the tongue or as dialectal variations. Describe the metathetic pronunciation of the following words, which are given following each word, and discuss anything that surprises you about these pronunciations.

integral /ɪntrəgəl/	foliage /foyləǰ/
cavalry /kælvəri/	relevant /rɛvəlɪnt/
comfortable /kʌmftərbəl/	strategy /stræǰəti/

Also look up the older forms of each of the following words, whose Present-Day English pronunciation is the result of metathesis. Give the older form of the words.

horse, run, frost

And finally, consider the word *iron.* How is metathesis at work in the standard pronunciation of this word?

RPE 4.13 > Slips of the Tongue

Slips of the tongue involve accidental manipulation of the building blocks of language: phonetic, phonological, morphological, and syntactic. For the following phonological slips, describe what happened from the intended utterance to the actual utterance, using the terminology from syllable structure.

	Intended Utterance	Actual Utterance
a.	play with fire	fay with plire
b.	stoke the fire	stike the foire
c.	take off your snowpants	snake off your toepants
d.	fish net	fit nesh
e.	I would name it . . .	I nould wame it . . .

RPE 4.14 > Where's the Stress?

Remember that the English stress system is quite complicated. In the following words, for example, the words in data set A and those in data set B follow two different stress rules. What are the two rules that determine which syllable is stressed in these groups of English nouns? The accent mark ´ indicates the primarily stressed syllable for most English speakers.

Data Set A	Data Set B
synópsis	cábinet
veránda	América
agénda	cínema
consénsus	aspáragus
amálgam	metrópolis
uténsil	jávelin

It will be useful to divide the words into syllables. Then examine the structure of the syllables that receive primary stress. Write a rule that describes which syllable receives primary stress.

RPE 4.15 ⟩ Da DUM da DUM da DUM da DUM da DUM

Do you recognize iambic pentameter? Recall that an iambic foot (one iamb) is an unstressed syllable followed by a stressed syllable, such as in the words *today* and *undo*. Shakespeare, among many other poets, used a lot of *iambic pentameter*, in which a poetic line consists of five iambic feet. Find or invent some examples of iambic trimeter (three sets of iambs), tetrameter (four sets of iambs), and pentameter (five sets of iambs).

Other terms from poetry of varied stress patterns are the following:

a. **Trochee** two syllables, stressed–unstressed, as in the words *lamppost* and *standard*
b. **Anapest** three syllables, unstressed–unstressed–stressed, as in the words *unperturbed* and *disengage*
c. **Dactyl** three syllables, stressed–unstressed–unstressed, as in the words *probably* and *imbecile*

Find examples of each of these in poetry as well.

RPE 4.16 ⟩ Watch Your Tone!

Place the intonation nucleus in at least two places in the following sentences, then describe the way the meaning changes when the intonation changes.

a. I don't remember his name.
b. Did you forget to lock the door?
c. I hope she isn't too disappointed.
d. I think we've run out of pullover sweaters.
e. How can we persuade them to help?
f. Her secretary wouldn't say where the client was.

RPE 4.17 ⟩ Rules of a Language Game

Here's an English-speaking children's language game called Pet. Using your knowledge of syllable structure, figure out and explain the rules of this language game.

/bɛtpɛtərpər letpet ðænpæn nɛvpɛv ərpər/

Betpetterper latepate thanpan nevpeverper.

Morphology: Words and Their Parts

Key Concepts

- We all have unconscious knowledge of word structure.
- Words can be divided into two basic classes: content words and function words.
- Morphemes are pieces of words that express their own meanings.
- Morphology helps us recognize words and possible words.
- Morphemes come in a variety of types; some can stand alone as words themselves, and others can't.
- *Affixes* attach to other morphemes according to specific rules.

Did You Know . . . ?

Pooh on Pronouns
Linguists in Hollywood

Language Alive!

Embiggen His Soul!
What about *Cranapple*?
Word-*orama*!
The Battle over *Whom*
Ain't Ain't Had It Easy!

Linguistics in the News   Arkansas's Apostrophe

Accent on   Field Linguistics

Morphemes and Meaning
   Morphemes and Syllables
   Recognizing Morphemes
Word Classes
   Content Words
   Function Words
   Word Classes and Our Mental Lexicon
Free and Bound Morphemes
   Affixes
   Roots
Derivational Affixation
Affixation and Our Mental Lexicon
   Drawing Word Trees
   Word Trees and Ambiguity
Inflectional Affixation
   Inflectional Affixation of English
   Nouns
   Inflectional Affixation of English
   Verbs
   Suppletive Verbs and Adjectives
Summary
Sources and Resources
Review, Practice, and Explore

> *When ideas fail, words come in very handy.*
>
> —JOHANN WOLFGANG VON GOETHE

morphology study of the system of rules underlying our knowledge of the structure of words

In this chapter and the next, we will investigate **morphology**, which, you might remember from Chapter 1, is the study of words and parts of words. As in the previous chapters, we will focus on uncovering unconscious knowledge, revealing what you don't know that you already know about the structure of words in your language.

What exactly do we know about words? What *is* a word? Knowing words includes knowing the meanings attached to combinations of sounds, but it is much more. Speakers share some kind of common knowledge that allows us to recognize words as English even when we don't all use the same vocabulary. We recognize nonsense words as English, and we recognize a child's words as English even though these words do not conform to those we use as adults. We even recognize words from earlier varieties of English that are no longer spoken. This understanding of "what is a word" comes from a vast amount of unconscious knowledge about the structure of words in our language. Morphology includes the study of the system of rules underlying our knowledge of the structure of words; the word *morphology* is from the Greek words *morph-* 'form/structure' and *-logy* (study). Morphology is closely

lexicon our mental dictionary; stores information about words and the lexical rules that we use to build them

linked to the study of our mental dictionary, or **lexicon**. The operations and systems we use to form words are called *word formation rules* or *lexical rules*.

As we discussed in Chapter 1, the pieces or elements of any communication system are called signs. Signs can be iconic or non-iconic, where the relation between the form and the meaning of the sign is arbitrary. For example, English speakers call a domesticated feline *cat*; a Spanish speaker calls it *gato*; a Japanese speaker, *neko*; and a Witsuwit'en (spoken in northern British Columbia, Canada) speaker, *dus*. The words have the same meaning, but their forms are all distinct. Most words

onomatopoeia use of a word for which the connection between sound and meaning seems nonarbitrary because the word's sound echoes its meaning

in a language, with the exception of **onomatopoeic** words, are non-iconic. The most obvious sign (in Saussure's sense, introduced in Chapter 1) in human language is the word, and though we all can recognize words, and we can certainly use them, it's actually rather difficult to come up with a definition of *word*. What would you say in response to the question, What is a word? You would probably find it much easier to simply provide examples— we all agree that *cat* is a word and that *eat*, *drive*, *xylophone*, and *flabbergasted* are, too. A working definition of *word* in oral language, then, might be

© Dragana Gerasimoski/Shutterstock.com

This iconic symbol indicates the location of an up escalator to people regardless of the language they speak.

ƕæȶ!

The onomatopoeic words for a dog's barking aren't the same in all languages; English = *woof, arf, bow-wow, ruff;* Arabic = *haw haw;* Indonesian = *guk guk;* Catalan = *bup bup;* Estonian = *auh auh;* and Russian = *gav gav.* Hear children making onomatopoeic sounds in their language at http://www.bzzzpeek.com.

"a sound or combination of sounds to which speakers attach meaning." It's a good definition as far as it goes—but we'll amend this definition in the next section. A similar definition of *word* applies in signed languages: a word is a sign or combination of signs to which meaning is attached. In English and many other languages, words in print are separated by spaces, and it can be difficult to visually distinguish the words when the spaces are not there.

Iwonderifyoucanreadthiswithoutspacesaseasilyasyoucanwhentherearespacesbetweenthewords.

And of course, there are no spaces when we speak, and some languages' writing systems do not consistently separate words (Old English, Old Russian). Many languages of the world have no written version at all, but they all have words.

So, one way to try to get at the definition of a word is by meaning. We all know that words have meaning—*peace, elephant, rancor*—but we also know that many pieces of words have meaning too: *un-, -s, non-, -ed.* Once again, although explaining what a word is might be difficult, it's pretty clear that we nevertheless can identify not only the words in our language but other units within words that also have meaning. We call these meaningful pieces **morphemes**. Let's explore this concept in more detail in order to come up with a clearer definition of *word.*

Morphemes and Meaning

morpheme smallest unit of meaning in a word

Consider the following nonsense sentence:

The minnly erks yodded both thunkish blonks.

Speakers of English immediately recognize *the* and *both* in this sentence as English words. Though we don't know what the other words in the sentence mean, we can nevertheless deduce quite a bit about them. We would recognize *minnly* and *thunkish* as words in the same category as *lovely* and *pinkish*—namely, as adjectives—because of their *-ly* and *-ish* endings and because of their position in the sentence preceding *erks* and *blonks*, respectively. We know that *erks* and *blonks* are plural nouns because of their positions and because of their *-s* endings. We know that *yodded* is a verb, again because of its position but also because it ends in the past-tense suffix *-ed.* The form of a word, its suffixes and prefixes, therefore helps us determine the **syntactic category**, or part of speech (noun, verb, adjective, adverb, preposition, etc.) of the word. We return to syntactic categories later in the chapter. (And we discuss syntactic categories in more detail in Chapter 7.)

syntactic category set of words that share a significant number of grammatical characteristics (nouns, verbs, etc.)

ƕɯæᴄ!

We love word games! *Scrabble*, for example, is now produced in thirty languages as well as in Braille; it's also available on a CD and online (free). Go to http://www.mattelscrabble.com to read the fascinating story about the invention of *Scrabble* more than 50 years ago.

This nonsense sentence illustrates that we have knowledge of morphemes—of words and meaningful parts of words—and that we use this knowledge to determine a number of things: the syntactic category of the word, whether the word is plural or singular, or whether it is in the past or present tense.

A morpheme is often described as the smallest unit of meaning in a word. On this logic, there are two morphemes in the word *pancake*, namely, *pan* and *cake*, both of which have rather obvious, recognizable meanings, and both of which are words by themselves. Other morphemes have meaning, too, though perhaps not in the dictionary sense. English speakers would probably all agree that there are three morphemes in *waspishness* (*wasp*, *-ish*, and *-ness*). We can say that the morphemes *-ish* and *-ness* have meaning because we recognize them as parts of words we easily combine with other parts to create words such as *pinkish* and *happiness*, and we also know that *-ish* and *-ness* can't be combined with *run* or *work* to create **runnish* or **workness*. So, although we might have difficulty defining the term *word*, we certainly know what a morpheme is, and we also know a complex set of rules that allow us to combine morphemes to create larger, meaningful units.

Morphemes and Syllables

Be sure not to confuse morphemes with syllables; *Mississippi* has more than one syllable but is only a single morpheme, at least to speakers who are unaware that its origin, or **etymology**, is that it comes from the Ojibwa *misisipi* 'big river'. English speakers know that *miss* and *sip* in this word are not related to the English uses of those words.

etymology
historical origin of a word

monomorphemic
consisting of a single (free) morpheme

polymorphemic
consisting of more than one morpheme

Words can be **monomorphemic**, or made up of a single morpheme, such as *car* and *brown*, or **polymorphemic**, made up of more than one morpheme, such as *grammaticality*, *anthropomorphic*, *linguistics*, and *racehorse*.

Other examples of monomorphemic words (with more than one syllable) are *paper*, *pizza*, *Google*, *river*, and *catapult* (in this last word, *cat* is a syllable but not a morpheme—it is not related to the feline).

Recognizing Morphemes

We use a variety of clues to identify morphemes. English has borrowed many morphemes from Latin and Greek, but as we saw previously with the discussion of *Mississippi*, we don't need to speak the language a word comes from in order to analyze its morphology. Take, for example, the word *transmission*. We may know that *trans-* is a morpheme because it occurs in many other words: *translation*, *transport*, *translate*, and so on. We may also know that *mit-* (which ends up being spelled *mis-* in *transmission*) is a morpheme from its appearance in words like *transmit* and *permit*. And finally, we know that *-ion* is a morpheme because we find it in *nation* and *translation*. We may not, however, know that *trans-* means 'through' in Latin and that *mit* comes from the verb *mittere* 'to send'.

It may come as no surprise, then, that although all languages have words, speakers of all languages do not share the same morphological rules. Though we can apply our own English rules to words that come from other languages, it is much more difficult to identify morphemes in a language one does not speak. For this reason, the following Lushootseed sentence is difficult for a non-Lushootseed speaker to break up into morphemes. (Lushootseed is a Salish language of the Pacific Northwest.)

> ošuhlh čuhd t'uhbilhuhd
> made I rope
> 'I made rope'

Similarly, when we use the rules of one language to analyze a different language, the result can be a misanalysis. Consider, for example, the following place names in the Pacific Northwest, which are also the names of the Salish tribes in the region.

> stulegʷabš   (borrowed into English as *Stillaguamish*)
> s-tulegʷ-abš
> noun-making prefix—river—people of   'river people'

> sq'ixʷabš   (borrowed into English as *Skykomish*)
> s-q'ixʷ-abš
> noun-making prefix—located upstream—people of   'upstream people'

English speakers might think from the English spelling of these names that *-ish* is an adjectival suffix, the suffix that occurs in such words as *girlish* or *reddish* and also in such "nationality adjectives" as *Swedish* and *Spanish*. In Salish languages, however, *-abš* is completely different from English *-ish*; in Salish, it means 'people of'.

We often *don't* misanalyze words, even when we could. English speakers know that the *-s* at the end of *Massachusetts* is not the plural *-s* that occurs on English nouns because there is no singular *Massachusett*, nor do we treat *Massachusetts* as plural: **Massachusetts are beautiful in the fall*. (Recall that * indicates that the sentence or word is ungrammatical, odd-sounding.)

We can now amend our definition of *word*. Previously, we said that a word was "a sound or combination of sounds to which speakers attach meaning." We might now say, after this brief discussion of morphemes, that a word is "a morpheme (*cat*) or combination of morphemes (*waspishness*) to which we attach meaning." In the following section, we'll take a closer look at words and discuss how words can be broken down into two basic classes. We will then move on from there to discuss how words within those two classes can be broken down into morphemes in a variety of ways.

hwæt!
Keep your eye on the suffix *-ish*, which seems to be increasingly productive. *Suckish* is definitely a word now!

RPE 5.1

Word Classes

Traditional grammar identifies eight parts of speech: noun, verb, adjective, adverb, preposition, conjunction, article, and interjection. You may be familiar with these terms because they are often taught in school and are used in writing handbooks and dictionaries. However, there are actually more categories, and here, consistent with current grammatical theory and the approach to syntax we take in Chapter 7, we will divide words up into the following syntactic categories (parts of speech): noun, verb, adjective, adverb, preposition, auxiliary verb, modal, determiner, quantifier, numeral, pronoun, degree word, and conjunction. Syntactic categories can in turn be divided into two word classes: *content* words and *function* words.

Content Words

content words
words with lexical meanings (nouns, verbs, adjectives, adverbs)

open class category of words that accepts new members (nouns, verbs, adjectives, and adverbs)

Nouns, verbs, adjectives, and adverbs are all **content words**, words with meanings that we can look up in the dictionary (Table 5.1). Content words are **open class** words, meaning that they accept new members. For example, *textmessage*, *e-mail*, and *fax* are all verbs (with noun counterparts) that have been recently added to the language, and new(ish) nouns include *blog* and *tofurkey*. Recent adjectives include *crunk*, *fetch*, and *satellic*; and *awesome* has recently shifted from being only an adjective ("That band is awesome") to also being an adverb for many speakers ("That band plays awesome").

Table 5.1	Content Word Categories with Examples		
Noun	**Verb**	**Adjective**	**Adverb**
river, intelligence, Washington, scissors, furniture, fax, blog, hashtag	discuss, remember, annoy, feel, gallop, seem, textmessage	unhappy, fortuitous, beautiful, mad, tiny, crunk, chill, satellitic	hopefully, maddeningly, fast, still, now, often

Function Words

function words
words with functional meanings (determiners, auxiliary verbs, etc.)

closed class
category of words that does not accept new members (determiners, auxiliary verbs, and conjunctions, among others)

In contrast to content words, **function words**, such as determiners and auxiliary verbs (which we discuss more in Chapter 7), do not have "contentful" meanings; rather, they are defined in terms of their use, or function (Table 5.2). For example, the meaning of the auxiliary verb *is* in *Leo is running* is difficult to define, but we can say that the function of the auxiliary verb *is* in this case is to express present tense (to see this, compare *Leo was running*). Function words are **closed class** words. Though we freely add new members to open classes of words, we don't coin new determiners or conjunctions, nor do we come up with new pronouns, modal verbs, or auxiliary verbs (*have*, *be*, and *do*).

Table 5.2	Function Word Categories with Examples		
Determiner	the, a, this, that, these, those, his, my	Preposition	without, in, on, over, behind, above, around
Numeral	one, five, ten, second, eighth	Conjunction	and, or, yet, for, but, so, nor
Quantifier	all, each, every, both, some	Degree Word	very, so, quite, rather, too
		Auxiliary Verb	have, be, do
Pronoun	they, he, she, her, theirs, mine, yours	Modal	may, might, can, could, will, would, shall, should, must

Note that membership in a particular word class is not necessarily fixed. Just as words can belong to more than one syntactic category (such as a word that is both a verb and a noun—*e-mail*, for example—or an adjective and an adverb, like *fast*), some words share characteristics of both word classes. Prepositions are an example. We haven't added any new prepositions to the language in several hundred years, so in that sense prepositions form a closed class. And although their primary function seems to express information about the direction, location, and such of a following noun in English (*near/on* the table), many prepositions have quite complex, "contentful" meanings. Consider, for example, the meanings of the preposition *by*:

by the river   by myself
by Mark Twain   by mistake
by boat

Did You Know...?

Pooh on Pronouns

If the English language had been properly organized . . . then there would be a word which meant both "he" and "she," and I could write, "If John or Mary comes heesh will want to play tennis," which would save a lot of trouble.

— A. A. Milne, *The Christopher Robin Birthday Book*

Even though there have been attempts to introduce a gender-neutral pronoun (one example was *thon*) in order to avoid generic *he* (as in *Each child should read a book. Then he should discuss it.* and *The astronaut must be very dedicated. He must undergo hours of rigorous training*), such attempts have largely failed, not necessarily because of resistance to gender-neutral terms (though that is part of it) but simply because pronouns are a closed class. Note that an alternative strategy, namely, to use plural *they* instead of *he or she*, is widely accepted because it does not involve introducing a new pronoun.

So, although we will assume here that prepositions are function words, note that this distinction is not entirely clear and that prepositions present an interesting case of the possible overlap between function and content word classes.

Another example of words that don't fit neatly into one category or another is degree words. Degree words are traditionally classified as adverbs, but actually behave differently syntactically, always modifying adverbs or adjectives and expressing a degree: *very, rather, so, too*. This is a relatively fixed class and new members do not enter it frequently. But consider the word *hella*; like other degree words, it expresses degree and can be used to modify adverbs or adjectives: *She's very/hella/so tall*. *Wicked* is also used in some dialects as a degree word: *I am wicked hungry!*

RPE 5.2

Word Classes and Our Mental Lexicon

Though sometimes the difference between content and function word classes can be rather fuzzy, there is a great deal of evidence that this basic distinction exists and that this distinction among classes of words is part of our fundamental knowledge of language. The fact that content words can take affixes, primarily inflectional morphemes, but function words cannot (except, as Eric Hyman notes, metalinguistically as in *no ifs, ands, or buts*) demonstrates that they are distinct kinds of categories.[1] Also, as we discussed in Chapter 2, children go through a telegraphic stage of language acquisition in which they omit function words and morphemes, saying things such as *go store* and *baby cry*, omitting function words such as *to* and *the*. This omission of function words might be because they can only store so many whole words in their working memories, and therefore words with lexical content take priority because they allow children to convey the most meaning with limited vocabulary.

Aphasia provides additional evidence that we store function words in our mental lexicons differently from content words. Recall that sufferers of Broca's aphasia tend to have great difficulty speaking and omit function words such as determiners, prepositions, and the verb *be*. The following excerpt is from an interview between neuropsychologist Howard Gardner (1974: 60–61) and Mr. Ford, a Coast Guard radio operator who had suffered a stroke three months earlier.

Dr. Gardner: Why are you in the hospital, Mr. Ford?

Mr. Ford: Arm no good . . . speech . . . can't say . . . talk, you see.

Dr. Gardner: What happened to you to make you lose your speech?

Mr. Ford: Head, fall, Jesus Christ, me no good, str, str . . . oh Jesus . . . stroke.

And finally, recall that the earliest speakers of Nicaraguan Sign Language, or *Idioma de Señas de Nicaragua*, who developed language after puberty (and

---

1. Thanks to Eric Hyman for pointing this out.

thus after the critical period), created a form of language closer to a pidgin than signers who were exposed to a more developed version of ISN at an earlier age. One of the characteristics of pidgin ISN was the lack of classifiers, signs that can be regarded as functional rather than contentful.

We will discuss lexical and functional categories in Chapter 7 on syntax, where we'll explore some of the distinctions among them in more detail.

RPE   5.3

Free and Bound Morphemes

bound morpheme
morpheme that must attach to another morpheme

free morpheme
morpheme that can stand alone as a word

affix bound morphemes, including prefixes, suffixes, infixes, and circumfixes

Morphemes, like words, fall into different classes. Morphemes are either **bound** or **free**. The words *drink, cat,* and *butter* are all free morphemes; they are single morphemes (monomorphemic) and can stand alone as words. Bound morphemes, on the other hand, are morphemes that cannot stand alone and must be attached to another morpheme or word. Examples of bound morphemes include *trans-* and *-mit* in *transmit, -ize* in *materialize,* and *un-* in *unhappy.* Bound morphemes themselves come in different types: *-ize* is a suffix, and *un-* is a prefix. Suffixes and prefixes fall under the more general heading of **affixes**, morphemes that attach to other morphemes or words by a process called *affixation.*

Affixes

Let's take a look at affixes in more detail before we go on to discuss other types of bound morphemes. Some common examples of English prefixes and suffixes are the following:

> **prefixes:** dis-, un-, for-, anti-, semi-, hyper-, in-, en-
> **suffixes:** -ment, -ion, -er, -ing, -s, -able, -ize, -ship, -ity

Another type of affix is an *infix*, an affix that attaches within a word root. The Inuktitut language of Western Canada, a member of the Eskimo-Aleut language family, has an infix, *-pallia-*, which must be inserted into a verb root, resulting in a distinct form of the verb. The rough translation of this infix is *gradually.*

> *nungup + pallia + jut = nunguppalliajut*   'They are gradually disappearing'
>
> *ilinniaq + pallia + jugut = ilinniaqpalliajugut*   'We are gradually learning'

expletive infixation
process by which a morpheme is inserted inside another morpheme: *abso-bloomin'-lutely*

Although infixes occur in many other languages, there is only one basic type in English, **expletive infixation**. This infix has the effect of adding emphasis. The infix may only be inserted into words with more than two syllables, and it can range from the relatively tame *gosh darn* to the more powerful so-called F-word. In *My Fair Lady,* Eliza Doolittle sings about how nice it would be to sit *abso-bloomin'-lutely* still, where the infix is *bloomin'.* Native speakers of English have

Language Alive!

Embiggen His Soul!

Though *em-/en-* + *-en* is not commonly used as a circumfix in English, we are still able to understand its two pieces and use them to create new—though perhaps surprising—words. An example comes from *The Simpsons* TV show, in which the founder of the fictional town of Springfield, Jebediah Springfield, uses the word *embiggen*, appropriately attaching the affix to an adjective base when he sings "that a man might embiggen his soul."

_____

Thanks to Jason Cuniff for this example.

And one coining leads to another. Here's another bit of dialogue from the show:

> EDNA: Embiggen? I never heard that word before I moved to Springfield.
>
> Ms. HOOVER: I don't know why. It's a perfectly *cromulent* word.

_____

Thanks to Russell Hugo for this example.

intuitions about where in a word the infix is inserted. Consider where your favorite expletive infix goes in these words:

> fantastic, education, Massachusetts, Philadelphia, Stillaguamish, emancipation, absolutely, hydrangea

Most speakers agree on these patterns, though there are some dialectal variations as well. You likely found that the infix is inserted at the following points:

> fan-***-tastic, edu-***-cation, Massa-***-chusetts,
> Phila-***-delphia, Stilla-***-guamish, emanci -***-pation,
> abso-***-lutely, hy-***-drangea

The infix gets inserted before the syllable that receives the most stress, and it cannot be inserted anywhere else in the word.

> absolutely = abso-flippin'-lutely
>
>> but not *ab-flippin'-solutely, nor *absolute-flippin'-ly
>
> hydrangea = hy-freakin'-drangea
>
>> but not *hydrang-freakin'-ea

Now, what happens when the first syllable in the word is the one that receives the most stress, as in the following?

> basketball, underdog, Bellingham, institute, pickpocket

The rule is that when the first syllable is the one with the most stress, the infix is then inserted before the syllable that receives secondary stress in the word.

basket-***-ball, under-***-dog, Belling-***-ham, insti-***-tute, pick-***-pocket

Now, nobody ever taught you this rule! It's a striking display of your unconscious knowledge of the rules of language and of how phonology and morphology interact.

Yet another type of affix is the *circumfix* (from Latin *circum-* 'around'); this type of affix surrounds another morpheme. German has a very common circumfix, *ge- -t*, which creates the perfective form of certain verbs.

| kommen | 'to come' |
| Er ist <u>ge</u>komm<u>t</u>. | 'He has come.' (*ge* + komm + *t*) |

And Samoan has a circumfix *fe-* + *-aʔi* which indicates reciprocity:

| finau | 'to quarrel' |
| fefinauaʔi | 'to quarrel with each other' |

English does not use circumfixes as these languages do. Some researchers suggest that because the prefix *em-/en-* occurs only in words with the suffix *-en*, such as *embolden/enlighten*, that *em-/en-* and *-en* are not a prefix and a suffix but rather a circumfix. (The prefix *en-* becomes *em-* before /b/ for phonological reasons—can you explain why? What phonological process is at work here?) That we don't have words like *embold or *bolden provides additional evidence that in *embolden*, *em-/en-* plus *-en* is a circumfix; each affix must occur with the other. However, as *-en* does exist separately from *em-/en-* as a verbal suffix (*sharpen, tighten, sweeten*), *em-/en-* + *-en* may not be a true circumfix.

RPE 5.4

clitic morpheme that is grammatically independent but phonologically dependent on another word.

We add here a note on what are called **clitics**. A clitic is a morpheme that is phonologically dependent on another word but is grammatically independent, so in that way clitics are distinct from regular affixes. They involve at least some phonological reduction, as in the *not* of *do not* becoming /ənt/, written *n't*; the *to* of *want to* becoming /tə/ (and often written *wanna*); the *have* of *could have, would have, should have* becoming /ə/ (and often written *coulda, woulda, shoulda*). Clitics occur in a variety of languages and are the subject of much interesting debate since they are an interesting kind of hybrid between affixes and free morphemes.

Roots

root morpheme morpheme to which an affix can attach

Let's take a look now at the types of morphemes that affixes can attach to. Affixes can attach to words: *-less* can attach to *friend* to derive *friendless*. In this case, the word to which *-less* attaches is a free morpheme, *friend*. We call *friend* in this case a **root**, a morpheme to which an affix attaches. If we attach *-ness* to *friendless*, on the other hand, *-ness* attaches to a word that is made up of two morphemes and is therefore not a single morpheme and thus not a root: *friend* + *less*. Let's take another example. If we attach *un-* to *cool*, the prefix *un-* attaches to a root, *cool*. If we attach *un-* to *forgiveable*, *un-* attaches to a word that is not a root but rather a word made up of three morphemes, *for* + *give* + *able*.

Many of the roots of English words cannot occur alone like *friend* and *cool* can. Instead, they can occur *only* with prefixes or suffixes attached to them. For example, *-ceive* is a **bound root** because it occurs in words like *receive, perceive, deceive,* and *conceive,* in which it is clearly distinct from the *re-, per-, de-,* and *con-,* which all show up in other words, such as *return, permit, denote,* and *convince,* but *-ceive* cannot stand alone as a word. There is no word *ceive,* so we call it a bound root morpheme that must occur with another bound morpheme in order to be a word.

> **bound root morpheme** a non-affix morpheme that cannot stand alone

Morphological rules that regularly combine certain morphemes are called **productive rules.** So attaching *-ion* to verbs (*transmit + ion, communicate + ion, deactivate + ion*) is a *productive* rule of English morphology. Some morphological rules, on the other hand, are *not* productive: indeed, in English some morphological rules apply to create only a single word! To illustrate, consider the words *lukewarm, cranberry, inept,* and *unkempt.* We certainly recognize *warm, berry, in-,* and *un-* as regularly occurring morphemes in English because they occur in many other words (*rewarm/warming, huckleberry/strawberry/blueberry, inoperable/incredible/invincible, unthinkable/unhappy/unsafe*). The morphemes *luke-, cran-, -ept,* and *-kempt,* on the other hand, appear only in *lukewarm, cranberry, inept,* and *unkempt.* We don't use the term *lukecold,* nor do we use *cran-* anywhere other than attached to *berry,* and we don't ever say "He is an inept writer, but she is very ept" or "Her hair looked kempt". So the rules that attach *un-* to *-kempt* or *luke-* to *warm* are not productive; they derive only these words. We will also define morphemes such as *cran-, luke-, -ept,* and *-kempt* as bound roots because they cannot stand alone as free morphemes and because they don't occur as affixes in other English words.

> **productive rule** rule that regularly applies in the formation of new words or forms of words

So, to summarize this section, morphemes can be bound or free, and they can be roots or affixes. Roots can be free morphemes or bound ones, but affixes are always, by definition, bound morphemes. Affixes can attach to words in various ways, as prefixes, suffixes, circumfixes, and infixes. In the following section, we turn our attention to affixation in more detail, discussing another way in which we can distinguish affixes: by dividing them into two different types, with different properties— derivational affixes and inflectional affixes.

ƕæt!

The longest word in English is, purportedly, *pneumonoultramicroscopicsilicovolcanoconiosis,* a disease of the lungs.

RPE 5.5 ⟩

Derivational Affixation

Most of the examples of affixes in English that we have discussed so far have been of **derivational affixes,** affixes that attach to other morphemes to form new words that are separate entries in our mental dictionary, or lexicon. The affix *-able* attaches to verbs, deriving adjectives. The affix *-able* is therefore a derivational affix—an affix that derives a new word, a new dictionary entry.

> **derivational affix** affix that attaches to a morpheme or word to derive a new word

What about *Cranapple*?

You might be thinking that affixation of *cran-* to roots is a productive rule because you are familiar with the word *cranapple* or *crangrape*, advertising names for drinks that contain cranberry juice. Note, however, that this is the *only* place we see *cran-* attached to another morpheme, and one way to analyze this use of *cran-* is not as an affix attached to *apple*, nor even as a bound root, but rather as a *blend*. Blends are words that are combinations of two or more reduced words; a classic example is *smoke + fog = smog*. *Cranapple* can therefore be analyzed as a blend of *cranberry + apple* rather than as evidence that *cran-* affixation is productive, allowing *cran-* to be attached to roots other than *berry*.

Derivational Affixes

verb			adjective
read			readable
like	+ *-able* =		likeable
think			thinkable

The affix *-ity* is another derivational affix. This affix attaches to adjectives to derive nouns, as illustrated in the following examples.

adjective			noun
serene			serenity
divine	+ *-ity* =		divinity
obscene			obscenity

Here are some other common derivational affixes and some of the words derived from them.

verb + *ment* = noun		adjective + *ness* = noun	
excite	excitement	lonely	loneliness
realign	realignment	happy	happiness
deport	deportment	churlish	churlishness
appease	appeasement	bald	baldness

adjective + *ize* = verb		adjective + *ly* = adverb	
regular	regularize	fortunate	fortunately
sensational	sensationalize	possible	possibly
legal	legalize	quick	quickly

In addition to derivational suffixes, English has a number of derivational prefixes, which productively combine with bound or free morphemes to derive new words.

un + happy
dis + enchant
semi + soft

Derivational prefixes and suffixes both derive new words, but the attachment of derivational prefixes usually results in a word of the same category as the word to which the prefix attaches. So, *happy* and *unhappy* are both adjectives; the prefix *un-* doesn't change the category of *happy*. The attachment of derivational suffixes, on the other hand, usually does result in a change in the category of the word; the adjective *happy* becomes the noun *happiness* with the addition of the suffix *-ness*. But notice that even though prefixes don't change the category of a word, they do create words with different meanings. *Happy* and *unhappy* are each listed separately in our mental lexicon (and in the dictionary). So, although prefixes in English do not change the category of a word (they do in many other languages), prefixes are nevertheless derivational affixes, changing the meaning of the words they attach to.

Like derivational suffixes, prefixes in English attach to words or roots of a particular category. For example, *ex-* attaches to nouns to derive nouns. *Ex-* cannot attach to verbs or adjectives:

ex + **noun** = **noun**	*ex* + **verb** = *	*ex* + **adjective** = *
ex-president	*ex-mystify	*ex-modern
ex-friend	*ex-activate	*ex-fixable

Here are a few more examples of prefixes in English and the words they can attach to:

anti + **noun** = **noun**	*de* + **verb** = **verb**	*in* + **adjective** = **adjective**
anti-depressant	de-activate	in-eligible
anti-establishment	de-nude	in-competent

Language Alive!

Word-*orama!*

In Present-Day English, we use *-(o) rama* as an affix (from the Greek root *horama* 'sight', *horan* 'to see'). The earliest example seems to be *pan-orama* (where Greek *pan-* means 'all'), 'a view at a glance', which was coined by painter Robert Barker in 1787. Today, we have words like *diorama*, *striporama*, and *audiorama*. This affix is

Courtesy of Rag-O-Rama

also used to refer to something that is excessive or overdone. In either sense, we use it as a productive morpheme: "They gave you a trailer and all the donuts you wanted. It was a *donutorama*" (*Oxford English Dictionary*). For a Western Washington University student, "This week is *examorama*."

Because of the influence of other languages on English, derivational suffixes and prefixes in English typically fall into three basic etymological classes: Germanic, Latinate (including Latin and its descendants, primarily French), and Greek. Interestingly, although English is a Germanic language, Greek and Latin affixes are used far more productively than Germanic affixes to form new words. In fact, Present-Day English has more words with Latin and Greek roots and affixes than Latin and Greek had themselves! A few examples include _neo-Nazi_, _unibrow_, _pseudostudent_, _retrovirus_, _semisoft_, _autoimmune_, _Beatlemania_, _Ultrabrite_, _minivan_, _ex-boyfriend_, _megastar_, _metrosexual_, and booty_licious_.

RPE 5.6

RPE 5.7

Affixation and Our Mental Lexicon

Though our intuitions as speakers usually serve us well, there is sometimes variation in how words and morphemes may be stored in our lexicons. This variation is due in part to our varying knowledge of the etymologies of English words and our varying vocabularies based on our education and experience. Although most, if not all, speakers of English will recognize -_ed_ as a morpheme in _mommucked_, even if we are not familiar with the word (which means 'to harass or bother' in the English dialect spoken on Ocracoke Island, North Carolina), not all of us break up words the same way. For example, consider the words _panic_ and _pandemonium_. These seem to have a common root meaning something to do with terror or fear. In fact, _panic_ comes from the Greek _panikon_, 'pertaining to Pan', where Pan was a god who inspired fright. _Pandemonium_ was coined in the seventeenth century by John Milton in _Paradise Lost_ as the name of the palace built in the middle of Hell. The word is a blend of Greek _pan-_ 'all' (as in _panorama_) and Greek and Latin _demonium_ 'demon'. Though a Milton scholar might be aware that the _pan-_ in _pandemonium_ is not the same _pan-_ of _panic_, many people might assume they are the same _pan-_, given the meanings of the words.

Let's take a somewhat different example: _obscure_. Would you divide that word into two morphemes, or would you analyze it as monomorphemic? The word comes from _ob-_ 'over' and _scurus_ 'covered', a root that shows up in many Indo-European languages (it is the root of Germanic _sky_ and Latin _scutum_ 'shield'). But to divide this word up, we would expect to find other words with _ob-_ and other words with -_scure_. Can you think of any? If you can't, then for you the word is likely monomorphemic and cannot be broken down into component morphemes.

So although many words are quite easy to break into component morphemes and all speakers of the language would do so easily and in the same way, others are not so straightforward. How you go about breaking words into morphemes depends on your goals in doing so as well. If we are simply trying to recognize the pieces of the word that have meaning, we can research the etymology of the words and break them into the smallest units possible (for example, breaking *obscure* into *ob-* and *-scure*), but psycholinguists also aim to discover how we naturally store free and bound morphemes in our heads, and we likely do not store a bound morpheme such as *-scure*. Research shows that there is evidence that we build words up in our heads according to their meaningful component parts; for example, psycholinguistic experiments indicate that it takes subjects longer to respond to words that are made up of more than one morpheme than to words made up of a single morpheme, even when the words are matched for length and frequency (factors that could affect reaction time). There is in fact evidence that we form words in steps, "building them" beginning with the root and then attaching the prefixes and suffixes. There is even evidence that we attach the prefix and suffix in a particular order, which we'll explore in the next section.

ᚻᚹᚫᛏ!

If you like word games, check out http://crickler.com to find word puzzles for the computer age.

Also, consider words like *cupboard* and *breakfast*. These are each formed historically from two free morphemes: *cup* and *board*, *break* and *fast*. However, most speakers likely store these items as whole chunks. We don't think of *breakfast* as "breaking a fast" nor a cupboard as a board for cups. Even our pronunciation, with both vowels of *breakfast* altered from their pronunciation in the separate words *break* and *fast*, further suggests that the word is likely stored for most people as a single word in its entirety.

Drawing Word Trees

Before we talk about how we can illustrate the ways in which we build words in our mental lexicons, let's review some important information. As we have seen, when examining words made up of only two morphemes, we know two facts about the ways in which the affixes attach to other morphemes.

Affixes attach to certain syntactic categories: *-able* attaches to verbs (but not to nouns or adjectives), but *-ish* attaches to nouns (and some adjectives, but not to verbs):

> *readable, drivable, breakable* but not **greenable* or **catable*
> *girlish, selfish, longish* but not **readish, *breakish*

Affixes can determine the syntactic category of a word: Words that end in *-able* are adjectives, words that end in *-ish* are also adjectives, but words that end in *-ness* are nouns (*happiness, attractiveness, hopelessness*). These two facts are important for determining the steps by which words with more than one affix must be formed. Let's look first at the word *reusable* and what we know about the affixes *re-* and *-able*. The prefix *re-* attaches to verbs and creates new verbs: *reword, redo, retype*. The affix *-able* attaches to verbs and forms adjectives: *washable, stoppable*. Crucially, *re-* does not attach to adjectives: **rehappy, *regreen, *retall*.

We can visually represent the way words are built with *word tree diagrams*. We know that *re-* attaches to verbs, and we can draw *reword, redo,* and *retype* in the following way:

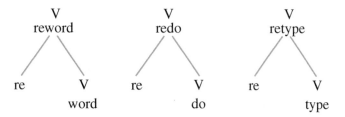

And we can draw *washable* and *stoppable*, too:

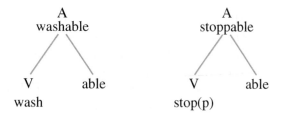

Now, let's consider how to draw a word formed in steps, such as *reusable.* The tree for this word requires different levels of structure if we are to represent how we store this word in our mental lexicon.

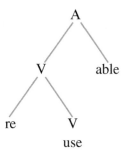

This is the only possible way to build this word; *re-* must attach first to *use* because *re-* attaches only to verbs. The suffix *-able* attaches to the verb *reuse* to form *reusable.* We know that this is the only one possible way to build this word, because *re-* cannot attach to adjectives (**rehappy*), and so we know that *re-* therefore cannot attach to *usable.* Thus, the following tree is not a possible structure that we build in our heads.

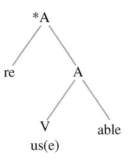

Take another example, the word *disengagement*. Does *-ment* attach to the word *disengage*, or does *dis-* attach to *engagement*? Both *disengage* and *engagement* are words, so how do we decide?

Evidence from other words with the affixes *dis-* and *-ment* can help clarify things. Consider, for example, the category of words that *dis-* attaches to.

dis- + *engage, trust, mount*

These examples suggest that *dis-* attaches to verbs, deriving other verbs. *Engage* is a verb, and that *dis-* attaches to it is exactly what we might expect. For *dis-* to attach to the noun *engagement*, however, violates this pattern. The evidence seems to suggest, then, that *dis-*, a prefix that attaches to verbs and verbal roots, attaches to *engage* rather than to *engagement*. On this logic, *-ment* must attach to *disengage*, a verb. In fact, the evidence supports the hypothesis that *-ment* attaches to verbs.

engage, excite, entrap, enchant, discourage, contain + *-ment*

The evidence from our analysis of *disengagement* suggests that complex words with more than one affix have internal, **hierarchical word structure** that reflects the order in which affixes attach. We illustrate with *disengagement*, supported by the evidence just discussed.

hierarchical word structure property of words whereby one morpheme is contained inside another.

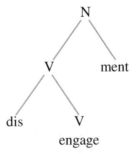

The morpheme *engage* in this example comes from the Latin morphemes *en* meaning 'make' and *gage* meaning 'pledge', so if your goal is to break the word into its smallest meaningful units, one could go this far; however, the word *engage* is an unanalyzable morpheme for most English speakers and so would be stored as such in our lexicons.

RPE 5.8

Word Trees and Ambiguity

One final note on word tree diagrams is that they provide a way to express word ambiguities that would otherwise seem completely mysterious. Consider, for example, the word *unlockable*. This word is ambiguous because of the two possible meanings of *un-*. The two meanings of *unlockable* are explained in (a) and (b).

a. *unlockable* 1: I can't lock the door because it is *unlockable*. = [un [lockable]]

b. *unlockable* 2: I can unlock the door because it is *unlockable*. = [[unlock] able]

We can diagram the meaning of *unlockable* 1 in (a) as follows:

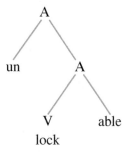

And a diagram of the meaning of *unlockable* 2 in (b) as follows:

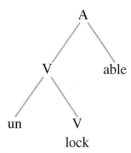

This word is fairly unusual, however, in having two possible meanings and two possible structures, and it is due to the fact that there are actually two distinct *un*s. English has one *un-* that means 'not', and it attaches to adjectives. This is the *un-* that appears in *unlockable* 1. The other *un-* means 'to reverse some action', and it attaches to verbs. This is the *un-* that appears in *unlockable* 2.

RPE 5.9

Inflectional Affixation

We've seen that we attach derivational affixes to words or roots to derive new words. Most derivational suffixes have the effect of changing the syntactic category, or part of speech, of a word. For example, *-ity*, added to

inflectional affix
affix that adds
grammatical
information to an
existing word

an adjective such as *divine*, creates a noun, *divinity*. A different class of affixes, **inflectional affixes**, do not change the category of the word to which they attach, nor do they create new dictionary entries. Rather, these affixes express grammatical information—information about case, tense, aspect, number, person, and so on, rather than changing meaning.

English has what is sometimes called a "poor" or "weak" inflectional system. This means that English has relatively little inflectional morphology compared to languages that have morphologically "rich" systems, systems that morphologically express case, gender, number, tense, and other grammatical relationships in productive ways.

English has only eight inflectional affixes, as shown in Table 5.3. As you can see, only English nouns, verbs, adjectives, and adverbs—all open classes of words—take inflectional affixes. Closed classes of words—prepositions, conjunctions, quantifiers, etc.—take no inflectional affixes in English.

Inflectional affixes always follow derivational ones if both occur in a word, which makes sense if we think of inflections as affixes on fully formed words. For example, the words *antidisestablishmentarianism* and *uncompartmentalize* each contain a number of derivational affixes, and any inflectional affixes must occur at the end: *antidisestablishmentarianisms* and *uncompartmentalized*.

We can also see from Table 5.3 that not only does English have few inflectional affixes but also that possessive, plural, and third-person singular are identical in form; they are all -*s*. The past participle affix -*ed* is also sometimes identical in form to the past tense affix -*ed*. This lack of distinction in form dates back to the Middle English period (1100–1500 CE), when the more complex inflectional affixes found in Old English were slowly dropping out of the language for a variety of reasons, discussed more in Chapter 11.

We might think that the overlap in forms of inflectional affixes would cause confusion and make English harder to learn than languages with unambiguous

Table 5.3	**English Inflectional Affixes**	
Nouns	**Verbs**	**Adjectives**
possessive -*s* Lee**'s** book	3rd person, singular -*s* Lee walk**s**	comparative -*er* Lee is tall**er.**
plural -*s* six book**s**	past tense -*ed* Lee walk**ed**	superlative -*est* Lee is tall**est**
	present participle -*ing* Lee is walk**ing**	
	past participle -*ed/-en* Lee has walk**ed** Lee has eat**en**	

inflectional endings. We might think, for example, that children would confuse verbs with nouns because both can be affixed with -s, but this is not the case. Children appear to have no problem mastering the English inflectional system. They also acquire inflectional affixes and function words in a particular order. For example, psychologist Roger Brown demonstrated that English-speaking children acquire inflectional affixes in the same general order; for example, the present progressive (aux + -ing, as in is running) is acquired before possessive inflections (-'s, as in the dog's ball), which is acquired before regular third-person forms (-s, as in She runs fast) and so on (Brown 1973).

Also, children's acquisition of the plural inflection -s underscores the productivity of this affixation rule in English over other possible plural formation rules. Children typically overgeneralize -s, producing forms such as gooses, deers, and childs, before they master the adult irregular forms geese, deer, and children. The "regular" inflectional rule for plural in English thus appears to be -s affixation, and it is no wonder that new words in the language take this inflection in the plural rather than through a change in the vowel (geese/mice) by some affix other than -s (-en in children or -i in foci), or by nothing at all (deer/elk). We send faxes (not faxi) and e-mails (not e-mailen), and we create blogs (not blog). (We discuss the ways English forms plural nouns in more detail in the section "Inflectional Affixation of English Nouns.")

Other experiments show not only that children can keep the inflectional affixes straight but also that children use information from inflectional affixes as clues to the syntactic category (part of speech) of a word. In an experiment with 3-year-old children (reported in de Villiers & de Villiers 1978), Roger Brown showed how children use grammatical clues to identify the part of speech of an unfamiliar (and in this case nonsense) word. Brown was interested in testing children's knowledge of the grammatical distinctions between count nouns (dogs, chairs), mass nouns (rice, mud), and verbs (kick, eat). He showed the children pictures that illustrated three unknowns: a person using a strange instrument to perform a strange action on a strange substance (for example, a person using a tool to knead a spaghetti-like substance). He explained each picture as follows:

> Here's a picture of a *sib*. (count noun)
> Here's a picture of *sibbing*. (verb)
> Here's a picture of *some sib*. (mass noun)

He then showed the children pictures of each unknown—the tool, the action, the substance—and asked them to point to the picture of a *sib/sibbing/some sib*, and the children were able to consistently pick out the right picture. This suggests that children use grammatical clues to make such determinations, clues that include word order (position of *sib* or *sibbing* in the sentence), morphology (the -ing affix on *sibbing*), and the distinction between *a*, a determiner that precedes only count nouns, and *some*, a quantifier that precedes mass nouns (nouns that don't take a plural -s, such as *furniture* or *jewelry*: some furniture/*furnitures, some jewelry/*some jewelries, some sib/*sibs).

Brown's experiment shows that we rely on morphological and syntactic clues to determine the syntactic category of a word. What about when morphological clues, such as inflectional affixes, aren't there?

In many varieties of English, inflections go unpronounced, but their meanings aren't lost because other clues help us recover them. In African American Vernacular English and Chicano/Hispanic English, for example, inflections can go unpronounced, as in *six bat flew over the barn* or *I read John book*. This "lack" of inflection is not really a lack at all; one way to analyze such constructions is that the inflection is deleted as the result of a regular phonological rule, consonant cluster simplification. Most speakers of English employ a version of this rule in phrases in which a consonant cluster precedes another consonant, such as in *band saw* and *cold cuts*, which are frequently pronounced as *ban saw* and *col cuts*. Utterances such as *six bat flew over the barn* or *I read John book* are stigmatized as "lazy" or "sloppy" English, but in fact the deletions here are the result of a systematic phonological rule. Moreover, consonant cluster simplification rarely results in ambiguity; speakers who employ this in some contexts do not reduce the cluster if doing so would result in ambiguity. For example, speakers would not delete the plural *-s* in *the bats*, because *the bat* would be ambiguous with respect to singular or plural. However, *six bat* is not ambiguous because the numeral already indicates plurality, so that *-s* would be more likely to be deleted.

We'll now take a look at each inflectional affix in English in more detail, beginning with the inflectional affixes that occur on nouns.

RPE 5.10

Inflectional Affixation of English Nouns

Nouns take several kinds of inflectional affix in English. In this section, we will learn about number, case, and gender as they are expressed in English nouns.

Number

number singular, plural, or other (dual) inflection

English nouns productively express **number** (plural or singular) in the form of *-s* (which may be dropped for speakers of dialects that include the consonant cluster reduction rule). As mentioned, new words coming into the language are typically inflected with *-s*, though plural inflection is expressed in a number of other ways in English. These other methods of marking plural come from earlier forms of English or from adopting other languages' (e.g., Latin, Greek) methods of marking plural, as the following words show:

inflectional affix -s: dogs, cats, hallucinations, decisions
Latin plurals: syllabus/syllabi, medium/media, ovum/ova
Old English mutated (vowel) plurals: goose/geese, tooth/teeth, mouse/mice, foot/feet
Old English zero (affix) plurals: deer/deer, sheep/sheep, fish/fish, moose/moose, elk/elk
Old English -*en* plurals: brethren, children, oxen

LINGUISTICS
IN THE NEWS

Arkansas's Apostrophe

Do people really care about punctuation? Well, yes, and some quite vehemently. Since the seventeenth century, when the notion of "correct" English was born, "correct" punctuation has been tied to "correct" behavior, which is in turn linked to education and social class. It matters a great deal to many people whether punctuation rules are followed or "violated."

One of the few remaining morphological case markers in English—the possessive -s affix on noun phrases—became the subject of a surprising amount of media attention, all because it involved a punctuation mark, the apostrophe.

In 2007, Representative Steve Harrelson, a Democratic member of the Arkansas legislature, introduced a resolution to declare, once and for all, the correct way to write the possessive form of the state's name—Arkansas's rather than Arkansas'. Harrelson proposed the resolution as a favor to a friend who felt very strongly about the issue. Expecting this resolution to pass without fanfare, Harrelson was surprised by the strength of the opposition. Apparently, the largest newspaper in Little Rock, the *Arkansas Democrat-Gazette*, fiercely opposed the resolution because it ran counter to the Associated Press's punctuation rules. Suddenly, the proposed resolution was a political hot potato and, although he did not want to alienate the *Gazette*, Harrelson persevered, and his resolution passed unanimously in March 2007. Such resolutions are nonbinding, but clearly this one touched a nerve; the controversy over the Arkansas "Apostrophe Act" was reported on many blogs and also made the national news, appearing in *The Boston Globe* and on FOXNews.

The furor over the apostrophe stems in part from the clash between spoken and written language. For example, in a "normal" possessive noun phrase, -s is affixed to a phrase ending in a consonant and, depending on the consonant, pronounced /z/ or /s/: *the dog's bone, the cat's paw*. When the noun is plural, the -s affix is pronounced the same way: *the dogs' bones, the cats' paws*.

If the possessive noun ends in a sibilant sound, such as /s/ or /z/, most style manuals give two options: *Ross' house* or *Ross's house* and *Roz' house* or *Roz's house*. Both forms are generally accepted (except, apparently, in Arkansas). However, no matter how we punctuate the possessive in writing, most of us pronounce the possessive morpheme /əz/ after a sibilant consonant: *Ross/əz/ house, Roz/əz/ house*.

So, it seems that *Arkansas*, which ends with the letter <s>, should be subject to the same (inconsistent) rule, and hence the debate. Perhaps the whole issue could be resolved if Arkansans based their punctuation on phonology rather than spelling. Arkansas ends in a vowel sound. From that viewpoint, the punctuation is clear; add -'s, as we would for any name ending in a vowel (*Gino's*). What does this mean for *Illinois*? And for *Texas* and *Kansas*? Given the way people feel about apostrophes, who knows?

For more information
Apostrophe Protection Society. http://www.apostrophe.fsnet.co.uk/. (14 January, 2008.)

DeMillo, A. 2007. Arkansas House backs Apostrophe Act. Associated Press. March 6.

Gambrell, J. 2007. Arkansas House to argue over apostrophes. Associated Press. *Boston Globe*, February 27. http://www.boston.com/ printer_friendly_news/ nation/articles/2007/02/27/ arkansas_house_to_argue_over_ apostrophes/

National Public Radio. 2007. Arkansans quibble over the possessive 's.' *All Things Considered*. February 28. http://www.npr.org/tem plates/story/story.php?storyId =7648711

What we now consider the regular way of forming plurals, adding an *-s*, was only one of several ways of pluralizing nouns in older forms of English. Many nouns that have adopted the *-s* pluralization did not start out with it; for example, *eyes* used to be *eyen*, *shoes* used to be *shooen*, *hands* used to be *handen*, and *ears* used to be *earen*. As we'll see in the discussion of the history of English in Chapter 11, plurality also comes to be expressed through **vowel mutation**[2] rather than through affixation. Mutated plurals are now considered irregular because we don't use the process of mutation to form plurals in Present-Day English, but historically mutations followed a predictable pattern. And sometimes words have been added to the "irregular" patterns that didn't originally form their plurals in that way. For example, *moose* is a word borrowed from an Algonquin language and did not exist in Old English; however, by analogy with the other zero plurals, we form its plural in the same way as *deer* or *sheep*. Similarly, some words that end in *-um* or *-us* but are not of Latin origin, such as *cactus* and *octopus*, can have the non-English plural: *cacti* and *octopi*, though the historically "correct" plurals of these are *cactuses* and *octopuses*.

There also exist words in English, called **pluralia tantum** (from Latin, meaning 'plural as such'), that have a plural *-s* but refer to a single object.

scissors, pants, trousers, pliers, (*scissor, *pant, *trouser, *plier)

The fact that these words are morphologically plural but refer to semantically singular objects (with two parts) results in some dialectal variation. Most speakers use *pair* to individuate these words: *a pair of scissors, a pair of pants*; but some speakers can use the singular indefinite article and say *a scissors* or *a pliers*, treating these words simply as singular nouns, regardless of their *-s* ending.

Case

Case can express the **grammatical function** of a noun phrase (the unit of words containing a noun, such as *the student, six dogs*, or *the Queen of England's crown*) as the subject, object, indirect object, or possessor (and some languages mark many other functions by case). In English, noun phrase subjects, objects, and indirect objects are not inflected for case at all.

a. The student bought a car. (nominative/subject)
b. Louise saw the student. (accusative/direct object)
c. Louise gave a book to the student. (dative/indirect object)

The noun phrase *the student* does not change its form, whether the noun phrase is in the subject position, as in (a), or in the direct object position, as in (b). The noun phrase *the student* also does not change its form when it is in the indirect object position, as in (c). In other languages, however, subjects are marked with **nominative case**, and direct objects are marked with **accusative case**. Indirect objects are marked with **dative case**. In German, for example, case inflection shows up on the determiner that precedes

vowel mutation change of inflection through a change in vowel structure rather than through affixation

pluralia tantum refers to a noun that is morphologically plural but semantically singular (*scissors*)

grammatical function function of a phrase in the sentence as subject, direct object, indirect object, and so on

nominative case case typically assigned to subject noun phrases

accusative case case typically assigned to direct object noun phrases

dative case case typically assigned to indirect object noun phrases

---

2. The term *mutation* here has nothing to do with hereditary or genetic change but is used as *Merriam-Webster's* first definition, "a significant and basic alteration."

a noun. In the following example, *der* is nominative, marking the subject; *den* is accusative, marking the direct object; and *dem* is dative, marking the indirect object.

<u>Der</u> Mann gibt	<u>den</u> Knochen	<u>dem</u> Hund
(nom./subj.)	(acc./dir. obj.)	(dat./ind. obj.)
the man gave	the bone	the dog

'The man gave the bone to the dog.'

Because case is so clearly marked in German by the forms of the determiners that precede nouns, there is less dependence on word order to interpret grammatical function. That is, the noun phrases in the preceding German example can be rearranged without any loss in meaning.

<u>Den</u> Knochen gibt	<u>der</u> Mann	<u>dem</u> Hund.
(acc./dir. obj.)	(nom./subj.)	(dat./ind. obj.)
the bone gave	the man	the dog.

'The man gave the bone to the dog.'

RPE   5.11
Word order in English, a language with little case morphology, is therefore more rigid than in languages with richer case morphology, like German.

Did You Know...?

Linguists in Hollywood

The language developed for the hit movie *Avatar*, called Na'vi, was created by linguist-turned-businessman Paul Frommer, Professor Emeritus of Clinical Management Communication, University of Southern California. Frommer developed a syntax for the language modeled on the structure of real languages; Na'vi is a case-marking language, which uses a system much like that found in Basque, Eskimo-Aleut languages, and Panoan languages of South America. The Na'vi language has quite a following, and continues to develop with the help of its "speakers." Become a follower by visiting Frommer's blog about the language http://naviteri.org/, and learn more about the structure of the language at http://www.learnnavi.org/navi-grammar/.

Na'vi was not the first language to be developed for a science fiction film. Klingon, the language used in many *Star Trek* films, was created by linguist Marc Okrand in the 1980s. He has since written two books on Klingon. And noted linguist Victoria Fromkin, who died in 2000, and is perhaps best known for her collection and analysis of slips of the tongue, developed the language Pakuni used by the primate-like creatures on the 1970s TV series *Land of the Lost*. So creating a language spoken by "aliens" is yet another interesting career option for someone with training in linguistics!

Pronouns and genitive case English expresses case distinctions in only two ways: on pronouns and in possessive (**genitive**) noun phrases.

genitive case case typically assigned to possessive noun phrases

Pronouns substitute for full noun phrases and, as you can see next, have different forms.

a. <u>She</u> bought a car.
b. Louise saw <u>her</u>.
c. Louise gave a book to <u>her</u>.

In (a), the subject pronoun *she* is in nominative case, and in (b), the pronoun *her*, a direct object, is in accusative case. There is no distinction between accusative and dative case in English, so direct object pronouns and indirect object pronouns, such as *her* in (c), have the same forms. This nominative/accusative difference is expressed in other pronouns in English, as the following examples illustrate.

Nominative case	Accusative case
<u>He</u> bought a car.	Louise saw <u>him</u>.
<u>They</u> bought a car.	Louise saw <u>them</u>.
<u>We</u> bought a car.	Louise bought a car for <u>us/them/him</u>.

The other way that English expresses case morphology is on possessive noun phrases and pronouns. First, look at how pronouns express possessive, or genitive, case:

<u>My/his/our</u> book
The book is <u>mine/his/ours</u>

RPE 5.12

Table 5.4 shows how English personal pronouns morphologically express case (as well as number and gender).

Genitive case is also marked by the affix *-s* on the noun phrase possessor in phrases such as *the Queen of England's crown*. This case marking shows up as *-'s* in written English.

Louise saw <u>the student's car</u>.

Table 5.4	English Personal Pronouns			
Person	**Number and Gender**	**Nominative**	**Accusative**	**Possessive**
1st	singular	I	me	mine
	plural	we	us	ours
2nd	singular	you	you	yours
	plural	you	you	yours
3rd	singular masculine	he	him	his
	singular feminine	she	her	hers
	singular neuter	it	it	its
	plural	they	them	theirs

Language Alive!

The Battle over *Whom*

Which are you more likely to say?

> Whom did you talk to?
> Who did you talk to?

If you answer *whom*, you probably do so because it is a form that you were taught (by grammar-conscious parents or teachers). But really, you probably rarely, if ever, use *whom* in your conversations.

"Use *who* for subjects and *whom* for objects." This prescriptive grammar rule has a long history beginning in the seventeenth century in England. But in spite of efforts to maintain *whom* as the object pronoun, its usage has been in decline for centuries. (Chaucer, author of the *Canterbury Tales*, which he wrote over a period of years between 1386 and 1400, did not even use it consistently and instead used *who*.) It is interesting to note, however, that while use of *whom* is declining, the use of other object pronouns, such as *me* and *him*, is not.

This is the only case marking that Present-Day English has on noun phrases.

Gender

grammatical gender masculine, feminine, or neuter inflection realized on words that has no relation to biological gender

Many languages distinguish nouns in terms of **grammatical gender**—as masculine, feminine, or neuter. Old English divided nouns in this way; for example, the noun *bāt* 'boat' was masculine, *scip* 'ship' was neuter, and *brycg* 'bridge' was feminine. Despite our inclination to think otherwise, grammatical gender is just that: grammatical rather than biological.

In Germanic languages, such as Old English and German, all nouns are specified as masculine, feminine, or neuter. Function words that introduce these nouns, as well as adjectives that modify the nouns, must also *agree* in inflection (gender, case, and number) with the noun. So, the Old English masculine, nominative, singular noun *bāt* must be introduced by a masculine, nominative, singular function word, namely *se* 'this/that'.

> *se* = masculine, nominative, singular
> *bāt* = masculine, nominative, singular
> *se bāt* = 'this/that boat'

The noun *scip*, on the other hand, is neuter, singular, and nominative, and the form of *this/that* that agrees with the inflection is *þæt*, and the adjective *gōd* must also agree, and so appears as *gōde*. (The runic symbol <þ> has been replaced by <th> in Present-Day English. See Chapter 11 for more discussion of runes.)

þæt scip 'this/that ship'

> *þæt* = neuter, nominative, singular
> *scip* = neuter, nominative, singular

þæt gōde scip 'this/that good ship'

> *gōde* = neuter, nominative, singular

French expresses grammatical gender in a similar way; nouns are either masculine or feminine (there is no neuter gender in French). Determiners and adjectives that modify nouns must agree in gender with the noun; note how the determiners vary (*la* is feminine and *le* is masculine) and also how the adjective for 'white' changes from *blanche* (feminine) to *blanc* (masculine) to agree with the gender of the noun.

la lune	la lune blanche
'the moon'	'the white moon'
le livre	le livre blanc
'the book'	'the white book'

Though *la lune* 'the moon' is feminine in French and masculine in German (*der Mond*), and though *fille* 'girl' is feminine in French, *Mädchen* 'girl' in German is neuter. This is what we might expect, given that grammatical gender is not equivalent to "real-world" notions of gender but is rather a grammatical inflection. This is not to say that words can't express **biological gender**; they most certainly can. English pronouns *he/him* and *she/her* express (masculine and feminine) biological gender, but other pronouns do not. *They/them, we/us, you,* and *it* are unspecified for biological gender. The words *man, woman, filly, bachelor, wife,* and *rooster* are each specified as masculine or feminine, but these specifications have no grammatical effect.

> **biological gender** masculine or feminine inflection that expresses biological gender of the object a word represents (*him/her*)

> RPE 5.13

Inflectional Affixation of English Verbs

The English verb system is surprisingly complex, even though verbs in English take only the following four different inflectional affixes. We will discuss the function of each affix and in doing so provide a overview of the different morphological forms of verbs in English.

third-person singular *-s*
past tense *-ed*
progressive *-ing*
past participle *-ed/-en*

> **infinitive** base form of the verb, in English preceded by *to* (*to walk*)

Infinitives, Present Tense, and Past Tense

The form of the verb that has no inflection at all is the **infinitive**. In English, infinitives can be preceded by *to*, as in *to go, to walk, to eat*. The only form of the verb in the present tense that expresses tense inflection is the third-person singular form, which is affixed by *-s*.

| I/you/they/we | sleep, collapse, run, eat |
| he/she/it | sleeps, collapses, runs, eats |

When we take a look at the past-tense forms of English verbs, things get a bit more complex. Many English verbs form the past tense with the affix *-ed*, as in *walked* or *chased*. Other verbs form the past tense by vowel mutation: by a change in the vowel rather than by adding an affix. Some examples of mutated forms include the past tenses of *run*, *sing*, and *drink*: *ran*, *sang*, and *drank*. Still other verbs form the past tense by both vowel mutation and affixation, as in *sleep/slept, keep/kept, buy/bought*.

We	walked, chased
	ran, drank, sang, ate
	slept, bought, kept

Though mutated forms are often called irregular, they follow regular patterns that you are very familiar with. In fact, you can easily make up mutated forms for past-tense verbs. The mutated past tense of *fling* could be *flang*, or that of *slink* could be *slank* (by analogy with other words: *sing/sang, drink/drank*). We can also make up examples of verbs with both mutated vowels and affixation: *bleek/blekt*.

Verbs that express inflection (such as tense) through vowel mutation alone are called **strong verbs**, and verbs that express inflection only through regular affixation (of *-ed*) or through vowel mutation and some other kind of suffix, such as *-t* (*buy/bought, keep/kept*), are called **weak verbs** (the terms *strong* and *weak* have nothing to do with the typical meanings we associate with these words!). Some of the formerly strong verbs that have became weak in Present-Day English (so they have acquired the "regular" affixation rather than a vowel change) include *bow/bowed, brew/brewed, burn/burned, climb/climbed, help/helped, mourn/mourned, row/rowed, step/stepped, and walk/walked*. The strong past tense form of *climb*, for example, used to be *clumban* in Old English, and that of *step* was *stop*. Look up the etymology of the others in the *Oxford English Dictionary*! And some verbs that used to be strong verbs have strong forms only as adjectives: from *cleave* we have *cloven*, from *melt* we have *molten*, and from *swell* we have *swollen*.

In contrast to English, many languages have far more inflectional affixes for verbs. This complexity is illustrated by the present tense of the Icelandic verb for 'buy' and by the present tense of the Old English verb 'love.' As you can see, both languages have a number of distinct affixes; these express tense, person, and number (singular or plural).

keypti	I buy	kepytum	we buy
keyptir	you (sg.) buy	kepytudh	you (pl.) buy
keypti	he/she buys	kepytu	they buy

strong verb verb that expresses inflection through vowel mutation

weak verb verb that expresses inflection through regular affixation and sometimes vowel mutation

RPE 5.14

lufian, to love

ic luf**ie**	I love
þu luf**ast**	you love
heo luf**aþ**	he/she loves
we luf**iaþ**	we love
ge luf**iaþ**	you love
hie luf**iaþ**	they love

Present and Past Participles

participle form of the verb that follows an auxiliary verb *have* or *be*

The affixes *-ing* and *-en/-ed/-t* occur on English **participles**, the forms of main verbs that occur with auxiliary verbs *have* and *be*.

Julia is <u>talking</u> to George. (talking = present participle)
Julia has <u>talked</u> to George. (talked = past participle)
George has <u>eaten</u> the apple. (eaten = past participle)

Though the auxiliary verb *be is* typically followed by a present participle (*V+ ing*), in the passive voice, the auxiliary *be* is followed by a past participle:

active: George <u>ate</u> the apple.
passive: The apple was <u>eaten</u> by George. (eaten = past participle)

When the past participle is formed with *-ed*, it is identical to the past-tense form. Remember that the difference is that the past participle occurs in construction with a form of *have* (*has, have, had*).

Julia <u>has talked</u> to George. (talked = past participle)
Julia <u>talked</u> to George. (talked = past tense)

As with the past tense, the past participles of some verbs are formed by vowel mutation, and others are formed by both vowel mutation and an affix.

Julia has <u>run</u>, has <u>drunk</u>, has <u>sung</u> . . .
Julia and George have <u>brought</u>, have <u>slept</u>, have <u>crept</u> . . .
George had <u>written</u>, had <u>bitten</u>, had <u>bought</u> . . .

RPE 5.15

Table 5.5 shows the different verb forms we've discussed here.

Table 5.5	Standard English Morphological Verb Forms				
Infinitive	(to) walk	(to) eat	(to) drink	(to) go	(to) bring
Present tense	walks	eats	drinks	goes	brings
Past tense	walked	ate	drank	went	brought
Present participle	walking	eating	drinking	going	bringing
Past participle	walked	eaten	drunk	gone	brought

Participles as markers of social class   When we stigmatize a way of speaking, a particular use of a word or an accent, claiming that certain usage is bad grammar or sloppy English, we are basing our opinions on social attitudes rather than on linguistic facts. Participles are often markers of social class (as reflected in the following quote from Carl Sandburg: *"I never made a mistake in grammar but once in my life and as soon as I done it I seen it'*). We'll see, though, that what we often label bad grammar is really the result of a linguistic pattern that has been around as long as the Old English epic poem *Beowulf*.

Because of the overlap in the past-tense and past-participial forms of many verbs (such as *walked*: *I walked. I have walked*), a common process in English is to extend this pattern to other verbs, even those whose past-participle form is different from the past tense. This pattern of regularization gives rise to two possible past participles, one that is identical to the past tense (following the same pattern as *walk*) and one that is not. For some verbs, neither form is particularly stigmatized for most North American English speakers. Consider these examples of verbs with two past-participle options: *I have sewn* or *I have sewed*, *I have shaven* or *I have shaved*, *I have mown* or *I have mowed*, *I have proven* or *I have proved*. But other verbs that follow exactly the same pattern are considered nonstandard and remain stigmatized: *I have sung* (more standard), *I have sang* (less standard); *I have drunk* (more standard), *I have drank* (less standard).

Yet another way in which past participles are changing and varying is that the past-participial form is used for the past tense. This variation is more highly stigmatized than the others we've discussed so far. *I saw* (more standard), *I seen* (less standard); or *I grew* (more standard), *I grown* (less standard).

The different forms of the past participle sometimes have different social uses. For example, the past participle of *strike* is *stricken* or *struck*, but the former is used primarily as a legal term (which is why *stricken* sounds bizarre in the context of baseball).

> The defendant's statement was stricken from the record.
> The defendant's statement was struck from the record.
> *The first baseman was stricken by the ball.
> The first baseman was struck by the ball.

The same is true of the verb *hang*: The past participial form *hanged* is preserved only in the context of capital punishment but not in everyday use applied, for instance, to hanging a picture.

> The defendant was hanged.
> The defendant was hung.
> *The picture was hanged on the wall.
> The picture was hung on the wall.

And finally, consider the following verb patterns, which illustrate yet another interesting fact about the strong verb system. Some speakers have created a new form of the past participle by affixing *-(e)n*, which is a common way to form a past-participial form, thus distinguishing the past participle from the past tense. *I have bought* (more standard) or *I have boughten* (less standard); *I have put* (more standard) or *I have putten* (less standard); *I have cut* (more standard) or *I have cutten* (less standard). These newly affixed forms are quite common and are becoming standard among many speakers in various parts of the country. (These forms seem more common when a vowel follows, so *I have cutten all the meat* is more likely than *I have cutten the meat*.[3])

All the variation that exists with respect to the past-participial forms of verbs suggests that we are torn right now (unconsciously, of course) about the past participle: either making a distinction where one has been lost (generalizing *-en* as a past-participle affix and attaching it to the past tense form) or letting go of the distinction (using the same form of the verb for the past tense and the past participle). Such examples illustrate well how the language that we usually see as quite fixed and standardized is indeed still changing, and such changes can even come into the standard language.

Suppletive Verbs and Adjectives

suppletion process of change whereby one form of a word has no phonological similarity to a related form of that word

Some verb forms seem to be completely unrelated to the infinitival form of the verb: *go/went*, for example. This is called **suppletion**: one form of the verb has no phonological similarity to another. Usually there is a historical reason for this; the current conjugation of *go/went*, for example, comes from two distinct Old English verbs, *gan* and *wendan* (related to the word *wend: I wended my way home*). It's hardly surprising that children produce *goed* before they learn suppletive *went*.

Suppletion is not confined to verbs; consider the comparative and superlative forms of the adjectives *good* and *bad*. These are also examples of suppletive forms.

good/better/best
bad/worse/worst

As we might expect, children acquire the basic form of the adjective and produce forms such as *gooder* and *goodest*, *badder* and *baddest* until they master the more idiosyncratic *better/best*, *worse/worst*.

And perhaps the most obvious example of suppletion in English is illustrated by the forms of the verb *be*, as you can see in Table 5.6.

The notoriously irregular forms of *be* have an interesting history. *Bēon* was used in the present tense, and the past-tense and present-participle forms derived from a different verb, *wesan*. These two distinct verbs led to the familiar but quite "irregular" pattern we have today. In most languages, the verb that means 'to be' is irregular because it is used so much. That makes it more susceptible to change. Some dialectal variations of *be* are common within other dialects, such as *I be working/they was working/I were working*. We discuss some of these patterns more in later chapters.

RPE 5.16

RPE 5.17

---

3. Thanks to Jason Cuniff for this insight. Subsequent data collection bears this out, at least among speakers in the Pacific Northwest.

Table 5.6	The English Verb *Be*	
Person	**Present**	**Past**
I	am	was
you	are	were
he/she/it	is	was
we	are	were
you	are	were
they	are	were
Past participle	been	
Present participle	being	
Infinitive	(to) be	

Language Alive!

Ain't Ain't Had It Easy!

Did you learn that *ain't* was a bad word and that if you used it, you'd sound uneducated or at least careless in the way you express yourself? Well, there ain't really nothing wrong with *ain't*.

Ain't first appeared in print with this spelling in the late 1700s, though it had been around long before that—at least a century—with the spelling *an't*. It seems to have started as a contraction for *amn't* (am not), but probably because it's awkward to say the two nasals (*m* and *n*), *amn't* was usually reduced to *an't*. Some other common contractions also appeared in the Early Modern English period—Shakespeare uses many—including *don't*, *won't*, and *can't*. And though most of them became quite standard, *ain't/an't* came under attack. In Present-Day English, *ain't* is stigmatized even though linguistically it is formed by the same rule speakers use to form *aren't* and other nonstigmatized contracted auxiliary verbs. Look at the gap that *ain't* fills, allowing contraction of the verb and *not*:

I am not	→	*I ain't*	we are not	→	we aren't
you are not	→	you aren't	you are not	→	you aren't
(s)he/it is not	→	she isn't	they are not	→	they aren't

Ain't can now be used not only with the first-person singular *I* but with other subjects as well. Though it is highly stigmatized, there is nothing linguistically wrong with it; in fact, *ain't* is used by many speakers in certain fixed expressions and to convey a certain rhetorical effect: *It ain't over yet! You ain't seen nothing yet. If it ain't broke, don't fix it.*

Accent on *Field Linguistics*

Farah Nosh/Getty Images

As you've probably figured out by now, in order to study language scientifically linguists rely on data from a wide range of languages and language families. Where does this data come from? And how do researchers gather such data, especially when they don't speak the language in question? What methods does a researcher use to gather data from a speaker who not only speaks a different language but may also come from a vastly different culture?

There are many sources of written, well-studied languages, but what happens when we want to study a language without written records—no audio recordings, grammar books, or dictionaries, and no classes? What if all we have is access to the language's native speakers? How do we go about studying a language "from scratch," and how in the world do we figure out the phonology, morphology, and syntax of a language that no one has ever studied before?

Studying a language "from scratch" is the focus of field linguistics, which is not a theory of language but a methodology (see Munro 2001).

Field linguistics is also called *descriptive* linguistics, the process of describing a language based on work with native speakers. It has long been associated with anthropology, and field linguists are often housed within anthropology departments. Linguists who do such work must not only be experts in language but must also be able to elicit data from speakers without violating cultural rules. They must also be able to determine whether that data is really representative of the speakers' natural language or whether it is shaped by, for example, what native speakers think the researcher wants to hear. This is no small feat! It sometimes takes years to achieve the trust and familiarity with native speakers required to really understand how the language works.

You don't need to travel to exotic places to do field linguistics, though many researchers do. Speakers of indigenous languages are not necessarily confined to inaccessible places, and many languages have yet to be described and analyzed. The photo shows linguists Erma Lawrence and Jordan Lachler in Alaska working to preserve the Haida language.

Computers and the Internet make gathering data and creating databases much easier, which contributes to cataloguing and, one hopes, preserving some of the world's disappearing languages—and in so doing, preserving disappearing cultures.

Field linguistics keeps linguists honest, often recovering data that challenges prevailing assumptions about language. For example, it was long assumed that the most basic orders of languages were SVO (subject, verb, object) and SOV, and that VSO and VOS were not found. But field linguists researching Amazonian languages found much evidence to the contrary, describing languages with both OSV and OVS order, giving rise to a shift in how we look at language typology (see Derbyshire & Pullum 1981 for discussion). Such discoveries shift and challenge conventional wisdom, an essential part of scientific study.

For more information

Anderson, S. 1976. On the notion of subject in ergative languages. In C. Li (ed.), *Subject and topic*, 1–24. New York: Academic Press.

Derbyshire, D. & G. Pullum. 1981. Object initial languages. *International Journal of American Linguistics* 47. 192–214.

Kasaan Haida Heritage Foundation. http://kavilco.com.

Max Planck Institute for Evolutionary Anthropology. Department of Linguistics. Typological tools for field linguistics. http://www.eva.mpg.de/lingua/tools-at-lingboard/tools.php. (15 October, 2008.)

Munro, P. 2001. Field linguistics. In M. Aronoff & J. Rees-Miller (eds.), *The handbook of linguistics*. Malden, MA: Blackwell.

The Society for the Study of the Indigenous Languages of the Americas (SSILA). http://www.ssila.org/. (30 October, 2008.)

Summary

In this chapter, we have explored our complex knowledge of words and how they are made up of one or more morphemes. We have examined different types of morphemes, how they can be bound or free, and how some are roots and some are affixes. We've looked at how words fall into two basic classes, content words and function words. We have closely investigated the internal structure of words and how they are built, particularly through derivational affixation. We have discussed how words express inflection through affixation, vowel mutation, suppletion, and even through their order in the sentence, and we've seen how morphology provides clues about a word's syntactic category as a noun, verb, adjective, and so on. We've seen that although not all of us share the same knowledge of morphology and etymology, we nevertheless all use morphological rules to break words into their component parts, and that each of us has a rich and complex store of words in our mental lexicons. All of these investigations have helped demonstrate the complexity of the morphological system of English as well as the enormous amount of unconscious knowledge we all have about words and their parts.

Sources and Resources

Anderson, S. 1976. On the notion of subject in ergative languages. In C. H. Li (ed.), *Subject and Topic*, 1–24. New York: Academic Press.

Apostrophe Protection Society. http://www.apostrophe.fsnet.co.uk/. (14 January, 2008.)

Ayers, D. 1986. *English words from Latin and Greek elements*, 2nd edn. Revised by T. Worthen. Tucson, AZ: University of Arizona Press.

Bauer, L. 1983. *English word formation*. Cambridge, UK: Cambridge University Press.

Brown, R. 1973. *A first language: The early stages*. Cambridge, MA: Harvard University Press.

DeMillo, A. 2007. Arkansas House backs Apostrophe Act. Associated Press. March 6.

Derbyshire, D. & G. Pullum. 1981. Object initial languages. *International Journal of American Linguistics* 47. 192–214.

Gambrell, J. 2007. Arkansas House to argue over apostrophes. Associated Press. *Boston Globe*, February 27. http://www.boston.com/news/nation/articles/2007/02/27/arkansas_house_to_argue_over_apostrophes/

Gardner, H. 1974. *The shattered mind: The person after brain damage*. New York: Vintage Books.

Harley, H. 2006. *English words: A linguistic introduction*. Malden, MA: Blackwell.

Matthews, P. 1976. *Morphology: An introduction to the theory of word structure*. Cambridge, UK: Cambridge University Press.

Max Planck Institute for Evolutionary Anthropology. Department of Linguistics. Typological tools for field linguistics. http://www.eva.mpg.de/lingua/tools-at-lingboard/tools.php. (15 October, 2008.)

Munro, P. 2001. Field linguistics. In M. Aronoff & J. Rees-Miller (eds.), *The handbook of linguistics*. Malden, MA: Blackwell.

National Public Radio. 2007. Arkansans quibble over the possessive 's.' *All Things Considered*. February 28. http://www.npr.org/templates/story/story.php?storyId=7648711

Oxford English Dictionary. "Orama." http://www.oed.com/. (20 October, 2008.)

The Society for the Study of the Indigenous Languages of the Americas (SSILA). http://www.ssila.org/. (30 October, 2008.)

Tolkien, J. R. R. 1999. *The fellowship of the ring*. Boston, MA: Houghton Mifflin.

Villiers, J. de & P. de Villiers. 1978. *Language acquisition*. Cambridge, MA: Harvard University Press.

Review, Practice, and Explore

RPE 5.1 ▷ OK, Break It Up!

Divide the following words into morphemes. If there are any you are not sure about—that you believe could be divided in more than one way—describe what is problematic and discuss any other issues that arise.

treehouses	equipment	massage
cabinets	freakishness	communism
shipment	turnip	nevertheless
gracious	begs	heated

Are any of these words monomorphemic? Give an example of how one of these words illustrates the difference between morphemes and syllables.

RPE 5.2 ▷ Finding Function Words

Find at least six (different) function words in the following text excerpt. Label each word's syntactic category. Also list and label at least six different content words. What kind of information is lost when function words are omitted?

> Bilbo was very rich and very peculiar, and had been the wonder of the Shire for sixty years, ever since his remarkable disappearance and unexpected

return. The riches he had brought back from his travels had now become a local legend, and it was popularly believed, whatever the old folk might say, that the Hill at Bag End was full of tunnels stuffed with treasure. (from *The Fellowship of the Ring* by J. R. R. Tolkien)

RPE 5.3 > What's Missing?

Find an example of a text that omits function words (the classified advertising section of any newspaper is a good place to look, and newspaper and magazine headlines provide good examples). Identify the syntactic category of each content word in your example, and list the function words that are missing. What effect does the lack of function words have on your understanding of the piece overall?

RPE 5.4 > Free and Bound Morphemes

Divide the following words into morphemes. Which morphemes are affixes? Which morphemes are free morphemes, and which are bound?

> legalize   prescription   distaste   sportsmanship   serenity   ridden   misinformation

RPE 5.5 > A Wieldy Task

Analyze the morphology of the following text excerpt, in which the author plays with morphological rules for comic effect. Using the terminology and concepts discussed in the chapter, explain each example of wordplay as explicitly as you can. Do you find any "cranberry" (bound root) morphemes?

> It had been a rough day, so when I walked into the party I was very chalant, despite my efforts to appear gruntled and consolate. I was furling my wieldy umbrella for the coat check when I saw her standing alone in a corner. She was a descript person, a woman in a state of total array. Her hair was kempt, her clothing shevelled, and she moved in a gainly way. I wanted desperately to meet her, but I knew I'd have to make bones about it since I was travelling cognito. Beknownst to me, the hostess, whom I could see both hide and hair of, was very proper, so it would be skin off my nose if anything bad happened. And even though I had only swerving loyalty to her, my manners couldn't be peccable. Only toward and heard-of behavior would do. (from "How I Met My Wife" by Jack Winter, *The New Yorker*, July 25, 1994.)

RPE 5.6 > Derivational Affixation

See if you can come up with at least two other words for each of the following suffixes. Label the syntactic category of the words or roots to which each suffix attaches, and label the category of the word created by affixation. (Ignore spelling differences—they don't affect the outcome.) Here's an example:

Word	Root/Word	+ Suffix	= Word
serenity:	serene	+ ity	= serenity
	adjective	+ ity	= noun

Do the same for the following; find words to which the following affixes are attached, and determine how affixation changes the syntactic category (the part of speech) of the word:

-ence/-ance (as in *avoidance*)
-en (as in *weaken*)
-ify (as in *simplify*)
-ness (as in *senseless*)

RPE 5.7 > It's Greek (or Latin?) to Me!

Recall that many words in English have Greek and Latin roots and affixes and that we use these parts of words productively to form new words. For example, the prefix *neo-* 'new' can be affixed to *conservative* to derive *neoconservative*. Some words with Latin and Greek affixes are the following:

Latinate suffixes
excite-ment, pens-ive, ecst-atic, appear-ance, peer-age, pleas-ure, leg-al, real-ize, read-able, seren-ity

Latinate prefixes
co-edit, de-frost, dis-belief, inter-national, non-skid, post-mortem, pre-cede, re-build, trans-mit, audio-phile, bi-lateral, circum-navigate

Greek suffixes
neur-algia, morpho-logy, micro-scope, colos-tomy, an-emia, the-ism, conform-ist, di-graph, kilo-gram, pan-demic, homo-phobe, franco-phone, kilo-meter, aero-gram

Greek prefixes
a-moral, anti-war, auto-mobile, bio-sphere, geo-graphy, hyper-ventilate, mono-chrome, neo-logism, thermo-meter, macro-biotic, acro-bat, techno-crat

A. Using these examples as well as a good dictionary, list at least five words (not on this list) currently used in English that have Greek or Latin affixes. Choose examples of words that are probably recent additions to the language (like *neoconservative*).

B. Create five words using Latin and Greek morphemes. Give each word a meaning consistent with its affix (if you choose *neo-*, for example, your words would include the meaning 'new', as in *neolingologist*).

RPE 5.8 > Word Trees

A. Draw trees for the following words, indicating the category of word at the top of the tree.

friendship   quickly   grievance   copilot

B. Now draw these more difficult word trees, showing the order in which each morpheme attaches.

reorganization   understatement   degradable   nonbeliever   deployment

RPE 5.9 > Word Trees and Meaning

A. *Remarkable* is ambiguous, meaning either 'notable' or 'able to be marked on again'. (One meaning is more common, but the other is possible nonetheless.) Draw tree structures illustrating these two meanings.

B. *Inflammable* is a word that has come to have two opposite meanings. The traditional meaning is 'able to catch on fire easily', while the more recent meaning is 'not flammable'. Draw tree diagrams that show the two possible meanings, and provide a brief discussion of what you have illustrated.

C. Draw the two word trees that represent the two distinct meanings of the noun phrase *toy car crusher*. Label each with an appropriate paraphrase of the meaning.

RPE 5.10 > Derivation or Inflection?

Label the following prefixes and suffixes as derivational or inflectional.

autumn*al*	gest*ation*	automa*ted*	fast*er*	fasten*er*
freak*s*	*de*compose	skipp*ing*	*non*compliant	

RPE 5.11 > Derivation and Inflection in Latin

Does the following data from Latin with rough English translations show that Latin marks case and number on its nouns? Are these examples of inflection or derivation?

vir	*man*	vir-i	*men*
vir-i	*of man*	vir-orum	*of men*
vir-o	*to man*	vis-is	*to men*

RPE 5.12 > Mine, Yours, and Thine

Possessive pronouns—*mine, yours*—vary among dialects of English and have been in flux for hundreds of years. The standard pattern is given in (a).

a.

mine	ours
yours	yours
his/hers/its	theirs

Some dialects, especially in Appalachian English and some Southern dialects, have the following pattern.

b.

mine	ourn
yourn	yourn
hisn/hern/its	theirn

Describe the pattern that the pronouns take in this dialect and why. Also consider the archaic form *thine*. Where does it fit into the paradigm?

RPE 5.13 > Masculine, Feminine, Neuter?

Conduct some research on Spanish, Welsh, Arabic, Tuvalu, and Russian, all of which mark grammatical gender in some ways. Show examples of gender marking in each language, and briefly explain how gender is indicated and how it contrasts among the different forms (masculine, feminine, and/or neuter).

RPE 5.14 > Where Have All the Strong Verbs Gone?

The following list of words used to be strong verbs and are now weak verbs. Look them up in the *Oxford English Dictionary* or another good etymological dictionary and give the older, strong form of each verb. Do any of these verbs have different forms in different dialects? Are strong forms maintained?

bow, brew, burn, climb, help, mourn, row, step, walk

RPE 5.15 > Been There. Done That.

A. Table 5.5 shows the five forms of an English verb. Using that table as a guide, label the form of each boldface verb in the following sentences. Another helpful resource is Table 5.6, which lists the different forms of the verb *be*.

1. Ferdinand has been **eating** dandelions.
2. Bees **are** buzzing around the flowers.
3. Have you **seen** the movie?
4. Lee **loves** chocolate.
5. I **want** to go home.
6. She hopes **to see** the movie tomorrow.
7. Elisabeth **lives** in Chicago.
8. They **have** been planning a trip.
9. Joseph **had** a dog named Bones.
10. Ferdinand has **been** stung by a bee.

B. Construct seven sentences that include (at least) one verb in the form specified for each sentence. Label the verb forms.

1. infinitive
2. past participle
3. present participle
4. past tense
5. present tense
6. present tense, past participle
7. past tense, present participle

RPE 5.16 > *Be* in Other Languages

Look up the word for *be* in at least two languages, and provide the verb's complete present-tense conjugation—all the forms of the verb for each person and number. Do these forms follow a regular pattern, or are they irregular compared to the way that other verbs are conjugated in the language? If they are irregular, discuss why you think this might be.

RPE 5.17 > *Be* in Spanish

If you have studied or are a speaker of Spanish, you are aware that there are two forms of the verb *be* in Spanish – and if you are not a speaker of Spanish, you can learn about these two verbs now! In Spanish, a different verb is used to express *to be* depending on whether the speaker is addressing a condition or an essential quality, illustrated, for example, as follows.

> La manzana *está* verde. 'The apple is green.' (condition)
> La manzana *es* verde. 'The apple is green.' (quality)

Come up with some other examples which use a form of *be* in English, and determine which verb would be used in Spanish. You should consult a speaker of Spanish or conduct some research to validate your answers.

Chapter at a Glance

Morphological Typology
    Synthetic Languages
    Analytic Languages
    Mixed Typological Systems
The Morphology of Other Languages
Word Formation Processes
    Slang versus New Words
    Recent New Words
    Coining
    Compounding
    Eponyms
    Retronyms
    Blends
    Conversions
    Acronyms
    Clipping
    Backformation
    Reduplication
Summary
Sources and Resources
Review, Practice, and Explore

Morphological Typology and Word Formation

Key Concepts

- Languages can be classified by morphological type as analytic or synthetic or on a continuum somewhere between these two types.
- English is mostly analytic but has some synthetic properties.
- We create new English words in a wide variety of ways.
- Through word formation processes, we are able to continually and creatively add words and alter the meanings and structures of existing ones.
- Word formation processes clearly illustrate our enormous capacity for creativity in language and that language is a dynamic, ever-changing system.

Did You Know . . . ?

>   Solid Roundish Objects and Mushy Matter
>   The Truth about *Truthiness*

Language Alive!   Blimey!
                     Ms.

Linguistics in the News   F***ing Brilliant! FCC Rulings on Profanity

Accent on   Lexicographers

> *Damn words; they're just the pots and pans of life, the pails and scrub brushes.*
>
> —EDITH WHARTON, 1932

In this chapter, we look at the inflectional morphology of other languages and show how languages fall into morphological classes, or typologies, with respect to the patterns of their affixes and word order. Although languages vary quite a bit in the way they express grammatical information, we find that some general properties of grammatical structure are at work in all languages, which provides further evidence for Universal Grammar.

We then turn to how we form words in ways other than affixation, through a variety of processes that give us such words as *blog, NASA, flip-flopper, schnoodle,* and *popemobile.* Languages have wonderful, built-in ways of creating new words. We make new words when we have a new concept, thing, or action that needs a label, when we give a new name to an existing thing (for political, social, ironic, or comic reasons), or when we just play with the language. To create words, regardless of why we do so, we exhibit our unconscious knowledge of the inner workings of our language. We know how to manipulate morphemes because we all have a great deal of knowledge of the meaningful units of our various languages.

Morphological Typology

We have already seen some of the ways morphological systems differ across languages. For example, in English we indicate that something will happen in the future by a modal verb and the infinitival form of the verb:

> I speak. I will speak.
>   (modal) (infinitive)

Spanish indicates the future by modifying the inflectional affixes within the verb.

> Habl<u>o</u>   I speak.
> Habl<u>aré</u>   I will speak.

In this section, we examine some of the various ways languages combine morphemes and how languages fall into **morphological typologies** based on their common morphological structures. We detail these language types and consider some examples of each.

We have seen that English uses a variety of morphological strategies to express grammatical tense, aspect, plurality, possession, comparative and

morphological typology classification of languages according to common morphological structures

superlative degrees, and other relationships. To express these relationships, English uses inflectional affixation (*cats, freezing, biggest*), as well as vowel mutation (*foot/feet, run/ran*) and suppletion (*go/went, good/better*), to show inflection on verbs, nouns, and adjectives. We have also seen that, relatively speaking, English expresses far fewer such grammatical relationships than many other languages do. For instance, as we learned in the previous chapter, pronouns in English express some case relationships, but other nouns do not express case morphologically except in the genitive, or possessive, case (*manatee's flipper*). Rather, English relies on word order to express case relationships (e.g., subject, direct object, and indirect object) and grammatical functions. English thus has what we call a mixed system: some grammatical relationships are expressed morphologically and some by word order.

Languages that express grammatical relationships morphologically are called **synthetic languages**. These languages' words are more complex, made up of content root morphemes with one or more affixes. Most European languages are synthetic and have both prefixes and suffixes. English, though it has some synthetic features, is more of an **analytic language**. In analytic languages, words tend to consist of free morphemes with very few affixes. We learn more about these two language types in the following sections.

Synthetic Languages

Synthetic languages form words by affixing morphemes to a root morpheme. Word order is less important in these languages because the affixes, rather than the position of the words in the sentence, indicate grammatical relationships.

Synthetic languages are typically further broken down into two subtypes: *agglutinative* and *fusional*. **Agglutinative languages** can have several morphemes that attach to a root morpheme, and each morpheme has only one meaning that is clearly distinct. Some agglutinative languages are Turkish, Swahili, Salish languages, Nahuatl, and Japanese, among many others. Here are examples of a Lushootseed (Salish) sentence and one from Swahili. Notice the many morphemes within the verb and that each has a unique meaning (illustrated by the hyphens separating the distinct morphemes):

sqʷ əbayʔ	tiʔəʔ	sugʷ əčəb
sqʷ əbayʔ	tiʔəʔ	s-u-gʷ əč- əb
dog	determiner	NOUN PREFIX-PUNCTUAL-look for-MIDDLE-3rd person object

'The one he is looking for is the dog.' (Hess, personal communication)

Hawàtasóma kitabu	
Ha-wà-ta-sóma	kitabu
negative-3rd person plural-FUTURE-read	book

'They will not read the book.'

synthetic language language in which syntactic relations are expressed by inflectional morphemes rather than by word order

analytic language language in which syntactic relations are expressed primarily by word order rather than by inflectional morphemes attached to words

agglutinative language language whose words have several morphemes that attach to a root morpheme, and each morpheme has only one distinct meaning

ʰwæɐc!

With more than 100,000 native speakers, Navajo has more speakers than any other Native North American language. This number has actually increased with time as language revitalization programs have gone into effect.

Another interesting fact about Swahili is that all noun roots are bound morphemes, so in the preceding example the root *-tabu* 'book' cannot stand alone and must have a prefix that marks the word class it belongs to. There is one prefix for trees, plants, and nature; another for names of humans; another for names of animals, and so on. (There are about thirteen classes.)

Another example of agglutinative languages are the Athabaskan languages spoken from Alaska through western Canada and all the way down to the American Southwest (thus including Navajo); they have about twenty different affixes that can attach to the verb root and that indicate grammatical functions and relationships (e.g., subject, object, and indirect object) or other grammatical information (e.g., tense, aspectual categories, and negation). (We discuss noun classes again in Chapter 10, on semantics.) Here is a sentence from the southern Alaskan language Ahtna, also called Tanaina:

Ts'anhdghulayał hyegh nuqulnix htsast'a.

Ts'anhdghulayał	qey-egh	nu-qe-ghe-l-nix	qe-tsas-t'a
name	him-about	ITERATIVE-it-PREFIX-CLASSIFIER-tell.stories	it-about-be

'A long time ago they used to tell stories about Ts'anhdghulayał.'

(Mithun 1999: 366)

It is not important for our purposes here that you know all of the terms used to describe the prefixes but rather that you see that the morphological system is quite complex, with most words containing many meaningful parts.

Such highly agglutinative languages, languages with a high number of morphemes per word, are also called **polysynthetic languages**. In addition to the Athabaskan languages, many other native North American languages are polysynthetic languages, as are many Australian languages. Here is another example, this one a single word from Yup'ik, a member of the Eskimo-Aleut language family, whose many languages are spoken in Siberia, Greenland, Alaska, and northeastern Canada.

polysynthetic language language with a high number of morphemes per word

kaipiallrulliniuk

kaig-piar-llru-llini-u-k

be.hungry-really-PAST-apparently-INDICATIVE-they.two

'The two of them were apparently really hungry.'

(Mithun 1999: 38)

When we see a language that forms its words this way, the question once again arises, What is a word, and how can we distinguish a word from a sentence in such languages? Since this single word in Yup'ik conveys the same information that would be expressed in a whole sentence in English, how do we know that this is, in fact, a word in Yup'ik? Our intuitions tell us a lot about whether something is a word in our own language, so native speaker judgments are the best way to determine whether clusters of morphemes are recognized as single words. This is true also in languages that are not written; speakers or signers of the language have intuitions about what constitutes a word, and the concept of *word* does seem to be psychologically real. Although speakers and signers do not pause between words, they can do so, indicating their awareness of word boundaries. This same awareness holds in polysynthetic languages in which the words are quite morphologically complex. Mithun (1999) points out, too, that speakers are not typically consciously aware of the meanings of individual morphemes within words but do know the meanings of the whole words, again giving evidence for the concept *word* (p. 38). And in many languages, stress patterns correlate with the concept of *word*; there is only one primary stress per word.

Consider that we recognize a word like *unconstitutionality* in English as a single word, even though we can divide it into its meaningful parts. None of those other bound morphemes can stand alone; thus, the word is a single word made up of several meaningful morphemes:

un-constitu-tion-al-ity

(And maybe *con-* is an affix, too? It appears in words such as *constrain* and *conserve,* where it comes from the Latin prefix *com-* 'together'. And it occurs in words such as *consternation,* where *con-* is a Latinate "intensive prefix.")

fusional language language in which morphemes have more than one meaning fused into a single affix

Agglutinative languages contrast with **fusional languages**, in which the morphemes attached to the root may fuse more than one meaning into a single affix. Some fusional languages are Spanish, German, Russian, and Semitic languages such as Hebrew, among others. Consider from this German example how a determiner alone can carry much distinct meaning:

der Hund 'the dog'
der = definite masculine nominative singular
Hund = dog singular

And here's another example from Russian, showing the various forms of the root *stol-*, meaning 'table'. In English, of course, the forms are the same, except for the genitive, to which *-'s* is added.

	Singular	**Plural**	**English examples of cases**
Nominative	stol	stol-y	The <u>table</u> is wooden ('table' is the subject)
Accusative	stol	stol-y	She saw <u>the table</u> ('table' is the direct object)
Genitive	stol-a	stol-ov	The <u>table's</u> legs ('table' is a possessive)
Dative	stol-u	stol-am	She gave <u>the table</u> new paint. ('table' is the indirect oject)

The *-a* on *stola* indicates both singular and genitive. Similarly, the *-am* on *stolam* means dative and plural.

Did You Know...?

Solid Roundish Objects and Mushy Matter

In Navajo, distinct verb stems classify an object by its shape or other physical characteristics and also describe the movement or state of the object. The eleven "handling" verb stems are the following:

Classifier + Stem	Explanation	Examples
-'á	solid roundish object	bottle, ball, boot, box
-yí	load, pack, burden	backpack, bundle, sack, saddle
-jool	noncompact matter	bunch of hair or grass, cloud, fog
-lá	slender flexible object	rope, mittens, socks, pile of fried onions
-tį'	slender stiff object	arrow, bracelet, skillet, saw
-tsooz	flat flexible object	blanket, coat, sack of groceries
-tłéé'	mushy matter	ice cream, mud, slumped-over drunk person
-nil	plural objects 1	eggs, balls, animals, coins
-jaa'	plural objects 2	marbles, seeds, sugar, bugs
-ká	open container	glass of milk, spoonful of food, handful of flour
-t'į	animate object	microbe, person, corpse, doll

(Young 2000: 3–7)

So, for example, Navajo does not have a single verb that corresponds to an English word like *give*. To say the equivalent of "Give me some hay," the Navajo verb *nítjool* (noncompact matter) must be used; for "Give me a cigarette," the verb *nítįįh* (slender stiff object) must be used. The English verb *give* is expressed by eleven verbs in Navajo, depending on the characteristics of the object. In addition to defining the physical properties of the object, Navajo verb stems can distinguish the manner of the object's movement. There are three manners of movement, described as *handling*, which include actions like carrying, lowering, and taking; *propelling*, which includes tossing, throwing, and dropping; and *free flight*, which includes falling and flying through space. For example, using a solid-roundish-object stem, the -'á affix means 'to handle (a round object)', -ne' means 'to throw (a round object)', and -ts'id means '(a round object) moves independently', as these words and their translations illustrate:

tsits'aa'náá'á	'I lowered the box down'
tsits'aa'náátne'	'I tossed the box down'
tsits'aa'náálts'id	'the box fell'

(Young 2000: 2)

For more information
Young, R. 2000. *The Navajo verb system: An overview*. Albuquerque: University of New Mexico Press.

Analytic Languages

In an analytic language, grammatical information is conveyed by word order and particles rather than by inflectional morphemes. In the analytic language—Vietnamese, for example—the form of the verb is the same regardless of the subject of the verb, and no tense or other agreement marking is expressed on the verb. Consider the verb *ăn*, meaning 'eat' in the following paradigm:

tôi ăn	I eat	chúng tôi ăn	we eat
anh ăn	you eat	các anh ăn	you (pl.) eat
anh â'y ăn	he eats	ho ăn	they eat
chi â'y ăn	she eats		
nó ăn	it eats		

As you can see, the verb *ăn* always has the same form.

As analytic languages have very few derivational or inflectional affixes, they often form words by combining free morphemes into compound words:

life
guard
lifeguard
lifeguard chair
lifeguard chair tan (you know, a tan someone might get sitting on a lifeguard chair)

Chinese, a largely analytic language, also has a great many compounds. (Although Chinese is a tone language, as discussed in Chapter 3, the tones are not indicated on the words shown here.)

dit ban
grand board
'floor'

lu kou
road mouth
'intersection'

And this one is a bit more metaphorical:

ming bai
bright white
'to understand'

RPE 6.1

Mixed Typological Systems

Although some languages fall into a clearly analytic or clearly synthetic system, many, like English, are mixed systems. Let's look first at the ways in which English is synthetic. English expresses plurality by the morpheme *-s* and past tense by the morpheme *-ed* and is thus synthetic in this regard. Vowel mutation used to express tense or aspect, as in English strong verbs, is also a property of synthetic languages. English relies on word order rather than morphology, however, to express future tense. In English, this tense is formed by the addition of *will, going to,* or sometimes *shall* to the verb phrase (*will visit, going to visit, shall visit*). To express negation, the morpheme *not* is added to the sentence, changing the positive sentence *The student is learning Old English* into the negated version, *The student is **not** learning Old English.* Future tense and negation are both examples of how grammatical relationships can be expressed by separate words and word order rather than morphologically on the verb, as it is in many synthetic languages. In this way, English is an analytic language.

Prepositions are words that express a grammatical relationship (of location, direction, etc.) that applies to a noun. A language with prepositions as separate words, such as English, is analytic in this regard. In many languages, however, prepositions show up as inflections on nouns, so they are not separate words but affixes. Old English had both types: prepositions as separate words and prepositions that were attached to other words; therefore, Old English had both analytic and synthetic properties.

Synthetic preposition
þæt entas woldon <u>aræran</u> ane burh
that giants would <u>up-raise</u> a city
'that giants would raise up a city'

(Anglo-Saxon Chronicle 22.318.14)

Analytic preposition
þæs cyninges þegnas þe <u>him beæftan</u> wærun
the kings thegns who <u>him behind</u> were
'the king's thegns (servants) who were <u>behind him</u>'

(Cynewulf and Cyneheard)

Incidentally, in Old English, prepositions usually preceded their objects when the object was a noun, but they usually followed the object when the object was a pronoun, as shown in the preceding example.

The history of the English language offers an excellent illustration of a shift from a highly synthetic language, Old English, to a largely analytic one, Present-Day English. As you can see by the examples in the previous chapter that illustrate the inflectional morphology of nouns, verbs, and adjectives in Old English, the language was primarily synthetic, even though it had certain analytic relationships as well (as illustrated by the mixed use of prepositions as separate words and as inflections). These inflectional affixes largely disappeared in the Middle English period (1100–1400 CE), and nouns, verbs, and adjectives became, in general, largely uninflected. The shift from a synthetic to an analytic language had the consequence of triggering a shift in word order; in Old English, word order was much freer (though not entirely without constraints), but in Middle English, word order became fairly rigid, as Subject–Verb–Object. Word order became crucial in order to interpret grammatical relationships that had been indicated by inflectional morphology.

Many other languages also exhibit mixed morphological systems. Though Chinese is usually given as an example of an analytic language, it does have some bound morphemes. And Japanese has a high degree of inflectional marking on verbs, so it is synthetic in that respect, but it has almost no affixes on nouns, so it is analytic in that respect.

RPE   6.2 >

The Morphology of Other Languages

Through a method of comparing and contrasting, you can discover a great deal about the morphology of languages you are not familiar with. Data organized in this way is called a *paradigm*. Paradigms are useful in working out the morphology of a language; they let you compare words that have different inflections so you can tell what the root is and what the affixes are. Consider the following data from Spanish:

amigo	'male friend'	perro	'male dog'
amiga	'female friend'	perra	'female dog'
amigos	'male friends'	perros	'male dogs'
amigas	'female friends'	perras	'female dogs'

From this data, you can see that the root *amig-* appears every time we have 'friend' in the translation, and the root *perr-* appears every time we have 'dog' in the translation. Thus, *amig-* and *perr-* must mean 'friend' and 'dog', respectively. Also, the suffix *-o* appears every time we have 'male' in the English translation, and *-a* appears when we have 'female'. Thus, *-o* and *-a* must mean masculine and feminine gender, respectively.

And consider the following words from Classical Greek and their English translations. (Recall that : after a vowel indicates a long vowel.)

grapho:	'I write'	uo:	'I lose'
grapheis	'you (sg.) write'	ueis	'you (sg.) lose'
graphei	'he/she/it writes'	uei	'he/she/it loses'
grapho:men	'we write'	uo:men	'we lose'
graphe:te	'you (pl.) write'	ue:te	'you (pl.) lose'
graphousi	'they write'	uousi	'they lose'

RPE   6.3 >

RPE   6.4 >

By simply comparing and contrasting, you can determine the roots of the Classical Greek verbs 'write' and 'lose' and the morphemes that correspond to the various pronominal agreement forms.

Word Formation Processes

The previous sections show some of the ways in which other languages build words. And in the previous chapter, we saw some of the many ways in which we create new words in English through derivational affixation. Derivational affixation is not our only option for creating new words, however. In these next sections, we will discuss a number of additional ways in which new words are formed and in which existing words take on new meanings.

We don't have to look very far to find examples of new words coming into the language—as completely new words, as old words that had fallen out of use and come back into the language, or as new words created from parts of existing words. New words come into languages all the time. Most will stick around, and others will cease to be used because they are no longer necessary (due to an obsolete item or a passing fad). Some remain slang, their use restricted to a particular group.

Slang versus New Words

slang an informal word or expression that has not gained complete acceptability and is used by a particular group

Let's explore the concept of slang in a bit more depth. **Slang** words or phrases are typically very informal, and they are usually restricted to a particular group—typically teens and young adults—as a marker of in-group status. Most are not new words but existing words that have acquired new meanings for some group. Slang is also characterized by having a fairly short life; most slang words do not last more than a generation. And those that do stick around soon cease to be slang; some former slang words include *dwindle, mob, hubbub,* and *rowdy.* There are a few exceptions: words that still are informal and colorful but are used by multiple groups and generations. *Cool* is one. Can you think of other words that still seem to be slang but are used by, say, you and your parents and maybe even your grandparents? While particular slang terms are sometimes viewed unfavorably by those who do not use them, slang is a feature of most languages and is an indicator of the ways in which language adapts for the purposes of those who use it. As Gilbert Keith Chesterton wrote way back in 1902, "The one stream of poetry which is continually flowing is slang."

jargon specialized vocabulary associated with a trade or profession, sport, game, etc.

Slang can be distinguished from **jargon**. Jargon is also words or phrases used by a particular group, but jargon is not as informal; rather, it is associated with particular professions, trades, sports, occupations, games, and so on. We have used lots of linguistics jargon in this book so far: *phoneme, diphthong, allophone, morpheme, bilabial.* Snowboarders have their own jargon: *air, carving, fakie, grind, jibbing, half-pipe.* (Look 'em up or ask a boarder!)

dialect variety of a language that has unique phonetics, phonology, morphology, syntax, and vocabulary

Slang is not the same as a **dialect**. Dialects have their own unique phonetics, phonology, morphology, syntax, and vocabulary. The same slang terms may be shared across dialects, and dialects are not short-lived like slang terms.

register manner of speaking that depends on audience (e.g., formal versus informal)

Slang should also not be confused with style or **register**. We all have different ways of speaking formally and informally, though these styles can vary a great deal across speech groups. We shift registers easily and unconsciously from a job interview to a conversation with close friends, using different vocabulary, more or less prescriptively correct forms, and even different intonation.

F***ing Brilliant! FCC Rulings on Profanity

What exactly is profanity? What do we mean when we call something profane, indecent, or obscene? The Federal Communications Commission (FCC), a U.S. government agency established by the Communications Act of 1934, is charged with regulating interstate and international communications by radio, television, wire, satellite, and cable, including material that is "obscene," "indecent," or "profane." Recent court cases demonstrate that determining what constitutes obscenity and profanity is not an easy matter.

The FCC website provides the following information: "Obscene speech is not protected by the First Amendment and broadcasters are prohibited, by statute and regulation, from airing obscene programming at any time. According to the U.S. Supreme Court, to be obscene, material must meet a three-prong test: (1) an average person, applying contemporary community standards, must find that the material, as a whole, appeals to the prurient interest (i.e., material having a tendency to excite lustful thoughts); (2) the material must depict or describe, in a patently offensive way, sexual conduct specifically defined by applicable law; and (3) the material, taken as a whole, must lack serious literary, artistic, political, or scientific value. The Supreme Court has indicated that this test is designed to cover hard-core pornography." And the FCC's

definition of profanity: "Profane language" includes those words that are so highly offensive that their mere utterance in the context presented may, in legal terms, amount to a "nuisance."

Not only is it difficult to define obscene and profane language, but the definitions themselves depend on possibly subjective notions of "prurient interest" and material that "lacks serious literary, artistic, political or scientific value," and so on.

In NBC's 2003 broadcast of the Golden Globe Awards show, the lead singer of U2, Bono, uttered the phrase *fucking brilliant*. In October 2004, the FCC ruled that the use of the word *fucking* as an adjective in this context was not indecent. The decision ruled that the broadcast had not violated the indecency prohibition, because Bono's use of the "*f*-word" had been "fleeting" and "in a nonsexual context." However, the FCC later overruled its own Enforcement Bureau's decision and put a new policy into place, the Golden Globe Awards Order, which warns broadcasters that "depending on context, it would consider the '*f*-word' and those words (or variants thereof) that are as highly offensive as the *f*-word to be 'profane language' that cannot be broadcast between 6 A.M. and 10 P.M." It also concluded that other cases holding that isolated or fleeting use of the *f*-word are not indecent are no longer good law. The commission further concluded that use of the *f*-word in the

context of the Golden Globe Awards was profane under 18 U.S.C. Section 1464.

Though no fines were issued for this incident—or for another involving Nicole Richie (who uttered the *f*-word during the Billboard Music Awards)—the FCC says that it will issue fines for future violations. Broadcasting companies FOX, ABC, NBC, and CBS challenged the new policy in an attempt to clarify the order to make sure they do not violate the rules.

In July 2010, the 2nd U.S. Circuit Court of Appeals ruled that the FCC's policy banning even a single "patently offensive" expletive and other profanity on television and radio violates the First Amendment. The three-judge panel said the FCC "will have to go back to the drawing board" if it wants a profanity policy that will survive scrutiny since the current policy is "unconstitutionally vague" and creates a "chilling effect that goes far beyond the fleeting expletives at issue here." (Hamblett 2010)

For more information
http://www.fcc.gov/eb/oip/welcome/
http://www.cbsnews.com/stories/2004/02/25/tech/main602251.shtml
http://www.cnn.com/2003/LAW/12/23/findlaw.analysis.hilden.indecency/
Hamblett, Mark, "2nd Circuit Strikes FCC Profanity Ban as Vague, Overly Broad," *New York Law Journal*, July 14, 2010, http://www.law.com/jsp/article.jsp?id=1202463506252

taboo word forbidden word or expression interpreted as insulting, vulgar, or rude in a particular language

And finally, slang should be distinguished from **taboo** words. Most (if not all) languages have taboo words, and they typically refer to things that are forbidden or unmentionable in the culture. Many languages have taboo words that refer to sex and excrement, for example. It also considered taboo or blasphemous (from the Greek word *blasphemia*, meaning 'profane speech, slander') to use words affiliated with religion or religious figures in a way that is offensive or shows lack of respect. It's interesting that the substitutes for the taboo words, which may have exactly the same meaning and are clearly a substitute, do not carry the same power as the taboo words themselves. Consider *shoot* for *shit*, *darn* for *damn*, *heck* for *hell*. Taboo words are also distinct from slang words because they have staying power; many of our taboo words have been around, with approximately the same meanings, for hundreds and hundreds of years.

RPE 6.5

Recent New Words

Now let's consider new words that have recently come into the language. Some may be slang, but others may become more permanent additions to the language.

Every year, the American Dialect Society (ADS), a professional group of linguists, holds an annual Word of the Year competition, which showcases new words. The ADS notes that the words do not have to be "brand new" but must be newly prominent or notable, much like *Time* magazine's Person of the Year. The Word of the Year is announced in January at the annual ADS meeting and posted on the ADS website, and even hits the front page of most newspapers (http://www.americandialect.org/).

> **ADS Word of the Year for 2010** *app:* (noun) an abbreviated form of *application*, a software program for a computer or phone operating system
>
> **ADS Word of the Year for 2009** *tweet:* (noun) a short message sent via the Twitter.com service, and (verb), the act of sending such a message
>
> **ADS Word of the Year for 2008**: *bailout:* the rescue by the government of companies on the brink of failure, including large players in the banking industry.

Another "word watcher" website is Word Spy, "dedicated to recently coined words and existing words revived into modern usage" (http://www.wordspy.com/). Here are a few of Word Spy's recent additions.

- **trypophobia** *n.* (2010) – An unusually strong fear of, or aversion to, holes, particularly tiny holes that appear clustered together
- **defriend** *v.* (2010) – To remove a person from one's list of friends on a social networking site
- **lifestreaming** *n.* (2007)—an online record of a person's daily activities, either via direct video feed or via aggregating the person's online content such as blog posts, social network updates, and online photos. lifestreamer *n.*, lifestream *v., n.*

- **gamification** *n.* (2011)—The use of game-related concepts in non-game websites and applications to encourage users to perform actions desired by the business. gamify *v.*

hwæt!

Visit the ADS website (http://www.americandialect.org/) to see which words were nominated for Word of the Year but didn't make it.

Other recent top words of the week, according to Word Spy: *rusticle, polyfidelity, municide, phishing, metrosexual, earworm,* and *spim.*

As you can see by examining the examples of new words from the American Dialect Society and Word Spy lists, we make great use of existing roots, stems, and affixes to create new words. For example, *metrosexual* is a combination of the Greek morpheme *metro* and the adjective *sexual,* following the same pattern as *homosexual* and *heterosexual,* which is also evident in the more recent *retrosexual* and *pomosexual.* The word *mash-up* follows a common pattern of making nouns of verb + particle (phrasal verb) constructions. Verb + particle constructions follow a particular syntactic pattern, as the following examples illustrate.

a. The teacher handed out the papers.
b. The teacher handed the papers out. Noun: *handout*

Did You Know...?

The Truth about *Truthiness*

The press likes to get in on the American Dialect Society's pick for Word of the Year. In a story about the 2005 winner, *truthiness,* a reporter neglected to mention that the term was made popular by Stephen Colbert of *The Colbert Report,* a TV show on Comedy Central. It was Colbert's sense of the word that caused it to be Word of the Year. Colbert explained, "We're not talking about truth, we're talking about something that seems like truth—the truth we want to exist" (Sternbergh 2006). Right after the American Dialect Society's selection of the word, the reporter interviewed a linguist who must not have known about the Colbert source, so he cited an older definition of *truthiness* from the Oxford English Dictionary; its use was rare even in the 1800s, when it was cited as a derivation of *truthy.* The word's oddity as a noun is due to the fact that because there is already a noun, *truth,* we do not expect another noun form, *truthiness,* to have the same meaning. But in fact, it doesn't have the same meaning as *truth,* and isn't Colbert's intended meaning—something like truth but not truth—appropriate in today's political context?

The term made a comeback in 2010 when it was used frequently during the campaign leading up to Jon Stewart and Stephen Colbert's "Rally to Restore Sanity and/or Fear," also dubbed the "Restore Truthiness" rally, held in Washington, DC.

For more information
Sternbergh, A. 2006. Stephen Colbert has America by the ballots. *New York Magazine,* October 16.

    a.   The farmer shooed in the cows.

    b.   The farmer shooed the cows in. Noun: *shoo-in*

In the (a) sentences, nothing comes between the verb (*hand, shoo*) and following the particle (*out, in*). In the (b) sentences, on the other hand, the particle appears to the right of the direct object (*the papers, the cows*). Syntactic details aside, verb + particle constructions are the source of nouns such as *handout, shoo-in, takeout, takeover, pickup,* and the recent additions *mash-up, meet-up,* and *drawdown.*

We will look in some detail at a few word formation processes, many of which illustrate our creativity with language, and also at the systematic nature of morphological rules.

Coining

**coining
(neologism)**
recently created
word; typically
refers to a word
not derived from
existing words

Coinings, or **neologisms,** are words that have been recently created. They often apply to new inventions or concepts. The word *neologism* means 'new word' and was, in fact, itself a neologism around 1800. True coinings, which are completely new words, are rather rare relative to the vast number of words we create by means of the other word formation processes.

Shakespeare is often credited with coining many words, such as *sanctimonious, fashionable, bedazzle, pander,* and *unearthly*; however, notice that these coinings have recognizably English morphology, including the affixes *-ous, -ly, -able,* and *un-*. Often, words that are called coinings are really not; they are formed from existing morphemes by existing word formation processes. For example, *blog* is listed as a coining on the Word Spy website, and though it is certainly a new word, it is a blend of existing words: *web* and *log*. *Sniglets* are new words so dubbed by comedian Rich Hall; they are words that he would like to see in the dictionary that fill a gap—words for things we don't have a word for. But even sniglets are usually formed by English word formation processes. His noun *backspackle,* for example, is a compound of *back* and *spackle,* meaning 'the markings on the back of one's shirt from riding a fenderless bicycle.'

True coinings include *googol* (invented by the then 9-year-old nephew of American mathematician Edward Kasner as the name for a very large number, ten to the power of one hundred) and *bling* (hip-hop slang for expensive or flashy jewelry). The British duo Douglas Adams and John Lloyd wrote *The Meaning of Liff,* a humorous dictionary of things there aren't words for but should be. These are distinguished from sniglets because all the words listed come from place names (mostly from the United Kingdom); place names, they say, because they are seldom used and could be fine words for all those things we don't have words for. Two examples are *oughterby,* which is defined as someone you don't want to invite to a party but feel you should, and *nottage,* a word for the things you find a use for right after you have thrown them away.

Compounding

compounding
combining one or
more words into a
single word

One very common way to form new English words is by **compounding**. A compound is formed when two or more words behave as a single word. English speakers know, for example, that *black bird* in the sentence *I saw a black bird* differs from the meaning of *blackbird* in *I saw a blackbird*. In the first sentence, *black bird* means a bird that is black, a bird of any possible species. In the second sentence, *blackbird* refers to a particular species of bird. In the first sentence, the adjective *black* modifies the noun *bird*, and together *black bird* is a noun phrase (NP). In the second, *blackbird* is a noun, and more specifically a compound noun, as illustrated schematically below.

    a. [black] + [bird] adjective + noun
    b. [blackbird] compound noun

Compounds can be of any open-class category—noun, verb, adjective, or adverb. There also exist compound prepositions, and prepositions form the parts of compounds of other categories (for example, *outsource* is a preposition + verb compound of the category verb). Pronouns can also occur in compounds (*whoever*), as can quantifiers such as *some* or *every* (*someone, everything*), and there exist a number of historical examples of compound adverbs such as *herewith* and *thereupon*. Table 6.1 lists more compounds from all of the major parts of speech categories, illustrating the wide variety of types.

Notice that there is no consistent spelling or punctuation of compounds; they can occur with hyphens, as separate words, or spelled out as a single word. As discussed in Chapter 4, one way to recognize many compounds is by stress patterns; typically, compound stress falls on the first word in the compound, allowing us to distinguish compounds from phrases.

    a. black bírd, bláckbird
    b. green hoúse, gréenhouse

Table 6.1	Common Compound Words by Type			
Nouns	**Adjectives**	**Verbs**	**Adverbs**	**Prepositions**
blackbird	childlike	blackmail	downward	into
horsefly	ready-to-wear	overact	upward	onto
peanut butter	well-off	downsize	therefore	without
six-pack	upright	update	however	toward
daughter-in-law	single-minded	outsource	furthermore	within

This is not always the case; here are a few interesting exceptions and dialectal variations:

    a. úpgrade, uplíft
    b. ápple cake, apple píe
    c. íce cream, whipped créam

Compounds are typically affixed just as any other words, providing evidence that we do store them in our mental lexicons as single words; they can take plural -s, possessive -'s, past tense -ed, present participle -ing, and so on.

    a. blackbirds, six-packs, horseflies
    b. whitewashing, outsourcing, downsized

Often-cited exceptions to this generalization include *sister-in-law, attorney general, master-at-arms,* and *heir apparent*. These compounds are unusual for English because they are "head-first" compounds, with the modifier of the head (the adjective or the prepositional phrase) following the head (the noun). Compounds are pluralized in two ways. The plurals in group (a) are perhaps more prescriptively correct, though the plurals in group (b) also oc-cur, particularly in oral language, and are perhaps more common.

a. three sister**s**-in-law	b. three sister-in-law**s**
six attorney**s** general	six attorney general**s**
two heir**s** apparent	two heir apparent**s**

Attorney-general is derived from French, where the adjective *general* follows the noun it modifies. English speakers, however, have English, not French, intuitions about morphological rules and thus treat *attorney general* just like *famous general*, where *famous* precedes *general* (not the other way around). The fact that both options for pluralization of such compounds exist can be accounted for by proposing that the group (b) plurals are "natural" and conform to speakers' descriptive rules of English but that the group (a) pluralization is learned the same way as other prescriptive rules, or are at least consciously analyzed by the speaker.

The meaning of many compounds is fairly transparent; a *blackbird* is a type of bird, and a *supermom* is a type of mom. The meanings of other compounds are not so obvious, however. A *blockhead* is not someone whose head is shaped like a block, nor is to *backstab* someone to physically harm them with a sharp implement.

German, in particular, uses compounds as a way of forming new words, ending up with some impressively long ones:

    a. Donaudampfschifffahrtsgesellschaftskapitän

    Donau - dampf - schiff - fahrt - gesellschaft - kapitän
    Danube steam   ship   operate society   captain
    'captain of a boat belonging to the Danube Steamship Company'

b. Ausländerbehördebürostunden

Aus	-	länder	-	behörde	-	büro	-	stunden
out		country (pl.)		officials		office		hours

‘hours of the immigration office’

c. Rehunterkieferbackenzahnteil

Reh	-	unter	-	kiefer	-	backen	-	zahn	-	teil
deer		lower		jaw		cheek		tooth		section

‘piece of the deer’s lower jaw with the teeth intact’ (in order to tell the age of the animal)

RPE   6.6

Eponyms

eponym word that comes from the name of a person associated with it

Another way we create new words is by creating **eponyms**, or words from names of (usually) famous people, and the words’ meanings relate to something specific about them or their experiences. Consider the Pythagorean theorem (a geometric equation named for the Greek mathematician Pythagoras), the system of Braille used for the blind (named for the Frenchman Louis Braille, who invented it), Morse code (a communication system invented by Samuel Morse for use with the telegraph), and hundreds more. Some examples of eponyms are obviously from names, even if we are not certain of their origins (Achilles’ heel, Reyes syndrome, Orwellian), but others are less so; *algorithm, bloomers, gerrymander, leotard,* and *saxophone* are all words that come from names.

Brand names are usually registered (like trademarks and copyrights) so that using them without the owner’s permission is illegal—but you’re not likely to get arrested for saying *Kleenex.*

Eponyms also come from brand names. For example, many of us refer to tissues of any brand as *Kleenex,* an original facial tissue brand name, to any petroleum jelly as *Vaseline,* to all cotton swabs as *Q-tips,* and to all MP3 players as *iPods.* Some brand-name eponyms are recognizable, but many are so integrated into the language that we aren’t aware they were ever brand names at all.

RPE   6.7

Retronyms

retronym word that provides a new name for something to differentiate the original word from a more recent form or version

Another type of word formation, called a **retronym** (a term first coined by journalist Frank Mankiewicz in 1980 and then popularized by *New York Times* columnist William Safire) provides a new name for something to differentiate the original word from a more recent form or version. The original word typically gains a modifier, rather than being completely replaced by a new word, to account for developments of the object or concept—for example, *analog watch* to differentiate from *digital watch,* or *acoustic guitar* as distinct from *electric guitar.*

Blends

blend (portman-teau) word made from putting parts of two words together

RPE 6.8

Another common word formation process involves telescoping two words together, as Lewis Carroll does in the nonsense poem "Jabberwocky," in which he creates *slithy* from *lithe* and *slimy*. Other examples of **blends**, also called **portmanteau** words, include the following: *apathetic* (from *apathy + pathetic*), *permafrost* (*permanent + frost*), *transistor* (*transfer + resistor*), *hassle* (*haggle + tussle*), *prissy* (*prim + sissy*), *blog* (*web + log*), *schnoodle* (*schnauzer + poodle*), and *brunch* (*breakfast + lunch*).

Conversions

conversion change of a word's syntactic category without changing form, such as a noun becoming a verb

ʰwæʧ!

Portmanteau, French for a kind of folding suitcase (a blend of *porter* 'to carry' and *manteau* 'coat'), was first used by Lewis Carroll in 1882 to refer to blended words, such as those he used in his poem "Jabberwocky."

RPE 6.9

Sometimes we create words by simply assigning them another syntactic category. For example, from the noun *mother* we have created the verb *mother* (and similarly *father* and *parent*), and from the noun *trash* we have the verb *(to) trash*. Such **conversions**, also called functional shifts, happen in a variety of ways; we can convert a noun to a verb as with *mother, trash, google,* or *friend*; or we can convert a verb to a noun, as in *impact, commute, blackmail, e-mail,* and *fax*. We also convert adjectives to verbs, as in *to savage* or *to total*, and adjectives to nouns, as in *a crazy*.

Some conversions induce a change in stress, though such stress patterns often vary dialectally.

verbs: transfér, permít, convért, pervért, commúne
nouns: tránsfer, pérmit, cónvert, pérvert, cómmune

Conversions are quite common in English. Both words often become established, and then it is not obvious which word came first unless you look them up in a dictionary. For example, the noun *electronic mail,* which soon became simply *e-mail,* almost immediately become a verb as well: *She e-mailed me about the meeting.*

CALVIN AND HOBBES © 1993 Watterson. Dist by Universal Uclick. Reprinted with Permission. All rights reserved.

Language

Blimey!

All of the following words were once longer phrases.

- *Howdy* came from *how do you do*.
- *Goodbye* came from *God be with you*.
- The word *blimey*, more common in British English, came from *God blame me* (or maybe *God blind me*).
- And the slightly archaic word *druthers* came from *would rather* as in *I would rather* and shifted from a verb phrase to a noun: *If I had my **druthers**, we wouldn't go to the fair.*

The process that reduces a longer phrase to a single word usually takes a long time, sometimes hundreds of years. You can see this process taking place over about 300 years with the word *goodbye* in the following quotes from the *Oxford English Dictionary* (given with the year they appeared in a text and the author's name):

1588 I thanke your worship, *God be wy you.* (William Shakespeare)
1591 *God b'uy* my Lord. (William Shakespeare)
1600 Gallants, *God buoye* all. (William Shakespeare)
1602 I so, *God buy' ye* (William Shakespeare)
1604 *God buy to you.* (William Shakespeare)
1607 *God b'y you* Mistresse Gallipot. (Thomas Middleton and Thomas Dekker)
1652 Heartily *Godbuy*, good Mr. Crasy. (Richard Brome)
1659 . . . his strength will scarce supply His Back to the Balcona, so *God b' wy* (Samuel Pepys)
1694 He flings up his tail . . . and so bids us *good-b'wy*. (John Cleveland)
1707 So to a Feast should I invite ye You'd stuff your Guts, and cry, *Good bwi't'ye*. (Edward Ward)
1719 *Good B' w"y*! with all my Heart. (Thomas D'Urfey)
1818 And so your humble servant, and *good-b'ye*! (George Gordon Byron)
1860 We then bade Ulrich *good-bye*, and went forward. (John Tyndall)
1874 Then he said *good-bye* to me . . . and so left me. (Francis Burnand)

And now we just say "bye!"

Acronyms

acronym word formed from abbreviations of other words

Acronyms are abbreviations that can be formed in two ways. First, words can be formed from initial letters of each part of a compound word or phrase and then pronounced as the words they become: *SARS* and *NASA* are examples.

SARS	severe acute respiratory syndrome
NASA	National Aeronautics and Space Administration

ℎwᴂᴄ!

A handy place to look up unfamiliar acronyms is the website all-acronyms.com. Beware, though, that it claims no absolute authority on the etymology and definitions.

Humvee	HMMWV (high-mobility multipurpose wheeled vehicle)
LARP	live action role-playing game
WASP	white, Anglo-Saxon Protestant
ROM	read-only memory
NIMBY	not in my backyard
FAQs	frequently asked questions

Some acronyms have become so ingrained in the language that we may no longer know what the letters once stood for; they have also usually lost their uppercase letters in the acronym.

laser	light amplification by the stimulated emission of radiation
radar	radio detecting and ranging
scuba	self-contained underwater breathing apparatus
snafu	situation normal all fouled up

initialism word formed from the initial letters of a group of words (*CD*)

The second type of acronym is the **initialism**, a word created by initial letters, which is pronounced with the letter names: DVD, FBI, CIA. Here are some familiar initialisms (also called *abbreviations*):

WMD	weapons of mass destruction
OMG	Oh my God
DVD	digital versatile/video disk
NCAA	National Collegiate Athletic Association
NPR	National Public Radio
brb	be right back (primarily used in online communication)
lol	laughing out loud (primarily used in online communication)

We can also distinguish *orthographic initialisms* or *abbreviations*, in which the written word is a shortening of some other word, but we pronounce the whole word rather than the abbreviated form:

Jr., Dr., Mrs., Mr., wt. (for *weight*), g (for *gram*), state names—AZ, TN, WA, NY

A subtype of initialism is a word formed from letters within a word rather than from separate words.

TV/tv   television

ℎwᴂᴄ!

Ever wonder why *lb.* is the abbreviation for *pound* and *oz.* is the abbreviation for *ounce*? *Lb.* is an abbreviation of the first word of the Latin phrase *libra ponda*, which was an equivalent measurement for the Romans. And *ounce* was spelled *onza* in fifteenth-century Italian, when it came into common use in Europe, and was thus abbreviated *oz.*

The initialism *ID*, taken from the first two letters of *identification*, has become a root word that can take an affix:

They were IDing everyone at the door.

Other languages also use a lot of acronyms and abbreviations. An example from French is SAMU, which comes from *Service d'Aide Médicale Urgent*, the agency people call in medical emergencies. And one from Spanish (which has a great many acronyms), is SEAT (pronounced [se-at]) for *Sociedad Español de Automóviles y Turismo*.

Language Alive!

Ms.

When you see *Ms.* written on something, how do you say it, and what does it mean? If you see it as a choice on a form along with *Mr.* and *Mrs.*, you might think it's an abbreviation. But it's not an abbreviation. The definition and etymology from the *Oxford English Dictionary* follows:

> **Ms,** *n.* A title of courtesy prefixed to the surname of a woman, sometimes with her first name interposed. *Ms* has been adopted esp. in formal and business contexts as an alternative to *Mrs* and *Miss* principally as a means to avoid having to specify a woman's marital status (regarded as irrelevant, intrusive, or potentially discriminatory).

Some examples from the *Oxford English Dictionary*, going as far back as 1932, show its various uses as well as the conscious attempt to integrate it into the language in order to treat women and men equally.

1932: In addressing by letter a woman whose marital status is in doubt, should one write 'M's' or 'Miss'? (*New York Times*, May 29)

1949: Feminists . . . have often proposed that the two present-day titles be merged into 'Miss' (to be written 'Ms.'), with a plural 'Misses' (written 'Mss.'). (Mario Pei, *Story of Language*)

1952: Use abbreviation Ms. for all women addressees. This modern style solves an age-old problem. (*Simplified Letter*, publication of the National Office Management Association, Philadelphia)

1974: The Passport Office yesterday conceded the right to women to call themselves Ms (pronounced Miz) on their passports instead of Mrs. or Miss. (*London Daily Telegraph*, May 21)

The creation of this word is an example of a successful attempt at word manipulation for a political or social reason.

German also has many acronyms, though it tends to take a letter or two more than the initial letter of the word to make the new word easily pronounceable. So, *haribo*, the name of a gummy bear candy company, comes from <u>Ha</u>ns <u>Ri</u>egel in <u>Bo</u>nn, the founder. And *KaDeWe* is a big, well-known department store in Berlin whose name comes from <u>Ka</u>ufhaus <u>de</u>s <u>We</u>stens.

Clipping

clipping making a word by omitting syllables in an existing word (e.g., *rad* from *radical*)

Another way to create words is to omit syllables (rather than morphemes). This process, called **clipping**, is the source of the following:

pantaloons	→	pants
streptococcus	→	strep

| brother | → | bro |
| mathematics | → | math |

It is typically the first syllable that becomes the word, but not always, as the following examples show.

| influenza | → | flu |
| chrysanthemum | → | mum |

Other languages also use clipping to form new words. The following examples of clipping are from German:

Mathemathik	→	Mathe	'math'
AutoBus	→	Bus	'bus'
Bibliothek	→	Bib	'library'
Extempore	→	Ex	'pop quiz'

RPE 6.10

Backformation

backformation
making a new word by omitting what appears to be a morpheme (usually a suffix or prefix) but actually isn't

Unless we know the history of a word, it is nearly impossible to tell which words are formed through **backformation**, even though many words enter the language in this way. Backformation is a process by which a word is formed by omitting what appears to be a morpheme but which in reality is not. For example, *edit* is a backformation from *editor*, and *scavenge* is backformed from *scavenger*. Both *editor* and *scavenger* came into English from other languages: *editor* from Latin *editus* and *scavenger* from Old French *scawager*. Note the /n/ that was inserted from the French word to the English word; this by analogy with other words like *messenger* (French, *messager*) and *passenger* (French, *passager*). Although each of these words ends in *-er*, this *-er* is not equivalent to the *-er* affix that means 'one who does X', as in *driver* and *teacher*, where the *-er* is affixed to the verbs *drive* and *teach*. However, English speakers, by analogy, nevertheless unconsciously analyzed *scavenger* and *editor* as ending in the familiar "agentive" *-er* and backformed the verbs *edit* and *scavenge*. Similar examples, from the same historical contact with French, include *cobble, hawk, swindle,* and *burgle,* from *cobbler, hawker, swindler,* and *burglar*. Another historical example is *pease*, originally a mass noun (a noun that can't be counted—much pease is in the pot) and now interpreted as count (so now many peas are in the pot is what we say). You may be familiar with the nursery rhyme "Pease porridge hot. Pease porridge cold. Pease porridge in the pot, nine days old," an example of the older form *pease*.

Still other, more recent examples of backformations include the following: *spectate, resurrect, enthuse, peoplewatch, backform, couth, statistic, intuit, babysit, televise, liaise, sightsee, typewrite, orientate*. Some may be more acceptable or standard, but all are formed by the same morphological process.

Reduplication

reduplication
making a word by
doubling an entire
free morpheme
(total reduplication)
or part of it (partial
reduplication)

Reduplication is the process of forming new words by doubling either an entire free morpheme (total reduplication) or part of it (partial reduplication). English doesn't use reduplication very productively to form new words, though it does use a version of reduplication in certain expressions and in baby talk to form words related to or derived from the original meaning of a word (e.g., *wa-wa* from *water*).

> knock knock, hocus-pocus, hoity-toity, tutti-frutti, bye bye, mama, dada, boo-boo, wawa (for *water*)

Other languages use reduplication much more productively. Indonesian uses total reduplication to form the plurals of nouns.

rumah	'house'	rumahrumah	'houses'
ibu	'mother'	ibuibu	'mothers'

Pangasinan, a language of the Philippines, uses partial reduplication to indicate plural.

baley	'town'	balbaley	'towns'
lupa	'face'	luplupa	'faces'
sondalo	'soldier'	sonsondalo	'soldiers'

Lushootseed, among other Salish language of the Pacific Northwest and British Columbia, uses reduplication in all sorts of ways. Let's look at two of them.

The *diminutive* morpheme doubles the initial consonant and vowel of the stem and results in a diminutive interpretation, as indicated by the following translations.

ʔálʔal	house	ʔáʔálʔal	hut
ʔúqʷ'ud	pull out	ʔúʔúqʷ'ud	pull part way out
híwil	go ahead	híhíwil	go on ahead a bit
q'íxʷ	upstream	q'íq'íxʷ	upstream a little bit

And the morphology of the so-called out-of-control form results from doubling the final consonant and vowel of the stem, resulting in interpretations like the following.

ʔáɬ	fast, quickly	ʔáɬáɬ	hurry up!
dᶻáq'	fall, topple	dᶻáq'áq'	stagger, totter
čəx̌	split	čəx̌əx̌	cracked to pieces
yúbil	starve	yúbúbil	tired out, sick

An example of reduplication that has come into English from Hawaiian is *wikiwiki*, meaning 'quick'. It is quickly gaining new meanings and functions (*We set up a wiki*; *Just wiki it*), however, and it is now used as a prefix, as in *wikipedia* and *wiktionary*. Or are these blends?

RPE   6.11

RPE   6.12

Accent on *Lexicographers*

© Amerika Haus/SZ Photo/The Image Wor

Who writes dictionaries? Lexicographers provide the definitions, etymologies, clues to pronunciation, examples of use, and even syntactic uses. They are well educated and interested, even expert, in many areas—language and languages, history, culture, and so on. The job has changed quite a bit since the seventeenth century, when lexicographers were starting their work.

Commissioned to 'fix' and improve English, Samuel Johnson published pretty much single-handedly the *Dictionary of the English Language* in 1755. Noah Webster, pictured above, labored alone to publish *A Compendious Dictionary of the English Language* in 1806; one of his goals was to distinguish American from British English. He created many American spellings: *color, center, program,* and *catalog,* among others.

James Murray strove to compile a dictionary that would map out, with scientific accuracy, the history and meaning of English words, not only in England and America but around the world. Editors working with him collected 3.5 million citation slips submitted by a small army

of volunteers for the *Oxford English Dictionary*. The *OED* was published in installments from 1884 to 1928. When Murray died in 1915, after thirty-seven years as its editor, the *OED* had only reached the letter *T*.

The *OED's* editors helped change the lexicographer's role from prescriptive to much more descriptive, aiming to discover and document the language real people use, though it was still based on written, not spoken, language.

It might be surprising to learn that the *Dictionary of Slang and Unconventional English* was first published in 1937. Its editor, Eric Partridge, devoted his life to writing about some of the more curious aspects of language and thus perpetuated an interest in documenting *all* aspects of language, both standard and nonstandard.

The current editors are at work on the last volume of the *Dictionary of American Regional English*, which documents those ways in which our regional language varieties are distinct from each other; it focuses on the spoken rather than the written language. Lexicographer Frederic Cassidy was chief editor of this dictionary from its inception in 1965 until his death in 2000.

A distinct kind of dictionary has emerged that focuses more directly on usage. *Merriam-Webster's Dictionary of English Usage*, for example, arranges in dictionary format a collection of "common problems of confused or disputed English usage from two perspectives: . . . historical background . . . and . . . present-day usage" (preface). It tackles such things as the distinction between *infer* and *imply*, *indubitably* and *undoubtedly*, *orientate* and *orient*.

Mass literacy, global communication, and technology have guaranteed the ongoing demand for dictionaries and have changed the

Erin McKean

We don't always know today's lexicographers by name; there are so many of them working on diverse dictionary projects. They all, however, maintain a fascination with words, their histories, and their use.

For more information
AskOxford.com. http://www.askoxford.com/worldofwords/oed/wordsearchers/?view=uk.
Dictionary of American Regional English. http://polyglot.lss.wisc.edu/dare/dare.html.
Green, J. 1996. *Chasing the sun: Dictionary makers and the dictionaries they made.* New York: Henry Holt.
Merriam-Webster OnLine. 2008. Noah Webster and America's first dictionary. http://www.merriam-webster.com/info/noah.htm.
Merriam-Webster's dictionary of English usage. 1994. Springfield, MA: Merriam-Webster.
Oxford English dictionary. http://www.oed.com/.
Winchester, S. 1998. *The professor and the madman: A tale of murder, insanity, and the making of the Oxford English Dictionary.* New York: HarperCollins.

way in which lexicographers compile and we retrieve information; search engines seek words or phrases from thousands of sources in a matter of seconds. Erin McKean, pictured here, has used all of these modern tools as an editor for American dictionaries at Oxford University Press and founder of Wordnik.com.

Summary

In this chapter, we've gone beyond the borders of English affixation to look at the morphological properties of other languages. We've seen that languages can be classified by their morphological type as analytic or synthetic or on a continuum between these two types. English, in fact, is mostly analytic but has some synthetic properties, too. We've also discussed a wide range of morphological processes other than affixation, processes that allow us to continually and creatively add new words to our language and alter the meanings and structure of existing ones. Our discussion of regular word formation rules, such as compounding, as well as other nonsystematic ways of adding new words, such as eponyms and acronyms, clearly illustrates our enormous capacity for creativity in language and that language is a dynamic, ever-changing system.

Sources and Resources

Adams, D. & J. Lloyd. 1983. *The meaning of liff*. London: Pan Books. Also available at http://folk.uio.no/alied/TMoL.html

All-acronyms.com. 2010. http://www.all-acronyms.com (20 December, 2010.)

American Dialect Society. 2008. http://www.americandialect.org/ (9 June, 2008.)

Aronoff, M. 1976. *Word formation in generative grammar*. Cambridge, MA: MIT Press.

AskOxford.com. http://www.askoxford.com/worldofwords/oed/wordsearchers/?view = uk

Chesterton, G. 1902. *The defendant*. London: J. W. Dent & Sons.

Comrie, B. 1982. *Language universals and linguistic typology*. Chicago: University of Chicago Press.

Dictionary of American Regional English. http://polyglot.lss.wisc.edu/dare/dare.html

Green, J. 1996. *Chasing the sun: Dictionary makers and the dictionaries they made*. New York: Henry Holt.

Hess, T. 1993. *Lushootseed reader with introductory grammar*, 1. Marysville, WA: Tulalip Tribes.

Hess, T. Personal communication.

Jensen, J. 1990. *Morphology: Word structure in generative grammar*. Amsterdam: John Benjamins.

Lovin, A. 1997. *An introduction to the languages of the world*. New York: Oxford University Press.

Merriam-Webster OnLine. 2008. Noah Webster and America's first dictionary. http://www.merriam-webster.com/info/noah.htm.

Merriam-Webster's dictionary of English usage. 1994. Springfield, MA: Merriam-Webster.

Mithun, M. 1999. *The languages of native North America*. Cambridge, UK: Cambridge University Press.

Oxford English dictionary. http://www.oed.com/

Sternbergh, A. 2006. Stephen Colbert has America by the ballots. *New York Magazine*, October 16.

Winchester, S. 1998. *The professor and the madman: A tale of murder, insanity, and the making of the Oxford English Dictionary*. New York: HarperCollins.

Word Spy. 2010. http://www.wordspy.com/index.asp.

Wright, C. 1990. A journal of English days. In *The world of the ten thousand things*, 132. New York: Farrar Straus & Giroux.

Wright, C. 1995. Black and blue. In *Chickamauga*, 44. New York: Farrar Straus & Giroux.

Wright, C. 1995. Chickamauga. In *Chickamauga*, 47. New York: Farrar Straus & Giroux.

Wright, C. 2000. Meditation on song and structure. In *Negative blue*, 120. New York: Farrar Straus & Giroux.

Wright, C. 2002. Looking around II. In *A short history of the shadow*, 7. New York: Farrar Straus & Giroux.

Young, R. 2000. *The Navajo verb system: An overview*. Albuquerque: University of New Mexico Press.

Review, Practice, and Explore

RPE 6.1 ▷ Analytic? Synthetic?

A. In the Lushootseed (dxʷləšucid) language, the place name *Skykomish* can be broken down into the following morphemes. Based on this word, would you classify this language as more analytic or synthetic?

Skykomish

sq'ixʷabš

s-q'ixʷ- abš

nominalizer—located upstream—people of

'upstream people'

B. Explain how this example from Chinese is illustrative of an analytic rather than a synthetic language.

我	所有	的	朋友	都	要	吃	才	蛋
wǒ	suǒyǒu	de	péngyou	dōu	yào	chī	jī	dàn
I	all	possessive	friend(s)	all	want	eat	chicken	egg(s)

'My friends all want to eat eggs.'

C. Conduct some research on a language—perhaps one that you have studied—and determine what type of language it is. Is it more analytic or synthetic? Does it exhibit characteristics of a fusional language? An agglutinative language? Be sure to give examples and to label the morphemes.

RPE   6.2   〉 Japanese as Synthetic and Analytic

Japanese has agglutinative (synthetic) verbs but analytic nouns. Conduct some research on Japanese, collect examples of verbs and nouns, and illustrate those aspects that are synthetic and those that are analytic. If you find other examples of languages that share features of more than one language type, discuss those as well.

RPE   6.3   〉 Analyzing Yoruba Nasals

Recall the discussion in Chapter 4 of the various phonological processes that change one sound into another. Such processes are at work in Yoruba, leading to several different forms, called allomorphs, of the progressive morpheme. Based on the following data, what is the form of the progressive morpheme (equivalent to English –ing) in each set of Yoruba verbs? The English translations are given only in the infinitive. (Adapted from Cowan & Kakušan, 1985: 79)

present	progressive	
bá	ḿbá	'to meet'
bɛ́	ḿbɛ́	'to cut off'
bérò	ḿbérò	'to fear'
bò	ḿbò	'to cover'
bù	ḿbù	'to cut'

progressive morpheme =

dà	ńdà	'to pour'
dé	ńdé	'to arrive'
dì	ńdì	'to tie'
dìkpò	ńdìkpò	'to replace'
dúró	ńdúró	'to stand'

progressive morpheme =

kà	ŋkà	'to fold'
kàn	ŋkàn	'to touch'
kó	ŋkó	'to gather'
kù	ŋkù	'to remain'

progressive morpheme =

What kind of phonological process accounts for the different forms, or *allomorphs,* of the progressive morpheme in Yoruba?

RPE 6.4 > Analyzing Iraqi Arabic Noun Stems

Based on the data in Set 1, what is the possessive morpheme in Iraqi Arabic? (Adapted from Cowan & Kakušan 1985: 88-89)

Set 1

Nonpossessive	possessive (my)	
walad	waladi	'son'
qalam	qalami	'pencil'
balad	baladi	'town'
tanak	tanaki	'tin'
ǰaras	ǰarasi	'bell'

possessive morpheme =

Now consider the following data. Assume that the form of the possessive morpheme doesn't change, and that a phonological process applies to the nouns in Set 2 to derive their forms (which are different from the forms of the nouns in Set 1). What is that process and why does it occur?

Set 2

Nonpossessive	possessive (my)	
šaʕar	šaʕri	'hair'
bayʲal	bayʲli	'mule'
laḥam	laḥmi	'meat'
taxat	taxti	'bench'
šaʕab	šaʕbi	'people'

RPE 6.5 > Slang

A. Using the slang dictionaries in your library and online, discuss the origins and evolution of three slang words. If the words are still in use and the current meaning is related to or derived from the older meaning, discuss how their meanings have changed.

B. Define and discuss three slang terms that you and your friends know and use. Are they listed in the slang dictionary? If they are, do they have the same meaning as your definitions? Do you think your slang words will be around in 10 years? Twenty years? Why or why not? See if you can determine the origins of your slang terms.

In your discussion, try to answer the following questions:

- What criteria do we use to define a word as slang?
- What role do dictionaries play in defining a word as slang?
- What is the difference between slang terms and dialect variation?

RPE   6.6 > Compounds

Sometimes it isn't obvious whether a group of words is a compound word or not. Consider the following:

cab ride
iron gate
paperback book
paperback novel
life insurance premium
barking dog

Are these compound nouns? Why or why not? What kinds of tests can you use to find out whether they are compounds or not?

RPE   6.7 > Eponyms

A. Choose at least five of the following eponyms, look them up in a good etymological dictionary such as *A New Dictionary of Eponyms* (Oxford University Press), and write a summary of each word's meaning and origin.

> badminton, cardigan, derringer, forsythia, gorilla, hollandaise, jodhpurs, limousine, mackinaw, tuxedo, volt, welch, zeppelin, Amber alert, Enronomics, Casanova, Dear John, Dear Abby, jack-of-all-trades, boycott, Martha moment, Starbucks, John Hancock, quisling, John Doe, bogart, Uncle Tom, Aunt Jemima, Electra, oedipal, Ophelia, the Atkins, (to be) borked

B. Consider the following words, which all originally came from brand names. Which of these do you use as the generic name for the item?

> escalator, granola, cellophane, zipper, yo-yo, linoleum, kerosene, jungle gym, dumpster, frisbee, chapstick, port-a-potty, xerox, Q-tip, band-aid, taser, ping-pong

RPE   6.8 > Blends

What do the following words mean, and what words did they come from?

skullet, pomo, modem, spork

Come up with two other blends, and give the words that they are blended from.

RPE   6.9 > Creative Morphology in Poetry

Poet Charles Wright employs a number of word formation processes in his work. One such process in particular is illustrated in the following boldface words from his poetry. What is the word formation he uses? Explain briefly.

A. From "Black and Blue":

> Like deer in a leafy light,
> window and looking glass,
> Yesterdays flash and reflect,
> Ready to bolt, ready to empty out.
> **Horizon** them black and blue.

B. From "Chickamauga":

> History handles our past like spoiled fruit.
> Mid-morning, late-century light
> **calicoed** under the peach trees.
> Fingers us here. Fingers us here and here.

C. From "Meditation on Song and Structure":

> In North Carolina, half a century ago,
> Bird song over black water,
> Lake Llewellyn **Bibled** and night-colored,
> mockingbird
> Soul-throated, like light, a little light in great darkness.

D. From "Meditation on Song and Structure":

> The afternoon breaking away in little pieces,
> Siren's squeal from the bypass,
> The void's tattoo, *Nothing Matters,*
> **mottoed** across our white hearts?

Below are two more examples from the poetry of Charles Wright of a word formation process discussed in the chapter. What process is Wright using in excerpts E and F?

E. From "A Short History of the Shadow":

> Now into June, cloverheads tight, **Seurating**[1] the yard.

F. From "Journal of English Days":

> November's my favorite month,
> the downside of autumn
> And winter in first array, the sky
> **Constabled**[2] now and again
> Over Kensington Gardens:
> north of the Serpentine,

RPE 6.10 > Clippings

Here are a few clippings not mentioned in the chapter:

> jag, memo, typo, lab, gas

Determine what words each of these came from. Come up with three more examples of words formed by clipping.

RPE 6.11 > Duplicate Reduplication

A relatively recent phenomenon in English is the doubling of certain words and phrases to create a new meaning. So someone might say, "No, I don't like like him" or "Yes, she's my girlfriend girlfriend," which seem to be used to contrast one meaning of a word with another. Come up

---

1. Reference is to Georges Seurat's pointillist paintings (e.g., *Le Pont de Courbevoie*).
2. Reference is to John Constable.

with several other examples of words that can do this kind of reduplication, and explain how the doubling of these words changes the meaning of the original word. Describe any limitations on the reduplication (which words can do it, which can't) and therefore how productive a process it is.

RPE 6.12 > Forming New Words

Recall the following word formation processes used in English: affixation, compounding, blending, clipping, acronyms, eponyms, conversions, backformations, and reduplication.

Now, consider the following words from Word Spy and previous nominees for the American Dialect Society's Word of the Year.

chugger, bridezilla, NIMBY, manscaping, crittercam, nanopublishing, furkid, tofurkey, refudiate

Explain which process of word formation has applied in each word. Look up the meaning of each word; if you can find no meaning, make one up!

Chapter at a Glance

Nouns and Noun Phrases
  A Phrase Structure Rule for Noun
  Phrases
Verbs and Verb Phrases
  A Phrase Structure Rule for Verb
  Phrases
  Evidence for the Aux Position
  A Phrase Structure Rule for Clauses
Adjectives and Adjective Phrases
  Adjective Phrase Positions
  A Variable Phrase
Adverbs and Adverb Phrases
  Adverb Phrase Positions
Prepositions and Prepositional Phrases
  Prepositional Phrase Positions
Summary of Phrase Structure Rules
More Clauses
  Subjects and Predicates
  Independent and Subordinate
  Clauses
  What Is a Sentence?
Summary
Sources and Resources
Review, Practice, and Explore

Syntax: Heads and Phrases

Key Concepts

- Words are organized into phrases and clauses.
- Each phrase is of a particular syntactic category (noun phrase, verb phrase, adjective phrase, etc.), and each has a head (noun, verb, adjective, etc.).
- Phrase structure rules provide us with a way to draw, or diagram, phrases and to capture certain important generalizations about how syntactic structure is organized.
- The largest phrase is the clause, a syntactic unit consisting of a subject and a predicate.
- Clauses are independent or subordinate, depending on whether they are contained in larger phrases.

Did You Know . . . ?

  The Root of Trees
  Syntax in the "Real" World

Language Alive!   How Many Modals?

  Don't Use Double Negatives. NOT!
  English Didn't Always *Do*

Linguistics in the News   What's the Right Answer?

Accent on   Teaching with Trees

> *What did I learn in school? The most valuable thing by far was grammar.*
>
> —NORTHROP FRYE

syntax system of rules and principles that describe how we organize words into phrases and phrases into larger units, the largest being the clause; also, the study of this system

In this chapter, we will explore our knowledge of yet another system, namely, the system of rules and principles that allows us to combine words into larger units. This system of rules is called **syntax**. For example, we know that words must be organized in a certain order in the sentence (just as affixes and roots occur in certain orders in words). In fact, the position of a word in the sentence is often the only way we know its syntactic category (part of speech). For example, the word *walks* can be either a verb or a noun, and we know how to interpret this word only when we see where it occurs in the sentence.

The girl goes on many long *walks*.
The girl *walks* the dogs.

In which sentence is *walks* a noun? In which is it a verb? It's a noun in the first sentence because of its position; it occurs to the right of *long*, the adjective that modifies it. In the second sentence, on the other hand, *walks* is a verb; it occurs after the subject, *the girl*, and before its object, *the dogs*. Put more simply, we know that *walks* in the first sentence is different from *walks* in the second, regardless of whether we have the technical vocabulary we're using here to explain that difference.

Another thing we know about syntax is that words can be grouped or combined in certain ways. For example, we'd all probably agree that the boxed part in the following sentence is a possible word group. We'll soon describe more specifically what we mean by *word group* and give you some tests for identifying such groups, but you do have some intuitions about which words go together to form such phrasal units.

Six hungry gorillas | spotted the sandwiches.

We'd also probably agree that the boxed group of words in the following sentence is not a possible unit:

Six hungry | gorillas spotted the | sandwiches.

So, it appears that sentences are not simply "flat" strings of words; they have some kind of internal structure, structure about which we have pretty strong intuitions.

So far, we've referred to long strings of words as sentences. But as we'll see, we actually know that *sentence* is a general term for a long string of words but that sentences can be made up of one or more *clauses*, syntactic units that we are fully, if unconsciously, aware of. We know, for example, that if we combine *spotted the sandwiches* with *six hungry gorillas*, we have a complete syntactic unit, namely, a clause. And we also know that the following sentence is (one big) clause but that it also contains two smaller clauses inside it:

> The gorillas thought that *they spotted the sandwiches* when *they were strolling through the jungle.*

In this chapter, we explore a specific aspect of your intuitive knowledge of syntax, in particular your knowledge of syntactic categories such as nouns, verbs, and so on, and how those categories can be combined with other words to form larger categories, or **phrases**. We will also discuss the largest syntactic unit, the clause, and how some clauses are independent and others are subordinate. We'll also take a brief look at how clauses differ from sentences (and how they can be the same!). We will introduce you to phrase structure rules, a notation that allows us to express this knowledge of syntactic units. We will also explore a possible parameter based on language variation over space (looking at evidence from modern French) and also over time (looking at evidence from earlier varieties of English). We'll see that our knowledge of categories is likely part of Universal Grammar.

phrase syntactic unit (NP, VP, etc.) headed by a syntactic category (N, V, etc.)

Nouns and Noun Phrases

Many children learn in school that a noun is a "person, place, or thing." While this semantic definition is useful, it tells us nothing about the fact that we use a great deal of information, other than meaning, to identify nouns. For example, we can recognize nouns even though we have no idea what they mean. We know that in the phrase *the granflons*, the nonsense word *granflons* is a noun because we know that in English nouns usually follow a certain set of words (in this case, the determiner *the*). In Chapter 5, we identified these words as quantifiers, numerals, and determiners, all of which are functional categories. Though these categories are distinct in a number of important ways, for simplicity here we'll assume that they are all members of a single functional category, determiner (Det).

ˈhwæt!

Not all languages have determiners, which is one reason that people who learn English as a second language often omit them in English.

Determiners: *the, these, this, all, some, six,* etc.
Six houses, all dogs, few people

Nouns can also be introduced by more than one determiner—*the six houses, all eight dogs, a few people*—and these elements must also occur in a particular order. We know, for example, that **eight all dogs* is ungrammatical but that *all eight dogs* is fine. We also know that certain nouns need no determiner at all; generic nouns and mass nouns can occur without them.

Lions roar. (generic plural noun)
Lou makes lovely *jewelry*. (mass noun)

And proper names usually occur without determiners, too:

> *Mary* walked in the door. (proper name)
> *The Mary walked in the door.

(We can say *I know a lot of Marys*, but in this sense *Mary* has become a common noun. We'll talk more about the proper/common distinction in Chapter 9, on semantics.)

Some proper nouns do take determiners, however:

> The *Chunnel* is an amazing innovation.
> The *New York Mets* played a game yesterday.

The English determiner system is therefore very complex, and a full description of it (if we could even give one) is beyond our scope here. Simply observe that, typically, a good test for whether a word is a noun or not is to see if it can occur after one of the function words from the category D. We can turn this statement around into a generalization about the syntax of D: this functional category introduces nouns.

A Phrase Structure Rule for Noun Phrases

Descriptions and generalizations about the syntax of nouns and of the categories that introduce nouns are aspects of **phrase structure** and can be expressed by phrase structure rules for the larger syntactic unit, the noun phrase, or NP.

phrase structure system of rules that organizes words into larger units or phrases

In phrase structure rules, items in parentheses are optional. The following rule means that although NP must contain a noun, the determiner element is optional. (The phrase structure rule for NP is of course much more complex than the one we provide here, which allows N to be preceded by only a single, optional determiner.) You can read the following phrase structure rule as "an NP can contain a determiner (optional) and must contain a noun."

> NP → (Det) N
> Det → *these, six, all, every, the/a*

RPE 7.1

Phrase structure rules provide a way to express some of the basic properties of syntactic structure. Phrase structure is actually very complex, and how to represent it most accurately is a subject of constant debate among linguists who study syntactic theory. The simple phrase structure rules we will use in this chapter express the basic syntactic concepts that any notation must capture, namely, that syntactic structure is divided into phrases and that each phrase must have a **head**. For example, a noun phrase (NP) must include at least a noun, and a verb phrase must include at least a verb, and so on. The head of the phrase is the most important part because it determines the category of the phrase. All the elements that combine to form a phrase are called **constituents**. So, N is the head of NP, a phrase that can also include D. Both D and N are constituents of NP. Heads combine with other elements to make up phrases.

head word whose syntactic category determines the category of the phrase

constituent group of words that forms a larger syntactic unit

We can draw tree diagrams, a graphic representation of phrase structure, for simple noun phrases using the phrase structure rule for NP. Some examples are given here. The constituents of the noun phrase are *these* and *mangoes* in one diagram, *four* and *mangoes* in another, and *all* and *mangoes* in another. The noun *mangoes* is the head of each NP. All of the following NP tree structures are built from the phrase structure rule NP → (D) N.

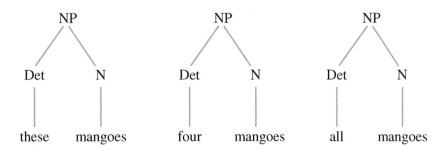

This simple phrase structure rule captures the syntax of the simplest noun phrases. We will modify this rule shortly to provide a more accurate description of other English noun phrases (such as *the delicious mangoes* or *the mangoes from Florida*).

Verbs and Verb Phrases

Continuing our discussion of phrases, we turn now to the verb phrase (VP), one of the basic building blocks of the sentence. First, let's review some important facts about verbs that we discussed in Chapter 5.

Recall that verbs in English have as many as five forms: *infinitive, present tense, past tense, present participle,* and *past participle*. The forms of the verbs are morphological. Syntactically, verbs can be divided into three groups: **auxiliary, main,** and **modal.**

auxiliary verb form of *have, be,* or *do* that occurs in Aux, a syntactic position preceding V

main verb verb that occurs under V and is head of VP

modal verb class of verbs (*can/could, may/might*, etc.) that occur in Aux

Main verbs: *feel, go, eat, run, hope*
Horatio *feels* happy.
       went on a trip.
       ate breadfruit.
       ran the Boston Marathon.
       hopes to win the election.

Auxiliary verbs: *have, be*
Horatio *has* eaten too much candy.
       is running for his life.

Modal verbs: *may, might, shall, should, will, would, can, could, must*
Horatio *may, might, shall, should, will, would, can, could, must* go on a cruise.

Auxiliary, main, and modal verbs occur in a certain order in English. The following sentences illustrate the various combinations of the main verb *read* with auxiliary and modal verbs. These combinations follow a particular syntactic pattern, shown by the fact that the first four sentences are grammatical and the next three sentences, in which orders are rearranged, are ungrammatical.

Scarlett *should have been reading* under the umbrella.
Scarlett *should be reading* under the umbrella.
Scarlett *should read* under the umbrella.
Scarlett *read* under the umbrella.
*Scarlett *have should been reading* under the umbrella.
*Scarlett *should reading be* under the umbrella.
*Scarlett *read should* under the umbrella.

In addition to a main verb, the verb phrase can include as many as three other verbs. These options include a modal (which, if present, must come first) and as many as two auxiliary verbs, forms of *have* or *be*. Examples of each possible order are given here.

modal + *have* + *be* + main verb	might have been sleeping
modal + *have* + main verb	might have slept
modal + *be* + main verb	might be sleeping
modal + main verb	might sleep
have + main verb	has slept
have + *be* + main verb	has been sleeping
be + main verb	is sleeping
main verb	slept

Language Alive!

How Many Modals?

Speakers of other varieties of English, primarily in the southeastern United States, routinely produce sentences with two modals and find this double modal construction completely natural. Which modals they are varies from person to person and across subregions of the Southeast:

We *might could sing* at the concert.
    modal modal main verb
I *may should apply* for a new job.
    modal modal main verb

Two modal verbs is the limit, however. No variety of English allows sentences like the following:

*We *might could would sing* at the concert.
    modal modal modal main verb

From these data, we can see that main verbs are not optional in the sentence (which makes sense, because you can't have a sentence without a verb or verb phrase), and they can be preceded by as many as three other verbal elements. These elements must occur in a specific order; modals precede auxiliary *have, have* precedes *be,* and last is the main verb. These three elements are optional, but the main verb is not. So, we can state the order of verbal elements as follows, with modals and auxiliary verbs in parentheses:

RPE   7.2 >

(modal) (have) (be) main verb

A Phrase Structure Rule for Verb Phrases

Because the main verb is required in the verb phrase, it is the *head* of the verb phrase (VP). Just as in NP, the elements that precede the main verb are functional categories, namely, auxiliary verbs and modals. Auxiliary verbs and modals are distinct from each other, but for simplicity we'll refer to them as members of a single functional category, Aux. As we did with NP, we'll also only diagram sentences with a single Aux element, to keep things simple.

The following phrase structure rule captures the generalization that V in English is optionally preceded by an Aux element, namely an auxiliary verb or modal.

VP → (Aux) V
Aux → modal, *have, be*

RPE   7.3 >

With this rule, we can draw the following trees:

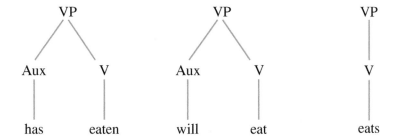

Again, this rule is very simple and allows us to generate only one kind of VP, namely, a VP that is made up of only a main verb, or of one auxiliary verb or modal and a main verb. We'll elaborate this rule later when we consider the phrase structure of other categories that can occur in VP.

Evidence for the Aux Position

So far, we've simply assumed, based on the order of verbs in the verb phrase, that auxiliary verbs and modals occur in Aux and main verbs occur in V. In this section, we'll look at some syntactic puzzles that provide evidence for this distinction. We'll then see

hwæt!

Tree diagrams are also used in other fields to help sort out complex ideas by organizing them on paper or onscreen; for example, math and probability, genealogy, management and planning (workload and schedules), sports ratings, and biological classification (species, genus, family, order, etc.).

that we need to revise our rule for VP in order to capture some significant differences between main verbs and those that occur in Aux.

When we look at how **negation** works in English, we see a clear difference between modal and auxiliary verbs and main verbs. Auxiliary verbs and modals, which here we refer to collectively as Aux verbs, typically occur before the negative adverb *not*.

negation a logical operation—when the negation of a proposition is true, that proposition is false, and vice versa

Negation: *have/be/modal + not*
Joachim <u>is</u> *not* playing a game of chess.
Joachim <u>has</u> *not* played a game of chess.
Joachim <u>must</u> *not* play a game of chess.

Main verbs can't occur in this position:
*Joachim <u>played</u> *not* a game of chess.

Language Alive!

Don't Use Double Negatives. NOT!

Most of you were probably taught to avoid using double negatives, as in *You don't know nothing*, even though they might sound just fine to you. Double negative constructions are highly stigmatized because they occur in dialects whose speakers are stigmatized, namely, speakers of southeastern U.S. English, African American English, and Hispanic English. Double negatives are also more common among blue-collar speakers than among white-collar ones. But double negatives are not only very common among the world's languages (French is an example, with *ne-pas*), they were also very common in earlier varieties of English. In fact, triple and even quadruple negatives were not uncommon!

Spanish:	Juan no sabe nada.
	'Juan no knows nothing.'
English:	Juan don't know nothing.
Middle English:	He nevere yet no vileynye ne sayde
	'he never yet no villainy not said'

—Chaucer, *Canterbury Tales*

subject-auxiliary inversion movement of an auxiliary verb to sentence-initial position (preceding the subject) to form a question

Subject-Auxiliary Inversion

Another difference between auxiliary and modal verbs and main verbs is that Aux verbs appear in sentence-initial position in yes/no questions. This question formation rule is called **subject-auxiliary inversion**, or SAI, a process by which Aux verbs *move* over the subject NP. (We discuss syntactic movement more in Chapter 8.)

Minerva *is* singing the aria.
Is Minerva singing the aria?

Joachim *has* played an excellent game of chess.
Has Joachim played an excellent game of chess?
Joachim *can* play an excellent game of chess.
Can Joachim play an excellent game of chess?

Main verbs in English cannot undergo SAI. If we try to invert the main verb and the subject, we get a completely ungrammatical sentence in English (though the order is perfectly grammatical in some languages).

Minerva *sings* the aria.
*Sings Minerva the aria?

Another difference between English main verbs and Aux verbs is that only Aux verbs can occur in tag questions, questions that are added on to the end of the sentence by a rule we'll refer to as **tag question formation**.

tag question formation syntactic rule that "copies" the subject and an auxiliary or modal verb in sentence-final position: *Bert should leave, shouldn't he?*

Minerva is singing the aria, *isn't she?*
Joachim can't play chess, *can he?*
Joachim has played an excellent game of chess, *hasn't he?*

Main verbs cannot occur in tag questions, which is why we never produce sentences such as this one:

*Joachim played an excellent game of chess, *playedn't he?*

Summarizing, it appears that there is a lot of evidence for a distinction between Aux verbs and main verbs in English:
Only Aux verbs

- undergo SAI
- occur to the left of *not*
- show up in tag questions

We can explain this syntactic distinction by hypothesizing that auxiliary verbs and modals occur in a syntactic position, what we call Aux, to the left of (optional) *not*. Main verbs occur in a different position, V, to the right of *not*.

RPE 7.4

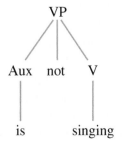

English Do Insertion

So far, it seems quite clear that there is a distinction in English between the Aux and V positions. But what if there is no auxiliary element in a sentence? What happens in these sentences? Is there an Aux position present or not?

> Minerva sings/sang the aria.
> Joachim plays/played a game of chess.

We are now faced with a *theoretical* question because the answer is not yet something we can see; we need to find data that support or refute our hypothesis about the phrase structure of VP.

We might simply say that in these sentences, Aux, which is optional anyway, is simply omitted. But in fact, there is evidence that even in such sentences, Aux is still there. This evidence comes from a syntactic phenomenon called **do insertion.**

When you read about negation, SAI, and tag questions above, you may have noticed that the ungrammatical sentences we discussed with only a main verb (we repeat them below), become grammatical when we insert the pleonastic auxiliary verb *do.*

> *Joachim played not a game of chess. (negation)
> *Sings Minerva the aria? (SAI)
> *Joachim played an excellent game of chess,
> > *playedn't he*? (tag question formation)
> Joachim *didn't* play a game of chess.
> *Does* Minerva sing the aria?
> Joachim played a game of chess, *didn't he*?

do **insertion**
insertion of pleonastic do into empty Aux to form questions, tags, or negative sentences

These data illustrate a syntactic pattern that seems peculiar to English, namely, the insertion of a *dummy*—or in more technical terms, **pleonastic**— auxiliary verb *do.* This *do* insertion occurs in sentences without an auxiliary or modal verb, in contexts in which such an auxiliary or modal is needed to form a question or negate the sentence.

pleonastic *do*
"dummy," or semantically empty, auxiliary verb

Another way to look at *do* is in terms of the Aux position itself. We can say that in sentences that express tense but that do not have auxiliary verbs, the Aux position is nevertheless still there. When such sentences are negated or questioned, *do* shows up in Aux to do the work of an auxiliary verb. This suggests that English speakers' knowledge of syntax includes a *do* insertion rule that can be informally stated this way:

Do **insertion**
To perform subject-auxiliary inversion, negation, and tag question formation, insert *do* in Aux if Aux is otherwise empty.

It appears, then, that there is very good reason to assume that in English, the Aux position is there in all tensed clauses, even if it isn't filled with an actual verb. It also appears that English, unlike other languages, has a pleonastic auxiliary that can be inserted in Aux to do the work of an auxiliary verb under certain conditions.

Language Alive!

English Didn't Always *Do*

English has not always had an auxiliary verb *do*. Old English lacked *do* altogether. Auxiliary *do* began to appear in negatives and questions in Middle English (1100–1400), though we still also find examples of such constructions without *do*. (Examples are from Millward 1996: 186.)

> My maister did not graunt it. ('My master did not grant it.')
> Fader, why do ye wepe? ('Father, why do you weep?')
> Gaf ye the child any thing? ('Give you the child any thing?')

Also in Middle English, nonemphatic *do* appears:

> Unto the mayde that hir doth serve
> To the maid that her doth serve

That *do* is inconsistent during this period suggests that English was still in transition and that *do* insertion was not (yet) an obligatory rule.

It seems that in Early Modern English (1500–1800), *do* insertion was optional. (Shakespeare sometimes used both constructions in the same play!)

> Why do you look on me?
> Why look you so upon me? (*As You Like It*)

And we also find both negative sentences with negation following the main verb and negative sentences with auxiliary *do*.

> I doubt it not. (*Romeo and Juliet*)
> I do not doubt you. (*Hamlet*)

Not until very late Early Modern English did *do* insertion become an obligatory rule in English, and speakers began to form questions and negatives the way we do today.

A scene from the 2006 film *As You Like It* based on Shakespeare's play, directed by Kenneth Branagh.

BBC FILMS/HBO FILM/SHAKESPEARE FILM COMPANY/THE KOBAL COLLECTION

Emphatic and Main Verb Do

The pleonastic auxiliary *do* is sometimes inserted in sentences for other reasons. For example, in sentences that lack an auxiliary or modal, we might insert *do* to emphasize something. This emphatic *do* is stressed.

> But I *did* clean my room!
> So you *did* eat that last piece of cake! You rat!

The sentences sound very odd if *do* is not emphatic and is pronounced with level intonation.

> But I did clean my room.
> You did eat that last piece of cake.

And there is yet another place where we find *do* in English:

> I *did* my homework./I am *doing* my homework./I have *done* my
>   homework.
> They *did* a good job on the project.
> You *do* the dishes every night.

In these examples, *do* is the main verb in the sentence. We know this because if we want to negate or question such sentences, *do* insertion applies, just as it does in other sentences with main verbs and no Aux verb.

> *Did* I do my homework? (SAI)
> They *didn't* do a good job on the project. (negation)
> You do the dishes every night, *don't* you? (tag question formation)

A Phrase Structure Rule for Clauses

We have seen that there is quite a bit of evidence that the Aux position is not part of VP, but rather a separate constituent altogether. Let's consider one more piece of evidence, illustrated by the following sentences.

> Joachim played a game of chess but Minerva didn't.
> Minerva won't sing the aria but Joachim will.

These sentences illustrate a phenomenon called VP deletion, which we discuss in more detail in Chapter 8. What's important to notice here is that VP deletion seems to operate only on VP, but not on Aux:

> Joachim played a game of chess but Minerva didn't ~~play a game of chess~~.

> Minerva won't sing the aria but Joachim will ~~sing the aria~~.

The evidence from VP deletion, together with the other evidence we have discussed, supports the hypothesis that Aux is actually separate from VP. To capture this distinction, we revise our rules for VP and Aux as follows, where Aux is a separate node, optionally filled with a modal or auxiliary.

> VP → V
> Aux → (modal) *(have) (be)* or *(do)*

We can now propose a phrase structure rule for the clause, or CL, where Aux is separate from VP (and present, even if it is not filled with an actual word).

CL → NP Aux VP

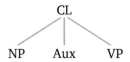

Using these rules, we draw the following simple tree diagrams:

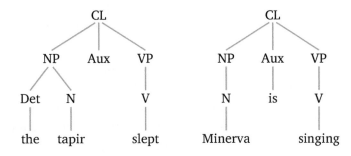

We will need to amend our phrase structure rules in order to draw more complex sentences (such as *Minerva is singing the aria* and *The tapir feels sleepy* and others). We will explore how we can extend our simple phrase structure rules to draw more complex tree diagrams below.

RPE 7.5

Adjectives and Adjective Phrases

Adjectives are words that describe nouns: *tall* trees, *happy* child, *enormous* hogs. Adjectives (Adj) can themselves be modified by members of the functional category Deg, which stands for *degree*, such as *so, too, very, rather,* and *quite.*

the *rather enormous* hog
    Deg   Adj

a *very happy* child
  Deg Adj

These examples suggest that a simple phrase structure rule for Adjective Phrase is the following:

AP → (Deg) A
Deg → *very, so, rather*

We can now draw simple trees for the adjective phrase (AP):

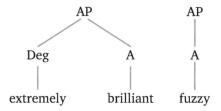

Adjective Phrase Positions

Because adjective phrases modify nouns, they occur in certain positions in the sentence where they can do just that. One position is called *prenominal* position, the position before a noun in a noun phrase. The adjective phrases in the two preceding examples occur in prenominal position, as do those in the following noun phrases:

hwæt!

In Romance languages, adjectives occur before and after the noun, but in different ways than in English. Descriptive adjectives such as color adjectives occur after the noun (French: *le chat noir* 'the black cat'), but other adjectives occur before the noun (*mon vieil ami* 'my longtime friend'.)

> the *enormous* hog
> six *enormous* hogs
> all *very happy* children

Adjective phrases can also occur after certain nouns in English, in *postnominal* position, right after the noun in a noun phrase:

> something *wicked*
> the options *available*
> the heir *apparent*

We can now elaborate our phrase structure rule for NP to include prenominal and postnominal adjective phrases:

RPE   7.6

> NP → (Det) (AP) N (AP)

Adjective phrases also occur in what we call *predicate* position, immediately following what are called **linking verbs**—verbs that link the subject with an adjective phrase that describes it. Linking verbs include *remain, appear, become, be,* and "sense" verbs such as *feel, taste, look, smell,* and *sound.* (In traditional grammar, adjective phrases in this position are called *predicate adjectives.*) The following italicized adjective phrases are in predicate position:

linking verb verb that "links" the subject of the sentence with a phrase that describes it, usually an adjective phrase

> The hog remained/appeared/became/is/seemed *enormous*.
> (subject)   (linking verb)   (adjective)

> The pork tasted/smelled very *funny*.
> (subject)   (linking verb)   (adjective)

To diagram these sentences, we need to elaborate our phrase structure rule for VP to include an optional AP after V. We can do this by revising the VP rule in the following way:

> VP   →   (Aux) V (AP)

Did You Know...?

The Root of Trees

Sentence diagrams have been around for a long time, though the "tree" diagrams we use here are a relatively recent version of graphic representations of the relationships among words in a sentence. Sentence diagrams date back to "balloon" diagrams of W. S. Clark, in his 1847 book A Practical Grammar: In Which Words, Phrases & Sentences are Classified According to Their Offices and Their Various Relationships to Each Another. Though we don't see balloon diagrams anymore, you may be familiar with their descendent, Reed-Kellogg diagrams, invented by Alonzo Reed and Brainerd Kellogg, and first presented in their 1877 book Higher Lessons in English. Rather than balloons or trees, Reed-Kellogg diagrams use horizontal, vertical, and slanted lines to express relationships among constituents in the sentence. A vertical line divides the subject from the predicate for example, and modifiers, such as adjectives, are drawn on slanted lines connected with the word or phrase they modify.

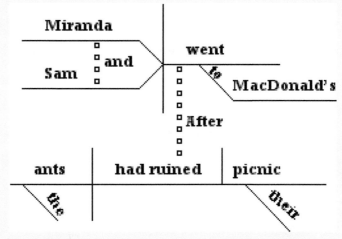

Source: http://www.utexas.edu/courses/langling/e360k/handouts/diagrams/
diagram_basics/basics.html—accessed 10-01-11. Used by permission.

Within generative grammar, the approach we take in this book, there are a number of theories of phrase structure and diagramming: Head-driven Phrase Structure Grammar (HPSG), Generalized Phrase Structure Grammar (GPSG), Tree-adjoining Grammar, Relational Grammar, Lexical Functional Grammar (LFG), among others. Though each theory differs in significant ways from the others, all strive to represent the relationships among constituents in the clause, relationships that cannot be captured by a linear, or "flat" structure.

Author Kitty Burns Florey gives the history of diagramming sentences and tells of her experiences in sixth grade in her popular 2006 memoir *Sister Bernadette's Barking Dog: The Quirky History and Lost Art of Diagramming Sentences*.

A Variable Phrase

We all know, however, that AP isn't the only kind of phrase that can follow a verb; at this point, our phrase structure rule is quite restrictive. It does not allow us to diagram the VPs in such sentences as *The enormous hog talked to the goose* or *The enormous hog won a prize yesterday*. We can't even diagram the VP in the sentence *The enormous hog won the prize*, where the verb *won* is followed by a simple NP. We can remedy this situation, however, by simply saying that VP can be followed by a phrase of *any* category, not just AP. We can use a variable, X, to stand for any category (so XP can be NP, VP, AP, etc.). We can now write a more accurate rule for VP:

VP → V (XP)
XP = a phrase of any category (NP, AP, etc.)

Some tree diagrams that conform to our phrase structure rules so far are given here.

hwæt!

Words that are not typically adjectives can become adjectives, as evidenced by their pairing with degree words: *very now* and *so last year*.

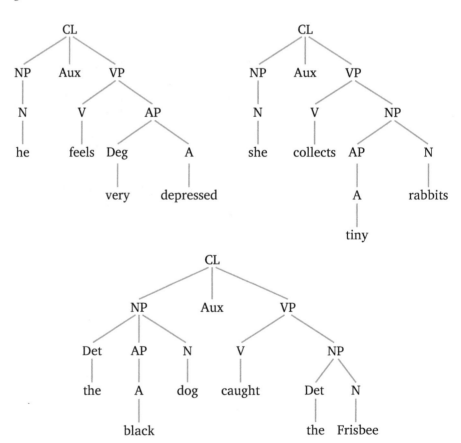

What's the Right Answer?

Did you have to take the Scholastic Aptitude Test (SAT) when you applied to colleges? Do you remember the grammar section of the test? How did you do?

In school, we learn that there is a difference between correct and incorrect grammar and that good speaking and writing depend on knowing the difference between the two. The SAT tests that knowledge. And the Educational Testing Service, which generates and scores the SAT, has all the right answers, right? Wrong. It turns out that "right" and "wrong" answers on the grammar section are somewhat controversial. In fact, there was quite a flap over one of the answers on the PSAT, the practice exam that prepares students for the SAT. The question was whether this sentence was grammatical or whether there was an error:

> Toni Morrison's genius enables her to create novels that arise from and express the injustices African Americans have endured.

What do you think?

The intended answer was "no error." But this answer was challenged by high school journalism teacher Kevin Keegan, who argued that, according to well-known rules of prescriptive grammar, the sentence is ungrammatical because the pronoun *her* cannot take the possessive phrase *Toni Morrison's* as its antecedent.

Keegan's claim sparked something of a grammatical firestorm, spawning articles in the *New Yorker* magazine, the *New York Times*, and the *Weekly Standard*, among others. In the face of the controversy, the Educational Testing Service felt obliged to convene a panel to decide what to do. In the end, the question was dropped from the test, the test was rescored, and scores overall improved as a result, which means that many students found an error in the test sentence and originally got the answer "wrong."

This controversy over pronouns and antecedents illustrates a number of issues about the politics of language and attitudes about grammar, summarized by linguist Geoffrey Nunberg in an article in the *New York Times*. One issue is that there is not a consensus on what is right or wrong even among style manuals; another is that *usage*, or how we actually use language (which is what students relied on when finding no error in the Toni Morrison sentence), often diverges from the rules and conventions of the authorities. Part of students' anxiety over grammar, then, comes from their uncertainty over how grammar errors are defined

and, in terms of testing, scored. It is no wonder that students are afflicted with "grammar anxiety"; they are taught that much hinges on some notion of grammatical correctness, but how grammatical correctness is defined remains something of a mystery! Perhaps, as linguist Mark Liberman suggests, SAT grammar questions should be created by a usage panel with a broader view of language and how we (actually) use it.

For more information

Lewin, T. 2003. College board corrects itself on test score. *The New York Times*. May 15.

Liberman, M. 2005. The SAT fails a grammar test. *Language Log*. January 31. http://itre.cis .upenn.edu/~myl/languagelog/ archives/001863.html

Nunberg, G. 2003. The nation: Parts of speech; the bloody crossroads of grammar and politics. *The New York Times*. June 1. http://query.nytimes .com/gst/fullpage.html?res=9E06 E2DC1430F932A35755C0A965 9C8B63

Skinner, D. 2003. The PSAT's genius grant: The Educational Testing Service gets a question wrong and reveals too much of its literary tastes. *The Weekly Standard*. May 15. http://www .weeklystandard.com/Content/ Public/Articles/000/000/002/ 681xnmqz.asp

Adverbs and Adverb Phrases

You may have learned that adverbs modify verbs and that most end in *-ly*, such as *quickly, happily, enormously,* and so on. Many adverbs do not end in *-ly*, however, and not all adverbs modify only verbs. (And some adjectives end in *–ly* too: *friendly, lovely, manly*). Here is a short list of adverbs, including many that do not end in *-ly*.

> still, never, often, fast, usually, just, perhaps, even, fortunately, once, twice, also, forcibly, sometimes

Certain adverb phrases (AdvP), like adjective phrases, can be modified by degree words (Deg). "Manner" adverbs (which can be paraphrased as "in X manner") can be modified in this way, as the following examples show:

> very *dejectedly*
> so *slowly*
> awfully *happily*

Other adverbs can't be modified by degree words. (As you can see with *awfully*, some degree words are actually degree *adverbs* themselves!)

> *very *once*
> *so *sometimes*
> *awfully *yet*

We can now write a phrase structure rule for adverb phrases in which the degree word modifier is optional:

> AdvP → (Deg) Adv

RPE 7.7

RPE 7.8

Unlike adjective phrases, which modify nouns, adverb phrases modify verbs and even entire clauses. They also differ from adjective phrases in that they contribute information about time, manner, reason, place, or cause (among other things).

> They marched *clockwise* around the field. (manner)
>   (modifies verb)

> *Luckily*, the beagle ate the dog food before the cat did. (speaker attitude)
> (modifies clause)

> That dog *always* runs around after he eats. (frequency)
>   (modifies verb)

> The dishes aren't done *yet*. (aspect: completion)
>   (modifies verb)

Adverb Phrase Positions

Adverb phrases also have the unique property of occurring in a number of different positions in the sentence. Most adverb phrases can occur at the beginning or at the end of the sentence, and many can also appear in positions internal to the sentence.

> *Happily/luckily/still*, the beagles like their dog food.
> The beagles *happily/luckily/still* like their dog food.
> The beagles like their dog food *happily/luckily/still.*

It is perhaps not surprising that adverb phrases can occur in so many positions, given that they modify a variety of phrases in the sentence. Because of the variability of the position of adverb phrases, we will not integrate them into our set of phrase structure rules (though there are ways to accommodate their syntactic behavior within syntactic theory). We'll assume that they can occur almost anywhere, with some restrictions. Here are some basic tree diagrams with AdvP.

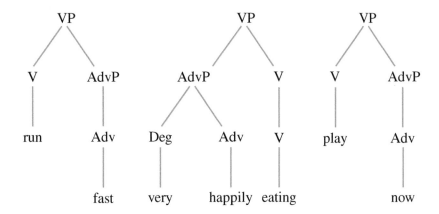

Prepositions and Prepositional Phrases

As we saw in Chapter 5, prepositions seem to be a functional category because they are a closed class; we don't add prepositions to the language. On the other hand, prepositions can have very complex meanings—compare the meanings of *near the table* and *on the table*—and for this reason, prepositions seem to be best categorized as a lexical category.

Syntactically, prepositions (P) are typically followed by NP objects:

> *in/on/under/over/around/above* the rocks
> P   + NP

Some prepositions, like adverbs and adjectives, can be modified by degree words; the following example has the degree words *right/ straight/clear* (there are interesting regional variants: in Alabama, for example, a squirrel can run *slap* up a tree, and in some varieties of American English someone can be *plumb* out of luck).

hwæt!

Which prepositions are used in certain phrases can vary across dialects. In New York you might wait *on line*, but in other places, you wait *in line*. In Washington (state), you might do something *on accident*, but in other places it's *by accident.*

She ran right/straight/clear *into/on/under/over/around/above* the rock.

Prepositions can also be followed by phrases other than NP. In these examples, P is followed by VP and by another prepositional phrase (PP):

You should never eat *before going on a run.*
             P   + VP

You can see wildflowers growing *over under a tree.*
             P   + PP

We can capture the basic syntax of PP with the following phrase structure rule. As with our rule for VP, we will use XP to indicate a phrase of any category.

     PP → (Deg) P (XP)

RPE 7.9 ▷ And here are some tree diagrams of PP that we can draw.

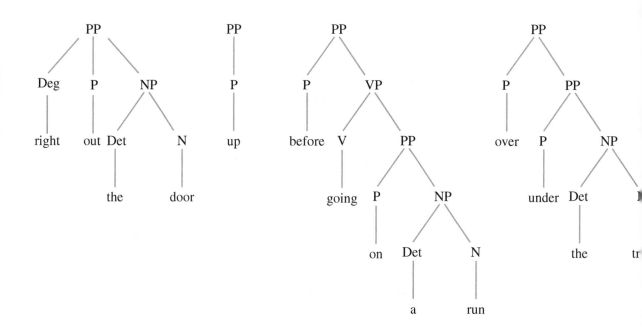

Prepositional Phrase Positions

Prepositional phrases can occur in a number of different positions in the clause. They can occur after verbs in a VP:

She [slept [*under the stars*]].
     VP   PP

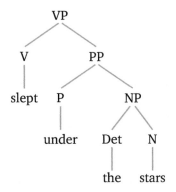

Another common position in which we find PP is in NP, as a modifier of N.

She chose [the kitten [*with white paws*]].
NP   PP

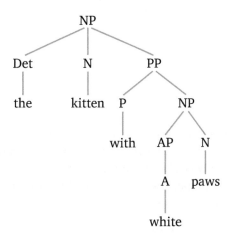

We need to now revise our rule for NP to include PP modifiers, but this is fairly easy to do. Recall that N can be followed by a postnominal AP, as in *something* <u>*wicked*</u>. Recall the phrase structure rule for NP that we came up with to account for this:

NP → (Det) (AP) N (AP)

We can see here that N can also be followed by PP, so we need to revise our phrase structure rule accordingly:

NP → (Det) (AP) N (XP)

According to the second version of our rule, the modifier that follows N in NP can be AP, PP, or a phrase of another category.

RPE 7.10

Did You Know...?

Syntax in the "Real" World

The language developed for the hit movie *Avatar*, called Na'vi, was created by linguist-turned-businessman Paul Frommer. The language has quite a following and continues to develop with the help of its "speakers." Frommer developed a syntax for the language modeled on the structure of real languages; Na'vi is a case-marking language, which uses a system much like that found in Basque, Eskimo-Aleut languages, and Panoan languages of South America. Become a follower by visiting Frommer's blog about the language http://naviteri.org/ and learn more about the structure of the language at http://www.learnnavi.org/navi-grammar/.

Na'vi was not the first language to be developed for a science fiction film. Klingon, the language used in many Star Trek films, was created by linguist Marc Okrand in the 1980s. He has since written two books on Klingon. And noted linguist Victoria Fromkin, who died in 2000, and is perhaps best known for her collection and analysis of slips of the tongue, developed the language Pakuni used by the primate-like creatures on the 1970s TV series "Land of the Lost."

Summary of Phrase Structure Rules

We now have phrase structure rules for the syntactic categories introduced in Chapter 5. Once again, remember that these phrase structure rules are just a way of representing some of the basic unconscious knowledge we all have as speakers of English. Here are the basic phrase structure rules we've come up with so far.

CL → NP Aux VP
NP → (Det) (AP) N (XP)
Det → *that, ten, some, the*
VP → V (XP)
Aux → (modal) *(have) (be)* or *(do)*
AP → (Deg) A
AdvP → (Deg) Adv
PP → (Deg) P (XP)
Deg → *very, so, too, clear, etc.* *

*Remember that although we lump them all together here, the members of the category Deg that modify prepositions are a little different from those that modify adjectives or adverbs.

We are now ready to see how we combine phrases into even larger units: clauses and sentences.

RPE 7.11

More Clauses

clause syntactic phrase made up of at least a subject (NP) and a predicate (VP)

subject syntactically, the NP in the clause [NP VP]

predicate syntactically, the VP in the clause [NP VP]

In this section, we examine in a bit more detail the syntax of the **clause**. We'll discuss the basic building blocks of the clause, subjects and predicates, and we'll talk about how a clause is different from a sentence. We'll introduce the difference between independent and subordinate clauses to set the stage for a more detailed discussion of the syntax of clauses in Chapter 8.

As we've seen, a clause is made up of NP Aux VP and is the largest syntactic phrase. The NP is the **subject**, and the VP is the **predicate**. Given the phrase structure rules we already know, we can diagram a number of different clauses. Here are two examples.

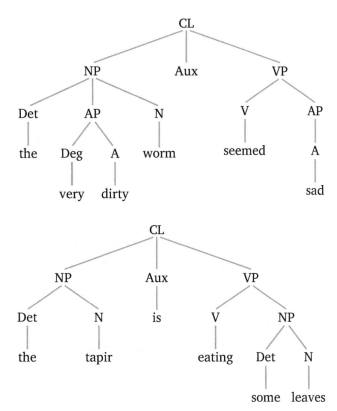

hwæt!

"All that glitters is not gold." "Love is blind." "He was dead as a doornail." Shakespeare (1564–1623) created these and many other sayings that we see, read, and hear every day.

Subjects and Predicates

As you may note, the subjects of the above clauses are *the tapir* and *the very dirty worm*. You've probably learned that a subject is the doer of the action or something similar, but not all subjects are agentive in this way. Though we might say this of *the tapir* in the clause just shown (because it is eating the leaves), we can't really say this of *the very dirty worm* unless we consider *seeming* an action. We can look at other examples and see that subjects of the clauses aren't necessarily agents of an action:

> *It* is raining.
> *There* is a mouse in the hallway.
> *That* is simply ridiculous!

The subjects of these clauses are not even animate, much less agents, so the semantic definition of *subject* (what we might call the logical subject) is very different from the syntactic one. Consider these sentences:

> The cat chased the mouse.
> The mouse was chased by the cat.

In the first clause, called an *active* sentence, *the cat* is the subject and the agent of the action (chasing). In the second clause, a *passive* sentence, *the cat* is still the chaser and *the mouse* is the chasee, but the NP *the mouse* is in the syntactic subject position. (We discuss passive sentences more in Chapter 8.) This again illustrates that when we talk about the subject of a sentence, we're talking about a syntactic *position*, not about meaning.

RPE 7.12

You may have learned in school that the predicate is *what the subject did.* So, in the sentence 'The cat chased the rat', the predicate is what *the cat* (the subject) did, which is *chase the rat.* This definition gets tricky once again because not all subjects are agents of an action, and so the predicate is often difficult to describe in terms of an action performed by the subject. Think about *That is simply ridiculous!* Here, the subject—*that*—isn't *doing* anything, nor can we say that *is ridiculous* describes an action. So, the predicate of a sentence is rather difficult to describe in terms of meaning, but it is fairly simple to describe it syntactically: the predicate is the VP of the clause.

> [The cat] [chased the mouse].
> subject   predicate

> [The mouse] [was chased by the cat].
> subject   predicate

RPE 7.13

Independent and Subordinate Clauses

In the following sentence are several clauses, each of which is italicized. The entire sentence is also a clause because it consists of an NP (the subject, *I*) and a very large VP (the predicate, which starts with *think* and ends with *clams*).

> I think [that Wiley claimed [that Joachim believes [that Daria detests clams.]]]

subordinate clause
clause that is
contained in
another constituent

We call a clause that is contained inside another constituent (either another phrase or another clause) a **subordinate clause** (also called a *dependent*

RPE 7.14 >

clause or an *embedded clause*). All the italicized clauses in the example sentence are subordinate. We've diagrammed this sentence; each subordinate clause is represented by a triangle (a shortcut we'll use rather than draw out each clause in detail).[1]

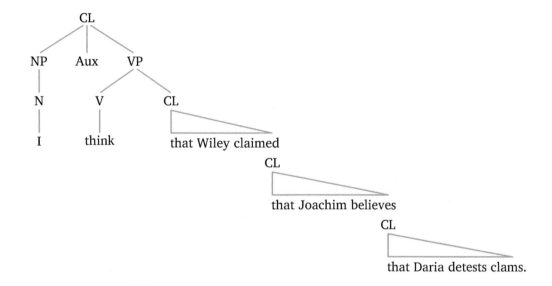

Subordinate clauses come in a variety of types, but all have in common that they consist of a subject and a predicate and that they are contained inside some larger constituent. Here are some examples of different types of subordinate clauses. See if you can pick out the subject and predicate in each.

The teacher thinks *that Mary is very intelligent.*
We wonder *who took the exam.*
The students believe *the teacher to be crazy.*
That pigs have wings is a proven fact.
A person *whom I know from work* was on the news yesterday.

independent clause clause that is not contained in another constituent

The entire (largest) clause is called an **independent clause** because it is not contained inside another constituent.

RPE 7.15 >

What Is a Sentence?

Let's now consider the definition of *sentence*. A clause is a syntactic unit, namely, the unit [NP VP]. A sentence, on the other hand, is more abstract; it

___
1. As you may have noticed, certain subordinate clauses in English can be optionally introduced by *that*. We will ignore *that* when diagramming clauses, for simplicity.

could be a single clause, two clauses, or much more. A sentence can include any number of clauses (both independent and subordinate) and, when written, can be of any length. Using different types of punctuation (colons, semicolons, dashes), it's possible to string together any number of clauses and call the entire thing a "sentence. Here's a very long sentence that clearly includes many clauses. The whole excerpt is punctuated as a single sentence.

Don Quixote and Sancho Panza after jousting with windmills.

About this time, some rain began to fall, Sancho proposed that they should shelter themselves in the fulling-mill; but, Don Quixote had conceived such abhorrence for it, on account of what was past, that he would by no means set foot within its wall: wherefore, turning to the right-hand, they chanced to fall in with a road different from that in which they had traveled the day before: they had not gone far, when the knight discovered a man riding with something on his head, that glittered like polished gold: and scarce had he descried this phenomenon, when turning to Sancho, "I find," said he, "that every proverb is strictly true; indeed, all of them are apophthegms dictated by experience herself; more especially, that which says, 'Shut one door, and another will soon open': this I mention, because, if last night, fortune shut against us the door we fought to enter, by deceiving us with the fulling-hammers; today, another stands wide open, in proffering to us, another greater and more certain adventure, by which, if I fail to enter, it shall be my own fault, and not imputed to my ignorance of fulling-mills, or the darkness of the night." (Cervantes: 148)

We can easily read this sentence, breaking it down into understandable units (clauses, for example). So, we might say that a sentence is (at least) a clause and sometimes more. A very short sentence, then, could be something like *Leave!* and a very long one could be something like the Cervantes excerpt. In any case, it's clear that there is not a one-to-one correspondence between sentences and clauses, and there is no simple way to define *sentence*, because it seems to be more of an abstraction than a syntactic unit. Table 7.1 contains some definitions of *sentence* that give you some idea of the complexity involved in defining this concept.

We talk more about sentences in Chapter 9, on semantics, and in Chapter 13, on written language. For now, we will leave the definition rather fuzzy and concentrate on clauses rather than the more abstract term *sentence*.

© Mary Evans Picture Library/Alamy

Table 7.1	Definitions of *Sentence*

- A string of words satisfying the grammatical rules of a language: "He always spoke in grammatical sentences" (OneLook Dictionary Search: http://www.onelook.com/cgi-bin/cgiwrap/bware/dofind.cgi?word=sentence)

- A word, clause, or phrase or a group of clauses or phrases forming a syntactic unit which expresses an assertion, a question, a command, a wish, an exclamation, or the performance of an action, that in writing usually begins with a capital letter and concludes with appropriate end punctuation, and that in speaking is distinguished by characteristic patterns of stress, pitch, and pauses. (http://www.merriam-webster.com/dictionary/sentence)

- A series of words in connected speech or writing, forming the grammatically complete expression of a single thought; in popular use often such a portion of a composition or utterance as extends from one full stop to another. (Oxford English Dictionary Online. http://www.oed.com.)

- In linguistics, a sentence is a unit of language, characterized in most languages by the presence of a finite verb. For example, "The quick brown fox jumps over the lazy dog." (http://en.wikipedia.org/wiki/Sentence)

Accent on *Teaching with Trees*

Hugh Conroy

You probably know many traditional grammar rules whether you stick to them or not. They include rules that tell you where to place punctuation marks, when to use *whom* rather than *who*, not to say *ain't* and *I don't know nobody*, and to watch your spelling (don't mix up *they're*, *there*, and *their*). You might have had to diagram sentences, too.

A growing number of linguists (including us; see photo) are collaborating with teachers to improve teaching about language in the schools. Their goals include using students' intuitive knowledge of grammar to learn about reading and writing, encouraging students to investigate language itself, and creatively using technology to make it real and include all students.

One teacher using linguistics and technology in the classroom is Beth Keyser, who uses tree diagrams to teach her seventh-graders about language. Rather than relying on traditional definitions (e.g., a noun is a person, place, or thing), Keyser teaches parts of speech by encouraging students to investigate the morphological, syntactic, and semantic properties of words (e.g., nouns follow words such as *the*, *some*, and *a/an*). Diagramming sentences helps her students learn more about phrases and categories and also helps them discover on their own such things as the difference between transitive and intransitive verbs. Through an ingenious use of *smartboard* technology, Keyser's students first diagram simple sentences with intransitive verbs (*the boy laughed*). Parts of speech are color coded. Once students are independently able to create sentences with intransitive verbs, students move on to sentences with transitive verbs (e.g., *ate* in *the boy ate the apple*), discovering that transitive verbs differ from intransitive ones in having a relationship to another phrase (namely, NP) in the tree. Other exercises that Keyser does with her students include exploring the difference between prepositions and particles (*the girl ran up a big hill* versus *the girl ran up a big bill*) and discovering how adverbs can occur at the edges of most phrases but not inside them (*up the tree quickly* but not *up quickly the tree*, for example).

Keyser (2008) observes that having students diagram sentences this way levels the academic playing field. All students (without language disorders) can recognize units of language. Work such as Keyser's moves education about language away from traditional, rote rules to exploration and discovery and focuses not on what students need to learn about grammar but on what they already know!

For more information

Adger, C., C. Snow & D. Christian (eds.). 2002. *What teachers need to know about language.* McHenry, IL: Delta Systems.
Denham, K. & A. Lobeck (eds.). 2005. *Language in the schools: Integrating linguistic knowledge into K-12 teaching.* Mahwah, NJ: Lawrence Erlbaum Associates.
Denham, K. & A. Lobeck (eds.). 2010. *Linguistics at school: Language awareness in primary and secondary education.* New York: Cambridge University Press.
Keyser, B. 2008. Enriching language awareness through linguistics. Linguistic Society of America (LSA) Symposium on Linguistics and Education. Chicago, IL.

Summary

In this chapter, we have explored the basic elements of phrase structure and introduced phrase structure rules as a way to illustrate syntactic structure and some important generalizations about it. We have seen that heads combine with other words to form phrases (NP, VP, AP, etc.), and that there are various syntactic "tests" we can use to determine the categories of words, even nonsense words. We've examined the English verb system in some detail and investigated the syntactic distinction between main verbs and auxiliary verbs, including the syntax of pleonastic *do*, all of which suggests that the Aux position in English is separate from VP and obligatory in tensed clauses, even if it seems to be "empty." We've explored the basic phrase structure of the clause, the largest syntactic phrase, and discussed how clauses can be independent or subordinate and how they differ from sentences.

Sources and Resources

Adger, C., C. Snow & D. Christian (eds.). 2002. *What teachers need to know about language.* McHenry, IL: Delta Systems.
Baker, C. 1995. *English syntax*, 2nd edn. Cambridge, MA: MIT Press.

Carnie, A. 2002. *Syntax: A generative introduction*, 1st edn. Malden, MA: Blackwell.

Cervantes, M. 1755. *The history and adventures of the renowned Don Quixote*. T. Smollett, trans. Published 1986 as *Don Quixote de la Mancha*, 2nd edn. New York: Farrar, Straus & Giroux.

Chomsky, N. 1965. *Aspects of the theory of syntax*. Cambridge, MA: MIT Press.

Denham, K. & A. Lobeck (eds.). 2005. *Language in the schools: Integrating linguistic knowledge into K-12 teaching*. Mahwah, NJ: Lawrence Erlbaum and Associates.

Denham, K. & A. Lobeck (eds.). 2010. *Linguistics at School: Language awareness in primary and secondary education*. New York: Cambridge University Press.

Freedman, R. 1963. *The lyrical novel: Studies in Hermann Hesse, André Gide and Virginia Woolf*. Princeton, NJ: Princeton University Press.

Hersey, J. 1963. *Here to stay*. New York: Alfred A. Knopf.

Keyser, B. 2008. Enriching language awareness through linguistics. Linguistics Society of America (LSA) Symposium on Linguistics and Education. Chicago, IL.

Lewin, T. 2003. College board corrects itself on test score. *The New York Times*. May 15.

Liberman, M. 2005. The SAT fails a grammar test. *Language Log*. January 31. http://itre.cis.upenn.edu/~myl/languagelog/archives/001863.html

Lobeck, A. 2000. *Discovering grammar*. New York: Oxford University Press.

Merriam-Webster OnLine Dictionary. http://www.merriam-webster.com/dictionary/sentence. (24 October, 2008.)

Millward, C. 1996. *Workbook to accompany A biography of the English language*, 2nd edn. Boston: Thomson Wadsworth.

Nafisi, A. 2003. *Reading Lolita in Tehran: A memoir in books*. New York: Random House.

Napoli, D. 1993. *Syntax: Theory and problems*. New York: Oxford University Press.

Nunberg, G. 2003. The nation: Parts of speech; the bloody crossroads of grammar and politics. *The New York Times*. June 1. http://query.nytimes.com/gst/fullpage.html?res=9E06E2DC1430F932A35755C0A9659C8B63

OneLook Dictionary Search. 2008. http://www.onelook.com/cgi-bin/cgiwrap/bware/dofind.cgi?word=sentence. (30 October, 2008.)

Oxford English Dictionary Online. http://www.oed.com. (24 October, 2008.)

Pollard, C. & I. A. Sag. 1994. *Head-driven phrase structure grammar*. Chicago: University of Chicago Press.

Pullman, P. 1996. *The golden compass*. New York: Alfred A. Knopf.

Pullum, G. 2003. Menand's acumen deserts him. *Language Log*. October 3. http://158.130.17.5/~myl/languagelog/archives/000027.html

Skinner, D. 2003. The PSAT's genius grant: The Educational Testing Service gets a question wrong and reveals too much of its literary tastes. *The Weekly Standard*. May 15. http://www.weeklystandard.com/Content/Public/Articles/000/000/002/681xnmqz.asp

Tufte, V. 2006. *Artful sentences*. Cheshire, CT: Graphics Press.

Wikipedia. http://en.wikipedia.org/wiki/Sentence. (24 October, 2008.)

Review, Practice, and Explore

RPE 7.1 Nouns and Noun Phrases

Find all the nouns in the following excerpt. Identify any members of the category Det (as we've defined it here, to include determiners, numerals, and quantifiers) that introduce each noun. There may be other words that precede the noun too. See if you can tell what they are, if they are not members of the category Det.

Lyra and her dæmon moved through the darkening hall, taking care to keep to one side, out of sight of the kitchen. The three great tables that ran the length of the hall were laid already, the silver and the glass catching what little light there was . . . The places here were laid with gold, not silver, and the fourteen seats were not oak benches but mahogany chairs with velvet cushions. (Pullman 1995: 3)

Can you identify four NPs in this excerpt? List them and underline the head noun of each.

RPE   7.2 ⟩ Verbs and Verb Phrases

Write out the following sentences, and circle all the main verbs in each. Underline auxiliary verbs and modals.

a. I might never have seen you if you had not taken this class.
b. Who are you buying that magazine for?
c. Shakespeare wrote many plays and would have written more if he had lived longer.
d. You always seem to be happy about something.
e. Were they with you on the trip?
f. Ned must leave before he gets into trouble.

RPE   7.3 ⟩ More Verbs and Verb Phrases

In a text of your choice, find examples of verb phrases that conform to each of the following patterns. Write out each of your example sentences, and label each verbal element.

a. modal + *have* + *be* + main verb
b. *have* + main verb
c. *have* + *be* + main verb
d. modal + *be* + main verb
e. *be* + main verb
f. main verb (no auxiliaries or modals)

RPE   7.4 ⟩ The Verbs *Have* and *Be*

This section looks at a number of ways that auxiliary verbs differ from main verbs. Many of our examples have included *have* and *be* as auxiliary verbs.

A. Consider the following data, and then try to answer the questions below.

Lucinda *has* a ferret.

Lorenzo *is* obnoxious.

- What is the main verb in each sentence? On what do you base your conclusion?
- What happens when you apply SAI?
- What happens when you negate the sentences or form tag questions?
- Do *have* and *be* in these sentences behave in exactly the same way? If not, how are they different? (*Hint:* The difference has to do with *do* insertion.)
- Are *have* and *be* in these sentences main or auxiliary verbs? Why?

B. Now consider the following sentences.

Lucinda *has had* a ferret.

Lorenzo *is being* obnoxious.

What is the main verb in each of these sentences? What is the auxiliary verb?

C. Finally, consider the following sentences.

Baa, baa, black sheep, have you any wool?

Has Mary a new car?

These sentences probably sound odd to speakers of U.S. English, but they are natural for most speakers of contemporary British English and some varieties of Canadian English. Can you explain how this use of *have* differs from U.S. English *have*, based on these data?

RPE   7.5   ▷   **Which *Do* Is It? Main Verb or Auxiliary?**

Each of the following sentences includes some form of the verb *do*. Using the tools of analysis in the chapter, identify each form of *do* as pleonastic ("dummy") auxiliary *do* or as main verb *do*. (Note: Some sentences may have both, so be careful!) Explain why you label each *do* the way you do, and give any relevant examples (of SAI, tag question formation, and negation) to support your hypotheses.

   a. I never could do yoga!
   b. Did you get a new puppy?
   c. I didn't do it!
   d. You ate my dessert!
      I did not!
   e. You ate my dessert.
      Yes, I did eat your dessert.
   f. I don't do dessert.
   g. Just do the job, will you?

RPE   7.6   ▷   **Finding Adjective Phrases**

The following text excerpt contains several adjective phrases. (Remember, a phrase, as we've defined it, consists minimally of a head but can include other material.) So, *tall* can be an adjective phrase (AP) but so can *very tall*.

   a. List at least five adjective phrases that you find in the excerpt.
   b. List two noun phrases from the excerpt that include prenominal adjective phrase modifiers.

I had never seen Sanaz without her uniform, and stood there almost transfixed as she took off her robe and scarf. She was wearing an orange T-shirt tucked into tight jeans and brown boots, yet the most radical transformation was the mass of shimmering dark brown hair that now framed her face. She shook her magnificent hair from side to side, a gesture that I later noticed was a habit with her; she would toss her head and run her fingers through her hair every once in a while, as if making sure that her most prized possession was still there. (Nafisi 2003: 16)

RPE   7.7   >   Adverb Phrases

The following is a (very uninteresting) text that includes no adverb phrases.

> I was sitting at my desk, staring out the window. A car raced by and I wondered where it was heading. A police car sped by. A child riding her bike down the street stopped to watch the exciting chase.

Add at least six adverb phrases to the text to make it more interesting and descriptive. (To make this a little more challenging, use only three adverbs that end in -*ly*.) How do the adverb phrases change the text? What information do they add?

RPE   7.8   >   Not all -*ly* Words are Created Equal(ly)

As we mentioned in the text, some adverbs have -*ly* endings, and some don't. We also mentioned that some adjectives also end in -*ly*. You can tell -*ly* adjectives and -*ly* adverbs apart based on the category of word they attach to. What category does -*ly* attach to to form adjectives? What category does it attach to to form adverbs?

Adjectives	Adverbs
knightly	happily
manly	softly
friendly	possibly
lovely	obviously

RPE   7.9   >   Finding Prepositional Phrases

Try to find all the prepositional phrases in the following poem, "Of Mere Being" by Wallace Stevens.

> The palm at the end of the mind,
> Beyond the last thought, rises
> In the bronze decor,
>
> A gold-feathered bird
> Sings in the palm, without human meaning,
> Without human feeling, a foreign song.
>
> You know then that it is not the reason
> That makes us happy or unhappy.
> The bird sings. Its feathers shine.
>
> The palm stands on the edge of space.
> The wind moves slowly in the branches.
> The bird's fire-fangled feathers dangle down.

("Of Mere Being," from *Opus Posthumous* by Wallace Stevens, edited by Milton J. Bates, copyright (c) 1989 by Holly Stevens. Preface and selection copyright (c) 1989 by Alfred A. Knopf, a division of Random House, Inc. Copyright (c) 1957 by Elsie Stevens and Holly Stevens. Copyright renewed 1985 by Holly Stevens. Used by permission of Vintage Books, a division of Random House, Inc.)

Can you find a PP that modifies a noun? What kinds of information do the PPs add to the poem?

RPE 7.10 〉 Nouns, Verbs, or Adjectives?

We've seen that the position of a word can help us identify its syntactic category. For example, if we say *Mary is walking*, we identify *walking* as a verb because of its position after the auxiliary verb *is*. In the sentence *Brisk walking is good for you*, we identify *walking* as a noun. Here, it is modified by an adjective, *brisk*, and occurs in the subject position of the sentence, a position in which we often find NPs. Using the tools introduced in the chapter to help you identify the syntactic category of a word, label the category of each of the following italicized words. Explain your answers by showing how the word behaves morphologically and syntactically like other words in a particular category (such as the position in which the word occurs or whether the word can take affixes).

    a. Horatio was very *disappointed* when he found out that he couldn't *father* children.
    b. A very conscientious *father*, Horatio tried not to *disappoint* his children by missing their birthdays.
    c. Loudly *playing* the drums is Horatio's only means of relaxation.
    d. Horatio was *playing* the drums when the hurricane hit.
    e. Loud *playing* of drums disturbs the neighbors.
    f. Those *annoying* drums should be off limits to people like Horatio.
    g. We should *videotape* Horatio *playing* the drums.
    h. We could get a lot of money on eBay for that *videotape*.

RPE 7.11 〉 Jabberwocky Syntax

Following are a few stanzas from the nonsense poem "Jabberwocky" by Lewis Carroll.

    a. Choose six nonsense words in the poem, and label them N, V, P, A, or Adv. Explain why you labeled them as you did and what syntactic (and other) evidence you used.
    b. Find six function words in the poem. How do they contribute to the meaning of the poem and help you make sense of it?
    c. What clues, other than grammatical ones, help you derive meaning from the poem? Can you tell what's going on? On what do you base your interpretation?

> "Beware the Jabberwock, my son!
> The jaws that bite, the claws that catch!
> Beware the Jubjub bird, and shun
> The frumious Bandersnatch!"
>
> He took his vorpal sword in hand:
> Long time the manxome foe he sought—
> So rested he by the Tumtum tree,
> And stood awhile in thought.
>
> And, as in uffish thought he stood,
> The Jabberwock, with eyes of flame,
> Came whiffling through the tulgey wood,
> And burbled as it came!

> One, two! One, two! And through and through
> The vorpal blade went snicker-snack!
> He left it dead, and with its head
> He went galumphing back.

RPE 7.12 > A Test for Subjects

In school, you learn different ways to identify the subject of a sentence. As we've mentioned, one is to identify the doer of the action, but this semantic definition is problematic in that although it may help you identify the *logical* subject of the sentence, it may not help you identify the *syntactic* subject of the sentence, the NP in the subject position. There is a very good test for syntactic subjects, however, namely, the rule of subject-auxiliary inversion. SAI has the effect of inverting or moving the modal or auxiliary verb over the subject to sentence-initial position to form a question to which the answer would be *yes* or *no*.

> *The grizzly bear population in Yellowstone National Park* is dwindling rapidly.

> Is *the grizzly bear population in Yellowstone National Park* dwindling rapidly? (SAI)

Here, the auxiliary verb *is* has moved not over a single noun but over the entire NP, *the grizzly bear population in Yellowstone National Park*, the subject NP.

Another test for the subject is tag question formation. Only subjects and auxiliary verbs (and modals) occur in tags.

> *The spider crept up the wall.*

> *The spider crept up the wall,* didn't *it*? (tag question formation)

> it = the spider (subject)

Using these two tests, find the subjects in the following sentences. What is interesting about the subjects you find? Are they what you expect?

   a.   The shadow crept up the wall.
   b.   There were six linguists at the lecture.
   c.   It is very hot outside.
   d.   The giant chased Jack.
   e.   Jack was chased by the giant.

RPE 7.13 > Diagramming Clauses

   A.   Diagram the clause *The wind is rocking the boat,* and answer the following questions.

      a.   What are the constituents of the subject NP?
      b.   What are the constituents of the VP (the predicate)?

   B.   Diagram the following clauses for practice.

      c.   Several important dignitaries are visiting.
      d.   The audience clapped for the actors.
      e.   Hortense seems depressed.
      f.   Two ducks with yellow beaks will eat the stale bread.

RPE 7.14 > Subordinate Clauses

Find the subordinate clauses in each of the following independent clauses. (*Hint:* Subordinate clauses can occur in various positions.)

   a. Lucinda thinks that ferrets are excellent pets.
   b. That ferrets can be smelly doesn't bother Lucinda.
   c. I wonder whether Lucinda likes ferrets.
   d. My friend met the woman who likes ferrets.
   e. I never believed that Lucinda knew that ferrets made good pets.

RPE 7.15 > Diagramming Practice

We've repeated our set of phrase structure rules below, along with some sentences to diagram for more practice.

        CL → NP Aux VP
        NP → (Det) (AP) N (XP)
        Det → *that, ten, some, the*
        VP → V (XP)
        Aux → (modal) *(have) (be)* or *(do)*
        AP → (Deg) A
        AdvP → (Deg) Adv
        PP → (Deg) P (XP)
        Deg → *very, so, too, clear,* etc.

   a. The schnauzer was eating his food.
   b. Seven chickens scurried under the porch.
   c. Children can be very loud.
   d. Elizabeth ate apples.
   e. Those students headed right out the door.
   f. Each person remained quite calm.
   g. The fly on the wall is cleaning his wings.
   h. The six hungry boys walked to the market on the corner.
   i. Cats with long tails sauntered along the fence.

The cat is chasing the mouse and the dog is chasing too.

Syntax: Phrase Structure and Syntactic Rules

Hierarchical Structure and Ambiguity
  Ambiguity
  Recursion
Silent Syntax
Evidence for Phrases and Clauses
  Substitution
  Pronoun Reference
  Conjunctions and
  Coordination
Movement and Deletion
  Deep and Surface Structure
  Deletion Rules
  Reordering Phrases:
  Movement
Summary
Sources and Resources
Review, Practice, and Explore

Key Concepts

- Phrase structure is recursive, which allows infinitely long phrases and sentences.
- Our unconscious knowledge of syntax includes the ability to interpret ambiguous sentences and unpronounced, yet understood, phrases.
- That we know how to relate pronouns to their antecedents provides evidence for our knowledge of clauses and the boundaries between them.
- That we know how phrases can be moved, coordinated, and deleted within the clause provides evidence for syntactic structure and the rules that apply to it.

Did You Know . . . ?

Who Are *They*, Anyway?
"Does She . . . or Doesn't She?"
Passive Should Be Avoided?

Language Alive!   Silent Pronoun?
Pronouns, Prestige, and Illogical Rules
Sex and Syntax

Linguistics in the News   Starling Syntax?

Accent on   Psycholinguists

> *A word after a word after a word is power.*
>
> —MARGARET ATWOOD

In the previous chapter, we explored the basic structure of phrases and clauses, and we introduced phrase structure rules, the notation we use to graphically represent syntactic structure. In this chapter, we investigate additional properties of phrase structure, and we also take a look at some other syntactic phenomena. We'll examine the evidence for phrases and phrase structure and discover that our knowledge of syntax includes a complex understanding of how to interpret, reorder, and even omit material in a sentence. We'll go beyond phrase structure to discuss a variety of syntactic rules that apply to phrases.

To preview some of the syntactic puzzles we will discuss in this chapter, consider the following sentence:

Six hungry gorillas spotted the sandwiches *in the tree.*

Who spotted what where? We understand this sentence to mean that *in the tree* is where the gorillas spotted the sandwiches, or that the sandwiches in the tree are the ones the gorillas spotted (maybe while sitting under the tree). How do we know this? It turns out that this sentence has two possible structures, one for each meaning.

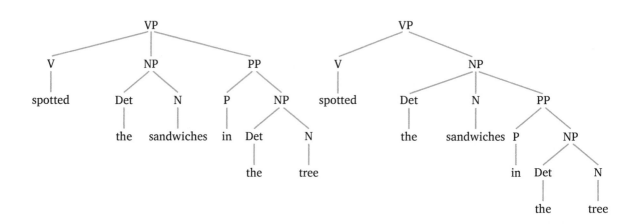

Phrase structure helps us explain how we understand *ambiguity*—when a sentence, phrase, or word has more than one meaning.

Our phrase structure rules also allow us to draw this (very long) NP.

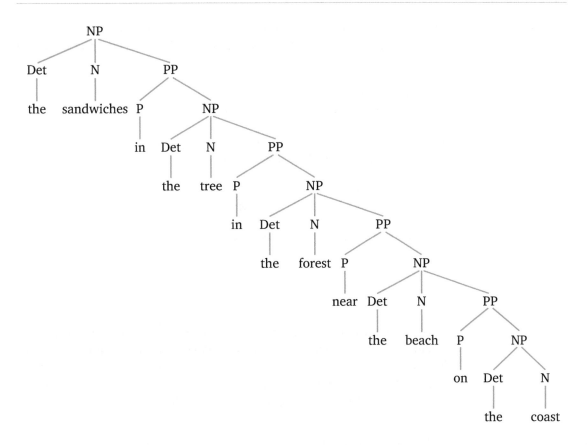

We could make this NP even longer; phrase structure rules allow unlimited extension (even though our memories might not). We'll talk about this property, called *recursion*, in this chapter. We'll also talk about how we understand the meaning of this sentence:

Mary loves her children, and so does Sue.

We understand that Sue loves either Mary's children or her own; how do we know that? And consider the following sentence:

Lee thinks that Cary loves her.

Why can the pronoun *her* refer to *Lee* but not to *Cary*? And why, in the following sentence, can the pronoun *herself* refer only to *Cary*?

Lee thinks that Cary loves herself.

What do we know about the structure of these sentences that allows us to distinguish between these meanings?

Finally, we'll look at a variety of syntactic puzzles that involve moving phrases around in ways that are governed by a complex system of rules.

For example, we know we can transform the following *active* sentence into a *passive* sentence by simply reordering *Beowulf* and *Grendel* and changing the form of the verb:

Beowulf killed *Grendel*. (active)
Grendel was killed by *Beowulf*. (passive)

But we can't form a passive sentence from the following sentence, where we've replaced the verb *kill* with *resemble*:

Beowulf resembled *Grendel*.
*Grendel was resembled by *Beowulf*.

Why not? Read on, and you'll find out!

Hierarchical Structure and Ambiguity

So far, we've illustrated the order of constituents in a particular phrase (phrase structure) with tree diagrams, and we've labeled heads and phrases. We've also seen that one phrase can contain, or *dominate*, another. For example, a clause (CL) dominates a noun phrase (NP) and a verb phrase (VP), as the tree diagrams for the following two sentences illustrate:

The tree seemed so tall.
Each child rolled down the hill.

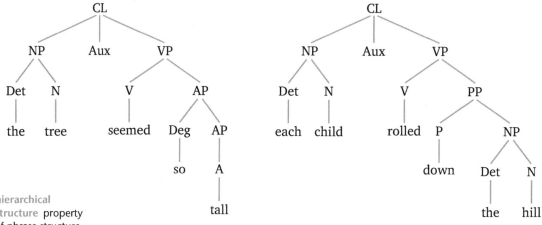

hierarchical structure property of phrase structure whereby one phrase is contained inside another: one phrase dominates another phrase

The tree diagrams illustrate **hierarchical structure**; one phrase dominates another. In addition to CL dominating NP, Aux, and VP, VP dominates V and AP in one sentence and V and PP in the other, and so on.

Ambiguity

Consider the following sentence:

Templeton is a rat.

This sentence is ambiguous; it has more than one meaning. Templeton can be either a furry rodent or an unsavory person. This kind of ambiguity is called **lexical ambiguity**: a sentence is ambiguous because a word—here, the noun *rat*—has more than one meaning.

Now consider this sentence:

The cat chased the rat with a knife.

This sentence is ambiguous; who has the knife, the cat or the *rat*? Let's assume that none of the words in the sentence is ambiguous: the cat is a furry feline, and the rat is a rodent. Two tree diagrams can illustrate the ambiguity, and we call this kind of ambiguity a **syntactic ambiguity**. One possible structure is the following, where the PP *with a knife* is dominated by NP and modifies the noun *rat*:

lexical ambiguity
word that has more than one meaning

syntactic ambiguity
clause or phrase has more than one meaning because it has more than one syntactic structure

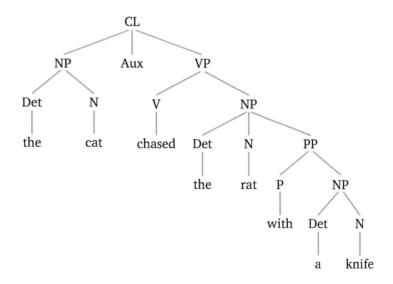

And here is the other, where the PP is in a completely different position. It is a constituent of the VP and modifies the verb *chased*. (Notice that this tree does not conform to the simple phrase structure rules we discussed in Chapter 7. Can you tell why not?)

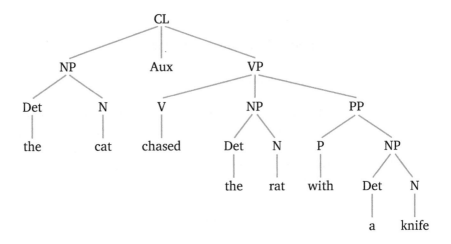

The tree diagrams here are one way of graphically representing the hierarchical structure that is a part of human language. Understanding that language has hierarchical structure allows us to explain, among other things, why certain sentences are ambiguous, even though they have no ambiguous words. They are syntactically ambiguous; the sentences have more than one possible structure.

RPE   8.1

Recursion

Recall from the previous chapter that clauses can contain other clauses, a property called *subordination*. Take, for example, the independent clause (from Chapter 7) that contains a number of subordinate clauses:

> I think *that Wiley claimed that Joachim believes that Daria detests clams.*
> *that Joachim believes that Daria detests clams.*
> *that Daria detests clams.*

We can keep make this independent clause even longer by adding more subordinate clauses:

> I think *that Sue hopes*
> *that Pat said*
> *that Wiley claimed*
> *that Joachim believes*
> *that Daria detests clams.*

hwæt!

Recursion is also an essential tool in computer science, used to break down and build very complex algorithms. A recursive function can repeat itself an infinite number of times.

Even though this independent clause is grammatical, it's awkwardly long. It could be even longer, though; you can imagine how to add onto this clause even more than we have here. If we ever heard someone utter such a long clause, we'd probably lose our train of thought (or get bored or lose interest). This is because of the difference between our linguistic *competence*, our unconscious knowledge of language (which includes recursive rules), and our linguistic *performance*, our actual language use in a given situation. We certainly have the ability to produce sentences of infinite length, but we don't because our memories can only process so much before we get confused.

recursion property that allows phrase structure rules to generate phrases of infinite length

The grammatical property of unlimited extension of phrases is called **recursion**. Recursion is what makes subordination (generating a clause within a clause) possible. More technically, we can say that our phrase structure rule for the clause is a recursive rule. Let's look at why, beginning with the rule itself.

CL → NP AUX VP

Recall that the rule for VP is

VP → V (XP)

Suppose that XP in VP is a clause (CL). Then the phrase structure rule for CL would allow for a VP that dominates a clause that dominates a VP that dominates a clause—you get the idea. The tree diagram for this sentence is given here, and it shows how a CL can include another CL, which can include another CL, and so on. (The rule for CL is recursive, and the rule for VP is, too; can you explain why?)

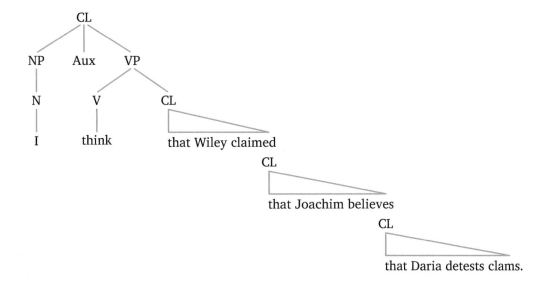

The rule for NP is also recursive. This is because NP includes a possible PP (the XP in the phrase structure rule for NP), which can include another NP (the XP in the phrase structure rule for PP), which can include a PP, which can include an NP, and so on.

NP → (Det) (AP) N (XP)
PP → (Deg) P (XP)

Recursion explains why we can have NPs that are relatively short, such as *the rat* or *the rat with the knife*, but we can also generate very long ones, such as

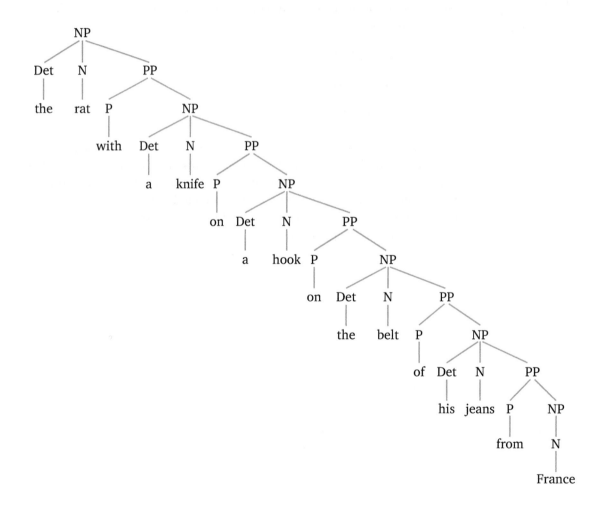

This diagram illustrates that it is possible (indeed, quite common) for one NP to dominate another NP. This means that an NP could (in theory) go on forever, which is why we could (in theory) produce NPs of infinite length!

The evidence that our mental grammar includes recursive phrase structure rules helps explain why we can generate clauses of great complexity and length quite effortlessly. This is one reason why we call grammar generative; it is a system that allows us to produce, or generate, very complex units of language.

RPE   8.2

LINGUISTICS IN THE NEWS   Starling Syntax?

Many people delight in recognizing a bird by its song. A robin sings the robin song, and a blackbird sings like a blackbird. Birds sing the songs they're programmed to sing, and that's it, right? Well, some scientists think that birds might know more than we think they do and that birds might even understand recursion.

Hauser, Chomsky, and Fitch (2002) argue that recursion is unique to human language. Fitch and Hauser created a way to test whether humans understand recursion by using sounds. They came up with a "language" with only two categories of words: short sounds, such as *mo* and *li*, made by men, and the same sounds, made by women. The male and female were distinguished by voice pitch. They created sentences in which sounds were combined in ways that did not involve recursion (so, the sentence pattern might involve male sounds, A, following female sounds, B: ABAB) and sentences that did involve recursion, by embedding a female–male sound pair within another pair, A-AB-B. Humans can figure out

both patterns easily, but tamarin monkeys could figure out only ABAB.

Gentner and colleagues (2006) tried this sound-pattern recognition experiment on male starlings. They created artificial starling songs that followed the ABAB and AABB patterns and then attempted to train starlings by having them listen to the songs. After 40,000 tries, nine of eleven starlings recognized the AABB pattern.

Some scientists have concluded that the starlings' ability to recognize the pattern means that recursion might be part of birds' evolutionary history, too. Chomsky and other linguists remain skeptical, suggesting that the birds were using other criteria (relying on numbers of sounds to recognize a pattern) and that recognizing the pattern may involve short-term memory rather than any real ability to recognize recursion.

Another key difference from human language is that the new patterns for the starlings still had the same meaning, just a different sound. Humans can think of endless pickup lines, but for birds,

as Hauser put it, "It's still, 'I'm Fred, I'm a male.'"

Hauser, Chomsky, and Fitch's work has sparked a debate among linguists about what is unique to human language. (Is it only recursion? What about other aspects of grammar and speech perception and the vocal tract?) It has also sparked great interest among scientists about the ability of other species to recognize sound patterns and what this means about the ingredients and origins of language.

For more information

Gentner, T., et al. 2006. Recursive syntactic pattern learning by songbirds. *Nature* 440. 1204–1207.

Hauser, M., N. Chomsky, & W. Fitch. 2002. The faculty of language: What is it, who has it, and how did it evolve? *Science* 298(5598). 1569–1579.

Zimmer, C. 2006. Starlings' listening skills may shed light on language evolution. *The New York Times*. May 2.

To read about the linguists' arguments, go to http://itre.cis.upenn.edu/~myl/languagelog/archives/002422.html

Silent Syntax

Not all syntactic ambiguity can be explained in terms of hierarchical structure. Other ambiguities arise in sentences in which material is missing but nevertheless understood. Phrase structure again helps us explain why we understand such sentences the way we do.

The following sentence is ambiguous, but not because there are two possible positions for a PP modifier:

The crab is too hot to eat.

Do you understand the sentence as having two meanings? There are no lexical ambiguities here; the noun *crab*, whether the living creature or your dinner, has the same meaning; *hot* indicates temperature, and *eat* means *consume*. In syntactic terms, the ambiguity can be stated in this way: Who or what is the subject of *eat*—the crab or someone else? And who or what is the **complement** of *eat*—crab food or the crab itself? Complements are phrases that combine with heads to form (or "complete") a larger phrase. So, *eat* is a verb that typically is followed by an NP complement (because we typically eat *something*). Here, the complement is understood but not overt or pronounced.

What all this boils down to is that in order to interpret this sentence, we must assume that there is an unpronounced subject of the (infinitival) verb *eat* and also an unpronounced complement of that verb. These two "invisible" NPs are represented by the delta symbol, Δ.

The crab is too hot [Δ to eat Δ].
The crab is too hot (*for someone*) to eat (*the crab*).
The crab is too hot (*for the crab*) to eat (*something*).

We explain the syntactic ambiguity of this sentence by proposing not that the sentence could have two different structures but that there is an "understood" or "silent" subject of *eat* and also a silent complement of *eat*.

> **complement**
> phrase that combines with a head to form a larger phrase

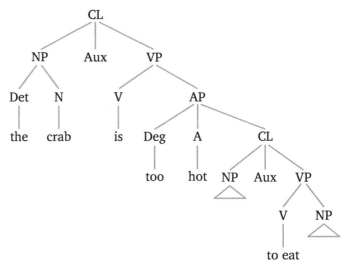

The two silent syntactic positions in this tree diagram can be interpreted in two ways (as the crab or as someone else). If there were no such understood positions, we wouldn't be able to explain why the sentence has more than one meaning.

To further convince you of the existence of **silent syntax**, or structure that is somehow there but unpronounced, consider some more examples:

silent syntax
unpronounced yet
understood syntactic material in
sentences

> Julio is easy to please.
> Julio is eager to please.

Once again, we have sentences that look exactly the same in terms of word order and differ only in the adjective phrases *easy* and *eager*. We interpret these sentences quite differently, however, as illustrated here:

> Julio is easy [Δ to please Δ].
> Julio is easy (*for someone*) to please (*Julio*).
> Julio is eager [Δ to please Δ].
> Julio is eager (*for Julio*) to please (*someone*).

We can't explain the different interpretations of these sentences unless we propose that they include phrase structure that we understand to be there, even though those understood elements are not pronounced.

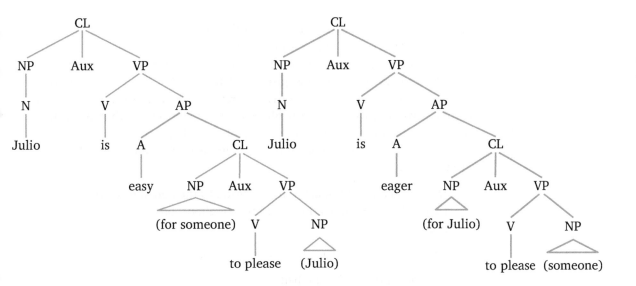

You may have noticed that we have diagrammed the clause here with an Aux node, even though the clause is not tensed (it is an infinitive). There is actually quite a bit of evidence that the Aux node exists in infinitival clauses as well as in tensed clauses, and it may even be the case that *to* is in Aux, rather than in V.

As we can see from the properties of phrase structure, there is a great deal of evidence that our knowledge of phrase structure is quite complex. This knowledge is not at all obvious, particularly in our representations of sentences in writing as linear strings of words rather than as (recursive) phrases with hierarchical structure and understood, yet unpronounced, structure.

RPE 8.3

Evidence for Phrases and Clauses

So far, we've relied mainly on our intuitions about what a phrase is, coming up with phrase structure rules that reflect our syntactic knowledge of the structure of AP, NP, VP, and so on. We haven't yet provided any other *evidence* for phrases or clauses. To study language scientifically, we need to test the data and find evidence that supports or refutes our hypotheses—in this case, about phrase structure. In this section, we'll investigate some of the syntactic evidence for phrases and clauses. We'll introduce a number of important syntactic concepts, and we'll explore the syntax of two functional categories we haven't said much about yet: pronouns and conjunctions.

Substitution

substitution
process by which we replace a phrase with a pronoun (or other proform)

We've seen that NP can be made up of the head N along with an optional determiner (Det) and other optional phrases, including AP and PP modifiers. We assumed that these elements together form a constituent, a syntactic unit. There is evidence beyond just our intuitions that this is the case; NPs can be replaced by *pronouns*, words that replace noun phrases, by a process called **substitution**. You've probably learned in school that pronouns replace nouns, but you'll see here that that is not the case!

The italicized NP in the following sentence has been replaced by the pronoun *they*:

The new houses will make a fine addition to the neighborhood.
They will make a fine addition to the neighborhood.
They = the new houses.

The NP *that mouse* is replaced by the pronoun *it*.

That mouse ran under the bed.
It ran under the bed.
It = that mouse.

Even very large NPs can be replaced by pronouns:

The mouse that Jill found in her pocket when she put her coat on yesterday ran under the bed.

It ran under the bed.
It = the mouse that Jill found in her pocket when she put her coat
on yesterday.

Now, look at the evidence in this next set of sentences. From this evidence, we might conclude that what you learned in school is true: pronouns really do replace nouns. The pronouns *they* and *he* seem to replace the nouns *students* and *Bob*, respectively.

Students ran through the park.
They ran through the park.
Bob ran through the park.
He ran through the park.

But if pronouns replace nouns (rather than noun phrases), then why can't we replace *house* (a noun) with a pronoun?

The new *houses* will make a fine addition to the neighborhood.
*The new *they* will make a fine addition to the neighborhood.

And why can't we replace *mouse*, also a noun, with a pronoun?

*The *it* that Jill found in her pocket when she put her coat on
yesterday ran under the bed.

The answer is that pronouns replace noun phrases, not nouns. The italicized phrases *students* and *Bob*, respectively, are not only nouns but full noun phrases. Here's where phrase structure rules come in handy; by drawing tree diagrams, we can show how *students* and *Bob* are noun phrases, just like *the new houses* and *the mouse that Jill found in her pocket when she put her coat on yesterday*.

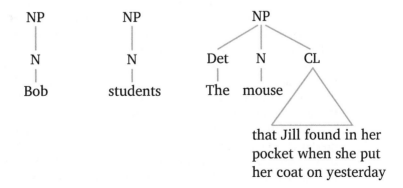

In these tree diagrams, the NPs *students* and *Bob* consist only of a head N. These are therefore the smallest possible noun phrases we can have, those with only N. The more complex NPs (*the new houses, the mouse that Jill found in her pocket when she put her coat on yesterday*), on the other hand, consist of a head N and other material (Det, an AP modifier, and in one case a very large modifier of the noun *mouse*). Even though these NPs are larger than the NP *Bob* and *students*, they are all nevertheless NPs. If we assume that pronouns replace only NPs but not Ns, we explain why all of these NPs can be replaced by pronouns. We also explain why the NPs in which we tried to replace only the head N are ungrammatical; pronouns do not replace nouns. Substitution, therefore, provides evidence for noun phrases as syntactic units.

Silent Pronoun?

Linguists have found much evidence in support of silent pronouns and even for different types of silent pronouns with distinct syntactic behavior. Certain silent pronouns occur regularly in Spanish, Italian, and other languages, but not in English (examples here are from Italian).

> Son il tricheco.
> Δ am the walrus.
> 'I am the walrus.'
> Parla.
> Δ speaks.
> 'He/she/it speaks.'

It is possible in *null subject* languages such as Spanish and Italian to routinely produce sentences in which the subject is missing but interpreted. One reason for this might be that in Spanish and Italian, the inflection on the verb provides enough information for the hearer to interpret the missing subject (as a third person pronoun, for example), but it's not entirely clear that this is the only reason. French, also a Romance language with verbs that express inflection in a way similar to verbs in Spanish and Italian, does not appear to be a null subject language. One can say *Je suis le morse/Je parle* ('I am the walrus'/'I speak') with a subject pronoun *je*, but if that subject pronoun is silent, the result is ungrammatical **Suis le morse/*Parle*.

Although exactly what makes a language a null subject language is the topic of a great deal of study, linguists generally agree that whether a language has this property or not follows from the *null subject parameter* that we briefly discussed in Chapter 1. In English and French, the "switch" for this parameter is set to "off," but in Spanish and Italian, it is "on."

So far, we've talked only about pronouns substituting for NP, but in fact, other **proforms** can substitute for other phrases (that aren't NP) as well. For example, the proform *do so* replaces VP, again showing that VP forms a constituent:

proform word that substitutes for a phrase (AP, PP, or even a clause)

The mouse <u>ran down the hall</u>, and the cat *did so*, too.
VP

Mary wanted to <u>go to Hawaii</u>, but she couldn't *do so* because she didn't have the money.   VP

The proform *so* can replace AP, and *there* can replace PPs that express location:

That giraffe is <u>extremely tall</u>, and *so* is that elephant.
VP

I left the book <u>on the table</u>, but now it's not *there*.
PP

So can even replace an entire clause:

I thought <u>that the movie was terrific</u>, even though you didn't think *so*!
CL

Pronouns and Ambiguity

Pronouns also provide us with evidence for hierarchical structure. Let's look again at the ambiguous sentence we discussed earlier: *The cat chased the rat with a knife*. Remember that this ambiguous sentence has two possible structures. Here's one of them:

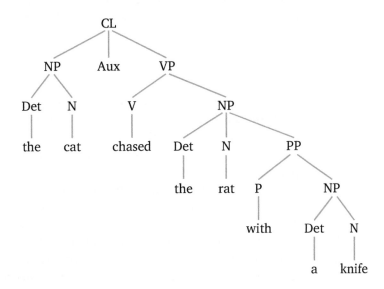

In this tree, the PP *with a knife* is a constituent of NP. We can replace this NP with a pronoun *him*.

The cat chased *him*.
him = the rat with a knife

Now, let's look at the second tree for this sentence.

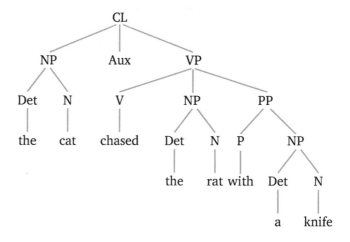

Here, the PP *with a knife* is a constituent of VP, not NP. We can replace the NP *the rat* with *him*, but the PP *with a knife* is not included:

The cat chased *him* with a knife.

So, pronoun substitution provides us with further evidence for our two tree structures, and it is also a good way to tell whether a phrase (here, PP) is a constituent of another phrase (here, of NP or VP) when you diagram a sentence.

RPE 8.4

Pronoun Reference

antecedent phrase to which a proform refers; can be linguistic (spoken, written, or signed) or pragmatic (interpreted from context)

pronoun reference relates a pronoun to its antecedent, the phrase to which the pronoun refers

Pronouns provide evidence for phrases in another way as well. Their syntactic properties tell us that we have very clear intuitions about clauses and the boundaries between them. The evidence we will discuss here has to do with the syntactic relationship between pronouns and their **antecedents**, the phrases to which they refer. This phenomenon is called **pronoun reference**.

It's fairly obvious that pronouns must refer to something; the pronoun *she*, for example, is impossible to interpret unless we can hook it up with an antecedent. (In the random phrase *she's not here*, we have no idea who *she* is, without some kind of linguistic or contextual clue.) The antecedent of a pronoun can be in another sentence, what we call a *linguistic antecedent*, or it can be implied by the context, a *pragmatic* antecedent. For instance, in the following sentence, the antecedent *a student* precedes *she* in the sentence, providing the pronoun with a linguistic antecedent:

A *student* came in, and *she* sat down.

In the description of the following scene, on the other hand, there is no linguistic antecedent for the pronouns *him* and *he*. Instead, the speakers understand the antecedent for these pronouns from the context: they take the child on the bike as the referent for the two pronouns. This is an example of a pragmatic antecedent.

Two children are watching a third child race down the street on a bike.
Child A: Look at *him* go!
Child B: Wow! *He*'s going really fast!

RPE   8.5

Did You Know...?

Who Are *They*, Anyway?

They said it's not supposed to rain tomorrow. They say that ferrets make good pets. Who are *they*—the ones who seem to know everything and to be responsible for all kinds of things? There is no linguistic antecedent for *they* in such sentences, but we nevertheless understand these sentences perfectly well. And it's not just *they* we can use this way. Look at the use of pronouns in the following sentences:

In the future, *we'll* have cars that run on alternative energy, and *you'll* be able to avoid standing in line at the gas pump.

Is this sentence really about you and me? When we use pronouns in this way, they are called *impersonal*, as opposed to *personal*, because they refer to, well, no one in particular. We might say they have pragmatic antecedents, antecedents that are understood but not linguistically expressed. Such pronouns are similar in some ways to *it* in sentences such as *it's raining*, where *it* doesn't have an antecedent (pragmatic or linguistic).

Now, let's look in a bit more detail at the syntax of pronoun reference. Reflexive pronouns (the *-self* pronouns) and personal pronouns (*he/him, she/her, it, we/us,* etc.) differ in an interesting way with respect to the syntactic position of their linguistic antecedents. To illustrate, consider the following set of sentences:

John likes *him*. (*him* cannot refer to John)
John likes *himself*. (*himself* must refer to John)

These data illustrate that although *himself* requires an antecedent in the same clause, the opposite is true of *him*; the antecedent of this pronoun *cannot* be in the same clause.

Pronouns, Prestige, and Illogical Rules

Many of us learned (in school, from our parents, or elsewhere) that the first of the following sentences is correct, and the second is incorrect.

Jane and I went to the store.
*Jane and me went to the store.

We're taught that the second sentence is incorrect because we're supposed to use *I*, the nominative case form of the first person pronoun, rather than the accusative form *me*. As "proof" of the incredible logic of this rule, we are presented with

I/*me went to the store.

The reasoning is that *I* is correct because only *I*, and not *me*, is grammatical when there is only a single subject.

Hmm. According to Emonds (1986), this logic is not really logical, however; nor does it explain why, in natural speech, many people are likely to say "Jane and me went to the store" or "Me and Jane went to the store" even if they would never say "Me went to the store." So, the nominative pronoun sounds odd when there's only one subject, *Me went to the store*, but fine when there are two, *Me and Jane went to the store*. And to make matters worse, what about the following sets of sentences?

We went to the store. / Jane and *we* went to the store. / Jane and *us* went to the store.

They went to the store. / Jane and *they* went to the store. / Jane and *them* went to the store.

According to the logic that tells us to use *Jane and I*, the second sentence in each of the foregoing sets of sentences is supposed to be correct, with nominative *we* and *they*. What about the third sentence in each set, with accusative *us* and *them*? They are still odd but perhaps better than the nominative pronouns. What does this mean? That the prescriptive rule we are taught that may keep us from saying "John and me went to the store" is in fact not logical at all and cannot be generalized to pronouns other than *I*!

The way we use pronouns can mark us as standard or nonstandard speakers. Pronouns still show morphological case in English, and prescriptive rules of pronoun usage depend on using the "correct" case form of the pronoun. But these rules are often quite inconsistent and arbitrary and don't conform to rules of natural language (and therefore must be consciously learned).

The evidence from pronoun reference also tells us that we know what clauses are (even though we might have trouble identifying them in written English). Otherwise, we'd have no way to explain our very clear intuitions about the possible antecedents for *him* and *himself* in the preceding examples. We even seem to have a very clear understanding of subordinate clauses, clauses contained inside larger ones. Consider the following examples:

> Elmer thinks <u>that Irma must know *him*</u>.
> *Elmer thinks <u>that Irma must know *himself*</u>.

In the first sentence, *him* occurs in a subordinate clause (the underlined section). *Him* can refer to *Elmer* because in this case *Elmer* is outside of the clause containing *him*. The second sentence shows that the reflexive pronoun *himself*, on the other hand, can't take *Elmer* as an antecedent because *Elmer* is outside the (underlined) clause containing the reflexive. This evidence again suggests not only that we are very much aware of clause boundaries in general but also that we can easily (unconsciously, at least) distinguish between independent and subordinate clauses. We can informally state the rules of pronoun reference, which depend on our understanding of clause boundaries, as follows:

> A personal pronoun must have an antecedent *outside* of the (immediate) clause that contains it.

> A reflexive pronoun must have an antecedent *inside* of the (immediate) clause that contains it.

RPE   8.6

The syntax of pronouns, then, provides evidence not only for the constituent structure of NP but also for our knowledge of clauses and clause boundaries.

Conjunctions and Coordination

Conjunctions, a class of function words that we introduced in Chapter 5, allow us to connect phrases in a variety of ways, a syntactic process called **coordination**. As the following examples illustrate, phrases of any category can be coordinated, and so can clauses. What is interesting about coordination is that the coordinated phrases usually have to be of the same category.

coordination
joining phrases (of the same category, usually) with a conjunction (*for, and, nor, but, or, yet,* and *so*)

> Amelia left *this team* <u>for</u> *that one*. (NP + NP)
> Amelia both *loves* <u>and</u> *hates* soccer. (V + V)
> *Amelia doesn't like soccer,* <u>nor</u> *can she play very well.* (CL + CL)
> Amelia saw not *seven* <u>but</u> *six* soccer games. (D + D)
> Amelia *won't* <u>or</u> *can't* play soccer. (Aux + Aux)
> *Amelia plays soccer,* <u>yet</u> *she likes softball better.* (CL + CL)
> *Amelia left early,* <u>so</u> *they played the game without her.* (CL + CL)

parallelism constraint on coordinating like categories (NP and NP, VP and VP, etc.)

This same-category requirement is sometimes referred to as **parallelism.** Coordination that violates parallelism sounds odd, if not ungrammatical, and we are more apt to find examples in written English than in speech. We return to parallelism in more detail in Chapter 13, where we discuss written representations of English. Here are some examples to illustrate this phenomenon:

> *Amelia plays *the guitar* <u>and</u> *in the woods.* (NP + PP)

(Compare: Amelia plays the guitar and the banjo.)

> *Amelia saw not *seven* <u>but</u> *thrilling* soccer games. (Det + AP)

RPE 8.7 >

(Compare: Amelia saw not *boring* <u>but</u> *thrilling* soccer games.)

It is useful here to point out the difference between coordination and subordination. Remember that a *subordinate* clause is one that is contained inside another phrase. Here is an example of an independent clause that contains a subordinate clause:

> John believes *that Wiley told a lie.*

This sentence is very different in meaning and in structure when we coordinate rather than subordinate the clauses:

RPE 8.8 >

> *John believes in honesty* and *Wiley told a lie.*

hypotaxis subordinate clause structure

parataxis coordinate clause structure

We can think of subordination as a syntactic way of subordinating one idea to another; the subordinate clause *Wiley told a lie* is not the main idea but is subordinate to the larger idea, what John believes. In the coordinate clauses, on the other hand, neither clause is subordinate (in structure or meaning) to the other. In traditional grammar, subordination is called **hypotaxis,** and coordination is called **parataxis.**

Coordination and Ambiguity

Coordination also provides some interesting evidence for constituency in other ways. For example, consider the following ambiguous sentence:

> We ate chocolate-covered grasshoppers and flies.

Did we eat chocolate-covered grasshoppers and chocolate-covered flies, or just plain old flies? Phrase structure and coordination allow us to explain why this sentence is ambiguous. Each meaning can be represented by a different tree diagram, as the following trees illustrate.

We can now see that the AP *chocolate-covered* modifies only the N *grasshoppers,* or it modifies the coordinated Ns *grasshoppers and flies.*

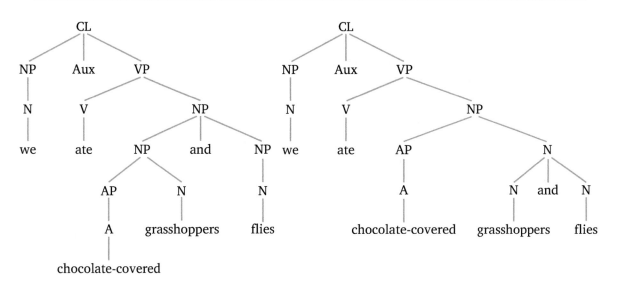

Language Alive!

Sex and Syntax

Otto Jespersen (a great early twentieth-century linguist) is rather famous for his claims about the differences between men's and women's speech. In his influential book *Language: Its Nature, Development and Origin*, first published in 1922, he wrote an entire chapter titled "The Woman," in which he says,

> In learned terminology we may say that men are fond of hypotaxis and women of parataxis. Or we may use the simile that the male period [read *sentence*] is often like a set of Chinese boxes, one within another, while a feminine period is like a set of pearls joined together on a string of *ands* and similar words. (251–252)

Jespersen also claimed that women often produce half-finished sentences, a claim he used as evidence to support the then widely held perception that women don't think before they speak! As you might expect, there is no evidence for Jespersen's claim in terms of natural, spoken language. Interestingly, however, claims about "women's language" based on social perceptions have persisted. For example, Robin Lakoff, in her 1975 book *Language and Women's Place*, suggests that women use a variety of conversational strategies that men do not, based on women's lower social status and their need for acceptance. Lakoff's claims, though an important first step in language and gender studies, have since been shown to be based on anecdotal evidence rather than scientific investigation and to reflect, as Jespersen's do, expectations and assumptions about gender and language rather than linguistic fact.

Movement and Deletion

So far, we've focused mainly on phrase structure and on the internal structure of different phrasal categories and clauses. We've shown how phrase structure rules express many aspects of our knowledge of syntax:

- the basic order of words in a sentence
- syntactic categories, heads, and phrases
- hierarchical structure
- recursion
- silent syntax

Phrase structure reflects the basic structure, what linguists refer to as the *base order,* of phrases and clauses in a language, as well as properties of those base orders. Syntax is more than just phrase structure, however. For example, consider the following sentences:

Lorraine *has* emptied the garbage.
Has Lorraine emptied the garbage?

hwæt!

Chomsky's ideas have often been controversial, even sparking what have been called the "Linguistics Wars." These were the 1960s disputes between Chomsky and some of his students about aspects of grammatical theory, including the concepts of deep and surface structure.

movement
syntactic operation by which phrases can be rearranged in a sentence under specific conditions or constraints

This pair of sentences illustrates the operation of subject-auxiliary inversion (SAI), which we discussed in our investigation of the English auxiliary verb system. In Chapter 7, we assumed that the auxiliary verb moved from its basic position (to the right of the subject NP *Lorraine*) to sentence-initial position (to the left of the subject NP). This suggests an important relationship between the first sentence and the second: we actually *derive* the second one from the first by **movement**—in this case, by SAI.

This relationship between base order and derived order is one of the foundations of Noam Chomsky's theory of generative grammar. As you may recall from our discussion in Chapter 1, Chomsky proposed that to account for the human ability to create and understand novel sentences, we must assume that knowing a language doesn't mean knowing all the sentences in that language. Rather, it means knowing a grammar, the system of rules and operations that allow us to generate possible sentences in the language. Movement rules are examples of the rules and operations that allow us to generate sentences. Put slightly differently, these rules and operations allow us to derive one sentence from another. A child, then, acquires the rule of SAI and can then use that rule to form questions from any sentence she hears. She can generate a novel question without ever having heard it before.

deep structure
clause in its base word order (in English, SVO) before syntactic rules such as movement or deletion apply

Deep and Surface Structure

Originally, Chomsky proposed that the base order of the sentence is the **deep structure** and that derived orders (derived by the application of

surface structure clause in its derived order after movement and deletion rules have applied

movement rules such as SAI) are **surface structures**. The ways in which we can rearrange phrases and words in a sentence are part of our knowledge of syntax beyond our knowledge of phrase structure rules. Phrase structure rules provide a roadmap of the basic orders and structures of the language, but they don't explain how these orders can be rearranged.

The deep and surface structure model, or theory (illustrated schematically below) captures the generalization that acquiring a language involves acquiring rules rather than memorizing a (vast and limitless) list of sentences:

DEEP STRUCTURE

↓

Application of rules

↓

SURFACE STRUCTURE

We won't go into the particulars of the theory here, but in this section we will investigate some of the basic syntactic puzzles that have motivated the deep and surface structure model (though in its current incarnation the model looks quite different from Chomsky's original version). We will investigate some syntactic operations that apply to base orders, operations that, however they are described, must be part of our unconscious knowledge of language. We will also show how the basic concepts we've introduced so far—such as subordination, coordination, and understood, or silent, syntax —play a significant role in those rules and operations.

Deletion Rules

There are many kinds of silent syntax, syntactic structure that is not pronounced but nevertheless understood. Earlier, we discussed some examples of silent yet understood subjects and complements. Here, we'll look at some other examples of silent syntax and show how they can be explained by proposing that part of our knowledge of syntax includes knowledge of the syntactic operation of **deletion**.

deletion process by which constituents are deleted in a sentence under certain syntactic conditions

Verb Phrase Deletion

The following are examples of sentences in which deletion has applied:

Alfie is riding his motorcycle across the desert, and Ziggy is Δ, too.
Sally said she would get a llama, and she did Δ.
Even though she shouldn't Δ, Violet will stay out late tonight.

Did You Know...?

"Does She . . . or Doesn't She?"

A popular 1960s television commercial for Clairol hair color products shows a young woman running across the screen with her beautiful hair flying behind her. The voiceover says, "Does she . . . or doesn't she? Hair color so natural only her hairdresser knows for sure!" Knows what? Does she or doesn't she what? Well, it was pretty obvious from the context that the missing phrase is *color her hair*, and the point was that Clairol products were desirable because they were so natural looking no one could tell whether a woman colored her hair.

Image Courtesy of The Advertising Archives

Besides being a groundbreaking advertising slogan (it began in the 1950s and ran for 18 years), the phrase *does she or doesn't she* became somewhat controversial among linguists who studied VP deletion; does this phrase constitute evidence that VP deletion takes a pragmatic antecedent? Or does the advertising context make this an unnatural example?

For more information

Hankamer, J. & I. Sag. 1976. Deep and surface anaphora. *Linguistic Inquiry* 7. 391–426. Cambridge, MA: MIT Press.

Polykoff, S. (Clairol ad originator). http://www.ciadvertising.org/studies/student/00_spring/theory/kwilliam/public_html/polykoff/ads.html. (26 October, 2008.)

Schachter, P. 1977. "Does she or doesn't she?" *Linguistic Inquiry* 8. 763–767. Cambridge, MA: MIT Press.

In each of these examples, the Δ is (unambiguously) interpreted as identical to another constituent in the sentence:

Alfie is *riding his motorcycle across the desert*, and Ziggy is Δ, too.
(Δ = riding his motorcycle across the desert)

Sally said she would *get a llama*, and she did Δ.
(Δ = get a llama)

Even though she shouldn't Δ, Violet will *stay out late tonight.*
(Δ = stay out late tonight)

VP deletion
syntactic operation in which a verb phrase is deleted but understood as referring to an antecedent verb phrase (*I don't jog, but Olivia does.*)

The missing constituent in each case is a VP. This phenomenon, very common in English, is called **VP deletion**. VP deletion involves deleting a VP when it is identical to another VP somewhere close by, not necessarily in the same sentence. In the following exchange, for example, the deleted VP is in a completely different utterance.

> Speaker A: Did Sally buy a llama?
> Speaker B: She did Δ.

VP deletion is in a certain way similar to pronoun reference. For instance, remember that a pronoun has to have an antecedent, something to which it refers. *It* in the following sentence takes *her llama* as an antecedent, and the antecedent of *her* is *Sally*.

> <u>Sally</u> loves <u>her llama</u>, and *it* loves *her* too.

The deleted VP also seems to have an antecedent, namely some other (pronounced) VP in the surrounding discourse. The antecedent of Δ is *buy a llama* in the preceding clause.

RPE   8.9

Gapping

gapping deletion operation that applies in coordinate clauses (*Sam likes halibut, and Cary, salmon*)

Below we give some examples of another deletion rule, called **gapping**. As with VP deletion, we have no trouble interpreting the missing material:

> Ziggy bought a Harley, and Alfie bought a Yamaha.
> Ziggy bought a Harley, and Alfie Δ a Yamaha.
> Δ = *bought*

> Sally likes llamas, but Sam likes alpacas.
> Sally likes llamas, but Sam Δ alpacas.
> Δ = *likes*

This phenomenon differs in several ways (some of which we discuss below) from VP deletion. It is similar, however, in deleting some element (here, a verb) when it is identical to another element in the preceding discourse.

hwæt!

Shirley Polykoff is the ad agency copywriter who wrote "Does she . . . or doesn't she?"—one of the top ten slogans of the twentieth century. This ad campaign for Clairol sent the marketing industry in new directions and increased the use of hair color, which led to phenomenal profits in that industry

Constraints on Deletion

Both VP deletion and gapping are strictly constrained rules. That is, they operate only under certain conditions. Put more simply, we don't delete a VP or a V just anywhere we want to, another example of our (quite complex) unconscious knowledge of syntax.

VP deletion can operate in either a subordinate clause (introduced here by *even though*) or a coordinate clause (preceded by *and*):

Violet will stay out late tonight even though *she shouldn't* Δ.

subordinate clause

Violet will stay out late tonight, and *she shouldn't* Δ.

coordinate clause

In these examples, the deleted VP follows its antecedent. The deleted VP can also precede its antecedent, as in the following sentence:

Even though *she shouldn't* Δ, Violet will *stay out late tonight.*
deleted VP   antecedent

A gap, on the other hand, can't occur in a subordinate clause, only in a co-ordinate clause:

*Ziggy bought a Harley even though *Alfie* Δ *a Yamaha.*
                                                subordinate clause

Ziggy bought a Harley, and *Alfie* Δ *a Yamaha.*
                                        coordinate clause

And a gap can only follow, but never precede, its antecedent:

Alfie Δ *a Yamaha,* and Ziggy *bought* a Harley.
gapped V   antecedent V

Complexities aside, the important point here is that the ungrammaticality of these sentences tells us that VP deletion and gapping operate only under certain conditions. In addition to the rules of VP deletion and gapping, our unconscious knowledge of syntax includes an understanding of where these rules can operate and where they can't.

Let's look now at these syntactic phenomena in terms of deep and surface structure. There is evidence for a rule of VP deletion that deletes a VP under certain syntactic conditions. This rule applies to deep structures to derive surface structures (where VP will be missing).

DEEP STRUCTURE   Sally wanted to buy a llama, and she did buy a llama.

↓

Application of rule   VP deletion

↓

SURFACE STRUCTURE   Sally wanted to buy a llama, and she did Δ.

Similarly, for gapping we can say that the rule deletes V under certain conditions.

DEEP STRUCTURE   Sally likes llamas, but Sam likes alpacas.

↓

Application of rule   gapping

↓

SURFACE STRUCTURE   Sally likes llamas, but Sam Δ alpacas.

If we assume that VP deletion and gapping rules are part of our knowledge of English syntax, we can then expect a child acquiring the language to acquire the rules and to then be able to apply them, producing novel examples of these phenomena that he or she may not have uttered before.

Reordering Phrases: Movement

We'll now turn to a discussion of movement rules in more detail. One movement rule that we are already familiar with is subject-auxiliary inversion (SAI). This rule has the effect of moving an auxiliary verb to sentence-initial position:

DEEP STRUCTURE	Minerva is singing the aria.
↓	
Application of rule	SAI
↓	
SURFACE STRUCTURE	Is Minerva singing the aria?

passive syntactic operation in which an active sentence (*Beowulf killed Grendel*) is reordered: the object moves to the subject position, and the subject occurs in a prepositional phrase (*Grendel was killed by Beowulf*)

We also talked about the *active* and *passive* sentences below.

Beowulf killed *Grendel*.
Grendel was killed by *Beowulf*.

hwæt!

Despite the challenges of reading and interpreting more than 3,000 lines of Old English poetry, the epic poem *Beowulf* has lasted more than a thousand years, evolving from oral traditions to manuscripts to books to audio recordings and, in 2007, to a popular film.

We know intuitively that the active sentence is related to the passive one; they mean the same thing, even though the word order has been rearranged. We can therefore propose that the passive is derived from the active. The active sentence is therefore the deep structure, and the passive, a possible surface structure, is derived by the application of a rule that moves *Beowulf* to the end of the sentence and *Grendel* to the subject position. We'll call this rule **passive**.

DEEP STRUCTURE	Beowulf killed Grendel.
↓	
Application of rule	passive
↓	
SURFACE STRUCTURE	Grendel was killed by Beowulf.

RPE 8.10

Did You Know...?

Passive Should Be Avoided?

You are likely familiar with the old adage "Avoid passive in writing." According to Sherry Roberts, in *11 Ways to Improve Your Writing and Your Business* (1992),

> A sentence written in the active voice is the straight-shooting sheriff who faces the gunslinger proudly and fearlessly. It is honest, straightforward; you know where you stand. A sentence written in passive voice is the shifty desperado who tries to win the gunfight by shooting the sheriff in the back, stealing his horse, and sneaking out of town. (para. 27)

Such descriptions are typical of traditional ideas about the use of the active and passive voice in writing. Arnold Zwicky (2006) wrote in a *Language Log* posting about this kind of objection to passive, noting that "[It] is an appeal to metaphorical values attached to the two voices: active as energetic, strong, and emphatic, passive as inert, weak, and reserved." But passive sentences have the same meanings as their active counterparts; *Grendel was killed by Beowulf* means exactly the same thing as *Beowulf killed Grendel*. The difference is that in the passive sentence, Grendel, the logical object, is highlighted or focused. So, when you want to highlight the object, passive is perfectly appropriate and often a better choice. Zwicky notes that although pronouncements about the "weakness" of passive voice abound in writing handbooks, very few authors discuss the actual grammatical structure and semantics of the construction.

For more information
Pullum, G. 2006. Passive aggression. *Language Log*. July 18. http://itre.cis
.upenn.edu/~myl/languagelog/archives/003366.html
Roberts, S. 1992. *11 ways to improve your writing and your business*. Greensboro,
NC: The Roberts Group. http://www.editorialservice.com/11ways.html
Zwicky, A. 2006. How long have we been avoiding the passive, and why?
Language Log. July 22. http://itre.cis.upenn.edu/~myl/languagelog/
archives/003380.html
Zwicky, A. 2007. Evil passive voice. *Language Log*. May 1. http://itre.cis.upenn
.edu/~myl/languagelog/archives/004456.html

Constraints on Movement

As we might by now expect, there are constraints, or restrictions, on movement rules. For example, passive can apply only in clauses with certain verbs. Passive is impossible in clauses with stative verbs, such as *resembled*, *become*, and *remain*. It is perfectly acceptable in clauses with active verbs, however, such as *meet* and *discuss*. (We return to semantic classes of verbs and how they interact with syntax more in Chapter 9.)

The child met an adult.
An adult was met by the child.
The girls discussed old friends.
Old friends were discussed by the girls.

The child became an adult.
*An adult was become by the child.
The girls remained old friends.
*Old friends were remained by the girls.

There are also constraints on SAI. One is that although the rule applies freely in main clauses, it cannot apply in subordinate clauses:

Minerva is singing the aria → Is Minerva singing the aria?
I think Minerva is singing the aria → *I think is Minerva singing the aria?

A key part of the scientific study of language involves investigating why rules operate in some contexts but not in others. Linguists construct theories that attempt to explain (rather than simply catalogue) data such as those presented here.

Wh-Movement

wh-movement
movement rule in which an interrogative phrase is moved to sentence-initial position
(*Who did Mary meet yesterday?*)

Another movement rule is **wh-movement**. *Wh*-movement can be described as operating in two steps. First, a noun phrase is replaced by an interrogative *wh*-phrase (*who, what, when, where, how, why*) or a *wh*-phrase (*which car, how many teeth, what in the world,* etc.). Then, the phrase is fronted to clause-initial position. (*Wh*-movement also sometimes involves subject-auxiliary inversion, as in the example here.)

DEEP STRUCTURE	You talked to Bill.
Rule 1: substitution of *wh*-phrase:	You talked to who(m)?
Rule 2: movement of *wh*-phrase:	Who(m) did you talk to ____?
SURFACE STRUCTURE	Who(m) did you talk to?

Here's another example:

DEEP STRUCTURE	Marcy bought a car.
Rule 1: substitution of *wh*-phrase:	Marcy bought which car?
Rule 2: movement of *wh*-phrase:	Which car did Marcy buy ____?
SURFACE STRUCTURE	Which car did Marcy buy?

We can question not only NPs in this way but other phrases as well. First, we substitute the phrase with a *wh*-word or phrase, then we front it to sentence-initial position. Can you tell which phrase the *wh*-word substitutes for in the following sentences?

> The students wrote their term papers quickly yesterday so they could go swimming.

> <u>What</u> did the students write _____ quickly yesterday so they could go swimming?

> <u>How</u> did the students write their term papers _____ yesterday so they could go swimming?

> <u>When</u> did the students write their term papers quickly _____ so they could go swimming?

> <u>Why</u> did the students write their term papers quickly yesterday _____?

RPE 8.11

Wh-movement is subject to a number of constraints, and we'll explore a few well-known examples. Here is another example of a sentence in which *wh*-movement has applied, moving the object of a subordinate clause to the front of the sentence:

> You think [that Willard likes pickles].
> What do you think [that Willard likes ___]?

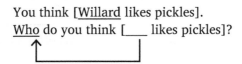

The *that* in this kind of sentence is optional, so the following sentence with *that* omitted is grammatical:

> What do you think [Willard likes ___]?

Now let's consider another example in which *wh*-movement has applied, this time moving the subject of a subordinate clause to the front of the sentence:

> You think [<u>Willard</u> likes pickles].
> <u>Who</u> do you think [___ likes pickles]?

The subordinate clause can also optionally be introduced by the word *that*. However, when *that* is present in this case, *wh*-movement is apparently blocked from applying (because if we do apply it, the result is ungrammatical):

> You think [*that* Willard likes pickles].
> *Who do you think [*that* ___ likes pickles]?

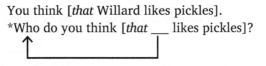

It seems, then, that *wh*-movement of the subject of a subordinate clause is possible only if *that* is absent. *Wh*-movement of the object in a subordinate clause, on the other hand, seems unaffected by the presence or absence of *that*.

Let's look at another constraint on *wh*-movement. The first sentence below contains two coordinate clauses. The second sentence contains a subordinate clause, introduced by *that*.

> *Sharks eat meat,* but *whales like plankton.*
> coordinate clause   coordinate clause

> Stefan thinks *that whales like plankton.*
>   subordinate clause

We know (from the discussion of *wh*-movement over *that*) that the object NP *plankton* can undergo *wh*-movement in the second sentence, moving over *that*.

> What does Stefan think that whales like _____?

But *plankton* can't undergo *wh*-movement in the coordinate clause:

> *What do sharks eat meat and whales like _____?

These data raise two important questions. One is, Why can *wh*-movement apply to move *plankton* out of a subordinate clause but not out of a coordinate clause? The second, even larger, question is, How do we explain that a child seems to already know this distinction (children never make this kind of error)? In each sentence, *plankton* is in exactly the same position, namely, as the object of *like*. But somehow children understand clause boundaries, in particular the difference between subordinate and coordinate clauses. And they also know that rules that apply to one do not necessarily apply to the other. This is a good example of our unconscious knowledge of syntax and also of our ability to acquire language without instruction; certainly children are never taught the difference between subordinate and coordinate clauses and how *wh*-movement operates (or does not operate) in each!

Of course, we don't actually hear or see this movement (or deletion either, for that matter); it all must happen in our heads before we actually say the sentence out loud. Nevertheless, the evidence from *wh*-movement that we've presented here is good evidence that producing the sentences we actually utter involves complex grammatical operations—what we might think of as computations, much like those performed by your computer.

RPE 8.12

RPE 8.13

Accent on *Psycholinguists*

© Deco / Alamy

Psycholinguists are not linguists who have gone off the deep end! They are linguists who study how we acquire, process, and produce language. We use language every day, all day, in many ways, without even thinking about it. Psycholinguists think about it. And observe it. And test it.

While neurolinguists study the physical mechanisms in the brain that underlie speech comprehension and production, psycholinguists investigate the unconscious processes that underlie our language abilities, primarily the production and processing of speech. Psycholinguistic research overlaps with other scientific research in psychology, linguistics, cognitive science, communication sciences and disorders, computer science, and neuroscience, and research findings contribute to the diverse and growing knowledge of human language ability.

Psycholinguistics involves all aspects of grammar. Psycholinguists study how the brain processes and understands sounds and prosody (phonology), how words and their parts are stored in our mental lexicons, and how we put them together to produce, process, and comprehend words (morphology). Psycholinguists study how we understand meaning and interpret sentences (semantics) and how we produce and process sentences (a subfield known as *sentence processing*, which focuses on syntax).

Researchers who study sentence processing investigate the segmentation of sentences into smaller syntactic units (finding evidence for phrases), how these units might be combined to produce sentences, and also how we process *empty categories*, those empty spaces in a sentence left by movement or deletion. For example, when we encounter a sentence such as *Which car will Marcy buy?* linguists assume that the noun phrase *which car* begins (at deep structure) after the verb—*Marcy will buy which car*—and then moves to the front of the sentence. And in fact, psycholinguistic experimentation shows that this is not a purely theoretical claim: using electroencephalogram (EEG) recordings (shown in the photo), functional magnetic resonance imaging (fMRI), and other methods of experimentation, they find evidence that the moved phrase is *reactivated* at the original site: *Which car will Marcy buy which car*. Psycholinguistic investigation can therefore validate some of the proposals from linguistic theory and helps us to understand better how language is processed and produced in our brains, which can then lead to improved methods of helping people who have language disorders.

Many psycholinguists work at universities where they teach and research. Some psycholinguists conduct research that can help people who suffer from aphasia or people with language disorders such as specific language impairment (SLI). Others work as specialists in assessing, diagnosing, and treating people, often children, who have language delays or disorders. We find people with training in psycholinguistics working in schools, hospitals, early intervention programs, or private practice.

For more information
Haskins Laboratories. http://www.haskins
.yale.edu/

Journal of Psycholinguistic Research. http://
www.springerlink.com/content/104271/
(30 October, 2008.)
McKinnon, R. 2006. Rick McKinnon, Ph.D.:
educator and elearning specialist.
http://rickmckinnon.com/services
(20 October, 2008.)

Summary

In this chapter, we've delved a little more deeply into syntax, going beyond the basic phrase structure rules and syntactic categories we investigated in Chapter 7. We've looked at how phrases are organized hierarchically and how recursion accounts for our ability to generate phrases within phrases within phrases. We've seen that we understand a great deal more about syntax: we can (effortlessly) interpret ambiguities and unpronounced, silent material; we know how to find the antecedents of pronouns; we are fully aware of clause boundaries. We've explored a few of the complex yet constrained ways in which phrases can be moved, deleted, and coordinated. And finally, we've shown one way that this range of syntactic phenomena can be expressed within a theoretical framework in terms of the abstract concepts of deep and surface structure.

Sources and Resources

Cook, V. & M. Newson. 1996. *Chomsky's universal grammar: An introduction*, 2nd edn. Oxford, UK: Blackwell.

Eagleton, T. 1983. *Literary theory*. Minneapolis: University of Minnesota Press.

Emonds, J. E. 1986. Grammatically deviant prestige constructions. In *A Festschrift for Sol Saporta*, M. Brame, H. Contreras, F. Newmeyer (eds.), 93–129. Seattle: Noit Amrofer.

Gentner, T., et al. 2006. Recursive syntactic pattern learning by songbirds. *Nature* 440. 1204–1207.

Haegeman, L. 1997. *Elements of grammar: A handbook of generative syntax*. Dordrecht: Kluwer Academic Publishers.

Hauser, M., N. Chomsky & W. Fitch. 2002. The faculty of language: What is it, who has it, and how did it evolve? *Science* 298(5598). 1569–1579.

Jespersen, O. 1922. *Language: Its nature, development and origin*. London: Allen & Unwin. Reprinted 1934. New York: Holt.

Lakoff, R. 1975. *Language and women's place*. New York: Harper Colophon Books.

Liberman, M. 2005. JP versus FHC + CHF versus PJ versus HCF. *Language Log*. August 25. http://itre.cis.upenn.edu/~myl/languagelog/archives/002422.html

Napoli, D. 1993. *Syntax: Theory and problems*. New York: Oxford University Press.

Niedzielski, N. & D. Preston. 2000. *Folk linguistics*. New York: Mouton de Gruyter.

O'Connor, P. 1996. *Woe is I: The grammarphobe's guide to better English in plain English.* New York: G. P. Putnam.

Pullum, G. 2006. Passive aggression. *Language Log.* July 18. http://itre.cis.upenn.edu/~myl/languagelog/archives/003366.html

Radford, A. 2004. *Syntactic theory and English syntax.* Oxford, UK: Blackwell.

Roberts, S. 1992. *11 ways to improve your writing and your business.* Greensboro, NC: The Roberts Group. http://www.editorialservice.com/11ways.html

Zimmer, C. 2006. Starlings' listening skills may shed light on language evolution. *The New York Times.* May 2.

Zwicky, A. 2006. How long have we been avoiding the passive, and why? *Language Log.* July 22. http://itre.cis.upenn.edu/~myl/languagelog/archives/003380.html

Zwicky, A. 2007. Evil passive voice. *Language Log.* May 1. http://itre.cis.upenn.edu/~myl/languagelog/archives/004456.html

Review, Practice, and Explore

RPE 8.1 > Syntactic Ambiguity: Drawing Trees

Draw tree diagrams for the following sentences, paying special attention to where each PP is attached. Some (but not all!) of the sentences are ambiguous. If there is ambiguity, draw two trees to represent the two meanings; be sure to indicate the meaning of each tree in this case.

a. The boy with the hat sat on a mushroom with green spots.
b. The white horse ran out the door on Monday.
c. Bill likes pieces of cabbage with sauce.
d. The ladybug with six spots sees the grasshopper on the branch.
e. Seven large sloths climbed up the tree on the hill.
f. The largest manatee chased the smallest manatee into a cave.
g. Students from six states in the country attended the luncheon.

RPE 8.2 > Recursion

Some of the following sentences include phrases that are recursive. Can you identify the category of the recursive phrase(s) (PP, NP, CL, etc.)?

a. The house on the corner by the bank is for sale.
b. A few people came to the party, and everyone left early.
c. I don't think that Barry was happy that Sam won the raffle.
d. Cheese that you can buy at stores that import goods from overseas is usually pretty expensive.
e. I jumped up and ran home.

In a text of your choice, find at least three examples of recursion (of any category you choose, but common examples include NP, PP, and clause recursion). Label the recursive categories.

RPE 8.3 > Silent Syntax

Each of the following sentences or exchanges includes a silent phrase, which is marked with Δ. What syntactic material is missing in each sentence?

a. I just bought three new textbooks, and Avery bought six Δ!
b. You might want to go to the party, but I don't Δ.
c. The book wasn't interesting enough Δ to finish Δ.
d. I promised Jane Δ to take out the garbage.
e. The mountaintop is hard Δ to see Δ in the fog.
f. Δ Eat your dinner!

RPE 8.4 ⟩ Nouns, Noun Phrases, and Pronoun Substitution

Find all the noun phrases in the following sentences. (Some include only a head noun; others are much larger.) Then, show how the pronoun substitution test provides evidence that those phrases are in fact noun phrases, even if they consist of only one word. Are any of the sentences ambiguous? How can pronoun substitution help you explain the two meanings?

Example: Dogs on leashes are allowed in this park.
They are allowed in *here.*
They = dogs on leashes, *here* = this park

a. Dogs are free to run and jump and play with the toys in the park.
b. My neighbor brings seven dogs to the park every day.
c. The schnauzer and the cocker spaniel bark a lot.
d. The schnauzer, the cocker spaniel, and the border collie like to play together.
e. People who have dogs and like to take them out for exercise use the park often.
f. Mary loves the park.

RPE 8.5 ⟩ Pronouns and Antecedents

Find all the pronouns and their antecedents in the following excerpt. Do any of the pronouns seem to lack antecedents? What about *it*? Are there any pronouns with pragmatic antecedents?

The meaning of the text is not just an internal matter: it also inheres in the text's relation to wider systems of meaning . . . It is obvious that literary criticism has come a long way from the days when we had little to do but thrill to the beauty of the imagery. (Eagleton 1983: 89)

RPE 8.6 ⟩ A Pronoun Puzzle

Recall that a personal pronoun can't have an antecedent in the same clause and that a reflexive pronoun *must* have an antecedent in the same clause.

Irma loves her. (*her* cannot refer to *Irma*)
Irma loves herself. (*herself* must refer to *Irma*)

Now, consider the following sentences. What are the possible antecedents of *her* and *herself*, and how does this evidence complicate our rules of pronoun reference? Think about the structure of the sentence, in particular the structure of the phrase *Irma's mother.*

Irma's mother loves her.
Irma's mother loves herself.

RPE 8.7 > Coordination and Parallelism

Coordination seems to require parallelism: the conjoined constituents must be of the same syntactic category.

A. Label the category of the italic phrases or words in the following examples of coordination.

1. Artichokes are *in season* but *out of stock*.
2. Olivia heard *that schnauzers don't shed* and *that they make great pets*.
3. I've never seen *a unicorn* or *a hippogriff*.
4. *Each* and *every* candidate attended the rally.
5. *Maurice saw the bus*, and *his son got on it*.
6. We saw lots of nice cars, but only *two* or *three* were in our price range.

B. Which of the following examples violate parallelism? Why or why not? Is it accurate to say that parallelism *always* requires the coordination of the same syntactic category? Under what circumstances can this requirement be relaxed?

1. Artichokes are *in season* and *very delicious*.
2. Olivia heard *about schnauzers* and *that they make great pets*.
3. I've never seen *a unicorn talk* or *a hippogriff sing*.
4. *Each voter* and *every candidate* attended the rally.
5. Maurice saw *the bus* and *that his son got on it*.
6. Lucy was *grumpy* and *in a funk*.

RPE 8.8 > Conjunction and Subordination

We've seen that coordination involves linking constituents in various ways. Subordination, on the other hand, involves embedding one constituent in another. For example,

Wiley will order seafood tonight because *he loves it*.

Here, the clause *he loves it* is subordinate and introduced by *because*, a member of a large set of *subordinating conjunctions* (also called *subordinating prepositions*), words that introduce subordinate clauses. Others in this class include *although, even though, since, while, when, before,* and *after*.

Wiley ate the shrimp *after* <u>he ate the mussels</u>.

Make up a pair of clauses. First, coordinate them with one of the coordinating conjunctions (*for, and, nor, but, or, yet, so*). Then try to use the same clauses, but this time subordinate one of the clauses to the other using a subordinating conjunction. How does subordination affect the meaning of the sentence?

Example   The children wanted to go swimming. It was a cool and breezy day.
            The children wanted to go swimming, *but* it was a cool and breezy day.
            The children wanted to go swimming *although* it was a cool and breezy day.

| RPE | 8.9 | > | The Good, the Bad, and the Ugly |

Are these words (*good, bad,* and *ugly*) nouns or adjectives? They are introduced by a determiner (*the*), which suggests they are nouns. Let's look at more evidence and see if this hypothesis is correct. Consider the following sentences:

> The poor are always with us.
> The poor's power is always marginal.
> The very poor are always with us.

Is *poor* in these sentences a noun or an adjective? Why or why not? Apply the tests for different categories (discussed in Chapter 7), and see what you find. (*Hint:* Silent syntax may be involved.)

What are some other examples of words like *poor* that we use in this way? What do they have in common? What words don't work in this context?

| RPE | 8.10 | > | Particle Shift |

Certain prepositions have the interesting syntactic property of being able to move around the direct object of the verb.

a.   You should hand <u>out</u> *the papers.*
b.   You should hand *the papers* <u>out</u>.

Prepositions with this property (the ability to move) are called *particles*. The movement rule illustrated in items (a) and (b) is called *particle shift*.

Which of the prepositions in items (c)–(f) are particles? Use particle shift as a test.

c.   Louise ran up a big hill.
d.   Louise ran up a big bill.
e.   Franz turned on the lights.
f.   Franz turned on the corner.

Write down three sentences with particles (use different examples from those given here). Show how they undergo particle shift. Also, write down three sentences with prepositions, and show how these do *not* undergo particle shift.

| RPE | 8.11 | > | Deep and Surface Structure |

In the following sentences, one or more of these rules may have applied: SAI, passive, and *wh*-movement. Write out the deep structure for each sentence, list the rules that have applied, and write out the surface structure. In some cases, more than one rule might apply, so list them both.

Example:	Will it rain?	DEEP STRUCTURE	It will rain.
		Application of rules	SAI
		SURFACE STRUCTURE	Will it rain?

a.   Is *The Lord of the Rings* your favorite movie series?
b.   The window was broken by the baseball.

 c. Which letter did the secretary mail?
 d. Should we go home?
 e. A letter was mailed by the secretary.
 f. Was your stolen jewelry ever recovered by the police?

RPE 8.12 > **A Cross-Linguistic Look at *Wh*-Movement**

Wh-Questions in Chinese

We have seen that English has *wh*-movement:

 a. Jack can see *the rabbit.* = basic word order
 b. *What* can Jack see? = question word order

Some languages have no *wh*-movement. The basic word order is the same in declaratives and in questions. Chinese is an example:

Ta	yao	xiaobing	(basic word order)
she/he	want	bread	

'She/he wants some bread.'

Ta	yao	shenme	(question word order)
she/he	want	what	

'What does she/he want?'

In English, the movement of the *wh*-phrase to the front of the clause marks the clause as a question. How do you think Chinese speakers know that a question is being asked?

Wh-Questions in Aleut

Aleut is a language spoken on the Aleutian Islands off the coast of Alaska. Look at the following pairs of sentences in Aleut and their translations, and determine whether or not Aleut has *wh*-movement.

 a. Piitrax Ivaanax ilagulix.
  Peter John help
  'Peter is helping John.'

 b. Piitrax kiin ilagulix?
  Peter who help
  'Who is Peter helping?'

 a. Tayagux qax qalix.
  man fish eat
  'The man is eating a fish.'

 b. Tayagux alqutax qalix?
  man what eat
  'What is the man eating?'

RPE 8.13 ⟩ Another Constraint on *Wh*-Movement in English

Here are some more sentences in which *wh*-movement in English appears to be blocked.

a. Whose book did you read _____?
b. *Whose did you read _____ book?

Why is (b) ungrammatical?

Here are some similar examples in which *wh*-movement is grammatical. Can you make up the ungrammatical sentences patterned in the same way as (b) from these examples? Can you state (informally) the constraint on *wh*-movement that blocks the ungrammatical sentences from being generated?

a. Which person did you meet yesterday?
b. What class does John have in the morning?
c. Whose dog are you taking care of?

Chapter at a Glance

Making Meaning
    Semantic Deviance
Lexical Semantics
    Meaning Classifications: Semantic
    Features
    Meaning Subclassifications:
    Semantic Fields
Meaning Relationships: The Nyms
    Opposite Meanings: Antonymy
    Similar Meanings: Synonymy
    Meaning Categories: Hyponymy
    Related Meanings: Polysemy
    Different Meanings: Homonymy
    Many Meanings: Lexical Ambiguity
Meaning Change: Semantic Shift
Making New Meanings: Figurative
Language
    Connecting Meanings: Metaphor
    Comparing Meanings: Simile
    Idioms
Summary
Sources and Resources
Review, Practice, and Explore

Semantics: Making Meaning with Words

Key Concepts

- Words have arbitrary meanings that we can express in terms of semantic features.
- Word meanings are also constructed through a variety of relationships, which we refer to here as the *nyms*.
- Word meanings change over time; meanings broaden and narrow and sometimes become more positive or more negative.
- Words have many nonliteral, or figurative, meanings, which are often quite complex and abstract, but we understand and use them effortlessly in speech and writing every day.
- The various ways in which we construct meaning out of words tells us something about how we think and about how we understand the world.

Did You Know . . . ?

   Can Something Be *Very Dead*?
   Hearing Colors

Language Alive!   *Is* the Team Playing? *Are* the Team Playing?

   Shifts in Meaning: Progress or Decay?

Linguistics in the News   Talking Right . . . and Left

Accent on   Linguistics and Computers

In this chapter, we will explore our unconscious knowledge of the semantics of words and the system of rules that underlies this knowledge. Understanding and creating meaning out of words is not a simple matter but rather involves a complex system of linguistic rules that interact with other grammatical systems, including syntax, phonology, and morphology. **Semantics** is the study of how we construct and understand the meanings of words and groups of words (clauses, sentences, etc.). Our complex knowledge of word meaning encompasses a wide range of phenomena and overlaps with other fields of study, including philosophy (in particular, logic) and mathematics (algebra and set theory), and it is central to the study of literature, humor, gender, politics, advertising, and law.

We will see in this chapter that meaning can in fact be meaningless and that meanings can deviate from expected meaning but still be meaningful. How can that be? A good starting point for the discussion of word meaning is, in fact, to discuss what it means for a word or sentence to be meaningless.

semantics system of rules underlying our knowledge of word and sentence meaning

Making Meaning

We have seen in other chapters that even sentences made up of nonsense words have some kind of meaning. Consider this sentence:

She yarped that canzos spleeked the batoids.

We can tell that whatever the canzos are, they are doing something to the batoids, and whoever she is, she's yarping about that. We know that there is more than one canzo, more than one batoid, and that the yarping and spleeking happened in the past. All this information comes from the syntax and morphology of the words in the sentence. We therefore derive some meaning from this sentence even though we don't know what any of the words really mean.

Speakers would also probably conclude that the following sentence (invented by Noam Chomsky to illustrate the semantic phenomenon we are discussing here) is English but, again, is odd:

Colorless green ideas sleep furiously.

English speakers know that there is something deviant about this sentence and also something completely grammatical about it. This sentence is well formed in terms of syntax and morphology but odd because the meanings of the words don't fit together.

Semantic Deviance

anomaly deviation from expected meaning

Sentences like *Colorless green ideas sleep furiously* are **anomalous**, which means they deviate from expected meaning. This sentence therefore provides important evidence that the grammar of our language includes a system of meaning rules. Even though Chomsky's sentence breaks no syntactic or morphological rules, it breaks meaning rules. Our meaning rules are therefore somehow separate from (although they interact with) other rule systems in our grammar. Speakers of a language not only have complex knowledge of meaning that allows them to interpret words and sentences, assigning them grammatical meanings, but this knowledge also gives speakers the ability to recognize anomaly. Knowledge of meaning, then, is just like syntactic, morphological, and phonological knowledge in this way: we know what is grammatical and what is not, but lack of grammaticality doesn't always preclude us from coming up with some kind of interpretation.

To take another example, recall that we can understand child language, even though the grammatical rules the child employs may deviate from those of adult grammar, leading children to produce such sentences as *What time it is?* or *We holded the baby rabbits.* The first sentence deviates syntactically from the adult version, *What time is it?* in which the auxiliary verb *is* inverts with the subject *it.* The second sentence deviates morphologically from adult grammar by affixing *hold* with the past tense affix *-ed* rather than using the adult form *held.* We understand phonological deviations in child language as well when, for example, a child calls a *spider* a *pider* and a *spoon* a *poon.*

The same is true of semantic deviance: when we hear a child refer to a horse as a *dog*, we can probably figure out what the child means, just as when we hear someone make a slip of the tongue, saying, "You have too many irons in the smoke" instead of "You have too many irons in the fire." We often find such semantic errors amusing; in fact, humor is frequently based on deviations from expected meanings. Henriksson (2003: 54, 75) offers the following gaffes in his collection of errors made by college students in their history papers:

> British paternalists were motivated by "noblesse oblique."
> St. Teresa of Avila was a Carmelized nun.

Often, such errors are created for comic effect and are referred to as *malapropisms* (French for *mal à propos*), after Mrs. Malaprop, a character created by Richard Sheridan in his 1775 Restoration comedy *The Rivals.* Some examples, in lines uttered by the infamous Mrs. Malaprop:

> . . . promise to forget this fellow, to *illiterate* him, I say, quite from your memory.

> I have since laid Sir Anthony's *preposition* before her.

> I'm sorry to say, Sir Anthony, that my *affluence* over my niece is very small.

Poetry is often based on deviations from expected meanings as well, as this poem by Shel Silverstein (1981) shows:

What Did?

What did the carrot say to the wheat?
" 'Lettuce' rest, I'm feeling 'beet.' "
What did the paper say to the pen?
"I feel quite all 'write,' my friend."
What did the teapot say to the chalk?
Nothing, you silly . . . teapots can't talk! (*Light in the Attic*, p. 16)

These deviations from expected meaning, whether expressed in slips of the tongue or child speech or designed for comic effect, all illustrate not only the complexity of meaning but also that our understanding of semantics includes knowledge of both meaning and anomaly.

RPE 9.1 >

Lexical Semantics

In the ancient Western world, a central question about language was whether it is *natural* (not under human control) or *conventional* (under human control). In Plato's *Cratylus*, Socrates, Cratylus, and Hermogenes argue at length over whether names of things are chosen by individuals, communities, or some higher "reality" outside human control. In the Bible, God charges Adam with naming all things, and in this way meanings are assigned to words. Such approaches to word meanings, however, assume a monoglot (single-language) view of the world and do not take into account evidence from other languages. From such evidence, we find that the connection between a word and its meaning is *arbitrary*: there is no intrinsic reason why the word *dog* best represents the meaning we attach to it. In French, this animal is a *chien*; in German, a *Hund*; and in Japanese, an *inu*. This arbitrariness is reflected not only across languages but also within a particular language; a speaker from Alabama might put things in a *poke*, but a speaker from Montana would use the term *sack*, and a speaker from Wisconsin, *bag*.

Nevertheless, there is a class of words for which the connection between sound and meaning is nonarbitrary—namely, onomatopoeic words (*onomatopoeia* is Greek for 'name making'), words that sound like their meanings. These words are also called *echoic* words.

buzz, clang, splash, purr, kapow, boom
moo, cock-a-doodle-do, oink oink

Though there are some interesting similarities among onomatopoeic words across cultures (cows in Turkish, Greek, Albanian, Estonian, French, Hebrew, and English all say something very much like *moo*), much cross-cultural variation in onomatopoeia still exists. In Albanian, a horse says *hihi hi* but in Finnish, *ii-hahahaa*; in Korean, *hi-hing*; and in Hindi, *hin hin hin*. In English, horses *neigh* and *whinny*. Though a Portuguese rooster says *cocorococo*, a Russian one says *ku-ka-re-ku*, and a Thai one says *ake-e-ake-ake*. Onomatopoeia nevertheless is a useful way to use sound to *suggest* meaning, and many authors invoke onomatopoeia for just this purpose.

Jose Elias da Liva Neto/Shutterstock.com

> Hear the sledges with the bells-
> Silver bells!
> What a world of merriment their melody foretells!
> How they tinkle, tinkle, tinkle,
> In the icy air of night!
>
> From "The Bells" by Edgar Allen Poe

The pronunciation of onomatopoeic words can provide clues to their meanings (so Poe uses *tinkle* here instead of *clang* to suggest a light, merry sound), though this relationship between sound and meaning is still somewhat arbitrary. We can gather other clues about meaning from the morphology of a word and also from its syntactic position. We also use *etymological* clues to unlock meaning—we draw on our knowledge of the origins of words and of *cognates*: words that have common ancestors such as *Hund* in German and *hound* in English. (We discuss cognates in more detail in Chapter 11.) *Context* also provides important clues to meaning, and we draw on our knowledge of the world and our experience to unlock meanings of words we don't know (meaning constructed from context is discussed in the next chapter).

RPE   9.2 ▷

Suppose, for example, that you hear the following sentence, and you don't know the meaning of the word *defenestrated*.

About to be caught in the act, the burglars defenestrated the jewelry.

Even if you don't already know what *defenestrated* means, you can pick up some clues from morphology and syntax. You know that the word is a verb because of its position, and you know that it is in the past tense because of the *-ed* inflectional suffix. Its *-ate* derivational suffix also tells you this word is probably a verb. You might also figure out that it means to not *fenestrate* in some way because of the negative prefix *de-*, which you might recognize as similar in meaning to the *de-* in *declaw* and *deforestation*. Some of you may infer that *defenestrate* has something to do with windows, based on etymological information: you may know that 'window' in French is *fenêtre*, and you might also be familiar with the cognate words *Fenster* in German or *fenestra* in Latin. Context can also help us determine the meaning of a word. For example, the following sentences includes more information about what happens when one *defenestrates*, helping us infer that *defenestrate* means 'to fall out of a window'.

> About to be caught in the act, the burglars defenestrated the jewelry.
> The heavy sack fell two stories and landed on the lawn, spilling its contents into the bushes.

Your knowledge of the world tells you that in order for something to fall two stories, it must fall from a building, and it would typically fall out of a window or perhaps off a balcony. The reference to a lawn suggests the burglars are in a house. Thus, you may conclude that *defenestrate* means 'to throw from a window', which would be correct.

So, sometimes we make meaning out of words we don't know, using various clues and strategies and a variety of semantic rules. The formal study of the conventions of word meaning is called **lexical semantics.**

lexical semantics
formal study of the conventions of word meaning

RPE   9.3

Meaning Classifications: Semantic Features

Some aspects of meaning can be represented in terms of oppositions expressed by binary features. These features allow us to divide words into different semantic categories. For example, part of our understanding of words includes our understanding of **semantic features** inherent in many words, features such as [+/–human], [+/–animate], [+/–young], [+/–married]. To illustrate, consider the following sentences, all of which are in some way semantically deviant but otherwise completely well formed.

semantic features
classifications of meaning that can be expressed in terms of binary features [+/–], such as [+/–human], [+/–animate], [+/–count]

> The *bachelor* is married.
> *The baby* drove to town in a Ford pickup.
> *The rock* combed its hair.

We understand the oddity of the first sentence to follow from our understanding of the word *bachelor* as [–married]. The second sentence is strange because *baby* is [+young] and only adults, typically, drive. The third is bizarre because humans, not rocks, comb their hair, so we expect the subject of *comb* to be [+human]. In each of these sentences, then, inherent semantic features have a grammatical function or effect.

Noun Classes

In addition to the nouns we've considered so far, verbs, adjectives, and other syntactic categories of words can be divided into semantic classes. *Go* and *chase* are both verbs of motion, for example, but differ in that only *chase* implies pursuit of something. Part of the study of semantics involves analyzing and describing such semantic classifications. In this section, we will explore the semantic features of nouns in yet more detail to give you an idea of how semantic features interact with other principles of grammar.

hwæt!

In British English, *mathematics* is shortened to *maths* rather than *math*, though it's still a mass noun: 'maths is fun!' But in French, the related word *les mathématiques* is morphologically plural: *les mathématiques sont amusantes!*

Concrete and abstract nouns Concrete nouns are names for things in the physical world (they name things we can point at). Abstract nouns are not physical objects.

concrete: dog, car, the Empire State Building, rice
abstract: love, attitude, terrorism, indignation

Some words have two (related) meanings and can, therefore, belong to more than one category; *light*, for example, is both abstract (*I need more light! The light in the eastern sky is purple.*) and concrete (*Turn on the light.*).

Count and noncount nouns Count nouns are those that we can, well, count. Count nouns can therefore be pluralized, preceded by numerals and certain quantifiers such as *each, both, every, few(er),* and *several*. Noncount nouns cannot be pluralized, nor can they occur with numerals or the quantifiers just listed. They can, however, occur with quantifiers *much, most, all,* and *less*.

count nouns: dog, car, puppy, country
noncount nouns: rice, jewelry, furniture, fruit, love, terrorism, mud, indignation

Some noncount nouns in U.S. English are morphologically plural, a relationship that we can also see reflected by the verb through subject–verb agreement.

mathematics/ethics/linguistics *is/*are* fun to study.

Notice that many nouns can be both count and noncount. For example, beer and paper can be count or noncount.

Etienne drank six *beers*. Etienne likes *beer*.
Etienne bought six *papers*. Etienne bought *paper*.

RPE 9.4

Common and proper nouns Common nouns are nouns that have more than one *referent*, or entity to which the noun refers. Proper nouns, on the other hand, have only one referent; they are the names of unique entities.

common: tulip, baseball, brother, horseradish, language, school, anger
proper: Etienne, Harry Potter, the Kentucky Derby, Halloween, Lake Victoria, the Kremlin

Language Alive!

Is the Team Playing? *Are* the Team Playing?

Collective nouns name groups that act as a single unit of some kind, such as *team*, *family*, *committee*, *herd*, *fleet*, *group*, and *class*. In U.S. English, such nouns are count nouns and can be pluralized: *teams*, *families*, and so on.

> The team *is* going to win.
> The teams *are* going to win.
> Six teams *were* at the competition.

In most dialects of British English, on the other hand, collective nouns are semantically plural but not morphologically so. That is, collective nouns lack a plural suffix *-s*, but subject–verb agreement is plural, not singular. The same is true of singular "nouns of multitude," (referring to the German soccer team as *Germany*, for example).

> The team *are/*is* going to win.
> The Royal Family *live/*lives* in Buckingham Palace.
> Germany *are* in first place.

Interestingly, several U.S. athletic teams have names that are treated as "nouns of multitude" in the British way by those in the sports community. (You may or may not be aware of this usage, depending on your familiarity with sports.) These nouns are morphologically singular but (always) semantically plural, triggering plural subject–verb agreement.

> The Utah Jazz *is/are* going to play tonight.
> The Seattle Storm *is/are* an excellent basketball team.

Sometimes the same word can function as both a proper and a common noun. Proper nouns have only a single referent and therefore can't be plural, so they are by definition count nouns (because there is only *one* of them). So, if someone says, "I just saw Etienne at the movies," the proper noun *Etienne*, which refers to a particular person, is also a count noun: there is one *Etienne* to which this noun refers. In the sentence *I know many Etiennes*, *Etienne* is arguably no longer a proper noun but a common (count) noun because it refers to a member of a set of more than one.

RPE 9.5

entailment
inclusion of one aspect of a word's or sentence's meaning in the meaning of another word or sentence

Entailment and Markedness

Semantic features can also be useful in expressing **entailments**, or the inclusion of one aspect of the meaning of one word in the meaning of another word. For example, the word *man* has the semantic features

[+human, +male, +adult], and the meaning of the word *bachelor* includes the features [+human, +male, +adult, –married]. The meaning of *bachelor* thus overlaps—or more specifically, *entails*—the meaning of *man*. We will return to entailment in later sections because it is part of other semantic relationships among words.

Though all languages share certain semantic features (animate/inanimate, human/nonhuman), not all languages divide words into the same semantic categories. For example, in Swahili, which is a Bantu language spoken in Africa, nouns are divided into about thirteen classes according to morphological and semantic criteria. Trees, plants, and nature fall into one class; names of human beings and names of animals into another; and names of fruits, mass nouns, everyday life objects, persons, and names of Arabic origin into another. In Navajo, a member of the Athabaskan language family, nouns are also divided into different semantic classes, including animate, round object; long, stiff object; and granular object.

Some problems arise with defining meaning in terms of semantic features alone when we consider a wider range of examples. One problem with semantic features is that binary oppositions by definition depend on positive and negative values. An obvious case where this becomes problematic is in the feature specification of biological sex as [+/–male]. This specification assumes that biological sex is binary, an opposition that fails to account for a more complex and inclusive view of biological sex that includes, for example, transgendered people. Another issue that arises with this feature specification is that gender can be expressed only in positive/negative terms, with *female* as negative, [–male], and *male* as positive, [+male], which is inconsistent with social attitudes about gender equity. Nor do binary features necessarily capture socially defined meanings, which can carry positive or negative connotations. For example, consider the different feature specifications of the opposition *spinster/bachelor*:

spinster = [+adult, –married, –male]
bachelor = [+adult, –married, +male]

The only distinction between these terms is the feature of maleness or lack thereof. However, we are all familiar with the negative connotations of *spinster* and the positive connotations of *bachelor*, a socially defined distinction that is not captured by semantic features.

A case in which semantic features are actually defined in terms of social attitudes is illustrated by *nurse/male nurse*. The opposition between *nurse* and *male nurse* suggests that for many people *nurse* is specified as [+female] (or as [–male]) based on social expectations and that the adjectival modifier *male* is required in order to indicate a deviance from the typical interpretation of the term. The semantic feature for which *nurse* is specified is therefore based on cultural expectations about career paths for women rather than on grammatical properties.

Similarly, we all "know" a number of oppositions that are not clearly explained by binary features and that can have positive and negative social values attached to them. The idea of **markedness** can help us describe just such distinctions. Markedness occurs in phonological, morphological, syntactic, and semantic relationships, defining them in terms of marked and unmarked opposites; the dominant term is known as the unmarked term and the secondary term as the marked one. This concept of asymmetry has been extended to the analysis of sets of linguistics concepts and to grammatical constructions, and it has also been applied to various cultural relationships as well, with background cultural categories. Markedness has been the subject of much discussion in linguistics. (See, for example, Battistella 1990, 1996.)

In semantic relationships, markedness is based on how we consider one member of a pair of words "typical" and the other "marked."

> right/left, white/black, rich/poor
> knife/fork, salt/pepper

In English, the term *nurse* is unmarked (based on cultural expectations); the term *male nurse* deviates from the typical meaning of *nurse* and is marked.

It is probably impossible to explain all the nuances of meaning in terms of binary features; nevertheless, the semantic features that do have a grammatical function must be part of our mental lexicon. How this information is encoded in our lexicons is unclear; do we, for example, list *Mom* (*Mom went to work today*) as a proper noun and also as a count noun (*All the moms were at the game*), or do we simply know a rule that allows us to make proper nouns count nouns? And how are gendered words listed in our lexicons? How does culture affect the meanings of those words and how they are stored? We won't attempt to answer these questions here but will simply point out the complexity involved in understanding what words mean.

Meaning Subclassifications: Semantic Fields

Another thing we know about word meaning is that words can be divided into semantic categories called **semantic fields**. Semantic fields are classifications of words associated by their meanings. There is a great deal of evidence that words are stored in semantic fields in our mental dictionaries. Semantic fields could be CLOTHING, PARTS OF THE BODY, EMOTIONS, OLD BOYFRIENDS; the fields may vary across speakers, and words may belong to more than one category. The meaning of the word *pig* in the semantic field FARM ANIMALS overlaps the meaning in the semantic field MEAT and even (possibly) PETS.

Slips of the tongue provide interesting evidence for semantic fields. The word substituted for the intended word in the following slips of the tongue

---

markedness
opposition that differentiates between the typical form of a word and its "marked" opposite ("right" is unmarked, and "left" is marked)

semantic fields
basic classifications of meaning under which words are stored in our mental lexicons (FRIENDS, for example)

is a semantically related one (adapted from the Fromkin Speech Error Database):

Intended Utterance	Actual Utterance
he's going *up*town	he's going *down*town
you have too many irons in the *fire*	you have too many irons in the *smoke*
that's a horse of another *color*	that's a horse of another *race*

See the link on the Max Planck Institute for Psycholinguistics website: http://www.mpi.nl/cgi-bin/sedb/sperco_form4.pl.

The semantic field including both *up* and *down* might be DIRECTIONS; for *fire* and *smoke*, THINGS HAVING TO DO WITH FIRE, and so on. Speakers rarely, if ever, make random substitutions when producing a slip of the tongue (though we know from other chapters that some slips are phonetic, some phonological, and some morphological, as well as semantic).

In addition to slips of the tongue, aphasia provides us with evidence of how words might be stored in the brain. Many people who suffer from aphasia (language deficit as the result of trauma to the brain, introduced in Chapter 2) suffer from lexical access problems and are not able to produce the word they intend but often select a related word—for example, *table* for *chair*, *boy* for *girl*, *knife* for *fork*—suggesting that words that are semantically related are stored together in the brain.

RPE 9.6

Meaning Relationships: The Nyms

nyms meaning relationships among words—antonyms, synonyms, homonyms, etc.

Part of knowing the meaning of a word includes knowing the semantic relations among words. These same relationships, which we'll call **nyms**, exist across languages.

Opposite Meanings: Antonymy

antonyms words that we think of as opposites, though oppositions may be relational (*doctor/ patient*), complementary (*alive/ dead*), or gradable (*hot/cold*)

We all learn, early on, that *rich* is the opposite of *poor*, *awake* is the opposite of *asleep*, and *teacher* is the opposite of *student*. These opposites, or **antonyms**, seem based on fact: if you are rich, you can't be poor; if you are awake, you can't be asleep; and in class, the "opposite" roles of teacher and student seem well defined and obvious. (If you ask someone what the opposite of *pepper* is, they'll probably say *salt*.) Nevertheless, there are important differences among these pairs. Some antonyms are *gradable*; that is, the antonyms are two ends on a scale, and there can be various gradations of each term. So, what is considered *rich* or *poor* varies from person to person.

What *rich* means to Tevye in the musical *Fiddler on the Roof* as he sings "If I Were a Rich Man" is quite different from what *rich* means to Donald Trump; for someone who used to weigh 300 pounds, weighing 200 pounds might

Table 9.1	Antonym Types		
Gradable	**Relational**	**Complementary**	
smart/stupid	teacher/student	dead/alive	
often/rarely	friend/enemy	before/after	
fat/thin	question/answer	permit/prohibit	
most/least	doctor/patient	precede/follow	
up/down	mother/father	send/receive	
tall/short	parent/child	beginning/end	
rich/poor	lawyer/client	day/night	

hwæt!

Some words can have two diametrically opposed meanings: *cleave* can mean either to adhere closely or to divide. Look up some other "contra-nyms": *sanction, oversight, moot.*

RPE   9.7

RPE   9.8

be thin, but not everyone would share this interpretation. These antonyms therefore express degree in various ways: by comparative and superlative morphology (*smarter, thinner*) or syntactically (*more gigantic, extremely minuscule*). *Complementary antonyms* are another subtype of antonymy: if you are one, you cannot be the other; these are "absolute" opposites. That is, if you are dead, you cannot also be alive; if you are asleep, you are not awake, and so on. Similar pairs of this sort include *legal/illegal* and *beginning/end*. *Relational antonyms* are a third type; these are pairs in which each member describes a relationship to the other: *teacher/student, father/mother, lawyer/client, doctor/patient.* All languages have antonyms as well as these subtypes of antonyms. (See Table 9.1.)

Did You Know...?

Can Something Be *Very Dead*?

Although it may seem obvious that *dead* and *alive* and other antonyms are complementary, it doesn't mean we always use them that way. We say such things as "Downtown is completely dead by 8 p.m." and "That plant is quite dead" and "She's *really* pregnant," where we modify *dead* and *pregnant* with degree words even though these adjectives by definition should not be modifiable (because you either are or aren't dead or pregnant). We also say *very unique*, a phrase that rubs many language purists the wrong way but which is nevertheless quite common even among the most educated speakers. Our colleague Eric Hyman explains such examples as morphosyntax "outranking" meaning—adjectives can always take degree words precisely because they are adjectives. Our unconscious knowledge of lexical categories allows us to use degree words with adjectives regardless of prescriptive, meaning-based edicts.

Similar Meanings: Synonymy

synonyms words that have similar meanings (*purse/handbag*)

Words that are different in form but similar in meaning are called **synonyms**. Synonyms are derived from a variety of sources, and we make choices among synonyms for a variety of reasons.

One source of synonyms is dialectal variation. In some dialects of North American English, a long, upholstered seat is called a *couch*, but speakers of another dialect call the same piece of furniture a *sofa*. Canadian English speakers might call this item a *chesterfield*, and still other speakers might call it a *divan*. Though these words all mean the same thing and are therefore synonyms, they tend to be dialect specific and may not be shared across dialect boundaries.

Synonyms can also cross dialect boundaries; most North American English speakers are familiar with the synonyms *professor/instructor*, *doctor/physician*, and *lawyer/attorney*. Still other synonyms arise as a result of language change over time. For example, your grandparents might use a particular term that seems old fashioned to you, and you might use a more modern term. For example, what might be a *pocketbook* for your grandmother is called in current fashion circles a *handbag* or a *bag* or a *purse*. An older term for *dress* is *frock*, and what used to be called a *baby carriage* or *perambulator* is now a *stroller* or *jogger*; we are less likely now to refer to women as *gals*.

hwæt!

Isn't it fun when antonyms come to be synonyms? *Bad* is bad and it's good. It's bad to be sick, but *sick* can mean 'good'.

Two other, closely related sources for synonyms are style and register. In casual speech, a speaker might say, "That's a nice ride," but in more formal speech, "That's a nice car."

For a variety of historical reasons (discussed elsewhere in this book), we attach social value and prestige to words with Latin or Greek roots. We therefore might choose a Latinate synonym over its native English (Anglo-Saxon) counterpart in formal, academic writing. Table 9.2 shows some pairs of synonyms or at least close synonyms. (Exact synonyms are quite rare.)

RPE   9.9

Euphemisms

euphemism word or phrase used to avoid offending or to purposely obscure (*collateral damage* for 'civilian deaths')

English has a vast number of synonyms, more than most languages, largely because of borrowing from other languages, especially French and Latin. Though synonymy allows for a variety of ways to express ideas, it can also be the source of **euphemisms**. Euphemisms are words and phrases used to avoid offending (by directly addressing taboo subjects) or to deliberately obscure actual (usually unpleasant) meanings. Government terminology provides a good source of examples. *Area denial munitions* are 'landmines', and *physical persuasion* means 'torture'. *Operational exhaustion* means 'shell shock', and *wet work* is 'assassination'. We use euphemisms to avoid talking about bodily functions: *sweat* can be replaced by *perspire*, *genitalia* by *privates*, and *urinate* by *go to the bathroom*. Still another source of synonyms

Table 9.2	Synonyms of Anglo-Saxon and Latin/Greek Origin
Anglo-Saxon Origin	**Latin/Greek Origin**
land	alight
try	attempt
hard	difficult
talk (about)	discuss
crazy	insane
ghost	spirit
clean	sanitary
dirt	soil
go	advance
see	visualize
holy	sacred
space	cosmos
heavenly	celestial

is *politically correct language,* terminology specifically intended to limit use of certain terms in favor of more socially and culturally acceptable ones in public discussion. Common examples include *Native American* for *Indian, firefighter* for *fireman, differently abled* rather than *disabled* or *handicapped,* and *mail carrier* rather than *mailman.* The use of politically correct language can be the source of some controversy because politically correct terms can be—not surprisingly—political, which raises questions about the accuracy of their meanings and the implications of those meanings.

RPE 9.10

Meaning Categories: Hyponymy

hyponym word whose meaning is included, or entailed, in the meaning of a more general word (*tulip/ flower*)

Another word-meaning relationship is hyponymy. A **hyponym** is a word whose meaning is included, or entailed, in the meaning of a more general word. For example, *thoroughbred* is a hyponym of *horse,* and *house* is a hyponym of *building.* A hyponym can itself have hyponyms, as shown in this diagram:

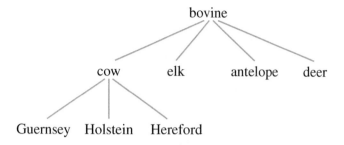

The entailments expressed by hyponymy can be illustrated as follows:

Guernseys are cows.
Bossie is a Guernsey.
Bossie is a cow.

Hyponymy expresses how we assign meaning to larger categories and to smaller categories included in these larger ones. We use hyponymy in language to make general statements more specific:

What are you reading?
A book/a Russian novel/*War and Peace*

RPE   9.11

Related Meanings: Polysemy

polysemy refers to words with two or more related meanings (*lip* = of a cliff or part of the mouth)

Words that are **polysemous** have two or more related meanings (Greek *poly* 'many', *semy* 'meanings'). For example, *lip* is polysemous because we can use it not only to refer to a part of one's mouth but also in phrases such as *lip of the cliff* or the *lip of a cup,* and we also have the expression *don't give me any lip.* We call a furry, burrowing animal a *mole,* and *mole* can also refer to a spy who pretends to be a legitimate member of the group on which he or she is spying. *Foot* is polysemous as well: in addition to meaning 'the lowest part of the body' (with the top being the *head*), we have *foot/head of the bed,* as well as *foot of the stairs* and *foot of the mountain.* Body parts are often polysemous; we use *leg* to refer to the leg of a chair and the leg of a table, *arm* to refer to the arm of a chair, and *eye* to refer to the eye of a storm. We return to a discussion of polysemy in the section on figurative language; most polysemy makes use of figurative, or nonliteral, meanings.

retronym new word or phrase created to distinguish an original word from a more recent meaning of the word (*analog watch/ digital watch*)

Another meaning relationship, which can perhaps also be considered a type of polysemy since the two terms have related meanings, is also called a **retronym**. A retronym is a new word, compound word, or phrase created to distinguish an original word from a more recent meaning of the word: for example, *analog watch* to distinguish from *digital watch, acoustic guitar* to distinguish from the newer *electric guitar,* or *film camera* to distinguish from *digital camera.*

RPE   9.12

Different Meanings: Homonymy

homonyms words with the same sound and spelling but different, unrelated meanings (*saw/saw*)

Words that sound the same but have different (unrelated) meanings are called **homonyms** (Greek *homeos* 'same', *onoma* 'name'). The verb *bear* can mean 'to have children' or 'to tolerate'. So, *She can't bear children* is ambiguous because *bear* is a homonym. **Homophones** do not necessarily share the same spelling (*sole/soul, gorilla/guerilla, to/too/two*), but they sound the same; **homographs** have different meanings, the same spelling, but different pronunciations (the *bow* of a ship versus a *bow* and arrow).

homophones words that do not share the same spellings or meanings but sound the same (*sole/soul*)

homographs words that have the same spelling, different meanings, and different pronunciations (*bow/bow*)

homonyms
sound the same, same spelling
cleave, bear, saw

homophones
sound the same, different spelling
sole/soul, gorilla/guerilla

homographs
same spelling, sound different
bow, wind, wound, abuse

RPE 9.13 >

Many Meanings: Lexical Ambiguity

We've already talked about how sentences can be ambiguous; the following example of syntactic ambiguity is explained by two different phrase structure trees. No actual words in this sentence are ambiguous.

Six hungry gorillas spotted the sandwiches in the tree.

Polysemes and homonyms are therefore, by definition, ambiguous because both polysemes and homonyms have more than one meaning. For example, the sentence *She met a guerilla* is ambiguous (in speech) because of the homonyms *gorilla/guerilla*, and the sentence *The area around the mouth is rather uninteresting* is also ambiguous because of the polysemous *mouth* (human or river or cave). In speech, then (where spelling can't offer clues to meaning), we must rely on context to decipher ambiguity. Clues can be nonlinguistic (pragmatic): if we were to hear the sentence *The area around the mouth is rather uninteresting* in a classroom with someone pointing at a map of the Mississippi River, the sense of *mouth* would be quite clear. Clues can also be linguistic: were we to hear the sentence *She met a guerilla* with a linguistic clue attached, as in *She met a guerilla, and he has a Ph.D.*, we would infer that the guerilla in question is not only male but human rather than simian.

Vagueness

Ambiguity is different from vagueness, though the difference between the two can sometimes be hard to see. One way to think about it is that an

Talking Right . . . and Left

Linguistic analysis of political discourse has come more and more into the public eye. Two linguists in particular have received a lot of press. Geoffrey Nunberg, "the NPR linguist," appears regularly on National Public Radio's *Fresh Air* with Terry Gross, often discussing the language of politics. George Lakoff, professor of linguistics at UC Berkeley, is well known for his work on metaphor and is also founder of the progressive think tank The Rockridge Institute. Both linguists' work has appeared in a number of publications, including the *New York Times*.

In his book *Talking Right*, Nunberg looks at the language of conservatives and liberals—the political Right and the political Left. The conservative Right, he claims, is more skilled than the liberal Left in coining catchphrases and shaping convincing political discourse. Two examples are conservatives' use of *climate change* instead of *global warming* and *death tax* instead of *estate tax*. He also argues that conservatives are more successful at

shaping public interpretations of core vocabulary: *values* really means 'conservative values', for example.

In his book *Moral Politics*, George Lakoff suggests that his ideas about the mind and its conceptual structure are central to understanding the political process and political views. Like Nunberg, Lakoff believes that the Left is linguistically less powerful in its message than the Right. Lakoff has been an advisor to the Democratic Party, so his analysis and proposals are gauged to help the Democrats develop their message and to frame the political debates.

Nunberg's and Lakoff's work shows that the study of political language has gone far beyond anecdotal observation. This use of language can now be tracked in online discussions, press databases, broadcast transcripts, and even advertising. Linguists can now analyze and document this body of evidence, construct hypotheses about it, and even test their hypotheses against additional evidence. The work

of these linguists illustrates an important way in which linguistic science can shed light on our everyday lives and shows how linguists themselves are increasingly entering the domain of public discourse.

For more information
   Lakoff, G. 2002. *Moral politics: How liberals and conservatives think*. Chicago: University of Chicago Press.
   Lakoff, G. 2006. Staying the course right over a cliff. *New York Times*. October 27. http://www.nytimes.com/2006/10/27/opinion/27lakoff.html?_r=1&oref=slogin
   Nunberg, G. 2004. Political language. *Fresh air*. National Public Radio. September 1. http://www.npr.org/templates/story/story.php?storyId=3883628
   Nunberg, G. 2006. *Talking right: How conservatives turned liberalism into a tax-raising, latte-drinking, sushi-eating, Volvo-driving, New York Times–reading, body-piercing, Hollywood-loving, left-wing freak show*. New York: Public Affairs.

ambiguous word has more than one possible meaning and that (as with *mouth* and *guerilla*) the appropriate meaning is quite obvious, given a context. *Vague words,* on the other hand, aren't so easily clarified by context. In fact, what it means for a word to be vague is rather, well, vague. *Vague* is defined in dictionaries as 'obscure', 'undefined', or 'lacking in clarification' and is the subject of much discussion in philosophy. We therefore won't pursue a precise definition of vagueness here because it is actually quite complicated. Rather, we'll provide one example of a linguistic argument for distinguishing vague words from ambiguous ones; it involves VP deletion, which we talked about in Chapter 8. Remember that VP deletion has the effect of deleting a VP that refers to an identical antecedent VP.

Mary bought a Ferrari, and John *did* Δ, *too*.

Speakers interpret the phrase *did* Δ, *too* as identical in meaning to a previous phrase: *bought a Ferrari.*

Kempson (1977) made up a test using VP deletion to distinguish ambiguous words from vague ones. Consider what happens when we construct sentences with *did* Δ, *too* and ambiguous words:

The student pointed at the mouth, and the teacher *did* Δ, *too*.

Here, whichever interpretation of *mouth* jumps into your mind (mouth of a river or a human mouth, say), the phrase *did* Δ, *too* must have the same interpretation. That is, the sentence can mean (a) or (b) but not (c) (where * indicates an unacceptable sentence).

a. The student pointed at the mouth (of the river), and the teacher did, too (pointed at the mouth of the river).
b. The student pointed at the mouth (human), and the teacher did, too (pointed at the human mouth).
c. *The student pointed at the mouth (of the river), and the teacher did, too (pointed at the human mouth).

When words are simply vague, such an interpretation, where the meaning of an ambiguous word must match that of the *did too*-phrase, is not required. For example, the verb *contact* is not ambiguous but just vague, as illustrated in the following examples:

Margaux contacted him (by phone, e-mail, post, telepathy).
Margaux contacted him (by phone) and Sue did Δ, *too* (by e-mail).

hwæt!

The Sorites paradox (from the Greek word for 'heap') stems from the inability to define a thing precisely and can be applied to syntactic vagueness; for example, when grains of sand are removed from a heap of sand, at what point does it stop being a heap? When does blue stop being blue? Or old, old? Or young, young? Many words involve such vagueness.

RPE   9.14

Meaning Change: Semantic Shift

semantic shift change in the meaning of words over time

shift in connotation change in words' general meanings over time

So far, we've talked about some of the meaning relationships among words. Here, we turn to how word meanings (and thus their meaning relationships) can change over time. These **semantic shifts** happen in a variety of (sometimes overlapping) ways. They can be **shifts in connotation**, or changes in general meanings associated with a word. In Old English, the word *Hund* meant 'dog', but in modern English, *hound* refers to a particular type of dog. This process is called **narrowing**. In Old English, *gōme* meant 'jaw, palate, inside of the mouth', but the meaning narrows in Middle English, in which *gome*

narrowing change in words' meanings over time to more specific meanings

broadening change in words' meanings over time to more general or inclusive

amelioration shift of words' meanings over time from neutral or negative to positive

pejoration shift of words' meanings over time from neutral or positive to negative

shift in denotation complete change in words' meanings over time

means 'gum'. In Early Modern English, the word *acorn*, which formerly meant 'fruits', narrows to 'fruit of an oak tree', and *courage*, which meant 'heart, mind, disposition, nature, bravery, valor', narrowed to 'bravery, valor'.

The Old English word *dogge*, on the other hand, referred to a particular breed of dog and today refers to domestic canines in general, through a process called **broadening**. In Old English, *bridd* meant 'young bird', but the meaning of this term broadened in Middle English, and *bird* came to mean 'fowl of any age'. (Note the phonological *metathesis* that occurred here, too: *bridd* → *bird*.) The word *twist* used to mean 'twig, tendril, or branch', but after the seventeenth century, its meaning broadens to mean 'the action of twisting something', and 'anything that has been twisted' (such as a slice of lemon, a wire, yarn). *Decimate*, for the Romans, meant 'to kill every tenth person', but now its meaning has broadened to mean 'destroy, utterly wipe out, annihilate'.

Word meanings also undergo **amelioration**, a shift to a more positive connotation. The word *croon*, for example, which in English means 'to sing softly', comes from Dutch *kronen*, which means 'to groan or lament'. Word meanings can also undergo **pejoration**, shifting to a more negative connotation. The Old English word *ceorl* meant 'peasant, freeman, layman', but during Middle English degenerated in meaning; it occurs in Present-Day English as *churl*, 'a rude or ill-bred person'.

Words can also **shift in denotation**, eventually shifting to mean something else entirely. For example, *blush* used to mean 'look' or 'gaze'. In Early Modern English, this word came to mean 'to redden in the face (from shame or modesty)'. The term *moody* in Old English meant 'brave' and now means 'given to changeable emotional states'. Although the current meaning of a word may not seem related at all to its original meaning, such shifts are usually not arbitrary. The modern English word *bead* comes from the Old English word *gebed* 'prayer'. The shift in meaning here came from beads threaded on a string to count prayers (a rosary), but without knowledge of the word's history, *bead* and *prayer* seem completely unrelated in meaning.

In the morphology chapter, we discussed how we bring new words into the language through the morphological processes of coining, blending, compounding, clipping, and so on. We are equally creative in assigning new meanings to words or shifting meanings of words in the ways just outlined. Some current innovations are *bad* for 'good' and *sweet* for 'exceptional'. *Awesome*, which used to mean 'inspiring awe' or 'full of awe', usually means in current speech 'remarkable, great, fantastic'. Though shifts in meaning are inevitable, change can sometimes cause some confusion. For example, *aggravate*, which originally meant 'to worsen', is often now used to mean 'irritate'; *anxious*, which meant 'filled with anxiety', is now used to mean 'eager'. Because these changes are not complete—and many people still have only the first meanings—confusion and lack of precision of meaning may result. When one meaning truly takes over the other, the language changes.

RPE 9.15

RPE 9.16

RPE 9.17

Making New Meanings: Figurative Language

figurative language
nonliteral language;
language that shifts
meaning from the
primary meaning of
the word

Often, particularly in discussions of literature, we talk about language being **figurative**, or expressing *nonliteral* meanings, meanings that do not conform to the *primary meaning* of a word. Primary meanings of words are listed first in dictionary definitions and are the most typical or common meanings we associate with a word. And though we may think that the use of figurative language is confined to stories and poems, in fact, *most* of our everyday language use is nonliteral, from what we say in casual conversation to what we hear in a weather report on the news to political speeches. We think of objective writing and speaking, conveying "just the facts," as less figurative than literary language. On some level, this might be true, but as C. S. Lewis points out in his short treatise on language, *Studies in Words* (1990), "By his metaphor [discussed in next section] the speaker is trying to communicate what he believes to be a fact." That is, we can still express "facts" figuratively. When we say "He was madder than a hornet" or "I bombed that test," we are using nonliteral meanings of *hornet* and *bombed*. And what about when we say "Why the long face?" We aren't commenting on the length of someone's jaw but rather on their mood; and when we say "I see what you mean," we are using *see* to mean 'to understand' rather than 'to perceive with the eye'.

Language Alive!

Shifts in Meaning: Progress or Decay?

Though semantic shift is inevitable and very common, some language purists see it as a kind of language decay. Two examples of shifts that are often thought of this way are *imply/infer* and *affect/effect*. The verb *imply* traditionally meant 'to suggest without explicitly stating', and *infer* meant 'to arrive at a conclusion based on evidence.' So, when someone says, "We'd better go," he or she is *implying* that it is time to leave. If someone says, "I missed my bus," you can *infer* that he or she did not get to the bus stop on time. Due to their similarity in meaning, *imply* and *infer* are often used interchangeably. And *affect* and *effect*? The verb *affect* (with stress on the second syllable) traditionally meant 'to influence', as in 'The new process affects how we make cheese.' The verb *effect* means 'to create', as in 'The new process will effect a change in how we make cheese.' The fact that these words are pronounced identically by most speakers contributes to their tendency to be used interchangeably. Also, both words can be nouns with different meanings, but we don't mix these up as often as we do the verbs, though we do often misspell them.

Many writers are even commended for their use of figurative language to convey scientific (and presumably objective) ideas. Physician Lewis Thomas, well known for his lyrical essays on the human condition, describes the relationship between sea anemones and crabs in the following way:

> The anemones who live on the shells of crabs are precisely finicky; so are the crabs. Only a single species of anemone will find its way to only a single species of crab. They sense each other exquisitely, and live together as though made for each other. (1979: 4)

By describing the relationship between sea anemones and crabs figuratively, Thomas conveys not just his thoughts on the habits of marine creatures but also his thoughts on human relationships.

Contrast Thomas's description of the behavior of the sea anemone with the following description from *The Columbia Electronic Encyclopedia* (2005), which is more technical and relies on primary meanings:

> Most sea anemones attach temporarily to submerged objects; a few thrust themselves into the sand or live in furrows; a few are parasitic on other marine organisms . . .

It might be argued, then, that the distinction between figurative language and objective, factual language is rather fuzzy, and it is perhaps not surprising that the linguistic properties of figurative language are a topic of some debate. For Aristotle, figurative language is a rhetorical device that is distinct from the standard use and meaning of language. Philosopher John Searle takes a similar view in his 1979 article "Metaphor." For the Romantics, on the other hand, figurative language is part of the imagination, central to how we see the world. From this perspective, there is no distinction at all between literal and nonliteral language. Still another view of figurative language, somewhere between the Aristotelian and Romantic models, is the position taken by linguists George Lakoff and Mark Johnson (1980: 4), who argue that figurative language reflects much about our cognition and conceptual structure but that there is still a distinction, though not as great a one as Aristotle or Searle would propose, between literal and nonliteral language.

The role of figurative (nonliteral) language in creating and reflecting how we conceive of our world is complex and relevant to the larger question of the relationship between language and thought (something we take up in more detail in the following chapter). On the one hand, figurative language provides a tool to express a vast range of meaning beyond the primary meanings of words (if, in fact, we can designate certain meanings as primary, a proposal to which a Romantic might object). On the other hand, not all meaning can be expressed through language; some meaning is better expressed visually, through physical movement, drawing, and so on. (For example, try to describe the meaning of the word *spiral* or the way scissors work without using your hands.) Below, we examine some of the ways in which we use figurative language and discuss how such language creates meaning.

Connecting Meanings: Metaphor

metaphor nonliteral meaning of one word or phrase describes another word or phrase (*My car is a lemon.*)

Perhaps the most recognizable use of figurative language is **metaphor**. A metaphor, as Aristotle conceived it and as we still understand it, is a figure of speech that sets up an analogy between two words or phrases: *something is something else.* The word ultimately comes from the Greek *metaphero*, meaning 'to carry over' or 'transfer.'

As mentioned, Lakoff and Johnson (1980) take the position that there is no real distinction between metaphors and literal speech because metaphorical meanings actually reflect our conceptual structures, how we view the world. Lakoff and Johnson also argue that these metaphorical conceptual structures influence how we behave. Metaphor for Lakoff and Johnson is not a rhetorical device but rather a way of perceiving the world that is woven throughout ordinary language. They provide examples of metaphors such as the following to support this claim:

Time is money

we spend it, waste it, save it, don't have it, invest it, budget it,
lose it

Argument as war

your claims are indefensible

you attacked every weak point in my argument

your criticisms were right on target

I've never won an argument with you

you shot down all my arguments

hwæt!

The word *lemon*, used to refer to a malfunctioning vehicle, narrowed in meaning from the early 1900s slang meaning of *lemon*: something bad or undesirable or which fails to meet one's expectations. It has now expanded again to mean any item that is unsatisfactory or defective.

To what extent, if at all, do you think such metaphors shape our perspective and our behavior?

Types of Metaphors

dead metaphor metaphor that is so common that it goes unnoticed as a metaphor (*I see your point.*)

Dead metaphors   **Dead metaphors** are those that are so conventionalized in everyday speech that we don't even realize they are metaphors. Metaphors of sight provide some examples: *I see your point. I'll take a look at your paper for you. He is blind to new ideas.* These uses of *see, look,* and *blind* have nothing to do with visual perception; we use *see* as a synonym for *understand, blind* to express intentional lack of understanding, and *take a look* to mean 'investigate'. (Lakoff and Johnson argue that because these metaphors are so commonly used, they are not really dead at all but very productive.)

Another example of a truly dead metaphor is *broadcast*, which began as a metaphorical use of the casting of seeds broadly; today, it is not likely that anyone makes a connection with the spreading of seed.

We do have to *learn* that these are dead, however, as evidenced by some children's use and understanding of these words. A child who overhears the sentence *He can be so blind sometimes!* might ask, "Is he really blind?" And one child, knowing that *say* means 'to utter', said about a sign: "The sign wrote . . ." rather than "The sign said . . ." She had not yet learned the metaphorical meaning of *say*.

mixed metaphor
metaphor that comprises parts of different metaphors: *hit the nail on the jackpot* combines *hit the nail on the head* and *hit the jackpot*

Mixed metaphors   **Mixed metaphors** are those in which parts of different metaphors are telescoped into one utterance. This mixing can occur for a variety of reasons. The following examples were taken from the University of Illinois at Chicago website (http://tigger.uic.edu/~rramakri/Readings/Fun/Mixed-Metaphors.htm):

She grabbed the bull by the horns, and ran with it.
I've hit the nail on the jackpot.
I'm shooting from the seat of my pants.
You're pulling my leg over my eyes.
I'm flying by the edge of my seat.
Beware my friend . . . you are skating on hot water.
I would not trust him with a ten-foot pole.
We're robbing Peter to pay the piper.
I can see the carrot at the end of the tunnel.

We might come up with "hit the nail on the jackpot" because the two source metaphors ("hit the nail on the head" and "hit the jackpot") overlap in meaning ('to achieve a goal of some kind') and/or because they both include the verb *hit*. We might produce "flying by the edge of my seat" because both "flying by the seat of my pants" and "on the edge of my seat" have related meanings (unplanned action that may include fear and anxiety) and/or because both metaphors include the word *seat*.

RPE   9.18 ▷

personification
attribution of human qualities to something that is not human

Personification   **Personification**, another subtype of metaphorical language, gives human attributes to something that is not human. (For some, there is overlap between personification and *anthropomorphism*, but others argue that anthropomorphism is more specific, ascribing human qualities to gods, while others believe anthropomorphism to be more general that just language use; for example, ascribing human characteristics to nonhuman form in art.)

The steeples swam in the mist.
The gates opened their arms.
The project ate up all my time.
The cold knocked me out.

The idea died a natural death.
His theory explained . . .
These facts suggest . . .

RPE 9.19

synesthesia
metaphorical language in which one kind of sensation is described in terms of another; for example, a smell described as *sweet* or a color as *loud*

Synesthesia   **Synesthesia** is a type of metaphorical language in which one kind of sensation is described in terms of another (color is attributed to sounds, odor to color, sound to odor, etc.). Examples include "sweet" smells (taste attributed to smell), "loud" colors (sound attributed to color), and so on. In the following lines from Charles Baudelaire's poem "Correspondances," "perfumes" (smells) are described in terms of touch, "fresh like the skin of infants." The sense of touch is described in terms of sound ("sweet like oboes"). Finally, perfumes are described in terms of color ("green like prairies").

There are perfumes fresh like the skin of infants
Sweet like oboes, green like prairies . . .

metonymy
description of something in terms of something with which it is closely associated: *The pen is mightier than the sword* (pen = the written word/ diplomacy, sword = violence/force)

Metonymy   Another type of figurative speech is **metonymy**; we refer to something by describing it in terms of something with which it is closely associated. A well-known example of metonymy is *The pen is mightier than the sword*, in which *pen* refers to writing or diplomacy and *sword* to action or war. Additional examples are the following:

The Pentagon/The White House/Congress issued a statement yesterday.
The law is after her.

We often use metonymy to create verbs from nouns.

They *limousined* to the prom last night.
We *Taco Belled* for lunch today.

Synecdoche is a specific type of metonymy in which we use a part of something to refer to the whole thing. A physician may refer to a patient as *the tonsillectomy* rather than *the patient in 4B or Mary Jones*. We may refer a car as *wheels* or a *ride*.

head (of cattle), threads (clothing), skirt (woman), suit (man)
Sometimes synecdoche is more abstract:

Give me *a hand* = help
Lend me *an ear* = your attention
Two heads are better than one = cooperation

Synecdoche can also involve referring to something by manufacturer, product, material, or color.

I like my *Honda* = producer for product
Natural fibers are all the rage these days = cotton clothes
Do you take *plastic*? = credit cards

Did You Know...?

Hearing Colors

Synesthesia (related to the Greek word for 'sensation') is more than just a literary device; it is also a neurological phenomenon in which stimulation of one sensory or cognitive pathway leads to automatic, involuntary experiences in a second sensory or cognitive pathway. For example, one common form of synesthesia is grapheme → color synesthesia, in which letters or numbers are perceived as inherently colored. Writer Patricia Lynne Duffy reports, in her book *Blue Cats and Chartreuse Kittens*,

"One day," I said to my father, "I realized that to make an 'R' all I had to do was first write a 'P' and then draw a line down from its loop. And I was so surprised that I could turn a yellow letter into an orange letter just by adding a line."

Russian writer Vladimir Nabokov also had grapheme → color synesthesia, though it was likely actually phoneme → color since when he writes "letter'" he means phoneme because it's aural.

Another form of synesthesia is music → color synesthesia, in which synesthetes experience colors when they hear certain tones, timbres, or keys.

For more information

Duffy, P. 2001. *Blue cats and chartreuse kittens*. New York: Henry Holt.

Nabokov, V. 1966. *Speak, memory: An autobiography revisited*. New York: Putnam.

van Campen, C. 2010. *The hidden sense: Synesthesia in art and science*. Cambridge, MA: MIT Press.

Some theorists suggest that all language is metonymic since words stand for things. (See Lakoff 1987, for example.)

Comparing Meanings: Simile

simile comparison, usually of two unlike things, in order to create a nonliteral image (*run like a deer*)

Similes differ from metaphor and metonymy in that they involve a comparison of two unlike things and usually involve the words *like* or *as*.

He eats like a pig.
She's big as a house.
We're happy as clams.
My brain is like a sieve.

Here are some famous similes:

Suspicion climbed all over her face, like a kitten, but not so playfully. (Raymond Chandler)

Exuding good will like a mortician's convention in a plague year. (Daniel Berrigan)

As good as gold. (Charles Dickens)

Death hangs on her like an untimely frost. (William Shakespeare)

Solitude . . . is like Spanish moss which finally suffocates the tree it hangs on. (Anaïs Nin)

A woman without a man is like a fish without a bicycle. (attributed to Gloria Steinem)

Idioms

idiom collocation of words or phrases with nonliteral meaning (*kick the bucket* = die)

Another type of figurative speech is **idiom**. Like other kinds of figurative language, idioms are collocations of words or phrases with nonliteral meanings.

a chip on one's shoulder, dodge the bullet, champing at the bit, foaming at the mouth, push the envelope, pull the wool over someone's eyes, tongue in cheek, pull one's leg

Idioms in other languages can be completely distinct from those in English, though some have English counterparts, sometimes with interesting twists.

Idioms in Portuguese

Macacos me mordam! (monkeys bite me) 'to be intrigued or surprised'
botar um ponto final em (put the final dot in) 'bring the curtain down'
encurraldado (cornered) 'in a corner'
cair em si (to fall in oneself) 'to become aware'
andar na boa vai ela (to go in the good goes she) 'to be out on a spree'

Idioms in French

faire d'une pierre deux coups (to hit twice with a stone) 'to kill two birds with one stone'
avoir le cafard 'to have the blues'
casser les couilles 'break one's balls/piss one off'
mort de rire 'to die laughing'
se taper la cloche (to tap/ring the bell) 'to eat very well'

Idioms in German

RPE 9.20

RPE 9.21

Hans hat den Vogel abgeschossen. (Hans has shot off the bird.) 'Hans stole the show.'
Er hat ins Gras gebissen. (He has bitten into the grass.) 'He died.'

Accent on *Linguistics and Computers*

Courtesy of Apple

Does your spell-checker save or confuse you? Does your grammar-checker help or hinder your writing? Does your speech-recognition software make funny mistakes? Do you get frustrated or amazed by these computer programs? Well, have you ever wondered who invented and programmed them? Computational linguists have a major role here.

To program these computer features that we use every day required development of software that provides the computer with the grammatical rules of our language. Imagine the complexity! For example, how do you program a computer to recognize and understand ambiguity? Consider these two sentences:

They gave the monkeys the bananas because they were hungry.

They gave the monkeys the bananas because they were overripe.

They are syntactically identical, but they crucially differ in who or what *they* refers to. And this ambiguity is different from the one in the following "garden path" sentence:

The horse raced past the barn fell.

A garden path sentence is one that misleads us because we begin to decode (or parse) it one way but then have to backtrack to decipher its actual meaning. (We are led down the wrong garden path, so to speak.) How do we get a machine to decode it to [*The horse (who was) raced past the barn*] *fell*? To complicate it more, there are sentences with the same syntactic structure that are not ambiguous:

The horse ridden past the barn bucked.

How does one create a software program that understands both the ambiguity of the garden path sentence and the lack of ambiguity of the second sentence, which has the same syntactic structure? This is the kind of challenge that draws many linguists into *computational linguistics,* the study of language and computers. This field is very broad and includes the following subfields:

- Natural language processing: Design software that (ideally) gives computers the capability to analyze, decode, and produce "natural" language.
- Machine translation: Design software that allows computers to translate from one language to another.
- Speech generation: Use computers to program telephones, cars, elevators, GPSs, and games to produce speech (and this involves getting intonation right!). Apple's new Siri app (see photo) does all this and more!
- Speech recognition: Use computers to transform spoken language into written language.
- Corpus linguistics: Use computers to study large collections of spoken or written language (a collection is a *corpus*; plural *corpora*) statistically for frequency of patterns and so on.

(continued)

Computational linguistics extends beyond the borders of linguistics and computer science to include psychology (which provides models of how we think and solve problems), information theory (which provides models of communication), and mathematics and statistics (which provide tools for analyzing such models).

It is possible now to specialize in computational linguistics and then find rewarding employment with technology giants all over the world—AT&T Labs, General Electric, IBM, Lucent Technologies, Bell Labs, Microsoft, Xerox, SRI International in the United Kingdom, XRCE in France, DFKI in Germany, and IRST in Italy, to name just a few.

For more information
Professional organizations
Association for the Advancement of Artificial Intelligence. 2011. http://www.aaai.org/home.html

Association for Computational Linguistics (ACL). 2011. http://www.aclweb.org/
Manning, C. & H. Schütze. 1999. *Foundations of statistical natural language processing.* Cambridge, MA: MIT Press.
Microsoft Research. 2011. Natural language processing. http://research.microsoft.com/nlp/.

Professional journals
Computational Linguistics. 2011. MIT Press Journals. http://mitpress.mit.edu/journal-home.tcl?issn=08912017. (25 May, 2011).
Computer Speech and Language. 2011. Elsevier Press. http://www.elsevier.com/wps/find/journaldescription.cws_home/622808/description#description. (25 May, 2011).
Speech Technology Magazine. 2010–2011. http://www.speechtek.com/2011/

Summary

We now know that to know what a word means is not a simple thing; our understanding of word meanings involves a complex semantic rule system. In this chapter, we've examined some of the parts of that system. We've seen that the meanings of some words can be expressed in terms of binary features and that word meanings fall into different categories, or semantic fields, that tell us something about how we view the world. Word meanings can also include the meanings of other words (entailment), and other meaning relationships among words can be described by the nyms, the complex relationships that we bring into play in our everyday language. We've explored how the meanings of the words we use (euphemisms and metaphors, among other examples) may reflect how we think and perceive things and how word meanings change and shift over time in various ways. And finally, we've discussed in some detail how much of what we say is actually figurative in meaning, which provides us with yet another example of our unique ability to use language creatively.

Sources and Resources

American heritage dictionary of the English language, 4th edn. 2000. Boston: Houghton Mifflin.

Battistella, E. 1990 *Markedness: The evaluative superstructure of language*. Albany, NY: SUNY Press.

Battistella, E. 1996. *The logic of markedness*. New York: Oxford University Press.

Browning, R. 1888. *The pied piper of Hamelin*. New York and London: Frederick Warne & Co.

Canin, G. 1964. Conversations with Felix. *Reader's Digest* 84(506). June.

Chierchia, G. & S. McConnell-Ginet. 2000. *Meaning and grammar: An introduction to semantics*. 2nd edn. Cambridge, MA: MIT Press.

Cruse, D. 1986. *Lexical semantics*. Cambridge, UK: Cambridge University Press.

Duffy, P. 2001. *Blue cats and chartreuse kittens*. New York: Henry Holt.

Fromkin Speech Error Database. 2011. Max Planck Institute for Psycholinguistics. http://www.mpi.nl/cgi-bin/sedb/sperco_form4.pl. (22 April, 2011).

Hall, J. (ed.). 2002. *Dictionary of American regional English*, 4. Cambridge, MA: Belknap Press.

Henriksson, A.2003. *Non campus mentis: World history according to college students*. New York: Workman.

Hurford, J. & B. Heasley. 2007. *Semantics: A coursebook*, 2nd edn. Cambridge, UK: Cambridge University Press.

Kempson, R. 1977. *Semantic theory*. Cambridge, UK: Cambridge University Press.

Lakoff, G. 2002. *Moral politics: How liberals and conservatives think*. Chicago: University of Chicago Press.

Lakoff, G. 2006. Staying the course right over a cliff. *New York Times*. October 27. http://www.nytimes.com/2006/10/27/opinion/27lakoff.html?_r=1&oref=slogin

Lakoff, G. 1997. *Women, fire and dangerous things*. Chicago: University of Chicago Press.

Lakoff, G. & M. Johnson. 2003. *Metaphors we live by*, 2nd edn. Chicago: University of Chicago Press.

Lewis, C. S. 1990. *Studies in words*, 2nd edn. London: Cambridge University Press.

Nunberg, G. 2004. Political language. *Fresh air*. National Public Radio. September 1. http://www.npr.org/templates/story/story.php?storyId=3883628

Nunberg, G. 2006. *Talking right: How conservatives turned liberalism into a tax-raising, latte-drinking, sushi-eating, Volvo-driving*, New York Times–*reading, body-piercing, Hollywood-loving, left-wing freak show*. New York: Public Affairs.

Saeed, J. 2008. *Semantics*, 3rd edn. Oxford, UK: Blackwell.

Sea anemone. *Columbia electronic encyclopedia*, 6th edn. 2001–2007. New York: Columbia University Press.

Searle, J. 1979. Metaphor. In Andrew Ortony (ed.), *Metaphor and thought*, 92–123. Cambridge, UK: Cambridge University Press.

Silverstein, S. 1981. *A light in the attic*. New York: HarperCollins.

Thomas, L. 1979. *The medusa and the snail: Notes of a biology watcher*. New York: Viking Press.

University of Illinois at Chicago. http://tigger.uic.edu/~rramakri/Readings/Fun/Mixed-Metaphors.htm

van Campen, C. 2010. *The hidden sense: Synesthesia in art and science*. Cambridge, MA: MIT Press.

Review, Practice, and Explore

RPE 9.1 Deciphering Meaning: American English Vocabulary

We can derive meaning from the morphology and syntax of a word even if we've never seen it before. We can also derive meaning from context. Here are some words from different dialects of English, words you may or may not be familiar with (these are words taken from the *Dictionary of American Regional English*). Can you match each word with its meaning? Check your answers with the key at the end of this section. How did you came up with your answers? What clues did you use? Which words were the most difficult to match to meanings, and why? (To explore the DARE website, go to http://polyglot.lss.wisc.edu/dare/dare.html.)

pinkie	**a.** a tomato
princeton	**b.** a man's short hairstyle
poison apple	**c.** a nickname for an unimportant or out-of-the-way place
pirok	**d.** a water faucet placed on the outside of a building
sill cock	**e.** a main-dish pie, frequently containing fish and rice
Skunk's Misery	**f.** a trick, deception
prairie	**g.** a vacant lot or city block
sandy	**h.** a small sailing vessel with a sharp stern

RPE 9.2 Onomatopoeia

Onomatopoeia can be used as a rhetorical device to create the illusion of sound in a text, as in the following example:

> And ere three shrill notes the pipe he uttered, / You heard as if an army *muttered*; / The *muttering* grew to a *grumbling*; / And the *grumbling* grew to mighty *rumbling*; / And out of the house the rats came tumbling. (Browning 1888)

Find at least three examples of onomatopoeia in poetry or prose. You might find examples in unlikely places such as the newspaper and e-mails.

RPE 9.3 Etymological Clues

Sometimes we use etymology (word origins) to help us decipher meanings. As you know, many English words have Latin and Greek roots. Below is a list of Greek and Roman gods' names. See if you can list words that have these names as roots. How does the meaning of the god's name help you decipher the meaning of the words on your list?

Luna—goddess of the moon. At one time, people believed that the moon had the power to drive some people out of their minds.

Hypnos—Greek god of sleep

Somnus—Roman god of sleep

Nox—goddess of darkness of night

Lethe—means 'forgetfulness'; the river in Hades where the spirits of the dead drink and then forget their former lives and become listless ghosts

Phobos—son of Ares, the Greek god of war. His name means 'fear'.

Pan—god of fields, forests, wild animals. Part man and part goat, he often caused serious trouble. The belief that he was nearby caused people to run in terror.

Gaea—goddess of the earth; Greek word for earth

Terra—Roman goddess of the earth

Gratiae—the Graces, three sisters who were goddesses of all that is charming in women

Hygeia—Greek goddess of health

Pysche—the maiden who fell in love with Eros, the Greek god of love. Her name means 'soul'.

Hydra—a water serpent slain by Heracles

Helios—god of the sun

Sol—Roman god of the sun

Morta—Roman sister of Fate

RPE 9.4 ⟩ **Count or Noncount Nouns?**

Many nouns can have both count and noncount interpretations. For example:

noncount: <u>Love</u> is patient.
count: She had two <u>loves</u>: philosophy and poetry.

noncount: <u>Rice</u> is good for you.
count: There are many <u>rices</u> to choose from: arborio, jasmine, basmati—to name a few.

Consider whether the following words are count or noncount, and give evidence (use them in sentences) to support your analysis.

truth, courage, music, fish, money

RPE 9.5 ⟩ **Semantic Features of Nouns**

Write out the feature specifications of each of the following nouns. Remember that each noun is specified for three features: concrete/abstract, count/mass, and proper/common. Be prepared to justify your answers, as not all of you will agree on the features you assign to each noun.

kitten, homework, beer, the president of the United States, music, river, light, Santa Claus

RPE 9.6 > Children's Semantic Fields

Children do an amazing job of acquiring word meanings quickly and accurately. However, most children do make errors; most commonly, they overgeneralize the meaning of a word. Here are some typical examples:

Word	Child's Meaning
sweet	all things sweet (syrup, cookies, doughnuts, sugar, etc.)
apple	all fruits that are recognizable to child (round)
hot	light, bright objects (fire, lights, lamps, etc.)

Describe how these examples illustrate how the children are constructing semantic fields and how those are different from adult versions.

RPE 9.7 > Antonyms: Find the Opposites

Give antonyms for the following terms, and label each pair as gradable, relational, or complementary. Compare your answers. Did everyone come up with the same pairs? Discuss why or why not.

a. over
b. hello
c. quickly
d. now
e. chicken
f. near
g. black
h. give

RPE 9.8 > Antonymy and Markedness

Antonyms come in different forms: gradable, relational, and complementary. Nevertheless, we tend to think of antonyms as opposites. Markedness is a related concept involving binary oppositions, highlighting how we tend to consider one member of a pair of antonyms typical and the other marked. Markedness is illustrated by the following pairs of antonyms, with the "typical" member of the pair on the left and the "marked" member on the right.

a. How high/*low is it? (height)
b. How long/*short is it? (length)
c. How wide/*narrow is it? (width)
d. How heavy/*light is it? (weight)
e. How deep/*shallow is it? (depth)

What are three or four other pairs of adjectives that illustrate this markedness relation?

RPE 9.9 > Synonyms

Write a short paragraph (four or five sentences) on a topic of your choice. Use at least four Anglo-Saxon terms from Table 9.2. Then rewrite the paragraph, replacing the Anglo-Saxon terms with their Latin or Greek synonyms. How does this substitution change your paragraph? Explain briefly.

RPE 9.10 > Ethnic Slurs

Research the origins of four or five ethnic slurs you are familiar with. Trace how those terms have evolved in meaning over time. Why do you think such terms are so powerful? Do you think that by changing terms (by using politically correct language or euphemisms) we can also change attitudes and reduce discrimination? Will changing how we talk also change how we think about ourselves and about groups other than our own?

RPE 9.11 > Hyponymy

Here are four semantic categories:

CARS   STUDENTS   JOBS   DOGS

Come up with at least four hyponyms for each category. What criteria did you use to decide? Are your hyponyms distinguishable in terms of semantic features? Compare notes with your classmates. Why might your hyponyms for these categories differ from person to person?

RPE 9.12 > Polysemy

Explain how each of the following words is polysemous. The first example is done for you.

a. finger (lift a finger, give someone the finger, finger something—steal or touch)
b. lip
c. heart   f. butt
d. face   g. hand
e. toe   h. ear

Now, find as many examples of polysemy in the following poem as you can.

Things

What happened is, we grew lonely
living among the things,
so we gave the clock a face,
the chair a back,
the table four stout legs
which will never suffer fatigue.
We fitted our shoes with tongues
as smooth as our own
and hung tongues inside bells
so we could listen
to their emotional language,
and because we loved graceful profiles
the pitcher received a lip,
the bottle a long, slender neck.
Even what was beyond us
was recast in our image;
we gave the country a heart,
the storm an eye,
the cave a mouth
so we could pass into safety.

(Reprinted by permission of Louisiana State University Press from *Alive Together*, by Lisel Mueller. Copyright ©1996 by Lisel Mueller.)

RPE 9.13 > Homonyms

Recall the following distinctions between homonyms, homophones, and homographs:

homonyms: sound same, same spelling
homophones: sound same, different spelling
homographs: same spelling, sound different

Supply a homonym, homophone, or homograph for each of the following words. Label your examples.

compact, bat, see, pupil, refuse, aisle, pail, bank, race, job, entrance, alter, braid

RPE 9.14 > Ambiguity

Label each of the following newspaper headlines as *lexically* ambiguous (ambiguous because of a word) or *syntactically* ambiguous (ambiguous because of the structure of the sentence). Briefly explain each of your answers. If the sentence is both lexically and syntactically ambiguous, label it as such and explain why.

a. Grandmother of Eight Makes Hole in One
b. Quarter of a Million Chinese Live on Water
c. Police Begin Campaign to Run Down Jaywalkers
d. Two Convicts Evade Noose, Jury Hung
e. Safety Experts Say School Bus Passengers Should Be Belted
f. Milk Drinkers Are Turning to Powder
g. Iraqi Head Seeks Arms
h. Two Sisters Reunite after Eighteen Years at Checkout Counter
i. Doctor Testifies in Horse Suit
j. Police Discover Crack in Australia

Also, choose two lexically ambiguous words that you find in these headlines. How do you know these words are ambiguous rather than simply vague?

RPE 9.15 > Meaning Change in Progress

The *American Heritage Dictionary* gives the following definitions for *aggravate*:

1. To make worse or more troublesome
2. To rouse to exasperation or anger; provoke

Many usage experts believe only the first definition should be used. Here's the dictionary's usage note: "*Aggravate* comes from the Latin verb *aggravare*, which meant 'to make heavier,' that is, 'to add to the weight of'." It also had the extended senses 'to annoy' and 'to oppress.' Some people claim that *aggravate* can only mean 'to make worse', and not 'to irritate', on the basis of the word's etymology. But in doing so, they ignore not only an English sense in use since the seventeenth century but also one of the original Latin ones. Sixty-eight percent of the *American Heritage* Usage Panel approves of its use in *It's the endless wait for luggage that aggravates me the most about air travel.* Look up the following words to see what the experts have to say about them; then discuss your own usage and attitudes about the words and their meanings.

anxious

hopefully

orientate

comprise

literally

RPE 9.16 > Historical Shifts in Meaning

Below are a number of words from Old English (and a few that came into Old English from Old French) that still exist in Present-Day English, though each has shifted in meaning. Identify the type of meaning shift for each word. Choose from amelioration, pejoration, narrowing, broadening, and shift (in denotation—a completely new meaning).

PDE Word	Original Word	Meaning
dream	dréam	'mirth'
moody	mōdig	'brave'
deer	déor	'beast/animal'
knight	cniht	'boy, lad'
gum	góma	'inside of mouth or throat'
bead	bedu	'prayer'
dizzy	dysiȝ[1]	'foolish'
bird	bridd	'young bird'
tide	tíd	'time'
uncouth	uncúþ[2]	'unknown'
witch	wicca	'male or female sorcerer'

PDE Word	Old French	Meaning
butcher	bocher	'one who slaughters goats'
accident	accident	'an event'
carry	carier	'transport by cart'

RPE 9.17 > Shifts in Meaning: Slang Words

The changes in meanings of English slang and taboo words are particularly interesting to study because these meanings have often changed rather dramatically over time. For example, the slang word *crapper* has its origin in one Thomas Crapper, who was in some way associated with the originator of the flush toilet (the "Silent Valveless Water Waste Preventer" patented in 1819, by Albert Giblin).

Choose four slang terms and look up their meanings. Explain how the meaning of each word has shifted over time. Illustrate with examples, and identify examples of broadening,

---

1. This symbol (ȝ), called *yogh*, was used in Middle English to represent /y/ and sometimes other velar phonemes.
2. This symbol, þ, called *thorn*, was used in Old and Middle English to represent either of the interdental fricatives, /θ/ and/or /ð/.

narrowing, pejoration, amelioration, and shift in denotation. (Slang dictionaries are excellent resources for this exercise.)

RPE 9.18 > Metaphors We Live By?

What are some of the metaphors we use in talking about the following concepts, and do they fall into a particular category? If so, do you think that category accurately represents our cultural perceptions of that concept? Explain briefly.

love   marriage   illness   life

RPE 9.19 > Human Qualities: Personification

Personification involves ascribing human attributes to inanimate or abstract concepts:

> High gas prices are *killing us,* and they are the *enemy* of commuters.

> The bad weather is truly *treacherous* and might *cheat* farmers out of some of the growing season.

In a text of your choice, find five examples of personification. Examples can come from a newspaper, poem, story, TV news report, magazine, radio program, or other medium. (*Hint:* sports commentary abounds with personification and metaphor.)

RPE 9.20 > Semantic Classes of Idioms

Idioms can be classified by the concepts they express. For example, there are many idiomatic expressions for anger, work, love, and sex.

> *Anger:* flip your lid, blow your stack, bite someone's head off, let off steam

> *Love:* fall for, be crazy about, dig, have a crush on, hit it off with, get hung up on, make eyes at someone

Come up with two classes of idioms on your own, and give three or four examples of idioms that fall into each class.

RPE 9.21 > The Semantics of Jokes

Many jokes are funny for semantic reasons, relying on ambiguous words, synonyms, antonymy, and various types of figurative language to create humor. We also use our knowledge of other grammatical components (syntax, morphology, phonology) to create humor. Explain the humor in each of the following jokes using your grammatical knowledge. What contributes to the humor in each joke? Be as specific and detailed as you can.

> Q: What's the difference between Cheerios and Georgia Tech (insert team of your choice)?
> A: Cheerios belong in a bowl.

> Q: What lies at the bottom of the ocean and twitches?
> A: A nervous wreck.

> Q: Why do chicken coops have two doors?
> A: Because if they had four doors, they would be chicken sedans.

Q: What does a skeleton get when he goes to a bar?
A: A beer and a mop.

Q: How many men does it take to wallpaper a room?
A: About two, if they're thinly sliced.

Q: How many ears did Davy Crockett have?
A: Three—his left ear, his right ear, and his wild front ear.

Q: Why don't cannibals eat clowns?
A: Because they taste funny.

Answers to RPE 9.1
pinkie (h), princeton (b), poison apple (a), pirok (e), sill cock (d), Skunk's Misery (c), prairie (g), sandy (f).

That's not what I said!

Semantics and Pragmatics: Making Meaning with Sentences

Chapter at a Glance

Sentence Semantics: The Linguistic Meaning of Sentences
  Propositions and Truth Conditions
  When Meanings Overlap: Entailment and Paraphrase
  When Semantics and Syntax Overlap: The Structure of Meaning

Pragmatics: How Context Shapes Meaning
  Saying What You Mean and Meaning What You Say: Speech Acts
  Cooperative Talk: Conversational Rules
  The Power of Politeness
  When Semantics and Pragmatics Overlap

Language and Thought
  Linguistic Relativity and the Sapir-Whorf Hypothesis

Summary

Sources and Resources

Review, Practice, and Explore

Key Concepts

- Like words, sentences also have meaning, derived both from their structure and from the context in which they are uttered.
- Though we may think otherwise, our conversations actually follow rules. We are experts at manipulating these rules, maintaining them, violating them, and sometimes just ignoring them to express meaning.
- Cultural politeness conventions also shape how we talk to each other.
- Our language may (or may not) influence how we think.

Did You Know . . . ?

  The Cooperative Principle and Language Acquisition
  Does Culture Count?
  Lost in Translation

Language Alive! Culture Clash and Pragmatic Failure

  Register as a Literary Device

Linguistics in the News Watson the Computer Plays "Jeopardy!"

Accent on Forensic Linguistics

> *Words differently arranged have a different meaning, and meanings differently arranged have a different effect.*
>
> —BLAISE PASCAL (1623–1662)

I n the previous chapter, we discussed word meanings and meaning relationships such as hyponymy, metaphor, antonymy, and so on. Our discussion concerned semantics, the study of the complex set of rules by which we assign meanings to linguistic sounds or signs. One way of thinking about semantics is that it is the study of meanings encoded in words regardless of their context. In this chapter, we will discuss the meaning encoded in sentences, or **sentence meaning**. Like the word meanings we discussed in Chapter 9, sentence meaning is the meaning of a sentence on its own regardless of its context. Consider, for example, the sentence *Have you quit smoking?* This sentence encodes more than just a question; it has the additional meaning that you smoked at some point in the past. We extract this meaning from the sentence regardless of the context in which the sentence is uttered—the meaning is encoded in the sentence itself. And what about this sentence: *Jones was killed, but he didn't die.* The oddity of this sentence, a contradiction, comes from the fact that it is both false and true at the same time. We understand this as a contradiction regardless of context, just from the meanings of the words.

sentence meaning meaning of a sentence regardless of context or knowledge of the world (its linguistic meaning)

hwæt!

Blaise Pascal was a French philosopher, mathematician, and physicist in the seventeenth century. He was a strong supporter of the scientific method and made important contributions in diverse areas, including geometry, mechanics, and probability theory.

The meanings encoded in words and sentences are not the only way we make meaning out of language, however. Sentences, like words, can also have nonliteral meanings. The sentence *I want to be a linguistics major* conveys exactly what it seems to—that you have a desire to be a linguistics major (sentence meaning). But not everything we say is so straightforward. What about when you say "How are you doing?" when you greet someone on the street? Are you really asking for information about someone's well-being, or are you simply saying *hello* in a nonliteral way? (We know it's usually the latter because if someone actually gives us a detailed description of how they are doing in response to this question, it's usually far more than what we wanted to know.) We will discuss the unspoken or indirect meaning of sentences here, what we'll call **utterance meaning**, and how these unspoken meanings differ from "direct," or literal, meanings.

utterance meaning meaning of utterances in context; their unspoken or indirect meaning

We will look at how we make conversational choices, such as to use *please* or *thank you;* to call someone by his or her first name, a nickname, or a formal title; to say *yes* in some contexts but *yeah* in others. We'll also look at the rules of conversation that are shared by most speakers, rules that we use to construct meaningful exchanges. We'll discuss how much information we convey and in what way, and how we know not only how to follow the rules of conversation but how to break them in order to express meaning. For example, when someone asks "What are you reading?" you might say, "My linguistics textbook," or you might say "A book!" Each response conveys a different meaning and has a different purpose.

The study of the meaning of language in context (utterance meaning) is called **pragmatics**. Pragmatics overlaps semantics (and utterance meaning overlaps sentence meaning) to provide us with a bigger picture of how we construct meaning out of language. We close the chapter with a discussion of the influence of language on how we think. Do the meanings we construct out of language reflect our view of the world? Does language reflect how we think? And if so, what does this mean about different languages and different cultures? How much does language influence our view of the world and vice versa?

pragmatics study of the meanings of sentences in context (utterance meaning)

Sentence Semantics: The Linguistic Meaning of Sentences

The first thing we have to do before pursuing sentence meaning in any detail is to briefly consider once again what we mean by *sentence*. And how does a sentence differ from an *utterance*? Do we need to make a distinction between the two?

Recall from Chapter 7 that a sentence is not the same thing as a clause; a sentence can contain many clauses, as in the following example:

I think that Louise told me that someone said that a train is coming.

A sentence can also be made up of a single clause:

A train is coming!

This sentence is not an utterance; you are reading it rather than saying it out loud or hearing someone say it to you. Its meaning, then, is based not on context but on the meaning encoded in the sentence itself. But if someone uttered or, even more specifically, *yelled* into your ear, "A train is coming!" your reaction might be very different from what it is here as you read the sentence on the page. You may take the meaning of this sentence to be a warning. So, in this case, the meaning of what we might call an utterance is determined in part by the context, by the speaker, and by the hearer.

So the distinction between sentence and utterance is rather fuzzy, and we will not attempt to pursue a precise definition here. But we will distinguish between *sentence meaning* and *utterance meaning*. We will define *sentence meaning* as the literal meaning of a sentence, regardless of context.

Utterance meaning is the meaning of a sentence in context, where the speaker's intention and hearer's interpretation contribute to meaning. In the next section, we look at sentence meaning in more detail, and we take up utterance meaning later in the chapter.

Propositions and Truth Conditions

proposition
assertion expressed by a sentence regardless of context or real-world facts

Think again about the sentence *A train is coming!* Regardless of context, this sentence has a meaning; it expresses a **proposition**, namely, that a train is coming. Whether a train is or is not really barreling down the track at this moment is irrelevant to how we assess sentence meaning; rather, propositions are meanings derived from sentences regardless of the facts of the world or the context in which the sentence is uttered. The principles of logic studied by philosophers and formal semanticists give us the framework for the study of the propositions expressed by a sentence. Key in this study is whether a proposition is logically true or false, its **truth condition**. Consider the following:

truth condition
whether a proposition is logically true or false regardless of context or real-world facts

A train is coming.
A train is not coming.

In logical terms, we can say that the proposition expressed in the first sentence (namely, that a train is coming) is true, but that same proposition is false in the second: It is not the case that a train is coming. This general property of sentence meaning holds across languages: Sentences can express propositions—assertions that are either true or false.

Interestingly, truth conditions hold regardless of whether the proposition expressed is really possible. For example, we understand that the proposition expressed in *A unicorn is in my garden* is true (in the logical sense), and we know that this proposition is false in the sentence *A unicorn is not in my garden*. This understanding of propositions holds regardless of whether we believe in unicorns and regardless of whether we have gardens.

When Sentences Don't Express Propositions

Not all sentences contain propositions. More specifically, not all sentences have truth conditions. Take, for example, the sentence *Is there a unicorn in my garden?* The proposition *There is a unicorn in my garden* does not follow from this sentence. Similarly, in the negative sentence *Isn't there a unicorn in my garden?* it does not follow that *There is not a unicorn in my garden*. This is because in interrogative sentences, propositions are questioned rather than asserted. A similar situation arises with commands, or imperative sentences. The sentence *Get out of here!* does not assert a proposition; the proposition *You will get out of here* does not follow.

RPE 10.1

Analytic and Synthetic Sentences

Take a look at the following sentences. Are they true or false? Why?

George's uncle is a man.
She is her daughter's mother.
Sue met a bachelor who is unmarried.

Such sentences are *necessarily* true because their truth derives from linguistic meaning, not from any actual facts. For example, you don't have to know George's uncle to know that the proposition *George's uncle is a man* is true, and you don't have to know anything about Sue or the person she met to know that *Sue met a bachelor who is unmarried* is also true (and redundantly so). Such necessarily true sentences are called **analytic sentences.**

analytic sentence sentence that *must* be true regardless of real-world facts

Now, think about sentences whose truth conditions depend on our knowledge of the world. The sentence *That dog is brown* expressess the proposition that there is a dog that is brown, but it is quite different from *That dog is a canine.* This second proposition is true because of its meaning relationships; as we saw in Chapter 9, the meaning of *dog* includes the meaning of *canine.* But the meaning of *dog* does not include the meaning *brown,* so the truth of *That dog is brown* depends not on the meaning relationships within the sentence itself but on meanings we gather from our knowledge of the world. Sentences that are true because they accord with the facts of the world are called **synthetic sentences.**

RPE   10.2 ⟩

synthetic sentence sentence that is true because it accords with real-world facts

When Meanings Overlap: Entailment and Paraphrase

Let's take a closer look at how sentences can include the meanings of other sentences. You may remember from Chapter 9 the meaning relationship called entailment. For example, the word *thoroughbred* entails the meaning of *horse.* This entailment relationship is called *hyponymy.* When we construct sentences with hyponyms, the sentence will also express those entailments. So, the meaning of the sentence *Seabiscuit is a thoroughbred* entails the meaning of the sentence *Seabiscuit is a horse.*

ƕæꞇ!

Seabiscuit was a champion racehorse in the 1940s—an unlikely champion who became a symbol of hope for many Americans during the Great Depression. He's been the subject of a 1949 film, a 2001 book, and a 2003 film, *Seabiscuit,* which was nominated for an Academy Award for Best Picture.

Thoroughbreds are horses.
Seabiscuit is a thoroughbred.
Seabiscuit is a horse.

Entailment can be logically expressed in the following way:

Entailment: A proposition X entails a proposition Y if the truth of Y follows necessarily from the truth of X.

paraphrase
(sentence
synonymy)
sentence with the
same entailments as
another sentence

Recall that words are synonymous when they share the same basic meanings. Sentences can also be synonymous when they express the same entailments: when the truth of one sentence entails the truth of the other. Some examples of synonymous sentences, or **paraphrases**, are given below.

> Seabiscuit beat War Admiral.
> War Admiral lost the race against Seabiscuit.
> Mary sold her house to Sue.
> Sue bought Mary's house.

In these examples, paraphrases are created by using different words and phrases that have the same entailments. Paraphrases can also be created by syntactic movement (such as by passive construction), as illustrated below. Both of these sentences entail that Seabiscuit beat War Admiral.

> Seabiscuit beat War Admiral.
> War Admiral was beaten by Seabiscuit.

Subtle differences in word meaning can affect entailments. For example, the words *unmarried man* and *bachelor* entail each other (and are synonymous), and their meanings can be expressed by semantic features.

> Mary met an unmarried man. [+male, +adult, –married]
> Mary met a bachelor. [+male, +adult, –married]

The following two sentences do not have the same entailments, which illustrates the difference between *kill* and *assassinate*, a distinction that is difficult to express in terms of semantic features.

> Booth killed Lincoln.
> Booth assassinated Lincoln.

Both sentences entail that Lincoln died and that Booth was the agent of his death. The word *assassinate*, however, also entails that Booth's killing of Lincoln was politically motivated. It is difficult to see how semantic features could handle this. (Is there a feature [+politically motivated]?) These two terms overlap in meaning but aren't synonymous.

And finally, ambiguous sentences (discussed in Chapters 8 and 9) are those in which there is more than one set of entailments. Consider, for example:

> She wrote a book on Fifth Avenue.
> He should lose those ugly polyester shirts.

The first sentence is syntactically ambiguous: one interpretation entails that she wrote a book while she was located on Fifth Avenue (she wrote a book, say, on dinosaurs); the other entails that she wrote a book *about* Fifth Avenue and says nothing about where she was when she did so. The second sentence is lexically ambiguous because of the verb *lose*, which can mean either 'misplace' or 'discard'. Each sentence has more than one meaning and, therefore, more than one set of entailments.

RPE 10.3 >

Sentences That *Can't* Be True: Contradictions

contradiction
sentence that can't
be true

Sentences that logically can't be true are called **contradictions**. For example, *The man is canine* can't be true (in contrast to the analytic sentence *The man is human*, which is necessarily true). Consider the following sentences, each of which contains more than one clause. Are any of them contradictions?

(1) Seabiscuit is a thoroughbred, and Seabiscuit is not a thoroughbred.
(2) Either Seabiscuit is a thoroughbred or Seabiscuit is not a thoroughbred.
(3) If Seabiscuit is a thoroughbred, Seabiscuit is a thoroughbred.
(4) If every racehorse is here, no racehorse is not here.
(5) If some racehorse is here, then no racehorse is here.

You probably figured out that (1) and (5) can't be true and are contradictions. You can probably also see that the truth conditions of these connected sentences depend in part on the logical relationships expressed by *and*, *either*, *or*, *if*, *every*, *some*, and *no*—members of the functional categories *conjunction* and *quantifier* (discussed in Chapters 5 and 7). In logic, *and*, *either*, *or*, and *if* are **logical connectives**, and they interact with quantifiers (such as *every*, *some*, and *no*) and negation (*not*) to affect sentence meaning in crucial ways. A full discussion of the interaction of these words would take us far into the realm of logic, so we won't pursue it here, but note that we have no trouble interpreting the meanings of these connected sentences, another piece of evidence for our (very complex) unconscious knowledge of language.

logical connectives
words that express
logical relationships,
such as *either*, *or*,
and *if*

RPE   10.4

Presupposition

presupposition
assumption that is
implied by a word
or sentence based
on world knowledge

We have seen so far that words and sentences can express entailment relations in a variety of ways. Entailments depend on the complex interplay of propositions, truth conditions, and logical connectives and do not, crucially, seem to depend on our knowledge of the world. Another type of entailment is **presupposition**, wherein we infer, or assume, certain propositions based on a particular sentence.

Have you stopped kissing Seabiscuit?
> Presupposition: You used to kiss Seabiscuit.

I regret that Seabiscuit lost the race.
> Presupposition: Seabiscuit lost the race.

I would love to go to another race.
> Presupposition: I have been to at least one race already.

Presupposition on one level seems exactly like entailment: a logical conclusion follows from a particular proposition. There is some controversy, however, about whether presupposition, in contrast to entailment, relies on context rather than being strictly confined to sentence meaning. The argument is that a particular sentence will always express the same entailment(s) but not always the same presuppositions. Linguist Stephen Levinson (1983: 187) provides the following sentences to illustrate:

> She cried before she finished her thesis.
> Entailment: She was working on her thesis.
> Presupposition: She finished her thesis.

> She died before she finished her thesis.
> Entailment: She was working on her thesis.
> Presupposition: She finished her thesis.

When we change the verb in the sentence from *cry* to *die*, the proposition *she finished her thesis* is no longer presupposed because of what we know about dead people and their ability to complete projects. If we assume that presuppositions do not depend on contextual knowledge, then this difference should not arise. Presupposition, then, is often considered a part of pragmatics, in which context rather than semantics plays a role.

RPE 10.5 >

When Semantics and Syntax Overlap: The Structure of Meaning

In this section, we'll investigate the overlap of sentence meaning (semantics) and sentence structure (syntax). This overlap is illustrated by the Chomsky's well-known sentence:

> Colorless green ideas sleep furiously.

Remember that this sentence is syntactically well formed but semantically deviant. For this sentence to make sense, we have to change the words, coming up with a sentence such as the following:

> Colorful red flags wave furiously.

or

> Shoeless small children peer curiously.

You get the idea, and it's pretty straightforward. But a slightly different problem arises in sentences such as the following, and something else must be fixed to make them grammatical.

> *She slept the baby.
> *Jude met that Sam is smart.
> *The doctor seemed singing the blues.

These all sound very weird, but changing the words doesn't help: *She slept the bed* is also ungrammatical, as is *Jude met that the bus is on time*. These sentences are ungrammatical

hwæt!

Some normally intransitive verbs can take complements, but they are nearly always lexically related to the verb, and they have a poetic quality: *sleep a deep sleep, dream a dream, die a slow death.*

because they violate syntactic rules, which is different from the violation we see in *Colorless green ideas sleep furiously*. We can fix them by changing the syntax:

> She slept.
> Jude met Sam.
> The doctor seemed cheerful.

Here, we've eliminated the NP *the baby* from the first sentence and changed the clause *that Sam is smart* to an NP, *Sam,* in the second. In the third sentence, we've replaced the VP *singing the blues* with the AP *cheerful*. In the first example, we've eliminated the *complement* of the verb altogether, and in the other two we've replaced the complement of the verb with a complement of a different syntactic category: We've replaced a clause (CL) with NP, and VP with AP.

That changing the syntax makes these sentences meaningful tells us that syntax overlaps semantics. These data also suggest that part of our grammatical system includes rules that determine the syntactic configurations in which a particular verb can occur. *Sleep* is intransitive, for example, which means that it takes no complement at all. But *met*, on the other hand, is transitive and must take an NP (specifically, a direct object) as a complement. Semantic rules tell us what kinds of meanings go together: The subjects of the verbs *sleep* and *meet* must be things or entities that can sleep and meet something or someone (eliminating *colorless green ideas* as a candidate for the subject of *sleep,* for example). Syntactic rules require that the subjects of these verbs are of the category NP and also that the complement of *meet* is an NP as well (excluding the clause *that Sam is smart* in this position).

This overlap between syntax and semantics is one of linguistics' gray areas; it is not always easy to determine whether certain properties of language are best described as semantic, syntactic, or both. For example, does the fact that *meet* requires an NP complement rather than a clause complement follow from the fact that *meet* must be followed by a thing, namely, something that can be met? Is it semantics that determines the category of that complement, or is it the other way around? We will outline some of the central ideas that linguists have advanced to explain this complex relationship.

arguments set of phrases that occur with a verb and are assigned certain semantic roles by the verb

thematic roles semantic roles, including *agent, patient, source, goal,* etc., that the verb assigns to its arguments

Thematic Roles and Argument Structure

To explain the evidence that verbs seem to "select" semantically appropriate phrases with which they occur, linguists have proposed that these phrases, or **arguments** of a verb, are assigned certain semantic roles, or **thematic roles,** by the verb. Table 10.1 lists some common thematic roles assigned to different phrases.

Table 10.1	Typical Thematic Roles

Agent: Initiator of the action (capable of volition)*

The puppy chewed up the shoe.

Marty played chess.

Patient: Entity undergoing the effect of some action or change of state

The ice melted.

The sun melted *the ice*.

Marty cooked *the bacon*.

Theme: Entity moved by the action or whose location is described (with no change of state)

The horse is in the stable.

Juanita passed *the ball* to Jake.

Marty gave Leo *a book*.

Experiencer: Entity that is aware of the action or state described by the verb but is not in control of that action or state

Marty felt happy.

The referee observed the game.

The deer heard the hunter in the woods.

Beneficiary: Entity for whose benefit the action was performed

Marty gave *Leo* the book.

We baked a cake for *Lorian*.

Instrument: Means by which an action is performed or by which something comes about

She flipped the pancakes with *a spatula*.

Miss Scarlet killed Colonel Mustard with *a lead pipe*.

Location: Place in which something is situated or takes place

We ate *at Denny's*.

John sprinted *to the goal*.

Goal: Entity toward which something moves, either literally or metaphorically

Marty gave the book *to Leo*.

She gave a speech *to the club*.

Source: Entity from which something moves, either literally or metaphorically

The water bubbled *from the spring*.

They came all the way *from New Orleans*.

*Definitions from Saeed, J. 2003. *Semantics*, 2nd edn. Oxford: Blackwell. 149–150.

The verb *sleep*, for example, assigns the thematic role *patient* to one argument, but the verb *meet* two arguments and assigns the role *agent* to one and *theme* to the other.

sleep: patient
meet: agent, theme

As stated here, the relationship between the verb and its arguments is purely semantic; what's lacking, however, is the information about where each argument occurs in the sentence and the category of the argument itself as NP, PP, and so on. Nothing in the above information about *sleep* and *meet* tells us, for example, that *meet* assigns the agent's thematic role to an NP in the subject position and the theme's thematic role to an NP in the object position. This syntactic information must be included somewhere in our grammatical knowledge, in what we will refer to as **argument structure**. Our knowledge of syntax and semantics includes not only the thematic roles that a verb assigns but also principles and rules that determine the syntactic categories and positions of those arguments.

argument structure
set or arguments
of a verb and their
syntactic categories

This concludes our discussion of sentence meaning. In the following section, we turn to meaning in context, or pragmatics. Just as semantics and syntax overlap, we'll see that there is some overlap between semantics and pragmatics and that both contribute to how we understand and use language.

RPE 10.6 >

Pragmatics: How Context Shapes Meaning

If you were to hear an urgent, adult voice utter "A train is coming!" while you were standing on a railroad track not paying much attention to the proximity of trains, you would, under typical circumstances, quickly move off the track to safety. The meaning of this utterance is bound up with the context in which you hear it—where you are, what you are doing, who says it, what kind of experiences you've had, your cultural expectations, and so on. It's a warning. Now consider a different scenario. You are on the train track again. A child comes up with her mother and, laughing, says, "A train is coming!" You don't flinch; you smile benignly and remain where you are. In this case, the meaning of the utterance is quite different. You know from the situation that there is no danger (the parent, for example, doesn't seem concerned about you getting off the track), and the speaker is a laughing child whose intention is not to warn but to amuse. So, the social context within which a sentence is uttered can affect its meaning (here, what is a warning under certain circumstances becomes a joke under others), as can the speaker's intention and the hearer's interpretation. How speaker intention and hearer interpretation affect meaning is the subject of pragmatics, the study of *utterance meaning*, or how the meanings of the things we say

Watson the Computer Plays "Jeopardy!"

© Jeopardy/Landov

"What is Toronto?????" In a bout with human "Jeopardy!" champions Ken Jennings and Brad Rutter, Watson the IBM computer was first to buzz in. The answer was "Its largest airport is named for a WWII hero, its second largest for a WWII battle" in the category "U.S. Cities." The correct response was Chicago. Does this mistake mean that Watson isn't as smart as he's supposed to be? It seemed like a pretty major mistake, but Watson was smart enough to wager only $947 and win the game.

IBM's Watson is a "question-answering" machine, designed to understand questions put to it in natural language and respond (through a voice synthesizer) with a factual answer. So Watson, unlike a search engine, doesn't simply point a user to a document that contains the answer. Rather, Watson produces an answer itself, as a human would in conversation. Watson's abilities are particularly put to the test on a game show such as "Jeopardy!", where clues to questions require complex decoding of language (such as witty puns and other wordplay based on cultural experience)

rather than on logic. It was logic that led another IBM computer, Deep Blue, to beat chess champion Gary Kasparov at chess in 1997. Watson, it seems, brings us one step closer to being able to program computers to understand language in the way that humans do.

Watson was developed by David Ferrucci, senior manager of IBM's Semantic Analysis and Integration department. IBM gave Ferrucci three to five years and a team of fifteen people to develop a question-answering system that could win at "Jeopardy!" Ferrucci and his colleagues fed millions of documents into Watson's memory (including dictionaries, thesauruses, bibles, and encyclopedias) and programmed it with hundreds of algorithms so that Watson can "think" in hundreds of directions at a time. Algorithms rank the plausibility of answers, providing Watson not with a "right" answer but with many possibilities, ranked in order of plausibility. So Watson is basically programmed to find the answer that is "more right" than the others and to be able to cross-check answers. (For example, when Watson analyzed the clue "In 1594 he took a job as a tax collector in Andalusia," two most likely answers emerged: "Thoreau" and "Cervantes." Cross-checking "Thoreau" revealed his birth date was 1817, ruling out that answer.)

IBM hopes to market computers like Watson to companies to help decision makers sort through huge amounts of data quickly and efficiently and, based on this information, to get answers quickly. Some argue, however, that Watson's "intelligence" is based only on knowable facts gleaned from written English texts. Human knowledge involves mathematical reasoning and judgment, and understanding language involves not simply semantics but also pragmatics: decoding meaning based on context. Nevertheless, Watson's abilities may tell us something about how our brains process language and how we make educated guesses about meanings of words and sentences.

For more information
O'Connor, A. Watson dominates 'Jeopardy' but stumbles over geography. *New York Times*. 15 February 2011. http://artsbeat.blogs.nytimes.com/2011/02/15/watson-dominates-jeopardy-but-stumbles-over-geography/

Watch Watson play "Jeopardy!" at http://www.collegehumor.com/video/6195785/watson-the-computer-that-could-play-jeopardy

IBM's Deep QA Project: http://www.research.ibm.com/deepqa/deepqa.shtml

are shaped by context. In the following sections, we discuss some of the major topics of study within pragmatics: speech acts, conversational rules, and politeness. We conclude this section with a discussion of *definiteness* and *deixis*, which illustrate how pragmatics and semantics overlap.

Saying What You Mean and Meaning What You Say: Speech Acts

Before we delve more deeply into utterance meaning, let's return briefly to syntax. We use certain kinds of syntactic structures, called *sentence types*, when speaking: interrogatives (questions), imperatives (commands), and declaratives (statements).

> Is it raining? (interrogative)
> Get out! (command)
> I'd like a sandwich. (statement)

In pragmatic terms (recall the train example), each utterance we make carries communicative force and can be thought of as performing a particular act, what we call a **speech act**. If you were to say "Is it raining?", you would have performed a speech act. When sentence type corresponds with our intention, it is a **direct speech act**. The speech act *Is it raining?* is a direct speech act if uttered with the intention of asking a question about the truth or falsity of the current level of precipitation. Direct speech acts are the sum of the meanings of their parts. You typically ask a question when you don't know something, and you ask someone so you can have an answer; for example, "Can you juggle?" The appropriate answer would be either *yes* or *no*. In a direct speech act, the intention and effect are predictable; a question is a request for information to which a particular reply is appropriate.

Now, what about this sentence:

Have you cleaned your room yet?

This sentence is also an interrogative in terms of sentence type, but does it have to be a question? Not necessarily. What if you have asked your daughter repeatedly to clean her room and told her that if she doesn't, she won't be allowed to go the movies as planned? Uttering this interrogative sentence type actually conveys a (mild) threat: If you don't clean your room, then no movies for you! This sentence (which we'll also assume is an utterance) is an **indirect speech act**: Its meaning depends on context rather than on sentence type.

This is just a simple illustration of the complexity of speech acts and of how sentence type does not always correspond to speaker intention (nor, for that matter, to hearer interpretation). **Speech act theory** tries to explain more precisely how meaning and action are related to language. Speech act

---

speech act
utterance intended to convey communicative force

direct speech act
utterance whose meaning is the sum of its parts, the literal meaning

indirect speech act
utterance whose meaning depends on context rather than on literal meaning

speech act theory
theory dealing with the construction of meaning in conversation by direct and indirect speech acts

theory (originally introduced by Austin in 1962) is concerned with the communicative intentions of speakers and how they achieve their communicative goals. John Austin proposes that communication is a series of communicative acts that are used systematically to accomplish particular purposes and that all utterances perform actions by having a specific force assigned to them. Austin offers three basic kinds of acts that are simultaneously performed by an utterance. They can be informally described as follows:

locutionary act: an utterance with a particular sense and reference (closest to meaning in the traditional sense, the sum of its parts)

illocutionary act: the act (defined by social convention) that is performed by making the utterance: a statement, offer, promise, bet, etc.

perlocutionary act: the (not necessarily intentional) effects on the audience, whether intended or unintended, brought about by the utterance

Examples are useful here. Say that a teacher says, "Jo, would you like to read your poem first?" The locutionary speech act is the literal meaning of the question, namely, whether Jo is interested in reading her poem. The illocutionary speech act is, by social convention, a request that Jo read her poem. The perlocutionary act is its effect on Jo, who might agree or refuse to read her poem.

The philosopher John Searle proposed that the basic unit of human communication is the illocutionary act, more specifically, the indirect speech act, which he says is "[when] the speaker communicates to the hearer more than he actually says by way of relying on their mutually shared background information, both linguistic and nonlinguistic, together with the general powers of rationality and inference on the part of the hearer" (1975: 61).

What are some ways that the following question, statement, and command sentence types can be interpreted? In what contexts can these sentences be indirect speech acts?

Can you pass the salt?
Open the door!
Do you know where the museum is?
Tell me why you're never on time!
Is there a bathroom near here?
I'd like one ticket, please.
You left the light on.

Many other factors contribute to how we understand speech acts. Who are the participants in the conversation, and what is their relationship to one another? Under what conditions is a particular utterance made? If you make a promise, for example, it's only a promise if you can follow through on it or think you can and intend to do so. If you know you can't, it isn't a promise. What do such social factors as age, ethnicity, gender, and religious and political beliefs contribute to utterance meaning? We often violate social conventions, causing miscommunication or worse; sometimes we say things that are insulting, insensitive, or even hateful based on our world knowledge (or lack thereof). Think about humor, too; an utterance might be funny in one context and downright insulting in another, again illustrating that meaning is shaped by context in crucial and often powerful ways.

RPE   10.7
RPE   10.8

Cooperative Talk: Conversational Rules

So far, we've talked about the importance of context, speaker intention, and listener interpretation in determining the meanings of utterances. As speakers, we also share certain implicit conversational rules for how to communicate spoken and unspoken messages. These conversational rules are crucial for successful communication, and we are well aware of how to follow them, or in some cases how to ignore them, in order to convey a particular message. We'll also see that these rules of conversation can vary across languages and cultures, and the lack of shared knowledge regarding these rules can lead to communication breakdown.

The philosopher Paul Grice (1975, 1989) proposed the following **maxims of conversation**, which continue to be an accurate description of the shared rules that speakers use in interactions.

> **Grice's maxims of conversation** rules of conversation that describe the shared rules speakers use in interactions; they include *quantity*, *quality*, *relevance*, and *manner*

Maxim of Quantity

- Make your contribution to the conversation as informative as necessary.
- Do not make your contribution to the conversation more informative than necessary.

Maxim of Quality

- Do not say what you believe to be false.
- Do not say that for which you lack adequate evidence.

Maxim of Relevance

- Say only things that are relevant.

Maxim of Manner

- Avoid obscurity of expression.
- Avoid ambiguity.
- Be brief (avoid unnecessary wordiness).
- Be orderly. (1989: 27)

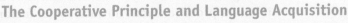

Did You Know...?

The Cooperative Principle and Language Acquisition

Part of acquiring a language is acquiring the pragmatics of the language, not just in order to participate in conversations but, as Brian MacWhinney (2003) proposes, to learn the meanings of words. Suppose a child is presented with three items—a glass, a teacup, and a demitasse—and is asked to pick out each item ("Which is the teacup?" "Which is the glass?"). The child will match the known terms to the known items. The child will also correctly infer that the remaining term, *demitasse*, is the name of the leftover item. MacWhinney proposes that this is not simply because of the process of elimination but because the child is actually relying on the cooperative principle, assuming that the questioner is reasonable and using a new name for a new object. Learning new words and their meanings, according to MacWhinney, involves not only semantics but pragmatics and mutual cooperation.

Grice's cooperative principle
assumption that in conversation speakers will make a sincere effort to collaboratively exchange information

speaker meaning
meaning beyond the words alone, which the speaker assumes the hearer can interpret based on communicative context

The conversational maxims go hand in hand with Grice's **cooperative principle**, another principle of conversation, which assumes that the participants in a conversation will make a "conversational contribution such as is required, at the stage at which it occurs, by the accepted purpose or direction of the talk exchange" (Grice 1989: 26). At its core, the cooperative principle means that in conversation, we don't lie, nor do we assume our conversational partners lie—we are sincere, and for the most part, we contribute relevant information. Grice recognized the difference between sentence meaning and speaker intention (similar to direct and indirect speech acts). He proposed that speakers assume that the hearer can interpret additional meaning based on the context or communicative situation and does not rely on the meanings of the words alone. Grice refers to this kind of meaning as **speaker meaning**.

Manipulating Maxims

Grice also discusses the fact that speakers can violate maxims, often because of *maxim clash*, wherein if one maxim is to be maintained, another must be violated. Even when we violate maxims, meaning is typically conveyed by *implicature* in such cases, and the cooperative principle is maintained. Speakers can also ignore the maxims or flout them, in some cases, as when they are attempting to deceive or are being intentionally obtuse. Flouting a maxim can also involve an implication that creates meaning. Under normal circumstances, however, speakers expect other conversation partners to follow the maxims.

Here are examples of utterances in which the maxims are followed, violated, and then flouted.

> (1) Speaker A: Have you been to a baseball game lately?
> Speaker B: No, but I'm going to go to a game this weekend.

Here, the maxims are followed: Speaker A has asked for information, and Speaker B has supplied it in the relevant manner and amount. Now, consider this next exchange:

> (2) Speaker A: When is your next class?
> Speaker B: Sometime this afternoon.

Here, Speaker B is violating the maxim of quantity, not providing enough information. But if we assume Speaker B is not doing this deliberately and really doesn't know when the class is, Speaker B is not violating the cooperative principle. Speaker B doesn't want to lie or guess, which would violate the maxim of quality, so has to stick with this uninformative but truthful statement. The interplay of the two maxims (quality and quantity) causes a maxim clash.

Now, look at this third exchange:

> (3) Speaker A: So, do you think Maria will make it to the wedding?
> Speaker B: Well, she told me she was taking off work that day.

Here, Speaker B's statement is obscure and doesn't provide the information requested by Speaker A. The maxim of manner is flouted—Speaker B deliberately chooses not to observe it. But Speaker B clearly *implies* an answer to Speaker A's question and so is not being deliberately obscure. Speaker B is therefore following the cooperative principle in this case as well.

And finally, consider this (odd) exchange:

> (4) Speaker A: So, do you think Maria is having a baby?
> Speaker B: I have a train to catch.

Here, Speaker B is flouting several maxims by responding to Speaker A's question with a statement that seems completely irrelevant (violating the maxim of relevance), obscure (violating the maxim of quality), and uninformative (violating the maxim of quantity). But, because the cooperative principle is so strong, a possible interpretation of Speaker B's statement here is that Speaker B is refusing to participate in gossip about Maria. By flouting maxims, Speaker B is actually making an interpretable and meaningful conversational move.

RPE 10.9 ⟩

The Power of Politeness

The most common reason for an indirect rather than direct speech act is politeness. Politeness takes many linguistic forms and is somewhat

A Buddhist monk and a European girl greet each other with Namaste.

Ernst Haas/Getty Images

difficult to define. Politeness expresses concern for others but also carries the intention of having this concern reciprocated; we're polite because we want to make others feel at ease, and this in turn makes us more comfortable, too. Politeness also crosses social boundaries; adults and small children can be polite to each other, and the president of the United States would be expected to be polite to a citizen he or she meets on the street, even though their social status is dramatically different. So, politeness is not restricted by social distance, and how we perform polite speech acts depends on our gauging and evaluating this social distance (or lack of it). To be considered polite, a speech act must fit the social expectations of politeness in the particular context—expectations that are culturally defined.

positive politeness politeness strategy based on the speaker's constructing solidarity with the addressee

negative politeness politeness strategy based on the speaker's minimizing imposition on the addressee

We can break politeness down into **positive politeness** and **negative politeness** (Brown & Levinson 1987). In positive politeness, the speaker and the addressee have the same needs, and the speaker indicates that to the addressee (expressing solidarity with the addressee). In negative politeness, the speaker appreciates the addressee's needs but may not share them (expressing the need to be free from imposing on the addressee). Table 10.2 lists the features of positive and negative politeness.

Is Speaker B's utterance a positive politeness strategy or a negative one?

(5) Speaker A: I'm so disappointed that I missed the game!
    Speaker B: I bet you are! They should have told you they'd rescheduled it!

Speaker B is using positive politeness, expressing solidarity with Speaker A, sympathizing with Speaker A, and assuming common ground by asserting that missing the game is an unfortunate occurrence and agreeing that Speaker A should have been informed of its being rescheduled.

Table 10.2	Features of Positive and Negative Politeness

Positive Politeness

Speaker	claims common ground with the hearer
	conveys a sense of cooperation with hearer
	tries to meet or appreciate hearer's needs and desires
	may offer sympathy, a compliment, optimism, promise, offer, and so on

Negative Politeness

Speaker	makes no assumptions about hearer's needs, desires, or abilities to cooperate
	doesn't assume or attempt to coerce, is direct, and tries not to impose his or her needs on hearer
	is often pessimistic, deferential, and impersonal

Now, consider the next exchange. Is Speaker A using positive politeness or negative politeness?

(6) Speaker A: I know you have a lot of students asking you this, but I was hoping you'd let me register for your class; I'd love to take it!

   Speaker B: Well, I'll be happy to if space becomes available, and I'm sorry if it doesn't work out.

This exchange illustrates negative politeness; Speaker A is asking a question of B, trying to minimize the possible imposition on B, and is being very deferential and apologetic. Speaker B responds with a polite, but possibly negative, message: that space may not become available in the class, and Speaker A's needs may not be met.

RPE   10.10

RPE   10.11

Honorifics and Forms of Address

Some languages encode pragmatic distinctions about formality, politeness, and social status more directly in their grammatical system than does English. **Honorifics** are grammatical forms, usually words or affixes, that express the relative social status of the speaker to the addressee. For example, German, Spanish, and French have distinct pronouns for *you* that reflect status and formality.

honorifics
grammatical forms, usually words or affixes, that express the relative social status of the speaker to the addressee

German	du	informal you (singular)
	ihr	informal you (plural)
	Sie	formal/polite you (singular or plural)

Culture Clash and Pragmatic Failure

When the pragmatic differences across cultures collide, communication can break down because speaker intentions are badly misunderstood. The result is *pragmatic failure* (Thomas 1983).

As English becomes the second language of younger generations of Hmong speakers, certain pragmatic practices are lost, causing miscommunication among the younger speakers and their elders. Expectations of what is considered polite, for example, begin to diverge, causing pragmatic failure and social distance. Take the following example, from Lillian Faderman's *I Begin My Life All Over* (1998), a collection of narratives by Hmong immigrants from Laos. Here, Loco Vang, a young gang member, tells the story of how resentment grew between him and his father.

> When I go home, I know my mother cares about me a little. But I don't really talk to her. I just say "Hi, hello." Every time I used to help out my dad, he never showed respect to me for it. If he needed me to help him carry, I'd help him. But he never said "Thank you," or "You're welcome." So I got mad. Whenever he tells me what to do now, I don't even bother to do it. (p. 193)

You may recognize Loco Vang's expectations about politeness as similar to your own; in North American culture, speakers explicitly thank each other in a variety of situations, which is not the case among the Hmong. Loco Vang's adoption of American politeness strategies and his father's lack of familiarity with those strategies has led to pragmatic failure and miscommunication. Burt and Yang's (2005) study of pragmatic failure emphasizes the need not only for English language instruction in immigrant communities but also for instruction in cross-cultural pragmatics to minimize the potential for pragmatic failure.

For more information

Burt, S. & H. Yang. 2005. Growing up shifting: Immigrant children, their families, and the schools. In K. Denham & A. Lobeck (eds.), *Language in the schools: Integrating linguistic knowledge into K-12 education.* Mahwah, NJ: Lawrence Erlbaum.

Faderman, L. with G. Xiong. 1998. *I begin my life all over: The Hmong and the American immigrant experience.* Boston: Beacon Press.

Thomas, J. 1983. Cross-cultural pragmatic failure. *Applied Linguistics* 4(2). 91–112.

Spanish	tú	informal you (singular)
	usted	formal/polite you (singular)
	ustedes	formal/polite you (plural)
French	tu	informal you (singular)
	vous	formal/polite you (singular or plural)

Honorifics are used in many languages, including Korean, Javanese, Tibetan, Samoan, and Sudanese. An example from Japanese (Harada 1976: 514) is the series of affixes that can attach to names:

-sama	used to address people of high rank
-san	title of respect, quite common
-chan	a diminutive, informal version of -san, used with children and pets. Used more by women and girls and also to refer to women and girls.
-kun	informal honorific, used primarily for males
-sensei	used to address someone of authority, usually someone who has a particular skill or capability: teachers, doctors, politicians, etc.

ƕƿæꞇ!

You may recognize the word *sensei* and the phrase "bow to your sensei" from *The Karate Kid* and other movies; it's used to address teachers and other professionals.

Also, many Japanese words take a different form depending on their relative honorific status, and words are grouped into *sonkei-go* (respectful words), *teinei-go* (polite words), and *kenzyoo-go* (humble words). Japanese also employs three levels of politeness: plain, used among friends; polite, used among strangers or to show respect to superiors; and formal, used in formal situations such as speeches. The forms differ not only in vocabulary but also in the addition of certain affixes. Also, there are two respectful forms for each level of politeness, indicated by distinct verb endings. *Sonkei-go*, the respectful language, shows respect to the subject of the sentence, while *kenzyoo-go*, the humble language, shows respect to the direct or indirect object, primarily by humbling the speaker.

plain:	Jon san ga Sato san wo *matsu*
	'John is waiting for Sato.'
respect for subject:	Sensei ga o-machi-ni-naru.
	'The teacher is waiting.'
respect for object:	Sensei wo omachi-suru.
	'We are waiting for you, Teacher.'

Javanese is another language that demonstrates respect (based on age, gender, kinship relationships, wealth, etc.) by employing different levels of language. For example, a single expression, *Are you going to eat rice and cassava now?* results in five distinct utterances, depending on the status of the person being addressed, as illustrated by these examples from Geertz (1968: 282–295):

high status:	Menapa pandjenengan bade ḍahar sekul kalijan kaspé samenika?
	'Are you going to eat rice and cassava now'?

high with honorific:	Menapa sampéjan bade neḍa sekul kalijan kaspé samenika?
	'Are you going to eat rice and cassava now'?
middle status:	Napa sampéjan adjeng neḍa sekul lan kaspé saniki?
	'Are you going to eat rice and cassava now'?
low status:	Apa sampéjan arep neḍa sega lan kaspé saiki?
	'Are you going to eat rice and cassava now'?
low with honorific:	Apa kowé arep mangan sega lan kaspé saiki?
	'Are you going to eat rice and cassava now'?

Though all languages have ways of conveying respect and politeness, some languages have encoded this feature into the grammatical system with honorifics.

Though systems like the Japanese or Javanese may seem complex to English speakers, we all make similar choices about vocabulary and style all the time, based on social status, comfort level, and degree of formality. In English, we vary our language by varying terms of address, such as *Mr.* or *Ms.*; by using tags of camaraderie or endearment, such as *dear*, *sweetie*, or *hon*; by making decisions about word choice, such as *however* versus *but*, *perhaps* versus *maybe*; and even by altering the pitch of our voices. We use euphemisms (discussed in Chapter 9) to avoid taboo words and topics that may cause discomfort; for instance, we may use *rest room* rather than *john* in a particular context, or *sleep together* rather than *have sex*.

RPE 10.12

Register

Even though we think of politeness as "being nice to people"—opening doors for people, offering to help, letting someone go first—politeness has everything to do with power and solidarity. We are polite because we want to create or maintain solidarity, and no matter who we talk to, we are constantly aware of social distance (which we may want to widen or narrow depending on our intentions). Because it is so important in negotiating and maintaining social relationships, we are often insecure about our language. We may use formal language for this purpose in certain contexts but informal language in others—we all are adept at switching **registers**, or speech styles, unconsciously and often to assert our power and status in certain contexts and to minimize it in others. A doctor talking to a patient with a serious illness will use a different register from the one used to discuss the patient with another physician; you most likely talk to your friends during lunch in a register different from the one you use when talking to your teacher or to a small child.

register speech or writing style adopted for a particular audience

Language Alive!

Register as a Literary Device

The images of a novel's characters that we conjure up in our mind's eye are often created by how they talk. Dialogue can reflect differences in register (*sez* rather than *says*, *dunno* rather than *don't know*) and tells us not only about a character but also about social perceptions of language—what is considered lofty and what is considered low. Register in literature also offers us a window into how language, and the social perceptions about it, changes over time. The writing of Geoffrey Chaucer, the great fifteenth-century author of *The Canterbury Tales* and other works, provides not only a rich repository of both the most vulgar and the most sophisticated terms of the time but also of the perceptions about language and how they were linked to class. In addition to *ferte, erse, pisse, shiten, queynte,* and *swive* (meaning 'to copulate'), in Chaucer's work we also find such archaic terms as *maat* (Arabic for 'dead' or 'defeated') and *dulcarnoun* 'a puzzle', as well as a range of highly technical terms (such as *solsticium*). The lowbrow but cunning Miller in *The Canterbury Tales* is described almost entirely in Anglo-Saxon vocabulary (Anglo-Saxon and Norse vocabulary in italics):

> The Millere was a stout *carl* for the nones;
> Ful byg he was of *brawn,* and eek of *bones.*
> That proved well, for over al there he cam
> At *wrastlynge* he wolde have alwey the ram
> He was short-sholdred, *brood,* a thikke *knarre.* (lines 545–550)

But the Prioress, who fancies herself sharp and sophisticated, is described in terms borrowed from French, which at this point was a language of diminishing social prestige. Her association with French thus makes her character pretentious and absurd (French vocabulary in italics):

> And likely she was of greet *desport,*
> And ful *pleasant* and *amiable* of *port,*
> And *peyned* hire to *countrefete cheere*
> Of *court,* and to been *estatliche* of *manere,*
> And to ben holden *digne* of *reverence.*
> But, for so speken of hire *conscience,*
> She was so *charitable* and so *pitous*
> She would wepe, if that she saugh a mous
> Kaught in trappe, if it were deed or bledde. (lines 137–145)

Examples from Hughes (2000: 125–130).

Register differences show up in various ways. One is word choice; we may use a euphemism (*restroom* versus *john*) depending on audience, and we might use contractions (*gonna, wanna*) around our friends but not in a high-intensity job interview. We write in different registers, too; think about the register you use in e-mail compared to the one you use in a research paper.

RPE 10.13

RPE 10.14

When Semantics and Pragmatics Overlap

Suppose your teacher walked into class and said "She won the race!" You wouldn't have any idea who *she* was, but you would know that whoever she was, she was female, and there was only one of her. So the semantics of *she* would tell you something, but the word alone would not provide enough information for you to interpret this sentence. You'd also need information about who or what *she* refers to. This information could be supplied by a previous conversation (about, say, your teacher's sister, who is running in the Boston Marathon) or by another utterance by your teacher ("My sister won the Boston Marathon!") or even by someone directing you to a newspaper with a picture of a woman winning a race. In other words, the interpretation of pronouns relies on more than just semantics; pragmatics, or context, also plays a role. In this section, we look at how semantics and pragmatics overlap in constructing meaning.

Definiteness

As we saw in Chapter 7, the determiners *the* and *a* express grammatical information of number; *the* is either singular or plural (*the dog/dogs*), and *a* (*a dog/*dogs*) is singular. The interpretation of these words also relies on context. To illustrate, consider the following:

> *The woman* sent me a letter.
> *A woman* sent me a letter.

What is the difference in interpretation between *the woman* and *a woman* here? What do the different determiners tell us about the speaker and the hearer of these sentences?

The first utterance assumes that both speaker and hearer know to whom the NP *the woman* refers, but this is not the case in the second sentence, where the NP *a woman* does not refer to a particular woman known to both the speaker and the hearer. This distinction is called **definiteness** and is typically expressed in English on words that introduce nouns. Definiteness is the means by which the speaker indicates to the hearer that they share knowledge of the referent of a particular noun phrase.

definiteness means by which the speaker indicates to the hearer that they share knowledge of the referent of a particular noun phrase

Proper names are also definite NPs; when we use a name in conversation, we typically assume that the hearer understands who we're talking about.

> *Mabel* came in.

Certain quantifiers, such as *every*, *each*, and *all*, are definite as well and perhaps obviously so. The following sentences assume that both the speaker and the hearer (or the writer and the reader, in this case) know to whom the underlined noun phrases refer (and in the case of the quantified noun phrases, we have no choice, given that the noun phrase refers to all the women who exist!).

Each/every woman came in.

NPs with the quantifiers *some*, *several*, and *many* are indefinite and don't assume the kind of shared knowledge expressed by definite NPs.

Some/many women came in.

How languages express definiteness is quite complex and not something we can always predict based on the determiner. For example, though noun phrases with *the* are typically definite in reference, this is not always the case.

The elephant does not make a good pet.
An elephant does not make a good pet.
Elephants do not make good pets.

The noun phrase *the elephant* here can have a *generic* interpretation and does not refer to a particular referent. It is semantically equivalent to *an elephant* in the second sentence and to *elephants* in the third one, both of which also have generic interpretations and are indefinite in reference.

Sometimes indefinite determiners appear to be semantically definite. Consider, for example, the following sentence from Heim (1982: 8):

A dog came in. It lay down under the table.

In this sentence, the indefinite pronoun *it* appears to refer to the indefinite noun phrase *a dog*. This suggests that the phrase *a dog* is definite and is the antecedent for the pronoun *it*. Philosophers of language provide complex arguments, however, that suggest that *a dog* in this case is indefinite and that the relationship between *a dog* and *it* is very different from the relationship between the definite noun phrase *the dog* and the pronoun *it* in the following example (see, for example, Evans 1977: 467–536).

The dog came in. It lay down on the floor.

RPE 10.15

Do you see a difference in definiteness?

Deixis

deictic words words whose meanings can be interpreted only with reference to the speaker's position in space and time (context); the noun *deixis* refers to the pointing or specifying function of such words

Definiteness plays an important role in the larger set of words in the language that are **deictic** (from the Classical Greek word *deiknymi* 'pointing'), words whose meanings can only be interpreted with reference to the speaker's position in space and time; that is, they need context in order to be interpreted appropriately. All languages have deictic words, though some have more than others, and they break down into three main types: personal deictics (first- and second-person pronouns such as *my*, *yours*, and *us*), temporal deictics (*now, yesterday, tomorrow*, and verb tenses: *ate* versus *eat*), and spatial deictics (*there, behind, left, right, here*). Even verbs can be deictic. Consider the difference between *Don't go in* versus *Don't come in*. *Go* in the first sentence tells us about the speaker's location, namely, outside the location in question, but in the second, the speaker is inside that location. The meanings of these sentences depend on context. Consider another example: *I left it there*. In this sentence, the interpretation of *there* depends on context, as does the interpretation of the pronoun *I*, whose referent is completely dependent on context. Similarly, in *My book will be published next month*, the interpretation of *next month* depends on context—in April, it will be different from what it was in January. The same is true of the expression *my book*; who *my* refers to depends entirely on context.

Demonstratives (*this/that, these/those*) are also definite; both of the following sentences assume shared knowledge of the referent of the italicized phrase.

> *That woman* sent me a letter.
> *Those students* did well on the exam.

Demonstratives differ from other determiners because they are also deictic; part of their meaning is based on the context in which they are uttered. More specifically, demonstratives indicate *proximity* of certain items distinct from others, what is also called *spatial deixis* (the context of the physical surroundings, often accompanied by pointing).

> This book was really good. I've never read that one.
> Do you like these flowers?
> No, but I like those daffodils over there.

The concepts of definiteness and deixis illustrate the overlap between semantics and pragmatics. Definite and deictic terms have grammatical meanings, but their meanings cannot be construed in the absence of context.

RPE 10.16

Language and Thought

As you've probably gathered by now, the notion of *context* is enormously complex and involves power relationships among speakers that are influenced by a vast array of factors, including age, gender, political and religious beliefs, and knowledge of the world. There clearly is a link, then, between language and culture, between how we talk and how we perceive the world. One question about language that has perpetually fascinated philosophers, linguists, anthropologists, and many others (even you?) is how language influences our thinking. Put slightly differently, how does culture influence language and vice versa? Does one determine the other?

Did You Know…?

Does Culture Count?

Because we live in different cultures and speak different languages, do we think in different ways? This question has been stirred up by studies of Amazonian tribes who have words that might mean 'one' or 'two' and words that might mean 'a lot' or 'many' but no words for all the numbers that we have. Some scholars claim this is an issue of culture, not language—these tribes don't need exact numbers because they don't use money.

A new study (Spaepen et al. 2011) shows that without access to language, people will not develop a full number system, even though they live in a numerate culture (e.g., holding jobs and using money). Spaepen's team studied Nicaraguan homesigners, deaf people who have not had access to oral language (Spanish) or signed language (Nicaraguan Sign Language), and found that they do not develop a counting system in the same way as people do who have acquired an oral or signed language. To test for numeration, the researcher would knock one, two, or three times on the signer's fist and look for the same number of knocks in return. Though signers would consistently knock twice for two and once for one, for more than three knocks, the researcher might get four or five knocks on her fist.

This study suggests that language, not culture, is at the core of our ability to comprehend and manipulate large quantities of countable things. Although the human brain can assess small numbers (1, 2, 3) and approximate values (20,000 is a lot more than 10), it needs a counting system to specify the difference between 10 and 11 or between 20,204 and 20,207. It is language, not culture, that unlocks this ability.

For more information
Hamilton, J. "Without language, large numbers don't add up." National Public Radio.
http://www.npr.org/2011/02/09/133601966/language-essential-for-understanding-large-numbers. (9 February 2011).
Spaepen, E., et al. "Number without a language model." Proceedings of the National Academy of Sciences of the United States of America. http://www.pnas.org/content/early/ 2011/01/31/1015975108. (7 February 2011).

Linguistic Relativity and the Sapir-Whorf Hypothesis

Sapir-Whorf hypothesis Benjamin Whorf's claim that language determines our perceptions of the world

A well-known example of the "strong" form of this hypothesis, that language *determines* how we think, was proposed by Benjamin Whorf in the 1950s. Whorf was a student of the linguist and anthropologist Edward Sapir, who also was interested in this question; Whorf's version of this idea is now called the **Sapir-Whorf hypothesis**. Whorf claimed, based on his study of several languages, that the language of a culture provides a window into how the members of that culture think. More specifically, he claimed that language determines how a culture looks at the world and that cultures that speak different languages as a result think about the world in different ways.

The general idea that language and culture influence each other is called **linguistic relativity**. One common example of linguistic relativity is the idea that if we use gender-neutral language, it will mitigate against sexism in the culture. So, if we use the term *mail carrier* instead of *mailman*, we might be less apt to think of those in this line of work as male. Here's another example of culture reflected in language: We use the terms *male nurse* and *woman doctor*; attaching gendered modifiers to the terms *nurse* and *doctor* because we think of these occupations as female (nurse) and male (doctor), which reflects our (sexist) perceptions of the world. The language of war is another case in point; references to indigenous peoples as *savages* during periods of colonization or to Jews as *vermin* during the

linguistic relativity theory that language and culture influence or perhaps even deter-mine each other

Did You Know...?

Lost in Translation

How exactly do we translate ideas expressed in one language into an-other? The answer lies in how we learn the meanings of words. Do we learn the meanings of words simply by connecting them with the objects they refer to? How do we learn the word *kitty*, for example? We might learn it through *ostention*—the meaning of the word is defined by example. Someone says, "Look, it's a kitty!" and we'd figure, from the way this sentence is constructed, that the word *kitty* is the label attached to the object in question. But philosopher W. V. O. Quine (1960) argues that ostention only works along with our understanding of other facts about the language, namely, our understanding of the frame *It's a ____,* and so ostention itself depends on some kind of prior knowledge of the language.

What about when we do not have language to help us determine the meaning of a word? In Quine's famous example, hunters are out with a guide. The guide points to a rabbit that is running by and says, "Gavagai!" What does this utterance mean? It is unfamiliar to the hunters, so what would they think? They might assume that *gavagai* means *rabbit*, but it could mean *long ears, tail, Look out!* or *There will be a storm tonight* (suppose the guide is superstitious). To find out the meaning of *gavagai*, the hunters would have to do some exten-sive investigation, examining other uses of the word in order to determine its meaning. What kinds of knowledge would this require?

For more information
Fodor, J. 1975. *The language of thought*. New York: Crowell.
Quine, W. 1960. *Word and object*. Cambridge, MA: MIT Press.

Holocaust dehumanized those groups, (ostensibly) licensing their oppression. And using euphemisms (discussed in Chapter 9) such as the term *collateral damage* rather than *civilian deaths* seems to mask the horror of war; what one person might call a *freedom fighter*, another might call a *mercenary* and yet another, a *terrorist*.

Examining the Evidence

Linguistic relativity is in counterpoint to the idea that language and thought are related but rely, in the end, on different cognitive processes. Consider, for example, the fact that we don't always know how to say what we're thinking. As Steven Pinker (1994) points out, we often remember the gist of what was said but not the exact words; there has to be a gist, and this meaning doesn't rely on the original set of words (pp. 55–82). Perhaps more important, Whorf's claims have been soundly debunked by further research into his evidence for strong connections between language and how we think. His conclusions were based on his own perceptions of languages and cultures he knew very little of and on faulty translations of sentences. For example, Whorf claimed that, based on the evidence that the Hopi have no way of grammatically expressing past or future time, their worldview did not include these concepts. Anthropologist Ekkehart Malotki (1983) shows, however, that Hopi has a number of ways of indicating time (through tense, metaphors about time, words for days, weeks, etc.) and that Whorf's claim was completely without merit. This misinterpretation of another culture's language illustrates how our own cultural perceptions can bias our research; the fact that Whorf's idea was (and continues to be) very popular is testament to how hard our cultural perceptions of language are to dislodge, even in the face of contradictory evidence.

So, if language doesn't determine how we think, at least to the degree that Whorf claimed, what is its role in shaping or influencing how we think? First of all, it is clear from what we've discussed so far that language *underspecifies* meaning. That is, we often mean something quite different and more complex from what we actually say based on the meanings of our words. Second, think of the examples of children, aphasics, savants, and others we discussed in Chapter 2. We saw that children acquiring language (and thus without it, at least in its full form) certainly think and communicate. Broca's aphasics are often frustrated precisely because they have many things on their minds that they can't convey given their speech impairments. They are, however, *thinking*, even without language. The opposite is true as well; remember, children with Williams syndrome can talk fluently and with great expression, but their ability to perform other very simple cognitive tasks that require reason are dramatically impaired. And then there's Christopher, the linguistic savant who can

hwæt!

In 2010 Hofstra University began offering the first master's degree program in the USA that specializes in forensic linguistics. http://www.hofstra.edu/Home/News/PressReleases/ 112210_MAinForensicLinguistics.html

speak several languages fluently but whose other cognitive abilities are severely impaired. Also, just consider actual grammatical differences. Does the fact that a French speaker puts adjectives after the noun rather than before it, as we English speakers do, indicate a difference in perception of the world? How would that perception be characterized? Where do we draw the line between where language does or does not influence thought? Does each grammatical difference among languages illustrate some kind of difference in perception, and if so, why can we translate ideas from one language into another?

Mentalese

If language doesn't shape our thought, what does? Researchers such as Jerry Fodor (1975) and Neil Stillings and colleagues (1995) argue for a "language of thought," what Steven Pinker calls *mentalese*. All of us, as humans, have the same basic program and use the same basic processes of memory and reasoning, regardless of culture. Some have argued that these mental representations have a sort of grammar of their own, a system based on propositional meanings such as those discussed earlier in the chapter. So, we actually think in mentalese rather than in language, and this accounts for the similar ways in which we construct meaning, regardless of language, and for the fact that language doesn't always capture what we mean. In the words of Pinker (1994: 82): "Knowing a language, then, is knowing how to translate mentalese into strings of words and vice versa."

RPE 10.17

© LAIF/Redux

Accent on **Forensic Linguistics**

Because so much of the legal system depends on language both oral and written, it is not surprising that linguistics can provide great insights into the nature and interpretation of legal language and the law. Forensic linguistics is a subfield of linguistics that focuses on the interface of language, the law, and crime. Peter Tiersma (1999) discusses a number of ways in which language and law intersect. One area of study is the history of legal language in English and the influence of Latin and French—in such terms as *quid pro quo*, *habeas corpus*, *post-mortem*, and *pro bono*, as well as many more common legal terms such as *court*, *justice*, *judge*, *jury*, *decision*, *legal*, *dismiss*, and *jurisdiction*. Tiersma also analyzes lawyers' syntax, including the avoidance of pronouns in legal documents (*the respondent agrees that the respondent will pay . . .*); the use of passive voice to foreground, for example, the victim of an alleged crime and (sometimes purposely) to obscure the perpetrator (*the vehicle was stolen at 5:30 p.m.*); the purpose of archaic terms such as *aforesaid* and *to wit*; and the use of ritualistic language (*All rise . . .*) in order to be precise and to avoid ambiguity. Lexical semantics can be key in deciding a case; for example, whether something is interpreted as *obscene* or *profane* depends on how those terms are defined.

In another branch of forensic linguistics, the language of legal process, experts examine language as it is used in cross-examination, police interviews, the questioning process in court, and evidence presentation, among other contexts. Pragmatics is an essential part of interpreting courtroom discourse; much of what we mean is implied rather than stated, and differences between literal and nonliteral meaning can complicate what it means to tell the truth. Whether a witness is considered believable can also depend on that person's social status, which can be conveyed by accent or dialect just as much as by clothing and appearance.

And finally, linguists like Roger Shuy, Robert Leonard (who used to sing in the doo-wop band Sha Na Na!), and Robert Rodman provide evidence and expert testimony in cases involving trademark disputes, identification of authors of anonymous texts (such as ransom notes or letters of threat), tracing a speaker's linguistic origins (in the cases of asylum seekers), acoustic analysis of audio-recorded evidence, cross-cultural communication facilitation, and a number of other areas. The photo shows a German federal officer analyzing the grammar in a blackmail letter.

The study of language and the law includes a vast array of topics, such as the language of perjury, language rights (language policies such as the official English movement, bilingual issues, and language preservation), how to improve jury instructions, and even lawyer jokes!

For more information

Dumas, B. (ed.). 2000. Language in the judicial process. http://www.ljp.utk.edu. (3 April 2006).

The International Journal of Speech, Language and the Law. http://www.equinoxpub .com/IJSLL. (27 May 2011).

Leonard, R. Robert Leonard Associates. http://www.robertleonardassociates. com/publications.html. (27 May 2011).

Shuy, R. 2008. http://rogershuy.com/. (27 May 2011).

Tiersma, P. 1999. *Legal language*. Chicago: University of Chicago Press.

Tiersma, P. Welcome to LANGUAGE*and*LAW .org. http://www.languageandlaw.org/. (27 May 2011).

Summary

We've seen that beyond the meanings of words, we also construct meaning from sentences and from the context in which sentences are uttered. Understanding and using a language involves a complex interplay of social and linguistic factors, including our cultural expectations, attitudes about power and solidarity, social conventions, and much more. We've discussed in previous chapters how children acquire a complex grammatical system, and now you can see that in addition to that system, another aspect of language that we seem to acquire is social—how to interact in conversations, manipulate politeness conventions, produce and understand direct and indirect speech acts, and so on. Learning to *use* language may be as complex a process as acquiring the language itself, and both are essential components of our linguistic knowledge. The interaction between meaning and context raises the question of how context, or culture, shapes meaning and language. We've explored here some of the research on the ways in which language might (and might not) shape how we think and view the world.

Sources and Resources

Austin, J. 1962. *How to do things with words.* Oxford, UK: Oxford University Press.

Bloomer, A., et al. 2005. *Introducing language in use: A coursebook.* New York: Routledge.

Brown, P. & S. Levinson. 1987. *Politeness: Some universals in language usage.* Cambridge, UK: Cambridge University Press.

Burt, S. & H. Yang. 2005. Growing up shifting: Immigrant children, their families, and the schools. In K. Denham & A. Lobeck (eds.), *Language in the schools: Integrating linguistic knowledge into K-12 education.* Mahwah, NJ: Lawrence Erlbaum.

Cameron, D. 2007. *The myth of Mars and Venus: Do men and women really speak different languages?* New York: Oxford University Press.

Chomsky, N. 1957. *Syntactic structures.* The Hague: Mouton.

Dumas, B. (ed.). 2000. Language in the judicial process. http://www.ljp.utk.edu. (3 April 2006). Eckert, P. & S. McConnell-Ginet. 2003. *Language and gender.* New York: Cambridge University Press.

Else, L. & L. Middleton. 2008. Interview: Out on a limb over language. *New Scientist.* January 19. http://www.newscientist.com/channel/opinion/mg19726391.900-interview-out-on-a-limb-over-language.html.

Evans, G. 1977. Pronouns, quantifier and relative clauses. *Canadian Journal of Philosophy 7.* 467–536.

Everett, D. 2007. Welcome to Daniel L. Everett's website. http://www.llc.ilstu.edu/dlevere/. (20 October 2008.)

Everett, D. 2008. *Don't sleep, there are snakes: Life and language in the Amazonian jungle.* New York: Pantheon.

Everett, D. 2008. Out on a limb over language. Video. http://uk.youtube.com/watch?v=v7Spzjh9QgA.

Faderman, L., with G. Xiong. 1998. *I begin my life all over: The Hmong and the American immigrant experience.* Boston: Beacon Press.

Fodor, J. 1975. *The language of thought.* New York: Crowell.

Geertz, C. 1968. Linguistic etiquette. In J. Fishman (ed.), *Readings in the sociology of language,* 282–295. The Hague: Mouton.

Grice, P. 1975. Logic and conversation. *Syntax and semantics,* 3. New York: Academic Press.

Grice, P. 1989. *Studies in the way of words.* Cambridge, MA: Harvard University Press.

Harada, S. 1976. Honorifics. In M. Shibatani (ed.), *Syntax and semantics,* 5, 499–561. New York: Academic Press.

Hauser, M., N. Chomsky & W. Fitch. 2002. The faculty of language: What is it, who has it, and how did it evolve? *Science* 298(5598). 1569–1579.

Heim, I. 1982. *The semantics of definite and indefinite noun phrases.* Amherst, MA: University of Massachusetts dissertation.

Hughes, G. 2000. *A history of English words.* Malden, MA: Blackwell.

The International Journal of Speech, Language and the Law. 2008. http://www .equinoxjournals.com/ojs/index.php/IJSLL. (30 October 2008).

Leonard, R. Robert Leonard Associates. http://www.robertleonardassociates.com/ leadership.htm. (20 October 2008).

Levinson, S. 1983. *Pragmatics.* Cambridge, UK: Cambridge University Press.

MacWhinney, B. 2003. First language acquisition. In M. Aronoff & J. Rees-Miller (eds.), *The handbook of linguistics*, 466–487. Malden, MA: Blackwell.

Malotki, E. 1983. *Hopi time: A linguistic analysis of temporal concepts in the Hopi language.* Berlin: Mouton.

Mey, J. 1993. *Pragmatics: An introduction.* Oxford, UK: Blackwell.

Pinker, S. 1994. *The language instinct: How the mind creates language.* New York: William Morrow.

Pullum, G. 1991. *The great Eskimo vocabulary hoax and other irreverent essays on the study of language.* Chicago: University of Chicago Press.

Quine, W. 1960. *Word and object.* Cambridge, MA: MIT Press.

Russell, B. 1919. *Introduction to mathematical philosophy.* London: Allen & Unwin.

Saeed, J. 2003. *Semantics*, 2nd edn. Oxford, UK: Blackwell.

Searle, J. 1975. Indirect speech acts. In P. Cole & J. Morgan (eds.), *Syntax and semantics*, 3, 59–82. New York: Academic Press.

Shuy, R. 2008. http://rogershuy.com/

Stillings, N., et al. 1995. *Cognitive science: An introduction*, 2nd edn. Cambridge, MA: MIT Press.

Tannen, D. 2006. Language and culture. In R. W. Fasold and J. Connor-Linton. *An introduction to language and linguistics.* New York: Cambridge University Press.

Thomas, J. 1983. Cross-cultural pragmatic failure. *Applied Linguistics* 4(2). 91–112.

Tiersma, P. 1999. *Legal language.* Chicago: University of Chicago Press.

Tiersma, P. Welcome to LANGUAGEandLAW.org. http://www.languageandlaw.org/. (20 October 2008).

Wolfram, W. & N. Schilling-Estes. 1998. *American English.* Oxford, UK: Blackwell.

Review, Practice, and Explore

RPE **10.1** > **Propositions and Truth Conditions**

Which of the following sentences contain propositions? Which propositions are true, and which are false?

a. Eat your cereal!
b. Did you eat your cereal?
c. I ate cereal this morning.
d. I didn't eat cereal this morning.
e. The dog ate cereal this morning.
f. The dog ate cereal this morning, didn't he?
g. Should dogs eat cereal?
h. Dogs never eat cereal.

RPE 10.2 › Analytic and Synthetic Sentences

Label the following sentences as analytic (A) or synthetic (S).

    a. Lions are felines.
    b. Lions are carnivores.
    c. Lions can be fierce.
    d. Lions live only in certain parts of the world.
    e. Lions are animals.
    f. I like lions.
    g. You don't like lions.

RPE 10.3 › Entailment

Write down as many entailments as you can for the following sentences. A sentence may have more than one entailment or may have no entailments.

    a. Lions are animals.
    b. Lions live only in certain parts of the world.
    c. Lions are carnivorous.
    d. Lorraine is my mother's sister.
    e. Lorraine is my friend.

Do the following sentences have the same entailments? Why or why not?

    f. The puppy devoured the pizza.
    g. The puppy ate the pizza.

What entailments are expressed by the following ambiguous sentence?

    h. The movie star met the journalist in a tux.

Paraphrase the following sentences. Remember that paraphrases have the same meaning but different word order, and any entailments remain the same.

    i. Lorraine loves going to the Bahamas in the winter.
    j. The baby gave the rattle to his mother.
    k. The students handed in their papers.
    l. The ball rolled under the bed.

RPE 10.4 › Contradictions

Make up three sentences that are contradictions because of the interplay of words that express logical relationships, such as *all, every, some, and, or, but,* and *if.*

RPE 10.5 › Presupposition

Some of the following sentences include presuppositions. Write the presupposition down for each sentence. What propositions do we infer or assume in each sentence?

    a. Do you want to go bowling again?
    b. Her husband is a banker.
    c. Have you stopped eating meat?

    d. Do you eat meat?
    e. Why did you steal the money?
    f. Einstein discovered relativity.
    g. I have already donated to the cause.

RPE   **10.6** >   Thematic Roles

Assign the most appropriate thematic role to each of the underlined NPs:

    a. Francine rode her bike to the party.
    b. Elvis ate peanut butter with a spoon.
    c. Bess gave the waitperson a nice tip.
    d. Ariadne saw the dog at the pound.

Make up sentences in each of which *the child* is the subject but in which it has a different thematic role in each case. You'll have to change the verb in each sentence you make up.

    a. *The child* saw the teacher leave the building.
        experiencer

    b. *The child*
        agent

    c. *The child*
        patient

    d. *The child*
        goal

RPE   **10.7** >   Direct and Indirect Speech Acts

Identify each of the following as a direct or an indirect speech act. Explain briefly why you identify them as you do. Does sentence type correlate with meaning?

    1. Please read the assigned reading by Monday.
    2. Could you pick up the trash over there?
    3. Did you see the movie last night?
    4. I would like to know how many of you finished the assignment.
    5. Do your chores!
    6. Do you want that window open?
    7. Move your car out of the way!
    8. Can you please move your car?
    9. Please move your car.
    10. Your car is in the way.

RPE   **10.8** >   Performative Speech Acts

Speech acts are called *performative* when uttering them is an act in itself rather than reporting on an act. For example, if someone says "I saw a cat run under the porch," they are asserting that they saw this event and are reporting on it. If a judge in court says "I order you to spend six days in jail," that statement performs an action: It legally binds you to serve your jail time. Which of the following speech acts are performative? (*Hint:* You can usually insert *hereby* in performative speech acts but not in nonperformative ones.) What conditions must be satisfied for these acts to be performative? Are there conditions under which the sentence would *not* be performative? Explain briefly.

    a. John hopes to be there on time.
    b. SAFE! (yelled by the umpire in a baseball game)
    c. I christen you the H.M.S. *Titanic*.
    d. I will pay you the money I owe you.
    e. I promise to pay you the money I owe you.
    f. Yesterday, Joe promised to pay the money he owes Jack.
    g. Did Joe promise to pay Jack the money he owes him?
    h. Louise knows that pigs can fly.
    i. Joachim decreed that pigs can fly.

Performatives can be rather tricky. Discuss some of the issues that are raised when we try to determine whether the following sentences are performative.

    j. Checkmate! (spoken by a player in a chess game who has checkmated his opponent)
    k. Checkmate! (spoken by a player in a chess game who has not checkmated his opponent)
    l. Checkmate! (spoken in a context other than a chess game)

RPE 10.9 > Grice's Maxims of Conversation

    A. Make up a (plausible) conversational exchange in which Grice's maxims are followed. Explain briefly how each maxim is satisfied.
    B. Come up with a (plausible) conversation in which at least one of Grice's maxims is violated. Explain why the violation might take place and what inferences the speakers and hearers could use to make sense of the utterances. (Remember that a violation doesn't necessarily mean that the conversation breaks down; it is often the result of *maxim clash*, wherein a maxim is violated but the cooperative principle maintained.)
    C. Now, come up with an example of a conversational exchange in which at least one of Grice's maxims is flouted. Does the conversation break down or not? Explain briefly.

RPE 10.10 > Positive and Negative Politeness

Referring to Table 10.2, make up one conversation in which a speaker uses positive politeness and one in which a speaker uses negative politeness, and then answer the following questions:

    A. How does context influence the situation?
    B. What is the relationship between the two speakers, and does that matter?
    C. In what kinds of situations are we more likely to use positive politeness, and in what situations might we use negative politeness?
    D. In your conversations, what are some examples of direct and indirect speech acts?

RPE 10.11 > Gender Differences in Conversation

It has long been argued that men and women have different speech styles and conversational practices. More recent work in language and gender studies has shown, however, that generalizations about men and women are impossible and that gender interacts with a number of other variables, such as age, ethnicity, social class, and sexual orientation, in shaping our speech styles and practice. What are some current issues and arguments about gendered language? Is it possible to claim that men and women talk differently and use different conversational and politeness strategies? (Some good resources include Cameron 2007, Tannen 2006, Eckert & McConnell-Ginet 2003, and Wolfram & Schilling-Estes 1998.)

RPE 10.12 > Terms of Address

One way to express status and respect in English is with terms of address. Perhaps as a reflection of changing attitudes about such relationships, however, this system is in a state of flux, leaving many of us unsure of how to address certain people. These days, more adults are likely to be called by their first names by children; use of the terms *Mr.* and *Ms.* is waning. Even in elementary and secondary schools, teachers are asking their students to call them by their first names. For many, this confusion about what to call someone can result in "no-naming," calling that person by no name at all! College professors frequently experience this situation if they haven't told their students what they would like to be called. Discuss what factors you use when trying to determine how to address someone; consider age, gender, occupation, and level of schooling, among other factors. Is there a situation in which you choose the no-naming strategy? Why? Is politeness at work?

RPE 10.13 > Style-Shifting: Conversational Register

We shift registers often and unconsciously, depending on where we are, who we're talking to and why, and so on. Describe three different registers you might use and the context in which you would use each. Describe the context, the speakers involved, and any other factors that you think contribute to your choice of register. What kinds of vocabulary, sentence structure, accent, and so forth do you use in shifting from one register to another? Give examples to illustrate. (*Hints:* Do you use contractions such as *gonna* or *wanna* in one register but not another? When would you choose a more formal term over a more informal one? In what situations would you use euphemisms? When do you say *yeah*, and when are you careful to say *yes* or maybe even *yes, ma'am*?)

RPE 10.14 > Cross-Cultural Conversations

What are some of the conversational practices of a culture other than your own? Do the maxims of conversation seem to apply as they do in your own speech community? Give examples of how maxims might be violated, flouted, or even maintained in different ways in another cultural context. Discuss cross-cultural differences in politeness conventions such as honorifics, terms of address, and other conversational practices. Are direct and indirect speech acts used in different ways?

RPE 10.15 > Definiteness and Geographical Place Names

Do you say *Rocky Mountains* or *the Rocky Mountains*? Most native English speakers agree that *the Rocky Mountains* sounds better than *Rocky Mountains* when referring to the geographical location. Likewise, *Lookout Mountain* somehow sounds better than *the Lookout Mountain*. For the following list of place names and your local landmarks, do they sound better with or without the definite determiner *the*?

Great Salt Lake
Lake Whatcom
Colorado River
Mississippi River
Nooksack River
Black Hills
Nob Hill
Eagle Lake
Whatcom Creek
Heron Creek

What is the rule that determines whether *the* occurs with a proper name for a natural landmark? Discuss why you think this might be.

RPE 10.16 > Deixis

Explain how each of the following sentences uses deixis.

   a.   We're going on vacation this summer.
   b.   I walked to the store.
   c.   I walked from the store.
   d.   I walk to the store.
   e.   Come on over here!
   f.   John bought that new car.
   g.   The cat is over there behind the couch.

RPE 10.17 > Language and Thought

Pullum (1991) outlines the development of the myth, based on "research" by Benjamin Whorf, that "Eskimos" (a misnomer right there) have "bucketloads" of words for snow and that this is evidence for the Sapir-Whorf hypothesis. Research this myth (using resources in addition to Pullum's book). What evidence is there against Whorf's claim?

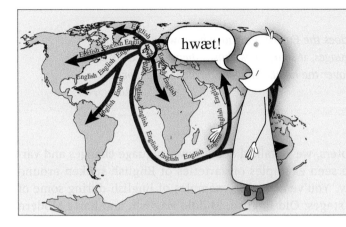

hwæt!

The Early Story of English

Key Concepts

- Indo-European, one language family among many, includes languages spoken across Europe and into Asia, including English.
- We can trace the development of English from Old English (449–1100) to Middle English (1100–1500) to Early Modern English (1500–1800) to Present-Day English.
- The stages of English can be identified by syntactic, morphological, phonological, and lexical differences, as well as by differences in spelling.
- As English changes, so do attitudes about language and language authority, and we see the rise of the idea of "correct" English and prescriptive grammar in eighteenth-century England.

Did You Know . . . ?

Pretty Grimm Tales
Why Was Alfred So Great?
Runic Writing and the *Futhorc*
The Black Death, Rats, and Fleas
The Word According to Johnson

Language Alive!   False Cognates

Pagan Fossils

Linguistics in the News   Languages and Land Bridges

Accent on   Philologists

Finding Families: The Comparative Method
   Indo-European Language Families
   Beyond Indo-European: Other Language Families
   The Germanic Branch of Indo-European

English Emerges in the British Isles
   Old English Vocabulary
   Old English Morphology
   Old English Syntax
   Old English Phonetics and Phonology

English Meets French: Middle English
   Middle English Vocabulary
   Middle English Morphology
   Middle English Syntax
   Middle English Phonology

English Established
   The Birth of "Correct" English and Prescriptive Grammar
   Early Modern English Grammar
   The Early Modern English Vocabulary Explosion

Summary

Sources and Resources

Review, Practice, and Explore

> *Not only does the English language borrow words from other languages, it sometimes chases them down dark alleys, hits them over the head, and goes through their pockets.*
>
> —EDDY PETERS

In previous chapters, we've talked about how language changes and varies, and you've seen examples of varieties of English spoken around the world today. You've also seen examples of English during some of its developmental stages: Old English, Middle English, and Early Modern English.

Here, we'll explore how languages change over time, with special attention to the history of English, its origins in the British Isles over a thousand years ago, and how Present-Day English (PDE) can be traced back to Old English, a language that looks completely foreign to speakers of today's English. We'll see how Old English developed over time into Middle English and then into Early Modern English, and we'll discover how this development was shaped by a series of political and cultural events and also, sometimes, by nothing obvious at all.

Proto-Indo-European reconstructed parent language of members of the Indo-European language family, which spans Eastern and Western Europe and parts of Asia

historical linguistics study of how languages change over time

We'll also study the ways in which other languages are related to one another and to English, and we'll look at the evidence for language families, related languages that can be traced back to a common ancestor. We'll see evidence that many languages, spoken from Europe to India, have evolved from a single ancestor—or "mother"—language called **Proto-Indo-European**, and that English is a member of this family, part of the subfamily of Germanic languages. We will introduce you to some of the other language families that have been discovered through the study of language change over time, or **historical linguistics**, and we will take a look at the kinds of evidence and methodology that historical linguists use to determine how languages develop, change, and branch off from one another.

Finding Families: The Comparative Method

The year 1786 is often given as the year of the beginning of the study of historical linguistics. In that year, Sir William Jones gave a speech at the Royal Asiatic Society in Calcutta, India. Though his paper was primarily about the culture, religion, and people of India, what he had to say about language has had a lasting effect. Most notably, Jones discussed Sanskrit (from which most languages of India are descended) and the commonalities among Sanskrit, Greek, Latin, and Gothic (more broadly understood now as Germanic). Others had noticed these similarities, but Jones went further than they had, saying that these languages must have come from a common source language (what is now known as Proto-Indo-European). The ideas put forth in Jones's lecture formed the basis for the *comparative method* of linguistics. From that point forward, the study of language was no longer a branch of religion or philosophy but a legitimate area of study in its own right, which paved the way for modern linguistics.

The **comparative method** is a technique of linguistic analysis that compares lists of related words in a selection of languages. **Cognates** are words descended from a common ancestor, not just words that happen to look like each other. For example, the word for 'father' in Latin is *pater*; in French, *père*; and in Spanish, *padre*. This similarity suggests that all these words come from a common root language (Latin) and are in the same language family (the Italic family). The word for 'father' in English is related to *Vater* in German (*v* is pronounced as /f/ here). This suggests that English and German are related in a similar way and are part of the Germanic language family. Taking this comparison a step further, when we find that other words that begin with *p* in Italic languages show up in Germanic languages beginning with *f*, then we have what is called a **regular sound correspondence**. So, for example, the words for 'fish' in Latin, French, and Spanish (*pisces*, *poisson*, and *pescado*, respectively) all begin with *p*, and the words for 'fish' in German and English begin with *f* (*Fisch* and *fish*, and *fisk* in Danish, another Germanic language). This suggests that the Italic and Germanic language families themselves may descend from a common root language. Further, scholars have shown that Italic and Germanic are members of the larger language family Indo-European, and that languages in this family descend from a common root language, Proto-Indo-European. It's important to remember that there are nearly 7,000 languages spoken and signed in the world today, and that Indo-European is only one of about a hundred language families. The Indo-European languages are the most widely studied in the world, and more than half the world's population speaks an Indo-European language as a first or second language.

Table 11.1 gives examples of words in five Indo-European languages and then the reconstructed Proto-Indo-European (PIE) root word. From lists like these, regular sound relationships are established and a possible proto-form (hypothetical word) is proposed (traditionally indicated by the asterisk).

Table 11.2 shows the words for numbers from one to three in both Indo-European and non-Indo-European languages. Can you pick out the non-Indo-European one(s)?

As you may have guessed, L1 (Italian), L4 (Avestan), and L5 (Wendish) are Indo-European, but L2 (Mongolian) and L3 (Vietnamese) are not.

comparative method technique of linguistic analysis that compares lists of related words in a selection of languages to find cognates

cognates words (with the same basic meaning) descended from a common ancestor

regular sound correspondences predictable sound changes across languages that show they are related

RPE 11.1

Table 11.1	Proto-Indo-European Word Roots					
Sanskrit	**Greek**	**Latin**	**Gothic**	**English**	**PIE Root**	**Meaning**
pita	pater	pater	fadar	father	*pater-	father
padam	poda	pedem	fotu	foot	*ped-	foot
bhratar	phrater	frater	brothor	brother	*bhrater-	brother
bharami	phero	fero	baira	bear	*bher-	carry
jivah		wiwos	qius	quick	*gwei-	live
sanah	henee	senex	sinista	senile	*sen-	old
virah		wir	wair	were	*wiro-	man

PIE = Proto-Indo-European; * = possible protoform

Table 11.2	Numbers in Indo-European and Non-Indo-European Languages			
L1	**L2**	**L3**	**L4**	**L5**
uno	nigen	mot	aeva	jedyn
due	khoyar	hai	dva	dwaj
tre	ghorban	ba	þrayo	tři

hwæt!

Russian Empress Catherine the Great sent scholars to all parts of Russia to collect words in the late eighteenth century. She then compiled many of the word lists herself, which scholars still use today.

hwæt!

Grimm called the sound change a law because he believed there were principles governing these changes that were similar to the laws of other sciences, such as physics.

Several other scholars made important contributions to historical linguistics and the comparative method. The Danish linguist Rasmus Rask (1787–1832) worked out many of the relationships among the languages now known as members of the Indo-European language family. He died fairly young, however, and never received much credit (so we will give him some here!).

Jacob Grimm (1785–1863) took things much farther than Rask—he talked about natural classes of sounds, or sounds that share similar features (remember natural classes from Chapter 3?). He worked out some of the systematic sound changes among the languages. He agreed that the reason for the similarities across the languages he was studying was their common ancestor.

Grimm is best known in linguistics for coming up with what is now known as Grimm's Law, a sound shift that took place in all the Germanic languages, distinguishing them from the other non-Germanic Indo-European languages. Grimm noticed that everywhere certain sounds occurred in both Sanskrit and Latin, certain other sounds occurred in Germanic (and now in English).

Did You Know...?

Pretty Grimm Tales

You might recognize Jacob Grimm when you know he and his brother Wilhelm are responsible for compiling the famous collection of more than a hundred fairy tales. In the early nineteenth century, when the Grimm brothers lived and wrote, there was not yet a Germany as we know it but rather a collection of smaller countries. Part of what motivated the Grimm brothers' work was a desire to establish a German identity. The Grimms didn't do their linguistic work and their tale collecting to entertain; both endeavors involved studying the past to find out more about the present.

The Brothers Grimm recorded the old stories as they knew them, but the stories were too scary for many readers and listeners so there was a movement to revise the fairy tales so they wouldn't promote nightmares across the land! The edited versions, though they might end happily ever after, are said to maintain the meat of the messages.

Indo-European Language Families

A tree of the Indo-European language family and the languages that came from PIE is given in Figure 11.1. The Indo-European language family tree that we have today is thought to quite accurately reflect the relationships among the languages indicated. Realize, however, that it is some-what misleading in the way that it suggests that each language branched off from a parent language at the same time. It is not, of course, the case that one day—bam!—everyone who had spoken one language suddenly began to speak a different language. Each branch developed very slowly over hundreds to thousands of years. However, the tree remains a very useful way of graphically representing the relationships among languages.

hwæt!

The regular sound correspondences are at work in the naming of *Star Wars'* Darth Vader, the evil father of Luke Skywalker, don't you think?

Celtic

The Celtic languages likely dominated Western Europe around 400 BCE; the people then migrated to what became the British Isles about 2,000 years ago. When Germanic tribes arrived in the British Isles, they pushed the Celtic-speaking people into what is now Wales, Ireland, and Scotland and to Brittany in France. Though these languages still have some speakers, other Celtic languages are now extinct: Cornish, Gaulish, Manx, Cumbrian, Pictish, and Galatian.

Italic

From the Italic language family, also known as Latin or Romance, we get Italian and Portuguese (these two are the most like the original Latin), Spanish, French, Romanian, Rhaeto-Romansch (a language still spoken in

Language Alive!

False Cognates

Cognates can be very tricky because we often assume words are related which aren't. For example, German *Ratte* and English *rat* are indeed cognates and historically related. But the German *Rat* (pronounced with a long a sound) is a *false cognate* of English *rat*; the words look the same but are historically unrelated. German *Rat* means 'council'.

False cognates can get you into trouble. The Parker Pen Company's slogan "It won't leak in your pocket and embarrass you" was translated into Spanish for the Latino market. The translation incorrectly used the false cognate *embarazar* for *embarrass*; the message became "It won't leak in your pocket and *impregnate* you." The Spanish verb *embarazar* means 'to impregnate', not 'to embarrass'. The Spanish verb meaning 'embarrass' is *avergonzar*.

For more information
Serva, S. 2003. iLanguage: Translations for global research. *EContent, Digital Content, Strategies and Resources* 26(1). 51. http://www.econtentmag.com/Articles/ArticleReader.aspx? ArticleID=1038

ʰwæʈ!

The dog breed Dalmatian was bred to guard the borders of Dalmatia (now in Croatia), the homeland of the speakers of the extinct Dalmatian language.

Switzerland), Ladino (a language spoken by Jews from Spain who were exiled in the fifteenth century and now live in Turkey and Israel), Walloon (a variety of French spoken in Belgium), Sardinian, and Canadian French. Catalan, spoken in the northern part of Spain, and Provençal, spoken in the south of France, round out the Italic languages that are still spoken. Extinct languages include Dalmatian, Oscan, Faliscan, Sabine, and Umbrian.

Hellenic

The only language still spoken from the Hellenic branch is Modern Greek. Ancient Greek is believed to be one of the oldest languages of the Indo-European family, with three well-established stages: Archaic, or Ancient, Greek (ninth–sixth centuries BCE), Classical Greek (fifth–fourth centuries BCE), and Hellenistic Greek (third century BCE–sixth century CE). This Hellenistic stage is known as Koine, meaning 'common', or Biblical, Greek. Mycenaean, for which there are a great number of inscriptions on clay tablets, was spoken about 1300 BCE, and we know that the Ancient Greek epic *The Iliad* was written around 700 BCE. The main varieties of Ancient Greek were Doric, Ionic, Aeolic, and Attic; this last one is also known as Classical Greek. Today's Modern Greek stems from the medieval period's language variety, which in turn descended from Koine.

Figure 11.1   Indo-European Language Family Tree

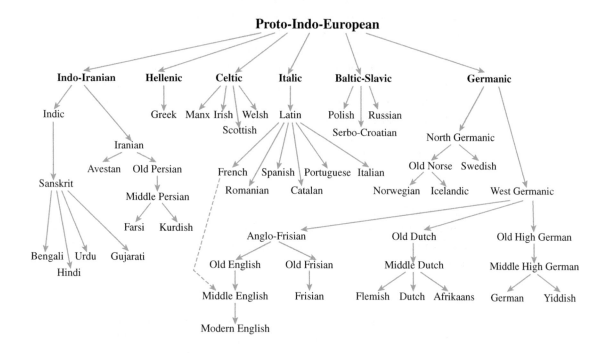

Baltic

The two languages of the Baltic family that are still spoken are Lithuanian and Latvian, spoken in Lithuania and Latvia, respectively. Lithuanian and Latvian diverged from each other around 800 CE and likely continued as mutually intelligible dialects until at least the fifteenth century. Old Prussian is an extinct member of this family.

Slavic

The Slavic languages, spoken in Eastern Europe, are believed by some to be so closely related to the Baltic language family that they form a single branch, the Balto-Slavic family. The Slavic languages include Bulgarian, Russian, Polish, Czech, Slovak, Slovene, Macedonian, Bosnian, Ukrainian, Byelorussian, Kashubian (spoken in Poland), and Sorbian (spoken in parts of eastern Germany).

Indo-Iranian

The languages of the Iranian subfamily are all descended from Ancient Persian, which was the literary language of the Persian Empire and one of the great classical languages alongside Greek, Latin, and Sanskrit. Currently, the most widely spoken language is Farsi, spoken in Afghanistan and Iran and also known as Persian, Iranian, or Dari. Kurdish is spoken in Turkey, Iran, Iraq, and Syria by the Kurds. Baluchi is spoken in Iran, Afghanistan, and Pakistan; Pashto is also spoken in Afghanistan and parts of Pakistan; Ossetian is spoken in Georgia; Tadzhik is spoken in Tadzhikistan and northern Afghanistan.

The languages of the Indic branch of the Indo-Iranian family are spoken primarily in India and are all descended from Sanskrit, the classical language of Hinduism. Hindi and Urdu are very similar languages, but Hindi is spoken by Hindus and is written in the Sanskrit writing system called Devanagari (which means 'writing of the gods'), while Urdu is spoken by Muslims and is written in Arabic script.

Armenian

Armenian is a language, not a family, but it is thought to be the only surviving language of what was once a larger family. Armenian is spoken in Armenia and Nagorno-Karabakh in Azerbaijan. Extinct languages include Dacian, Thracian, and Phrygian.

Albanian

Albanian is another sole survivor of what was once a larger language sub-family. Albanian is also known as Shqip. Illyric and Mesapian, which used to be spoken in parts of Italy, are two extinct members of this family.

Germanic

A language variety we now call Germanic was probably spoken in the mid-first century BCE. Those who spoke Germanic didn't write their language, so we really don't know much about it. Proto-Germanic is to German, Dutch, the Scandinavian languages, and English what Latin is to Italian, French, and Spanish. And while there is a great deal written in Latin, and Latin records go back about 2,500 years, there is nothing written in Proto-Germanic. Written records in Germanic begin only about 300 CE with a few Scandinavian inscriptions, and the earliest written records in English are from about 700 CE. Proto-Germanic gradually divided into what are now known as North Germanic, West Germanic, and East Germanic, as indicated in Figure 11.1. (The East Germanic branch does not appear in the figure because all of its members, including Gothic, are now extinct.)

Beyond Indo-European: Other Language Families

Nearly 7,000 languages are spoken today, and many of them are from language families other than Indo-European; the *Ethnologue* website lists 116 language families (Lewis 2009; http://www.ethnologue.com/family_index.asp). We list only a few of the families in Table 11.3; it is important to note that not everyone agrees on the classifications presented here, and you may find some

Table 11.3	Some Language Families of the World	
Family	**Sampling of Members**	**Main Areas Where Spoken**
Uralic	Hungarian, Finnish, Siberian language, Mordvin	Europe
Altaic	Turkish, Uzbek, Mongolian, Korean, Japanese	Europe, Central Asia, Mongolia, Far East
Sino-Tibetan	Mandarin and Cantonese	Asia
Malayo-Polynesian	Malay, Indonesian, Maori, and Hawaiian	Island nations of Southeast Asia and the Pacific Ocean, continental Asia, Madagascar
Iroquoian	Mohawk, Seneca, Huron	North America
Afro-Asiatic	Arabic and Hebrew	North Africa and Middle East
Caucasian	Georgian and Chechen	Caucasus Mountains
Dravidian	Tamil, Malayalam, and Kannada	India
Austro-Asiatic	Vietnamese and Khmer	India to Vietnam
Niger Congo	Swahili, Shona, Xhosa, Yoruba, and Zulu	Africa, south of the Sahara Desert
Nilo-Saharan	Luo, Songhay, Dinka, Nubian	North Africa, Upper Nile region
Khoisan	Nama, Sandawe, Hadza	Southern and eastern Africa
Eskimo-Aleut	Inuit, Yupik, Aleut, Atka, Inupiaq	American Arctic
Uto-Aztecan	Hopi, Comanche, O'odham	Western U.S., Mexico
Mayan	Ch'olan, Quiche, Yucatec	Northern Central America, Meso-America

Source: Lewis, M. P. (ed.). 2009. *Ethnologue: Languages of the world,* 16th edn. Dallas, TX: SIL International. Online version: http://www.ethnologue.com/. Used by permission of SIL International.

RPE 11.2

of these languages classified differently elsewhere. (There is some controversy, for example, over whether Japanese is a member of the Altaic family.)

The Germanic Branch of Indo-European

Though scholars rely a great deal on regular sound correspondences to discover the relationships among languages, this is only one type of evidence for such relationships. Many linguistic changes resulted in a unique branch distinguishing Germanic from the other Indo-European languages. Tense and aspectual inflections on verbs came to be expressed by separate words except in two tenses, past and present. So, in Present-Day English, we can say *walks*

Grimm's Law
system of regular
sound correspon-
dences, discovered
by Jacob Grimm,
that distinguishes
Germanic languages
from others in the
Indo-European
family; also called
the First Sound Shift

or *walked*, but other tense and aspectual distinctions are made up of verb phrases: *will walk, have been walking*. Other branches of Indo-European use a single word to express some of these other tenses and aspects (in French, for example, 'will walk' is a single word: *marchera*). Another factor that distinguishes Germanic from other Indo-European languages has come to be known as **Grimm's Law** (also called the First Sound Shift). This generalization about sound change shows that where certain sounds occurred in both Sanskrit and Latin (represented here as *IE*, or Indo-European), certain other sounds occurred in the Germanic languages (*Gmc*), including English.

Grimm's Law

IE Gmc	IE Gmc	IE Gmc
b → p	p → f	bh → b
d → t	t → θ	dh → d
g → k	k → x (→ h)	gh → g

voiced stops → voiceless stops   voiceless stops → voiceless fricatives   aspirated stops → unaspirated stops

If one compares, say, modern French and Spanish words with English ones, you can see the evidence for these sound changes. For example, consider the word *deux* in French or *dos* in Spanish, both meaning 'two'. The Indo-European <d> became <t> in Germanic (*zwei*, in which the initial sound is actually /t/, *two* in English, *twee* in Dutch). Another example is the word *père* in French or *padre* in Spanish, both meaning 'father'; here, the Indo-European <p> became <f> in Germanic. Also, because English has borrowed many words from Latin, Greek, French, and Spanish, a great many English words that are of non-Germanic origin did not, therefore, undergo the Grimm's Law sound shift. Consider pairs such as *horn/cornucopia, heart/cardiac,* and *tooth/dental*; the second word in each pair is borrowed from a non-Germanic Indo-European language and therefore did not undergo the shift.

The sound changes associated with Grimm's Law are an example of a change for which there is no apparent reason. This doesn't mean it is a *linguistically* random change, however. There is a systematicity to the sound changes: voiced stops become voiceless, aspirated stops become unaspirated. One would not find sound changes in which features of sounds acted unpredictably; for example, we never find that voiced stops become voiceless nasals. So, even though we don't know why such changes happen, we do know that they happen in predictable ways with respect to phonetic features and phonological rules.

In addition to the sound changes and the two-tense (past and present) verb system, several other features distinguish the Germanic branch of Indo-European from other branches of that family:

- a common, distinctive vocabulary
- an alveolar suffix for the past tense

- "strong" versus "weak" adjectives
- a fixed stress accent

We discuss these features in later sections.

Interestingly, English exhibits some of these features, but the language has undergone so many changes since its origins in the British Isles that not all of these features are still present in the language. We will see how these features did exist in earlier varieties of English, however.

Such systematic differences allow scholars to distinguish certain languages and certain families from others, as illustrated in the family tree model. So, from Proto-Indo-European (which comprised several hundred languages) to Germanic (with about fifty languages) to West Germanic (which includes German, English, and Dutch), we arrive at the branch that includes English. This branch is sometimes called the Anglo-Frisian branch. Never heard of Frisian, the closest relative of English? We'll see where Frisian is spoken and why it is related to English as we investigate the primary historical events that led to English as we know it.

RPE   11.3 ⟩

English Emerges in the British Isles

As far as we know, Celtic people lived in what is now the British Isles for many centuries—even before Julius Caesar's invasions in 55 BC and 54 BC. Contact with the Romans continued, and about a hundred years later, the Romans were firmly established in Britain. The Roman occupation of England lasted for several hundred years. Despite the long occupation, the British Celts continued to speak their own languages. The Celtic languages still spoken in Britain are Welsh, Irish Gaelic, and Scots Gaelic. We know from an account called *Ecclesiastical History of the English People* (*Historia ecclesiastica gentis Anglorum*, written in Latin by a monk named Bede and completed around 730—almost three centuries after the events!) that in 449 the Anglo-Saxon adventurer-warriors from what is now Germany and Holland landed in the British Isles. (What we don't know is how accurate Bede's account is, written so long after the fact; it's likely that what happened was a bit more complicated and more gradual than Bede's account suggests.) Bede wrote that word reached the continent of the cowardice of the Celtic peoples and the fertility of the island, and in the course of the next hundred years or so, more and more Angles, Saxons, and Jutes, "from the most powerful nations of Germania," arrived in the British Isles. In addition to the tribes known as the Angles and the Saxons, there were also the Frisians and probably other tribes as well, likely all speaking a number of closely related, probably mutually intelligible dialects of a single Germanic language. (Aha! There are the Frisians, whose descendants still live in Friesland, off the coast of the Netherlands, and who speak a language closely

Language Alive!

Pagan Fossils

The following names for the days of the week derive from the names of Scandinavian gods:

Monandæg	the moon
Tiwesdæg	Tiw, god of war
Wodnesdæg	Woden, supreme deity
Thorsdæg	Thor, god of war
Frigedæg	Frige, goddess of love

Saturday, however, means simply 'day of the planet Saturn,' and Sunday, of course, means day of the sun. These words, along with *Yule*, the name of the midwinter festivities celebrated by the Anglo-Saxons and now synonymous with *Christmas*, are some words taken from pagan religions, absorbed into Christian culture, and then given Christian meanings. The Old English word *god* also has its roots in pagan rites of sacrifice.

related to English.) The descendants of these people, it seems, only about a century and a half later, were already beginning to think of themselves and their speech as English (*englisc*). The name of a single tribe was adopted as a national name, *Engle*, and 'the land of the Angles' was *Englalond*.

The time now known as the Old English period is usually assumed to extend from 449, the date Bede gives as the first landing of the Anglo-Saxons, to about the year 1100. Historians differ over the nature of the interactions between the Germanic invaders and the Celtic-speaking Britons. The fact that the remaining Celtic languages are spoken in the borderlands—in Wales and Cornwall, in Ireland, and across the water in France (in the area now known as Brittany)—suggests that the English did not simply absorb the Celts. DNA analysis confirms that there was not a great deal of assimilation among the groups. However, because most Anglo-Saxons were not literate, we do not have any written accounts of what actually took place.

Old English Vocabulary

One of the ways we determine whether languages are members of a particular branch of Indo-European is to see whether those languages share a distinctive vocabulary. Here, as we trace the origins of English, we'll also trace the development of Old English vocabulary, the words Old English has in common with other Germanic languages, as well as the words borrowed into Old English from non-Germanic languages.

Even though the Anglo-Saxons were in contact with Celts in England for many years, there are only a few Celtic **loanwords**, or words borrowed from

loanwords words borrowed into a language from another language

Celtic languages, in English. The Old English word *cros* comes from the Irish (Celtic) *cross*, (the cognate in Latin is *crux*), and other loanwords include *bin*, *bog*, *dun*, and *hog*. A few Celtic place-names made their way into English (in their modern forms): *Thames, Dover, Cornwall, Carlisle, York, Rochester,* and *Avon*. Place-names of Anglo-Saxon origin include those with *-sex, -ford, -ham, -shire, -bridge,* and *-bury,* among others: *Sussex, Wessex, Oxford, Nottingham, Berkshire, Cambridge,* and *Canterbury*. Latin had a huge impact on English vocabulary, contributing many of the terms associated with the Christian religion, including *abbot, alter, mæsse* ('mass'), *candel* ('candle'); and the Old English words *nunne, biscop, engel* ('angel'), and *deofol* ('devil') all derive from Latin or Greek words. English words also made their way into religious vocabulary, giving rise to synonym pairs that exist today. The Latin *sanctus* ('holy'), *deus* ('god'), and *spiritus* ('spirit/ghost') have the Old English synonyms *hālig, god,* and *gaāst*.

From the eighth to the eleventh centuries, Viking raiders—Swedes, Norwegians, and Danes who spoke a related Germanic language now called Old Norse—repeatedly attacked the English. They targeted monasteries and their libraries along the coast, destroying many books in Old English and Latin. The legendary King Alfred was king of Wessex at the time. Aware that his forces could not defeat the Vikings, Alfred allowed them to settle in the northern part of the country in an area called the **Danelaw**.

> **Danelaw** northern region of England decreed by King Alfred and the Danes to be a legitimate Norse settlement under Norse, not English, law

Over time, the people began to live peaceably together. Their languages, formerly Old English and Old Norse, which were already quite similar, began to merge. A great many words of Old Norse origin were borrowed during this time and thus became English words.

Several things are noteworthy in this list of borrowings from Old Norse. One is the borrowing of the pronouns *they, them,* and *their,* which replaced the Anglo-Saxon *hie, hiera, him.* When languages come in contact, they very rarely borrow pronouns but rather borrow nouns, verbs, or adjectives; scholars aren't

Did You Know...?

Why Was Alfred So Great?

Alfred was the king of Wessex from 871 to 899. He is best known for his defense of the Anglo-Saxon kingdoms in the south of England against the Vikings, but he was also the only English monarch to be dubbed 'the Great' for his promotion of education and of the English language, which many believe helped unite all of England. King Alfred encouraged his subjects to learn to read English and had many books from Latin and French translated into English. He even learned Latin and translated some important works into English himself, including *The Consolation of Philosophy* by Boethius. It is also thought that King Alfred ordered the important *Anglo-Saxon Chronicle*, which was begun about 890 and maintained by generations of anonymous scribes until the middle of the twelfth century.

sure what led to the borrowing of these pronouns. Also notable is the borrowing of the auxiliary verb form *are*, another type of word rarely borrowed. And notice all of the words that begin with [sk]: *scant, scare, scrap, scrape, skill, skin, skirt, sky*. We know that these are all of Norse origin because this sound combination [s] + [k] existed in early Old English but had changed to the [š] sound: *shin, shirt*. In fact, *shirt* and *skirt* derive from the same Proto-Germanic word: **skurtijon* 'a short garment', which then became *scyrte* (and later *shirt*) in Old English and *skyrta* in Old Norse (and later English *skirt*). Though the number of words borrowed from Old Norse is small compared to the number that English would later borrow from French and Latin, these borrowed words are very much a part of everyday English speech.

The Danelaw (Figure 11.2) part of England is still filled with place-names of Scandinavian origin. And many Old Norse suffixes have become

Figure 11.2 Places with Names of Scandinavian Origin

The Danelaw is an area of northeast England, where the Danes (or Vikings) were allowed to settle in the later ninth century.

Did You Know...?

Runic Writing and the *Futhorc*

Some Old English words have odd-looking letters that are no longer part of our writing system. These letters, some of which were incorporated into Old English writing in the Latin alphabet, are *runes*, from the runic alphabet, or *Futhorc*, a Scandinavian writing system named for its first six letters: *feoh* ('movable property'), *ūr* ('bison'), *þorn* ('thorn'), *ōs* ('god'), *rād* ('road'), *cēn* ('pine' or 'torch'). These first six letters correspond to the following runes:

ᚠ ᚢ ᚦ ᚠ ᚱ ᚻ

Runes have the shape they do because they were usually carved into wood or stone. Each runic letter (except two, *eolh* and *Ing*) corresponds to a noun and represents the sound at the beginning of that noun.

---

part of place-names throughout the English-speaking world. The suffix *-wick* or *-wich* likely came from the Scandinavian *-vik*, meaning 'creek' or 'bay' (and gives us *Keswick, Greenwich,* and the word *Viking*). The most common Scandinavian suffix in the Danelaw was *-by* (*Grimsby, Whitby, Derby*), which originally meant a farmstead; *-thorpe* (*Bishopsthorpe*) meant 'a smaller settlement', a sort of suburb of a village; *-holme* or *-holm* (*Holmhill, Reed's Holme*) indicated land reclaimed from marshland and is often associated with island names; *-kirk* meant 'church' and occurs as both a prefix and suffix in place-names (*Kirkbridge, Ormskirk*); and the suffix *-thwaite* (*Bassenthwaite*) originally meant 'a smaller farmstead on a larger farm'.

Though Old English vocabulary includes borrowings from other languages through language contact, the vocabulary of the language was still overwhelmingly Germanic. It has been estimated, though, that about 85 percent of the 30,000 Anglo-Saxon words died out after contact with the Scandinavians and the French, which means that only about 4,500 Old English words survived. However, among those surviving words are some of the most common and basic words in English: *and, at, brother, but, child, drink, eat, fight, for, house, in, on, live, love, man, sister, sleep, to,* and *wife,* for example. In fact, the one hundred most common words in contemporary English are words of Old English origin.

Old English Morphology

Someone who studies Old English today has to learn it as a foreign language. What makes the study of Old English grammar even more challenging is that there are no longer any native speakers around, and all we have to study are surviving texts. Nevertheless, we still know quite a bit about the language, and we'll talk about some of the major morphological, syntactic, and phonological differences between Old English and Present-Day English.

Strong and Weak Nouns

Old English is a case-marking language, indicating nominative, accusative (marking direct objects), genitive (marking possessives), dative (marking indirect objects), and (some) instrumental cases on its nouns. Nouns were also classified as **strong** or **weak**, and each noun had grammatical gender: masculine, feminine, or neuter. The following table shows the inflectional morphology of the strong neuter noun *scip* 'ship'. (You may want to go back to the discussion of inflectional morphology in Chapter 5 to review case and grammatical gender.)

strong and weak nouns classification of Old English nouns depending on how they are inflected to show case, gender, and number

	Singular	Plural
nominative	scip	scipu
accusative	scip	scipu
genitive	scipes	scipa
dative	scipe	scipum

Weak nouns had another pattern altogether. Here is the declension of the masculine noun 'name':

	Singular	Plural
nominative	nama	naman
accusative	naman	naman
genitive	naman	namena
dative	naman	namum

Strong and Weak Adjectives

strong and weak adjectives in Old English, the differential expression of case, number, and gender of adjectives, according to whether or not they are preceded by a determiner (weak adjectives are preceded by a determiner, and strong ones are not)

Like nouns, adjectives in Old English were also **strong** or **weak**, but this relationship shows up in a different way than it does on nouns. Adjectives in Old English express gender, case, and number and must agree with the noun they modify in these features. An adjective that is not preceded by a determiner is "strong," and one that is preceded by a determiner is "weak." This distinction exists in many Germanic languages today.

For example, the adjective *good* must agree with the noun *ship*, a neuter, nominative, singular noun. When preceded by the demonstrative *þæt* ('that'), the adjective is in its weak form, *gōde*; when not preceded by an article or demonstrative, the adjective is in its strong form, *gōd*.

þæt gōde scip 'that good ship' (*gōde* is weak)
gōd scip 'a good ship' (*gōd* is strong)

Strong and Weak Verbs and a Two-Tense System

Verbs had more inflectional information in Old English. Here are the various forms for the verb meaning 'love', which had four distinct endings for the present tense, depending on what the subject was (notice the **runes**!):

runes Norse alphabet of figures carved into wood or stone; each runic letter corresponds to a noun and represents its initial sound

ic lufie	'I love'
þu lufast	'you love'
heo lufaþ	'he/she loves'
we lufiaþ	'we love'
ge lufiaþ	'you love'
hie lufiaþ	'they love'

Old English had a two-tense system typical of Germanic languages. Verbs were inflected for past and present tense but not for future (future tense was expressed with adverbs and/or with verbs in the present tense: *I go tomorrow*, for example). Old English had no progressive form of the verb (no verbs ending in -*ing* in combination with *be*, as in *I am going*) and no complex tenses expressed as they are today, as in *I will have left* or *I had been eating*.

When we look at the past tense of Old English verbs, we see that they express a feature common among Germanic languages, a *dental preterite*, or past-tense form of the verb that ends with a dental consonant /d/ or /t/ (still seen today with our -*ed* past-tense ending; remember, it is pronounced as both /d/ and /t/).

fremede 'did'
bærende 'burned'
lōcode 'looked'

Not all verbs in Old English had dental preterites, though as the language developed this feature became more and more common. Contrast these past-tense verbs with those above:

clēaf 'cleave'
wæs 'was'

strong and weak verbs in Old English, the differential expression of inflection through a vowel change (strong verbs) or through a regular affix (weak verbs)

Old English verbs could also be **strong** or **weak**; again, this strong/weak distinction is a bit different from that described for nouns and adjectives. A strong verb is one in which tense is expressed by an internal vowel change, and a weak verb is one in which tense is expressed by a regular affix. So, Old English *love* is weak, but Old English *singan* 'to sing' is strong: *singþ, sang, gesungen* ('sing', 'sang', 'sung'). This strong/weak distinction exists in verbs in Present-Day English as well, as we can see by the translation of *sing*, and also by such verbs as *drink/drank/drunk* and *ring/rang/rung*.

Recall from Chapter 6 that languages can be synthetic or analytic. Synthetic languages encode inflectional information in affixes that include more than one grammatical feature (so, for example, an affix that expresses case, number, and gender). Inflection expressed through vowel changes is also a feature of synthetic languages. Analytic languages, on the other hand, express inflection through regular affixes, through word order, and/or through separate words that express grammatical information. The suffix -*ed* in Present-Day English is an analytic affix. Old English is therefore largely synthetic, having affixes that express more than one grammatical feature (case, number, *and* gender, for example) and also using vowel changes to express inflection.

Old English Syntax

Old English was more synthetic than Present-Day English. This difference is responsible in part for the fact that Old English had somewhat freer word order than Present-Day English does because grammatical information is expressed morphologically rather than syntactically.

Old English Word Order

In Old English, the sentence meaning *The cat chased the rat* could also have the order *The rat chased the cat*, where *the cat* is still understood as the subject (the one doing the chasing), and *the rat* as the object (the one being chased). This is because in Old English *the cat* would have nominative case, telling us that it is the subject (no matter where it is in the sentence), and *the rat* would have accusative case and be marked as the object regardless of its position. In Present-Day English, we depend on word order to interpret subject/object relationships, and so the only possible order for this sentence is *The cat chased the rat.*

The following examples of Old English sentences illustrate some of the possible word orders in which the subject (S), verb (V), and object (O) could occur: SVO, OVS, and SOV.

S V O

[He] hæfde þa oþ he [ofslog] [þone aldormon].
   S   *V*   *O*
'He had it until he killed the elderman.'

O V S

[þa stowe] [habbaþ giet] [his ierfenuman]
    O   *V*   *S*
that place have still his successors
'his successors still have that place'

In dependent clauses, word order was typically SOV, as it is in many modern Germanic languages.

S O V
þæt [hie] [þone Godes mann] [abitan scolden]
     S   O   V
that they the God's man devour should
'in order that they should devour the man of God'

Interrogative and Negative Sentences

In Old English, the auxiliary *do* was not used in negative or interrogative sentences as it is today. In negative sentences, *ne* was simply inserted before the verb, and interrogatives were formed by inverting the subject and the verb. (Notice also the example of multiple negation *nān . . . ne*, also common in Old English.) Forming negatives in this way, by adding separate words, is one of the ways in which Old English was an analytic language.

Hē cwæþ þæt nān man ne būde be norðan him.
He said that no man not lived north of him.
'He said that no one lived north of him.'

Hwilce fixas gefēhst þu?
Which fishes catch you?
'Which fishes did you catch?'

Hæfst ðu hafocas?
Have you hawks
'Do you have any hawks?'

Old English Phonetics and Phonology

Even though there is no record of what Old English sounded like, scholars have come up with reasonable hypotheses about the phonology of the language based on spellings, puns, rhymes, pronunciations in related languages, and knowledge of how language sounds typically change. Old English had much the same consonant system as Present-Day English, though /r/ was trilled, and consonants that we don't pronounce today were pronounced in Old English. So the initial consonants in *cnāwan* and *cnafa* ('know' and 'knave') and *gnæt* and *gnagan* ('gnat' and 'gnaw') were pronounced in Old English. And remember the Great Vowel Shift from Chapter 3? Old English was spoken long before this shift occurred, so words were pronounced quite differently because of their different vowel sounds. Recall that an Old English speaker would say [hu:s] for *house* and [fo:d] for *food*. These examples also illustrate that vowel length (marked with :) was distinctive in Old English; that is, it could make a difference in meaning. And because of vowel mutation (a different process, which occurred during the

ƕƿæꞇ!

The several surviving manuscripts of the *Anglo-Saxon Chronicle*, most written in Old English with some in Middle English, are a rich source of historic and linguistic information.

time Old English was spoken), the plural of *mūs* ('mouse'), *mūsiz* ('mouses') became *mys*. After the Great Vowel Shift, *mys* is pronounced as in Present-Day English, [mays]. (Vowel mutation, or *ablaut*, is also the process that gives us *foot/feet* and *goose/geese*, among other pairs.) Also, final vowels were pronounced and occurred in many words that no longer have them, such as *sōna* 'son' and *nama* 'name'.

The following text excerpt from *The Battle of Maldon* (http://faculty.uca.edu/jona/texts/maldon.htm) illustrates the "otherness" of Old English compared to Present-Day English. How many words look familiar to you? Study the text to find examples of the grammatical aspects of OE we've discussed.

Hige sceal þe heardra,	Thought must be the harder,
heorte þe cenre,	heart be the keener,
mod sceal þe mare,	mind must be the greater,
þe ure mægen lytlað.	while our strength lessens.
Her lið ure ealdor	Here lies our prince
eall forheawen,	all hewn,
god on greote.	good one on grit.
A mæg gnornian	He may always mourn
se ðe nu fram þis wigplegan	who from this war-play
wendan þenceð.	thinks now to turn.
Ic eom frod feores;	My life is old:
fram ic ne wille,	I will not away;
ac ic me be healfe	but I myself
minum hlaforde,	beside my lord,
be swa leofan men,	by so loved a man,
licgan þence.	think to lie.

Source: Bodleian MS Rawlinson B 203. Oxford.
Translation copyright © 1982, Jonathan A. Glenn.

Did you notice the negative marking: *ne wille* where the negation precedes the modal verb? Also, the adjective *god* in "god on greote" is a strong adjective, and the word order in the line *Her lið ure ealdor* has the verb *lið* 'lies' preceding the subject *ure ealdor* 'our elder (prince)'. Some words are clearly cognates: *men, heort*; can you find others? Notice the prefix *for-* in *forhewean*.

Now let's consider the phonology of this Old English text. Listen to the audio of the passage at the following link (3: "Birhtwold's Speech" from *The Battle of Maldon*, anonymous, date unknown): http://www.wwnorton.com/college/english/nael/noa/audio.htm.

As you listen, note the following: <sc> is pronounced /š/, as in *sceal*; <g> is pronounced when it precedes a consonant, as in *gnornian*, as is <h> before another consonant, as in *hlaforde*; <c> is pronounced /k/;

the <f> coming between two voiced sounds becomes voiced /v/, though there was not yet a phoneme /v/, as in *leofum*.

In Old English, words were stressed on the first syllable, as in other Germanic languages, unless that syllable was a prefix. In that case, stress migrated to the following syllable. For example, *feores* is stressed on the first syllable: *féores*, while the verb *forheawen*, which begins with the prefix *for-*, is stressed on the second syllable: *forhéawen*. We still find vestiges of Old English stress in Present-Day English, particularly in words with Germanic prefixes such as *be-, for-, forth-, after-,* and *under-,* as in *becóme, forgét,* or *forthcóming*.

RPE   11.4 ⟩

English Meets French: Middle English

In 1066, the Normans, from the northern part of France, invaded and conquered England at the Battle of Hastings, on the southeastern coast of England. With the French-speaking rulers in power, French gradually became the language of the land until around the second half of the fourteenth century, but English would remain entrenched as the language of the common people. The variety of English spoken from around 1100 to around 1500 is called Middle English.

A series of events led to the rise and fall of French in England and to the eventual establishment of English as the national language. A short time after William the Conqueror (and Duke of Normandy) vanquished the Anglo-Saxon king, Harold Godwineson, at Hastings, Anglo-Saxon nobles were replaced with Norman ones, and England came fully under William's rule. The language of the court became French. William also brought with him a feudal system, creating a social division between the French nobility and the English-speaking peasants. Though English was greatly affected over time by contact with French, it remained the language of the English peasants, who had very little contact with courtly life conducted in French.

Another reason that French did not become the language of England was that in 1204 King John of England finally lost all of England's Norman lands to the French (and to Philip II, the French king). This effectively broke the political ties between France and England, and the Norman nobles in England, known as Anglo-Normans, had to choose between staying in England and giving up their French lands, or going back to France. Most Anglo-Normans chose to stay in England, and interest in and connections to France waned. The variety of French that the Anglo-Normans spoke wasn't well accepted among continental French speakers either, which further isolated the two countries and cultures from each other. School came to be taught in English, and over time English became the language of the court. The off-and-on battle for power between France and England (1337–1453) known as the Hundred Years' War resulted in further separation between the two countries and their languages.

Black Death
bubonic plague,
carried by rodents
(and their fleas),
which wiped out
two-thirds of the
population of
Europe in the four-
teenth century

Another blow dealt to French was the **Black Death** (bubonic plague), which struck around 1348; by 1351, it had killed approximately two-thirds of Europe's population and about one-third of England's. As you can imagine, one effect of the plague was a massive labor shortage, and English-speaking peasants moved to the towns, working for higher pay for French merchants and guildsmen and sometimes moving into positions of economic power themselves. This helped break down the social division between French speakers and English speakers, and English gained in prestige.

Did You Know...?

The Black Death, Rats, and Fleas

We know now that the Black Death (so called because of the black spots it caused to appear on the skin), or bubonic plague, is carried by rats and mice and that humans became infected with the disease when bitten by fleas from rodent carriers. Because rat infestation was higher in urban areas than in rural areas, medieval towns and cities were hit harder by the disease, causing economic havoc. The disease struck with great speed; in the words of Boccaccio, the great Italian writer of the time, victims "ate lunch with their friends and dinner with their ancestors in paradise" (Boccaccio 1351: Day 1).

By all accounts, everyone in England spoke English by the end of the fourteenth century, even the Norse speakers north of the Danelaw. As you might imagine, there were great dialectal differences across the country, and the English spoken in London, the seat of economic and political power and a major seaport, became the standard dialect. Until the late Middle Ages, there had been no real standard version of English; scribes producing books wrote in whatever dialect they spoke, spelling words sometimes radically differently. When William Caxton brought the printing press to London in 1476 and printed the first books in English, he not only revolutionized bookmaking but set in motion the process of standardizing spelling (to avoid resetting type for different spellings). (We will discuss spelling the language in more detail in Chapter 13.)

Middle English Vocabulary

Though Old English looks unfamiliar to speakers of Present-Day English, it's easy to tell that Middle English is English, and we can even understand a lot of it when we read it or hear it. Perhaps the most obvious change in the language after the Norman Conquest was in vocabulary; English borrowed thousands of French words, many of which we still use today. French was the language of government, so it's not surprising that many words having to do with government and administration are from French: *administer, attorney, chancellor, country, court, crime, judge, jury, noble, royal,* and *state,* to name just a few. And French, along with Latin, was used in the Church, so many of those words are of French origin: *clergy, preach,* and *sacrament.* And also from French are words having to do with food and cooking, or *cuisine: beef, mutton, pork,* and *veal.* Compare the Old English words for these same foods: *cow, sheep, pig,* and *calf.* Because languages generally avoid exact synonyms, these words came to have different meanings from the French borrowings. And because the French-speaking people were, for the most part, being served by the English, the creature in the field (the English word) and the item on the table (the French word) came to have these different meanings. We also see this distinction in status in words borrowed from French, such as *tax, estate, pay, religion, savior,* and *pray* and the culinary terms *roast, serve,* and *dine.*

Fashion terms were introduced (including the word *fashion* itself)— among them *dress, coat, pantaloons, bonnet, boots, satin, ribbon, pleat, pearl,* and *bracelet.* Terms for sports, art, education, medicine, government, and law were borrowed from French during this period: *tournament, park, dance, chess, tennis, amusement, art, portrait, color, music, romance, tragedy, ball, study, pupil, copy, pen, pencil, paper, grammar, noun, subject, surgeon, pain, remedy, cure, plague, poison, government, rule, reign, public, crown, tax, citizen, appeal, accuse, pardon, prison, innocent.* Many Middle English words were also borrowed from Scandinavian languages: *anger, bag, cake, call, hit, husband, kid, race, rag, down, flag,* and *freckle,* among many others.

Middle English Morphology

The biggest morphological change from Old English to Middle English is that many inflectional affixes disappeared (remember that Present-Day English has only eight inflectional affixes, but in Old English, nouns, adjectives, and verbs were much more highly inflected). For example, the *-an* and *-um* endings on the Old English nouns in the tables shown earlier (for *scip* and *nama*) were reduced to /ə/. Infinitival verbs in Old English, such as *drivan* 'drive', lost the final syllable and thus the infinitival inflectional affix, becoming *drive* in Middle English (where the final < e > was pronounced for a while, then finally dropped as well). Similar loss of inflectional affixes occurred on adjectives, which lost most of their case, number, and gender inflections and, with that, the loss of distinction between weak and strong forms.

Loss of Inflection

Scholars do not agree on what motivated the loss of inflectional endings during the Middle English period, especially the loss of case-marking, though it is not thought that the influence of French directly produced the changes. One explanation is that speakers were exposed to and confused (unconsciously) by the combination of English, Old Norse, and French and so abandoned all the endings. However, the loss of inflectional markings was already occurring before the Norman Conquest. Also, Scandinavian influence was felt only in certain parts of the country, though the loss of inflectional endings seems to have happened across the board. Another more likely explanation is that the phonological reduction of unstressed final vowels to /ə/ meant that many distinctions were no longer heard. Another factor was that the language already had a generalized word order, so information could be used to indicate grammatical function instead of inflectional morphemes, making the inflections redundant.

Middle English Syntax

With the loss of inflection came more fixed word order and increased use of words such as auxiliary verbs rather than inflections to convey grammatical information.

Fixed SVO Order

Word order, as you recall, was fairly flexible in Old English, but in Middle English the typical order in main clauses came to be SVO. Both SVO and SOV orders appeared in dependent clauses, where in Old English the order was typically SOV, but SVO had become the more common pattern by this time.

> Thyn Astolabie hath a ring to putten on the thombe
>   S   V   O
> 'Your astrolabe has a ring to put on the thumb'

This change appears to be a result of the loss of inflection because grammatical relations were no longer clearly expressed morphologically. Instead, syntactic position became more important and the means by which relationships such as subject and object were conveyed.

Middle English Auxiliary and Modal Verbs

The loss of inflection also resulted in words rather than affixes being used to convey grammatical information. In Middle English, perfect aspect (expressed with the auxiliary *have*) began to show up (remember that this didn't exist in Old English).

> þou *hauset don* oure kunne wo
> 'You have done our family woe'

In Middle English, we see an increased use of modal verbs, again to reflect meanings that were previously indicated with inflections:

> þat y *mowe* riche be
> 'that I may rich be'

The modal verbs with *shall* and *will* began to be used to express future tense (whereas in Old English the present tense was used to express the future, using adverbs and other words to provide the right context).

> And swiche *wolle* have the kingdom of helle, and not of hevene
> 'And such will have the kingdom of hell, and not of heaven'

Interrogative and Negative Sentences

Also in contrast to Old English, in Middle English we see a great rise in the use of auxiliary *do*, and for the first time it appears in negative and interrogative sentences:

> My maister dyd not graunt it.
> Fader, why do ye wepe?

And as in Old English, multiple negation existed in Middle English, as you can see in the following sentence from the great Middle English author Geoffrey Chaucer's *The Canterbury Tales*, "The General Prologue" (Hallissy 1995: 24):

> He *never* yet *no* vileynye *ne* sayde
> 'He never yet no villainy not said'

Middle English Phonology

Phonology continued to change, but not too much, during the Middle English period; most of the consonants and vowels of Old English were maintained in Middle English. Remember, though, that vowels were to undergo a huge shift (the Great Vowel Shift) at the end of the Middle English period, so Middle English vowels were pronounced very differently from how we pronounce them today. Also during this period, /w/ was lost before /o/, so *swa* became *so*; and /h/ was lost before other consonants, so *hring* became *ring*, and *hlaford* became *lord*. Old English *acsian* 'ask' became *asken* in Middle English (so in modern dialects of English, *aks* rather than *ask* is actually closer to the original pronunciation), an example of metathesis that you learned about in Chapter 3, and the Old English prefix *ge-* became /ɪ/, so *genōg* became *inough* 'enough'. Certain vowels lengthened unless followed by another syllable, which is where we get the vowel distinction in pairs like *children* and *child*. And as we mentioned in the discussion of morphology, final unstressed vowels were lost, which led to Old English *heorte* being pronounced in Early Middle English as *herte* and in later Middle English as *hert* ('heart'). Old English *sōna* was pronounced *sōne* in early Middle English and in late Middle English *son* 'son'.

Stress in Middle English began to diverge from the Old English (predictable) pattern. Though English word stock maintained its Germanic stress patterns (patterns that are with us today), the influx of French vocabulary—in which stress fell, typically, on the final syllable (*medicíne*)—brought with it a shift in stress patterns that depends on the arrangement of stressed and unstressed syllables in a word. So, though we stress *grammar* on the first syllable, stress migrates depending on the number of syllables:

grámmar   grammátical   grammaticálity

Here is another excerpt (lines 43–55) from Chaucer's "General Prologue" to *The Canterbury Tales*. Can you pick out some of the French vocabulary, as well as some of the grammatical properties of Middle English we talked about earlier?

A knyght ther was, and that a worthy man,
That fro the tyme that he first bigan
To riden out, he loved chivalrie,
Trouthe and honour, fredom and curteisie.
Ful worthy was he in his lordes werre,
And therto hadde he riden, no man ferre,
As wel in cristendom as in hethenesse,
And evere honoured for his worthynesse.
At Alisaundre he was, whan it was wonne.
Ful ofte tyme he hadde the bord bigonne
Aboven alle nacions in Pruce;
In Lettow hadde he reysed, and in Ruce,
No Cristen man so ofte of his degree.

RPE 11.5 >

From Synthetic to Analytic

Many of the changes we've discussed chronicle the way that English gradually developed from a synthetic to a more analytic language. In Middle English, we see the loss of inflection and a subsequent dependence on SVO word order to express grammatical relationships. We see the rise of the auxiliary elements *have* and *be* and the modals *shall* and *will* to construct complex tenses (perfect, progressive, and future) and an increased use of auxiliary *do* to form interrogative and negative sentences. In Old English, word order was much freer because grammatical relationships were expressed morphologically instead (on strong and weak nouns, adjectives, and verbs).

RPE 11.6 >

English Established

The next phase in the development of English is Early Modern English, spoken from about 1500 to about 1800 (remember that these dates are not intended to suggest that the language changed from one version to another overnight). Early Modern English is quite recognizable to contemporary

LINGUISTICS
IN THE NEWS

Languages and Land Bridges

Evidence from bones, tools, and DNA shows that our North American continent was settled by people from northern Asia over 10,000 years ago. The DNA comes from recently discovered human feces that date back 14,300 years. DNA analysis reveals that people who lived in caves in Oregon were closely related to modern Native Americans and to people across the Bering Strait in Siberia and eastern Asia.

A link between the languages of northern Asia and those of North America had been suspected for some time since the similarities in words had been noticed. However, such similarities can occur by borrowing or by chance, so establishing definite family relationships must go beyond word resemblances.

Edward Vajda, a professor of linguistics at Western Washington University in Bellingham, recently demonstrated a convincing kinship between a Siberian language family called Yeniseic and a Native North American language called Na-Dene. The Na-Dene family includes the many Athabaskan languages, including languages of Alaska, Canada, the Pacific Northwest, and Navajo in the Southwest, as well as the Tlingit language. Vajda presented a paper at the University of Alaska

in Fairbanks and convinced fellow linguists, who work on many of the languages on both sides of the Bering Sea, of a shared ancestor. Vajda's clinching evidence came from his work of more than fifteen years on Ket, an endangered language spoken in central Siberia. Vajda says that features of the Ket verb reminded him of Navajo, so he got down to serious comparison. He determined that verbs in Ket, in its Yeniseic family, and in the Na-Dene family all contain a complex series of prefixes, and he showed that the form, order, and meanings of these prefixes were very much the same in both families. Vajda also established relationships in the sound systems of the two language families, as well as a great many cognates in the various languages.

The comparisons were made possible by the work of linguists at the University of Alaska, Fairbanks: Jeff Leer's analysis of Tlingit; Michael Krauss's work on the extinct language Eyak and on comparisons of various Athabaskan languages; and James Kari's work on Athabaskan words and verb structure. Working independently, Vajda and the Alaska linguists have discovered too many parallels to be explained by anything other than a common ancestor.

The distance from the Yeniseian range to the most distant Athabaskan languages in the southwestern United States is the greatest overland distance covered by any known language spread not using wheeled transport or sails.

For more information
Doughton, S. 2008. Fossilized feces found in Oregon suggest earliest human presence in North America. *Seattle Times.* April 3. http://seattletimes. nwsource.com/ html/localnews/ 2004324975_weboldpoop04m .html

Kari, J. 2008. Notes from the Dene-Yeniseic Symposium, February 26–27. University of Alaska, Fairbanks. http://www .uaf.edu/anlc/docs/Kari-DY-intro-3.pdf

Nichols, J. 2008. Linguists demonstrate Siberian-North American link. *Linguist List.* http://www. linguistlist.org/issues/19/19-717. html. (3 March 2008).

Solis, M. 2008. Tongue ties: A language bridge across the Bering Strait. *Crosscut.com: News of the Great Nearby.* http://www. cross cut.com/tribes/13846/. (30 April 2008).

Vajda, E. 2008. Dene-Yeniseic in past and future perspective. http:// www.uaf.edu/anlc/dy2008.html

English speakers, mostly because we are familiar with it from literature, and of course because it isn't as "old" as Old or Middle English. Shakespeare's writing is in Early Modern English, as is the King James version of the Bible. There are, however, quite a few differences in phonology, morphology, and syntax, compared to any contemporary dialect of English.

Remember that right at the end of the Middle Ages the printing press had been introduced to England; however, most people were still illiterate. Mass production of books and pamphlets did mean that literacy gradually was becoming more widespread. The spread of books in English had several consequences. One is that English became even more entrenched as the national language of Britain; it was now a literary language (in addition to French and Latin) as well as being the most widely spoken one. Another important consequence is that readers now had access to works written in the variety of different dialects of English spoken in Britain, such as *Sir Gawain and the Greene Knight*, written in West Midlands English, as well as Chaucer's works, written in London dialect (East Midlands). Because London dialect appeared in print, other dialects came to be seen as less prestigious because they were not written down anymore. As we saw in the earlier discussion of Caxton and the printing press, the London dialect became the standard dialect of England and is the foundation of other standard varieties of the language in the United States, Canada, Australia, New Zealand, South Africa, and India.

Despite becoming the language of Britain, English still had some challenges to its popularity. During the Renaissance, there was a revival of interest in classical learning. Many works by Caesar, Virgil, Homer, and others were translated into English, though scholars also experimented with English and were sometimes defensive and even apologetic about using the language in their work. English was still viewed as inferior to the classical languages, and some writers—among them Elyot, Spenser, Thomas More, Sidney, Shakespeare, and Jonson—tried to "improve" English by introducing new words and defending the English language and its literature quite directly. The substantial body of poetry and prose that was being written at this time was beginning to put people at ease that English was a "worthy" language.

One major event in the history of English was the separation of the English Church from Rome in 1536, when Henry VIII broke with the Catholic Church. This event led to a rise in status of English as the language of religion and learning (the position previously held by Latin). The Anglican Protestants believed that everyone should have access to the Bible in English, and many people began to learn to read English so they could read the Bible in their own language.

RPE 11.7

The Birth of "Correct" English and Prescriptive Grammar

The increased literacy and the increasing number of printed texts in English gradually led to an increased standardization of the language, which in turn gradually led to the idea of correctness in language. People began to want dictionaries to help them read, write, and spell in the same manner, and some became intent on fixing the language in what they viewed as a polished, perfect, and permanent form. Scholars attempted to reduce the language to a finite set of teachable and learnable rules and to set up a standard correct usage, but there were no dictionaries and no real authoritative governing bodies on language (such as a language academy) to "fix" the language. John Dryden wrote in 1660 that "we have yet no prosodia, not so much as a tolerable dictionary, or a grammar, so that our language is in a manner barbarous" (Stackhouse 1731: 187).

Some half-hearted attempts were made to set up a language academy that would codify how the language should be used and spoken, but no academy ever really got off the ground (the Académie Française, in contrast, is alive and well in France but not very powerful). There was agreement, however, that a good dictionary of English was needed. Samuel Johnson's *Dictionary of the English Language*, published in 1755, revolutionized reference books and all English dictionaries that followed. Although a great improvement over anything they had, it was inadequate by modern standards, with only 50,000 entries (compared to two to three times that many in most dictionaries today), few pronunciations, and quite a few incorrect etymologies.

RPE   11.8 ⟩

Did You Know...?

The Word According to Johnson

Can you tell what these definitions from Johnson's dictionary define?

- grain, which in England is generally given to horses but in Scotland supports the people (*oats*)
- an allowance made without equivalent, which in England "is generally understood to mean pay given to a state hireling for treason to his country" (*pension*)
- female cant (*gossip*)
- hateful tax levied upon commodities, and adjudged not by the common judges of property, but wretches hired by those to whom excise is paid (*excise*)
- a convulsion of the lungs, vellicated by some sharp serosity. And this word is pronounced *coff*. (*cough*)

Though some of Johnson's definitions are funny, politically biased, or sexist, his work also set high standards for lexicographical research. Johnson continued the emerging practice of using literary quotations to illustrate word meanings, a practice still in use today by the *Oxford English Dictionary*, among others. Some of Johnson's quotations come from the writings of Shakespeare, Milton, and Dryden, among other literary and political luminaries of the day.

This period also sees the rise of grammars of English, breaking the tradition of grammar study based solely on the grammar of Latin. One such grammar of English was Joseph Priestley's *The Rudiments of English Grammar*, published in 1761 (with a second edition in 1768). Priestley defined grammatical rules in terms of **usage**, or how people use language, rather than in terms of *prescription*, how they "should" use language. He wrote, "The general prevailing custom where ever it happen to be, can be the only standard for the time it prevails." This is a quite progressive attitude about language change and language standards for the time, and Priestley is often hailed as being unique in his descriptive, rather than prescriptive, approach to grammar.

usage language that is accepted as standard and that may or may not follow prescriptive rules

And here's another early quotation on usage from Scottish rhetorician George Campbell (1776):

> Language is purely a species of fashion . . . It is not the business of grammar, as some critics seem preposterously to imagine, to give law the fashions which regulate our speech. On the contrary, from its conformity to these, and from that alone, it derives all its authority and value. For, what is the grammar of any language? Good usage is national and reputable and present.

Because Latin was for so long the language of religion and education in England, it was seen as more prestigious than English, and some even went so far as to suggest that English grammar should conform to the grammar of Latin, even though the two languages are grammatically quite different (and from two different language families, Romance and Germanic). Priestley responded to such attempts, remarking, "We have no more business with a future tense in our language, than we have with the whole system of Latin moods and tense; because we have no modification to our verbs to correspond to it . . ." (Priestley 1761, cited in Beal 2004: 110).

Another well-known English grammarian of the time, Bishop Robert Lowth, is often portrayed as a staunch prescriptivist, guilty of imposing the rules of Latin grammar on English. Lowth was author of the very popular *A Short Introduction to English Grammar*, of which at least twenty-two editions appeared during the eighteenth century. He is often cited as the source of such prescriptive rules as "Never end a sentence with a preposition" (*Who did you talk to?*) and "Never split an infinitive" (*She wants to quickly run into the store.*), based on the fact that in Latin both constructions are impossible. It turns out, however, that both of these rules can be traced to sources other than Lowth, and that while some of Lowth's rules were certainly prescriptive, others were based on usage, much like Priestley's. Lowth makes the point, for example, that "stranding" prepositions is informal but not necessarily to be condemned (Beal 2004: 111).

Regardless of these grammarians' dependence on usage or on prescription, the Early Modern period sees the rise of the notion of correct versus incorrect English and the clear perception that certain ways of talking are more prestigious than others. Typically, the speech that is highly valued is that of speakers who have higher social status. For example, J. Greenwood, author of *An Essay Towards a Practical English Grammar* (1711), claimed that the double negative construction (*I don't know nobody*) should be avoided (p. 160), a stance that Lowth adopts in his second edition. It's probably not accidental that by this time, speakers of double negative dialects were stigmatized as lower class.

Early Modern English Grammar

As we mentioned previously, although we can easily read and understand Early Modern English, it nevertheless differs in several ways from Present-Day English. Phonologically, Early Modern English is close to Present-Day English because it was spoken after the Great Vowel Shift (discussed in Chapter 3). During this period, all the remaining final schwas that were still pronounced in Middle English words were dropped; for example, the words *trouthe* and *hadde*, with final <e> pronounced, became *truth* and *had*. In this period, the consonant /l/ was lost after low back vowels and before labial or velar consonants, so speakers pronounced *half, palm, folk,* and *talk* without /l/, but *film, silk,* and *hulk* with /l/. By this period, too, the initial /g/ and /k/ that were pronounced in Old English become silent, so *gnaw* and *knee* were pronounced as we pronounce them today. And this period is when /r/ drops in certain environments (a process that started in Middle English), leading to "r-less" pronunciations of the <r>s following vowels in words such as *quarter, march, brother, car,* and *farm.*

Morphologically, Early Modern English looks much like English today, though some *-en* plurals still existed (*housen, hosen, eyen*), and other nouns were not always affixed with *-s,* so we find *a team of horse* but also *a brace of horses.* Comparative adjectives showed up with both a comparative word and an affix, as in *most stillest night,* and the comparative and superlative affixes *-er* and *-est* showed up on adjectives different from those we affix today, as in *violentest* and *certainer.* The language retained some verb inflections in the present tense (*-est, -eth*), though not consistently, and the formal *you*/informal *thou* distinction also persisted into this period, though again not consistently.

Syntactically, modals and the auxiliary verb *do* were used as we use them today, although nonemphatic *do,* which we discussed in Chapter 7, still existed until late in this period. Nonemphatic *do,* remember, is pronounced without stress (which makes it different from emphatic *do,* which is stressed, as in *I DID do my homework!*).

Juliet: I have forgot why I did call thee back. (*Romeo and Juliet*)
That handkerchief did an Egyptian to my mother give. (*Othello*)

In Early Modern English, we find questions formed both by inverting the main verb with the subject and by inserting the pleonastic auxiliary *do* (indicating that *do*-insertion was optional during this stage of the development of English).

> Why do you look on me?
> Why look you so upon me? (both from *As You Like It*)

Also, as we discussed in Chapter 7, we find negative sentences with negation following the main verb but also negative sentences with auxiliary *do*.

> Came he not home tonight? (*Romeo and Juliet*)
> I do not sue to stand. (*Richard II*)

In other syntactic developments, SOV order was still around, even though the language was by now predominantly SVO.

> As the law should them direct.
>   S   O   V

And we find much evidence of English as an analytic language, with phrases such as *be going to* and the modal *will* + main verb to indicate future tense (*will go*).

RPE 11.9

The Early Modern English Vocabulary Explosion

The Renaissance was an age of exploration, and as a result, English became infused with a number of loanwords, not just from other Indo-European languages but for the first time from non-Indo-European languages as well. Below are some examples, which also illustrate the parts of the globe to which English was exported, often through colonization (Millward 2012: 287–288).

Italian: adagio, alto, aria, opera, solo, balcony, bandit, ghetto, macaroni, malaria, artichoke, tariff, belladonna, vermicelli
Amerindian: moose, hickory, moccasin, papoose, tomahawk, pecan, skunk, terrapin
German: cobalt, meerschaum, quartz, zinc, halt, knapsack, noodle, swindle, veneer, waltz
Celtic: banshee, brogue, galore, cairn, plaid, shamrock, trousers
Russian: beluga, steppe, mammoth
Norwegian: fiord, troll, lemming
Dutch: commodore, cruise, deck, reef, scow, sloop, blunderbuss, uproar, sleigh, snuff, drill, yacht
Turkish: dervish, divan, jackal, pasha, pilaf, sherbet, turban
Arabic: ghoul, harem, hashish, henna, sheik
Hindi: bandanna, bungalow, cheetah, dungaree, guru, jungle, seersucker, shampoo, veranda
African: chigger, marimba, okra
Chinese: ginseng, ketchup, kumquat, pekoe, sampan, tea, typhoon

RPE 11.10

Accent on *Philologists*

J. R. R. Tolkien was a philologist. His first job, in fact, was as a lexicographer on the *New English Dictionary* (which was the precursor to the *Oxford English Dictionary*). His training in language and his positions, first as a professor of English language at the University of Leeds and later as professor of Anglo-Saxon at Oxford University, gave him the knowledge to create the languages he used in his books. Tolkien (pictured) created the languages spoken by the Elves before even writing his famous *Lord of the Rings* trilogy. The phonology, vocabulary, and grammar of two of the languages, Quenya and Sindarin, were based largely on Finnish and Welsh, two of the languages Tolkien studied.

Philologists are linguists—or at least they used to be. Though today's philologists remain concerned about language, the meaning of the word, and therefore what philologists do, has changed quite a bit over time. For example, the American Philological Association was founded in 1869 by "professors, friends, and patrons of linguistic science"; now, the organization is the "principal learned society in North America for the study of ancient Greek and Roman languages, literatures, and civilizations." Most of its current members are classics teachers, and philology, when it is understood to refer to the study of classics, is sometimes called classical philology. Traditionally, language study in the West meant the study of Greek and Latin, and language study throughout the eighteenth and nineteenth centuries was the study of the historical development of language (diachronic linguistics). When language study shifted in the twentieth century to the study of a language at a particular point in time (synchronic linguistics), the term *philology* came to be contrasted with *linguistics*. The meaning of philology also varies today depending on where you live. In British English, philology still is synonymous with the study of historical linguistics, while in the United States, it means either the study of classics or,

AP Photo

more broadly, the study of a language's grammar, history, and literary tradition.

For philologists, both historically and currently, the study of language and literature are usually intertwined. In addition to classical philologists, those who study other languages and their literatures, such as the medievalists in English departments, can be considered philologists. Medievalists today study the literature of the Middle Ages, but to do so, they must learn the language or languages themselves, so they are usually quite adept at the Old and Middle English languages.

Today if you're a philologist, you can study and teach Greek or Latin, you can study and teach Old English or Middle English language and literature, and you can work in the overlap between the study of language and the study of literature. And, like Tolkien, you could invent your own language!

For more information

American Philological Association. 2008. http://www.apaclassics.org/APA-MENU. html. (17 October 2008).

Green, J. 1996. *Chasing the sun: Dictionary makers and the dictionaries they made.* New York: Henry Holt.

Summary

In this chapter, we've discussed how scholars began to study language and language change in the eighteenth and nineteenth centuries. We have seen that languages are members of language families, with both ancestors and descendants (metaphorically speaking, of course). We've introduced the language family to which English belongs, Indo-European, and the particular branch of the family that English is a member of, Germanic. We've discussed characteristics of Germanic languages and how they are reflected in the developmental stages of English, although English today has lost some of those features. We've traced the history of English from its beginnings in the British Isles to the brink of its expansion across the world during the age of exploration.

As we've seen, the developmental stages of English are Old English, Middle English, and Early Modern English, and each stage has certain phonological, morphological, and syntactic characteristics, as well as unique vocabulary and spelling differences. We've observed the development of English from a synthetic language (Old English) to a more analytic one (Middle English and onward), with fixed word order and the use of regular affixes and separate words to express grammatical relationships.

An integral part of the history of English includes the rise of prescriptive grammar and the notion of grammatical correctness. We've briefly explored prescriptive grammar and the idea of language authority: who decides what is correct, what is not, and why. We've seen that prescriptive rules are often arbitrary and that a more moderate approach to language norms is to base rules on usage, or how language is actually used in the community.

In the next chapter, we investigate the spread of English to other parts of the globe. We will explore contemporary varieties of English and will look at their origins, their characteristics, and where they're spoken and by whom, all around the world.

Sources and Resources

Algeo, J. & C. Acevedo Butcher. 2005. *Problems in the origins and development of the English language*, 5th edn. Boston: Thomson Wadsworth.

American Philological Association. 2008. http://www.apaclassics.org/APA-MENU.html (3 June 2011).

Baugh, A. & T. Cable. 1993. *A history of the English language*, 4th edn. London: Routledge.

Beal, J. 2004. *English in modern times: 1700–1945*. London: Arnold.

Boccaccio, G. (written 1351). 1996. *The Decameron*. New York: Penguin Classics.

Campbell, G. 1776. *The philosophy of rhetoric*. Edinburgh: Creech.

Doughton, S. 2008. Fossilized feces found in Oregon suggest earliest human presence in North America. *Seattle Times*. April 3. http://seattletimes.nwsource.com/html/localnews/ 2004324975_weboldpoop04m.html.

Fennell, B. 2001. *A history of English*. Malden, MA: Blackwell.

Green, J. 1996. *Chasing the sun: Dictionary makers and the dictionaries they made*. New York: Henry Holt.

Greenwood, J. 1711. *An essay towards a practical English grammar*. London: R. Tookey.

Hallissy, M. 1995. *A companion to Chaucer's* Canterbury Tales. Westport, CT: Greenwood Press.

Hughes, G. 2000. *A history of English words*. Malden, MA: Blackwell.

Johnson, S. 1755. *A dictionary of the English language*. London: J. McGowan.

Kari, J. 2008. Notes from the Dene-Yeniseic Symposium, February 26–27. University of Alaska, Fairbanks. http://www.uaf.edu/anlc/docs/Kari-DY-intro-3.pdf

Lewis, M. P. (ed.), 2009. *Ethnologue: Languages of the world,* 16th edn. Dallas, Tex.: SIL International. Online version: http://www.ethnologue.com/

Lowth, R. 1762. *A short introduction to English grammar*. London: R. Dodsley.

McCrum, R., et al. 1986. *The story of English*. New York: Penguin.

Millward, C. & M. Hayes. 2012. *A biography of the English language*, 3rd edn. Boston: Wadsworth.

Millward, C. M. & M. Hayes. 2012. *Workbook to accompany A biography of the English language,* 3rd edn. Boston: Wadsworth.

Nichols, J. 2008. Linguists demonstrate Siberian-North American link. *Linguist List*. http://www.linguistlist.org/issues/19/19–717.html. (3 March 2008).

Priestley, J. 1761. *The rudiments of English grammar*. London: Griffiths.

Serva, S. 2003. iLanguage: Translations for global research. *EContent, Digital Content, Strategies and Resources* 26(1). 51. http://www.econtentmag.com/Articles/ArticleReader.aspx?ArticleID=1038.

Solis, M. 2008. Tongue ties: A language bridge across the Bering Strait. *Crosscut.com: News of the Great Nearby*. http://www.crosscut.com/tribes/13846/. (30 April 2008).

Stackhouse, T. 1731. *Reflections on the nature and property of language in general, on the advantages, defects, and manner of improving the English tongue in particular*. London: J. Batley.

Vajda, E. 2008. Dene-Yeniseic in past and future perspective. http://www.uaf.edu/anlc/dy2008.html

Review, Practice, and Explore

RPE 11.1 Regular Sound Correspondences

A. Which of the following languages is/are Indo-European?

B. On what do you base your answer? Can you identify any regular sound correspondences?

C. Can you identify the non-Indo-European languages? What language family are they members of?

A key to this exercise appears at the end of this section.

L1	L2	L3	L4	L5
ichi	ekas	jedyn	en	egy
ni	dvau	dwaj	twine	két
san	tryas	tři	thria	három
shi	catvāras	štyri	fiuwar	négy
go	pañca	pjeć	fīf	öt
rocku	şaş	šěsć	sehx	hat
shichi	sapta	sedm	sibun	hét
hachi	aşţau	wosm	ahto	nyolcz
ku	nava	dżewjeć	nigun	kilencz
jū	daça	dżesać	tehan	tíz
hyaku	çatam	sto	hunderod	száz

(Adapted from Algeo and Butcher 2005: 84.)

RPE 11.2 > Non-Indo-European Languages

Choose a non-Indo-European language and research it (you can choose from the list of non–Indo-European languages we provide in the chapter). A good source is the *Ethnologue* website, http://www.ethnologue.com/. Write a summary of your research in which you answer the following questions:

A. Where is the language spoken, and by how many speakers?

B. What language family is the language a member of? What are some related languages? Or is it an isolate, a language with no other existing family members?

C. What are two other facts about the language that you find particularly interesting or striking and that you didn't know before (pronunciations, morphology, word order, vocabulary, interesting facts about its origins)?

RPE 11.3 > Major Changes from Indo-European to Germanic

All Germanic languages in their oldest forms share characteristics that distinguish them from other Indo-European languages. These six features unique to Germanic languages are given on pages 375–377.

A. Choose a Germanic language (other than English), conduct some research, and then explain and illustrate how it exhibits *two* of these characteristics. Give the characteristic, an example, and a brief explanation.

Characteristic: alveolar suffix for the past tense

Example: Old English: ic sēce 'I seek'

ic sōhte 'I sought'

ic temme 'I tame'

ic temede "I tamed'

Explanation: In Old English, the past tense verbs *sōhte* and *temede* end in an alveolar sound (/t/ and /d/) in the past tense.

B. Now, choose a non-Germanic language and show that it *doesn't* exhibit the two characteristics you illustrated in A. For example, verbs in Latin, a Romance language, do not have alveolar suffixes in the past tense.

Example: Latin: sagiō 'I perceive'

sāgivi 'I perceived'

domō 'I tame'

domui 'I tamed'

Explanation: The Latin verbs *sāgivi* and *domui* do not have alveolar suffixes in the past tense.

RPE   11.4   › Old English Grammar

Discuss differences in vocabulary and syntax that you can identify in the following Old English sentences. What are some of the different word orders that you can identify? What prefixes or suffixes, if any, do you find? What words look familiar to you? Which are completely unfamiliar, and what do they mean? What differences in spelling do you find?

a. þa geseah ic beforan unc onginnan ðeostrainða stowe.
'then saw I before us begin to darken that place'

b. Her is seo bot, hu ðu meaht þine æ ceras betan gif hie nellaþ wel weaxan.
'here is the remedy, how you can your fields restore if they will not well grow'

c. Ic ahsige eow, forhwi swa geornlice leorni ge?
'I ask you, why so eagerly study you?'

d. Hwæt sægst þu, fugelere?
'what say you, bird-hunter?'

e. ond þæs oþrew þone mæstan dæl hie geridon ond him to gecirdon buton þæm cyninge Elfrede.
'and of the rest the greatest part they seized and (to) them submitted except the king Alfred'

f. Her for se here to Cirenceastre of Cippanhamme. One þy geare gegadrode an hloþ wicenga
'here went the army to Cirencester from Chippenham. And in that year assembled a troop (of) Vikings'

RPE   11.5   › Old English to Middle English Spelling

The following words are given in their Old English and Middle English spellings. Examine the list, and describe the spelling environments that determined the change in spelling of the Old English letter *c* during the Middle English period (from Millward 2012: 132).

Old English	Middle English	Present-Day English
candel	candel	'candle'
castel	castel	'castle'
cese	chese	'cheese'
cest	chest	'chest'
ciele	chile	'chill'
cild	child	'child'
clag	clay	'clay'
cleofan	cleven	'cleave'
cnif	knif	'knife'
cniht	kniht	'knight'
cuppe	cuppe	'cup'
cwacung	quakinge	'quaking'
cwealm	qualm	'qualm'
cwellan	quell	'quell'
cweorn	quern	'quern'
cycene	kichene	'kitchen'
kynd	kind	'kind'
cyrnel	kernell	'kernel'

a. In what environments did OE *c* remain ME *c*?
b. In what environments did OE *c* become ME *ch*?
c. In what environments did OE *c* become ME *k*?
d. In what environments did OE *c* become ME *q*?

RPE 11.6 > **Middle English Grammar**

Although the word order of Middle English is similar to that of Present-Day English, the sentences below illustrate some important differences. The first five were written in the first half of the twelfth century (and are therefore closer to Old English). The second five were written in the last half of the fourteenth century (and are closer to Early Modern English).

A. For each sentence, describe how the word order differs from present-day use.
B. What morphological differences (prefixes and suffixes, both inflectional and derivational) from Present-Day English do you notice in each sentence? What similarities?
C. What words are familiar to you in each sample? Can you identify any vocabulary that may have come from French?
D. What are some spelling differences?
E. How are these two samples different? In what way is the first sample "older" than the second? (In what ways is the first sample closer to Old English than the second?)

From *The Peterborough Chronicle* (early Middle English)

a. his gear heald se kyng Heanri his hird æt Cristesmæsse on Windlesoure.
'This year King Henry held his court at Christmas in Windsor.'

b. And him com togæ es Willelm eorl of Albamar.
'And William, Earl of Aumale, came against him'

c. þerefter come ðe kinges dohter Henries, ðe hefde ben emperice in Alamanie.

'Thereafter came King Henry's daughter, who had been empress in Germany.'

d. þe King him sithen name in Hamtun.

'The King afterwards captured him in Hampton.'

e. Sume he iaf up, and sume ne iaf he not.

'Some he gave up, and some he did not give.'

From Chaucer's *Canterbury Tales,* "Tale of Melibee" (late Middle English)

f. Thre of his olde foes han it espyed.

'Three of his old foes have noticed it.'

g. Wepyng is not thing deffended to hym that sorweful is.

'Weeping is by no means forbidden to him that is sorrowful.'

h. And whan this wise man saugh that hym wanted audience, al shamefast he sette hym down agayn.

'And when this wise man saw that audience was lacking for him, all ashamed he sat down again.'

i. My lord, I you biseche as hertely as I dar and kan, ne haste yow nat to faste.

'My lord, I beseech you as heartily as I dare and can, don't move too fast.'

j. But seyeth and conseileth me as you liketh.

'But tell and counsel me as it pleases you.'

RPE **11.7** Semantic Change

Remember that the meanings of words shift over time and that many words in contemporary English originally meant something entirely different. Look up the following words, and find out what their meanings were both before and after the Early Modern English period. Explain whether their meanings have *ameliorated, pejorated, narrowed,* or *broadened* (you may have to go back to Chapter 9 for a quick review!).

lust, battle, carp, harlot, scant, jolly, luxury, sermon, read, knave, boy

RPE **11.8** Etymology of English Words

Using a good etymological dictionary, choose at least three of the following words and determine what Indo-European language the word comes from. Is the word borrowed into English or native to the language? You can find this out by seeing whether the dictionary lists a date of entry into English from another language. If the word is native to English, the dictionary will usually list Old English or Anglo-Saxon as the source language. Also try to determine if there are other English words that derive from the same root.

bath, charity, cheer, clerk, clue, companion, hell, host, guest, corn, doom, fantasy, fee, galore, genius, gentle, glisten, group, holy, humor, kind, know, lace, liberal, maniac, manure, mild, mood, napkin, nausea, nature, nice, outlaw, pain, pity, sad, silly, soap, virtue, wit

RPE 11.9 > **Early Modern English Syntax**

When you examine Early Modern English texts, the differences are not as obvious as they are in Middle English, but they are still notable. Find a text excerpt (or more than one) written during the Early Modern English period (1500–1800), and see if you can find and record at least three of the following syntactic features typical of the language of the day. Explain how each is different from Present-Day English. (You may use the excerpts provided in textbooks on the history of the English language, but Shakespeare's plays and sonnets are an excellent resource, as is the King James version of the Bible.) Write down your examples (and where you found them) to share with the class.

a. adjectival double comparatives: *most unkindest*

b. pronouns: especially look for *thou* and *you*

c. questions without auxiliary *do*: *Know you?*

d. negation without auxiliary *do*: *If I become not?*

e. Orders other than SVO

f. plurals without *-s*: *a brace of horse, shoen*

Feel free to discuss aspects of grammar other than those listed here. There are many more differences between Early Modern English and Present-Day English grammar than these!

RPE 11.10 > **The Etymology of Names**

A. Look up the etymology of your first name. A good source is the *Behind the Name* website: http://www.behindthename.com/.

B. What language does it come from? Is it Indo-European?

C. What does it mean?

D. What are cognates of your name in other languages? For example, Irish *Sean* is a cognate of English *John* and Scottish *Ian*. All descend originally from Latin *Iohannes*.

E. Compile a list of the languages of origin of your first names. Which languages do most names come from? Why?

F. How do English first names reflect the history of the language? What languages are represented, and why?

Answers to Exercise 1

Non-Indo-European languages: L1 = Japanese (Altaic family), L5 = Hungarian (Finno-Ugric or Uralic family)

Indo-European languages: L2 = Sanskrit (Indic family), L3 = Wendish (Slovenian-Slavic family), L4 = Old Saxon (Germanic family)

English Goes Global

Key Concepts

- The study of language change over time (historical linguistics) overlaps the study of language variation over space (sociolinguistics).
- American dialects, based on dialects of British English, differ according to a wide range of complex factors, including region, ethnicity, race, gender, and social class.
- Certain dialects and languages have higher status than others, which does not mean that any language variety is better linguistically but is simply a reflection of society's attitudes.
- Standard English is in large part an idealization of the language that we perceive to be most prestigious or preferred.

Did You Know . . . ?

    The Ann Arbor Trial
    Aladdin Speaks Standard English?

Language Alive!   German Goes from Good to Bad

    Urban Dictionary

Linguistics in the News   Linguistic Profiling

Accent on   Dialect Coaches

What Is a Dialect?

The Origins of American English
    British English Goes to the New
    World

American Regional Dialects
    Dialects and Settlement Patterns
    Drawing Dialect Boundaries
    Appalachian English
    New England English
    American "English" Vocabulary

Ethnic Dialects
    African American English
    Native American English
    Chicano English

Social Dialects
    Social Networks
    Communities of Practice
    Social Class and Language Attitudes

English Keeps Traveling
    Australian English
    Caribbean English
    English in Asia
    English in Africa
    English as a Global Language

Language Variation and Language Discrimination
    Standard English and "General American"
    Dialect Pride

The Future of English Dialects

Summary

Sources and Resources

Review, Practice, and Explore

> *Words, like fashions, disappear and recur throughout*
> *English history, and one generation's phraseology, while*
> *it may seem abominably second-rate to the next, becomes*
> *first-rate to the third . . .*
>
> —VIRGINIA GRAHAM

language variation
language change in progress, such as the Northern Cities Vowel Shift

sociolinguistics
study of how language varies over space (by region, ethnicity, social class, etc.)

In Chapter 11, we introduced you to the major discoveries of historical linguistics, namely, that relationships among languages can be determined through the study of regular sound correspondences and that these relationships provide evidence for language families that can be traced back to common ancestors. In this chapter, we address the study of language change that occurs not over time but right now, what is also called the study of **language variation**, the focus of the field of **sociolinguistics**.

As you might imagine, historical linguistics (language change) and sociolinguistics (language variation) overlap: Both concern the study of grammatical patterns that differentiate one language variety from another. Consider, for example, the vowel shifts that we discussed in Chapter 3. Recall the Northern Cities Vowel Shift that is affecting the accents of English speakers in Chicago, Detroit, Rochester, Cleveland, and Buffalo. Another vowel shift, referred to as the Great Vowel Shift, occurred long ago during the Early Modern period. The first is a change in progress (and at the moment, a variation) that allows us to see how different varieties of English are developing over a particular geographical region, developing *over space* in the United States. The second is a change that occurred in the past; it developed *over time* and became established in the language. Variation overlaps with change when a particular variation is adopted by the speech community and passed on to following generations. At that point, we say that the language has changed.

In this chapter, we discuss language variation over space in some detail. Why do languages merge and diverge, and how do different varieties, or dialects, of a single language come to be? As we'll see, geographical separation is a major factor leading to language variation (and ultimately to language change). Language variation often results when people are isolated on islands or separated by mountains or rivers. To this day, for example, many speakers in areas east of the Connecticut River, including New York and New England, do not pronounce [r] following a vowel in a word such as *car* ("cah"), but speakers west of the river do.

Geographical barriers and boundaries are only part of the story of language variation, however. Speakers' age, gender, occupation, social class, religion, and even politics can influence language variation. Another important factor is speakers' attitudes about how they and others talk, what they consider good and bad language, and what is considered standard and nonstandard.

So, the study of language variation involves not only determining what linguistic features distinguish language varieties but also what kinds of geographical and social factors lead to language variation. In this chapter, we will discuss some of the factors that give rise to the diverse dialects of American English, and we'll also take a look at different "Englishes" that have developed around the globe.

What Is a Dialect?

In our discussion of what a language is in Chapter 1, we pointed out that this concept is not always easy to define because, although we may say that different speech communities speak English, the varieties of English spoken in each community (and even among individuals, to some extent) might be quite different, making it difficult to draw the line between a dialect and a language. It can also sometimes be difficult to decide at what point two language varieties are distinct enough to be distinct languages.

Recall that linguists generally consider two language varieties to be *dialects* of the same language if the speakers of each can understand each other, if the language varieties are **mutually intelligible**, and if each has systematic grammatical differences from the other. By "systematic grammatical differences," we mean differences in grammar, pronunciation, and vocabulary. Languages, on the other hand, are varieties that are not mutually intelligible. Keep in mind, however, that many language varieties fall somewhere in the middle of a language–dialect continuum. And it's also important to remember that a dialect is much more than just an accent, though this is often how we recognize speakers of dialects different from our own. Accent is only one (phonological) way in which we distinguish one dialect from another. As you'll see as we explore dialects of English in this chapter, differences among dialects involve much more.

mutually intelligible
language varieties
that can be
understood by
speakers of the two
(or more) varieties

The Origins of American English

Before we turn to specific grammatical distinctions among American dialects, we'll first provide a brief overview of how they came to be and how English spread from the British Isles, where we left it in Chapter 11, to what became the United States.

British English Goes to the New World

The first permanent English settlements in the New World were on the east coast of North America: Jamestown, Virginia, in the south in 1607 and Plymouth, Massachusetts, in the north in 1620. We know they were settled by people from England. It is impossible, however, to trace the origins of most of these settlers, for there are no records of where they came from in England, only the port from which the ship sailed (London, in most cases). Many people came in search of religious freedom—the Puritans in New England, the Catholics in Maryland, and the Quakers in Pennsylvania. Others were fleeing economic disaster, and most did not have a lot of education. Though we can say that they spoke Early Modern English, they did not all speak the same dialect; British English of the time was (and still is) made up of many regional and social varieties.

British English Influences on American English

The linguistic effects of different British settlement groups that landed up and down the coast can still be heard in American dialects today. One of those features is the pronunciation of the [r]s after vowels, called **post-vocalic [r]**. While everyone who speaks English pronounces [r] word-initially, as in *rock* and *red*, some dialects "drop" [r] after vowels and before consonants, pronouncing *park* and *work* more like "pahk" and "wuk." Several "*r*-less" dialects of English exist all up and down the coastal United States (in eastern New England but also in parts of the southern coast all the way to Florida) and are attributed to settlement of these areas by *r*-less speakers from southeastern England. Well-known examples of *r*-less dialect areas include Boston, Massachusetts, and Tidewater, Virginia. Tidewater was also part of the Southern plantation agricultural system, and *r*-lessness spread to the English eventually spoken by slaves, influencing what was to become African American English (discussed in more detail in a later section). Not all coastal areas of the eastern United States are *r*-less; speakers of "*r*-ful" dialects of British English also settled along the coast, as did *r*-ful Scots-Irish from Northern Ireland, who greatly influenced the speech of upland Virginia colonists.

Another feature of seventeenth-century British speech is the [æ] sound in words like *fast* and *dance*, which was abandoned (in favor of [a]) in southern England at the end of the eighteenth century but continues in North America. Another difference between British and American English is the use of the past participial form *gotten* instead of *got*: Americans typically say "She has gotten hit by the ball," whereas most British speakers say, "She has got hit by the ball." The use of *gotten* sounds quite archaic to British speakers today, though it was common in Britain two centuries ago. In fact, many of the distinctions in pronunciation and grammatical structure that distinguish American dialects from each other have British origins.

post-vocalic [r] distinctive feature of many dialects of English (which pronounce [r] in words such as *car* and which don't: "cah")

hwæt!

African American English has more speakers than any other variety of post-vocalic r-dropping dialect. See http://www.pbs.org/speak/seatosea/americanvarieties/southern.

RPE 12.1

American Regional Dialects

During the seventeenth century, many more immigrants came to North America, settling all along the Eastern seaboard. These settlements soon dotted the east coast of the New World. Between 1620 and 1640, more than 15,000 new immigrants arrived in New England from Britain. Only 150 years later, according to the first census in 1790, the population of the newly formed United States had grown to about four million. At this point, however, most European settlers still lived east of the Appalachians and were still of British ancestry (Svartvik & Leech 2006: 80). Through the next century, diverse dialects and as well as distinct languages began to blend, and some of the earlier distinctions were lost. This process continued throughout the nineteenth and twentieth centuries as people migrated westward.

Dialects and Settlement Patterns

Three main dialects existed at the time of the American Revolution: New England, Midland, and Southern. Soon, as the settled areas grew crowded, people began to move in search of new land and new opportunity. New Englanders moved westward into upper New York State and beyond into the Great Lakes region. Midlanders moved west along the Shenandoah Valley and then into what is now the Midwest and beyond to the western coast. Southerners moved west and south down to the Gulf Coast but no farther west than Texas. These three main dialects still exist today; and a fourth, Western, came into existence after the long process of westward expansion began.

The dialect communities and settlement patterns are not quite that simply defined, however. The three great westward movements were not always along horizontal parallels, and some interior regions in the western part of the country were settled after the growth of settlements on the Pacific Coast. Dialect communities that spread in horizontal bands across the country began to be disturbed by second waves from the east and by new waves of immigrants from Europe and elsewhere. All of this means that it is very difficult to draw dialect boundaries west of the Appalachians.

The Rocky Mountain area is full of individual settlements that date from several periods of migration. Some settlements were left behind by pioneers of the earlier period, first by those who went south into California and later by some who went northwest into Oregon. The area around the Rocky Mountains has mostly Midland dialect features but includes a number of Northernisms, probably carried by the early Californians who returned eastward.

The Northwest region, including Washington, Oregon, and Idaho, was only sparsely settled before 1846, when the western end of the boundary between the United States and Canada was finally drawn. In 1853, a separate Washington Territory was created, and the population increased. Some settlers arrived directly from the East over the Rockies; others took a more northerly route,

Figure 12.1   U.S. Regional Dialects

Source: From map 11.15, Labov, W., S. Ash, & C. Boberg. 2006. *The atlas of North American English* (New York: Mouton de Gruyter). Reprinted by permission of Professor William Labov.

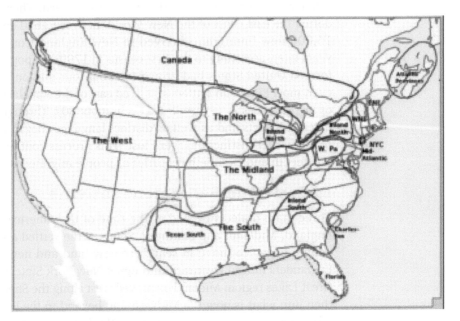

the first leg of which was along the Erie Canal; and still others came from the coast of California (see Figure 12.1).

Drawing Dialect Boundaries

dialectologist sociolinguist who focuses on cataloguing and mapping dialects

How do linguists come up with dialect maps? **Dialectologists** (sociolinguists who focus on cataloguing and mapping dialects) typically conduct extensive interviews with speakers in a particular region, attempting to elicit information about pronunciation, grammar, and vocabulary. Interviewers often use detailed questionnaires, collecting and compiling data over a long period of time. These data are then plotted on a map.

Hans Kurath, a pioneer in what we might call dialect cartography, published *A Word Geography of the Eastern United States* (1949) as part of a larger project, the *Linguistic Atlas of the United States and Canada,* begun in 1931 (and only partially completed and never published). Kurath's original dialect boundaries are still largely considered intact, though some changes have occurred. Figure 12.2 shows how Kurath plotted the distribution of the terms *pail* and *bucket,* one of the distinctions between dialects in southern and northern Pennsylvania.

As you can see, Kurath's map shows where each term was more widely used—way back in the 1930s and 1940s—and also the line of demarcation between the two, illustrating that speakers in southern Pennsylvania said *bucket,* and those in the north part of the state said *pail.* This boundary is called an **isogloss,** and in early dialect research, dialect areas were determined by large "bundles" of such isoglosses.

isogloss geographical boundary of a particular linguistic feature

Figure 12.2 Pennsylvania Dialect Boundaries

Source: Fig 66 from *A Word Geography of the Eastern United States*, by Hans Kurath (Ann Arbor: The University of Michigan Press, 1949)/University of Michigan Press.

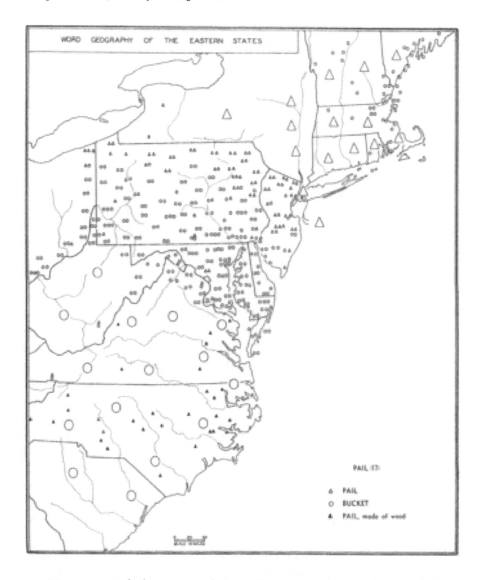

More recent dialect research investigates much more than variations in vocabulary, of course. Several noteworthy projects have been devoted to mapping the features and distribution of dialects across the United States, including Frederic Cassidy's *Dictionary of American Regional English* (begun in the 1960s and still in progress), and William Labov, Sharon Ash, and Charles Boberg's *The Atlas of North American English* (ANAE), published in 2005. ANAE grew out of Labov and colleagues' TELSUR project, in which linguistic data was gathered from extensive telephone surveys (hence, the name TELSUR) of speakers across the country. (You can visit the TELSUR website at http://www.ling.upenn. edu/phono_atlas/home.html.)

We'll now look at two examples of American regional dialects in a bit more detail, Appalachian English and New England English, to give you an idea of what are called **regionalisms**, or features that distinguish one regional dialect from another regional dialect.

regionalism feature that distinguishes one regional dialect from others

Appalachian English

The Scots-Irish (so called because they came from Scotland, stopped in Ireland, then settled in America) were the largest group to settle in the area known as Appalachia, which they did in great numbers in the late 1700s. The Appalachian Mountains stretch from Maine to Georgia, but the heart of Appalachia is in the mountainous parts of Georgia, South Carolina, North Carolina, Tennessee, Virginia, West Virginia, Kentucky, Ohio, and Maryland. The Scots-Irish settlers mingled with the earlier settlers, the Germans who had settled mostly in Pennsylvania (known as the Pennsylvania Dutch), though some moved on south, and with settlers from England, Holland, and other parts of Europe. This blend of languages and dialects in the eighteenth century led to the dialect we now know as Appalachian English. Once permanent settlements were established, two basic lifestyles developed: small-scale farming (often in mountainous areas) and then later, when the country grew rapidly in the nineteenth century, small-scale industry, mostly lumber and coal mining. The later decline of these industries left many people in poverty, which persists to this day throughout much of Appalachia.

hwæt!

Many people know of Appalachia and its mountains because of the Appalachian Trail, stretching some 2,000 miles from Maine to Georgia and hiked by an estimated 3 to 4 million people each year.

We have seen some of the linguistic features of the dialect in other chapters. As with any dialect, there are distinct features of phonology, morphology, syntax, and vocabulary. We discussed the Southern Vowel Shift (Chapter 3), which is typical of Appalachian vowels as well. The deletion of /l/ (Chapter 4), which is in transition in the speech of most Americans (with the /l/ coming back into the pronunciation of words like *caulk*, *palm*, and *folk*), is unpronounced in the speech of many Appalachians in such words as *wolf*, *shelf*, and *help*, as it was in many dialects in England before the eighteenth century. Syntactically, the past tense form of *be* with the second person singular, *you*, is *you was* rather than *you were*. This verb form is common in many contemporary English dialects and also has a long history. Until the seventeenth century, *thou* (the nominative form when used as a subject) and *thee* (the accusative form when used as a direct object) were used for second-person singular pronouns. When these forms were lost and *you* was substituted, the singular verb *was* was still used, resulting in a neat paradigm for the past tense of *be*:

I was	we were
you was	you were
he/she/it was	they were

You was was still used in literature up till the 1800s and has always been common in speech. Noah Webster tried to defend it, though its usage began to decline in the nineteenth century, probably due to the analogy with the second-person plural *you were*.

Ain't (discussed in Chapter 5, "*Ain't* Ain't Had It Easy") is another word with quite a long history; *ain't*, like *you was*, has not always been such a stigmatized verb form. It is still very common in Appalachian English as it is in many other dialects. Another feature of the dialect is the use of what linguists call "positive *anymore*." The word can be used to mean something like 'nowadays', and it can appear without another negative: *Things are getting worse anymore. She's so rude anymore.* In other dialects, *anymore* means 'no more' and can only be used with another negative (resulting in double negation! Egads!): *She doesn't do yoga anymore. She is not nice anymore.* The positive *anymore* has now spread to other dialects of American English.

Some colorful words and phrases of Appalachian origin have now expanded into General American; these include *spitting image of* (from *spirit and image of*), *snickerdoodles, varmint, tacky,* and *three bricks shy of a load*.

Though the Appalachian dialect does maintain some features of older English, it is not, as is sometimes mistakenly assumed, a relic of Elizabethan English. Like many dialect communities that remain more isolated than others due to their remoteness in the mountains or on islands, it may retain features of older versions of the language. However, it has just as many new features, or innovations. So it is not the case that the Appalachian dialect is closer to the language of Elizabethan England than other dialects.

New England English

hwæt!

Why is a clam happy? The entire phrase is "happy as a clam at high tide" because clams are dug at low tide. At high tide, they're safe. For meanings and origins of sailing and other common sayings, go to PhraseFinder.com.

Some features of the speech of the Puritans, who settled in New England after arriving mostly from East Anglia in England in the early 1600s, can still be heard in the speech of many who live in New England. Some of those features are the pronunciation of a mid back vowel /ɔ/ in words like *caught* and *fought*; the r-dropping after vowels (discussed earlier and in Chapter 4); and the low fronted /a/ of words like *car* and *father*, which gives the dialect what some call a nasality. The early speech of these settlers influenced American speech primarily in vocabulary, including idioms. Many idioms associated with sailing (long prominent in the waters of New England) come from this dialect: *three sheets to the wind* and *take the wind out of your sails,* as well as others including *cool as a cucumber, don't know beans about . . . , wouldn't touch it with a ten-foot pole,* and *happy as a clam*.

RPE 12.2

American "English" Vocabulary

Many languages have left their mark on English as immigrants from non-English-speaking countries have come to the United States over the last two centuries. The Spanish occupied parts of the Southwest and the West, leaving their mark mainly with place-names and more recently with many words for foods (*burrito, tamale, taco, salsa, cilantro, guacamole, enchilada, oregano*). There have also been borrowings from German (*pretzel, streudel, quartz, dachshund, hamburger, kindergarten*), Italian (*confetti, crescendo, gondola, motto, pizza, regatta, lasagna, salami, zucchini, piccolo*), Yiddish (*glitz, bagel, nosh*), Czech (*polka, robot*), Russian (*babushka, borscht, borzoi, samovar, troika, tundra*), Dutch (*boss, bushwhack, cruller, snoop*), French (*suede, trousseau, camouflage, chauffeur, coupon*), Celtic languages (*blarney, brogan, slew, colleen*), Japanese (*jujitsu, kamikaze, karaoke, origami, sukiyaki, tsunami*), Hawaiian (*aloha, hula, lei, ukulele, wiki*), and African languages (*goober, gumbo, safari, impala*). Native American languages had very little influence on English; however, Tables 12.1 and 12.2 show vocabulary items borrowed from various Native American languages.

RPE 12.3

RPE 12.4

Table 12.1	English Words of Native American Origin
Native American	**English**
Abenaki	wigwam
Algonquian	caucus
Algonquian, Abenaki?	skunk
Algonquian, Narragansett?	moose
Algonquian, Powhatan?	muskrat, opossum, hickory
Algonquian, Cree, Ojibwa, or Narragansett	woodchuck
Algonquian, Cree, or Ojibwa	pecan
Carib	potato
Chinook	potlatch
Chippewa	moccasin
Choctaw	bayou
Dakota	teepee
Inuit	kayak
Micmac	toboggan, caribou
Nahuatl	chocolate
Narragansett	powwow, squash, succotash, papoose
Ojibwa	totem, chipmunk
Powhatan	hominy, pone, raccoon, tomahawk
Quechua	jerky

Table 12.2	U.S. State Names and Native American Origins
Alabama	Creek word for 'tribal town'
Alaska	Russian version of Aleutian word, *alakshak*, 'peninsula', 'great lands', or 'land that is not an island'
Arizona	Spanish version of O'odham (formerly called Papago) word for 'little spring place' or perhaps Aztec *arizuma*, 'silver-bearing'
Arkansas, Kansas	Sioux word meaning 'south wind people'
Connecticut	From Mohican or other Algonquian words meaning 'long tidal river'
Illinois	French for Illini or land of Illini, an Algonquian word for 'men' or 'warriors'
Indiana	Not a Native American word but means 'land of the Indians'
Michigan	From Chippewa words *mici gama*, 'great water', after the lake of that name
Minnesota	From Dakota Sioux word meaning 'cloudy water' or 'sky-tinted water' of the Minnesota River
Mississippi	Probably from Chippewa *mici zibi*, 'great river'
Missouri	An Algonquian term meaning 'river of the big canoes'
Nebraska	From Omaha or Otos word meaning 'broad water' or 'flat river', describing the Platte River
North and South Dakota	*Dakota* is Sioux for 'friend' or 'ally'
Ohio	Iroquois word for 'good river'
Oregon	Of unknown origin but may come from an Algonquian word for 'good, beautiful'
Texas	Variant of Caddo word meaning 'friends' or 'allies' and applied to them by the Spanish in eastern Texas; also written *texias*, *tejas*, *teysas*
Utah	From a Navajo word meaning 'upper' or 'higher up' as applied to a Shoshone tribe called Ute

Ethnic Dialects

Thus far, we have discussed dialects that differ primarily due to geographical location. People who live in one place talk differently from people in another place due largely to the settlement patterns of that area—the linguistic characteristics of the people who settled there are the primary influence on that dialect, and the speech of most people in that area shares similar dialect features. However, the next dialect we discuss, African American English, is spoken primarily by Americans of African descent; its unique characteristics were due initially to settlement patterns as well but now persist due to the social isolation of African Americans and the historical discrimination against them. African American English is therefore more accurately defined as an ethnic dialect than as a regional one. We then turn to another ethnic dialect of English, Native American English, which, like African American English, became established as a result of shared cultural identity and social isolation from other groups.

African American English

African American English (AAE), also known as Black English, Ebonics, and African American Vernacular English (AAVE), developed in the Southern states when speakers of dozens of distinct West African languages were brought to the United States as slaves and forced to learn English. Slave masters deliberately separated slaves who spoke the same or related languages so that they couldn't communicate with one another. But since the Africans and the whites on the plantations needed to communicate, a pidgin language, and then likely a creole language, developed. That early African-influenced, English-based creole developed by the slaves greatly influenced today's African American English. This variety was also influenced by and shares characteristics with the speech of Southern white speakers. And in turn, the Southern dialect was influenced by the speech of African Americans; one of the main influences of the slaves' language on the Southern white speakers was via the speech of the white children of the aristocratic slave owners. Their primary caretakers were typically the black nannies, and their playmates were the black children of slaves.

hwæt!

The term *Ebonics* (a blend of *ebony* and *phonics*) was coined by Robert Williams in 1973, but it wasn't until the Oakland Ebonics controversy in 1996 that the term became a household word.

Some of the features of the current African American dialect are thought by some scholars to come directly from West African languages. One of these features is the use of aspect rather than tense: *He sleepin'* (meaning 'right now') versus *He be sleepin'* (meaning 'regularly, all the time'). This kind of aspectual marking is found in many West African languages. Another is the use of *done* as a verbal aspect marker: *He done gone.* (This word may have been borrowed from the West African language Wolof word *doon*.) Linguist Lisa Green (2002: 45–47) provides a detailed analysis of the AAE aspectual markers *be*, *bin*, and *done*, showing that although they appear similar in form to auxiliary verbs in Standard American English, in AAE these words have quite different meanings. See Table 12.3.

RPE 12.5

Some phonological features, such as the voiced interdental /ð/ which becomes /d/ in initial position—*this* as *dis*, *they* as *dey*—may have come from African languages' distinct phonological systems.

Table 12.3	African American English Aspectual Markers		
REGULAR	**EMPHATIC AFFIRMATION**	**NEGATIVE**	
Habitual			
be eating	*do* be eating	don('t) be eating	
'am usually/always eating' or 'usually eats'	'*am* usually/always eating or '*do* usually eat'	'am not usually eating' or 'don't usually eat'	
Remote Past (state or habit)			
bin eating	*have bin* eating	ain('t)/haven't *bin* eating	
'have been eating for a long time'	*have* been eating for a long time'	'hasn't/haven't been eating for a long time'	
Remote Past (completion)			
bin ate	*have bin* ate	ain('t)/haven't *bin* ate	
'ate a long time ago'	'*did* eat a long time ago'	'didn't eat a long time ago'	
Regular Resultant State			
done ate	*have* done ate	ain't done ate	
'has/have already eaten'		'hasn't/haven't already eaten'	

(Adapted from Green 2002: 45–47.)

A large number of West African words came into American English: *tote* ('carry' in Kikonongo), *bug* ('to annoy', perhaps from Kikonongo), *mumbo jumbo* (a West African god's name), *jazz* (perhaps from Arabic *jazib* via Bantu, meaning 'one who allures'), *chigger* (from Wolof or Yoruba), *okra* (from Akan), *yam* (from Twi *anyinam*), *banana* (from Wolof), and others.

The speech of African Americans gradually became more like the speech of their Southern white neighbors through what may have been **decreolization**, the process by which a creole over time takes on more and more features of the language it is in contact with (usually a language with more social prestige, such as the speech of Southern whites, in this case). African American English spread rapidly around the country as black people began moving first to the Northern cities in the 1920s and then to other urban centers across the country. Despite the dispersal of African Americans across the country throughout the twentieth century, most speakers still share enough linguistic features that the dialect is still

decreolization process by which a creole language becomes more like the superstrate language

considered a single dialect. So in this case, it is not geographical isolation but social and ethnic identity shared by the speakers that maintains the language variety.

Did You Know...?

The Ann Arbor Trial

In 1977, a case was brought by the parents of some children of the Martin Luther King Elementary School in Ann Arbor, Michigan, against the Ann Arbor school board. The parents claimed that the school failed to take into account their children's racial, sociocultural, and linguistic background. They argued that a linguistic barrier impeded their children's academic performance because their home language diverged from the school language so much that they were prevented from having equal educational opportunities. Their case depended on whether African American English was shown to be so different from some Standard English that it constituted a barrier to learning. Recordings were played of the children, and a team of linguistic experts testified to the extent to which the language was different, to the history of the dialect as a creole with African origins, which suggested that the differences were the result of racial segregation, an important aspect of the case. The plaintiffs won the case, so the school board had to take steps to help the teachers better instruct the African American–speaking children in their use of academic English. Since this historic case, other districts (e.g., in Los Angeles and Oakland, California) have developed similar programs with excellent results, though they remain controversial.

For more information
Joiner, C. 1979. *The Ann Arbor decision: Memorandum opinion and order and the educational plan.* Washington, DC: Center for Applied Linguistics.
Labov, W. 1982. Objectivity and commitment in linguistic science: The case of the black English trial in Ann Arbor. *Language in Society* 11(2).165–201.

Native American English

The speech of another minority group in the United States, Native Americans, has not been very well represented in the descriptions of English dialects in the United States. Native American English, like African American English, is best defined as an ethnic rather than a regional dialect, influenced by a range of social factors beyond race. The language varieties that fall under the umbrella of Native American English are quite diverse and vary depending on a number of factors. For example, some varieties are influenced by the native languages spoken by the older adults while others are not; some varieties are native languages (first languages), and others are learned as second languages and incorporate features of the native language. Leap (1993) argues for some "pan-Indian English" features that all varieties have in common and which arose from the social segregation of Native Americans from the white community.

One feature shared by varieties of Native American English across North America and Canada is a prosodic rhythm that is syllable timed rather than stress timed as is typical of the prosody of most dialects of English (Coggshall 2007). In a syllable-timed language, each syllable has equal stress, which gives the language what might be called a machine-gun rhythm. In a stress-timed language, some syllables are longer than others, and stressed syllables have approximately the same length (sometimes described as a "Morse code" rhythm). French is a syllable-timed language, and English is a stress-timed one. Though researchers aren't certain why Native American English is syllable timed, it is thought to be an influence from bilingual speakers of many Native American languages west of the Mississippi who speak syllable-timed languages such as Cherokee. That feature of their language has transferred to English. And interestingly, it has transferred now even to monolingual English speakers in tribes all across the country.

Another widely shared feature of Native American English is the absence of the verb *be* in certain structures. Here are some examples from Isletan English, spoken in Isleta, New Mexico, by people for whom Tiwa is the ancestral language (Leap 1993: 70).

> She [ ] a Red Corn people.
> They [ ] just goin' by the old ways, yet.

Leap provides many examples of how variations in different varieties of Native American English can be attributed to a number of factors, including speakers' age, influence of ancestral language, gender, and so on. The syntax and semantics of Navajo, for example, seem to account for the use of the following prepositional phrases in Navajo English. (Examples from Cook & Sharp 1966: 28, cited in Leap 1993: 74.)

> Got to downtown
> At store
> All kinds from birds

Flanigan (1984: 92) makes a similar argument for deletion of prepositions in Lakota English (cited in Leap 1993: 75):

> I color [ ] this. (*with* is the missing preposition)
> We like to ride [ ] horse.
> You wanna go [ ] bathroom?

Flanigan suggests that this variation comes from the influence of French-Indian Creole, a trade language spoken during the eighteenth and early nineteenth centuries in which preposition deletion was used. (Leap suggests that this pattern could also be age related, occurring in the speech of younger speakers, who were the only ones interviewed.)

Lumbee English

Sociolinguists Walt Wolfram and Natalie Schilling-Estes (2006: 206–209) present a fascinating example of an ethnic Native American dialect that seems to have emerged without an ancestral language at all. The Lumbee are the largest Native American group east of the Mississippi River, with more than 55,000 members, more than 45,000 of whom live in Robeson County, North Carolina. The Lumbee make up 40 percent of the county population; African Americans, 25 percent; and European Americans, 35 percent. Each group speaks a different language variety (a result of ethnic segregation). There have been no speakers of the Lumbee heritage language for five generations, and it is unclear if there ever *was* a Lumbee heritage language; the Lumbee likely emerged from an aggregate of Iroquoian, Siouan, and Algonquian tribes, and no records exist of a distinct Lumbee language. Nevertheless, their very strong ethnic identity has led to the emergence of a Lumbee Vernacular English that is most likely based on English sources rather than ancestral ones, with unique innovations.

One unique feature of Lumbee English is the use of the verb *be*. Rather than saying "I have been to the store," Lumbee speakers say "I'm been to the store." They also use "negative *weren't*," or the form *were* rather than *was* in negative sentences: *I weren't there. She weren't there.* Although this use of *weren't* occurs in other varieties of English along the coast of North Carolina, it does not occur in the varieties of African American English or Standard English that surround the Lumbee in Robeson County. The Lumbee also seem to have incorporated a unique use of *be* that occurred in Scots and Scots-Irish English but which became obsolete in those varieties: *I hope it bes a girl. They bes doing all right.* This is a use of *be* distinct from the habitual *be* of AAE speakers in the community, again illustrating Lumbee English innovation.

Chicano English

The United States has been populated by people of Spanish heritage since the fourteenth century. According to the U.S. Census Bureau, as of July 2006, 44.5 million Hispanics were living in the United States, and Spanish speakers make up the majority of current immigrants to the United States (http://www.infoplease.com/spot/hhmcensus1.html).

Hispanic is an umbrella term the government uses to refer to a variety of groups, and *Hispanic English* is a cover term for a wide range of Spanish-influenced varieties of English. Just as the term *Native American*

English fails to capture the diversity of varieties of English spoken by people of Native American heritage, the term *Hispanic English* obscures the diversity of dialects of Spanish-influenced English in the United States. This umbrella term also fails to capture the diverse social, ethnic, and other factors that influence the language of different groups who have in common only an association with Spanish language.

Subcategories of Hispanic English are themselves difficult to define. For example, *Latino English*, the English spoken by people of Latin American descent, is really best described as a continuum that includes monolingual English speakers, bilingual Spanish and English speakers, and speakers with only limited English proficiency. According to Wolfram and Schilling-Estes (2006), no specific dialect features connect all varieties into unified "Latino English." Varieties of Spanish-influenced English are also spoken by people of Puerto Rican and Dominican descent in New York City, by immigrants to the Northwest from Central America, by the Cuban American population in South Florida, particularly Miami, and by Mexican Americans throughout the United States.

hwɑɛꞇ!

The terms *Latino* and *Chicano English* are controversial not just because of the diverse heritage of speakers but also because the labels are in the masculine form, not the feminine *Latina* and *Chicana*.

Although *Hispanic English* is not a single language variety, we can still identify certain varieties based on shared features. For example, Chicano English, spoken throughout the American Southwest in California, Arizona, New Mexico, and Texas, has some distinguishing linguistic features. As we saw with other ethnic dialects, however, we can also identify features specific to certain varieties of Chicano English, features which arise from contact with other dialects, among other factors.

One of the most interesting features of Chicano English is that it does not depend on bilingualism. As Carmen Fought (2003) explains, "You don't need to know Spanish to speak Chicano English." Chicano English is not "learner English," and though it does exhibit many influences of Spanish, it is a fully developed variety of English, the native English of many of its speakers.(http://www.pbs.org/speak/seatosea/americanvarieties/chicano/; see also Santa Ana 1993, Mendoza-Denton 1997, Fought 2003.)

Chicano English is distinctive because of its vowels (based on Spanish pronunciation), particularly the merger of [i] and [ɪ]. So, *beet* and *bit* are both pronounced *beet*, *sheep* and *ship* are pronounced *sheep*, and the *-ing* suffix is pronounced with [i] as well (*talking* is pronounced something like /tɔkin/, for example). Sounds usually described as interdentals (*this, then*) are made with the tongue touching the back of the teeth, rather than between the teeth. Chicano English is also syllable timed, like Spanish, rather than stress timed, like English. The influence of Spanish can also be seen in the use of prepositions: *She's on fifth grade* or *She told the truth for she won't feel guilty*. Chicano English also shares many features with other American English dialects that are not influenced by Spanish, including consonant cluster deletion (*test* is 'tes', and *end* is 'en'), double negation (*She don't know* *nobody*), irregular past tense (*Yesterday he come to visit*), and *was* for *were*: *We was there* (examples from Wolfram & Schilling-Estes 2006: 198–199).

As we saw in the discussion of other ethnic dialects, ethnicity is not the only factor influencing Chicano English. Wolfram and Schilling-Estes report that Chicano English speakers in Southern California have adopted habitual *be* (*The news be showing it too much.*) from African American English. Speakers have also adopted "quotative" *be like* and *be all* (*She's like, "You don't leave the house."* and *He's all, "I'm working for you."*), a characteristic attributed to Valley Girl Talk, shared now by younger speakers across the United States (Wolfram & Schilling-Estes 2006: 199).

RPE 12.6 >

Social Dialects

As you've seen with the examples of African American English, Native American English, and Chicano English, dialects are shaped not only by geography but by other factors as well, including shared cultural identity and isolation from other groups. Sociolinguists have also found that regardless of region, certain generalizations about language variation seem to hold. Urban speakers are more likely than rural speakers to adopt or initiate changes in the language, probably because rural speakers are more conservative and less mobile than urban speakers and because there are fewer of them. In the United States, certain speech patterns appear to be linked with social class. And women, regardless of their social class, appear to generally be more likely than men to conform to prestige norms. Sociolinguists have also found that these generalizations are actually much more complex; in-depth study reveals a much more nuanced picture of factors that shape language variation.

Social Networks

social network
social relationships
that characterize a
group of speakers

Sociolinguists have found that **social network** plays a crucial role in whether speakers maintain a particular language variety or initiate or adopt change. Speakers with denser social networks will be more likely to maintain their language variety even though they are aware that it is stigmatized and lacks social advantage.

hwæt!

The 2010 film *The Social Network*, about the founding of Facebook, illustrates that the term *social network* now has a meaning distinct from the sociolinguistic one.

Patricia Nichols (1983) found that speakers in an African American community in South Carolina used three language varieties: Gullah (an English creole originated by slaves in the region), a variety of African American Vernacular English, and a variety of English considered standard in the region. Nichols found that older women and men used more Gullah forms, and among the younger generation, males used more Gullah features than young women. Gullah use in this community therefore could not be attributed simply to gender differences. Nichols found that, in fact, Gullah use correlated with social networks. Men in the community tend to work in construction and to be in social contact with each other, part of a dense social network. Similarly, older women worked as farm laborers or maids, again as part of a social network. Younger women, however, had begun to take up service jobs that brought them in contact with more Standard English speakers outside of their community, and their social networks became less dense. These young women became the instigators of language change not simply because they were women but because of their social networks.

Communities of Practice

Most sociolinguists agree that no single variable (race, class, gender, ethnicity, etc.) can be held responsible for language variation or change. Rather, it appears that **communities of practice** (Eckert & McConnell-Ginet 1992) are key; people's reasons for coming together and their shared activities, beliefs, and perceptions all seem to play a crucial role in language variation and change. Communities of practice are defined not by external factors (number of members in one's social network, whether a speaker is urban or rural) but rather by speakers' sense of membership and active participation in a group.

> community of practice group whose members come together and share activities, beliefs, and perceptions

Mallinson and Childs's 2005 study of women in a small African American community in Appalachia provides a good example of how a community of practice—rather than (in this case) gender alone—explains language variation. They found that "church ladies" (women who attended church and participated in other activities associated with propriety) spoke a dialect that included more features of Standard American English than the "porch sitters," a group of women in the community whose socializing revolved around conversations on the porch and participation in activities more tied to African American culture (listening to music, for example). The porch sitters tended to use more features of African American English. It is the shared values of each community in this case that plays a role in shaping their language variety.

Social Class and Language Attitudes

Another factor that shapes language variation is speaker attitudes; what one considers good and bad language, attitudes about social class, politics, and religion all influence our linguistic choices. William Labov, who has studied the dialects of New York City for more than forty years, is well known for his analysis of how the insertion or deletion of [r] in certain dialects is tied to speakers' perceptions of social class. In New York City, r-less dialects are stigmatized (post-vocalic [r] is dropped in words such as *four, here*, etc., as we saw earlier), and r-full dialects have social prestige. Labov designed an ingenious study in which he elicited the phrase *fourth floor* from salespeople in three department stores: Saks 5th Avenue (high prestige), Macy's (mid-prestige), and S. Klein (low prestige). Salespeople in Saks pronounced [r]

LINGUISTICS IN THE NEWS

Linguistic Profiling

Is it racist to say that you recognize someone's voice as black, white, Hispanic, or Asian? Is it sexist to say that the voice on the other end of the line is a woman or a man? Well, only if you use that information to discriminate, according to John Baugh, a professor of linguistics and education at Stanford University. What if, for example, you use that information to decide against a loan application or an apartment rental?

Baugh, an African American, has conducted research on linguistic profiling, the racial identification of a speaker based on the way he or she talks, and the use of that information to make legal decisions based entirely on race. Baugh has conducted numerous experiments using himself as a guinea pig, calling landlords in his "white" voice, his "black" voice, and his "Latino" voice. Typically, his black voice gets about half as many

callbacks as his white voice. And if he calls in his white voice and shows up as a black man? You got it. No rental.

The ABC News program *20/20 Downtown* did a show on linguistic profiling (University of Iowa 2002); you can hear some of the voices used in that program and test your ability to identify someone's race based on their voice at the following link: http://www .uiowa.edu/~c103112/lingprof. html. Most people get it correct between 75 and 90 percent of the time.

Baugh's concerns about linguistic profiling are not simply theoretical. In 1999, a Kentucky Supreme Court judge ruled that it was acceptable for a white police officer to identify a suspect as African American based only on the voice heard in an audio transmission from a wired cop. Though Baugh would not disagree that someone can "sound black," using this as concrete

evidence that this identifies the defendant is where Baugh would disagree, and it is what makes such assumptions profiling rather than fact.

If such profiling is admissible as evidence in court, then it sanctions profiling of African Americans or Hispanics who call about apartments, jobs, or loans and never get a callback. The National Fair Housing Act makes it illegal to deny housing to anyone on the basis of race. Baugh has worked with the National Fair Housing Alliance (NFHA), a civil rights organization that works to reverse this trend.

For more information
  Baugh, J. 2000. Racial identification by speech. *American Speech* 75(4). 362–364.
  Johnson, P. 2002. Linguistic profiling. *The Black Commentator* 1. April 5. http://www.blackcom mentator.com/linguistic_profiling. html.

62 percent of the time; in Macy's, 51 percent; and in S. Klein, 20 percent. Labov's study shows that the salespeople adjusted their speech style (unconsciously) depending on perceptions of prestige (Labov 1966).

English Keeps Traveling

English did not stop in North America, of course, but spread to other parts of the globe, including Australia and New Zealand toward the end of the eighteenth century, leading to distinctive varieties of the language there. British colonization in parts of Africa, Asia, and the South Pacific led to unique varieties of English in these places. We discuss next a few of the many dialects of English that are spoken worldwide.

Australian English

The Dutch began to settle in Australia during the first half of the seventeenth century, but the English came not long after that. They began settling prisoners in penal colonies in New South Wales in the late eighteenth century, and this continued until about 1840. The convicts and the personnel assigned to them were primarily from southern England; many convicts spoke Cockney English, a stigmatized dialect spoken in London's East End. Then there was another wave of immigration from Scotland at the end of the eighteenth century and yet more immigration during the Australian gold rush of 1850.

Australian English borrowed little vocabulary from the aboriginal languages (aboriginal people now make up only 1 percent of the population), though a number of place-names are of aboriginal origin (*Illawarra, Coolaburragundy River*). Although Australian English was originally based on British English, meanings have shifted over time: for example, *paddock* means 'field' in Australian English but 'small enclosure for livestock' in British English. Australian English has also borrowed from American English, and the words *truck, elevator,* and *freeway* exist, as do British *petrol, boot* (of a car), and *tap* (Crystal 1988: 240).

Distinctive vowels mark the Australian dialect. One rather noticeable difference, to American ears, is that the mid and low, front, lax vowels are raised and tense in Australian English; so, /æ/ (as in *sat*) and /ɛ/ (as in *set*) sound more like /ɛ/ and /e/, respectively. And what's rather striking about Australian English is that it is remarkably consistent throughout the country. In an area about the same size as the continental United States (though with a much smaller population), there is very little regional variation, and the subtle distinctions that do exist are based on class and educational factors, not region. There are very few morphological or syntactic differences from other standard varieties of English, though Australian English does share many features of British English that are distinct from American, such as the use of singular verbs with collective nouns: *the government hear, the jury decide, the team win.* Words that originated in Australia, too, have been borrowed into English, mostly to refer to the flora and fauna encountered by Europeans for the first time: *koala, kookaburra, kangaroo, wallaby, wombat,* as well as the word *boomerang*, borrowed from an extinct aboriginal language formerly spoken in the New South Wales area.

Caribbean English

Caribbean English, also called Western Atlantic English, is a general term for the English used in the Caribbean archipelago and on the Caribbean coast of Central America (including Nicaragua, Panama, and Guyana). The term *Caribbean English* is problematic because in a narrow sense it can refer to a dialect of English alone, but in a broader sense it covers English and the many

hwæt!

The United States does not have an official language, though many states do. Alongside English, Hawaiian is an official language of Hawaii, and French is an official language of Louisiana.

English-based creoles (discussed more in Chapter 14) spoken in this region. Traditionally, Caribbean creoles have been (incorrectly) classified as dialects of English, but more and more varieties are being recognized as unique languages. Also, there is often a continuum of usage by speakers between some variety of English and a creole. And although English is the official language of the area that is sometimes called the Commonwealth Caribbean, only a small number of the people in each country speak what we might consider regionally accented standard English as a native language. In many Caribbean countries, however, some standard version of (mostly) British English is the official language and is taught in schools.

One syntactic feature shared by many West Atlantic Englishes is the use of *would* and *could* where British or American English uses *will* and *can*: *I could swim* for *I can swim*; *I would do it tomorrow* for *I will do it tomorrow*. Another is the formation of *yes/no* questions with no inversion of auxiliary and subject: *You are coming?* instead of *Are you coming?* A phonological similarity is that the prosody tends to be syllable timed. The study of all of these language varieties is in its infancy (though more work has been done on Jamaican English), and much work remains to be done to properly describe the many features of the languages, dialects, and creoles of the Caribbean.

English in Asia

English is studied widely as a second language in many Asian countries, including Japan, China, and Korea. However, in other countries, English is used much more widely as a second language, and many speakers are quite fluent in English. In Singapore, English is commonly learned as a second language and is one of four official languages. (The others are Mandarin Chinese, Tamil, and Malay.)

In many Asian countries in which English is gaining prominence as a second language, unique linguistic features have developed that are becoming standard and are resulting in new standard varieties. In India, for example, Indian Standard English has gained some acceptance, though it is still a matter of debate whether Indian Standard English or British English is a more appropriate standard variety for use in India. Many features of this variety of English are typical of the kinds of variation that nonnative speakers of English make, but given that they are the primary users of the language, these variations (which would be considered errors by native speakers) have become accepted and are becoming standardized. Linguist David Crystal (1995) provides the following examples of features of Indian English. Mass nouns can be used as count nouns: *Bring in the mails*. Progressive aspect can be used with verbs that traditionally denote states: *I am liking it. I am understanding.* There is variation in the use of prepositions, compared to other varieties of English: *stand at line, pay attention on*.

There is some variation in basic word order: *Who you have come for? My all friends are waiting.* And among the unique words Crystal includes are *cousin-brother* (male cousin), *opticals* (eyeglasses), and *crore* (ten million) (p. 360).

RPE 12.7

Did You Know...?

Aladdin Speaks Standard English?

In 1993, the American Arab Anti-Discrimination Committee (AAADC) complained that *Aladdin* discriminated against Arabs. The 1992 Disney film *Aladdin*, set in a "mythical" Arabian kingdom, depicts the main character, Aladdin, and his love interest, Jasmine, speaking American English with a standard accent, while the villains, all Arab characters too, speak heavily Arab-accented English. Michael Precker wrote, "[The use of dialect in the movie] pounds home the message that people with a foreign accent are bad." Also, after the release of the film in 1992, the AAADC pressured Disney to change the lyrics of the opening song in the film to be less discriminatory. Originally, the lines read, "Oh, I come from a land/From a faraway place/Where the caravan camels roam./Where they cut off your ear/If they don't like your face/It's barbaric, but hey, it's home." For home video release, the fourth and fifth lines were replaced with lyrics that describe the desert climate and geography, though the last line, with *barbaric*, remained.

For more information
Lippi-Green, R. 1997. *English with an accent: Language, ideology, and discrimination in the United States.* New York: Routledge.
Precker, M. 1993. This Aladdin is rated PC. *Dallas Morning News.* October 2.

English in Africa

hwæt!

Zulu is the most common of South Africa's eleven official languages. In 2011, a new Zulu–English dictionary, the first in forty years, was published to facilitate South Africans' ability to participate and compete in our global economy.

English is an official language in many African countries, not because there are many native speakers of English there (except in South Africa, where about 10 percent of the population are native speakers of English) but because of the complex history of most African nations. Due to the many unrelated languages and due to the colonization of most of Africa by European nations throughout the nineteenth and twentieth centuries, English (as well as French and Portuguese) is an official language in many nations, though many of them have from five to ten official languages. As English is used more and more as a second language in Gambia, Liberia, Ghana, Nigeria, Uganda, Swaziland, Zambia, and other countries, it has many unique linguistic features that are becoming standardized in each country and will likely eventually lead to more standardized forms—Nigerian English, Zambian English, and so on.

RPE 12.8

English as a Global Language

Today, fewer than one-fifth of native English speakers live in the British Isles. Just to give you an idea of where English ranks as a language worldwide, let's consider the following figures. The question of which are the world's most widely spoken languages is actually rather difficult to answer with certainty, because estimates of the numbers of people speaking a language vary quite a bit. Estimates of the number of people who speak English, for instance, range from 300 million to more than 450 million. Also, we can count either only native speakers of a language or include those who use the language regularly or even primarily but for whom it is not their native language. Bernard Comrie, in an article for *MS Encarta Encyclopedia* of 1998, estimated the native speakers of languages by population:

Mandarin Chinese	836 million
Hindi	333 million
Spanish	332 million
English	322 million
Bengali	189 million
Arabic	186 million
Russian	170 million
Japanese	125 million
German	98 million
French	72 million

Weber (1997) offers a similar breakdown of the top languages by population but includes native speakers and nonnative speakers who use the language regularly or primarily:

Mandarin Chinese	1.12 billion
English	480 million
Spanish	320 million
Russian	285 million
French	265 million
Hindi/Urdu	250 million
Arabic	221 million
Portuguese	188 million
Bengali	185 million
Japanese	133 million

In Weber's estimates, the totals for Chinese, Arabic, and French include more than one variety.

Another interesting set of numbers (Weber 1997) is the number of countries in which the top-ranking languages are widely spoken. Here, English tops the list: English, 115; French, 35; Arabic, 24; Spanish, 20; Russian, 16; German, 9; Mandarin, 5; Portuguese, 5; Hindi/Urdu, 2; Bengali, 1; and Japanese, 1.

The prominence of English as a worldwide language is due primarily to the expansion of British colonial power in the nineteenth century and to the emergence of the United States as the leading economic power in the twentieth century. Given a different set of historical circumstances, another language could have been as prominent as English is now; and in the future, another language could possibly become more prominent.

Language Variation and Language Discrimination

As we have seen throughout the text, all languages and all dialects have equally systematic phonological, morphological, and syntactic rules; and all languages and all dialects have the same expressive power. Nevertheless, we allow certain dialects and languages more status than others, which has nothing to do with one variety being better linguistically but simply with a society's attitude toward the speakers of that variety. If the speakers are viewed negatively, then the dialect is viewed negatively. If the speakers are viewed positively, then the dialect is viewed positively. Why do we view certain groups in negative ways? It has to do with power: in the United States, the language or dialect of those who are poor, who are nonwhite, who do not speak English, and whom we consider uneducated is less preferred. But when we discriminate against someone based on the way he or she talks, we discriminate against that person.

We make all kinds of assumptions about each other based on the way we dress, the kind of car we drive, where we live, and how we talk. The way we talk, our dialect, is intertwined with our identity. It remains somewhat acceptable in our society to criticize people's speech—their accents, their vocabulary choice, their syntax. We can find numerous examples of people making judgments about others' speech: "[He spoke with a] working-class accent thicker than the sludge at the bottom of a can of baked beans" (Newman 2004). This discrimination is most obvious with two of the most stigmatized American dialects: Southern dialects and African American dialects (there are several subtypes of each variety). Consider the assumptions underlying this sentence from a newspaper. "For 37 years, Charles Kuralt has shown us what network news can be—calm, thoughtful, perceptive. Beneath that deceptive North Carolina drawl, there's a crisp intelligence" (*Daily Guide* 1994). The assumption is that a Southern dialect indicates that someone is likely a bit slow, not very smart; thus, it is surprising if they are smart. Edward Ayers (1996) tells of a Virginian who attended Harvard in the early 1980s and wished he could just put a sign around his neck to stave off the questions that came up, or that he thought people were at least wondering about, when they heard him speak: "Yes, I am from the South. No, I do not know your uncle in Mobile . . . Both of my parents are, in fact, literate . . . No, I do not own slaves. No, I do not want any." The stereotype of Southerners as uneducated, gullible slave owners continues to play out in the media, in books, and in schools. It remains quite prevalent even when recognized as unfair and untrue.

hwæt!

Stephen Colbert, host of the popular "news" show *The Colbert Report*, changed his Southern accent (he's from Charleston, South Carolina). Why? Because he didn't want to appear stupid?

This kind of linguistic discrimination is not easy to fix because it is connected to so many complex social issues. However, an important first step, at least, is to recognize where our attitudes about language variation and language change come from and then to contextualize them within our current culture.

RPE   12.9 >

German Goes from Good to Bad

Immigrant groups in the United States have met with various degrees of tolerance with respect to maintenance of their languages and cultures. Such tolerance depends on changing attitudes toward the people and is influenced by political and social events. For example, in the eighteenth and nineteenth centuries, German was the primary language of instruction in many schools. Language policy expert James Crawford (1996) notes that in 1839, Ohio became the first state to pass a law allowing German–English instruction when it was requested by parents. But even without authorization, many public schools throughout the East used the languages of the immigrant communities, including Czech, Danish, Dutch, Italian, Norwegian, Polish, and Swedish. However, when attitudes toward speakers of a language change, so do the policies governing that language. During World War I, public use of German was banned in many communities and even in some states. Once the most prestigious modern language, studied by one-fourth of all U.S. high school students in 1915, German was banned in most schools in the country. Historian Carl Wittke (1936) documented the burning of German textbooks sponsored by some schools.

For more information

Crawford, J. March 1996. Anatomy of the English-Only movement. *Conference on Language Legislation and Linguistic Rights.* University of Illinois at Urbana-Champaign. http://ourworld.compuserve.com/homepages/jWCRAWFORD/anatomy.htm

   Wittke, C. 1936. *German-Americans and the World War: With special emphasis on Ohio's German-language press.* Columbus: Ohio State Archaeological and Historical Society.

Standard English and "General American"

The term *Standard English* is often defined as a preferred variety of English that we all take for granted. As we saw in Chapter 11, the idea that one language variety is better than another has its roots in seventeenth-century England and is our legacy today. Given what we now know about language variation and change, let's examine the notion of Standard English in more detail.

   We cannot deny the role of a standard language. Certainly, having some standard variety of English is important in teaching the language, especially to nonnative speakers of English. And certainly, having a standard written form of the language is important, too—communication problems would inevitably increase if we allowed words to be spelled in different ways and abandoned punctuation rules. (However, such rules are typically abandoned in texting, some e-mail, chat rooms, etc., so, arguably, communication problems do not inevitably result, especially for those who are part of the group.)

We have mentioned throughout the text the pull of a standard language variety, and we will discuss this more in Chapter 13. However, we have certainly seen that no single language variety is *the* standard. There are various regional standards within the United States; what most people say in one part of the country can vary from what most people say in another part of the country. In Chapter 7 on syntax, for example, we mentioned that using more than one modal verb is quite standard in many Southern varieties: *I might should go to the store.* And the preferred words (lexical choices) vary across dialects: *bag/sack, wait on line/wait in line, knapsack/backpack,* and so on. We have also seen throughout the text, however, that other linguistic features are quite stigmatized outside the community that uses them—*ain't,* the use of double negatives (*I don't have none*), the use of certain past-tense and past-participial verb forms (*I seen him. She hasn't came in yet*), for example. We have also seen that all such variations are linguistically sound—they are patterned and systematic. However, they are stigmatized outside the community because of the attitudes toward the people who speak them; stigmatized dialects and dialect features are spoken only by stigmatized groups.

Some propose that we can identify a language variety called **General American**, a variety of English that is not associated with a particular city or region but rather is defined by what it *doesn't* include, namely, stigmatized features or obvious regionalisms. This variety is fairly phonologically flexible, too, and not identified with a particular accent. *R*-full dialects are typically perceived as more neutrally American than *r*-less dialects, however. General American, like Standard English, is still an idealization, and what we consider standard or mainstream is perhaps more accurately characterized as speech that one perceives as including few, if any, stigmatized forms.

General American an idealized variety of English that speakers perceive as neutral, with few stigmatized forms or regionalisms

RPE 12.10 ⟩

Dialect Pride

Attitudes about nonstandard dialects are definitely not always negative; in fact, dialect pride is on the increase. As public awareness of dialect discrimination increases and as linguists have taken note of the importance of the disappearance of languages and dialects (discussed more in Chapter 14), we see efforts to reclaim dialects whose numbers are declining. For example, the North Carolina Language and Life Project (NCLLP) (http://www.ncsu.edu/linguistics/ncllp/), established by Walt Wolfram of North Carolina State University, has the following aims:

- To gather basic research information about language varieties in order to understand the nature of language variation and change.
- To document language varieties in North Carolina and beyond as they reflect varied cultural traditions.

Language  Alive!

Urban Dictionary

The Urban Dictionary, a web-based dictionary of slang words and phrases, has at the top of its page: "The slang dictionary you wrote. Define your world." It was started by Aaron Peckham at California Polytechnic Institute in San Luis Obispo in 1999. Anyone can submit words or phrases and their definitions, which are then edited by volunteers and rated by users. Submissions come from all over the English-speaking world. As of February 2011, 5,621,495 definitions have been submitted since the site's founding in 1999, and the number is constantly updated. Go to http://www .urbandictionary.com and add your own, if you haven't already!

- To provide information about language differences for public and educational interests.
- To use research material for the improvement of educational programs about language and culture.

According to the NCLLP's website, some results of this work include the following:

- A growing collection of more than 1,500 recorded sociolinguistic interviews
- The development of new technologies for language analysis and preservation
- The establishment of an extensive program of community-based sociolinguistic research that includes linguistic descriptions of Outer Banks English, African American English, Southern Appalachian English, Native American English, and Hispanic English
- The production of local, statewide, and national TV documentaries on language variation in North Carolina and on particular dialects that include Outer Bank English, Appalachian English, Lumbee English, and Hispanic English
- The production of CD collections of local narratives and published trade books on particular varieties of English
- The construction of museum exhibits for local communities and for the citizens of and visitors to North Carolina
- The development of a dialect awareness curriculum for middle school students in social studies and language arts throughout the state

Such programs, resulting in increased awareness of the importance of diverse dialects, will lead to more such programs in other parts of the country.

The Future of English Dialects

In the 1950s, when people were exposed to mass media via radio and television and began to hear the somewhat standard broadcast English, it was thought that that would be the end of English dialects. Interestingly, that has not been the case; there are just as many dialect distinctions as before the advent of radio and television, and perhaps even more.

And though dialects are alive and well, sometimes we do adapt our speech to be like that of those around us, even if it is not the way we typically speak. You may have experienced social pressure to change your language. This can happen when, say, you modify your speech to match that of your peers: they say /eprɪkat/ though you grew up saying /æprɪkat/, but you change the way you say it when you're with them. Why do you do this? Because the point of language is communication. Variation in language can distract from communication, so we sometimes avoid linguistic distractors and instead modify our speech to conform to those around us.

Throughout this book, we have seen ways in which our attitudes about language are not linguistically determined but socially determined. That is, there is nothing linguistically better or worse about any linguistic form or construction, but the social positions of various groups in our society mean that their language varieties share that same social position. It's all about power.

Accent on *Dialect Coaches*

Have you seen these films: *Snatch* starring Brad Pitt, *Sophie's Choice* starring Meryl Streep, *The Deer hunter* with Meryl Streep, and *The Lord of the Rings*? How did Brad Pitt, who was raised in Missouri, learn the dialect of Irish traveler Mickey O'Neil? How did accent chameleon Meryl Streep so convincingly portray Sophie, a Polish Jew escaping the Nazis, and Linda, from a working-class family in western Pennsylvania? And who taught all those *Lord of the Rings* actors to speak in Middle-Earth accents? The photo shows dialect coach Andrew Jack, who coached Elijah Wood in *The Lord of the Rings*.

Though we may take them for granted, accents and dialects in film and on stage are as important in shaping a character as costumes, sets, and lighting. And the wrong

Courtesy of Andrew Jack

accent or dialect can be distracting—it's very important to get it right. And that's the job of the dialect coach.

(continued)

Dialect coaches were originally dialogue coaches, experts who helped actors make the transition from silent movies to "talkies." Today, they are everything from dialogue coaches (how to learn and deliver your lines) to voice teachers (working on breath, sound, tone) to experts on accent and dialect. Their training varies as much as their jobs, but most are trained as actors, some have professional training in speech and voice, and much of their training is also on the job.

Not all dialect coaches confine their work to training actors. Sam Chwat, "speech therapist to the stars," specializes in helping clients (actors, but also many corporate clients) "eliminate" their accents and learn Standard American English. Chwat defines SAE as an accent and, more specifically, "'the accent without an accent,' . . . which does not distract the listener with, or reveal any, regionalisms. It comprises forty-four vowels and consonants, many of which do not occur in non-English languages."

Sam Chwat's Speech Center employs state-licensed speech–language therapists with at minimum a master's degree in speech–language pathology. The center is responsible for teaching Julia Roberts, from Smyrna, Georgia, and Andie McDowell, from Gaffney, South Carolina, to eliminate their Southern accents.

Dialect coaches are aware that language changes, and though many teach American Theatre Standard (ATS), there is some controversy over whether this variety accurately reflects mainstream American English. A similar debate arises in Britain with Received Pronunciation (RP), long assumed to be the standard accent for British English (and spoken by such actors as Dame Judi Dench and Jeremy Irons). The status of RP is waning, and regional accents are considered more and more standard.

For more information

Chwat, S. 2008. Sam Chwat Speech Center. http://www.samchwatspeechcenter .com. (23 October 2008).

Eckert, G. 2002. Bay Area dialect coaches. *Theater Bay Area.* August. http://www/ theatrebayarea.org/mag/article.jsp; jsessionid=1967A2040400FD151A51 FA8810F550F9D?thispage=archives. jsp&id=36&hi=1.

Goldes, J. 2007. Joel Goldes: The dialect coach. http://www.thedialectcoach .com/content.asp?contentid=530 (23 October 2008).

Jack, A. 2008. Andrew Jack: International dialogue coach: Accent and dialect. http://www.andrewjack.com.

Summary

In this chapter, we've explored how language is changing right before our eyes (and ears); we've learned that wherever there are speech communities, there are different language varieties. Different varieties of a single language, or dialect, arise for a number of different reasons; in the United States, dialects of British English imported to the eastern seaboard shifted and changed to become uniquely American. English traveled across the country with European settlers, and regional dialects of American English emerged— dialects that are shifting and changing all the time. We've also seen that dialects can be influenced by a number of factors other than geography.

Race, ethnicity, social networks, communities in which we live, work, and play—these all shape our language and our language identity. Our attitudes about language and dialect lead to language variation and also to language discrimination. Judgments about language are really judgments about the people who speak them, and knowing more about the natural inevitability of language change and variation may lead to less stereotypical attitudes about good and bad language, what is standard or not, and may also lead us to take a livelier interest in the richness and diversity of language around us.

Sources and Resources

Ayers, E. 1996. What we talk about when we talk about the South. In E. Ayers et al. (eds.), In E. Ayers et al. (eds.), *All over the map: Rethinking American regions*. Baltimore, MD: Johns Hopkins University Press.

Baugh, J. 2000. Racial identification by speech. *American Speech* 75(4). 362–364.

Cassidy, F. (ed.). 1985. *The dictionary of American regional English*. Cambridge, MA: Belknap Press.

Chwat, S. 2008. Sam Chwat Speech Center. http://www.samchwatspeechcenter.com. (23 October 2008).

Coggshall, E. October 2007. The prosodic rhythm of two varieties of Native American English. *New Ways of Analyzing Variation (NWAV)* 36. Philadelphia, PA.

Cook, M. & M. Sharp. 1966. Problems of Navajo speakers in learning English. *Language Learning* 16. 21–29.

Crawford, J. March 1996. Anatomy of the English-Only movement. Conference on Language Legislation and Linguistic Rights, University of Illinois at Urbana-Champaign. http://ourworld.compuserve.com/homepages/jWCRAWFORD/anatomy.htm

Crystal, D. 1988. *The English language*. New York: Penguin Books.

Crystal, D. 1995. *The Cambridge encyclopedia of the English language*. Cambridge, UK: Cambridge University Press.

Daily Guide. 1994. *Lansing State Journal*, April 3, 1. Cited in Lippi-Green, 210.

Eckert, G. 2002. Bay Area dialect coaches. *Theater Bay Area*. August. http://www/theatrebayarea.org/mag/article.jsp;jsessionid=1967A2040400FD151A51FA8810F550F9D?thispage=archives.jsp&id=36&hi=1

Eckert, P. & S. McConnell-Ginet. 1992. Think practically and look locally: Language and gender as community-based practice. *Annual Review of Anthropology* 21. 461–490.

Flanigan, B. 1984. Bilingual education for Native Americans: The argument from studies of variational English. In J. Handscome (ed.), *On TESOL '83*, 81–93. Washington, DC: TESOL.

Fought, C. 2003. *Chicano English in context*. New York: Palgrave/MacMillan.

Fought, C. 2005. Interview: Do you speak American? Talking with Mi Gente. Public Broadcasting System (PBS). http://www.pbs.org/speak/seatosea/american varieties/chicano/

Goldes, J. 2007. Joel Goldes: The dialect coach. www.thedialectcoach.com/content.asp?contentid=530. (23 October 2008).

Green, L. 2002. *African American English: A linguistic introduction*. Cambridge, UK: Cambridge University Press.

Holm, J. 1994. English in the Caribbean. In R. Burchfield (ed.), *The Cambridge history of the English language* 5, 328–381. Cambridge, UK: Cambridge University Press.

Honda, M. et al. 2009. On promoting linguistics literacy: Bringing language science to the English classroom. In K. Denham & A. Lobeck (eds.), *Linguistics at school: Language awareness in primary and secondary education*. Cambridge, UK: Cambridge University Press.

Jack, A. 2008. Andrew Jack: International dialogue coach: Accent and dialect. http://www
.andrewjack.com

Johnson, P. 2002. Linguistic profiling. *The Black Commentator* 1. April 5. http://www
.blackcommentator.com/linguistic_profiling.html

Joiner, C. 1979. *The Ann Arbor decision: Memorandum opinion and order and the educational
plan.* Washington, DC: Center for Applied Linguistics.

Kurath, H. 1949. *A word geography of the Eastern United States.* Ann Arbor: University of
Michigan Press.

Labov, W. 1966. *The social stratification of English in New York City.* Washington, DC: Center
for Applied Linguistics.

Labov, W. 1982. Objectivity and commitment in linguistic science: The case of the black
English trial in Ann Arbor. *Language in Society* 11(2). 165–201.

Labov, W., S. Ash & C. Boberg. 2006. *The atlas of North American English.* New York: Mouton
de Gruyter.

Lawton, D. 1984. English in the Caribbean. In R. Bailey & M. Görlach (eds.), *English as a
world language,* 251–280. Cambridge, UK: Cambridge University Press.

Leap, W. 1993. *American Indian English.* Salt Lake City: University of Utah Press.

Lippi-Green, R. 1997. *English with an accent: Language, ideology, and discrimination in the
United States.* New York: Routledge.

Mallinson, C. & B. Childs. 2005. Communities of practice in sociolinguistic description:
African American women's language in Appalachia. *Penn Working Papers in Linguistics*
10(2). Philadelphia: University of Pennsylvania.

McArthur, T. 1998. Caribbean English. *Concise Oxford companion to the English language.*
Oxford, UK: Oxford University Press.

Mendoza-Denton, N. 1997. *Chicana/Mexicana identity and linguistic variation: An ethnographic
and sociolinguistic study of gang affiliation in an urban high school.* Palo Alto, CA: Stanford
University dissertation.

Newman, A. 2004. Outsourcing comes to summer camp. *The New York Times.* July 9. D1, 5.

Nichols, P. 1983. Linguistic options and choices for black women in the rural South. In B.
Thorne et al. (eds.), *Language, gender, and society,* 54–68. Rowley, MA: Newbury House.

North Carolina Language and Life Project (NCLLP). North Carolina State University
Linguistics Program. http://www.ncsu.edu/linguistics/ncllp/. (23 October 2008).

Peckham, A. 1999. *The urban dictionary.* http://www.urbandictionary.com. (23 October 2008).

Precker, M. 1993. This Aladdin is rated PC. *Dallas Morning News.* October 2.

Preston, D. 1986. Five visions of America. *Language in Society* 15(2). 221–240.

Preston, D. 1989. Standard English spoken here: The geographical loci of linguistic norms.
In U. Ammon (ed.), *Status and function of languages and language varieties,* 324–354.
Berlin: Walter de Gruyter.

Santa Ana, O. 1993. Chicano English and the Chicano language setting. *Hispanic Journal of
Behavioral Sciences* 15(1). 1–35.

Svartvik, J. & G. Leech. 2006. *English: One tongue, many voices.* New York: Palgrave Macmillan.

University of Iowa. 2002. *103:112 Phonological analysis.* http://www.uiowa.edu/~c103112/
lingprof.html. (13 February 2002).

U.S. Census Bureau. 2008. Hispanic Americans by the numbers. *Infoplease.* http://www
.infoplease.com/spot/hhmcensus1.html. (3 June 2011).

Weber, G. 1997, updated 2008. Top languages: The world's 10 most influential languages.
In *Language Today,* 2. http://www.andaman.org/BOOK/reprints/weber/rep-weber.htm.

Wittke, C. 1936. *German-Americans and the World War: With special emphasis on Ohio's
German-language press.* Columbus: Ohio State Archaeological and Historical Society.

Wolfram, W. et al. 1999. *Dialects in schools and communities.* Mahwah, NJ: Lawrence
Erlbaum.

Wolfram, W. & N. Schilling-Estes. 2006. *American English,* 2nd edn. Malden, MA: Blackwell.

Review, Practice, and Explore

RPE 12.1 › British versus American English

Conduct some research to find at least five ways in which British English and American English differ. Give examples from vocabulary, pronunciation, and syntax.

RPE 12.2 › Explore a Dialect

Research an American dialect of your choice. Provide at least five examples of vocabulary, pronunciation, and syntax unique to this dialect. Trace its history; is it a regional, social, or ethnic dialect, or something else entirely? Who speaks this dialect and where? What factors led the variety to develop its unique characteristics? Among the many dialects you may want to consider are General Southern, Midland, Upper Midwest, West, Pacific Northwest, and Canadian.

RPE 12.3 › Recent Borrowings

Look up the etymologies of at least six of the following words in a good etymological diction-ary (*The Online Etymological Dictionary*, *The Oxford English Dictionary*), and determine from what language the word was borrowed, when it was borrowed, and whether the meaning has changed since the borrowing. Where possible, determine what historical, political, social, and/or geographical factors led to the borrowing of the word. Also note spelling or pronunciation differences from the original language.

   slalom, caravan, jitters, gingham, ketchup, chess, shampoo, icon, klutz, bum, studio, spool, waffle, mosquito, bigot

RPE 12.4 › Etymologies of Place-Names

Choose five place-names in your state and research their origins, including the language of ori-gin and the meaning.

RPE 12.5 › The Ebonics Controversy

What was the 1996–1997 Ebonics controversy, and who was involved? What was the Oakland school board's intent, and what factors contributed to the media frenzy? Do you think this controversy could have been avoided? How would knowledge of language variation have played a role?

RPE 12.6 › Research an Ethnic Dialect

Ethnic dialects arise for a variety of reasons, chief among them social isolation and cultural identity. Research an ethnic dialect of your choice. Where did the dialect originate and why? What are some of its grammatical features? Why would you say this is an *ethnic* dialect rather than a regional one? (Some ideas: Pacheco, Cajun, New York Jewish.)

RPE 12.7 > **Language Stereotypes on Television**

TV cartoons are a good place to look for the use of dialect as a way to build character. Watch some cartoons (*Looney Tunes*, *South Park*, *The Simpsons*), and pay attention to the use of language. Consider who speaks foreign-accented English, who speaks a nonstandard American dialect, who speaks British English, and so forth. Is the use of language appropriate? Is it fair? Is it discriminatory? Is it simply a shortcut to typify a character so that the audience can make assumptions? Compare cartoons aimed at children and adults. Provide an overview of your research and your reflections on it.

RPE 12.8 > **Global Varieties of English**

Research a global variety of English (spoken in a region other than the United States, Canada, or the United Kingdom). What is its history, and what are some unique features of the variety? Choose from the varieties discussed in the chapter, and go into more depth (East Indian English, Caribbean English, South African English, Singapore English) or branch out; what about Barbadian English or Jamaican English? There are many others to choose from.

RPE 12.9 > **Is Your English "Pleasant"?**

Do the exercise on language attitudes found at http://www.pbs.org/speak/speech/mapping/map.html.

Linguist Dennis Preston researches people's attitudes toward dialects of American English. In this exercise, you'll determine whether various pronunciations from around the world are "correct" or "pleasant." Summarize your reactions to the exercise and to the other information linked there.

RPE 12.10 > **Your Version of General American?**

Here are some sentences from different American English dialects. Which are familiar to you? Do you think these are features of General American? If not, why not? Compare your answers with your classmates' answers. Do you all agree on what is considered General American? If you don't, can you explain why?

a. I'm really liking the new house.

b. It's fixin' to rain.

c. So she's like "when will we get there?"

d. They answered wrong.

e. I wonder who all will be there.

f. The bullet went clean through the door.

g. Y'all better get some sleep.

h. Youse better get some sleep.

i. I like those ones over there.

Representing Language: The Written Word

Key Concepts

- Only 25 percent of the world's languages have written forms.
- There are a great many differences between written and spoken language.
- Humans have created writing systems based on phonemes, on syllables, and on meaning.
- The English spelling system is only partially phonetic; its nonphonetic features reflect a great deal about the history of the language.
- The spelling conventions of English influence language acquisition in our highly literate society.
- Written language plays a large role in the standardization of language.

Did You Know . . . ?

Hieroglyphics
Cuneiform
Autocorrect Isn't Always
The Oxford English Dictionary

Language Alive! Ye Olde Confusion
Smileys
Are You Ever Alright?

Linguistics in the News The CSIs of Language

Accent on Copy Editors

A Brief History of Writing
  Logograms and Phonograms
  Alphabets

The Development of English Spelling
  Old English Writing and
    Spelling
  Middle English Spelling
  Toward Modern English
    Spelling
  Attempts at Spelling Reform

The Development of English Punctuation
  Early Punctuation
  Modern Punctuation
  Punctuation "Errors"

Writing Rules, Standardization, and Authority
  The Power of the Dictionary
  Writing Registers and Forms
  Electronic English
  Written Standards in Flux
  The Effects of Print

Summary

Sources and Resources

Review, Practice, and Explore

> *Words, once they are printed, have a life of their own.*
>
> —CAROL BURNETT

Think about your world without printed words. No signs, libraries, e-mail, research papers to write; no movie tickets, road maps, recipes, textbooks, birth certificates, words on cereal boxes. Even names for things are based on writing: *S-curve, T-shirt, A-list*. In Western culture, print is everywhere. In fact, print is so pervasive in our lives that you might not even think of oral language and written language as different. One big difference, however, is that oral (or signed) language comes without instruction—it's part of what makes us human, as we've discussed throughout this book, but writing is a human invention. Linguists have estimated that only 25 percent of the world's languages have written forms.

We begin our discussion of the graphic representation of language with a look at a variety of writing systems that humans have created over time, including systems based on phonemes, systems based on syllables, and ideographic systems based on meaning, among others. Also, we will explore the English spelling system in some detail to see what it tells us about the history of the language and how spelling influences language acquisition in a highly literate society. We will then discuss some of the differences between writing and speech and how writing is similar to but also distinct from speech. Throughout the chapter, we will reflect on the issue of authority in language and the role of writing in language standardization.

A Brief History of Writing

When linguists talk about and study language, they typically mean the study of spoken language. This is the form of language that emerges naturally; as we've seen, children acquire spoken (or signed) language without instruction simply by being exposed to it. Writing and reading, however, must be taught. From this perspective, writing is a secondary form of language based on the spoken version.

Writing is a fairly recent invention. We really don't know when people started speaking (estimates range from somewhere between 50,000 and 100,000 years ago; we will return to this question in the next chapter), but we have a fairly good idea of when people started making conventionalized marking on stone, wood, clay, metal, parchment, and paper to symbolize their speech. The invention of the first writing system is believed to have been around the fourth millennium BCE.

This pictogram clearly warns of the danger of crushing fingers in the gears.

Clipart.com

logogram/ logograph symbol that represents a word or a morpheme

pictogram pictures or symbols that represent an object or idea

ideogram symbol that represents an idea

phonogram symbol based on sound

syllabary system of writing based on syllable sounds

Logograms and Phonograms

The two broad systems of writing languages are logographic and phonographic. A **logogram**, or **logograph**, is a symbol that represents a word or a morpheme. Two subtypes of logographic systems, for which there is some degree of overlap, are *ideograms* and *pictograms*. **Pictograms** are pictures or symbols that represent an object or idea and may communicate a message, but they are not direct representations of speech. The pictogram to the left depicts the result of fingers getting caught in some gears in a very direct way (ouch!).

Ideograms (from Greek *idea* 'idea' and *grapho* 'to write') are symbols that communicate or represent an idea, though they are not necessarily pictures of actual objects or events. When a picture becomes conventionalized, it may be an ideogram, like the peace sign. Pictograms and ideograms are often used in public places where people speak many languages.

Pictograms and ideograms are not complete writing systems for any language because they are unable to represent all aspects of a language. Rather, all writing systems that fully represent the language are partly or completely phonemic; this makes sense since writing systems represent language, and (spoken) language is composed of sounds. Some systems, however, also have characters based on meaning rather than sound.

As its name suggests, a **phonogram** is a symbol based on sound rather than meaning. Phonographic systems include **syllabaries**, based on syllables,

Did You Know...?

Hieroglyphics

The key to deciphering Egyptian hieroglyphics came in 1799 with the discovery of the Rosetta Stone by French soldiers (near the city of Rosetta near the Nile River). The stone had three languages on it. One was Greek, which they could read, and the other two were hieroglyphic forms of Egyptian languages. After twenty years of trying to break the code, French Egyptologist Jean-François Champollion, building on work by Briton Thomas Young, discovered that the characters stood for sounds, making it a phonographic system rather than a purely logographic one as had been assumed.

For more information
The British Museum. http://www.britishmuseum.org/search_results.aspx?search Text=hieroglyphics

alphabet system of writing based on individual sounds

and **alphabets,** based on sounds. Such systems do not represent meaning directly but instead represent the sounds in the spoken language. Some languages that use syllabaries are Cherokee (developed by Sequoyah), Japanese, Ojibwe, Blackfoot, Cree, and Mende. A lot of other languages use an alphabetic system, and we take a look at a variety of related alphabetic systems here.

An important syllabary is that developed by Sequoyah, a Cherokee chief, in the early part of the nineteenth century. After Sequoyah developed the syllabary, he spent the rest of his life teaching people to read and write in the language. In 1828, the first issue of the newspaper *Tsa la gi Tsu lehisanunhi*, meaning 'Cherokee Phoenix', was printed in both Cherokee and English. It was the first Indian newspaper ever published.

RPE 13.1

Did You Know...?

Cuneiform

Cuneiform (from Latin *cuneus*, meaning 'wedge', as the symbols were wedge-shaped) is one of the earliest known examples of writing, created by the Sumerians maybe as long ago as 3400 BCE. It began as a pictographic system and gradually became more abstract. It was used throughout Mesopotamia for thousands of years by the Akkadians, the Elamites, the Assyrians, and the Hittites to write their own languages; it evolved to become more like an alphabet or a syllabary in some systems while retaining logographic characteristics in most systems. Cuneiform was also used to write Aramaic (an endangered Semitic language formerly widespread in the Middle East and believed to be the language that Jesus spoke) but was later replaced by the Aramaic alphabet.

Alphabets

In alphabetic systems, each symbol represents a sound. Most scholars believe that the first writing system was the Sumerian script, a cuneiform which formed the basis of all alphabetic writing. Sumerian script was gradually replaced by the Phoenician alphabet, a consonantal system, or *abjad*. Semitic writing today (for example, the Arabic and Hebrew writing systems) still represent consonant sounds only (for the most part). The Phoenician system had certain consonantal sounds not found in other languages, and when Greeks adopted the system, these symbols were used to represent vowels. The Phoenician system is therefore the ancestor of both Semitic writing systems (Arabic and Hebrew) and the Greek system, which in turn is the ancestor of the Latin, Cyrillic, and Coptic systems.

The Greeks even used the Semitic names of the symbols, which they adapted to Greek phonetic patterns; so *aleph* 'ox' and *beth*

hwæt!

Nushu 'woman's writing,' is a Chinese writing system developed and used exclusively by women in a remote corner of Hunan province. The only known system of its kind, it is no longer in use since the last woman proficient in the system died in 2004.

'house' became *alpha* and *beta* because words ending in consonants (other than *n*, *r*, and *s*) do not follow Greek syllable structure, which is primarily consonant–vowel (CV) syllables. The forms of the Greek letters changed somewhat over time, and the Romans introduced other changes when they borrowed the Greek alphabet to write Latin.

hwæt!

Serbian, Croatian, Bosnian, and Montenegrin are all really based on the same language, which used to be referred to as Serbo-Croatian, the official language of the former Yugoslavia.

The Slavic Russians, Bulgarians, and Serbs were Christianized by the Eastern Greek Orthodox Church, whose members spoke Greek. These Slavic groups borrowed their alphabet, called Cyrillic, from Greek in the ninth century. Those Slavs whose Christianity stems from Rome—the Poles, the Czechs, the Slovaks, the Croats, and the Slovenians—use the Roman alphabet. Other alphabetic systems include Arabic and the Brahmi system of scripts, the ancestor of those systems of Southeast Asia as well as the ancestor of the Arabic numerals now used all over the world.

Chinese, though often described as logographic, uses a combination of systems. Every Chinese word originally had a symbol based not on the phonetic structure of the word but on its meaning. The symbol 山 is the Chinese character for *mountain*. Though you can perhaps see the resemblance between the symbol and an actual mountain, it would be difficult to determine the meaning from the character.

RPE 13.2 ⟩

The Development of English Spelling

We discuss here some of the kinds of changes in the written language that have taken place in English over the last 1,300 years or so. We will explore the changes through the three traditional historical periods of the language: Old English, Middle English, and Early Modern English. The changes in the written language have slowed since the written language has become more standardized, but change is still taking place. A host of reasons exist for the seemingly chaotic spelling system of English. When you understand the history of writing and spelling, the current spelling system, with all its seeming idiosyncrasies, makes a great deal more sense.

Old English Writing and Spelling

In the early Middle Ages, various script styles developed in lands that had been provinces of the Roman Empire. The Romans invaded the Celtic peoples living in what later became the British Isles in the first century BCE and stayed approximately until the fifth century BCE. The Romans introduced Latin writing and therefore the Latin alphabet; both all but disappeared when the Romans left. As you know from Chapter 11 on the history of English, Germanic invaders arrived in the late fifth century after the Romans had departed. These Germanic invaders were largely illiterate, and any writing

Language Alive!

Ye Olde Confusion

The shape of the thorn, þ, grew less and less distinctive, with the letter losing the top part and therefore looking more like the wynn, <p>, which had fallen out of use by about 1300 (perhaps due to the influence of French, which did not use that letter); instead, <w> was used. The handwritten thorn, then, became fairly indistinguishable from the letter <y>, and so *the* and *ye*, for example, began to look very much alike. Sometimes scribes would place a dot over the *y* to distinguish it from the thorn, but when they didn't, these symbols were sometimes confused. So all those quaint shops whose names begin with "Ye Olde" are based on a mixup!

was rare, but when they did write their language (as it was at that time, both in the British Isles and back on the continent), they used a system clearly related to and derived from the Latin alphabet. This alphabet, called the *futhorc* or *futhark* (see the "Did You Know . . . ?" box on page 377), consisted originally of twenty-four letters; between five and nine letters were added during the early Old English period. The letters are angular, likely due to the fact that they were made by cutting or scratching into wood or stone.

Several of the runic letters were used throughout the Old English period: the æ, called *ash*; the ð, called *eth*; the þ, called *thorn*; the p, called *wynn*; and the ʒ, called *yogh*.

In Old English, more words were spelled as they were pronounced than in Present-Day English. For example, the initial "silent" letters in words now spelled with <kn>, <gn>, and <wr> were all pronounced in Old English (*cneow*, 'knee', *gnæt* 'gnat', and *wrœcca* 'wretch'). Both vowels were pronounced in combinations such as <eo> (*feohtan* 'fight') and <ea> (*eald* 'old'). Old English also had variable spellings: the letter <c> was pronounced [k] before back vowels (*carfulnes* 'anxiety') but as [č] before front vowels (*cild* 'child'). Old English books were written on vellum, or sheets of carefully prepared calfskin. Most of the letter forms were different from their current forms. An Old English text called *Sermo Lupi ad Anglos* (*The Sermon of the Wolf to the English*), written about 1050, toward the end of the Old English period, can be viewed at Melissa Bernstein Ser's site: http://english3.fsu.edu/~wulfstan/noframes.html. (Though the title is Latin, still regarded as a "superior" language by many writers, the work is written in Old English.) You can also take a look at a great many Old English texts at

"Knot Just Yarn"

Jackie Ricciardi/The Augusta Chronicle

RPE 13.3 > the Labyrinth Library collection from Georgetown University: http://www8
.georgetown.edu/departments/medieval/labyrinth/library/oe/oe.html.

Middle English Spelling

The Norman Conquest of England in 1066 brought influence from French
(and Latin) to the language. A great many words were added from French
(as discussed in Chapter 11), and French-speaking scribes introduced a
number of spelling changes into English. For example, the French letters
<j> and <v> were introduced into English, alternating with <i> and
<u>; so, for example, *time* could show up spelled as *tijm* or *tiim*, and *judge*
could be *iuge* or *juge*. Also, the letters <q> and <z> were borrowed from
French, so the Old English letter combination <cw> gave way to <qu>
(*cwen* became *quene* 'queen'). Now, it would be much handier for kids learning to spell to have that old <cw> back! There was a greater tendency
to match spelling to sound; for example, <z> was often used in plurals
when the sound was voiced, so a word like *days* was written *daiz*. Also due
to French, the letter <c> came to be pronounced [s] (rather than [k] as
it had been in Old English) in some words borrowed from French, such as
city and *cellar*, and then even spread to such native Old English words as
lice and *mice*. The letter <k> replaced Old English <c> before high and
mid vowels (*keen, kiss*), but <c> was retained before low vowels and consonants (*cat, cool, cut, clean*). Old English long vowel [ū] came to be spelled
<ou> or <ow>: *hus* became *house*, and *hu* became *how*. And on and on.

Sometimes, spelling changes were introduced in order to distinguish
letters that looked quite similar in the old slanting script. The up and down
pen strokes used by the scribes, called *minims*, could be difficult to distinguish, so the scribes would simply change the letters. For example, several
words spelled with <u> in Old English, such as *lufian* 'love' and *cumin*
'come', were spelled with <o> in Middle English since <u> was difficult
to distinguish from the pen strokes of the neighboring <f> and <m>,
respectively. This also happened with the words *monk* (Old English *munuc*),
some (Old English *sum*), and *worm* (Old English *wurm* and *wyrm*).

The letter *yogh*, <ʒ>, was replaced in Middle English by the French
<g>, and words spelled with <hw> were mostly switched to <wh> in the
spelling: *where, when, why, what*. The pronunciation remained /hw/ for many
speakers, but this pronunciation is being lost (as discussed in Chapter 3). And
note the pronunciation of the other *wh-* word *who*: /hu/, while *how* is both
spelled and pronounced with /h/, though both of these words used
to be spelled and pronounced with /hw/ in Old English.

hwæt!

Johannes Gutenberg was
a German goldsmith who
invented movable type and thus
mechanized printing in 1439.

Toward Modern English Spelling

William Caxton, who introduced the printing press to England in
1476, and other early printers are responsible for many spelling
idiosyncrasies. Sometimes, they would simply change the spelling

of a word to make it fit on a line. During Caxton's time, not a great deal of attention was paid to consistency of spelling; Caxton, for example, spelled one word several ways within the same text.

Sometimes, printers and scribes inserted letters in words to reflect the origin of a word. Renaissance scholars, obsessed with the ideas and traditions of ancient Greece and Rome and hoping to bolster the reputation of English as a worthy language, altered words' spellings to reflect their Latin origins. For example, English got the word *debt* via French *dette*. However, it had originally come from Latin *debere* 'to owe', so the <b> was inserted into the English spelling sometime after 1400. The King James Bible (from the early seventeenth century) has *detter* three times, *debter* three times, *debtor* twice, and *debtour* once. Sometimes the respellings had no effect on pronunciation, as in the <b> in *debt* and *doubt* or the <c> in *indict* (which came to English via French *enditer* but was respelled with the <c>— "re-Latinized"—around 1600). Other times, the new spelling did alter pronunciation such that the modern spelling and pronunciation correspond; for example, *adventure* came from Middle English *aventure*, but the <d> (from Latin *aduentas*) was reinserted in spelling and later in speech. Similarly for *falcon*, which came to English from French *faucon* but Latin *falco*; the [l] was not originally pronounced but was reinserted to Latinize the word and is in most speakers' pronunciations of the word now.

The pronunciation of [l] before another consonant is in quite a state of flux. Consider the letter <l> in such words as *half, calf, walk, salmon, palm, folk, wolf, talk*. This [l] before a consonant had disappeared in pronunciation across the board by Early Modern English (1500–1800). However, the [l] has returned in certain words for certain speakers due to spelling pronunciations. Another spelling pronunciation is the [t] in the word *often*. It went unpronounced for several hundred years, but speakers have begun to pronounce it more frequently, and it is becoming a standard pronunciation, mentioned in many dictionaries as an alternative pronunciation.

hwæt!

What about *Bratz* dolls? Why the <z>? This is not a spelling pronunciation, but it does capture your attention, which is probably the point!

In some cases, we find "incorrect" Latin spellings based on what are called false etymologies. A well-known example is the word *island*, from Old English *igland* and related cognate *ealand*, meaning 'water-land'. The <s> was inserted in the fifteenth century because scholars thought the word was related to the similar but unrelated word *isle*, which came from the Latin word *insula*.

Sometimes spellings were changed to make them match words that were pronounced similarly but had distinct origins. For example, words spelled with <gh>, such as *light* and *knight*, had the uvular fricative [x] in Old English, which eventually dropped out of the language, and <gh> in some words (but not others, such as *enough* and *rough*) became silent. *Delite*, spelled as such until the sixteenth century, was respelled *delight* by analogy with similarly pronounced words.

hwæt!

Ever wonder why we pronounce the names of the famous authors William Butler Yeats and John Keats differently? Yeats was Irish (where there was no Great Vowel Shift) but Keats was English, as his name reflects.

Another major effect on our modern spelling system was the Great Vowel Shift. Recall from Chapter 3 that at the tail end of the Middle English period, sometime between 1400 and 1600, the seven tense vowels of English shifted to become seven different vowels for most speakers of English. The primary reason that we know this shift occurred is that it greatly affected our spelling system. When Caxton introduced the printing press to England and began to print books, a gradual standardization process began that continued steadily over the next hundred years or so (and does still, but at a much slower rate). This standardization process had begun before the vowel shift was complete; thus, many of our spellings represent pre–Great Vowel Shift pronunciation. For instance, words such as *cheat, plead, wreath,* and *leaf* all used to be pronounced with [e], but shifted to [i] as a result of the Great Vowel Shift. Perhaps because of dialectal variation, not all words with this pronunciation shifted; we still have *threat, head, death,* and *deaf.* And what about *break, steak,* and *great*? Here, [ɛ] shifted to [e] but didn't shift all the way to [i].

We can see that although the English spelling is often characterized as chaotic and rife with irregular patterns, an investigation of the many patterns in English spelling and of the history of individual words provides important insights into the nature of sound change, word origins, the effects of print on pronunciation, and a wealth of examples of language change at work.

The introduction of the printing press and the first English dictionaries that soon followed resulted in fairly rapid standardization of spelling. By about the mid-sixteenth century—only one hundred years after the introduction of the printing press to England—many of the features of current spelling were established. Prior to that, printers, scribes, and other literate people spelled as they spoke, using various methods and various dialects.

RPE   13.4

Attempts at Spelling Reform

Numerous attempts have been made to alter the English spelling system, beginning in the eighteenth century and continuing up to the present, with The Simplified Spelling Society, based in the United Kingdom, founded in 1908.

Samuel Johnson's *Dictionary of the English Language,* published in 1755, is often called the first English dictionary, though it had several predecessors. Johnson's dictionary, however, became the authority for spelling and was fairly widely accepted as the definitive source. Across the Atlantic, Benjamin Franklin began to create a new phonetically based English writing and spelling system in the late 1700s. Franklin's system got rid of some letters and added new ones. It never gained any ground but seemed to spur Noah Webster's interest in a new, uniquely American spelling system. Webster (1789: 41) proposed the removal of all silent letters and regularization of certain other common sounds. So, *give* would be *giv, built* would be *bilt, speak* would be *speek*, and *key* would be *kee*. Though these suggestions obviously didn't take hold, many of Webster's American English spellings did: *colour* → *color*, *honour* → *honor*, *defence* → *defense*, *draught* → *draft*, and *plough* → *plow*, to name a few.

Melville Dewey was another American interested in spelling reform. In 1876, he created the Spelling Reform Association and dedicated himself not only to spelling reform but also to a new system for cataloguing library collections. The cataloguing worked; the spelling reform did not.

In 1897, the National Education Association came up with new spellings for twelve words: *catalog, decalog, demagog, pedagog, prolog, program, tho, although, thoro, thorofare, thru,* and *throughout*. Only a few of these remain with us.

The American Simplified Spelling Board, founded in 1906, proposed a list of 300 newly spelled words. Andrew Carnegie supported the Simplified Spelling Board both philosophically and financially, and President Theodore Roosevelt was very much in favor of its suggestions. However, Roosevelt's successor, President William Howard Taft, was less enthusiastic. Carnegie's death and the resultant lack of funding also slowed the spelling reform movement, though it enjoyed a brief resurgence in the 1930s when a Swedish philologist, R. E. Zachrisson, proposed a new spelling system called Anglic. This system never got off the ground, due to World War II and Zachrisson's death. The following is a portion of Lincoln's Gettysburg Address in Zachrisson's Anglic:

hwæt!

Divergent spelling is the deliberate spelling of a word in a nonstandard way. It's often used in product and brand names: Krispy Kreme, Froot Loops, Bi-O-Kleen.

> Forskor and sevn yeerz agoe our faadherz braut forth on this kontinent a nue naeshon, konseevd in liberti, and dedikaeted to the propozishon that aul men ar kreaeted eequel.

When the playwright George Bernard Shaw died in 1950, his will provided for the development of a new alphabet and spelling system for English. Quite a bit of his fortune was spent on inventing and promoting what came to be called the Shaw, or Shavian, Alphabet, a system developed by Kingsley Read, a typographer who won the contest held by the trustees of Shaw's estate to develop the best system. The Shaw Alphabet is phonemic, with each symbol representing a unique sound. The fact that you have likely never even heard of this alphabet, much less used it, is a clue to the success—or lack thereof—of Shaw's dream. (However, you can find lots of links to the Shavian alphabet, including http://www.shawalphabet.com/index1 .html, http://www.omniglot.com/writing/shavian.htm and http://www .spellingsociety.org/journals/j31/shawbett.php.)

The spelling reform movement is still alive and well, concentrated in the Simplified Spelling Society. Its goals are "to raise awareness of the problems caused by the irregularity of English spelling and to promote remedies to improve literacy, including spelling reform" (Bett 2002). It is not likely

> ## LINGUISTICS IN THE NEWS
> # The CSIs of Language
>
> In the late 2000s, a forensic linguist, Tim Grant, appeared on the BBC News Channel and spoke about his evidence in a case involving a terrorist suspect in the United Kingdom. He had sifted through piles of documents, comparing them to other pieces that the suspect, Dhiren Barot, was known to have written. Grant compared consistent spelling and grammatical variations to see if it was likely that the suspect had written the papers. He found that it was indeed likely, and that evidence contributed to the decision to charge Barot with the crime. Barot pleaded guilty in 2006 to conspiracy to murder and was sentenced to at least forty years in jail.
>
> Forensic linguists were also essential in the capture of the Unabomber, Theodore Kaczynski. His brother first recognized his writing style, and linguists then corroborated that the Unabomber's threat letters contained many words and phrases common in Kaczynski's known writings.
>
> Forensic linguists provide expert evaluations of written items (whether on paper or onscreen) involving murders, kidnappings, fraud, and other crimes. Sometimes, their expertise is so critical to a legal case that they are called upon to testify in court.
>
> *For more information*
> Edwards, K. 2008. Reading between the lines. *BBC News.* May 23. http.//news.bbc. co.uk/1/hi/england/west _midlands/7411388.stm
>
> Zimmer, B. 2006. Forensic linguistics, the Unabomber, and the etymological fallacy. *Language Log.* January 14. http://itre.cis .upenn.edu/~myl/languagelog /archives/ 002762.html

ever to have more than minor success in fulfilling its aims, however. The logical, practical, and social reasons for maintaining our current spelling system are numerous. Here are some of them:

- Language continues to change, so whatever spelling system is introduced will have to continue to adapt to the spoken language.
- What system would be used?
- What dialect would be followed?
- Would kids learn both the old and the new systems (to be able to read pre–spelling reform literature and documents)?

Some countries, including Germany, Japan, Ireland, and Norway, have introduced spelling reforms that have been fairly successful.

Any spelling reform that attempted to create a closer match between sound and symbol would perhaps result in children having an easier time decoding text; however, a great deal of semantic information, which is obviously an extremely important piece of literacy, would be lost. Consider words that share a root but have distinct pronunciations—how would spelling reform affect such word groups?

RPE 13.5

RPE 13.6

sign	signal, signature	logic	logician
bomb	bombard	reduce	reduction
hymn	hymnal	design	designation
part	partial	critical	criticize, criticism

The Development of English Punctuation

As any child in the U.S. school system knows, writing involves much more than learning the alphabet and the spellings of words. Along with learning how to spell, English-speaking children also learn how to arrange words on the page—from left to right with spaces between words. Sentences begin with a capital letter and end with a period, and shifts in topic are indicated by indenting the first word of a new paragraph. Though this system may seem completely logical to those of us who are familiar with it, it has been in use in English writing only since about the seventeenth century. Here, we will explore a bit of the history of punctuation. We will also see that some features of written English reflect features of oral language (helping us read written language out loud), but others perform a different purpose, and rather than reflecting grammatical features of oral language, they are part of the "grammar" of writing.

hwæt!

Frustrated by his own inability to write (though he could read), the Emperor Charlemagne is credited with initiating many reforms in the written system, including placing a space between letters, a bigger space between words, and an even bigger one between sentences.

Early Punctuation

Early punctuation was related more closely to speaking than to reading. Latin texts were originally written without spaces between words. Punctuation marks began as a guide to reading texts aloud, and word spaces were finally introduced around the eighth century BCE. Early Old English texts needed marks to indicate when the speaker should pause to give emphasis or indications or to breathe. In elementary school, punctuation is still often taught by asking students to think of how a sentence is spoken; children are taught, for example, to put commas where they would pause (though this can also lead to what are considered "errors," such as separating two clauses with a comma rather than a period). Because Old English texts were handwritten and because there were not yet standards for punctuation, it is not surprising that there is great variability in the punctuation used; some used no punctuation at all. Most scribes used the *point* (a period) to mark a rhetorical break of some kind or a suggestion for where to breathe when reading aloud. Points were written on the line or above the line. Semicolons indicated longer breaks, and *punctus elevatus*, something like our modern comma, marked a shorter break. Question marks (*punctus interrogativus*) were sometimes used, but not required, in questions.

Spaces occurred between words in compounds, between prefixes and suffixes and the roots or words to which they were attached, and sometimes between syllables. Prepositions, pronouns, and adverbs were typically attached to following words, and word breaks at the end of a line were often at syllable breaks, sometimes marked with a hyphen, sometimes not. Proper names were not capitalized, and although some scribes capitalized the first letter of the word beginning a sentence, not all did. Nouns were often written with the determiners and prepositions with which they formed constituents, with no spaces between the words.

Middle English punctuation is similarly sparse; a point or period sometimes appears but not necessarily to mark the end of a sentence, and there is some use of hyphens to mark the breaking of a word at the end of a line. Question marks are not consistently used, and neither are commas. Comma use becomes much more consistent during the Early Modern English period (1500–1700) but capitalization is still inconsistent; most other modern marks of punctuation (apostrophes, semicolons, and contracted spellings) appear during this period, though they are used somewhat differently than we use them today.

Modern Punctuation

Although the rules of English punctuation were pretty much established by the end of the eighteenth century, they are still not fixed. After the invention of printing, punctuation conventions came to be associated more with grammatical structure than with sound, though some current punctuation is based on phonological aspects of language. We place a period at the end of an independent clause, a syntactic unit. A period can also suggest an intonational pause when reading text aloud. A comma can also suggest a pause and, more often, a certain intonational contour, such as the one we find separating the subordinating prepositional phrase *before he goes to bed* from the main clause *Joshua always brushes his teeth* when a sentence like the following is read aloud:

Before he goes to bed, Joshua always brushes his teeth.

Other punctuation marks are based on grammatical information and do not reflect aspects of oral language. Hyphens in words like *mother-in-law* mark the morphological boundaries between words in a compound, for example, but these punctuation marks tell us nothing about intonation (indeed, the rules for hyphen placement in compounds are quite inconsistent, and many compounds have no hyphens at all: *houseboat, highjack, uptick*). Other punctuation is useful only to indicate something specific to the conventions of writing. For example, we might use capital letters in a sign to catch shoppers' attention:

SHOE SALE TODAY

Alternatively, we might capitalize letters to indicate word stress:

I said you should bring a COAT, not a GOAT!

hwæt!

The Coop is the campus bookstore serving Harvard and MIT in Cambridge, Massachusetts. It was originally the Harvard Cooperative Society, founded in 1882 by students to supply books and other materials (including coal and wood) to college students.

Sometimes we use punctuation to prevent misreading or mispronouncing of words. An example of this is words in which a prefix that attaches to a root morpheme might lead to mispronunciation: *co-op, re-evaluate, re-examine*. Usually a hyphen is used to separate the prefix from the root, though some editors or publishing companies use other techniques: *The New Yorker* magazine, for example, uses a diaeresis (¨) over the second vowel, indicating that two adjacent vowels are in separate syllables: *coöp, reëvaluate*; elsewhere, it is written with no hyphen or diaeresis, letting the context suggest the appropriate word and pronunciation: *coop, reevaluate*.

Though change in punctuation rules tends to be slower than other changes in our written system, some are in flux. For example, the use of apostrophes is definitely in a state of transition, though their use has been quite varied since they began to be used in the seventeenth century. Apostrophes set off the *-s* morpheme in possessives:

Alicia's Bridal Shop

We also commonly see, especially in signage:

Alicias Bridal Shop

Apostrophes are also commonly used to mark plurals in what is known as the "greengrocer's apostrophe" because it is used frequently on grocery store signs:

plum's $1.29/lb.

Apostrophes are also commonly used to mark plural proper names (on a mailbox or in an address):

The Jones'   The Talbot's

Using an apostrophe to mark a plural is typically considered an error, and although such errors enjoy a lot of popular press time (the *New York Times* bestseller *Eats, Shoots and Leaves* is a screed of just such punctuation errors), most of them are founded on a certain amount of linguistic logic and are not just laziness. It is now considered standard to use apostrophes in plural acronyms and in dates:

CD's, DVD's, 1900's, 1000's of years

There is also inconsistency in rules of apostrophe use, particularly in possessives with names ending in <s>:

James' car   James's car

We can also use apostrophes to mark plurals in possessives:

The Jones' car   the Jones's car

So perhaps it's no wonder that apostrophes are used more and more to mark plurals as well as possessives, both of which involve the affix *-s*. And what about *its* and *it's*? It is the possessive here that *lacks* the apostrophe:

> It's raining.   The dog ate its food.

Apostrophe rules are therefore actually quite a bit more complicated than we might think. Whether we like it or not, we seem to be moving toward using apostrophes to set off *-s* affixes (plural or possessive), which is probably no surprise, given the overlap. Use is therefore much more complicated than what we consider an error; and what we consider a rule, for that matter, can be can often be the result of language change in action.

RPE 13.7 >

Punctuation "Errors"

Some punctuation rules make linguistic sense; they are designed in a way that is consistent with our intuitions about syntax and clause structure. As we've seen, we have fairly clear intuitions about what constituents are. We can see this play out in our writing by the fact that we very rarely make the mistake of putting parentheses around nonconstituents in our writing; parentheses are therefore a graphic representation of our unconscious knowledge of phrase boundaries. For example, we would probably all agree that the "right" place for parentheses in sentence (1) would be (2b) but not (2a):

1. The two students took a grammar test that they both failed.
2. a. The two students took a grammar (test that they both failed).
   b. The two students took a grammar test (that they both failed).

When we write (formally), we are supposed to follow the conventions of writing and indicate sentence boundaries with capital letters at the beginning and periods at the end. It turns out that we have pretty good intuitions about clause boundaries. But our spoken language lacks punctuation, of course, and though we sometimes use intonational pauses to indicate clause boundaries, we do not pause between sentences or even speak in sentences in most situations.

run-on/fused sentence writing error in which two or more independent clauses are joined without punctuation

Therefore, because we intuitively know where clause boundaries are, but because we must learn the rules of punctuation, we can create **run-on**, or **fused, sentences**,[1] such as the following:

> The movie was filmed in Wyoming in winter it must have been very cold.

---

1. Run-on sentences are not always clearly defined. Computer grammar-checkers, for example, underline sentences of a certain length, categorizing them as too long, or run-on. Given the grammatical possibility for recursion, there is no linguistic equivalent of a sentence that is too long. Our grammatical rules allow us to generate clauses of infinite length; what keeps us from producing such constructions in speech has to do with the limitations of our memories rather than with the limitations of our grammar.

In this example, there are two independent clauses, which are not separated by any kind of punctuation. This lack of punctuation is typically viewed as a rather egregious writing error, but most students, if asked to insert a period, would have no problem doing so, creating either (a) or (b). (If you read the example sentence about the movie aloud, you naturally pause at the end of the first independent clause.)

a. The movie was filmed in Wyoming. In winter it must have been very cold.
b. The movie was filmed in Wyoming in winter. It must have been very cold.

That we know where to put the period (once reminded) is not surprising, given our intuitions about clause boundaries. Omitting a period therefore doesn't mean we don't understand clause structure but rather that we must learn to graphically represent clause boundaries. The writing error known as a **comma splice** comes from putting a comma rather than a period (or semicolon) between two independent clauses:

> The movie was filmed in Wyoming in winter, it must have been very cold.

comma splice writing error in which two or more independent clauses are joined with a comma rather than a period

These examples illustrate a fundamental distinction between our unconscious knowledge of spoken language and conscious knowledge of how that spoken language is to be visually represented. Moreover, though run-on sentences and comma splices are considered serious errors in writing, they do not reflect an error in our real understanding of language.

The writing error known as a **sentence fragment** is another excellent example of the mismatch between oral and written language and of the difficulty we sometimes have in transferring oral language to the page. In writing, we are taught to use sentences rather than pieces of them, or fragments, even when our meaning is quite clear. Consider, for example, the following representation of a perfectly natural oral discourse exchange:

sentence fragment phrase or clause that is punctuated as a sentence (with a capital letter and a period) but is not a complete sentence

> Speaker A: What kind of car did Alonzo buy?
> Speaker B: A Toyota.

Though it is natural to reply as Speaker B does, in writing (except in representation of dialogue) we are encouraged to avoid fragments and to fill in what we call "old" information, or information that is known to both speakers. We typically learn that the desired written version of speaker B's reply, if it is not written as a dialogue, is *Alonzo bought a Toyota* rather than the fragment *A Toyota*. Learning to write formally, therefore, often involves overriding our patterns of speech to create a document or record that can be read and interpreted without the benefit of clues available to us when we speak face to face.

We have not, of course, detailed all the punctuation conventions or even all those that correlate with linguistic knowledge. We mean to show only that some punctuation conventions do reflect aspects of the linguistic system: phonological, morphological, and syntactic. Sometimes, however, our intuitions do not correspond to the written form of the language. When we learn how to write sentences, we also learn about punctuation, capitalization, and so on—what teachers sometimes refer to as mechanics or writing conventions—such things as using commas in dates (e.g., September 12, 2014) and using periods in abbreviations (Mr. Schuyler Jensen). These kinds of rules for representing sentences in print do not correspond to our intuitive knowledge and must simply be learned and memorized.

As you probably know, rules of punctuation are not the same in all languages. The quotation marks used to enclose direct quotation in English, for example, are not used by the French, who use either a dash (—) at the opening of a quotation or angled brackets called *guillemets* (« ») to surround it. Where English would use underlining or italics to indicate emphasis, English quotation marks are sometimes used in other languages, like Spanish. In British English, it is standard to put the end punctuation outside of quotation marks, whereas inside is preferred in American English.

RPE 13.8

Writing Rules, Standardization, and Authority

Punctuation and spelling are both important aspects of language standardization. Writing rules and conventions are taught fairly uniformly in the U.S. school system; we all learn to capitalize the first letter of the first word of every sentence, for example, and to end each sentence with a period. Spelling is also standardized (and enforced by computer spell-checkers), as are certain grammatical constructions (we are taught to avoid double negation in print, and grammar-checkers point that out as well) and vocabulary (we also avoid *ain't* and *yeah*, even though we may commonly use them in speech). Though this standardization certainly influences our oral language (e.g., we might start avoiding double negation and *ain't* in oral speech, too), our oral language system is relatively less vulnerable to standardization than our written system. This in turn leads us to issues of language authority; if the writing system is the primary locus of language standardization, who is in charge of the writing system, and who decides what is standard? Who writes grammar-checkers for computers, grammar handbooks for use in schools, dictionaries, and other usage guides?

Writing a language down does have the effect of beginning the standardization process, and the introduction of the printing press to England in 1476, which allowed mass production of texts, began the standardization process for English in earnest. So, how does such standardization typically take place? A group of factors typically co-occur that can gradually result in the standardization of a language. Some of these factors are publication of dictionaries, suggesting standardized spellings and pronunciations; universal schooling, resulting in the teaching of standardized spellings and rules of writing; the teaching of the language to speakers of other languages,

Language Alive!

Autocorrect Isn't Always

Do you do what your grammar checker tells you? Does it seem like your smartphone has a mind of its own? Are we a little too trusting of these electronic authorities? Ben Zimmer tells the story of Hannah, who received the text message from her father: "Your mom and I are going to divorce next month." Hannah's dad thought he had texted "Disney," but autocorrect had stepped in, and the result was communication melt-down. David Pogue blogs about other autocorrect debacles, such as "sorry about your feces" rather than "sorry about your fever." For more examples, visit DamnYouAutoCorrect.com, which is dedicated to cataloging such errors.

Are autocorrect mishaps the result of our typing, or "fat-finger" errors? Not always. Autocorrect errors are particularly difficult to predict because the kinds of corrections our technology "learns" to make are actually based on patterns of individual users, so not all errors are reproducible.

For more information

Zimmer, B. Auto(in)correct. *On Language. New York Times*, 13 January 2011.

Damn You Auto Correct! http://damnyouautocorrect.com/category/best-of-dyac

Pogue, D. *Pogue's Posts. New York Times*, 21 June 2010. http://pogue.blogs.nytimes .com/2010/06/21/autocorrect-follies/?scp=1&sq=autocorrect%20follies &st=Search

necessitating a relatively uniform version of the language; and a canon of literature. In some countries, the selection of a standard language is a social and political issue, and laws are drawn up declaring the official status of a particular language. (English, for example, is the official language and the standard language of schooling in many countries, including the following in Africa: Botswana, Cameroon, Ethiopia, Gambia, Kenya, Malawi, Namibia, Nigeria, Sierra Leone, Swaziland, Tanzania, Uganda, Zambia, and Zimbabwe.) It is the native language of very few people in any of those places but is chosen as a neutral language of government. (Note that English is not the official language of the United States, though it is the official language in about twenty-nine of the states. (See Chapters 12 and 14 for more discussion of the Official English movement.)

RPE 13.9

RPE 13.10

The Power of the Dictionary

One of the major ways in which a language is codified and standardized is through the compiling of a dictionary. Lexicographers, or dictionary makers (see "Accent on Lexicographers" in Chapter 6), determine how a word should be spelled, pronounced, and defined. Today's lexicographers make their decisions based on usage; that is, they observe how the language is actually used and then offer the spelling, definition, and usage that is the most common and "preferred." The dictionary then forms the basis of what we think of as the correct spellings, pronunciations, and definitions of words. Lexicographers also make choices about whether words should be labeled *archaic*, *slang*, *regionalism*, and so on. We might not all agree on how to pronounce *praline* or *aunt*, and an accurate dictionary must take such differences into account. Dictionaries must also reflect how language changes over time; though spelling may remain the same, we've seen in previous chapters how the meaning and pronunciation of words can change, sometimes quite dramatically, over time. Nevertheless, we usually trust that the information in a dictionary is accurate and up to date, and we tend to defer to its advice.

RPE　13.11 ▷

Did You Know...?

The Oxford English Dictionary

The *Oxford English Dictionary* is the most comprehensive historical dictionary of English, providing not only words and their definitions but also the history of words and their meanings.

The history of the *OED* itself is fascinating. About 150 years ago, the London Philological Society proposed this new dictionary, recruited James Murray as its editor, and convinced Oxford University Press to support the project. This huge undertaking depended on scores of readers, who combed though all the print material they could get their hands on, laboriously cataloguing every appearance of a word, a quote in which the word appeared, its date, and its meaning at that time.

One notorious and prolific contributor to the dictionary was W. C. Minor, a surgeon and soldier and murderer confined to the Broadmoor Asylum for the Criminally Insane. Minor invented an ingenious tracking system to find words and collect quotations (Winchester 1999).

Contemporary *OED* editors still visit the "quotations room," a vast repository of print material, but they have access to an enormous range of electronic and print material—magazines, cookbooks, film scripts, Internet blogs, zines, and so on. To date, the *OED* contains some 3 million quotations! And it's growing—*OED Online* publishes updates every 3 months. Recent additions include *taquito*, *muffin top*, the verb *to heart* (as in *I heart my golden retriever*), *couch surfing*, and many Internet acronyms like *LOL* and *OMG*.

For more information

Winchester, S. 2004. *The meaning of everything: The story of the Oxford English Dictionary*. New York: Oxford University Press.

Winchester, S. 1999. *The professor and the madman: A tale of murder, insanity, and the Making of the Oxford English Dictionary*. New York: Harper Perennial.

The Oxford English Dictionary website: http://www.oed.com/public/about

Writing Registers and Forms

Discussion of a standard written form for a language should not imply that all versions of the written language follow one set of standardized rules. Indeed, as in speech, writing has different registers. We represent speech in writing (called *indirect speech*) with quotation marks, as in the following examples:

> Linguist Michael Krauss (1992) wrote, "Any language is the supreme achievement of a uniquely human collective genius, as divine and unfathomable a mystery as a living organism."

> "No matter how eloquently a dog may bark, he cannot tell you that his parents were poor but honest," wrote Bertrand Russell (1948).

The words on this page are not a transcription of speech, yet we do have many ways in which we represent conversations, and certain forms of writing are more reflective of speech than others. Obviously, the conventions of written language (punctuation, spacing, capitalization, spelling) are absent in oral language, but there are connections between the two. Think about reading aloud; what cues does written language give us so that we can read text aloud in a way that makes sense and is even expressive? We also write in ways that move closer to reflecting the patterns and features of oral discourse. Consider, for example, the following short text, which you might see in an e-mail message or on a sticky note:

> hi j
> WOW great job on the pres REALLY kool
> u rock
> b

Several features in this short note are used to approximate conversation. Uppercase words indicate changes in intonation for emphasis, lowercase greetings (*hi*) and closing set an informal, conversational tone. Nonstandard spellings (*kool*), abbreviations (*u*, *pres*), and lack of punctuation reflect an informal, personal register, as do initials (*j*, *b*) rather than full names, and the use of lowercase letters. This kind of informal communication, which more closely captures certain aspects of our oral language, has increased since the advent of e-mail, instant messaging (IMing), chat room speak, text messaging, and other keyboard and keypad communication. These modes are beginning to result in new ways of spelling and different standards that govern these new, informal, written conventions.

RPE 13.12

Electronic English

The newest form of communication, via the Internet, has allowed for instantaneous written communication in real time or almost in real time. Although it is written, this "electronic language" is much more like spoken language than any other form of written language. Ways of conveying tone and emotion—so much a part of communication in speech but sometimes absent from written communication—have even become part of it. Crystal (2001) uses the term *netspeak* to refer to all of the varieties of written language of the Internet. He notes other terms in use: *netlish, weblish, internet language, cyberspeak, electronic discourse, electronic language, interactive written discourse,* and *computer-mediated communication* (CMC), among others. All do not refer to the same written language transmitted on the Internet, but *netspeak* is a useful term to refer generally to the more informal, unique, written conventions of much of the writing of the Internet.

This electronic communication in all its many forms is often criticized, and fear runs high, primarily among educators and newspaper pundits, that netspeak will ruin children's ability to write correctly, leading to poor spelling, ignorance of the rules of formal writing, and even the decline of morality! For example, an Arizona father quoted in *USA Today* says that he knew there was a problem when his 15-year-old son's summer job application said, "i want 2 b a counselor because I love 2 work with kids" (Friess 2003). Though it's not clear that this sort of genre mixing is indeed a widespread problem, fear of new forms of communication is not new. Crystal (2001) notes that in the fifteenth century, the invention of the printing press was thought by the Church to be a tool of the devil because it would allow the spread of uncensored ideas, which would lead to a breakdown in social order and religious authority.

We will first look at some conventions of writing that are fairly unique to e-mail (the term *e-mail* or *email* comes from *electronic mail*). One feature of this kind of communication is a higher level of tolerance for typos and misspellings. No one is going to be misled by misspellings like the following:

The meeting willb e at 4 in teh main conference room.

The reader of this e-mail may or may not make social judgments about the writer's level of education or attention to detail; but in either case, the reader is likely to be more tolerant of misspellings in e-mail but less so of such errors in more formal writing, such as in a memo or business letter. The writer would likely never allow such typos to go unedited in other print forms. (There are clearly varying degrees of formality in e-mail as well. Now that e-mail and the Internet are replacing many things formerly done only in hard copy—such as job applications, letters of recommendation, and the like—the same degree of editing is expected in those electronic documents as in printed documents.)

Capitalization is also considered somewhat optional in much of e-mail, whether at the beginning of a sentence or for proper names. Here are some examples taken from our own e-mail:

hey! That grant thing looks cool. i'll check it out and get more details.
wanna schedule the mtg for 6?
love ivy
cheers, ben

Most e-mail addresses, URLs, and user names are not case sensitive, which may have led to the lack of capitalization in general, as well as what Crystal calls the "save a keystroke" principle—Internet communication is fast. Crystal says that the "save a keystroke" principle means that any use of capitalization is more marked. When something is written in all caps, it is taken as anger, as if the writer were shouting:

DO YOU THINK THIS IS FUNNY?

Now, there is a good bit of variation in the ways we ignore spelling and writing conventions in e-mail communication. Some e-mail users capitalize everything according to convention; and of course, there are different registers of e-mail communication, too. Now that so much of our daily communication happens by e-mail—from chatting with friends or family to applying for college and jobs—many registers are available to the writer.

Another interesting feature of netspeak is its use of abbreviations, many of which appear most frequently in chat groups and virtual worlds, though they have spread to e-mail, web pages, and even into non-Internet print forms and occasionally into speech. Here is a sampling:

hwæt!

In *A Prayer for Owen Meaney*, John Irving's main character is a dwarfish person who speaks only in CAPITAL LETTERS. Is Irving trying to express anger with all those caps, or humor, or power, or irony?

lol	laughing out loud
b4	before
cul8r	see you later
idk	I don't know
f2f	face to face
oic	oh I see
imho	in my humble opinion
wu	what's up
tx	thanks
4yeo	for your eyes only
2d4	to die for
ta4n	that's all for now

emoticon typographic symbol or combination of symbols used to convey emotion: :-)

RPE 13.13

Another feature of netspeak is its use of **emoticons**, symbols used to express emotion. This innovative feature of the written language allows some conveying of emotion, a feature that the written language has been hard-pressed to do until now.

hwæt!

It seems that online abbreviations are here to stay since the venerable and authoritative *OED* now includes them in the dictionary.

Written Standards in Flux

Informal representations of language that violate standardized rules are not restricted to e-mails and sticky notes; the McDonald's fast-food restaurant chain recently based its entire advertising campaign on the phrase *i'm lovin' it*. The image created by this phrase, with its lowercase *i* and its dropped *g*, gives the idea that

Language Alive!

Smileys

:-) ;-) :-(:-o You understand these symbols, of course, to express joking, flirting, distress, and surprise. These and many other emoticons appear often in electronic communications. Unlike other means of written communication, they stand not for words but for feelings (hence, emotion icons). This unique feature of Internet language uses not letters of the alphabet but combinations of punctuation marks to make faces. They are so common that many word-processing programs and websites automatically turn certain combinations of keystrokes into emoticons. And the simple black-and-white smileys of more than twenty-five years ago have evolved to include colorful, dancing icons.

The first documented appearance of a smiley was in 1982 as the result of misunderstandings in conversations on electronic billboards (precursors to chat rooms and blogs). Professor Steve Fahlman of Carnegie Mellon University proposed them as a means to clarify written words that, in the absence of such conversational clues as intonation and facial expression, might be misunderstood.

For more information

Fahlman, S. History. Carnegie Mellon Computer Science Department. http://www.cs.cmu.edu/smiley

Lovering, D. 2007. Digital 'smiley face' turns 25. *The Washington Post*. September 18. http://www.washingtonpost.com/wp-dyn/content/article/2007/09/18/AR2007091800517.html

---

McDonald's is, indeed, your kind of place: an informal, happy restaurant with your best interests at heart. Such deviations from the written standard abound not only in advertising but in other representations of language.

Often words are misspelled—or *respelled*, as it's sometimes called when it is done intentionally—not only in informal e-mail messages but in more public, "edited" spaces. These respellings, such as in the following examples, also known as **allegro speech**, indicate informality.

allegro speech informal respelling of a word

> gonna, dunno, wanna
> nite, lite, thru

The spellings of these words are all in a state of transition with respect to their acceptability as standard spellings. At this time, most people view them as nonstandard but intentional spellings; thus, they differ from simple misspellings. However, their usage is restricted mostly to informal writing or print situations. We can also think about this kind of variation as a snapshot in time; language change is quite gradual, and written recognition of those changes comes even more slowly. The variations usually coexist for some time before one becomes dominant and the other drops out. For example, the use of *nite* remains fairly restricted right now; its use may increase over time, and eventually the spelling *night* could drop out of the language.

Another example of written standardization change in progress is the way we write compounds. Whether we write words with spaces or hyphens between them or join them with nothing between them is another way in which we find variation across writers, among usage guides, and across time. So, can *lowfat* be written as a single word, or must there be a space in between: *low fat*? And is it *high end stereo* or *high-end stereo* or *highend stereo*? Often, dictionaries are not much help here. They may offer a preferred form but acknowledge the alternatives. And what the dictionary offers may differ from the way you read it most often in other published works. The trend for writing compounds seems to be that frequently used word combinations go from two words to one, sometimes passing through a hyphenated stage, though the hyphen appears to be used quite a bit less now than it used to be. (In the nineteenth century, writers routinely, though not consistently, hyphenated such words as *rail-road, to-morrow, to-day, in-to*, and so on. Herman Melville wrote the title of his most famous work as *Moby-Dick*.

We now write many *compound prepositions* as single words:

into, onto, heretofore, therefore, nevertheless, whereas, whereupon

Compound prepositions are common in English, as well as in other languages—the Romance languages, Germanic languages, and Japanese (though in Japanese they are postpositions since the "preposition" follows the noun it is associated with), but even these compound prepositions are not written consistently without spaces. Consider the following example, in which the two prepositions *out* and *of* actually function as a single word:

Read to me *out of* that book.

We also represent dialectal language variation in print, for different purposes and with different results. When we listen to the recorded speech of someone whose dialect is different from our own, we may draw inferences about the speaker's race, ethnicity, education, age, class, and so on. We draw these inferences from print representations as well, and we can even manipulate such representations for rhetorical effect. For example, nonstandard spellings can be used to influence readers' attitudes about the speaker represented, sometimes in negative and discriminatory ways.

For example, think about the difference between these two sentences:

He sez.
He says.

eye dialect inten-
tional nonstandard
spelling that reflects
character more than
pronunciation

This kind of respelling, known as **eye dialect**, often uses a nonstandard spelling not to reflect pronunciation but to reflect other aspects of a character. In this case, it could suggest that the character or narrator is illiterate or

Language  Alive!

Are You Ever Alright?

Is it all right to use *alright*? *Merriam-Webster Online* offers the following:

> The one-word spelling *alright* appeared some 75 years after *all right* itself had reappeared from a 400-year-long absence. Since the early 20th century some critics have insisted *alright* is wrong, but it has its defenders and its users. It is less frequent than *all right* but remains in common use especially in journalistic and business publications. It is quite common in fictional dialogue, and is used occasionally in other writing: 'The first two years of medical school were *alright*— Gertrude Stein.'

However, Wilson (1993), in the *Columbia Guide to Standard American English*, is a bit more blunt: "*All right* is the only spelling Standard English recognizes." But Bergen and Cornelia Evans (2000), in *The Dictionary of Contemporary Usage*, point out that there's a case to be made for *alright*. "Using 'alright' as a synonym for 'O.K.' or 'satisfactory'," they say, "would allow us to make the distinction between 'the answers are alright' (satisfactory) and 'the answers were all right' (every one of them)." Hmm. So, you decide!

For more information

Evans, B. & C. Evans. 2000. *The dictionary of contemporary usage*. New York: Random House.

Merriam-Webster Online. 2011. http://www.merriam-webster.com/

Wilson, K. 1993. *Columbia guide to standard American English*. New York: Columbia University Press.

uneducated. Eye dialect is also used in representations of different (usually considered nonstandard) dialects. Here's a line from Zora Neale Hurston's story "Spunk":

> "Looka theah, folkses!" cried Elijah Mosley, slapping his leg
> gleefully, "Theah they go, big as life an' brassy as tacks."

Other well-known users of eye dialect in American literature include Joel Chandler Harris, author of the *Uncle Remus* stories, Mark Twain, and Cormac McCarthy.

RPE 13.14

The Effects of Print

The printed word is very strong indeed and seems to have the potential to affect our language acquisition. Children who are learning to read see that there is not a one-to-one correspondence between sound (pronunciation) and symbol. A child says /no/ but writes *know*. One child says /dæt/ while another says /ðæt/, but both learn to spell the word *that*. So we are not as likely to change pronunciation to match spelling because, as we begin to learn to read, we realize that it is not a wholly phonemic system. However, the lack of correspondence between our pronunciation and our writing system is less evident in morphological and syntactic examples; a child would not be likely to say *bringed* and then represent that as *brought* on the page without recognizing that there is a mismatch between the word as the child says it and the way it is written. And utterances in which the morphology or syntax does not conform to the written version are less likely to persist for kids who are exposed to lots of print early (since such variations do not appear in print very often). These factors are the primary reason that morphological and syntactic variations are more stigmatized than phonological ones.

The idea that early exposure to print correlates with success in reading and writing has been accepted in some very broad ways, resulting in, for example, pediatricians giving out free books and national ad campaigns that attempt to get the message out about the importance of early literacy and exposure to books (such as the oldest literacy organization in the United States, Reading Is Fundamental [RIF]).

The enormous importance that we place on literacy is intertwined with our notions of correctness, standard English, and dialect. There are words and phrases that are seen largely in print and occur in formal or archaic speech that children pick up not from speech but from being read to; examples are *for instance, inasmuch as, however,* and narrative syntactic patterns such as *said she*. And as mentioned, we all have "spelling pronunciations" in which pronunciation is modified after seeing the word in print. Every first-grade classroom is full of examples.

> "Oh, it's *pump*kin!" says a six-year-old upon seeing the word written, thus modifying her former (and very typical) pronunciation without the medial [p].

> Another six-year-old child pronounces *because* with an initial [p] and writes *pekose*. When the teacher corrects his spelling, he also changes his pronunciation of the word.

But it happens to adults as well. You have probably seen a word in print and been surprised at the spelling because it didn't match your pronunciation:

> Pronouncing the <n> in *hypnotize* rather than the assimilated [m], so *hyp̲motize* becomes *hyp̲notize*.

> Or changing the perhaps naturally acquired *undoubteb̲ly* or *supposeb̲ly* to *undoubted̲ly* and *supposed̲ly* after seeing them in print.

RPE 13.15

Other times, however, we do not alter our natural pronunciation to match spelling, particularly if doing so would require us to deviate from an

hwæt!

Benjamin Franklin wrote,
"Write with the learned,
pronounce with the vulgar."

accepted pronunciation. For example, no one would pronounce *know* with a [k] or *colonel* with the first [l] because these pronunciations would sound very odd, outside the norm.

Before we end this chapter, let's consider here how a language makes the transition from an unwritten language to a written one. Though there is no consensus on the exact figures, linguists estimate that only about 25 percent of the world's languages have written forms. If a language has not been written, it causes no problems at all for the language; the complex rules and principles that underlie linguistic systems do not depend on writing; nor does child language acquisition, for which only exposure to naturally occurring language is required. Representing language in writing, however, has a number of possible cultural and political effects.

Writing systems for many languages—for example, many Native American languages—have been developed within the last fifty years. Given what we now know about phonetics, and given how difficult it can be to learn to read and write using a writing system that has so many inconsistencies (such as the system used for English), a newly written language would appear to be a perfect opportunity to develop a phonetically based writing system that has a one-to-one correspondence between sound and symbol. And while the International Phonetic Alphabet has been employed to some extent to write many languages that did not have written forms until recently, there are some practical hurdles to adopting the IPA as a writing system: the unfamiliarity of the symbols and a familiarity with—and thus, a bias toward—the spelling conventions of English. Also, speakers of endangered languages face so many hurdles that a new alphabetic system is typically not deemed worthwhile by the members of the community. Also, bear in mind that a language will continue to change, so even if there is a one-to-one match between sound and symbol at first, that match will not last very long.

It is important to understand our biases as a literate society. We often take it for granted that to be educated is to be literate, so it can be hard to understand the different ideas about education, intelligence, and culture in the hundreds of communities with oral rather than written literary traditions. Though many Native American languages, for instance, were not written down until relatively recently, the oral traditions in many of these languages and their communities are very complex and sophisticated. There is an emerging new study of the literary principles and qualities of oral literature, its narrative structure, and literary patterning, based on examples from many such communities. Such formal analyses show these oral traditions in the context of the world's literary heritage and seek to represent the texts in a way that reflects how the stories are appreciated and understood by members of the cultures from which they came.

Accent on *Copy Editors*

We all have ideas and attitudes about language that are sometimes based on social factors rather than on linguistic fact. Some ideas about language reflect discriminatory attitudes about other social groups. The very notion of a standard language can be discriminatory, especially to those who speak nonstandard language varieties.

But language standards are not always discriminatory or unnecessary. Though there certainly exist language mavens who promote one form of the language over another, there are others, namely copy editors, whose expertise lies in a more balanced approach.

A copy editor's job varies depending on the copy to be edited and the intended readers. Copy editors check all of the written material that goes into books, magazines, journals, newspapers, websites, dissertations, marketing brochures, corporate reports, and other published material—anything that requires putting words together to convey a message. Copy editing includes correcting errors of spelling, usage, and grammar and checking format. Some copy editors are also fact-checkers or reporters, and some do layout and design. Copy editors check texts for libel, errors of fact, and plagiarism.

Beyond these "technicalities," copy editors polish material for coherence (tone, vocabulary, level of formality, etc.) while respecting the author's personal writing style and allowing the author's "voice" to come through. Copy editors are not usually expected to rewrite and, if they do their job well, you will never notice their work. Other copy editors might notice, though. The American Copy Editors Society awards its annual Robinson Prize for all-around excellence based on "a combination of elements, including editing, design, mentoring and training, fostering teamwork and pride among colleagues,

American Copy Editors Society

conflict resolution, creative problem solving, and anything else that furthers the craft of professional editing." Andy Angelo of the Grand Rapids Press (pictured above) won the prize in 2010.

Copy editing requires a complete knowledge not only of publishing but of traditional prescriptive rules of writing and style, spelling, and various copy editing marks. Copy editors must be aware of language conventions, how the standards change over time, and how the changes are reflected in written language. For example, the casual tone of this book would not likely have been allowed in an academic text even a few years ago. We often start sentences with conjunctions such as *and*, and we use contractions such as *don't* and *can't*—practices that would have been discouraged, if not "corrected," had we written this book several decades ago.

Excellence in copy editing relies on a flexible rather than dogmatic approach to language usage. Writing style varies dramatically not only among individual writers but also by field, topic, and type of publication. Lest you think there is only one right way to write, here are some style guides that authors and copy editors use; each includes the rules of grammar, usage, spelling, and punctuation, and some are targeted at a particular genre or field: *The Chicago Manual of Style, The Associated Press Stylebook, The Elements of Typographic Style, The Modern Language Association Style Handbook, The Oxford Guide to Style, The Publication Manual of the American Psychological Association, Modern Humanities Research Association Style Guide, The New York Times Manual, The ACS (American Chemical Society) Style Guide, The Manual of Style for Technical Publications, The American Medical Association Manual of Style,* and the list goes on.

Copy editors have degrees in linguistics, journalism, communications, English or other languages, and other disciplines. They sometimes specialize in fields such as medicine, technical writing, computer science, and law. And most copy editors read a wide range of material; they get paid to read!

For more information

The American Copy Editors Society. http:// www.copydesk.org/

Society of Professional Journalists. http:// www.spj.org/

Walsh, B. 1995. The slot: A spot for copy editors since 1995. http://www.theslot .com/

Website of any publication or professional organization

Summary

In this chapter, we have examined the written representation of language. Though language itself is something humans come prewired with, writing down those languages is a human invention that only about one-quarter of the world's languages have. A variety of writing systems have been created over the last few thousand years, including systems based on phonemes, systems based on syllables, and ideographic systems based on meaning. We have seen that though we often equate spoken and written language, there are actually a great many differences between them. We have seen that the English spelling system is only partially phonetic but that its nonphonetic features reflect a great deal about the history of the language. We have also looked at the systems of spelling and punctuation and how both writing and punctuation standards are still changing, illustrating the ways in which a print system can affect our ideas about language and about standardization in our highly literate society.

Sources and Resources

Ager, S. 2011. Alphabets. Omniglot: Writing Systems and Languages of the World. http://www.omniglot.com/writing/alphabets.htm

Ager, S. 2011. Shavian alphabet. Omniglot: Writing Systems and Languages of the World. http://www.omniglot.com/writing/shavian.htm

The American Copy Editors Society. 2011. http://www.copydesk.org/

Baron, N. 1998. Letters by phone or speech by other means: The linguistics of email. *Language and Communication* 18. 133–170.

Baron, N. 2000. *Alphabet to email: How written English evolved and where it's heading.* New York: Routledge.

Beason, L. 2001. Ethos and error: How business people react to errors. *College Composition and Communication* 53. 33–63.

Bett, S. 2002. Introduction to the Shaw Alphabet. *Journal of the Simplified Spelling Society* 2. 23–24. Available at http://www.spellingsociety.org/aboutsss/aims.php

Brians, P. Common errors in English usage. http://public.wsu.edu/~brians/errors/

The British Museum. http://www.thebritishmuseum.ac.uk/

Crystal, D. 2001. *Language and the Internet.* Cambridge, UK: Cambridge University Press.

Damn You Auto Correct! http://damnyouautocorrect.com/category/best-of-dyac

Edwards, K. 2008. Reading between the lines. *BBC News.* May 23. http://news.bbc.co.uk/1/hi/england/west_midlands/7411388.stm

Evans, B. & C. Evans. 2000. *The dictionary of contemporary usage.* New York: Random House.

Fradkin, R. 2000. Evolution of alphabets. http://terpconnect.umd.edu/~rfradkin/alphapage.html

Friess, S. 2003. Yo, can u plz help me write English? *USA Today.* March 31.

Hairston, M. 1981. Not all errors are created equal: Nonacademic readers in the professions respond to lapses in usage. *College English* 43. 794-806.

Irvine, M. & D. Everhart. 2001. Labyrinth library: Old English literature. http://www8.georgetown.edu/departments/medieval/labyrinth/library/oe/oe.html

Krauss, M. 1992. The world's languages in crisis. *Language* 68(1). 4–10.

Lawless, J. "OMG! Online abbreviations make the OED." *Boston Globe.* March 25, 2011. http://articles.boston.com/2011-03-25/business/29360418_1_new-words-publishers-doubt-oxford-english-dictionary

Merriam-Webster Online. 2011. http://www.merriam-webster.com/

Ong, W. 1984. *Orality and literacy: Technologizing the word.* London: Methuen.

Pogue, David. *Pogue's Posts.* New York Times. June 21, 2010. http://pogue.blogs.nytimes.com/2010/06/21/autocorrect-follies/?scp=1&sq=autocorrect%20follies&st=Search

Pullum, G. 2004. Sidney Goldberg on NYT grammar: Zero for three. *Language Log.* September 17. http://158.130.17.5/~myl/languagelog/archives/001461.html

Purcell-Gates, V. et al. 2006. *Print literacy development: Uniting cognitive and social practice theories.* Cambridge, MA: Harvard University Press.

Russell, B. 1948. *Human knowledge: Its scope and limits.* London: Allen & Unwin.

Ser, M. 2004. The electronic *Sermo Lupi ad Anglos.* http://english3.fsu.edu/~wulfstan/noframes.html

Shaw Phonetic Alphabet. http://shawalphabet.com/index1.html

Society of Professional Journalists. http://www.spj.org/

The Oxford English Dictionary website. http://www.oed.com

Trigiani, A. 2001. *Big stone gap.* New York: Ballantine Books.

Truss, L. 2004. *Eats, shoots and leaves: The zero tolerance approach to punctuation.* New York: Gotham.

Walsh, B. 1995. The Slot: A Spot for Copy Editors Since 1995. http://www.theslot.com/. (6 June 2011).

Webster, N. 1789. *Dissertations on the English language.* Boston: Isaiah Thomas.

Wilson, K. 1993. *Columbia guide to standard American English.* New York: Columbia University Press.

Winchester, S. 1999. *The professor and the madman: A tale of murder, insanity, and the making of the Oxford English Dictionary.* New York: Harper Perennial.

Winchester, S. 2004. *The meaning of everything: The story of the Oxford English Dictionary.* Oxford University Press.

Zimmer, B. Auto(in)correct. *On Language.* New York Times, 13 January 2011.

Zimmer, B. 2006. Forensic linguistics, the Unabomber, and the etymological fallacy. *Language Log.* January 14. http://itre.cis.upenn.edu/~myl/languagelog/archives/002762.html

Review, Practice, and Explore

RPE 13.1 〉 Logograms

Consider the following symbols, and determine whether they are logograms or ideograms or both. Is it clear what each indicates, or might there be more than one interpretation? Describe what meaning you think each is intended to convey. What other interpretations might exist?

a.

Stocksnapp/
Dreamstime LLC

b.

Feng Yu/Shutterstock

c.

Last Resort/Getty Images

RPE 13.2 〉 Writing Systems

A. Go to the website http://www.wam.umd.edu/~rfradkin/alphapage.html and carefully examine the transition of the various alphabetic systems as graphically represented by Robert Fradkin. Are there any in which the "leap" from one symbol to the next does not seem likely? What kinds of things might account for the changes?

B. Consider the variation in handwriting systems. The way we are taught to form letters in school blends into a unique system by the time we are adults; many people develop a blend of printing and cursive, taking features of each into their own unique style. Consider letters like α/a, and make a list of other variations that you notice. Think about your own handwriting and the ways in which it varies from the handwriting of other people you know. Write a paragraph summarizing the issues raised here, focusing on the variations from a standard that are allowed in handwriting and why you think we generally allow them.

RPE 13.3 > Old English Pronunciation Leaves Spelling Remnants

Our spelling conventions offer us a glimpse into the phonological history of the language. Notice the inconsistencies we have with the pluralization of words that end in /f/:

> wolf: wolves, dwarf: dwarfs/dwarves, scarf: scarves, roof: roofs, leaf: leaves, waif: waifs, wharf: wharfs/wharves

Some words that end in /f/ form their plural in the "regular" way. In Chapter 4, we saw that our regular rule of pluralization is that if a word ends in a voiceless consonant, add /s/; so, *roof* /ruf/ → /rufs/. Why, then, do we have forms like *wolves* and *scarves* instead of *wolfs* and *scarfs*? Because in Old English, the vowel before the final *s* was pronounced, and a phonological rule of Old English was that when a fricative came between voiced sounds, it, too, became voiced: the plural of *wulf* 'wolf' was [wulvas] phonetically, though it would be spelled *wulfas*. Old English had no voiced fricatives as phonemes, so [f, θ, s] did not have [v, ð, z] as voiced counterparts phonemically, though they did occur as allophones quite early in Old English. Later on in the Middle English period, after influence from French, we began to use the letter *v*. So our current state of pluralization of words that end in /f/ illustrates the conflict between our natural phonological rule of pluralization and the influence of spelling on pronunciation.

Determine the plural of each of the following words, and then look them up in a dictionary. Determine whether any of the plurals differ for British speakers and American English speakers. Also, determine which of them have two accepted, standard spellings:

> belief, leaf, roof, scarf, cuff, wolf, loaf, dwarf, brief, cliff, reef, hoof, proof, chief, knife, half, calf, life, thief, wharf, chef, plaintiff, wife, shelf, handkerchief, giraffe, sheriff, whiff

RPE 13.4 > Spelling Flukes

Mishearing and, therefore, misspelling happens more frequently with idiomatic phrases like these:

> *laughing stock* as *laughing stalk*
> *nick picky* for *nit picky*
> *I would just assume* for *I would just as soon*
> *all intensive purposes* for *all intents and purposes*
> *segue* as *segue way*

Why do you think the mishearings and consequent misspellings happen? Find examples of some other typical mishearings that lead to misspellings.

Here are two historical misanalyses; that is, the words *nickname* and *apron* used to be *ekename* (with separate vowel changes) and *napron*:

> an ekename
> a napron

Look up these words in the *Oxford English Dictionary* and summarize their etymologies. Also consider the contemporary phrase *a whole nother*, in which the word *another* is separated. Do you think *nother* is likely to emerge as its own word? Why or why not?

RPE   13.5   ⟩   **Spelling Reform**

Write a letter to the Simplified Spelling Society outlining the pros and cons of spelling reform; make a recommendation for a modest reform or a complete overhaul of English spelling.

RPE   13.6   ⟩   **Spelling Reform in Other Languages**

Conduct some research on the spelling reform movements for other languages that have enjoyed somewhat more success than those for English, including German, Japanese, Irish Gaelic, Norwegian, Russian, Spanish, or Portuguese. In what ways was the reform successful? In what ways did it fail? Were there features of the language and spelling system that made it easier to reform compared to English? What sort of support (governmental, educational, etc.) seems to be required for reforms to succeed?

RPE   13.7   ⟩   **Punctuation Fluctuation**

Some punctuation conventions have more than one accepted standard. Use several online or printed usage guides to see their recommendations for the following:

- commas with items in a series
- punctuation with quotations
- possessive apostrophes with words, especially names, already ending in <s>:
  - *Jones' house, Jones's house, Joneses' house*

Summarize the recommendations and the reasoning behind each explanation.

RPE   13.8   ⟩   **Comma Rules**

Find rules about comma usage from a usage guide, and list them. Which of the rules can a conscious awareness of grammar help you with, and which are simply conventions of writing that must be learned? Are all of the rules useful? If so, what purpose(s) do they serve?

RPE   13.9   ⟩   **The Teaching of Standard English**

Though most would agree that there do need to be standards for written English, there is no agreement about whether to teach a *spoken* standard and, if so, how to go about doing so. To discover where your feelings lie, consider the following questions regarding Standard Written versus Standard Spoken (and their roles in education):

- What is the role of the teacher or school in the teaching of Standard Written English? What are the goals?
- What is the role of the teacher or school in the teaching of some Standard Spoken English? What sorts of differences exist between the spoken and written standards?
- Is simply modeling an effective way to teach a spoken standard?
- Is talking about dialect, register, style, formality, appropriateness, and so forth directly a way to approach teaching (about) a spoken standard?
- In your own experience, what features of a standard spoken dialect were you explicitly taught? If you weren't taught them, how did you acquire them? How might that differ across dialect groups or speech communities?
- What's the difference between shifting register and shifting dialects?

RPE 13.10 > Survey of Writing Errors

Conduct a writing error survey by interviewing teachers and asking them to list their top five writing errors. Also ask teachers how they grade errors of writing on written work. Do they consider these grammatical errors? And more generally, what does the term *grammar* mean to them? You will likely find that teachers don't all agree on what is considered an error. Why? How is *error* defined then? Some good resources on perceptions of writing error include Beason 2001, Hairston 1981, and http://public.wsu.edu/~brians/errors/.

RPE 13.11 > The *Oxford English Dictionary*

Conduct some research on the *Oxford English Dictionary*. Explore the website http://www.oed.com/. What do "new word" editors do? What are some current additions to the dictionary? Read entries for some words, count the number of quotations, and list the dates that they appear. What kinds of texts are the quotations from? The website is full of interesting information and even includes short videos on different topics. Write a one-page description of what you find.

RPE 13.12 > Conversation Transcription

A. Record 2 to 5 minutes of casual conversation. (You must have permission to do so from the people you record. However, try to make the recording as unobtrusive as possible—you don't want their speech to be stilted or formal as a result of the recording. Tell them you're recording them, but then try to get them to forget about it.) Now, transcribe the recording, taking down everything that was said, including "ums" and "ahs," false starts, and so on. (You can leave out names or substitute fake ones if you'd like.) Then answer the following questions:

- Did you include any pseudophonetic spellings: *-in'*, *dunno*, and so on?
- If so, which words did you do it with, and why? Do you know what guided your decisions to select those words?
- How did you indicate interruptions and utterances that trailed off?
- Did you edit out anything besides names? Why?
- Are all the transcriptions of very casual conversations? Are any somewhat formal?
- What factors seem to affect the number of interruptions, unfinished utterances, or the use of slang?

B. Assume you're a newspaper reporter who is selecting quotations from the conversation for an article you're writing. Which would you select, and how, if at all, would you alter them? Would you put them in quotation marks?

RPE 13.13 > Electronic English

Conduct some research and write a brief essay on the potential effects of IMing, text messaging, and other e-mail and chat room communication. Consider questions such as these, among others: Is there potential for some of these conventions to come into other genres of more formal writing? If so, would that be detrimental to the written standard? How might teachers deal with such questions?

RPE   13.14   Dialect in Literature

In the following selections from Adriana Trigiani's *Big Stone Gap*, the author uses various techniques in her representation of language to convey something about the various characters. Some of the names of her characters are listed, followed by a brief description of the character. The underlined words and phrases are typical of a Southern dialect, while the bolded examples convey the informality of speech but aren't unique to a specific dialect. Consider also how the age, socioeconomic status, and education level are reflected here in the representation of language.

Fleeta Mullins—works at the counter in the pharmacy, lived in the Gap all her life:

"<u>Hi-dee</u>, Ave Maria," she barks . . . I need to <u>declare me</u> some sort of moratorium on these damn fund-raising jars," Fleeta complains. "I <u>can't hardly</u> ring up a sale without **flippin'** one over. . . .You're too much of a soft touch. Let me handle <u>them</u> kids that come in here. If it <u>wasn't</u> for me, **people'd** run all over you all day long. I'll tell them **damn** kids to take their jars to the <u>Piggly Wiggly</u>. We <u>ain't</u> got the room; they do . . ." (p. 16)

Teena Lee—a second-grader:

"Miss Mulligan, my <u>mamaw</u> said you'd put my jar on the counter **'cause** we trade here . . ." (p. 16)

Iva Lou Wade—librarian, driver of the bookmobile, in her 40s:

"<u>Y'all</u> scoot. And here's my number when you get the information. . .Well, ***honey-o***, somebody's got to put a fire under your **butt**." (pp. 98–99)

Ave Maria Mulligan—35-year-old pharmacist, college-educated:

"Good. Right. **See there**? Iva Lou gets what I'm talking about. Sooner or later everybody has to ask the big questions of themselves. Some of us ignore the truth, and some of us gut the interior of our lives and attempt to reinvent it. I am doing the latter." (p. 182)

Find a text that uses respellings of different types as well as other indications of dialect, and do an analysis similar to the one here, in which you indicate features of dialect, informal features, and any others you notice that the author may be using to indicate age, socioeconomic status, or education level of the characters via their speech.

RPE   13.15   Spelling Pronunciations

Remember that a spelling pronunciation is a pronunciation that reflects a word's current spelling, which differs from the way it was pronounced in previous generations. The following words have undergone some kind of pronunciation change based on their spelling for many speakers of American English. Research the etymologies and pronunciations of the following words, and describe how they exhibit spelling pronunciations.

forehead, victuals, figure, ye, wainscoting, tsk tsk

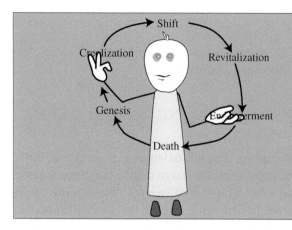

The Life Cycle of Language

Key Concepts

- There are many stories and theories about the origins of language and why the human language system differs from other species' communication systems.
- The origins of language could tell us something about why our brains are organized for language as they are.
- Not all languages descend from a parent language; the life cycles of languages include pidgins and creoles.
- The loss of a language is a loss of cultural identity and can happen through colonization or as one language supplants another over time.
- Language policy can help erode or promote preservation of language and cultural identity.

Did You Know . . . ?

Chinook Jargon
Ketchup-Only Law
Language Preservation in Action

Language Alive! The Origins of American Sign Language

Esperanto: A Failed Lingua Franca

Linguistics in the News Sundance Features *The Linguists*

Accent on What Linguists Can Do

Language Origins
  A Mother Tongue?
  A Linguistic Big Bang?
  Why Don't Apes Do It?
Language Genesis
  Creoles Revisited
  Jamaican Creole
  Hawaiian Creole English
  Tok Pisin
  Gullah and African American English
Language Shift
  Latin
  Native American Languages
  Norman French in England
  Language Planning
  English-Only Laws
Language Revitalization
  Hebrew
  Welsh
  Hawaiian
  Native American Languages
Summary
Sources and Resources
Review, Practice, and Explore

> *Language is power, life and the instrument of culture, the instrument of domination and liberation.*
>
> —Angela Carter

In this final chapter, we discuss the life cycle of languages—language birth, language and dialect endangerment, language death, language maintenance and survival—and what factors lead to each phase of the cycle. An important issue we discussed in Chapter 1 was the ways in which human language differs from the communication systems of other species. In this chapter, we will delve more deeply into the origins of human language—what we know about those origins and what remains a mystery. Did all languages descend from one *proto-language*? Does Proto-Indo-European, which we discussed in Chapter 11, share with other proto-languages an ancestor from which the world's language families descend?

Investigating the origins of language also brings us back to themes we discussed in Chapter 2, namely, how our brains are organized for language. When did that organization occur, and why? What biological adaptations led to human language, adaptations not shared by other species?

Remember that not all languages appear because they descend from a parent language. The life cycle of languages includes pidgins and creoles, languages that arise through language contact or sometimes virtually out of nothing, as is the case of Nicaraguan Sign Language (introduced in Chapter 2). Here, we will investigate the origins and grammar of a wider range of creoles in more detail to see what these relatively young languages have to tell us about how languages emerge, which in turn sheds light on how our minds are organized for language.

In previous chapters, we touched on how language and culture are intertwined and how our language provides insights into how we think about the world. We saw in Chapter 10 that pragmatic rules (of conversation, politeness, speech style) vary from culture to culture and that our language is an integral part of how we identify ourselves. In this chapter, we'll explore how languages supplant one another gradually over time or as the result of colonization and imperialism. Such changes can have a dramatic effect on cultural identity and can lead to efforts to revitalize language in order to preserve and protect speakers' identity.

Language shift, death, and revitalization are closely tied to power and authority; the dominant language is typically the most powerful one. We've seen how language authority emerged in seventeenth-century England with the rise of prescriptive grammar and led to what we consider standard English today. We will probe language standardization in more depth here—how it applies to oral and written language and how it can lead to linguistic discrimination.

We will look at some examples of language policies that sometimes protect and sometimes erode speakers' right to their own language.

Language Origins

Where did language come from? And when did it start? Did it happen all at once or more gradually, in stages? These are all questions that we humans are very curious about, but they are all impossible to answer with any degree of certainty. In this section, we'll discuss the origins of language. Is there such a thing as a single language from which *all* languages descend—a "mother tongue"?

A Mother Tongue?

Remember that the large Indo-European language family discussed in Chapter 11, containing about 450 languages, is one of some 116 language families in the world, resulting in about 7,000 languages spoken and signed today. Table 14.1 is the list of language families from *Ethnologue*, "an encyclopedic reference work cataloging all of the world's 6,909 known living languages" (Lewis 2009). The numbers in parentheses indicate the number of living languages in each family.

Language Alive!

The Origins of American Sign Language

In 1817 Thomas Gallaudet and Laurent Clerc founded the first school for the deaf in North America, in Hartford, Connecticut. Gallaudet had learned much about teaching the deaf from visiting a school in Paris that had been set up in 1755 by Abbé Charles Michel de L'Eppe, who founded the first free school for the deaf there. De L'Eppe recognized that a sign system was already being used by a group of deaf people in Paris, so he developed a system based on the existing signs. At the school in Connecticut, the French sign language combined with the students' own sign systems and with a sign language that had been used on the island of Martha's Vineyard, from which many of the students came. (The island had a high rate of deafness.) American Sign Language eventually emerged from this situation to become the dominant sign language in the United States and Canada. Because of the early influence of the French sign language, contemporary French Sign Language and American Sign Language share about half of their vocabulary; however, they are not really members of a language family. In fact, developing a family tree for sign languages proves challenging due to the complex ways in which sign languages are acquired and taught.

For more information
Lane, H. 1989. *When the mind hears: A history of the deaf.* New York: Vintage Books.

Table 14.1	World Language Families

Afro-Asiatic (374)*
Alacalufan (2)
Algic (44)
Altaic (66)
Amto-Musan (2)
Andamanese (13)
Arafundi (3)
Arai-Kwomtari (10)
Arauan (5)
Araucanian (2)
Arawakan (59)
Arutani-Sape (2)
Australian (264)
Austro-Asiatic (169)
Austronesian (1257)
Aymaran (3)
Barbacoan (7)
Basque (1)
Bayono-Awbono (2)
Border (15)
Caddoan (5)
Cahuapanan (2)
Carib (31)
Central Solomons (4)
Chapacura-Wanham (5)
Chibchan (21)
Chimakuan (1)
Choco (12)
Chon (2)
Chukotko-Kamchatkan (5)
Chumash (7)
Coahuiltecan (1)
Constructed language (1)
Creole (82)
Deaf sign language (130)†
Dravidian (85)
East Bird's Head-Sentani (8)
East Geelvink Bay (11)
East New Britain (7)
Eastern Trans-Fly (4)
Eskimo-Aleut (11)
Guahiban (5)
Gulf (4)

Harakmbet (2)
Hibito-Cholon (2)
Hmong-Mien (38)
Hokan (23)
Huavean (4)
Indo-European (439)
Iroquoian (9)
Japonic (12)
Jivaroan (4)
Kartvelian (5)
Katukinan (3)
Kaure (4)
Keres (2)
Khoisan (27)
Kiowa Tanoan (6)
Lakes Plain (20)
Language isolate (50)
Left May (2)
Lower Mamberamo (2)
Lule-Vilela (1)
Macro-Ge (32)
Mairasi (3)
Maku (6)
Mascoian (5)
Mataco-Guaicuru (12)
Mayan (69)
Maybrat (2)
Misumalpan (4)
Mixed language (23)
Mixe-Zoque (17)
Mongol-Langam (3)
Mura (1)
Muskogean (6)
Na-Dene (46)
Nambiquaran (7)
Niger-Congo (1532)
Nilo-Saharan (205)
Nimboran (5)
North Bougainville (4)
North Brazil (1)
North Caucasian (34)
Oto-Manguean (177)
Panoan (28)

Pauwasi (5)
Peba-Yaguan (2)
Penutian (33)
Piawi (2)
Pidgin (17)
Quechuan (46)
Ramu-Lower Sepik (32)
Salishan (26)
Salivan (3)
Senagi (2)
Sepik (56)
Sino-Tibetan (449)
Siouan (17)
Sko (7)
Somahai (2)
South Bougainville (9)
South-Central Papuan (22)
Tacanan (6)
Tai-Kadai (92)
Tarascan (2)
Tequistlatecan (2)
Tor-Kwerba (24)
Torricelli (56)
Totonacan (12)
Trans-New Guinea (477)
Tucanoan (25)
Tupi (76)
Unclassified (73)
Uralic (37)
Uru-Chipaya (2)
Uto-Aztecan (61)
Wakashan (5)
West Papuan (23)
Witotoan (6)
Yanomam (4)
Yele-West New Britain (3)
Yeniseian (2)
Yuat (6)
Yukaghir (2)
Yuki (2)
Zamucoan (2)
Zaparoan (7)

*Numbers in parentheses indicate the number of languages in the family.
†*Ethnologue* categorizes all sign languages in a single group here, though most of these languages are unrelated.
Source: Lewis, M. Paul (ed.), 2009. *Ethnologue: Languages of the world*, 16th ed. Dallas, Tex.: SIL International. Online version: http://www.ethnologue.com/. Used by permission of SIL International.

When we look at this vast number of language families containing thousands of languages, you may wonder how they all came about. People seem to have always wondered that; most cultures of the world have myths about the origin of language as well as how and why languages change and vary.

For example, a Salish myth tells how an argument led to the divergence of a language into two languages. Two people were arguing whether the high-pitched whistling noise made by ducks in flight is from air passing through the bill or from the flapping of wings. The argument is not settled by the chief, who then calls a council meeting of neighboring villages' leaders. This breaks down in argument when nobody can agree, and eventually the dispute leads to a split where some people move far away. Over time, they slowly began to speak differently, to need words for new objects, and eventually new dialects and languages were formed (Boas 1917: 111–112).

Was there originally a single language from which all of the world's languages descended? This is a question not easily answered, and it is one that can never be answered with complete certainty. Languages leave no fossil record, and the written information we do have about language goes back only several thousand years, not a long time in terms of human history. Archeological evidence seems to indicate that modern humans, *Homo sapiens*, emerged within the last 150,000 years. Some have wondered whether the success of our species over other extinct hominids may be related to our language abilities. Those with language could organize, plan, plot, and convey all sorts of information that would have given them an advantage over other hominids. We don't know for sure that extinct hominids did not have language, but it is a common supposition that they did not.

The comparative method (described in Chapter 11) has led to construction of family trees much like the Indo-European family tree. Historical linguists have also been at work since the early twentieth century on reconstructing **proto-languages** for these families—a single parent language for each of these families from which all members of the family may have originally descended. Proto-Indo-European is that proto-language for the Indo-European language family. Written records from some members of the Indo-European family go back only about 6,000 years for the oldest (Sanskrit) and are far more recent for other languages in the family (Latin, Greek, Old English). Most linguists would agree that the reconstruction of language families is good science, though there are ongoing scientific debates about some of the details. However, some suggest that it is possible to go back further, reconstructing the language that Proto-Indo-European came from, and trying to determine what other language families may have also come from this proto-proto-language family. Though most linguists agree that there simply isn't enough evidence for such a hypothetical reconstructed language, this idea has enjoyed a certain amount of attention in the popular press and has shown up on several magazine covers over the last few decades. While it's

hwæt!

Ninety-two percent of the world's countries have at least one official language. English is the sole official language in 31 nations.

proto-language
single parent language from which all members of a language family may have descended

an intriguing idea that may well be true, most agree that there just isn't enough data to go back 50,000 to 100,000 years to reconstruct the language or languages that humans may have been speaking (or signing?).

RPE   14.1

A Linguistic Big Bang?

We really have no idea when humans began using language. Most scientists agree there was probably some sort of linguistic "big bang" (50,000 to 100,000 years ago?) that resulted in a change in the structure of the brain, resulting in the ability to acquire language as we know it. Researchers in various other fields have done a great deal of investigation into the questions of when humans began using language and what their speech was like. Paleontologists studying fossils, bones, and artifacts have shed light on early humans' life, giving insight into their possible speech capacity as well. Primatologists try to determine how much humanlike behavior and communication various apes can learn, and come up with theories about how language may have evolved. Neurologists and neurolinguists study the brain to determine the current shape and how it has evolved, comparing this information to that of other primates, for example, and then making hypotheses about language's development in the brain.

A promising piece of evidence has recently emerged that may eventually shed some light onto how human language ability has evolved. In Chapter 2, we discussed a mutation in a gene called FOXP2 that has been shown to lead to deficits in language as well as a loss of control of facial muscles, including those involved in speech production. This gene is only a slightly altered version of a gene found in apes, but it seems to have achieved its present form between 200,000 and 100,000 years ago. Though it is very tempting to call this gene a language gene (indeed, the media has done so, as this research was reported in the popular press over the last few years), but that is oversimplifying. However, further investigation into the human genome is undoubtedly going to reveal more about human linguistic ability.

hwæt!

Primatologist Jane Goodall has been studying the behavior, including the communication, of chimpanzees in the wild since 1960. She has received numerous awards and honorary degrees, and the Jane Goodall Institute strives to "advance the power of individuals to take informed and compassionate action to improve the environment for all living things."

Why Don't Apes Do It?

Scientists think that humans have adapted genetically to facilitate spoken language. We did this, in fact, at a great cost—an increased risk of choking and greater likelihood of death. For such an evolutionary adaptation to take place, it must have been worth that risky trade-off. The throat—the pharynx—of *Homo sapiens* is elongated compared to that of earlier hominids, and the larynx is lower. The illustrations in Figure 14.1 illustrate these differences that are still present between today's apes and today's humans.

Figure 14.1   Adaptation of the Pharynx for Language

Source: Figure 11.4, from *The symbolic species: Co-evolution of language and the brain*, by Terrence W. Deacon. Copyright © 1997 by Terrence W. Deacon./Used by permission of W. W. Norton & Company, Inc.

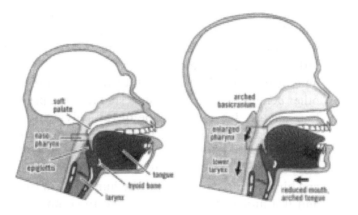

The result of these changes is that our tongues can move forward and backward and up and down in ways that create a great variety of resonant cavities in a lot of different places in the vocal tract. The stretching out and lowering of the pharynx, however, means that the epiglottis can no longer make contact with the soft palate. In primates and extinct hominids, the epiglottis can do so, and this arrangement results in two separate pathways—one for air and one for food and liquid. But in humans, because the respiratory and the digestive tracts intersect at the pharynx, food can become lodged in the larynx, making it impossible to breathe. It is this descent of the larynx, however, that makes us able to produce speech sounds. (And interestingly, human infants are born with the larynx higher in their throats, making it impossible for them to produce speech sounds until they are at least 3 months old.)

Another difference between humans and apes is brain size. This is not, of course, due simply to language, but Ralph Holloway (1983), who researches the evolution of the human brain, discusses how some of the changes in the human brain do correlate with language. Of the four major reorganizational changes that have occurred during hominid brain evolution, three correlate with language: (1) reduction of the visual cortex area with relative increase in the posterior cortex, where Wernicke's area (involved in language comprehension and lexical access) is located; (2) reorganization of the frontal lobe, where Broca's area (involved in syntactic processing and production and speech motor control) is located; and (3) the development of strong lateralization (localization of language in the dominant—typically left—hemisphere of the brain).

Like the changes to the vocal tract that resulted in the risk of choking, the changes in the human brain have had drawbacks as well. Holloway discusses how brain size typically correlates with gestation period—the larger the brain, the longer the gestation. If humans' brain size and weight were consistent with that of other animals, the gestation period would be about 17 months. However, human infants are born at about 9 months, making them, in a sense, quite premature and, therefore, virtually helpless and completely dependent on the mother—a considerable burden, really, but one that we have traded for language (among other benefits). It has been suggested that the premature births of modern humans are due to the shape of the pelvis and the birth canal, which allows us to walk upright. In all nonhuman primates, the birth canal is essentially a straight tube, wider from front to back than from side to side; the newborn's head fits in the birth canal with room to spare, so an ape birth is fairly simple. But the human birth canal is a complex tunnel, and if a human fetus were allowed to complete its brain development in utero, it would be too large to be born! The rapid brain growth that in most primates occurs only before birth continues in infancy for modern humans. Only when a baby is a year old does brain growth slow down; so, in terms of brain development, human gestation lasts 21 months. (Holloway also notes that the ways in which the feet evolved, allowing for bipedalism, meant that the feet could no longer grasp with a thumb-like big toe, which meant big changes for the early human mothers and babies. While ape infants cling to their mothers with muscular hands and grasping toes, the human infants now had to be carried, lessening the mother's ability to provide for herself.) Our large brains, which allowed us language, among other things, and our upright walking ability have resulted in difficult births and helpless infants. Though it has complicated our lives in some ways, the linguistic big bang nevertheless seems to have been a worthwhile evolutionary trade-off.

Many have asked what the course of this pressure for language might have been and why our distant ancestors made such a big investment in talking. Biological anthropologist Terrence Deacon (1997) suggests that the motivation for language was social; that hominid brains and human language coevolved over the past 2 million years, driven by the imperative of "representing a social contract" (p. 401), which was required in order to take advantage of the resources available via systematic hunting and gathering. Evolutionary biologist and anthropologist Robin Dunbar (1998) also suggests that the motivation for language was primarily social, but he claims that it is the need to gossip that is behind language, arguing that gossip became a more efficient substitute for the grooming behavior (you can talk and do other things at the same time) that other primates use to establish and maintain social relationships.

Language Genesis

The family tree models of language relations allow us to see how groups of languages share certain linguistic features with each other and are thus likely descended from a common parent language. We discussed in Chapter 11 some of the grammatical features of members of the Indo-European language family as well as some of the features and patterns that distinguish the various branches of a family. For example, all members of the Germanic branch of the Indo-European family have a two-tense verbal system (past and present tense, but not aspect, are marked on the verb). That is, in modern English, for example, we can say *walk* and *walked*, but other combinations of tense and aspect must be expressed by a combination of auxiliary and modal verbs: *will have walked, could have walked, might have been walking.* Non-Germanic branches of the Indo-European family use a single word with distinct affixes to express these semantic variations. It is this difference, along with other distinctions, that has led historical linguists to separate the Germanic language family from the other Indo-European subgroups.

Here, we take another look at some creoles of the world, languages that are not always easily represented in a family tree model because they are "brand-new" languages, though they share features of other languages. Recall from the discussion in Chapter 2 that creole languages are exciting examples of **language genesis**, and because they share so many grammatical similarities (regardless of who speaks them, where they are spoken, or what languages they share features with), they are perhaps a window into the mind, giving us clues to the structure of human language. Creoles can also give us clues to what the earliest language(s) may have been like.

language genesis how languages come to be, descending from another language or coming about from language contact and creolization

Creoles Revisited

Grammatical similarities across creoles may indicate that the human brain is hardwired to create particular patterns of language. Over time, these similar patterns may change in different ways, but each time a language is created, it tends to follow certain patterns. This idea, however, is met with some skepticism because there often is not a great deal of recorded material on early creoles. Creoles were long thought of as bastardized versions of the superstrate language from which each took much of its vocabulary. Also, the study of creoles was neglected because many creoles were spoken by less powerful, dominated peoples; many pidgins and then creoles arose out of the slave trade.

In the nineteenth century, when slaves from Africa were brought over to North America to work on the plantations, those who spoke the same or related languages were intentionally separated from each other so that the difficulty in communication would make it harder to plan a revolt. Therefore, in order to finally communicate with their peers on the

Figure 14.2 Creoles Around the World

As a result of colonization, shipping, and trade, many creoles grew up in coastal areas all around the world. This map shows many, but not all, areas where pidgins and creoles are or were spoken.
Source: http://lingweb.eva.mpg.de/apics/ index.php/Image:Creole_map1.jpg/APiCS/Max Planck Institute

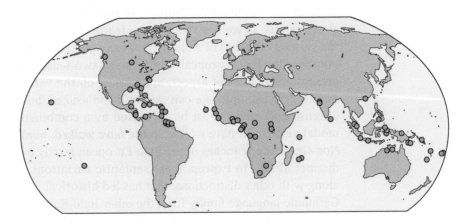

plantations and with their owners, they needed a language. Such languages are thought to be the origin of what have been called Plantation Creole and Gullah, discussed more later. Pidgins also arose because of colonization. Prominent languages such as French, Spanish, Portuguese, English, and Dutch were the languages of the colonizers. The colonizers traveled around the world (see Figure 14.2) and set up ports in coastal towns where shipping and trading routes were accessible, and pidgins formed between the colonists and the indigenous peoples.

The traditional linguistic understanding of a creole is that it has developed from a pidgin (discussed in Chapter 2). The primary way in which this happens is that a child is exposed to a pidgin as a first language and develops it into a fully formed, completely explicit language. This kind of brand-new language is a creole. In contrast to a pidgin, which typically has reduced morphology and syntax, tolerance of considerable phonological variation, reduction in the number of functions for which the pidgin is used (usually not a written language), extensive borrowing from local languages, and much variability across speakers, creoles have all the features of a complete language.

So if adults in a community don't speak a common language, they speak with each other in the pidgin; then the children use it, too, but they fill in all the grammatical and lexical holes. In an amazing demonstration of the hardwired language capabilities that humans possess, children create a complete, new language. Nicaraguan Sign Language (*Idioma de Señas de*

Nicaragua, ISN), developed by deaf children, is an example of such a "new" language.

Some of the most thorough descriptions we have of creoles are of the creolized languages of the Caribbean. Creoles often arose on slave plantations where Africans who spoke different languages used pidgins to communicate; their children created creoles such as Haitian Creole, Jamaican English, and Gullah (spoken on the islands off the coast of Georgia and South Carolina).

Because most creoles are spoken in close proximity to a more powerful or dominant language, the original form of the creole is often greatly affected by that dominant language. For example, the creole Gullah, though likely not originally mutually intelligible with English, is now much closer to English in terms of phonology, morphology, syntax, and vocabulary.

Creoles are languages like any other languages; the term *creole* just refers to the way the language came into being and emphasizes its relative youth. A factor in the struggle of creoles to be recognized as legitimate languages is that these young languages do not always have a written form. (But bear in mind that neither do many languages that have been around for thousands of

Did You Know...?

Chinook Jargon

Chinook Jargon was a language used in what is now Oregon, Washington, British Columbia, and Alaska throughout the 1800s. The language takes vocabulary from various tribes of the Pacific Northwest, including the language of the Chinook tribe, with some borrowings from French and English. It was used primarily as a trade language between speakers of different languages, both between Native American groups and between Europeans and Natives. The language is nearly extinct, though it was used well into the twentieth century; its use was documented in Seattle until World War II, according to novelist Nard Jones (1972). It was also a written language, unlike many other pidgins and creoles. In Kamloops, British Columbia, a missionary publication, *Kamloops Wawa*, was published in the language for some twenty years, from the 1890s on. Dictionaries and other texts were also published in the language during that time.

For more information
Jones, N. 1972. *Seattle*. Garden City, NY: Doubleday.
  Lewis, P. 2009. Chinook Wawa: A language of Canada. In *Ethnologue: Languages of the world*, 16th edn. Dallas, TX: SIL International. Online version: http://www.ethnologue.com/show_language.asp?code=chn.

years.) In many societies today, the writing down of a language has the effect of legitimizing and standardizing it. Recently, speakers of various English-based creoles are choosing to spell words differently from the way they are spelled in their English cousins, to emphasize the different meaning and the fact that it is a part of a distinct language. (Recall *bin* and *bai* of Tok Pisin, discussed in Chapter 2. We'll see more examples in the next section.)

Another way in which creoles are marginalized, even by linguists, is that the family tree method of categorizing language cannot accurately represent the ways in which creole languages develop. Hugo Schuchardt (1885) pointed out in the late nineteenth century that creoles were a problem for the comparative method because one could wrongly reconstruct something like Proto-French-Haitian. That is, if we knew nothing about the history of Haiti, we might assume Haitian Creole and French had a common ancestor when, in fact, Haitian Creole developed because of contact between French and African languages. In the same way, English-based creoles are not technically descendants of English, though they share much vocabulary. Their syntax and morphology is often completely new, so it would not be accurate to represent them on the same family tree. Because of these difficulties in representing them in the family tree model, creoles are often simply left off such tree diagrams, contributing to the notion that they are not real or complete languages.

Let's consider some features of several English-based creoles. We will focus on the complexity of the grammatical systems as well as the similarities among these unrelated languages.

Jamaican Creole

Slave labor came from Africa to Jamaica in the seventeenth century. An English-based pidgin and then a creole developed. Jamaica was a British colony until 1948, when it gained independence. Some version of Standard English is the official language and is used in schools, though most people speak Jamaican Creole at home. (There is a dialect of English known as Jamaican English, which is distinct from the creole.)

Consider the pronoun system of Jamaican Creole. Although the vocabulary of the pronouns is borrowed from English, they are now distinct, as Table 14.2 indicates.

Jamaican Creole also differs from English in the way tense and aspect are marked. In Jamaican Creole, tense is indicated by *ben* before the main verb. Though *ben* is borrowed from English *been*, it has a distinct meaning and grammatical function in Jamaican Creole.

hwæt!

Jamaica was inhabited by the Arawaks when the Spanish arrived in 1494. The Arawaks were soon all dead, and so was their language.

    past tense = *ben* + verb stem
    If me *ben waak* huom . . .
    'if I *had walked* home . . . '

Table 14.2	Jamaican Creole and English Pronouns			
	Jamaican Creole		English	
Person	**Singular**	**Plural**	**Singular**	**Plural**
1st	mi	wi	I	we
2nd	yu	unu	you	you
3rd	im/i	dem	he/she/it	they

Aspect, which marks duration, intensity, completion, or frequency of verbs, is indicated in the following examples:

progressive aspect = *a* + verb stem
Why yu *a dhu* out yah?
'What *are* you *doing* out here?'

completive aspect = *done* + verb stem
Mi jus a *done tell* me two pickney dem sehh . . .
'I *have just* finished *telling* my two children that . . . '

You can see from these few examples that even though much of the vocabulary is borrowed from English, the meanings and grammatical functions of those borrowed words is quite different in Jamaican Creole.

RPE 14.2

Hawaiian Creole English

Hawaiian Creole English, known to most Hawaiians simply as "pidgin," has a long history in Hawaii and has been influenced by many languages, including English, Hawaiian, Portuguese, Chinese (primarily Cantonese), and later by plantation workers who were speakers of Japanese, Tagalog, and Korean. Similar to the grammar of Jamaican Creole, Hawaiian Creole English marks what is called the anterior tense with *bin*, similar to the past perfect in English, so *bin walk* in Creole would translate to 'had walked' in English.

The irrealis aspect (similar to conditional) is marked with *go*. It distinguishes possible actions from actual ones:

irrealis: If I *bin* get car, I go drive home.
              'If I had a car, I would drive home.'

The habitual aspect, indicating that something occurs regularly, is marked by *stay*:

habitual: I *stay* run in Kapiolani Park.
              'I regularly run in Kapiolani Park.'

hwæt!

Hawaii, which became the fiftieth state in 1950, was first inhabited more than 1,500 years ago by Polynesian peoples. It was ruled by a monarchy until 1893, when the last monarch (and the only queen), Lili'uokalani, a speaker of Hawaiian, was deposed.

An interesting feature of Hawaiian Creole English, pointed out by Derek Bickerton (1981), is that it has a way to distinguish actions that have been completed from those that haven't. Consider the following English sentence.

Kai went to Hilo to see Alena.

In English, we don't know whether Kai saw Alena or not, but in Hawaiian Creole, that must be specified.

Kai bin go Hilo go see Alena

means that Kai saw Alena. But

Kai bin go Hilo for see Alena

This means either that Kai didn't see Alena or the speaker doesn't know whether he did or not. Here again, we see that although superficially these English-based creoles seem very similar to English, they are, in fact, quite different grammatically and lexically and can even offer more information and more details than can be expressed grammatically by their English equivalents.

Tok Pisin

This language, also known as Melanesian Creole or New Guinea Pidgin, is a creole language spoken in Papua New Guinea, where 800 languages are spoken. It is one of three official languages spoken there. (The other two are English and Hiri Motu.) Tok Pisin began as a pidgin when Pacific Islanders, speaking many languages, were sent to work in the sugarcane fields in Queensland, Australia, and other neighboring islands in the late 1800s. The pidgin used much vocabulary from English but had influences from German, Portuguese, and various Austronesian languages. It developed into the primary language of the descendants of these people. There are related creoles elsewhere in the South Pacific: Bislama, spoken in Vanuatu, and Pijin, spoken in the Solomon Islands.

Though about 80 percent of the vocabulary of Tok Pisin is derived from English, many grammatical features of the language are quite distinct from those of English and are also features that Tok Pisin shares with many other creole languages. One example is the **transitivity marker**; like many creoles, Tok Pisin has an affix that indicates transitivity of verbs. So, if a verb can take an object, the suffix -*im* must attach to the verb: *luk* means 'look', but *lukim* means 'to see something' and must be accompanied by a noun phrase. Another feature is the distinction between inclusive and exclusive personal pronouns. For example, Tok Pisin distinguishes between *mipela*, meaning 'we' but excluding the addressee, and *yumi*, meaning 'we' and including the addressee. Tense and aspect are indicated by separate words borrowed from English but exhibiting novel meanings: *bai* indicates future,

transitivity marker affix that indicates transitivity of verbs

bin indicates past, and the progressive aspect is indicated by *stap*. Redupli-cative morphology is another feature of Tok Pisin and of other creoles: for example, a repeated action can be expressed by reduplication of the verb: *tok* means 'talk', but *toktok* means to continue talking, and *smalsmal* means 'very smal' in Jamaican Creole.

Gullah and African American English

Gullah, also called Sea Islands Creole, is spoken on the islands off the coast of South Carolina and Georgia. Enslaved Africans continued to arrive at the islands until the early twentieth century; because they were isolated on the islands and thus cut off from the outside world, their language remained fairly distinct. Linguists have speculated that Gullah is an exam-ple of the early creoles that many slaves spoke in North America from the 1600s on, and Gullah is likely descended from what lin-guists call Plantation Creole. The variety of Gullah that is spoken today is for the most part mutually intelligible with English and is, therefore, perhaps best classified as a dialect rather than a cre-ole, though it was most certainly a separate language earlier in its development.

hwæt!

You can take a Gullah tour in Charleston, South Carolina, and learn all about Gullah history, culture, and language from one of their own.

Recall from Chapter 12 that scholars have proposed that African American English (or African American Vernacular English, AAVE) may have origi-nated as a creole. Some of the grammatical features of the language variety spoken by many African Americans are also characteristic of various African languages that would have been spoken by the ancestors of the speakers of the modern variety of the dialect (the use of grammatical aspect, for example). Whether these grammatical features came directly from lan-guages of Africa or came about independently is nearly impossible to prove. There is almost no recorded information on the language that the slaves and their owners spoke. But we can be more certain that the grammar of African American English is distinct from the grammar of other varieties of English; perhaps this is due to its creole origins (where grammatical aspect does often play a larger role).

Table 14.3 compares the aspectual marking of Hawaiian Creole English (HCE) to African American English (AAE). As we discussed in Chapter 2,

Table 14.3	Aspectual Marking in HCE and AAVE*		
	Anterior	**Irrealis**	**Nonpunctual**
HCE	bin	go	stay
AAVE	been, done	be gon' be	be steady

*HCE = Hawaiian Creole English; AAVE = African American Vernacular English

these grammatical markers for anterior, irrealis, and nonpunctual recur in creole after creole, and they do so in the same order. The similarities in these unrelated languages, HCE and AAE, are rather remarkable.

We have seen that pidgins and creoles are new languages. Though they often share features of the superstrate language, these similarities are primarily restricted to lexical borrowings. The process of creolization, however, results in new meanings for that vocabulary and in unique grammatical structures. Watching creoles develop allows us to witness the birth of new languages, and the similarities that exist across unrelated creoles suggest that we may be witnessing the births of languages much as it may have happened tens of thousands of years ago, when it happened for the very first time.

RPE 14.3 >

Language Shift

language shift shift of a speech community from speaking one language to another

When a speech community shifts from speaking one language to another, the process is known as **language shift**. Language shift happens for a variety of reasons. You learned in Chapter 12 about the spread of English worldwide and the factors that led to this: first, the power of England as a result of colonial expansion, and then the growth of the United States and its economic and political power. This expansion of English led to the deaths of Native American languages, Australian aboriginal languages, and many languages of the Caribbean, as well as to the decrease in use or loss of Celtic languages in Britain.

Other colonizing languages have had similar effects: Spanish and Portuguese wiped out perhaps hundreds of indigenous languages of Mexico and Central and South America, French colonization in the West Indies and in parts of Canada led to the disappearance of the indigenous languages spoken in those places, and Dutch took over those parts of the Caribbean that were colonized by the Dutch (the Dutch Antilles, the Virgin Islands, and Tobago, as well as parts of South America colonized in the seventeenth and eighteenth centuries). Where there is a colonizing power, there is a language that will become the dominant language.

Though you may be aware that some languages are no longer spoken and are thus "dead," some of the languages mostly commonly thought of as dead languages didn't actually die out but slowly changed into other related languages. We look at several examples of language shift in this section, both those with descendants and those without, and examine the causes of the shift.

endangered language language in danger of becoming extinct because it has very few remaining speakers

Michael Krauss (1992), an expert on **endangered languages**, has proposed that, in this century, as many as 95 percent of the nearly 7,000 languages currently spoken and signed in the world may become extinct, and that they are dying out at the highest rate ever. The remaining 5 percent

LINGUISTICS
IN THE NEWS
Sundance Features *The Linguists*

It's not often (ever?) that linguistics is featured in a major motion picture—but perhaps that trend is beginning to change. *The Linguists*, a documentary film featuring linguists David Harrison and Gregory Anderson, premiered in 2008 at the Sundance Film Festival. The film follows Harrison and Anderson to jungles, mountains, and remote villages in India, Bolivia, and Siberia as they document endangered and disappearing languages. In pursuit of their goal, they encounter fascinating and dangerous circumstances while finding their way through difficult geography and unfamiliar cultural mores.

These two linguists have traveled extensively to interview the last speakers of critically endangered languages. Many of the world's languages (some say half) are in danger of extinction. When a language dies, the knowledge, history, and culture of its speakers is lost to all.

Harrison and Anderson have established the Living Tongues Institute for Endangered Languages, a nonprofit organization dedicated to the documentation, revitalization, and maintenance of endangered languages.

The National Geographic's Enduring Voices Project, in conjunction with Harrison and Anderson's Living Tongues Institute, identifies what they call language hotspots, the regions of the world with the greatest linguistic diversity, the greatest language endangerment, and the least-studied languages. So far, they have isolated five hotspots: eastern Siberia, northern Australia, central South America, and, in North America, Oklahoma and the Pacific Northwest. When invited, the project assists people in these indigenous communities in their efforts to revitalize and maintain their threatened languages.

News of the team's research and the film *The Linguists* made headlines around the world, appearing in *The New York Times*, *The Washington Post*, *Guardian UK*, and *The Australian*, among many others. Harrison appeared on the television programs *The Colbert Report* and *Good Morning America*.

The publicity is all in an attempt to raise public awareness about language endangerment and language loss and to document and prevent language extinction.

For more information
Harrison, K. D. 2010. *The last speakers: The quest to save the world's most endangered languages*. Washington, DC: National Geographic Books.
   Harrison, K. D. http://www.swarthmore.edu/SocSci/dharris2/. (31 May 2011).
   Ironbound Films. *The Linguists*. http://www.ironboundfilms.com/newsroom.html#linguists.
   Living Tongues Institute for Endangered Languages. 2011. http://livingtongues.org/ enduringvoices.html.
   National Geographic. 2011. Enduring Voices Project. http://www.nationalgeographic.com/mission/enduringvoices/.
   YouTube. http://www.youtube.com/enduringvoices.

will belong to at most twenty language families, and more than half of the remaining languages will belong to just two families, Indo-European and Niger-Congo. How does this rapid language decline happen? In some rare cases, speakers of a language have all died from disease or genocide, as happened with some Native American tribes upon contact with Europeans. More often, languages die gradually as a speech community adopts a language spoken by others.

While it is true that new languages are being born as creoles, they are not emerging nearly as fast as other languages are dying out. And though we

hwæt!

In January 2008 an earthquake in India killed about 30,000 people who spoke the endangered language Kutchi; now there are only some 700,000 speakers left.

can think of language change as natural—all languages undergo change, and it is difficult to prevent change—language change that results in a language's disappearance can have powerful cultural consequences. For example, if communities with different languages come together by choice (migration), those languages might affect each other and change. However, when there is colonization, forced assimilation, or some other prohibition against a community's language, there is a natural reluctance—or even overt resistance—to let go of a language and the accompanying culture.

Latin

Latin is now considered a dead language because it is not spoken as a native language by anyone. However, it didn't really die; it simply slowly morphed into Spanish, Portuguese, French, Italian, Romanian, Catalan, and the other Romance languages, much as Old English changed into Present-Day English. At the time these languages were changing, no one would have noticed the shifts any more than we notice today's language changes (and just as happens today, such changes were likely viewed as language degradation at the time). Thus, Latin is not really an example of language shift as we've defined it since it was not replaced by another language. However, we discuss it here because it is a ubiquitous example of a dead language. We'll contrast its story to that of other dead languages to see the different factors at work.

Latin was a common and widespread language throughout the Roman Empire (including Europe, North Africa, and the Middle East) for many hundreds of years. It was used throughout the Empire as the language of government and law and, in many places, as the language of the common people.

Because literacy was common among citizens of Rome and then throughout its growing empire, the works of Latin authors were read by many. Many of the other languages spoken throughout the Empire did not have written forms, so the fact that Latin had a literary tradition gave it more power.

The Roman Empire collapsed in 476 CE, but Latin continued to be used as a literary language throughout western and central Europe. It wasn't until the fifteenth century that Latin began to lose its powerful position as the primary language of scholarly work and of religion throughout Europe. It was replaced there by what were slowly becoming the standardized languages of Europe, many of which were languages that descended from Latin (French, Italian, Spanish, Catalan).

Latin was used by the Roman Catholic Church in its religious services and texts until the middle of the twentieth century and is still used in many traditional services all over the world. Latin is one of the official languages of Vatican City and is used in Catholic services conducted there.

Latin was taught in schools in the United States throughout the twentieth century and was, and still is to some extent, one indicator of an educated citizen. Though its teaching has declined, it is still taught in many schools in the United States and so remains quite "alive" as a second language (though the focus is typically not on speaking it but on the language's structure and on learning to read and write it).

In English, Latin words and word roots are still used by scientists to name new species and specimens (*Patholops hodgsonii* 'Tibetan antelope', named after Hodgson; *Escherichia coli*, a bacterium; *Xenos vesparum*, a type of wasp; *Passer domesticus*, 'house sparrow'). Many Latinate terms are still used in the law (*affidavit, habeas corpus, pro bono, pro forma*), in academic writing (*ibid.* is the abbreviation for the Latin *ibidem* 'in the same place' and is used in bibliographical references to refer to the previous source references; also *etc., emeritus*, and others [or *et al.*!]), and in medicine. In fact, many medical schools recommend their students take Latin to understand the names for diseases, symptoms, and anatomy.

The power of Latin established during the Roman Empire lasted for centuries, long after the Empire itself had disappeared. The fact that Latin has remained for so long has to do with the power of the people who used it, not with anything about the language itself. However, its eventual disappearance as a native language also illustrates that the use of language is driven by who uses it; after the Roman Empire collapsed, the power centers were more localized, and the languages that developed reflect that (French in France, Spanish in Spain, Italian in Italy, and so on).

RPE 14.4 >

Native American Languages

The native languages of North America are examples of true language shift. The languages didn't slowly change into other languages; they were almost completely wiped out fairly rapidly. Beginning in the latter half of the nineteenth century, Native American languages were targeted by the U.S. government as part of the "assimilation" of Native Americans. In 1868, a federal commission on making peace with the Plains Indians concluded, "In the difference of language today lies two-thirds of our trouble . . . Schools should be established, which children should be required to attend; their barbarous dialects should be blotted out and the English language substituted" (Atkins 1887). These boarding schools did more than anything else to kill off scores of Native American languages. Students were taken from their homes, often sent hundreds of miles away, and made to attend military-like schools and government-subsidized, church-run mission schools. The students were routinely punished, sometimes quite severely, for speaking their languages. The force that lay behind these prohibitions is readily seen upon reading this statement from the commissioner of Indian affairs, E. A. Hayt, in 1879: "I [have] expressed very decidedly the idea the Indians should be taught in the English language only. . . . There is not an Indian pupil whose tuition is paid by the United States Government who is permitted to study any other language than our vernacular—the language of the greatest, most powerful, and enterprising nationalities under the sun. The English language as taught in America is good enough for all her people of all races" (cited in Jaimes 1992: 380). Given these attitudes and policies, it is of course no surprise that use of the languages began to diminish, quickly eradicating many languages but also chipping away at the very identity of many Native Americans, alienating them from their cultural roots and from their tribes while also not allowing them full access to the dominant (white) society. The twentieth century saw the death of perhaps hundreds of Native American languages.

James Crawford, a language policy expert, writes that the pressures that induced many Native American tribes to adopt a new language include changes in values, rituals, or economic and political life resulting from trade, migration, intermarriage, religious conversion, or military conquest.

> Modern cultures, abetted by new technologies, are encroaching on once-isolated peoples with drastic effects on their way of life and on the environments they inhabit. Destruction of lands and livelihoods; the spread of consumerism, individualism, and other Western values; pressures for assimilation into dominant cultures; and conscious policies of repression directed at indigenous groups—these are among the factors threatening the world's biodiversity as well as its cultural and linguistic diversity. (Crawford 1995: 22)

In the sections on language revitalization, we will see how some Native American communities have begun to fight—perhaps too late—to save their languages.

Norman French in England

In Chapter 11, you learned about the Norman Conquest, the conquering of England by the Norman French in 1066. This takeover led to French becoming the language of the ruling class, of the government, and of the courts. Was this an example of language shift? We have learned how the language of power typically becomes the dominant language; why, then, don't we speak French instead of English? Why didn't language shift take place for the people of England? We discussed this rise and fall of French in Chapter 11 and the events that led to its eventual demise as the language of England. Recall that William the Conqueror ruled under a feudal system in which there was a huge social and practical division between the French-speaking ruling class and the English-speaking peasants. Despite hundreds of years of rule by the French, English remained the language of the masses. Other practical matters discussed in Chapter 11, such as the Black Death

Language Alive!

Esperanto: A Failed Lingua Franca

Esperanto is an invented language, created in the 1870s by Ludovic Zamenhof, an Ashkenazi Jew from what is now Poland. It was developed as a lingua franca for use between speakers of different languages; Zamenhof hoped it would become a language used around the world. He spent years creating the language and then translating literature into the language, as well as writing a grammar book. Throughout the twentieth century, it was taught in schools and universities around the world but did not receive acceptance as an international language. Its grammar and vocabulary are based primarily on various Indo-European languages, and it is intended to be quite easy to learn.

Today, *Ethnologue* reports that there are between 200 and 2,000 Esperanto speakers; it is used in about 115 countries, mostly in Central and Eastern Europe, China, and other countries in eastern Asia, certain areas of South America, and Southwest Asia.

For more information

Lewis, M. Paul (ed.). 2009. *Ethnologue: Languages of the world*, 16th ed. Dallas, TX: SIL International. Online version: http://www.ethnologue.com/.

Grigorjevskij, A. 2011. Esperanto.net. http://www.esperanto.net/info/index_en.html.

(which killed both English and French speakers but led to an increase in the number of English speakers in positions of power), eventually led to the demise of French in England.

RPE   14.5

Language Planning

Sometimes the use of a particular language is more carefully planned, with official, governmental policies developed to ensure that the language is spoken and/or taught in schools. Such deliberate efforts to influence the selection and promotion of a community's language use and acquisition are known as **language planning**.

Language planning and policy arise out of sociopolitical situations where, for example, speakers of various languages compete for resources or where a particular linguistic minority is denied access to basic rights. One example is the U.S. Court Interpreters Act of 1978, which provides an interpreter to any victim, witness, or defendant whose native language is not English. Another is the Voting Rights Act of 1975, which provides for bilingual ballots in areas where more than 5 percent of the population speak a language other than English (see Robinson 1988 for more information).

language planning official (usually governmental) efforts to influence the selection and promotion of a community's language use

Other language planning decisions attempt to meet needs by *reducing* linguistic diversity, as in instances where a language is declared a national language in a multilingual country (such as Bahasa Indonesia, "language of Indonesia") or where a single language or a single variety of a language is declared the standard or official one to promote linguistic unity in a country where divergent dialects or languages exist. For example, although many dialects of Chinese exist, the promotion of a single variety as the national language (Mandarin) contributes to a sense of national unity.

English-Only Laws

Contrary to popular belief, the United States does not have an official language. English-only legislation was proposed in 1981 by Senator Hayakawa of California as a constitutional amendment called the English Language Amendment. If approved, it would have banned all uses of languages other than English in federal, state, and local government. However, the measure has never come to a congressional vote. Since then, however, twenty-four states have adopted English as an official language, though many of these laws are simply symbolic, stating that English is the official language of the state.

These various laws and proposed laws regarding making English an official language are quite controversial, sometimes pitting basic rights against linguistic unity. As Robinson (1988) writes,

> As the recent proliferation of efforts to legislate problems of language difference attests, language planning is becoming more and more essential in an increasingly multilingual society. A coherent and informed legislative response to the social and political questions raised by the changing composition of the population is needed so that legislators and educators can make informed choices about language policy in areas such as educational policy and access to basic services. (para. 15)

RPE 14.6

RPE 14.7

Did You Know...?

Ketchup-Only Law

In 1996, U.S. House of Representatives delegate Robert Underwood of Guam proposed in a letter to Congress a "ketchup-only" bill, which would make ketchup the national condiment, making it mandatory in government food agencies and prohibiting salsa, soy sauce, and other condiments. It turns out that the bill was a tongue-in-cheek ploy to express his disdain for the English-only bill sponsored by Representative Toby Roth of Wisconsin.

Language Revitalization

If language shift resulting in language death is of concern, then in theory, reviving some of those languages and then maintaining both the dominant language and the threatened language within these communities seems like a good solution to prevent loss of native languages and the accompanying culture. Such attempts to bring back the spoken use of a language that is no longer in daily use are known as **language revitalization**.

language revital-
ization attempt to
bring back spoken
use of a language

What are the benefits and consequences of trying to preserve languages and fend off their disappearance? For linguists, the loss of linguistic data is a great loss of the material for the field of linguistics. This is not trivial, for that data and the consequent analysis of it can be, as Chomsky has put it many times, a partial window on the human mind. The value of preserving languages goes far beyond linguistics. James Crawford writes,

> We should care about preventing the extinction of languages because of the human costs to those most directly affected. . . . Along with the accompanying loss of culture, language loss can destroy a sense of self-worth, limiting human potential and complicating efforts to solve other problems, such as poverty, family breakdown, school failure, and substance abuse. After all, language death does not happen in privileged communities. It happens to the dispossessed and disempowered, people who most need their cultural resources to survive. (Crawford 1995: 34–35)

ħwæt!

In 1992, a Turkish farmer's death marked the end of Ubykh, a language from the Caucasus region that had the most consonants on record.

We'll see in this section some of the attempts to revive lost languages or to revitalize languages that are waning, and we'll learn about some issues that affect such attempts.

Hebrew

Ancient Hebrew, though it was not spoken for about 2,000 years, was able to be revived and modified, resulting in Modern Hebrew; however, because of all the written records and because it remained alive in religious contexts, there was a great deal of material (as well as a unique political and social situation—and a lot of sheer will), enabling the language to again be spoken by children as a first language.

Hebrew had been "dead" for nearly 2,000 years when it was brought back to life in Israel about sixty years ago; it now has several million speakers. Hebrew is a member of the Semitic family of languages, related to Arabic and to a lesser extent Amharic. The language and alphabet go back more than 3,000 years. The language became extinct as a spoken language after about the second century BCE, when Aramaic (a closely related Semitic language) became the dominant language of the Middle

East. However, Jews continued to learn Hebrew as a literary and religious language, even when the Jewish population was scattered by the Romans in the year 70 CE. So, for 2,000 years, Hebrew was not a spoken language. In the late nineteenth century, a Lithuanian-Jewish medical student named Eliezer Perelman (later Ben-Yehuda) became interested in the revival of the Hebrew language and devoted the rest of his life to the cause. He coined nearly 4,000 new Hebrew words based on original Hebrew roots in order to make Hebrew a modern, practical language for everyday usage. The language was adopted by the early Zionist settlers in Palestine around the turn of the twentieth century and became the official language of Israel in 1948 when the state was established. Today, Hebrew is spoken by about 5 million Israelis both in Israel and abroad and is the language of prayer for Jews throughout the world. A native speaker of Modern Hebrew is able to read the Bible (Old Testament) in its original Hebrew much as an English speaker can read Shakespeare. Hebrew is an inspiration to many people trying to revive languages today.

Welsh

Welsh, spoken for centuries in the southwest of what is now England, has been a threatened language for hundreds of years. Speakers of various Celtic languages existed in England when the Anglo-Saxons invaded in the fifth century. Pushed to the edges of the territory (Wales, Ireland, Scotland, and over to Brittany in France), the Welsh people and its speakers coexisted fairly peacefully with English speakers for hundreds of years. But English, the language of the conquerors, gained the upper hand, and speakers of Welsh decreased steadily over time. Morgan (2001) writes that in 1911 there were nearly a million Welsh speakers, a quarter of whom spoke only Welsh. Today, the half-million speakers of Welsh are all bilingual speakers of Welsh and English. In the latter half of the twentieth century, however, support for both Welsh culture and its language began to develop and have an effect on the use of Welsh in schools and in the public realm (p. 110).

hwæt!

In 2010 linguists discovered a new language, Koro, in northeastern India. Only about 800 people still speak this endangered language.

Before the 1950s, language choice was a nonissue for the British government. Schools were run locally, not nationally, so Welsh was used in the areas in which it seemed relevant. However, English was viewed as the language that allowed children to climb up the social ladder, so all official business—legal, governmental, higher education—was conducted in English. World War II brought many non-Welsh-speaking children from other English cities into Wales, and much more intermingling of Welsh and English speakers began to occur. This led to renewed interest in maintaining the Welsh language and culture, and in the 1950s Welsh-speaking primary schools were established; but secondary schools and higher education still were conducted in English only. Probably the most important milestone in recent history was the Welsh Language Act of 1993, which asserts that Welsh and English are equal by law. Also on the governmental level, *Cymdeithas yr Iaith Gymraeg* (the Welsh Language Society) and *Plaid Cymru* (the Welsh political party) have worked since the 1960s to bring issues related to the Welsh language to public (governmental) attention. *Ethnologue* (Lewis 2009) estimates that 19 percent of the Welsh population now speaks the language, and 33 percent understand it. And Morgan (2001) writes that 80 percent of Welsh-speaking couples bring up their children with Welsh as their first language. The passion and commitment of this tiny part of Britain have led to an increase in speakers (according to the 2001 census) for the first time in a hundred years (p. 112).

Hawaiian

Hawaii, the isolated island chain in the Pacific, is united by its Polynesian language and culture. Throughout the twentieth century, when Hawaii was first a U.S. territory and then a U.S. state, it was locally controlled politically by multiracial speakers of Hawaiian or Hawaiian Creole English, and the Hawaiian language was given special legal status. However, the power of English has proved very strong indeed, and the number of speakers of Hawaiian has been steadily declining at a rapid rate. According to Wilson and Kamana (2001), a count of traditional native-speaking elders born before 1930 resulted in 200 speakers—fewer than 0.01 percent of the 230,000 native Hawaiians now in Hawaii and fewer than 0.002 percent of the island population of just over a million (p. 148). A small, isolated island, Ni'ihau, however, still has native speakers of the language among its 130 inhabitants. Though Benton (1981) predicted Hawaiian to be the first Polynesian language to be completely replaced by a European language, it is today in a better position than many other Polynesian languages due to the determination and commitment of the 'Aha Punana Leo, an organization that has worked tirelessly for more than twenty years to have Hawaiian fully integrated into K–12 education as the language of instruction. Also, the University of Hawaii at Hilo has a college of Hawaiian language, called Ka Haka 'Ula O Ke'elikolani ('Royal Standard of Ke'elikolani'), which strives to reestablish the Hawaiian language and culture, and all courses are taught in Hawaiian. Though the number of native-speaking Hawaiian children may not be increasing, many children are now coming out of the school system completely fluent in Hawaiian, and the language is being used in daily public functions as well. In the Hawaiian situation, as in other language revitalization programs, it has taken an enormous amount of dedication, commitment, and relentless pressure on education institutions and the government, as well as a lot of money, to begin to turn the language decline around.

Figure 14.3 Native American Language Families in the United States

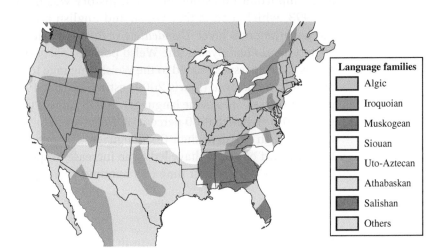

Language families
- Algic
- Iroquoian
- Muskogean
- Siouan
- Uto-Aztecan
- Athabaskan
- Salishan
- Others

Native American Languages

Recall that there used to be hundreds of Native American languages spoken in the United States. Figure 14.3 shows the major language families. Most of the languages are extinct or will be soon. However, in the last couple of decades, interest has increased in preserving or revitalizing many of these languages.

Many Native American communities are trying to bring back a language that no one speaks (at least fluently) anymore, but the challenges these communities face in that task are enormous. In some communities, there are no speakers left. Some have only a few elderly speakers. The languages vary somewhat in how much material has been documented, but they often lack a dictionary or grammatical description of the language. And the languages that do have documentation may not have educational materials to make the often quite technical linguistic description and explanation useful for the classroom. So, although the community may desire to have their children speak the language, it is not easy to accomplish. Teacher training is a huge task that is complicated because remaining speakers of a language often lack academic credentials, while outsiders lack essential cultural and linguistic knowledge. Also, language renewal projects must compete with other, usually more pressing, priorities like health care, education, housing, and economic development.

Cherokee

The Cherokee Preservation Foundation is trying to bring Cherokee back into the daily lives of its people. The Cherokee's original homelands were in the southern Appalachian Mountains, but in the 1830s, all the Native Americans living in the South, including the Cherokee, were forcibly removed from their homes and marched as far as a thousand miles south to Oklahoma's new Indian Territory. This march has become known as the Trail of Tears. Today most Cherokee live in eastern Oklahoma, though the Eastern Cherokee maintain their reservation in western North Carolina.

Cherokee, though in danger of becoming extinct, is still one of the healthier languages of Native North America. One reason for its relative health is the number of texts being published in the language. Sequoyah, the son of a Virginia fur trader and a Cherokee chief's daughter, developed a written form of Cherokee (discussed in Chapter 13) in the early 1800s, and there is an established body of literature written in this form today. However, Cherokee suffered the same fate as other Native American languages because of government policies that forced the removal of Cherokee-speaking children from their homes to boarding schools where only English was allowed until the 1950s. *Ethnologue* reports that, today, out of an ethnic population of 308,132, only 130 are monolingual in Cherokee.

The Cherokee Preservation Foundation (http://www.cherokeepreservationfdn.org/) is working to change those numbers. The organization raises money for various language preservation programs that teach children and adults to speak and read the Cherokee language. They coordinate language preservation and revitalization programs in preschools and elementary schools, as well as developing teacher education programs to prepare teachers to teach the language while becoming fluent themselves. They are also at work on curriculum materials for use at all levels.

Lushootseed

Lushootseed is a member of the Salish language family, which is spread throughout the Pacific Northwest and lower British Columbia. It is a nearly extinct language; there are, perhaps, six speakers left, all in their 80s and 90s. Vi Hilbert (see "Did You Know . . . ? Language Preservation in Action") was an elder in the Upper Skagit tribe in northwestern Washington who worked tirelessly for almost forty years to document her language. Largely because of her work and her willingness to share it, there is renewed interest in the language at local reservations (Tulalip Elementary School on the Tulalip Reservation in Marysville, Washington; Chief Leschi School on the Puyallup Reservation; and Muckleshoot Tribal School on the Muckleshoot Reservation near Auburn, Washington, all have incorporated Lushootseed into their curricula). Many local tribes throughout Washington State have developed language programs aimed at both documenting what is left of the languages and teaching the language to children. Though Lushootseed and other members of the Salish family are not likely to ever have native speakers again, the efforts to document, promote, and teach the language will

ƛ̣ʷɑɛɔ!

The last speaker of Nooksack, a Salish language in Washington state, died in 1977.

Language Preservation in Action

Vi Hilbert, one of the last speakers of Lushootseed, died in December 2008. She worked for some forty years recording, documenting, and transcribing her language. In the 1960s, she began working with linguist Tom Hess (of the University of Victoria, British Columbia) to become literate in her language. She worked with Hess to develop teaching materials, and she taught the language at the University of Washington. She then worked with numerous schools to document and revitalize the language through teaching the language and sharing the tribe's culture, history, and stories. In 1989, Hilbert was named a Washington State Living Treasure and received a National Heritage Fellowship from the National Endowment of the Arts, which was presented to her by President Bill Clinton. A nonprofit organization she founded can be found at http:// www.lushootseed.org/.

allow members of the community to retain a part of their culture. You can see some of the Lushootseed teaching and how it is integrated throughout the curriculum of one school by visiting the Tulalip Elementary School site: http://www.msvl.k12.wa.us/elementary/tulalip/home.html.

Navajo

Navajo is perhaps the single Native American language whose extinction is not imminent. However, its use has been declining continually for the past 50 years. *Ethnologue* (Lewis 2009) reports that of 178,000 Navajos (in the 2000 census), 7,616 were monolingual in Navajo. They also report that first-language speakers among first graders were 30 percent in 1998 compared to 90 percent in 1968. Despite this rapid decline, the language revitalization and maintenance programs on this large reservation are active and enjoying a great deal of success in fluency among second language learners. Part of the reason that Navajo is ahead of some other Native American languages in terms of maintenance of the language is an early and continuing emphasis on literacy. Robert Young and William Morgan published a Navajo dictionary in 1943, and they also published a monthly newspaper in Navajo into the 1950s. The emphasis on literacy led to the publication of a number of children's books during this time as well. Navajo also became celebrated during and following World War II because of the Navajo codetalkers, and it became somewhat easier to acquire public funds to aid in school programs. Another reason for the relative success of the maintenance of Navajo language is the foresight demonstrated at Rough Rock Demonstration School (discussed in Hale 2001), which embraced the idea in 1966 that Navajo children should be educated in their native language. Children were therefore taught in Navajo, and the school was used as a model for other successful programs in places as far away as Australia. In spite of all these positive steps, the 1950s Indian language eradication programs mentioned previously took their toll on Navajo as well, and Navajo is still fighting its way back. There are several dual-language and Navajo immersion programs spread throughout the Navajo territory; Diné College in Shiprock, New Mexico, on the Navajo reservation, has a Navajo Language Program in which students can receive an associate's degree in Navajo Language (http://www.dinecollege.edu/cds/).

Accent on *What Linguists Can Do*

By now it's clear to you that some solid knowledge of linguistics can be professionally advantageous. There are loads of possibilities. Here's a roundup of some things we've mentioned.

- Computer industry: Linguists work on speech recognition, search engines, and artificial intelligence.

Courtesy of Apple

- Higher education: A graduate degree in linguistics allows you to teach in college departments of linguistics, philosophy, psychology, speech/communication sciences, anthropology, English, computer science, and foreign languages. At the university level, many applied linguists are involved in teacher education and educational research.

- Education: People with a background in linguistics and education develop curricula and materials, train teachers, and design tests and other methods of assessment, especially for language arts and second language learning.

Monkey Business Images/ Shutterstock.com

- English as a Second Language: To teach ESL in the United States, you will probably need additional training in language pedagogy, such as a master's degree in education or TESOL. Many teaching positions abroad require only an undergraduate degree, but at least some specialized training in the subject will make you a much more effective teacher. Linguistics can give you a valuable cross-language perspective.

- Translation or interpreting: Skilled translators and interpreters are needed everywhere, from government to hospitals to courts of law. A high level of proficiency in the relevant language(s) is necessary, and specialized training may be required. Nonetheless, linguistics can help you understand the issues that arise in communicating across languages.

- Language documentation or fieldwork: A number of projects and institutes around the world are looking for linguists. Some organizations engage in language-related fieldwork,

(continued)

including documenting endangered languages, conducting language surveys, establishing literacy programs, and translating documents of cultural heritage. This is a great way to interact with speakers of diverse languages representing communities around the world.

Farah Nosh/
Getty Images

- Teaching a foreign language: Students will benefit from your knowledge of language structure and your ability to make certain aspects of the language especially clear. You will need a high level of proficiency in the relevant language and possibly additional training.

- Publishing: The verbal skills and knowledge that linguists develop are ideal for numerous positions in editing, publishing, and writing.

American Copy
Editors Society

- Testing agency: Linguists help prepare and evaluate standardized exams and conduct research on assessment issues.

- Dictionaries: Knowledge of phonology, morphology, historical linguistics, dialectology, and sociolinguistics is key to becoming a lexicographer.

Erin McKean

- Consultant on language in professions (e.g., law, medicine): Forensic linguistics involves studying the language of legal texts, linguistic aspects of evidence, issues of voice identification, and so on. Agencies such as the FBI and police departments, law

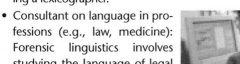

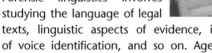

LAIF/Redux

firms, and the courts hire linguists for these purposes.

- Product naming: Companies that name products do extensive linguistic research on the associations that people make with particular sounds and classes of sounds.

© South West
Images Scotland/
Alamy

- Government: The federal government hires linguists for the Foreign Service, the FBI, and so on.

- Acting or training actors: Actors need training in pronunciation, intonation, and different elements of grammar to sound like real speakers of a language or dialect. They may even need to know how to make mistakes to sound like an authentic nonnative speaker.

Courtesy of Andrew
Jack

The skills and abilities of those who major in linguistics are being recognized by many employers and professional schools. Studying linguistics develops critical thinking, careful analysis, research skills, and powerful communication skills. It's the best possible major!

For more information

The Linguist List. 2011. http://www.linguistlist .org/. (large, searchable site for all things linguistic; includes job postings)

Macaulay, M., & K. Syrett. Why major in linguistics? Linguistic Society of America. http://www.lsadc.org/info/ling-faqs-whymajor.cfm.

Summary

This chapter has given you the "big picture" of language, bringing together many of the themes and concepts discussed throughout this book. We have seen that the entire life cycle of a language—language birth, language and dialect endangerment, language death, language maintenance and survival—is affected by people and the choices we make. While many questions about language (its origins in humans, and why only in humans, for example) remain hard (and maybe impossible) to answer, what we do know is that the more we learn about language, the better equipped we are to make informed rather than discriminatory decisions about our own language and the language(s) around us.

Sources and Resources

Atkins, J. 1887. *Annual report of the commissioner of Indian affairs to the secretary of the interior for the year 1887.* Washington, DC: U.S. Government Printing Office.

The Atlas of Pidgin and Creole Language Structures Project. http://lingweb.eva.mpg.de/apics/index.php/The_Atlas_of_Pidgin_and_Creole_Language_Structures_%28APiCS%29. (31 May 2011).

Benton, R. 1981. *The flight of the Amokura: Oceanic languages and formal education in the South Pacific.* Wellington: New Zealand Council for Educational Research.

Bickerton, D. 1981. *Roots of language.* Ann Arbor, MI: Karoma.

Boas, F. 1917. *Folk tales of Salishan and Sahaptin tribes.* Lancaster, PA, and New York: American Folk-Lore Society.

Center for Diné Studies. 2004. Navajo Language Program and Diné Studies. http://www.dinecollege.edu/cds/.

Cherokee Preservation Foundation. 2011. http://www.cherokeepreservationfdn.org/languagerevitalization.html.

Christiansen, M. & S. Kirby (eds.). 2003. *Language evolution.* New York: Oxford University Press.

Crawford, J. 1995. Endangered Native American languages: What is to be done and why? *The Bilingual Research Journal* 19(1). 17–38.

Crawford, J. 1998. Endangered Native American languages: What is to be done, and why? *Language and Politics in the United States and Canada: Myths and Realities*, ed. by Thomas Ricento and Barbara Burnaby. Mahwah, NJ: Lawrence Erlbaum Associates.

Deacon, T. 1997. *The symbolic species: The co-evolution of language and the brain.* New York: W. W. Norton.

Dunbar, R. 1998. *Grooming, gossip, and the evolution of language.* Cambridge, MA: Harvard University Press.

Grigorjevskij, A. 2011. Esperanto.net. http://www.esperanto.net/info/index_en.html.

Hale, K. 2001. The Navajo language II. *The green book of language revitalization in practice*, ed. by L. Hinton and K. Hale, 199–201. New York: Academic Press.

Harrison, K. 2008. http://www.swarthmore.edu/SocSci/dharris2/. (31 May 2011).

Hinton, L. & K. Hale (eds.). 2001. *The green book of language revitalization in practice.* New York: Academic Press.

Holloway, R. 1983. Human paleontological evidence relevant to language behavior. *Human Neurobiology* 2. 105–114.

Holloway, R. 1996. Evolutionary of the human brain. *Handbook of human symbolic evolution*, ed. by A. Locke and C. Peters, 74–108. Oxford, UK: Oxford Science Publications.

Ironbound Films. 2011. *The Linguists.* http://www.thelinguists.com/

Jaimes, M. (ed.). 1992. *The state of Native America: Genocide, colonization, and resistance.* Boston, MA: South End Press.

Jones, N. 1972. *Seattle.* Garden City, NY: Doubleday.

Keesing, R. 1988. *Melanesian pidgin and the Oceanic substrate.* Palo Alto, CA: Stanford University Press.

Krauss, M. 1992. The world's languages in crisis. *Language* 68(1). 4–10.

Krauss, M. 1998. The condition of Native North American languages: The need for realistic assessment and action. *International Journal of the Sociology of Language* 132. 9–21.

Lane, H. 1989. *When the mind hears: A history of the deaf.* New York: Vintage Books.

The Linguist List. 2011. http://www.linguistlist.org/.

Lewis, P. 2009. Chinook Wawa: A language of Canada. *Ethnologue: Languages of the world,* 16th ed. Dallas, TX: SIL International. Online version: http://www.ethnologue.com/show_language.asp?code=chn.

Lewis, P (ed.). 2009. *Ethnologue: Languages of the world,* 16th ed. Dallas, TX: SIL International. Online version: http://www.ethnologue.com/.

Living Tongues Institute for Endangered Languages. 2011. http://livingtongues.org/enduringvoices.html.

Lushootseed Research. 2011. http://www.lushootseed.org/.

Macaulay, M. & K. Syrett. 2011. Why major in linguistics? Linguistic Society of America. http://www.lsadc.org/info/ling-faqs-whymajor.cfm.

Morgan, G. 2001. Welsh: A European case of language maintenance. *The green book of language revitalization in practice,* ed. by L. Hinton and K. Hale, 107–113. New York: Academic Press.

National Geographic. 2011. Enduring Voices Project. http://www.nationalgeographic.com/mission/enduringvoices/.

Robinson, D. 1988. Language policy and planning. *ERIC Digest.* Washington, DC: ERIC Clearinghouse on Languages and Linguistics. ERIC Identifier: ED303051. http://www.ericdigests.org/pre-9210/planning.htm.

Schuchardt, H. 1885. *Uber die Lautgesetze Gegen die Junggrammatiker.* Berlin: Robert Oppenheim.

Smith, G. 2002. *Growing up with Tok Pisin: Contact, creolization, and change in Papua New Guinea's national language.* London: Battlebridge Publications.

Wilson, W. & K. Kamana. 2001. *'Mai Loko Mai O Ka 'I'ini:* Proceeding from a dream: The 'Aha Punana Leo connection in Hawaiian language revitalization. *The green book of language revitalization in practice,* ed. by L. Hinton and K. Hale. New York: Academic Press.

Young, R. & W. Morgan. 1943. *The Navajo language.* Republished in 2003 as *The Navajo language: A grammar and colloquial dictionary,* 2nd ed. Flagstaff, AZ: Salina Bookshelf, Inc. University of New Mexico Press.

Review, Practice, and Explore

RPE 14.1 > Language Origins

Research the language origin stories of a culture other than your own. What do the stories about where language comes from tell us about the culture itself and about language? Some to consider are the myths of Bantu, Hindu, Ancient Greek, or Aztec cultures.

RPE 14.2 > Cape York Creole Pronouns

Consider the following data illustrating some aspects of the pronominal system of Cape York Creole, an English-based creole spoken in Australia. Using these data to illustrate your point, present an argument to someone who claims that this creole is just bad English.

dual and plural, 2nd and 3rd persons

dual, 2nd person	yutu (pela)
dual, 3rd person	tupela
plural, 2nd person	yu (pela)
plural, 3rd person	ol, dempela

dual and plural pronouns, 1st person

dual, inclusive	yumi, yumtu (speaker plus one addressee)
dual, exclusive	mitu (speaker plus one other, not the addressee)
plural, inclusive	mipela, wi (speaker plus addressee)
plural, exclusive	mitupela, wi (speaker plus others, not addressee)

a. If A says to B, "*Yumi go nau*," A is saying that the two of them will go but not C.
b. If A says to B, "*Mitu go nau*," A is saying that A and C will go but not B.
c. If A says to B and C, "*Mipela go nau*," A is saying that all three of them will go.

RPE   14.3 ▷ Creole Transitivity Markers

Many unrelated creoles have a grammatical marker for *transitivity* (marked TRN below); that is, if a verb is transitive, the transitive morpheme must be attached. Consider the transitivity markers in the following languages.

Solomons Pidgin

luk	'look'
lukim	'see something'
hamar	'pound, hammer'
hamarim	'pound, hammer something'
sut	'shoot'
sutim	'shoot something'

Mi no luk-im pikipiki bulong iu
I no see (TRN) pigs belong you
'I didn't see your pigs.'

And the same sentence is ungrammatical if the transitivity marker is not attached:

*Mi no luk pikipiki bulong iu.

Kwaio (an Oceanic creole language)

aga	'look'
agasi	'see something'
gumu	'pound, hammer'
gumuri	'pound, hammer something'
fana	'shoot'
fanasi	'shoot something'

Conduct some research to find another creole language that uses a transitivity marker. Illustrate with examples. Then, using these data, construct an argument for someone who claims that creoles are simplified and/or illogical versions of a more standardized language. (Data from Keesing 1988: 119)

RPE 14.4 > **Latin Lives On**

Look up the following Latin words and phrases, and determine original Latin meanings of at least six. Have the meanings changed, or do they hold their original meanings in Present-Day English?

> ad infinitum, alter ego, alumni, A.D. (anno Domini), bona fide, circa, de facto, e.g. (exempli gratia), ergo, extant, facsimile, in vitro, inter alia, m.o. (modus operandi), nota bene (n.b.), per capita, per se, post mortem, pro bono, pro forma, quorum, re, sic, status quo, subpoena, tabula rasa, terra firma, veto, vice versa

RPE 14.5 > **Language Death**

Using *Ethnologue* (http://www.ethnologue.org) and other sources, conduct some research to discover at least five languages that have fewer than one hundred speakers and therefore may soon be extinct. Determine which language has replaced the endangered language. What factors led to that replacement? Summarize your findings.

RPE 14.6 > **English-Only Laws**

Many websites are devoted to the pros and cons of the English Only/Official English movement (some are listed here). Research the pros and cons of the English Only movement. What are the central arguments for each position? Which arguments are supported by statistics and research, and which are based on social attitudes about language and national identity? Where do you stand on this issue and why?

> U.S. English: http://www.us-english.org/.
> James Crawford's website: http://www.languagepolicy.net/archives/home.htm.
> English First: http://www.englishfirst.org/.
> English Plus: http://www.massenglishplus.org/mep/engplus.html.
> Pro-English: http://www.proenglish.org/notenglishonly.html.
> Center for Applied Linguistics: http://www.cal.org/resources/digest/lewell01.html.
> Linguistic Society of America Resolution, drafted by Geoff Nunberg: http://www.lsadc.org/info/lsa-res-english.cfm.

RPE 14.7 > **English as a Second Language**

Using *Ethnologue* (http://www.ethnologue.org) and other sources, conduct some research to discover at least five countries in which English is an official language but is not a native language of most speakers. Determine, if you can, what factors have led to the prominence of English in these countries.

Credits

These pages constitute an extension of the copyright page. We have made every effort to trace the ownership of all copyrighted material and to secure permission from copyright holders. In the event of any question arising as to the use of any material, we will be pleased to make the necessary corrections in future printings. Thanks are due to the following authors, publishers, and agents for permission to use the material indicated.

Chapter 1

pp. 1, 22
© Cengage Learning 2013
Figure 1.1, p. 16
From *A Basic Course in American Sign Language* by Tom Humphries, Carol Padden, and Terrence J. O'Rourke (1994). Used by permission of the authors.

Chapter 2

pp. 31, 42, 57
© Cengage Learning 2013
Drawings, p. 34
Berko-Gleason, J. 1958. The child's learning of English Morphology. *Word*, 14, 150–177; Jean Berko-Gleason. Reprinted by permission.

p. 40
Table 52, Page 358 "Acquisition order (children's) and frequencies for the 14 morphemes plus passives and perfectives in the three sets of parents" reprinted by permission of the publisher from *A First Language: The Early Stages* by Roger Brown, p. 358, Cambridge, Mass.: Harvard University Press, Copyright © 1973 by the President and Fellows of Harvard College.

p. 42, Table 2.2
Data from Lenneburg, E. 1967. *Biological Foundations of Language.* New York: Wiley.

p. 52, Table 2.3
Source: From Bickerton, D. "Creole Languages." In V. Clark, P. Escholz, & A. Rosa (eds.), *Language: Introductory Readings*, 4th edn. New York: St. Martin's.

p. 66
"Grammar Alive," from *Non-Native Speakers in the English Classroom* by B. Haussamen et al., 2003. Reprinted by permission of National Council of Teachers of English.

p. 67
"Creole Grammar," from page 65 from Honda, Maya / O'Neil, Wayne, Thinking Linguistically: A Scientific Approach to Language, November 2007. Wiley UK. Used with permission.

Data from Curtiss, S. 1977, "Genie: A Psycholinguistic study of a modern-day "wild child" (perspectives in neurolinguistics and psycholinguistics)." NY: Academic Press, p. 31.

Chapter 3

pp. 69, 83, 85(2), 91, 94, 101
© Cengage Learning 2013

p. 70
Reprinted by permission of Neal Whitman.

p. 74, Table 3.1, Table 3.2
Source: The International Phonetic Alphabet, International Phonetic Association (Department of Theoretical and Applied Linguistics, School of English, Aristotle University of Thessaloniki, Thessaloniki 54124, Greece)

Source: The International Phonetic Alphabet, International Phonetic Association (Department of Theoretical and Applied Linguistics, School of English, Aristotle University of Thessaloniki, Thessaloniki 54124, Greece)

p. 75
Used by permission of Russell Hugo.

p. 92
Data from William Labov, "The Organization of Dialect Diversity in North America." Paper presented at the Fourth International Conference on Spoken Language Processing, Philadelphia, PA, October 6, 1996.

p. 93
Data from William Labov, "The Organization of Dialect Diversity in North America." Paper presented at the Fourth International Conference on Spoken Language Processing, Philadelphia, PA, October 6, 1996.

Chapter 4

pp. 103, 105, 106, 113, 123(2)
© Cengage Learning 2013

p. 121
Reprinted from *Going Nucular: Language, Politics, and Culture in Confrontational Times* by Geoffrey Nunberg, published in 2004 by PublicAffairs. © 2004 by Geoffrey Nunberg.

p. 129
Data from D. Deutsch, et al. 1999. Tone language speakers possess absolute pitch. Acoustical Society of America (ASA) 138. Columbus, OH.

p. 135(2)
Cowan, W. & J. Rakušan. 1985. Source book for linguistics. John Benjamins Publishing, Philadelphia/Amsterdam. p. 42.

Chapter 5
pp. 141, 146, 147, 157(3), 158(2), 159(2), 160, 166, 170, 173
© Cengage Learning 2013

pp. 177
"How I Met My Wife" by Jack Winter as appeared in *The New Yorker*, July 25, 1994, p. 82. Reprinted by permission.

p. 176–177
From Tolkien, J.R.R. 1999. *The Fellowship of the Ring*. Boston: Houghton Mifflin.

Chapter 6
pp. 183, 197
© Cengage Learning 2013

p. 211–212
A. *Chickamauga* by Charles Wright, p. 44 (New York: Farrar, Straus and Giroux, 1995); B. *Chickamauga* by Charles Wright, p. 47 (New York: Farrar, Straus and Giroux, 1995); C. *Meditation on Song and Structure* by Charles Wright, p. 120 (New York: Farrar, Straus and Giroux, 1997); D. *Negative Blue* by Charles Wright, p. 120 (New York: Farrar, Straus and Giroux, 1997); E. *A Short History of the Shadow* by Charles Wright, p. 7 (New York: Farrar, Straus and Giroux, 2002); F. *The World of the Ten Thousand Things* by Charles Wright, p. 132 (New York: Farrar, Straus and Giroux, 1990) Adapted from Source Book for Linguistics, by William Cowan and Jaromira Rakusan. John Benjamins Publishing Company, Philadelphia/Amsterdam. 1985. p. 79. Adapted from Source Book for Linguistics, by William Cowan and Jaromira Rakusan. John Benjamins Publishing Company, Philadelphia/Amsterdam. 1985. pp. 88–89. From Mithun, M. 1999. The Languages of Native North America. Cambridge: Cambridge UP, pp. 366, 38.

p. 188
From *The Navajo Verb System* by Robert W. Young, pp. 3–7. Copyright © 2000. Reprinted by permission of the University of New Mexico Press.

p. 201, 203
Oxford English Dictionary

Chapter 7
pp. 215, 219, 221, 223, 227(2), 228, 229, 232, 233, 234(2), 237, 239
© Cengage Learning 2013

p. 235
From Millward, C. M. *A Biography of the English Language*, 2nd edn. © 1996 Heinle/Arts & Sciences, a part of Cengage Learning, Inc. Reproduced by permission. www.cengage.com/permissions.

p. 240
Vol. 1, Book 3, Ch. 8, p. 148 from *Don Quixote de la Mancha* by Miguel de Cervantes, translated by T. Smollett. Copyright © 1986. NY: Farrar, Straus and Giroux.

p. 241
Excerpts from dictionaries

p. 244
From Pullman, P. 1995. *The Golden Compass*. NY: Knopf, p. 3.

p. 245
From Nafisi, A. 2003. *Reading Lolita in Tehran: A Memoir in Books*. NY: Random House, p. 16.

p. 246
"Of Mere Being," from *Opus Posthumous* by Wallace Stevens, edited by Milton J. Bates, copyright © 1989 by Alfred A. Knopf, a division of Random House, Inc. Copyright © 1957 by Elsie Stevens and Holly Steven. Copyright renewed 1985 by Holly Stevens. Used by permission of Vintage Books, a division of Random House, Inc.

pp. 247–248
Jabberwocky

Chapter 8
pp. 251, 252, 253, 254, 255, 256, 257, 258, 260, 261, 263, 265, 266, 271
© Cengage Learning 2013

pp. 278
Short paragraph (paragraph 27) from brochure by Roberts, S. 1992. "11 Ways to Improve Your Writing and Your Business." Greensboro, NC: The Roberts Group. http://www.editorialservice.com/11ways.html

Chapter 9
pp. 291, 302, 304, 305, 306
© Cengage Learning 2013

p. 293
Quotes from Mrs. Malaprop

p. 294
"What Did?" from *A Light in the Attic* by Shel Silverstein. Copyright © 1981 by Evil Eye Music, Inc. Used by permission of HarperCollins Publishers.

p. 295
"The Bells," Edgar Allen Poe from http://tigger.uic.edu/~rramakri/Readings/Fun/Mixed-Metaphors.html.

p. 320
Verses from Browning, R., 1888, from *The Pied Piper of Hamelin*. NY: Frederick Warne & Co.

p. 323
Lisel Mueller, *Alive Together: New and Selected Poems*. © 1996 by Lisel Mueller. Reprinted by permission of Louisiana State University Press.

Chapter 10
p. 329
© Cengage Learning 2013

p. 336
Source: Levinson from Faderman, L. with G. Xiong. 1998. *I Begin My Life All Over: The Hmong and the American Immigrant Experience*. Boston: Beacon Press.

p. 338
Definitions from Saeed, J. 2003. Semantics, 2nd edn. Oxford: Blackwell. pp. 149–150.

p. 343
Source: Grice 1989.

p. 347, Table 10.2
"Linguistic etiquette" from *Readings in the Sociology of Language* by Joshua A. Fishman. Copyright © 1968. Published by Walter de Gruyter. Reprinted by permission of the author.

p. 349
Harada 1976: 514.

pp. 349–350
Geertz 1968: 282–295.

p. 351
Hughes 2000: 125–130.

Chapter 11
pp. 367, 370(2), 373, 380
© Cengage Learning 2013

p. 375, Table 11.3
Source: Lewis, M. P. (ed.). 2009. *Ethnologue: Languages of the World*, 16th edn. Dallas, TX: SIL International. Online version: http://www.ethnologue.com/ Used by permission of SIL International.

pp. 391–392
Excerpts from Johnson, Samuel, 1755, *The Dictionary of the English Language*. London: Richard Bentley.

Chapter 12
pp. 407, 416, 417
© Cengage Learning 2013

Chapter 13
p. 441
© Cengage Learning 2013

p. 475
From Trigiani, A. *Big Stone Gap*. NY: Ballantine Books.

Chapter 14
pp. 477, 489, 491, 502
© Cengage Learning 2013

p. 480
Source: Lewis, M. Paul (ed.), 2009. *Ethnologue: Languages of the World*, 16th edn. Dallas, TX: SIL International. Online version: http://www.ethnologue .com/ Used by permission of SIL International. Figure 14.1, p. 483

Source: Deacon, T. 1997. *The Symbolic Species: The Co-evolution of Language and the Brain*. New York: W. W. Norton, 356. http://wwwens.uqac.ca/ ~flabelle/socio/larynx.htm

Bibliography

Adams, D. & J. Lloyd. 1983. *The meaning of liff*. London: Pan Books. Also available at http://folk.uio.no/alied/TMoL.html

Adger, C., C. Snow & D. Christian (eds.). 2002. *What teachers need to know about language*. McHenry, IL: Delta Systems.

Ager, S. Alphabets. Omniglot: Writing Systems and Languages of the World. http://www.omniglot.com/writing/alphabets.htm. (8 November 2011.)

Ager, S. Shavian alphabet. Omniglot: Writing Systems and Languages of the World. http://www.omniglot.com/writing/shavian.htm

Algeo, J. & C. Acevedo Butcher. 2005. *Problems in the origins and development of the English language*, 5th edn. Boston: Thomson Wadsworth.

All-acronyms.com. http://www.all-acronyms.com

American Academy of Pediatrics. http://www.aap.org

The American Copy Editors Society. http://www.copydesk.org

American Dialect Society. http://www.americandialect.org

American heritage dictionary of the English language, 4th edn. 2000. Boston: Houghton Mifflin.

American Philological Association. http://www.apaclassics.org/APA-MENU.html

Anderson, S. 1974. *The organization of phonology*. New York: Academic Press.

Anderson, S. 1976. On the notion of subject in ergative languages. In C. Li (ed.), *Subject and Topic*, 1–24. New York: Academic Press.

Apostrophe Protection Society. http://www.apostrophe.org.uk/. (8 November 2011.)

Aronoff, M. 1976. *Word formation in generative grammar*. Cambridge, MA: MIT Press.

AskOxford.com. http://www.askoxford.com/worldofwords/oed/wordsearchers/?view=uk

Association for the Advancement of Artificial Intelligence. http://www.aaai.org/home.html

Association for Computational Linguistics (ACL). http://www.aclweb.org

Atkins, J. 1887. *Annual report of the commissioner of Indian affairs to the secretary of the interior for the year 1887*. Washington, DC: U.S. Government Printing Office.

The Atlas of Pidgin and Creole Language Structures Project. https://lingweb.eva.mpg.de/apics/index.php/The_Atlas_of_Pidgin_and_Creole_Language_Structures_%28APiCS%29. (8 November 2011.)

Austin, J. 1962. *How to do things with words*. Oxford: Oxford University Press.

Ayers, D. 1986. *English words from Latin and Greek elements*, 2nd edn. Revised by T. Worthen. Tucson: University of Arizona Press.

Ayers, E. 1996. What we talk about when we talk about the South. In E. Ayers et al. (eds.), *All over the map: Rethinking American regions*. Baltimore: Johns Hopkins University Press.

Baker, C. 1995. *English syntax*, 2nd edn. Cambridge, MA: MIT Press.

Ball, M. 1993. *Phonetics for speech pathology*, 2nd edn. London: Whurr.

Ball, M., et al. (eds.). Forthcoming. *The handbook of clinical linguistics*. Malden, MA: Wiley-Blackwell.

Banks, M., et al. 1975. Sensitive period for the development of human binocular vision. *Science* 190(4213). 675–677.

Baron, N. 1998. Letters by phone or speech by other means: The linguistics of email. *Language and Communication* 18. 133–170.

Baron, N. 2000. *Alphabet to email: How written English evolved and where it's heading*. New York: Routledge.

Bauer, L. 1983. *English word formation*. Cambridge: Cambridge University Press.

Baugh, A. & T. Cable. 1993. *A history of the English language*, 4th edn. London: Routledge.

Baugh, J. 2000. Racial identification by speech. *American Speech* 75(4). 362–364.

Beal, J. 2004. *English in modern times: 1700–1945*. London: Arnold.

Benton, R. 1981. *The flight of the Amokura: Oceanic languages and formal education in the South Pacific*. Wellington: New Zealand Council for Educational Research.

Berko, J. 1958. The child's learning of English morphology. *Word* 14. 150–177.

Bett, S. 2002. Introduction to the Shaw Alphabet. *Journal of the Simplified Spelling Society* 2. 23–24. Available at http://www.spellingsociety.org/aboutsss/aims.php

Bickerton, D. 1981. *Roots of language*. Ann Arbor, MI: Karoma.

Bickerton, D. & commentators. 1984. The language bioprogram hypothesis. *Behavioral and Brain Sciences* 7. 173–221.

Bickerton, D. 1985. Creole languages. In V. Clark, P. Escholz & A. Rosa (eds.), *Language: Introductory readings*, 4th edn., 134–151. New York: St. Martin's.

Bloomer, A., et al. 2005. *Introducing language in use: A coursebook*. New York: Routledge.

Boas, F. 1917. *Folk tales of Salishan and Sahaptin tribes*. Lancaster, PA, and New York: American Folk-Lore Society.

Bower, B. 2005. The Pirahã challenge: An Amazonian tribe takes grammar to a strange place. *Science News*. December 10. http://findarticles.com/p/articles/mi_m1200/is_24_168/ai_ n16029317

Bocaccio, G. (written 1351). 1996. *The Decameron*. New York: Penguin Classics.

The British Museum. http://www.thebritishmuseum.ac.uk/compass/ixbin/goto?id=OBJ67

Brown, P. & S. Levinson. 1987. *Politeness: Some universals in language usage*. Cambridge: Cambridge University Press.

Brown, R. 1973. *A first language: The early stages*. Cambridge, MA: Harvard University Press.

Browning, R. 1888. *The pied piper of Hamelin*. New York and London: Frederick Warne & Co.

Burt, S. & H. Yang. 2005. Growing up shifting: Immigrant children, their families, and the schools. In K. Denham & A. Lobeck (eds.), *Language in the schools: Integrating linguistic knowledge into K–12 education*. Mahwah, NJ: Erlbaum Associates.

Campaign for a Commercial-Free Childhood. http://www.commercialexploitation.org

Campbell, G. 1776. *The philosophy of rhetoric*. Edinburgh: Creech.

Canin, G. 1964. Conversations with Felix. *Reader's Digest* 84(506). June.

Caplan, D. 1987. *Neurolinguistics and linguistic aphasiology*. New York: Cambridge University Press.

Carnie, A. 2002. *Syntax: A generative introduction*, 1st edn. Malden, MA: Blackwell.

Cassidy, F. (ed.). 1985. *The dictionary of American Regional English*. Cambridge, MA: Belknap Press.

Center for Diné Studies. 2004. Navajo Language Program and Diné Studies. http://www.dine college.edu/cds/

Cervantes, M. 1755. *The history and adventures of the renowned Don Quixote*. T. Smollett, trans. Published 1986 as *Don Quixote de la Mancha*, 2nd edn. New York: Farrar, Straus & Giroux.

Cherokee Preservation Foundation. http://www.cherokeepreservationfdn.org/language revitalization.html

Chesterton, G. 1902. *The defendant*. London: J. W. Dent & Sons.

Chevalier, T. 2001. *The girl with a pearl earring*. New York: Plume.

Chierchia, G. & A. McConnell-Ginet. 1990. *Meaning and grammar*. Cambridge, MA: MIT Press.

Chomsky, N. 1957. *Syntactic structures*. The Hague: Mouton.

Chomsky, N. 1965. *Aspects of the theory of syntax*. Cambridge, MA: MIT Press.

Chomsky, N. 1981. *Lectures on government and binding: The Pisa lectures*. Dordrecht: Foris Publications.

Chomsky, N. 2006. *Language and mind*, 3rd edn. New York: Cambridge University Press.

Chomsky, N. & M. Halle. 1968. *The sound pattern of English.* New York: Harper & Row.

Christiansen, M. & S. Kirby (eds.). 2003. *Language evolution.* New York: Oxford University Press.

Chwat, S. Sam Chwat Speech Center. http://www.samchwatspeechcenter.com. (8 November 2011.)

Clark, H. & E. Clark. 1977. *Psychology and language: An introduction to psycholinguistics.* New York: Harcourt Brace Jovanovich.

Clark, J. & C. Yallop. 1990. *An introduction to phonetics and phonology.* Oxford: Blackwell.

Coggshall, E. October 2007. The prosodic rhythm of two varieties of Native American English. *New Ways of Analyzing Variation (NWAV)* 36. Philadelphia, PA.

Colapinto, J. 2007. The interpreter: Has a remote Amazonian tribe upended our understanding of language? *The New Yorker.* October 20. http://www.newyorker.com/reporting/2007/04/16/070416fa_fact_colapinto

Cole, P. & J. Good (eds.). Typological tools for field linguistics. Max Planck Institute for Evolutionary Anthropology Department of Linguistics. http://www.eva.mpg.de/lingua/tools-at-lingboard/tools.php. (8 November 2011.)

Computational Linguistics. MIT Press Journals. http://mitpress.mitpressjournals.org/los/coli

Computer Speech and Language. 2008. Elsevier Press. http://www.elsevier.com/wps/find/journaldescription.cws_home/622808/description#description

Comrie, B. 1982. *Language universals and linguistic typology.* Chicago: University of Chicago Press.

Comrie, B. 1998. Language. In *MSN Encarta Encyclopedia.* http://encarta.msn.com/encyclopedia_761570647_4/Language.html#s36

Cook, M. & M. Sharp. 1966. Problems of Navajo speakers in learning English. *Language Learning* 16. 21–29.

Cook, V. & M. Newson. 1996. *Chomsky's universal grammar: An introduction*, 2nd edn. Oxford: Blackwell.

Crain, S. & D. Lillo-Martin. 1999. *An introduction to linguistic theory and language acquisition.* Oxford: Blackwell.

Crain, S., R. Thornton & G. Tesan. How children ask questions. Video. On LSA: Videos on the Web. http://www.uga.edu/lsava/Crain/Crain.html. (8 November 2011.)

Crawford, J. 1995. Endangered Native American languages: What is to be done and why? *The Bilingual Research Journal* 19(1). 17–38.

Crawford, J. March 1996. Anatomy of the English-Only movement. *Conference on Language Legislation and Linguistic Rights.* University of Illinois at Urbana-Champaign. http://ourworld.compuserve.com/homepages/jWCRAWFORD/anatomy.htm

Crawford, J. 1998. *Language and politics in the U.S. and Canada.* Mahwah, NJ: Lawrence Erlbaum Associates.

Cruse, D. 1986. *Lexical semantics.* Cambridge: Cambridge University Press.

Crystal, D. 1988. *The English language.* New York: Penguin Books.

Crystal, D. 1995. *The Cambridge encyclopedia of the English language.* Cambridge: Cambridge University Press.

Crystal, D. 2001. *Language and the Internet.* Cambridge: Cambridge University Press.

Crystal, D. 2003. Clinical linguistics. In M. Aronoff & J. Rees-Miller (eds.), *Handbook of linguistics*, 673–682. Malden, MA: Blackwell.

Curtiss, S. 1977. *Genie: A psycholinguistic study of a modern-day "wild child" (Perspectives in neurolinguistics and psycholinguistics).* New York: Academic Press.

Daily Guide. 1994. *Lansing State Journal*, April 3, 1. Cited in Lippi-Green, 210.

Deacon, T. 1997. *The symbolic species: The co-evolution of language and the brain.* New York: W. W. Norton.

DeMillo, A. 2007. Arkansas House backs Apostrophe Act. Associated Press. March 6.

Denham, K. 2005. Ludlings teach language diversity and change. *National Council of Teachers of English (NCTE) Annual Meeting.* Pittsburgh, PA.

Denham, K. & A. Lobeck (eds.). 2005. *Language in the schools: Integrating linguistic knowledge into K–12 teaching.* Mahwah, NJ: Lawrence Erlbaum Associates.

Denham, K. & A. Lobeck (eds.). 2009. *Linguistics at school: Language awareness in primary and secondary education.* Cambridge: Cambridge University Press.

Department of Human Communication Sciences, University of Sheffield. http://www.shef.ac.uk/hcs/research/clinling

Derbyshire, D. & G. Pullum. 1981. Object initial languages. *International Journal of American Linguistics* 47. 192–214.

Deutsch, D., et al. 1999. Tone language speakers possess absolute pitch. *Acoustical Society of America (ASA)* 138. Columbus, OH.

Deutsch, D., et al. 2006. Absolute pitch among American and Chinese conservatory students: Prevalence differences, and evidence for a speech-related critical period. *Journal of the Acoustical Society of America* 119. 719–722.

de Villiers, J. (see Villiers)

Dictionary of American Regional English. http://polyglot.lss.wisc.edu/dare/dare.html

Doughton, S. 2008. Fossilized feces found in Oregon suggest earliest human presence in North America. *Seattle Times.* April 3. http://seattletimes.nwsource.com/html/localnews/2004324975_weboldpoop04m.html

Duffy, P. 2001. *Blue cats and chartreuse kittens.* New York: Henry Holt.

Dumas, B. (ed.). 2000. Language in the judicial process. http://www.ljp.utk.edu/. (8 November 2011.)

Dunbar, R. 1998. *Grooming, gossip, and the evolution of language.* Cambridge, MA: Harvard University Press.

Eagleton, T. 1983. *Literary theory.* Minneapolis: University of Minnesota Press.

Eckert, G. 2002. Bay Area dialect coaches. *Theater Bay Area.* August. http://www/theatre bayarea.org/mag/article.jsp;jsessionid=1967A2040400FD151A51FA8810F550F9Dthis page=archives.jsp&id=36&hi=1

Eckert, P. & S. McConnell-Ginet. 1992. Think practically and look locally: Language and gender as community-based practice. *Annual Review of Anthropology* 21. 461–490.

Edwards, K. 2008. Reading between the lines. *BBC News.* May 23. http.//news.bbc.co.uk/1/hi/england/west_midlands/7411388.stm

Else, L. & L. Middleton. 2008. Interview: Out on a limb over language. *New Scientist.* January 19. http://www.newscientist.com/channel/opinion/mg19726391.900-interview-out-on-a-limb-over-language.html

Emmorey K. & H. Lane (eds.), *The signs of language revisited,* 103–114. Mahwah, NJ: Lawrence Erlbaum Associates.

Enard, W., et al. 2002. Molecular evolution of FOXP2, a gene involved in speech and language. *Nature* 418. 869–872.

Evans, B. & C. Evans. 2000. *The dictionary of contemporary usage.* New York: Random House.

Evans, G. 1977. Pronouns, quantifier and relative clauses. *Canadian Journal of Philosophy* 7. 467–536.

Everett, D. 2005. Cultural constraints on grammar and cognition in Pirahã: Another look at the design features of human language. *Current Anthropology* 46(4). 621–646. http://www.llc.ilstu.edu/dlevere/docs/currentanthroarticle.web.pdf

Everett, D. 2008. *Don't sleep, there are snakes: Life and language in the Amazonian jungle.* New York: Pantheon.

Everett, D. 2008. Out on a limb over language. Video. http://uk.youtube.com/watch?v=v7Spzjh9QgA

Faderman, L., with G. Xiong. 1998. *I begin my life all over: The Hmong and the American immigrant experience.* Boston: Beacon Press.

Fahlman, S. History. Carnegie Mellon Computer Science Department. http://www.cs.cmu .edu/smiley

Fennell, B. 2001. *A history of English.* Malden, MA: Blackwell.

Fillmore, L. & C. Snow. 2002. What teachers need to know about language. In C. Adger, C. Snow & D. Christian (eds.), *What teachers need to know about language*, 7–53. McHenry, IL: Delta Systems.

Fisher, S., et al. 1998. Localisation of a gene implicated in a severe speech and language disorder. *Nature Genetics* 18. 168–170.

Flanigan, B. 1984. Bilingual education for Native Americans: The argument from studies of variational English. In J. Handscome (ed.), *On TESOL '83*, 81–93. Washington, DC: TESOL.

Fodor, J. 1975. *The language of thought.* New York: Crowell.

Foss, D. & D. Hakes. 1978. *Psycholinguistics.* Englewood Cliffs, NJ: Prentice-Hall.

Fought, C. 2003. *Chicano English in context.* New York: Palgrave/MacMillan Publishers.

Fought, C. 2005. Interview: Do you speak American? Talking with Mi Gente. Public Broadcasting System (PBS). http://www.pbs.org/speak/seatosea/american varieties/ chicano/

Fradkin, R. 2000. Evolution of Alphabets. http://www.wam.umd.edu/~rfradkin/alphapage .html. (10 February 2000.)

Freedman, R. 1963. *The lyrical novel: Studies in Hermann Hesse, André Gide and Virginia Woolf.* Princeton, NJ: Princeton University Press.

Friess, S. 2003. Yo, can u plz help me write English? *USA Today.* March 31.

Fromkin Speech Error Database. 2002. Max Planck Institute for Psycholinguistics. http:// www.mpi.nl/resources/data/fromkins-speech-error-database. (8 November 2011.)

Fry, D. 1979. *The physics of speech.* Cambridge: Cambridge University Press.

Gambrell, J. 2007. Arkansas House to argue over apostrophes. Associated Press. *Boston Globe.* February 27. http://www.boston.com/news/nation/articles/2007/02/27/ arkansas _house_to_argue_over_apostrophes/

Gardner, H. 1974. *The shattered mind: The person after brain damage.* New York: Vintage Books.

Gardner, H. 1978. What we know (and don't know) about the two halves of the brain. *Harvard Magazine* 80. 24–27.

Gardner, R., B. Gardner & T. Van Cantfort (eds.). 1989. *Teaching sign language to chimpanzees.* Albany: State University of New York Press.

Gazzaniga, M. 1970. *The bisected brain.* New York: Appleton-Century-Crofts.

Geertz, C. 1968. Linguistic etiquette. In J. Fishman (ed.), *Readings in the sociology of language*, 282–295. The Hague: Mouton.

Gentner, T., et al. 2006. Recursive syntactic pattern learning by songbirds. *Nature* 440. 1204–1207.

Geschwind, N. 1979. Specializations of the human brain. *Scientific American* 206. 180–199.

Goldes, J. Joel Goldes: The dialect coach. http://www.thedialectcoach.com/content .asp?contentid = 530. (8 November 2011.)

Gordon, R. 2005. Chinook Wawa: A language of Canada. In *Ethnologue: Languages of the world*, 15th edn. Dallas, TX: SIL International. Online version: http://www.ethnologue .com/show_language.asp?code = chn

Gordon, R. (ed.). 2005. *Ethnologue: Languages of the world*, 15th edn. Dallas, TX: SIL International. Online version: http://www.ethnologue.com

Green, J. 1996. *Chasing the sun: Dictionary makers and the dictionaries they made.* New York: Henry Holt.

Greenwood, J. 1711. *An essay towards a practical English grammar.* London: R. Tookey.

Grice, P. 1975. Logic and conversation. In P. Cole & J. Morgan (eds.), *Syntax and semantics*, 3. New York: Academic Press.

Grice, P. 1989. *Studies in the way of words*. Cambridge, MA: Harvard University Press.

Grigorjevskij, A. 2005. Esperanto.net. http://www.esperanto.net/info/index_en.html

Grundy, K. (ed.). 1995. *Linguistics in clinical practice*, 2nd edn. London: Whurr.

Haegeman, L. 1997. *Elements of grammar: A handbook of generative syntax*. Dordrecht: Kluwer Academic Publishers.

Hale, K. 2001. The Navajo language II. In L. Hinton & K. Hale (eds.), *The green book of language revitalization in practice*, 199–201. New York: Academic Press.

Hall, J. (ed.). 2002. *Dictionary of American Regional English*, 4. Cambridge, MA: Belknap Press.

Hallissy, M. 1995. *A companion to Chaucer's* Canterbury Tales. Westport, CT: Greenwood Press.

Hankamer, J. & I. Sag. 1976. Deep and surface anaphora. *Linguistic Inquiry* 7. 391–426. Cambridge, MA: MIT Press.

Harada, S. 1976. Honorifics. In M. Shibatani (ed.), *Syntax and semantics*, 5. 499–561. New York: Academic Press.

Harley, H. 2006. *English words: A linguistic introduction*. Malden, MA: Blackwell.

Harrison, K. http://www.swarthmore.edu/SocSci/dharris2/

Haskins Laboratories. http://www.haskins.yale.edu/research.html

Hauser, M., N. Chomsky & W. Fitch. 2002. The faculty of language: What is it, who has it, and how did it evolve? *Science* 298(5598). 1569–1579.

Haussamen, B., et al. 2003. Non-native speakers in the English classroom. In *Grammar alive! A guide for teachers*, 53–55. Urbana, IL: NCTE.

Heim, I. 1982. *The semantics of definite and indefinite noun phrases*. Amherst, MA: University of Massachusetts dissertation.

Henriksson, A. 2002. *Non-campus mentis: History according to college students*. New York: Workman.

Hersey, J. 1963. *Here to stay*. New York: Alfred A. Knopf.

Hess, T. 1993. *Lushootseed reader with introductory grammar*, 1. Marysville, WA: Tulalip Tribes.

Hess, T. Personal communication.

Hinton, L. & K. Hale (eds.). 2001. *The green book of language revitalization in practice*. New York: Academic Press.

Hockett, C. 1960. The origin of speech. *Scientific American* 203. 88–96.

Hoffman, H. 1996. *Amorous turkeys and addicted ducklings: The science of social bonding and imprinting*. Boston, MA: Authors Cooperative.

Holloway, R. 1983. Human paleontological evidence relevant to language behavior. *Human Neurobiology* 2. 105–114.

Holloway, R. 1996. Evolution of the human brain. In A. Locke & C. Peters (eds.), *Handbook of human symbolic evolution*, 74–108. Oxford: Oxford Science Publications.

Holm, J. 1989. *Pidgins and creoles, vol. 1: Theory and structure*. Cambridge: Cambridge University Press.

Holm, J. 1994. English in the Caribbean. In R. Burchfield (ed.), *The Cambridge history of the English language*, 5. 328–381. Cambridge: Cambridge University Press.

Honda, M. & W. O'Neil. 2008. *Thinking syntactically*. Malden, MA: Wiley- Blackwell.

Honda, M., et al. 2009. On promoting linguistics literacy: Bringing language science to the English classroom. In K. Denham & A. Lobeck (eds.), *Linguistics at school: Language awareness in primary and secondary education*. Cambridge: Cambridge University Press.

Hughes, G. 2000. *A history of English words*. Malden, MA: Blackwell.

Hurford, J. & B. Heasley. 1983. *Semantics: A coursebook*. Cambridge: Cambridge University Press.

Interlandi, J. 2007. Learning: Turn it off, baby. *Newsweek*, August 20–27. http://www.news week.com/id/32243

The International Journal of Speech, Language and the Law. http://www.equinoxpub.com/ IJSLL. (8 November 2011.)

Ironbound Films. 2008. *The Linguists*. http://www.thelinguists.com

Irvine, M. & D. Everhart. Labyrinth library: Old English literature. http://www.8 .georgetown.edu/departments/medieval/labyrinth/library/oe/oe.html

Jack, A. 2008. Andrew Jack: International dialogue coach: accent and dialect. http://www .andrewjack.com

Jaimes, M. (ed.). 1992. *The state of Native America: Genocide, colonization, and resistance*. Boston, MA: South End Press.

Jensen, J. 1990. *Morphology: Word structure in generative grammar*. Amsterdam: John Benjamins.

Jespersen, O. 1922. *Language: Its nature, development and origin*. London: Allen & Unwin. Reprinted 1934. New York: Henry Holt.

Johnson, P. 2002. Linguistic profiling. *The Black Commentator* 1. April 5. http://www .blackcommentator.com/linguistic_profiling.html

Johnson, S. 1755. *A dictionary of the English language*. London: J. McGowan.

Joiner, C. 1979. *The Ann Arbor decision: Memorandum opinion and order and the educational plan*. Washington, DC: Center for Applied Linguistics.

Jones, N. 1972. *Seattle*. Garden City, NY: Doubleday.

Journal of Psycholinguistic Research. http://www.springerlink.com/content/104271/

Jusczyk, P. 1993. From general to language-specific capacities: The WRAPSA model of how speech perception develops. *Journal of Phonetics* [Special issue on phonetic development], 21(1–2). 3–28.

Kaminski, J., J. Call & J. Fischer. 2004. Word learning in a domestic dog: Evidence for "fast mapping." *Science*, June 8. 1682–1683.

Kari, J. 2008. Notes from the Dene-Yeniseic Symposium, February 26–27. University of Alaska, Fairbanks. http://www.uaf.edu/anlc/docs/Kari-DY-intro-3.pdf

Kasaan Haida Heritage Foundation. http://kavilco.com

Keesing, R. 1988. *Melanesian pidgin and the Oceanic substrate*. Palo Alto, CA: Stanford University Press.

Kegl, J. 1994. The Nicaraguan Sign Language Project: An overview. *Signpost* 7(1). 24–31.

Kegl, J., et al. 1999. Creation through contact: Sign language emergence and sign language change in Nicaragua. In M. DeGraff (ed.), *Comparative grammatical change: The intersection of language acquisition, creole genesis, and diachronic syntax*, 179–237. Cambridge, MA: MIT Press.

Kempson, R. 1977. *Semantic theory*. Cambridge: Cambridge University Press.

Kenneally, C. 2001. First language gene found. http://www.wired.com. (3 October 2001.)

Kenstowicz, H. 1995. *Phonology in generative grammar*. Oxford: Blackwell.

Keyser, B. 2008. Enriching language awareness through linguistics. *Linguistic Society of America (LSA) Symposium on Linguistics and Education*. Chicago, IL.

Klima, E. & U. Bellugi. 1979. *The signs of language*. Cambridge, MA: Harvard University Press.

Kopp, J. 2007. Directory to on-line Jargon dictionaries and other references. http://chinookjar gon.home.att.net/dictnote.htm. (26 October 2007.)

Krauss, M. 1992. The world's languages in crisis. *Language* 68(1). 4–10.

Krauss, M. 1998. The condition of Native North American languages: The need for realistic assessment and action. *International Journal of the Sociology of Language* 132. 9–21.

Kuhl, P., et al. 1997. Cross-language analysis of phonetic units in language addressed to infants. *Science* 277. 684–686.

Kurath, H. 1949. *A word geography of the Eastern United States*. Ann Arbor: University of Michigan Press.

Labov, W. 1966. *The social stratification of English in New York City*. Washington, DC: Center for Applied Linguistics.

Labov, W. 1982. Objectivity and commitment in linguistic science: The case of the black English trial in Ann Arbor. *Language in Society* 11(2). 165–201.

Labov, W., S. Ash & C. Boberg. 2006. *The atlas of North American English.* New York: Mouton de Gruyter.

Ladefoged, P. 2001. *A course in phonetics*, 4th edn. Toronto: Harcourt.

Ladefoged, P. & I. Maddieson. 1996. *The sounds of the world's languages.* Cambridge, MA: Blackwell.

Lai, C., et al. 2001. A forkhead-domain gene is mutated in a severe speech and language disorder. *Nature* 413. 519–523.

Lakoff, G. 2002. *Moral politics: How liberals and conservatives think.* Chicago: University of Chicago Press.

Lakoff, G. 2006. Staying the course right over a cliff. *New York Times.* October 27. http://www.nytimes.com/2006/10/27/opinion/27lakoff.html?_r=1&oref=slogin

Lakoff, G. & M. Johnson. 1980. *Metaphors we live by.* Chicago: University of Chicago Press.

Lakoff, R. 1975. *Language and women's place.* New York: Harper Colophon Books.

Lane, H. 1975. *The wild boy of Aveyron.* Cambridge, MA: Harvard University Press.

Lane, H. 1989. *When the mind hears: A history of the deaf.* New York: Vintage Books.

Lawton, D. 1984. English in the Caribbean. In R. Bailey & M. Görlach (eds.), *English as a world language*, 251–280. Cambridge: Cambridge University Press.

Leap, W. 1993. *American Indian English.* Salt Lake City: University of Utah Press.

Lenneberg, E. 1967. *Biological foundations of language.* New York: John Wiley.

Leonard, R. Robert Leonard Associates. http://www.robertleonardassociates.com/leadership.htm. (8 November 2011.)

Levinson, S. 1983. *Pragmatics.* Cambridge: Cambridge University Press.

Lewin, T. 2003. College board corrects itself on test score. *The New York Times.* May 15.

Lewis, C. 1967. *Studies in words*, 2nd edn. London: Cambridge University Press.

Liberman, M. 2005. JP versus FHC+CHF versus PJ versus HCF. *Language Log.* August 25. http://itre.cis.upenn.edu/~myl/languagelog/archives/002422.html

Liberman, M. 2005. The SAT fails a grammar test. *Language Log.* January 31. http://itre.cis.upenn.edu/~myl/languagelog/archives/001863.html

Lillo-Martin, D. 1991. *Universal Grammar and American Sign Language: Setting the null argument parameters.* Dordrecht: Kluwer Academic Publishers.

The Linguist List. http://www.linguistlist.org/

Lippi-Green, R. 1997. *English with an accent: Language, ideology, and discrimination in the United States.* New York: Routledge.

Living Tongues Institute for Endangered Languages. http://www.livingtongues.org/enduringvoices.html

Lobeck, A. 2000. *Discovering grammar.* New York: Oxford University Press.

Lovering, D. 2007. Digital 'smiley face' turns 25. *The Washington Post.* September 18. http://www.washingtonpost.com/wp-dyn/content/article/2007/09/18/AR2007091800517.html

Lovin, A. 1997. *An introduction to the languages of the world.* New York: Oxford University Press.

Lowth, R. 1762. *A short introduction to English grammar.* London: R. Dodsley.

Lushootseed Research. http://www.lushootseed.org. (8 November 2011.)

Macaulay, M. & K. Syrett. Why major in linguistics? Linguistic Society of America. http://www.lsadc.org/info/ling-faqs-whymajor.cfm. (8 November 2011.)

MacGregor-Mendoza, P. 2005. Bilingualism: Myths and realities. In K. Denham & A. Lobeck (eds.), *Language in the schools: Integrating linguistic knowledge into K–12 teaching.* Mahwah, NJ: Lawrence Erlbaum Associates.

MacWhinney, B. 2003. First language acquisition. In M. Aronoff & J. Rees-Miller (eds.), *The handbook of linguistics*, 466–487. Malden, MA: Blackwell.

Mallinson, C. & B. Childs. 2005. Communities of practice in sociolinguistic description: African American women's language in Appalachia. *Penn Working Papers in Linguistics* 10(2). Philadelphia: University of Pennsylvania.

Malotki, E. 1983. *Hopi time: A linguistic analysis of temporal concepts in the Hopi language.* Berlin: Mouton.

Manning, C. & H. Schütze. 1999. *Foundations of statistical natural language processing.* Cambridge, MA: MIT Press.

Matthews, P. 1976. *Morphology: An introduction to the theory of word structure.* Cambridge: Cambridge University Press.

Max Planck Institute for Evolutionary Anthropology. Department of Linguistics. Typological tools for field linguistics. http://www.eva.mpg.de/lingua/tools-at-lingboard/tools.php. (8 November 2011.)

McArthur, T. 1998. Caribbean English. In *Concise Oxford companion to the English language.* Oxford: Oxford University Press.

McCrum, R., et al. 1986. *The story of English.* New York: Penguin.

McKinnon, R. 2006. Rick McKinnon, Ph.D. Educator and eLearning Specialist. http://rick mckinnon.com/services. (20 October 2008.)

McMahon, A. 2002. *An introduction to English phonology.* Oxford: Oxford University Press.

Meltzoff, A. & R. Borton. 1979. Intermodal matching by human neonates. *Nature* 282. 403–404.

Mendoza-Denton, N. 1997. *Chicana/Mexicana identity and linguistic variation: An ethnographic and sociolinguistic study of gang affiliation in an urban high school.* Palo Alto, CA: Stanford University dissertation.

Merriam-Webster OnLine. http://www.merriam-webster.com

Merriam-Webster OnLine. Noah Webster and America's first dictionary. http://www .merriam-webster.com/info/noah.htm. (9 June 2008.)

Merriam-Webster OnLine Dictionary. http://www.merriam-webster.com/dictionary/ sentence

Merriam-Webster's dictionary of English usage. 1994. Springfield, MA: Merriam-Webster.

Mey, J. 1993. *Pragmatics: An introduction.* Oxford: Blackwell.

Microsoft Research. 2008. Natural Language Processing. http://research.microsoft.com/nlp/

Millward, C. 1996. *A biography of the English language,* 2nd edn. Boston: Thomson Wadsworth.

Millward, C. 1996. *Workbook to accompany* A biography of the English language, 2nd edn. Boston: Thomson Wadsworth.

Mithun, M. 1999. *The languages of native North America.* Cambridge: Cambridge University Press.

Morgan, G. 2001. Welsh: A European case of language maintenance. In L. Hinton & K. Hale (eds.), *The green book of language revitalization in practice,* 107–113. New York: Academic Press.

Mueller, L. 1996. *Alive together.* Baton Rouge: Louisiana State University Press.

Munro, P. 2001. Field linguistics. In M. Aronoff & J. Rees-Miller (eds.), *The handbook of linguistics.* Malden, MA: Blackwell.

Nafisi, A. 2003. *Reading* Lolita *in Tehran: A memoir in books.* New York: Random House.

Napoli, D. 1993. *Syntax: Theory and problems.* New York: Oxford University Press.

National Geographic. 2011. Enduring Voices Project. http://www.nationalgeographic.com/ travel/enduringvoices/

National Public Radio. 2006. Behaves so strangely. *Radio lab.* Show #202. April 21. http:// www.wnyc.org/shows/radiolab/episodes/2006/04/21

National Public Radio. 2007. Arkansans quibble over the possessive 's.' *All things considered.* February 28. http://www.npr.org/templates/story/story.php?storyId=7648711

Newman, A. 2004. Outsourcing comes to summer camp. *The New York Times.* July 9. D1, 5.

Newman, A., et al. 2002. A critical period for right hemisphere recruitment in American Sign Language processing. *Nature Neuroscience* 5. 76–80. http://www.nature.com/ neuro/

Newmeyer, F. 1986. *Linguistic theory in America*. Orlando, FL: Academic Press.

Newport, E. 1990. Maturation constraints on language learning. *Cognitive Science* 14. 11–28.

Newport, E. & T. Supalla. 2000. Sign language research at the Millennium. In

Nichols, J. 2008. Linguists demonstrate Siberian-North American link. *Linguist List*. http://www.linguistlist.org/issues/19/19-717.html. (8 November 2011.)

Nichols, P. 1983. Linguistic options and choices for black women in the rural South. In B. Thorne, et al. (eds.), *Language, gender, and society*, 54–68. Rowley, MA: Newbury House.

Niedzielski, N. & D. Preston. 2000. *Folk linguistics*. New York: Mouton de Gruyter.

North Carolina Language and Life Project (NCLLP). North Carolina State University Linguistics Program. http://www.ncsu.edu/linguistics/ncllp/. (8 November 2011.)

Nunberg, G. 2003. The nation: Parts of speech; the bloody crossroads of grammar and politics. *The New York Times*. June 1. http://query.nytimes.com/gst/fullpage .html?res=9E06E2DC1430F932A35755C0A9659C8B63

Nunberg, G. 2004. Going nucular. *Fresh air*. National Public Radio. October 2. Published in *Going nucular*. 2004. New York: Public Affairs.

Nunberg, G. 2004. Political language. *Fresh air*. National Public Radio. September 1. http://www.npr.org/templates/story/story.php?storyId=3883628

Nunberg, G. 2006. *Talking right: How conservatives turned liberalism into a tax-raising, latte-drinking, sushi-eating, Volvo-driving, New York Times–reading, body-piercing, Hollywood-loving, left-wing freak show*. New York: Public Affairs.

Oakbog Studios. 1997. Synesthesia and the synesthetic experience. http://web.mit.edu/synesthesia/www/

Obler, L. & K. Gjerlow. 1999. *Language and the brain*. Cambridge: Cambridge University Press.

O'Connor, P. 1996. *Woe is I: The grammarphobe's guide to better English in plain English*. New York: G. P. Putnam.

OneLook Dictionary Search. http://www.onelook.com/cgi-bin/cgiwrap/bware/dofind .cgi?word=sentence. (8 November 2011.)

Ong, W. 1984. *Orality and literacy: Technologizing the word*. London: Methuen.

Oxford English dictionary. http://www.oed.com

Oxford English Dictionary Online. http://www.oed.com

Peckham, A. *The urban dictionary*. http://www.urbandictionary.com. (8 November 2011.)

Pinker, S. 1994. *The language instinct: How the mind creates language*. New York: William Morrow.

Pinker, S. 2001. Talk of genetics and vice versa. *Nature* 413. 465–466.

Pirahã. *Language Log*. http://itre.cis.upenn.edu/~myl/languagelog/archives/003125.html

Polykoff, S. (Clairol ad originator). http://www.ciadvertising.org/studies/student/00_spring/theory/kwilliam/public_html/polykoff/ads.html. (26 October 2008.)

Precker, M. 1993. This Aladdin is rated PC. *Dallas Morning News*. October 2.

Preston, D. 1986. Five visions of America. *Language in Society* 15(2). 221–240.

Preston, D. 1989. Standard English spoken here: The geographical loci of linguistic norms. In U. Ammon (ed.), *Status and function of languages and language varieties*, 324–354. Berlin: Walter de Gruyter.

Priestley, J. 1761. *The rudiments of English grammar*. London: Griffiths.

Pullman, P. 1996. *The golden compass*. New York: Alfred A. Knopf.

Pullum, G. 1991. *The great Eskimo vocabulary hoax and other irreverent essays on the study of language*. Chicago: University of Chicago Press.

Pullum, G. 2003. Menand's acumen deserts him. *Language Log*. October 3. http://158.130.17.5/~myl/languagelog/archives/000027.html

Pullum, G. 2004. Sidney Goldberg on NYT grammar: Zero for three. *Language Log*. September 17. http://158.130.17.5/~myl/languagelog/archives/001461.html

Pullum, G. 2006. Passive aggression. *Language Log.* July 18. http://itre.cis.upenn
.edu/~myl/languagelog/archives/003366.html

Purcell-Gates, V., et al. 2006. *Print literacy development: Uniting cognitive and social practice theories.* Cambridge, MA: Harvard University Press.

Quine, W. 1960. *Word and object.* Cambridge, MA: MIT Press.

Radford, A. 2004. *Syntactic theory and English syntax.* Oxford: Blackwell.

Ritchie, W. & T. Bhatia (eds.). 1996. *The handbook of second language acquisition.* San Diego, CA: Academic Press.

Rizzi, L. 1982. *Issues in Italian syntax.* Dordrecht: Foris Publications.

Roberts, S. 1992. *11 ways to improve your writing and your business.* Greensboro, NC: The Roberts Group. http://www.editorialservice.com/11ways.html

Robinson, D. 1988. Language policy and planning. *ERIC Digest.* Washington, DC: ERIC Clearinghouse on Languages and Linguistics. ERIC Identifier: ED303051. Available at http://www.ericdigests.org/pre-9210/planning.htm

Robinson, J. (ed.). 1990. *The Nag Hammadi Library,* rev. edn. San Francisco: HarperCollins.

Russell, B. 1905. On denoting. *Mind* 14(56). 479–493.

Russell, B. 1919. *Introduction to mathematical philosophy.* London: Allen & Unwin.

Russell, B. 1948. *Human knowledge: Its scope and limits.* London: Allen & Unwin.

Rymer, R. 1993. *Genie: An abused child's flight from silence.* New York: HarperCollins.

Saeed, J. 2003. *Semantics,* 2nd edn. Oxford: Blackwell.

Santa Ana, O. 1993. Chicano English and the Chicano language setting. *Hispanic Journal of Behavioral Sciences* 15(1). 1–35.

Savage-Rumbaugh, E. 1986. *Ape language: From conditioned response to symbol.* New York: Columbia University Press.

Schachter, P. 1977. "Does she or doesn't she?" *Linguistic Inquiry* 8. 763–767. Cambridge, MA: MIT Press.

Schuchardt, H. 1885. *Uber die Lautgesetze Gegen die Junggrammatiker.* Berlin: Robert Oppenheim.

Sea anemone. *Columbia Electronic Encyclopedia,* 6th edn. 2001–07. New York: Columbia University Press.

Searchinger, G. 1995. *The human language series,* part 2. Video. New York: Ways of Knowing.

Searle, J. 1975. Indirect speech acts. In P. Cole & J. Morgan (eds.), *Syntax and semantics,* 3, 59–82. New York: Academic Press.

Searle, J. 1979. Metaphor. In Andrew Ortony (ed.), *Metaphor and thought,* 92–123. Cambridge: Cambridge University Press.

Selinker, L. 1972. Interlanguage. *International Review of Applied Linguistics (IRAL)* 10(3). 209–231.

Sentence. Wikipedia. http://en.wikipedia.org/wiki/Sentence. (8 November 2011.)

Ser, M. 2004. The electronic *Sermo Lupi ad Anglos.* http://english3.fsu.edu/~wulfstan/ noframes.html

Serva, S. 2003. iLanguage: Translations for global research. *EContent, Digital Content, Strategies and Resources* 26(1). 51. http://www.econtentmag.com/Articles/ ArticleReader .aspx?ArticleID=1038

Shaw Phonetic Alphabet. http://shawalphabet.com/index1.html. (8 November 2011.)

Shuy, R. 2008. http://rogershuy.com

Silverstein, S. 1981. *A light in the attic.* New York: HarperCollins.

Skinner, D. 2003. The PSAT's genius grant: The Educational Testing Service gets a question wrong and reveals too much of its literary tastes. *The Weekly Standard.* May 15. http:// www.weeklystandard.com/Content/Public/Articles/000/000/002/681xnmqz.asp

Slobodchikoff, C. 1998. The language of prairie dogs. In M. Tobias & K. Solisti-Mattelon (eds.), *Kinship with the animals,* 65–76. Hillsboro, OR: Beyond Words Publishing.

Smith, G. 2002. *Growing up with Tok Pisin: Contact, creolization, and change in Papua New Guinea's national language.* London: Battlebridge Publications.

Smith, N., with I.-M. Tsimpli. 1995. *The mind of a savant.* Oxford: Blackwell.

Society of Professional Journalists. http://www.spj.org

The Society for the Study of the Indigenous Languages of the Americas (SSILA). http://www.ssila.org

Solisti-Mattelon K. (eds.), *Kinship with the animals,* 65–76. Hillsboro, OR: Beyond Words Publishing.

Solis, M. 2008. Tongue ties: A language bridge across the Bering Strait. *Crosscut.com: News of the great nearby.* http://www.crosscut.com/tribes/13846/. (8 November 2011.)

Speech Technology Magazine. 2007–2008. http://www.speechtek.com/2008/

Sperry, R. 1968. Mental unity following surgical disconnection of the cerebral hemisphere. In *The Harvey Lectures,* Series 62, 293–323. New York: Academic Press.

Sperry, R. 1974. Lateral specialization in the surgically separated hemispheres. In F. Schmitt, et al. (eds.), *Neuroscience 3rd study program,* 5–19. Cambridge, MA: MIT Press.

Springer, S. & G. Deutsch. 1981. *Left brain, right brain.* San Francisco: W. H. Freeman.

Stackhouse, T. 1731. *Reflections on the nature and property of language in general, on the advantages, defects, and manner of improving the English tongue in particular.* London: J. Batley.

Stemmer, B. & H. Whitaker (eds.). 1998. *The handbook of neurolinguistics.* San Diego, CA: Academic Press.

Sternbergh, A. 2006. Stephen Colbert has America by the ballots. *New York Magazine,* October 16.

Stillings, N., et al. 1995. *Cognitive science: An introduction,* 2nd edn. Cambridge, MA: MIT Press.

Struhsaker, T. 1967. Behavior of vervet monkeys and other cercopithecines. *Science* 156(3779). 1197–1203.

Svartvik, J. & G. Leech. 2006. *English: One tongue, many voices.* New York: Palgrave Macmillan.

TELSUR Project. http://www.ling.upenn.edu/phono_atlas/home.html. (8 November 2011.)

Terrace, H. 1979. *Nim.* New York: Alfred A. Knopf.

Thomas, J. 1983. Cross-cultural pragmatic failure. *Applied Linguistics* 4(2). 91–112.

Thomas, L. 1979. *The medusa and the snail: Notes of a biology watcher.* New York: Viking Press.

Tiersma, P. 1999. *Legal language.* Chicago: University of Chicago Press.

Tiersma, P. Welcome to LANGUAGE*and*LAW.org. http://www.languageandlaw.org. (8 November 2011.)

Tolkien, J. 1999. *The fellowship of the ring.* Boston, MA: Houghton Mifflin.

Treiman, R. 2003. Linguistics and reading. In M. Aronoff & J. Rees-Miller (eds.), *The handbook of linguistics,* 664–672. Malden, MA: Blackwell.

Trigiani, A. 2001. *Big stone gap.* New York: Ballantine Books.

Trivedi, B. 2001. Scientists identify a language gene. *National Geographic Today.* http://news.nationalgeographic.com/news/2001/10/1004_TVlanguagegene.html. (8 November 2011.)

Truss, L. 2004. *Eats, shoots and leaves: The zero tolerance approach to punctuation.* New York: Gotham.

Tufte, V. 2006. *Artful sentences.* Cheshire, CT: Graphics Press.

UCLA Phonetics Lab Archive. (With sound.) http://archive.phonetics.ucla.edu. (8 November 2011.)

University of Illinois at Chicago. http://tigger.uic.edu/~rramakri/Readings/Fun/Mixed-Metaphors.htm

University of Iowa. 2002. *103:112 Phonological analysis*. http://www.uiowa.edu/~c103112/lingprof.html. (8 November 2011.)

U.S. Census Bureau. 2008. Hispanic Americans by the numbers. *Infoplease*. http://www.infoplease.com/spot/hhmcensus1.html. (23 October 2008.)

Vajda, E. 2008. Dene-Yeniseic in past and future perspective. http://www.uaf.edu/anlc/dy2008 .html

Vargha-Khadem, F., et al. 1995. Praxic and nonverbal cognitive deficits in a large family with a genetically transmitted speech and language disorder. *Proceedings of the National Academy of Sciences USA* 92. 930–933.

Villiers, J. de & P. de Villiers. 1978. *Language acquisition*. Cambridge, MA: Harvard University Press.

von Frisch, Karl. 1967. *The dance language and orientation of bees*. Cambridge, MA: Harvard University Press.

Walsh, B. The Slot: A Spot for Copy Editors Since 1995. http://www.theslot.com. (8 November 2011.)

Wanner, E. & L. Gleitman (eds.). 1982. *Language acquisition: The state of the art*. New York: Alfred A. Knopf.

Weber, G. 1997. Top languages: The world's 10 most influential languages. In *Language Today*, 2. http://www.andaman.org/BOOK/reprints/weber/rep-weber.htm

Webster, N. 1789. *Dissertations on the English language*. Boston: Isaiah Thomas.

Wei, L. (ed.). 2000. *The bilingualism reader*. London: Routledge.

Werker, J. & R. Desjardins. 1995. Listening to speech in the first year of life: Experiential influences on phoneme perception. *Current Directions in Psychological Sciences*, 4(3). 76–81.

Wheeler, R. 1999. *Language alive in the classroom*. Westport, CT: Praeger.

White, L. 2003. *Second language acquisition and universal grammar*. New York: Cambridge University Press.

Wikipedia. http://en.wikipedia.org/wiki/Sentence. (8 November 2011.)

Wilson, K. 1993. *Columbia guide to Standard American English*. New York: Columbia University Press.

Wilson, W. & K. Kamana. 2001. *'Mai Loko Mai O Ka 'I'ini*: Proceeding from a dream: The 'Aha Punana Leo connection in Hawaiian language revitalization. In L. Hinton & K. Hale, *The green book of language revitalization in practice*. New York: Academic Press.

Winchester, S. 1998. *The professor and the madman: A tale of murder, insanity, and the making of the Oxford English Dictionary*. New York: HarperCollins.

Wittke, C. 1936. *German-Americans and the World War: With special emphasis on Ohio's German-language press*. Columbus: Ohio State Archaeological and Historical Society.

Wolfram, W., et al. 1999. *Dialects in schools and communities*. Mahwah, NJ: Lawrence Erlbaum Associates.

Wolfram, W. & N. Schilling-Estes. 2006. *American English*, 2nd edn. Malden, MA: Blackwell.

Word Spy. http://www.wordspy.com/index.asp. (8 November 2011.)

Wright, C. 1990. A journal of English days. In *The world of the ten thousand things*, 132. New York: Farrar Straus & Giroux.

Wright, C. 1995. Black and blue. In *Chickamauga*, 44. New York: Farrar Straus & Giroux.

Wright, C. 1995. Chickamauga. In *Chickamauga*, 47. New York: Farrar Straus & Giroux.

Wright, C. 2000. Meditation on song and structure. In *Negative blue*, 120. New York: Farrar Straus & Giroux.

Wright, C. 2002. Looking around II. In *A short history of the shadow*, 7. New York: Farrar Straus & Giroux.

Young, R. 2000. *The Navajo verb system: An overview*. Albuquerque: University of New Mexico Press.

Young, R. & W. Morgan. 1943. *The Navajo language*. Republished in 1987 as *The Navajo language: A grammar and colloquial dictionary*, rev. edn. Albuquerque: University of New Mexico Press.

Zimmer, B. 2006. Forensic linguistics, the Unabomber, and the etymological fallacy. *Language Log*. January 14. http://itre.cis.upenn.edu/~myl/languagelog/archives/002762.html

Zimmer, C. 2006. Starlings' listening skills may shed light on language evolution. *The New York Times*. May 2.

Zimmerman, F., et al. 2007. Association between media viewing and language development in children under age 2 years. *Journal of Pediatrics* 151. 364–368.

Zwicky, A. 2006. How long have we been avoiding the passive, and why? *Language Log*. July 22. http://itre.cis.upenn.edu/~myl/languagelog/archives/003380.html

Zwicky, A. 2007. Evil passive voice. *Language Log*. May 1. http://itre.cis.upenn.edu/~myl/languagelog/archives/004456.html

Glossary

accusative case case typically assigned to direct object noun phrases

acronym word formed from abbreviations of other words

affix bound morpheme, including prefixes, suffixes, infixes, and circumfixes

agglutinative language language whose words have several morphemes that attach to a root morpheme, and each morpheme has only one distinct meaning

agrammatism disorder caused by trauma to Broca's area such that word order does not conform to grammatical rules of the language

allegro speech informal respelling of a word

allophone predictable phonetic variant of a phoneme

alphabet system of writing based on individual sounds

amelioration shift of words' meanings over time from neutral or negative to positive

analogy learning rules and applying them to other similar expressions; learning through comparison

analytic language language in which syntactic relations are expressed primarily by word order rather than by inflectional morphemes attached to words

analytic sentence sentence that *must* be true regardless of real-world facts

anomaly deviation from expected meaning

antecedent phrase to which a proform refers; antecedents can be linguistic (spoken, written, or signed) or pragmatic (interpreted from context)

antonyms words that we think of as opposites, though oppositions may be relational (*doctor/ patient*), complementary (*alive/dead*), or gradable (*hot/cold*)

aphasia language disorder resulting from trauma to the brain

arguments set of phrases that occur with a verb and are assigned certain semantic roles by the verb

argument structure set of arguments of a verb and their syntactic categories

articulators parts of the human body involved in speech production: tongue, teeth, lips, glottis, velum, vocal folds

aspiration puff of air that accompanies the initial voiceless consonants in such words as *pat* and *tick*

assimilation process of making one sound more like a neighboring one with respect to some feature

auxiliary verb form of *have, be,* or *do* that occurs in Aux, a syntactic position preceding V

backformation making a new word by omitting what appears to be a morpheme (usually a suffix or prefix) but actually isn't

bilingualism (bilingual language acquisition) native ability to express oneself in two languages, acquired simultaneously, usually at a very young age

biological gender masculine or feminine inflection that expresses biological gender of the object a word represents (*him/her*)

Black Death (1348–1351) bubonic plague, carried by rodents (and their fleas), which wiped out two-thirds of the population of Europe

blend (portmanteau) word made from putting parts of two words together

bound morpheme morpheme that must attach to another morpheme

bound root morpheme a non-affix morpheme that cannot stand alone

broadening change in words' meanings over time to more general or inclusive

Broca's aphasia form of aphasia characterized by labored speech and general agrammatism (see also *Wernicke's aphasia*)

clause syntactic phrase made up of at least a subject (NP) and a predicate (VP)

clipping making a word by omitting syllables in an existing word (e.g., *rad* from *radical*)

closed class category of words that does not accept new members (determiners, auxiliary verbs, and conjunctions, among others)

coda consonant(s) at the end of the rime

codeswitching switching between two languages during one conversation

cognates words (with the same basic meaning) descended from a common ancestor; *two*, *deux* (French), and *zwei* (German) are cognates

coining (neologism) recently created word; typically refers to a word not derived from existing words

comma splice writing error in which two or more independent clauses are joined with a comma rather than a period

community of practice group whose members come together and share activities, beliefs, and perceptions

comparative method technique of linguistic analysis that compares lists of related words in a selection of languages to find cognates, or words descended from a common ancestor

complement phrase that combines with a head to form a larger phrase

compounding combining one or more words into a single word

consonant sound characterized by closure or obstruction of the vocal tract

constituent group of words that forms a larger syntactic unit

content words words with lexical meanings (nouns, verbs, adjectives, adverbs)

continuum of language varieties grammars that share enough of a historical and grammatical relationship to be recognized as varieties of one language

contradiction sentence that can't be true

conversion change of a word's syntactic category without changing form, such as a noun becoming a verb

coordination joining phrases (of the same category, usually) with a conjunction (*for, and, nor, but, or, yet,* and *so*)

creole native language with full grammatical complexity that develops (over time) from a pidgin

critical period for language acquisition early childhood to prepuberty; according to some, the best, maybe only, time in which humans can acquire a first language

Danelaw northern region of England decreed by King Alfred and the Danes to be a legitimate Norse settlement under Norse, not English, law

dative case case typically assigned to indirect object noun phrases

dead metaphor metaphor that is so common that it goes unnoticed as a metaphor (*I see your point.*)

decreolization process by which a creole language becomes more like the superstrate language

deep structure clause in its base word order (in English, SVO) before syntactic rules such as movement or deletion apply

definiteness means by which the speaker indicates to the hearer that they share knowledge of the referent of a particular noun phrase

deictic words words whose meanings can be interpreted only with reference to the speaker's position in space and time (context); the noun *deixis* refers to the pointing or specifying function of such words

deletion process by which constituents are deleted in a sentence under certain syntactic conditions; process causing a segment present at the phonemic level to be deleted at the phonetic level of a word

derivational affix affix that attaches to a morpheme or word to derive a new word

descriptive grammar set of grammatical rules based on what we say, not what we *should* say according to some language authority

descriptive linguists researchers whose main interest is in observing and cataloguing languages

design features of language proposed by Hockett, the features that distinguish human language from other communication systems

dialect variety of a language that has unique phonetics, phonology, morphology, syntax, and vocabulary and is spoken and understood by a particular group

dialectologist sociolinguist who focuses on cataloguing and mapping dialects

dichotic listening method of testing processing of linguistic stimuli, wherein people hear different sounds in two ears simultaneously

diphthong two-part vowel sound consisting of a vowel and a glide in one syllable

direct speech act utterance whose meaning is the sum of its parts; the literal meaning

dissimilation process causing two neighboring sounds to become less alike with respect to some feature

_do_ insertion insertion of pleonastic _do_ into empty Aux to form questions, tags, or negative sentences

ease of articulation making something easier to say

emoticon typographic symbol or combination of symbols used to convey emotion: :-)

empiricism philosophy based on the idea that we gain knowledge not through reason but through experience and that the mind starts out as a blank slate

endangered language language in danger of becoming extinct because it has very few remaining speakers

entailment inclusion of one aspect of a word's or sentence's meaning in the meaning of another word or sentence

eponym word that comes from the name of a person associated with it

etymology historical origin of a word

euphemism word or phrase used to avoid offending or to purposely obscure (_collateral damage_ for 'civilian deaths')

exchange error (spoonerism) common type of slip of the tongue involving the exchange of one part of a syllable for another in two different words

expletive infixation process by which a morpheme is inserted between other morphemes: _abso-bloomin'-lutely_

eye dialect intentional nonstandard spelling that reflects character more than pronunciation

figurative language nonliteral language, language that shifts meaning from the primary meaning of the word

flap manner of consonant articulation similar to a stop, but with no air pressure build-up and therefore no air release

free morpheme morpheme that can stand alone as a word

fronting process causing a segment produced in the back of the mouth to change to a segment produced at the front of the mouth

function words words with functional meanings (determiners, auxiliary verbs, etc.)

fused sentence see _run-on sentence_

fusional language language in which morphemes have more than one meaning fused into a single affix

gapping deletion operation that applies in coordinate clauses (_Sam likes halibut, and Cary, salmon_)

General American idealized variety of English that speakers perceive as neutral, with few stigmatized forms or regionalisms

generative grammar system of grammatical rules that allow speakers to create possible sentences in a language

genitive case case typically assigned to possessive noun phrases

grammar linguistic rule system that we use to produce and understand sentences

grammatical function function of a phrase in the sentence as subject, direct object, indirect object, and so on

grammatical gender masculine, neuter, or feminine inflection realized on words that has no relation to biological gender

graphotactic related to the spelling and writing system

Grice's cooperative principle assumption that in conversation speakers will make a sincere effort to collaboratively exchange information

Grice's maxims of conversation rules of conversation that describe the shared rules speakers use in interactions; they include _quantity, quality, relevance,_ and _manner_

Grimm's Law system of regular sound correspondences, discovered by Jacob Grimm, that distinguishes Germanic languages from others in the Indo-European family; also called the First Sound Shift

head word whose syntactic category determines the category of the phrase

hierarchical structure property of structure of words and phrases, which are constructed in levels; property of phrase structure whereby one phrase is contained inside another: one phrase dominates another phrase

historical linguistics study of how languages change over time

homographs words that have the same spelling, different meanings, and different pronunciations (_bow/bow_)

homonyms words with the same sound and spelling but different, unrelated meanings (*saw/saw*)

homophones words that do not share the same spellings or meanings but sound the same (*sole/soul*)

honorifics grammatical forms, usually words or affixes, that express the relative social status of the speaker to the addressee

hyponym word whose meaning is included, or entailed, in the meaning of a more general word (*tulip/flower*)

hypotaxis subordinate clause structure

ideogram symbol that represents an idea

idiom collocation of words or phrases with nonliteral meaning (*kick the bucket* = die)

independent clause clause that is not contained in another constituent

indirect speech act utterance whose meaning depends on context rather than on literal meaning

infinitive base form of the verb, in English preceded by *to* (*to walk*)

inflectional affix affix that adds grammatical information to an existing word

initialism word formed from the initial letters of a group of words

insertion process causing a segment not present at the phonemic level to be added to the phonetic form of a word

interlanguage grammar intermediate grammar that is influenced by both a person's native and second languages

intonation variation in pitch across an utterance

intonation nucleus most prominently stressed syllable in an utterance

isogloss geographical boundary of a particular linguistic feature

jargon specialized vocabulary associated with a trade or profession, sport, game, etc.

language acquisition natural, unconscious process of language development in humans that occurs without instruction

language genesis how languages come to be, descending from another language or coming about from language contact and creolization

language learning process of gaining conscious knowledge of language through instruction

language planning official (usually governmental) efforts to influence the selection and promotion of a community's language use

language revitalization attempt to bring back the spoken use of a language no longer in daily use

language shift shift of a speech community from speaking one language to another

language variation language change in progress, such as the Northern Cities Vowel Shift

langue in structural linguistics, the set of organizing principles of signs, including rules of combination

lateralization idea that cognitive functions reside in or are controlled by either the left or the right side of the brain

lexical ambiguity word or phrase that has more than one meaning

lexical semantics formal study of the conventions of word meaning

lexicon our mental dictionary; stores information about words and the lexical rules we use to build them

linguistic competence unconscious knowledge of grammar that allows us to produce and understand a language

linguistic parameters binary ("on/off") settings of universal grammatical principles proposed to account for differences among languages

linguistic performance the language we produce, including slips of the tongue and other missteps

linguistic relativity theory that language and culture influence or perhaps even determine each other

linguistic savant person who is linguistically gifted but whose other cognitive abilities are below average

linguistics the scientific study of language

linking verb verb that "links" the subject of the sentence with a phrase that describes it, usually an adjective phrase

loanwords words borrowed into a language from another language

localization theory that different parts of the brain are associated with or control particular behaviors and functions

logical connectives words that express logical relationships, such as *either*, *or*, and *if*

logogram/logograph symbol that represents a word or a morpheme

main verb verb that occurs under V and is the head of a VP (verb phrase)

markedness opposition in meaning that differentiates between the typical meaning of a word and its "marked" meaning or opposite (*right* is unmarked, and *left* is marked)

metaphor nonliteral meaning of one word or phrase describes another word or phrase (*My car is a lemon.*)

metonymy description of something in terms of something with which it is closely associated: *The pen is mightier than the sword* (*pen* = the written word/diplomacy, *sword* = violence/force)

minimal pair pair of words that differ only in one sound in the same position (pit, /pɪt/, and bit, /bɪt/)

mixed metaphor metaphor that comprises parts of different metaphors: *hit the nail on the jackpot* combines *hit the nail on the head* and *hit the jackpot*

modal verb class of verbs (*can/could, may/might,* etc.) that occur in Aux

modification adjustment, change, and modification of grammatical systems based on various social factors

monomorphemic consisting of a single (free) morpheme

morpheme smallest unit of meaning in a word

morphological typology classification of languages according to common morphological structures

morphology study of the system of rules underlying our knowledge of the structure of words

movement syntactic operation by which phrases can be rearranged in a sentence under specific conditions or constraints

mutually intelligible language varieties that can be understood by speakers of the two (or more) varieties

narrowing change in words' meanings over time to more specific meanings

nasalization production of a speech sound with the velum lowered so that most of the airflow passes through the nose rather than the mouth

natural class set of sounds that have certain phonetic features in common

negation causing a statement to have the opposite meaning by inserting *not* between Aux and V

negative politeness politeness strategy based on speaker's minimizing imposition on the addressee

neologism see *coining*

neurolinguistics study of the mechanisms of the brain that underlie how we acquire, produce, and understand language

nominative case case typically assigned to subject noun phrases

nucleus vowel that is the minimum unit of the rime

number singular, plural, or other (dual) inflection

nyms meaning relationships among words—antonyms, synonyms, homonyms, etc.

onomatopoeia use of a word for which the connection between sound and meaning seems nonarbitrary because the word's sound echoes its meaning

onset consonant(s) at the beginning of a syllable

open class category of words that accepts new members (nouns, verbs, adjectives, and adverbs)

overextension use of words to apply to things beyond their actual meaning

overgeneralization application of a grammatical rule more broadly than it is generally applied

palatalization process that results from an interaction between either front vowels or a /y/ glide and a neighboring alveolar consonant, resulting in a palatal fricative or affricate palatal consonant

parallelism constraint on coordinating like categories (NP and NP, VP and VP, etc.)

paraphrase (sentence synonymy) sentence with the same entailments as another sentence

parataxis coordinate clause structure

parole in structural linguistics, the physical utterance itself; the use of a sign or a set of signs

participle form of the verb that follows an auxiliary verb *have* or *be*

passive syntactic operation in which an active sentence (*Beowulf killed Grendel*) is reordered: the object moves to the subject position, and the subject occurs in a prepositional phrase (*Grendel was killed by Beowulf*)

pejoration shift in words' meanings over time from neutral or positive to negative

personification attribution of human qualities to something that is not human

phoneme unit of sound that makes a difference in the meaning of a word

phonemic transcription written recording of sounds using the distinctive phonemes of a language, resulting in a one-to-one correspondence between a sound and a symbol

phonetics study of speech sounds

phonogram symbol based on sound

phonological rule description of when a predictable variation of a particular sound occurs

phonology system of rules underlying the sound patterns in a language

phonotactics branch of phonology dealing with natural and unconscious restrictions on the permissible combinations of phonemes in a language

phrase syntactic unit (NP, VP, etc.) headed by a syntactic category (N, V, etc.)

phrase structure system of rules that organizes words into larger units or phrases

pictogram picture or symbol that represents an object or idea

pidgin a simplified, non-native "contact" language that develops to enable speakers of distinct languages to communicate

pleonastic *do* "dummy," or semantically empty, auxiliary verb

pluralia tantum refers to a noun that is morphologically plural but semantically singular (*scissors*)

polymorphemic consisting of more than one morpheme

polysemy refers to words with two or more related meanings (*lip* = of a cliff or part of the mouth)

polysynthetic language language with a high number of morphemes per word

portmanteau see *blend*

positive politeness politeness strategy based on speaker's constructing solidarity with the addressee

post-vocalic [r] distinctive feature of many dialects of English (which pronounce [r] in words such as *car* and which don't: "*cah*")

poverty of the stimulus argument position that children do not receive enough data to acquire language simply from what they hear

pragmatics study of the meanings of sentences in context (utterance meaning)

predicate syntactically, the verb phrase (VP) in the clause [NP VP]

prescriptive grammar set of grammatical rules prescribed by a language authority

presupposition assumption that is implied by a word or sentence based on world knowledge

productive rule rule that regularly applies in the formation of new words or forms of words

proform word that substitutes for a phrase (AP, PP, or even a clause)

pronoun reference process that relates a pronoun to its antecedent, the phrase to which the pronoun refers

proposition assertion expressed by a sentence regardless of context or real-world facts

Proto-Indo-European attested parent language of members of the Indo-European language family, which spans Eastern and Western Europe and parts of Asia

proto-language single parent language from which all members of a language family may have descended

psycholinguistics study of how we acquire, produce, and understand language

rationalism philosophy based on the idea that we use innate knowledge, or reason, to make sense of the world

recursion property that allows phrase structure rules to generate phrases of infinite length

reduplication making a word by doubling an entire free morpheme (total reduplication) or part of one (partial reduplication); doubling of a syllable, a common syllable structure in children's language

regionalism feature that distinguishes one regional dialect from others

register manner of speaking or writing style adopted for a particular audience (e.g., formal versus informal)

regular sound correspondences predictable sound changes across languages that show they are related (words that begin with /t/ in Germanic languages, such as *tooth/tame*, show up beginning with /d/ in Romance languages: *dental/domestic*)

rime vowel and any consonants following it at the end of the syllable

root morpheme morpheme to which an affix can attach

runes Norse alphabet of figures carved into wood or stone; each runic letter corresponds to a noun and represents its initial sound

run-on/fused sentence writing error in which two or more independent clauses are joined without punctuation

Sapir-Whorf hypothesis based on Edward Sapir's claim that language and thought mutually influence each other; refined by Benjamin Whorf, who claimed that the grammatical structure of a language determines speakers' perceptions of the world

scientific method formation of hypotheses that explain data and the testing of those hypotheses against further data

semantic features classifications of meaning that can be expressed in terms of binary features [+/−], such as [+/−human], [+/−animate], [+/−count]

semantic fields basic classifications of meaning under which words are stored in our mental lexicons (FRIENDS, for example)

semantic shift change in the meaning of words over time

semantics system of rules underlying our knowledge of word and sentence meaning

sentence fragment phrase or clause that is punctuated as a sentence (with a capital letter and a period) but is not a complete sentence

sentence meaning meaning of a sentence regardless of context or knowledge of the world (its linguistic meaning)

sentence synonymy see *paraphrase*

shift in connotation change in words' general meanings over time

shift in denotation complete change in words' meanings over time

sibilants natural class of "hissing" or "hushing" sounds in a language, which includes alveolar and palatal fricatives and affricates

sign the abstract link that connects sound and idea

signified in structural linguistics, the concept, idea, or meaning of the signifier

signifier in structural linguistics, a spoken or signed word or a word on a page

silent syntax unpronounced, yet understood, syntactic material in sentences

simile comparison, usually of two unlike things, in order to create a nonliteral image (*run like a deer*)

slang an informal word or expression that has not gained complete acceptability and is used by a particular group

social network social relationships that characterize a group of speakers

sociolinguistics study of how language varies over space (by region, ethnicity, social class, etc.)

speaker meaning meaning beyond the words alone, which the speaker assumes the hearer can interpret based on communicative context

Specific Language Impairment (SLI) disorder in which children do not acquire language in the normal way but are otherwise not generally cognitively impaired

speech act utterance intended to convey communicative force

speech act theory theory dealing with the construction of meaning in conversation by direct and indirect speech acts

split brain severed corpus callosum, usually to relieve epileptic seizures

spoonerism see *exchange error*

stress relative emphasis given to syllables in a word

strong and weak adjectives in Old English, the differential expression of case, number, and gender of adjectives, according to whether or not they are preceded by a determiner (weak adjectives are preceded by a determiner, and strong ones are not)

strong and weak nouns classifications of Old English nouns depending on how they are inflected to show case, gender, and number

strong and weak verbs in Old English, the differential expression of inflection through a vowel change (strong verbs) or through a regular affix (weak verbs); for example, *sing, sang, sung* (strong) and *walk, walked, walked* (weak)

strong verb verb that expresses inflection through vowel mutation (see also *strong and weak verbs*)

structural linguistics study of the relationship between signifier and signified and of how signs get their meaning from structure

subject syntactically, the noun phrase (NP) in the clause [NP VP]

subject-auxiliary inversion movement of an auxiliary verb to sentence-initial position (preceding the subject) to form a question

subordinate clause clause that is contained in another constituent

substitution process by which we replace a phrase with a pronoun (or other proform)

suppletion process of change whereby one form of a word has no phonological similarity to a related form of that word

suprasegmentals phonological phenomena that are larger than a single sound; includes syllables, stress, and intonation

surface structure clause in its derived order after movement and deletion rules have applied

syllabary system of writing based on syllable sounds

syllable basic unit of speech generally containing only one vowel sound (*nucleus*) and possibly an *onset* and a *coda* (called the *rime*)

synesthesia metaphorical language in which one kind of sensation is described in terms of another; for example, a smell may be described as *sweet* or a color as *loud*

synonyms words that have similar meanings (*purse/handbag*)

syntactic ambiguity a clause or phrase that has more than one meaning because it has more than one syntactic structure

syntactic category set of words that share a significant number of grammatical characteristics (nouns, verbs, etc.)

syntax system of rules and principles that describe how we organize words into phrases and phrases into larger units, the largest being the clause; also, the study of this system

synthetic language language in which syntactic relations are expressed by inflectional morphemes rather than by word order

synthetic sentence sentence that is true because it accords with real-world facts

taboo word forbidden word or expression interpreted as insulting, vulgar, or rude in a particular language

tag question formation syntactic rule that "copies" the subject and an auxiliary or modal verb in sentence-final position: *John left, didn't he?*

thematic roles semantic roles, including *agent, patient, source, goal,* etc., that the verb assigns to its arguments

tone variation in pitch that makes a difference in the meaning of words

transitivity marker affix that indicates transitivity of verbs

truth condition whether a proposition is logically true or false, regardless of context or real-world facts

underextension use of words to apply to things more narrowly than their actual meaning

Universal Grammar (UG) set of linguistic rules common to all languages; hypothesized to be part of human cognition

usage language that is accepted as standard and that may or may not follow prescriptive rules

utterance meaning meaning of utterances in context; their unspoken or indirect meaning

voicing vibration of the vocal folds

vowel sound characterized by an open vocal tract, with no closure or obstruction

vowel mutation change of inflection through a change in vowel structure rather than through affixation

VP deletion syntactic operation in which a verb phrase (VP) is deleted but understood as referring to an antecedent verb phrase (*I don't jog, but Olivia does.*)

weak verb verb that expresses inflection through regular affixation and sometimes vowel mutation (see also *strong and weak verbs*)

Wernicke's aphasia form of aphasia characterized by fluent speech that makes little sense (see also *Broca's aphasia*)

wh-movement movement rule in which an interrogative phrase is moved to sentence-initial position (*Who did Mary meet yesterday?*)

Williams syndrome rare genetic disorder that involves severe retardation, distinct physical characteristics, and uniquely expressive language ability

Index of Languages

A

Abbish/Obbish, 132
Adyghe, syllable structure, 126
African American Vernacular English. *See* English, African American Vernacular English
Ahtna (Tanaina), 186
Akan, 419
Albanian, 295
American Sign Language (ASL)
  displacement, 17
  grammar, 16–17
  morphology, 16
  origin, 479
  phonology, 16
  semantics, 16
  syntax, 16
Arabic, stress-timed language, 128
Aramaic, 444
Athabaskan languages
  agglutinative language, 186
  polysynthetic language, 186
Australian aborigine, semantics, 9

B

Bahasa Indonesia, 498
Bantu, 419
Blackfoot, syllabary, 444
Braille, 199
Bulgarian, 13

C

Cherokee
  revitalization of, 502–503
  syllabary, 444
  timing, 421
Chinese, 13
  alphabet, 445
  analytic language, 189
  Cantonese, 13
  Mandarin, 13, 90
  Mandarin, and pitch, 129
  mixed morphological system, 191
  tone language, 90
Chinook jargon, 487
Coptic, 71
Cree, syllabary, 444

E

English, 3–4, 80, 82
  in Africa, 429
  African American English (AAE), 410, 418–420
  African American Vernacular English (AAVE), 162, 491–492

allophones, 106
alveolar nasal assimilation, 109
American, effect on by British English, 410
American, effect on by Native American language, 415–417
American, impact by immigrants, 415–416
American, origin, 409–410
American accent, 87
American regional dialects, 411–417
American Theatre Standard (ATS), 436
analytic language, 185
Appalachian English, 414–415
in Asia, 428–429
aspiration, 94–95
assimilation rules, 109–113
Australian English, 427
auxiliary verb *do,* history, 225
British dialects, 106
British dialects, punctuation, 457
British dialects and collective nouns, 298
Caribbean English, 427–428
Chicago/Hispanic English, 162
Chicano English, 422–424
circumfix, 151
codeswitching, 49
compounding, 197–199
compound prepositions, 464
consonant insertion, 115
consonant phonemes, 74
consonant phonemes with additional natural classes, 83
consonant phonemes with sibilants, 113
consonants, 72–84
"correct" English and prescriptive grammar, 394–397
deletion rules, 116–118
derivational affixation, 152–155
descriptive and prescriptive grammar rule overlap, 11
diphthongs, 86–87
dissimilation rules, 113–114
and double negatives, 9–10, 11

Early Modern English, 12, 309, 392, 394
Early Modern English grammar, 397–398
Early Modern English vocabulary, 398
electronic, 460–462
emergence, 377–398
exchange rules, 119–120
fronting rules, 118–119
General English, 433
global speakers, 430–431
Great Vowel Shift, 91–92
Hispanic dialects, 93
history of, 190
impact of time and space on, 12–13
Indian Standard English, 428
inflectional affixes, 160–162
influence on by Celtic languages, 379
influence on by Old Norse, 379–381
insertion rules, 114–116
intonation, 130
Isletan English, 421
Lakota English, 421
loanwords, 378–381, 398
Lumbee English, 422
Middle English, 12, 114, 115, 190, 309, 387–392
Middle English and French, 387–392
Middle English interrogative and negative sentences, 391
Middle English loss of inflection, 389–390
Middle English morphology, 389–390
Middle English phonology, 391–392
Middle English punctuation, 453
Middle English spelling, 447
Middle English syntax, 390–391
Middle English verbs, 390–391
Middle English vocabulary, 388–389
mixed typological system, 189–190
Modern English spelling, 447–449
monophthongal vowel phonemes, 85
morphemes, 144–145
morphology, 9
multiple-rule processes, 120–122

nasal assimilation, 109
Native American English, 420–422
New England English, 415
Nigerian English, 429
Northern California Vowel Shift, 93
Northern Cities Chain Shift, 92
Old English, 12, 89, 108, 114, 143, 169, 190, 308, 378
Old English, grammatical gender, 167
Old English adjectives, 382
Old English interrogative and negative sentences, 385
Old English morphology, 381–384
Old English nouns, 382
Old English phonetics and phonology, 385–387
Old English punctuation, 452–453
Old English syntax, 384–385
Old English verbs, 383–384
Old English vocabulary, 378–381
Old English word order, 384–385
Old English writing and spelling, 445–447
overgeneralization, 33
palatalization, 110
parentese, 43
participles, 170
personal pronouns, 166
phonemes, 105
phonetics, 8, 70–101
productive rule, 152
pronouns and genitive case distinctions, 166
punctuation development, 452–457
roots, 152
semantics, 9
Southern drawl, 87
Southern vowel shift, 92–93
spelling, development of, 445–451
spelling system, 71–72
Standard English, 432–433
stress, 128
struggle for dominance of, 50
suppletion, 172
suprasegmentals, 122–132
syllabic consonants, 88
syntax, 9
timing, 421
verb *be,* 173

English, *Continued*
  verb forms, 170
  verbs, 220–226
  vowel distinctions, 88–90
  vowels, 85–93
  word order, 165
  Zambian English, 429
Esperanto, 497

F
Finnish, 295
  stress, 127
  vowel distinctions, 88–89
French
  acronyms, 202
  grammatical gender, 168
  honorifics, 348
  idioms, 316
  nasalization of vowels, 90
  Norman French in England,
    496–497
  punctuation, 457
  syntax, 9
  timing, 421

G
Georgian, syllable structure,
  126
German
  acronyms, 203
  case, 164–165
  clipping, 204
  compounding, 198–199
  consonants, 82
  fusional language, 187
  grammatical gender, 168
  honorifics, 347
  idioms, 316
  and language
    discrimination, 432
  morphology, 9
Greek, 444–445
  Classical Greek, 191
Gullah, 487, 491–492
  and social networks,
    424–425

H
Haitian Creole, 51, 52, 487,
  488
Hawaiian, 72
  allophones, 106
  phonetics, 8
  reduplication, 205
  revitalization of, 501
Hawaiian Creole, 51, 52,
  489–490
Hebrew
  fusional language, 187
  revitalization of, 499–500

Hindi, 295
  aspiration, 104–105
  phonemes, 104–105
Hiri Motu, 490
Hopi expression of time, 357
Hungarian
  stress, 127
Hupa, 72

I
Icelandic, inflectional affixes,
  verbs, 169–170
Ijo, nasalization of vowels, 90
Indonesian, 13
  reduplication, 205
Italian
  null subject language, 15,
    264
  silent pronoun, 264

J
Jamaican Creole, 488–489
Jamaican English, 487
Japanese
  agglutinative language,
    185
  allophones, 106
  compound prepositions,
    464
  consonants, 82
  diphthongs, 86
  honorifics, 349
  and interlanguage
    grammar, 47
  mixed morphological
    system, 191
  syllabary, 444
  syllable structure, 125–126
  vowel distinctions, 89
Javanese, honorifics, 349–350

K
Kikonongo, 419
Klingon, 165
Korean, 295
  allophones, 106
  aspiration, 104–105
  honorifics, 349
  phonemes, 104–105
  tone language, 90

L
Latin, 11
  circumfix, 151
  and language shift, 494–495
Lushootseed
  morphemes, 145
  phonemes, 107
  reduplication, 205
  revitalization of, 503–504

M
Macedonian, 13
Malaysian, 13
Maori, syllable structure, 125
Mazatec, consonants, 82
Melanesian Creole. *See* Tok
  Pisin
Mende, syllabary, 444
Mohawk, 72
Morse code, 199

N
Nahuatl, agglutinative
  language, 185
Navajo
  agglutinative language, 186
  "handling" verb stems, 188
  nasalization of vowels, 90
  revitalization of, 504–505
  semantic categories, 299
  vowels, 90
Na'vi, 165
  syntax, 236
New Guinea Pidgin. *See* Tok
  Pisin
Nicaraguan Sign Language
  (ISN), 45–46, 148–149,
    355, 486–487
  and creolization, 52–53
Norwegian, 13
Nthlakampx, 107
Nupe, tone language, 90

O
Ojibwa, 144
  syllabary, 444

P
Pangasian, reduplication, 205
Pig Latin, 131
Pirahã, 72
Polish, stress, 127
Portuguese, 295
  idioms, 316

Q
Quechua, stress, 127

R
Russian, 295
  fusional language, 187
  Old Russian, 143
  parentese, 43
  stress-timed language, 128

S
Salish languages, agglutinative
  language, 185
Samoan, circmfix, 151
Samoan, honorifics, 349

Signed Exact English (SEE), 17
Spanish, 191
  acronyms, 202
  allophones, 106
  codeswitching, 49
  consonants, 82
  diphthongs, 87
  fusional language, 187
  honorifics, 348
  null subject language, 264
  punctuation, 457
  silent pronoun, 264
  syllable-timed language,
    128
Sranan, 51, 52
Sudanese, honorifics, 349
Swahili, 186
  agglutinative language,
    185
  semantic categories, 299
  stress, 127
  tone language, 90
Swedish, 13
  parentese, 43

T
Telugu, syllable-timed
  language, 128
Thai, tone language, 90
Tibetan, honorifics, 349
Tiwa, 421
Tok Pisin, 50–51, 490–491
Tsonga, consonants, 82
Turkish, agglutinative
  language, 185
Twi, 419

U
Ubby Dubby, 132
Ubykh, syllable structure, 126

V
Vietnamese
  and pitch, 129
  tone language, 90

W
Welsh, revitalization of,
  500–501
Wolof, 418, 419

X
!Xu, 72

Y
Yoruba, 419
  syllable-timed language,
    128
Yup'ik, polysynthetic
  language, 186

Index

A

absolute pitch, 129
abbreviations, 201
abstract nouns, 297
accusative case, 164, 166, 187, 268
acquisition of language, 4, 32–46
 analogy, 36–37
 babbling stage, 38, 42
 bilingualism, 48–49
 in children, 32–33. *See also* children's
  language
 children's mistakes, 33
 critical period, 42, 44–46
 early multiword stage, 40–41, 42
 first language, 37–46
 holophrastic stage, 39
 interlanguage grammar, 46–47
 and isolation, 45–46
 later multiword stage, 41–42
 one-word stage, 38–39, 42
 overgeneralization, 33, 34
 poverty of the stimulus argument, 33
 prelinguistic stage, 37–38, 42
 second language acquisition (SLA),
  46–48
 sign language, 45–46
 two-word stage, 39, 42
acronyms, 201–203
abbreviations, 202
acting, 506
active sentence, 238
Adams, Douglas, 196
address, forms of 343–346
Adger, C., 48
adjectives (ADJ), 146
 adjective phrase, variable, 230
 adjective phrase and linking verbs, 228
 adjective phrase positions, 228
 adjective phrases, syntax, 227–230
 conversions, 200
 Old English, 382
 strong, 378
 suppletive, 172–173
 syntax, 227
 weak, 378
adverbs, 146
 adverb phrase positions, 232, 233
 adverb phrases and syntax, 232, 233
 syntax, 232
affixation, 149
 derivational affixation, 152–155
 inflectional affixation, 159–173
 and mental lexicon, 155–159
 suppletion, 172–173
 word trees, 156–159
affixes, 148–172
affricates, 74, 79, 82
agglutinative languages, 185–186
agrammatism, 57–58
agraphia, 57
'Aha Punana Leo, 501
Aigner-Clark, Julie, 44

ain't, 415
Aladdin (film), 429
Alexia, 57
Alfred, King, 375
allegro speech, 463–464
allophones, 94, 104–108
alphabets, 444–445
 Chinese, 445
 Cyrillic, 444
 Futhorc, or *futhark,* 446
 International Phonetic Alphabet, 72,
  74, 75, 80, 467
 Roman, 445
 Shaw, or Shavian, alphabet, 450
alveolar consonant, 108, 113
alveolar nasal, 107, 116, 122
alveolar ridge, 73, 75, 80, 103
alveolar sounds, 72–75, 111
alveolar stop, 103, 107, 108, 113, 122
ambiguity, 252, 254–270, 284, 306, 317,
  324
amelioration, 309
American Arab Anti-Discrimination
  Committee (AAADC), 429
American Dialect Society (ADS), 194, 195
American Simplified Spelling Board, 449
analogy, 36–37
analytic languages, 189, 380
analytic sentences, 329
Anderson, Gregory, 493
Angelo, Andy, 468
Angles, 373
Anglo-Frisian language branch, 373
Anglo-Normans, 383
animal communication, 4–7
 apes, 482–484
analogy, 36–37
anapest, 138
Ann Arbor Trial, 420
anomaly, 292
anomia, 57, 59
antecedents, 266–267
anterior marker, 51, 52
anthropological linguistics, 23
anthropomorphism, 313
antonyms, 301–302
apes and language, 482–484
aphasia, 56–59, 301
 Broca's, 56–58, 148, 353
 and mental lexicon, 148
 and storage of words in brain, 301
 Wernicke's, 57, 58–59
apostrophe, 163, 450–451
Arkansas' Apostrophe Act, 163
archaic, 459
argument structure, 339
Aristotle, 311
Arkansas' Apostrophe Act, 163
articulation, ease of, 122
articulation, manner of, 78, 80–82
articulation, places of, 75, 76–78

articulators, 74
aspiration, 94–95
assimilation rules, phonology, 109–113
Atkins, J., 495
The Atlas of North American English (ANAE,
  Boberg), 413
Atwood, Margaret, 252
Austin, J., 338
authority, language and, 457–467
autocorrect, 458
AUX position, 221, 224, 226, 254
auxiliary verbs, 147, 219, 221–225
Ayers, Edward, 431

B

babbling stage, 38–42
Baby Einstein, 44
baby talk, 43
backformation, 204
Banks, M., 44
Battistella, E., 300
The Battle of Maldon, 386
Baugh, John, 426
Beal, J., 396
Bede, the Venerable Saint, 377
Bell, Alexander Melville, 75
Benton, R., 501
Beowulf, 3, 12, 171, 254, 277, 278
Bergen, Cornelia, 465
Bett, S., 450
bias, 467
Bible, 290, 390, 448
Bickerton, Derek, 51, 490
bilabial sounds 74, 76, 82–84, 97
 fricative 74, 76, 78, 79, 82, 83, 95–97,
  108 110, 112–119, 126
 nasal 74, 81–84, 88, 109, 113–115,
  118, 121, 124
bilingualism, 48–49
biological behavior, characteristics of, 43
biological gender, 168
Black Death, 384
blends, 200
Boas, F., 481
Boberg, Charles, 413
body language, 17–18, 28
Bono, 193
bound morphemes, 149, 152, 156, 177
borrowing, 49
Braille, Louis, 199
brain, 54–62
 aphasia and, 56–59
 Broca's aphasia, 56–58
 hemispheres, 59–60
 intonation and, 130
 language areas of, 32, 55–62
 language disorders and, 56–59
 lateralization, 57, 59–62
 localization, 56
 psycholinguistics and, 282
 size, 479–480
brain imaging, 56, 59, 61, 63

brand names, 199, 211
British Isles, 373–374
broadening, of meaning, 309
Broca, Paul, 56–57
Broca's aphasia, 56–58, 148, 353
Brothers Grimm, 367
Brown, P., 342
Brown, Roger, 40, 161
bubonic plague, 384
bunched liquid, 80
Burnett, Carol, 438
Bush, George, W., 121

C

Call, Joseph, 7
Campbell, George, 392
Carnegie, Andrew, 446
Carter, Angela, 474
case, 163–166, 185, 187, 378, 380, 385
Cassidy, Frederic, 206, 409
Caxton, William, 384, 443–444
Celtic languages, 367, 373, 374–375
Cervantes, M., 240
Champollion, Jean-François, 439
Chaser, the dog, 7
Chaucer, Geoffrey, 347
Cherokee Preservation Foundation, 498
children's language, 289. *See also*
        language acquisition
    Abbish vs. Ubby Dubby, 132
    games, 2
    mistakes, 33
    rules, 63
    inflectional affixation, 161
    and intonation, 130
    ludlings, 131–132
    and pitch, 129
    overgeneralization, 33–34, 40, 42, 322
    pluralization, 136
    reading and, 459
    stages of speech production, 37, 41–42,
        46, 58, 65, 67
    syllables, 124–125
    syntactic categories, 161
Childs, B., 421
Chimpsky, Nim, 6–7
Chinese alphabet, 445
Chomsky, Noam, 18–20, 128, 255, 268,
        288, 289, 332, 495
    and generative grammar, 18–20
    language acquisition, 33
    linguistic competence vs. linguistic
        performance, 21
Chomskyan revolution, 20
Christian, D., 48
Chwat, Sam, 432
circumfix, 151
Clark, Bill, 44
Clark, E., 40
Clark, H., 40
Clark, W. S., 229
clauses (CL), 14–15, 216. *See also* phrases
        and clauses
    defined, 216–217
    dependent, 42, 380
    independent, 239
    phrase structure, 226, 227
    subordinate, 238–239, 252
    syntax, 237–241
Clerc, Laurent, 475
clinical linguistics, 61–62

clipping, 203–204
clitics, 151
closed class words, 146
coda, 123
codeswitching, 49
Coggshall, E., 417
cognates, 291, 365
    false cognates, 368
coining, 196
Colbert, Stephen, 195
collection nouns, 298
colonization, 482
comma, 448, 449
comma splice, 446,
common nouns, 297–298
comparative method of linguistics, 365
*"A Compendious Dictionary of the English
        Language,"* 206
competence, linguistic, 21, 253
complement, 260, 336–337
compounding, 197–199
computational linguistics, 23, 317–318
computers and linguistics, 317–318, 505
Comrie, Bernard, 430
conjunctions, 269–271
conjunctions and coordination, 269–271
connotation, 308
consonants, 72–73
    articulation of, 75, 76–78
    defined, 70
    deletion of, 114–116
    exchange rules, 117–118
    fronting rules, 116–117
    groupings of sounds, 82–84
    insertion of, 115
    labials, 83
    long, 87
    manner of articulation, 73, 78, 80–82
    natural class, 73
    obstruents, 83
    simplification of clusters, 117–118
    sonorants, 83
    syllabic, 88
    voiced/voiceless, 73–74
constituents, 218–219, 229, 248
consultants and linguistics, 506
content words, 40, 146
context, 304
    semantics and, 295, 327–328, 331
    pragmatics and, 339–354
contradictions, 326, 331, 358
conversation, maxims of, 343–345
    maxim clash, 344
    maxim of manner, 343
    maxim of quality, 343
    maxim of quantity, 343
    maxim of relevance, 343
conversions, 200
Cook, M., 421
cooperative principle, 344
coordination, 42, 269–271
copy editors, 468–469
corpus callosum, 59
corpus linguistics, 321
"correct" English, 390
count nouns, 297
Crain, Stephen, 35
Crawford, James, 432, 496, 499
creaky voice, 82, 100
creating language, 49–53
Creoles, 49–53, 485–492

critical period for language acquisition,
        42, 44–46
Cyrillic alphabet, 444
Crystal, David, 61–62, 427, 428, 461
cuneiform, 444
Curtiss, Susan, 45

D

dactyl, 138
Danelaw, 383, 384
dative case, 164, 187, 378
days of the week names, 378
Deacon, Terrence, 484
dead languages, 494
dead metaphors, 310
decreolization, 419
deep structure, 272–273, 276, 277, 279,
        282, 287
definiteness, 352–353, 354
degree (Deg),148, 221, 223, 225, 227
deixis, 353–354
demonstratives, 354
deletion rules, 116–118, 273–277, 308
    of fricative next to fricative, 117
    of like sounds or syllables, 117
    of /r/ after vowels, 116
    simplification of consonant clusters,
        117–118
    of verb phrase 273, 275, 308
demonstratives, 354
Denham, K., 132
denotation, 309
dependent clauses, 42, 380
Derbyshire, D., 174
derivational affixation, 152–155
de Saussure, Ferdinand, 20, 21
descriptive grammar, 9–11
design features of language, 4–5, 6
Desjardins, R., 107
determiners (D), 146, 213,–214, 260.
        See also tree diagrams in Chapter 8
Deutsch, Diana, 129
Dewey, Melville, 450
dialect boundaries, 411, 412–414
dialect coaches, 439–441
dialect in literature, 471
dialect pride, 437–438
dialectical variation, 301
dialects, 13, 192
    African American English, 418–420
    American regional, 411–417
    Appalachian English, 414–415
    Australian English, 427
    Caribbean English, 427–428
    Chicano English, 422–424
    defined, 409
    diphthongs and, 84
    ethnic, 417–424
    eye, 464–465
    Lumbee English, 422
    Native American English, 420–422
    New England English, 415
    social, 424–426
    vocabulary, 413–414
    Western Atlantic English. *See* dialect,
        Caribbean English
dialectologists, 408
dichotic listening, 60
dictionary, 457, 458–459, 506
    power of, 453
    Navajo, 504

Oxford English Dictionary (OED), 459
Urban Dictionary, 434
Zulu–English, 429
Dictionary of American Regional English (Cassidy), 206, 413
Dictionary of Slang and Unconventional English (Partridge), 206
Dictionary of the English Language (Johnson), 206, 395
diphthongs, 86–87
direct speech act, 341
discreteness of language, 5
discrimination, language, 431–434
displacement of language, 5, 17
dissimilation rules 113–114
do-insertion, 224–226
double negatives, 9–10, 11, 226
duality of patterning, 5
Duffy, Patricia Lynn, 315
Dunbar, Robin, 484
duplicate reduplication, 212

E
Early Middle English, 12, 387, 400, 537
Early Modern English, 12, 29, 118, 138, 173, 225, 309, 388–390, 393–394, 400, 401, 402, 410, 445, 448, 453, 537
early multiword stage, 40–41
ease of articulation, 122
Ebonics, 418
education and linguistics, 505
Educational Testing Service, 226
eggcorn, 14
ejectives, 82
electroencephalography (EEG), 56, 61, 280
electronic language, 460–462
e-mail, 461
Emonds, J.E., 268
emoticons, 462
empiricism, 20
endangered languages, 492–493
English, 537–538
    emergence in British Isles, 377–387
    global language, 430
    influence by French, 387–392
    influence by Old Norse, 380–381
    influence on by Celtic languages, 379
    Middle English morphology, 389–390
    Middle English syntax, 390–391
    Middle English vocabulary, 388–389
    Old English morphology, 381–384
    Old English vocabulary, 378–381
English as a Second Language (ESL), 505
English-only laws, 498
entailments, 298–299
epenthesis, 114
epiglottis, 483
eponyms, 199
An Essay Towards a Practical English Grammar (Greenwood), 397
etymology, 144, 291
euphemisms, 303–304
Evans, Bergen, 465
exchange error, 126
exchange rules, phonology, 119–120
    exchanging /r/ and a vowel, 120
    exchanging /s/ and a consonant, 119–120
    exchanging syllable onsets, 120

expletive infixation, 149–151
eye dialect, 464–465

F
Faderman, Lillian, 348
Fahlman, Steve, 463
family tree models, 485
    and creoles, 488
fast mapping, 39
Federal Communications Commission (FCC), 193
Feruuci, David, 340
field linguistics, 174–175
figurative language, 310–316
Fillmore, L., 62
first language acquisition, 33, 37–43
First Sound Shift, 376. *See also* Grimm's Law
Fischer, Julia, 7
Fitch, W., 259
Flanigan, B., 422
flap, 106
Florey, Kitty Burns, 229
fluent aphasia, 58
Fodor, Jerry, 358
foreign language teaching, 506
forensic linguistics, 358–359, 451
Foss, D., 40
Fought, Carmen, 423
Franklin, Benjamin, 449–450
free morphemes, 149, 151, 152, 153, 156, 177
Freudian slips, 84
fricatives, 72, 76, 78, 80, 81, 94, 117
Friess, S., 461
Frisch, Karl von, 5
Frisians, 377
Fromkin Speech Error Database, 301
Frommer, Paul, 165, 236
fronting rules, 118–119
functional magnetic resonance imaging (fMRI), 56, 282
functional shifts. *See* conversions
function words, 40, 42, 59, 146–148
fused sentence, 455
fusional languages, 185, 187
futhorc, 381

G
Gage, Phineas, 57
Gall, Franz Joseph, 56
Gallaudet, Thomas, 479
Gardner, Allen, 6
Gardner, Beatrix, 6
Gardner, Howard, 148
Gazzaniga, Michael, 60–61
Geertz, C., 349
gender, 167–168
gender, grammatical, 167–168, 339, 345, 350, 352, 360–361
generative grammar, 8, 18, 19
genes and language, 53, 482
genesis of language, 485–492
    creoles, 485–492
genitive (possessive) case, 166, 185, 187, 378
Gentner, T., 259
Germanic languages, 375–377
    and Grimm's Law, 376
gestation time, 484
Gleason, Jean Berko, 34

glide sounds, 81
global language, 430
glottal sounds, 74, 78, 83, 106, 107, 113
Goodall, Jane, 482
government and linguistics, 506
Graham, Virginia, 404
grammar, 7–18, 23
    categorical , 22
    clauses, 14–15
    components of, 8–9
    defined, 7–8
    descriptive, 10–11, 13
    generative, 18–20
    grammar checker, 458
    grammaticality, 9–10
    head-driven phrase structure, 22
    across time and space, 12–13
    interlanguage , 46–47
    lexical functional, 22
    linguistic parameters, 15
    modification of, 11–12
    morphology, 8, 9, 16
    nongenerative theories, 22
    phonetics, 8
    phonology, 8, 16
    prescriptive, 10
    relational, 22
    semantics, 8, 9, 16
    sign language, 7, 16–17
    syntax, 8, 9, 16
    See also Universal Grammar
grammatical function, 164
grammatical gender, 167
grammatical rules 33–34, 36–37, 40, 46–47, 55, 58, 62, 65, 67
Grant, Tim, 451
graphotactic, 124
Great Vowel Shift, 91–92, 397, 408, 449
Green, Lisa, 418, 419
Greenwood, J., 397
Grice, Paul, 343, 344
Grimm, Jacob, 370, 371
Grimm's Law, 366, 370–372
Gross, Terry, 307
Gutenberg, Johannes, 447

H
Hakes, E., 40
Hale, K., 505
Halle, M., 128
Hamblett, Mark, 193
Harada, S., 349
Harrelson, Steve, 163
Harris, Joel Chandler, 465
Harrison, David, 493
Hauser, M., 259
Hayakawa, Senator, 498
Hayt, E.A., 495
head, of phrase, 214–215, 217
head-first compounds, 198
Hellenic languages, 372
Henriksson, A., 293
Henry VIII, King, 394
hierarchical structure, 158, 254, 256, 260, 262, 265, 272
hieroglyphics, 443
higher education and linguistics, 505
Hilbert, Vi, 503, 504
Hispanic, 418–419
historical linguistics, 23, 368, 408, 481
Hockett, Charles, 4, 6

Hoffman, H., 44
Holloway, Ralph, 483, 484
holophrastic stage, 36
home signs, 52
homesigners, 355
homograph, 306
homonym, 306
homophone, 127, 306
honeybees and displacement, 5
honorifics, 347–350
hotspots, 493
human language, 32–68
human language, uniqueness, 259
Hume, David, 20
Hundred Years' War, 387
hyponym, 304–305
hypotaxis, 270, 271

I

iconic signs/symbols, 142
ideograms, 443, 471
idioms, 316
imitation, language acquisition and, 36, 65
implicature, 344
independent clauses, 239, 249, 256, 269, 270
indirect speech, 341
Indo-European language families, 367–370
infix, 149–151
inflectional affixation, 159–173
  case, 164–165
  and English nouns, 162–168
  of English verbs, 168–172
  gender, 167–168
  number, 162
inflectional endings, 59
initialism, 202
insertion
  of consonants, 115
  do, 220–222
  voiceless stop, 115
  vowels, 114–115
  of schwa, 134
  of /y/, 115–116
insertion rules, 114–116
interdental sounds, 74, 77, 83
International Phonetic Alphabet (IPA), 74, 75, 467
Internet, 460–462
interrogatives, 337, 381
intonation, 128, 130–132
  and the brain, 139
  intonation nucleus, 130
  and language acquisition, 37, 39, 41, 43, 58
  and stress, 130
invented spelling, 110, 111
IPA. See International Phonetic Alphabet
irreal marker, 51, 52
isogloss, 412
isolation and language acquisition, 45–46
Italic languages, 371–372
Itard, Jean Marc, 45

J

Jaimes, M., 496
jargon, 192
Jennings, Ken, 340
"Jeopardy!", 340
Jespersen, Otto, 271

John, King, 387
Johnson, Mark, 311
Johnson, Samuel, 395, 449
jokes, 326
Jones, Nard, 487
Jones, William, 367–369
Jusvzyk, P., 107
Jutes, 373

K

Kamana, K., 501
Kaminski, Juliane, 7
Kari, James, 393
Kasner, Edward, 196
Kasparov, Gary, 340
Keegan, Kevin, 231
Kegl, Judy, 53
Kellogg, Brainerd, 229
Kempson, R., 308
Ketchup-Only Law, 498
Keyser, Beth, 241–242
Krauss, Michael, 393, 492
Kuhl, P., 43
Kuralt, Charles, 431
Kurath, Hans, 412

L

L1. See first language
L2. See second language
labial sounds, 96
labiodental sounds, 74, 77, 83
Labov, William, 92, 93, 425, 473
Lachler, Jordan, 174
Ladefoged, Peter, 79
Lakoff, George, 307, 310, 315
Lakoff, Robin, 271
land bridges, 393
language acquisition
  in children, 20
  critical period for, 4
  defined, 2–3
  first, 33, 37, 40, 42, 43–44
  scientific study of, 18–22
  second, 46–48
language attitudes, 425, 440
language change, 408, 425,432, 436, 494
language death, 478, 499, 510
language discrimination, 431–434
language endangerment, 493
language families, 364, 367, 370–371, 389, 392, 396, 478–481, 493, 502
language hotspots, 493
language intelligence, 54
Language Log, the, 14
language loss, 493, 499
language revitalization, 499–505
language shift, 492–498
language variation, 408–440
langue vs. parole, 21
larynx, 73, 483
lateralization of brain, 59–62, 487
later multiword stage, 37, 41, 42
Lawrence, Emma, 174
Leap, W., 421
Leer, Jeff, 393
Lenneberg, Eric, 20, 42, 43, 44
Leonard, Robert, 359
Levinson, S., 346
Lewis, C.S., 310
Lewis, P., 479, 501, 504
lexical ambiguity, 306–308

lexical semantics, 294–301
lexicographers, 206–207, 458–459
lexicon, 142, 148–149
Liberman, Mark, 14, 231
life cycle of language, 477–510
  endangered languages, 492–493
  language genesis, 485–492
  language revitalization, 499–505
  language shift, 492–498
  origin of language, 479–484
Lincoln, Abraham, 450
linguistic competence, 21, 257
linguistic parameters, 15
linguistic performance, 21, 257
linguistic profiling, 426
linguistic relativity, 356–358
linguistic savants, 54–55
Linguistic Atlas of the United States and Canada (Kurath), 412
linguistics, 18
  anthropological, 23
  clinical, 61–62
  computational, 23, 317–318
  corpus, 321
  descriptive, 268, 302, 392
  field, 174–175
  forensic, 358–359, 451
  historical, 23, 368, 412, 485
  modern , 22
  prescriptive, 231, 392, 468, 478
  structural, 21
  subfields of, 23
Linguistic Society of America (LSA), 23–24
The Linguists, 493
linking verbs, 228
liquid sounds, 74, 81–83, 88
literacy, 465–467
Living Tongues Institute, 493
Lloyd, John, 196
loanwords, 378, 398
localization, 56, 58
locutionary act, 342
logical connectives, 335
logogram/logograph, 443
Lorenz, Konrad, 44
Lowth, Robert, 396
ludlings, 131–132

M

MacGregor-Mendoza, P., 48
machine translation, 317
magnetic resonance imaging (MRI), 56, 61
MacWhinney, Brian, 344
malapropisms, 293–294
Mallinson, C., 425
Malotki, Ekkehart, 357
Mankiewicz, Frank, 199
manner of articulation, 73, 78, 82, 97, 98
markedness, 300
maxims of conversation, 339–340
McKean, Eric, 207
meaning. See pragmatics; semantics
Meltzoff, Andrew, 38
mental lexicon, 148–149
mentalese, 358
Merriam-Webster's Dictionary of English Usage, 206
metalanguage, 47
metaphor, 312–315
meter, in poems, 128
metonymy, 314

Middle English, 12, 114, 115, 118, 190, 309, 387–392, 400, 447, 453, 537
migration and language, 393
Millward, C.M., 398
Milne, A.A., 147
minimal pair, 73
Minor, W.C., 459
Mithun, M., 186, 187
mixed metaphor, 313
mixed typological systems, 189–191
monoglot view, 294
monophthongs, 86–87, 99
monomorphemic words, 144
Morgan, G., 500
Morgan, William, 504
morphemes, 143–145
    affixation, 149
    affixation and mental lexicon, 155–159
    bound, 149
    circumfix, 151
    clitics, 151
    defined, 144
    derivational affixation, 152–155
    expletive infixation, 149–151
    free, 149
    infix, 149–151
    monomorphemic words, 144
    polymorphemic words, 144
    productive rules, 152
    recognizing, 144–145
    root, 151–152
    and syllables, 144
    word trees, 156–159
morphological typology, 184–191
morphology, 141–181, 282
    affixation, 155–159
    defined, 142
    derivational affixation, 152–155
    inflectional affixation, 159–173
    Middle English, 389–390
    word classes, 146–152, 148–149
    word trees, 156–159
morphology, of grammar, 8, 9, 26
Morse, Samuel, 199
movement, 272–283
Ms., 203
multiple-rule processes, phonology, 120–122
multiword stages, 40–42
Munro, P., 174
Murray, James, 206

N
Nabokov, Vladimir, 315
narrowing, of meaning, 308–309
nasal sounds, 81, 107, 116, 122
nasalization, 90, 109
National Education Association, 450
National Geographics's Enduring Voices Project, 493
Native American languages, 495–496
    effect on names of states, 417
    impact on American English, 416–417
    language families, 502
    revitalization of, 502–505
natural classes of sounds, 73, 83–84, 95, 98
natural language processing, 317
negation, 222
negative politeness, 346
negative sentences, 41, 55, 224, 225, 381, 387, 388, 394

negative utterances, 65
neologisms, 196
netspeak, 461
neurolinguistics, 23, 32, 55–62, 482
Newman, A., 45
Newport, E., 45
new words 190–191, 196, 201, 202
Nichols, Patricia, 424
nominative case, 164, 166–168
nonarbitrary sign, 142
nonemphatic do, 225
nonpunctual marker, 51, 52
Normans, 387, 447
North Carolina Language and Life Project (NCLLP), 433–434
Northern California Vowel Shift, 93
Northern Cities Chain Shift, 92
Northern Cities Vowel Shift, 408
noun classes, 296–298
noun phrases, 218–219
nouns, 146
    abstract, 295
    case of, 164–165
    collective, 298
    common, 297–298
    concrete, 297
    conversions, 204
    count, 297
    gender of, 167–168
    inflectional affixation, 162–168
    nonconcrete, 297
    noncount, 297
    number, 162
    Old English, 382
    proper, 297–298
    strong, 382
    and syntax, 217–218
    weak, 382
null subject languages, 15, 264
number, in nouns, 162
Nunberg, Geoffrey, 121, 231, 307
nyms, 301–308

O
object, of a phrase, 376, 380, 386
obscene language, 193
obstruents, 83
Old English period, 12, 89, 108, 114, 143, 167, 169, 190, 308, 378–385, 387, 400, 445–447, 452–453, 537
one-word stage, 38–39, 41
onomatopoeic words, 142, 294–295
open class words, 146
origin of language, 479–484
    genes, 482
    human adaptation, 482–484
    linguistic "big bang," 482
    mother language, 479–482
    Salish myth, 481
    social motivation, 484
    world language families, 480
overextension, 39
overgeneralization, 33, 34
Oxford English Dictionary (OED), 206, 459

P
pagan fossils, 374
palatal sounds, 77
palatalization, 110–111
parallelism, 270
parameters, linguistic, 15

paraphrase, 329–330, 358
parataxis, 274, 275
parentese, 43
parole. See langue vs. parole
participles, 170–171
particle shift, 287
parts of speech, 146
passive sentence, 238, 254, 277, 278
past participles, 160, 168, 170–173, 180
past tense, 143, 160, 168–172, 180
Patridge, Eric, 206
Peckham, Aaron, 434
pejoration, 309
Perelman, Eliezer, 500
perfect pitch, 129
performance, linguistic, 21, 257
perlocutionary act, 342
personal pronouns, 267, 269, 285
personification, 313–314
pharynx, 482, 483
philologists, 399
phonemes, 72, 73, 104–108
phonemic awareness, 133
phonemic transcription, 73
phonetics, 69–101
    Old English, 385–387
    phonemes, 72
    and spelling system, 71–72
phonetics, or grammar, 8
phonics, 110
phonogram, 443–444
phonological rule, 104
phonology, 103–140, 282
    assimilation rules, 109–113
    defined, 104
    deletion rules, 116–118
    dissimilation rules, 113–114
    ease of articulation, 122
    exchange rules, 119–120
    fronting rules, 118–119
    insertion rules, 114–116
    Middle English, 391–392
    multiple-rule processes, 120–122
    Old English, 385–387
    phonemes and allophones, 104–108
    suprasegmentals, 122–132
phonology, or grammar, 8, 16
phonotactics, 123–124
phrases, 216. See also phrases and clauses; phrase structure
phrases and clauses, 262–282
phrase structure, 252–259
    adjectives, 227–229
    adverbs, 230–232
    ambiguity, 255–256, 265–266
    base order, 272
    clauses, 216–217, 225–227, 237–239
    constituents, 218
    domination, 254
    head, 218
    hierarchical, 254–259, 265–266
    movement and deletion, 272–281
    nouns, 218–219
    prepositional, 232–234
    recursion, 256–259
    summary of rules, 236
    syntactic ambiguity, 255
    verbs 219–227
phrenology, 56
physiology and language, 482–484
    brain size, 483–484

physiology and language, *Continued*
   epiglottis, 483
   gestation, 484
   larynx, 483
   pharynx, 482, 483
   tongue, 483
pictograms, 443
pidgins, 50–51, 486
Pilley, John, 7
Pinker, Steven, 41–42, 55, 357, 358
pitch, 87, 102, 126–127, 129
Plato, 294
pleonastic *do*, 224
pluralia tantum, 164
pluralization, 164
plurals,162, 164
Poe, Edgar Allen, 295
Pogue, David, 458
politeness, 341–347
politics and language, 231, 307
polymorphemic words, 144
polysemy, 305
polysynthetic languages, 186
portmanteau words, 200
positive politeness, 346
possessive case, 160–161, 163, 166
post-vocalic [r], 410, 425
poverty of the stimulus argument, 33
pragmatic antecedent, 266, 267, 274, 285
pragmatic failure, 344
pragmatics, 23, 331, 339–354
predicate, 237–238
prefix, 143, 145, 149, 153–158, 178, 179
prelinguistic stage, 37–38
prepositional phrases, 234–235
prepositions, 147, 190
   analytic prepositions, 190
   literary, 233, 234, 236, 242, 246
   syntax, 233–234
   synthetic prepositions, 190
prescriptive grammar, 231, 392,
   468, 478
Present-Day English, 12, 364, 371,
   378–385, 393, 400, 402
Priestley, Joseph, 396
primates, 6–7
printing press, 394, 447–448, 457
productive rules, 152
productivity of language, 5
product naming, 95–96, 109, 199, 506
profanity, 193
proficiency, 46
profiling, linguistic, 426
proform, 265
pronouns
   ambiguity, 265–266
   gender-neutral, 147
   and genitive case, 166
   and nonstandard English, 268
   nominative, 187
   personal, 267
   possessive, 179
   reference, 266–269. *See also*
      antecedent
   reflexive, 267
   silent, 264
   substitution, 262–266
propositions, 332
Proto-Indo-European (PIE) language
   family, 368, 369, 370
proto-languages, 481–482
psycholinguistics, 23, 32

psycholinguists, 282–283
publishing and linguistics, 510
Pullum, Geoff, 14, 174
punctuation, 452–457, 464
Pythagoras, 199

Q
questions, 34–36, 40–41, 43, 46, 48, 53,
   54, 62, 68
Quine, W.V.O., 356

R
Rask, Rasmus, 370
rationalism, 20
reading, and linguistics, 132–133
Reading Is Fundamental (RIF), 466
recursion, 253, 256–259, 272, 284
reduplication, 205
Reed, Alonzo, 229
Reed-Kellogg diagrams, 229
regionalism, 459
register, 192, 350–351
regular sound correspondence, 369
relativity, linguistic, 356–358
retronym, 199, 305
revitalization of language, 499–505
Richie, Nicole, 193
Rico the dog, 7
Ried, Allison, 7
rime, 123
Roberts, Sherry, 278
Robinson, D., 497, 498
Rodman, Robert, 359
Romance languages. *See* Italic languages
Roman Empire, 494–495
Roosevelt, Theodore, 450
roots, of words151–152
Rosetta Stone, 443
Roth, Toby, 498
Royal Standard of Ke'elikolani, 501
The Rudiments of English Grammar
   (Priestley), 396
runes, 381
run-on sentence, 455–456
Rutter, Brad, 340

S
Safire, William, 199
SAI. *See* subject-auxiliary inversion
Sapir, Edward, 355
Sapir-Whorf hypothesis, 355–356
savants, linguistic, 54–55
Saxons, 377
Schilling-Estes, Natalie, 422, 424
Scholastic Aptitude Test (SAT), 231
Schuchardt, Hugo, 488
scientific method, 18
Searle, John, 311, 342
second language acquisition (SLA), 46–48
Selinker, L., 47
semantic deviance, 292–294
semantic features, 296–300
semantic fields, 300–301
semanticity, 4, 5
semantics, 282, 291–327, 329–366
   defined, 292
   figurative language, 310–316
   of grammar, 8, 9, 16
   lexical, 294–301
   nyms and, 301–308
   and pragmatics, 352–354
   semantic deviance, 292–294

semantic shift, 308–309
sentence, 331–339
semantic shift, 308–309
semitic family of languages, 499
sentence, 216
   active, 277
   analytic, 333
   contradictions, 335
   definitions, 245
   entailment, 333–334
   fragment, 456
   fused, 455–456
   interrogative, 381, 387, 388
   meaning, 326–329
   negative, 381–382, 387–388, 393–394
   paraphrase, 330, 358
   passive, 254, 277, 278, 287
   presupposition, 331–332, 358
   processing, 282
   syntax, 247–249
   semantics, 326–340, 348
   synthetic, 329, 358
Sequoyah, 444, 503
Ser, Melissa Bernstein, 446
settlement patterns, 411, 417–418
Shakespeare, William, 196, 394
Sharp, M., 421
Shaw, George Bernard, 450
Sheridan, Richard, 293
shifts
   semantic, 308–309, 310
   vowel, 86, 90–93, 96, 100
Shuy, Roger, 359
sibilants, 112
signs, 21, 142
signifier, 21
simile, 315–316
Simplified Spelling Society, 449, 450
slang, 192, 193, 459
Slavic languages, 373
slips of the tongue, 84–85, 300–301
smileys, 459
Smith, Neil, 54–55
sniglets, 196
Snow, C., 48, 62
social dialects, 424–426
social network, 424–425
social value, 21–22
sociolinguistics, 23, 408
sonorants, 83
sounds of language, 74, 77, 78
Southern Vowel Shift, 92–93
SOV. *See* Subject Object Verb
Spaepen, E., 355
specific language impairment (SLI), 54
speech act, 341–343, 345–347
speech generation, 317
speech recognition, 317
spelling, 445–451
split-brain patients, 60–61
Spooner, William, 126
spoonerism, 126–127
Stackhouse, T., 395
standardization of language, 394–397,
   449, 457–467
Sternburgh, A., 195
stereotypes, language, 28
Stewart, Jon, 195
stop sounds, 78, 80
stress, 90, 127–128, 130
stress-timed languages, 128
strong adjectives, 382

strong nouns, 388
strong verbs, 169, 171, 180, 388
structural linguistics, 21
Struhsaker, T., 5
Subject-Auxiliary Inversion (SAI), 222–224, 272
subject of clause, 241–242
Subject Object Verb (SOV), 381–381, 386, 394
Subject Verb Object (SVO), 380, 386, 388, 394, 402
subordinate clauses, 256, 269–270, 275–276, 280–281, 286
substitution, 262–264, 279, 285
substrate language, 50
suffixes, 143, 145, 149, 151–159, 169, 177, 178, 179
Sumerian script, 444
superstrate language, 50
suppletion, 172–173
suprasegmentals, phonology, 122–132
surface structure, 273
SVO. See Subject Verb Object
syllabaries [ch 13]
syllables, 122–132, 144
    children's syllables, 124–125
    definition, 122
    nucleus, 123
    onset, 123
    structure, 123, 125–126
syllable-timed languages, 128
synedoche, 314–315
synesthesia, 314, 315
synonyms, 303–304
syntactic category of words, 143
syntax, 215–253, 251–289
    adjectives and adjective phrases, 231–234
    adverbs and adverb phrases, 232, 233
    ambiguity and clauses, 237–241
    defined, 216
    Middle English, 390–391
    movement and deletion, 272–281
    nouns, 217–219
    Old English, 384–385
    phrases and clauses, 262–282
    phrase structure, 218, 252–259
    prepositions and prepositional phrases, 233–235
    and sex, 271
    silent syntax, 260–262, 273–277
    verbs, 220–221
synthetic languages, 185–188, 384
synthetic sentences, 329, 358

T
taboo words, 194
tag questions, 223
Taft, William Howard, 450
TELSUR project, 413
tense vowels, 449
Terrace, Herb, 6–7
Tesan, Gabriela, 35
text messaging, 460, 474
The Canterbury Tales, 351
thematic roles, 337–339
Thomas, J., 348
Thomas, Lewis, 311
Thornton, Rosalind, 35
thought and language, 354–358

and culture, 355–356
    linguistic relativity, 356–358
    mentalese, 358
    Sapir-Whorf hypothesis, 355–356
Tiersma, Peter, 358
Tolkien, J.R.R., 399
tone languages, 90
tongue, 483
transcription, , 73, 99, 474
transitivity marker, 490
translation, 505
translation of ideas, 356
tree diagrams, 219, 221, 223, 227–230, 233–235, 237, 239, 252–258, 260, 261, 263, 265, 266, 271
trochee, 138
truth conditions, 328–329, 331, 357
two-word stage
typology, morphological, 184–191

U
UG. See Universal Grammar
underextension, 39
Underwood, Robert, 498
uniqueness of human language, 259
United States settlement patterns, 411–412
Universal Grammar (UG), 13–15, 34–35, 48, 55
Urban Dictionary, 434
utterance meaning, 330, 331–332, 339
uvula, 75

V
V. See verbs
vagueness, lexical, 306–307
Vajda, Edward, 393
Vang, Loco, 348
variation, language, 408–440
velar sounds, 74, 76, 79
velum, 74–78, 81, 90, 109
verbs (V), 146
    Aux, 221–226
    auxiliary, 146, 219–220, 221, 390–391
    forms, 219–220, 82, 83, 97
    "handling" stems, 188
    infinitive, 168–169
    inflectional affixation, 168–172
    intransitive, 332, 333
    linking, 228
    main, 219–220, 224–226
    modal, 219–220, 221, 390–391
    Old English, 383
    participles, 170–172
    past tense, 169
    phrases, 226–227, 273–275, 308
    strong, 169, 383
    suppletive, 172
    syntax, 219–220
    thematic roles, 337–339
    transitive, 337
    two-tense system, 383
    verb phrases, 220–221
    weak, 169, 383
Vikings, 379
visible speech, 75
vocabulary, early modern English, 398
voiced/voiceless consonants, 73–74
voiceless stop,115
voicing, 73
voicing assimilation, 111–113
vowel mutation, 164

vowels, 72, 85–93
    deletion and, 116
    diphthongs, 86–87
    distinctions, 88–90
    exchange rules and, 119–120
    insertion rules, 114–115
    lax vowels, 86
    length variations, 88
    monophthongal, 85
    nasalization, 109
    as nucleus of syllable, 123
    syllabic consonants, 88
    shifts, 90–93
    tense, 86

W
Washoe, 6
Watson, the computer, 340
weak adjectives, 378
weak nouns, 382
weak verbs, 169, 383
Weber, G., 430
Webster, Noah, 206
Welsh Language Society, 501
Werker, J., 107
Wernicke's aphasia, 57, 58–59
Wernicke's area, 483
wh-movement, 283–285
White, L., 47
who and whom, 10
Whorf, Benjamin, 355, 357
Williams syndrome, 55
Wilson, K., 465
Wilson, W., 501
Wolfram, Walt, 422, 424, 433
word, defined, 142–143, 145
word classes, 146–152
word formation, 191–205
A Word Geography of the Eastern United States (Kurath), 412
Word of the Year, 194
Word Spy, 194–195
word trees, 156–159
written language, 441–475
    alphabets, 444–445
    authority and, 10
    cuneiform, 444
    dictionaries and, 457, 458–459
    forms of, 445, 460–462
    history of, 442–445
    oral language and, 451–454
    print and, 447–448, 457, 465–467
    punctuation and, 452–457
    registers, 192
    rules and, 453–463
    spelling and, 445–451
    standardization, 457–458, 462–465
    Sumerian script, 444
    syllabaries, 443–444
    registers and forms, 460
wugs, experiment, 34

Y
Young, Robert, 504
Young, Thomas, 443

Z
Zachrisson, R.E., 450
Zamenhof, Ludovic, 497
Zimmer, Ben, 458
Zwicky, Arnold, 278

PCL ANTH 341 #1
Linguistics for everyone :
an introduction